Law ⠿ CONNECTIONS

Media ⠿ CONNECTIONS

SOCIAL
PSYCHOLOGY

SOCIAL PSYCHOLOGY

CATHERINE A. SANDERSON
AMHERST COLLEGE

JOHN WILEY & SONS, INC.

Vice President & Publisher	Jay O'Callaghan
Executive Editor	Christopher Johnson
Senior Editor	Leslie Kraham
Assistant Editor	Eileen McKeever
Executive Marketing Manager	Danielle Torio
Production Manager	Dorothy Sinclair
Senior Production Editor	Sandra Dumas
Designer	Brian Salisbury
Media Editor	Melissa Edwards
Illustration Editor	Anna Melhorn
Photo Department Manager	Hilary Newman
Senior Photo Editor	Elinor Wagner
Media Editor	Lynn Pearlman
Production Management Services	Ingrao Associates
Cover Photo	Clockwise from top left: iStockphoto; Blend Images/Getty Images, Inc.; Westend61/SuperStock; Digital Vision/Getty Images, Inc.; Image Source/Getty Images, Inc.; Photodisc/Getty Images, Inc.; Frida Marquez/Getty Images, Inc.; Blend Images/Getty Images, Inc.; Tim Klein/Stone/Getty Images, Inc.

This book was typeset in 10/12 Sabon Regular by Prepare and printed and bound by Courier/Kendallville. The cover was printed by Courier/Kendallville.

The paper in this book was manufactured by a mill whose forest management programs include sustained yield harvesting of its timberlands. Sustained yield harvesting principles ensure that the number of trees cut each year does not exceed the amount of new growth.

This book is printed on acid-free paper. ∞

ISBN 13   978-0471-25026-5
ISBN 13   978-0470-55646-7

Printed in the United States of America.
10 9 8 7 6 5 4 3 2 1

To Andrew Reese,
Robert Parks, and
Caroline Kenton

CATHERINE A. SANDERSON is an Associate Professor of Psychology at Amherst College. She earned her A.B. at Stanford University and her M.S. and Ph.D. at Princeton University. While at Princeton, she received the Psychology Department's First Year Merit Prize, a National Science Foundation Fellowship, and a Dissertation Research Award from the American Psychological Association.

Sanderson's research, which has received funding from the National Institute of Health, is based in social-personality psychology and specifically on issues within close relationships and health-related behavior, such as the interaction of individuals in close relationships; individuals' accuracy in perceiving others' attitudes and behavior; and why individuals learn more when they receive personally-relevant or "matching" messages. Sanderson is the author of *Slow and Steady Parenting: Active Child-Raising for the Long Haul* as well as a textbook entitled *Health Psychology*. She has served on the Editorial Boards for *Health Psychology,* the *Journal of Personality and Social Psychology, and the Journal of Research in Personality*. In addition, Sanderson writes a "Body Talk" blog for *Psychology Today.*

In her introductory psychology and social psychology courses at Amherst College, Sanderson's teaching emphasizes providing students with general information and skills in interpreting and understanding research that can then be explored in more detail in future classes as well as be used in some way in their day to day lives. She also teaches more specialized classes that focus in depth on health psychology, close relationships, and sports psychology. These classes offer a different type of challenge, namely working with students to critically examine, discuss, and write about empirical research in particular areas.

Catherine Sanderson's *Social Psychology* helps open students' minds to a world beyond their own experience so that they will better understand themselves and others. Sanderson's uniquely powerful program of learning resources was built to support you in moving students from passive observers to active course participants.

Go further in applying social psychology to everyday life.

Sanderson includes six application boxes on business, law, media, environment, health, and/or education in every chapter right as the relevant material is introduced, rather than at the end of the book. This allows students to make an immediate connection between the concept and the relevant application – and provides a streamlined 13-chapter organization that helps you cover more of the material in a term.

Go further with research.

Help your students understand and appreciate the importance of research in social psychology and how social psychologists know what they know.

Go further with culture.

More than any other book, Sanderson's *Social Psychology* helps students understand how key social psychological concepts in each chapter of the book apply to people from other cultures. The last section of each chapter reviews the topics in the chapter in the context of other cultures.

Go further with homework and study materials

with a robust set of end-of-chapter activities and our powerful media resource, WileyPLUS. This online teaching and learning environment integrates the entire digital textbook with the most effective instructor and student resources to fit every learning style.

THE PURPOSE OF THIS BOOK

Students vary considerably in their backgrounds, interests, experiences, and personal and professional aspirations. This book brings social psychology to all of these students—students who will continue their interest in social psychology in graduate programs, students who will become educators, business people, or health professionals, and students who take this course out of sheer curiosity about social psychology.

Through a combination of a lively and current introduction to social science research, a uniquely accessible approach to thinking scientifically, and online teaching and learning resources that immerse students in social psychology in the world today, this book will help you open students' minds to a world beyond their own experience so that they can better understand themselves and others. My primary goal is to help students see the many intersections of social psychology in everyday life. An appreciation of the scientific processes behind these connections will enable them to develop the skills to become critical consumers of information in the world around them.

To reach every student, the writing about social psychology must be accessible, the research presented with clarity, and the content stimulating and comprehensive, but not overwhelming. This text is therefore written in a light and engaging style, to appeal to every student—non-majors and majors. Both classic and contemporary research is described in a clear and vivid way, with examples of research studies throughout specifically chosen to be interesting and relevant for the college student reader.

Students benefit as they see themselves reflected in the discussion of social psychology and are given the opportunity to connect to this discussion and see social psychology through the lens of their daily lives. In addition, the diversity of the student population is mirrored in the evolving and diverse views in the field of social psychology (which has growing research on culture, gender, and neuroscience). The role of culture in social behavior is incorporated in every chapter of this book, reflecting the growth of research in this field and encouraging cultural awareness in students.

FEATURES

Social Psychology helps students learn to think critically, to apply social psychology to everyday life, and to address the central role of diversity, in the student population, the world at large, and even in the field of social psychology. It frames content coverage with five key ideas, designed to get students actively participating in the study of social psychology.

- Think Critically
- Make Connections
- Understand the Big Picture
- A Picture Is Worth a Thousand Words
- Culture Matters

These ideas are carefully interwoven throughout the narrative and pedagogy. The Illustrated Book Tour on the following pages provides a guide to the innovative features contributing to Social Psychology's pedagogical plan.

THINK CRITICALLY

Social Psychology shows students the many ways that social psychology helps them to think about the world. It provides the tools they need to actively engage in critical thinking and analysis.

- A separate chapter on research methods describes the strengths and weaknesses of different methods, as well as strategies for increasing validity of research studies.

Media
CONNECTIONS
The Growing Use of
Web-based Experiments

Environment
CONNECTIONS
The Hazards
of Hot Weather

Health
CONNECTIONS
Evaluating Abstinence-
only Sex Education

Law
CONNECTIONS
The Challenges of Studying
Drinking and Driving

2

Research Methods

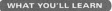
WHAT YOU'LL LEARN

How do researchers in social psychology test their ideas?

What are the types of correlational research methods?

RESEARCH FOCUS ON NEUROSCIENCE
Facial Movements as a Measure of Discrimination

How do you conduct experimental research?

What are the ethical issues involved in conducting research?

How does CULTURE influence research findings?

Did you ever wonder?

Several highly publicized studies have shown that SUVs are responsible for more deaths in car accidents each year than smaller, lighter cars, including subcompacts (Volkswagen Jettas, Honda Civics) and mini-vans (Ford Windstar, Chevrolet Venture; Gladwell, 2004). For example, per million cars on the road, drivers of Volkswagen Jettas cause 70 deaths a year, drivers of Ford Windstars cause 72 deaths per year, and drivers of Ford Explorers cause 148 deaths per year. These statistics are often used to emphasize the inherent danger of SUVs compared to other cars. However, can you think of another explanation for this association? How about the typical person who drives each of these cars? Well, a typical driver of a mini-van is probably a mother with children—who just might be a slower and more cautious driver than the typical driver of an SUV—who might be male, younger, and single (all of which are associated with higher rates of accidents). In fact, if you look at deaths caused by drivers of less expensive subcompact cars, they are even worse than those caused by SUVs: drivers of Chevrolet Cavaliers cause 186

deaths each year, drivers of Dodge Neons cause 199 deaths each year, and drivers of Pontiac Sunfires cause 202 deaths each year. This illustrates the important difference between a correlation between two variables and research that shows that one variable caused the other. This chapter will examine research methods such as correlational studies. Later in the chapter, you'll find out why SUVs may not be as dangerous as you think. In addition, you'll find out . . .

Q A Why are children who watch violent cartoons more likely to hit their siblings?

Q A Why do people underestimate their risky behavior when answering surveys?

Q A Why do women eat less when they are talking with an attractive man?

Q A Why can college students who pretend to act as prison guards become violent very quickly?

Q A Why do women in the United States give more extreme answers to questions about dating than women in Iran?

These are typical questions examined within the field of social psychology using different types of research methods.

NewsCom

28

- **QUESTIONING THE RESEARCH** queries in each chapter prompt students to actively question the results and implications of particular research studies. For example, if you find that college students who come to a workshop entitled "stopping binge drinking" are shown to drink less than their peers, can you be sure that the workshop caused this change? Why or why not? These features encourage critical thinking and facilitate students' awareness of the many ways that social psychology helps them to think about the world.

ide explana-
orisingly lead
e, stu-
n aca-
man,
may
ing a
done
Steele
gative
r per-
negatively by
)95).

?

Questioning the Research

Can you think of another explanation for the finding that people who self-handicap report having worse study habits and lower GPAs? Hint: Is this correlation or causation?

MAKE CONNECTIONS

Social Psychology helps students learn to think critically, to apply social psychology to everyday life, and helps students make critical connections to real life and to their own lives. Students will be most willing to commit time and energy to a topic when they believe that it is relevant to their own life or to their future career. There is no better way to demonstrate relevance than to ground discussion in the real world.

Media CONNECTIONS

What Happens When Barbies Get Smaller and GI Joes Get Bigger?

Virtually all media images of women in the United States show women as thin. This includes women in movies, on television shows, in music videos, and on magazine covers. Some would say that women are portrayed as dangerously thin: Miss America contestants, for example, have body weights 13 to 19% below the expected weight for women of their height, which meets one of the criteria for diagnosing the eating disorder anorexia nervosa (Wiseman, Gray, Mosimann, & Ahrens, 1992). Movie and magazine depictions of women have become consistently thinner in the past twenty years (Silverstein, Perdue, Peterson, & Kelly, 1986): Between 1959 and 1978 the weight of Miss America contestants and *Playboy* centerfold models decreased significantly (Garner, Garfinkel, Schwartz, & Thompson, 1980), and women's magazines have increased the number of articles on weight loss they publish, presumably in an attempt to "help" women reach this increasingly thin ideal (Andersen & DiDomenico, 1992; Garner et al., 1980).

What are the consequences of this focus on the thin ideal in the media? Not surprisingly, women who are of normal weight often feel too heavy. Nearly half of women of average weight are trying to lose weight (Biener & Heaton, 1995), as are 35% of normal-weight girls, and 12% of underweight girls (Schreiber, Robins, Striegel-Moore, Oberzanek, Morrison, & Wright, 1996). One study of teenage girls found that the "ideal girl" was seen as 5 feet, 7 inches tall and weighing 100 pounds. This translates into a body mass index of less than 16, which is clearly anorexic (Nichter & Nichter, 1991). Women who rate advertisements featuring female models in popular women's magazines—who presumably are thin and attractive—feel more depressed, especially if they are already unsatisfied with their own appearance (Patrick, Neighbors, & Knee, 2004).

Although most research on social pressures leading to dissatisfaction with body image has focused on the prevailing thin ideal for women, men are also increasingly feeling pressure to conform to a similarly unrealistic, overly muscular ideal (Pope, Olivardia, Gruber, & Borowiecki, 1999). To test the evolution of the "muscular male ideal" over time, researchers examined the measurements of GI Joe action toys (the action toy with the longest continuous history) produced in 1973, 1975, and 1994. This review revealed a disturbing trend. As shown in this photo, the GI Joe action figure became much more muscular over time: although there was no change in the height of the figure, the circumference of the biceps increased from 2.1 inches (1973) to 2.5 inches (1975) to 2.7 inches (1994). These may seem like small differences, but if you translate these changes to adult male bodies, biceps circumference would increase from 12.2 inches to 16.4 inches. And the latest GI Joe (the GI Joe Extreme, introduced in 1998) has biceps that translate into 26.8 inches in adult males—larger than those of any bodybuilder in history.

REUTERS/Mike Blake/Landov
Daniel Acker/Bloomberg News, /Landov

• **CONNECTIONS BOXES** apply topics in each chapter to the broader themes of Health, Law, Environment, Business, Education, and Media. These applications are uniquely integrated directly with the topics as they are discussed, instead of being grouped in chapters at the end of the book. This organization responds to the preference expressed by a vast majority of reviewers.

• **RATE YOURSELF QUIZZES** occur in each chapter to encourage students to become active participants in the material they are learning and see how their personal results or reactions to the material compare with those discussed in the text. Several of these occur in each chapter as a way to encourage the reader to make a connection to the topic and to increase awareness of their own thoughts and perceptions.

Interestingly, such comparisons seem to occur at an automatic level (Stapel & Blanton, 2004). In one study, participants viewed a picture of either a baby girl or an elderly woman at a subliminal level (meaning they saw the picture very quickly and below the level of conscious awareness). Participants then rated their own age on a scale of one to seven, with one meaning "young" and seven meaning "old." As expected, participants who saw the picture of the baby revealed

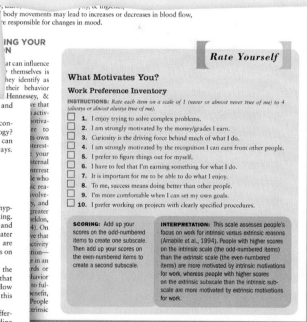

body movements may lead to increases or decreases in blood flow, ...re responsible for changes in mood.

Rate Yourself

What Motivates You?

Work Preference Inventory

INSTRUCTIONS: *Rate each item on a scale of 1 (never or almost never true of me) to 4 (always or almost always true of me).*

- ☐ **1.** I enjoy trying to solve complex problems.
- ☐ **2.** I am strongly motivated by the money/grades I earn.
- ☐ **3.** Curiosity is the driving force behind much of what I do.
- ☐ **4.** I am strongly motivated by the recognition I can earn from other people.
- ☐ **5.** I prefer to figure things out for myself.
- ☐ **6.** I have to feel that I'm earning something for what I do.
- ☐ **7.** It is important for me to be able to do what I enjoy.
- ☐ **8.** To me, success means doing better than other people.
- ☐ **9.** I'm more comfortable when I can set my own goals.
- ☐ **10.** I prefer working on projects with clearly specified procedures.

SCORING: Add up your scores on the odd-numbered items to create one subscale. Then add up your scores on the even-numbered items to create a second subscale.

INTERPRETATION: This scale assesses people's focus on work for intrinsic versus extrinsic reasons (Amabile et al., 1994). People with higher scores on the intrinsic scale (the odd-numbered items) are more motivated by intrinsic motivations for work, whereas people with higher scores on the extrinsic subscale than the intrinsic subscale are more motivated by extrinsic motivations for work.

1. Describe each of the steps in the scientific method.
2. Describe two advantages and two disadvantages of each of the three major methods of conducting research in social psychology: naturalistic/observation, self-report/survey, and experiments.

3. What are two ways of increasing internal validity and two ways of increasing external validity?
4. What are four ways researchers manage ethical concerns when conducting research in social psychology?
5. Describe how people from different cultures can respond to the same questionnaire in different ways.

TAKE ACTION!

1. After observing that whenever your brother goes for a run, he seems to be in a great mood, you wonder whether exercise makes people feel good. How could you do this study using self-report methods? How could you do this study using experimental methods?
2. Dr. D'Angelo is a dentist who wants to get feedback from her patients about their satisfaction with office policy and wait times. She was planning on mailing an anonymous survey to all of her patients, but then decided that this would be too much work. Instead she is planning on asking patients for their thoughts about their dental care when they come in for the appointment. What is the problem with this approach?
3. Your roommate Darren wants to know if his new hypnosis tape is actually effective in helping people

stop smoking. He decides to ask his closest friends to help him determine whether hypnosis is a good way of helping people stop smoking. He gives his five male friends the hypnosis tape, and his five female friends a music tape. One week later he asks each person how many cigarettes they are smoking. When Darren asks you for your thoughts on his study, what problems do you see?
4. As part of a class project, you want to measure the effects on self-esteem of telling college athletes that they have failed a test of "sports intelligence." How could you design a study to ethically test this question?
5. You are interested in designing a study to test differences in attitudes towards human rights, including women's rights and gays' rights, across cultures. How could you conduct such a study? What do you think

• **TAKE ACTION** queries at the end of each chapter ask students to take an active role in applying social psychology to their own lives.

UNDERSTAND THE BIG PICTURE

To help students appreciate the connections between the broad range of topics covered throughout the book and understand how each topic contributes to the whole of social psychology, the first chapter describes three central themes of social psychology:

- The social world influences how we think about ourselves
- The social world influences our thoughts, attitudes, and behaviors
- Our attitudes and behavior shape the social world around us

A Big Picture summary table at the end of each chapter connects the specific material learned in each chapter to these key ideas in the course.

and emphasized the tone of the delivery of the word over the word's meaning in making their explanation. Once again, this study provides evidence of cultural differences in the importance of different types of communication.

The Big Picture

SOCIAL PERCEPTION

This chapter included many applications of the three "big ideas" studied in social psychology. The examples below should help you see the connection between Social Perception and these big ideas, and contribute to your understanding of the big picture of social psychology.

THEME	EXAMPLES
The social world influences how we think about ourselves.	<ul><li>Contestants in a quiz bowl-type game give themselves lower ratings of intelligence than questioners.</li><li>Prisoners see their own criminal behavior as caused by situational factors.</li><li>People who watch a videotape of themselves engaging in a conversation see their behavior as caused by dispositional factors.</li></ul>
The social world influences our thoughts, attitudes, and behaviors.	<ul><li>We believe persuasive essays are more effective when they are written by someone who agrees with the position they are supporting than someone who doesn't.</li><li>We see a teaching assistant as more responsible for adding false information to a teaching evaluation when he or she is given a reward for doing so than punishment for refusing to do so.</li><li>People are more accurate at detecting lies told by a person from their culture than lies told by someone from a different culture.</li></ul>
Our attitudes and behavior shape the social world around us.	<ul><li>People who are distracted when they judge a child's behavior are more likely to make errors in rating that child's behavior.</li><li>Each spouse sees the other as responsible for initiating conflict, and sees his or her own behavior as caused by the situation.</li><li>We see people who engage in negative nonverbal behavior as less likeable and self-assured than those who use more natural nonverbal behavior.</li></ul>

A PICTURE IS WORTH A THOUSAND WORDS

In *Social Psychology*, art is a true learning tool! This text features a completely unique new approach to research-based graphs throughout all chapters.

Graphs are annotated to help students interpret the key findings in the research and to help students understand the Independent and Dependent variables in the research studies through consistent reinforcement of these concepts.

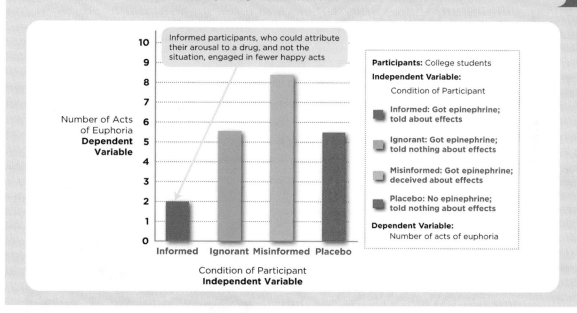

attribute their arousal to the drug as opposed ... west levels of happy mood and behavior.

One of the interesting aspects of the two-factor theory of emotion is that we can interpret the exact same feeling of arousal in very different ways, depending

FIGURE 3.4

HOW DOES COGNITION AFFECT OUR LABELING OF AROUSAL?

Participants received shots and information about its side effects, and then waited with a confederate who modeled euphorically happy actions. As predicted, participants in the ignorant, misinformed, and placebo conditions behaved more euphorically than those in the informed condition, who could attribute their arousal to the drug, rather than to the situation.

Source: Schacter, S., & Singer, J. (1962). Cognitive, social, and physiological determinants of emotional state. *Psychological Review*, 69, 379-399.

Informed participants, who could attribute their arousal to a drug, and not the situation, engaged in fewer happy acts

Number of Acts of Euphoria
Dependent Variable

Condition of Participant
Independent Variable

Participants: College students

Independent Variable:
Condition of Participant

Informed: Got epinephrine; told about effects

Ignorant: Got epinephrine; told nothing about effects

Misinformed: Got epinephrine; deceived about effects

Placebo: No epinephrine; told nothing about effects

Dependent Variable:
Number of acts of euphoria

78   CHAPTER 3   SELF-PERCEPTION AND SELF-PRESENTATION

CULTURE MATTERS

How Does Culture Influence…? sections at the end of each chapter review chapter topics with a focus on how the findings and theories that have been presented might in fact differ in various cultures. These sections simultaneously review prior material from the chapter and engage students meaningfully with cultural issues. Through this consistent approach, students will better appreciate the role of culture in social behavior. For example, students will learn that some expressions that are extremely popular in American culture (e.g., "Be Yourself") might not work so well in countries that value connection and interdependence over individualism.

CULTURE

HOW DOES CULTURE INFLUENCE SELF-PERCEPTION AND SELF-PRESENTATION?

Imagine that you are assigned to work with a group of fellow students on a project for the entire semester. At the end of this project, you are asked to rate yourself, and each of your classmates, on their attributes, including sociability, intellect, and assertiveness. This method allowed researchers to examine whether individuals' self-reports were the same as, higher, or lower than the reports of other group members. How do you think your own self-ratings would compare to those given to you by your peers? Given what you've already learned in this chapter about individuals' tendency to see themselves in overly positive ways, I hope you believe that people tend to rate themselves higher than do others (and this is precisely what researchers have demonstrated, with American samples). However, when Chinese college students participated in this same study, they rated themselves lower than group members (Yik, Bond, & Paulhus, 1998). Although 56% of North American students rated themselves better than did group members, only 43% of Chinese participants showed this type of self-enhancement. In other words, the general tendency to see oneself in extremely positive ways seems to hold true for people in individualistic cultures, but not those in collectivistic cultures. This section will examine how culture impacts self-perception and self-presentation, including the factors that influence the self-concept, the self-perception of motivation, the strategies used to maintain a positive self-concept, and the strategies of self-presentation.

FACTORS INFLUENCING THE SELF-CONCEPT

As described in Chapter 1, people in different cultures see themselves in very different ways: in individualistic cultures, such as the United States, Canada, and England, people view themselves in terms of their attitudes, skills, and traits (Bochner, 1994; Cousins, 1989; Dhawan et al. 1995; Rhee, Uleman, Lee, & Roman, 1995). When people are asked to respond to the question "Who am I?", those from individualistic cultures often describe their personal attributes and traits, such as "smart," "funny," or "shy." In contrast, in collectivistic cultures, such as Japan, Korea, and India, people tend to see themselves in terms of their group and family affiliations. They also describe themselves in terms of their social roles, interpersonal relationships, and group memberships, such as "a college student," "a daughter," or "a member of the Catholic church."

How people think about themselves. This difference in how people define their self-concepts extends to how people think about and reflect on their experiences in the world. People in individualistic cultures are more likely to think about themselves in the first person, and to project their needs and feelings onto others, than are those from communalistic cultures (Cohen & Gunz, 2002). For example, when asked to describe a memory, those from individualistic cultures are much more likely to recall being at the center of the event, whereas those from collectivistic cultures are much more likely to recall someone else being the focus. Americans, and those from other individualistic cultures, are also more likely to show an egocentric projection of their own emotions onto others. These cultural differences are reflected in how

People from collectivistic cultures, such as India, tend to describe themselves in terms of their social roles and interpersonal relationships.

FOCUS ON GENDER AND NEUROSCIENCE

- **RESEARCH FOCUS ON GENDER** sections in most chapters examine a particular issue related to gender in depth. This information will help students understand how research in social psychology contributes to our understanding of gender differences and similarities.

- **RESEARCH FOCUS ON NEUROSCIENCE** sections in most chapters examine specific neuroscience research studies in depth. This information will help students understand how the rapidly growing field of neuroscience contributes to our knowledge about social psychological theories in a way that is not currently seen in other books.

participants who had first been asked for directions agreed to watch the bag. These people looked at their behavior and determined that they were indeed helpful people. They had tried to provide directions when asked, and they were now willing to help yet another stranger by watching her luggage.

RESEARCH FOCUS ON GENDER
Gender Differences in Self-Definition

Although we all have a distinct view of our own strengths and weaknesses, one relatively consistent difference that has emerged in various studies is that men and women tend to differ in their views of themselves (Cross & Madson, 1997; Gabriel & Gardner, 1999; Josephs, Markus, & Tafarodi, 1992). Specifically, women tend to define themselves in part by their interpersonal relationships—their status as a mother, wife, sister, friend, and so forth. Compared to men, they are more likely to agree with statements such as " My close relationships are an important reflection of who I am," and "When I think of myself, I often think of my close friends or family also." In turn, women gain self-esteem from feeling connected to and interdependent with others. On the other hand, men tend to define themselves in terms of their individual achievements and to gain self-esteem from those accomplishments. Although men may also define themselves in part by their relationships, these relationships tend to be broader and more focused on group memberships (e.g., sports teams, larger friendship groups, fraternities). These differences appear relatively early in life, when girls tend to play in small groups with one or two other girls, and boys tend to play in larger groups.

Gahan Wilson/The CartoonBank

"How are the smu

2000). If you've ever been on a diet, you have undoubtedly struggled to control the urge to eat something "forbidden" (e.g., cheesecake), and have probably been unable to resist on at least one occasion. This failure to match your actual behavior to your ideal standards occurs because it is exhausting to constantly try to exercise such restraint; sooner or later you may simply "use up" your willpower and give in to temptation (Pennebaker, 1989; Wegner, 1994). As described in Research Focus on Neuroscience, recent research in neuroscience suggests that different parts of the brain are activated when we make decisions about an immediate reward (e.g., eating that cheesecake right now) versus a delayed reward (e.g., promising ourselves a piece of cheesecake in a few weeks, after we've lost those stubborn 10 pounds).

RESEARCH FOCUS ON NEUROSCIENCE
Different Parts of the Brain Make Different Types of Decisions

Recent research in neuroscience suggests that different parts of the brain are responsible for making decisions regarding immediate rewards versus delayed rewards (McClure, Laibson, Loewenstein, & Cohen, 2004). In one study researchers used functional magnetic resonance imaging (fMRI) to examine which parts of the brain were active when participants made different types of decisions. When participants made decisions about an immediate reward—such as whether to receive $10 immediately or $11 tomorrow—the part of the brain influenced by neural systems associated with emotions was activated. On the other hand, when participants made decisions about a delayed reward—such as receiving $5 in two weeks or $40 in six weeks—the part of the brain involved in abstract reasoning and calculation was activated. This study provides convincing evidence that different parts of the brain are used to make different types of decisions. As one of the authors of this study describes, "Our emotional brain wants to max out the credit card, order dessert and smoke a cigarette. Our logical brain knows we should save for retirement, go for a jog and quit smoking."

The limits of self-control. Once we've spent energy on controlling our thoughts and desires, we have difficulty doing so again. In one study by Roy Baumeister and colleagues (1998), participants, who had signed up for a "taste perception" study and were specifically told not to eat for three hours before the experiment, came into a laboratory room and saw a table with two types of food: a bowl of freshly baked chocolate chip cookies and chocolate candies and another bowl of red and white radishes. Participants were then randomly assigned to one of the two food conditions (chocolate or radishes), and

Brand X/SUPERSTOCK

HOW DO PERSONAL FACTORS INFLUENCE THE SELF-CONCEPT? **67**

BRING SOCIAL PSYCHOLOGY TO LIFE

- **SOCIAL PSYCHOLOGY IN ACTION** The accompanying online WileyPLUS course offers materials for both students and instructors that are fully integrated, not tacked on as an afterthought. The built-in study material is tied to learning objectives in each chapter and is fully assignable and assessable.

- **RESEARCH CONNECTIONS** activities take students from passive observers to active participants in the process of "doing" social psychology and will help to ensure their mastery of core concepts and ideas. The on-line environment allows students the freedom to accomplish things they couldn't do otherwise, such as participating in research studies, testing research hypotheses, designing their own social psychology experiments, manipulating data, and analyzing their results.

← RESEARCH CONNECTIONS →

Try some of these research activities to gain experience in conducting and evaluating research, and to increase your understanding of research methods and techniques in social psychology.

Visit WileyPLUS for more activities and interactive research tools! (www.wileyplus.com)

Participate in Research

Activity 1 Forming a Research Question: Research questions can be inspired by your daily experiences. Spend a day examining your own behavior. Focus on a specific behavior from that day and think about factors that may have influenced that behavior. Turn your observation into a research question that you can bring to class, post on your class discussion board, or share with others.

Activity 2 Understanding Correlation: Why do first born children tend to show higher levels of academic achievement? This chapter has described the distinction between correlation and causation, and the possibility of a third variable accounting for the association between two variables. Describe two or three different third variables that may be responsible for the association of birth order and achievement.

Activity 3 The Importance of Internal and External Validity: No study is perfect. To test the impact of internal and external validity in experimental research, go to WileyPLUS to read about some studies and determine if they have problems with internal validity, external validity, or both.

Activity 4 Understanding the Ethics of Research: Imagine you are the chair of an institutional Review Board. As such, you must insure that research is conducted in an ethical way. Go to WileyPLUS to see a series of proposed studies in social psychology that you will approve or deny based on issues of informed consent, deception, confidentiality, or debriefing.

Activity 5 The Role of Context: The culture you grew up in determines a lot about you, even how you respond to research questions. To examine the impact of culture on research, complete a survey on WileyPLUS and see how your answers compare to someone of a different culture.

Test a Hypothesis

One of the findings discussed in this chapter was whether students, who receive better grades in a class, like the professor more than those who receive worse grades. To test whether this hypothesis is true, design a survey to ask other students about their grade in a class and their liking of the professor. Do your findings support or refute the hypothesis?

Design a Study

To design your own study to test the influence of exposure to aggressive models on acts of aggression, decide on a research question you would like to answer. Then decide what type of study you want to conduct (self-report, observational/naturalistic, or experimental), choose your own independent and dependent variables, and operationally define each by determining the procedures or measures you will use. Form a hypothesis to predict what will happen in your study (the expected cause and effect relationship between your two variables) and collect the data.

ORGANIZATION AND PEDAGOGICAL PLAN

The book moves logically from beginning to end, starting with how we see ourselves and others, and then moving to address how we interact with others in group settings, including both positive and negative interactions. The chapters can be covered in any order, depending on the organization of a particular course. The table of contents has been kept to 13 chapters so that instructors are more likely to be able to cover the entire book.

I encourage readers to ask themselves these questions as they read each chapter, and chapters are organized to facilitate this:

- What does the research say about this topic?
- How can I think critically about the research?
- How does this concept relate to everyday life?
- How does culture influence this concept?

Each chapter follows a carefully developed pedagogical approach designed to help students master the material. Chapters are organized around five central topics, listed on the opening page of the chapter under the heading *What You'll Learn*, and each of these topics is introduced via a specific research study with compelling and highly relevant findings. *Did You Ever Wonder?* questions at the start of the chapter introduce these high-interest findings which are then described in detail at the start of each of the five sections throughout the chapter. Then, at the end of each of these major sections comes a *Concepts in Context* summary table. These section summaries help students synthesize the material, but more importantly, understand its real-world applications. Finally, at the end of the chapter comes *What You've Learned*, a summary of the material in the chapter, organized around each of the five main chapter headings. The chapter concludes with *Review Questions*, *Take Action* activities and *Research Connections* activities, all organized around the five main chapter headings and designed to help students review and apply core concepts while, at the same time, allowing them to take the material further through real world applications and opportunities to experience social psychological research first hand.

WileyPLUS

This online teaching and learning environment integrates the entire digital textbook with the most effective instructor and student resources to fit every learning style.

WITH WileyPLUS:

- Students achieve concept mastery in a rich, structured environment that's available 24/7.
- Instructors personalize and manage their course more effectively with assessment, assignments, grade tracking, and more.

  WileyPLUS can complement your current textbook or replace the printed text altogether.

FOR STUDENTS

PERSONALIZE THE LEARNING EXPERIENCE

Different learning styles, different levels of proficiency, different levels of preparation—each of your students is unique. *WileyPLUS* empowers them to take advantage of their individual strengths:

- Students receive timely access to resources that address their demonstrated needs, and get immediate feedback and remediation when needed.

- Integrated, multi-media resources—including audio and visual exhibits, research activities, and much more—provide multiple study-paths to fit each student's learning preferences and encourage more active learning.
- *WileyPLUS* includes many opportunities for self-assessment linked to the relevant portions of the text. Students can take control of their own learning and practice until they master the material.

FOR INSTRUCTORS

PERSONALIZE THE TEACHING EXPERIENCE

WileyPLUS empowers you with the tools and resources you need to make your teaching even more effective:

- You can customize your classroom presentation with a wealth of resources and functionality from PowerPoint slides to a database of rich visuals. You can even add your own materials to your *WileyPLUS* course.
- With *WileyPLUS* you can identify those students who are falling behind and intervene accordingly, without having to wait for them to come to office hours.
- *WileyPLUS* simplifies and automates such tasks as student performance assessment, making assignments, scoring student work, keeping grades, and more.

STUDENT AND INSTRUCTOR SUPPORT

Social Psychology is accompanied by a host of ancillary materials designed to facilitate a mastery of social psychology.

WILEYPLUS www.wileyplus.com

This online teaching and learning environment integrates the entire digital textbook with the most effective instructor and student resources to fit every learning style.

RESEARCH CONNECTIONS ACTIVITIES

These interactive online activities created by Catherine Sanderson and Katherine Dowdell of Des Moines Area Community College, and available in WileyPLUS, take students from passive observers to active participants in the process of "doing" social psychology and will help to ensure their mastery of core concepts and ideas. These online activities allow students to participate in research studies, test hypotheses, and design their own research studies.

VIDEOS (UPON ADOPTION)

Wiley partners with the Films for the Humanities to offer an outstanding selection of videos (including Roger Bingham's series on the brain). Perfect for introducing new topics, enlivening your classroom presentations, and stimulating student discussion.

INSTRUCTOR RESOURCE WEBSITE

This comprehensive website is uploaded with resources to help you prepare for class, enhance your presentations, and assess your students' progress. The textbook's Test Bank, Instructor's Resource Guide, Power Points, and Image Gallery can be accessed directly from the website.

TEST BANK (AVAILABLE IN RESPONDUS FORMAT, AND IN WORD FORMAT)

Prepared by Robin Musselman of Lehigh Carbon Community College, the test bank to accompany Social Psychology is available in printed form as well as online. Instructors can customize exams by adding new questions or editing existing ones.

INSTRUCTOR'S RESOURCE GUIDE

Prepared by Chris Mazurek of Columbia College, this comprehensive resource includes a wealth of resources for instructors. For each text chapter in the text, this comprehensive resource includes:

- chapter outline
- lecture launchers
- key points the student should know,
- key terms
- discussion stimulators

POWER POINT PRESENTATIONS

Prepared by Brian Parry of Mesa State College of Colorado, this full set of dynamic and colorful PowerPoints for each chapter highlights the major terms and concepts.

POWER POINT IMAGE GALLERY

Online electronic files are available for most figures and tables in the text, which allow you to easily incorporate them into your Power Point presentations or to create your own overhead transparencies and handouts.

STUDENT LEARNING RESOURCES

Student Resources, such as flashcards, self-quizzes (prepare by Andrea Mercurio of Boston University), and chapter objectives are available on the student website to provide a wealth of support materials that will help students develop their understanding of class material and master the material.

ACKNOWLEDGMENTS

Writing a textbook is a labor of love, and hence I want to acknowledge and thank the numerous people who have contributed in large and small ways over the year.

To the reviewers and focus group participants, I offer my sincere appreciation. Thank you for taking time away from your own research and teaching to read drafts of my book or evaluate the art and media programs, and provide thoughtful and constructive feedback. I am deeply indebted to all of the individuals listed below.

MANUSCRIPT REVIEWERS

Allison Abbe, *George Washington University*
Mark Agars, *California State University, San Bernardino*
Joan Bailey, *New Jersey City University*
Daniel Barrett, *Western Connecticut State University*
Frank Barrios, *University of Northern Iowa*
Carolyn Becker, *Trinity University*

Shawn Bediako, *University of Maryland, Baltimore County*
Melinda Blackman, *California State University, Fullerton*
Jennifer Brennom, *Kirkwood Community College*
Justin Buckingham, *Towson University*
Melissa Burkley, *Oklahoma State University*
Melissa Cahoon, *University of Dayton*
Judith Chapman, *Saint Joseph's University*
Tsu-Ming Chiang, *Georgia College & State University*
Nicholas Christenfeld, *University of California, San Diego*
Chante Cox-Boyd, *Carnegie Mellon University*
Don Corriveau, *University of Massachusetts Dartmouth*
Kellina Craig-Henderson, *Howard University*
Layton Curl, *Metropolitan State College of Denver*
Deborah Davis, *University of Nevada, Reno*
Jennifer Devenport, *Western Washington University*
Lynda Dodgen, *Lone Star College-North Harris*
Amanda Dykema-Engblade, *Northeastern Illinois University*
Steve Ellyson, *Youngstown State University*
James Evans, *Louisiana State University-Shreveport*
Sharon Fair, *University of St. Augustine for Health Science*
Kimberly Fairchild, *Manhattan College*
Phillip Finney, *Southeast Missouri State University*
Phyllis Freeman, *State University of New York, New Paltz*
Bill Gabrenya, *Florida Institute of Technology*
David Gersh, *Houston Community College*
Eugene Gilden, *Linfield College*
William Goggin, *University of Southern Mississippi*
Penny Green, *Colorado State University-Pueblo*
Christina Grimes, *Duke University*
Judith Harackiewicz, *University of Wisconsin-Madison*
Mark Hartlaub, *Texas A&M University, Corpus Christi*
Helen Harton, *University of Northern Iowa*
Elaine Hatfield, *University of Hawaii, Honolulu*
Misty Hook, *Texas Women's University*
Kathy Howard, *Harding University*
Maria Hunt, *Avila University*
Karen Huxtable-Jester, *University of Texas at Dallas*
Matthew Isaak, *University of Louisiana*
Julia Jacks, *Guilford College*
Richard Jenks, *Indiana University Southeast*
Susan Johnson, *University of North Carolina at Charlotte*
Nancy Karlin, *University of Northern Colorado*
Cynthia Kernahan, *University of Wisconsin-River Falls*
Gagan Khera, *George Washington University*
Suzanne Kieffer, *University of Houston*
Jennifer Knack, *University of Texas at Arlington*
Randi Koeske, *University of Pittsburgh at Greensburg*
David Kopplin, *Baylor University*
Catalina Kopetz, *University of Maryland*
Robin Kowalski, *Clemson University*
Neil Kressel, *William Paterson University*
Suzanne Kurth, *University of Tennessee*
Alan Lambert, *Washington University in St. Louis*
Travis Langley, *Henderson State University*
Marvin Lee, *Tennessee State University*
Deborah Long, *East Carolina University*
Amy Lyndon, *East Carolina University*
Teresa Lyons, *Salem State College*
Jeffrey Martin, *Wayne State University*

Stephen Mayer, *Oberlin College*
Kelly McGonigal, *Stanford University*
J. Mark McKellop, *Juniata College*
Jo Meier Marquis, *University of Houston-Clear Lake*
Eric Miller, *Kent State University*
Leslie Minor-Evans, *Central Oregon Community College*
Daniel Molden, *Northwestern University*
Melanie Moore, *University of Northern Colorado*
Robin Morgan, *Indiana University Southeast*
Janet Morgan Riggs, *Gettysburg College*
Joel Morgovsky, *Brookdale Community College*
Michael Nielsen, *Georgia Southern University*
Virginia Norris, *South Dakota State University*
Kerth O'Brien, *Portland State University*
Carol Oyster, *University of Wisconsin-LaCrosse*
Neophytos Papaneophytou, *Baruch College*
Terry Pettijohn, *Ohio State University at Marion*
Steven Phillips, *Broward Community College*
Jason Plaks, *University of Toronto*
Gregory Pool, *St. Marys University*
Jackie Pope-Tarrence, *Western Kentucky University*
Sharon Presley, *California State University, East Bay*
Douglas Price, *Tulsa Community College*
Mary Pritchard, *Boise State University*
Chemba Raghavan, *New College of Florida*
Michelle Rainey, *Purdue University*
Pamela Regan, *California State University, Los Angeles*
Elizabeth Rhodes, *Florida International University*
Bob Ridge, *Brigham Young University*
Rosann Ross, *University of Northern Colorado*
Laurie Rudman, *Rutgers University*
Michael Sakuma, *Dowling College*
Cory Scherer, *Northern Illinois University*
Wesley Schultz, *California State University, San Marcos*
Catherine Schuman, *University of Vermont*
Fred Shaffer, *Truman State University*
Marne Sherman, *University of Missouri-Kansas City*
Ellen Shupe, *Grand Valley State University*
Christine Smith, *Antioch College*
Margaret Snooks, *University of Houston-Clear Lake*
Matthew Spackman, *Brigham Young University*
Emily Sweitzer, *California University of Pennsylvania*
Alexander Takeuchi, *University of Northern Alabama*
Rowena Tan, *University of Northern Iowa*
Ronald Thrasher, *Oklahoma State University*
Nancy Tosh, *Ventura College*
Loren Toussaint, *Luther College*
Dana Tucker, *Brigham Young University*
Jocelyn Turner-Musa, *Morgan State University*
Eric Vanman, *Georgia State University*
Chris Verwys, *Rensselaer Polytechnic Institute*
Kathleen Vohs, *University of Minnesota*
T. Joel Wade, *Bucknell University*
Naomi Wagner, *San Jose State University*
Patricia Wallace, *Northern Illinois University*
George Whitehead, *Salisbury University*
Aaron Wichman, *Ohio State University*
Sara Wilcox, *University of South Carolina*
Carol Wilkinson, *Whatcom Community College*

Larry Williams, *Midwestern State University*
Judy Wilson, *Palomar College*
Ann Winton, *John Jay College*
William Woody, *University of Northern Colorado*
Marcel Yoder, *University of Illinois at Springfield*

ART REVIEWERS

Joan Bailey, *New Jersey City University*
Jennifer Brennom, *Kirkwood Community College*
Justin Buckingham, *Towson University*
Nicholas Christenfeld, *University of California, San Diego*
Kellina Craig-Henderson, *Howard University*
Steve Ellyson, *Youngstown State University*
Elaine Hatfield, *University of Hawaii, Honolulu*
Nancy Karlin, *University of Northern Colorado*
Suzanne Kieffer, *University of Houston*
Travis Langley, *Henderson State University*
Neophytos Papaneophytou, *Baruch College*
Mary Pritchard, *Boise State University*
Bob Ridge, *Brigham Young University*
Rowena Tan, *University of Northern Iowa*
T. Joel Wade, *Bucknell University*
George Whitehead, *Salisbury University*

RESEARCH CONNECTIONS (MEDIA) REVIEWERS

Justin Buckingham, *Towson University*
Nicholas Christenfeld, *University of California, San Diego*
Mark Hartlaub, *Texas A&M University Corpus Christi*
Kathy Howard, *Harding University*
Maria Hunt, *Avila University*
Richard Jenks, *Indiana University Southeast*
Travis Langley, *Henderson State University*
Terry Pettijohn, *Ohio State University at Marion*
Jason Plaks, *University of Toronto*
Sharon Presley, *California State University, East Bay*
Pamela Regan, *California State University, Los Angeles*
Alexander Takeuchi, *University of Northern Alabama*
T. Joel Wade, *Bucknell University*
George Whitehead, *Salisbury University*

FOCUS GROUP PARTICIPANTS

Amy Buddie, *Kennesaw State*
Natalie Ciarocco, *Monmouth University*
Vera Dunwoody, *Chaffey College*
William Fry, *Youngstown State University*
Eugene Gilden, *Linfield College*
Omri Gillath, *University of Kansas*
Judith Karackiewicz, *University of Wisconsin*
Lisa A. Harrison, *California State University, Sacramento*
Chris Long, *Ouachita Baptist University*
Chris Mazurek, *Columbia College*
Kathryn Oleson, *Reed College*
Courtney Rocheleau, *Appalachian State University*
Robin Vallacher, *Florida Atlantic University*
Jason Young, *Hunter College, CUNY*

SUPPLEMENTS TEAM

Katherine Dowdell, *Des Moines Area Community College*
Chris Mazurek, *Columbia College*
Andrea Mercurio, *Boston University*
Robin Musselman, *Lehigh Carbon Community College*
Brian Parry, *Mesa State College of Colorado*

PROFESSIONAL FEEDBACK

I am also thankful to the following instructors who took the time to have
detailed conversations with us and provide feedback on the approach of this
book. I really appreciate your feedback and ideas.

Frank Adair, *Louisiana State University*
Stephanie Afful, *Fontbonne College*
Deb Belle, *Boston University*
Bob Blodgett, *Buena Vista University*
Kim Brown, *Ball State University*
Mindy Burgess, *Southwestern Oklahoma State University*
Nicholas Christenfeld, *University of California-San Diego*
Laurie Couch, *Morehead State University*
Kristy Dean, *California State University, San Bernardino*
Jennifer Devenport, *Western Washington University*
Steve Ellyson, *Youngstown State University*
Phillip Finney, *Southeast Missouri State University*
Cindy Frantz, *Oberlin College*
David Gersh, *Houston Community College*
William Goggin, *University of Southern Mississippi*
Josh Greene, *Harvard University*
Judith Harackiewicz, *University of Wisconsin-Madison*
Gene Indenbaum, *State University of New York at Farmingdale*
Billy Jones, *Abilene Christian University*
Nancy Karlin, *University of Northern Colorado*
Marika Lamoreaux, *Georgia State University*
Angela Lipsitz, *Northern Kentucky University*
Sterling McPherson, *Washington State University*
Andrea Mercurio, *Boston University*
David Morgan, *Spalding University*
Jan Ochman, *Inver Hills Community College*
Steven Phillips, *Broward Community College*
Gregory Pool, *St. Mary's University*
Jackie Pope-Tarrence, *Western Kentucky University*
M. Christine Porter, *College of William and Mary*
Mary Pritchard, *Boise State University*
Erin Richman, *University of North Florida*
Bob Ridge, *Brigham Young University*
Tamara Rowatt, *Baylor University*
Natalie Shook, *Virginia Commonwealth University*
Susan Kay Sprecher, *Illinois State University*
Emily Stark, *Minnesota State University, Mankato*
Rowena Tan, *University of Northern Iowa*
Ronald Thrasher, *Oklahoma State University*
Stephanie Tobin, *University of Houston*

PERSONAL ACKNOWLEDGMENTS

Many people at John Wiley & Sons, Inc. contributed tremendous time and energy to this book, and the book is much better for their efforts. I'd like to thank Jay O'Callaghan, Vice President and Publisher, for his support of this project over many years. I am very thankful to all of those who contributed to what I believe is an excellent design and art program for my book, including Brian Salisbury (Designer), Jeof Vita (Art Director), Elle Wagner (Photo Researcher), and Sheralee Connors, as well as to those who worked diligently on producing my book, including Sandra Dumas (Production Editor) and Suzanne Ingrao (Freelance Production Manager). My thanks also go to Ann Greenberger, Freelance Development Editor, who provided thoughtful and constructive guidance about how best to frame and present my ideas. Suzanna Zeitler, Associate Director of Market Development, Danielle Torio, Marketing Manager, and, especially, Barbara Heaney, Director of Product and Market Development, were extremely helpful in determining how best to market my book, which was no small task given the competition in the social psychology textbook market. I also want to thank Eileen McKeever, Assistant Editor, and Media Editors Lynn Pearlman and Bridget O'Lavin, for their considerable work on the supplements for my book, which I think will be invaluable to students and professors.

I owe particular thanks to two people without whom this book would simply not have been possible: Chris Johnson, Executive Editor, and Leslie Kraham, Senior Development Editor. Chris provided thoughtful guidance in creating the overall vision for this book, and helped me to understand the importance of developing features that would truly make a contribution to the field. I appreciate the considerable time and energy he has brought to this project over the years, and the book is much better precisely because at times he pushed me to go in new directions with this project. Leslie, who has probably devoted almost as many hours over the last several years to this book as I have, has provided thorough feedback—both general and specific—about numerous aspects of this book. Her comments about virtually all aspects of the book—writing, art program, photographs, figures, research ideas—have improved the nature of this book in multiple ways, and I am extremely lucky to have had her guidance and support.

I also want to thank several people at Amherst College who helped with this book in various ways and at various stages. Early in the project, Darren Yopyk was very helpful in gathering research articles and cartoons, and made my initial writing much easier. Later in the project, Jack Grein went to considerable lengths to track down and alphabetize every single reference in the entire book. Throughout the project, Isabel Margolin assisted with mailing (many) drafts to Wiley as well as copying and scanning figures and cartoons. I am very grateful for all of their efforts.

Finally, I'd like to thank my husband, Bart Hollander, for his tremendous support of this project ... which included allowing me to take over (at times) our study and our dining room, entertaining the kids on weekends and evenings while I frantically wrote and revised, and commiserating over numerous highs and lows as this project progressed over the years.

The point of this book, obviously, is to share my love of the field of social psychology with students across the country, so I'd be very interested in hearing thoughts from students (and faculty) about how this book has worked for you (or your students). So, please drop me an email (casanderson@amherst.edu) and let me know what you think.

Catherine A. Sanderson
Amherst College

BRIEF CONTENTS

CONTENTS

3 Self-Perception and Self-Presentation 62

4 Social Perception 110

5 Social Cognition 144

8 Social Influence: Norms, Conformity, Compliance, and Obedience 248

11 Aggression 376

12 Interpersonal Attraction and Close Relationships   412

13 Altruism and Prosocial Behavior **460**

1

Introducing Social

WHAT YOU'LL LEARN

What is social psychology?

How has social psychology evolved over time?

Is social psychology really just common sense?

 RESEARCH FOCUS ON GENDER
Understanding Gender Differences in Sexual Behavior

How is social psychology connected to other fields?

 RESEARCH FOCUS ON NEUROSCIENCE
How Rejection Looks in the Brain

How does social psychology apply across CULTUREs and subcultures?

Did you ever wonder?

If you read a magazine, or watch a news program on television, you'll learn about numerous acts of human behavior. Just over the last few months, the following stories have been widely reported in the media:

- A man jumps onto subway tracks to pull a stranger to safety.
- People stop eating peanut butter, following concern about salmonella.
- A gunman opens fire in a church, killing four people.
- Same-sex couples get married in California.

These examples illustrate a range of human behavior, from altruism to reasoning to aggression to love. But what do you really learn about these people from these media reports? How well do you understand the person who is described in these stories, and what drives his or her behavior? How accurately could you predict this person's behavior in the future? This chapter will explore these, and other questions, about how we think about people in the social world and

2

Study Organizer To help you make connections between research in social psychology and real-world issues, each chapter will include four Connections boxes that illustrate how principles in social psychology relate to Education, Law, Health, Business, the Media, or the Environment.

Psychology

the impact of the social world on our attitudes, thoughts, and behavior. In addition, you'll find out ...

Q **A** **Why do college students often fail to ask questions during class?**

Q **A** **Why did many German people stand by and watch as the tragic events of the Holocaust unfolded?**

Q **A** **Why may eating dinner as a family lead teenagers to have better grades?**

Q **A** **Why should parents be more worried about car seats than kidnappers?**

Q **A** **Why do Americans see themselves in terms of their personal traits, whereas Malaysians see themselves in terms of their group memberships?**

These questions all address issues that are examined within the field of social psychology.

Stop/SUPERSTOCK

What do these rather different examples—about college students, the Holocaust, family dinners, and parents—have in common? They all describe topics in the real world that are examined by social psychologists—and this book will describe these, and other issues, related to how people interact in, influence, and are influenced by the social world. This chapter will first define social psychology, and the specific topics examined within this part of psychology. Next, you'll learn about how social psychology has evolved over time, and how it connects to other disciplines. You'll also learn about the basis of this field in the scientific method, and about the impact of culture on theory and research in social psychology.

WHAT IS SOCIAL PSYCHOLOGY?

Social psychology is the scientific study of how people's thoughts, attitudes, and behaviors are influenced by factors in the social world. For example, social psychologists study how people's thoughts about the attractiveness of their dating partner vary depending on whom they are comparing this partner to, how people's attitudes might change after hearing a particular advertising message, and why people behave more aggressively when they are in a group setting than when they are alone. Table 1.1 illustrates the chapters in which these, and other, topics will be described in this book.

This book will focus on three distinct, but inter-related, topics addressed by social psychologists:

- How we think about ourselves
- How we think, feel, and act in the social world
- How our attitudes and behavior shape the social world

These three topics within social psychology will be highlighted in The Big Picture table at the end of each chapter so that you can see how the topics addressed in each chapter relate to these broad themes and contribute to an understanding of the big picture of social psychology. Let's examine each of these pieces in turn.

social psychology the scientific study of how people's thoughts, attitudes, and behaviors are influenced by factors in the social world

self-perception how we think about ourselves

How we see ourselves is often strongly influenced by the type of comparison we are making to other people.

Bonnie Kamin/PhotoEdit

HOW WE THINK ABOUT OURSELVES

Social psychology examines how we think about ourselves, or **self-perception**, and in particular, how our views about ourselves depend on our environment. Many students arrive at college feeling rather good about themselves. They may have been one of the smartest, or most athletic, or most artistic, members of their high school class. However, students quickly realize that in the college environment, the comparison group is different. Once you are surrounded by hundreds, or thousands, of people who themselves were the smartest, or most athletic, or most artistic, members of their own high school class, you suddenly don't feel so good about yourself. Similarly, you may feel quite confident about your own appearance. But after skimming through a *Cosmopolitan* or *Maxim,* you may feel rather insecure. These are

TABLE 1.1 PREVIEW OF COMING ATTRACTIONS

CHAPTER	WHAT YOU'LL FIND OUT
Chapter 2: Research Methods	Why asking people how often they read *Penthouse* isn't a good way to get accurate information
Chapter 3: Self-Perception and Self-Presentation	Why everyone thinks he or she is a better-than-average driver
Chapter 4: Social Perception	Why giving your dating partner the benefit of the doubt is a good idea
Chapter 5: Social Cognition	Why getting a bronze medal can make you happier than getting a silver medal
Chapter 6: Attitude Formation and Change	Why college students who are drunk are less likely to use condoms
Chapter 7: Persuasion	Why ads for laundry detergents feature homemakers and ads for toothpaste feature dentists
Chapter 8: Social Influence: Norms, Conformity, Compliance, and Obedience	Why teenagers should ask their parents for a 3 AM curfew
Chapter 9: Group Influence: The Impact of Group Processes	Why many students dread group projects
Chapter 10: Stereotypes, Prejudice, and Discrimination	Why we see Caucasian athletes as worse than African American athletes, even when their performance is the same
Chapter 11: Aggression	Why spanking your child is a bad idea
Chapter 12: Interpersonal Attraction and Close Relationships	Why you should take dating partners to scary movies instead of out to dinner
Chapter 13: Altruism and Prosocial Behavior	Why CD clubs "give" you five CDs for just a penny

This table describes just a few of the exciting topics you'll read about in this book.

just some of the ways in which factors in the social world influence how we think about ourselves.

Social psychology also examines **self-presentation**, or how we present ourselves to others. We use many strategies to convey impressions about ourselves to others—the car we drive, the clothes or jewelry we wear, even the size of our cell phone or television. Even the casual references we make in conversations—about where we are going on vacation, parties we've attended, and items we've bought—convey information about our habits, interests, and resources.

self-presentation how people work to convey certain images of themselves to others

HOW WE THINK, FEEL, AND ACT IN THE SOCIAL WORLD

social perception how people form impressions of and make inferences about other people and events in the social world

Social psychology also examines how people form impressions and make inferences about other people and events in the social world, a process called **social perception**. We form these impressions easily and frequently—we decide why our favorite baseball team won the game, why a grade on a test was lower than we expected, and why our best friend's dating relationship probably won't last.

But we often make mistakes when deciding the cause of another person's behavior. Social psychologists provide insight into this phenomenon. Although understanding and predicting someone's attitudes and behavior may seem like a very rational and straightforward process, we often make mistakes in assessing the cause of another person's behavior. One of the common errors we make is to focus too much on the role of personal factors, while ignoring, or minimizing, the often considerable influence of the situation. Imagine that you see a person acting rudely to a sales clerk, who seems to be taking a long time to ring up an order. Many people in this situation would quickly make an assumption about the person's personality, and judge him or her as rude, aggressive, and/or obnoxious. These are all *internal traits* or *characteristics*.

fundamental attribution error the tendency to overestimate the role of personal causes, and underestimate the role of situational causes in predicting behavior

social cognition how we think about the social world, and in particular how we select, interpret, and use information to make judgments about the world

However, we are much less likely to think about *external*, or *situational*, *factors* that may have influenced this person's behavior. Perhaps the customer was running late for a job interview. Perhaps he or she was worried about a child who was very sick. Perhaps this person was concerned about receiving a parking ticket. Each of these situational factors could potentially explain this person's rude behavior, and yet we often ignore such variables and instead attribute the behavior to the person's internal traits (a phenomenon called the **fundamental attribution error**).

A particular type of social perception, **social cognition**, describes how we think about people and about the social world. In some cases, we see the world in an accurate, or realistic, way. For example, you might assume that expensive restaurants serve better food than cheap restaurants—and this is a pretty good assumption. But in other cases, we make errors in our judgments about people and events in the world. For example, many people are more afraid of travel by airplane than travel by car. In reality, more people each year die in car accidents than in airplane accidents, suggesting that our fear of airplane travel isn't very realistic.

social influence the impact of other people's attitudes and behaviors on our own thoughts, feelings, attitudes, and behavior

Another central issue examined by social psychology is **social influence**, meaning the impact of other people's attitudes and behaviors on our own thoughts, feelings, attitudes, and behavior. In some cases social influence is quite direct: advertising messages are a good example of deliberate efforts to influence attitudes and behavior. In other cases, however, social influence is very subtle. We are, for example, less likely to help a person in need if we are in a large group than if we are alone with the person, in part because we don't feel personally responsible for helping.

Social psychology examines not only the impact of the real people's attitudes and behavior—that is, the attitudes and behavior of our friends, classmates, parents, celebrities, and so on—but also the impact of our perceptions of these people's attitudes and behaviors. Let's take an example that occurs frequently in college classes. Imagine that your professor finishes a section of the lecture and asks whether anyone has a question. You might have a question that you'd like to ask about the material that was just presented, but when you look around the room, you notice that no one else has a hand raised. You therefore decide not to ask your question, because you fear looking stupid for being the only person with a question. In this case, you assume that no other students have questions, and therefore believe that they must have understood all the material. This perception of their knowledge—regardless of whether it is accurate—influences your own behavior. Our beliefs about the social world can influence our attitudes and behavior even when these beliefs are inaccurate, as described in the Health Connections box.

Why College Students Drink Less Than You Think They Do

To help you make connections between research in social psychology and real-world issues, in each chapter this book will feature boxes that illustrate how principles in social psychology relate to education, law, health, business, the media, or the environment. As you'll learn in Chapter 8, social norms, and errors we make in perceiving such norms, influence alcohol use by college students. In one of the first studies of this effect, Deborah Prentice and Dale Miller at Princeton University examined students' own comfort with the frequency of alcohol use on campus as well as their beliefs about their peers' comfort with alcohol use (1993). Their findings revealed that many students felt uncomfortable with the amount of drinking on campus—they believed that there was too much drinking. However, these students also tended to believe that other students were quite comfortable with the amount of drinking. Unfortunately, students who believe (even wrongly) that other students approve of high levels of drinking may start drinking more in order to fit in with their perceptions of what others are doing. In this way, beliefs about the frequency of and comfort with alcohol use on campus can actually increase such behavior, even when such beliefs are based on inaccurate information.

Image Source/SUPERSTOCK

Social psychology examines the impact of events on our attitudes and behaviors. Have you ever noticed that when you are in a bad mood you are more likely to act rudely? Would you believe that just feeling really hot can lead you to behave more aggressively, or that smelling a cinnamon bun baking could lead you to be nicer to others? We'll talk about these and other ways in which aspects of the social world influence how we feel and how we think and even how we behave.

HOW OUR ATTITUDES AND BEHAVIORS SHAPE THE SOCIAL WORLD

Finally, social psychology also examines how our own attitudes and behaviors can shape the social world. In the process called **self-fulfilling prophecy**, people's expectations about someone else's traits influence how they act toward that person. In turn, these actions elicit the behavior that is expected. Self-fulfilling prophecy therefore leads people to confirm whatever beliefs they have, and makes it very difficult for these beliefs to be disconfirmed.

Self-fulfilling prophecy can have dramatic consequences in real-world situations. In Chapter 5, you'll learn about a study in which researchers told elementary school teachers that a test had revealed that certain students in their class would show a rise in intelligence scores in the upcoming school year (Rosenthal & Jacobson, 1968). In reality, these students who were identified as likely to show an increase in intelligence were chosen at random by the experimenters. However, students whose teachers believed they would show an increase in intelligence improved their scores by as much as 30 points. This is just one example of the power of self-fulfilling prophecy on creating behavior in real-world situations.

self-fulfilling prophecy the process by which people's expectations about a person lead them to elicit behavior that confirms these expectations

WHAT IS SOCIAL PSYCHOLOGY?

Concepts in Context

THEME	EXAMPLE
How we think about ourselves	DeShandra feels smarter when spending time with her high school friends than when spending time with her college friends.
How we think, feel, and act in the social world	Julio is very afraid of flying, even though his mother has assured him that flying is a safer way of traveling than driving.
How our attitudes and behaviors shape the social world	Pam believes her new co-worker is aloof and distant. She therefore doesn't ask him to join the other staff members for their regular after-work happy hour on Fridays. Pam then notices that he seems even more aloof and distant—thereby confirming her original opinion of him.

HOW HAS SOCIAL PSYCHOLOGY EVOLVED OVER TIME?

The field of social psychology is a relatively new one within the discipline of psychology; it was first established as a unique discipline within psychology only at the start of the twentieth century, with the publication of the first textbook in social psychology, written by Floyd Allport (1924). Early research in social psychology was heavily influenced by three major factors: behaviorism, Gestalt psychology, and historical events. Let's review each of these factors.

BEHAVIORISM

behaviorism a theory of learning that describes people's behavior as acquired through conditioning

In the early 20th century, psychologists who were interested in understanding people's behavior focused on the impact of positive and negative events on behavior. This discipline of **behaviorism** described people's behavior as determined in a very straightforward way. Behavior that was followed with a reward would continue. Behavior that was followed by punishment would not. This perspective was very influential in much of the early work understanding animal behavior. For example, renowned behaviorist B. F. Skinner trained pigeons to engage in various behaviors, such as turning in a circle, nodding, and "playing" the piano, using a reward to reinforce the behavior.

The behaviorist approach is still influential in social psychology today. As you'll learn in Chapter 6, the social learning perspective describes how people form attitudes and behaviors through both receiving reinforcements for their own attitudes and behaviors and watching other people's attitudes and behaviors. Children who watch movies where people are smoking are more likely to form positive attitudes toward smoking (as you'll learn in Chapter 6), children whose parents show prejudice toward people form negative attitudes about others (as you'll learn in Chapter 10), and children who watch aggressive cartoons are more likely to behave aggressively (as you'll learn in Chapter 11).

Although the behaviorist approach clearly explains some behavior, it ignores the role of people's thoughts, feelings, and attitudes, and thereby is too simplistic to explain other behaviors. Giving a child a reward for reading a book, for example, can actually backfire and reduce his or her interest in reading—because the child then sees reading as driven only by the prospect of a reward, and not as driven by the pure enjoyment of reading. This is one example of how people's interpretation of their behavior matters, as you'll learn in Chapter 3.

GESTALT PSYCHOLOGY

In part due to the limitations inherent in the behaviorist approach, other psychologists in the early 1900s examined the influence of people's *perceptions* of objects and events in the world, not simply their objective appearance. This subfield, called **Gestalt psychology**, emphasized the importance of looking at the whole object and how it appeared in people's minds, as opposed to looking at specific objective parts of the object. For example, in the classic *Dog Picture* example shown in the photo here, people don't recognize the dog by individually identifying all of its parts (head, paws, tail, and so on). In fact, if you focus on any specific part of the picture, it is very difficult to determine that these seemingly random marks are part of a dog. However, when you look at the picture all together, you simply perceive the dog as a single object all at once.

In the 1930s and 1940s, several psychologists who were trained in the Gestalt approach migrated to the United States in order to avoid the atrocities committed by the Nazis during World War II. These psychologists had a keen sense of the importance of perception in determining attitudes and behaviors, as well as first-hand experience in the dangers of social influence. One of these psychologists, Kurt Lewin, is often considered the founder of modern social psychology.

Lewin was born into a Jewish family in Poland, and served in the German army during World War I. Following a war injury, he attended the University of Berlin and received a PhD in 1916. Lewin initially worked within the schools of behavioral psychology, and then Gestalt school of psychology, but his largely Jewish reading group was forced to disband when Hitler came into power in Germany in 1933. Lewin then moved to the United States. Lewin's commitment to applying psychology to the problems of society led to the development of the M.I.T. Research Center for Group Dynamics. His research focused on the role of social perception in influencing people's behavior, the nature of group dynamics, and the factors contributing to stereotyping and prejudice (and you'll learn more about his work on these topics in Chapters 8, 9, and 10).

This picture is a classic example of the Gestalt perspective: it is virtually impossible to recognize the object by looking individually at a specific piece of the picture. But when you look at the picture all together, it is quite easy to recognize that these individual pieces together form a picture of a dog.

Gestalt psychology a theory that proposes objects are viewed holistic

HISTORICAL EVENTS

Historical events also influenced other young social psychologists. Muzafer Sherif grew up in Turkey, and then came to the United States to attend graduate school. He received a PhD in psychology in 1935 from Columbia University, and then returned to Turkey to teach at Ankara University. Sherif's outspoken opposition to the Nazi movement during World War II led to his imprisonment in a Turkish prison. Following complaints from colleagues in the United States Sherif was released from prison after four months, and he was then allowed to return to the United States. This personal experience with the dangerous powers of groups during times of war led to a series of studies on group influence, and in particular how introducing tasks that required cooperation between groups could reduce inter-group conflict. You'll read about Sherif's work on group processes and group conflict in Chapter 9.

Similarly, Stanley Milgram, a social psychologist who began his work in the late 1960s, was deeply affected by the events of Nazi Germany. Although many people blamed these events on the cruel and evil German people, Milgram wondered whether the people themselves were less to blame for the atrocities of Nazi Germany than the situation. While a professor at Yale University, Milgram conducted a series of experiments demonstrating the powerful role of the authority in leading to obedience. This research, which was greeted by much controversy when its results were first published, is one of the most famous studies in social psychology, and has been used to explain many real-world events, including mistreatment of prisoners during times of war. You'll read about Milgram's research on the power of authority in leading to obedience in Chapter 8.

Kurt Lewin, a German-Jewish professor living in Germany in the 1930s, is often considered the founder of social psychology.

In the 1940s, research by social psychologists Kenneth and Mamie Clark revealed that African American girls preferred playing with a Caucasian doll to playing with an African American doll. This study provided additional evidence for the dangers of segregation, and may have contributed to the famous Brown v. Board of Education decision in 1954 that led to school desegregation.

Laura Dwight/PhotoEdit

positive psychology a recent branch of psychology that studies individuals' strengths and virtues

| TABLE 1.2 | SIX VIRTUES AND COMPONENT CHARACTER STRENGTHS |

VIRTUES	COMPONENT CHARACTER STRENGTHS
Wisdom and knowledge	Creativity, curiosity, open-mindedness, love of learning, perspective
Courage	Bravery, persistence, integrity, vitality
Humanity	Love, kindness, social intelligence
Justice	Citizenship, fairness, leadership
Temperance	Forgiveness, humility, prudence, self-regulation
Transcendence	Appreciation of beauty and excellence, gratitude, hope, humor, spirituality

Source: Peterson, C., & Seligman, M. (2004). *Character Strengths and Virtues: A Handbook and Classification*. Washington, DC, New York, NY: American Psychological Association.

Social psychologists in the United States were also influenced by a series of legal decisions on racial segregation, culminating with the famous 1954 Brown v. Board of Education decision requiring integration of public schools (Pettigrew, 2004). Social psychologists served as expert witnesses about the psychological consequences of segregation as well as on how school desegregation should best be accomplished (see photo). Chief Justice Warren noted Kenneth Clark, a social psychologist who, with his wife, performed a series of studies on the detrimental effects of segregation on African American children's self-concepts, as one of the "modern authorities" on which the decision was based. This was the first time that psychological research was cited in a Supreme Court decision and was seen as influential in the Court's decision.

In part because early theory and research in social psychology was sparked by truly horrific events, such as the Holocaust, much of the early work in social psychology focused on explaining evil behavior, including aggression, stereotyping and prejudice, and obedience to authority. Recent research in social psychology focuses on positive behaviors, such as altruism, attraction, and leadership. In fact, a new subfield within social psychology, **positive psychology**, was established in 1998 to focus specifically on people's virtues and strengths (Peterson & Seligman, 2004). As shown in Table 1.2, researchers in this field examine the traits that are associated with life satisfaction and the predictors of healthy human functioning. Then, researchers design interventions to improve well-being.

Social psychologists continue to be interested in examining, and solving, real-world issues, including decreasing prejudice and discrimination, helping communities regulate the use of natural resources, and improving group decision making. To give you a sense of the multiple applications of social psychology to real-world issues, each chapter features several boxes that describe applications of social psychology to various domains, including education, the media, the law, health, and business. For example, in Chapter 6 you'll read about how people decide which candidate to vote for—and whether they actually vote. In Chapter 7 you'll read about the effects of media's images of smoking and drinking on such behaviors in real-world settings. In Chapter 10 you'll read about the effects of affirmative action on the education system.

HOW SOCIAL PSYCHOLOGY EVOLVED OVER TIME

Concepts in Context

INFLUENCE	EXAMPLE
Behaviorism	Liam's older brother always watches wrestling on television. Liam now also enjoys watching wrestling.
Gestalt psychology	Ricardo is not comfortable with the homophobic slurs that he often hears one of his friends use. However, Ricardo believes that his other friends aren't bothered by this offensive language, so he decides not to speak up about his concerns.
Historical events	After allowing her 2nd grade students to sit wherever they'd like in the classroom, Ms. O'Shea noticed a clear separation, and increased conflict, between the boys and the girls. She then created smaller groups, composed of boys and girls, to work on particular shared tasks. This effort decreased conflict, and increased cooperation, between the sexes.

IS SOCIAL PSYCHOLOGY REALLY JUST COMMON SENSE?

This focus on practical and real-world issues is one of the earliest tenets of social psychology, in part because initial research in this field was prompted by horrific real-world events, such as Nazi Germany. In fact, Kurt Lewin, the founder of modern social psychology, saw the inherent connection between social psychological theory and application as one of its greatest strengths: "There is nothing so practical as a good theory." Unfortunately, this ready application of social-psychological theories and research to daily life can also be a curse, in that people may view social psychology as simply "common sense." This section will describe the biases that lead people to see the field in this simplistic way, and the importance of using the scientific method and engaging in critical thinking to combat such tendencies.

THE "I KNEW IT ALL ALONG" PROBLEM

If I told you that scientific research suggests "opposites attract," you'd probably believe me. But you'd have had the same confidence, and agreement with the statement, if I'd said the reverse—"birds of a feather flock together." Similarly, if I told you, "absence makes the heart grow fonder," that would probably sound pretty plausible. But once again, so would the opposite expression, "out of sight, out of mind."

These examples illustrate a bias that people fall prey to frequently—the **hindsight bias**. Hindsight bias, or the "I knew it all along" phenomenon, refers to people's tendency to believe, once they've learned the outcome of something, that that particular outcome was obvious. Unfortunately, this bias can lead people to see social psychology as little more than commonsense because once they've heard something, they see it as obvious (Richard, Bond, & Stokes-Zoota, 2001; Slovic & Fischoff, 1977). What they don't recognize is that the exact opposite statement would also have sounded believable.

Here's an example of this problem. Let's say I offered to pay you either $20 to do something, or $1.00 to do the same behavior; which reward would make you like that behavior more? The behaviorist tradition believed that people would like engaging in behavior that was reinforced with a big reward more than behavior that was reinforced with a small reward—and you'd probably agree with this principle (surely you'd rather receive $20 than $1). But the results of

hindsight bias the tendency to see a given outcome as inevitable once the actual outcome is known

Social psychology has many applications to the legal system. Social psychologists have studied the influence of group pressures on jury deliberations, the effects of order in which information is presented in a trial, and cognitive errors that can lead to mistaken identifications of suspects.

Corbis/SUPERSTOCK

a classic experiment on the phenomenon of cognitive dissonance revealed the reverse; at least in some cases, people who receive $1 for engaging in a behavior report liking that behavior more than those who receive $20. You'll learn more about this experiment by Festinger and Carlsmith (1959) in Chapter 6.

USE OF SCIENTIFIC METHOD

scientific method a technique for investigating phenomena, acquiring new knowledge, and/or correcting previous knowledge

hypothesis a testable prediction about the conditions under which an event will occur

To examine the accuracy of these and other seemingly commonsense beliefs, social psychologists use the **scientific method**, a research method for investigating phenomena, acquiring new knowledge, and evaluating and integrating previous knowledge. Social psychologists form an educated guess, called **hypothesis**, about the relationship between events, and then examine the accuracy of this guess by collecting data, through observation and/or experimentation, to determine whether this belief is accurate or false (as you'll read about in Chapter 2). Social psychology therefore uses the same approach to evaluate hypotheses as other scientific fields, such as biology, chemistry, and physics.

This research process helps us find objective answers to questions about why people feel and think and behave the way that they do.

In some cases this research leads us to conclusions that are quite surprising. If, for example, I told you that people who receive a bronze medal (meaning third place) are happier than those who receive a silver medal (meaning second place), you might be quite puzzled. But this is exactly the finding of considerable research on errors we make in social cognition, as you'll read about in Chapter 5. Similarly, although we often assume that children from upper-class families will face fewer problems than those from low-income backgrounds, some research suggests exactly the opposite: one study found that adolescents from high-income communities actually report significantly more anxiety and depression than those from inner-city (and low-income) communities (Luthar & Latendresse, 2005). Moreover, adolescents from high-income communities also reported higher rates of substance abuse, including alcohol, cigarettes, marijuana, and other illegal drugs. Using the scientific method is therefore crucial, because it allows researchers to test whether our beliefs are actually correct.

However, in these cases this testing leads researchers to accept unsurprising findings as true. For example, a widely accepted finding within the field of social psychology is that men are more interested in casual sex than are women (read more about this in Chapter 12)!

To help you examine how research in social psychology contributes to our understanding of gender differences and similarities, most chapters will feature a Research Focus on Gender section that examines a particular issue related to gender in depth. For example, some intriguing research even suggests that economic principles can explain many of the often-noted gender differences in sexual behavior (Baumeister & Vohs, 2004). According to this view, men are interested in buying sex, because sex for men is largely a no-cost proposition. For women, the potential cost of sex is high (disease, pregnancy, even death from childbirth), and so women are interested in using sex to gain other resources. This view of sex as a resource that is "bought" by men and "sold" by women explains a number of gender differences in sexual attitudes and behavior, including the significant gender imbalance in prostitution (women just aren't interested in paying men for sex), the tendency for men to desire sex at earlier stages of relationships than women, and men's greater interest in "one-night-stands." For example, in one study researchers approached attractive men and women on campus and asked if they would be interested in engaging in sexual intercourse that evening (Clark & Hatfield, 1989). Although none of the women agreed to this proposition, 75 percent of the men agreed!

EMPHASIS ON CRITICAL THINKING

This focus on the scientific method also means that you should carefully and critically examine research findings presented in this book, and especially those that are presented in the media. In other words, don't just casually believe what you read or hear, but really think about the information and whether you can think of alternative explanations.

Imagine that you learn happy people make more money—which is true; you need to carefully examine what factors lead to this association. One possibility is that happy people engage in certain behaviors that lead them to experience greater work success—such as getting along better with colleagues or persisting through difficulties—which in turn leads to more financial success. But another, equally likely, possibility is that making more money leads to greater happiness. Still another possibility is that another factor altogether—perhaps optimism or social support—leads to both happiness and income.

Let's take another example. One study published in *The Archives of Pediatrics and Adolescent Medicine* reported that adolescents who frequently had dinner

Although research reveals that teenagers who have dinner with their family have better health habits and better grades, this finding does not prove that eating dinner together as a family *caused* those beneficial effects.

with their families reported lower levels of smoking, drinking, drug use, and depressive thoughts. These adolescents also had better grades (Eisenberg, Olson, Neumark-Sztainer, Story, & Bearinger, 2004). The media widely reported this study, and urged parents to have dinner with their kids as a way of preventing drug use and increasing grades. But let's think about whether this study demonstrates that having dinner as a family really has such a strong impact. Can you think of other explanations for this finding?

First, remember that this study shows that two things are *related* to each other, but it doesn't demonstrate that one thing, such as eating dinner together, *causes* another, such as less smoking and higher grades. One possibility is that parents who eat dinner with their children differ in some other way from those who don't eat dinner with their children, and that this other factor leads to this relationship. For example, maybe parents who are wealthier, or more religious, or more conscientious, spend more time with their children, and these other factors (wealth, religiosity, conscientiousness) lead to better grades and less smoking.

Another possibility is that simply spending time with children is associated with better outcomes, regardless of whether that time is during dinner specifically. In turn, research might show that parents who spend more time with their children each day, or each week, have children who have better grades and healthier behavior. In this case, it would be the amount of time that would influence these behaviors, not whether that time was during dinner.

Still another possibility is that children who engage in unhealthy behavior and show poor academic performance are less interested or willing to eat dinner with their families. Perhaps children who are "acting out" in some way refuse to eat dinner with their parents, even if their parents are home during the dinner hour. This example illustrates the principal of reverse causality, in which two factors are related in precisely the opposite direction than is hypothesized.

To help you learn how to critically examine information, Chapter 2 will describe various methods for conducting research in social psychology as well as various factors that influence research findings and the conclusions that can be drawn. Beginning with Chapter 3, each chapter will include a series of Questioning the Research queries that present a specific question about the results of a research study. Think carefully about your answers—this is an opportunity to sharpen your critical thinking skills.

WHY SOCIAL PSYCHOLOGY IS NOT JUST COMMON SENSE

Concepts in Context

THEMES	EXAMPLE
The "I knew it all along" problem	After reading a newspaper article describing very aggressive behavior by players during a football team, Jeremy comes to the conclusion that these players must be very aggressive kids. His older sister, however, then points out that many situational factors—such as high levels of physical arousal and the anonymity of the football uniform—may have contributed to this behavior, meaning that we can't assume the athletes were generally aggressive. Both of these explanations sound equally plausible to Jeremy.
Use of the scientific method	Mei-Mei learns in her psychology class that women typically eat more when they are with other women than when they are eating with men. Mei-Mei is surprised by this finding, and therefore decides to measure how much she notices female students eating in these two situations.
Emphasis on critical thinking	Naomi hears about a new book that profiles a number of highly successful people who were C-average college students. Although this book claims that C-average students are particularly successful in life, Naomi is skeptical about whether these students are actually more successful than those with a higher average.

HOW IS SOCIAL PSYCHOLOGY CONNECTED TO OTHER FIELDS?

As described at the start of this chapter, the field of social psychology examines how people think about themselves; how people think, feel, and act in the social world; and how people's attitudes and behavior shape the social world. But these, and related, questions are also examined both within different disciplines in the larger field of psychology as well as within other disciplines outside of psychology. Let's learn about some of these connections.

LINKS TO FIELDS WITHIN PSYCHOLOGY

Social psychology is closely connected to several disciplines within the field of psychology, including personality psychology, clinical psychology, and cognitive psychology.

Personality psychology.   Personality psychologists focus on the role of *individual differences*, meaning aspects of people's personality that make them different from other people, in explaining how different people feel and behave in distinct ways. We often use personality descriptions to describe other people in our social world—my friend Darren is extraverted, my co-worker Deirdra is arrogant, my boss Duane is neurotic.

Whereas personality psychologists emphasize the role of individual differences between people in influencing attitudes, thoughts, and behaviors, social psychologists emphasize the role of the situation. For example, if you observe a person driving very aggressively, you might immediately judge that person's personality in a not-very-nice way ("She's a careless person." "She only thinks about herself."). A social psychologist, on the other hand, would try to examine the role of situational factors in producing that behavior; perhaps the person is late for a job interview, or perhaps that person is taking a sick child to the hospital. When you consider the situation (the woman was taking her sick child to the hospital), that might influence your attitude toward the aggressive driver. Do you still judge her personality as careless or self-centered?

Social psychologists examine how different people react to different situations in distinct ways. This part of social psychology focuses specifically on the role of aspects of personality, such as self-esteem, need for cognition, and prosocial orientation, in influencing behavior in a given situation. Issues of personality will be addressed throughout this book. For example, in Chapter 7 you'll read about how different people are persuaded by different types of advertising messages, and in Chapter 13 you'll read about how people with high levels of empathy are more likely to donate money to someone in need.

Clinical psychology.   Clinical psychology is probably the best-known field within the larger field of psychology. When people think about the field of psychology, they often think about the role of clinical psychologists in diagnosing and treating mental health problems. Clinical psychology focuses on understanding and treating people with psychological disorders such as schizophrenia, depression, and phobias.

Social psychology also examines issues that are highly relevant for clinical psychology. Some social psychologists examine

Social psychology examines factors that predict interpersonal attraction and relationship satisfaction.

Photosindia.com/SUPERSTOCK

how the presence of very thin female models in the media can influence women's attitudes about their own bodies and thereby contribute to eating disorders (Chapter 3). In Chapter 4 you'll learn why people who blame their failures on themselves are at greater risk of experiencing depression than those who blame their failures on other people. Other social psychologists examine strategies for promoting better psychological and physical health, including ways of reducing rates of smoking (Chapter 6), strategies of increasing condom use (see Chapter 7), and methods of increasing relationship satisfaction (see Chapter 12).

Cognitive psychology. Cognitive psychology examines mental processes, including thinking, remembering, learning, and reasoning. For example, a cognitive psychologist might examine why people are more likely to buy a $200 sweater that is on sale for $50 than a sweater that is simply priced at $50, why some people have higher IQs than others, and why we sometimes "remember" things as having happened when they really didn't happen.

The *social cognitive perspective* is a combination of social psychology and cognitive psychology. This perspective refers to how people think about themselves and the social world, with a particular focus on how they make judgments and decisions about the world. In some cases our thoughts can lead us to make good and accurate decisions. In other cases, however, our thinking can lead us astray. For example, which of the following poses the greatest threat to children's safety: kidnapping by strangers or car accidents? Although many parents worry most about the first event, many, many more children are killed in motor vehicle accidents each year (often because they are not wearing a seatbelt or riding in a car seat) than are killed by a kidnapper. We'll learn more about this and other errors in thinking in Chapter 5.

LINKS TO OTHER FIELDS

Social psychology is a distinct field within psychology, but it shares a number of features with other fields within psychology as well as with other disciplines. This section will examine the links between social psychology and sociology, biology, anthropology, and economics.

Sociology. Sociology examines general rules and theories about groups, ranging from very small groups to large societies, and specifically how such groups affect people's attitudes and behavior. Sociologists are likely to focus on broad group-level variables such as culture, social class, and ethnicity. For example, a sociologist might examine why rates of homicide in the United States are much higher than in other countries.

Similarly, social psychologists study how individual people behave in groups, as well as how one's group or culture can influence a person's behavior. In Chapter 11 you'll learn why homicide rates are higher in some subcultures within the United States than in others. However, social psychologists are more likely to focus on the effects of immediate and specific variables, such as mood, temperature, and other people, on attitudes and behaviors, and to examine the influence of the group on the individual, not simply the effect of the group in general.

WOULD YOU BELIEVE... Our Genes Can Influence Our Attitudes Toward the Death Penalty and Frequency Aggression? Throughout this book these Would You Believe queries will present a surprising finding demonstrated by research in social psychology. The two examples posed in this box are examples of contributions to social psychology made by the relatively new field of biology called *behavioral genetics*, which studies how genetics influences human behavior. You will learn about new research showing how behavioral traits may be based in our genes, and thus can be inherited from one's parents. In Chapter 6, you'll learn about the influence of genetics on our attitudes, and in Chapter 11 you'll learn about the influence of genetics on rates of aggression.

Biology. The field of biology examines the structure, function, growth, origin, and evolution of living things. Biologists examine how species evolve over time, the role of genes in influencing traits and attributes, and how individuals grow and develop over time. A biologist might examine how a parent's level of aggression influences his or her child's level of aggression, and why men and women look for different characteristics in sexual partners.

The link between social psychology and biology has received increasing attention in recent years as research in social psychology has examined the role of biology in influencing such factors as aggression, altruism, and attraction. The subfield of *evolutionary psychology* examines how biological factors can influence people's behavior; it proposes that certain types of behaviors are "selected for" and hence have survived over time. In Chapter 11, you'll learn how evolutionary pressures influence rates of aggression, and why men tend to show higher levels of aggression than women. In Chapter 12 you'll read about how evolutionary psychologists explain gender differences in preferences for different characteristics in a dating partner as well as why men and women may find that different types of infidelity trigger their jealousy. Chapter 13 examines the influence of evolutionary pressures on whom people help—and why, in an emergency, we favor young people over older ones, and genetically close relatives (siblings, children, parents) over more distantly related ones (cousins, aunts and uncles, grandparents).

The influence of biology on people's thoughts and feelings is also studied within the subfield of **social neuroscience**, an interdisciplinary field that emerged in the early 1990s. This field examines how factors in the social world influence activity in the brain, as well as how neural processes influence attitudes and behavior (Cacioppo et al., 2007; Harmon-Jones & Devine, 2003; Heatherton, Macrae, & Kelley, 2004). This increased focus on the role of the brain in influencing people's attitudes, thoughts, and behavior is driven in part by the increasing availability of new techniques for studying brain activity, including positron emission tomography (PET) and functional magnetic resonance imaging (fMRI). Both of these techniques measure blood flow to particular parts of the brain (which is thought to reflect activity), but the fMRI technique does not involve radioactive materials (as the PET scan does) and provides clearer images.

As a result of technological advances, an increasing number of social psychologists are investigating the interaction between brain activity and experiences in the social world. For example, in Chapter 10, you'll learn that different parts of the brain are activated when people look at faces of those who are their same race versus a different race (Hart, Whalen, Shin, McInerney, Fischer, & Rauch, 2000). In Chapter 12, you'll learn that particular parts of the brain are most active when people are thinking about people they love (Fisher, Aron, Mashek, Li, & Brown, 2002). Given the growing importance of the field of social neuroscience in social psychology, each chapter in this book will describe a specific research study that uses such techniques. The Research Focus on Neuroscience box describes a study showing that physical and social pain both activate the same part of the brain.

social neuroscience a subfield of social psychology examining how factors in the social world influence activity in the brain, as well as how neural processes influence attitudes and behavior

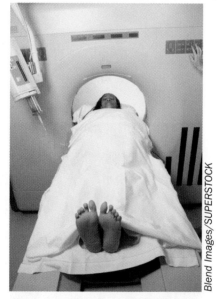

The technique used for fMRI imaging involves measuring the blood oxygen level in a given part of the brain, with the assumption that more blood oxygen level is a sign of greater activity. Imagine that you are picking up a stack of heavy books, or groceries, in your arms. This muscular activity would lead to a greater flow of blood oxygen to your arms, because your arms need assistance to manage this level of exertion *(Cacioppo et al., 2003)*.

RESEARCH FOCUS ON NEUROSCIENCE
How Rejection Looks in the Brain

To help you understand how the rapidly growing field of neuroscience contributes to our knowledge about social psychological theories, most chapters will feature a Research Focus on Neuroscience section that examines a particular research study in neuroscience in depth. For example, one compelling example of how techniques in neuroscience can help psychologists understand social processes comes from a clever research study conducted by Naomi Eisenberger and her colleagues (Eisenberger, Lieberman, & Williams, 2003). Participants in this study underwent brain scans (participants were in fMRI machines) while they played a virtual ball-tossing game (called "CyberBall") in which they believed they were tossing a ball to two other participants. After a few trials, the other two participants suddenly stopped throwing the ball to the one participant, which led that participant to feel he or she was being ignored and excluded. Interestingly, the part of the brain that was active when participants experienced these negative emotions was precisely the same part of the brain that is activated when people experience physical pain. This research suggests that both social and physical pain share a common neurological basis.

"Hey, I'm just happy to be making an obscene amount of money."

Anthropology. Anthropology examines the concept of culture, and specifically the role of culture in influencing people's attitudes and behavior. For example, anthropologists study the social significance of food in different cultures, the impact of culture on gender differences, and how cultures vary in their interpretations of the links between health and illness.

Social psychology originated in Western cultures, and hence much of the early work in this area was conducted by Western researchers using people living in Western cultures. However, in the last two decades social psychologists have shown increasing interest in examining the impact of culture on people's thoughts, feelings, and behaviors. The impact of culture on theory and research in social psychology will be described in detail in the final section of each chapter. For example, you'll learn about the impact of culture on rates of aggression (Chapter 11), definitions of love (Chapter 12), and frequency of helping behavior (Chapter 13).

Economics. Economics studies how people make trade-offs between scarce resources and how they choose between various alternatives. For example, an economist might examine how people choose between two different jobs, or the factors that lead a person to spend money now versus save it for the future. Economists also examine why people make choices that do not maximize their well-being—such as giving money to charitable causes instead of using it themselves—and why people make cognitive errors. For example, a person may choose one medical treatment when it's presented as the numbers of years of life to be gained but turn down that medical treatment if it's presented in terms of years lost.

In particular, the field of *behavioral economics* applies research on social, cognitive, and emotional biases to understand how people make economic decisions (Ariely & Norton, 2007; Thaler, 1980). In 2002, Professor Daniel Kahneman of Princeton University received the Nobel Prize in Economics (although his field is psychology) in large part due to his focus on issues at the intersection of psychology and economics, including fairness in the marketplace (Kahneman, Knetsch, & Thaler, 1986a, 1986b, 1990). In Chapter 5 you'll learn about Kahneman's research on errors in social decision making.

Social psychologists also focus on how people make particular choices as well as the costs and benefits of various alternatives. In Chapter 9, you'll learn how people make decisions that will benefit themselves versus benefit their broader group. In Chapter 12, you'll learn that physically attractive people experience many benefits that others do not, including higher starting salaries and bigger raises. In Chapter 13 you'll learn about the cost-benefit analysis people perform before they decide to help a person in need.

Professor Daniel Kahneman of Princeton University won the Nobel Prize in 2003 for his work, in collaboration with the late Amos Tversky, on decision making.

EXAMPLES OF THE LINK BETWEEN SOCIAL PSYCHOLOGY AND OTHER FIELDS

FIELDS WITHIN PSYCHOLOGY	SAMPLE RESEARCH QUESTION
Personality psychology	Do people who are high in neuroticism hold more negative attitudes toward others?
Clinical psychology	Do depressed people see the world in a more pessimistic way?
Cognitive psychology	Do people remember more negative behaviors performed by out-group members than by in-group members?

FIELDS OUTSIDE OF PSYCHOLOGY	SAMPLE RESEARCH QUESTION
Sociology	How do divorce rates differ as a function of ethnicity?
Anthropology	How do cultures vary in their views of ideal body shape and size?
Biology	How do evolutionary factors predict altruistic behavior?
Economics	How does paying students for reading influence frequency of reading in the future?

CULTURE

HOW DOES SOCIAL PSYCHOLOGY APPLY ACROSS CULTURES AND SUBCULTURES?

Most of the early research in social psychology was conducted almost entirely by researchers in Western cultures, such as the United States, Canada, Australia, and Western Europe. These researchers studied people and events in their own country, largely for convenience, and assumed that their general findings would apply equally well to people and events across different cultures. However, more recent research reveals that culture can have a dramatic impact on how people think about themselves and the social world (Matsumoto & Yoo, 2006). This **sociocultural perspective** describes people's behavior and mental processes as shaped in part by their social and/or cultural contact, including race, gender, and nationality. This section will examine the distinction between different types of cultures and how culture can impact theories and findings in social psychology.

sociocultural perspective a perspective describing people's behavior and mental processes as shaped in part by their social and/or cultural contact, including race, gender, and nationality

INDIVIDUALISTIC VERSUS COLLECTIVISTIC CULTURES

The United States and other Western cultures, such as Canada, Australia, and Great Britain, are **individualistic** or independent cultures, meaning cultures in which independence, self-reliance, autonomy, and personal identity are prided (Markus & Kitayama, 1991, 1994; Triandis, 1989). Independent cultures describe the self as a unique set of attributes and traits, and see people's behavior as emerging largely from such traits. A person may, for example, be described as hostile, optimistic, and/or conscientious, and these traits, in turn,

individualistic a view of the self as distinct, autonomous, self-contained, and endowed with unique attributes

"Excuse me. We're Americans. Would you give us your table?"

collectivistic a view of the self as part of a larger social network, including family, friends, and co-workers

lead to specific patterns of behavior. Individuals in individualistic cultures focus on expressing their own needs, goals, and preferences. American culture, including historical events (e.g., American independence from Britain, the ending of slavery in the United States) and popular culture (e.g., *Good Will Hunting*, *The Firm*, *John Q Public*), emphasize the strength of the individual against the group. People are told to follow their dreams, struggle against blind conformity and obedience, and be all they can be. Groups are often seen as destructive forces that pressure and intimidate individuals.

Other cultures, in contrast, are **collectivistic** or interdependent in their orientation, and are focused on interdependence, harmony, cooperation, and social identity (Markus & Kitayama, 1994; Triandis, 1989). Many Eastern countries, such as Japan, Thailand, Korea, and India, are collectivistic. In these cultures, the self is viewed as fundamentally integrated with one's relationships and social group, and people focus on maintaining interdependence with others. One's thoughts, feelings, and behaviors are all influenced by those of one's group. In many collectivistic cultures a desire for independence is seen as unnatural and immature, and people may even fear being separated and different from others. Asserting one's unique needs and desires interrupts feelings of group solidarity and harmony, and hence people are willing to sacrifice their own particular wants in favor of the group. These distinctions are illustrated in Table 1.3.

TABLE 1.3	DIFFERENCES BETWEEN INDIVIDUALISTIC AND COLLECTIVISTIC VIEWS OF THE SELF

INDIVIDUALISTIC	COLLECTIVISTIC
Be unique	Belong, fit in
Express self	Occupy one's proper place
Realize internal attributes	Engage in appropriate action
Promote own goals	Promote others' goals
Be direct; "say what's on your mind"	Be indirect; "read other's mind"

These examples illustrate the distinction between how people from individualistic versus collectivistic cultures see themselves.

Source: Markus, H., & Kitayama, S. (1991, April). Culture and the self: Implications for cognition, emotion, and motivation. *Psychological Review*, 98, 224-253.

Culture influences how people see and act in the social world, and even how people see themselves. In one study Malaysian, Australian, and British adults were asked to complete the "Who are you?" test (Bochner, 1994). This test simply asks people to respond 20 times to the open-ended prompt "Who are you?" and is a commonly used approach for measuring how someone sees oneself. Sixty-one percent of the British responses and 68% of the Australian responses focused on personal qualities and traits, such as "I am tall," "I am outgoing," and "I want to be a nurse." Only 48% of the Malaysian responses described personal qualities and traits. In contrast, 41% of the Malaysian responses referred to group memberships, including family relationships, religious group memberships, and occupational group memberships. These responses included "I am the youngest child in my family," "I am a member of a tennis club," and "I am a student."

What's Your Cultural Orientation?

Self-Construal Scale

INSTRUCTIONS: *Rate your agreement with each of these items on a 1 to 7 scale, with 1 meaning "strongly disagree" and 7 meaning "strongly agree."*

☐ **1.** My happiness depends very much on the happiness of others.

☐ **2.** It is important for me to maintain harmony within my group.

☐ **3.** The well-being of my co-workers is important to me.

☐ **4.** I feel good when I cooperate with others.

☐ **5.** Winning is everything.

☐ **6.** It annoys me when other people perform better than I do.

☐ **7.** I enjoy working in situations involving competition with others.

☐ **8.** It is important for me to do my job better than others.

SCORING: Add up your scores on items #1 to #4. Then add up your scores on items #5 to #8.

INTERPRETATION: The first four items measure orientation toward collectivism. The last four items measure orientation toward individualism. People with a higher score on the first set of items than the second are more oriented toward collectivism, whereas people with a higher score on the second set of items are more oriented toward individualism (Singelis et al., 1995).

Only 18% of the British and 19% of the Australian responses described group memberships.

Research comparing statements made by Americans versus Indians reveals similar findings (Dhawan, Roseman, Naidu, & Rettek, 1995). The majority of statements (65%) made by Americans describe their own attributes and traits. Only 34% of those made by Indians describe themselves. Moreover, even within the general category of self-evaluation, Americans describe feelings of self-worth and psychological attributes. In contrast, Indians are more likely to write about positive states. Table 1.4 describes another example of the distinction in self-description by culture.

Not surprisingly, culture also influences the prevalence of different types of messages (Morling & Lamoreaux, 2008). One recent study analyzed whether the wording used in products across different cultures reflected individualism (such

TABLE 1.4 SELF-DESCRIPTIONS IN DIFFERENT CULTURES

CULTURE	SIX-YEAR-OLD SELF-DESCRIPTION
American response	I am a wonderful and very smart person. A funny and hilarious person. A kind and caring person. A good-grade person who is going to go to Cornell. A helpful and cooperative girl.
Chinese response	I'm a human being. I'm a child. I like to play cards. I'm my mom and dad's child, my grandma and grandpa's grandson. I'm a hard-working good child.

These two quotes illustrate the differences in self-description that are seen in six-year-olds from the United States and from China. The first quote describes the child's own traits and attributes, whereas the second quote describes the child's social roles and relationships.

Source: Wang, Q. (2006). Earliest recollections of self and others in European American and Taiwanese young adults. *Psychological Science, 17*, 708–714.

Hazel Markus, a professor of psychology at Stanford University, is one of the leading experts in the field of cultural psychology.

as uniqueness, goals, self-knowledge, privacy) or collectivism (such as belonging, harmony, relatedness, hierarchy). The products examined included popular song lyrics, advertisements, and children's books. As predicted, products that came from Western cultures, such as the United States, used more individualistic, and less collectivistic, words than products that came from collectivistic cultures, such as Korea, Japan, China, and Mexico.

THE IMPACT OF CULTURE

Cross-cultural research, meaning research examining similar theories and findings across different cultures, sometimes reveals that people across different cultures see the world in largely the same way. For example, people in different cultures share views about what is attractive. Across different cultures, prominent cheekbones, thin eyebrows, and big eyes are commonly viewed as attractive (Cunningham, Roberts, Barbee, Druen, & Wu, 1995; Langlois, Kalahonis, Rubenstein, Larson, Hallam, & Smoot, 2000).

In other cases, findings from research in Western cultures, such as the United States, differ dramatically from those in other cultures. For example, in addition, and as described previously in this chapter, the personality traits associated with attractiveness vary considerably across different cultures. In the United States "what is beautiful is good," whereas in Korea "what is beautiful is honest." One of the common findings in research conducted in Western cultures is that people tend to focus on the role of the person in influencing behavior more than on the role of the situation. As you'll learn in detail in Chapter 4, the fundamental attribution error explains why if we notice a car following too closely behind us or driving too fast, we tend to make a personal or dispositional attribution for this behavior ("that driver is a jerk!"), and not a situational attribution ("that driver must be in a hurry").

People across cultures share relatively common views about what is attractive. Across different cultures, prominent cheekbones, thin eyebrows, and big eyes are commonly viewed as attractive (Cunningham, Roberts, Barbee, Druen, & Wu, 1995; Langlois, Kalahonis, Rubenstein, Larson, Hallam, & Smoot, 2000).

AN EXAMPLE OF CROSS-CULTURAL DIFFERENCES IN DEFINING SUCCESS

A boat docked in a tiny Mexican village. An American tourist complimented the Mexican fisherman on the quality of his fish and asked how long it took him to catch them.

"Not very long," answered the fisherman.

"But then, why didn't you stay out longer and catch more?" asked the American.

The Mexican explained that his small catch was sufficient to meet his needs and those of his family.

The American asked, "But what do you do with the rest of your time?"

"I sleep late, fish a little, play with my children, and take a siesta with my wife. In the evenings, I go into the village to see my friends, have a few drinks, play the guitar, and sing a few songs . . . I have a full life."

The American interrupted, "I have an MBA from Harvard and I can help you! You should start by fishing longer every day. You can then sell the extra fish you catch. With the extra revenue, you can buy a bigger boat."

"And after that?" asked the Mexican.

"With the extra money the larger boat will bring, you can buy a second one and a third one and so on until you have an entire fleet of trawlers. Instead of selling your fish to a middle man, you can then negotiate directly with the processing plants and maybe even open your own plant. You can then leave this little village and move to Mexico City, Los Angeles, or even New York City! From there you can direct your huge new enterprise."

"How long would that take?" asked the Mexican.

"Twenty, perhaps twenty-five years," replied the American.

"And after that?"

"Afterwards? Well, my friend, that's when it gets really interesting," answered the American, laughing. "When your business gets really big, you can start selling stocks and make millions!"

"Millions? Really? And after that?" said the Mexican.

"After that you'll be able to retire, live in a tiny village near the coast, sleep late, play with your children, catch a few fish, take a siesta with your wife, and spend your evenings drinking and enjoying your friends."

This story illustrates differences in how different cultures define success—is success gaining financial wealth or spending time with family and friends? People in individualistic cultures are more likely to define success in terms of individual accomplishments, such as acquiring great wealth, whereas those in collectivistic cultures are more likely to define success in terms of interpersonal relationships.

Although this general tendency was assumed to represent a general perceptual bias, cross-cultural research indicates that this bias is not commonly seen across all cultures. In fact, in many collectivistic cultures, people focus more on the role of the situation in influencing behavior than on the role of the person (Choi, Nisbett, & Norenzayan, 1999). This is just one example of how the knowledge we gain from studying one culture may not apply equally well in a different culture, and hence researchers need to test theories across different cultures instead of simply assuming that people in different cultures will all respond in the same way. The following example describes how cultures may differ in other ways as well, such as in how they define success.

THE IMPACT OF SUBCULTURE

Other research on culture examines not differences between people who live in different countries, but rather people who live in different subcultures within a given country. These subcultures, or different groups, could be based on region of a given country, socioeconomic status, or religion (Kashima, Kokubo, Boxall, Yamaguchi, & Macrae, 2004; Kitayama, Mesquita, & Karasawa, 2006). For example, you'll learn about the impact of the Southern versus Northern subculture on rates of aggression in Chapter 11.

Another subculture that could impact individuals' attitudes and behavior is level of education. In line with this view, research indicates that level of education does impact how people see and interact in the world in multiple ways. For example, in one study, researchers examined data collected from over 17,000 people in the U.S. Census Bureau's Survey of Public Participation in the Arts (Snibbe & Markus, 2005). This survey asked about participants' level of education as well as their liking of different types of music. As shown in Figure 1.1, college-educated Americans liked rock music more than country music, whereas Americans with less than a high school degree liked country music more than rock music.

Why should level of education influence the type of music a person likes? These researchers hypothesized that different types of music include different themes,

FIGURE 1.1

DOES LEVEL OF EDUCATION ATTAINED INFLUENCE MUSIC PREFERENCE?

Researchers examined responses to U.S. Census survey questions about people's education levels and what kind of music they liked. The researchers expected that the individualistic themes common in rock music might appeal to those with high education, while the themes of honesty and loyalty common in country music might appeal to those with lower education. The hypothesis was confirmed: The percentage of participants who liked rock music generally increased by level of educational attainment, whereas the percentage of participants who liked country music generally decreased by level of educational attainment.

Source: Snibbe, A., & Markus, H. (2005). You can't always get what you want: Educational attainment, agency, and choice. *Journal of Personality and Social Psychology, 88*, 703–720.

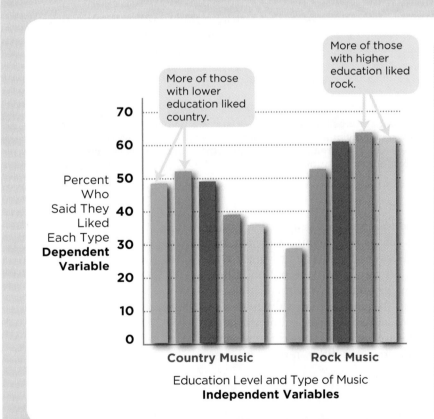

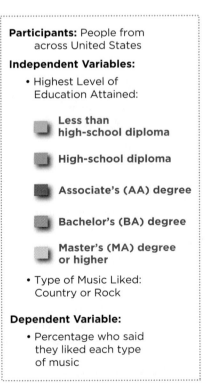

TABLE 1.5 THEMES OF COUNTRY AND ROCK SONGS

TYPE OF MUSIC	THEME	LYRIC
Country	Honesty, loyalty	"Stand by your man." "Never gonna let you down, never gonna run around."
Rock	Uniqueness	"Everyone could see what a prize he was." "I'll be your hope, I'll be your dream, I'll be your fantasy."

These lyrics from country and rock songs clearly reflect different themes, which may help explain why individuals with different levels of education may have distinct music preferences.

Source: Snibbe, A., & Markus, H. (2005). You can't always get what you want: Educational attainment, agency, and choice. *Journal of Personality and Social Psychology, 88*, 703–720.

and that these themes appealed to people with different types of orientations. As shown in Table 1.5, country songs are more likely to include themes related to interpersonal relationships, such as honesty and loyalty. Rock songs, on the other hand, are more likely to include themes related to uniqueness.

To help students understand how culture impacts the findings of social psychology, each chapter in this book ends with a section describing how research findings may differ across cultures. These sections will help you see which facts in social psychology are truly universal and which ones are largely a function of culture.

The Big Picture

INTRODUCTION

As described at the start of this chapter, social psychology examines three distinct but interrelated topics:

How the social world influences how we think about ourselves

How the social world influences our thoughts, attitudes, and behaviors

How our attitudes and behavior shape the social world around us

Study organizer. To help you focus on these broad themes within social psychology, each chapter will end with "The Big Picture" table giving specific examples of how the topics addressed in each chapter relate to these broad themes and contribute to an understanding of the big picture of social psychology.

This chapter has described the nature of social psychology, including the topics addressed within this field, how it has evolved over time, and how it is connected to other fields.

YOU LEARNED **What is social psychology?** This section examined the definition of social psychology, and the topics addressed within this discipline. These topics include how we think about ourselves; how we think, feel, and act in the social world; and how our attitudes and behaviors shape the social world.

YOU LEARNED **How has social psychology evolved over time?** This section described how the field of social psychology has evolved over time. This discipline was heavily influenced by behaviorism, Gestalt psychology, and historical events.

YOU LEARNED **Is social psychology really just common sense?** This section examined whether social psychology is just "common sense." You learned about the "I knew it all along" problem, and the importance of using the scientific method to test theories and hypotheses within this field. This section also described how to use critical thinking to test information you are given.

YOU LEARNED **How is social psychology connected to other fields?** This section examined how social psychology is connected to fields within and outside of psychology. First, it described the connection between social psychology and other fields within psychology, including personality psychology, clinical psychology, and cognitive psychology. Next, you learned how social psychology is connected to fields outside of psychology, including sociology, biology, anthropology, and economics.

YOU LEARNED **How does social psychology apply across cultures and subcultures?** This section examined the impact of culture on theory and research in social psychology. You learned about the impact of culture as well as the distinction between individualistic and collectivistic cultures.

KEY TERMS

behaviorism 8

collectivistic 20

fundamental attribution error 6

Gestalt psychology 9

hindsight bias 11

hypothesis 12

individualistic 19

positive psychology 10

scientific method 12

self-fulfilling prophecy 7

self-perception 4

self-presentation 5

social cognition 6

social influence 6

social neuroscience 17

social perception 6

social psychology 4

sociocultural perspective 19

QUESTIONS FOR REVIEW

1. Describe three distinct issues examined by social psychology.
2. How have historical events influenced theory and research in social psychology?
3. Describe the "I knew it all along" phenomenon, and one strategy for critically examining information.
4. How is social psychology connected to two disciplines within psychology, and two disciplines outside of psychology?
5. Describe the major distinction between individualistic and collectivistic cultures.

TAKE ACTION!

At the end of each chapter, you'll read about five distinct ways in which you could put the information you've learned to practical use in the real world. These Take Action! ideas could include strategies for helping motivate your child to clean his or her room (Chapter 3), improving the effectiveness of sales techniques (Chapter 7), or working effectively with other students on a group project (Chapter 9).

RESEARCH CONNECTIONS

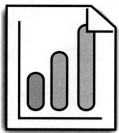

To help you gain experience in conducting and evaluating research, each chapter will end with a series of activities that will give you exposure to research methods and techniques in social psychology. Additional activities and interactive tool are available on Wiley plus. These activities will fall into three categories: "Participate in Research"; "Test a Hypothesis"; and "Design a Study."

WILEY PLUS

Participate in Research

These activities will give you research experience as a participant—meaning the person who participates in a study. In these cases, you will complete a study in social psychology from the perspective of the participant, which will help give you a sense of exactly what participants themselves experience.

Test a Hypothesis

These activities will give you experience from the perspective of a researcher. In these activities, you'll be given a specific hypothesis to test that relates to a topic described in that chapter.

Design a Study

This final type of activity will give you a chance to create your own study. You'll be able to choose the type of study you want to conduct (self-report, observational/naturalistic, or experimental, and form your own hypothesis and approach to testing this hypothesis. This type of hands-on experience with research will help you better understand the challenges of conducting research in social psychology.

Media
CONNECTIONS
The Growing Use of
Web-based Experiments

2

Research Methods

WHAT YOU'LL LEARN

How do researchers in social psychology test their ideas?

What are the types of correlational research methods?

 RESEARCH FOCUS ON NEUROSCIENCE
Facial Movements as a Measure of Discrimination

How do you conduct experimental research?

What are the ethical issues involved in conducting research?

How does CULTURE influence research findings?

Did you ever wonder?

Several highly publicized studies have shown that SUVs are responsible for more deaths in car accidents each year than smaller, lighter cars, including subcompacts (Volkswagen Jettas, Honda Civics) and mini-vans (Ford Windstar, Chevrolet Venture; Gladwell, 2004). For example, per million cars on the road, drivers of Volkswagen Jettas cause 70 deaths a year, drivers of Ford Windstars cause 72 deaths per year, and drivers of Ford Explorers cause 148 deaths per year. These statistics are often used to emphasize the inherent danger of SUVs compared to other cars. However, can you think of another explanation for this association? How about the typical person who drives each of these cars? Well, a typical driver of a mini-van is probably a mother with children—who just might be a slower and more cautious driver than the typical driver of an SUV—who might be male, younger, and single (all of which are associated with higher rates of accidents). In fact, if you look at deaths caused by drivers of less expensive subcompact cars, they are even worse than those caused by SUVs: drivers of Chevrolet Cavaliers cause 186

Environment
CONNECTIONS
The Hazards
of Hot Weather

Health
CONNECTIONS
Evaluating Abstinence-
only Sex Education

Law
CONNECTIONS
The Challenges of Studying
Drinking and Driving

deaths each year, drivers of Dodge Neons cause 199 deaths each year, and drivers of Pontiac Sunfires cause 202 deaths each year. This illustrates the important difference between a correlation between two variables and research that shows that one variable caused the other. This chapter will examine research methods such as correlational studies. Later in the chapter, you'll find out why SUVs may not be as dangerous as you think. In addition, you'll find out . . .

NewsCom

Q A Why are children who watch violent cartoons more likely to hit their siblings?

Q A Why do people underestimate their risky behavior when answering surveys?

Q A Why do women eat less when they are talking with an attractive man?

Q A Why can college students who pretend to act as prison guards become violent very quickly?

Q A Why do women in the United States give more extreme answers to questions about dating than women in Iran?

These are typical questions examined within the field of social psychology using different types of research methods.

Social psychology is a science, and therefore findings in social psychology are based on the scientific method. Scientific research describes a phenomenon (are people more aggressive when it is very hot outside?), makes *predictions* about it (will the rate of homicide increase during the summer?), and *explains* why it happens (why do people act more aggressively when it is hot?). In this chapter, you'll learn how to design research studies to examine questions in social psychology. You will learn the advantages and disadvantages of different research methods, ethical issues to consider when conducting research, and how culture can influence research findings.

HOW DO RESEARCHERS IN SOCIAL PSYCHOLOGY TEST THEIR IDEAS?

What are the effects on children of watching violence on television? This is a question of great importance to parents, and this question can be answered by research in social psychology. In a classic study, researchers were interested in examining the power of modeling on aggressive behavior (Bandura, Ross, & Ross, 1963). Children were shown a video of an adult throwing around, punching, and kicking an inflatable Bobo doll. The video was very unusual and specific in terms of the behavior and words modeled (e.g., the adult sat on the doll, punched it in the nose, hit him with a wooden mallet, and said "Sock him in the nose" and "Hit him down"). The researcher then observed the children's behavior following a frustrating event—such as being shown some very attractive toys but then being told that these toys were being saved for another child, and given some less desirable toys to play with. As expected, children who'd watched the adult aggress against the Bobo doll replicated much of that behavior, even using the same words and actions. This study provides powerful evidence that children model what they see on television (and you'll read more about this in Chapter 6).

This study, and other studies within the field of social psychology, was designed using the scientific method. This section will describe each of the steps involved in the research process (see Figure 2.1):

- Step 1: Form a question
- Step 2: Search the literature
- Step 3: Form a hypothesis
- Step 4: Create an operational definition
- Step 5: Collect and analyze data
- Step 6: Propose and/or revise a theory

FORM A QUESTION

All research in social psychology as well as in other scientific fields starts with a question. Many studies in social psychology start with a question based on observation of a real-world event. In Chapter 13 you'll learn about the murder of Kitty Genovese, which occurred while other people were watching, yet failed to call the police. Why didn't anyone call for help? This tragic event led to numerous studies on the factors that predict helping (or, in this case, not helping). Sometimes people form these questions based on their own experiences or observations. For example, you might observe that you feel fat after watching *Dancing With the Stars* or that you run faster when you are running with friends than alone. In other cases, these questions are formed based on intuition, or a "gut feeling."

Photodisc/SUPERSTOCK

FIGURE 2.1

STEPS IN THE RESEARCH PROCESS.

This figure describes each of the steps in the research process.

Source: Huffman, K.C. *Psychology in Action*, 8/e. Figure 1.5, p. 18. John Wiley & Sons. Reprinted with permission of John Wiley & Sons, Inc.

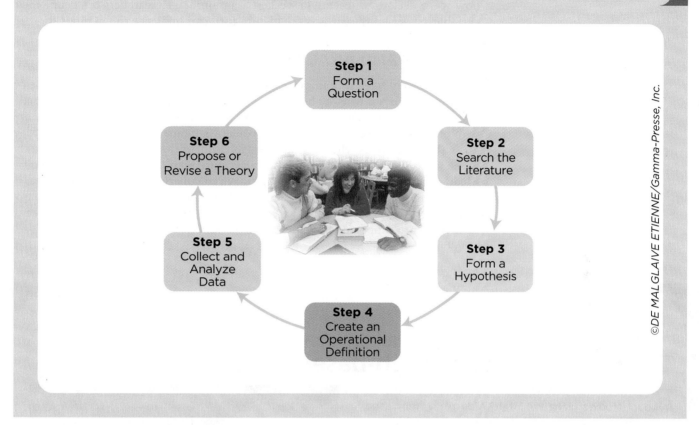

©DE MALGLAIVE ETIENNE/Gamma-Presse, Inc.

Sometimes these questions are designed to test established theories in psychology. For example, researchers who examined the predictors of prejudice and discrimination initially believed that conflict between people in different groups led to such behaviors—a theory known as Realistic Conflict Theory. You'll learn more about this theory in Chapter 10.

SEARCH THE LITERATURE

Because some ideas that you have are likely to have been studied by others, it is a good idea to start investigating these ideas by figuring out what other people might have found about the same, or similar, ideas. Go to the library and read journal articles about research, or search for topics on the Web. Use online databases, such as PsychINFO and PsychLIT, that let you search for articles by a particular topic or author. Check out the library homepage at your school or ask a librarian for access.

FORM A HYPOTHESIS

A **hypothesis** is a testable prediction about the conditions under which an event will occur. It is a statement about the expected cause and effect relationship between two variables, but has greater specificity than the original question you asked. Because a hypothesis could be directly tested, it includes a specific prediction. For example, you could have a hypothesis that children who watch a lot of television will engage in more aggressive behavior against their peers during recess than those who watch less television.

hypothesis a testable prediction about the conditions under which an event will occur

CREATE AN OPERATIONAL DEFINITION

operational definition a specific procedure or measure that one uses to test a hypothesis

An **operational definition** describes a specific procedure or measure of how you will test this hypothesis. If you want to test whether absence makes the heart grow fonder, you need to decide how you will classify fonder (Is it what people report on a survey? Is it how often they touch and kiss when they are together?), and how you will classify absence (a weekend? a month?). Researchers can define their variables in very different ways, which in turn can influence the findings.

COLLECT AND ANALYZE DATA

Data can be collected in a number of different ways—by observation, surveys, or experiments. To test whether heterosexual women eat less when they are with male dating partners, you could go to restaurants and see what women eat when they are with other women versus men. Or you could ask women what they eat when they are with a date versus when they are with a friend, or design a "food tasting" study to see whether women in same-sex pairs eat more than those in opposite-sex pairs. Media Connections describes a new approach to collecting data on the Internet.

After the data are collected, the next step is to analyze the data. For many researchers, this is the best part of conducting research because they get to see if their ideas are supported by data.

Media
:::: CONNECTIONS

The Growing Use of Web-based Experiments

Recently, social psychologists have started to conduct studies using the World Wide Web. Web-based research has a number of advantages over traditional methods, particularly when collecting self-report surveys. One of the greatest advantages is the ability to collect large amounts of data from many people at low cost. Web-based surveys also allow researchers to collect data from a more diverse group of participants than the typical college student sample because Web-based surveys tend to attract participants from a broader range of ages and backgrounds. Despite the appeal of Web-based research, several large scale studies of Web-based research reveal a number of problems (Gosling, Vazire, Srivastava, & John, 2004; Johnson, 2005).

Jason Smalley/Alamy

First, Web-based studies are very likely to include repeat participants. In one study, approximately 4% of the responses were resubmitted by the same participants, meaning people completed the survey more than once. For example, people with more than one email account could complete the same survey using different email addresses. This means that certain types of responses will appear more common than they actually are—which naturally decreases the accuracy of the study.

Second, participants who are completing a survey on the Web may read items carelessly—or not at all—in part because they are not being watched by an experimenter. In fact, approximately 3.5% of the responses to Web-based studies were submitted by individuals who had not read the response options. This error occurs in fewer than 1% of cases in pencil-and-paper self-reports.

Third, participants who complete Web-based studies may skip items, either intentionally (they are bored) or unintentionally (they don't see the instructions at the top of the screen). In line with this view, the rate of missing data in Web-based surveys, while low (1.2%), is much higher than that in standard self-reports. In sum, although Web-based research has a number of advantages, researchers should be aware of its potential limitations and should take steps to minimize these common errors.

PROPOSE AND/OR REVISE A THEORY

The final step in the research process is proposing a **theory**, meaning an organized set of principles used to explain observed phenomena. Although hypotheses are specific predictions about the association between two events (such as watching television and engaging in aggressive behavior), they do not explain how or why these two events are connected. In contrast, theories provide potential explanations. According to social learning theory, exposure to violence on television leads to aggression (as you'll see in Chapter 11). Sometimes the results from a study lead to the revision of a particular theory, if the findings suggest modification of the theory, and other times they could even refute the theory altogether. Because theories provide one type of explanation for a given phenomena, they also generate questions for future research—which in turn starts the research process over again.

theory an organized set of principles used to explain observed phenomena

Concepts in Context

STEPS INVOLVED IN THE RESEARCH PROCESS

STEP	EXAMPLE
Form a question	Does watching aggression on television lead children to act aggressively?
Search the literature	What have other researchers done to examine this question?
Form a hypothesis	Children who watch adults act aggressively on television will behave more aggressively than children who do not watch such aggression.
Create an operational definition	Aggression will be measured as the number of acts of physical aggression and verbal aggression in the 15 minutes following exposure to the aggression on television.
Collect and analyze data	Researchers will observe children's behavior following exposure to the aggression on television. Researchers will examine whether rates of aggression are higher in children who watched the aggression on television than in children who did not watch this television.
Propose and/or revise a theory	Researchers will propose a social learning theory of aggression stating that exposure to aggression leads to modeling this behavior.

WHAT ARE THE TYPES OF CORRELATIONAL RESEARCH METHODS?

Imagine that you participate in a psychology study and are asked questions about your alcohol use and sexual behavior. These questions ask for highly personal information, including whether you've had sex without a condom, whether you've consumed alcohol, and whether you've had sex after drinking. Students in one condition were asked to check which of these statements were true for them—a direct approach. In another condition, students were asked to read a group of statements and rate how many of the statements were true for them *without* having to indicate which specific statements were true—an indirect approach. (Researchers were then able to compare how many total statements were rated as true in each of these two conditions.)

As predicted, researchers found that fewer students were willing to directly acknowledge risky behavior than were willing to indirectly acknowledge such behavior (LaBrie & Earleywine, 2000). For example, only 36% of students admitted to having engaged in sex without a condom after consuming alcohol when they were given a standard self-report questionnaire that directly asked about this behavior. However, 65% admitted to engaging in this behavior when they were given a questionnaire that asked this question indirectly. This study illustrates some of the challenges in designing surveys and self-report measures, one type of correlational research method for examining issues in social psychology. Correlational research methods examine the association, or **correlation**, between two or more variables (e.g., height and weight are highly correlated). This section will examine the two major types of correlational research used in the field of social psychology—observational/naturalistic methods and self-reports/surveys—and the advantages and disadvantages of each approach.

OBSERVATIONAL/NATURALISTIC METHODS

Observational or naturalistic methods are used to describe and measure people's behavior in everyday situations. In this approach, researchers observe behavior and systematically record that behavior. The sociologist Emile Durkheim

correlation a technique that examines the extent to which two or more variables are associated with one another

observational/naturalistic methods a research approach that involves the observation and systematic recording of a particular behavior

"So we figured why explore Mars when, closer to home, there's still so much we don't know about the Petersens."

(1951) conducted naturalistic research by examining the records of people who had committed suicide between 1841 and 1872. His findings indicated suicide was more frequent in people who were single than married, and was more common during the week than on weekends. Through this investigation, he hypothesized that alienation from others was a predictor of suicide.

Some researchers collect these data observing interactions and rating them in various ways. For example, if you were interested in examining whether boys or girls are more aggressive, you could watch children playing on a playground and count their aggressive behaviors (e.g., hitting, name calling, kicking, throwing, etc.). Researchers who use this approach try to be as unobtrusive as possible to avoid influencing the behavior of the people who were being observed.

You can also collect naturalistic data without directly observing people's behavior. If you were interested in examining the association between living in a fraternity and alcohol use, each week you could count the number of beer cans in the garbage at a fraternity and at a different type of housing situation (e.g., a dorm). If you found that fraternities had many more beer cans and bottles each week than dorms, you might conclude that there is a link between drinking and fraternity life. Researchers in one clever study on the factors leading to the common cold gathered and weighed used tissues as a way of measuring mucus produced (Cohen, Doyle, Skoner, Rabin, & Gwaltney, 1997). Can you think of an experiment you might do that involves collecting naturalistic data?

Another observational approach is **archival research**, in which researchers use already recorded behavior, such as divorce rates, death rates, sports statistics, crime rates, or weather reports. In Chapter 4 we will look at a famous archival study in which researchers examined newspaper quotations from famous baseball players to form theories about their personalities and then measured their life expectancies (Peterson & Seligman, 1987). In Chapter 8 we will look at an archival study on the effects of publicizing suicides on rates of suicide later on (Phillips, 1982). Environmental Connections describes the use of archival research to examine whether hot temperatures are associated with higher crime rates.

Literature reviews comprise a variety of studies that have been done on a given topic, such as television violence and aggression, and attempt to reach an overall conclusion. This approach is often used when different studies have revealed different findings. A literature review that also analyzes data that come from many different studies is called a **meta-analysis**. Meta-analyses use a statistical technique for combining data that have been collected by different researchers, and therefore the strengths and weaknesses of particular studies even out when they are all considered simultaneously.

Meta-analyses have been used to examine a number of issues in social psychology, including attitudes toward rape (Anderson, Cooper, & Okamura, 1997), gender differences in the attributions people make for success and failure (Swim & Sanna, 1996), the link between attitudes and behavior (Kraus, 1995), and the impact of extrinsic rewards on intrinsic motivation (Deci, Koestner, & Ryan, 1999).

DNY59/iStockphoto

archival research a research approach that uses already recorded behavior

meta-analysis a literature review that also analyses data from many different studies

Environment

The Hazards of Hot Weather

Researchers who examine the impact of climate on rates of aggression often rely on archival data. In one study, Craig Anderson and colleagues examined the association between the number of hot days (days the maximum temperature reached 90 degrees) in a given summer and the rate of violent crimes in 50 different American cities (Anderson, Bushman, & Groom, 1997). As predicted, hotter summers were associated with more violent crimes, including assault, property crime, and rape. Other research reveals that aggressive crimes occur more frequently in the hotter geographic regions of countries (e.g., the South versus the North in the United States) and that violent crimes occur more frequently in the summer than in the winter (Anderson, 1989). Hot weather is also associated with riots, such as the one of summer 2008 in India (see photo).

afp/NewsCom

Advantages.   What are the advantages of using naturalistic or observational methods? Because these methods are based in the observation of real-world phenomena, they help researchers develop hypotheses and theories. These methods are also relatively easy to conduct. They usually rely on either observing naturally occurring situations, or analyzing already collected data, and hence do not require extensive laboratory space, equipment, and assistance.

Also, naturalistic methods can provide data about rare events that researchers would be unable to examine in other settings. For example, researchers have used archival data to examine the link between temperature and rates of homicide, which would be impossible to gather in any other way.

Naturalistic methods can provide large amounts of data that researchers would never be able to collect on their own. This is particularly important when researchers are interested in examining how something has changed over time: it is unlikely a researcher would ever be able to design a study and then follow the participants for 20 years (and you'll read about just such a study examining the link between exposure to violence on television as a child and levels of adult aggression in Chapter 11).

Limitations.   One problem with the observation approach is that the presence of the observer is likely to influence behavior. People are likely to behave in different ways when they know that they are being watched. When my cousin Jon joined a fraternity during college, his parents were understandably worried about the potential negative effects of such an environment. They were quite reassured, however, when during Parent's Weekend, a Dean told parents that as an "experiment" he had actually moved into the frat for a weekend, and was pleased to report that the men were well-behaved, attentive to cleanliness, and very studious! (Can you spot any problems with this study?)

The observer's own biases can also influence how he or she interprets the behavior observed. One person might interpret pushing between children on a playground as normal behavior. Another person might see such behavior as a sign of aggression or hostility. To help limit the problems of observer bias, researchers often have at least two people do the ratings independently, and then measure how often they agree. This is called **inter-rater reliability**.

inter-rater reliability the extent to which two or more coders agree on ratings of a particular measure

The most important limitation of all observational methods is that while such approaches can show whether two variables are *correlated,* or associated, with each other, they cannot tell us which variable causes the other. For example, if we find—as research shows—that students who receive better grades in a class give their professor better ratings, what can we conclude? We know there is an association, or **correlation**; students who receive higher grades in a class give that professor more positive teaching evaluations (*a positive correlation*). But even though we know there is a correlation between these two events or variables (grades, evaluations), we still don't know which one causes the other. Does having a better professor cause you to get better grades? Or do students who are doing well in class come to like their professor more? Similarly, if you find that people who are more hostile have fewer friends (*a negative correlation*), you can't tell if people who are mean to others have trouble making friends, or if people who don't have many friends grow to be hostile over time (see Figure 2.2).

In some cases we don't have to worry about the direction of the association between two variables. First, if one of the variables is fixed, we can be certain that it was not caused by the other variable. For example, if we conduct a naturalistic observation study and find that men are more aggressive than women, we can be sure that the aggression did not lead to their gender. Second, if the data regarding the two variables were collected at two different periods of time, we can be certain that the second variable could not have caused the first variable (e.g., your love for your spouse could not have caused your feelings for that person when he was your boyfriend).

FIGURE 2.2

TYPES OF CORRELATION

Figure A shows a positive correlation (as student grades increase, professor evaluations increase), Figure B shows a negative correlation (as hostility increases, number of friends decreases), and Figure C shows no correlation (as physical attractiveness increases, number of colds doesn't change).

Source: Kowalski & Weston, *Psychology*, John Wiley & Sons. Figure 1.5, page 50. Reprinted with permission of John Wiley & Sons, Inc.

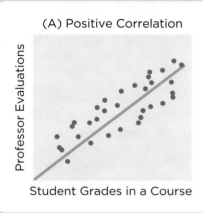

(A) Positive Correlation — Professor Evaluations vs. Student Grades in a Course

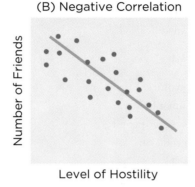

(B) Negative Correlation — Number of Friends vs. Level of Hostility

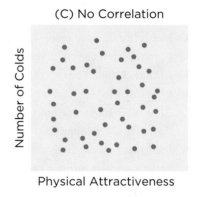

(C) No Correlation — Number of Colds vs. Physical Attractiveness

However, even in these cases we can't be certain that one variable caused the other, because it is possible that a third variable explains the observed association between the two variables. For example, hair loss and coronary heart disease are positively correlated: people who are bald are more likely to have coronary heart disease. However, it would be inaccurate to say that balding *causes* coronary heart disease because actually both balding and coronary heart disease are the result of getting older (the "third variable" in this example).

Questioning the Research

One possibility is that smoking by mothers during pregnancy leads to behavior problems in toddlers. Can you think of any other alternative explanations for this association?

In Chapter 1, you learned that adolescents who eat dinner with their family have lower levels of smoking, drinking, and drug use (Eisenberg et al., 2004). You also learned about several possible alternative explanations for this association. Similarly, a recent study revealed that two-year-olds whose mothers smoked during pregnancy are seven times more likely to have disruptive behavior problems than those whose mothers refrained from smoking during pregnancy (Wakschlag, Leventhal, Pine, Pickett, & Carter, 2006). But is this convincing evidence that mothers' smoking itself leads to behavior problems in children?

SELF-REPORT OR SURVEY METHODS

Self-report or survey methods rely on asking people questions about their thoughts, feelings, desires, and action. These questions could be asked directly by the experimenter in an interview either in person or on the telephone, or participants could complete written surveys. The Rosenberg Self-Esteem Scale is one commonly used measure that assesses whether people generally have positive feelings about themselves (Rosenberg, 1965; see "Rate Yourself" for an example). Researchers could give people this scale as well as a questionnaire assessing their health behaviors to determine if people with high self-esteem engage in more healthy behaviors than those with low self-esteem.

How Do You Feel About Yourself?

Self-Esteem Scale

INSTRUCTIONS: *Rate your agreement with each of these items on a 1 to 4 scale, with 1 meaning "strongly disagree" and 4 meaning "strongly agree."*

- ☐ **1.** I feel that I'm a person of worth, at least on an equal plane with others.
- ☐ **2.** On the whole, I am satisfied with myself.
- ☐ **3.** I wish I could have more respect for myself.
- ☐ **4.** I certainly feel useless at times.
- ☐ **5.** At times I think I am no good at all.
- ☐ **6.** I feel that I have a number of good qualities.
- ☐ **7.** All in all, I am inclined to feel that I am a failure.
- ☐ **8.** I am able to do things as well as most other people.
- ☐ **9.** I feel that I do not have much to be proud of.
- ☐ **10.** I take a positive attitude toward myself.

SCORING: Indicate whether you strongly agree, agree, disagree, or strongly disagree with each of these statements. For statements 1, 2, 6, 8, and 10 give yourself 4 points for strongly agree, 3 points for agree, 2 points for disagree, and 1 point for strongly disagree. For statements 3, 4, 5, 7, and 9 give yourself 1 point for strongly agree, 2 points for agree, 3 points for disagree, and 4 points for strongly disagree. Then add up your total number of points.

INTERPRETATION: People with a higher score on this scale have higher self-esteem, meaning they see themselves in an overall more positive light than those with lower scores on this scale (Rosenberg, 1965).

---

event-recording measure a particular type of self-report or survey data where participants report various experiences they have at regular time intervals

One particular type of self-report or survey data is **event-recording** or *experience sampling measures* (see Table 2.1; Reis & Wheeler, 1991). In these measures, respondents report various experiences they have at regular intervals. In some cases, respondents report on a designated set of events, such as social interactions, particular moods, etc., and they simply fill out a brief form whenever they are in these situations (noting mood, describing the event, etc.). In other cases, respondents carry a programmed watch or beeper, and write down various pieces of information (e.g., mood, describing the event) after they are signaled (usually several times a day).

Advantages. Survey measures have many advantages and are commonly used to collect information about the link between people's attitudes and behaviors. Surveys enable researchers to collect data from many participants at the same time, so this is a very inexpensive way to gather data. Researchers could, for example, recruit many college students to complete a written survey on their attitudes toward love and their experience in romantic relationships to see if their dating experience was associated with their views of love.

Surveys also let researchers ask questions about a range of topics, including actions, feelings, attitudes, and thoughts, that could not be assessed simply by observing people's behavior. You can't directly measure variables such as love, empathy, or prejudice, but you can infer them indirectly by observing people's actions.

WOULD YOU BELIEVE? . . . Politicians Who Are Listed First on the Ballot Are More Likely to Win? Some intriguing research by Jon Krosnick at Stanford University reveals that candidates who are listed first on the ballot get about two percentage points more votes than they would have if they were listed later (Miller & Krosnick, 1998). How can you tell the impact of order on voting? In California, the order of candidates' names is randomly assigned in each of the 80 districts. In 1996, Bill Clinton received four percent more votes in California districts in which his name was listed first than in the ones in which his name was listed last. In 2000, George Bush received nine percentage points higher in California districts in which his name was listed first than in the ones in which his name was listed last. This means that the order in which names appear could mean the difference between winning and losing an election—such as the 2000 presidential election, in which George Bush was listed first on every Florida ballot (because in this state, candidates from the governor's party automatically get listed first).

Limitations. Self-report or survey methods also have their limitations. Let's examine some factors that limit the reliability of this method.

TABLE 2.1 — THE ROCHESTER INTERACTION RECORD

Intimacy	Superficial	1	2	3	4	5	6	7	Meaningful
I disclosed	Very little	1	2	3	4	5	6	7	A great deal
Other disclosed	Very little	1	2	3	4	5	6	7	A great deal
Quality	Unpleasant	1	2	3	4	5	6	7	Pleasant
Satisfaction	Less than expected	1	2	3	4	5	6	7	More than expected
Initiation	I initiated	1	2	3	4	5	6	7	Other initiated
Influence	I influenced more	1	2	3	4	5	6	7	Other influenced more

The Rochester Interaction Record is a commonly used event-recording measure in which participants record information about their daily interactions shortly after they occur. This measure has been used to examine frequency of conflict with a dating partner, intimate discussions, and feelings of loneliness (Reis & Wheeler, 1991).

Source: Reis, H.T., & Wheeler, L. (1991). Studying social interaction with the Rochester Interaction Record. In M. P. Zanna (Ed.), *Advances in Experimental Social Psychology* (Vol. 24, pp. 270–318). San Diego: Academic Press.

Question Wording. First, survey methods can lead to biased findings if they use leading questions. Leading questions are those questions that provide some evidence of the "right answer" based on how they are phrased. For example, polls consistently reveal that asking if the government is spending too much on welfare reveals a different answer (53%) than asking if the government spends too much on assistance to the poor (23%). In a *New York Times*/CBS News poll in 2004, a majority of respondents agreed with both of the following questions: "I am in favor of a constitutional amendment allowing marriage only between a man and a woman," and "Defining marriage is not an important enough issue to be worth changing the Constitution for." Why did people tend to agree with both of these statements, even though they clearly mean directly opposite things? Pollsters assume that the phrase "changing the Constitution" sounds more radical to most people than adding an "amendment," even though adding an amendment would in fact change the Constitution.

Nationwide surveys of abortion often reveal conflicting results about how Americans feel about legalized abortion. This difference is caused at least in part by question wording. People are more likely to support abortion when asked, "How much are you in favor of allowing an abortion for a teenager who becomes pregnant following a rape?" than when they are asked, "How much are you in favor of allowing a woman to murder an innocent baby in her womb?" This is an extreme example, but it is not far from what happens in some surveys (see Table 2.2 for some additional examples).

Even subtle wording differences can lead to different results. Some research indicates that the order in which questions are asked can influence the response (Schwarz, Strack, & Mai, 1991). People who are asked how happy they are with their life, and then asked how happy they are with their marriage give very different answers than those who are asked the same two questions, but in the opposite order. The preceding question influences our interpretation of the second question,

TABLE 2.2 — EXAMPLES OF LEADING SURVEY QUESTIONS

QUESTION 1	QUESTION 2
Given the importance to future generations of preserving the environment, do you believe the Clean Air Act should be strengthened, weakened, or left alone?	Given the fact that installing scrubbers at utility plants could increase electricity bills by 25%, do you believe the Clean Air Act should be strengthened, weakened, or left alone?
Do you prefer your hamburgers flame-broiled or fried?	Do you prefer a hamburger that is grilled on a hot stainless steel grill or cooked by passing the raw meat through an open gas flame?

Can you see how people would answer these pairs of questions in very different ways based on their wording? Most people are more in favor of the Clean Air Act in the first question than in the second question, and prefer flame-broiled hamburgers more in the first question than in the second (Goodwin, 1998).

Source: Goodwin, C.J. (1998). *Research in Psychology: Methods and Design*. 2nd ed. New York: Wiley.

and hence impacts the answer we give. Similarly, people have higher scores on self-esteem measures when the questions are phrased positively, such as "I feel that I have a lot of good qualities," than when they are framed negatively, such as "I certainly feel useless at times" (Schmitt & Allik, 2005). These findings suggest that people tend to show higher levels of agreement with positively worded items than negatively worded ones, which could lead to biases in survey responses.

Finally, providing information about who is conducting the research influences responses. More people are in favor of the statement, "People should have the freedom to express their opinions publicly," when this question is asked by the Catholic Church than by the American Nazi Party (Ottati, Riggle, Wyer, Schwarz, & Kuklinski, 1989).

Response Options.　Similarly, the response options given in a survey can influence the results. The responses provided give people an idea of what the "normal" or "typical" behavior is, and people often don't want to appear very different from others. (And they *really* don't want to appear worse than others.) Therefore, they are likely to choose one of the mid-level choices as opposed to one of the more extreme (high frequency or low frequency) choices. So, if you ask someone if he smokes fewer than 1 cigarette a day, 1 to 2 cigarettes a day, 3 to 5 cigarettes a day, or more than 5 cigarettes a day, he will give lower estimates about their cigarette smoking than if you ask if they smoke fewer than 10, 10 to 20, 20 to 30, or more than 30 cigarettes a day. In this first example, people will be likely to report smoking between 1 and 5 cigarettes a day (the two mid-level choices in this set of answers), whereas in the second example, people are likely to report smoking 10 to 30 cigarettes a day, again because these responses are the mid-level options. Table 2.3 provides another example of how response options can influence people's reports of how much television they watch (Schwarz, Hippler, Deutsch, & Strack, 1985). Chapter 4 on social perception describes a study showing that people strongly prefer a food that is 75% fat-free to one that is 25% fat (Sanford, Fay, Stewart, & Moxey, 2002).

TABLE 2.3 — REPORTED DAILY TELEVISION WATCHING AS A FUNCTION OF RESPONSE OPTIONS

LOW-FREQUENCY OPTIONS	DAILY USE	HIGH-FREQUENCY OPTIONS	DAILY USE
Up to ½ hour	7.4%	Up to 2 ½ hours	62.5%
½ hour to 1 hour	17.7%	2 ½ hours to 3 hours	23.4%
1 hour to 1 ½ hours	26.5%	3 hours to 3 ½ hours	7.8%
1 ½ hours to 2 hours	14.7%	3 ½ hours to 4 hours	4.7%
2 hours to 2 ½ hours	17.7%	4 hours to 4 ½ hours	1.6%
More than 2 ½ hours	16.2%	More than 4 ½ hours	0.0%

Only 16.2% of people report watching more than 2 ½ hours of television (the highest response option given) in the low-frequency condition, but 37.5% of people report watching this much television in the high-frequency condition.

Source: Schwarz, N., Hippler, H., Deutsch, B., & Strack, F. (1985). Response scales: Effects of category range on reported behavior and comparative judgments. *Public Opinion Quarterly, 49*, 388–395.

Response options can have an even stronger impact on answers when participants must choose between a set of very limited response options. A story in the *New York Times Magazine* described the somewhat surprising results of a survey showing that 51% of Americans think "primates are entitled to the same rights as human children" (Pollan, 2002). However, the actual survey listed only four choices: primates should be treated "like property," "similar to children," "the same as adults," or "not sure." Given these four options, some respondents may have chosen the "similar to children" answer not because this choice expressed their true feelings, but because this choice was the option closest to their true feelings, given the rather limited options.

Inaccuracy of Responses. Surveys methods are also limited by the possibility of inaccurate reporting. In some cases, people might believe they are telling the truth, but they simply may not be able to accurately recall the necessary information. For example, people may not remember how much money they donated to charity last year or how often they flossed their teeth.

Researchers who use event-recording measures are less likely to encounter problems caused by their participants' forgetfulness. However, all types of self-report measures can experience problems if people are motivated to give inaccurate information. Why would people provide inaccurate information? People are concerned with the social desirability of their answers, particularly in cases in which the research examines highly personal or controversial topics. For example, students often report to their parents and professors that they studied and attended class more frequently than perhaps

"What I drink and what I tell the pollsters I drink are two different things."

covert measures measures that are not directly under a person's control

Michael Newman/PhotoEdit

The number of pornographic magazines purchased based on sales reports is considerably higher than the number of pornographic magazines purchased based on surveys. Can you guess why?

Questioning the Research

Some researchers have criticized the use of the IAT as a measure of prejudice. In particular, these researchers suggest that responses on the IAT may not reflect participants' own endorsement of a prejudicial attitude, but rather familiarity with a given stereotype, the salience of particular types of pairings, and/or cultural knowledge about a given belief (Blanton & Jaccard, 2006). What do you believe the IAT likely measures? How could you test your belief?

TABLE 2.4	WORD COMPLETION TEST		
SAMPLE FRAGMENT	**PREJUDICED RESPONSE**	**NON-PREJUDICED RESPONSE**	
_ I C E	RICE	NICE	
P O L I _ E	POLITE	POLICE	

This table shows three types of word completions tasks that could be used to test prejudiced reactions. In one study, participants who watched a tape of an Asian woman completed the word fragments in ways that are stereotype consistent.

Source: Gilbert, D., & Hixon, J. (1991). The trouble of thinking: Activation and application of stereotypic beliefs. *Journal of Personality and Social Psychology, 60,* 509–517.

they really did. Remember the study described at the start of this section? It revealed that students' reports of frequency of condom use (a highly personal topic) were less accurate if the question was asked with a more direct approach compared to a less direct approach. Similarly, sexual behavior data reported in retrospective self-reports tends to be much lower than sexual behavior data reported in a daily diary approach (McAuliffe, DiFranceisco, & Reed, 2007).

To minimize the problems associated with socially desirable responding, some researchers rely on **covert measures**, meaning measures that are not directly under a person's control. Covert measures are particularly likely to be used in cases in which participants might not want to be honest in their responses. In one study, researchers examined heterosexual men's arousal in response to erotic material that featured either heterosexual couples, lesbian couples, or homosexual couples (Adams, Wright, & Lohr, 1996). Because heterosexual men would likely report little arousal in response to material featuring homosexual men, researchers used "penile cuffs" to measure erection strength in response to the three different types of material. Interestingly, heterosexual men who were homophobic, meaning they reported having negative feelings toward gay men, were the only participants who showed an increase in erection strength in response to the homosexual material. This study illustrates the advantages of using covert measures when studying sensitive topics such as sexual behavior.

Because people are often reluctant to admit to racial prejudice on self-report measures, many researchers who study stereotyping use various types of covert measures (as you'll read about in detail in Chapter 10). One commonly used covert measure is the Implicit Association Test (IAT), which is based on the assumption that it is easier—and hence faster—to make the same response to concepts that are strongly associated than those that are more weakly associated (Nosek, Greenwald, & Banaji, 2005). In this test, people respond to two different types of stimulus words: the first set is attitudinal words (e.g., pleasant, peace, ugly, happy, etc.), and the second set is the list of stereotypic target words (e.g., Caucasian names and Black names, women's names and men's names, etc.). People press one key when they see a pleasant word and another key when they see an unpleasant word. Research generally shows that people are faster at responding to the compatible blocks than the incompatible ones, which suggests an implicit linking of Caucasian and good and Black and bad. For example, students often respond more quickly to the pairing of the words "old" and "bad" (which are often closely linked in people's mind) than the words "old" and "young" (which are typically less closely linked). Other covert measures to assess prejudice include word completion tasks (see Table 2.4), reaction times, and facial expressions (see Research Focus on Neuroscience).

What other types of covert measures do researchers use? Researchers have measured participants' nodding in response to a persuasive communication, timed how long participants take to walk down a hallway following exposure to neutral versus "old" words, or observed their behavior toward another person behind a one-way mirror after they've seen a violent television program. In one study, participants came in to complete a two-part study that examined the association between personality and impression formation as well as personality and taste preferences (Lieberman, Solomon, Greenberg, & McGregor, 1999). First, participants read an essay on politics that was supposedly written by another student (their partner in this study). For half of the participants, this essay criticized their prevailing political orientation. The other half of the participants read an essay that supported their political views. Next, participants were told that this day the taste the researchers were examining was "spicy," and that they should pour some spicy sauce into a small cup for their partner to drink. (They were also told that their partner did not particularly like spicy foods.) As predicted, participants who read the criticizing essay gave significantly more hot sauce to their partner than those who read a supportive essay. Thus, the amount of hot sauce given was a covert way of testing level of aggression.

RESEARCH FOCUS ON NEUROSCIENCE
Facial Movements as a Measure of Discrimination

Researchers in this study used facial movements as a way to measure racial prejudice (Vanman, Saltz, Nathan, & Warren, 2004). Caucasian students were asked to read three folders supposedly from graduate students who were applying for a teaching fellowship. Each folder contained information about the applicant's grades and standardized test scores, a letter of recommendation from a professor, and a photograph of the applicant. Two of the three folders included a photo of a Caucasian student and the other folder included a photo of an African American student. All participants were equally qualified (researchers varied which information was presented with each phase for different participants). Participants were then asked to choose an applicant for the fellowship. Three weeks later, supposedly as part of a different study, these participants were recruited to take part in a study on "neural responses." In this part of the study, researchers attached electrodes to participants' faces and recorded their reactions while they viewed a series of 16 photos (8 African Americans, 8 Caucasians).

As predicted, participants who showed a higher level of facial movement when viewing photos of Caucasians as compared to African Americans were more likely to choose a Caucasian applicant for the fellowship. In contrast, participants who showed no facial bias were much more likely to choose the African American applicant than a Caucasian applicant. This research shows that facial reactions—a type of covert measure—are related to discrimination.

EXAMPLES OF EACH RESEARCH APPROACH

Concepts in Context

Let's say you want to examine whether exposure to very thin media images of women leads to eating disorders in women. This table describes how both naturalistic and survey methods could be used to examine this hypohesis.

RESEARCH METHOD	EXAMPLE
Naturalistic/ observation methods	Analyze archival data to rate the thinness of women appearing in magazines and on television over time, and the rate of diagnosed eating disorders.
Survey/ self-report methods	Give women a questionnaire that asks them to rate how frequently they read magazines featuring thin models and how frequently they engage in various symptoms of disordered eating.

HOW DO YOU CONDUCT EXPERIMENTAL RESEARCH?

 Researchers conducted a study to find out if women eat less when they want to appear attractive (Mori, Chaiken, & Pliner, 1987). They brought in female college students to have a "get acquainted" conversation (designed to simulate a dating situation), and examined the effects of the "quality of the dating partner" on the amount women ate. Women in one condition were told that they were interacting with a very desirable man; he was described as interested in travel, athletics, photography, going to law school, and single. Those in another condition were told they were interacting with a less desirable man; he was described as having no interests other than watching TV and no plans other than making money. Researchers then measured how many M&Ms women ate during the conversation. As predicted, women who were talking with the undesirable man ate significantly more than those who were talking with the desirable man. In contrast, men ate about the same amount regardless of whether their partner was attractive. These results suggest that women present an image to men in certain situations: when they want to appear attractive, they don't eat much.

This section will examine issues in experimental methods (such as the study just described) as well as two factors that influence the quality of experimental research methods: internal and external validity.

EXPERIMENTAL METHODS

experimental methods a research approach that involves the manipulation of one or more independent variables and the measurement of one or more dependent variables

independent variable the variable that is manipulated in experimental research

dependent variable the factor that is measured to see if it is affected by the independent variable

In **experimental methods**, researchers manipulate one or more **independent variables** and then measure the effects of such manipulations on one or more **dependent variables** (the factor that is measured to see if it is affected by the independent variable). In the study just described, the independent variable was the desirability of the man (highly desirable versus relatively undesirable) and the dependent variable was the number of M&Ms eaten.

This approach lets us determine systematically whether the independent variable caused the dependent variable, and therefore provides evidence of causation as opposed to correlation. For example, if you want to test whether people who are injured get more help if they are alone or in groups, you could fake an emergency in front of either one other person or in front of a large group, and then see in which situation people got help the fastest. In this case the independent variable is the size of the group, and the dependent variable is the speed of help.

Similarly, let's say you have an internship with an advertising agency and are asked to test whether people who see a particular television advertisement will develop more positive attitudes toward that product. You could show one group of people that advertisement, and show another group of people no advertisement, and then measure the attitude toward that project in people in both groups. If people in the group who saw the advertisements liked the product more than those who did not see the advertisement, your findings would suggest that the advertisement was effective in increasing positive attitudes.

random assignment a technique used in experimental research meaning every participant has an equal opportunity of being selected for any of the conditions in a particular experiment

Random assignment. As the first step in conducting experiments, researchers assign people to the different experimental conditions. **Random assignment** means that every person had an equal chance of being in either of the conditions: they did not get to choose which condition they wanted nor did the experimenter use any type of selection process to assign people to conditions (e.g., putting the first 10 people in one condition and then the next 10 people in the second condition, etc.). Instead, researchers use a truly random method of assigning people to groups, such as flipping a coin, drawing slips out of a hat, or using a table of random numbers. This random assignment to condition means you have greater confidence that there is not a third variable that may cause both the independent and dependent variables, and therefore explains your findings.

What would happen if you ran an experiment on the effects of watching violent television on aggression but instead of randomly assigning children to watch a particular show, you let children choose whether they'd like to watch a violent television show or a funny sitcom? If you then find that those who watch violent television are more aggressive than those who don't, can you be certain that watching this type of television show caused the aggression? No, because it is likely that kids who <u>chose</u> to watch violent television differ from those who did not want to watch it. Perhaps these kids are more aggressive in general, or they don't get to watch violent television much at home. Therefore, we can't tell whether your independent variable (watching a violent television show) caused your dependent variable (intensity of aggression). This may seem like an obvious point, but some research studies do rely on such flawed designs, as illustrated in Health Connections.

Control.   Researchers have a lot of *control* over what happens to the participants in their experiment. Researchers choose what happens to whom and when and how. Therefore they do not have to worry about other factors influencing their findings, such as the participants' personalities, attitudes, and/or experiences. In the nonexperimental research described earlier, the researcher only measures—but does not manipulate—the independent variable. For example, the gender of the participants or the type of school they attend (large versus small) could serve as an independent variable, but these factors are only measured. In experiments, the researchers manipulate one or more independent variables, and therefore have control over exactly what happens to the participants.

Health
::: **CONNECTIONS**

Evaluating Abstinence-only Sex Education

Many research studies have examined the effectiveness of abstinence-only education, meaning programs in which students learn only about strategies for abstaining from sexual intercourse before marriage, and not about contraceptive use. Researchers have often reported beneficial effects of these programs, such as reductions in early sexual activity (Kirby, 2002). However, these research studies often have problems that limit what we can learn. For example, one study found that an abstinence-only program led to an increase in age at first sexual encounter—but researchers eliminated girls who had sex during the program from inclusion in their analyses. Other studies have included only adolescents who had taken a pledge to refrain from sexual activity before marriage—but adolescents who make such a pledge probably differ in many ways from those who don't. Still other studies didn't evaluate the effectiveness of abstinence-only education on sexual behavior, but rather on attitudes toward sexual behavior. Would you be surprised to know that following an abstinence-only program many adolescents report more positive attitudes about abstinence? However, these studies don't measure whether such attitudes actually lead to abstinent behavior. So, what do well-designed studies on abstinence-only

Mary Kate Denny/PhotoEdi

education—including random assignment, inclusion of all research participants, and evaluation of sexual behavior—reveal? Those who receive abstinence-only education are no more likely than those in a control group to abstain from sexual activity or delay the start of sexual activity (Trenholm, Devaney, Fortson, Clark, Bridgespan, & Wheeler, 2008).

FIGURE
2.3

A MODEL OF EXPERIMENTAL DESIGN

As shown in this figure, experiments include random assignment and the use of a control condition. These two features, which are not used in naturalistic/obervation and self-report/survey methods of research, help researchers determine whether the independent variable caused the dependent variable.

```
          Randomly
       assign participants
          to condition

    Treatment              Control
    Condition              Condition

  Give participants      Do not give
   the treatment         participants
                         the treatment

                Measure
              the outcome
```

Because experiments contain multiple conditions and people are randomly assigned to these conditions, this type of research method gives us greater confidence that the effects of the independent variable cause the effects on the dependent variable. This is an advantage over the other research methods discussed that show correlation, but not causation (see Figure 2.3).

INTERNAL VALIDITY

Because experimenters use random assignment and can control exactly what happens to the participants, this research approach is the only one that provides answers about causality. (Remember the important distinction between correlation and causation?) In order to be confident that the effects on the dependent variable were caused by the independent variable, we need to design experiments that are high on **internal validity**, meaning the degree to which one can validly draw conclusions about the effects of the independent variable on the dependent variable. For example, let's say we are conducting an experiment about the effects of peer tutoring on grades, and you randomly assign some people to receive such tutoring and other people to get nothing extra. If the results show that those who received peer tutoring have better grades than those who do not, can we be sure that this effect is caused by the tutoring? Maybe those who didn't receive the tutoring were disappointed and therefore felt especially badly toward the class and simply stopped studying at all. Maybe the experimenter assumed that those who received the tutoring would do better in the class, and therefore was nicer to those people. In turn, perhaps those people who received the tutoring felt better because they were treated well by the experimenter, not due to the effects of the tutoring itself. Maybe people who received the tutoring talked about how great it was, which made those who didn't get the tutoring feel badly. In other words, there could be a variety of alternative explanations for the findings, which therefore weakens their internal validity.

Researchers often try to increase internal validity by reducing or eliminating the **demand characteristics**, meaning cues in a research setting that may guide participants' behavior (Aronson, Wilson, & Brewer, 1998; Orne, 1962).

internal validity the degree to which one can validly draw conclusions about the effects of the independent variable on the dependent variable

demand characteristics the features introduced into a research setting that make people aware they are participating in a study

Participants are often focused on trying to "figure out" the goal of the study, and sometimes try to "help the researcher" by behaving in the desired way. This behavior decreases the internal validity of the experiment because participants' behavior is then influenced by these demand characteristics and not merely by the variables the experimenter is manipulating. There are ways of decreasing such cues, including providing a good cover story, providing a high quality control condition, minimizing experimenter expectancy effects, and designing studies with high experimental or psychological realism.

Provide a Good Cover Story.   Participants in an experiment often want to figure out the purpose of the study. If participants know the purpose of the research experiment, they might act either in a way to support it or sometimes to discredit it. Therefore, researchers often try to hide the exact hypotheses of the study. For example, if you are conducting a study on how low self-esteem leads to aggression, you obviously couldn't tell your subjects that or this knowledge would influence their behavior. Some studies even use deception by providing false information to subjects to minimize the impact of participant expectancy effects (we will talk more about the use of deception at the end of this chapter). In one study you'll read about in Chapter 13, researchers told participants the study was examining personality variables, but in reality the researchers were measuring how students reacted when smoke began pouring into the room as they completed their questionnaire (Darley & Latane, 1968).

Provide a High Quality Control Condition.   In some cases researchers can't completely disguise the nature of the study, but they can reduce demand characteristics by making sure that participants don't know exactly which condition they are in. For example, in research examining persuasion, all participants may hear the same persuasive message on the value of mandatory community service programs for college students. Some participants will be told the message is being delivered by a high school debate student. Others will be told the message is being delivered by a highly respected professor. If the researchers later find that those in the "professor condition" are more persuaded by the message, we can be relatively confident that the speaker influenced the power of the message. Why? Because the study was absolutely identical in all respects except for the one variable—speaker—that differed.

Compare this study design to one in which researchers did not use a high quality control condition. Imagine that these researchers asked half of the participants to listen to a persuasive message by an education speaker and then asked them to report their attitudes toward mandatory community service for college students. The other half of the participants don't hear any message, but just report their attitudes about mandatory community service for college students. Why is this an invalid study? Because there are too many variables to know what might be the cause of each group's attitudes. Did the groups have different attitudes because of the arguments in the message, because of the expertise of the speaker, or both? This illustrates why it is so important to provide a high quality control condition that differs from the experimental condition in only a single way.

Minimize Experimenter Expectancy Effects.   Another type of demand characteristic is the experimenter's own behavior. **Experimenter expectancy effects** are produced when an experimenter's expectations about the results of the experiment influence participants' behavior toward the subject, and thereby the results. For example, if I have a theory (which I don't, but anyway) that students from California aren't as intelligent as others, I might treat them differently when they come to office hours (e.g., give simple questions, provide more basic answers, challenge them less). Similarly, if you are conducting a study on smoking cessation, and you know that some students are listening to a tape that provides strategies to help them stop smoking, whereas others are only listening to music, you may treat subjects in these two conditions differently. For example, you might ask some people, "Don't you feel like you could go through the rest

experimenter expectancy effects a phenominon in which an experimenter's expectations about the results of the study influence participants' behavior and thereby affect the results of the study

of the day without another cigarette?" and others, "How much do you think you'll want to smoke tonight?."

Experimenter expectancy effects can even influence behavior in animals. In one clever study, an experimenter told some students that they were merely replicating a well-established finding that some rats are "maze-bright" and that other rats are "maze-dumb," and thus would have more trouble learning to navigate a maze (Rosenthal & Fode, 1963). The researcher then told half of the students they were working with smart rats. The other half of students were told they were working with dumb rats. Then, students placed their rats at the start of the runway and timed them. On Day 1, the times were pretty close, but over time, the "bright" rats ran faster and faster than the dumb rats (see Figure 2.4).

Researchers typically take a number of steps to avoid introducing experimenter expectancy effects. One approach is to minimize interaction between participants and experimenters. For example, participants may receive all of their instructions

Questioning the Research
Although this study clearly demonstrated that people's expectancies influenced the rats learning, it didn't examine why. How do you believe participants' expectancies may have influenced the rats' running speed?

FIGURE 2.4

CAN EXPERIMENTERS' EXPECTATIONS INFLUENCE RATS' BEHAVIOR?

In a study to test the strength of experimenter expectancy effects, researchers asked psychology students to count the correct responses of rats as they ran through mazes. Although the rats were all the same at the beginning of the study, researchers told some students that their rats were "maze smart," and others that their rats were "maze dumb." As predicted, rats labeled as "smart" made more correct responses than those labeled as "dumb" every day of the study. In addition, the difference between numbers of correct responses increased over time, meaning the difference between the rats' scores was greater on Day 5 than on Day 1. The researchers believe that the students' expectations about the rats may have led them to treat the rats differently in subtle ways that influenced the rats' performance.

Source: Rosenthal, R., and Fode, K. (1963). The effect of experimenter bias on the performance of the albino rat. *Behavioral Science, 8*, 183–189.

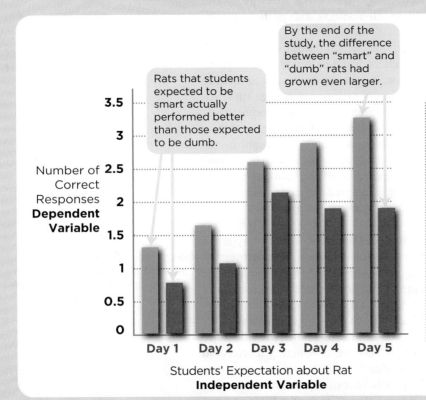

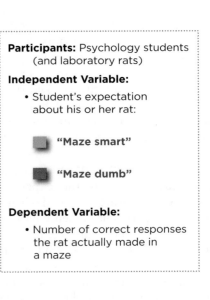

Participants: Psychology students (and laboratory rats)

Independent Variable:
• Student's expectation about his or her rat:

    "Maze smart"

    "Maze dumb"

Dependent Variable:
• Number of correct responses the rat actually made in a maze

in a standardized form, such as on the computer. Another strategy to protect against such problems is to keep the experimenter *blind*, meaning that the experimenters who are interacting with the participants do not know which condition the participants are in.

Design Studies That Are High in Experimental Realism.

Another way to reduce, or at least minimize, demand characteristics is to design experimental procedures with high **experimental realism**, meaning those studies that are engaging for subjects and hence lead them to behave naturally and spontaneously.

experimental realism the extent to which participants are engaged in a particular study and hence act in more spontaneous and natural ways

Some researchers who study marital interaction, for example, ask couples to re-enact a conflict they have had previously and then videotape that conflict. But it is certainly possible that couples who know that their fight will later be watched by psychologists do not act in the same way that they might if they were alone.

Creating studies with high experimental or psychological realism is particularly important when experiments take place in laboratory or research settings in which experimenters have their equipment, such as video cameras, one-way mirrors, and other materials needed for the study. In these settings, participants' attitudes and behavior may be influenced by the artificial setting, instead of by the independent variable. This can lead to problems in the study if participants who are asked to do an unusual procedure in the lab may act how they think they should act, as opposed to what they would normally do.

Pixland/SUPERSTOCK

Researchers who are interested in examining conflict often ask couples to re-enact a conflict they have had previously so they can code this interaction. But can you imagine that knowing researchers are observing their conflict could influence behavior?

However, even under laboratory conditions researchers can design studies that participants find very realistic and engaging. A famous study by Stanley Milgram in which people were directed to give painful electric shocks to other subjects, for example, was very involving—even gripping—for participants, and therefore it is assumed that their behavior was genuine (and you'll learn more about this study in Chapter 8).

EXTERNAL VALIDITY

In order to provide useful information about real-world events and processes, research studies also need to have **external validity**, meaning confidence that the same results would be obtained for other people and in other situations. One famous study on the link between attachment styles in infancy and later experience in romantic relationships collected data by asking readers of a newspaper to complete a "love quiz" (Hazan & Shaver, 1987). It seems likely that those who bother to complete and mail in the quiz would have characteristics that differ (more romantic attitudes? worse relationships?) from those who wouldn't bother to take the quiz. So, the study would be low in external validity. However, other researchers have replicated these findings about the link between attachment styles and relationship interaction (as you'll learn about in Chapter 12). But in other cases researchers may find that results from a particular study, using a particular finding, can't be obtained for other people and in other situations (meaning the study is low in external validity). There are, fortunately, several ways of increasing external validity.

external validity the degree to which there can be reasonable confidence that the same results would be obtained for other people in other situations

Design Studies That Are High in Mundane Realism.

Research studies need to have **mundane realism**, meaning to resemble places and events that exist in the real world, so the findings can be applied from an experiment to the real world. Some research has examined how susceptible college students are to getting a cold during exam period (Jemmott & Magliore, 1988). Obviously, this type of situation occurs several times during the academic year, and therefore findings from this type of research approach are likely to apply to other similar situations. However, imagine an experiment in which students completed an exam

mundane realism the extent to which the conditions of the study resemble places and events that exist in the real world

and were given an electric shock each time they gave a wrong answer. Although this type of situation would probably be extremely stressful (as well as ethically questionable), it would have low mundane realism, and hence might not give us accurate information about how stress can influence health in situations that are more realistic.

Conducting **field experiments** (experiments conducted in a natural setting) is an effective way of increasing mundane realism. For example, in Chapter 3 you'll read about a study researchers conducted on Halloween that measured how many candies children took from a bowl as a function of whether there was a mirror above the bowl (Diener, Fraser, Beaman, & Kelem, 1976). Experiments that are conducted in the field are less likely to be influenced by the particular setting in which they take place (in part because participants may not even know they are taking part in a study; more about this issue later in the chapter).

Use a Random or Representative Sample.

Many research studies are conducted using a *convenience sample*, meaning a sample that is selected because it is readily accessible to the researcher (this is often college freshmen who are taking an introduction to psychology course!). In fact, 75% of all published articles in psychology use college student as participants (Sherman, Buddie, Dragan, End, & Finney, 1999). Because students tend to be more educated, wealthier, and younger than the majority of the population, it is not clear whether findings based on such a sample would hold true for other people. Similarly, the majority of research in psychology is based largely in white, male, middle-class samples (Gannon, Luchetta, Rhodes, Pardie, & Segrist, 1992; Graham, 1992). We can be relatively confident that the findings from this type of study would apply to those in such a population in the real world. But we should be less confident that these findings would apply to populations that differ in terms of age, race, gender, income, and so on. Can we say that studies on relationship satisfaction that are done with college students in relatively short-term dating relationships will have real similarity to what happens in marriages? Probably not.

Another problem with the use of convenience samples is that those who take the time to participate in a study might also differ from those who do not respond. Therefore, their responses may not be applicable to the general population (Bradburn & Sudman, 1988). For example, a study of sexual behavior was conducted by researchers at the University of Chicago (Laumann, Gagnon, Michael, & Michaels, 1994). This study included a number of personal topics, such as frequency of masturbation, marital affairs, and homosexual behavior. But who is most likely to respond to these types of questions? Probably those who are relatively comfortable discussing such sensitive issues, and with revealing personal information to strangers; people who lack this comfort may have simply refused to participate

If you want to measure the impact of fraternity life on alcohol use, collecting data from a sample of men in fraternities would be a great approach. But if you want to study the frequency of drinking on college campuses in general, it would be better to use a random or a representative sample.

in the survey. However, individuals who are comfortable discussing such topics might also be more likely to engage in such behaviors. Thus, this type of survey approach might lead to an overestimate of the frequency of these behaviors.

Let's say that you are asked to evaluate the quality of your Social Psychology course. If you really like your professor, you are probably highly motivated to complete the survey to let others know how great this class is. Similarly, if you really hated this course (which I know is hard to imagine, but try), you are likely to want to warn others about this class, and so you would complete the survey. However, if you have mixed feelings about the class (you like some parts, you don't like other parts, but you don't generally feel strongly), you may not be very motivated to complete a survey at all.

Research studies should try to use a **representative sample**, meaning a sample that reflects the characteristics of the population at large. So, if you are interested in examining the frequency of drinking on college campuses, it would be a mistake to simply survey students who live in a fraternity or sorority, because research shows that these students drink more alcohol than those who live in residence halls or off-campus (Wechsler, Dowdall, Davenport, & Castillo, 1995). Instead, you might want to call every tenth person in the student directory to try to recruit a sample that represents all of the students at the school (e.g., an equal mix of males and females, athletes and non-athletes, etc.).

representative sample a sample that reflects the characteristics of the population at large

Make Participation Convenient.
Another way of increasing external validity is to make participation in a research study as convenient as possible. For example, if you recruit people to participate in a smoking cessation intervention that requires them to spend every Saturday for a month traveling to a faraway place, you are probably just influencing those who are very motivated to quit and hence the results may not be generalizable, or applicable, to the average smoker (who likely lacks such extreme motivation). On the other hand, if you find that attending one 2-hour workshop is helping people to stop smoking, that result would probably be very generalizable to lots of other smokers. Many people would be willing to attend this type of program, and therefore the researchers should feel more confident that their approach could work with other people.

Conduct Replications.
Finally, you should conduct the same study in different populations or locations. For example, if you conduct the same study in a small rural high school, a medium-sized suburban high school, and a large inner-city high school, and you find that in all three locations students who are lonely have poorer social skills, then you can have reasonable confidence that adolescents

"I don't usually volunteer for experiments, but I'm kind of a puzzle freak."

who have poor social skills are at greater risk of feeling lonely. However, you might not be able to tell if loneliness and poor social skills are connected in college students or for adults.

WHAT IS THE BEST APPROACH?

How do you decide which research technique to use to answer a particular question? There is no single best method, and all methods have strengths and weaknesses. Because experiments are the only technique that randomly assigns people to conditions, this approach is the best method for examining whether a specific factor is likely to cause another. However, because experiments are somewhat artificial, this approach does not give us as much information about what happens in real-life situations. While naturalistic observation methods give us very accurate information about what happens in the "real world," they tell us more about how two (or more) different variables are connected than about whether one variable causes the other.

As noted, experiments are the only research method that determines whether one variable causes another. However, there are some cases in which practical and/or ethical concerns make it impossible to conduct true experiments. For example, you can't randomly assign some people to get divorced in order to determine the effects of this stressor on children's own relationship satisfaction. Researchers who are interested in the impact of divorce might examine differences between children whose parents are divorced versus those whose parents remain married.

In sum, different methods are best for providing different types of information and for answering different questions. For example, you might want to use naturalistic observation to examine whether boys tend to play in larger groups than girls, because obviously you could not answer this question using a true experimental design. On the other hand, if you are interested in examining the effectiveness of a prosocial videotape on increasing cooperation, conducting a true experiment is probably the best approach.

Finally, we can be more confident about scientific findings if researchers using different types of research methods all produce the same answer. For example, if researchers using many different approaches all examine the link between alcohol use and risky sexual behavior and reach the same conclusion, we can be quite confident that drinking alcohol does lead to risky sexual behavior (and it does). Concepts in Context describes how researchers could use each of the three major approaches to examine a particular topic in social psychology, that is, the link between exposure to thin ideals in the media and disordered eating.

EXPERIMENTAL METHODS AND STRATEGIES FOR IMPROVING INTERNAL AND EXTERNAL VALIDITY

FACTOR	EXAMPLE
Experimental methods	Randomly assign some women to read a magazine featuring thin models and others to read a magazine featuring more neutral photographs, and then rate how much they eat during a supposed "ice cream taste-test" in the second part of the study.
Internal validity	Keep experimenters blind to which types of magazines the women read, so that any differences that emerge are clearly a function of the type of magazine read.
External validity	Recruit participants without referencing the specific focus of the study on ice cream tasting, and conduct the study with high school students, college students, and adult women.

WHAT ARE THE ETHICAL ISSUES INVOLVED IN CONDUCTING RESEARCH IN SOCIAL PSYCHOLOGY?

It is mandatory for researchers to attend to ethical issues involved in conducting research. Here is one of the reasons why. In 1973, Phillip Zimbardo, a professor at Stanford University, conducted a study to examine the impact of the prison environment on behavior (Haney, Banks, & Zimbardo, 1973; Haney & Zimbardo, 1998). Twenty-one college men were randomly assigned to either the "guard" or the "prisoner" role, and then literally lived in a make-believe prison (set up in the basement of the psychology building). Guards were given uniforms, whistles, and billy clubs, and were instructed to enforce various prison rules. Prisoners were given uniforms and spent most of their time locked in their cells. Although all participants had completed measures of psychological well-being prior to the study, after only a few days the prison environment became highly disturbing: guards forced prisoners to perform cruel and humiliating tasks, and prisoners became extremely passive and, in some cases, highly depressed. Although the original experiment was planned to last for two weeks, Zimbardo called off the study after only eight days, given the extreme behavior observed.

The Zimbardo prison study raised a number of concerns in the psychology community, in large part because participants clearly experienced psychological—and even physical—harm. Researchers therefore question whether this study should have been done, and whether the benefits of what was learned in this study outweigh the costs for the participants. To avoid conducting ethically questionable studies in the future, there are now careful procedures researchers must follow when conducting scientific research. This section will examine ethical issues involved in conducting research in social psychology, including review by an institutional board, informed consent, deception, confidentiality, and debriefing.

In Zimbardo's study, the consequences of participating in this study were substantial for both the "prisoners," who were subjected to unpleasant physical conditions and psychological pressures, and the "guards," who learned how cruel they could be to other students under particular conditions.

Dr. Philip Zimbardo

REVIEW BY AN INSTITUTIONAL REVIEW BOARD

First, studies now undergo an extensive review by an *Institutional Review Board* before they are implemented. This review of research plans for ethical concerns by a panel is required by virtually all organizations in the United States, including hospitals, colleges, universities, and government agencies. These boards review whether the potential benefits of the research are justifiable in light of possible risks or harms, including physical risks (e.g., receiving painful electric shocks, experiencing extreme heat, having to run on a treadmill) as well as psychological risks (e.g., having to give a speech, learning you are low in creativity, wearing an

©AP/Wide World Photos

In the NEWS **Abu Ghraib.** In 2004, some American soldiers forced their Iraqi prisoners to engage in degrading and humiliating behavior. Research in social psychology provides important information about the factors that led to this behavior.

embarrassing t-shirt). These boards may force experimenters to make changes in the design or procedure of the research, or they may deny approval for a particular study altogether. You might wonder about the effects of (falsely) telling someone his or her spouse was having an affair. However, a research review panel would never allow this type of study because of the high potential for psychological harm to the poor unsuspecting participant (and his or her spouse).

PROVIDE INFORMED CONSENT

informed consent all participants must sign a form stating their deliberate, voluntary decision to participate in research

Research studies now require participants to give **informed consent**. This consent refers to an individual's deliberate, voluntary decision to participate in research, based on the researcher's description of what such participation will

APA GUIDELINES FOR CONDUCTING RESEARCH WITH HUMANS

Informed Consent

Using language that is reasonably understandable to participants, psychologists inform participants of the nature of the research; they inform participants that they are free to participate or decline to participate or to withdraw from the research; they explain the foreseeable consequences of declining or withdrawing; they inform participants of significant factors that may be expected to influence their willingness to participate; and they explain other aspects about which the prospective participants inquire.

When psychologists conduct research with individuals such as students or subordinates, psychologists take special care to protect the prospective participants from adverse consequences of declining or withdrawing from participation.

When research participation is a course requirement or opportunity for extra credit, the prospective participant is given the choice of equitable alternative activities.

Deception in Research

Psychologists do not conduct a study involving deception unless they have determined that the use of deceptive techniques is justified by the study's prospective scientific, educational, or applied value and that equally effective alternative procedures that do not use deception are not feasible.

Psychologists never deceive research participants about significant aspects that would affect their willingness to participate, such as physical risks, discomfort, or unpleasant emotional experiences.

Reprinted by permission of American Psychological Association, 1995.

involve. Participants don't need to hear about every single aspect of the research, but do need to hear enough to make an educated decision about whether they would like to participate.

In some cases researchers can't provide participants with accurate information about the study because giving even a few details would ruin the study. For example, in one study, researchers were interested in examining honesty (Bersoff, 1999). Participants came into the lab to complete some questionnaires, and then, as they were leaving, the experimenter gave them the wrong amount of money (too much). The dependent variable was whether participants would return the money or just take it and leave. (As they predicted, most participants just took the extra money and left.) But obviously, participants in this study could not give full consent to their participation because telling them the study was examining honesty would of course have changed participants' behavior. These studies therefore use **deception**, in which they give false information to participants. Law Connections describes another type of study that involves tricky ethical considerations.

deception false information given to participants in a research study

PROTECT CONFIDENTIALITY

Participant confidentiality needs to be protected from unauthorized disclosure, and hence surveys often use a code number instead of the person's name. Data also

Law
CONNECTIONS

The Challenges of Studying Drinking and Driving

When researchers study real-life behavior that could have serious legal and/or health implications, they must take precautions to ensure participants' safety. In one study, researchers were interested in examining whether alcohol use affects people's attitudes and intentions toward drinking and driving (MacDonald, Zanna, & Fong, 1995). Male participants were randomly assigned to the sober or the intoxicated condition (and all participants were of legal drinking age). Those in the intoxicated condition drank enough alcohol to reach a blood alcohol concentration of .08 (the legal limit for driving while intoxicated in most states). All participants then completed a questionnaire assessing their attitudes and intentions to drink and drive in a number of situations. Results indicated that when asked general questions about their future intentions, sober and intoxicated participants were equally negative about this behavior. However, when a contingency was embedded in the question (e.g., "Would you drink and drive only a short distance?"), intoxicated participants were significantly less negative about drinking and driving than sober participants. Given the researchers' concern that intoxicated participants could leave the study and drive while intoxicated—an illegal and dangerous behavior—all participants in this condition were required to stay in the laboratory for one hour after completing the study. If a participant's blood alcohol concentration remained above .05% after one hour,

the experimenter then either accompanied the participant home (if he lived on campus) or provided a taxi ride home (if he lived off campus). This experiment also used only male participants, given the concerns about exposing females, if pregnant, to alcohol.

Ingram Publishing/SUPERSTOCK

need to be stored in a locked room with restricted access. When reports using the data are made, only group-level information is presented, as opposed to individually describing how particular people did. So, you would say that "most students who received the alcohol prevention workshop drank less," instead of "most students who received the alcohol prevention workshop drank less except for Bart Simpson, who surprisingly doubled his beer intake over the next month."

PROVIDE DEBRIEFING

debriefing a disclosure made to participants after research procedures are completed in which the researcher explains the purpose of the study, answers questions, attempts to resolve any negative feelings, and emphasizes the contributions of the research to science

Following participation in a research study, participants are given a **debriefing**. This refers to a disclosure made to subjects after research procedures are completed. The researcher explains the purpose of the study, answers any questions, attempts to resolve any negative feelings, and emphasizes the contributions to science of the research. This is especially important in cases in which deception has been used (as illustrated in The Downside of Using Deception box).

My husband can testify to the importance of a careful debriefing. One summer when I was in school, the graduate students in my department were desperate for subjects, so he ended up serving as a participant for several of my friends. He had had only one psychology class, and it was on Abnormal Psychology, so he was not aware of many of the techniques in social psychology. One day he participated in a study on cooperation in which he was told that he was hooked up with a partner who was working on a computer in the next room and they had to make some decisions. At the end of the study, after he had described how he and his partner got into a good rhythm, they told him "well, actually it was just you; the computer is programmed to respond to your answers in a given way." Then later in the summer, he participated in another study on learning in which he needed to teach another subject (who was in the next room) some word pairs. At the end of the study he described how he felt the learner really got the pairs, and he thought his teaching was effective. Then he learned there was no learner—it was just a tape recording. So how did he feel? Stupid. Tricked. And that is often people's experience, or fear, about participating in psychology experiments.

So what can we do as researchers to make sure people who serve as participants in our studies feel good about the experience? First, emphasize that the study is carefully designed to trick people and that everyone pretty much believes it (so the participant doesn't feel that he or she is particularly stupid or gullible). Second, explain the contribution their participation makes to science, and offer to send them a letter explaining the results or giving more information. When these procedures are followed, most participants hold positive beliefs about their experience, and believe the benefits of such participation outweigh the costs (Sharpe, Adair, & Roese, 1992).

THE DOWNSIDE OF USING DECEPTION IN PSYCHOLOGICAL RESEARCH

I was having a drink with my friend Justin when he spotted an attractive woman sitting at the bar. After an hour of gathering his courage, he approached her and asked, "Would you mind if I chatted with you for a while?" She responded by yelling at the top of her lungs, "No, I won't come over to your place tonight!" With everyone in the restaurant staring, Justin crept back to our table, puzzled and humiliated. A few minutes later, the woman walked over to us and apologized. "I'm sorry if I embarrassed you," she said, "but I'm a graduate student in psychology and I'm studying human reaction to embarrassing situations." At the top of his lungs Justin responded, "What do you mean, two hundred dollars?"

STRATEGIES FOR MANAGING ETHICAL ISSUES IN CONDUCTING RESEARCH

FACTOR	EXAMPLE
Review by an institutional review board	Dr. Rosenberg submits his research proposal to an institutional board. He then changes several aspects of study design following the board's request.
Provide informed consent	Dr. Rosenberg describes the goals and procedures to all participants before the study begins. She also reviews the benefits and costs of participating. Finally, she lets participants know they can stop the study at any time.
Protect confidentiality	Danny and Lisa, two research assistants in Dr. Rosenberg's lab, enter all data using participants' code numbers only. The forms that match participants' names and code numbers are stored in a separate lab.
Provide debriefing	After participants have completed the study, Dr. Rosenberg describes the study's goals and procedures. She emphasizes the contributions of this research to psychology theory, and the normality of the participants' actions.

CULTURE

HOW DOES CULTURE INFLUENCE RESEARCH FINDINGS?

Imagine that you are asked a series of questions about your own attitudes. These questions include "On a date, the boy should be expected to pay all expenses," "It is all right for a girl to want to play rough sports like football," and "Petting is acceptable on a first date." How would women from different cultures respond to these questions? Researchers examined precisely this question by asking female students in the United States from different cultural backgrounds (including Japan, Taiwan, Indonesia, and the Middle East as well as the United States) each of these, and other, questions (Gibbons, Hamby, & Dennis, 1997). As predicted, women from the United States gave more extreme answers—meaning both high and low answers—than women from other cultures, who tended to give more moderate answers—meaning those in the middle of the responses. The researchers assume that these moderate answers reflect, in part, the lack of meaning of many of these questions for those from different cultures. After all, in cultures in which arranged marriages are the norm (and dating thus does not occur) and in those cultures in which women are not allowed to engage in sports, such questions simply aren't meaningful. Participants are therefore much more likely to give neutral answers because they don't know how to interpret or respond. This study demonstrates one of the many challenges of conducting research across different cultures, as we'll discuss throughout this textbook. This section will examine how culture influences three particular issues in research design and methodology: the impact of question wording, question order, and language used.

THE IMPACT OF QUESTION ORDER

In one study, researchers asked German students at the University of Heidelberg and Chinese students at Beijing University identical questions (Haberstroh, Oyserman, Schwarz, Kuhnen, & Ji, 2002). Students were asked two questions:

(1) How happy are you with your studies? and (2) how happy are you with your life as a whole? However, half of the students at each school were asked the questions in that order, and half of the students were asked these questions in the opposite order. How did question order matter? Well, for German students, the correlation between these two answers was higher when they were asked about their academic lives first. For Chinese students, question order had no impact on the correlation between their responses.

How can culture impact the effect of order? For German students, academic performance plays a stronger role in self-esteem because academic achievement reflects their accomplishments. Thus, when German students first think about their academic achievements, they report having a somewhat higher overall life satisfaction. In other words, academic life satisfaction has a stronger impact on life satisfaction for German students than for Chinese students.

THE IMPACT OF QUESTION WORDING

How questions are worded in surveys can also influence responses in different ways across cultures. In one study, Canadian and Japanese participants were asked to complete a survey in which questions were worded in three distinct ways (Heine, Lehman, Peng, & Greenholtz, 2002). Participants in one condition read the question with no reference ("I have respect for the authority figures with whom I interact."); participants in another condition read the question with a reference to Japanese others ("Compared to most Japanese, I think I have respect for the authority figures with whom I interact."); and participants in yet another condition read the question with a reference to North Americans ("Compared to most North Americans, I think I have respect for the authority figures with whom I interact").

As predicted, the reference group included in the question had a significant effect on people's responses. Although there was no overall cultural difference in responses when no reference group was included, significant effects of culture occurred when reference groups were included. When comparing themselves to people in the other culture, Canadians saw themselves as less interdependent than the Japanese. In contrast, Japanese people saw themselves as more interdependent than Canadians. These findings indicate that question wording, and in particular the type of comparison noted in the question, impacts responses in different ways for people in different cultures.

THE IMPACT OF LANGUAGE

Another subtle factor that can influence findings in cross-cultural research is the language used during testing. In one study, researchers examined differences in how Chinese and European Americans organized sets of three words (Ji, Zhang, & Nisbett, 2004). Participants were given three words, and were asked to indicate which two words were most closely related and why. For example, if participants were given the words "monkey," "panda," and "banana," they would group "monkey" and "panda" because they were both animals, or they could group "monkey" and "banana" because monkeys eat bananas. Although in general, Chinese people organized objects in a more relational way than European Americans (meaning they were more likely to group together "monkey" and "banana" than "monkey" and "panda"), the responses of bilingual Chinese people were more relational when they were tested in Chinese than when they were tested in English. Other research supports this finding that the language used during testing can influence the accessibility of different types of thoughts, which in turn can impact the research findings (Trafimow, Silverman, Fan, & Law, 1997).

This chapter has examined five key issues involved in conducting research in social psychology.

YOU LEARNED **How do researchers in social psychology test their ideas?** This section examined the specific steps involved in the research process, including forming a question, searching the literature, forming a hypothesis and an operational definition, collecting and analyzing data, and proposing and/or revising a theory. You also learned why exposing children to images of aggression in the media is a bad idea.

YOU LEARNED **What are the different types of correlational research methods?** This section described two distinct types of correlational research methods— observational/naturalistic methods and self-report or survey methods—as well as the strengths and limitations of each approach. Also, you discovered that how you ask college students about their alcohol use and sexual behavior can influence their response.

YOU LEARNED **How do you conduct experimental research?** This section described specific features of experimental methods, including random assignment and control. It also described the importance of designing studies with high internal and external validity. You also learned that women eat fewer M&Ms when they are talking with an attractive man than when they are talking with someone who is less attractive.

YOU LEARNED **What are the ethical issues involved in conducting research in social psychology?** This section described how researchers manage the ethical issues involved in conducting research in social psychology, including review by an institutional board, informed consent, deception, confidentiality, and debriefing. You learned that college students can behave like prison guards (and indeed prisoners) very quickly when they are put in this situation.

YOU LEARNED **How does culture influence research findings?** The last section in this chapter described the role of culture in influencing research findings in social psychology. You discovered how question order, question wording, and language used can all impact responses in different ways for people from individualistic versus collectivistic cultures. You also learned that women in the United States give much more extreme answers to questions about dating than women in Iran.

KEY TERMS

archival research 35

correlation 34

covert measures 42

debriefing 56

deception 55

demand characteristics 46

dependent variable 44

event-recording measure 38

experimental methods 44

experimental realism 49

experimenter expectancy effects 47

external validity 49

field experiments 50

hypothesis 31

independent variable 44

informed consent 54

inter-rater reliability 36

internal validity 46

meta-analysis 35

mundane realism 49

operational definition 32

observational/naturalistic methods 34

random assignment 44

representative sample 51

theory 33

QUESTIONS FOR REVIEW

1. Describe each of the steps in the scientific method.
2. Describe two advantages and two disadvantages of each of the three major methods of conducting research in social psychology: naturalistic/observation, self-report/survey, and experiments.
3. What are two ways of increasing internal validity and two ways of increasing external validity?
4. What are four ways researchers manage ethical concerns when conducting research in social psychology?
5. Describe how people from different cultures can respond to the same questionnaire in different ways.

TAKE ACTION!

1. After observing that whenever your brother goes for a run, he seems to be in a great mood, you wonder whether exercise makes people feel good. How could you do this study using self-report methods? How could you do this study using experimental methods?
2. Dr. D'Angelo is a dentist who wants to get feedback from her patients about their satisfaction with office policy and wait times. She was planning on mailing an anonymous survey to all of her patients, but then decided that this would be too much work. Instead she is planning on asking patients for their thoughts about their dental care when they come in for the appointment. What is the problem with this approach?
3. Your roommate Darren wants to know if his new hypnosis tape is actually effective in helping people stop smoking. To test its effectiveness, he asks ten of his closest friends to help him determine whether hypnosis is a good way of helping people stop smoking. He gives his five male friends the hypnosis tape, and his five female friends a music tape. One week later he asks each person how many cigarettes they are smoking. When Darren asks you for your thoughts on his study, what problems do you see?
4. As part of a class project, you want to measure the effects on self-esteem of telling college athletes that they have failed a test of "sports intelligence." How could you design a study to ethically test this question?
5. You are interested in designing a study to test differences in attitudes towards human rights, including women's rights and gays' rights, across cultures. How could you conduct such a study? What do you think you would find?

RESEARCH CONNECTIONS

Try some of these research activities to gain experience in conducting and evaluating research, and to increase your understanding of research methods and techniques in social psychology.

Visit WileyPLUS for more activities and interactive research tools! (www.wileyplus.com)

Participate in Research

Activity 1 **Forming a Research Question:** Research questions can be inspired by your daily experiences. Spend a day examining your own behavior. Focus on a specific behavior from that day and think about factors that may have influenced that behavior. Turn your observation into a research question that you can bring to class, post on your class discussion board, or share with others.

Activity 2 **Understanding Correlation:** Why do first born children tend to show higher levels of academic achievement? This chapter has described the distinction between correlation and causation, and the possibility of a third variable accounting for the association between two variables. Describe two or three different third variables that may be responsible for the association of birth order and achievement.

Activity 3 **The Importance of Internal and External Validity:** No study is perfect. To test the impact of internal and external validity in experimental research, go to WileyPLUS to read about some studies and determine if they have problems with internal validity, external validity, or both.

Activity 4 **Understanding the Ethics of Research:** Imagine you are the chair of an institutional Review Board. As such, you must insure that research is conducted in an ethical way. Go to WileyPLUS to see a series of proposed studies in social psychology that you will approve or deny based on issues of informed consent, deception, confidentiality, or debriefing.

Activity 5 **The Role of Context:** The culture you grew up in determines a lot about you, even how you respond to research questions. To examine the impact of culture on research, complete a survey on WileyPLUS and see how your answers compare to someone of a different culture.

Test a Hypothesis

One of the findings discussed in this chapter was whether students, who receive better grades in a class, like the professor more than those who receive worse grades. To test whether this hypothesis is true, design a survey to ask other students about their grade in a class and their liking of the professor. Do your findings support or refute the hypothesis?

Design a Study

To design your own study to test the influence of exposure to aggressive models on acts of aggression, decide on a research question you would like to answer. Then decide what type of study you want to conduct (self-report, observational/naturalistic, or experimental), choose your own independent and dependent variables, and operationally define each by determining the procedures or measures you will use. Form a hypothesis to predict what will happen in your study (the expected cause and effect relationship between your two variables) and collect the data.

3

Self-Perception and

Did you ever wonder?

In January 2005, one of the hottest celebrity couples, Jennifer Aniston and Brad Pitt, announced their separation and, soon after, their divorce. Although initial reports portrayed this split as a "mutual decision," rumors of Brad's involvement with a recent co-star, Angelina Jolie, quickly surfaced. Initially neither Angelina Jolie nor Brad Pitt would comment on whether they in fact had a relationship, but tabloid photographs revealed the couple together in private settings, and in January 2006, the couple announced they were expecting a child. Although Jennifer Aniston embarked on a new romantic relationship herself during this time, many articles and interviews focused on how very difficult this experience must be for her—seeing her ex-husband date such a very attractive woman and start a family with her. So, why exactly did people assume that Jennifer Aniston—a wealthy and beautiful movie star—must feel so bad? This chapter will explain why people's own feelings of self-worth are influenced not only by their own

Media
CONNECTIONS
What Happens When
Barbies Get Smaller
and GI Joes Get Bigger?

Health
CONNECTIONS
The Downside of Too
Much Optimism

Law
CONNECTIONS
The Impact of
Feedback on
Eyewitness Confidence

Self-Presentation

attributes, but also by their comparisons with others. In addition, you'll find out ...

Q A Why are people who get fired just as happy as those who stay hired?

Q A Why can reading about Pamela Anderson make you feel smarter?

Q A Why do people see themselves as more virtuous than others?

Q A Why don't you need to worry about wearing an embarrassing t-shirt?

Q A Why do people in individualistic cultures tend to rate themselves as better than others, whereas people in communal cultures tend to see others as better than themselves?

What do these statements have in common? All of these describe findings from research in social psychology on how we see ourselves and how we present ourselves to others.

Eamonn McCormack/Getty Images, Inc.

If someone asks you what you're like, what would you say? You might say "smart," or "friendly," or "athletic." All of these describe your self-concept, meaning your overall beliefs about your own attributes. The self-concept is made up of distinct beliefs that we hold about ourselves and that influence what we notice about the world as well as how we process self-relevant information (Markus, 1977). People who see themselves as artistic are likely to focus on the aesthetic aspects of what they encounter in the world, such as the outfits their friends are wearing, the arrangement of flowers in a vase, or the combination of colors in a spectacular sunset. On the other hand, those who, like myself, are not schematic for art would be unlikely to notice such aesthetic details. If your overall evaluation of your attributes is positive, then you have high self-esteem. The self is an integral part of social psychology because—as you'll learn—social factors influence how we think about ourselves, and how we think about ourselves influences how we see and interact in the world.

HOW DO PERSONAL FACTORS INFLUENCE THE SELF-CONCEPT?

Imagine that you're an assistant professor of psychology approaching the tenure decision—meaning the decision by your department and your university regarding whether you will have basically guaranteed lifetime employment (if you are given tenure) or whether you will be, in effect, fired (if you are denied tenure). Which of those situations would make you feel better, and how long would that feeling (good or bad) last? This is precisely the study that was done by researchers at the University of Texas – Austin to examine people's accuracy in predicting their future emotional states (Gilbert, Pinel, Wilson, Blumberg, & Wheatley, 1998). In this study, researchers asked all former assistant professors who had achieved or failed to achieve tenure in the last 10 years to rate how happy they were. Then they asked current assistant professors—who were about to come up for tenure—how they thought they'd feel a few years later if they did or did not get tenure. Although current assistant professors predicted that they'd feel worse overall later on if they didn't get tenure, reports from those who'd lived through this experience don't support this belief: in fact, several years later those who did and did not have tenure were found to be equally happy. This is just one example of how people's thoughts about themselves—and the factors that influence their **self-concept**—can have unexpected results. This section will explain how the self-concept is influenced by a variety of factors within ourselves. What kinds of things do we do that make up our self-concept? We think about our thoughts, we focus on self-awareness, we regulate ourselves, we examine our own behavior, and we interpret our motivation.

self-concept an individual's overall beliefs about his or her own attributes

THINKING ABOUT YOUR THOUGHTS

Imagine you are trying to choose classes for next semester. You might think about English classes you've taken in the past, or about how you feel about reading literature, to help you make your decision. You are thinking about how you feel and this gives you insight into the choice you should make. This process of thinking about your thoughts or feelings is called introspection. Introspection is often seen as influencing the self-concept.

The hazards of introspection. Despite the common-sense belief that thinking about why we like something can help us understand our true attitudes, introspection is actually not a very effective way of gaining insight into our true attitudes (Dijksterhuis, 2004; Levine, Halberstadt, & Goldstone, 1996). In fact, people who analyze the reasons why they have a particular attitude (e.g., why they like their dating partner, why they prefer certain classes) show a lower correlation between their attitudes and their behavior, meaning that their attitudes aren't very good at predicting their actual behavior, than those who don't engage in this type of self-reflection. In one study, participants were asked to choose a poster to take home as a thank-you gift (Wilson, Lisle, Schooler, Hodges, Klaaren, & LaFleur, 1993). They were asked to base their selection either on the reasons why they preferred a given poster or on their "gut feeling" about a poster. When researchers contacted the students several weeks later, those who had relied on their gut feelings in making the choice reported feeling happier with their selection than those who had focused on the reasons.

Westend61/SUPERSTOCK

You might think that carefully weighing the costs and benefits of each dessert would lead you to make the best decision... but research actually suggests the opposite—just go with your gut instinct!

Why does thinking about their preferences lead people to make decisions that aren't necessarily in their best interest? First, in many cases our feelings are a better predictor of our true preferences and even our future behavior (Wilson, Dunn, Bybee, Hyman, & Rotondo, 1984; Wilson & LaFleur, 1995). This is why you may feel a tremendous attraction for someone whom it doesn't make sense for you to like—your heart is guiding your behavior, not your head (perhaps much to your parents' dismay). As Sigmund Freud noted, "When making a decision of minor importance, I have always found it advantageous to consider all the pros and cons. In vital matters, however ... the decision should come from the unconscious, from somewhere within our selves."

Overestimation of the impact of events. We often believe that various factors will influence our mood much more than they actually do (Gilbert & Wilson, 2000; Stone, Hedges, Neale, & Satin, 1985; Wilson, Laser, & Stone, 1982). In reality, however, people are very inaccurate in their **affective forecasting**, meaning that they greatly overestimate the impact that both positive and negative events will have on their mood (Wilson, Wheatley, Meyers, Gilbert, & Axsom, 2000). The example I gave at the start of this section on how assistant professors who do and do not receive tenure feel is one example of how affective forecasting is not so accurate. Similarly, college students expect that they will experience negative feelings for a long time following the break-up of a romantic relationship (Gilbert et al., 1998). But in reality, students whose relationships end are just as happy later on as those whose relationships continue. These findings suggest that people expect to feel much greater regret than they actually do, which could lead us to make faulty decisions—meaning those which are motivated primarily by our anticipation of great and long-lasting regret—which we never actually experience.

affective forecasting the process of predicting the impact of both positive and negative events on mood

It's not just that people are wrong about how they'll feel after experiencing relatively minor good or bad events, such as missing a train or winning a football game: we also tend to believe that major events will have a much longer lasting effect on our mood than they actually do (Wilson et al., 2000). Many people believe they'd be happier if they lived in California—given the warm climate—than in the Midwest, but overall, people who live in the Midwest are just as happy as those who live in California (Schkade & Kahneman, 1998). What does this mean at a practical level? Don't play the lottery (winning won't make you happy for long).

FOCUSING ON SELF-AWARENESS

self-discrepancy theory a theory that our self-concept is influenced by the gap between how we actually see ourselves and how we want to see ourselves

Another factor that can influence the way we see ourselves is how we compare ourselves to our own standards of behavior. The problem of self-discrepancy. According to **self-discrepancy theory**, our self-concept is influenced by the gap between how we see ourselves (our actual self) and how we want to see ourselves (our ideal self; Higgins, 1996). Everyone feels some discrepancy between their actual and ideal selves, but people who perceive a large discrepancy feel less good about themselves than people who see a small discrepancy. If you see yourself as a C-level student in organic chemistry but hope someday to be a world-class surgeon, you may experience a large gap between your actual and ideal selves and therefore feel very negative about yourself. On the other hand, a person who sees herself as a strong varsity tennis player and hopes to be the captain of the tennis team may perceive a relatively small gap between actual and ideal.

The impact of self-awareness. Self-discrepancy theory suggests that the self-concept is influenced by the gap between our actual and ideal selves. However, other researchers believe that people rarely think about such a discrepancy, and that, as a result, the presence of such a discrepancy would affect the self-concept only when a person is paying attention to it (Duval & Wicklund, 1972). Specifically, according to **self-awareness theory**, people notice self-discrepancies only when they focus on their own behavior. A variety of factors can lead to self-awareness, such as standing in front of a crowd, looking in a mirror, or hearing one's voice on tape. In turn, if you are forced to be self-aware, you will be motivated to either change your behavior (in order to match your behavior to your own personal standards) or try to escape from self-awareness (so that you don't notice this contradiction; see Figure 3.1).

self-awareness theory a theory that when people focus on their own behavior, they are motivated to either change their behavior (so their attitudes and behavior are in line) or escape from self-awareness (to avoid noticing this contradiction)

Research generally supports the idea that people who are self-aware are more likely to match their behavior to their own personal standards. In one study, Halloween trick-or-treaters were greeted at a researcher's door and left alone to help themselves from a bowl of candy (Beaman, Klentz, Diener, & Svanum, 1979). They were all asked to take only one piece. For half the children there was a full-length mirror right behind the bowl (which should clearly increase self-awareness), whereas

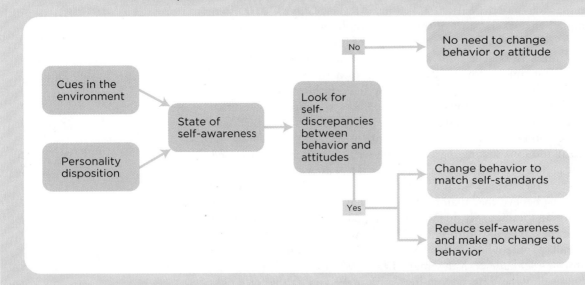

FIGURE 3.1

MODEL OF SELF-AWARENESS THEORY

According of self-awareness theory, environmental cues or personality factors can lead people to become more aware of their thoughts, feelings, and behavior. This increase in self-awareness, in turn, leads people to think about discrepancies between their attitudes and behavior. If self-discrepancies are found, we have one of two options: match our behavior to our internal attitudes or reduce self-awareness.

for the other half there was no mirror. Thirty-four percent of those without the mirror took more than one piece of candy, compared to only 12 percent of those with the mirror. And self-awareness doesn't just improve children's behavior; laboratory research with adults demonstrates that people who are looking at themselves in a mirror are less likely to use stereotypes (Macrae, Bodenhausen, & Milne, 1998) and more likely to behave in a moral way (Batson, Thompson, Seuferling, Whitney, & Strongman, 1999; Duval, Duval, & Neely, 1979).

REGULATING THE SELF

Although self-focused attention can lead us to try to match our behavior to our ideals, we can't always control our behavior to reach this standard (Baumeister, Bratslavsky, Muraven, & Tice, 1998; Muraven, Tice, & Baumeister, 1998; Vohs & Heatherton, 2000). If you've ever been on a diet, you have undoubtedly struggled to control the urge to eat something "forbidden" (e.g., cheesecake), and have probably been unable to resist on at least one occasion. This failure to match your actual behavior to your ideal standards occurs because it is exhausting to constantly try to exercise such restraint; sooner or later you may simply "use up" your willpower and give in to temptation (Pennebaker, 1989; Wegner, 1994). As described in Research Focus on Neuroscience, recent research in neuroscience suggests that different parts of the brain are activated when we make decisions about an immediate reward (e.g., eating that cheesecake right now) versus a delayed reward (e.g., promising ourselves a piece of cheesecake in a few weeks, after we've lost those stubborn 10 pounds).

RESEARCH FOCUS ON NEUROSCIENCE
Different Parts of the Brain Make Different Types of Decisions

Recent research in neuroscience suggests that different parts of the brain are responsible for making decisions regarding immediate rewards versus delayed rewards (McClure, Laibson, Loewenstein, & Cohen, 2004). In one study researchers used functional magnetic resonance imaging (fMRI) to examine which parts of the brain were active when participants made different types of decisions. When participants made decisions about an immediate reward—such as whether to receive $10 immediately or $11 tomorrow—the part of the brain influenced by neural systems associated with emotions was activated. On the other hand, when participants made decisions about a delayed reward—such as receiving $5 in two weeks or $40 in six weeks—the part of the brain involved in abstract reasoning and calculation was activated. This study provides convincing evidence that different parts of the brain are used to make different types of decisions. As one of the authors of this study describes, "Our emotional brain wants to max out the credit card, order dessert and smoke a cigarette. Our logical brain knows we should save for retirement, go for a jog and quit smoking."

The limits of self-control. Once we've spent energy on controlling our thoughts and desires, we have difficulty doing so again. In one study by Roy Baumeister and colleagues (1998), participants, who had signed up for a "taste perception" study and were specifically told not to eat for three hours before the experiment, came into a laboratory room and saw a table with two types of food: a bowl of freshly baked chocolate chip cookies and chocolate candies and another bowl of red and white radishes. Participants were then randomly assigned to one of the two food conditions (chocolate or radishes), and

Brand X/SUPERSTOCK

were asked to take about five minutes to taste at least two pieces of the assigned food. After this period of tasting, the experimenter returned to give the participant the second portion of the study—a problem-solving task in which participants had to trace a geometric puzzle without retracing any lines. However, this puzzle was specifically designed to be impossible to solve in order to create a frustrating situation. The experimenter then left the room, and timed how long the participant worked on the task prior to giving up (which was signaled by ringing a bell). As predicted, participants who were in the radish condition—and thus had to exercise great willpower in resisting eating chocolate—gave up working on the frustrating puzzles after only 8-1/2 minutes, whereas participants who were in the chocolate condition—and hence may not have "used up" all of their self-control when it comes time to work on the puzzles—worked an average of nearly 19 minutes before giving up.

Questioning the Research
Although Baumeister et al. (1998) describe their findings as caused by participants' lack of self-control in a second task once they've already had to exercise considerable self-control in the first task, can you think of another explanation for their findings?

One alternative explanation for these results is that participants in the radish condition were simply hungrier than those who were in the chocolate condition; after all, chocolate chip cookies and chocolates are certainly more filling than radishes. However, the results of a no-food control condition, in which participants simply worked on the frustrating puzzles without seeing either of the foods, revealed that participants in this condition—who clearly would be quite hungry—spent nearly 21 minutes working on the puzzles before giving up. Thus, we can be rather confident that the results of this study are not simply due to different levels of hunger in the different conditions. Figure 3.2 describes another example of the downside of exercising high levels of self-control.

FIGURE 3.2 DOES DEPLETING MENTAL ENERGY MAKE SELF-CONTROL MORE DIFFICULT?

Experimenters asked participants to solve various word starts, for example adding letters to "BU—" to create a word. Starts could be solved with sexual words, such as BUTT, or neutral words, such as BUGS. Some students had to complete a challenging mental task before completing the word starts. As predicted, a higher percentage of students whose energy and attention were depleted completed the word starts to make sexual words.

Source: Gaillot, M.T., & Baumeister, R.F. (2007). The physiology of will power: Linking blood glucose to self-control. *Personality and Social Psychology Review*, 11, 303–327.

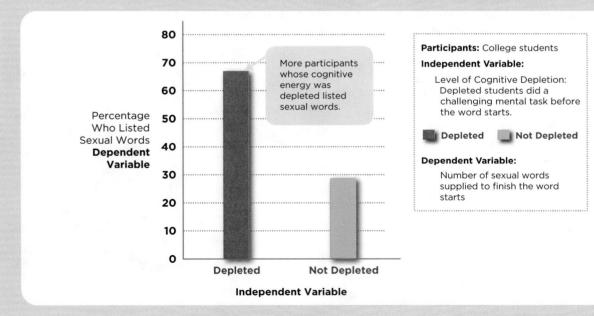

Trying to control or suppress our thoughts can also backfire and make these thoughts particularly salient (Major & Gramzow, 1999; Wegner & Gold, 1995; Wegner, Shortt, Blake, & Page, 1990). Have you ever tried to not think about something (e.g., an ex-boyfriend, a particularly gruesome scene from a movie, a failed test)? If so, then you most likely found that thoughts about this "forbidden" topic dominated your mind. Trying to suppress our thoughts can even influence our behavior. In one study, students were shown a picture of a "skinhead" named Hein, and were asked to spend five minutes describing a typical day in his life (Gordijn, Hindriks, Koomen, Dijksterhuis, & Knippenberg, 2004). (This study was conducted in The Netherlands, where skinheads, people with shaved heads and Nazi symbols on their clothing, are commonly seen as aggressive, racist, dumb, unhealthy, and unemployed.) Some participants were specifically told not to use stereotypes (the "suppression condition") whereas others were not given any instructions. Later, participants completed a second part of the study. It was a word recognition task in which strings of letters were presented together and participants had to decide whether this list of letters contained an actual word. Those who had tried to suppress their skinhead stereotypes recognized words that were related to the stereotype faster than did participants who were not given the suppression instructions. Do you see the downside of trying to control our thoughts?

Escape from self-awareness. Although in some cases self-awareness leads people to match their behavior to their internal standards, in other cases people choose to escape from this self-awareness and the discomfort it can bring. Efforts to escape from self-awareness can be relatively harmless. For example, dieters may choose to distract themselves from thoughts of food by reading a book or talking on the phone. But in other cases people's efforts to reduce self-awareness can have dangerous consequences. In a study by Jay Hull and Richard Young (1983), college students were given either negative or positive feedback about their IQ and then given an opportunity to taste and rate different kinds of wine. As predicted, students who were told they had low IQ scores drank more wine than those who received success feedback. These findings are in line with other findings showing that people often use alcohol to avoid thinking about themselves (Cooper, Frone, Russell, & Mudar, 1995; Steele & Josephs, 1990).

EXAMINING YOUR BEHAVIOR

Another factor that influences how we see ourselves is our own behavior—and research demonstrates that we look to our own behavior in particular ways as a way of understanding our self-concepts.

Self-perception theory. According to Daryl Bem's (1972) **self-perception theory**, we look at our own behavior to determine our attitudes and beliefs, in just the same way that we may examine other people's behavior to see what they are like. If you take a number of psychology classes, you look to your behavior and assume that you really like psychology. If you regularly choose the chocolate cake from a dessert tray, you assume that you must like chocolate. People who are led to believe that in the past they've supported a given policy tend to express positive attitudes toward that policy, whereas those who believe that they've opposed such a policy in the past tend to express negative attitudes toward it (Albarracin & Wyer, 2000; Schlenker & Trudeau, 1990).

Self-perception theory explains why asking people to perform a behavior, especially with little pressure, can lead them to experience a change in self-concept. Imagine that you are with a group of friends and they decide to go bowling. Even if you haven't enjoyed bowling in the past, if you go with your friends and participate, you may find yourself feeling more positive about bowling in the future. Self-perception theory predicts that you will experience this change in attitude because you will look at your behavior (e.g., "Here I am bowling.") to determine your belief about bowling (e.g., "I must like bowling").

BananaStock/SUPERSTOCK

self-perception theory the theory that people infer their attitudes by simply observing their behavior

In one test of self-perception theory, researchers approached random people on the street and asked them for help with finding a nonexistent address (the street did not exist; Dolinski, 2000). Virtually everyone (94%) responded (typically: "I don't know"). Participants were then approached a few blocks away by a woman carrying a huge suitcase and asked if they would watch the bag for a few minutes while she went up to visit a friend who lived on the 5th floor. Although only 34% of participants in the control condition agreed to watch the suitcase, 58% of the participants who had first been asked for directions agreed to watch the bag. These people looked at their behavior and determined that they were indeed helpful people. They had tried to provide directions when asked, and they were now willing to help yet another stranger by watching her luggage.

RESEARCH FOCUS ON GENDER
Gender Differences in Self-Definition

Although we all have a distinct view of our own strengths and weaknesses, one relatively consistent difference that has emerged in various studies is that men and women tend to differ in their views of themselves (Cross & Madson, 1997; Gabriel & Gardner, 1999; Josephs, Markus, & Tafarodi, 1992). Specifically, women tend to define themselves in part by their interpersonal relationships—their status as a mother, wife, sister, friend, and so forth. Compared to men, they are more likely to agree with statements such as " My close relationships are an important reflection of who I am," and "When I think of myself, I often think of my close friends or family also." In turn, women gain self-esteem from feeling connected to and interdependent with others. On the other hand, men tend to define themselves in terms of their individual achievements and to gain self-esteem from those accomplishments. Although men may also define themselves in part by their relationships, these relationships tend to be broader and more focused on group memberships (e.g., sports teams, larger friendship groups, fraternities). These differences appear relatively early in life, when girls tend to play in small groups with one or two other girls, and boys tend to play in larger groups.

"How are the smiling exercises coming along?"

Facial feedback hypothesis. Although Bem's self-perception theory focused specifically on people's tendency to judge how they feel based on their behavior, other researchers suggest that a similar process can influence our emotions (Laird, 1974). According to the **facial feedback hypothesis**, changes in facial expression can lead to changes in emotion. For example, people who hold their faces in a smile feel happier than those who maintain a frown (Kleinke, Peterson, & Rutledge, 1998). Changes in body posture and activity can have a similar effect on mood: people who sit slumped over feel less pride than those who sit upright; people who clench their fists feel more anger than those who relax their hands; and people who lift their hands up feel more positive than those who push their hands down (Duclos, Laird, Schneider, Sexter, Stern, & Van Lighten, 1989; Stepper & Strack, 1993). Similarly, people who nod while listening to a persuasive message show more attitude change than those who shake their heads (Briñol & Petty, 2003).

facial feedback hypothesis
the hypothesis that changes in facial expression can lead to changes in emotion

How could simply changing one's facial expression or body posture affect one's mood? One explanation is that changes in emotion that are caused by facial (and body) feedback are simply a result of self-perception (Kleinke et al., 1998). For example, people who are smiling may perceive themselves as happy, but those who are frowning see themselves as angry. Another explanation is that facial expressions and body movements influence emotions by producing physiological changes in the brain (Hennenlotter, Dresel, Castrop, Ceballos, Baumann, Wohlschläger, & Haslinger, 2009; Izard, 1994; Zajonc, Murphy, & Inglehart, 1989). Particular facial expressions and body movements may lead to increases or decreases in blood flow, which in turn are responsible for changes in mood.

INTERPRETING YOUR MOTIVATION

Another factor that can influence how people view themselves is the motivation they identify as the reason for their behavior (Amabile, Hill, Hennessey, & Tighe, 1994). If you believe that you are engaging in a given activity based on intrinsic motivation—namely, the desire to engage in the activity for its own sake, because we find it interesting or enjoy it—you see your behavior as motivated by internal factors, such as the sheer interest you have in this task. People who work on a task for intrinsic reasons report greater task involvement, enjoyment, curiosity, and interest. They also report greater psychological well-being (Sheldon, Ryan, Deci, & Kasser, 2004). On the other hand, if you believe that you engage in a given activity based on extrinsic motivation—namely, the desire to engage in an activity for external rewards or pressures—you see your behavior as motivated by the desire to fulfill obligations, receive a benefit, or avoid a punishment. People who work on a task for extrinsic

Rate Yourself

What Motivates You?
Work Preference Inventory

INSTRUCTIONS: *Rate each item on a scale of 1 (never or almost never true of me) to 4 (always or almost always true of me).*

☐ **1.** I enjoy trying to solve complex problems.
☐ **2.** I am strongly motivated by the money/grades I earn.
☐ **3.** Curiosity is the driving force behind much of what I do.
☐ **4.** I am strongly motivated by the recognition I can earn from other people.
☐ **5.** I prefer to figure things out for myself.
☐ **6.** I have to feel that I'm earning something for what I do.
☐ **7.** It is important for me to be able to do what I enjoy.
☐ **8.** To me, success means doing better than other people.
☐ **9.** I'm more comfortable when I can set my own goals.
☐ **10.** I prefer working on projects with clearly specified procedures.

SCORING: Add up your scores on the odd-numbered items to create one subscale. Then add up your scores on the even-numbered items to create a second subscale.

INTERPRETATION: This scale assesses people's focus on work for intrinsic versus extrinsic reasons (Amabile et al., 1994). People with higher scores on the intrinsic scale (the odd-numbered items) than the extrinsic scale (the even-numbered items) are more motivated by intrinsic motivations for work, whereas people with higher scores on the extrinsic subscale than the intrinsic subscale are more motivated by extrinsic motivations for work.

reasons report feeling concerned with recognition, competition, and tangible rewards or benefits. The pursuit of extrinsically focused goals, such as achieving financial success, can have negative consequences on overall life satisfaction and psychological well-being (Nickerson, Schwartz, Diener, & Kahneman, 2003; Sheldon, 2005).

The dangers of overjustification.   To determine why we are engaging in a particular behavior, we tend to examine the factors that lead to that behavior. Receiving external rewards can undermine our intrinsic interest in engaging in the behavior for intrinsic reasons, a phenomenon called **overjustification**. Unfortunately, this means that sometimes activities that should be intrinsically motivating, such as reading books, getting good grades, and attending classes, become less enjoyable once external motivations for such behaviors are provided. Some high schools have policies that require students to engage in a volunteer activity prior to graduation. These policies were developed in part to expose students to the benefits of volunteering (for themselves and for their communities). But some research shows that after being forced to volunteer, students become less interested in volunteering in the future, compared to students who were given a choice about volunteering (Stukas, Snyder, & Clary, 1999). This is presumably because, while volunteering should be fun (e.g., intrinsically

overjustification the phenomenon in which receiving external rewards for a given behavior can undermine the intrinsic motivation for engaging in that behavior

Business
CONNECTIONS

Does Giving Bonuses Enhance or Undermine Motivation?

Many businesses try to motivate their employees to work hard by providing specific incentives for good performance, such as bonuses. However, research on overjustification suggests that providing extrinsic motivation for completing a task can undermine intrinsic motivation and thereby reduce performance levels. Research with both children and adults reveals that those who receive an expected reward (e.g., are told that they will get to do a fun activity if they do three other activities first) are less creative than those who get no reward or get an unexpected reward (Amabile, Hennessey, & Grossman, 1986). Similarly, people who are motivated to make money primarily for extrinsic reasons (e.g., comparing well with others) are more depressed than those who are motivated by more intrinsic reasons (e.g., doing work one enjoys).

What can businesses do to motivate employees? Some companies have explored nonfinancial perks, such as "dressdown Fridays," more vacation days, or more flexible work schedules. However, other research suggests that people who are paid for meeting a performance standard show greater enjoyment of the task and higher performance levels (Eisenberger, Rhoades, & Cameron, 1999). Providing extrinsic motivation for vague tasks (e.g., creativity) may therefore undermine interest and performance, yet such rewards may improve performance on tasks for which clear, high standards are established.

Radius/SUPERSTOCK

rewarding), when you are forced to do it, you assume that the only reason you are doing it is for extrinsic reasons (e.g., fear of not graduating). See Business Connections for some important exceptions to the overjustification effect.

In one of the first experimental studies to demonstrate overjustification, Mark Lepper and his colleagues at Stanford University visited a nursery school and measured children's overall interest in drawing with magic markers (Lepper, Greene, & Nisbett, 1973). Some of the children were then asked to participate in a fun study of drawing. Some children were told that they would get a reward if they drew pictures with magic markers for the experimenter (and they did receive a reward). Others were simply asked to draw pictures for the experimenter (and did not receive a reward). Finally, a third group of children was asked to draw pictures for the experimenter and then received a "surprise reward" (meaning that they did not know they would receive a reward until after they had finished drawing). The researchers then measured the amount of time children in each group spent drawing with markers during the next class period. As predicted, children who had received the expected reward spent only 8.6% of their time drawing, compared to 16.7% for those who did not expect or receive a reward and 18.1% for those who received an unexpected reward. These findings suggest that providing a reward in advance of doing an activity undermines intrinsic motivation, but that providing an unexpected reward has no impact on such motivation.

Overcoming overjustification. Although the presence of external rewards can undermine intrinsic motivation in some cases, in many cases, rewards can work very well to stimulate interest in a given activity (Eisenberger & Cameron, 1996). For example, providing rewards for finishing a task and/or showing high quality work can be quite effective. Even in cases in which external pressures are present, there are ways to avoid, or at least minimize, their negative consequences. One study demonstrated that people who impose even more stringent deadlines on themselves for completing a task than are imposed by an external source show more task enjoyment than those who simply follow the externally imposed deadline (Burgess, Enzle, & Schmaltz, 2004). In other words, you can avoid dampening your intrinsic motivation to finish writing your psychology lab report that is due in two weeks by setting your own earlier deadline.

"All right, everybody, recess is over!"

PERSONAL INFLUENCES ON THE SELF-CONCEPT

FACTOR	EXAMPLE
Thinking about your thoughts	To choose which summer job to take, Carlo made a list of the costs and benefits of each option.
Focusing on self-awareness	Although the sign says, "Please take just one," Amy is tempted to help herself to many free samples on display at the new candy store, until she looks up and sees her own reflection in the mirror above the counter.
Regulating the self	Javier really misses his ex-girlfriend, so to help himself forget about her, he deliberately tries not to think about her—yet the more he forces himself not to think about her, the more he finds thoughts of their relationship creeping into his mind.
Examining your behavior	Daniel spends a lot of time playing chess with friends, so he thinks he really likes chess.
Interpreting your motivation	Samantha was always eager to play basketball until her new coach decided to reward each player with a dollar for each basket she scores.

HOW DO SOCIAL FACTORS INFLUENCE THE SELF-CONCEPT?

Imagine that you come to the psychology department one day to participate in a study on general knowledge. First, you read a brief paragraph about a famous woman, in which you learn about that person's behavior, lifestyle, and attributes. If you are in one condition, you read about Marie Curie, a scientist in the late 1800s who was the first woman to win a Nobel Prize. If you are in the other condition, however, you read about a very different famous woman, Pamela Anderson, a woman who is most commonly known for her frequent appearances in *Playboy* and her bad taste in men. Next, you complete a 16-question general knowledge test based on the game of Trivial Pursuit, in which you must answer questions such as "Who painted La Guernica?" (Dali, Miro, Picasso, or Velasquez) and "What is the capital of Bangladesh?" (Dacca, Hanoi, Yangon, or Bangkok). How does reading about one of the two (very different) women influence your score on the knowledge test? As predicted, those who read about Marie Curie performed worse on the trivia test than those who read about Pamela Anderson, presumably because they saw their own knowledge very differently depending on whether they were comparing to someone very smart or to someone not so smart (Stapel & Suls, 2004). This study is just one example of how factors in the social world—including actual as well as hypothetical comparison targets—can influence our own feelings and behavior. This section will describe two theories that show the impact of social factors on the self-concept: social comparison theory and the two-factor theory of emotion.

SOCIAL COMPARISON THEORY

social comparison theory a theory that people evaluate their own abilities and attributes by comparing themselves to other people

According to **social comparison theory**, people evaluate their own abilities and attributes by comparing themselves to others (Festinger, 1954). This tendency to use social comparison is especially likely in situations of uncertainty, in which it may be difficult to assess our ability in a purely objective way. If you are told that you received an 83 on an exam, you may want information on how other students performed so that you understand how your performance compared to others. I guarantee that you will feel much better if the average grade was 73 than you would if it was 93. Social comparison theory explains why so many first-year college students suddenly feel not-so-smart: many college students at selective schools were the academic stars of their high school, but all of a sudden they find themselves surrounded by students who were the stars of their own high schools, and in turn experience a drop in **self-esteem** (meaning one's overall evaluation of one's self; Marsh, Kong, & Hau, 2000). Similarly, and as discussed at the start of this chapter, Jennifer Aniston probably felt not so good about her own life—which probably seems extremely desirable to many of us—when she compared it to Angelina Jolie's life (that included a romantic relationship and new baby with Jennifer Aniston's ex-husband).

In one of the first studies of social comparison on self-concept, researchers advertised a part-time job in the campus newspaper and set up appointments for students to interview for the position (Morse & Gergen, 1970). When students showed up for the interview, they sat in the waiting room with another job applicant (who was actually a confederate of the experimenters). In one condition, the other supposed job applicant seemed quite impressive. He wore a suit, appeared well-groomed and confident, and carried an expensive briefcase stocked with several sharp pencils. In the other condition, the applicant seemed much less impressive. He wore a smelly sweatshirt with ripped pants and no socks. He completed the application with a small, dull pencil he managed to locate after digging through his pockets, and he seemed to have great trouble even completing the application. After a few minutes the experimenter returned to the waiting room with a final form, which was a self-esteem measure. As predicted, participants' self-esteem was much higher if they had sat in the waiting room with the weak applicant than if they had sat with the impressive applicant.

"Big deal, an A in math. That would be a D in any other country."

Social comparison theory thus explains why we think about ourselves in very different ways depending on the nature of the comparison we are making. In one study, men and women either saw a photo of a highly attractive person or read a description of another person (Gutierres, Kenrick, & Partch, 1999). Women received information (photo or description) about a woman, and men received information about a man. Then they were asked to rate themselves. Women who see photos of highly attractive women feel worse about their value as a marriage partner, whereas their self-concepts are unaffected by reading about highly dominant women. Men, on the other hand, feel worse about themselves as potential marriage partners after reading about socially dominant men but are not affected by reading about highly attractive men. This gender difference makes sense, given the considerable research showing that men place more value on attractiveness in a partner than do women, who in turn place more value on resources in a partner. Similarly, women in the study described at the start of this section felt much smarter—and in fact performed better on the trivia test—when they compared their own intelligence to that of Pamela Anderson than to that of Marie Curie. The Media Connections box provides another example of the hazards of such comparisons.

Media
CONNECTIONS

What Happens When Barbies Get Smaller and GI Joes Get Bigger?

Virtually all media images of women in the United States show women as thin. This includes women in movies, on television shows, in music videos, and on magazine covers. Some would say that women are portrayed as dangerously thin: Miss America contestants, for example, have body weights 13 to 19% below the expected weight for women of their height, which meets one of the criteria for diagnosing the eating disorder anorexia nervosa (Wiseman, Gray, Mosimann, & Ahrens, 1992). Movie and magazine depictions of women have become consistently thinner in the past twenty years (Silverstein, Perdue, Peterson, & Kelly, 1986): Between 1959 and 1978 the weight of Miss America contestants and *Playboy* centerfold models decreased significantly (Garner, Garfinkel, Schwartz, & Thompson, 1980), and women's magazines have increased the number of articles on weight loss they publish, presumably in an attempt to "help" women reach this increasingly thin ideal (Andersen & DiDomenico, 1992; Garner et al., 1980).

What are the consequences of this focus on the thin ideal in the media? Not surprisingly, women who are of normal weight often feel too heavy. Nearly half of women of average weight are trying to lose weight (Biener & Heaton, 1995), as are 35% of normal-weight girls, and 12% of underweight girls (Schreiber, Robins, Striegel-Moore, Oberzanek, Morrison, & Wright, 1996). One study of teenage girls found that the "ideal girl" was seen as 5 feet, 7 inches tall and weighing 100 pounds. This translates into a body mass index of less than 16, which is clearly anorexic (Nichter & Nichter, 1991). Women who rate advertisements featuring female models in popular women's magazines—who presumably are thin and attractive—feel more depressed, especially if they are already unsatisfied with their own appearance (Patrick, Neighbors, & Knee, 2004).

REUTERS/Mike Blake/Landov   *Daniel Acker/Bloomberg News./Landov*

Although most research on social pressures leading to dissatisfaction with body image has focused on the prevailing thin ideal for women, men are also increasingly feeling pressure to conform to a similarly unrealistic, overly muscular ideal (Pope, Olivardia, Gruber, & Borowiecki, 1999). To test the evolution of the "muscular male ideal" over time, researchers examined the measurements of GI Joe action toys (the action toy with the longest continuous history) produced in 1973, 1975, and 1994. This review revealed a disturbing trend. As shown in this photo, the GI Joe action figure became much more muscular over time: although there was no change in the height of the figure, the circumference of the biceps increased from 2.1 inches (1973) to 2.5 inches (1975) to 2.7 inches (1994). These may seem like small differences, but if you translate these changes to adult male bodies, biceps circumference would increase from 12.2 inches to 16.4 inches. And the latest GI Joe (the GI Joe Extreme, introduced in 1998) has biceps that translate into 26.8 inches in adult males—larger than those of any bodybuilder in history.

Interestingly, such comparisons seem to occur at an automatic level (Stapel & Blanton, 2004). In one study, participants viewed a picture of either a baby girl or an elderly woman at a subliminal level (meaning they saw the picture very quickly and below the level of conscious awareness). Participants then rated their own age on a scale of one to seven, with one meaning "young" and seven meaning "old." As expected, participants who saw the picture of the baby rated themselves as older than did those who saw the picture of the elderly woman. This finding is particularly surprising in that the participants had no conscious awareness of having seen a picture at all prior to rating their age.

We also choose particular people to serve as relevant comparison models against which to assess our own behavior. A college baseball player would likely compare himself or herself with strong players on his or her own team, not with a player on a major league baseball team. However, people often, perhaps for ease, rely on readily available comparisons to others to assess their own performance (Mussweiler & Ruter, 2003). In fact, people often think about and compare themselves to their best friend when they are evaluating their own performance. Ironically, we make this comparison even when this friend is very different from oneself on a given measure. These comparison standards are particularly important, and informative, when you are near the top of a given ability or group (Garcia, Tor, & Gonzales, 2006). For example, the second and third winners in a race will likely use each other as helpful way to evaluate their own performance more than will those who come in 41st and 42nd place.

THE TWO-FACTOR THEORY OF EMOTION

Another theory that describes the impact of other people on our own beliefs is the **two-factor, or cognitive-arousal, theory of emotion** (Schachter & Singer, 1962). According to this theory, the experience of a distinct emotion is determined by two distinct factors—the presence of physiological arousal (e.g., racing heart, heavy breathing, sweating, etc.) as well as the cognitive label a person gives to that arousal (see Figure 3.3). In other words, when we feel physiologically aroused, for whatever reason, we interpret that arousal in a particular way based on the cues present in the situation. According to this theory, all types of emotions feel physiologically the same, so we look to the situation we are in to find a specific cognitive label to give to the arousal, which determines the emotion we feel. So, if we feel physiologically aroused and we are standing near an attractive person, we interpret that feeling as love (or lust), but if we feel that arousal and we're in close proximity to a lion, we interpret that emotion as fear.

two-factor, or cognitive-arousal, theory of emotion a theory that the experience of emotion is determined by two distinct factors: the presence of some type of physiological arousal and the cognitive label a person gives to that arousal

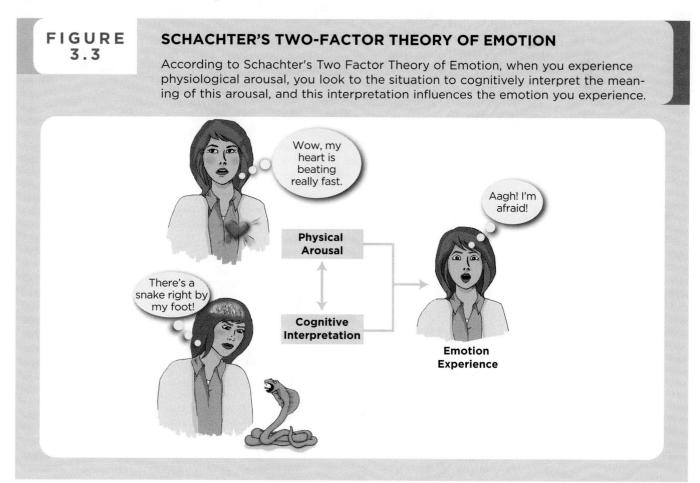

FIGURE 3.3

SCHACHTER'S TWO-FACTOR THEORY OF EMOTION

According to Schachter's Two Factor Theory of Emotion, when you experience physiological arousal, you look to the situation to cognitively interpret the meaning of this arousal, and this interpretation influences the emotion you experience.

Stanley Schachter and Jerome Singer (1962) conducted the original research study demonstrating the two-factor theory of emotion. Participants who came into the lab to participate in a study on vision were divided into four groups. One group was told that they would get epinephrine, which would make them feel aroused (e.g., racing heart, flushed skin, trembling hands, etc.), and they did get epinephrine ("epinephrine informed"). One group was told that they would get epinephrine but did not hear about any potential side effects, and they did get epinephrine ("epinephrine ignorant"). One group was told that they would get epinephrine but did not hear about any side effects, but they got a saline solution that had no side effects ("placebo"). Finally, one group was told that they would get epinephrine and that the side effect might be numb feet, and they did get epinephrine ("epinephrine misinformed").

The participants were then placed in a room with a confederate to complete a questionnaire while they waited for the drug to take effect so they could participate in the vision test. The confederate behaved joyously, flying paper airplanes, bouncing a ball, and so forth. The experimenter then came back into the room and said it was time for the vision test, but first it was necessary to rule out any possible effects of mood on vision, so the participants needed to complete a brief mood inventory. What was the participants' mood at the end of the study? Participants in the ignorant, misinformed, and placebo conditions felt happier and behaved more happily, which makes sense because they were with a happy confederate (see Figure 3.4). This effect was particularly strong in the misinformed conditions. However, participants who were in the informed condition, and therefore could attribute their arousal to the drug as opposed to the situation, had the lowest levels of happy mood and behavior.

One of the interesting aspects of the two-factor theory of emotion is that we can interpret the exact same feeling of arousal in very different ways, depending

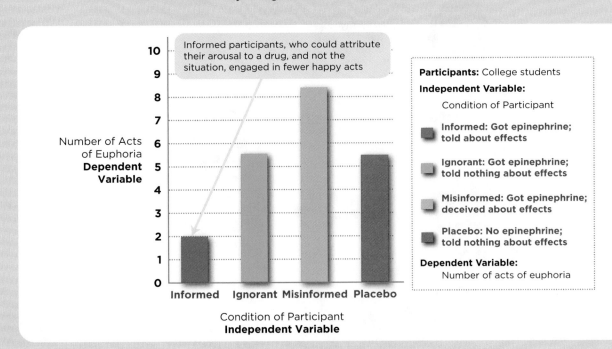

FIGURE 3.4

HOW DOES COGNITION AFFECT OUR LABELING OF AROUSAL?

Participants received shots and information about its side effects, and then waited with a confederate who modeled euphorically happy actions. As predicted, participants in the ignorant, misinformed, and placebo conditions behaved more euphorically than those in the informed condition, who could attribute their arousal to the drug, rather than to the situation.

Source: Schacter, S., & Singer, J. (1962). Cognitive, social, and physiological determinants of emotional state. *Psychological Review*, 69, 379-399.

Polka Dot Images/SUPERSTOCK

Steve Granitz/Wire Images/Getty Images

If the emotion we experience is determined by the cognitive label we give to our physiological arousal, we should experience the same type of arousal in response to seeing a fear-inducing stimulus and a sexually desirable stimulus.

on the cues present in our environment. During my first year of graduate school, I attended a three-hour class every Tuesday morning. To help me stay alert during this class, I brought a huge cup of coffee with me each time. But after a few weeks I noticed that about an hour into the class, I started to feel very nervous. I would then scan my thoughts to find a reason for my nervousness: Was I feeling anxious about an upcoming test? Was I mad at my boyfriend? Did I have an upcoming presentation? One day I mentioned my massive anxiety to a friend in the class, who tactfully suggested that the tremendous amount of coffee I drank during class could lead to some physiological symptoms that I might be interpreting as anxiety. Now that I had this explanation for my arousal, I no longer worried about the various things that could be going wrong in my life as a way of explaining it. (Of course, switching to decaf coffee also helped.)

The two-factor theory of emotion is rooted in the misattribution of arousal, meaning that we attribute the arousal we feel from one source to another. This phenomenon, which is also referred to as excitation transfer theory, has implications for a variety of real-life experiences, such as attraction and aggression, as we'll discuss in later chapters. In some cases the misattribution of arousal can even lead to positive outcomes. In one study, participants who were preparing to perform a task were encouraged to attribute their arousal (which was in reality caused by nervousness) to another source (supposedly some subliminal noise in the room; Savitsky, Medvec, Charlton, & Gilovich, 1998). Participants who made this misattribution had greater confidence in their likelihood of performing well at the task. Presumably this is because they saw their arousal as caused by something other than nervousness.

SOCIAL INFLUENCES ON THE SELF-CONCEPT

Concepts in Context

FACTOR	EXAMPLE
Social comparison theory	Ellen was thrilled with the grade of 91 on her organic chemistry midterm, until her roommate reported her own grade of 98.
Two-factor theory of emotion	Antonio just finished a five-mile run, so his heart was beating very fast when he noticed his new neighbor getting into her car. He was surprised to notice how attractive she seemed, and decided to ask her out on a date.

HOW DO PEOPLE MAINTAIN A POSITIVE SELF-CONCEPT?

Imagine that you are a student at a California school, and you are asked to follow water conservation practices during a drought—a not uncommon experience. For example, you might be asked to shower only every other day and to flush the toilet less frequently. Then if you are asked by researchers whether you are following the recommended water conservation practices—and whether you believe most other students are following such recommendations—what will you say? One recent study revealed that students see their own behavior as better than those of their peers (Monin & Norton, 2003). Specifically, although only 33% of students reported taking daily showers during the drought, students estimate that about 47% of other students are showering. When the ban is lifted, students still view their own behavior as especially good. Although at this point 84% of students are showering daily, they believe that only 72% of their peers have returned to taking a daily shower. This study is an example of a common principle in social psychology. It is called the **false uniqueness effect**, meaning that we see our own desirable behavior as less common. The false uniqueness effect is just one of several self-serving strategies that we will examine in this section. Other self-serving strategies that people use to maintain positive beliefs about themselves include self-serving biases, self-serving beliefs, self-serving comparisons, and self-serving behavior.

false uniqueness effect the tendency to underestimate the extent to which other people are likely to share our positive attitudes and behaviors

SELF-SERVING BIASES

How well did you do on the SATs or ACTs? If you are like most college students, you will remember your scores on these standardized tests (as well as your high school grades) as higher than they actually were (Bahrick, Hall, & Berger, 1996; Shepperd, 1993). This tendency to misremember events in a particular direction is one of the strategies that people use to feel good about themselves. In one study, participants were first led to believe that either extraversion or introversion was a good predictor of success in college and in the workplace (Sanitioso & Wlodarski, 2004). Participants then received feedback about their own personalities and were later asked to recall this feedback for the experimenter. As expected, those who thought that extraversion was a positive trait remembered the feedback related to extraversion more accurately than the feedback related to introversion, yet those who believed that introversion predicted success showed the opposite pattern.

Misremembering. This tendency to remember things in a self-serving way can also lead us to see change over time, even when no change has occurred. For example, people who are doing poorly in a class and get a tutor often report that their scores have improved, and they attribute this improvement to the tutor. But in reality students who do very poorly initially are likely to show some improvement over time simply because extreme values tend to become less extreme over time. In one study, researchers collected data from 101 dating couples on their love, commitment, and satisfaction at that time, as well as how these features had changed over the last year (Sprecher, 1999). These couples were then asked these same questions every year for the next four years, so that researchers could see how relationships changed over time. Couples that stayed together throughout this time reported that their love, commitment, and satisfaction had increased over time. However, there was no evidence from the yearly reports that these features did in fact increase. Other studies with married couples show similar patterns, namely, that people report increasing love for their spouse over time, whereas there is no such change when you look at actual relationship satisfaction ratings over time (Karney & Coombs, 2000).

What causes these biases in memory? This misperception occurs in part because we ignore the statistical phenomenon of regression to the average (Tversky & Kahneman, 1974), meaning that things that are initially at extreme (positive or negative) points are likely to become less extreme over time. For example, a student who gets a 100 on the midterm exam is much more likely to receive a lower score on the next exam (particularly because a higher score is impossible), but seeing this student as doing worse over time if he or she receives a 95 on the next exam would be silly.

Making beneficial attributions.

Although in some cases people misremember the outcome of events as a way of maintaining a positive self-concept, in some situations people must acknowledge a less-than-desirable outcome (e.g., failing a test, losing an important game, having a fight with a loved one; Sedikides, Campbell, Reeder, & Elliot, 1998; Lau & Russell, 1980). In the face of negative events, people make **self-serving attributions**—they maintain their positive self-views by blaming their failure on external events (Brown & Rogers, 1991; Grove, Hanrahan, & McInman, 1991). In contrast, when we experience success, we usually attribute the outcome to internal factors. When athletes win a game, both the athletes and their coaches see the victory as due to skill and effort. Losses are blamed on external factors such as bad officiating. Similarly, when you do well on a test, you probably see the outcome as due to your skill and effort, whereas when you do poorly, you attribute the outcome to unfair grading or poor test design. We also give ourselves the benefit of the doubt in another creative way: when we don't carry out our good intentions, we still give ourselves credit for at least having formed these intentions (Kruger & Gilovich, 2004). But we don't give others similar credit for their own failed intentions.

> **self-serving attributions** the tendency to blame failure on external factors while crediting success on internal factors

We also maintain our positive self-views by perceiving ourselves as having a disproportionately large role in past (positive) events. For example, when basketball players are asked to describe a turning point in their games, 80% refer to plays initiated by their own teams (Ross & Sicoly, 1979). Similarly, if husbands and wives are asked separately what percent of the housecleaning they do, although both spouses report that the wife does more, the percentages add up to well over 100%. Naturally, we see ourselves as responsible only for positive events, not for negative ones: divorced individuals see their former spouse as primarily responsible for the breakup and see themselves as having been more interested in reconciliation than their spouse (Gray & Silver, 1990).

Seeing our views as shared by others.

Another way in which people see themselves in a biased way is by assuming that their views and behavior are

How do you feel about Barack Obama's presidency and Kiefer Sutherland's television show *24*? According to the false consensus effect, you assume that most others share your feelings (positive or negative).

normative—that is, that their views and behaviors are shared by most other people. The **false consensus effect** refers to the tendency to overestimate the extent to which other people share our opinions, attitudes, and behaviors. In sum, people generally assume that anything they think or do, many other people must also think or do (Ross, Greene, & House, 1977). The false consensus effect explains why you are surprised when your preferred presidential candidate doesn't win, or why you can't believe it when your favorite television show is canceled: surely, if you feel strongly about a given candidate or program, many other people must share your (excellent) taste. Why do we make this mistake? In part, because we usually surround ourselves with people who share our beliefs.

In one of the first demonstrations of the power of the false consensus effect, Lee Ross and his colleagues at Stanford University asked students to wear a large cardboard sign that said "Eat at Joe's" around campus for 30 minutes and note the reactions they received (Ross et al., 1977). What percentage of students do you think agreed to wear the sign? Exactly 50%. Ross then asked all students what percentage of students they thought would agree to wear the sign. Those who had agreed to wear the sign believed that the majority of students would also agree (58%), whereas those who had refused to wear the sign believed that most other students would also refuse (77%).

People also see their own skills and abilities as relatively normative, meaning similar to that of others in their social group. For example, in one study, participants were given a bogus test of "social sensitivity," which supposedly was used to assess the progress of students who were interested in careers in clinical or counseling psychology (Alicke & Largo, 1995). This test included a number of tasks, including rating how people's traits fit together, predicting how another person would answer particular questions, and rating which word does not fit with other words in a given set. Participants were then told either that they had passed this test or that they had failed. When participants were then asked how they thought most other students would perform on this test, those who were told they had failed believed most of their peers would also perform poorly, but those who were told that they performed well believed that most others would also do well.

As mentioned earlier in this section, although people typically see their attitudes and undesirable behavior as normative, we tend to see ourselves as different—and particularly as better—than others on desirable abilities and behavior (Suls & Wan, 1987). The false uniqueness effect refers to the tendency for people to see themselves as more likely to perform positive acts than others, and to see ourselves as less biased, and more accurate, than others (Ehrlinger, Gilovich, & Ross, 2005). The bias occurs in part because people underestimate the number of people who engage in positive actions (e.g., donating blood) while overestimating the number of people who engage in negative actions (e.g., littering). In the water conservation study described previously, although only 33% of students were actually taking daily showers during the drought, participants estimated that 47% were showering daily (Monin & Norton, 2003).

WOULD YOU BELIEVE... People Named George Are Likely to Live in Georgia? A subtle type of self-enhancement that people often use is implicit egotism, meaning a preference for things that are connected to themselves (Pelham, Mirenberg, & Jones, 2002). A number of clever studies have shown that people's preference for personally relevant letters and numbers leads to some very surprising effects. In one study, researchers compared the first letters in people's names with the first letters of their home cities and states, and found that people appear to gravitate toward cities with names similar to their own (Pelham et al., 2002). For example, Philips are disproportionately likely to live in Philadelphia, while Mildreds are disproportionately likely to live in Milwaukee! Moreover, people are disproportionately likely to live in cities whose names began with their birthday numbers (e.g., Two Harbors, MN), and disproportionately likely to choose careers whose labels resemble their names (e.g., people named Dennis or Denise are overrepresented among dentists). They are also more likely to marry people whose first or last names resemble their own, meaning Patrick is more likely to marry Patricia than Michelle, who should marry Michael (Jones, Pelham, Cavrallo, & Mirenberg, 2004). Although these findings have been challenged by some psychologists (e.g., Gallucci, 2003), other researchers have replicated these effects and have extended them by showing that people are more likely to live on streets that share their name (Pelham, Carvallo, DeHart, & Jones, 2003). More recent research indicates that those with names that start with "C" or "D" have lower GPAs than those with names that start with "A" or "B," and that baseball players whose names begin with "K" strike out more often than other players (Nelson & Simmons, 2007).

SELF-SERVING BELIEFS

People also maintain positive self-concepts by seeing themselves as more likely than other people to experience good events, and as less likely than other people to experience bad events. This phenomenon, known as **unrealistic optimism**, explains why we see ourselves as "better-than-average" across multiple dimensions, including having more positive personality traits (e.g., honesty, intelligence, maturity), experiencing better relationships, and being less at risk of experiencing negative events (e.g., getting divorced, experiencing an unintended pregnancy, suffering a heart attack, having a car accident; Weinstein, 1980). See Table 3.1 for a vivid example of this tendency.

unrealistic optimism a phenomenon in which people see themselves as more likely than other people to experience good events, and less likely than other people to experience bad events

We even see ourselves as more likely to win even when the benefits that would generally help everyone's performance equally are shared by all group members (Windschitl, Kruger, & Simms, 2003). In one study, participants in the "benefit condition" were told that the instructor would spend the last two class days going over the terms on the review sheet for the final exam whereas those in the "adversity condition" were simply told they would receive a sheet listing the terms, but that students would be responsible for learning the terms on their own. Although everyone in the class benefits from going over the terms together in class, and suffers from having to learn the terms on their own, students in the adversity condition expected to rank in the 60th percentile in their final grade whereas those in the benefit condition expected to rank in the 71st percentile.

How do we maintain such optimistic illusions? In part, by describing our traits in ways that allow us to appear good (Dunning, Meyerowitz, & Holzberg, 1989; Dunning, Perie, & Story, 1991). Specifically, we see our traits in a particularly positive way, and seek out and view information that flatters us as particularly valid (Glick, Gottesman, & Jolton, 1989; Kruger, 1998). For example, if you are very artistic, you are likely to pay more attention to an article that suggests creativity is a great predictor of future success than one that suggests no correlation between creativity and future success. We also assign greater importance to things we are good at than to things we are bad at. For example, students who receive a high grade in an introductory computer science course later see computer skills as more important than those who receive a low

TABLE 3.1	ESTIMATES OF THE LIKELIHOOD OF EVENTS OCCURRING TO US AND OTHERS		
AVERAGE EVENT		**SELF**	**AMERICAN**
Be hurt in a terror attack		10	50
Have trouble sleeping because of the situation with terror		10	45
Be the victim of violent crime (other than terror)		10	40
Die from any cause (crime, illness, accident)		25	50

Two months after 9/11/01, Americans were asked to estimate the probability that they, as well as the average American, would experience various events within the next year. In line with the phenomenon of unrealistic optimism, Americans felt they were less likely to experience negative events than others.

Source: Lerner, J., Gonzalez, R., Small, D., & Fischhoff, B. (2003). Effects of fear and anger on perceived risks of terrorism: A national field experiment. *Psychological Science*, 14, 144–150.

The Life-cycle of a Chicago Cubs Fan

©Ken Krimstein

grade (Hill, Smith, & Lewicki, 1989). Although holding optimistic illusions has many benefits for psychological well-being, these beliefs can also lead to negative consequences, as described in the Health Connections box.

Having High Perceived Control.

In addition to seeing ourselves as more likely to experience positive events, we also have high levels of **perceived control**. This means that we see uncontrollable events as at least partially under our control (Thompson, 1999). For example, people tend to assume that they can control random events (e.g., picking lottery numbers), which is why people lose money in bets. (You almost always bet on "your" team to win, and believe that they will.) In one study, participants either chose a particular set of lottery numbers to play or were assigned specific numbers, and paid $1 for each ticket regardless of how numbers had been picked (Langer, 1975). They were then told that the tickets were all sold, but that someone who had not had a chance to purchase one wanted to do so. Would they be willing to sell their ticket to that person? Among those who had been assigned a number, the mean amount for which they sold the ticket was $1.96, but for those who had chosen the number, the mean amount was $8.17! Apparently people believed that if they chose a number, it was more likely to win, and therefore the ticket was worth more money.

We even believe that we have control in situations in which it is clearly impossible for us to have control. For example, sports fans often come to believe that their actions are influencing the outcome of a game; my husband will leave the room if his team is losing, for fear that his watching of the game on television is influencing the players' performance. We may form such beliefs about our control simply because we did something one time (e.g., drink coffee, wear a certain shirt, watch the game from a particular chair) and our team won, even though the association between the two events was purely a coincidence.

Making overconfident judgments.

Perhaps due to our overly optimistic feelings of control over the world, we are also overconfident in our judgments (Vallone, Griffin, Lin, & Ross, 1990). In one study conducted by Justin Kruger and David Dunning (1999), college students interacted briefly with a stranger and were then asked to predict how that person would behave in a particular situation and how their roommate would behave in the same situation. In both cases, students thought they would be pretty accurate in their predictions, even though it is extremely unlikely that they would be as accurate about strangers' behavior as about the behavior of those they know well.

perceived control the tendency to see uncontrollable events as at least partially under our control

The Downside of Too Much Optimism

Although optimism is generally associated with better health (Peterson, Seligman, Yurko, Martin, & Friedman, 1998; Scheier & Carver, 1993), some intriguing research suggests that optimism can also have some costs. Specifically, research by Neil Weinstein (1984, 1987) indicates that people who are unrealistically optimistic about their risk of experiencing various health problems can actually put their health at risk. For example, people generally believe that they are at less risk of experiencing many types of problems than other people, including car accidents, alcohol problems, sexually transmitted diseases, and drug addiction. Basically, people tend to believe that although risks do exist, "it won't happen to me." This tendency may be especially common in college students, who generally believe (wrongly!) that they are invulnerable to many types of problems. Unfortunately, these unrealistically positive beliefs can lead people to fail to protect themselves adequately from such problems—and thus bicycle without a helmet, refuse to wear a seatbelt, or drive under the influence. In fact, a longitudinal study by Friedman, Tucker, Tomlinson-Keasey, Schwartz, Wingard, & Criqui (1993) found that optimists had a higher mortality rate. This research suggests that while optimism in general is a good thing, too much optimism can have some serious drawbacks.

ThinkStock/SUPERSTOCK

Person biking without a helmet.

We are even overconfident in predicting our own behavior—which explains why we use up our cell-phone minutes each month (but don't increase our monthly plan) and why we pay for yearly gym memberships (but don't regularly use the gym). In one study, students made a number of predictions about their own behavior, such as how often they would call their parents or whether they would acquire a steady dating partner (Vallone, Ross, & Lepper, 1990). Although students estimated their accuracy at 82%, when researchers followed up throughout the year, the true rate of accuracy was only 68%. This tendency toward overconfidence means that sometimes others' predictions about our behavior are more accurate than our own (MacDonald & Ross, 1999). For example, people in a dating relationship typically believe that their current dating relationship will last for some time. However, the predictions of family and friends about how long this relationship will last are more accurate than those of the dating couple.

Amazingly enough, those who are least competent are most overconfident about their abilities. When students are asked to rate their own abilities in logic, grammar, and humor as compared to those of their peers, those whose actual scores placed them in the bottom 12% estimated that they were in the top 62% (Kruger & Dunning, 1999)! In sum, people who are most overconfident in their abilities are actually least competent in a given task.

Although the examples described thus far have focused on the relatively minor consequences of overconfidence, this type of self-serving belief can have substantial negative consequences. When President Bush declared war on Iraq in the spring of 2002, one of the major justifications of this war was the supposed presence of

The Impact of Feedback on Eyewitness Confidence

People's overconfidence is particularly strong in cases in which they are given feedback confirming their original views, a phenomenon that can have substantial consequences for the legal system. Specifically, eyewitnesses who are very confident in their judgments are, not surprisingly, particularly influential with juries (Cutler, Penrod, & Dexter, 1990; Fox & Walters, 1986). One factor that increases people's confidence in their judgments, regardless of their accuracy, is receiving confirmatory feedback. After an eyewitness identifies a particular person in a lineup or mug shot, he or she may receive feedback from a police officer regarding the selection (e.g., "Oh, good. I noticed on your identification sheet that you identified the actual murder suspect"). In one study of this effect, participants watched a videotape from an actual in-store camera recording a robbery in which a security guard was shot and killed (Wells & Bradfield, 1999). Then they were asked to identify the shooter from one of five pictures (none of which was the actual shooter). Those who received confirming feedback on their identification were later much more confident about their selection of the actual shooter than those who did not receive such feedback.

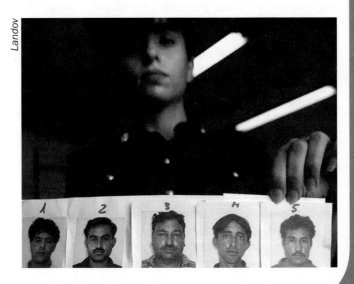

"weapons of mass destruction" that were being hidden from United Nations inspectors. However, more recent evidence indicates that Iraq was in fact not hiding weapons. In this case, the overconfidence of President Bush and his advisors led to war. The Law Connections box describes how eyewitness's overconfidence can also lead to negative consequences.

SELF-SERVING COMPARISONS

Another strategy that people use to maintain their positive self-concepts is strategically associating with successful others, a phenomenon known as **"basking in reflected glory" (or BIRGing)**. One study found that after a college football team won a weekend game, 32% of the students at that school described the outcome as "we won," whereas after their college football team loses, only 18% described the loss as "we lost" (Cialdini, Borden, Thorne, Walker, Freeman, & Sloan, 1976). Students are strategically making a connection between themselves and a good outcome, but distancing themselves from a poor outcome. In another study, researchers simply counted the number of people wearing clothes with their school name or another school's name at a number of large universities (Notre Dame, Ohio State University, Arizona State University, Michigan, University of Southern California, and Pittsburgh) on the Mondays after football games (Cialdini et al., 1976). On the Monday following a win by the football team, 64% of those observed were wearing school colors, compared to only 44% after a loss. As Cialdini eloquently notes, "We avoid the shadow of defeat and bask in the glow of victory. Even if it's reflected glory, you still get a tan."

basking in reflected glory (BIRGing) associating with successful others to increase one's feelings of self-worth

downward social comparison comparing ourselves to people who are worse than we are on a given trait or ability in an attempt to feel better about ourselves

The benefits of downward comparison. We can also use social comparison for other reasons, including making ourselves feel better and providing means for self-improvement (Helgeson & Mickelson, 1995). In the strategy known as **downward social comparison**, people compare themselves to those who are worse off than themselves on a particular trait or attribute (who are less successful, less happy, less fortunate, etc.) as a way of making themselves feel better. For example, Bill Klein's research (1997) demonstrates that students feel much better knowing they are at a lower risk of contracting a disease than their friends, even when they learn that their odds of contracting the disease are relatively high. In this case we feel better about ourselves even after learning something potentially upsetting, simply because we see ourselves as better off than others. Similarly, women with early-stage breast cancer often choose to compare themselves to other breast cancer patients who are worse off than they themselves are; making this type of downward comparison leads women to feel better (Bogart & Hegelson, 2000; Taylor, 1989).

People are generally quite good at choosing comparisons partners who will make them feel good about themselves. In one study conducted by Wendy Wood and her colleagues at Texas A & M, participants were given either success (12 or 13 out of 15) or failure feedback (3 or 4 out of 15) on a practice "social perception" test (Wood, Giordano-Beech, & Ducharme, 1999). Then they were asked to take a second test, which they would take along with another person in the experiment. However, they were able to choose which test they (and the other person) would take—one that the other person had already done well on ("superior" rating) or one that the other person had already done "OK" on ("average" rating). As shown in Figure 3.5, people who had just done well on a test were most

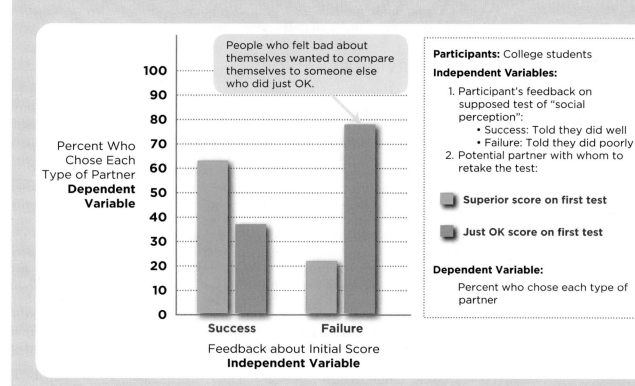

FIGURE 3.5

WHEN DO WE CHOOSE DOWNWARD SOCIAL COMPARISONS?

Participants in this experiment took a fake test that they were told measured their social perception skills and were given feedback intended to make them either feel good or bad about their social skills. They were then told they could take the test again, this time with a partner. As predicted, a higher percentage of people who were told they did poorly on the first test chose a partner who did just OK compared to those who were told they did well.

Source: Wood, J.V., Giordano-Beech, M., & Ducharme, M.J. (1999). Compensating for failure through social comparison. *Personality and Social Psychology Bulletin*, 25, 1370-1386. Used by permission of Sage Publications.

interested in comparing themselves on a second test to someone who had done well. Those who had done poorly on the first test were most interested in comparing themselves to someone who had just done OK. In sum, people are particularly interested in engaging in downward comparison when they are feeling bad about themselves.

Overcoming threatening comparisons. There are, however, some cases in which you are forced to compare yourself to people who are clearly better than you. Thus it becomes impossible to make self-enhancing comparisons. Although in some cases this type of comparison leads to jealousy and resentment (as when a close friend experiences a better outcome than you do), we have several ways of "fighting back" when these self-esteem threats occur. First, we may emphasize various advantages the other person may have had that led him or her to outperform us (Shepperd & Taylor, 1999). When my older son was having great trouble mastering toilet training, I focused on how many of his peers had older siblings who served as built-in models of this behavior.

Second, we may acknowledge that person as being extremely impressive in one domain, but derogate their abilities in other domains to compensate (Parks-Stamm, Heilman, & Hearns, 2008). In one study, women read a description of a highly successful woman who was the CEO of a company, and then rated her on various traits. Although women recognized this woman as highly competent, they rated her as unlikable and interpersonally hostile, which presumably helps minimize the self-evaluation consequences of this type of social comparison.

Third, we may exaggerate the other person's ability and see him or her as unusually good at a given behavior. This means that we can also be good at this behavior—even if not quite as good. In a study by Mark Alicke and his colleagues, participants and confederates both participated in an IQ test that was very difficult (students on average got 3 out of 10 items right; Alicke, LoSchiavo, Zerbst, & Zhang, 1997). The confederate was always given a score of 7. The participants knew both their scores and the confederates' scores, as did some observers (supposedly participants who were waiting to participate in the study). Observers rated the confederates' intelligence as higher than the participants', which makes sense based on what they had observed. However, participants rated the confederates as even smarter than did the observers. Once again, this strategy of "seeing the person who outperforms us as a genius" protects us from feeling the negative effects of having to make an unfavorable comparison.

SELF-SERVING BEHAVIOR

Because of our desire to feel good about ourselves, we often use strategies to help maintain our positive self-views. One such strategy is **self-handicapping**: creating obstacles to success so that potential failure can be blamed on these external factors as opposed to internal traits (Berglas & Jones, 1978). For example, the night before an exam students can avoid studying and stay out really late. Then, if they do badly, they can blame their poor performance on their lack of preparation, which protects their own view of their intelligence. On the other hand, if they happen to do well, what do people say? "Wow, they must be really smart to not have studied and still done so well." This is one reason that some people choose to procrastinate on a given assignment (and then pull an all-nighter). This strategy may cost them in terms of performance, but it also sets up a ready excuse for failure that protects self-esteem. After all, if you can get a C on a paper you wrote the night before, just imagine how well you could do if you'd really tried your hardest? By creating such obstacles, individuals free themselves from the pressure to perform well and as a result actually enjoy the task more (Deppe & Harackiewicz, 1996). Remember, however, that self-handicapping refers to setting up obstacles to success before an event, not giving excuses after the fact.

In the first study to demonstrate use of the self-handicapping strategy, Stephen Berglas and Edward Jones (1978) randomly assigned male students to complete

self-handicapping a strategy in which people create obstacles to success, so that potential failure can be blamed on these external factors

either solvable or unsolvable anagrams. All of the participants were then told that they had done well on the test, but this positive feedback was clearly confusing to those who had attempted to solve anagrams that in reality had no solution. Participants were then asked to choose whether they would prefer to take a performance-enhancing or a performance-inhibiting drug before they took another similar test. Of those who had received success feedback but had no idea why, 70% chose the drug that would hurt performance, as compared to 13% of those who knew why they had done well. These findings indicate that participants who are confident in their ability on a task typically prefer to take a drug that should help them perform even better. Those who lack this confidence are much more likely to choose to take the drug that should hurt their performance—and thereby give them a ready excuse for a poor outcome.

Pulling "all-nighters" to finish school work can be used as a self-handicapping strategy to help explain poor performance.

Self-handicapping can lead to a number of negative consequences. People who self-handicap use strategies to provide explanations for less-than-successful performance, which in turn cannot surprisingly lead to poorer performance (Hirt, Deppe, & Gordon, 1991). For example, students who tend to self-handicap report spending less time per week on academic work and engaging in less efficient studying for exams (Zuckerman, Kieffer, & Knee, 1998). They also have lower GPAs. Similarly, they may also use alcohol before engaging in a difficult task as a way of creating a face-saving explanation for poor performance (e.g., "I would have done much better on the test, but I was drunk"; Higgins & Harris, 1988; Steele & Josephs, 1990). Finally, the use of self-handicapping can have negative effects on interpersonal relations. People who make excuses for poor performance, such as low effort or drug impairment, are rated more negatively by their peers (Rhodewalt, Sanbonmatsu, Tschanz, Feick, & Waller, 1995).

Questioning the Research

Can you think of another explanation for the finding that people who self-handicap report having worse study habits and lower GPAs? Hint: Is this correlation or causation?

THE DOWNSIDE OF OVERLY POSITIVE SELF-VIEWS

This section has described a variety of strategies that people use to feel good about themselves, and in general these strategies are beneficial because people who feel good about themselves experience numerous benefits, including better physical and psychological well-being (Lipkus, **Dalbert, & Siegler,** 1996; Strauman, Lemieux, & Coe, 1993; Taylor & Brown, 1988). However, feeling good about yourself can have drawbacks. Under certain circumstances, people who hold overly positive views of themselves can behave more aggressively toward others and see them in a more negative light (Beauregard & Dunning, 1998; Bushman & Baumeister, 1998). They may also have poor social skills and be seen less positively by others, in part because they have difficulty responding well to any form of criticism and rejection and are seen as antagonistic (Colvin, Block, & Funder, 1995; Heatherton & Vohs, 2000; Paulhus, 1998). People who are high in self-esteem and receive failure feedback are more likely to denigrate others and exaggerate their superiority over others (Brown & Gallagher, 1992; Gibbons & McCoy, 1991). People with overly positive self-views can also engage in very destructive behavior. Although pessimists reduce their expectations and bet smaller amounts of money after repeatedly losing when they gamble, optimists continue to have positive expectations about their likelihood of winning, even after repeatedly losing, and continue to bet large sums of money (Gibson & Sanbonmatsu, 2004).

Finally, although research in social psychology has emphasized the benefits of having perceived control for psychological and even physical well-being (e.g., Lang &

Heckhausen, 2001), in some cases holding such beliefs can actually have negative consequences. For example, among women who experienced a sexual assault, their believing that they had control over the rape, such as feeling they used poor judgment or should have resisted more, leads to greater distress (Frazier, 2003). Similarly, women who believe they can control whether they are assaulted again in the future also experience higher rates of distress. Women who believed they had control over the recovery process, however, did report lower levels of distress. In sum, although perceived control is usually beneficial for psychological as well as physical well-being, in some cases this illusion of control can have quite negative consequences.

STRATEGIES PEOPLE USE TO MAINTAIN A POSITIVE SELF-CONCEPT

FACTOR	EXAMPLE
Self-serving biases	After Emilia's softball team loses a game, most of her teammates complain about poor officiating; however, after a win, the team views the officials as having done a good job.
Self-serving beliefs	Because Jamal is very confident that his safe driving will prevent an accident from occurring, he often neglects to wear his seatbelt.
Self-serving comparisons	Jenny plays on her high school basketball team, but isn't one of the better players. However, she consoles herself by remembering all the people who tried out and didn't make the team.
Self-serving behavior	Robert just got another C on his midterm exam—but this low grade doesn't really bother him because he knows he would have done much better if he had had time to study before the test.

HOW DO PEOPLE PRESENT THEMSELVES TO OTHERS?

Imagine you arrive at the psychology department to participate in a study of "incidental memory" (Gilovich, Medvec, & Savitsky, 2000). At the start of the experiment, the researcher pulls you aside from the other group members, and asks you to put on a relatively embarrassing t-shirt. In one condition the shirt features a picture of Vanilla Ice as well as the words "Ice, Ice, Baby." In another condition the shirt features a picture of Barry Manilow. After you put on the shirt (and all participants agreed to do so), you are then sent into a room where four or five other students are already sitting to get a questionnaire to fill out. You complete and turn in your questionnaire, and are then asked by the experimenter to estimate how many of the people in the room had noticed the t-shirt they were wearing. What would you say? Participants estimated that about 48% of the others would notice the embarrassing t-shirt, but the actual number was 23%. Why do people assume (wrongly) that more people would notice their embarrassing shirt than actually do? This error is caused largely by individuals' motivation not only to think of themselves in positive ways, but also to have others in their social world think of them in such ways (Paulus, Bruce, & Trapnell, 1995). In turn, this motivation influences our behavior in a variety of ways, such as the way we dress, the car we drive, where we go on vacation, the job we want to have, and much more. This section will examine self-presentation or **impression management**

impression management
strategies that people use to create positive impressions of themselves

strategies, meaning people's efforts to create positive impressions of themselves, including self-promotion, ingratiation, and self-verification, as well as both positive and negative aspects of our tendency to focus on self-presentation.

SELF-PROMOTION

The strategy of **self-promotion** focuses on making other people think you are competent or good in some way (Godfrey, Jones, & Lord, 1986). People who use self-promotion tend to appear with such statements as "I strive to look perfect to others," and "I try to keep my faults to myself" (Hewitt et al., 2003). Athletes who brag about how much they can bench press, and nerds who casually mention their 1600 SAT scores are trying to make you respect them.

In one study, students were asked to imagine that they were trying out for the part of Scrooge in *A Christmas Carol* (Quattrone & Jones, 1978). Some of the students were told to imagine that they had been through an audition, after which they received enthusiastic applause from the director; others were not asked to imagine such an audition. Then students were asked how likely they would be to mention that they had recently received rave reviews for their performance as a lovable, generous sucker in another play (a character who is a direct opposite of the Scrooge character). Those who were confident that they had done well (i.e., those who had imagined the applause) were much more likely to comment on their prior performance, presumably to show how much more difficult their stellar performance had been. On the other hand, those who were not told how the audition had gone were very unlikely to divulge this information, presumably because it would hurt their efforts to convince the director that they could effectively play Scrooge.

What are the drawbacks to using self-promotion? First, competence often speaks for itself, so people who try hard to convince others that they are competent may seem less so than those who "prove it" through their actions. Bragging about your golf game, for example, may be a sign that your game could use some work. Otherwise, why would you have to try so hard to convince others of your skill?

Second, there are more reasons to explain a negative performance than there are to explain a positive one. If you fail to do something well, you can blame it on various external causes, such as a difficult task, lack of effort, or illness. However, if you do something well, your performance is likely to be attributed to your ability.

Finally, self-promotion can have substantial personal consequences; although people who self-promote are seen as more competent, they are also viewed as less likeable (Godfrey et al., 1986). Self-promotion is particularly hazardous for women: women who self-promote are seen as more competent, but less likeable

self-promotion a strategy that focuses on making other people think you are competent or good in some way

J. SCOTT APPLEWHITE/©AP/Wide World Photos

In the NEWS **President Bush.** Although President Bush announced the successful accomplishment of the war in Iraq in 2003, this self-promotion was ridiculed by critics in the months to come as the war continued.

FIGURE 3.6

THE DANGERS OF SELF-PROMOTION ... FOR WOMEN

Which of these statements makes you like her better? Which one would you hire to design a new game? Although men who self-promote are seen as positively as those who are self-effacing, women who self-promote are seen as more competent but less likeable and less hirable than those who are more modest in their self-presentation.

Source: Rudman, L. A. (1998). Self-promotion as a risk factor for women: The costs and benefits of counterstereotypical impression management. *Journal of Personality and Social Psychology*, 74, 629–645.

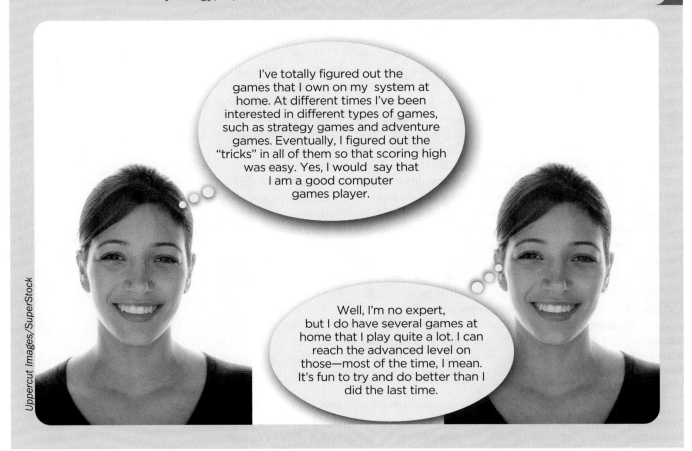

I've totally figured out the games that I own on my system at home. At different times I've been interested in different types of games, such as strategy games and adventure games. Eventually, I figured out the "tricks" in all of them so that scoring high was easy. Yes, I would say that I am a good computer games player.

Well, I'm no expert, but I do have several games at home that I play quite a lot. I can reach the advanced level on those—most of the time, I mean. It's fun to try and do better than I did the last time.

Uppercut Images/SuperStock

and less hirable, whereas men don't experience such problems with self-promotion (Rudman, 1998). This suggests that self-promotion is a "double-edged sword" for women, in that self-promoting leads to higher competence but lower "hire-ability" (see Figure 3.6).

INGRATIATION

ingratiation a strategy in which people try to make themselves likeable to someone else, often through flattery and praise

People who use the self-promotion strategy are trying to present themselves as competent. However, those who use the **ingratiation** strategy are trying to be liked (Gordon, 1996; Jones, 1990). This strategy often involves complimenting or flattering someone on their clothes, their golf game, or whatever.

One problem with ingratiation is that the more you need someone to like you, the more obvious this strategy is. If a student comes by my office to tell me what a brilliant lecture I just gave, and then asks for an extension on a term paper, I'm quite likely to suspect that the comment on my lecture was insincere. However, more subtle forms of ingratiation can be effective (e.g., "what a cute baby you have—can I have an extension on the due date for my term paper?").

Ingratiation can lead other people to dislike you because they see your behavior as insincere and as caused by an ulterior motive (e.g., desire for a promotion, a raise, or other benefits). If you ingratiate to your boss while being rude to your subordinates, you might have trouble getting along with colleagues (Vonk, 1998). We quickly notice, and especially dislike, a phenomenon sometimes referred to as "the slime effect." This is one reason why likeable behaviors are seen less positively when they are enacted toward a superior than toward a subordinate, namely, because people recognize the possibility that the behavior is influenced by other motives (e.g., ingratiation; Vonk, 1999).

SELF-VERIFICATION

So far we have focused on how people try to present themselves positively. But according to **self-verification theory**, people typically want others to perceive us the way we perceive ourselves (Chen, English, & Peng, 2006; Sedikides, 1993; Swann, 1987; Swann & Hill, 1982). However, if we perceive ourselves positively, we want others to see us this way, whereas if we see ourselves negatively, we actually want others to see us negatively. This preference for self-verification leads us to prefer to interact with those who see us as we see ourselves, even in cases in which we see ourselves negatively.

Participants in one study completed a questionnaire about themselves and indicated the extent to which they viewed themselves as likable and competent (Swann, Pelham, & Krull, 1989). (Although 80% of the participants saw themselves this way, about 20% saw themselves less positively.) A few months later, and supposedly as part of a different experiment, the participants had an opportunity to interact with one of two people who had read their original questionnaire. The participants were told that one of those people had described them as seeming socially competent and skilled whereas the other had described them as seeming less competent. Although 77% of the participants who saw themselves in a positive light wanted to interact with the person who saw them as highly competent, only 22% of those who saw themselves in a negative light preferred to interact with someone who saw them positively. In addition, the majority of those with a low self-image preferred to interact with someone who saw them in this same negative light. Although this study was conducted in a lab setting, research in more naturalistic settings reveals that roommates and married couples show similar preferences. In sum, people are more satisfied

self-verification theory a theory that people want others to perceive them as they perceive themselves, regardless of whether they see themselves in a positive or negative light

Creatas/SUPERSTOCK

Your level of self-monitoring influences the types of features you look for in a dating partner as well as how you present yourself.

and committed to their relationships with those who see them as they see themselves, regardless of whether their view of themselves is positive or negative (Swann, Hixon, & De La Ronde, 1992).

Our desire to have other people see us as we see ourselves leads us to act in even more extreme ways if we are "misread" by someone, as a way of "correcting" the wrong impression (Swann, 1987). In one study, 46 women rated themselves on dominance versus submissiveness; they then played a game with a confederate of the experimenter (Swann & Hill, 1982). The confederate gave them either dominant or submissive feedback (e.g., "You seem like a leader, someone who likes to take charge," or "You seem like someone who likes to follow others' lead and hold back somewhat"). Then the participant was videotaped while interacting with the confederate for two minutes. When this interaction was rated by independent observers, participants who received disconfirming feedback resisted it more strongly than those who received confirming feedback and behaved even more in line with their own self-perception. That is, those who saw themselves as dominant were especially dominant in the interaction. But those who saw themselves as submissive were especially submissive in the interaction. In short, if the description you receive matches your own self-view, you accept it. On the other hand, if this description is not in line with how you view yourself, you are motivated to change it by going out of your way to interact differently (e.g., being even more dominant or even more submissive) the next time you interact with the person.

Although people generally are concerned with self-presentation, they differ in **self-monitoring**, that is, how much they change their behavior in response to such concerns (Snyder, 1974; Snyder & Gangestad, 1986). Those who are high self-monitors readily and easily modify their behavior in response to the demands of the situation, whereas those who are low self-monitors care little about modifying their behavior in response to the situation and tend to maintain the same opinions and attitudes regardless of the situation. A person who is a high self-monitor is likely to behave in very different ways when with different people. For example, he or she may express support for one view when with a group of people who support that particular view, but express support for the exact opposite view when with another group of friends who oppose it. A low self-monitor, in contrast, tends to maintain the same views and behavior regardless of the views of others, and hence shows greater consistency across situations.

These differences in personality have a number of consequences for how people behave in their interpersonal relationships. Compared to those who are low in self-monitoring, people who are high in self-monitoring have more dating and sexual partners, are more interested in having sex with people they are not in love with, and are more likely to have had sex with someone only once (Snyder, Simpson, & Gangestad, 1986). High self-monitors are also more willing to deceive potential romantic partners. In one study, participants were given information about two prospective dating partners and specifically information about what the other person was looking for in a romantic partner (e.g., independent, gentle, self-confident, kind; Rowatt, Cunningham, & Druen, 1998). Participants then prepared their own descriptions for each of these potential partners (so the researchers could determine how much they would change their descriptions based on the preferences of potential partners). As predicted, high self-monitors were much more willing to change their presentations than low self-monitors.

Finally, when selecting a dating partner, high and low self-monitors show very different preferences (Snyder, Berscheid, & Glick, 1985). In one study, male college students had to choose between two interaction partners with very different strengths and weaknesses. One potential partner was a very attractive woman (she was rated 5.75 on a 7-point scale of attractiveness). But she was described as having a reserved attitude toward strangers and being more comfortable with friends, as being more concerned with herself than with others, and as having a tendency toward moodiness. The other potential dating partner was quite unattractive (she was rated 1.88) but had a number of very positive personality traits. She was described as highly sociable, outgoing, open, good at interacting with others,

self-monitoring the extent to which one adjusts one's self-presentation in different situations

Questioning the Research
The study on the influence of self-monitoring on preferences in a dating partner was conducted only with men. How do you think the findings would differ if it were conducted with women?

FIGURE
3.7

HOW DOES SELF-MONITORING IMPACT CHOICE OF DATING PARTNERS?

In this study, male college students who were either high or low in self-monitoring read descriptions of two potential dating partners (one physically attractive but with a negative personality, one physically unattractive but with a positive personality), and then selected one of these partners for a date. As predicted. high self-monitors preferred the physically attractive, but unsociable, partner, whereas low self-monitors chose the physically unattractive, but sociable, partner.

Source: Snyder, M., Berscheid, E., & Glick, P. (1985). Focusing on the exterior and the interior: Two investigations of the initiation of personal relationships. *Journal of Personality and Social Psychology*, 48, 1427–1439.

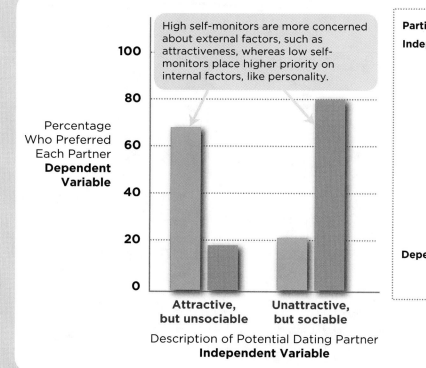

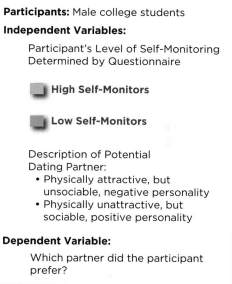

emotionally stable, having a good sense of humor, and willing to listen to others and get along. As shown in Figure 3.7, high self-monitors were more likely to choose the attractive person with the negative personality, whereas low self-monitors were more likely to choose the unattractive person with the positive personality.

THE GOOD—AND BAD—NEWS ABOUT SELF-PRESENTATION

Although people go to great lengths to present themselves in particular ways, some evidence suggests that we are overly concerned with self-presentation. Specifically, other people aren't paying as much attention to us as we often believe. So, we can relax and stop worrying about how we appear to others. In fact, people overestimate the extent to which their own appearance and behavior are obvious to others, a phenomenon called the **spotlight effect** that was described at the start of this section (remember the study on the Vanilla Ice t-shirt; Gilovich et al., 2000; Savitsky, Epley, & Gilovich, 2001). Similarly, although we often believe that our internal states are readily apparent to others, others typically have less access to our feelings than we think they do (Vorauer & Ross, 1999). So while you may

spotlight effect the tendency to overestimate the extent to which one's own appearance and behavior are obvious to others

think that the interviewer noticed your sweaty palms and could tell how nervous you were, rest assured—your secret is probably safe.

On the other hand, concerns with self-presentation sometimes lead people to engage in crazy and potentially dangerous behaviors, such as substance abuse (Sharp & Getz, 1996). Refusing to use sunscreen because you believe you'd look more attractive with a good tan can lead to skin cancer, and failing to use condoms because you are afraid you'll appear promiscuous to a partner can lead to unintended pregnancy or even infection with an STD or AIDS (Leary, Tchividijian, & Kraxberger, 1994; Martin & Leary, 1999).

"I can't walk in these shoes, which is a problem, because I can't sit down in this skirt."

STRATEGIES OF SELF-PRESENTATION

Concepts in Context

FACTOR	EXAMPLE
Self-promotion	In her bid to become class president, Denise continues to discuss her immense leadership skills with all of her classmates.
Ingratiation	Bill, who is one of several candidates for a promotion in his office, regularly compliments his boss on his great selection of ties.
Self-verification	Jill, who sees herself as very introverted and quiet, is trying to change roommates for next semester, because her current roommate, Pam, sees Jill as extraverted and outgoing.

HOW DOES CULTURE INFLUENCE SELF-PERCEPTION AND SELF-PRESENTATION?

Imagine that you are assigned to work with a group of fellow students on a project for the entire semester. At the end of this project, you are asked to rate yourself, and each of your classmates, on their attributes, including sociability, intellect, and assertiveness. This method allowed researchers to examine whether individuals' self-reports were the same as, higher, or lower than the reports of other group members. How do you think your own self-ratings would compare to those given to you by your peers? Given what you've already learned in this chapter about individuals' tendency to see themselves in overly positive ways, I hope you believe that people tend to rate themselves higher than do others (and this is precisely what researchers have demonstrated, with American samples). However, when Chinese college students participated in this same study, they rated themselves lower than group members (Yik, Bond, & Paulhus, 1998). Although 56% of North American students rated themselves better than did group members, only 43% of Chinese participants showed this type of self-enhancement. In other words, the general tendency to see oneself in extremely positive ways seems to hold true for people in individualistic cultures, but not those in collectivistic cultures. This section will examine how culture impacts self-perception and self-presentation, including the factors that influence the self-concept, the self-perception of motivation, the strategies used to maintain a positive self-concept, and the strategies of self-presentation.

FACTORS INFLUENCING THE SELF-CONCEPT

As described in Chapter 1, people in different cultures see themselves in very different ways: in individualistic cultures, such as the United States, Canada, and England, people view themselves in terms of their attitudes, skills, and traits (Bochner, 1994; Cousins, 1989; Dhawan et al. 1995; Rhee, Uleman, Lee, & Roman, 1995). When people are asked to respond to the question "Who am I?", those from individualistic cultures often describe their personal attributes and traits, such as "smart," "funny," or "shy." In contrast, in collectivistic cultures, such as Japan, Korea, and India, people tend to see themselves in terms of their group and family affiliations. They also describe themselves in terms of their social roles, interpersonal relationships, and group memberships, such as "a college student," "a daughter," or "a member of the Catholic church."

How people think about themselves. This difference in how people define their self-concepts extends to how people think about and reflect on their experiences in the world. People in individualistic cultures are more likely to think about themselves in the first person, and to project their needs and feelings onto others, than are those from communalistic cultures (Cohen & Gunz, 2002). For example, when asked to describe a memory, those from individualistic cultures are much more likely to recall being at the center of the event, whereas those from collectivistic cultures are much more likely to recall someone else being the focus. Americans, and those from other individualistic cultures, are also more likely to show an egocentric projection of their own emotions onto others. These cultural differences are reflected in how

People from collectivistic cultures, such as India, tend to describe themselves in terms of their social roles and interpersonal relationships.

Digital Vision Ltd./SUPERSTOCK

TABLE 3.2 A WORLDWIDE RANKING OF CULTURES

INDIVIDUALISTIC CULTURES	INTERMEDIATE CULTURES	COLLECTIVISTIC CULTURES
United States	Israel	Hong Kong
Australia	Spain	Chile
United Kingdom	India	Singapore
Canada	Argentina	Thailand
Netherlands	Japan	West Africa region
New Zealand	Jamaica	El Salvador
Italy	Arab world	Taiwan
Belgium	Brazil	South Korea
Denmark	Turkey	Peru
France	Uruguay	Costa Rica
Sweden	Greece	Indonesia
Ireland	Philippines	Pakistan
Norway	Mexico	Columbia
Switzerland	Hungary	Venezuela
South Africa	Austria	Guatemala

As shown in this table, cultures vary considerably in the relative emphasis placed on individualism versus collectivism (Hofstede, 1991).

parents and caretakers encourage different types of behavior: American kids are encouraged to speak up and use words to describe their feelings, whereas Japanese children are encouraged to try to understand others' emotions, intentions, and motivations (Kanagawa, Cross, & Markus, 2001). In sum, individualists see the world from the perspective of themselves looking out; collectivists see the world from the perspective of others looking at themselves.

Individualistic cultures also place a stronger emphasis than collectivistic cultures on having a consistent and stable self-concept, in part because Western cultures describe the self predominantly in terms of one's internal traits, abilities, and attributes (Campbell, Trapnell, Heine, Katz, Lavallee, & Lehman, 1996; Suh, 2002). In line with this belief, people from individualistic cultures are more likely to agree with statements such as "In general, I have a clear sense of who I am and what I am," and "I seldom experience conflict between different aspects of my personality" (Campbell et al., 1996). Those from collectivistic cultures,

CULTURAL DIFFERENCES IN FIRST MEMORIES

American: "I have a memory of being at my great aunt and uncle's house. It was some kind of party; I remember I was wearing my purple-flowered party dress. There was some sort of crib on the floor, shaped kind of like this: [a sketch]. I don't know if it was meant for me or for one of my younger cousins, but I crawled into it and lay there on my back. My feet stuck out, but I fit pretty well. I was trying to get the attention of people passing by. I was having fun and feeling slightly mischievous. When I picture the memory, I am lying down in the crib, looking at my party-shoed feet sticking out of the end of the crib."

Chinese: "I used to play with friends when I was little. We went to the bush to pick up wild fruits to eat. And I watched them catch birds."

When American and students were asked to describe their earliest childhood memory, Americans described, specific, self-focused, and emotionally elaborative memories, with a focus on individual attributes in describing themselves. In contrast, Chinese memories were brief and focused on collective activities, general routines, and emotionally neutral events. They were also more likely to describe social roles in their self-descriptions.

Source: Wang, Q. (2001). Culture effects on adults' earliest childhood recollection and self-description: Implications for the relation between memory and the self. *Journal of Personality and Social Psychology*, 81, 220–233.

on the other hand, are more likely to agree with statements such as "My beliefs about myself often conflict with one another," and "Sometimes I think I know other people better than I know myself."

Similarly, culture also influences how interested people are in engaging in social comparison. Those from collectivistic backgrounds are more interested in engaging in social comparison information than those from individualistic backgrounds

Rate Yourself

Are You Consistent in Different Situations?

Self-Consistency Scale

INSTRUCTIONS: *Rate each item on a scale of 1 (strongly disagree) to 5 (strongly agree).*

☐ **1.** In general, I have a clear sense of who I am and what I am.

☐ **2.** My beliefs about myself often conflict with one another.

☐ **3.** I seldom experience conflict between different aspects of my personality.

☐ **4.** Sometimes I think I know other people better than I know myself.

☐ **5.** I spend a lot of time wondering about what kind of person I really am.

☐ **6.** My beliefs about myself seem to change very frequently.

☐ **7.** Sometimes I feel that I am not really the person that I appear to be.

SCORING: For items 1 and 3, give yourself the number of points equal to the rating that you assigned to the statement. Items 2, 4, 5, 6, 7, and 8 are reverse-scored, so higher scores are converted to lower numbers (and vice versa). In other words, if you rated the statement a 5, give yourself 1 point. If you rated the statement a 2, give yourself 4 points.

INTERPRETATION: This scale assesses individuals' beliefs about their consistency across different situations (Campbell et al., 1996). Higher scores reflect greater consistency (typical of individualistic cultures), whereas lower scores reflect greater variability (typical of collectivistic cultures).

(White & Lehman, 2005). This greater interest in social comparison is likely a result of people with a more interdependent self-concept having an overall greater focus on the thoughts, feelings, behaviors, and goals of others.

Culture also is linked with self-concept clarity: Canadians and Americans have higher self-concept clarity than Japanese people, meaning that Canadians see themselves as more consistent across situations (Campbell et al., 1996). In one study, both Japanese and American college students were asked to complete the "Who am I?" test either alone, with a peer, in a large group of peers, or with a higher status person (such as a faculty member; Kanagawa et al., 2001). Both Canadians and Americans reported having a clear sense of who they are, showing consistency from day to day as well as across different situations (e.g., with a faculty member, with a peer, in a group, alone). In contrast, Japanese people reported differences in self-concepts across these distinct situations, because their self-concepts are more influenced by the situation. This patterning makes sense, given the individualistic emphasis on individual achievement and attributes, and the collectivistic emphasis on relationships and interdependence with others. The situation simply matters more for those in collectivistic cultures.

Questioning the Research

Although this section describes the impact of culture on how people answer the "Who Am I?" test, can you think of other factors that might influence how people answer this question? (Hint: What other demographic factors might influence responses?)

How people experience psychological well-being. Although consistency among different aspects of the self is an important predictor of well-being in individualistic cultures, such consistency is often not associated with well-being in collectivistic cultures (Suh, 2002). East Asians are less concerned with consistency because they see the self as more of a social product, in which the person is naturally different in different situations and with different people. Moreover, in collectivistic cultures consistency may represent rigidity and a lack of flexibility. In sum, what is psychologically good and healthy is determined by one's culture: consistency predicts well-being in Western cultures, because people are expected to orchestrate their behavior, but in Eastern cultures, well-being is a result of the fit between the person and the culture, and hence consistency is not associated with well-being.

One explanation for why consistency is a weaker predictor of well-being in collectivistic than in individualistic cultures is that these different cultures view the likelihood, direction, and cause of change in distinct ways see Table 3.3; (Choi & Nisbett, 2000; Ji, Nisbett, & Su, 2001; Peng & Nisbett, 1999). In collectivistic cultures, reality is seen as dynamic and changeable, and so change is a normal and natural part of life. In contrast, individualistic cultures expect consistency over time, and are thus surprised when change occurs. For example,

TABLE 3.3	COMMON PROVERBS IN DIFFERENT COUNTRIES

Chinese	American
"Beware of your friend, not your enemy."	"The apple doesn't fall far from the tree."
"Be prepared for danger while staying in peace."	"Fool me once, shame on you; fool me twice, shame on me."
"When you succeed, don't be conceited; when you fail, don't be dejected."	

Common Chinese proverbs reflect the view that change is likely. In contrast, common American proverbs reflect a view of stability and consistency over time (Kanagawa et al., 2001).

Americans are more surprised than Koreans when a "good person" (e.g., a seminary student) doesn't help someone, as well as when a "bad person" helps someone. They are also more surprised when a study's hypothesis is not supported and evidence is found instead for an alternative hypothesis. In sum, people in collectivistic cultures have a more fluid and open view of people. They do not hold the view "once a criminal, always a criminal," as is often true in individualistic cultures.

SELF-PERCEPTION OF MOTIVATION

Culture also impacts how people think about their motivation for engaging in behavior (Ivengar & Lepper, 1999). Remember the "magic marker study," described earlier in this chapter, in which children's intrinsic interest in drawing with magic markers was undermined when researchers gave children rewards for such drawing (which in turn decreased intrinsic motivation; Lepper et al., 1973)? As described previously, for American children intrinsic motivation is undermined when they do a task for extrinsic reasons (such as getting a reward or following their parent's wishes). In collectivistic cultures, on the other hand, the focus is on the family and social unit, and following the preferences of others, as opposed to those of oneself, does not necessarily undermine intrinsic interest.

In one study, researchers asked both European American and Asian American elementary school children to solve a series of anagrams (puzzles in which letters are unscrambled to form words; Iyengar & Lepper, 1999). In some conditions the children were told to choose a category of anagrams (and the color marker to work with), in others they were told the experimenter wanted them to solve a certain set of categories, and in still another they were told their mother wanted them to solve a certain category. As shown in Figure 3.8, Caucasian children solved slightly more anagrams when they could make their own choices, which is in agreement with other research showing the importance of intrinsic motivation in individualistic samples. Among Asian children, however, anagram solving was highest when the children followed their mother's choices, showing that intrinsic motivation remains high among Asian children even when children's choices are guided by an extrinsic factor.

STRATEGIES FOR MAINTAINING A POSITIVE SELF-CONCEPT

Earlier in this chapter you read about the strategies people use to maintain positive self-concepts, such as holding unrealistic beliefs about their ability to control events, making self-serving attributions, and seeing themselves in a particularly positive light. But many of these so-called "truths about human nature" may in fact best describe people in individualistic cultures, and may have little relevance for those from collectivistic cultures. For example, individuals from individualistic cultures are more likely than those from collectivistic cultures to believe they have some control over how objects work together, even when the objects are interacting in a completely random way (Ji, Peng, & Nisbett, 2000). Americans and others from individualistic cultures are also more likely to idealize or glorify their daily experiences than those individuals in collectivistic cultures. Although daily diary studies reveal no differences between European Americans and Asian Americans in how they describe their moods, in retrospective reports—meaning over time—European Americans report that they are happier overall than do Asians (Oishi, 2002). What causes this difference? Americans have a theory that "life is good," whereas Asians have a theory that "life is good and bad."

Use of self-serving attributional biases. People in individualistic cultures are much more likely to use self-serving attributional biases than those in collectivistic cultures. In fact, people in collectivistic cultures often make pessimistic explanations for events, by giving stable, global, and internal causes to negative

FIGURE
3.8

HOW DOES CULTURE IMPACT INTRINSIC MOTIVATION?

In this experiment, elementary-school children were asked to solve a series of anagrams. The choice of which anagrams to work on was made either by the child, the experimenter, or the child's mother. Anglo American children worked the longest when they chose the anagrams to work on, whereas Asian American children worked the longest when anagrams were chosen by their mother.

Source: Iyengar, S., Lepper, M. (1999). Rethinking the Value of Choice: A Cultural Perspective on Intrinsic Motivation. *Journal of Personality and Social Psychology, 76*, 349–366. Copyright © 1999 by the American Psychological Association. Reproduced. The use of APA information does not imply endorsement by APA.

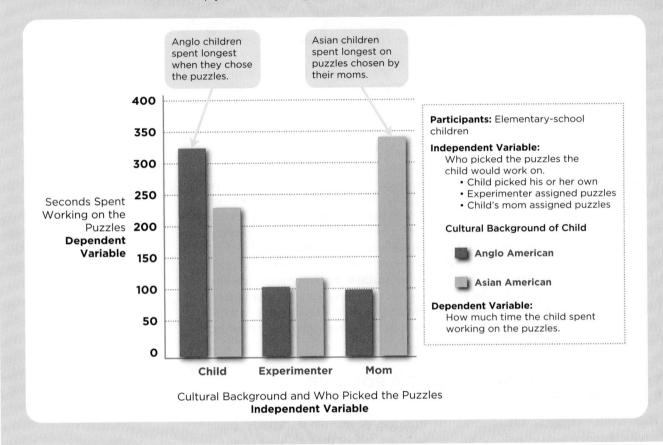

events and unstable, specific, and external causes to positive events (see Table 3.4; Morris & Peng, 1994). For example, in one study both American and Chinese college students imagined themselves in a series of situations (some positive—such as getting an A on an exam—and some negative—such as breaking up with a dating partner; Anderson, 1999). They were then asked to rate the cause of this situation (e.g., ability, effort, external circumstances, etc.). As predicted, Chinese students take more responsibility for failures, and take less credit for their successes relative to American students.

Use of false uniqueness bias. Similarly, the false uniqueness bias (people's tendency to see themselves as especially talented and better than others) is much more common in individualistic cultures than in collectivistic ones (Chang, Asakawa, & Sanna, 2001; Heine & Lehman, 1995; Markus & Kitayama, 1991; Stigler, Smith, & Mao, 1985). For example, Canadians tended to evaluate their own university in an unrealistically positive way—meaning as much better than students from another university see it. However, Japanese students show self-effacing biases—meaning they actually rate their own university less positively than

TABLE 3.4	EXAMPLES OF POSITIVE AND NEGATIVE EXPLANATIONS REGARDING THE OLYMPIC GAMES

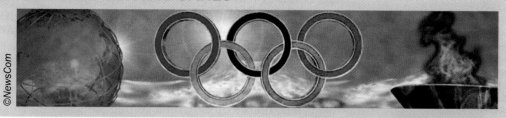

©NewsCom

	Positive events	Negative events
Typical Optimistic Explanations	We are in good spirits because we know we have greatly improved.	She fell yesterday because an avalanche of snow from nearby trees covered the visor of her helmet.
Typical Pessimistic Explanations	We succeeded because our competitors had been drinking all night before.	The disaster came because she is in such bad shape.

These descriptions of events were taken from newspaper reports about the 1984 Winter Olympic Games in Sarajevo, Yugoslavia, and revealed that newspaper reports were more pessimistic in tone in East Berlin than in West Berlin (Oettingen & Seligman, 1990). These findings are particularly remarkable because East Germany won 24 medals and West Germany won only four!

do students who attend another school (Heine & Lehman, 1997). In fact, individuals from individualistic cultures tend to see themselves as particularly good at a task when they receive objective information that their own performance was lower than that of other students.

These cultural differences in self-enhancement are also seen in research on individuals' expectancies for positive versus negative events. In one study, researchers asked European American college students attending the University of Michigan and Japanese students attending Shikoku Gakuin University in Japan to rate the likelihood of experiencing various events (Chang & Asakawa, 2003). Some of these events were positive, such as "meeting someone new with whom you expect to be close friends," and others were negative, such as "fail a test." They were then asked whether each event was more likely to happen to them than their sibling, more likely to happen to their sibling than to them, or equally likely to happen to both them and their sibling. Americans saw positive events as much more likely to happen to themselves than to a sibling, and negative events as much more likely to happen to a sibling than to themselves. In contrast, Japanese people saw positive events as equally likely to happen to themselves and a sibling, and negative events as much more likely to happen to themselves than their sibling. Again, this study shows that European Americans have an optimistic bias for both positive and negative events, whereas Japanese have a pessimistic bias for negative events.

Causes of cultural differences in self-enhancement. What leads to these cultural differences in tendency to self-enhance versus self-criticize? Some intriguing research by Shinobu Kitayama and his colleagues suggests that American situations are relatively conducive to self-enhancement, whereas Japanese situations are relatively conducive to self-criticism (Kitayama, Markus, Matsumoto, & Norasakkunkit, 1997). Americans see success situations (e.g., getting a good grade on a paper, passing other runners in a race) as more relevant to their self-esteem than failure situations (e.g., being jilted by a dating partner, receiving negative feedback from a boss). Americans believe that their self-esteem would increase more in success situations than it would decrease in failure situations. On the other hand, Japanese respondents show the reverse pattern, by selecting a greater number of failure situations than success situations as relevant to their self-esteem and seeing failure situations as having a greater impact on self-esteem than success situations.

Americans are relatively likely to engage in self-enhancement, whereas Japanese people are relatively likely to engage in self-criticism (Heine et al., 2001). For example, when North Americans fail at a task, they tend to give up much more quickly on a second, similar task compared to those who succeed (presumably because they fear receiving more negative information about their ability). Yet Japanese who fail at a task actually persist longer at a second task than those who succeed (again, presumably because they are focused on self-improvement). These findings suggest that people in collectivistic cultures tend to search for their weaknesses in an attempt to overcome them, and thus focus on what they don't do well.

Why do people in individualistic cultures use strategies to maintain a positive self-concept whereas those in collectivistic cultures do not? The commonly assumed belief that people need to have a positive self-regard seems to be unique to those in individualistic cultures (Heine, Lehman, Markus, & Kitayama, 1999). There is little evidence that Japanese people need a positive self-regard, and in fact, some research suggests that a self-critical focus is more common. One study with Japanese, Asian Canadian, and European Canadian students revealed that actual-ideal self-discrepancies were larger for Japanese than for either of the Canadian groups (Heine & Lehman, 1999). In other words, individuals' actual selves were more distant from their ideal selves for Japanese participants than for those in individualistic cultures, in part because feeling different from the person you'd like to be is more threatening to those in individualistic cultures than for those in collectivistic ones.

Finally, although people in individualistic cultures generally show more evidence of self-enhancement than do those in collectivistic cultures, researchers do find some evidence for self-enhancement even in collectivistic cultures. First, Japanese college students prefer letters that are included in their own name more than other letters, and these preferences are particularly strong for first letters of family names for males and first letters of their own first names for females (Kitayama & Karasawa, 1997). Japanese college students also prefer numbers that correspond to the day and month of their birthday more than other numbers, suggesting that even people in collectivistic cultures may show some preference for self-enhancement. Second, self-liking is higher in a highly collectivistic culture than in an individualistic one, in part because fitting in with one's group and pleasing others is highly valued, whereas individual achievement is not very celebrated or encouraged (Tafarodi & Swann, 1996). On the other hand, individualistic cultures prize assertiveness and self-promotion, and in turn, self-competence is higher in individualistic than in collectivistic cultures.

STRATEGIES OF SELF-PRESENTATION

These cultural differences in self-perception also lead people to present themselves to others in very different ways. In one study, Japanese Americans and European Americans completed a series of tasks (anagrams, perceptual reasoning, etc.) and were told they got 65% correct (Akimoto & Sanbonmatsu, 1999). They were also told that this was a very good score, and that they did better than 80–90% of other college students. When they were later asked about their performance by a confederate, Japanese students were less self-promoting and more self-effacing than European Americans, although such differences did not

Cornstock/SUPERSTOCK

Americans who fail at a task tend to give up relatively quickly when asked to work on that task again. In contrast, Japanese people who fail at a task tend to persist even longer when asked to work on that task again.

occur on their private, written questionnaire (meaning they don't actually see their performance in a less favorable light). Unfortunately, this modesty in their interaction leads them to be perceived as having performed less well, being less competent, and being less likely to be hired when such interactions are later rated. So, this collectivistic tendency for modesty, perhaps to promote in-group harmony and prevent jealousy, can have negative personal consequences.

The Big Picture

SELF-PERCEPTION AND SELF-PRESENTATION

This chapter included many applications of the three "big ideas" studied in social psychology. The examples below should help you see the connection between our discussion of the self and these big ideas, and contribute to your understanding of the big picture of social psychology.

THEME	EXAMPLES
The social world influences how we think about ourselves.	• Women who see photos of highly attractive women, and men who read descriptions of socially dominant men, feel worse about their own value as a marriage partner. • People who hold their faces in a smile feel happier than those who maintain a frown. • People who are physiologically aroused feel happy if they are with others who are happy.
The social world influences our thoughts, attitudes, and behaviors.	• Children who face a mirror while trick-or-treating are more likely to take only one piece of candy than those who don't face a mirror. • People who are given negative feedback about their IQ drink more wine than those who receive positive feedback. • Students whose college football team wins are more likely to wear clothes featuring their school name the following Monday than those whose football team loses.
Our attitudes and behavior shape the social world around us.	• Students who are initially required to volunteer are less likely to volunteer later on. • People who have overly positive views about themselves are more aggressive toward others. • People who are high in self-monitoring are more likely to deceive potential romantic partners than those who are low in self-monitoring.

This chapter examined five key principles of self-perception and self-presentation.

YOU LEARNED **How do personal factors influence the self-concept?** A variety of personal factors, including thinking about our thoughts, focusing on self-awareness, regulating the self, examining our behavior, and interpreting our motivation, can influence how we see ourselves. We also demonstrated that sometimes we make errors when assessing our attitudes and feelings: assistant professors think they'll be very sad—for a long time—if they don't get tenure, but in reality, they feel just as good as those who got tenure.

YOU LEARNED **How do social factors influence the self-concept?** Both social comparison theory and the two-factor theory of emotion demonstrate the influence of social factors on our self-concept. And you learned that comparing your intelligence to that of Pamela Anderson is a good idea.

YOU LEARNED **How do people maintain a positive self-concept?** We use a variety of strategies to maintain a positive self-concept, including self-serving biases, self-serving beliefs, self-serving comparisons, and self-serving behavior. For example, you learned that people see themselves as showering less frequently than others during a drought, but showering more frequently than others during normal conditions. All of these strategies help us feel good about ourselves, sometimes in the face of considerable evidence to the contrary.

YOU LEARNED **How do people present themselves to others?** People use a number of different strategies to present themselves to other people in a positive way. These strategies include self-promotion, ingratiation, and self-verification. However, we also learned that we don't need to focus quite so much on self-presentation—because other people are much less aware of our own behavior than we believe they are. In other words, it is truly OK to wear the Vanilla Ice t-shirt.

YOU LEARNED **How does culture influence self-perception and self-presentation?** The last section in this chapter described the role of culture in influencing both self-perception and self-presentation. We learned that individuals' tendency to self-enhance, meaning to rate themselves as particularly good—and certainly as better than most others—is highly influenced by culture. In sum, people from individualistic cultures tend to rate themselves in particularly positive ways, whereas those from collectivistic cultures show considerably more modesty.

KEY TERMS

QUESTIONS FOR REVIEW

1. Describe four ways in which personal factors influence the self-concept, including the limits of each factor.
2. Describe two distinct ways in which social factors influence the self-concept, and include a research example of each.
3. We all use a variety of strategies to maintain our positive self-views. Describe four specific ways in which people see themselves in a biased way, and at least one problem with the use of such self-presentational strategies.
4. Describe two strategies that we use to present ourselves to others. What are the advantages and disadvantages of each?
5. Describe two distinct cultural differences in strategies used to maintain a positive self-concept, and two explanations for this difference.

TAKE ACTION!

1. Suppose that you are trying to motivate your 8-year-old nephew to practice the guitar. What strategies might and might not work to accomplish this goal?
2. Your brother is an amazing athlete—he excels at basically every sport he tries. Unfortunately, you aren't quite as athletically gifted. What strategies can you use to avoid feeling bad about your own sports abilities in comparison to your brother's?
3. In the last year your best friend has experienced a number of negative events, including a rejection from a very desired job and the ending of a long-term dating relationship. Yet she continues to feel very positive about herself. What strategies should she use to maintain a positive self-concept in the face of disappointment?
4. You have an important job interview tomorrow morning. Given your knowledge about self-presentation, what strategies will you use (and avoid) in order to make a good impression?
5. Your sister will be spending a month in Japan this summer as part of a high school exchange program. What advice might you give her when she asks how Japanese people differ from Americans?

RESEARCH CONNECTIONS

Try some of these research activities to gain experience in conducting and evaluating research, and to increase your understanding of research methods and techniques in social psychology.

Visit WileyPLUS for more activities and interactive research tools! (www.wileyplus.com/college/sanderson)

Participate in Research

Activity 1 **Rating Cartoons:** Do we really look at our own behavior to determine our attitudes and beliefs? Go to WileyPLUS to rate a series of cartoons while holding your face in different expressions. See if your attitude changes as your facial expression does.

Activity 2 **Rating Yourself:** How you feel about yourself depends on the person standing next to you. Rate how you feel about yourself after looking at a magazine featuring more average-looking people. According to social comparison theory, we feel differently about ourselves depending on the types of comparisons we make. Did you?

Activity 3 **Testing BIRGing:** Do students at your school bask in reflected glory? To test the prevalence of BIRGing, follow the procedure used by Cialdini et al. Record the number of people you see on campus wearing school apparel the Monday following a football loss versus the Monday following a football win. Do your findings indicate students at your school BIRG(at least in relation to football)?

Activity 4 The Power of Self-Verification: we prefer others to see us as we see ourselves. Go to WileyPLUS to rate yourself across a series of dimensions. Do the two sets of ratings look the way self-verification theory suggests they should?

Activity 5 The Impact of Culture on Memory: Does culture influence the way we remember events? Take a few minutes to Write about one of your earliest memories. When you are finished, go to WileyPLUS to evaluate several features of your memory and see how another culture might compare.

Test a Hypothesis

One of the common findings in research on self-monitoring is that people with different levels of self-monitoring look for different things in a dating partner. To test whether this hypothesis is true, create several different descriptions of potential dating partners (varying such things as attractiveness, personality, income, and so on). Then ask your friends to complete the self-monitoring inventory and rate their interest in the different types of dating partners. Do your findings support or refute the hypothesis?

Design a Study

To design your own study testing the strategies people use to maintain a positive self-concept, decide on research questions you would like to answer. Then decide what type of study you want to conduct (self-report, observational/naturalistic, or experimental), choose your own independent and dependent variables, and operationally define each by determining the procedures or measures you will use. Form a hypothesis to predict what will happen in your study (the expected cause and effect relationship between your two variables), collect the data, and share what you find with others.

4

Social Perception

How do we think about why other people do what they do?

 RESEARCH FOCUS ON GENDER
Gender Differences in Attribution

What types of errors do we make in thinking about other people?

Why do we make errors when we think about other people?

How do we form impressions of people based on nonverbal behavior?

 RESEARCH FOCUS ON NEUROSCIENCE
The Special Processing of Eye Contact

How does CULTURE influence social perception?

Did you ever wonder?

On May 17, 2004, Massachusetts recorded the nation's first legal gay marriage when Marcia Kadish, 56, and Tanya McCloskey, 52, were married shortly after 9 A.M. by Cambridge City Clerk Margaret Drury. "Oh, my God, I'm speechless," said McCloskey, a massage therapist. "I'm so happy right now. This is a dream come true. To stand here in front of all these people makes us nervous but proud." "I'm glowing from the inside," said Kadish. "Happy is an understatement." Do you think same-sex marriage should be legal? Your opinion on same-sex unions is probably influenced by what you perceive is the cause of sexual orientation—whether you believe that people "choose" to be attracted to same-sex others or that people's sexual orientation reflects an innate preference (caused by biological and/or genetic factors). Although some people on both sides of this issue have very strong feelings about it, one of the predictors of attitudes toward same-sex marriage, as well as toward same-sex behavior in general, is how we think about a person's sexual orientation. People's perceptions about

Business
CONNECTIONS
Why Disserving
Attributions Can Be a
Good Idea

Law
CONNECTIONS
The Impact of Salience
on Perceived Guilt

Education
CONNECTIONS
Why Focusing on
Effort Over Ability Is a
Good Idea

the causes of a behavior have a strong impact on how we interpret that behavior. People who believe that sexual orientation can be attributed to controllable factors, such as a decision to prefer same-sex or opposite-sex partners, have more negative attitudes than those who believe that sexual orientation is caused by factors that can't be controlled, such as biological or genetic differences. This chapter will discuss this, and other, issues regarding how we interpret people's behavior, including:

Q A Why is giving your spouse the benefit of the doubt a good idea?

Q A Why do teenagers see their friends, but not themselves, as careless drivers?

Q A When is doing a good deed sometimes *not* a good idea?

Q A Why do people who lie talk really fast?

Q A Why are Americans likely to see murder as caused by crazy people, yet Chinese people are likely to blame the media?

©AP/Wide World Photos

These statements all describe findings from research on how we see other people and interpret their behavior.

Imagine that you're standing in line to buy tickets for a movie you've wanted to see, when you overhear the person in front of you describing how much they hated that movie. You now have to make a quick decision—should you see the movie you intended to see, or make an alternative choice? This decision will be driven largely by your inferences about the person whose conversation you overheard. This is just one example of **social perception**, meaning how we form impressions and make inferences about other people. Although the process of making attributions about someone's attitudes and behavior may seem like a very rational and straightforward process, we aren't always very accurate in assessing the cause of another person's behavior; we sometimes focus too much on the role of personal factors, while ignoring, or minimizing, the often-considerable influence of the situation.

HOW DO WE THINK ABOUT WHY OTHER PEOPLE DO WHAT THEY DO?

social perception how people form impressions of and make inferences about other people and events in the social world

Think about a time in which someone you were dating brought up a problem in your relationship, and how you reacted to this conflict. This reaction very likely influenced your satisfaction in the relationship. Researchers Thomas Bradbury and Frank Fincham (1992) conducted a series of studies with married couples in which they asked couples to discuss a problem in their relationship and then to make attributions for the cause of the problem. For example, a negative explanation for the problem of not spending enough time together might be "You stay up all night watching ESPN," whereas a positive explanation might be "Our schedules aren't really in synch." In turn, these different types of attributions, not surprisingly, can impact approaches to resolving the conflict as well as marital satisfaction. This section will examine three major theories that describe how we think about why people engage in particular types of behavior: attribution theory, correspondent inference theory, and the covariation model.

ATTRIBUTION THEORY

Imagine that while driving to work one day you notice that the driver behind you seems very aggressive: She is following your car very closely, honks her horn if you delay even a few seconds when the red light turns green, and finally swerves around to pass you. How will you make sense of, or *attribute*, this behavior? According to Fritz Heider (1958), often described as the "father of attribution theory," in some cases people make an **external attribution** about the causes of others' behavior. This means that they see the behavior as caused by the situation. For example, you could make a situational attribution (e.g., she is late for a job interview, in the car she has a sick child who needs to go to the hospital, she's had a bad day). In other cases, however, people make an **internal attribution** about the causes of others' behavior, meaning that they see the person's behavior as caused by personal factors (e.g., traits, ability, effort, or personality). For example, you could make a dispositional attribution about the driver's behavior (e.g., she is rude, she is hostile, she is very aggressive, etc.). We are motivated to try to figure out why a person acted in a given way so that we can predict how he or she will act in the future.

external attribution an explanation of a person's behavior as caused by situational, or external, factors

internal attribution an explanation of a person's behavior as caused by dispositional, or internal, factors

Ned Jones and his colleagues conducted one of the classic studies of the attribution process (Jones, Davis, & Gergen, 1961). Participants observed another person describing himself in either a very extroverted or very introverted manner during a job interview. Half of the participants were told that this applicant was

©AP/Wide World Photos

In the NEWS

Martha Stewart. Why did Martha Stewart allegedly lie to investigators about receiving advice to get rid of a particular stock? Attribution theories attempt to explain whether such behavior is caused by the person, meaning her internal traits and dispositions—or by the situation, meaning external factors. Do you think it was Martha Stewart's personal traits or the situation that caused her to behave this way?

interviewing for a job as a submariner (e.g., a job that requires considerable close contact with many others), and the other half, a job as an astronaut (e.g., a job that, at the time, required a person to spend long periods of time alone). Participants were then asked to rate the applicant's personality, and specifically his degree of extroversion. Those who saw an applicant acting in a predictable way—describing his extroversion when he was interviewing for a job as a submariner, describing his introversion when he was interviewing for a job as an astronaut—were quite reluctant to make this rating. They were reluctant because they (rightly) attributed the person's behavior to the situation (e.g., wanting to get the job). But when the person behaved in an unexpected way (e.g., the extravert wanting the astronaut job, the introvert wanting the submariner job), participants were very willing to make a dispositional attribution because they see the person's behavior as reflecting his true personality. (This behavior certainly isn't designed to help him win the job!). In turn, they rated the extravert as especially extraverted when he wanted the astronaut job and the introvert as especially introverted when he wanted the submariner job.

CORRESPONDENT INFERENCE THEORY

Edward Jones and Keith Davis (1965) developed a theory to explain why people make the attributions they do. Their **correspondent inference theory** is based on their observation that people often believe that other people's dispositions correspond to their behaviors. Specifically, this theory predicts that people try to infer whether an action is caused by internal dispositions of the person by looking at various factors related to that act. As with the covariation model, this theory proposes that there are three factors that influence the extent to which you attribute behavior to the person as opposed to the situation:

1. Does the person have the *choice* to engage in the action?
2. Is the behavior *expected* based on the social role or circumstance?
3. What are the *intended effects or consequences* of their behavior?

First, if you know that the person was forced to engage in a given behavior, obviously you infer that the action is due to the situation and not the person. For example, most students who major in psychology are required to take a course in statistics. If I know that a student who is majoring in psychology is taking statistics, can I infer that he or she must like statistics? No, because this behavior may have been caused by the situation (the requirements of the major). But if I find that an English major is taking statistics, can I probably assume

correspondent inference theory the theory that people infer whether a person's behavior is caused by internal dispositions of the person by looking at various factors related to that act

"*Which are you—a victim of society or a crook?*"

that he or she actually likes statistics? Yes, because in this case I have much greater certainty that the behavior was caused by the person.

Second, is the behavior *expected* based on the social role or circumstance? Behavior that is not necessarily required, but is largely expected due to a given situation, doesn't tell us much about the person. If you see someone wearing a tuxedo to a wedding, you shouldn't infer that he is a stylish and formal dresser because his outfit is quite likely to be a function of the situational requirement that he wear such attire. On the other hand, if you see a person wearing a T-shirt with a picture of a tuxedo on it to a formal wedding, you might very appropriately make a dispositional attribution for this unexpected behavior.

Third, what are the *intended effects or consequences* of their behavior? To make an attribution, Jones and Davis believe that you should look at the effects of a person's behavior that can be caused by *only one specific factor* as opposed to many factors. If there is only one intended effect, then you have a pretty good idea of why the person is motivated to engage in the behavior. If there are multiple good effects, it is more difficult to know what to attribute the behavior to. Another friend of yours decides to take a really boring job that pays $15,000 a year and is located in a small town near Vail, Colorado, an isolated place with cold weather, and she doesn't know anyone who lives there. Why did she take the job? Probably because she really likes to ski. Another friend of yours takes an interesting and challenging job that pays $80,000 and is located in San Francisco, where he has many friends. Why did he take the job? Who knows? In this case it is very difficult to make an attribution because the behavior could have been caused by a variety of factors.

In sum, according to correspondent inference theory we are best able to make a dispositional attribution, and see people's behavior as caused by their traits, when the behavior is freely chosen, is not a function of situational expectations, and has clear noncommon effects.

COVARIATION THEORY

covariation theory a theory explaining how people determine the causes of a person's behavior by focusing on the factors present and absent when a behavior does and does not occur, and specifically on the role of consensus, distinctiveness, and consistency

consensus information about whether other people generally behave in the same way toward the stimulus as the target person

An alternative theory of attribution was developed by Harold Kelley (Kelley, 1967). His **covariation theory** focuses on the factors that are present when a behavior occurs and the factors that are absent when it does not occur. Does your sister always fall madly in love with a potential romantic partner after the first date, regardless of that person's particular traits? If so, you probably make a dispositional or personal attribution (e.g., my sister gets infatuated easily). Did your sister ridicule most potential romantic partners but she feels very passionate about this one particular new partner? If so, you probably make a situational attribution (e.g., this person is very special). As shown in Figure 4.1, covariation theory has three main components: consensus, distinctiveness, and consistency.

The first component of covariation theory is the **consensus** of the attitude or behavior, that is, whether other people generally agree or disagree with a given person. If many people agree with that person or behave in a similar manner, we are more likely to make a situational attribution than we would if few people agreed with the target individual. In the case of your sister's dating life, we will likely make a situational attribution about the characteristics of the particular dating partner she likes if other people also really like that person. On the other hand,

MODEL OF COVARIATION

According to covariation theory, we use the level of consensus, distinctiveness, and consistency about a person's behavior to explain the behavior as mainly caused either by the person's situation or by the person's own characteristics or dispositions.

Consensus	Distinctiveness	Consistency	Attribution
High Other people all think your sister's boyfriend is great.	**High** Your sister is very picky about her dating partners. It is unusual for her to like one this much, so quickly.	**High** Your sister continues to like this person over time.	**Situational** This boyfriend really is special.
Low Other people think your sister's boyfriend is horrible.	**Low** Your sister quickly likes all her dating partners.	**High** Your sister continues to like this person over time.	**Dispositional** Your sister tends to fall in love quickly. This boyfriend is nothing special.
		Low Your sister quickly decides she doesn't like this guy.	**Uncertain** You can't tell if this boyfriend wasn't right or if your sister just falls in and out of love quickly.

if most other people find that person rude and annoying, we are less likely to make a situational attribution about this person.

Second, we consider the **distinctiveness** of the person's attitude or behavior, meaning whether the person's attitude or behavior in this situation is relatively unique or whether the person generally reacts in a similar way across different situations. Once again, your sister's liking of a particular partner, while ridiculing others, would make her attraction to that partner quite distinctive. In turn, we are more likely to make a situational attribution in this case.

Third, we consider the **consistency** of the person's attitude or behavior, that is, whether the person's attitude and/or behavior is similar over time. If a person's behavior is highly consistent over time and across situations (e.g., your sister likes a particular partner over time, even when they engage in different types of dating activities), we are likely to make a dispositional attribution. On the other hand, if a given behavior is unusual for a particular person, we are likely to make a situational attribution (e.g., your sister feels very attracted to a partner after their first date, but not so much after their third date).

Let's go through this process using another example. Imagine that you are trying to decide whether next semester you want to take a class in politics. You ask a friend, Joan, whether she would recommend the politics class she took last year. If Joan raves about this class, do you believe her and sign up? If you are smart, your decision about whether to take the politics class Joan recommends will be influenced by the three main components of covariation theory.

1. **Consensus:** Do her opinions have high consensus? Do many people like this class, or does only Joan like it? If everyone says it is a great class, then you can make a situational attribution (Joan liked the class because it was good), whereas if others say it is a really boring class, you should make a dispositional attribution for her attitude (Joan likes boring classes).

2. **Distinctiveness:** Next, consider the distinctiveness of Joan's attitude about this class. Does Joan rave about all of the classes she takes? If so, that doesn't tell

distinctiveness information about whether a person's behavior is generally the same toward different stimuli

consistency information about whether a person's behavior toward a given stimulus is the same across time

you much about this particular class because you should make a dispositional attribution for her attitude (it is just Joan, who likes all classes). But if Joan hates most of her classes, then her liking for this particular class should be attributed to the situation (the class).

3. **Consistency:** Finally, consider whether Joan's liking for this class is consistent over time. Maybe you asked Joan about the class on a day when she was in a particularly good mood, and later on she'll report a different opinion. To make a strong dispositional attribution for her attitude toward the class, you need to ask Joan about the class on more than one occasion to make sure that her attitude is consistently positive.

In sum, according to the covariation model, we make different attributions depending on the consensus, distinctiveness, and consistency of a person's attitude and/or behavior (Fiedler, Walther, & Nickel, 1999). If consensus and distinctiveness are low and consistency is high, we make an internal or dispositional attribution (Joan just loves this class). In contrast, if consensus, distinctiveness, and consistency are all high, we make a situational attribution (this class is really great). Finally, in any case in which a person's attitude or behavior is low in consistency, we can't make a dispositional or situational attribution.

RESEARCH FOCUS ON GENDER
Gender Differences in Attribution

Although the two theories of attribution present distinct pathways that lead to particular types of attribution, considerable evidence suggests that people consistently make different attributions for performance by men versus women (Swim & Sanna, 1996). In one meta-analysis (a summary of numerous different studies on the same issue), researchers found that observers tend to attribute men's successes to ability and women's successes to effort. This attribution pattern reverses in the case of failure. Observers seeing men's poor performance as caused by bad luck or low effort and women's poor performance as caused by lack of ability. One study of both 3rd graders and junior high school students revealed consistent gender differences in beliefs about the causes of both success and failure on a math exam (Stipek & Gralinski, 1991). Compared to boys, girls rated their ability lower, and the girls expected to do less well. Yet, even after doing well on this math test, girls were much less likely than boys to attribute this success to their ability.

THREE ATTRIBUTION THEORIES

Concepts in Context

THEORY	EXAMPLE
Attribution theory	Your sister has been especially rude to you on the phone recently—and given how unusual this type of behavior is, you assume she must be going through a hard time at work.
Correspondent inference theory	Your brother has decided to quit his well-paying job as an attorney to become a poet—much to your father's dismay. But you see this decision as the right one, because clearly your brother must be choosing a career that he truly wants to pursue.
Covariation theory	Juanita is certain she's going to enjoy reading Jackie Collins' new book. She's liked all of her other books; most of her friends rave about the book. Even her sister who doesn't like to read at all said this book was great.

Think back to when you first got your driver's license—and how well you drove. Although most teenagers have relatively high rates of risky driving, teenagers give very different explanations for their own risky driving versus that of their friends. In one study of teenagers with newly acquired drivers' licenses, researchers examined the attributions they made for their own and their friends' risky driving (Harré, Brandt, & Houkamau, 2004). As predicted, teenagers were much more likely to give situational explanations—"I was in a hurry, I was late"—for their own risky driving than for their friends' driving. But dispositional attributions—"He was showing off, acting cool"—were much more likely to be used to explain their friends' risky driving than their own. This section will describe two common errors people make in attributing the causes of people's behavior: the fundamental attribution error and the actor-observer bias.

FUNDAMENTAL ATTRIBUTION ERROR

The **fundamental attribution error** is a common type of attribution error in the United States and other Western cultures (Gilbert & Malone, 1995; Jones, 1979). Although people may use various pieces of information about the situation (e.g., choice, distinctiveness) to interpret behavior, we have a strong tendency to focus on the role of personal causes in predicting behavior, while ignoring situational influences.

fundamental attribution error
the tendency to overestimate the role of personal causes, and underestimate the role of situational causes, in predicting behavior

One study of the fundamental attribution error asked students to read a speech written by a college student that was either in favor of or opposed to Fidel Castro,

---

FIGURE 4.2

DOES CHOICE IMPACT USE OF THE FUNDAMENTAL ATTRIBUTION ERROR?

Experimenters asked students to read essays that either supported or opposed Fidel Castro and were supposedly written by students who either were given a choice about which side to write about or who had no choice. Surprisingly, participants in both conditions said that the writers were expressing true opinions, even when they were told the writer had no choice about the topic.

Source: Jones, E., & Harris, V. (1967). The attribution of attitudes. *Journal of Experimental Social Psychology, 3*, 1–24.

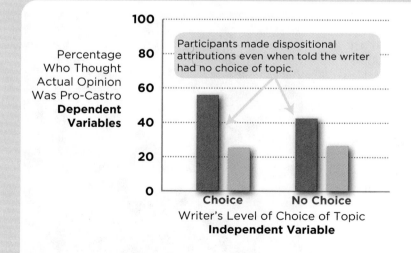

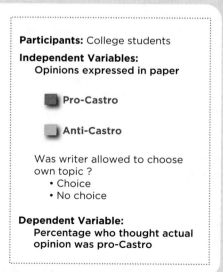

Percentage Who Thought Actual Opinion Was Pro-Castro **Dependent Variables**

Participants made dispositional attributions even when told the writer had no choice of topic.

Writer's Level of Choice of Topic
Independent Variable

Participants: College students
Independent Variables:
Opinions expressed in paper

■ Pro-Castro

□ Anti-Castro

Was writer allowed to choose own topic ?
• Choice
• No choice

Dependent Variable:
Percentage who thought actual opinion was pro-Castro

the communist leader of Cuba (Jones & Harris, 1967). Some of the participants were told that the student had been allowed to choose which position to take in the speech. Others were told that the professor had assigned the student which position to take. As predicted, participants who were told that a student who had written a pro-Castro speech had chosen the topic were more likely to assume that the student actually liked Castro (i.e., they made a dispositional attribution) than were those who were told that the student had been assigned the topic. As shown in Figure 4.2, interestingly (we will examine this more later) participants did assume that even in the assigned, no-choice condition, those who took the pro-Castro side were more pro-Castro than those who took the anti-Castro side.

Why do we make the fundamental attribution error? We believe that when people's behavior is caused by the situation, they give obvious clues that reflect this external pressure (Lord, Scott, Pugh, & Desforges, 1997). If a person who is strongly pro-choice is forced to argue the pro-life side for his or her high school debate team, we assume that the person's debate performance would be relatively weak (because he or she doesn't truly believe what he or she is arguing). We also believe that engaging in behavior that is in line with attitudes is easier. So, we are particularly likely to attribute strong performance to a person's true attitude. For example, essays that are described as in line with their writer's own attitude

Health

The Role of Attributions in Prejudice Against Obesity

Research reveals that obese people suffer a number of social and psychological consequences. Compared to normal-weight individuals, they are rated as less likable, have fewer dating partners, are less likely to get married, get lower grades, complete fewer years of education, earn less money, and are generally the subject of negative social attitudes (Miller, Rothblum, Barbour, Brand, & Felicio, 1990; Ryckman, Robbins, Kaczor, & Gold, 1989). One long-term study of obese and non-obese women found that those who were obese made less money, completed fewer years of education, and were less likely to be married than their normal-weight peers (Gortmaker, Must, Perrin, & Sobol, 1993).

Why do people who are obese experience such negative consequences? One reason is that obesity is often seen as something that is within a person's control. Obese people are seen as slow, lazy, sloppy, and lacking in willpower (Crandall, 1994). We often assume that if they wanted to lose weight, they could simply stop eating so much. In other words, we blame obese people for their weight. In one study, high school girls were shown a picture of a girl and read a short statement about her. Then they were asked to rate how much they thought they would like her (DeJong, 1980). Some of the girls saw a picture of an overweight girl, while others saw a picture of a normal-weight girl. Of those who saw the picture of the overweight girl, some were told that her weight was a result of a thyroid disorder. As predicted, participants who saw the normal-weight girl

liked her more than those who saw the overweight girl. But those who saw the overweight girl and were told that she had an acceptable reason for her weight (the thyroid condition) liked her just as much as those who saw the normal-weight girl. This study suggests that it is not just the weight that makes obese people seem unattractive, but the assumptions made about the causes of the weight, such as laziness.

Are obese people really different from others? No— the personality characteristics of obese and non-obese people are very similar (Poston, Ericsson, Linder, Nilsson, Goodrick, & Foreyt, 1999).

Alamy

are seen as stronger and more persuasive than essays that conflict with this attitude (Gawronski, 2003; Miller, Ashton, & Mishal, 1990). Unfortunately, and as described in the Health Connections box, the attributions we make about people's behavior can have negative consequences.

Interestingly, we even see our own behavior as driven by dispositional factors—even when the situation has clearly had a strong impact on this behavior. To demonstrate the power of this error, Ross and colleagues paired college students to play questioner and contestant in a quiz show game (Ross, Amabile, & Steinmetz, 1977). Participants drew cards to choose their role, and the questioners were then given 15 minutes to come up with questions to which they knew the answers but most people did not. For example, what do the initials in W.H. Auden's name stand for? How long is the Nile River? Which great lake is closest to the Gulf of St. Lawrence? Not surprisingly, the contestants could not answer very many of the questions. However, when questioners, contestants, and observers were asked how much general knowledge the questioners and the contestants had, only the questioners themselves seemed aware of the huge advantage of being able to come up with their own questions to ask. Questioners gave themselves and their partners about the same ratings of intelligence. On the other hand, contestants gave their partners higher ratings than themselves, and observers also saw the questioners as extremely knowledgeable and the contestants as about average.

ACTOR-OBSERVER EFFECT

Although we have a general tendency to see people's behavior as caused by dispositional factors, we are much less likely to see our own behavior as caused by such factors. In fact, we are very likely to focus on the role of the situation in causing our own behavior, a phenomenon called the **actor-observer effect** (Jones & Nisbett, 1971; Krueger, Ham, & Linford, 1996; Malle & Knobe, 1997). As described at the start of this section, teenage drivers attribute their own risky driving to situational factors, such as running late. But they attribute their peers' risky driving to personal factors, such as trying to "act cool" (Harré et al., 2004). Similarly, in one study, both prisoners and guards were asked to rate the cause of the prisoners' offenses (Saulnier & Perlman, 1981). As you might expect, prisoners

The fundamental attribution error helps explain why Alex Trebeck, the long-time host of *Jeopardy*, seems so smart. He always gives the right answers after contestants are wrong. But we tend to forget his distinct advantage—he has the answers in front of him.

actor-observer effect the tendency to see other people's behavior as caused by dispositional factors, but see our own behavior as caused by the situation

tend to see their crimes as caused by the situation, whereas guards tend to see these crimes as caused by dispositional factors. However, the Business Connections box describes an interesting exception to this general tendency to make self-serving attributions.

Access to internal thoughts and feelings.

Why does the actor-observer effect occur? One explanation is that observers can see other people's behavior, but do not have access to their internal thoughts or feelings. On the other hand, when we consider our own behavior as an actor, we obviously have access to our internal thoughts and feelings, but have little or no access to others' thoughts and feelings (Malle & Pearce, 2001). When you are in the midst of an important game, for example, you are likely to be highly aware of how your own nervousness is impacting your play. But you fail to consider how others' nervousness is impacting their own play. In line with this view, we are less likely to make the actor-observer error with our close friends than with strangers, presumably because we have greater access to our friends' internal thoughts and feelings.

Desire to maintain a positive self-image.

Motivational factors can also contribute to the actor-observer effect. As described in Chapter 3, we are highly motivated to see ourselves in positive ways. This tendency explains why women explain the success of attractive women (who presumably threaten their own self-concept) as due more to luck and less to ability compared to how they explain the

? **Questioning the Research**
Do the actor-observer differences seen in the risky driving study and prisoners' study reveal true differences or, alternatively, self-report or the desire to simply appear good to the experimenter? What do you think and why? How could you test whether this effect reflects true differences or simply differences in self-report?

Business
::: CONNECTIONS

Why Disserving Attributions Can Be a Good Idea

Attribution theory usually describes the benefits of making internal attributions for good events (e.g., "I'm smart, which is why I did well on my French test") and external attributions for bad events (e.g., "The teacher is unfair, which is why I did poorly on my math test"). But some recent research on the types of attributions made by business actually shows that making disserving attributions—making internal attributions for bad events—can sometimes be a good approach (Lee, Peterson, & Tiedens, 2004). In one study, researchers examined the types of attributions contained in the corporate annual reports from 14 companies during a 21-year period. Researchers counted the number of statements that focused on the company's own role in producing a negative outcome (e.g., "The unexpected drop in earnings this year is primarily attributable to some of the strategic decisions we made last year."). Researchers also counted the number of statements that focused on external factors (e.g., "The drop in earnings this year is primarily attributable to the unexpected downturn in the domestic and international environment."). Then they examined the change in average

stock price for each company one year later. Contrary to what attribution theory would generally suggest, companies that gave internal attributions for negative events reported greater increases in stock prices than those that gave external attributions. The authors suggest that because people expect organizations to be in control of their outcomes, making external attributions can lead to even worse expectations.

SUPERSTOCK

success of less attractive women (Försterling, Preikschas, & Agthe, 2007). We also use different explanations to describe our own behavior compared to others' behavior. For example, research with married couples demonstrates that each spouse tends to see the other as responsible for initiating the conflict (Schütz, 1999). And each spouse views his or her own behavior as caused by the situation.

This desire to maintain a positive self-image also leads us to interpret behavior caused by others in our group in a beneficial way, whereas we are less generous in interpreting the causes of other people's behavior. In one study, researchers asked both White and African Americans to explain the factors that led O.J. Simpson to murder his ex-wife, Nicole Simpson (only participants who believed that O.J. Simpson was guilty were included in this study; Graham, Weiner, & Zucker, 1997). As shown in Figure 4.3, Whites were much more likely to see the murder as caused by jealousy, a dispositional factor, whereas African Americans were more likely to see the murder as caused by his ex-wife's behavior.

Motivational factors can also lead us to blame others for their own misfortunes, again as a way of protecting ourselves from potentially experiencing such an outcome. In fact, we tend to assume that good things happen to good people and bad things happen to bad people. This phenomenon is known as **belief in a just world** (Lerner, 1980; Lipkus et al., 1996). This belief is another strategy that helps maintain our idealistic self-views because it lets us see ourselves as safe from harm—since surely we all see ourselves as good people.

"You can't blame everything on being home-schooled by bank robbers."

© New Yorker. P.C. Vey. from cartoonbank. Com. All Rights Reserved

belief in a just world the phenomenon in which people believe that bad things happen to bad people and that good things happen to good people

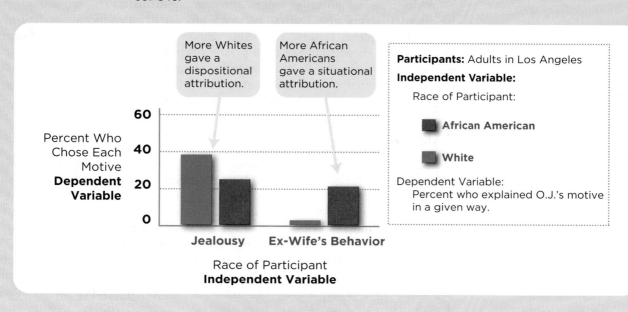

FIGURE 4.3

DOES THE ACTOR-OBSERVER BIAS EXTEND TO RACE?

People who believed that the former football star O.J. Simpson had murdered his wife were asked to explain the cause of the murder as reflecting either jealousy or his ex-wife's behavior. As predicted, race influenced the attributions people made: African American participants were more likely than Whites to blame O.J.'s behavior on the situation (and thus less likely to make the fundamental attribution error).

Source: Graham, S., Weiner, B., & Zucker, G. (1997). An attributional analysis of punishment goals and public reactions to O.J. Simpson. *Personality and Social Psychology Bulletin*, 23, 331–346.

More Whites gave a dispositional attribution.

More African Americans gave a situational attribution.

Participants: Adults in Los Angeles

Independent Variable:
Race of Participant:

■ African American

■ White

Dependent Variable:
Percent who explained O.J.'s motive in a given way.

Percent Who Chose Each Motive **Dependent Variable**

60
40
20
0

Jealousy   Ex-Wife's Behavior

Race of Participant
Independent Variable

People who have a strong belief in a just world are more likely to hold negative attitudes toward poor people, and therefore see them as deserving their plight (Furnham & Gunter, 1984). One study examined the attributions given to explain poverty among people in a "developed country" (Australia) versus a "developing country" (Malawi, a small country in sub-Saharan Africa; Campbell, Carr, & MacLachlan, 2001). As predicted, Australians were much more likely than Malawians to attribute poverty to dispositional characteristics of the poor—such as lack of intelligence, laziness, and lack of ability—rather than situational factors.

COMMON ATTRIBUTION ERRORS

Concepts in Context

ERROR	EXAMPLE
Fundamental attribution error	The car behind you honks as soon as the light turns green and then speeds up and passes you. You naturally assume this person is rude, inconsiderate, and impatient.
Actor-observer Effect	You have just received a "C" on a chemistry test and are furious because the professor was completely unclear about what material would be covered on the exam. But when you discuss this unfair testing practice with your advisor, you are shocked with her advice that you should have studied the information presented in lecture as well as in the textbook.

WHY DO WE MAKE ERRORS WHEN WE THINK ABOUT OTHER PEOPLE?

 Imagine that you are asked to read a brief story about a student ("Sara") who helped a professor move some heavy books and journals (Reeder, Vonk, Ronk, Ham, & Lawrence, 2004). Some participants were told that Sara helped voluntarily (e.g., she simply noticed the professor needed help). Other participants were told that Sara helped as part of her job in the psychology department. A third group of participants were told that Sara helped because she had an ulterior motive, namely, she needed a letter of recommendation from this professor. Participants rated Sara as much more selfish, and much less helpful, in the ulterior motive condition than in the other two conditions. When an ulterior motive is provided, participants then judge her seemingly altruistic behavior as motivated by external factors (the desire to receive a positive letter of recommendation) as opposed to internal factors. This study demonstrates one factor that influences how people make attributions for a person's behavior: the presence of an ulterior motive. This section will describe several explanations for why people can and do err when they attribute the causes of other's behavior, including salience, lack of cognitive capacity, belief about others' abilities, and self-knowledge.

SALIENCE

Different factors are *salient*, or obvious, for actors as opposed to observers (Storms, 1973; Taylor & Fiske, 1975). Specifically, if I *do* something, I am very aware of the situational factors that led to my behavior (for example, that I was able to choose the questions). If I am the *observer* of someone else's behavior, the person stands out as most salient. In turn, when salience of situational factors is high, we are less likely to make a dispositional attribution.

In one of the earliest studies to demonstrate the power of salience on attributions, Michael Storms (1973) conducted a study on the role of salience in which two students were asked to hold a conversation that was videotaped. Some students then watched the conversation from their own perspective (i.e., looking at the

FIGURE
4.4

THE IMPACT OF SALIENCE ON ATTRIBUTIONS

1. Participant's conversation with another student was videotaped.

2. Participant watched one of two versions of the video, either from the perspective of the other student (making her salient) or from her own perspective.

3. Participant was asked to make an attribution about the causes of his or her behavior in the conversation.

The conversation shows my true beliefs.

This conversation was influenced by both my beliefs and her questions.

When the participant was made salient, a dispositional attribution was more likely.

When the participant was not salient, dispositional and situational attributions were both likely.

other person). Others watched the conversation from their partner's perspective (i.e., looking at themselves; see Figure 4.4). Participants were then asked how much they attributed their own and the other person's behavior to dispositional versus situational effects. Participants who had watched from the same perspective (looking at their partner) saw their behavior as influenced by both dispositional and situational factors. Those who had watched the tape looking at themselves saw their behavior

The Impact of Salience on Perceived Guilt

The tendency to attribute another person's behavior to dispositional factors when that person is highly salient can have a substantial impact on real-life situations. Researchers in one study showed participants a videotaped police interrogation that focused in some cases on the "suspect," in other cases on the "detective," and in still other cases on both the suspect and the detective (Lassiter, Geers, Munhall, Ploutz-Snyder, & Breitenbecher, 2002; Lassiter & Irvine, 1986). As predicted, participants who watched the tape that focused only on the "suspect" were much less likely to see that person's confession as coerced than those who watched a videotape that focused on the "detective" or on both the suspect and the detective. Those who watched the videotape that focused on the suspect were also more likely to see the behavior as caused by dispositional factors. Other research supports this view, namely, that people attribute confessions to the person, not the situation, even when the power of the

situation is clear (Kassin & Sukel, 1997). Moreover, simply changing the perspective of the videotape influences jurors' verdicts, showing that an observer's perspective has substantial real-life implications (Lassiter, Geers, Handley, Weiland, & Munhall, 2002).

Spencer Grant/PhotoEdit

as caused by dispositional factors. These results show that the salience of the person influences our attributions, and that usually others are more salient to us than we ourselves. Law Connections describes a real-world example of the impact of salience on attributions in the criminal justice system.

The role of salience in influencing the types of attributions made can explain the findings from the Ross et al. (1977) study on quiz-game contestants. Although participants in this study tended to see the contestants as less bright than the questioners, contestants who missed difficult questions were seen as higher in knowledge than those who missed easy questions (Gawronski, 2003a). This effect suggests that question difficulty may be very salient for observers, and that at least in this case, they take this situational factor into account. On the other hand, question difficulty had little impact on the ratings of the questioners' general knowledge. So, when salience of the challenge of the situation (e.g., the difficulty of the questions posed by the questioners) is high, people take this external factor into account in attributing the cause of contestants' wrong answers.

LACK OF COGNITIVE CAPACITY

People may initially focus on the internal factors underlying a person's behavior, and only later adjust the weight of these factors by taking the situation into account (Gilbert & Malone, 1995; Krull, 1993). But people often give the situation insufficient weight and hence overestimate the impact of disposition. According to the **two-stage model of attribution**, you first automatically interpret another person's behavior as caused by his or her disposition, and only later do you adjust this interpretation by taking into account situational factors that may have contributed to the behavior. In line with this model's predictions, people who are busy or distracted when they must make an attribution are particularly likely to rely on dispositional factors and fail to take into account situational factors that may have contributed to the behavior (see Figure 4.5; Gilbert & Hixon, 1991; Gilbert & Osborne, 1989; Gilbert, Pelham, & Krull, 1988).

two-stage model of attribution
a model in which people first automatically interpret a person's behavior as caused by dispositional factors, and then later adjust this interpretation by taking into account situational factors that may have contributed to the behavior

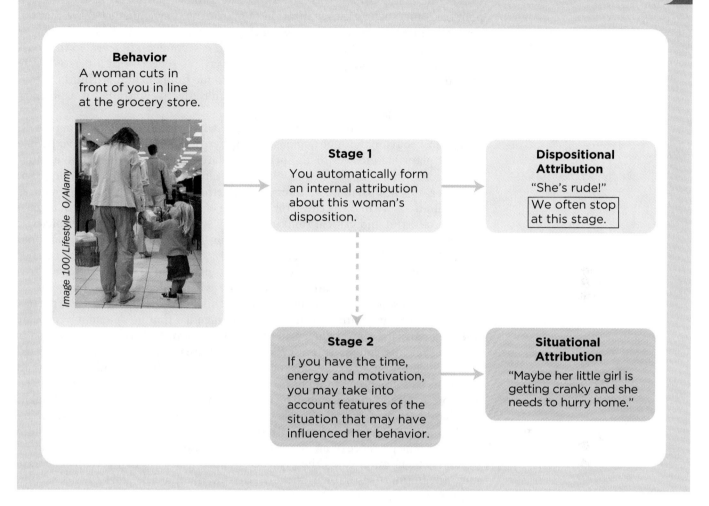

FIGURE 4.5 THE TWO-STAGE MODEL OF ATTRIBUTION

Source: Gilbert, D., Pelham, B., & Krull, D. (1988). On cognitive busyness: When person perceivers meet persons perceived. *Journal of Personality and Social Psychology*, 54, 733–740.

Behavior
A woman cuts in front of you in line at the grocery store.

Image 100/Lifestyle O/Alamy

Stage 1
You automatically form an internal attribution about this woman's disposition.

Dispositional Attribution
"She's rude!"
We often stop at this stage.

Stage 2
If you have the time, energy and motivation, you may take into account features of the situation that may have influenced her behavior.

Situational Attribution
"Maybe her little girl is getting cranky and she needs to hurry home."

In one study of the two-stage model of attributions, Stephanie Tobin and Gifford Weary (2003) examined the impact of distraction on people's judgments of a child's intelligence. First, participants watched a video of a child who either successfully completed a series of tasks on an IQ test (in the positive comparison condition) or failed these tasks (in the negative comparison condition). Next, all participants watched a second tape of another child's performance (the main video). Some of the participants were also given an extra task to distract them while they watched the main tape. They were told to remember an 8-digit code number that appeared on the bottom of the screen just before the main video started. As predicted, participants who were not distracted showed no difference in their rating of the child's ability regardless of which of the two comparison videos they had seen. This is because these participants had the ability to focus on the specific performance observed in the main video. In contrast, participants who were distracted while they watched the main video rated the child's ability as greater when they saw the negative comparison video first than when they saw the positive comparison video first. This difference in ratings occurred because participants who were distracted (by having to remember the number throughout the experiment) used the first video as a comparison to evaluate the child's performance in the main video.

BELIEFS ABOUT OTHERS' ABILITIES AND MOTIVATIONS

We tend to believe that people are unable to persuasively engage in counter-attitudinal behavior. Therefore we assume that a person's behavior must reflect his or her true attitudes (Gawronski, 2003b). In one study, participants were asked to imagine that a person was asked to write about a particular side of a given political topic, such as the legalization of marijuana. Participants believe that the essay would be more persuasive when the person agreed with the position he or she was taking than when he or she disagreed. A second study revealed that participants are more likely to see persuasive essays as reflective of a person's true attitude. In turn, one factor that contributes to the fundamental attribution error is our erroneous belief that people simply can't effectively argue for a position they do not support.

Although we have trouble understanding what would motivate a person to engage in behavior that goes against his or her true attitude, if you give people another plausible motive for the person's behavior, they are able to take situational factors into account (Fein, 1996; Fein, Hilton, & Miller, 1993; Hilton, Fein, & Miller, 1993). Providing an ulterior motive for a person's behavior influences the attributions we make because the presence of such a motive leads us to engage in more effortful and critical thinking. In one study, participants were told that a student, Rob, had written a speech arguing in favor of or against National Collegiate Athletic Association Proposition 42 stating that athletes who did not meet academic requirements were ineligible to play (Fein et al., 1993). Some students were told that Rob had no choice about which side to defend. Others were told that Rob was given a choice about which side to defend but that a professor he was working with had strongly recommended that he defend a particular side (i.e., participants were given an ulterior motive for Rob's choice). The results showed that inferring an ulterior motive did decrease participants' bias toward making dispositional attributions for the behavior. Specifically, students who read that Rob had no choice thought he was more in favor of the proposition when he wrote a pro speech than when he wrote an anti speech. But when they thought Rob had an ulterior motive for his choice, the difference disappeared, meaning they no longer believed they could tell exactly which side he favored. Although in this case the presence of an ulterior motive decreased participants' dispositional attributions, in other cases the presence of such a motive can actually increase such attributions—as shown in the study described at the start of this section about participants' evaluation of "Sara's" motives for helping a professor move some books.

Interestingly, we are more likely to make a dispositional attribution when we learn that a person received a positive incentive for engaging in a dishonest behavior than that a person received a negative incentive (Greitemeyer & Weiner, 2003). In one study, participants were told that a teaching assistant agreed to add false positive teaching ratings to a faculty member's course evaluation. In some cases the faculty member offered a reward for doing so (e.g., "I will write you a strong letter of recommendation"). In other cases the faculty member gave a threatened punishment for refusing to do so (e.g., "I will write you a weak letter of recommendation"). Participants saw the teaching assistant as more responsible for the transgression when a positive reward was given than when a punishment was threatened. These findings suggest that people see a positive incentive as motivating only certain people (e.g., those who already have certain dispositions). Yet a negative incentive is seen as a strong situational pressure that would influence most people's behavior.

Questioning the Research

All of the studies discussed in this section have used college student samples. Would you expect these findings to be the same in other populations? Why or why not?

SELF-KNOWLEDGE

We see ourselves behaving in different ways in different situations and with different people, but we typically see other people in relatively few situations. Because we have more information about our own behavior than we do about others' behavior, we assume that our behavior is more variable than do those who observe us (Krueger et al., 1996; Malle & Knobe, 1997). I may describe my own behavior as highly influenced by situational factors (e.g., I'm shy when trying to make small talk at crowded parties with my colleagues; I'm outgoing when giving a large lecture to students; I'm nervous when giving a professional address to other professors), but my students, who see me generally only in the classroom setting, are likely to see my outgoing nature as a reflection of my disposition.

Because we have access to our own internal attitudes and beliefs, we give ourselves credit for having good intentions, even when we don't carry them out (Kruger & Gilovich, 2004). In one study, participants rated how much weight should be placed on a person's intentions, as opposed to behavior, to get an accurate sense of whether a person actually possesses that trait. For example, if the trait was "thoughtful," participants would rate how important intentions alone were in determining whether someone was thoughtful. Participants rated each trait once for themselves, and once with another person in mind. As predicted, participants saw their own intentions to perform a given behavior as a stronger predictor of whether they actually had this trait compared to other people's intentions. The Education Connections box describes another example of the power of the attributions we make on our behavior.

Education
CONNECTIONS

Why Focusing on Effort Over Ability Is a Good Idea

Carol Dweck's research on implicit theories of intelligence reveals that the types of attributions people make for their success and failure influence academic motivation and performance (2006). Some people hold a "fixed" theory of intelligence, and believe their success is based on innate ability. Others, who hold a "growth" or "incremental" view of intelligence, believe their success is based on hard work and learning. People with these different mindsets show very different responses to both academic success and failure. In one study, fifth graders completed a set of problems, and were told they did very well (Mueller & Dweck, 1998). Then, children received different types of feedback attributions from the experimenter: some children were told, "You must be smart at these problems" (intelligence feedback), and others were told, "You must have worked hard at these problems" (effort feedback). On a later task, children who received praise for their intelligence showed less persistence, less enjoyment, and worse performance than children praised for effort. These findings suggest that there are significant downsides to having a "fixed" theory of intelligence, including how we react to failure: fixed-mindset individu-als tend to dread failure because they see it as a negative reflection on their basic abilities, while growth-mindset individuals don't mind failure as much because they realize their future performance can be improved. In turn, individuals with a growth theory may be more likely to continue working hard even in the face of some initial setbacks.

Christina Kennedy/PhotoEdit

FINAL THOUGHTS ON ATTRIBUTION ERRORS

Although this section has focused on common errors we make in understanding people's behavior, let me leave you with some good news … and some advice. First, the good news: we can overcome our tendency to make dispositional attributions when we are strongly motivated (either due to our personality or due to the situation we are in) to avoid making quick and easy judgments (Webster, 1993). In fact, people do understand that the situation impacts behavior, and most people even believe that others make more extreme dispositional attributions—meaning less situational correction—than they themselves do (Van Boven, White, Kamada, & Gilovich, 2003). This is similar to the self-enhancing biases described in Chapter 3; people want to see themselves as better than others.

Now, the advice: we tend to make dispositional attributions because such attributions are quick and easy: the person's behavior is immediately apparent although the situational factors that influenced the behavior may be much more subtle. So it is easier to make dispositional attributions, but they are not necessarily more accurate. We should therefore try to consider the role of the situation before jumping to dispositional conclusions. Is the dentist rushed and running late during your appointment? Instead of thinking she is rude and inconsiderate, perhaps you should think about situational factors that may have led to her behavior (e.g., concern about her son who is sick at home, another patient's appointment that ran late, an upcoming interview to hire a new dental hygienist).

Concepts in Context

CAUSES OF ATTRIBUTION ERRORS

ERROR	EXAMPLE
Salience	Although you feel pretty nervous during your practice job interview, you understand that this feeling is a normal reaction to the video camera taping the interview. But later on, when you watch the tape yourself, you are amazed at your very anxious appearance.
Lack of cognitive capacity	You are in the park reading the newspaper. You assume that the small child sitting alone at the playground must be shy. But after you finish your reading, you notice that some older children are building a fort in the sandbox and have forbidden the small children from participating in this game.
Beliefs about other's abilities and motivations	Jeff, a close friend of Hilary's, assumed that Hilary's newfound support of the death penalty reflected a change from her anti-death penalty views. But after he observed Hilary having a romantic late night dinner with Bill, the head of a local pro-death penalty group, he suddenly questioned whether her attitudes had truly changed.
Self-knowledge	Luke is very nervous during the spelling bee, and he is certain that his mistake was caused by the overwhelming pressure of the large audience.

HOW DO WE FORM IMPRESSIONS OF PEOPLE BASED ON NONVERBAL BEHAVIOR?

Q A Imagine that you are a high school student—and that once again, you've missed your curfew and must explain to your parents why you are 30 minutes late. How effectively could you lie to them about why you were late? Researchers who study

FIGURE
4.6

ARE THERE NONVERBAL CUES TO DECEPTION?

Participants watched a videotape and then answered questions (either lying or telling the truth) about what they had seen. Researchers then examined differences in the participants' nonverbal behavior, including the latency period (how long it took for the participants to start talking), speech hesitations (how frequently the participants said "ah" or "uhm"), and gesturing (how frequently the participants used hand or arm gestures to illustrate what they were saying). As predicted, participants who were lying took longer to start talking, hesitated more in their speech, and used fewer gestures compared to those who were telling the truth.

Source: Vrij, A., Edward, K., & Bull, R. (2001). Stereotypical verbal and nonverbal responses while deceiving others. *Personality and Social Psychology Bulletin*, 27, 899–909.

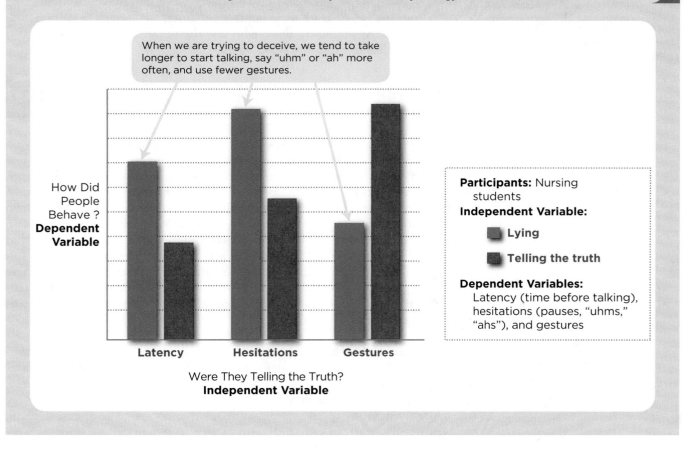

When we are trying to deceive, we tend to take longer to start talking, say "uhm" or "ah" more often, and use fewer gestures.

How Did People Behave ?
Dependent Variable

Latency   Hesitations   Gestures

Were They Telling the Truth?
Independent Variable

Participants: Nursing students
Independent Variable:
    Lying
    Telling the truth

Dependent Variables:
Latency (time before talking), hesitations (pauses, "uhms," "ahs"), and gestures

social perception have examined how people detect deception. In one study, students watched a video showing a theft and then answered three questions about the video (Vrij, Edward, & Bull, 2001). Some were told to tell the truth about the video while others were told to lie about it (and all answers were videotaped). Researchers then coded a number of dimensions from the video, including nonverbal and verbal behaviors: smiling, gaze aversion, gestures, speech hesitations, response latency, speech rate, and speech errors. As shown in Figure 4.6, people who lied were very different in several ways from those who told the truth. The differences included rate of speech, frequency of gesturing (e.g., use of arm or hand movements to modify or supplement what they said), and use of details (e.g., sights, sounds, smells, exactly where and when the event happened, and how they felt). Clearly, both verbal and nonverbal behavior communicate important information to others. This section will examine two distinct issues in nonverbal behavior: the effects of communicating in nonverbal ways, and how nonverbal behavior can aid in detecting deceptive communications.

"Say what's on your mind, Harris—the language of dance has always eluded me."

COMMUNICATING IN NONVERBAL WAYS

We typically think of communication as involving verbal expressions. However, in many cases people communicate in nonverbal ways—through body language, eye gaze, facial expressions, gestures, and even handshakes (Ambady & Rosenthal, 1993; Chaplin, Phillips, Brown, Clanton, & Stein, 2000; Gifford, 1991). In one study, participants watched a videotape of an attractive women giving a speech about the value of sororities and fraternities (Marsh, Hart-O'Rourke, & Julka, 1997). In one condition she used negative nonverbal behavior, including fidgeting and darting eye movements, and stroking her hair. In another condition she used more natural nonverbal behavior. As predicted, those who saw the negative nonverbal tape rated the speaker as less likeable and self-assured.

RESEARCH FOCUS ON NEUROSCIENCE

The Special Processing of Eye Contact

The power of eye contact as a social cue is very strong. In fact, research suggests that particular parts of the brain respond to receiving eye contact. In one study, participants watched a video of a person walking toward them (Pelphrey, Viola, & McCarthy, 2004). In some cases this person averted his eyes as he approached, whereas in other conditions the person shifted his gaze toward them so that eye contact occurred. Researchers then examined the parts of the brain that were activated during each of these two conditions. Findings indicated that the mutual gaze condition led to greater activity in the superior temporal sulcus (STS) region of the brain compared to the averted gaze condition. These results suggest that different parts of the brain are involved in processing general information about faces versus processing specific information about faces that facilitates communication.

The power of facial expressions. One of the most common and effective ways in which people communicate nonverbally is through facial expressions (Gosselin, Kirouac, & Doré, 1995; Izard, 1994; Wehrle, Kaiser, Schmidt, & Scherer, 2000). People in different cultures tend to use the same facial expressions to convey the major emotions—happiness, fear, sadness, anger, surprise, and disgust (Ekman, 1994; Russell, 1995). In one study, American and Indian college students were asked to recognize ten emotions (anger, disgust, fear, heroism, humor-amusement,

Happiness is clearly signaled by facial expression across diverse cultures.

love, peace, sadness, shame-embarrassment, and wonder) portrayed in videotapes (Hejmadi, Davidson, & Rozin, 2000). Participants from both countries showed a high level of recognition accuracy, indicating that emotions are interpreted in similar ways across cultures. This similarity provides strong evidence that the ability to use this type of nonverbal communication is universal. The finding that emotions are understood in the same way across cultures suggests an evolutionary basis for this consistency, and if so, "important emotions" should be understood more rapidly than less important ones (e.g., anger should be recognized more quickly than happiness)—which is exactly what the research shows.

Causes of errors in communication. Although nonverbal communication often provides important information about people's emotions, several factors can lead to lower accuracy. First, people may try to hide their emotions in order to avoid the consequences of letting others know how they are feeling (Gross, 1998; Gross & Levenson, 1993; Richards & Gross, 1999). For example, you may feel very angry with your boss but deliberately try to hide this emotion in order to avoid getting fired. Second, when facial expressions conflict with information about the situation, we interpret the emotion in line with the situation and not the expression (Carroll & Russell, 1996). For example, when a person's facial expression shows anger but he or she is in a frightening situation, we interpret the emotion as fear. Finally, people are more accurate when identifying emotions expressed by people within their same culture or by those with greater exposure to that culture (Elfenbein & Ambady, 2003).

DETECTING DECEPTION

As shown in Figure 4.7, people often conceal or even lie about their true thoughts—and they do so an average of one to two times per day (DePaulo & Kashy, 1998; DePaulo, Kashy, Kirkendol, Wyer, & Epstein, 1996). They may try to hide how much they dislike someone (e.g., the boss), or they may directly

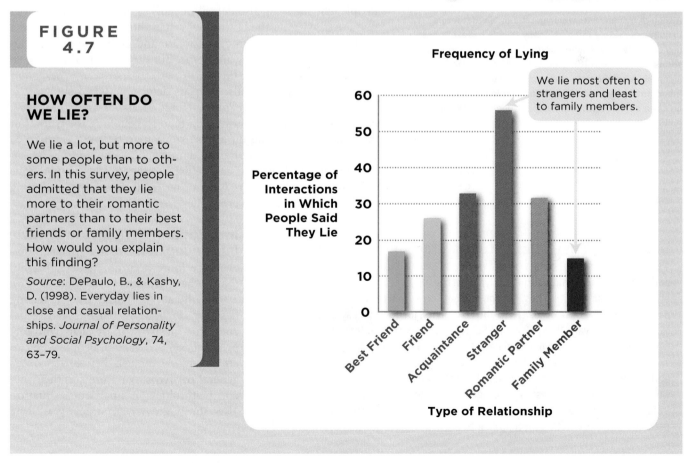

FIGURE 4.7

HOW OFTEN DO WE LIE?

We lie a lot, but more to some people than to others. In this survey, people admitted that they lie more to their romantic partners than to their best friends or family members. How would you explain this finding?

Source: DePaulo, B., & Kashy, D. (1998). Everyday lies in close and casual relationships. *Journal of Personality and Social Psychology, 74*, 63–79.

misrepresent what they feel (e.g., when you tell the boss that you really don't mind staying late or working on Saturdays). Yet we are often unable to detect exactly when someone is lying: we are accurate in distinguishing lies and truth only about 54% of the time (Bond & DePaulo, 2006).

One reason why we have trouble detecting lying is that we make the fundamental attribution error, and assume that people's statements reflect their honest and trustworthy dispositions (O'Sullivan, 2003). In one study, male participants were videotaped engaging in two types of deception: one involved committing a mock crime (e.g., stealing some money) and the other involved giving a false opinion (e.g., stating a belief about the death penalty that he did not endorse; Frank & Ekman, 2004). When these videotapes were later shown to two groups of observers (each group saw one of the two types of deception), the proportion of people who rated the participants as truthful in one situation was correlated highly with the proportion of people who rated the same participants as truthful in the other situation. This finding suggests that some people are simply better able to appear truthful than others, perhaps because some people are better able to control their facial actions.

Alamy

Although evidence from polygraphs or "lie detectors" isn't usually admissible in court, many people believe these devices provide valuable information about whether a person is telling the truth. Unfortunately, polygraphs are considerably less accurate than many people believe. Inaccurate polygraph information can lead guilty people to be seen as innocent, and innocent people to be seen as guilty.

Cues for detecting deception. Verbal cues can be useful for detecting deception (Ekman & Friesen, 1974). One study revealed that people who are lying make fewer references to the self (e.g., I, me, my), use more negative emotion words (e.g., hate, worthless, enemy), and use fewer "exclusive" words (e.g., but, except, without; Newman, Pennebaker, Berry, & Richards, 2003). This patterning suggests that people who are lying:

- try to distance themselves from the lie (and hence make fewer self-references),
- experience greater tension and guilt (and hence use more negative emotion words),
- focus their attention on creating a story (and hence use more simplistic, and less exclusive, language).

People who are lying also describe events in more general and brief ways (e.g., "I took the bus home") than those who are telling the truth, who tend to use more intricate and elaborate approaches (e.g., "I had planned to walk home, but then it started to rain, so I decided to wait for the bus").

Nonverbal cues can also help us determine when someone is trying to deceive us (DePaulo, 1992; Frank & Ekman, 1997). People who are genuinely smiling tend to be telling the truth, but those who are putting on a false smile may be lying (Ekman & Davidson, 1993). Physiological data, such as pulse and perspiration, is another type of nonverbal cue that can be used to detect whether someone is telling the truth. In sum, people who are lying differ from those who are telling the truth in both the verbal and the nonverbal cues they provide.

WOULD YOU BELIEVE... College Students Are as Accurate (or Inaccurate) as Police Officers at Detecting Lies Who is best at detecting lies? Perhaps surprisingly, expertise has little impact on people's effectiveness at detecting lies. College students do as well (or rather, as poorly) at detecting lies as police officers, FBI and CIA agents, judges, and psychiatrists (Ekman & O'Sullivan, 1991; Ekman, O'Sullivan, & Frank, 1999). Interestingly, Secret Service agents are better at detecting lies than other people, perhaps due to their highly specialized and intensive job training, considerable experience, and interest in detecting deception. In line with this view, clinical psychologists who are particularly interested in deception (namely, those who chose to attend a 2-day workshop on detecting deception) show greater accuracy than clinical psychologists without this specialized interest in deception (Ekman et al., 1999).

Individual differences in detecting deception. Some people, however, are more accurate at detecting lies than others (Frank & Ekman, 1997). Those who are most accurate at detecting lies rely on both verbal and nonverbal cues, in contrast to most of us who rely primarily on verbal cues. People who can effectively distinguish between people's general trustworthy nature and their specific truthfulness in a particular situation also show greater accuracy (see Rate Yourself).

How Accurate Are You at Detecting Deception?

INSTRUCTIONS: *Answer the following statements using a rating system of 1 (very uncharacteristic of me) to 9 (very characteristic of me).*

☐ **1.** When people lie to me, I often catch them because their voice and eyes give them away.

☐ **2.** I can usually see right through people's "acts."

☐ **3.** I tend to pay attention to the appearance or behavior of other people, from my own point of view.

☐ **4.** I can figure out a lot about people just by watching them interact in social situations.

☐ **5.** I like to observe and critique how others are acting in varying situations.

☐ **6.** I can tell by the way a person carries him/herself whether he/she is being genuine.

☐ **7.** I am alert to how other people manage their appearance.

☐ **8.** I can usually tell from others' body language when they are trying to hide something from me.

SCORING: Add up your total number of points on these eight items.

INTERPRETATION: This scale measures your belief in your own ability to judge other's behavior and determine deception. Higher scores indicate a greater belief in one's ability to detect other people's true intentions from their nonverbal communication (Sheldon, 1996).

Finally, yet another factor that helps in detecting lying is knowing a person's culture, presumably because some nonverbal cues for lying are culture specific. In one study, researchers videotaped college students in the United States and Jordan telling the truth (in some cases) or lies (in other cases) about their friends (Bond, Omar, Mahmoud, & Bonser, 1990). When these videotapes were shown to students in both cultures, people were better at detecting lies told by a person from their culture than lies told by someone from a different culture.

Concepts in Context

HOW NONVERBAL BEHAVIOR INFLUENCES IMPRESSIONS

FACTOR	EXAMPLE
Communicating in nonverbal ways	Jerry felt pretty confident about his speech delivery during his practice at home. However, his father suggested that he try to avoid fidgeting with his hands and shuffling his feet, which make him seem less trustworthy.
Detecting deception	Sara really wanted to believe her boyfriend's explanation about why her birthday present was late (once again). But his vague and general description of the supposed problem and the way he expressed it somehow made her doubt his story.

CULTURE

HOW DOES CULTURE INFLUENCE SOCIAL PERCEPTION?

Culture not only influences how people see themselves, but also how they see and make sense of the social world. Although the tendency to attribute behavior to dispositional factors is commonly seen in Western cultures, cross-cultural research reveals quite different findings. For example, in one cross-cultural study, both American and Chinese students read brief accounts of two murders that received

People from different cultures often make different types of attributions for the same behavior.

international attention (Morris & Peng, 1994). In one case, a Chinese physics student who had failed to get an academic job shot his adviser and several other people at the University of Iowa, and then killed himself. In another case, a recently fired postal worker shot his supervisor and several other people at a post office in Michigan, and then killed himself. As predicted, Americans generally blamed dispositional causes (the person was mentally imbalanced, had no grip on reality, had personality problems). The Chinese people generally blamed situational causes (e.g., America's selfish values, media's glorifying violence, an economic recession, unhelpful supervisors). In this section we will examine the impact of culture on the types of attributions people make, the factors that influence these attributions, and the expression of emotion.

TYPES OF ATTRIBUTIONS

Although the fundamental attribution error is one of the most commonly described biases within the field of social psychology, and until recently was thought to describe a universal human tendency, this error is much harder to find in collectivistic cultures than in individualistic ones (Choi & Nisbett, 1998; Choi et al., 1999; Krull, Loy, Lin, Wang, Chen, & Zhao, 1999). In one study, American and Asian Indian subjects were asked to describe the causes of positive and negative events that they had observed in their lives (Miller, 1984). Americans were much more likely to rely on dispositional factors than the Indians, who were much more likely than Americans to refer to situational factors. For example, in explaining a situation in which a motorcycle accident occurs and the motorcycle driver (an attorney) then takes his injured passenger to the hospital but then leaves to attend to his own work, an American said, "The driver is obviously irresponsible; the driver was in a state of shock; the driver is aggressive in pursuing career success" (p. 972, Miller, 1984). The Hindu, on the other hand, said, "It was the driver's duty to be in court for the client whom he's representing; secondly, the driver might have gotten nervous or confused; and thirdly, the passenger might not have looked as serious as he was" (p. 972, Miller, 1984). Although both Americans and Indians describe the driver's emotional state as partially at fault, the Indians are much more likely to also refer to situational factors, whereas Americans simply refer to additional individual factors. Similarly, and as described at the start of this section, Americans are much more likely to see a person as responsible for committing murder, whereas Japanese people are much more likely to take situational factors into account. In sum, although people in both cultures believe dispositions do impact behavior, those in collectivistic cultures see situations as a more powerful impact on behavior than do those in individualistic cultures (Choi et al., 1999).

These cultural differences in reliance on internal attributions are found not only in laboratory studies but also in naturalistic studies that use archival data. In one study, researchers analyzed newspaper articles describing various business scandals (e.g., unauthorized tradings; Menon, Morris, Chiu, & Hong, 1999). American newspapers made more references to the individual than the organization, whereas Japanese newspapers made more references to the organization. For example, the <u>New York Times</u> articles included quotes such as "Salomon's errant cowboy who attacked his work as aggressively as he hit tennis balls," whereas the Japanese newspaper wrote "somebody should have recognized the fictitious trading since documents are checked every day." The same patterns were found when responding to a hypothetical story about a maladjusted team member. Similarly, sports articles in newspapers in the United States are more likely to make dispositional attributions than such articles in Hong Kong, even when they are writing about the same sport (see Table 4.1; Lee, Hallahan, & Herzog, 1996; Markus, Uchida, Omoregie, Townsend, & Kitayama, 2006).

Questioning the Research

Where do these different attributional styles come from? Do you think they reflect biological differences, and/or what is taught in a given culture? How could you test these different theories?

FACTORS INFLUENCING ATTRIBUTIONS

What leads to the greater prevalence of the fundamental attribution error in individualistic cultures than in collectivistic ones? Research points to a variety of factors.

View of personality as changeable. One explanation is that in collectivistic cultures, personality is seen as more changeable than in individualistic cultures. In line with this view, those from collectivistic cultures are much more likely to disagree with such statements as "Someone's personality is something about them that they can't change very much," and "A person can do things to get people to like them but they can't change their real personality," (Choi et al., 1999). Cultures even have different beliefs about and ways of explaining physical causality, meaning how one event causes another (Peng & Knowles, 2003). For example, when people are asked to explain why an object moved in the way it did, Americans describe factors related specifically to that object—such as its weight, shape, energy—whereas Chinese people describe factors related to the background or context—such as friction, air/wind, or another object.

Stronger focus on the situation. Another explanation for the greater prevalence of the fundamental attribution error in individualistic cultures is that people in collectivistic cultures pay more attention to the impact of the situation on behavior, and therefore see more connection between events (Ji et al., 2000; Nisbett, Peng, Choi, & Norenzayan, 2001; Norenzayan & Nisbett, 2000). A clever study by Masuda and Nisbett (2001) asked students to watch underwater scenes that included fish, plants, rocks, and sand, and then to describe what they were seeing. Japanese participants described the background and relationships between the focal fish and the background much more than did Americans. For example, they were quite likely to note that "The water was green," or "The bottom was rocky." In contrast, Americans were much more likely to describe salient objects than Japanese—and were particularly likely to describe the biggest and/or fastest fish. Moreover, Japanese were more likely to recognize the focal object when presented with the same background than were Americans. But Americans were more

TABLE 4.1	ATTRIBUTIONS MADE FOR SUCCESSFUL PERFORMANCE BY OLYMPIC ATHLETES
ATHLETE	**QUOTE EXPLAINING THE WIN**
Misty Hyman (American)	I think I just stayed focused. It was time to show the world what I could do. I am just glad I was able to do it. I knew I could beat Suzy O'Neil, deep down in my heart I believed it, and I know this whole week the doubts kept creeping in, they were with me on the blocks, but I just said, "No, this is my night."
Naoko Takahasi (Japanese)	Here is the best coach in the world, the best manager in the world, and all of the people who support me—all of these things were getting together and became a gold medal. So I think I didn't get it alone, not only by myself.

These quotes reflect comments made by two athletes who won Olympic gold medals in the 2000 Summer Olympics in Sidney, Australia: Misty Hyman, an American, won the women's 200 meter butterfly event, and Naoko Takahasi, from Japan, won the marathon. Although both women achieved at the highest level in their respective sports, the explanations given for their success differ dramatically.

Source: Markus, H., Uchida, Y., Omoregie, H., Townsend, S., & Kitayama, S. (2006). Going for the gold: Models of agency in Japanese and American contexts. *Psychological Science, 17*, 103-112.

likely to recognize the focal object than Japanese when it was presented with no background or a novel background. This study shows the emphasis placed in these different cultures on the salient object versus the background (see Figure 4.8). In sum, collectivistic cultures engage in patterns of holistic thought and are more attentive to relationships and context, whereas individualistic cultures engage in analytical thought and focus on themselves.

Even in cases in which people from collectivistic cultures do make the fundamental attribution error, they are better able to overcome this bias than are those in individualistic cultures (Choi & Nisbett, 1998; Choi et al., 1999; Krull et al., 1999; Norenzayan & Nisbett, 2000). For example, when Choi and colleagues (1999) asked participants to read essays written by another person and rate that person's true attitude, both Americans and Koreans tended to assume that the essay reflected the person's true beliefs. However, when participants were first asked to rate an essay where the topic had been given to the essay writer by the experimenter, the Koreans were then much less likely to assume that the essay reflected the person's true beliefs, whereas the Americans' dispositional attribution did not change. Similarly, Americans continue to make the fundamental attribution error even when the no choice aspect is made salient (e.g., when they themselves are asked to write an essay on a topic under no choice conditions, when the essay by the target person is almost a direct copy of that written by the experimenter). On the other hand, increased salience leads to decreased fundamental attribution error in Korean participants (Norenzayan et al., 2002). In sum, although in the absence of situational information Koreans are as likely to make dispositional attributions as Americans, Koreans do make stronger situational attributions than Americans and are more responsive to salient situational information than are Americans.

The impact of distraction. Distraction also has a different impact on attributional errors in people from different cultures. As described earlier in this chapter, people tend to make more dispositional errors when they are distracted and therefore can't adjust for the situational pressure on behavior. But is this

FIGURE 4.8

HOW DOES CULTURE AFFECT FOCUS ON THE SITUATION?

What do you notice in this photo? According to research by Masuda and Nisbett (2001), Americans tend to remark on the fish, whereas Japanese people tend to remark on aspects of the background, such as the bubbles, rocks, and water.

Source: Masuda, T., & Nisbett, R. (2001). Attending holistically versus analytically: Comparing the context sensitivity of Japanese and Americans. *Journal of Personality and Social Psychology*, 81, 922–934.

equally true for those in collectivistic cultures? No. In one study, both American and East Asian students listened to a speech that was supposedly written by another student, who had been told by his professor to write about a particular side (Knowles, Morris, Chiu, & Hong, 2001). They were then asked to rate how much the speech reflected the student's true attitude. In some cases they also had to perform a challenging computer task (hitting a particular key every time a certain letter appeared on the screen) while listening to the speech. As shown in Figure 4.9, Americans do exactly what we've talked about before; when they are distracted, they make dispositional attributions even though the student had <u>no</u> <u>choice</u> about which side to write on. On the other hand, students from Hong Kong do not make this error, even when they are distracted.

EXPRESSION OF EMOTION

While the facial expressions associated with different emotions appear to be largely universal across cultures, different cultures do vary in their norms governing the expression of emotion (Aune & Aune, 1996; Eid & Diener, 2001). For example, people in individualistic cultures (e.g., America, Australia) are more comfortable expressing self-reflective emotions, such as pride and guilt, than those in communalistic cultures (e.g., China, Japan). Similarly, people from collectivistic cultures show more socially engaging emotions, such as friendliness and shame, whereas people from individualistic cultures show more socially disengaging emotions, such as anger and superiority (Kitayama et al., 2006).

FIGURE 4.9

HOW DOES DISTRACTION AFFECT ATTRIBUTIONS OF PEOPLE FROM DIFFERENT CULTURES?

Experimenters asked students from two cultures to listen to a speech. Participants were told that the student giving the speech was assigned to a particular topic and position by the professor. The results revealed that culture matters: Although distraction led to stronger dispositional attributions by Americans, it had no impact on the types of attributions made by people from Hong Kong.

Source: Knowles, E., Morris, M., Chiu, C., & Hong, Y. (2001). Culture and the process of person perception: Evidence for automaticity among East Asians in correcting for situational influences on behavior. *Personality and Social Psychology Bulletin, 27*, 1344–1356. Used by permission of Sage Publications.

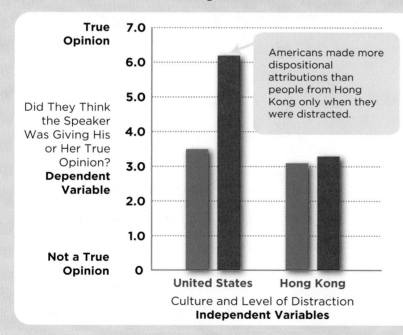

Participants: College students
Independent Variable:
Cultural Backround: United States (individualistic) or Hong Kong (collectivist)

Level of Distraction:

■ **Not Distracted– Just listening to the speech**

■ **Distracted– Doing another task while listening**

Dependent Variable:
Did they think the speaker was giving his or her true opinion?

Choice of words. Culture also influences how people talk about emotion. One study examined the words used during emotional events by people from various cultures. The study included European Americans, Chinese Americans who were highly oriented toward the American culture (e.g., born in the United States, not very proficient in Chinese), and Chinese Americans who were not oriented toward the American culture (e.g., born overseas, quite proficient in Chinese; Tsai, Simeonova, & Watanabe, 2004). All participants were then asked to describe their early relationships with their family, experiences of childhood rejection, and encounters with loss. Researchers then coded the different types of words:

- social words (e.g., friend, mother, give, advice),
- somatic words (e.g., heard, listen, ache, exhaust),
- positive emotion words (e.g., happy, good, fun), and
- negative emotion words (e.g., angry, miserable, hurt).

As predicted, European Americans used fewer somatic words and fewer social words than Chinese Americans who were not very oriented toward American culture (see Table 4.2). Interestingly, Chinese Americans who were oriented toward American culture used a pattern much more similar to European Americans than to Chinese Americans who were not oriented to American culture.

TABLE 4.2	EXAMPLES OF WORD USE BY EUROPEAN AMERICANS VERSUS CHINESE AMERICANS
NATIONALITY	**WORD USE**
Chinese Americans	"My parents would take me to the hospital, almost all the time. Both of them... One morning I woke up, I felt dizzy and light-headed, and they took me to the hospital." (somatic word use) "Cry a lot. I cry a lot! My mom ...would comfort me. When I was 7 years old ... I still cried, but at that time, I had a few friends. I had a few friends at a school, and we would spend a lot of time together, my friends, something like that. Each time when my dad punished me, he would say 'Hey, look at your brother, what, how excellent a job he did in school. Why can't you do that?' My brother, he was a genius." (social word use)
European American	"Um, if I got sick at school, my dad would usually come and get me—I would just kind of stay in bed and watch TV for the rest of the day usually—if it was like after lunch or whatever my dad would usually stay home for the rest of the day with me." (somatic word use) "Break things, yell, scream, threaten to kill myself, like when I was real little like before the age of 4. Yeah, uh, my mom says I don't remember it but when I was 2 1/2 I told her that I was going to cut my wrists with a butter knife if she didn't make me chicken and dumpling soup for lunch. Not one of my prouder moments." (social words)

These differences in how participants described emotional events reveal that Chinese Americans who are less oriented to American culture use more somatic and social words than European Americans.

Source: Tsai, J., Simeonova, D., & Watanabe, J. (2004). Somatic and social: Chinese Americans talk about emotion. *Personality and Social Psychology Bulletin, 30*, 1226-1238

Emphasis on tone. Finally, cross-cultural research reveals differences in focus on verbal content versus verbal tone. In one study, participants listened to either positive or negative words (e.g., grateful, satisfaction, pretty versus sore, dislike, anxiety) that were delivered in either a positive tone or a negative tone (Ishii, Reyes, & Kitayama, 2003). As predicted, Americans tended to focus on verbal content over verbal tone. Japanese participants showed the opposite pattern and emphasized the tone of the delivery of the word over the word's meaning in making their explanation. Once again, this study provides evidence of cultural differences in the importance of different types of communication.

The Big Picture

SOCIAL PERCEPTION

This chapter included many applications of the three "big ideas" studied in social psychology. The examples below should help you see the connection between Social Perception and these big ideas, and contribute to your understanding of the big picture of social psychology.

THEME	EXAMPLES
The social world influences how we think about ourselves.	• Contestants in a quiz bowl-type game give themselves lower ratings of intelligence than questioners. • Prisoners see their own criminal behavior as caused by situational factors. • People who watch a videotape of themselves engaging in a conversation see their behavior as caused by dispositional factors.
The social world influences our thoughts, attitudes, and behaviors.	• We believe persuasive essays are more effective when they are written by someone who agrees with the position they are supporting than someone who doesn't. • We see a teaching assistant as more responsible for adding false information to a teaching evaluation when he or she is given a reward for doing so than punishment for refusing to do so. • People are more accurate at detecting lies told by a person from their culture than lies told by someone from a different culture.
Our attitudes and behavior shape the social world around us.	• People who are distracted when they judge a child's behavior are more likely to make errors in rating that child's behavior. • Each spouse sees the other as responsible for initiating conflict, and sees his or her own behavior as caused by the situation. • We see people who engage in negative nonverbal behavior as less likeable and self-assured than those who use more natural nonverbal behavior.

This chapter has examined five key principles of social perception.

YOU LEARNED How do we think about why other people do what they do? We examined three theories that describe how we attribute people's attitudes and behavior either to the person or to the situation: attribution theory, correspondent inference theory, and the covariation model. Making beneficial attributions for your partner's behavior is an important part of both resolving relationship conflict and increasing marital satisfaction.

YOU LEARNED What types of errors do we make in thinking about other people? There are two distinct types of attributional errors—the fundamental attribution error and the actor-observer effect. These errors explain why prison guards focus on the dispositional causes of criminal behavior whereas prisoners focus on situational causes—and why teenage drivers see others' risky driving as caused by their dispositions, but their own risky driving behavior as caused by the situation.

YOU LEARNED Why do we make errors when we think about other people? There are several causes of attributional errors, including salience, lack of cognitive capacity, belief about other's abilities, and self-knowledge. Providing ulterior motives for good behavior influences how people make attributions for a person's behavior—meaning that good deeds make you seem good, unless people see this behavior as caused by selfish motives.

YOU LEARNED How do we form impressions of people based on nonverbal behavior? Nonverbal behavior includes facial expressions, gesturing, and even handshakes. Nonverbal behavior is very powerful in creating impressions and in detecting deception. Some important cues for detecting lying include a faster rate of speech, more speech hesitations, and less use of details (e.g., sights, sounds, smells, exactly where and when the event happened, and how they felt).

YOU LEARNED How does culture influence social perception? The role of culture in influencing social perception includes types of attributions, factors influencing attributions, and the expression of emotion. The tendency to attribute behavior to dispositional factors is common in individualistic cultures, but not in communal ones. Finally, we saw that Americans generally blamed dispositional causes for murder, though the Chinese people generally blamed situational causes.

KEY TERMS

QUESTIONS FOR REVIEW

1. Describe each of the three components of covariation theory and the three factors of correspondent inference theory, including how each of these factors impacts the attributions we make.
2. Describe the two different types of attribution errors we make in thinking about other people, using specific research examples.
3. Describe the four distinct factors that contribute to attribution errors.
4. Describe two ways in which people communicate in nonverbal ways, and two cues for detecting deception.
5. Describe two distinct ways in which one's culture influences the types of attributions they tend to make for people's behavior, as well as two explanations for these differences.

TAKE ACTION!

1. You've just received bad news—you weren't selected for the varsity soccer team. According to attribution theory, how would you explain this disappointing event?
2. Your uncle just returned from a camping trip in Yellowstone National Park, and is encouraging you to take a similar trip in the very near future … but somehow you just aren't sure if this trip is a good idea. According to covariation theory, what type of information would you need to make an external attribution for your uncle's enjoyment—and therefore lead you to take the trip yourself?
3. You are serving on a jury. Given your knowledge about factors that lead to attributional errors, what specific steps could you take to minimize the impact of these biases on your decision?
4. Your teenage son comes in over an hour past his curfew and claims that he ran out of gas on the way home. What are two verbal and two nonverbal cues that you could use to try to determine whether he is lying?
5. Your new boss is from India. How might you expect her cultural background to influence both the types of attributions she makes and the way in which she expresses emotion?

Try some of these research activities to gain experience in conducting and evaluating research, and to increase your understanding of research methods and techniques in social psychology.

Visit WileyPLUS for more activities and interactive research tools! (www.wileyplus.com)

Participate in Research

Activity 1 Testing the Covariation Model: Kelley's Covariation Model describes the role of consensus, distinctiveness, and consistency in making decisions. Ask three friends who are in the same class whether they would recommend that class to others, and whether they would recommend other classes they have taken. Then rate the information you receive on both consensus and distinctiveness to determine whether you should make a personal attribution or a situational attribution for their recommendation. Does your attribution match what theory predicts?

Activity 2 Understanding Attributional Errors: Think about a time in which you've engaged in a particular behavior and rate the potential cause of behavior. Then think about another person engaging in that same behavior, and rate the potential cause of his or her behavior. Are those causes based on the situation or the disposition of the person, and do the causes differ when rating yourself versus another person?

Activity 3 The Impact of Distraction on Attributions: Being distracted while determining the reasons why people do things impacts our conclusions. To test this idea, go to WileyPLUS to watch two interviews of job candidates. You will simply watch one and you will be distracted while watching the other. Rate the qualifications of each interviewee and compare your responses.

Activity 4 **Judging Emotion from Facial Expressions:** You've learned a lot in this chapter about the role of facial expressions, and other types of nonverbal behavior, in communicating emotion. Go to WileyPLUS to see a series of faces expressing universal emotions. See if you can correctly identify the emotions of happiness, anger, sadness, disgust, surprise, and fear.

Activity 5 **The Role of Context:** Your culture influences how you see and make sense of the world. To examine the impact of culture on the attributions we make, go to WileyPLUS to briefly look at a photograph, and then list all of the items you saw in that picture. Compare how your memory of items in the picture stacks up against those from people of other cultures.

Test a Hypothesis

One of the common findings in research on attribution theory is that people who win tend to take credit for their successes whereas people who lose tend to blame their failures on external factors. To test whether this hypothesis is true, find several recent articles that summarize games in the newspaper or on line. Then rate the types of attributions made by players following a win versus following a loss. Do your findings support or refute the hypothesis?

Design a Study

To design your own study testing the importance of nonverbal communication, decide on a research question you would like to answer. Then decide what type of study you want to conduct (self-report, observational/naturalistic, or experimental), select your independent and dependent variables, and operationally define each by determining the procedures or measures you will use. Form a hypothesis to predict what will happen in your study and collect the data.

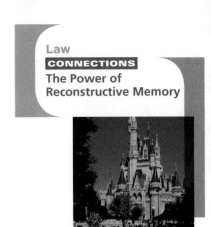
5

Social Cognition

WHAT YOU'LL LEARN

How can shortcuts lead to errors in thinking about the world?

How does presentation influence how we think about the world?

How do we form impressions of people?

 RESEARCH FOCUS ON NEUROSCIENCE
The Unique Processing of Social Information

 RESEARCH FOCUS ON GENDER
The Impact of Gender Stereotypes

How do beliefs create reality?

How does CULTURE influence social cognition?

Did you ever wonder?

Most of us will never actually compete in the Olympics, but we believe we'd be pretty happy with a silver medal—and that we'd rather get a silver medal than a bronze medal. But some research suggests that athletes who win a silver medal often don't have this reaction. In fact, in many cases the athlete who wins the bronze medal is happier than the one who wins the silver medal. In the 2008 Summer Olympics, American Natasha Liukin narrowly beat teammate Shawn Johnson for the gold medal in the All-Around. Shawn Johnson was generally viewed as the favorite, and presumably was disappointed to receive the silver. But Chinese gymnast Yang Yillin was clearly delighted to receive the bronze medal. Her best showing in international competition previously had been a 6th place finish in the All-Around at the 2007 Worlds, and her teammate, Jiang Yuyuan, was widely expected to be the Chinese gymnast who was most likely to receive a medal. In this chapter, you'll also find answers to the following questions:

Business
CONNECTIONS
The Impact of Mood
on Economic Decisions

Health
CONNECTIONS
The Power of Belief

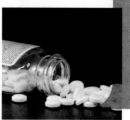

Education
CONNECTIONS
The Overwhelming
Power of Teachers'
Expectations

Q A Why do we remember an article titled "Opposites Attract" better than one titled "Researchers Examine Predictors of Attraction"?

Q A Why are men who "read" Penthouse less happy with their own dating partners?

Q A Why don't close relationships protect you from getting a sexually transmitted disease?

Q A Why can mothers' beliefs about how much their teenagers drink have dangerous consequences?

Getty Images, Inc.

Q A Why do people from individualistic cultures make judgments about an individual's personality much more quickly than those from collectivistic cultures?

These questions can all be answered by findings from research in social psychology on how we think about the social world.

Think about all the decisions you make in a given day—
what to eat, what to wear, who to see, and how to spend your time (and money). Although we naturally want to make good decisions, we are confronted with decisions almost constantly, and hence it is truly impossible to think about and process all of the relevant information in a careful and deliberative way. Instead, people often rely on **automatic thinking,** a type of decision-making process that occurs at an unconscious or automatic level and is entirely effortless and unintentional. This type of thinking relies on the use of shortcuts, or **heuristics,** which can save us time but can also lead to inaccurate judgments. However, in some cases people can and do use a more deliberate and careful type of thinking, namely, **controlled or effortful thinking,** which in turn can lead to more accurate judgments. We tend to use this type of thinking when we have the time and motivation necessary to make the considerable effort this type of thinking involves (Webster, Richter, & Kruglanski, 1996; Wegener & Petty, 1995). For example, when you chose which college or university to attend, you probably didn't make a snap judgment based on a pretty picture in a brochure. Rather, you evaluated the positive and negative features of different schools before ultimately reaching a decision. This chapter is about issues of **social cognition,** or how we think about the social world.

automatic thinking a type of decision-making process that occurs at an unconscious or automatic level and is entirely effortless and unintentional

Q A

heuristics mental shortcuts often used to form judgments and make decisions

controlled or effortful thinking thinking that is effortful, conscious, and intentional

social cognition how we think about the social world, and in particular how we select, interpret, and use information to make judgments about the world

intuition a decision-making shortcut in which we rely on our instinct instead of relying on more objective information

HOW CAN SHORTCUTS LEAD TO ERRORS IN THINKING ABOUT THE WORLD?

Imagine that as part of a psychology study you are asked to read 20 research summaries. Each of these summaries provides a title of the article, and describes a study on the link between similarity and attraction. However, sometimes the findings contradict each other. For example, some studies describe research showing that greater similarity leads to attraction, but others find the reverse. You are then asked to carefully review all of the evidence, and form your own belief about the link between similarity and attraction. How would you determine your answer? Rationally, you weigh the number of articles for and against each view in making your decision. However, participants in this study were heavily influenced by the titles of the studies (Bushman & Wells, 2001). Articles that had very salient titles (such as "Birds of a Feather Flock Together" and "Opposites Attract") were very influential on participants' judgments. Articles with less appealing titles ("Research Examines Similarity as a Source of Liking" and "Research Asks Who Likes Whom") were given less weight in participants' overall decision, even though the information contained in each research summary was the same (only the title changed). This study illustrates a particular type of shortcut, namely, *availability*, meaning the ease with which an idea comes to mind. This section will examine this and other cues that we rely on to quickly reach decisions, which in turn can lead to errors in perceiving the world: intuition, availability, representativeness, base-rate fallacy, anchoring and adjustment, and counterfactual thinking/simulation.

INTUITION

One of the most common shortcuts we use in making decisions about the world is relying on our instinct or **intuition,** instead of relying on more objective information. For example, employers often believe that they can do a better job of judging a person's future performance through interviews than they can through more objective measures, such as test scores, education, or prior experience. But in reality, this type of objective information is a better predictor of future job performance than interview ratings (Dawes, 2001). Yet employers (and medical schools,

SUPERSTOCK

HOW DO WE FORM IMPRESSIONS OF PEOPLE?

Although the last section focused on factors that lead to errors in perceiving the social world, some of our most important judgments are those we make about people. Imagine that you are asked to participate in a psychology study on "person perception," in which all you have to do is read a paragraph about a person and then rate the person's likelihood of having a sexually transmitted disease (STD; Conley & Collins, 2002). In some cases the person is single and has not been in a serious dating relationship for a long time. In other cases the person has been in a monogamous dating relationship for several months. However, in all cases the person described has had the exact same number of sexual partners (five) and has used condoms about half of the time. Although the relevant information (number of sexual partners and frequency of condom use) for STD risk is exactly the same in both conditions, participants overwhelmingly see the person in the relationship as less likely to have an STD than the person who is single. This example illustrates **implicit personality theory,** meaning that knowing that a person has a given trait leads us to assume that he or she also has certain other traits. This is one way in which we form impressions (sometimes wrongly) of others. This section examines factors that influence how we form impressions, including the ease of impression formation, beliefs about how traits go together, and the impact of mood.

implicit personality theory the theory that certain traits and behaviors go together

THE EASE OF IMPRESSION FORMATION

We form impressions about other people very quickly, and based on very little information, such as their facial expression, appearance, or even a single action (Berry, 1991; Hassin & Trope, 2000). For example, try to form a mental image of a person you are going to meet with each of the following names: Jennifer, Michael, Gertrude, Sigmund. I imagine that the impressions you formed differ greatly, because even something as subtle as a person's name can influence our expectations. Even these brief first impressions have a strong and lasting effect on our attitudes, beliefs, and behavior. In fact, we move quickly from forming our first impressions of a person to making various inferences about what the person is like, why he or she acts in a given way, and how he or she will behave in the future. However, some people make these decisions more quickly than others (see Rate Yourself).

The power of first impressions. Because we form impressions of people so quickly, information that we learn first has a strong influence on our overall judgment (yes, first impressions <u>do</u> matter). The **primacy** effect describes the phenomenon in which the traits that you hear about first influence your interpretation of other traits (Kelley, 1950). Solomon Asch (1946) demonstrated that people see certain traits as going together. In this well-known study, participants were randomly assigned to read one of two lists of words describing a target person. The words were exactly the same in the two conditions (e.g., intelligent, skillful, industrious, determined, practical, cautious), except that in one condition the word "warm" was added to the list and in the other condition the word "cold" was added to the list. Although only a single word was different in the two lists, participants who read the list that included the word "warm" saw the person being described as happier, funnier, more good-natured, and more generous than did those who read the list that included the word "cold." Similarly, would you believe that we form different impressions when a person is described as "intelligent, industrious, impulsive, critical, stubborn, and envious" than when a person is described as "envious, stubborn, critical, impulsive, industrious, and intelligent"? This is exactly what research by Solomon Asch suggests: The first trait we hear about exerts a particularly strong impact on the impressions we form.

primacy the tendency for information that is presented early to have a greater impact on judgments than information that is presented later

How Quickly Do You Form Impressions?

Need for Closure Scale

INSTRUCTIONS: *Rate each item on a scale of 1 (strongly disagree) to 6 (strongly agree).*

☐ **1.** When faced with a problem, I usually see the one best solution very quickly.

☐ **2.** I do not usually consult many different options before forming my own view.

☐ **3.** I tend to struggle with most decisions.

☐ **4.** When considering most conflict situations, I can usually see how both sides could be right.

☐ **5.** When thinking about a problem, I consider as many different opinions on the issue as possible.

☐ **6.** Even after I've made up my mind about something, I am always eager to consider a different opinion.

☐ **7.** I always see many possible solutions to problems I face.

☐ **8.** When trying to solve a problem, I often see so many possible options that it's confusing.

SCORING: For items 1 and 2, give yourself the number of points equal to the rating that you assigned to the statement. Items 3, 4, 5, 6, 7, and 8 are reverse-scored, so higher scores are converted to lower numbers (and vice versa). In other words, if you rated the statement a 6, give yourself 1 point. If you rated the statement a 2, give yourself 5 points. Then sum up your total number of points on all 8 items.

INTERPRETATION: This scale measures need for closure, meaning preference for quickly reaching (and maintaining) a conclusion as well as avoiding ambiguity. People with higher scores are more decisive, whereas those with lower scores are more comfortable with ambiguity (Webster & Kruglanski, 1994).

RESEARCH FOCUS ON NEUROSCIENCE
The Unique Processing of Social Information

Different parts of the brain are used when people engage in social tasks—such as when forming an impression of a person—versus nonsocial tasks—such as remembering the order in which information about a person is given (Mitchell, Macrae, & Banaji, 2004). In one study, researchers asked 17 participants to read a series of statements about personality traits (e.g., "at the party, he was the first to start dancing on the table"). Each of these statements was paired with one of 18 faces. In some cases, participants were asked to form an impression of the person, based on their picture and the information they read about the person. In other cases, participants were simply asked to memorize the order in which the information about a particular person was presented. Participants underwent functional magnetic resonance imaging (fMRI) scanning while performing their given task so that researcher could examine the type, and location, of brain activity that occurred in each case. The results revealed that participants used the dorsomedial prefrontal cortex (PRC) when engaging in the social task, meaning when they were asked to form an impression of a person, but used other parts of the brain (the superior frontal and parietal gyri, precentral gyrus, and the caudate) when engaging in the nonsocial task, meaning when they were asked to simply memorize the order of the information presented. This work shows that different parts of the brain are used to process social versus nonsocial information, suggesting that social cognition is a very distinct (and important) aspect of thinking.

©AP/Wide World Photos

Accuracy of first impressions.

Although you might question whether first impressions could be accurate, in many cases such impressions can be remarkably right. In one of the first studies to test the accuracy of first impressions, researchers asked students to rate themselves and rate their peers around them on the first day of class, before students had had any chance to interact (Norman & Goldberg, 1966). Students' self-ratings were positively correlated with others' ratings of them, particularly on the traits of "sociable" and "responsible." More recent research supports these findings (Albright, Kenny, & Malloy, 1988; Levesque & Kenny, 1993). For example, research by Nalini Ambady reveals that even very brief (six-second) silent video clips of teachers are associated with teachers' end-of-semester evaluations from students (Ambady & Rosenthal, 1993).

In some cases, we can even make fairly accurate predictions about a person based only on seeing a picture of the person's face. In one study, participants were shown photographs of two candidates who were running for Congress, and were asked to identify the face that displayed the most competence (Todorov, Mandisodza, Goren, & Hall, 2005). People's ratings of the face that was the most competent predicted the winner in the race about 70% of the time. Similarly, people's ratings of the power-related traits in the faces of chief executive officers (CEOs) are correlated with the company's profits (Rule & Ambady, 2008). In yet another study, participants looked at photos of men taken from online personal advertisements and guessed whether the person was gay or straight (Rule & Ambady, 2008). Would you believe that people are 70% accurate in determining someone's sexual orientation just from seeing his or her photo? That's exactly what these researchers found.

The power of negative traits.

The theory of primacy tell us that first traits influence our impression more than later traits. In addition, the type of trait influences our impressions in particular ways (Coovert & Reeder, 1990; Pratto & John, 1991; Vonk, 1993). People are more strongly influenced by negative traits than they are by positive traits, a phenomenon known as **trait negativity bias**. In other words, one bad trait can destroy someone's reputation much more than one positive trait can impress people (see Barry Bonds example). Trait negativity bias explains why negative information about a political candidate (e.g., inconsistent, short-tempered) has a greater effect on our impressions—and voting behavior—than does positive information (e.g., kind, intelligent; Klein, 1991).

Why do we pay so much more attention to negative traits than to positive ones? It is probably an adapted tendency based in our evolution—we need to react to negative information, such as potential threats to our safety—faster than to positive information. If you learn that a person is likely to hurt you, it is clearly more important to your survival than learning that a person is trying to help you.

trait negativity bias the tendency for people to be more influenced by negative traits than by positive ones

Research demonstrates that the brain reacts more strongly when evaluating negative information than when evaluating positive information (Ito, Larsen, Smith, & Cacioppo, 1998).

BELIEFS ABOUT HOW TRAITS FIT TOGETHER

When we form an overall impression of a person, we are also influenced by our general intuition or beliefs about how certain traits and behaviors go together. Therefore, we rely on implicit personality theory, and hence knowing that a person has a given trait leads us to assume that he or she also has certain other traits (Anderson & Sedikides, 1991; Sedikides & Anderson, 1994). For example, we often believe that highly attractive people also possess other positive traits, such as social skills, intelligence, and extraversion (Eagly, Ashmore, Makhijani, & Longo, 1991; Feingold, 1992; Langlois et al., 2000). In Chapter 12, we'll continue the discussion of implicit personality theory and how it relates to interpersonal attraction.

> **? Questioning the Research**
> Research demonstrates that attractive people do have other positive traits, such as greater social skills and higher levels of extraversion. Do you think this association reflects correlation or causation? How could you test these two hypotheses?

Implicit personality theory allows us to make judgments about the world in an efficient way, but it can also lead to some potentially dangerous errors. For example, many college students believe that people with a sexually transmitted disease must have certain other personality traits and behaviors, such as blatant promiscuity, an unhealthy appearance, and many sexual partners from high-risk settings (e.g., bars in cities; Williams, Kimble, Covell, & Weiss, 1992). This is why it can be difficult to believe that someone who goes to your own college or university could have AIDS. It just doesn't fit with our beliefs about how certain traits go together. And it is one reason why many college students put themselves—and their partners—at great risk when they fail to use condoms. As described at the start of this section, people tend to see those in close relationships as less likely to have a sexually transmitted disease.

RESEARCH FOCUS ON GENDER
The Impact of Gender Stereotypes

One of the drawbacks of using shortcuts when forming impressions of people is that these shortcuts can lead us to focus on general information about a person's group or category, and to pay much less attention to specific information about the particular person. In one study, participants read information about two male and two female students at their university (Stewart, Vassar, Sanchez, & David, 2000). The information included the names of the students and several personality traits. For example, some participants read about "Kathryn, who is careless, kind, irritable, and stable." Others read an identical description of "Thomas." Then they were asked to match the names of the four students with the personality descriptions they were given. Participants with progressive attitudes toward women—meaning those who tend to agree with statements such as "men should share in household tasks such as washing dishes and doing laundry"—made more errors in matching names to descriptions for female targets than for male targets. Those with more traditional attitudes toward women, on the other hand, showed the opposite tendency, and made more errors in matching names to descriptions for female targets than for male ones. These findings indicate, as predicted, that traditional men and women pay more attention to information about men and in turn are able to remember specific details about the target men described. In contrast, those with progressive values tend to focus on women's distinct features, and show greater accuracy when matching women's names and trait descriptions.

THE IMPACT OF MOOD

Our mood exerts a strong influence on how we think about the world (Mayer & Hanson, 1995; Seta, Hayes, & Seta, 1994). People who are in a positive mood are more likely than those in a neutral mood to rely on shortcuts in thinking. Imagine that you have just learned that you have been hired for a highly desirable summer job that you had wanted for some time; you and your friend then attend a class in which there is a guest lecturer. Because you are already in a good mood, you are likely to see the lecturer in a particularly positive way. Our mood can even influence how we see our own behavior (Forgas, Bower, & Krantz, 1984). In one study, researchers manipulated participants' feelings so that they were in either a good or a bad mood. They then showed them a videotape of themselves talking to someone else (the tapes had been made the day before). As predicted, participants who were in a good mood saw themselves more positively than those who were in a bad mood. Finally, and as described in Business Connections, mood can even impact our decisions in sometimes substantial ways.

Business
::: CONNECTIONS

The Impact of Mood on Economic Decisions

Mood can even have an impact on decision making when real money is at stake (Lerner, Small, & Lowenstein, 2004). In one study, participants were randomly assigned to watch one of three film clips:

- a sad clip (from *The Champ* describing the death of a boy's mentor),
- a disgusting clip (from *Trainspotting* showing a man using a disgusting toilet), or
- a neutral clip (from a National Geographic Special on the Great Barrier Reef).

Then participants were randomly assigned to one of two conditions. Some participants were in the "sell" condition—they were given a set of highlighters and had to choose to keep it or sell it. Other participants were in the "choice" condition—they had to choose between receiving the highlighter set or getting cash instead. Each participant was asked to rate a list of 28 choices (the amount of cash differed). Remember the other variables—participants saw either a sad movie, a disgusting movie, or a neutral movie. And participants were either in the "sell" condition or "choice" condition. This design allowed experimenters to judge whether mood impacts selling versus buying decisions. How did participants' mood affect their buying and selling? As predicted, mood had a dramatic impact on both types of decisions. Compared to those in the neutral condition, those in the disgust condition had very low buying and selling prices. Those in the sadness condition had higher buying prices but lower selling prices. In sum, different emotions can have quite different—and even opposing—effects on economic decisions. What does this mean for you? Be aware that your mood can influence the economic decisions you make: the price at which you'll sell your car, how much you are willing to spend on your spring break trip, and what you will pay for a ticket to the World Series.

Photononstop/SUPERSTOCK

Concepts in Context

FACTOR	EXAMPLE
Primacy	When Pete first met his new roommate, Leon, he was struck by how messy Leon kept his desk. Pete immediately decided that Leon was a very disorganized person.
Trait negativity bias	Denise's boss is considerate to and respectful of all of his employees. But after Denise learned her boss was arrested for driving under the influence (DUI), she decided that he was untrustworthy and selfish.
Implicit personality theory	Given Jordan's truly exceptional beauty, you are very surprised when she confides in you that she is very unhappy in her relationship with Brad. You've always assumed that people who are very attractive also have very satisfying personal relationships.

HOW DO BELIEFS CREATE REALITY?

Q A The factors described in the preceding section all refer to errors people make when observing the social world. In some cases, however, people's beliefs lead them to actually create the reality they expect. For example, in one study, researchers asked mothers how likely they thought it was that their 7th grade child would regularly drink alcohol as a teenager (Madon, Guyll, Spoth, Cross, & Hilbert, 2003; Madon, Guyll, Spoth, & Willard, 2004). They then collected data from both mothers and children 18 months later to examine children's actual alcohol use. As expected, mothers' expectations about whether their child would drink predicted children's actual drinking behavior later on. Specifically, mothers who expected their child would drink had children who were in fact drinking more than the children of those mothers who expected their child would not drink. This study describes the phenomenon of self-fulfilling prophecy, which is one way in which people's expectations can create the reality they expect. This section will examine three distinct ways in which people's beliefs can create such reality: through perceptual confirmation, belief perseverance, and self-fulfilling prophecy.

©AP/Wide World Photos

In the NEWS **Scott Peterson.** After the disappearance of Laci Roche Peterson in December 2003, her family initially insisted that her husband, Scott Peterson, had nothing to do with her disappearance. They attributed his somewhat odd behavior to his grief about her disappearance. But once her family learned that Scott was having an extramarital affair, they began to interpret his behavior in a very different light.

PEOPLE SEE WHAT THEY EXPECT TO SEE

One factor that leads us to create precisely the reality we expect is our tendency to see things in line with our initial expectations. Once we have a particular expectation, we interpret ambiguous events in line with our beliefs, look for information to support our view, and disregard information that contradicts it. Let's take a look at this process.

See events in line with their own beliefs. Considerable research in social psychology demonstrates that people tend to see things in line with their own beliefs and preconceptions, a phenomenon called **perceptual confirmation** (Klein & Kunda, 1992). For example, if you expect to work on a project with a person in a stigmatized group (e.g., one who is suffering from schizophrenia), you are likely to see him or her in a more positive way than you would if you didn't expect to work with that person. Why? Because if you believe you'll have to continue to interact with this person, you are very motivated to believe this person will be a good partner! This is just one example of our tendency to see what we want to see. (See the Health Connections box for an example of how people's expectations even influence how much pain they experience.)

perceptual confirmation the tendency for people to see things in line with their own beliefs and expectations

Health
:: CONNECTIONS

The Power of Belief

One of the most powerful examples of the power of belief on behavior is the placebo effect, in which physiologically inert medicines or treatments can produce very real, and even lasting, effects on physical health. The effects of placebos have been demonstrated on virtually every organ system in the body and on many diseases, including chest pain, arthritis, hay ~~fever~~, headaches, ulcers, hypertension, postoperative ~~...~~ and pain due to the common cold ~~...~~ 1997).

~~...~~ ortant factors predicting the ~~...~~ bos is patients' expectations ~~...~~ the treatment. Why? One reason is ~~...~~ expectations about how a treatment ~~...~~ ients to look for signs that confirm ~~...~~ (Skelton & Pennebaker, 1982). In ~~...~~ ants were told that they would be hearing a ~~noise~~ that might cause their skin temperature to either rise (in one condition) or fall (in another condition; Pennebaker & Skelton, 1981). As predicted, those who expected their skin temperature to rise reported feeling themselves get warmer; those who expected their temperature to fall reported feeling cooler!

People's expectations about how a treatment will work can even lead to changes in their own behavior. These changes in turn lead to some physical effect, such as the reduction of pain (Benedetti & Amanzio, 1997). If you have a bad headache and take an aspirin, which you believe will alleviate the headache, you may relax because you know the pain will soon disappear, and this relaxation will lead to a decrease in your headache.

Finally, the mere expectation of a physical change may lead to physiological changes in the body (Bandura, O'Leary, Taylor Gauthier, & Gossard, 1987; Benedetti & Amanzio, 1997). In a study with patients who were having their wisdom teeth removed, half were given real ultrasound therapy during their procedure (Hashish, Hai Harvey, Feinmann, & Harris, 1988). The others thought they were receiving this therapy but the machine was unplugged. Patients in both cases showed a decrease in pain, jaw tightness, and swelling, indicating that all these physical effects were caused simply by the expectation that they were receiving a pain-reducing therapy. This evidence suggests that the placebo effect occurs at least in part due to social-psychological principles such as perceptual confirmation and behavioral confirmation or self-fulfilling prophecy.

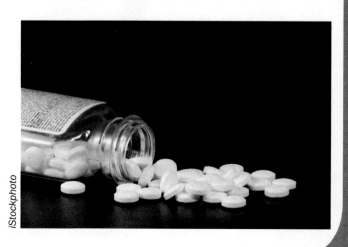

iStockphoto

In a unique demonstration of the power of our beliefs to influence how we see the world, David Rosenhan of Stanford University and several people without mental illness (e.g., a graduate student, a painter, a housewife, and a pediatrician) went to the admissions departments of local mental hospitals (Rosenhan, 1973). They all claimed that they were hearing voices, and they were all admitted to the hospitals with a diagnosis of schizophrenia. However, once they were in the hospital as patients, they acted in a completely normal manner. How did the professional staff treat them? They continued to see them as "sick" and even interpreted their normal behavior as symptoms of schizophrenia. For example, one "patient" kept a journal of his experiences in the hospital; this was described as "obsessive writing behavior" in his chart. Patients gathering outside the cafeteria before it opened (in a place where there was little to do) were said to be exhibiting "oral-acquisitive syndrome." In sum, once staff members believed that a given person was a patient, they interpreted the person's behavior according to their beliefs.

The phenomenon of perceptual confirmation helps explain why people can watch the same event but see it in very different ways. If you watch a presidential debate or a national football championship with someone who is rooting for a different person or team than you are, the bias in perception held by both of you will be evident (see Figure 5.3). People see their preferred candidate as making more intelligent points and see their favored athletic team as showing greater ability and morality. In fact, people feel even more supportive of their favored presidential candidate after watching

FIGURE 5.3

CAN OUR BELIEFS INFLUENCE WHAT WE SEE?

Researchers surveyed students who watched a football game between Princeton and Dartmouth, in which many episodes of rough play occurred. The researchers were interested in whether perceptual confirmation would affect spectators' interpretation of the episode, meaning that students would see the players on their team as less responsible for starting the rough play than players on the opposing team. In line with predictions, Princeton students saw Dartmouth students as much more at blame than Princeton students for starting the rough play (presumably because Princeton's star player left the game with a broken nose in the second quarter), whereas Dartmouth students saw players from both schools as starting the rough play.

Source: Hastorf, A.H., & Cantril, H. (1954). They saw a game: A case study. *Journal of Abnormal and Social Psychology*, 49, 129–134.

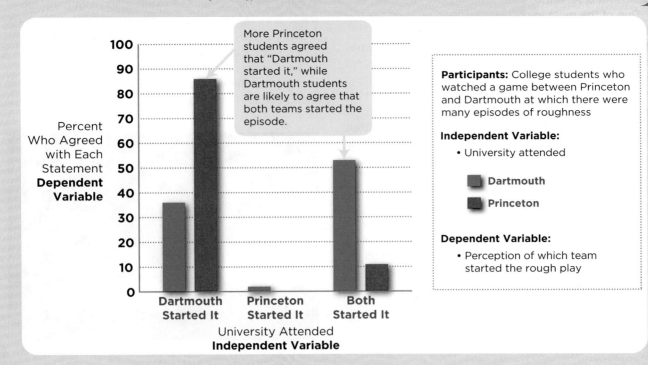

a debate. This suggests that such debates may do less to help candidates attract new supporters than to help their current supporters feel more positive toward them (and hence more likely to donate money and/or vote). The power of perceptual confirmation also helps explain a powerful effect in health psychology—the placebo effect (as described in Health Connections).

See uncorrelated events as correlated.

We tend to see the world in line with our expectations. This can lead us to see a correlation between two events when in reality no such association exists. This phenomenon is called **illusory correlation** (Hamilton & Gifford, 1976; McArthur, 1980). For example, people often see boy babies as more difficult than girl babies simply due to their stereotypes about the correspondence between sex and personality traits. One day I was talking with a friend who has an older son and a younger daughter. She described how very different boys and girls are, and specifically how, compared to her son, her daughter was much quieter, more obedient, and overall an easier baby. I then remarked that this description of her children was precisely how I would describe the difference between my older and younger sons.

> **illusory correlation** the tendency to see a correlation between two events when in reality, no such association exists

Why do we make this error? In part, because we tend to notice events that support our belief while ignoring those that do not. For example, if you believe that bad things happen on Friday the 13th, you will pay particular attention to such events on that day and in turn "see" bad things as happening with great frequency (e.g., you stub your toe, forget to bring your homework assignment to class, have an argument with a friend). If these events happened on another day, you would be unlikely to attribute them to the date on which they occurred.

Another factor that contributes to this error is our tendency to see two relatively rare attributes as associated, even if we have no expectation that these things should go together (Johnson & Mullen, 1994). In one study, participants read a series of sentences that described people in either Group A or Group B. More of the sentences described members of Group A than Group B, and more of the sentences described positive behaviors (e.g., "Arthur, a member of Group A, carved a statue for his town's park") than negative behaviors (e.g., "Dennis, a member of Group B, hit his pet dog because he was angry"). They then were given a list of sentences without the person's name included, and had to guess whether this sentence described a person from Group A or Group B. Although the number of sentences that described positive versus negative behavior was equivalent for those in both groups, participants were much more likely to choose negative behaviors as describing a person from Group B. This error occurs because people tend to attribute behavior that is more rare (in this case, the negative behavior) to those in smaller groups.

See a given outcome as inevitable.

Finally, we have a tendency to see a given outcome as inevitable once we are aware of the outcome. This **hindsight bias** (also called the *I-knew-it-all-along phenomenon*) means that we see whatever event occurs as completely in line with our expectations, even if we would have seen a completely different outcome as also in line with our expectations (Hawkins & Hastie, 1990). In a study designed to demonstrate the power of the hindsight bias, students read about a dating situation that ended in one of two ways—with a marriage proposal or a rape (Carli, 1999). Although the story was exactly the same in the two conditions (except for the last line), people saw the ending as rather predictable in both situations, based on the details of the story (which of course were the same in both conditions). Why do people make this error? In part because they misremember details that support their argument. In other words, we fill in blanks in our memory with things that seem to make sense.

> **hindsight bias** the tendency to see a given outcome as inevitable once the actual outcome is known

"I knew the woodpeckers were a mistake."

Hindsight bias also influences how we perceive numerous real-world events. In one study, researchers examined students' predictions about whether then-President Clinton would be convicted in his impeachment trial in 2001 (Bryant & Guilbault, 2002). As predicted, after his acquittal students reported having believed all along that he would not be convicted, even though before the announcement of his acquittal they saw conviction as rather likely. Similarly, after the tragic events of September 11th, many people saw the hijackings—and crashes—that occurred as caused by the now seemingly obvious need to lock cockpit doors on airplanes. But we need to remember that in all previous instances, hijackers were motivated by a desire to have the plane land safely...and people never imagined that hijackers would both be able to fly planes and intend to deliberately crash them.

PEOPLE MAINTAIN BELIEFS OVER TIME

Another factor that contributes to our ability to create precisely the reality we expect is our tendency to maintain our beliefs over time. We do this even when evidence suggests that these beliefs may be wrong.

belief perseverance the tendency to maintain, and even strengthen, beliefs in the face of disconfirming evidence

Explaining belief perseverance. **Belief perseverance** is the phenomenon in which people actively maintain and strengthen their attitudes even in the face of disconfirming evidence. For example, if you believe that swimming right after you've eaten will lead to a bad cramp, you are likely to continue to believe this even when evidence seems to refute it. This tendency to maintain our beliefs makes it very difficult to change a person's attitudes.

In one of the first studies to demonstrate belief perseverance, students were asked to read 25 supposed suicide notes and determine which ones were real and which ones were fake (Ross, Lepper, & Hubbard, 1975). Some of the students were led to believe that they were extremely good at distinguishing between the two types of notes. (They were told that they got 24 out of 25 right, whereas most students got only 16 right.) Others were led to believe that they were not very good (they were told that they got 10 right.) Still others were told that they got 17 right. Then the experimenter said that all this feedback had been made up in advance because the experiment involved deception, and that actually the participants' scores had nothing to do with their answers. The experimenter went on to say that some of the notes were indeed real and that others were fake. The experimenter asked the participants how many they thought they had gotten right. Those who had been told that they got only 10 right said about 13; those who had heard that they got 17 right said 15. Those who had been told that they got 24 right said 17. This shows that even though all of the participants heard that their scores were predetermined, these fake scores still influenced their assessment of their own abilities, illustrating the phenomenon of belief perseverance.

Questioning the Research

Given the findings of this study, should we believe the standard debriefing after participating in a deceptive psychology study is effective? Is there a better approach to letting participants know they were deceived?

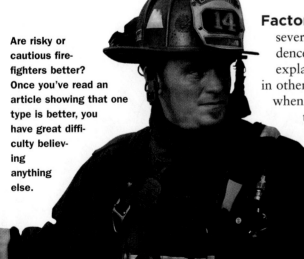

Are risky or cautious firefighters better? Once you've read an article showing that one type is better, you have great difficulty believing anything else.

iStockphoto

Factors leading to belief perseverance. Why does belief perseverance occur? First, we create causal explanations to explain the evidence. For example, students who were told that they did well may have explained their success to themselves by recalling their good intuition in other situations or the ease with which they understand people. Later, when their scores are shown to be false, they still recalled the reasons they had created to explain their success, and hence they had trouble believing that the evidence was really false.

Similarly, in another study, students read a fictitious report showing that good firefighters have either risk-seeking or cautious personalities (Anderson, Lepper, & Ross, 1980). Students then generated reasons for why this relationship might exist. For example, "You have to be willing to take risks to go into a burning building and save lives." Or "You have to be cautious so that you don't injure yourself and others by going into a burning building without really thinking of a plan." Then the students were told that the report was fake. However, they still believed the original (false) report they had read. What they did not understand was that they could just as easily have believed the reverse if they had read the other false report. These results demonstrate that the effects of belief perseverance are particularly strong when people generate their own causal reasons as opposed to when they read explanations provided by others (Davies, 1997).

People's Behavior Elicits What They Expect. Social perception involves not only interpreting situations or people in particular ways, sometimes based on biases. But social perception can even involve actively creating behavior in others based on biases and expectations (Darley & Fazio, 1980; Hilton & Darley, 1991; Rosenthal, 1994). Specifically, behavioral confirmation or self-fulfilling prophecy refers to the tendency to seek, interpret, and create information that verifies our own beliefs. If I believe that the woman my brother has just started dating is rude, I may initially behave in an aloof way toward her. In turn, when she acts rather distant from me, I will interpret her behavior as "proof" that my initial belief was correct, while ignoring the role that my own behavior played in eliciting her behavior (see Figure 5.4).

FIGURE 5.4 — MODEL OF A SELF-FULFILLING PROPHECY

In the cycle of behavioral confirmation or self-fulfilling prophecy, people's initial expectations about a target person actually elicit the behavior they expect.

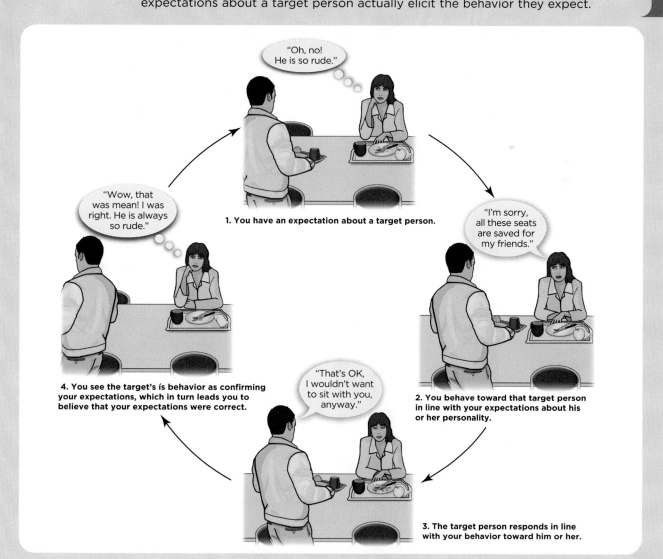

1. You have an expectation about a target person.

2. You behave toward that target person in line with your expectations about his or her personality.

3. The target person responds in line with your behavior toward him or her.

4. You see the target's is behavior as confirming your expectations, which in turn leads you to believe that your expectations were correct.

Explaining the process of self-fulfilling prophecy. How does this process of self-fulfilling prophecy work? First, and as shown in Figure 5.4, people form expectations about what another person is like (e.g., my new roommate will be very sophisticated because she's from Paris; my boyfriend's parents must be very wealthy because they live in New York City). As described at the beginning of this chapter, people form expectations about others based on even trivial and meaningless pieces of information such as a person's name, where they live, and what type of car they drive.

Second, these expectations influence how they act toward that person. We have a tendency to seek information that supports our views, which in turn can lead us to confirm these views even when the evidence doesn't support them (Snyder & Swann, 1978; Zuckerman, Knee, Hodgins, & Miyake, 1995). For example, if

---

FIGURE 5.5

HOW DO EXPECTATIONS ELICIT BEHAVIOR?

In this experiment, researchers led participants to believe that they would be talking either to a partner with an extroverted personality or to an introverted partner. Then, they noted how many questions participants asked that would elicit extroverted responses (such as "What is the most fun thing about working in groups?") or introverted responses (such as "When is the best time to work by yourself in the library?"). As predicted, participants who expected an extraverted partner asked many more extroverted questions than introverted questions, whereas those who expected an introverted partner asked somewhat more introverted questions than extroverted questions.

Source: Snyder, M., & Swann, W. (1978). Behavioral confirmation in social interaction: From social perception to social reality. *Journal of Experimental Social Psychology*, 14, 148–162.

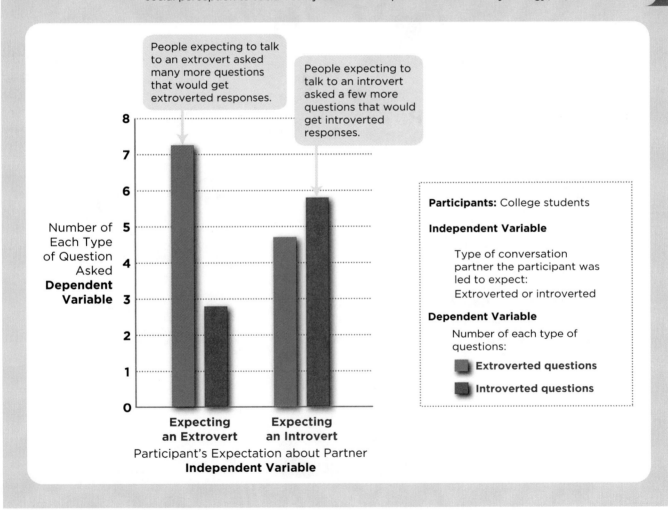

you are told that a new person in your dorm is introverted, you are more likely to ask questions that tend to confirm this impression (e.g., "What things do you dislike about large parties?" and "What factors make it hard for you to really open up to people?"). However, if you are told that he or she is extroverted, you are more likely to ask questions that confirm this very different impression (e.g., "What would you do to liven things up at a party?" and "What types of situations do you seek out if you want to meet new people?"). Figure 5.5 illustrates this tendency to ask questions that confirm our initial belief.

Third, this behavior may lead the person to act in ways that are consistent with the perceiver's expectations (e.g., not attending social events, talking about boring subjects). In a classic study, Mark Snyder, Elizabeth Tanke, and Ellen Berscheid (1977) asked male college students to have a phone conversation with a woman who they thought (based on a photograph they were shown) was either unattractive or attractive. Men who thought they were interacting with an attractive woman were friendlier and more outgoing. Later, researchers asked raters (who had no idea about the study's hypothesis or procedure) to evaluate the woman's responses. Researchers found significant differences as a function of whether the woman was thought to be attractive or not attractive. Not surprisingly, women who were treated in a friendlier manner responded in a more positive way.

Behavioral confirmation (self-fulfilling prophecy) can have major implications in real-world situations, including courtrooms, families, and education. For example, research by Allen Hart at Amherst College has shown that judges' beliefs influence juries' decisions even in cases in which jurors are specifically told to disregard the judge's behavior and form their own opinions (Hart, 1995). As mentioned earlier in the chapter, parents' overestimation of their child's alcohol use led to more alcohol use later on (Madon et al., 2003; Madon et al., 2004). The power of self-fulfilling prophecy can also be seen in the classroom, as described in Education Connections.

Education
CONNECTIONS

The Overwhelming Power of Teachers' Expectations

In a dramatic real-life demonstration of the power of self-fulfilling prophecies, researchers told teachers in a San Francisco elementary school that the results of an IQ test had revealed that 20% of their students were "late bloomers" and could be expected to do very well in the coming year (Rosenthal & Jacobsen, 1968). How effective was this manipulation? Students in this group (who were randomly assigned) improved their IQ scores by as much as 30 points. Although this study was conducted in the 1960s, more recent research reveals similar findings about the impact of teachers' expectations on students' performance. For example, teachers' expectations about students' grades were a strong predictor of those students' actual grades, even controlling for previous achievement and student motivation (Smith, Jussim, & Eccles, 1999). Such expectations are a particularly strong predictor of achievement for low-achieving students (Madon, Jussim, & Eccles, 1997). Teachers' expectations are also a stronger predictor of their own evaluations of students' performance—that is, the grades they assign—than of scores on standardized tests (Jussim & Eccles, 1992). This finding suggests that although teachers see (and grade) students' performance in line with what they expect, these expectations are not an accurate measure of students' true achievement. Why? Because these expectations do not predict more objective measures of performance (e.g., standardized test scores).

Can you break the links of self-fulfilling prophecy and thereby form accurate impressions? Yes, at least in some cases. First, behavioral confirmation is less likely to occur if the perceiver's goal is to be liked by the target person (Copeland, 1994; Neuberg, Judice, Virdin, & Carrillo, 1993; Snyder & Haugen, 1994). In cases in which one wants to be accurate about the target person, or wants to be liked by that person, one apparently tries hard to get to know the real person instead of relying on prior assumptions. In one study, participants were given a negative expectation about a person they would be interviewing, and then they were either given no particular goal for the interaction or told to try to be liked by the interviewee (Neuberg et al., 1993). Participants in the "no goal" condition acted in a distant and challenging way during the interview. In turn, they elicited less positive answers from the interviewee, thereby confirming the negative expectation. Participants in the "be liked goal" condition, on the other hand, were much warmer and less threatening and elicited more positive responses from the interviewee, thereby disconfirming the negative expectation.

The cycle of behavioral confirmation can also be broken if targets are aware of perceivers' expectations. In these cases the target will try actively to counter these expectations. This can help prevent self-fulfilling prophecies. In one study, pairs of students were assigned to have a conversation (Hilton & Darley, 1985). Half of the participants were told that their partner might be cold. The other half were not given any information about their partner. Moreover, half of the partners were told that their partner might think they were cold (i.e., they were given a forewarning). Who was most successful at refuting this (inaccurate) belief? Those who were aware that their partner might be likely to see them as cold. Thus, making a person aware of the perceiver's assumptions can work to decrease, or even eliminate, the effects of the perceiver's expectations.

The links of self-fulfilling prophecy can also be broken if the perceiver's assumptions are highly inaccurate, and the target therefore does not act in the expected way. Bill Swann and Robin Ely (1984) asked 128 women to interview individuals who were either certain or uncertain of their own extroversion. However, the perceivers were told that the target individuals were the opposite of what they actually believed about themselves (for example, introverted if they believed themselves to be extroverted). Perceivers were also told either that the target had been rated as extroverted by all of the other judges (high certainty) or by some of the other judges (low certainty). Perceivers then chose which five of twelve questions they would like to ask the target to judge his or her degree of extroversion. As predicted, those who expected the person to be extroverted and were very certain of this judgment asked more confirming questions than those who were less certain. Judges' ratings of the answers by the target individuals showed that behavioral confirmation does occur in interactions between high-certainty perceivers and low-certainty targets. However, when targets were quite firm in their beliefs about their own traits, they actively resisted the questions and eventually convinced the perceivers of their actual traits—thereby showing that behavioral confirmation is not inevitable.

The good news about self-fulfilling prophecy. Obviously, self-fulfilling prophecies can have many negative effects. (Chapter 10 describes some of the ways in which this cycle can lead to stereotypes and prejudice.) But here are a few encouraging words.

- We are better at judging friends and acquaintances than at judging strangers. We are better at making judgments about how people will act around us (e.g., our roommates, co-workers) than about how they will act in other situations. We are more accurate in these cases because we know the people and have lots of information about them (e.g., Madon et al., 2001).
- We can form more accurate impressions when we are motivated to be accurate and open-minded as well as when we are aware of the biases described in this chapter. For example, graduate students in psychology are less likely to make these errors.
- Finally, although I've described the power of self-fulfilling prophecies to lead to negative effects, such predictions can also lead to positive ones. For exam-

ple, people whose dating partners treat them as special and unique may try to live up to these idealized images. Therefore they become more like their partners' images of them over time (Snyder & Swann, 1978; Snyder et al., 1977), as in this excerpt from the book *Enchanted April*:

"The more he treated her as though she were really very nice, the more Lotty expanded and became really very nice, and the more he, affected in his turn, became really very nice himself; so that they went round and round, not in a vicious but in a highly virtuous circle" (von Arnim, 1922).

Concepts in Context

HOW BELIEFS CAN CREATE REALITY

FACTOR	EXAMPLE
Perceptual confirmation	After watching the presidential debate, you are delighted with the clearly superior performance of the candidate you prefer. But then you are shocked when the newspapers later report that both candidates performed equally well.
Belief perseverance	Although you drive a large SUV, in part because you believe this type of vehicle will protect you in the event of an accident, you decide to attend a talk on campus about the dangers of SUVs. Despite the evidence presented by the speaker on the dangers of SUVs (including their tendency to roll over and difficulty in coming to quick stops), you become even more strongly convinced that this vehicle is indeed the safest choice.
Self-fulfilling prophecy	Steven is babysitting for his 3-year-old niece, Sabrina, who he has heard is very shy and introverted. To avoid upsetting her, Steven keeps his distance and rarely talks to her or tries to engage her in play. Surely enough, Sabrina spends most of the time playing entirely on her own. At the end of the afternoon, Steven remarks to his brother that Sabrina sure is shy.

CULTURE
HOW DOES CULTURE INFLUENCE SOCIAL COGNITION?

Another factor that influences social cognition is culture. People from different cultures think about the social world in different ways. In one study, researchers asked both American and Mexican Americans to read a series of sentences describing a person's behavior, and then judge whether this person had a given trait (Zárate, Uleman, & Voils, 2001). For example, one sentence read "He took his first calculus test when he was 12" (and the trait they reacted to was "smart"). Another sentence read "She left a 25% tip for the waitress (and the trait they reacted to was "generous"). As predicted, Americans made the trait judgments much more quickly than did Mexican Americans. This reflects Americans' strong tendency to emphasize the role of traits in leading to behavior—as well as the tendency of those from collectivistic cultures to take situational factors into account. This section will examine the impact of culture on cognitive errors as well as beliefs about traits.

COGNITIVE ERRORS

Not surprisingly, culture influences the availability of different events/concepts. This is, in part, because one's country of origin influences what is known and therefore what is easily brought to mind. As a simple example, people in different cultures will think of different things if you ask them to name a food they like or a movie they've seen. This is simply because our culture influences what we are exposed to and therefore what types of experiences come easily to mind. Try the exercise in Figure 5.6 for a compelling example of how culture impacts availability.

FIGURE 5.6

AVAILABILITY EXERCISE

Follow the directions listed below very carefully. You'll be truly amazed at what you find.

1. Pick a number from 1 to 9.
2. Subtract 5 from that number.
3. Multiply that number by 3.
4. Square that number (meaning multiply that number by itself).
5. Add the digits in your number until you get only one digit (e.g., if you have the number 65, add 6 + 5 = 11, then add 1 + 1 = 2).
6. If the number is less than five, add five. If the number is greater than or equal to five, subtract four.
7. Multiply this number by two.
8. Subtract six from this number.
9. Now, map the digit of the number to a letter in the alphabet (1 = A, 2 = B, 3 = C, etc.)
10. Pick a country that starts with that letter.
11. Take the second letter in the country name and think of a mammal that begins with this letter.
12. Think of the color of that mammal.

Now, look at the bottom of the next page and see if I've correctly guessed your country and mammal!

Culture also impacts the frequency of counterfactual thinking (Morris & Peng, 1994). In one study, for example, students in the physics graduate program at the University of Michigan read a true story about a murder that had occurred on a college campus (in which a graduate student killed his advisor). They then read a series of scenarios that were similar to the scenario that actually occurred. These scenarios changed either a piece of information about the person or a piece of information about the situation. For example, in one condition participants were asked "What if Lu's advisor had worked harder to prepare him for the dissertation defense and job market?" (a change in situation). In another they were asked "What if Lu had not been mentally imbalanced?" (a change in person). Participants then rated how likely they believe the murder would have occurred in that (slightly new) scenario. As predicted, Chinese participants judged murder as much less likely to occur when the situation was changed in some way than did Americans. Because Americans focus on the person's disposition, they believed that this "murderous disposition" would have led to the killing regardless of the situational factors. In turn, people from collectivistic cultures are much more likely to engage in counterfactual thinking because they focus so intently on the situation—and they can see how features of the situation could change. In contrast, those from individualistic cultures focus intently on the person's internal disposition, which they see as largely fixed.

BELIEFS ABOUT TRAITS

As described in Chapter 4, people from collectivistic cultures are more likely to explain a person's behavior as caused by the situation. People from collectivistic cultures place relatively less emphasis, compared to those from individualistic cultures, on dispositional factors. This difference reflects, in part, cross-cultural differences in how individuals view traits. In other words, cultures differ in their beliefs about whether traits predict behavior as well as whether traits stay consistent over time. For example, an American college student would tend to see a

person's behavior, such as study habits, types of friends, and style of dress, as largely determined by his or her internal traits, and would see these traits as predicting behavior over time and across different situations. On the other hand, a college student from a collectivistic culture might see such behavior as heavily influenced by the person's immediate situation, and would therefore not believe such behavior would necessarily continue over time and in different situations.

In one study, researchers examined beliefs about personality in both American and Mexican college students (Church et al., 2003). Participants in both cultures reported holding strong beliefs about the stability of traits. Yet Americans held stronger beliefs about traits than did Mexicans. Specifically, Americans reported greater agreement with statements such as "People who are friendlier now than others will probably remain friendlier than others in the future as well" and "For most persons, success at their job will depend a lot on their personality characteristics." As described at the start of this section, this strong belief about the power of traits leads people from individualistic cultures to make judgments about people's personality much more quickly than those in collectivistic cultures (Zárate et al., 2001).

ANSWER TO THE AVAILABILITY EXERCISE

Did you guess a grey elephant from Denmark? This guess is very common due to reliance on the availability heuristic. The calculation (no matter what number you start with) leads to the number 4. Then, when you are asked to pick a country that start with the letter D, Denmark is the most available answer (although there are other countries one could choose, such as the Dominican Republic, Dominica, and Djibouti). Then, when you are asked to pick a mammal that starts with the second letter of the word ("E" if you've chosen Denmark), elephant is the most available answer (although there are other mammals one could choose, such as an elk or ewe).

SOCIAL COGNITION

This chapter included many applications of the three "big ideas" studied in social psychology. The examples below should help you see the connection between Social Cognition and these big ideas and contribute to your understanding of the big picture of social psychology.

Theme	Examples
The social world influences how we think about ourselves.	• A B+ grade feels much worse when we narrowly miss receiving an A- than when we narrowly miss receiving a B. • We see our performance on videotape more positively if we are in a good mood than if we are in a bad mood. • We see ourselves as less attractive after seeing photographs of highly attractive people of our same gender.
The social world influences our thoughts, attitudes, and behaviors.	• People who are subliminally cued with words related to the elderly walk more slowly than those who are cued with neutral words. • People are much more likely to choose a medical treatment with a 50% success rate than a 50% failure rate. • People are much more influenced by negative information about a political candidate than by positive information.
Our attitudes and behaviors shape the social world around us.	• Men who believe they are talking with an attractive woman elicit more positive behavior from her than those who believe they are talking with a less attractive woman. • People's expectations about the person they are talking to influence the types of questions they ask that person, which in turn confirms their initial expectation. • People whose dating partners treat them as special and unique over time grow to be more like their partners' images of them.

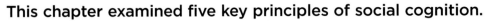

WHAT YOU'VE LEARNED

This chapter examined five key principles of social cognition.

YOU LEARNED **What errors do we make when we think about the world?** The first section described various errors, or shortcuts, we make when we think about the world. These shortcuts include intuition, availability, representativeness, base-rate fallacy, anchoring and adjustment, and counterfactual thinking. And you learned that people are more influenced by articles with catchy titles ("Opposites Attract") than by those with more neutral ones ("Researchers Examine Predictors of Attraction").

YOU LEARNED **How does presentation influence how we think about the world?** The next section examined various errors caused by presentation, and specifically how the same information can be seen very differently when it is described in different ways. We learned specific ways in which presentation can impact judgments, including the contrast effect and framing. This section revealed that spending a lot of time "reading" pornographic magazines makes your own (non-airbrushed) partner seem less sexually appealing, and that people prefer 90% fat-free food to food that is 10% fat.

YOU LEARNED How do we form impressions of people? This chapter also examined factors that influence the impressions we form of other people. These factors include the power of first impressions, the strength of negative information, and implicit personality theories. This section explained why people see those in close relationships as less likely to have an STD than those who are single, even when rates of lifetime sexual behavior are identical.

YOU LEARNED How do beliefs create reality? Next, we examined ways in which people's beliefs can create the reality they expect. These factors include perceptual confirmation, belief perseverance, and behavioral confirmation/self-fulfilling prophecy. You also learned that expecting your child will drink alcohol as a teenager can unfortunately predict whether they do drink.

YOU LEARNED How does culture influence social cognition? Finally, we examined the role of culture in predicting how we think about the world. This section described how culture influences what is easily accessible in our thinking as well as our beliefs about traits. These beliefs about traits lead people from individualistic cultures to make judgments about an individual's personality much more quickly than those from collectivistic cultures.

KEY TERMS

anchoring and adjustment 151	counterfactual thinking 152	perceptual confirmation 165
automatic thinking 146	framing 156	primacy 159
availability heuristic 147	heuristics 146	priming 148
base-rate fallacy 150	hindsight bias 167	representativeness 150
belief perseverance 168	illusory correlation 167	schemas 148
contrast effect 156	implicit personality theory 159	social cognition 146
controlled or effortful thinking 146	intuition 146	trait negativity bias 161

QUESTIONS FOR REVIEW

1. Describe four ways in which shortcuts can lead to errors in thinking about the world.
2. Describe two ways in which presentation influences how we think about the world.
3. Describe how we form impressions of other people, including the role of first impressions as well as the power of negative impressions.
4. Describe two distinct ways in which people's beliefs can create reality, and then two ways in which people can, at times, overcome the power of such beliefs.
5. Describe how one's culture influences both counterfactual thinking and beliefs about traits.

TAKE ACTION!

1. Your boyfriend has to travel across the country this summer for a family reunion. But unfortunately he's very afraid of flying because of the many news stories about the dangers of airplane crashes. What could you tell him about his errors in thinking to provide reassurance?
2. You have a summer internship with an advertising company. Your first assignment is to design a campaign to increase the sales of a new candy bar. How could you use framing to market this product?
3. This semester you are taking a course with Professor Adams, who your roommate warned you is a bad lecturer and an unfair grader. Although so far you have agreed with your roommate, after reading this chapter you are wondering whether some social cognitive biases might have influenced your reaction to this professor. Which biases do you think might be responsible for your negative impression?
4. Think of a time in which your initial expectations of a person may have led to their confirmation. What could you have done differently in this situation to avoid initiating the process of self-fulfilling prophecy?
5. Your sister is spending the summer on an exchange program with a Japanese family. What could you tell her to expect in terms of cultural differences in thinking about the social world?

Try some of these research activities to gain experience in conducting and evaluating research, and to increase your understanding of research methods and techniques in social psychology.

Visit WileyPLUS for more activities and interactive research tools! (www.wileyplus.com)

Participate in Research

Activity 1 The Impact of Counterfactual Thinking: This chapter has described how counterfactual thinking influences how we experience both positive and negative events. To test this theory, go to WileyPLUS to place yourself in a series of scenarios and rate how you think you'd feel in each situation. See if imaging a different outcome matters.

Activity 2 The Influence of Framing: Can the same information presented in a different way really change how we respond to it? Find information that could be presented in different ways in your daily life. Can you see how framing could influence the choices you make?

Activity 3 The Power of First Impressions: Our first impressions of others are surprisingly accurate. To test this idea, go to WileyPLUS to test whether your views of a candidate's competence accurately predict the winner of recent elections.

Activity 4 **The Hazards of Perceptual Confirmation:** How much of an influence do our expectations have on how we see things? Think about the expectations you hold about people based on particular characteristics, such as their sex, hair color, or home state. When interacting with these people, do you pay more attention to information that confirms your stereotypes?

Activity 5 **The Impact of Culture on Social Cognition:** People from different cultures vary in how strongly they believe in the power of people's personal traits. Go to WileyPLUS to rate your agreement with various statements about people's traits and see how people see how people of other cultures rate their own agreement.

Test a Hypothesis

One of the common findings in research on social cognition is that low probability events are much more likely to appear in the media (such as plane crashes and kidnapping) than high probability events (such as car crashes and drowning). To test whether this hypothesis is true, search your newspaper for the frequency of various health risks to see whether some types of events are more commonly reported than others. Bring your results to class or post on your class discussion board to share with others.

Design a Study

To design your own study testing how short-cuts in thinking can lead to errors, decide on a research question you would like to answer. Then decide what type of study you want to conduct (self-report, observational/naturalistic, or experimental), choose your own independent and dependent variables, and operationally define each by determining the procedures or measures you will use. Form a hypothesis to predict what will happen in your study (the expected cause and effect relationship between your two variables) and collect the data. Share what you find with others.

Media
CONNECTIONS
The Dangerous Impact of
Media Images of Smoking
and Alcohol Use

6

Attitude Formation and

WHAT YOU'LL LEARN

How do we form attitudes?

RESEARCH FOCUS ON NEUROSCIENCE
The Power of Negative Information

RESEARCH FOCUS ON GENDER
Gender Differences in Political
Attitudes

When do attitudes predict behavior?

**When does engaging in a behavior lead
to attitude change?**

**What are alternatives to cognitive
dissonance theory?**

**How does CULTURE impact attitude
formation and change?**

Did you ever wonder?

Obesity is a major problem in the United
States. An estimated 54% of adults are
overweight and 22% are obese (Flegal, Carroll,
Kuczmaraki, & Johnson, 1998). Moreover,
among American children ages 6 to 17, 16.5%
are overweight and another 15% are at risk of
becoming overweight (Hedley, Ogden,
Johnson, Carroll, Curtin, & Flegal, 2004). One
of the major contributors to this high rate of
obesity is the constant exposure of children to
unhealthy foods. For example, food and eating
references are presented nearly 5 times every
30 minutes of prime-time television (Story &
Faulkner, 1990). And these food ads aren't
promoting the benefits of fresh apples and
wheat bread. One study revealed that 83% of
the food ads featured during shows children
watch featured convenience/fast foods and
sweets (Harrison & Marske, 2005). In turn,
more than half of 9- to 10-year-old children
believe that Ronald McDonald knows what is
good for children to eat (Horgen, Choate, &
Brownell, 2001). How can we help children
form more positive attitudes about healthy
foods, and more negative attitudes about

Health
CONNECTIONS
How Cognitive Dissonance
Can Lead to Changes in
Health Behavior

Environment
CONNECTIONS
Using Cognitive
Dissonance to Increase
Water Conservation

Education
CONNECTIONS
How Self-Affirmation
Can Increase Academic
Achievement

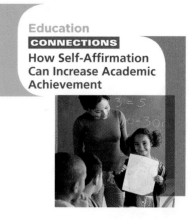

Change

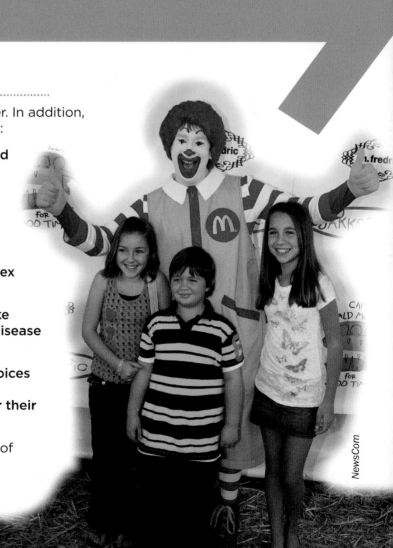

unhealthy ones? You'll find out later in this chapter. In addition, you'll discover answers to the following questions:

Q A Why does describing an elderly woman lead you to oppose sex and nudity on television?

Q A Why do people with prejudiced attitudes often not show prejudiced behavior?

Q A Why might you be really interested in participating in a group discussion on the sex lives of crickets?

Q A Why does describing a love of the arts make some people oppose research on chronic disease prevention?

Q A Why do European Canadians justify the choices they make for themselves, whereas Asian Canadians justify the choices they make for their friends?

What do these questions have in common? All of these describe findings from research in social psychology on attitude formation and change.

NewsCom

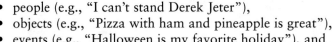

We quickly and constantly form attitudes, defined as the
positive and negative evaluations we hold about

- people (e.g., "I can't stand Derek Jeter"),
- objects (e.g., "Pizza with ham and pineapple is great"),
- events (e.g., "Halloween is my favorite holiday"), and
- ideas (e.g., "I am in favor of the death penalty").

As these examples illustrate, attitudes include three distinct components, namely, affect, cognition, and behavior (Rosselli, Skelly, & Mackie, 1995). Psychologists have long been interested in the link between attitudes and behavior, primarily because we tend to assume that attitudes lead to behavior (e.g., if I have a positive attitude toward President Bush, I will vote for him). But perhaps surprisingly, our attitudes are not always a very good predictor of our behavior (just think back to the resolutions you made last New Year's Eve). In some cases, changing our behavior can lead to changes in our attitudes, not the reverse.

HOW DO WE FORM ATTITUDES?

attitudes positive and negative evaluations of people, ideas, objects, and events

Although you probably don't realize it, attitudes are formed very quickly—and often without conscious awareness. Researchers in one study asked participants to write a description about a particular person, including this person's hobbies, personality traits, and general character (Kawakami, Dovidio, & Dijksterhuis, 2003). Some participants were told to describe an elderly woman and others were asked to describe a young woman. After finishing these descriptions, participants rated their own attitudes toward topics, such as feelings about spending more money on health care and beliefs about whether sex and nudity should be shown on television. As predicted, participants who described an elderly woman reported attitudes that were more consistent with those of elderly people than those who described a young woman. This example describes the impact of classical conditioning, a particular type of learning, on attitude formation. This section will examine ways in which people acquire attitudes—through information, classical conditioning, operant conditioning, and observational learning or modeling.

Information. One of the most common ways in which people form attitudes is through the information they receive from their social environment. Children, for example, often develop their initial attitudes based on the attitudes their parents and other role models express. On the positive side, this means that parents who love books, or enjoy gardening, are likely to pass these attitudes on to their children. On the negative side, this process can lead children to adopt their parents' negative attitudes as well; children who hear their parents express prejudiced views are very likely to adopt these same attitudes. As described in Research Focus on Neuroscience, negative information has a particularly strong impact on our attitudes.

RESEARCH FOCUS ON NEUROSCIENCE
The Power of Negative Information

Although both positive and negative information influences people's evaluations of a given object, negative information seems to have a stronger influence than does positive information—a phenomenon described as the negativity bias (Ito et al., 1998). One of the explanations for the negativity bias is that negative information should be more important to our survival than positive information; we should respond more quickly to painful stimuli, for example, than pleasant ones. In order to test whether the negativity bias occurs even at a neurological level, researchers in one study showed participants positive and negative pictures—such as photos of a bowl of chocolate ice cream and a dead cat, respectively. They then evaluated brain waves to measure electrocortical activity in response to each type of image. As predicted, participants showed larger brain waves, indicating greater brain activity, in response to the negative photos than in response to the positive photos. This research demonstrates that the negativity bias is seen even at a neurological level, which is one explanation for why this bias is so impactful.

CLASSICAL CONDITIONING

Attitudes can also be formed simply based on an association between an object or person and a pleasant or unpleasant event (Cacioppo, Marshall-Goodell, Tassinary, & Petty, 1992; Walther, 2002). This type of learning is called **classical conditioning**, and refers to learning in which a neutral stimulus leads to a given reaction, after it is repeatedly paired with another stimulus that naturally leads to that reaction (see Figure 6.1). As you may remember from your introduction to psychology course, classical conditioning was first demonstrated by Ivan Pavlov in his classic exper-

"They got extinct because they didn't listen to their mommies."

iment showing that dogs will start to salivate simply in response to hearing a bell ring, if that ring repeatedly occurs just before the presentation of food. For example, you may form a positive attitude toward a stranger who is wearing the perfume that your girlfriend wears, simply because you've repeatedly smelled this scent when you've experienced a positive mood (due to the presence of your girlfriend).

One way in which attitudes can be classical conditioned is through the **mere exposure** effect, meaning the more we are exposed to something, the more we like it (Abrams & Greenwald, 2000; Bornstein, 1989; Harmon-Jones & Allen, 2001; Moreland & Zajonc, 1982). Have you ever heard a song on the radio and really disliked it initially, but then, over time, as you hear it again, and again, and again, you actually grow to like it? This is an example of the power of mere exposure. This phenomenon helps explain why we prefer mirror-image pictures of ourselves, because that is how we normally see ourselves—whereas our friends prefer reverse-mirror-imaged pictures of us, because that is normally how they see us (Mita, Dermer, & Knight, 1977).

Although the examples described thus far refer to stimuli that people are exposed to in a conscious way, **subliminal persuasion** is mere exposure that influences liking below the level of consciousness (Bornstein, R. F. (1989), & D'Agostino, 1992; Murphy & Zajonc, 1993; Zajonc, 1968). In one study, participants saw a series of photographs of a woman engaging in various activities (e.g., getting into a car, sweeping a floor, sitting in a restaurant, studying, etc.; Krosnick, Betz, Jussim, & Lynn, 1992). Right before they saw two of the photographs, a picture was flashed subliminally (without the participants even being aware that they had seen it). In some cases, the picture was of something positive (a child with a Mickey Mouse doll, a couple in a romantic setting, a pair of kittens), and in other cases, the picture was of something negative (a bucket of snakes, a dead body on a bed,

classical conditioning a type of learning in which a neutral stimulus is repeatedly paired with a stimulus that elicits a specific response, and eventually the neutral stimulus elicits that response on its own

mere exposure the phenomenon by which the greater the exposure we have to a given stimulus, the more we like it

subliminal persuasion a type of persuasion that occurs when stimuli are presented at a very rapid and unconscious level

FIGURE
6.1

CLASSICAL CONDITIONING

Classical conditioning helps explain why a previously neutral stimulus, such as the smell of a given perfume, initially creates no reaction but over time, through pairing with something that does create a reaction, can lead to that reaction entirely on its own.

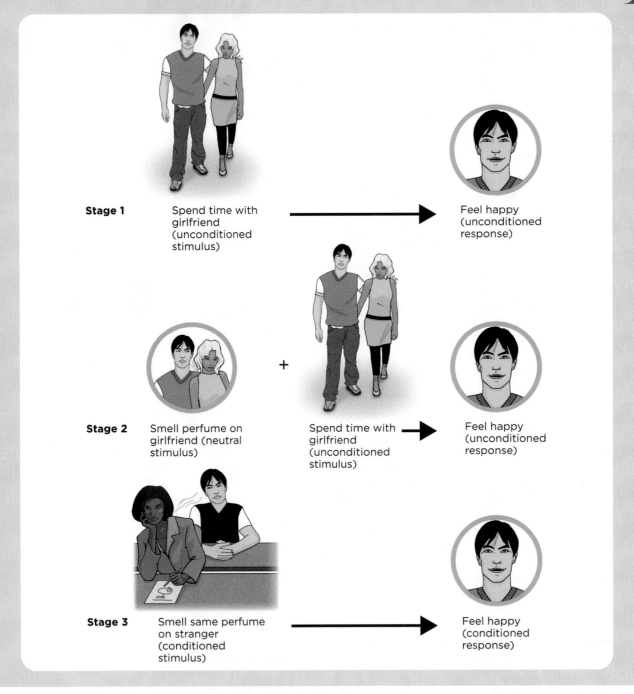

Stage 1   Spend time with girlfriend (unconditioned stimulus) → Feel happy (unconditioned response)

Stage 2   Smell perfume on girlfriend (neutral stimulus) + Spend time with girlfriend (unconditioned stimulus) → Feel happy (unconditioned response)

Stage 3   Smell same perfume on stranger (conditioned stimulus) → Feel happy (conditioned response)

a bloody shark). All participants were then asked to rate their attitude toward the woman and their beliefs about her personality. As predicted, those who saw positive pictures presented right before the pictures of the woman had a more positive attitude toward her than those who saw the negative pictures, even though the participants had no conscious awareness of having seen the pictures (see Figure 6.2).

Subliminal processing can also strengthen the attitudes we already hold. In one study, participants were subliminally primed with words related to either their political ingroup or their outgroup (Ledgerwood & Chaiken, 2007). For example, words that primed the Democrat group included "Democrats," "Bill Clinton," and "John Kerry," and words that primed the Republican group included "Republicans,"

FIGURE
6.2

CAN SUBLIMINAL PRIMING INFLUENCE ATTITUDES?

In this experiment researchers showed participants photos of a woman so quickly they could only perceive them subliminally. They later showed the participants another photo of the woman and asked them about their attitudes toward her and how they would rate her personality. People who saw positive photos subliminally rated the woman's attitudes and personally more positively than people who saw negative photos.

Source: Krosnick, J., Betz, A., Jussim, L., & Lynn, A. (1992). Subliminal conditioning of attitudes. *Personality and Social Psychology Bulletin, 18*, 152–162.

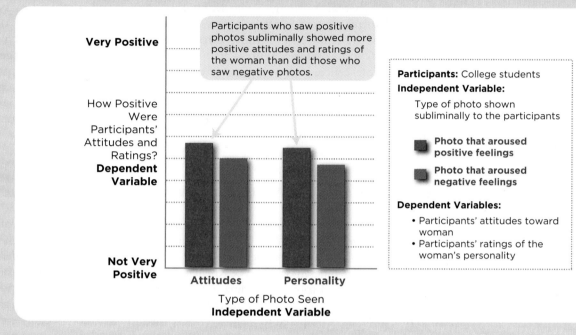

"George Bush," and "Dick Cheney." Participants in the control condition were primed with neutral words, including "headlight," "cork board," and "inhabitant." After the priming, participants rated their agreement with a series of items that reflected either the Democrat or the Republican positions (see Table 6.1). As predicted, participants who were primed with words related to their political ingroup showed higher levels of agreement with the ingroup positions and higher levels of disagreement with the outgroup positions than those who were primed with the neutral words.

TABLE 6.1 — SAMPLE STATEMENTS REFLECTING DEMOCRATS VERSUS REPUBLICANS

Democrat Statements	Republican Statements
"Funding social programs should be the government's top priority."	"The law must protect the lives of unborn babies."
"Gun control needs to be the top priority in our country."	"It is crucial for America to strengthen its defense capabilities."
"People always have a moral duty to look out for those who are less fortunate."	"It is important to find and secure more oil to avoid skyrocketing gas prices."

Source: Ledgerwood, A., & Chaiken, S. (2007). Priming us and them: Automatic assimilation and contrast in group attitudes. *Journal of Personality and Social Psychology, 93*, 940–956.

OPERANT CONDITIONING

Have you ever decided to wear your jeans in a particular way (maybe low-rise, or with a big rip in the knee) because you knew your friends would approve? Most of us have experience with conforming to the attitudes of our peers. This type of conditioning, **operant conditioning**, describes a type of learning in which people are rewarded or punished for engaging in a given behavior (Skinner, 1938). Operant conditioning can also influence attitude formation—and attitude expression. For example, if a little boy who wants a doll for Christmas is ridiculed by his parents, he is likely to form a negative attitude toward dolls, whereas a little girl who wants this present and is praised by her parents will form a positive attitude toward dolls. Parents initially have the power to form the children's attitudes through operant conditioning, which is one reason why most children express attitudes that are similar to those of their parents. By adolescence, however, peers often reward and punish particular attitudes—which is one of the factors that leads to high levels of conformity (e.g., of clothing, music preferences, and behaviors) in this age group. Research Focus on Gender describes gender differences in political attitudes as well as some potential causes of such differences.

RESEARCH FOCUS ON GENDER
Gender Differences in Attitudes Toward Politics

One area in which men and women may differ is in their attitudes toward social and political issues. To investigate gender differences in attitudes toward politics, researchers examined data from a large interview survey of approximately 1,700 respondents (Eagly, Diekman, Johannesen-Schmidt, & Koenig, 2004). Participants were asked their attitudes toward several topics, including gun control, the death penalty, abortion, reducing income differentials between the rich and the poor, gay rights, and the legalization of marijuana. Compared to men, women tended to have more socially compassionate attitudes, such as reducing income differentials between the rich and poor, and more morally traditional attitudes, such as opposing the legalization of marijuana. These differences may be a result of women's greater sense of family obligations and generally lower power in society, meaning they have a greater empathy with those in disadvantaged circumstances and a greater commitment for social equality. Interestingly, these gender differences do not simply line up in terms of liberalism versus conservatism: women are more liberal than men on issues of social compassion and rights, but more conservative than men on issues of traditional morality.

Operant conditioning influences people's attitudes—and behavior. It might even help you in your dating relationship. Researchers in one study examined the level of rewards received by each partner in a dating relationship, such as doing favors for one another, helping with projects, etc. (Berg & McQuinn, 1986). As predicted, couples who exchanged high levels of rewards were more likely to be still dating four months later than those who exchanged few rewards. Similarly, participants completed an activity and were thanked by the experimenter either with a pleasant tone of voice, smile, and direct eye contact (in one condition) or with a more neutral response (in the other condition; Deutsch & Lamberti, 1986). Those who receive the positive reinforcement for their participation were then more likely to later help another person (really a confederate of the experimenter's) when she dropped a pile of books and papers than those who did not receive this reinforcement.

Questioning the Research
This section describes the benefits of operant conditioning in influencing attitudes and behavior. Can you think of a drawback to this approach of influencing attitudes? (Hint: What did you learn in Chapter 3 about the dangers of overjustification?)

OBSERVATIONAL LEARNING/MODELING

Operant conditioning typically involves a direct or conscious transmission of attitudes, but attitudes can be formed in a more subtle way through **observational learning or modeling** (Bandura, 1986). This type of learning occurs when people form attitudes by watching how others act toward a given object, and in turn adopt those views themselves. This is one of the reasons why the frequent television advertisements for fast/convenient foods and sweets contribute to childhood obesity. So children may learn they should have a negative attitude toward broccoli, or a positive attitude toward Twinkies, simply by observing how others feel about these objects. In line with this view, children who are raised by an overweight mother have more positive attitudes toward overweight people, whereas those who are raised by a thin mother have more positive attitudes toward thin people (Rudman, Phelan, & Heppen, 2007). Similarly, children's intentions regarding their future safety

© MirosawTrembecki/PAP/EPA/Corbis

behavior (such as wearing a bicycle helmet, using a seatbelt, and wearing sunscreen) are heavily influenced by their observations of their parents' behavior on these topics (Morrongiello, Corbett, & Bellissimo, 2008).

Modeling is most effective at leading to attitude formation when it is done by someone who is similar to yourself. Why? Because those whom we identify with serve as more effective models for behavior. I experienced the power of a similar model several years ago when observing my older son Andrew learning how to swim. My husband spent several long months asking Andrew to watch him swim various strokes. Andrew would climb into the pool and swim "dog paddle." But he wasn't picking up on any of the swimming strokes. There was mounting frustration on the part of father and son. I signed Andrew up for a swimming class at our local gym. On the first day, Andrew initially resisted going into the water, but he then saw other kids his age who were learning to swim. He then quickly entered the pool and began to practice in earnest. One month later, he was swimming.

Al Bandura of Stanford University used the same strategy to try to help dog-phobic children become more comfortable with dogs (Bandura, Grusec, & Menlove, 1967). Nursery-school-age children who were scared of dogs watched a little boy play with a dog for 20 minutes a day. After only four days, 67% were willing to climb into the playpen with a dog and remain there confined while everyone else left the room. This comfort remained one month later. In fact, this study was even more effective when the children watched television clips that showed children interacting with these dogs.

Observational learning or modeling is most effective when we directly observe our parents, siblings, or friends engage in a behavior. However, it can also work to create attitudes even when we do not know the person who is expressing the attitude or engaging in the behavior (Bandura, 1986). Celebrities and other famous people, for example, are particularly likely to serve as models for our own behavior. When former First Lady Nancy Reagan had a mastectomy after developing breast cancer, many women followed this approach to treating their own disease (Nattinger, Hoffmann, Howell-Pelz, & Goodwin, 1998). One study found that compared to rates from the prior year, women were 25% less likely to undergo a lumpectomy (a breast-conserving surgical alternative to mastectomy) in the 6 months after Nancy Reagan's surgery.

Because attitudes are often influenced by what people observe in the media, including television, movies, and videos, some television campaigns feature celebrities promoting a particular cause, such as the importance of staying in school or engaging in volunteer work. In other cases, story lines on long-running television programs are used to influence people's attitudes. For example, in Mexico nearly one million

"I'm less a role model than a cautionary tale."

people enrolled in a literacy program after watching characters on a popular drama participate in such a program. In one particularly creative use of modeling, a television show targeted toward children in Africa now features an HIV-positive orphan named Kami, who is a Muppet. This character is a normal five-year-old child, who says things such as "I love to tell stories and fly kites. And even though I have HIV, my friends know it's OK to play with me!" Children who watch this show may therefore develop more positive attitudes about people who are infected with HIV. In Tanzania, story lines have emphasized the costs of having too many children, and have encouraged women to adopt methods of birth control. In Kenya, a radio soap opera includes fictional storylines on female circumcision and domestic violence.

On the other hand, the media can also lead to the formation of harmful attitudes. Children who watch more television request more toys than those who watch less television, presumably because more exposure to toy advertisements leads to more positive attitudes toward these products (Chamberlain, Wang, & Robinson, 2006). Non-smoking teenagers who watch movies in which characters smoke show a positive view of smokers' social status as well as greater intentions to smoke, compared to those who see the same films with the smoking edited out (Pechmann & Shih, 1999). The Media Connections box describes some potentially dangerous effects regarding the impact of media images of smoking and alcohol on young children.

Media
CONNECTIONS

The Dangerous Impact of Media Images of Smoking and Alcohol Use

The media play a substantial role in influencing people's attitudes toward smoking and alcohol use, and this influence is particularly impactful for young children. For example, smoking is often portrayed as glamorous and cool, even in films targeted to very young children. One study in the *Journal of the American Medical Association* examined the presence of tobacco products (cigarettes, cigars, and pipes) in 50 G-rated animated children's films, including Bambi, Lady and the Tramp, and The Lion King (Goldstein, Sobel, & Newman, 1999). Tobacco use was portrayed in 56% of the films, including all 7 films released in 1996 and 1997 (the latest years included in the study). "Good characters" were as likely to use tobacco as "bad" ones. Unfortunately, adolescents who view smoking in movies are more likely to start smoking themselves (Dalton et al., 2003). Similarly, television provides numerous examples of the link between fun and drinking (Grube & Wallach, 1994). Alcohol advertisements typically show young, attractive people drinking in appealing settings (e.g., at parties, on the beach, etc.) and having a very good time—they don't show senior citizens drinking while they play shuffle board. One study with 5th and 6th graders found that kids who had more awareness of television beer advertisements (e.g., could identify the type of beer advertised even when its name was blocked) had more favorable beliefs about the consequences of drinking and higher intentions to drink as an adult (Grube & Wallach, 1994). This research shows the strong influence of the media on children's attitudes toward smoking as well as alcohol use.

The Picture Desk

HOW MUCH DO ATTITUDES MATTER?

This section described ways in which attitudes are formed, including relatively direct methods, such as information and operant or instrumental condition. We also covered indirect methods for forming attitudes: mere exposure, classical conditioning, and observational learning or modeling. The Would You Believe feature describes another factor that can influence our attitudes—our genes.

But social psychologists are most interested in attitude formation as a way of predicting what people will do in the future—and as you might guess, our attitudes are not always a very good predictor of our behavior. Most of us are aware of many times in which our attitudes have not predicted our behavior. Early efforts at HIV prevention, for example, focused on providing people with straightforward information about the factors leading to the spread of HIV (e.g., unprotected sex, sharing needles), with the assumption that this information would lead to changes in attitudes, which in turn would lead to changes in behavior. In some cases, providing information led to changes in attitudes, but people's attitudes were often a poor predictor of their behavior. The next section examines when attitudes do, and do not, predict behavior.

WOULD YOU BELIEVE . . .   Our Attitudes Are Rooted in Our Genes?   A growing amount of research in personality psychology demonstrates that our genes can influence various aspects of our behavior, including intelligence and alcoholism. Yet some research in social psychology suggests that our genes can also influence our attitudes (Bouchard, 2004; Tesser, 1993). One study by Amy Abrahamson and her colleagues at the University of Southern California examined adopted and nonadopted children, and their biological and adoptive relatives (Abrahamson, Baker, & Caspi, 2002). Abrahamson's research asked the question, "Did these children hold certain religious attitudes or conservative ideas because of their genetics or their upbringing?" The findings suggest genetic factors have a strong impact on children's conservatism by age 12, and by age 15 are even a stronger influence than environmental factors on such attitudes.

Another study with pairs of adult twins revealed genetic factors influence a wide variety of attitudes, including attitudes toward support for the death penalty, enjoyment of roller coaster rides, and interest in playing organized sports (Olson, Vernon, Harris, & Jang, 2001). Although the exact genetic mechanism that influences attitudes is unknown, researchers believe broad genetic characteristics, such as sensation seeking and cognitive reasoning, may be responsible for these effects. In other words, our general genetic tendencies toward particular types of behaviors , such as a preference for highly arousing activities (e.g., rock climbing, car racing) , in turn may influence more specific attitudes.

HOW ATTITUDES ARE FORMED

Concepts in Context

METHOD OF ATTITUDE FORMATION	EXAMPLE
Information	Talia forms a love of the Mets because her parents are dedicated fans of the Mets.
Classical conditioning	You feel happy whenever you smell cinnamon because you associate this scent with your grandmother's kitchen.
Operant conditioning	Evan develops a negative attitude toward the pink bicycle he wanted after his grandmother ridicules that preference.
Observational learning/modeling	Jack forms a positive view of cigarettes because his older sister smokes.

WHEN DO ATTITUDES PREDICT BEHAVIOR?

In a classic study of the gap between attitudes and behavior, Richard LaPiere (1934), a sociologist at Stanford University in the 1930s, traveled around the United States with a young Chinese couple. During the time of LaPiere's study, widespread prejudice against Chinese people was quite common, and many restaurant and hotel managers expressed negative attitudes toward Chinese people. To test how well these attitudes would predict behavior, LaPiere took this couple on a 10,000-mile trip throughout the United States, which included visits to 251 restaurants, campgrounds, and hotels. What happened? In all 184 restaurants, the Chinese couple was accepted—and they were received with considerable hospitality in 72 of the restaurants. In visits to 66 hotels, they were refused only once. Two months after the trip, LaPiere wrote to all of the places they had visited and asked whether they would accept Chinese patrons. Of those who responded, 91% said they would not accept such guests, even though such a couple had clearly been served within the last few months. This study shows that the attitude-behavior link is not always as strong as we think. What are the factors that influence the attitude-behavior link? This section will examine each of these factors: strength, accessibility, specificity, and social norms.

STRENGTH

Attitudes vary in their strength, and strong attitudes are more likely to predict behavior than weak ones (Kraus, 1995; Krosnick, Boninger, Chuang, Berent, & Carnot, 1993). Stronger attitudes are highly important to the person, and are often formed on the basis of direct experience. Let's take a look at each of these elements.

Importance.   First, and not surprisingly, attitudes on topics that are highly *important* to us are more predictive of our behavior (see photo 6.7; Crano, 1997). Many people believe that children learn better in high-quality schools, and that having high-quality schools is important for our society. However, people who have young children who are in school, or will soon be in school, are probably more likely to act on these attitudes (e.g., vote to pay higher taxes, donate money to local school districts, etc.) than those who will not be affected directly by the quality of schools in their area. Similarly, 23.7% of people who see global warming as an important issue report contributing money on behalf of this cause, compared to only 8% of those who do not see this as an important issue (Visser, Krosnick, & Simmons, 2003).

Direct experience.   Second, attitudes that are formed on the basis of *direct experience* are likely to be stronger attitudes and therefore are a better predictor of behavior (Fazio & Zanna, 1981; Millar & Millar, 1996; Regan & Fazio, 1977). For example, if I ask you about your attitude toward reporting to the professor a student who you saw cheating on a final exam, your attitude will be more predictive of your behavior (meaning that your positive attitude would predict reporting, and your negative attitude would predict not reporting) if you have actually been in a situation in which you saw someone cheat and had to decide what to do. If you've never been in this situation, you might believe that you'd act in a certain way, but it is more difficult to predict what you'd do in reality.

In one study on the impact of direct experience on the attitude-behavior link, Russell Fazio and Mark Zanna (1981) gave two groups of participants a set of puzzles. One group actually worked on solving them, and the other group watched someone else work on them. Participants then rated their attitudes toward the puzzles, and were given 15 minutes to work on the puzzles. The link between attitudes and behavior was much stronger for those who had actually worked on the puzzles than those who had only watched (a .53 correlation versus only a .21 correlation). In the case of LaPiere's study, many people with negative attitudes toward Chinese people probably had never met a Chinese person, so their attitude was not

©AP/Wide World Photos

Mohamed Atta. Attitudes that are rooted in moral conviction are particularly strong, and therefore quite likely to influence behavior. This is one explanation for the willingness of those, such as the 9/11 terrorists, who feel very strongly about a given cause to martyr themselves for that particular cause. *(Skitka, Bauman, & Sargis, 2005).*

a good predictor of their behavior. Their image of Chinese people may have been very different from the Chinese people that were in front of them.

ACCESSIBILITY

The *ease* or *accessibility* with which one's attitude comes to mind can also influence the attitude-behavior link (Krosnick, 1989). People who are well-informed about a topic are likely to have greater attitude-behavior consistency than those who are poorly informed, because having a lot of information about a topic increases the accessibility of attitudes about this topic. For example, if I ask you to think about various political issues (e.g., abortion, capital punishment, global warming), the attitudes that come more quickly to your mind are likely to be a better predictor of your behavior toward these attitudes than if it takes some time for you to recall what you think about such issues. But for people with less accessible attitudes, when they encounter the attitude object (such as the Chinese couple), they may act before they have had time to access their attitudes and then their behavior won't be in line with these attitudes.

Situational factors can also influence accessibility, and in turn the attitude-behavior link. As described in Chapter 3, situational factors that increase self-awareness can lead people to engage in behavior that is in line with their attitudes, perhaps in part because factors that increase self-awareness may also increase the accessibility of one's attitude. For example, participants who are given a chance to think about their past behaviors prior to expressing their attitudes later show a higher correlation between these attitudes and their subsequent behavior (Zanna, Olson, & Fazio, 1981). Those who watch themselves in a mirror—which presumably reminds people of their own positive attitude toward honesty—engage in more moral behavior (Batson et al., 1999). Simply asking someone to express his or her attitude repeatedly increases accessibility of that attitude, which in turn should increase the likelihood that this attitude will predict behavior (Holland, Verplanken, & van Knippenberg, 2003).

On the other hand, situational factors that decrease self-awareness, and/or impair cognition, can weaken the attitude-behavior link (MacDonald, MacDonald, Zanna, & Fong, 2000; MacDonald et al., 1995). Tara MacDonald and her colleagues at the University of Waterloo conducted a study on the effects of alcohol use on intentions to use condoms (MacDonald, Zanna, & Fong, 1996). Fifty-four male undergraduates were randomly assigned to either the sober or the intoxicated condition. Those in both conditions watched a video and then answered some questions, but those in the intoxicated condition were first given three alcoholic drinks. (For those of you who are suddenly very interested in participating in psychology research, let me assure you that this study was conducted in Ontario, Canada, where the

"Susan, this might be just the wine talking,
but I think I want to order more wine."

drinking age is 19.) The 10-minute video featured a couple of undergraduates, Mike and Rebecca, who meet at a campus bar, dance and drink with friends, and then walk home to Rebecca's apartment. Mike and Rebecca then begin "hooking up," at which point they discuss that neither of them has condoms, and the only nearby store has recently closed. Rebecca discloses that she is on the pill, so pregnancy prevention is not the issue. At this point the video stops, and students are then asked to answer a series of questions as if they were experiencing the situations in the video.

The findings of this study provide strong (and scary) evidence for how alcohol impairs decision making. First, both sober and intoxicated students saw having unprotected sex in this situation as foolish. On a scale of 1 to 9, sober students rated this behavior as extremely foolish (8.08) as did intoxicated students (7.67). Similarly, sober students rated this behavior as extremely irresponsible (8.04) as did intoxicated students (7.83). However, while sober participants were fairly unlikely to report they would engage in sex in this situation (3.83), drunk students were very likely to report that they would indeed have sex in this situation (6.78). In fact, only 21% of the sober participants reported that they were even fairly likely to have sex in this situation, whereas 77% of the drunk participants did so. Although this study does not test what students would actually do in this situation, it suggests that alcohol use may lead people to engage in behavior that they recognize as foolish and irresponsible. Thus, in cases in which people are not so focused on or aware of their actual attitudes, people are less likely to show a strong correlation between their attitudes and behavior.

SPECIFICITY

Consider what might have happened if LaPiere had included a photograph of the young, well-dressed Chinese couple when he asked whether the restaurants and hotels would serve this particular couple. Would the link between attitudes and behaviors have been stronger? It is very likely. But why is this true? Attitudes toward a specific behavior show a stronger link to behavior than attitudes that are more general (Ajzen & Fishbein, 1977). The correlation between the attitude "how do you feel about using condoms?" and actual condom use is a lot lower than the correlation between the attitude "how do you feel about using condoms every time you have sex in the next month when you are with a new partner?" and actual condom use (Sheeran, Abraham, & Orbell, 1999).

SOCIAL NORMS

Social norms, meaning the informal rules a given group has for its members, can also influence whether our attitudes predict our behavior, in part because our behavior is often heavily influenced by others in our group (Trafimow & Finlay, 1996). For example, you may have a negative attitude toward smoking (and I certainly hope that you do), but you may choose to smoke when you are with certain friends who smoke. You may do this because you are worried that if you refuse to smoke, it will offend them, or you might be ridiculed. Social norms about a particular attitude are also more likely to lead to behavior because attitudes that are held by those in our social network are stronger, and thus more resistant to change (Visser & Mirabile, 2004). In terms of LaPiere's study, people's willingness to serve the Chinese couple might have been more strongly predicted by their attitudes if the social norms against Chinese people were particularly powerful.

Your attitude toward smoking might be negative. But you still might choose to smoke when with friends who smoke.

In one study, researchers examined the impact of exposure to sexual content on television on adolescents' perceived social norms regarding sexual activity (Martino, Collins, Kanouse, Elliott, & Berry, 2005). As predicted, adolescents who reported watching television shows that included high levels of sexual content (such as *Friends*, *Dawson's Creek*, and *Sex in the City*) believed that more of their friends were sexually active. Most importantly, adolescents who believed that more of their friends were sexually active were more likely to report engaging in sexual activity themselves one year later.

Two theories that emphasize the role of social norms in predicting behavior are the theory of planned behavior and the prototype/willingness model:

Theory of planned behavior. As shown in Figure 6.3, the **theory of planned behavior** developed by Icek Ajzen and Martin Fishbein (1977) describes behavior as influenced by *intentions*, meaning whether a person plans to engage in a given behavior. Intentions, in turn, are influenced by a combination of *attitudes* (positive or negative feelings about engaging in a particular behavior), *subjective norms* (individuals' beliefs about whether other people would support them in engaging in a new behavior), and *perceived behavior control* (the extent to which one believes he or she can successfully enact a behavior.) (See Rate Yourself for an example of how to rate one's perceived behavioral control, or self-efficacy.) For example, whether you wear sunscreen each time you go to the beach is influenced by whether you intend to wear sunscreen. These intentions, in turn, are influenced by your attitudes (how positively or negatively you feel

theory of planned behavior a theory that describes people's behavior as caused by their attitudes, subjective norms, and perceived behavioral control

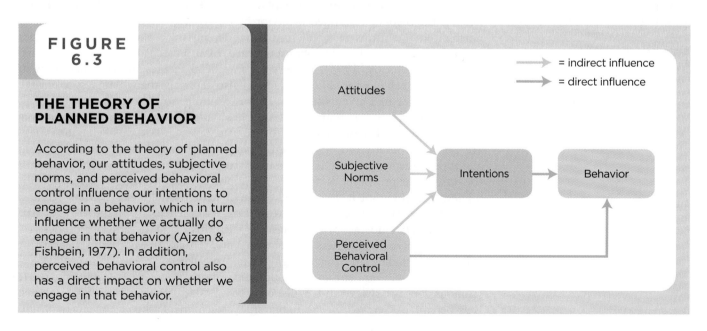

FIGURE 6.3

THE THEORY OF PLANNED BEHAVIOR

According to the theory of planned behavior, our attitudes, subjective norms, and perceived behavioral control influence our intentions to engage in a behavior, which in turn influence whether we actually do engage in that behavior (Ajzen & Fishbein, 1977). In addition, perceived behavioral control also has a direct impact on whether we engage in that behavior.

= indirect influence

= direct influence

Attitudes

Subjective Norms

Intentions

Behavior

Perceived Behavioral Control

The Condom Use Self-Efficacy Scale

INSTRUCTIONS: *These questions ask about your own feelings about using condoms in specific situations. Rate each item on the following scale: strongly disagree = 0, disagree = 1, undecided = 2, agree = 3, strongly agree = 4.*

☐ **1.** I feel confident in my ability to put a condom on myself or my partner.

☐ **2.** I feel confident in my ability to suggest using condoms with a new partner.

☐ **3.** I feel confident that I could remember to use a condom even after I have been drinking.

☐ **4.** I feel confident that I could stop to put a condom on myself or my partner even in the heat of passion.

☐ **5.** I feel confident in my ability to persuade a partner to accept using a condom when we have intercourse.

☐ **6.** I feel confident in my ability to use a condom correctly.

☐ **7.** I feel confident I could purchase condoms without feeling embarrassed.

☐ **8.** I feel confident that I could use a condom with a partner without "breaking the mood."

☐ **9.** I feel confident I could remember to carry a condom with me should I need one.

☐ **10.** I feel confident I could use a condom during intercourse without reducing any sexual sensations.

SCORING: Sum up your total number of points on all 10 items.

INTERPRETATION: This scale measures condom use self-efficacy, meaning confidence that one could effectively use condoms. People with higher scores are more confident in their ability to carry out this behavior, whereas those with lower scores are less confident (Brafford & Beck, 1991).

about wearing sunscreen), your subjective norms (how you think your friends and parents will feel about your wearing sunscreen), and your perceived behavioral control (your confidence in your own ability to actually put on sunscreen).

The theory of planned behavior is a particularly strong predictor of behavior when that behavior is relatively easy for a person to control (e.g., taking vitamins, voting, having a mammogram; Madden, Ellen, & Ajzen, 1992). This theory is less effective, however, at predicting more spontaneous behavior (e.g., smoking a cigarette at a party, putting on a seat belt, using a condom).

prototype/willingness model a model that describes the role of prototypes, or social images of what people who engage in the behavior are like, in influencing their willingness to engage in the behavior in a given situation

Prototype/willingness model. The **prototype/willingness model** extends the theory of planned behavior by describing not only the role of social norms and intentions in predicting behavior, but also the role of prototypes (Gibbons & Gerard, 1995; Gibbons, Gerrard, Blanton, & Russell, 1998; Gibbons, Gerrard, & McCoy, 1995). Prototypes are social images of what people who engage in the behavior are like. This model also describes the willingness to engage in the behavior in a given situation. If, for example, you see students who drink and drive as rather stupid and careless, you should be less likely to engage in this behavior yourself because your prototype of people who do this behavior is negative. On the other hand, if you see people who drink and drive as rather daring and independent, you may be more likely to engage in this behavior because, in this case, your prototype is positive. An important feature of the prototype/willingness model is that it describes the role of people's willingness to engage in a particular behavior. This willingness, in turn, is influenced by an individual's attitudes, subjective norms, prior experience with this behavior, and prototypes.

The prototype/willingness model is a good predictor of various health-risk behaviors, including smoking, engaging in unprotected sexual intercourse, and exercising (Blanton, VandenEijnden, Buunk, Gibbons, Gerrard, & Bakker, 2001; Gibbons, Gerrard, Cleveland, Wills, & Brody, 2004; Ouellete, Hessling, Gibbons, Reis-Bergan, & Gerrard, 2005). In one study, researchers asked teenagers to "think for a minute about the type of person your age who drinks alcohol frequently," and then rate your image of that person (e.g., smart, popular, boring, self-confident, independent, confused, etc.; Gerrard, Gibbons, Reis-Bergan, Trudeau, Vande Lune, & Buunk, 2002). Next, the participants rated their own willingness to drink alcohol in various situations. As predicted, those who did not drink alcohol rated the drinker prototype more negatively than those who did drink. This suggests that helping teenagers form negative images about those who choose to drink may be one avenue for decreasing underage drinking.

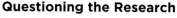

Questioning the Research

Most of the research on the prototype/willingness model has collected data on teenagers and young adults. Do you think this model would apply equally well to predicting behavior in older populations? Why or why not?

WHY (AND WHEN) ATTITUDES DO MATTER

This section described factors that influence the link between people's attitudes and their behavior. By understanding these factors, we can make a better guess about when a person's attitude will predict his or her behavior, and when it will not. Researchers can design strategies for increasing these factors as a way of changing someone's behavior. For example, the knowledge that accessibility of an attitude is an important predictor of behavior could lead health educators to design promotional materials (e.g., brochures, posters, signs, etc.) that are designed to increase the accessibility of various attitudes (e.g., driving sober, using condoms, smoking, etc.).

Concepts in Context

FACTORS INFLUENCING THE ATTITUDE-BEHAVIOR LINK

FACTOR	EXAMPLE
Strength	Reggie, who feels very passionately about the death penalty, is quite likely to volunteer his time with an organization devoted to this cause.
Accessibility	Although E.J. believes that it is a good idea to vote, he wasn't sure if he was going to make the time to vote in the presidential election. However, on Election Day, he was repeatedly asked by others whether he had voted, which finally led him to make a trip to his local polling place.
Specificity	Anna's attitude toward studying on a Saturday night while her friends are partying is a much stronger predictor of her studying behavior on Saturday night than her general attitude toward studying.
Social norms	Stefan's negative attitude toward drinking and driving typically leads him to refuse to drive after drinking. However, when he is with his high school friends, who do not share this attitude, he sometimes drives after drinking.

WHEN DOES ENGAGING IN A BEHAVIOR LEAD TO ATTITUDE CHANGE?

Although we often describe attitudes as leading to behavior, at least under some circumstances, the link between attitudes and behavior can go in both ways. In other words, in some cases our behavior can lead to our attitudes. In one of the first studies to demonstrate how effort justification can lead to attitude change, Elliott Aronson and Judson Mills (1959) conducted a study with college women on the impact of severity of initiation on liking for a group. Women were invited to participate in a discussion group on sex (which was seen as an exciting thing to do), but in order to be in the group, you had to go through a sort-of initiation (this initiation was supposedly just to make sure that everyone in the group would be comfortable talking). In the mild initiation condition, women read a list of 12 sexually oriented words (petting, kissing, necking)—a somewhat embarrassing task, but one that was not particularly unpleasant. In the severe initiation condition, on the other hand, participants read a list of highly sexually oriented words as well as two vivid sexual passages from various novels. Participants in the control condition got to be in the group without any initiation. Then, all participants were given headphones to listen to a portion of the group discussion (supposedly to prepare them for their own participation the following week). What did they hear? A very boring discussion of "secondary sex behavior in lower animals." But what did the women in the different conditions think? As predicted, those who had endured a lot to get into the group (the severe condition) liked the group discussion more than those in either of the other groups. In this section we will examine ways that behavior changes attitudes. First, we examine a very famous theory in social psychology, cognitive dissonance theory, and then describe revisions to this theory.

COGNITIVE DISSONANCE THEORY

cognitive dissonance theory a theory that describes attitude change as occurring in order to reduce the unpleasant arousal people experience when they engage in a behavior that conflicts with their attitude or when they hold two conflicting attitudes

One of the best-known and important theories in social psychology is **cognitive dissonance theory**, which was developed by Leon Festinger (Festinger, 1957). According to this theory, when a person holds two conflicting cognitions or engages in a behavior that conflicts with a cognition, he or she experiences a very unpleasant psychological state of arousal (or dissonance). Imagine that you are a member of a student organization that encourages recycling, but one day you toss an empty soda can into the nearest trashcan instead of carrying that can until you find a recycling bin (see Figure 6.4). This act should create the state of cognitive dissonance because you've engaged in a behavior (e.g., throwing a can into a trashbin) that is not in line with your attitude (e.g., recycling is very important).

FIGURE 6.4

COGNITIVE DISSONANCE THEORY

According to cognitive dissonance theory, engaging in an act that is not in line with your behavior creates unpleasant arousal, or dissonance, which can then lead you to change your attitude to match your behavior (Festinger, 1957).

In the NEWS **The Iraq War.** At the start of the Iraq war, most Americans supported this war because they believed that Iraq had weapons of mass destruction. However, once later information revealed that Iraq did not in fact have such weapons, many people continued to justify their original attitude, either by saying that Iraq could eventually have developed them or that liberating the Iraqi people from Saddam Hussein was also a good reason for going to war. People have difficulty admitting that their attitudes were wrong, and hence once they've stated an attitude, they often find ways to continue to justify that attitude as the correct one.

According to Leon Festinger (1957), people are highly motivated to reduce the arousal caused by holding inconsistent attitudes, or engaging in counter-attitudinal behavior. But how can we reduce such arousal? One way is by changing our behavior so that it is in line with our attitudes (e.g., you could go back and put the can in the recycling bin). However, it is often hard to "undo" behaviors once we've done them, and hence this method of reducing dissonance is relatively uncommon.

Another way to reduce the unpleasant arousal caused by inconsistency is to decide that this inconsistency isn't really a problem, because these attitudes and/or behaviors aren't very important (Simon, Greenberg, & Brehm, 1995). For example, if you engage in some type of counter-attitudinal behavior under conditions of high choice, then later you see your attitude and behavior as less important (e.g., well, I smoke, but that's not nearly as dangerous as driving without my seat belt). However, this strategy of *trivialization* isn't used very often because it isn't as effective with highly important decisions (e.g., "well, it really doesn't matter who I marry").

Finally, and most commonly, we can reduce feelings of inconsistency by changing our attitudes to match our behavior, or by changing one attitude to match another. For example, once you have stated an attitude—or engaged in a behavior—that goes against an attitude you hold, you are likely to change your initial attitude so that you feel consistent. If a smoker is trying to quit but she relapses, later she may see smoking as less risky (Gibbons, Eggleston, & Benthin, 1997). This section will examine four distinct ways that we might change our attitudes: insufficient justification, insufficient deterrence, effort justification, and post-decision dissonance.

Insufficient justification.   The first study to demonstrate the impact of cognitive dissonance on attitude change was conducted by Leon Festinger and his colleague Merrill Carlsmith (1959). Participants came into the lab to participate in a study on performance and were given an extremely boring task to complete: they were asked to move each of 48 spools of thread a 1/4 turn in one direction, then another 1/4 turn, then 1/4 turn, and then back again to their starting position, for an entire hour. Then, after participants were finally told they were finished with the experiment, the experimenter asked them for a favor. He explained that this task was not really on "measures of performance," as they had been told, but was actually on the influence of expectations about a task on how people see the task. Because the participant was in the control condition, he was not given any prior expectation about what to expect, but the next participant, who is supposed to arrive any minute, is in the "positive expectation" condition. However, the research assistant who is supposed to give the next student the positive expectations seems to be running late, and hence the experimenter asked if the participant would be willing to stay and just tell the next participant that the experiment is really fun and exciting. Some of the participants were offered $20

FIGURE
6.5

CAN RECEIVING A SMALL REWARD LEAD TO GREATER ENJOYMENT?

In a classic experiment, Festinger & Carlsmith (1959) had participants do a boring task. Then they paid each one to tell the next participant that the experiment was enjoyable. According to a behaviorist model, those who were paid $20 should find the task more enjoyable than those who were paid only $1. However, these findings showed the reverse: Participants who were paid $1 enjoyed participating in the study more than those who were paid $20, providing support for cognitive dissonance theory.

Source: Festinger, L., & Carlsmith, J. (1959). Cognitive consequences of forced compliance. *The Journal of Abnormal and Social Psychology, 58*, 203–210.

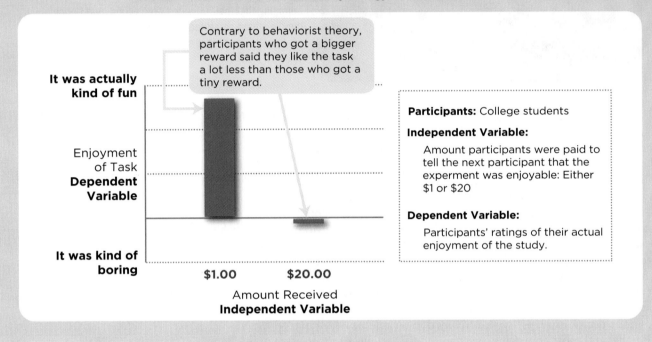

to lie to the next participants, whereas others were only offered $1 to tell this lie. All participants agreed to lie, and after doing so, they were asked by the experimenter what they thought of the experiment (on a 1-to-25 scale, in which 1 is very unenjoyable).

What do you think happened? Contrary to reward theory, those who were given $20 admit they found the task boring, as do those who were given no money. But what about those who are given the $1 to lie? As shown in Figure 6.5, they actually claimed they sort of liked the task!

This experiment demonstrates that receiving insufficient justification for engaging in an attitude-discrepant behavior leads to attitude change. In other words, if you engage in a behavior that is counter-attitudinal, you must make some kind of a justification. If the external justification is high ("well, I did get $20"), you will attribute your behavior to external factors and not change your attitude ("boy, that task really was boring), but if the external justification is low, people must explain their behavior using internal factors ("well, I must have at least liked the task a little").

Although the Festinger and Carlsmith (1959) study demonstrated the negative effects of insufficient justification—that is, that people convince themselves they like something they didn't really enjoy—this principle can also be used to promote positive behaviors. For example, Michael Leippe and Donna Eisenstadt (1994) found that asking White students to write an essay in favor of a policy doubling funds for academic scholarships for African American students (at the cost of such scholarships for White students) led the students to become more supportive of this policy. Similarly, and as described in the Health Connections box, cognitive dissonance can be used to promote health behavior change.

How Cognitive Dissonance Can Lead to Changes in Health Behavior

Jeff Stone and his colleagues at the University of California at Santa Cruz conducted a study using cognitive dissonance theory to change people's health-related behavior (Stone, Aronson, Crain, Winslow, & Fried, 1994). Seventy-two sexually active college students participated in a study on health and persuasion. Students were asked to write a persuasive speech about the importance of safer sex as a way of preventing HIV, and half of these students were then videotaped giving this speech (which would supposedly be shown to high school students). Finally, half of the students in each of these two conditions were asked to make a list of the times they had failed to use condoms in the past, as a way of making them feel hypocritical about their past behavior. Students who were made to publicly advocate the importance of using condoms and who were reminded of their own past failures to use condoms (which should create a feeling of dissonance) bought more condoms than those in the other conditions. In fact, 83% of the students in this condition bought condoms, but only 33 to 50% of students in the other conditions bought condoms.

More recent research used principles of cognitive dissonance theory to prevent eating disorders (Stice, Mazotti, Weibel, & Agras, 2000; Stice, Chase, Stormer, & Appel, 2001; Stice, Trost, & Chase, 2003). In one study, 148 adolescent girls (ages 13 to 20) were recruited from local high schools and universities to participate in a study on helping women improve their body image (Stice et al., 2003). Participants were then randomly assigned to a dissonance intervention group, a healthy weight control intervention group, or a control condition. Those in the dissonance group completed several activities designed to make participants aware of the inconsistency between their own attitudes (which were negative about their own body image) and their behavior as part of the group (which focused on helping other women avoid developing a negative body image). For example, they discussed how to help other women avoid body image problems, as well as the nature and consequences of the thin ideal portrayed in the media.

They also role played trying to convince someone not to adopt the thin ideal, and wrote an essay about the costs associated with the pursuit of the thin ideal. Findings at the three-month follow-up indicated that girls who received either the dissonance-based intervention or the healthy weight control intervention (who received general information on strategies for healthy eating and exercise) reported fewer bulimic symptoms than those in the control condition (who did not receive any information).

Getty Images, Inc.

Insufficient deterrence/punishment. Although offering an insufficient reward for a behavior is one way of creating attitude change, such change can also occur if you offer an insufficient deterrence for not doing something desirable (Aronson & Carlsmith, 1963; Freedman, 1965). In one study, children were brought into the lab and shown a bunch of toys. Most of the toys were pretty common (e.g., blocks, dolls, Etch-A-Sketch, etc.), but there was one really cool toy: Robby the Robot. Robby the Robot walked by himself, moved his arms, and made a noise, and this toy was novel for all of the children. After showing the children all of the toys, the experimenter said he needed to go get something from another room and he'd be back in five minutes. In one condition, he told the children that they could play with any of the toys except Robbie the Robot, and that if they played with Robbie, they would be in big trouble (severe deterrent). In the other condition, they were told to just play with any of the toys they wanted, except Robbie. What happened? Well, all children did avoid playing with Robbie the Robot, but when they were asked to rate the toys at the end of the study, evidence for self-persuasion occurred. As expected, those who received the severe threat still liked Robbie lots, but those who received only a mild threat didn't report liking Robbie that much at all. This study therefore shows the effect of *insufficient deterrence* on leading to attitude change.

The effects of insufficient deterrence on attitude change last over time. Six weeks after children participated in the "Robby the Robot" study, a different experimenter brought the same children into the lab to participate in a new study on creativity in drawing (Freedman, 1965). While she was scoring their drawing test, she said they could play with any toy in the room, including the robot. Of those who previously had received the strong threat, 77% played with the robot now, yet only 33% of those who previously had received the mild threat played with the robot. These findings suggest that the attitude change produced by the mild threat condition was indeed long-lasting and internally based.

Effort justification.   Have you ever spent a lot of time and energy on something and then ultimately achieved it, but found it wasn't worth the effort? Well, you probably haven't had this experience. Why? Because this kind of inconsistency arouses cognitive dissonance. So if you have this feeling, you work quickly to justify the effort you spent. This was demonstrated by the research described at the start of this section showing the impact of mild versus severe initiations on interest in participating in a (surprisingly boring) sex discussion group. Similarly, in a more recent study, students who are asked to perform an embarrassing task—in this case walking across a campus quad wearing a grass skirt, coconut bra, and hat featuring plastic fruit—estimate that the distance they have to travel is less under conditions of high choice than under conditions of low choice (Balcetis & Dunning, 2007). Our desire to justify our effort, and thus avoid the uncomfortable experience of cognitive dissonance, explains a variety of real-world phenomena, including why we stay in bad relationships far too long, why people are so attached to their fraternity/sorority, and why contestants on television report this highly embarrassing experience was so worthwhile.

Given what we know about cognitive dissonance, it shouldn't surprise you that people who have appeared on *Fear Factor* and other reality television shows are very likely to feel good about the experience—no matter what they had to suffer through at the time.

In line with the predictions of research on effort justification, simply forcing someone to undergo a challenging task can facilitate attitude and behavior change. One study with overweight participants examined the impact of engaging in high versus low effortful tasks on weight loss (Axsom & Cooper, 1985). Participants in this study completed several tasks that were completely unrelated to weight loss, but were high in effort in one condition and low in effort in the other condition. In the high effort condition, participants viewed a series of very similar (and nearly vertical) lines, determined which line is the most vertical, recited nursery rhymes, read a short story, and said the Pledge of Allegiance into a microphone, while they simultaneously listened to their own voices reflected back to them in earphones (a very difficult task). In contrast, those who engaged in easier versions of these tasks participated for much less time (13 minutes versus 50 minutes). However, those who completed the high effortful task lost an

Environment

Using Cognitive Dissonance to Increase Water Conservation

Eliot Aronson and his colleagues conducted a clever study in which they used cognitive dissonance to increase water conservation (Dickerson, Thibodeau, Aronson, & Miller, 1992). Female swimmers were asked to help with a water conservation project as they exited the pool and headed to the locker room. In one condition, participants were asked several questions about water conservation, including whether they took as short showers as they could. They were also asked to sign a flyer stating that they took short showers. In another condition, participants were asked the questions about water conservation and were asked to sign the flyer. Finally, in the control condition, participants did not answer questions or sign the flyer. Female researchers then followed the women into the locker room and surreptitiously timed the length of their showers. As predicted, participants who both signed the flyer and answered the questions took significantly shorter showers than those who did neither of these acts (220.5 seconds versus 301.8 seconds). Participants who did only one act (signed the flyer or answered questions) took showers that were midway between those in the control condition and those who completed both acts (148 seconds in both conditions). These findings demonstrate that reminding people of their past behavior that conflicts with their attitude (meaning that they have taken long showers but are in favor of water conservation) encourages behavior change (meaning shorter showers).

iStockphoto

average of 8.55 pounds at the six-month follow-up whereas those who completed the low effortful task showed no weight change. Similar results were found for those who were highly snake phobic and who anticipated voluntarily undertaking a high effort task involving snakes (Axsom, 1989; Cooper, 1980). The Environment Connections box describes yet another way in which cognitive dissonance theory can lead to behavior change.

Justifying decisions/postdecision dissonance. People often have to make difficult decisions, and after they do so, they may experience some dissonance because choosing one appealing option also means giving up another appealing option (Harmon-Jones & Harmon-Jones, 2002; Schultz, Léveillé, & Lepper, 1999; Simon, Krawczyk, & Holyoak, 2004). For example, people who are asked to choose between two jobs (each of which has some good features and some bad features) initially rate these jobs as rather equal in appeal (Simon et al., 2004). Once they have been forced to select one option—and reject the other—however, the difference in liking between the two jobs becomes significantly greater, as people justify their decision. Similarly, if you are torn between buying one of two cars, each of which has some pluses and some minuses, after you have bought one of the cars you may experience some discomfort because in making this decision you are very aware of what you have given up in the process.

People often resolve this dissonance by changing their attitudes toward both of the alternatives as a way of reducing this discomfort (Brownstein, Read, & Simon, 2004). Specifically, people increase their positive feelings toward the alternative they have chosen (e.g., "I am so happy driving this SUV because I feel so safe"). At the

Do you own an SUV? If so, you probably have convinced yourself that this vehicle is safer, even when objective evidence is less convincing.

same time, people increase their negative feelings toward the alternative they have rejected (e.g., "I can't believe anyone buys a mini-van; they just look so dorky"). Amazingly enough, this decrease in liking for highly rated alternatives we have rejected is seen in children as young as four years old and even in monkeys (Egan, Santos, & Bloom, 2007). This finding that attitude change occurs following rejection of an alternative even in these populations suggests that the drive to reduce dissonance may be a fundamental aspect of human psychology that occurs even without extensive experience in decision making and the ability to engage in highly sophisticated cognitive reasoning.

To test the impact of post-decision dissonance on evaluations of various alternatives, Jack Brehm recruited women to rate different consumer products (e.g., coffee pot, toaster, radio, etc.; Brehm, 1956). After the women rated the items, they were told they could take one of the items home. Participants in the high-dissonance condition were given a difficult choice—between two items that they rated very close together. Participants in the low-dissonance condition were given an easy choice—between items they rated pretty far apart. They then received their gift, read a few research papers about the products, and then re-rated the products. What do you think happened? In the low-dissonance condition, ratings didn't change very much. But in the high-dissonance condition, participants' ratings between the two objects they had chosen between (and rated very similarly) were now much farther apart.

REVISIONS TO DISSONANCE THEORY

Because cognitive dissonance theory is one of the most famous theories in the field of social psychology, researchers have continued to investigate the precise conditions under which attitude change through cognitive dissonance does and does not occur. Two of the most commonly discussed revisions to the original theory are the "new look" at dissonance theory and the self-standards models.

The "New Look." According to the "new look" at dissonance theory created by Joel Cooper and Russell Fazio (1984), four steps are necessary for people to experience attitude change following dissonance (see Figure 6.6). These four steps are

1. negative or aversive consequences,
2. personal responsibility,
3. physiological arousal and discomfort,
4. attribution of that arousal to his/her own behavior.

First, attitude change occurs only if a person experiences *negative or aversive consequence* for his or her behavior (e.g., lying to someone, doing something embarrassing, etc.; Johnson, Kelly, & LeBlanc, 1995; Scher & Cooper, 1989). For example, if you try to mislead someone into thinking the upcoming task is fun when it is actually boring (like the classic Festinger & Carlsmith study on peg turning), but the other participant is unconvinced, you don't experience negative consequences—and therefore don't experience dissonance and don't change your attitude (Cooper & Worchel, 1970).

Second, attitude change occurs only when a person takes *personal responsibility* for the negative consequences of his or her action. In one study, participants delivered a counter-attitudinal speech, which some were aware was going to be used to change others' opinions (e.g., a negative consequence), whereas others were not (Goethals, Cooper, & Naficy, 1979). Only those who were aware of the potential negative consequences of their action before they made the speech showed attitude change.

FIGURE
6.6

A NEW LOOK AT DISSONANCE

According to the "new look" at dissonance theory, engaging in a behavior that contradicts your attitude (such as throwing a can into a trash bin instead of a recycling bin if you are strongly pro-recycling) can lead you to change your attitude to match your behavior, but only if certain conditions are met. These conditions are experiencing negative consequences for engaging in the behavior, taking personal responsibility for engaging in the behavior, feeling uncomfortable arousal for engaging in that behavior, and, finally, attributing the arousal to engaging in that behavior. If, *and only if*, all of these conditions are met, you then experience dissonance and change your attitude to match your behavior (such as feeling that recycling isn't really that important; Cooper & Fazio, 1984).

Engage in a behavior that contradicts your attitude

Step 1. Experience negative or aversive consequences

Step 2. Take personal responsibility

Step 3. Experience physiological arousal and discomfort

Step 4. Attribute that arousal to his/her own behavior

Change attitude to match the behavior

Third, attitude change should occur only in cases in which a person experiences *physiological arousal and discomfort* (Elkin & Leippe, 1986; Elliot & Devine, 1994). To test this part of the new look at dissonance theory, researchers randomly assigned participants to one of three conditions (Steele, Southwick, & Critchlow, 1981). Here are the three conditions:

1. One group of participants gave their attitudes toward a tuition raise (the control condition).
2. Another group of participants wrote an essay in favor of raising tuition (which would lead to dissonance), and then tasted and rated different types of water.
3. The final group of participants wrote the same essay, but this time, they tasted and rated different types of vodkas.

As predicted, participants who tasted different types of water showed a significant increase in positive attitudes toward the tuition raise—the typical dissonance effect. However, participants in the dissonance alcohol condition showed almost no attitude change. These students reduced their arousal by drinking, so they didn't experience arousal, and had no need to change their attitude.

Fourth, attitude change should occur only when a person *attributes that arousal to his or her own behavior.* If you attribute your arousal to some external factor (e.g., seeing a funny cartoon, anticipating painful shocks, believing you have been given a stimulating drug, etc.), there is no dissonance and, in turn, no attitude change (Cooper, Fazio, & Rhodewalt, 1978; Croyle & Cooper, 1983; Pittman, 1975). In one study, all participants were given a pill (really just a placebo or sugar pill), which some students were told would probably lead them to experience some nausea (Zanna & Cooper, 1974). As expected, those who attributed their nausea to the pill did not show any attitude change following the dissonance-inducing task (writing that counter-attitudinal essay). Those who were not told about the pill's supposed tendency to cause nausea showed the predicted attitude change.

Although the new look at dissonance theory generated much interest among social psychologists, some recent research points to a few weaknesses in this theory. Specifically, the evidence now suggests that people can show attitude change following engaging in an attitude-inconsistent behavior even in the absence

FIGURE 6.7   CAN GREATER CHOICE LEAD TO GREATER ATTITUDE CHANGE?

In this experiment, participants were asked to taste either a delicious or a really nasty-tasting drink, and write a sentence saying they liked it. Some participants were given less freedom than others about writing the sentence. As predicted participants who had no choice about the position they took on the drink reported liking the unpleasant drink much less than those who "chose" to write they liked it.

Source: Harmon-Jones, E., Brehm, J., Greenberg, J., Simon, L., & Nelson, D. (1996). Evidence that the production of aversive consequences is not necessary to create cognitive dissonance. *Journal of Personality and Social Psychology, 70,* 5–16.

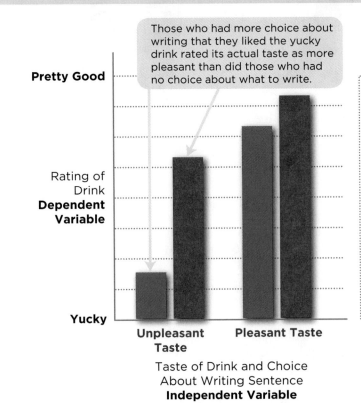

Those who had more choice about writing that they liked the yucky drink rated its actual taste as more pleasant than did those who had no choice about what to write.

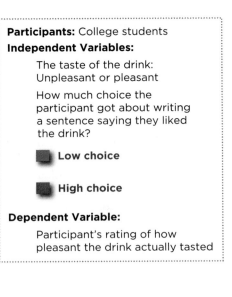

Participants: College students

Independent Variables:

The taste of the drink: Unpleasant or pleasant

How much choice the participant got about writing a sentence saying they liked the drink?

■ Low choice

■ High choice

Dependent Variable:

Participant's rating of how pleasant the drink actually tasted

of any aversive consequences (Harmon-Jones, 2000). In one study, participants drank an unpleasant-tasting beverage (Kool-Aid with vinegar) and then wrote a sentence saying they liked it under conditions of high choice (e.g., the person could choose which side to write on, although the experimenter pointed out that he was in need of more people to write that they liked the beverage) or low choice (the person was told that he or she had been randomly assigned to write about liking the beverage; Harmon-Jones, Brehm, Greenberg, Simon, & Nelson, 1996). Although participants in both choice conditions then simply threw the paper away (and hence didn't experience any negative consequences), those who wrote the sentence under conditions of high choice reported liking the beverage more than those who wrote under conditions of low choice (see Figure 6.7). In contrast, those who tasted a pleasant beverage showed no difference in rating in the two conditions.

Self-standards model. Jeff Stone and Joel Cooper (Stone & Cooper, 2001, 2003; Stone, 2003) have proposed a **self-standards model** of cognitive dissonance. This model proposes that people experience discomfort whenever they see their behavior as deviating from some type of important personal or normative standard, but that the strategy they use to reduce this dissonance will depend on what thoughts about the self are currently accessible. Attitude change will occur, as a way of reducing this dissonance, when no self-relevant thoughts are available or especially when self-relevant thoughts are available that are directly relevant to the behavior. For example, if you write an essay in favor of decreasing funding for handicapped services at your university, you then become even more in favor of this decrease if you are given positive feedback about your self-relevant attributes (e.g., your compassion) as a way of justifying your behavior. On the other hand, attitude change will not occur when you receive positive feedback about your personal attributes that are irrelevant to the given behavior (e.g., your creativity), because in this case your focus is shifted away from your own personal standards of behavior.

Can watching others engage in inconsistent behavior lead us to change our own attitudes? A recent research study shows exactly that. Students who see another student make a counter-attitudinal speech advocating for tuition increases become more supportive of that issue themselves (Norton, Monin, Cooper, & Hogg, 2003). This effect is particularly strong when participants know the speaker disagrees with the topic he

self-standards model a model that proposes people experience discomfort whenever they see their behavior as deviating from some type of important personal or normative standard, but that the strategy they use to reduce this dissonance will depend on what thoughts about the self are currently accessible

Questioning the Research
Should experiencing "vicarious dissonance" lead to as much attitude change as experiencing dissonance from our own actions? Why or why not?

Concepts in Context

COGNITIVE DISSONANCE THEORY AND REVISIONS TO DISSONANCE THEORY

THEORY	EXAMPLE
Cognitive dissonance theory	Joe goes through a humiliating and painful fraternity initiation. He then develops a tremendous love for his fraternity.
The "new look" at dissonance theory	As part of a class project, Linda writes an essay proposing a decrease in scholarship aid for college students (even though she disagrees with this proposal). Linda is relieved to learn that these essays would be immediately thrown out. She continues to oppose the reduction in scholarship aid.
Self-standards model	Todd wrote a paper proposing a decreased emphasis on recycling on campus as part of a business internship. Although he disagrees with this policy change, Todd was very pleased to receive an "A" on his paper—along with very positive comments on his writing. Todd continues to oppose this change in emphasis.

or she is speaking about. Apparently we can feel uncomfortable when we watch someone else engage in counter-attitudinal behavior, and this discomfort leads us to change our own attitudes to reduce this dissonance.

WHAT ARE ALTERNATIVES TO COGNITIVE DISSONANCE THEORY?

Q A Although dissonance theory has been around for a while, there are also other theories that attempt to explain why people change their attitudes. In one study designed to test self-affirmation theory, an alternative explanation for attitude change following dissonance, researchers asked participants to write an essay that opposed placing a high funding priority on research and treatment of chronic diseases and handicaps (Steele & Liu, 1983). Not surprisingly, writing this essay led students to experience dissonance. Next, all participants completed a measure in which they rated their appreciation of beauty in the arts, literature, architecture, and so on. Participants had been recruited to participate in this study based on their earlier scores on this measure: researchers chose participants who had very high scores on valuing the arts and students who had very low scores on valuing the arts. Finally, participants rated the strength of the essay opposing funding for research on disease prevention they had written. As predicted, participants who strongly valued arts rated their essays as very strong: an average of 24.4 on a 1-to-31-point scale. These participants had the opportunity to affirm an important part of themselves, their love and appreciation of the arts, and therefore resolve their dissonance (so, they didn't need to rate their essays as poor in quality to resolve their dissonance). On the other hand, participants who were low on valuing the arts, and therefore did not experience a self-affirmation boost from completing the measure of love and appreciation for the arts, rated their essays an average of 8.5. These participants needed to rate their essay as poor in quality to resolve the dissonance they experienced from writing a counter-attitudinal essay. This section will examine self-affirmation theory as well as two other theories—self-perception theory and impression management theory—that propose alternatives to cognitive dissonance theory.

self-perception theory the theory that people infer their attitudes by simply observing their behavior

SELF-PERCEPTION THEORY

According to Bem's (1967) **self-perception theory**, people don't actually change their attitudes, but simply look to their own behavior to determine what their attitudes are. In other words, we don't change our attitudes as a way of resolving tension or justifying our behavior, as posited by cognitive dissonance theory. Instead, we see our behavior as providing important information about our true attitudes. To test this theory, Daryl Bem told participants about the Festinger and Carlsmith study and asked them to guess participants' attitudes. As he predicted, those who were told participants said they liked the task and received $20 thought the participants just lied for the money. Those who were told participants said they liked the task for $1 thought participants must have actually liked the task (who would lie for just a dollar!). Similarly, people who are led to believe that they previously held a given attitude are more likely to engage in behavior that is in line with this attitude (Albarracín & Wyer, 2000).

Stuart Valins conducted a very clever study to test the effect of self-perception of attitudes on behavior (Valins, 1966). Male college students were shown "centerfold pictures" of beautiful naked women while they were "hooked up" to electrodes that supposedly measured their heartbeats. The experimenter actually controlled the pace of the heartbeats, and during one randomly selected photo, the heartbeats would speed up. The men then assumed that their heartbeat was fastest in response to one particular photo. When the experiment was over, the researcher let the men pick one of the pictures to take home: men

iStockphoto

Would you believe that learning about your physiological reactions to a stimulus influences your attitudes toward that object (even if this information is false)? That is precisely what research on self-perception theory suggests.

overwhelmingly chose the photo that they thought they liked the most, based on their perceived heartbeat rate. This study demonstrates the power of self-perception in determining our attitudes—participants clearly looked to their "behavior" (e.g., their supposed heart rate) to determine their attitude.

IMPRESSION MANAGEMENT THEORY

Impression management theory is based on the idea that individuals are not motivated to be consistent, but rather to appear consistent (Baumeister, 1982). In other words, individuals don't want to be seen as hypocritical. Therefore, we try to show others that our attitudes and behaviors are in line, even if they are not. In one study, participants who wrote a counter-attitudinal essay under "public conditions" (e.g., put their name, phone number, address, and major on the essay), even under no choice conditions, showed just as much attitude change as those who were exposed to the typical dissonance condition (e.g., high choice, but private; Baumeister & Tice, 1984). These findings suggest that self-presentational concerns can also influence attitude change.

Although there are cases in which stating attitudes anonymously decreases the effects of cognitive dissonance, impression management theory can't explain other research findings. For example, people are also more likely to change their attitudes following an interaction with an unattractive (e.g., rude and unpleasant) experimenter than an attractive one (Rosenfeld, Giacalone, & Tedeschi, 1984). This finding suggests, in line with cognitive dissonance theory, that people show more attitude change when they have to justify their reasons for engaging in a given behavior—and interacting with a rather unappealing experimenter should require more justification than interacting with a more pleasant one. In contrast, impression management theory would predict that greater attitude change occurs in front of the attractive experimenter, when you are more motivated to try to appear consistent. Similarly, it is difficult to explain why you'd get the results with children, such as in the Robby the Robot study. These children are too young to be motivated to appear consistent to the experimenter. Moreover, why then would they not play with Robby the Robot later on, with a different experimenter?

impression management theory a theory that individuals are not motivated to be consistent, but rather to appear consistent

SELF-AFFIRMATION THEORY

Claude Steele posits that engaging in attitude-discrepant behavior makes people feel badly about themselves, and so they are motivated to revalidate the integrity of their self-concept (Steele & Liu, 1983). Therefore, **self-affirmation theory** describes how people can reduce the arousal caused by cognitive dissonance by affirming a different part of their identities, even if that identity is completely unrelated to the cause of the arousal. Contrary to the original cognitive dissonance theory, this validation can be achieved in a number of ways, including but not limited to resolving dissonance. As described in the study at the start of this section, participants who valued the arts and were able to affirm this part of themselves rated their essays opposing research for chronic disease treatment as stronger than those who did not value the arts (and thus did not experience self-affirmation from rating their attitudes about the arts; Steele & Liu, 1983). So this theory suggests that the participants in Festinger and Carlsmith's study could have resolved their dissonance in a variety of ways (e.g., donating money to a charity, helping someone in distress, etc.). In these cases, participants would feel better about themselves, and then not feel the need to change their attitudes to be in line with their behavior. The Education Connections box describes the use of self-affirmation to increase academic achievement in students from traditionally disadvantaged groups.

In another study testing the self-affirmation theory, Steele and colleagues gave participants positive or negative feedback about a personality test (Steele, Spencer, & Lynch, 1993). Then they had participants rate 10 popular music albums. Participants were allowed to keep either their fifth- or their six-rated album, whichever they preferred. After they selected the album they'd like to keep, they

self-affirmation theory a theory that describes how people can reduce the arousal caused by cognitive dissonance by affirming a different part of their identities, even if that identity is completely unrelated to the cause of the arousal

Education

How Self-Affirmation Can Increase Academic Achievement

Self-affirmation can work to increase academic achievement in students from traditionally disadvantaged backgrounds, who are often at risk of underperforming. In one study, researchers randomly assigned both African American and Caucasian seventh graders to write about their values, such as relationships with friends or family or being good at art, for 15 minutes at the start of the fall semester (Cohen, Garcia, Apfel, & Master, 2006). Students in the affirmation condition were asked to write about values that were important to them, and to explain why these values were important to them. Students in the control condition were asked to write about values that were not particularly important to them, and to explain why these values might be important to other people. Researchers then examined students' grades over the fall term. African American students in the affirmation condition earned higher grades than those in the control condition—in fact, this condition was beneficial for nearly 70% of the African American students. Caucasian students didn't show any differences in grades. This study revealed that even a very subtle self-affirmation manipulation can lead to approximately a 40% reduction in the racial achievement gap.

Moreover, a two-year follow-up revealed long-term benefits of completing a series of these brief self-affirmation writing assignments, especially for low-achieving African American students (Cohen, Garcia, Purdie-Vaughns, Apfel, & Brzustoski, 2009). The grade point average of African Americans increased an average of .24 points, but low-achieving African-American students experienced an average increase of .41 points. In addition, low-achieving African American students who completed these self-affirmation exercises were much less likely to need to repeat a grade: only 5% compared to 18% of those in the control condition. These findings suggest that self-affirmation can be a powerful way to increase academic achievement.

SUPERSTOCK

re-rated the albums. What would dissonance theory predict? That after making a decision, you'd like the chosen album even more than the unchosen album (remember they were awfully close). This was true for most participants. However, and in line with the self-affirmation theory, those participants who received positive feedback did not change their ratings. This study was replicated using participants with high and low self-esteem, and half of the participants were given a test that made their self-esteem salient. Most people again increased their rating of their chosen album; those with high self-esteem who had this self-esteem made salient did not show this inflation.

Although self-affirmation may be a way to reduce dissonance without changing one's attitude, some evidence suggests that people don't prefer to indirectly get rid of dissonance (e.g., by self-affirming) when they can directly resolve inconsistency by changing their behavior to make it less inconsistent (Stone, Wiegand, Cooper, & Aronson, 1997). For example, if people are reminded of their failure to volunteer, and are then given an opportunity to resolve this discrepancy directly (e.g., donate money to the homeless) or indirectly (e.g., buy condoms to show you are a careful person), 67% of people donate, but only 11% purchase condoms.

WHICH THEORY IS RIGHT?

This is an ongoing question. Currently, cognitive dissonance theory and self-affirmation theory are seen as more likely explanations of behavior leading to attitude change than impression management theory and self-perception theory. However, and as described in this section, researchers continue to examine the specific conditions under which behavior change leads to attitude change.

ALTERNATIVES TO COGNITIVE DISSONANCE THEORY

THEORY	EXAMPLE
Self-perception theory	Selin realizes that she must be attracted to the teaching assistant in her English literature course because she tries to sit beside him every day in class.
Impression management theory	Darina is a vegetarian who agrees to eat veal during a psychology experiment on taste preferences. She falsely reports liking veal to the experimenter so that she appears consistent.
Self-affirmation theory	Harned feels bad about himself for littering his coffee cup on the ground. However, after he signs up to donate blood, he no longer sees littering as that big a deal.

CULTURE
HOW DOES CULTURE IMPACT ATTITUDE FORMATION AND CHANGE?

Another factor that influences attitude formation and change is culture. In one study, both European Canadians and Asian Canadians were asked to rate in terms of preference 10 types of dinner entrées available at nearby restaurants (Hoshino-Browne, Zanna, Spencer, Zanna, Kitayama, & Lackenbauer, 2005). Half of the participants were asked to think about their own preferences in making these ratings. The other half were asked to think about a close friend's preferences. They were then forced to make a difficult decision—to decide between receiving a gift certificate for their 5th or 6th favorite restaurant (a tough decision). They were then asked to re-rate the entrée options listed. In line with previous research, European Canadians showed a greater distinction in the two ratings (that clearly had been quite close) when they made the ratings based on their own preferences compared to their friend's preferences. Asian Canadians, on the other hand, showed a significantly greater distinction between the two ratings when they considered their friend's preferences compared to their own. In other words, European Canadians felt the need to justify the choices they made on their own behalf, and Asian Canadians felt the need to justify the choices they made on their friends' behalf. This section will examine the impact of culture on attitudes and cognitive dissonance.

ATTITUDES

Culture influences the factors that predict attitudes as well as attitude-behavior consistency. Let's look at each of these factors:

Factors predicting attitudes.   People in collectivistic cultures are more influenced by social norms (such as their beliefs about what their peers are doing) than people in individualistic cultures (Cialdini, Wosinska, Barrett, Butner, & Gornik-Durose, 1999). On the other hand, people in individualistic cultures are more influenced by information about what they have done in the past (e.g., consistency), presumably because dispositional traits should be stable.

Other people's behavior is a stronger influence on individuals' behavior in collectivistic cultures than in individualistic ones.

In one study, university students in the United States and Poland (a collectivistic culture) were asked about their willingness to complete a marketing survey without pay (Cialdini et al., 1999). Half of the students in each group were first asked to consider their own prior history of compliance with requests. The other half were first asked to consider information regarding other students' compliance. Although own prior history and others' history were both influences on compliance in students in both countries, own history had a greater impact on compliance for Americans whereas others' compliance had a greater impact on Polish students.

Attitude-behavior consistency.

People in different cultures also differ in the extent to which they show attitude-behavior consistency (Kashima, Siegal, Tanaka, & Kashima, 1992). As described previously, consistency between one's attitudes and behavior is seen as more important in individualistic cultures. Individualistic cultures emphasize the role of stable internal traits in predicting attitudes as well as behavior, but collectivistic cultures emphasize the power of the situation in influencing attitudes and behavior. In turn, Japanese people do not believe in attitude-behavior consistency as strongly as Australians do.

COGNITIVE DISSONANCE

Although the phenomenon of cognitive dissonance is one of the most famous theories in social psychology, the majority of research on this effect has been conducted in Western cultures. Because cognitive dissonance results from holding two inconsistent attitudes, or an attitude that conflicts with one's behavior, cultures in which such self-consistency is not valued may not experience cognitive dissonance so readily, or potentially not at all (Choi & Choi, 2002; Markus & Kitayama, 1991). Specifically, if one's self is based in one's social roles and relationships, then having inconsistencies between two attitudes, or between one's attitudes and behavior, simply may not lead to negative feelings about the self. Collectivistic cultures have a greater tolerance of ambiguity, and are likely to attribute inconsistencies in one's attitudes and behaviors to the situation as opposed to the person.

To examine the effects of creating two inconsistent attitudes in people in different cultures, Steve Heine and Darrin Lehman (1997) recruited Japanese and Canadians to participate in a "marketing study." Participants completed a personality test and were asked to evaluate various music CDs. Then they received feedback on their personality test, which was either positive (e.g., they scored better than 85% of others) or negative (e.g., they scored better than 25% of others). (Those in the control condition received no feedback.) Finally, they were allowed to choose between two closely rated CDs to take home as a "thank you," after which they again rated each CD (so the research could measure change in their ratings). (As described in research studies earlier in the chapter, asking people to choose between highly desirable items is a common way of creating dissonance.) As shown in Figure 6.8, Canadians who received no feedback or, especially, negative feedback showed a large change in ratings of the CDs. The ratings given by Japanese participants were not effected by the feedback, nor did it differ as a result of making a difficult choice between two closely rated CDs. Dissonance reduction, by changing ratings of the CDs, is simply not used by Japanese participants to counter self-esteem threats. Making a difficult choice just doesn't impact Japanese participants in the same way that it does those from Western cultures, such as Canada and the United States.

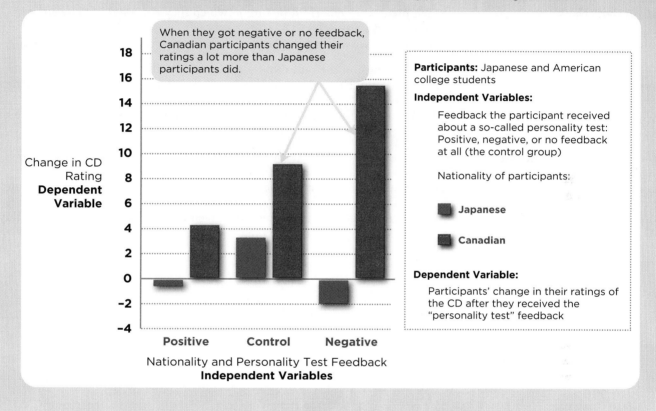

FIGURE 6.8   CAN NEGATIVE FEEDBACK LEAD TO ATTITUDE CHANGE?

In this experiment, Japanese and Canadian students were asked to listen to and rate a music CD. Then they took what they were told was a personality test. After researchers gave the feedback about their supposed results on the test, they asked students to rate the CD again. As predicted, Canadians who received no feedback or, especially, negative feedback showed a larger change in ratings of the CDs than those who received positive feedback, whereas the ratings given by Japanese participants were not affected by the type of feedback received.

Source: Heine, S., & Lehman, D. (1997). Culture, dissonance, and self-affirmation. *Personality and Social Psychology Bulletin, 23*, 389–400. Used by permission of Sage Publications.

Research also indicates that the factors that create cognitive dissonance are different in individualistic cultures and collectivistic ones. As described at the start of this section, European Canadians experience dissonance when they are forced to make a difficult decision for themselves (Hoshino-Browne et al., 2005). In contrast, Asian Canadians experience dissonance when they make a difficult decision about their friend's preferences.

Finally, the factors that lead to feelings of dissonance seem to differ as a function of culture. One series of studies used the standard free choice paradigm in which participants had to choose between two closely rated CDs, and then had to re-rate both the chosen and unchosen CD (Kitayama, Snibbe, Markus, & Suzuki, 2004). European American participants consistently showed the standard pattern, in which they rated the chosen CD much higher than the not chosen CD. However, Japanese Americans showed little difference in their rating of the two CDs unless they had also been forced to think about other people (in one study, to also rate how other students would rate the CDs; in another study, to also rate how someone they liked would rate the CDs). Thus, unlike the European Americans, Japanese Americans did not justify their choices by showing a spread of ratings unless they were primed to think about other people. This finding suggests that dissonance in European Americans is caused by a concern about their competence, but dissonance in Japanese people is caused by a concern about possible rejection from others.

The Big Picture

ATTITUDE FORMATION AND CHANGE

This chapter included many applications of the three "big ideas" studied in social psychology. The examples below should help you see the connection between attitude formation and change and these big ideas, and contribute to your understanding of the big picture of social psychology.

THEME	EXAMPLES
The social world influences how we think about ourselves.	• We like a boring task more if we get paid $1 to do it than if we get paid $20. • Men prefer the centerfold picture in which they *believe* they showed physiological arousal. • People who see a frowning picture of the Pope feel lower in self-esteem.
The social world influences our thoughts, attitudes, and behaviors.	• We like songs on the radio that we hear frequently. • Dating relationships with high levels of reward are more likely to continue over time. • Adolescents who watch television shows with high sexual content see their friends as more sexually active.
Our attitudes and behavior shape the social world around us.	• People who give high levels of rewards to their dating partners are more likely to maintain those relationships over time. • People who are concerned about global warming are more likely to donate to that cause. • Participants whose attitude toward a given presidential candidate are highly accessible are more likely to vote.

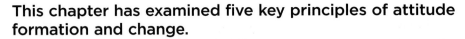

WHAT YOU'VE LEARNED

This chapter has examined five key principles of attitude formation and change.

YOU LEARNED How do we form attitudes? We initially form attitudes through information, mere exposure, classical conditioning, operant conditioning, and observational learning (or modeling). You also learned that even just describing an elderly person can lead you to form attitudes that are in line with those of a senior citizen.

YOU LEARNED When do attitudes predict behavior? There are several factors that influence the link between attitudes and behavior, and in particular when attitudes do—and do not—lead to behavior. We learned specific factors that strengthen the attitude-behavior connection, such as strength, specificity, and social norms. Even people who hold prejudiced attitudes won't necessarily behave in line with those beliefs, as demonstrated by the study with the Chinese couple visiting various hotels and restaurants.

YOU LEARNED When does engaging in a behavior lead to attitude change? This section described cognitive dissonance theory, factors leading to this theory, and several revisions to this theory. You learned about factors that lead to attitude change following dissonance, including insufficient justification, insufficient deterrence, effort justification, and justifying dissonance. You also learned about two revisions to this theory—the "new look" at dissonance theory and the self-standards model. You also learned that people who suffer through an embarrassing initiation to participate in a group discussion on sex (that in reality turns out to be very boring) report liking this group much more than those who only experience a mild initiation.

YOU LEARNED **What are alternatives to cognitive dissonance theory?** This section examined several theories that provide an alternative explanation for the findings seen in research that tests cognitive dissonance theory. These alternatives include self-perception theory, impression management theory, and self-affirmation study. You also learned that describing a love of the arts can make some people oppose research on chronic disease prevention.

YOU LEARNED **How does culture impact attitude formation and change?** This section described how culture influences the attitudes we form, as well as the factors that lead to cognitive dissonance. You learned that for people in collectivistic cultures, attitudes are more strongly influenced by social norms than they are for people in individualistic cultures. You also learned that cognitive dissonance is much more common in individualistic cultures than it is in collectivistic cultures. Finally, you learned why European Canadians justify the choices they make for themselves, whereas Asian Canadians justify the choices they make for their friends.

KEY TERMS

attitudes 182
classical conditioning 183
cognitive dissonance theory 196
impression management
  theory 207
mere exposure 183

observational learning/
  modeling 186
operant conditioning 186
prototype/willingness model 194
self-affirmation theory 207
self-perception theory 206

self-standards model 205
subliminal persuasion 183
theory of planned behavior 193

QUESTIONS FOR REVIEW

1. Describe two ways in which people acquire attitudes.
2. Describe two factors that increase the attitude-behavior link.
3. What are three different factors that can lead to cognitive dissonance?
4. Which explanation for self-persuasion do you find most convincing, and why? Which explanation is least convincing, and why?
5. Describe how culture impacts attitudes and cognitive dissonance.

TAKE ACTION!

1. You want your daughter to develop gender-neutral attitudes and behavior. What are three specific steps you could take to help accomplish this goal?
2. You are working with a local political organization to increase voting on college campuses. What strategies might you use to increase the likelihood that students' positive attitudes toward voting lead them to vote?
3. You are trying to get your niece to clean her room. How could you use principles of cognitive dissonance to accomplish this goal?
4. After writing a required term paper that argues for increasing college tuition, you experience dissonance. According to self-affirmation theory, how could you eliminate this arousal?
5. You have a summer internship with an international marketing company, and are asked to collect survey data from people in the United States and in Japan. What strategies should be most effective at increasing compliance with the request to complete a survey in each of these countries?

RESEARCH CONNECTIONS

Try some of these research activities to gain experience in conducting and evaluating research, and to increase your understanding of research methods and techniques in social psychology.

Visit WileyPLUS for more activities and interactive research tools! (www.wileyplus.com)

Participate in Research

Activity 1 The Power of Subliminal Processing: Can information we are not consciously aware of shape our attitudes? Find out at WileyPLUS where you will complete a brief task that includes subliminal processing information influences your attitude.

Activity 2 The Link Between Strength and Accessibility: When an attitude is strong, it tends to be more accessible. See if attitude strength and accessibility correlate for you. Think about various attitudes you hold, and whether the stronger attitudes are faster for you to come up with (a sign of accsssibility).

Activity 3 Using Cognitive Dissonance to Create Behavior Change: This chapter described how cognitive dissonance can lead to healthier behaviors, like increased condom use and healthier eating. Can you think of a time in which you experienced feelings of cognitive dissonance, in which your attitudes and behavior conflicted? Did this conflict lead to a change in your behavioral intentions?

Activity 4 **The Power of Self-Affirmation:** Test self-affirmation about one aspect of your life can help you resolve feelings of conflict about other aspects. Go to WileyPLUS to participate in an exercise that points out attitude-discrepant behavior, and then provides an opportunity for self-affirmation, to see the impact of self-affirmation on your attitudes.

Activity 5 **The Impact of Culture on Attitudes:** Does culture influences attitude formation and change? Complete an attitude survey on WileyPLUS to determine what factors influence your attitude. See how your answers compare to those from a different culture.

Test a Hypothesis

One of the common findings in research on attitude formation is that attitudes are often formed by images we see in the media. To test whether this hypothesis is true, watch two different children's programs—one designed to appeal to girls (such as *Hannah Montana*) and one designed to appeal to boys (such as *Mighty Morphin Power Rangers*), and count the number of gender stereotypic references in the advertisements shown during each program. Share your findings with fellow students in class or on your class discussion board.

Design a Study

To design your own study testing how and when attitudes can predict behavior, think of a research question you would like to answer, then decide what type of study you want to conduct (self-report, observational/naturalistic, or experimental), choose your own independent and dependent variables, and operationally define each by determining the procedures or measures you will use. Form a hypothesis to predict what will happen in your study (the expected cause and effect relationship between your two variables) and collect the data. Share your findings with others.

7

Persuasion

Did you ever wonder?

In the United States, the television commercial is generally considered the most effective mass-market advertising format—which explains why the Super Bowl is known as much for its commercial advertisements as for the game itself (with an average cost of over $2 million for a single thirty-second TV spot during the game). Because a single television commercial can be broadcast repeatedly over the course of weeks, months, and even years, companies often spend tremendous amounts of money to produce a single advertisement. Advertisements are used to sell virtually all goods and services, from breakfast cereals to cars to laundry detergents to candidates for president. Many television advertisements feature catchy jingles (songs or melodies) or catchphrases (e.g., "Where's the beef?" he "keeps going and going and going...") that generate sustained appeal, which may remain in the minds of television viewers long after the span of the advertising campaign. Other long-running ad campaigns catch people by surprise, such as the Energizer Bunny

Law
CONNECTIONS
The Benefits of
"Stealing the Thunder"

Health
CONNECTIONS
Why Having Wrinkles
is Worse Than Dying

Business
CONNECTIONS
How Waiters and
Waitresses Can
Increase Tips

advertisement series. This chapter examines factors that influence the persuasiveness of television commercials and other advertisements. In addition, you'll find out ...

Q A Why are people more convinced by familiar phrases than literal phrases that mean the same thing?

Q A Why are people who drink coffee highly critical of studies suggesting caffeine is bad for your health?

Q A Why do people tip better when their bill is placed on a tray with a credit card emblem?

Q A Why do warning labels about violence on a television program increase interest in watching this program?

Q A Why is "Ditch the Joneses" a more effective advertising slogan in the United States than in Korea?

Why do advertisements for beer feature young and highly attractive people? Why do we care what golf clubs Tiger Woods uses? Does having a 21-year-old age minimum for alcohol use increase teenagers' interest in drinking? This chapter examines each of these topics in **persuasion**, meaning communications that are designed to influence people's attitudes. These communications can be deliberate attempts to influence attitudes in general, such as through the advertisements we see on television, in magazines, and on billboards. These communications can also be less formal, such as the arguments you hear from a friend who wants you to vote for a particular presidential candidate. In this chapter, you'll learn about the factors that influence the effectiveness of persuasion techniques, the strategies of resisting persuasion attempts, and the influence of culture on persuasion.

HOW DO WE PROCESS PERSUASIVE MESSAGES?

Q A Imagine that you are asked to listen to a persuasive message, such as a speech by a politician or an advertisement for a car. Would you believe that the speed at which you heard the speech could be more impactful than the messages presented in the speech? In one study, researchers asked participants to listen to a speech supposedly made by another student (Smith & Shaffer, 1995). In one condition this speech included strong arguments. In another condition, the speech consisted of weak arguments. In addition, half of the participants in each condition heard the speech at a moderate rate of speech. The other half of participants heard the speech at a very high rate of speech. Who was most persuaded? Participants who heard weak arguments at a normal rate of speech were, not surprisingly, least persuaded. However, participants who heard weak arguments at a fast rate were just as persuaded as those who heard strong arguments at either normal or fast rate. This section examines two distinct routes to persuasion, the factors that influence the type of processing used, and the route that is most effective in leading to persuasion.

ROUTES TO PERSUASION

persuasion communication that is designed to influence one's attitudes

As described by the **elaboration likelihood model (ELM)** of persuasion, people focus on different aspects of a persuasive message as a function of their involvement in the message content (Petty & Cacioppo, 1986). When a person thinks carefully about a communication message and is influenced by the strength of the arguments, he or she is using the **central or systematic route**. Here's an example of the central route to persuasion. You are thinking about buying a car, and you read the latest issue of *Consumer Reports*, then test-drive several cars, evaluate the different features, etc.

elaboration likelihood model (ELM) a model describing two distinct routes of persuasion (central and peripheral) that are used to process persuasive messages

In contrast, the **peripheral or heuristic route** to persuasion is when a person does not think carefully about a communication message and is influenced by superficial characteristics. For example, if you see a television ad in which an attractive man or woman drives a new sleek car very fast in scenic areas, you might make your decision based on these superficial characteristics (see Figure 7.1).

central or systematic route a · type of processing of persuasive messages that occurs when people have the ability and motivation to carefully listen to and evaluate the arguments in a persuasive message

The difference in these two types of approaches to persuasion is illustrated by rival campaigns promoting toothpaste. One company created a series of advertisements for its new Crest Pro-Health toothpaste that emphasized the health benefits of their product in a belief that consumers will respond to receiving this type of information. These ads list the benefits of Crest Pro-Health and include the American Dental Association (ADA) seal. In contrast, advertisements for the rival toothpaste, Colgate Total, emphasize glamour and emotion. These print and television ads feature the actress Brooke Shields. In one television ad, Ms. Shields is playing with two children while soft music plays in the background. She then says, "Having a healthy smile is important to me. Not just as an actress, but as

peripheral or heuristic route a type of processing of persuasive messages that occurs when people lack the ability and motivation to carefully listen to and evaluate a persuasive message, and hence are influenced only by superficial cues

FIGURE 7.1   ELABORATION LIKELIHOOD MODEL OF PERSUASION

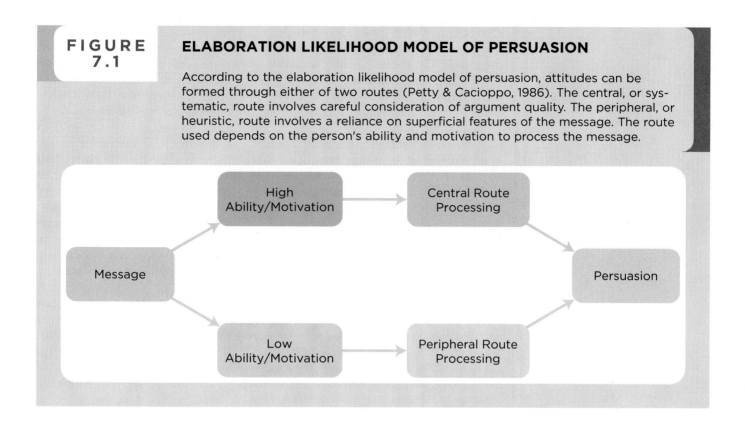

According to the elaboration likelihood model of persuasion, attitudes can be formed through either of two routes (Petty & Cacioppo, 1986). The central, or systematic, route involves careful consideration of argument quality. The peripheral, or heuristic, route involves a reliance on superficial features of the message. The route used depends on the person's ability and motivation to process the message.

a mom." These two distinct types of advertisements for toothpaste illustrate the differences between central messages and peripheral messages.

FACTORS THAT INFLUENCE TYPE OF PROCESSING USED

What factors influence which route of persuasion you use? There are two distinct factors—the ability to focus, and the motivation to focus.

Ability to focus. If you are distracted, and therefore have limited *ability to focus*, it is difficult to concentrate on central messages that require greater processing, and so you may rely on peripheral cues (Petty, Wells, & Brock, 1976). People tend to automatically accept information they receive, and only later do they process that information and decide whether to reject it (Gilbert, Krull, & Malone, 1990; Gilbert, Tafarodi, & Malone, 1993). For example, if a person is interrupted immediately after hearing some information, or is under intense time pressure, they are more likely to (incorrectly) accept this information as true simply because they lack the motivation and opportunity to engage in more careful processing.

In one study, students read either a strong or a weak argument in favor of a 20% increase in school tuition (Petty et al., 1976). The strong messages emphasized the benefits for education (e.g., improving teaching, lowering class sizes, hiring better teachers). The weak messages emphasized the benefits for the campus yards (e.g., hiring more gardeners,

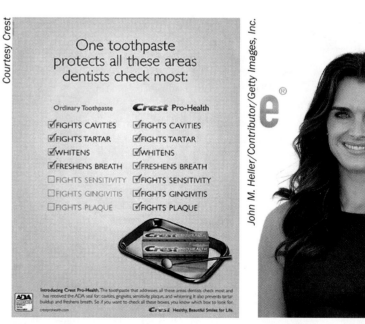

The two different approaches to persuasion are illustrated in advertisements for toothpaste. Ads for Crest use the central or systematic route and provide facts, whereas ads for Colgate use the peripheral route and feature actress Brooke Shields.

getting more flowers, etc.). Some students listened to these messages without distraction. Others listened to the messages while also performing a difficult computer task. Those who had no distraction were persuaded by the strong messages but not by the weak messages, as one would predict. Those who were distracted were somewhat persuaded by both types of messages, presumably because they did not have a chance to generate counterarguments to the weak messages.

Even subtle factors that increase people's ability to concentrate can lead to higher rates of central or systematic processing. In one study, half of the participants consumed an orange-juice drink that contained caffeine and the other half consumed the same drink but without the caffeine (Martin, Laing, Martin, & Mitchell, 2005). All participants then read a strong message opposing voluntary euthanasia and rated their agreement with this position. (Researchers selected participants for this study based on their positive attitude toward voluntary euthanasia, and thus this message opposed their current belief.) Which participants were most convinced? Those who had consumed caffeine—and were presumably more aroused and alert—were more persuaded by this counter-attitudinal message.

Motivation to focus. But even if you have the ability to focus, you may not have the *motivation to focus* on processing central messages if you are uninvolved or uninterested in the message (Chaiken, 1980; Fabrigar, Priester, Petty, & Wegener, 1998; Maheswaran & Chaiken, 1991). With no motivation, you are likely to rely on peripheral cues, such as the length of the message, the source of the message, and, as described at the start of this section, the speed at which the message is delivered (Smith & Shaffer, 1991, 1995).

Even the familiarity of the phrases used in a message can influence persuasion. In one study, researchers asked students to read two phrases and to rate their agreement with each phrase (Howard, 1997). Each of these pairs of phrases included one familiar phrase, and a second, more literal, statement that meant the same thing. For example, one pair of phrases was "Finding yourself between a rock and a hard place" (familiar phrase) and "Having to choose between undesirable alternatives" (literal phrase). Another pair of phrases was "Don't put all your eggs in one basket" (familiar phrase) and "Don't risk everything on a single venture" (literal phrase). Researchers manipulated participants' involvement with the task by providing different incentives for completing this study. In one condition, participants were told that their name would be entered in a drawing for a $200 bond that they could place in a tax-deferred individual retirement account (IRA) at the bank of their choice (these were all business school students, so this was a very desirable incentive). In the other condition, participants were told that their name would be entered in a drawing for $200 of free long-distance phone calls.

As predicted, message involvement influenced persuasion. People who were low in involvement with a message were more persuaded by familiar phrases than by the literal, but non-familiar, phrases that convey the same meaning. These participants relied on the peripheral cues, and therefore were more persuaded by the familiar phrases. On the other hand, high involvement participants were equally persuaded by both phrases. These participants weighed the meanings of the phrases—which were of course identical—in making their decision.

In a study by Richard Petty and his colleagues, students listened to a speaker promoting the benefits of mandatory exams for all students before college graduation (Petty, Cacioppo, & Goldman, 1981). This study included three distinct independent variables:

"Sorry, Pop, but your message is no longer relevant to the younger audience."

- Expertise of speaker: some students were told the person was an expert, an education professor at Princeton, whereas others were told he was a high school student;
- Message strength: some students heard a strong argument based on research, and others heard a weak argument based on personal anecdotes;
- Personal involvement: some students were very involved in the message because they were told the exams would start next year; others were told they would not be implemented for 10 years.

For those who were not very involved (motivated), the primary factor that predicted attitude was the expertise of the speaker. They were more positive about the exams when the message was delivered by a professor than by a high school student, regardless of the strength of the argument (peripheral processing). For those who were highly involved, the strength of the argument was the major predictor of attitudes (central processing).

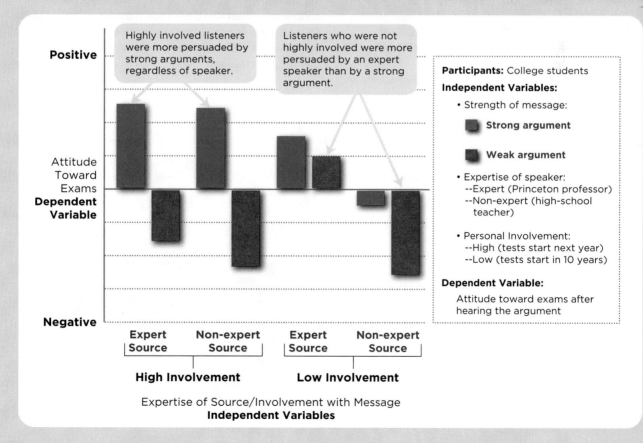

FIGURE 7.2

DOES PERSONAL INVOLVEMENT INFLUENCE THE TYPE OF PROCESSING USED?

In this experiment, college students listened to arguments in favor of requiring students to pass an examination in order to graduate from college. The hypothesis was that people who listen to a message that is highly personally involving will use central route processing, and hence are more persuaded by strong arguments than weak ones, regardless of who delivers the argument. In contrast, people who are less personally involved with the message will use peripheral route processing, and hence are more influenced by the expertise of the speaker than by the strength of the message. Both hypotheses were supported.

Source: Petty, R. E., Cacioppo, J. T., & Goldman, R. (1981). Personal involvement as a determinant of argument-based persuasion. *Journal of Personality and Social Psychology, 41*, 847-855.

Highly involved listeners were more persuaded by strong arguments, regardless of speaker.

Listeners who were not highly involved were more persuaded by an expert speaker than by a strong argument.

Participants: College students

Independent Variables:
- Strength of message:
  - **Strong argument**
  - **Weak argument**
- Expertise of speaker:
  - --Expert (Princeton professor)
  - --Non-expert (high-school teacher)
- Personal Involvement:
  - --High (tests start next year)
  - --Low (tests start in 10 years)

Dependent Variable:

Attitude toward exams after hearing the argument

Positive

Attitude Toward Exams
Dependent Variable

Negative

| Expert Source | Non-expert Source | Expert Source | Non-expert Source |

High Involvement   **Low Involvement**

Expertise of Source/Involvement with Message
Independent Variables

WHICH ROUTE IS MORE EFFECTIVE?

Is the central route or the peripheral route a more effective method of persuasion? Both are effective at changing people's attitudes, although these different types of processing are effective in different ways and for different people. Messages that are of high personal relevance motivate us to pay attention, and as long as we have the ability (i.e., no distractions), we process such messages centrally. On the other hand, messages that are of low personal relevance or that need to be processed while we have little attention to devote to them are processed peripherally. Interestingly, the same cue can be processed in different ways (depending on motivation and ability): white teeth in a toothpaste ad, for example, could be processed centrally (because white teeth could be a sign of an effective toothpaste) or peripherally (because white teeth are likely to be a cue of attractiveness). Finally, although persuasion can and does occur through both the central and the peripheral routes, attitude change that is based in central route processing is longer-lasting and more resistant to future persuasion efforts (Chaiken, 1980; Mackie, 1987). The Environment Connections box describes the benefits of persuasive messages that lead to central route processing.

Environment
::: CONNECTIONS

How Persuasive Messages Increase Recycling

Several studies have examined the use of persuasive messages to increase recycling of newspapers and aluminum cans (Werner, Byerly, White, & Kieffer, 2004; Werner, Stoll, Birch, & White, 2002). In one study, researchers placed one of two signs on all wastebaskets in classrooms and in the hallways of several large university buildings (Werner et al., 2004). Both signs requested that people refrain from putting their newspapers in the trash, and provided information about the location of the nearest recycling bin. Signs in the validation condition also included the following statement: "We are sorry for the inconvenience, but please recycle your newspaper." Signs in the persuasion condition read, "It is important, so please recycle your newspaper." The signs remained in place for three weeks and were then removed. The researchers counted the percent of newspapers that were recycled in each building by counting the number of newspapers placed in recycling bins and the number of newspapers that were placed in trash cans. This percentage was counted prior to the placement of the signs, during the period in which the signs were in place, and in the two-week follow-up period after the signs had been removed. The validation condition revealed a 9% increase in recycling and the persuasion condition revealed a 17% increase. Both of these increases were significantly higher than the increase observed in the control condition (3%), in which there were no signs. This research reveals how a simple persuasion attempt can have an impact on recycling, an important environmental improvement issue.

Daniel Hurst/GettyImages, Inc.

DIFFERENT ROUTES TO PERSUASION

ROUTE	EXAMPLE
Central route processing	Jan is deciding which college to attend. She visits the three schools she is considering, compares rates of tuition, and calls current students to ask their opinions.
Peripheral route processing	Jim is in a bar and is deciding which beer to order. He remembers a funny radio commercial he heard for one beer and decides to order that one.

WHAT FACTORS INFLUENCE PERSUASION?

Imagine that you read an article describing the link between coffee use and "fibro-cystic disease" (a fictional disease described as being associated with breast cancer). How would you react to this information? Researchers in one study tested precisely this question: For some participants, the article describes medical research suggesting a very strong link between caffeine use and this disease (a "strong report"; Liberman & Chaiken, 1992). For other participants, the article describes medical research that has disproved this link (a "weak report"). Participants—some of whom are regular coffee drinkers and others are not—are then asked to evaluate the article, including their beliefs about the link between caffeine use and this disease, the strength of the report, and their intention to reduce their own caffeine consumption. As predicted, those who drank coffee found both the strong and weak reports much less convincing than those who did not drink coffee. The researchers speculate that those who drink coffee—and hence found the information personally relevant—were threatened by any information describing problems with such consumption, and hence processed the message in a highly defensive way. This section examines the factors that influence the effectiveness of persuasive messages: the source who delivers the message, the content of the message, and the audience who receives the message.

SOURCE: WHO DELIVERS THE MESSAGE

The *source* of persuasion refers to the person or persons who deliver the message, such as the spokesperson for a given product, the actor who appears in an advertisement, or a person who gives a speech. In turn, the source's attractiveness, similarity, and credibility can each influence how persuasive people find the message.

Attractiveness.   First, and not surprisingly, *attractive* and *likable* sources are more persuasive than unattractive and less likable ones. Why? Because we assume if attractive people buy a particular car, or drink a particular soda, or use a particular shampoo, we might become more attractive by engaging in this same behavior! In one study, researchers recruited attractive and unattractive people to ask students to sign a petition (Eagly & Chaiken, 1975). Attractive people were successful in getting signatures 41% of the time, compared to only 32% of the time for the unattractive people. (See Chapter 12 to learn more about why attractiveness is so appealing.) Likable people are especially persuasive in videotaped and audiotaped messages, compared to written ones (Chaiken & Eagly, 1983). Unlikable people, on the other hand, are more persuasive in writing, suggesting that communicator likability is an especially important predictor of how people respond to television advertising.

Similarity.   Would you be more persuaded to buy a particular golf shoe if your good friend swears by it or if Tiger Woods swears by it? Research says your good friend is more similar to you and therefore more persuasive (Wilder, 1990).

BLACK ON BLACK

NEW EXTREME BLACK MAGNIF EYES MASCARA
Lash out BREAKTHROUGH EYE MAGNIFIER BRUSH
70% MORE VERTICAL LASHES Outstanding lash lift
DOUBLE HIT

RIMMEL
LONDON

It is not an accident that most advertisements feature highly attractive people; much research suggests that attractive sources are more persuasive than less attractive ones.

Because we have more in common with our friend, we believe the shoe is more likely to work for us. (Tiger could probably beat us wearing virtually any footwear.) This is why advertisements on TV try to feature people who are similar to the target audience (e.g., tired housewife, busy executive, etc.). In one study, students at the University of California at Santa Barbara (UCSB) read a strong speech about gun control or euthanasia (Mackie, Gastardo-Conaco, & Skelly, 1992). Some students were told the writer was a fellow UCSB student. Others were told the writer attended the University of Manitoba. Students' attitudes changed in the direction of the message they read when the speech was delivered by a student who supposedly attended their school. But they were not influenced at all when the message was delivered by someone who attended a different school. Why are similar sources more persuasive? One reason is that we remember messages presented by in-group members better than those presented by out-group members (Wilder, 1990).

Messages delivered by similar sources can be persuasive even if the message delivered feels somewhat coercive. In one study, students read an essay that was supposedly written by another student at their school (Silvia, 2005). This essay described the very negative attitude of their university toward its students, and included several strongly worded statements requesting agreement with these points (e.g., "*I know I will persuade you about this*"). Some of the participants were told the other student shared their first name and birthdate. Other participants were given the other student's first name and birthdate (that were intentionally different from their own). Researchers then asked participants for their agreement with the essay. Students who believed they shared a first name and birthdate with the author of the essay rated their agreement with the essay a 6.18 (with 1 = not at all and 7 = very much). Students who did not believe they had this similarity rated the essay a 4.19.

The power of similar sources in leading to persuasion is one explanation for the nearly $182 million in annual revenues by a company you've probably never heard of — Vector Marketing, which sells Cutco kitchen knives. The strategy this company uses is to recruit people (mostly college students) to attend an orientation session in which they learn how to make face-to-face sales calls to sell knives. Sellers are encouraged to sell the knives first to family members and friends (supposedly as a way of gaining experience in pitching the product). Then, at the end of these sales presentations, the sellers are told to ask for referrals of other people who might want to buy these knives—and what could be more persuasive than receiving a call about a product that your friend suggested you wanted to hear?

Credibility. Sources who appear *credible*, meaning competent and trustworthy, are more persuasive than those who lack credibility (Chaiken & Maheswaran, 1994; Maddux & Rogers, 1980; Priester & Petty, 1995; Verplanken, 1991). This is why doctors are often quoted in advertisements for health-related products, why Tiger Woods is featured in advertisements for golf clubs, and why packages of "Airborne" (a natural formula that supposedly protects against colds) proclaim "Created by a

School Teacher" (even though there is no scientific evidence indicating this product actually prevents colds).

We are also more convinced by sources that we believe are trustworthy, meaning those who do not have an ulterior motive for convincing us. Thus, if I try to convince you to join my health club, and you are aware that I will receive a month's free membership if you join, you should (wisely) question my credibility as a proponent of the club. Our concern about people's ulterior motives helps explain why we see expert witnesses who are paid for their testimony as less believable than those who volunteer (Cooper & Neuhaus, 2000).

People who argue unexpected positions—meaning those that seem to go against their own self-interests—are often especially persuasive because they are seen as highly credible (Wood & Eagly, 1981). Messages that are on a side that goes

"First off, by way of establishing some credibility, I'd like to note that twenty years ago I was living in a fur-lined van."

against participants' expectations are seen as more factually based than those that are on the expected side, and hence lead to greater attitude change. Alice Eagly and colleagues asked participants to listen to a political speech accusing a large company of polluting a local river (Eagly, Wood, & Chaiken, 1978). Some participants were told the speechmaker was a pro-environmental candidate who was addressing an environmental protection group. Others were told that he was a pro-business candidate addressing company supporters. When was the speech most persuasive? When it was delivered by the pro-business candidate, because in this case, he seemed most sincere and credible. The environmentalist was seen as biased.

The credibility of a speaker is particularly impactful when people have recently been exposed to another persuasive message (Tormala & Clarkson, 2007). Specifically, when people have just received a persuasive message from a source with low credibility, they are more persuaded by a message from a moderately credible source than if they had first received a message from a source with high credibility (see Table 7.1). This study indicates that how we evaluate the credibility of a source is influenced not just by his or her own credentials, but also by the credentials of

TABLE 7.1	EXAMPLES OF HIGH AND LOW CREDIBILITY SOURCES

HIGH CREDIBLE SOURCE	LOW CREDIBLE SOURCE
The passage you are about to read was taken from a message written by Professor Kenneth Sturreck, Ph.D. Dr. Sturreck is a Distinguished Professor of Education Sciences at Princeton University and is world renowned for his work in this area. The passage you will read is an editorial excerpt submitted by Dr. Sturreck to the Chronicle of Higher Education.	The passage you are about to read was taken from a message written by Kenneth Sturreck. Kenneth (age 14) is a freshman at Maude Johnson High School in Rosemont, West Virginia. The passage you will read is an editorial submitted by Kenneth to his high school newspaper.

Source: Tormala, Z.L., & Clarkson, J.J. (2007). Assimilation and contrast in persuasion: The effects of source credibility in multiple message situations. *Personality and Social Psychology Bulletin, 33,* 559–571.

Some advertisements are deliberately designed to blend in with the articles in a magazine, and therefore the "information" they present may seem more credible.

sleeper effect the phenomenon by which a message that is initially not particularly persuasive becomes more persuasive over time

other sources we have recently seen. (This is an example of the contrast effect, as discussed in Chapter 5: Social Cognition.)

Repeated exposure to a persuasive message can also lead individuals to attribute the message to a more credible source. In one study, researchers exposed some participants to a statement regarding a food legend five times, and other participants only two times (Fragale & Heath, 2004). All of the statements used were false. For example, one statement was "Star-Kist Tuna was recalled in Minnesota and Wisconsin after consumers found that the cans contained cat food and not tuna." Another statement was "Coca-Cola is just as effective as pain thinner at dissolving paint." Participants were then asked whether the statement was originally reported by *Consumer Reports* or by the *National Enquirer*. Those who heard the statement five times were more likely to believe it came from *Consumer Reports* than those who only heard the statement twice. In sum, simple repetition can lead information to be wrongly attributed to a more credible source.

Even noncredible sources can become more persuasive over time, a phenomenon known as the **sleeper effect** (Pratkanis, Greenwald, Leippe, & Baumgardner, 1988). This occurs because over time people may remember the message, but not remember the speaker. For example, you might read something in *Glamour* and initially discount it because of its source, but a few months later you might recall the information, but forget that you read it in *Glamour* and therefore believe it. In one study on the power of the sleeper effect, participants heard a message by a credible or a non-credible source, and then reported their attitude change (Hovland & Weiss, 1951). Immediately after the message, those who heard the credible speaker had much greater attitude change than those who heard the non-credible speaker. However, when participants reported their attitudes again four weeks later, there was no difference in attitude change between the high and low credibility speaker. Similarly, some advertisements in magazines appear as if they are articles. Although people may initially realize it is an advertisement, they may still read it and over time forget that it was just an ad.

CONTENT OF THE MESSAGE

The message content of the arguments presented (strong/weak) obviously influence persuasion. Some messages are based on providing information (e.g., this bleach will get your clothes their whitest). Other messages are based on positive emotion (e.g., don't these people drinking Coors look happy?), and still others are based on fear (e.g., public health ads against unsafe sex or smoking). So, which factors influence the effectiveness of a message?

Length. We often think that long messages are more persuasive than short ones, but the link between message *length* and persuasiveness is complex (Harkins

Questioning the Research

This section described factors that influence persuasion, but all of these factors can't be present at the same time. For example, similarity is often very different from expertise. Which of these source factors do you think is an especially strong influence on persuasion and why?

The Benefits of "Stealing the Thunder"

One common strategy in the legal system is for lawyers to volunteer the weaknesses in their own case, particularly if they believe their opponent will raise these issues in their own case. This approach, often referred to as "stealing the thunder," is seen as a highly effective way of reducing the impact of negative information. To test whether presenting both sides of the argument is indeed an effective strategy, researchers presented participants with one of three trial transcripts: "no thunder" (e.g., no hidden information), "thunder" (e.g., information presented by one side but not the other), and "stolen thunder" (e.g., information presented by both sides; Williams, Bourgeois, & Croyle, 1993). As predicted, those who read the "stolen thunder" version saw the lawyer who presented this damaging information about his own client as more credible, and were less likely to think the client was guilty than those who heard that information presented only by the other lawyer (although participants who read the "no thunder" version were the least likely to see the client as guilty). These findings suggest that presenting two-sided messages can be a very effective approach in the legal system, as long as one is reasonably confident that the opposing side will present the information anyway.

©Corbis /SUPERSTOCK

& Petty, 1981). Long messages are more effective if the message is strong and is processed centrally, but less effective if weak and processed peripherally (Petty & Cacioppo, 1984; Wood, Kallgren, & Preisler, 1985). But long messages that include weak or irrelevant messages can have less impact than short, strong, and focused messages, particularly if people are using central route processing (Friedrich, Fetherstonhaugh, Casey, & Gallagher, 1996). The Law Connections box describes another way in which message content can influence persuasion.

Discrepancy. The discrepancy of the message from the audience's original attitude can also impact its persuasiveness (Wegener, Petty, Detweiler-Bedell, & Jarvis, 2001). Messages that are too discrepant from people's attitudes are likely to be ignored, and messages that are right at people's current attitudes aren't effective in changing attitudes. For example, some messages about safer sex for high school students are ineffective because they say "no sex, ever" (see Would You Believe for a vivid example of the drawbacks to highly discrepant messages). Messages that say "always use a condom if you have sex" may be more realistic. Similarly, and as described at the start of this section, heavy coffee drinkers are more critical of a study supposedly showing a link between caffeine consumption and disease than those who didn't drink coffee. Presumably this is because coffee drinkers don't want to believe they are engaging in a health-damaging behavior (Liberman & Chaiken, 1992; Sherman, Nelson, & Steele, 2000).

This tendency to refute messages that are too discrepant from our original attitude helps explain why attitudes tend to become more extreme over time: because people gather support for their own beliefs and ignore disconfirming evidence (Miller, McHoskey, Bane, & Dowd, 1993; Pomerantz, Chaiken, & Tordesillas, 1995). In a classic study of this phenomenon, researchers asked students who were

WOULD YOU BELIEVE... Virginity Pledges Have No Effect on Rates of Sexually-Transmitted Diseases? One popular set of interventions to prevent the spread of sexually transmitted diseases (STDs) and unwanted pregnancy is to encourage adolescents to make a pledge to abstain from sex until marriage. This emphasis on virginity pledges is supported by federal policy and has been adopted by numerous organizations. In fact, it is estimated that over 2 million adolescents (approximately 12% of all adolescents) in the United States have taken such a pledge.

To examine the effect of making such a pledge on rates of STDs, researchers examined data collected from a sample of over 15,000 adolescents (Bruckner & Bearman, 2005). Participants were asked about their sexual behavior, including whether they had taken a pledge to remain a virgin until marriage, and, for those who had become sexually active, when they had first had sex and their number of sexual partners. In addition, researchers collected urine samples from the participants to test directly for STDs.

This data revealed several interesting findings. First, those who make a virginity pledge do become sexually active at a later age than those who don't make a pledge. On average, those who do not make a virginity pledge begin having sex at age 17, compared to age 19 for those who make a virginity pledge. Although those who make a pledge tend to have sex later than those who do not, the majority of both pledges and non-pledges do have sex prior to marriage: 88% of the pledgers and 99% of the non-pledgers. Most importantly, there are no differences in STD rates between those who make a pledge and those who do not. What explains this lack of difference in STD rates? Although those who make a virginity pledge start having sex at a later age and have fewer sexual partners than those who do not make a pledge, they are also less likely to use a condom when they first have sex and are less likely to see a doctor because they are worried about having an STD. This study indicates a potential downside to a reliance on virginity pledges: although they do delay the onset of sexual activity, they are not likely to lead to abstinence before marriage nor do they decrease the likelihood of contracting an STD.

either for or against the death penalty to read two fictitious studies: one that showed that the death penalty deterred homicides and one that showed no deterrent effect (Lord, Ross, & Lepper, 1979). After reading these studies, participants were asked what changes had occurred in their attitudes toward capital punishment. Even though everyone had read the same two studies, participants became more extreme in their attitudes: those who were somewhat in favor of capital punishment now strongly supported it, while those who were somewhat against it were now more strongly opposed to it. How does reading information about both sides of an issue lead to greater attitude extremity? One factor that contributes to this extremity is that people tend to see evidence that supports their view as quite strong, and evidence that opposes their view as quite weak (see Figure 7.3). Similarly, people who are high in prejudice against gays rate a (fake) scientific study that supports negative views about gay people as more convincing than a study that refutes these views (Munro & Ditto, 1997). People who are low in prejudice against gays make the opposite ratings. In sum, people rate information that supports their own views as more convincing than information that goes against those views (Biek, Wood, & Chaiken, 1996; Edwards & Smith, 1996; Giner-Sorolla & Chaiken, 1994, 1997).

Reed Saxon/©AP/WideWorld Photos

In the NEWS **The impact of discrepancy on persuasion.** Will exposure to the other side of an argument help people understand both sides and thereby reduce their support of their own position? No—in fact, such exposure typically strengthens a person's original views.

FIGURE
7.3

HOW PERSUASIVE ARE ARGUMENTS THAT CONTRADICT OUR INITIAL VIEWS?

In this experiment, participants were asked to read fictional studies that either supported or refuted their initial views about the death penalty. As predicted, participants rated an article that supported their initial view as stronger than an article that contradicted their initial view.

Source: Lord, C. G., Ross, L., & Lepper, M. R. (1979). Biased assimilation and attitude polarization: The effects of prior theories on subsequently considered evidence. *Journal of Personality and Social Psychology, 37*, 2098-2109.

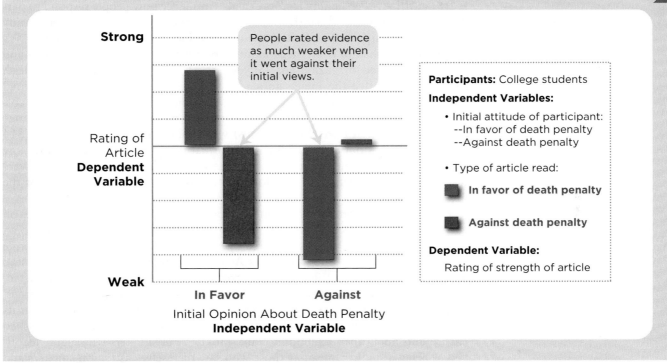

Strong

People rated evidence as much weaker when it went against their initial views.

Rating of Article
Dependent Variable

Weak

In Favor   Against
Initial Opinion About Death Penalty
Independent Variable

Participants: College students

Independent Variables:

- Initial attitude of participant:
  --In favor of death penalty
  --Against death penalty

- Type of article read:

  In favor of death penalty

  Against death penalty

Dependent Variable:

Rating of strength of article

AUDIENCE

Individual difference factors, such as age, gender, and personality traits, can influence the effectiveness of persuasive messages.

Demographic factors. People in their late adolescent and early adult years are most influenced by persuasive messages, which may in part explain why this demographic group is coveted by television executives (Krosnick & Alwin, 1989; Sears, 1986). Compared to adults, college students have less stable attitudes and a stronger tendency to comply with authority, which means their attitudes and behavior are more easily influenced. However, Penny Visser and Jon Krosnick (1998) found that people in early and late adulthood are more responsive to persuasive messages than those who are in middle adulthood. Recent research suggests that older adults are more persuaded by messages that focus on meaningful goals (e.g., "Take time for the ones you love" and "Capture those special moments"), whereas younger adults show no such preference (Fung & Carstensen, 2003). Research Focus on Gender describes gender differences in persuasion.

RESEARCH FOCUS ON GENDER
The Impact of Gender on Persuasion

Research on the impact of gender on persuasion overall suggests that women are more easily persuaded than men (Eagly & Carli, 1981). This difference is due in part to gender differences in social roles: men are often focused on demonstrating their independence from others, whereas women are often focused on fostering cooperation in their interactions. Another factor that may lead to gender differences in persuasion is the type of persuasion strategy used (Guadagno & Cialdini, 2002). Specifically, women tend to be more influenced by face-to-face persuasion attempts than by email persuasion attempts, perhaps because it is more difficult for women to resist agreeing with others during in-person communication than during a more distant persuasion attempt. On the other hand, men show no differences in how they respond to these two distinct types of communication.

Personality. Personality factors can also influence how people respond to particular persuasive messages (DeBono, 1987; Jarvis & Petty, 1996). One study examined the impact of *self-monitoring*—meaning the tendency to change one's attitudes and behavior to fit the situation—on responsiveness to both image- and information-based magazine ads (Snyder & DeBono, 1985). In ads for Irish Mocha Mint coffee the image ad said "Make a chilly night a cozy evening" whereas the information ad said "A delicious blend of three great flavors — coffee, chocolate, and mint." As predicted, high self-monitors (who tend to change their behavior to fit different situations) were willing to pay an average of $14 for the image ads but only $12 for the information ads. On the other hand, low self-monitors (who tend to stay the same regardless of their specific situation) were willing to pay an average of $13 for the information ads and only $11 for the image ads.

How people see themselves also influences the impact of persuasive messages on very serious topics, such as quitting smoking. In one study, smokers listened to an antismoking message that was delivered by either the World Public Health Institute or the Geneva Neighborhood Citizens Association (Invernizzi, Falomir-Pichastor, Muñoz-Rojas, & Mugny, 2003). (In Switzerland, where this study was conducted, neighborhood associations are very active social organizations that promote citizens' welfare.) This message was highly critical of the decision to smoke, and listed as its goal "to stop the damage of smoking by fighting smokers." Researchers then asked participants about their intention to quit smoking. For smokers who highly identified as being a smoker (meaning those who saw themselves as *typical* smokers and felt similar to other smokers), the antismoking message supposedly delivered by the neighborhood source was significantly more effective in increasing intentions to quit than the message delivered by the health institute. On the other hand, for smokers who did not identify as being smokers, messages that were delivered by the health institute led to greater intentions to quit smoking.

Another personality factor that can influence responsiveness to persuasive communications is people's need to think about things (Cacioppo & Petty, 1982; Jarvis & Petty, 1996). Those who are high in need for evaluating are less likely to give "no-opinion" responses on surveys, and are more likely to express evaluative thoughts when looking at new things (e.g., "I would not hang this in my home," and "I really like the colors"). Similarly, and as shown in Rate Yourself, the need for cognition scale measures people's enjoyment of engaging in careful and effortful processing of information. As you might predict, those who are high in need for cognition, namely, those who enjoy thinking carefully about information, tend to think about the information presented in a message more thoroughly (e.g., engage in central route processing). These high-cognition people are more persuaded by strong messages (Cacioppo, Petty, & Morris, 1983).

Those who are low in need for cognition, meaning those who like to conserve mental resources, are more persuaded by peripheral cues, such as the expertise of the speaker, the reaction of other people, and the length of the message (Cacioppo & Petty, 1982). In one study, students listened to audiotapes that contained either high or low quality arguments, and then rated their agreement with the message (Axsom, Yates, & Chaiken, 1987). Students who were low in need for cognition were more likely to be influenced by the reaction of others in the

© Radius/SUPERSTOCK

People who are low in cognition are especially likely to be influenced by how others react to a given message.

Do You Enjoy Thinking and Problem Solving?

Need for Cognition Scale

INSTRUCTIONS: *Rate each item on a scale of –4 (strongly disagree) to +4 (strongly agree).*

☐ **1.** I really enjoy a task that involves coming up with new solutions to problems.

☐ **2.** I appreciate opportunities to discover the strengths and weaknesses of my own reasoning.

☐ **3.** I would prefer my life to be filled with puzzles that I must solve.

☐ **4.** I enjoy thinking about an issue even when the results of my thought will have no effect on the outcome of the issue.

☐ **5.** I tend to set goals that can be accomplished only by expending considerable mental effort.

☐ **6.** I am usually tempted to put more thought into a task than the job minimally requires.

☐ **7.** I appreciate opportunities to discover the strengths and weaknesses of my own reasoning.

☐ **8.** I usually end up deliberating about issues even when they do not affect me personally.

SCORING: Sum up your total number of points on all 8 items.

INTERPRETATION: This scale assesses the extent to which people engage in and enjoy thinking about and carefully processing information (Cacioppo & Petty, 1982). People with higher scores are more interested in engaging in thinking, whereas those with lower scores are less interested.

audience (e.g., whether others seemed to support the argument) than were those who were high in need for cognition.

People who are low in need for cognition are also more influenced by other peripheral cues, such as the attractiveness or popularity of the speaker. In one study, researchers showed students a 20-minute clip of the film *Die Hard* (Gibson & Maurer, 2000). Half of the students saw a clip in which the lead character, played by Bruce Willis, smokes. The other half saw a clip in which he did not smoke. Among nonsmokers, those who were low in need for cognition and saw the lead character smoke reported more willingness to become friends with a smoker than those who were high in need for cognition.

FACTORS INFLUENCING PERSUASION

Concepts in Context

FACTOR	EXAMPLE
Source	Michelle was selecting a new toothpaste to buy. In making her decision, she remembered a recent advertisement about the kind of toothpaste used by most dentists.
Message	Alberto was persuaded to try a new cologne because the music playing in its advertisement was very catchy and appealing.
Audience	Bruce, who is a high self-monitor, was very persuaded by the car advertisement that featured an attractive model driving the car very quickly—even though he could barely see the car and learned nothing about its features.

HOW CAN SUBTLE FACTORS INFLUENCE PERSUASION?

Although thus far this chapter has focused on the presence of relatively obvious features of messages that impact persuasion, subtle cues can also lead to persuasion. In one study, diners at a restaurant were presented with their bill on one of two types of trays (McCall & Belmont, 1996). In one condition, the tray featured a credit card emblem, such as Visa or American Express. In the other condition, the tray was blank. Researchers then examined the size of tip left in each of these conditions—assuming that the presence of the credit card emblem would cue higher tips. As predicted, customers tipped on overage 4.29% more when their bill was presented on a tip tray with a credit card emblem than on a blank tray. This study provides strong evidence that even very subtle factors can influence our behavior—even without our knowledge. This section examines how two subtle factors influence persuasion: emotional appeals and subliminal processing.

THE IMPACT OF EMOTIONAL APPEALS

One strategy that is often used to influence people's attitudes and behavior is to create messages that try to arouse particular emotions. Two types of messages that illustrate the use of emotion are fear-based appeals and positive emotion appeals.

Would these ads scare you away from smoking? These warnings are required to appear on cigarette packages in Canada, and are much more fear-inducing than the warnings required to appear on cigarette packages in the United States.

Fear-Based Appeals. The use of negative emotion, and particularly *fear*, is common in some types of persuasive messages. One study of AIDS public service announcements on television found that 26% of the announcements used fear (Freimuth, Hammond, Edgar, & Monohan, 1990). Persuasive messages that use fear are designed to create the threat of impending danger or harm caused by engaging in a behavior (e.g., drug use, smoking) or by failing to engage in a behavior (e.g., not using a condom, not wearing a seatbelt). This is a common way to try to persuade people to change health-related behaviors (Higbee, 1969). These messages sometimes use scary verbal statements and may show graphic, even disgusting, images. One television ad promoting the use of seatbelts shows a young man backing his car out of the driveway to pick up ice cream for his very-pregnant wife, but failing to wear a seatbelt and then being hit by a speeding car. In countries such as Australia and Canada, television ads may include even more graphic images, for instance, dead bodies and crash survivors learning how to walk again.

Fear-based messages are designed to increase people's feelings of vulnerability to various health problems, and thereby motivate them to change their behavior. But most evidence suggests that this approach is not particularly effective. One study of Project DARE (Drug Abuse Resistance Education), a commonly used fear-based drug prevention program for children, found that this program has little effect on preventing or reducing drug use. It is often less effective than programs that focus simply on social skills (Ennett, Tobler, Ringwalt, & Flewelling, 1994). Similarly, a fear-arousing mass media campaign in Australia to promote condom use led to an increase in anxiety, but had little effect on knowledge or behavior (Rigby, K., Brown, M., Anagnostou, P., Ross, M.W., & Rosser, B.R.S., 1989; Sherr, 1990). Ironically, people who receive high fear messages often *report* that they are very influenced, but in reality show lower levels of attitude and behavior change than those who receive positive approaches (Janis & Feshbach, 1953).

But sometimes fear appeals can lead to behavior change, in part because such messages can increase feelings of vulnerability and thereby lead to more careful processing of the information presented (Baron, Logan, Lilly, Inman, & Brennan, 1994). In one study, participants rated their perceived likelihood of experiencing a stress-related illness, and then read a fictitious letter to a health journal describing the benefits of stress management training in reducing the risk of stress-related illnesses (Das, De Wit, & Stroebe, 2003). Participants who felt vulnerable to experiencing a stress-related illness were more persuaded by the letter, regardless of the quality of the arguments presented, and were more likely to intend to participate in stress management training. Similar results were found for participants who felt vulnerable to another type of injury, that is, RSI (repetitive strain injury, or "mouse arm"; De Hoog, Stroebe, & de Wit, 2005). Another study found that 86% of those who saw a scary video on lung cancer reported trying to stop or cut down their smoking, as compared to only 33% of those who saw a control video (Sutton & Eiser, 1984). The Health Connections box describes other factors that can increase the effectiveness of fear-based appeals.

Questioning the Research
This study suggests that people who see a scary movie on lung cancer report trying to quit more than those who don't see this movie. But are you confident that people are accurately reporting their behavior? Why or why not?

Fear messages are most likely to influence behavior change when they force people to actually imagine having a particular disease or problem, and thereby lead to heightened vulnerability. One public service announcement designed to enhance people's perceived vulnerability to HIV featured an attractive Hispanic man saying the following: "Do I look like someone who has AIDS? Of course not. I am Alejandro Paredes. I finished school. I have a good job. I help support my family. My kind of guy doesn't get AIDS, right? Well, I have AIDS, and I don't mind telling you it's devastating. If I had a second chance, I'd be informed. Believe me." (Freimuth et al., 1990, p. 788). This appeal is clearly designed to increase awareness of people's vulnerability to HIV, and to eliminate the use of various cognitive defenses against this information (e.g., only poor people get HIV, only people who look unhealthy have HIV, etc.).

The importance of feeling personally vulnerable to a disease helps explain why personal testimonials can be more effective than objective statistics at increasing risk perception and thereby motivating behavior change. In one study, researchers compared the effectiveness of two distinct types of messages describing risk of acquiring the hepatitis virus in promoting acceptance of risk among homosexual men (a group at high risk of acquiring this virus; de Wit, Das, & Vet, 2008). One of the messages emphasized statistical evidence about the prevalence of this virus, and the particularly large rates of hepatitis among gay men. The other message featured a person describing how he had been infected with this virus, even though he had believed he would not be vulnerable. Researchers then examined perceived risk and intention to receive a vaccination for hepatitis. The narrative message was more effective at increasing intentions to receive a vaccination than the statistical one, presumably because people are less likely to respond defensively to this approach.

Interestingly, providing the opportunity to self-affirm can also lead to greater acceptance of fear messages. In one study, women read a leaflet describing the link between excessive alcohol use and breast cancer (Harris & Napper, 2005). Half of these women were frequent drinkers (14 alcoholic drinks per week). The other half were infrequent drinkers. The women were randomly assigned to one of two conditions. In the self-affirmation condition, women wrote about their most important value and how this value influenced their behavior in daily life. In the control condition, women wrote about how their least important value might be important to another student. All participants then read the leaflet, which summarized recent research on the alcohol consumption–breast cancer link and emphasized that excessive drinking can be hazardous. Next, participants reported their personal risk of developing breast cancer, ease of imagining themselves developing breast cancer, and intention to reduce alcohol consumption. As predicted, women who were excessive drinkers and had the opportunity to self-affirm their most important value prior to reading the

Why Having Wrinkles Is Worse Than Dying

Because many people, especially teenagers, aren't very concerned about long-term consequences, fear-based messages that emphasize the long-term consequences of a behavior are usually ineffective. Many college students say that having an unplanned pregnancy would be worse than getting HIV, presumably because pregnancy leads to an instant problem, whereas developing HIV is a much more distant problem. This lack of concern about long-term consequences compared to short-term ones explains why people who learn that tanning can cause skin cancer still want to be tan because they are seen as healthier and more attractive (Broadstock, Borland, & Garson, 1992; Leary & Jones, 1993). Similarly, one study with 19 young drug sniffers (who often go on to use IV drugs) found that none gave concern about AIDS as a reason for not using IV drugs; they simply didn't want to lose control over their lives due to addiction (des Jarlais, Friedman, Casriel, & Kott, 1987).

On the other hand, fear appeals that focus on the short-term consequences of a behavior can be quite effective (Klohn & Rogers, 1991). For example, smoking prevention messages for teenagers emphasize the immediate physiological and social consequences of smoking, such as the financial cost of smoking, rejection by potential dating partners who don't like the smell of smoke, and having stained teeth and bad breath. Jones and Leary (1994) found that college students were more persuaded to use sunscreen after reading an essay describing the short-term negative effects of tanning on appearance (e.g., increasing wrinkles, scarring, aging, etc.) than an essay describing the long-term negative effects (e.g., the health risks of tanning, prevalence of different types of skin cancer). In fact, emphasizing minor but short-term consequences is more effective in changing attitudes toward smoking than emphasizing the serious long-term health consequences (Pechmann, 1997).

© medioblitzimages (uk)Limited/Alam

leaflet showed greater acceptance of the alcohol consumption–breast cancer link than those who were in the control condition. Similarly, smokers who write about important values, a commonly used way of triggering self-affirmation, are more accepting of information that smoking harms health (Crocker, Niiya, & Mischkowski, 2008).

The Power of Positive Emotion.   Although fear is one way to persuade people, so is using *positive emotion messages* (Janis, Kaye, & Kirschner, 1965; Mackie & Worth, 1989; Petty, Schumann, Richman, & Strathman, 1993). In fact, people who are in a good mood (e.g., eating snack foods, watching an upbeat program, listening to pleasant music) are more easily persuaded than those who are in a less good mood. The Business Connections box describes how putting people in a good mood can lead customers to tip more.

How Waiters and Waitresses Can Increase Tips

Creating positive emotions can persuade people to be more generous in one common daily life situation—tipping at a restaurant. Several studies demonstrate that small behaviors that activate positive moods in customers lead to significantly higher tipping. In one study, bartenders gave customers their bill accompanied by either a small advertisement card, a joke card, or no card (the control condition; Guéguen, 2002). As predicted, customers who received the joke card were more likely to tip than those who received no card or the advertisement card. In another study, waitresses left one of three messages on the checks after customers finished with their meals (Seiter & Gass, 2005). These messages all were designed to produce a good mood, but they varied in the specific content of the message: "Have a Nice Day," "United We Stand," or no message. People who received the "United We Stand" message left significantly higher tips (19%) than those who received no message (15%) or the "Have a Nice Day" message (16%). Simply learning the server's name increases tipping. In one study, couples that arrived at a restaurant were randomly assigned to one of two conditions (Garrity & Degelman, 1990). In one condition, the server introduced herself by name. In the other condition, she did not. The tipping rate was substantially higher when the customers learned the server's name—23%—than when they did not—15%. This research demonstrates that even subtle factors can increase persuasion.

Why do positive messages lead to persuasion? People who are in a good mood want to maintain this positive feeling, and thus are less likely to process information carefully. In turn, they tend to rely on shortcut peripheral cues, such as availability of a given argument, when evaluating a message (Ruder & Bless, 2003). If you are feeling very happy, you may simply agree with whatever message you hear, regardless of message quality. In fact, even nodding one's head—a type of cue of happiness or agreement—while listening to a persuasive message leads to greater persuasion than shaking one's head (Briñol & Petty, 2003). This tendency to rely on peripheral route processing is particularly likely when people are concerned that focusing on the message's content will disrupt their good mood (e.g., when the message is depressing), but not when the message is uplifting (Wegener, Petty, & Smith, 1995). As shown in Figure 7.4, students who are in a happy mood when they receive a positive message are more convinced by strong arguments than weak ones, yet argument strength has no impact on persuasion when those who are in a happy mood receive a negative message (e.g., a message involving a tuition raise).

"I forget the name of the product, but the jingle on TV goes something like 'Ya-dee-dum-dee-rah-te-dum-dee-rah-dee-dum.'"

In contrast, people who are in a sad mood tend to rely on the overall number of arguments they can generate for a given position. So, they rely on the content of the arguments generated in forming an attitude, not simply the ease with which these arguments came to mind. On the other hand, people who are in a sad or neutral mood are more likely to use the central route, and carefully evaluate the content of a persuasive message (Bless, Bohner, Schwarz, & Strack, 1990). The Research Focus on Neuroscience section describes how emotions can influence voting choices.

RESEARCH FOCUS ON NEUROSCIENCE
The Influence of Emotion in the Ballot Box

In one study conducted during the 2004 presidential election race, Emory University psychology professor Drew Westen examined the brain activity of participants as they listened to statements made by political candidates (Westen, Blagov, Harenski, Kilts, & Hamann, 2006). The brain areas responsible for reasoning did not show increased activity while they listened to these speeches, but the brain areas that controlled emotions did show increased activity. This finding suggests that unconscious feelings and emotions may have a stronger influence on our voting behavior than more conscious and rationale thoughts. As Westen writes, "In politics, the emotions that really sway voters are hate, hope and fear or anxiety. But the skillful use of fear is unmatched in leading to enthusiasm for one candidate and causing voters to turn away from another." The power of fear to influence voters' behaviors helps explain the common use of campaign advertisements that try to invoke danger, such as the pack of hungry-looking wolves that appeared in a 2004 advertisement for George Bush.

THE IMPACT OF SUBLIMINAL MESSAGES

You may have heard about a famous example of real-world persuasion in which Coke and popcorn sales at a movie theatre increased dramatically after the words "Eat Popcorn" and "Drink Coke" were flashed very briefly on the screen. Although this story was later determined to be a hoax, there is compelling evidence that at least in some cases, **subliminal persuasion**, meaning persuasion that occurs when stimuli are presented at a very rapid and unconscious level, can influence people's attitudes and behavior. In turn, advertisers continue to spend billions of dollars a year trying to increase people's exposure to certain products, in the belief that increased exposure should increase sales of such products. This belief in the power of subliminal persuasion explains why the character Eva Longoria plays on *Desperate Housewives* drives a Buick LaCrosse, Coke products are constantly on screen during *American Idol*, and a plot line on the soap opera *All My Children* involved character Erica Kane's cosmetic company competing with Revlon. All of these are examples of unconscious advertising.

This belief that subliminal priming can influence what people buy is supported by research studies in psychology (Strahan, Spencer, & Zanna, 2002). In one study, participants were asked to assist in a marketing study in which they would evaluate different types of products (Karremans, Stroebe, & Claus, 2006). During the first part of the study, participants completed a computer task in which they were primed with either the word "Lipton Ice" or a control word that contained the same letters (e.g., "Npeic Tol"). Next, participants were asked to indicate which of two brand names they would prefer if they were offered a drink now. One of those brand names was Lipton Ice and the other

subliminal persuasion a type of persuasion that occurs when stimuli are presented at a very rapid and unconscious level

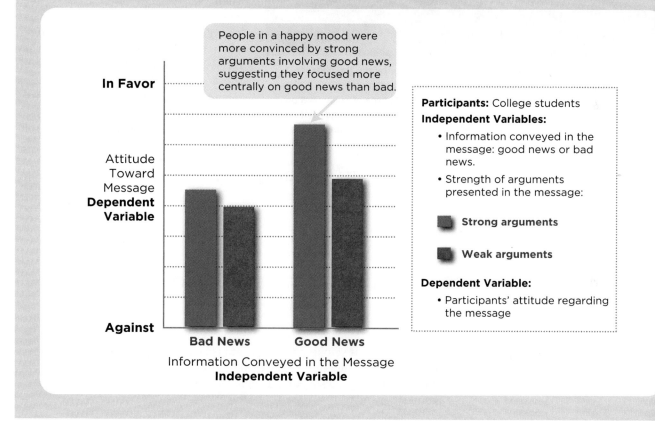

FIGURE 7.4

DOES MOOD IMPACT PROCESSING?

To study whether mood influenced the type of processing used to consider arguments, the researchers in this experiment had college students watch some funny television clips (such as from the David Letterman show) and then read messages involving either good news—a tuition decrease—or bad news—a tuition increase. As predicted, happy people were more convinced by strong arguments than weak arguments regarding a message that conveyed good news (suggesting central processing). However, strength of the argument had no effect on people's attitudes when the message conveyed bad news (suggesting a reliance on peripheral processing). Researchers suggested that using peripheral-route processing helps happy people avoid focusing too closely on depressing messages and allows them to maintain a good mood.

Source: Wegener, D. T., Petty, R. E., & Smith, S. M. (1995). Positive mood can increase or decrease message scrutiny: The hedonic contingency view of mood and message processing. *Journal of Personality and Social Psychology, 69*, 5-15.

People in a happy mood were more convinced by strong arguments involving good news, suggesting they focused more centrally on good news than bad.

In Favor

Attitude Toward Message
Dependent Variable

Against

Bad News   Good News

Information Conveyed in the Message
Independent Variable

Participants: College students

Independent Variables:

- Information conveyed in the message: good news or bad news.
- Strength of arguments presented in the message:

    Strong arguments

    Weak arguments

Dependent Variable:

- Participants' attitude regarding the message

was Spa Rood (a type of mineral water common in the Netherlands, where this study was conducted). Participants were also asked to rate how thirsty they were at that moment. There was no difference in intention to drink Lipton Ice as a function of prime condition for those who were not thirsty. However, among participants who were thirsty, those who received the Lipton Ice prime showed a strong preference for this brand over the other brand. This research reveals that subliminal persuasion can influence consumer preferences, at least in the short term.

However, there are limits to the effects of subliminal processing. Although you can buy many commercially produced self-help audiotapes, which claim they can help you stop smoking or improve your memory, research provides

The word "RATS" appeared in a television commercial paid for by the Republican National Committee and criticizing Al Gore's prescription-drug plan during the 2000 presidential campaign. Although people often believe that this type of subliminal processing can influence behavior, this type of processing has only limited and brief effects on behavior—and certainly didn't impact the 2000 election outcome.

no support for claims that subliminal processing can have such powerful effects. In one study, researchers gave students one of two types of tapes to listen to for the next three weeks (Greenwald, Spangenberg, Pratankis, & Eskenazi, 1991). Some participants received tapes they were told would improve their memory, whereas others received tapes they were told would improve their self-esteem. However, researchers gave half of the participants the type of tape they were not expecting—meaning some of those who thought the tape would help their memory was actually supposed to help their self-esteem. Researchers then measured memory and self-esteem changes three weeks later. Although participants believed that the tape they received had a positive impact, with those who believed they received a memory tape reporting better memory and those who believed they received a self-esteem tape reporting better self-esteem, there were no actual differences in self-esteem or memory after exposure to a particular tape. This research suggests that subliminal processing does not have long-term effects on behavior.

HOW SUBTLE FACTORS CAN IMPACT PERSUASION

Concepts in Context

FACTOR	EXAMPLE
Emotional appeals	Dupal knew that smoking was bad for his health but just couldn't seem to break the habit. But after seeing a photograph of a cancer-ridden lung, he immediately stopped smoking. Dupal hasn't had a cigarette in over six months.
Subliminal processing	Monique was not feeling particularly thirsty as she watched *American Idol*. But after repeatedly seeing Paula Abdul drink a Diet Coke on this show, Monique decided to go buy a Diet Coke herself.

HOW CAN YOU RESIST PERSUASION?

Although we have focused on factors that influence how people process persuasive messages, in some cases we are intent on resisting such attempts. In one study, students read descriptions of several fictitious made-for-television films (Bushman & Stack, 1996). Half of these articles described a violent film, and the other half described a nonviolent film. In addition, some of these movies included a warning label, such as "This film contains some violent content. Viewer discretion is advised." Other movies included only an information label, such as "This film contains some violence." Students then rated how interested they were in seeing each film. As predicted, participants were more interested in watching the violent films with the warning labels than those with the information labels. This study describes one example of the way in which attempts at persuasion can backfire. How can we resist persuasive messages? This section will describe four factors that influence our ability to resist persuasion: forewarning, reactance, inoculation, and attitude importance.

FOREWARNING

First, it is often easier to resist such attempts when people receive **forewarning** that others are trying to persuade them (Chen, Reardon, Rea, & Moore, 1992). For example, telling teenagers that they are going to hear a speech on "why teenagers should not drive" leads to less change than telling them they are going to hear a speech on driving in general (Freedman & Sears, 1965). Forewarning about an upcoming persuasion attempt allows people to construct counterarguments, and thus is particularly effective for resisting persuasion (Jacks & Cameron, 2003).

Forewarning about an upcoming persuasion attempt is especially useful if it includes specific training on evaluating features of persuasive messages. In one study, half of the participants received information on how to critically evaluate the legitimacy of the source that delivers a message (Sagarin, Cialdini, Rice, & Serna, 2002). For example, participants read the following:

> **Many ads use authority figures to help sell the product. But how can we tell when an authority figure is being used ethically or unethically? For an authority to be used ethically it must pass two tests. First, the authority must be a real authority, and not just someone dressed up to look like an authority. Second, the authority must be an expert on the product he or she is trying to sell (p. 530).**

Participants then rated six advertisements (three featuring legitimate authorities, three featuring illegitimate authorities). As predicted, participants who received the training rated the ads containing the illegitimate authorities as more manipulative and less persuasive than those in the control condition (who received no training).

REACTANCE

Knowing about an upcoming persuasion attempt also motivates us to resist whatever the message is; this is called **reactance** (or the boomerang effect; Brehm, 1966; Brehm & Brehm, 1981; Edwards & Bryan, 1997). Reactance refers to the feeling that people have when their freedom is threatened so that they want to restore freedom. If your parents really hate someone you are dating and try to break it off, how might you react? You might become even more attached to this person as a way of avoiding letting your parents restrict your freedom. In these cases, persuasion backfires, as described in the study at the start of this section on the use of warning labels on violent films. Reactance explains why banning television violence or using warning labels on particular television shows or movies can increase people's interest in watching these programs (Bushman & Cantor, 2003; Bushman & Stack, 1996; Pennebaker & Sanders, 1976). Reactance also explains why students drink more alcohol after receiving a high threat message about the dangers of alcohol consumption than after receiving a low threat message (Bensley & Wu, 1991).

forewarning making people aware that they will soon receive a persuasive message

reactance the idea that people react to threats to their freedom to engage in a behavior by becoming even more likely to engage in that behavior

© Richard Levine/Alamy

Could forbidding college students to drink actually increase alcohol use on college campuses? According to reactance theory, yes.

One factor that can lead people to react against a persuasive message is having the opportunity to engage in the behavior that is forbidden by the message (Albarracin, Cohen, & Kumkale, 2003). In one study, college students read one of two messages about an alcohol-type beverage. One of the messages urged students to completely abstain from consuming the beverage; the other message urged students to consume the beverage in moderate amounts. Some participants then had the opportunity to try the beverage. When participants later reported their future intentions regarding that beverage, those who had not tried the beverage reported similar levels of intending to consume the beverage in the future regardless of which message they had read. However, among those who had tried the beverage, those who had read the message urging complete abstinence reported stronger intentions to try the behavior again in the future than those who read the message urging moderate consumption. This research suggests that messages that emphasize moderation may be more effective than those that emphasize abstinence—because abstinence messages are much less effective than moderation messages if people do engage in the behavior.

INOCULATION

Another way to resist persuasion is for people to be exposed to a weak version of a persuasive message. People are better able to defend against messages if they have some practice defending their own views, a process called **inoculation** (as in having a measles inoculation; McGuire, 1964). This practice allows people to better defend against a stronger version of the message later on, and even increases attitude certainty (Tormala & Petty, 2004). For example, people who are first asked to write and then refute reasons opposing "equal opportunity for all" are then more resistant to an anti-equality message later on (Bernard, Maio, & Olson, 2003). If you are a college student who has been a Republican all your life, you will be more able to resist persuasive messages of the Democratic party if you were exposed to weak versions of these messages before and if you previously have responded to challenges to your view. But those who have never had to defend their views will be less able to offer such resistance.

inoculation the idea that exposure to a weak version of a persuasive message strengthens people's ability to resist that message later on

Persuasive messages may be particularly effective when they provide direct counterarguments to common reasons people give for failing to engage in the target behavior—meaning participants' initial opposition to the behavior is directly refuted. In one study, researchers created four different types of messages to promote organ donation (Siegel, Alvaro, Crano, Lac, Ting, & Jones, 2008). Counterargument messages refuted common myths about organ donation, emotional messages described the significant impact organ donors can have on the lives of others, motivating action messages emphasized the importance of acting on one's desire to sign up as a donor, and dissonance messages emphasized the inconsistency that results when people believe that organ donation is good to do, but then fail to sign up. Posters with these messages were placed at multiple locations, including a library, hospital, university setting, and community college, directly above a computer terminal on which people could register as organ donors. Researchers then counted the number of individuals who signed up in each location. In each location, the counterargument message led to the greatest number of registrations, indicating that this approach was particularly effective (see Figure 7.5). Thus, persuasive messages may be most effective, at least at increasing this type of altruistic health-related behavior, when they specifically refute arguments against engaging in the targeted behavior.

ATTITUDE IMPORTANCE

Finally, even in cases in which we are exposed to messages designed to change our attitudes, all attitudes are not created equal: attitudes that are important to us are more resistant to persuasion. In one study, people who were in favor of allowing gay people to serve in the military listened to a message that opposed this position (Zuwerink & Devine, 1996). People who considered this attitude highly important were more resistant to this attempt at persuasion than those who

FIGURE
7.5

CAN PROVIDING COUNTERARGUMENTS INCREASE PERSUASION?

In this experiment, researchers displayed in public places posters with four different types of messages promoting organ donation. As predicted, the counterargument message led to the greatest number of registrations, suggesting that refuting counterarguments can be a particularly effective persuasive approach.

Source: Siegel, J. T., Alvaro, E. M., Crano, W. D., Lac, A., Ting, S., & Jones, S. P. (2008). A quasi-experimental investigation of message appeal variations on organ donor registration rates. *Health Psychology, 27*, 170–178.

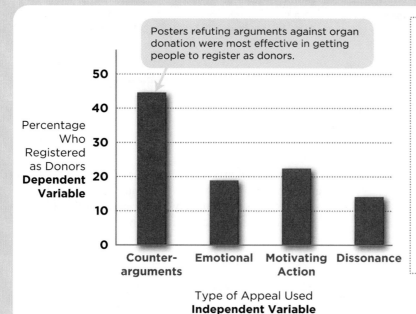

Posters refuting arguments against organ donation were most effective in getting people to register as donors.

Participants: General public

Independent Variable:

Type of appeal used

- **Counterarguments** - refuted organ-donation myths
- **Emotional** - described impact on the lives of others
- **Motivating Action** - emphasized acting on desire to sign up
- **Dissonance** - emphasized inconsistency of believing organ donation is good, but failing to sign up

Dependent Variable:

Percentage of people registered as organ donors

considered this attitude low in importance. Similarly, people who are highly aware of their attitudes and prior experiences are more resistant to persuasion than those who are less aware of their attitudes (Wood, 1982).

Similarly, people who consider a message in terms of how it relates to their important values show greater resistance to attempts to change these attitudes (Blankenship & Wegener, 2008). For example, people who read a persuasive message and reflect on how that message relates to their important values, such as loyalty, freedom, and self-respect, are more resistant to weak arguments than those who reflect on their less important values, such as social power, unity, and wealth.

However, even when we have important attitudes, resisting persuasion attempts takes effort—meaning that self-control plays a key role in determining whether we are influenced by persuasion attempts (Burkley, 2008). In one study, college students read an essay about a new university policy to shorten summer vacation to only one month, a policy that students generally rated as undesirable. Half of the students simply read this essay, and then rated their agreement with the new policy. The other students completed a challenging task that required considerable self-control prior to reading the essay. These students were asked to squeeze a handgrip shut for as long as possible, a task that becomes very difficult for the forearm to maintain, and thus requires considerable self-control to avoid releasing the grip. Students who first exercised self-control on the handgrip task rated the policy more positively than did those who simply read the essay, presumably because these students had already used up their ability to engage in self-control and thus were more persuaded by the essay.

Questioning the Research

This study suggests that important attitudes are more resistant to persuasion than less important ones. What other factors might explain the greater resistance of highly important attitudes? (Hint: How might important attitudes differ from less important attitudes?)

WAYS TO RESIST PERSUASION

FACTOR	EXAMPLE
Forewarning	Lily was looking forward to the school assembly until she learned that the topic was promoting abstinence. Lily is now certain that this assembly will present silly arguments and has already started developing counterarguments to refute this abstinence message.
Reactance	Andrew, who is 14 and a freshman in high school, was somewhat interested in seeing a new R-rated movie. After his father refused to allow him to see it, Andrew became extremely interested in seeing it.
Inoculation	Maya is president of the College Student Republicans at her school. In preparation for a speech she is giving to the student body, she asks her friends to criticize the points she will make in her speech. Maya is thereby able to practice defending her points.
Attitude importance	Mario is a strong proponent of affirmative action policies, and has assisted with several local and national initiatives to implement such policies. Although Mario is sometimes confronted with information that refutes the benefits of such policies, he remains convinced in his views about their benefits.

CULTURE
HOW DOES CULTURE IMPACT PERSUASION?

Have you ever looked at the advertisements in magazines from other countries? If not, you might be surprised at how culture affects persuasive messages. To test the impact of culture on the types of persuasive messages presented, Heejung Kim and Hazel Markus (1999) examined advertisements from popular American and Korean magazines. As shown in Table 7.2, they rated whether the advertisements

TABLE 7.2 **EXAMPLES OF AD SLOGANS IN THE UNITED STATES VERSUS KOREA**

ADS REFLECTING CONFORMITY	ADS REFLECTING UNIQUENESS
"Our ginseng drink is produced according to the methods of 500-year-old tradition."	"Choose your own view."
"Our company is working toward building a harmonious society."	"Ditch the Joneses."
"Seven out of ten people are using this product."	"The Internet isn't for everybody. But then again, you are not everybody."

Magazine advertisements in the United States appeal to individual benefits and preferences, and personal success and independence, to a greater extent than do advertisements in Korea. In contrast, Korean ads focused more on in-group benefits, harmony, and family integrity to a greater extent than do ads in the United States.

Source: Kim, H., & Markus, H. R. (1999). Deviance or uniqueness, harmony or conformity? A cultural analysis. *Journal of Personality and Social Psychology, 77*, 785-800.

appealed to conformity values (e.g., emphasizing tradition, group norms, social roles, trends) or uniqueness (e.g., rejecting tradition and group norms; emphasizing choices, freedom, and uniqueness). As predicted, although some ads from both countries emphasized both types of messages, advertisements in Korea were much more likely to focus on conformity whereas advertisements from the United States were much more likely to focus on uniqueness. This section will examine how culture impacts the types of persuasive messages used and the effectiveness of different persuasive messages.

TYPES OF PERSUASIVE MESSAGES USED

Commercial advertisements tend to reflect the distinct values and beliefs of a given culture (Aaker, Benet-Martinez, & Garolera, 2001). In one study, Jennifer Aaker and her colleagues at the Stanford University School of Business asked over 1,000 Japanese men and women to describe the personality attributes associated with various commercial brands (e.g., "If Coca-Cola was a person, how would you describe him/her?"). Although some of these attributes were similar to those found in ratings by Americans, such as excitement, competence, sophistication, and sincerity, a dimension of peacefulness emerged uniquely in the Japanese sample. Here are some additional findings from this study:

- The attribute ruggedness appeared in ratings by Americans, but not in Japan.
- Similar dimensions appear in ratings in Spain.
- Spain and America both included sincerity, excitement, and sophistication.
- Spain included the attributes of passion and peacefulness.
- The United States included competence and ruggedness.
- Both Japanese and Spanish cultures are more likely to rate commercial brands on harmony-oriented values (e.g., passion, peacefulness).
- The United States rates commercial brands on more individualistic values (e.g., competence, ruggedness).

Questioning the Research

This research suggests that people in different cultures respond in distinct ways to different types of advertising messages. But the research does not explain why this differential responsiveness occurs. For example, people may simply prefer advertisements that are familiar, regardless of whether those messages are in line with their cultural beliefs. How could you test the reason for people's distinct responsiveness to ads reflecting their own culture?

Similarly, advertisements tend to emphasize the prevailing themes of a given culture (Han & Shavitt, 1994). As described at the start of this section, magazine advertisements in the United States tend to emphasize uniqueness, whereas those in Korea tend to emphasize conformity (Kim & Markus, 1999).

THE EFFECTIVENESS OF DIFFERENT PERSUASIVE MESSAGES

Different types of persuasive messages are effective in different cultures. Specifically, advertising appeals that stress interdependence and togetherness lead to more favorable brand attitudes among Chinese people than do appeals that stress independence and autonomy (Wang, Bristol, Mowen, & Chakraborty, 2000). For example, Chinese participants reacted more positively to an advertisement for a watch that ended "The ALPS watch. A reminder of relationships" than to one that ended "The ALPS watch. The art of being unique." Americans, on the other hand, showed the reverse pattern, and found appeals stressing independence more appealing than those stressing interdependence.

People within subgroups within a broader culture can also be influenced in different ways by different types of persuasion messages (Marin, Marin, Perez-Stable, Otero-Sabogal, & Sabogal, 1990). In one study, researchers examined the impact of different factors on intentions to quit smoking among both Hispanic and non-Hispanic White smokers in the United States. Family-related attitudes were a greater influence on Hispanics' attitudes toward quitting, whereas the effects of withdrawal from cigarettes was a greater influence on Whites' attitudes toward quitting. This research points to the importance of designing persuasive messages that fit with individuals' cultural norms and values.

Culture influences how people respond to persuasive messages.

But the impact of culture on the persuasiveness of different messages is not always what you might predict. In one study, researchers asked both American and Chinese people to rate two advertisements for beer (Aaker & Williams, 1998). In one advertisement (the pride appeal), the caption read: "Acing the last exam. Winning the big race. Receiving deserved recognition. Ohio Flag Beer. Celebrating life's accomplishments." In the other advertisement (the empathy appeal), the caption read: "Reminiscing with old friends. Enjoying time together with family during the holidays. Relaxing near the fire with best friends. Ohio Flag Beer. Celebrating the relationships that matter most." Participants then rated how much they liked each advertisement.

Although researchers expected that the pride appeal would be seen more favorably in the United States, and the empathy appeal would be seen more favorably in China, they found the reverse. In the United States, messages that emphasize empathy and peacefulness are more effective at increasing helping. In contrast, in China, messages that emphasize pride and happiness are more effective. Do these findings surprise you? The researchers believe that people in each culture benefit more from hearing messages that are novel or unusual—so, in turn, people from individualistic cultures benefit from hearing messages that emphasize thoughts of the group, and people from collectivistic cultures benefit from hearing messages that emphasize personal thoughts.

The Big Picture

PERSUASION

This chapter included many applications of the three "big ideas" studied in social psychology. The examples below should help you see the connection between persuasion and these big ideas and contribute to your understanding of the big picture of social psychology.

THEME	EXAMPLES
The social world influences how we think about ourselves.	• Adolescents who make a "virginity pledge" see themselves (wrongly) as less at risk of having an STD. • Women who have the opportunity to self-affirm see their risk of developing breast cancer as higher than women who do not first self-affirm. • Women who rate how typical certain behaviors are for women rate themselves as less modest than women who rate how typical these behaviors are for college students in general.
The social world influences our thoughts, attitudes, and behaviors.	• People who hear a weak persuasive message at a fast rate are more persuaded than those who hear the message at a normal or slow rate. • People who hear persuasive messages delivered by highly attractive speakers are more persuaded than those who hear messages delivered by less attractive speakers. • People are more interested in seeing a movie that includes a warning label than those that include a label with information about the movie's content.
Our attitudes and behavior shape the social world around us.	• Our feelings about the death penalty influence how we perceive studies that describe research on this issue. • Coffee drinkers are more critical of a study supposedly showing a link between caffeine consumption and disease than those who don't drink coffee. • Waiters and waitresses who leave a patriotic message with their bills receive better tips.

This chapter has examined five key principles of persuasion.

YOU LEARNED How do we process persuasive messages? This section described two distinct routes to persuasion: central route and peripheral route. It also described the factors that influence which route we choose to use when processing a persuasive message, including the ability to focus and the motivation to focus, and which message is more effective in different cases. You also learned that messages delivered at a fast pace can be effective even if they consist of weak arguments.

YOU LEARNED What factors influence persuasion? This section described the factors that influence persuasion: the source, the message, and the audience. Source factors that influence persuasion include attractiveness, similarity, and credibility. Message factors include the length of the message, the discrepancy of the message, and the emotions aroused by the message. Audience factors that influence the persuasiveness of the message include demographic factors and personality. You also learned that people who drink coffee are much more critical of research describing health risks of caffeine than those who don't drink coffee. Therefore, they feel much less threatened by this information.

YOU LEARNED How can subtle factors influence persuasion? This section described how subtle factors can influence persuasion. You learned about how both negative appeals, such as those based in fear, and positive appeals, such as those based in happiness and positive emotion, can be persuasive. This section also described how subliminal processing can sometimes lead to persuasion. You also learned that providing a bill on a tray with a credit card emblem leads to higher rates of tipping.

YOU LEARNED How do we resist persuasive messages? This section described the strategies for resisting persuasion. You learned about forewarning (letting someone know a persuasion attempt is coming), reactance (the tendency to resist persuasion attempts), inoculation (the benefits of exposure to weak versions of a persuasive message in allowing us to overcome persuasion attempts), and attitude importance (the ability of important attitudes to resist persuasion attempts). You also learned that including warning labels on violent films leads to increased interest in seeing those films.

YOU LEARNED How does culture impact persuasion? This section described how culture influences persuasion. You learned that the types of persuasive messages used are different in different cultures, with messages in individualistic cultures emphasizing uniqueness and messages in collectivistic cultures emphasizing conformity. The effectiveness of different persuasive messages also differs across cultures, with novel messages being seen as more persuasive in a given culture. In turn, messages that emphasize uniqueness are seen as more persuasive in collectivistic cultures and those emphasizing conformity are seen as more persuasive in individualistic cultures. You also learned why "Ditch the Joneses" is a more effective advertising slogan in the United States than in Korea.

KEY TERMS

central or systematic route 218
elaboration likelihood model
    (ELM) 218
forewarning 239

inoculation 240
peripheral or heuristic route 218
persuasion 218
reactance 239

sleeper effect 226
subliminal persuasion 236

QUESTIONS FOR REVIEW

1. List the two routes to persuasion, and give an example of each.
2. Describe how message, source, and audience factors can influence persuasion.
3. Describe how both positive and negative emotions can influence persuasion.
4. Describe four ways in which we can resist persuasion.
5. Describe how culture impacts persuasion.

TAKE ACTION!

1. As part of a group project in your marketing class, you need to create advertisements for different types of products: a car, laundry detergent, beer, and a basketball shoe. Which route to persuasion, central or peripheral, would you recommend using for each product, and why?
2. Imagine you are asked to assist with a college-wide campaign to increase seatbelt use. How would you create a persuasive message for the college student audience? What source characteristics should be most effective? What types of messages would you recommend?
3. Your younger brother has decided to purchase a set of subliminal tapes to play while he sleeps to help him master Spanish. What would you tell him about the effectiveness of subliminal messages?
4. You are a principal at a local middle school, and you want to help your students resist being persuaded by all of the advertising messages for alcohol they see. What strategies might you use to help your students resist these persuasion attempts?
5. You are trying to get a summer internship with an advertising company, and are asked to submit a sample of an advertisement for a new car. What type of advertisement would you design to be shown in an individualistic culture? How would you change the advertisement if it were to be shown in a collectivistic culture?

RESEARCH CONNECTIONS

Try some of these research activities to gain experience in conducting and evaluating research, and to increase your understanding of research methods and techniques in social psychology.
Visit WileyPLUS for more activities and interactive research tools! (www.wileyxplus.com)

Participate in Research

Activity 1 The Impact of Message Relevance on Persuasion: This chapter describes how we process some messages in a central or systematic way, and others in a peripheral or heuristic way. Watch some advertisements on television and describe the type of processing designed to be used in each type of advertisement.

Activity 2 The Influence of the Source on Persuasion: One influence on the effectiveness of a persuasive message is the source who delivers that message. Go online to test the influence of the source on how persuaded you are by different messages.

Activity 3 The Power of Negative Information: This chapter describes how people's views about candidates for political office are more influenced by emotional factors than rational factors. Go to WileyPLUS to view campaign advertisements that rely on negative information and rate their effectiveness.

Activity 4 Strategies for Resisting Persuasion: You learned in this chapter about how we sometimes react against messages that try to change our behavior. Think about persuasive messages designed to stop you from doing a behavior, such as drinking or smoking. Which ones might you react against and why?

Activity 5 The Impact of Culture on Persuasion: The final section of this chapter describes how people from different cultures are influenced by different types of persuasive messages. Go online to rate how persuasive you find different advertising messages; then see how students from different countries rate these same messages.

Test a Hypothesis

One of the common findings in research on persuasion is that different types of messages are effective for different types of people. To test whether this hypothesis is true, find two different types of advertisements for the same product. Then, ask different people to rate how effective they find each of the advertisements.

Design a Study

To design your own study testing how various factors can influence persuasion, think of a research question you would like to answer. Then choose the type of study you want to conduct (self-report, observational/naturalistic, or experimental), choose your own independent and dependent variables, and form your own hypothesis.

Health
CONNECTIONS
Why Misperceiving
the Thinness Norm
Can Lead to Eating
Disorders

8

Social Influence: Norms, Conformity,

WHAT YOU'LL LEARN

How do social norms influence behavior?

What factors lead to conformity?

 RESEARCH FOCUS ON GENDER
Do Women Conform More Than Men?

What factors lead to compliance?

What factors lead to obedience?

How does CULTURE impact social influence?

Did you ever wonder?

Four days after his arrival at the Massachusetts Institute of Techology (MIT) as a freshman, Scott Krueger pledged and moved into the Phi Gamma Delta fraternity, known as "Fiji." As part of the initiation for this fraternity, Scott and 11 other pledges were told to gather together in a designated room of the fraternity, watch the movie *Animal House*, and collectively drink a prescribed amount of alcohol, including beer and a bottle of Jack Daniel's. Then the pledges each met with their "big brother," or mentor, who gave them more alcohol: Scott Krueger's big brother gave him a bottle of Bacardi spiced rum. Throughout the evening, Scott complained of nausea, and he eventually began to lose consciousness. At this time, two students carried Scott to his bedroom, placed him on his stomach, and put a trash can next to his bed. Ten minutes later, another fraternity member found Scott unconscious and covered in vomit. The fraternity member dialed the campus police, and paramedics rushed Scott to Beth Israel

Media
CONNECTIONS
Why Publicizing
Suicides May Be a
Bad Idea

Environment
CONNECTIONS
Why Conformity
Can Decrease
Littering

Law
CONNECTIONS
The Impact of
Compliance on False
Identifications and
False Confessions

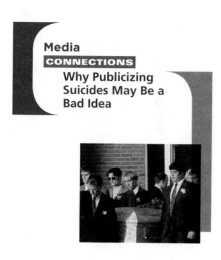

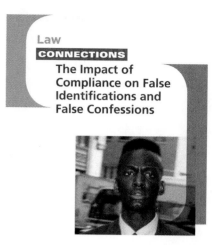

Compliance, and Obedience

Deaconess Medical Center, in Boston. He lingered in a coma for 40 hours, until he was pronounced dead on September 29, 1997. An autopsy determined that he died of alcohol poisoning and from suffocating on his vomit. How could an 18-year-old die during a fraternity initiation? Unfortunately this type of tragedy occurs several times a year. In this chapter, you'll learn how social psychological factors contributed to Scott Kruger's death. In addition, you'll find out ...

Q A Why is it a good idea to ask a question in class?

Q A Why do people sometimes ignore offensive remarks (when they shouldn't)?

Q A Why are we more helpful to someone who shares our birthday?

Q A Why are you likely to obey anyone who wears a uniform?

Q A Why do Americans prefer a pen with an unusual color, while Asians prefer a pen with a common color?

© Chuck Savage/©Corbis

Think about the clothes you are wearing, the music you listen to, and the way you wear your hair. All of these choices are influenced by **social norms**, meaning unspoken but shared rules of conduct within a particular formal or informal group. Although these examples describe relatively minor ways in which the social world impacts our attitudes and behavior, in some cases the social world exerts a powerful and direct impact on our behavior. For example, teenagers may feel pressure from others in their social groups to drink alcohol or smoke. This type of **conformity**, meaning changing our opinions or behaviors to meet perceived group norms, can occur because people fear the consequences of deviating from the norm. In some cases the social world can even lead us to obey orders that may harm or kill people—or ourselves (as described in the tragic case of Scott Kruger). This type of social influence describes **compliance**, meaning behavior that is elicited by direct requests, and **obedience**, meaning behavior that is produced by the commands of authority figures. This chapter will examine how these different types of social influence impact our attitudes and behavior.

HOW DO SOCIAL NORMS INFLUENCE BEHAVIOR?

Think about a time in which you were in a class and not understanding what the professor was describing. When he or she asked if there are any questions, how did you respond? If you are like many students, you did nothing. Why? Dale Miller and Cathy McFarland (1987) conducted a study to examine precisely this issue. They asked participants to read an article in preparation for taking part in a discussion with other students. The article was deliberately written in a confusing manner, and was virtually incomprehensible by anyone without considerable background in the area. Students were told to come see the experimenter if they had any serious problems in understanding the paper. After finishing the article, participants completed a survey in which they were asked questions about the clarity of the article and, most importantly, what percentage of other people in the study they believed would ask the experimenter questions about the article. Although no participants in the study asked the experimenter a question, students assumed that 37% of other students would ask questions. In a follow-up to this study, researchers examined participants' beliefs about the factors that inhibited themselves and others from asking a question. As predicted, participants believed their own behavior was motivated by fear of embarrassment, but saw other people's behavior as motivated by having a greater understanding of the article. This research provides one example of an error we can make in interpreting the social world—that is, we often see our own behavior as different from and caused by different factors than other people's behavior. This section will examine errors we make in perceiving social norms, as well as the power of norms and the pressure we feel to conform to them.

social norms unspoken but shared rules of conduct in a formal or informal group

conformity the tendency to change our perceptions, opinions, or behaviors in ways that are consistent with perceived group norms

compliance changes in behavior that are caused by a direct request

obedience behavior change produced by the commands of authority

THE POWER OF SOCIAL NORMS

Social norms are unspoken but shared rules of conduct within a particular formal or informal group (e.g., norms of dress, norms of greeting, norms of personal space, norms of eating). For example, when you came to college you may have found that people dressed differently, or listened to different types of music, or had different views about political or social issues than you did. It is also likely that at least in some ways you changed your own attitudes or behavior to conform to those that were the norm at your college. In many cases these norms serve as helpful guides to appropriate behavior: stopping at a red light, waiting your place in line at the post office, and raising your hand before asking a question in your psychology lecture. These are all examples of norms that regulate our behavior in socially acceptable ways.

Social psychologists distinguish between two kinds of social norms (Cialdini, Reno, & Kallgren, 1990; Reno, Cialdini, & Kallgren, 1993). **Descriptive norms** describe how people behave in a given situation. On many college campuses students follow a variety of descriptive norms of behavior. These norms might include how they spend Saturday nights, what types of clothes they wear, and how much they study. On the other hand, **injunctive norms** describe what people *ought* to do in a given situation, meaning the type of behavior that is approved of in a given situation. Reporting cheating to a professor might be an injunctive norm, even if this norm does not actually describe people's typical behavior.

Norms often influence our attitudes and behavior in very subtle ways. In one study, researchers at Columbia University examined how social norms influence teenagers' taste in music (Salganik, Watts, & Dodds, 2006). Over 14,000 teenagers were recruited from Internet sites and asked to participate in a study of music preferences. Half of the teenagers were simply asked to listen to some obscure rock songs and download the ones they liked; they received no information about the songs (which were taken from a Web site where unknown bands post their own music). The other teenagers were also asked to listen to these same obscure songs, but in this case they saw, in addition to the title of the songs, the number of times the songs had been downloaded by others (a measure of how popular each song was). Researchers found that simply knowing how many other people had downloaded a song influenced how likely others were to download the song, clearly showing that social norms influenced music ratings. The Would You Believe box describes another real-world example of the power of social norms.

People quickly acquire the norms of a new environment even if they do not know the norms when they first enter that environment. In fact, people are most likely to acquire norms when they are in new situations. They look to older and/or more established group members to form their own attitudes and behaviors. A classic study by Theodore Newcomb at Bennington College during the 1930s demonstrated the process of norm acquisition in a new environment (Newcomb, 1961). Most first-year students at Bennington at this time arrived with conservative political views, in line with their parents' views (over two-thirds of the parents of Bennington students were affiliated with the Republican Party). At Bennington, most faculty members held much more liberal political

In some cultures the greeting norm includes kissing on each check. In others the greeting norm includes shaking hands.

descriptive norms norms that describe how people behave in a given situation

injunctive norms norms that describe what people ought to do in a given situation, meaning the type of behavior that is approved of in a given situation

WOULD YOU BELIEVE... Just Hearing About an Illness Can Make You Sick? When I teach the abnormal psychology section in my Introduction to Psychology course, an amazing thing happens each semester. As I describe the various clinical disorders (depression, schizophrenia, etc.), many students suddenly recognize these relatively rare disorders in many of the people in their lives—their parents, siblings, friends, roommates, and sometimes even themselves. (This reaction is sometimes called medical student's disease because medical students, who learn about rare and unusual symptoms, often start diagnosing themselves with multiple disorders.)

This reaction can sometimes lead to the phenomenon of mass psychogenic illness, in which large numbers of people, typically in a relatively small and isolated group, all report similar symptoms. For example, students in a school may hear about a virus that is "going around" or a suspected case of food poisoning, and suddenly many will report experiencing related symptoms. This is not—at least not usually—just a case of students trying to get a vacation! Instead, researchers believe that drawing people's attention to a particular type of symptom leads them to engage in careful (even too careful) monitoring of their bodies and to interpret various minor symptoms, such as a headache or nausea, as caused by the suspected problem. In one case, a teacher at a Tennessee high school first noticed an odor and complained of various symptoms (headache, nausea, dizziness, shortness of breath; Jones, Craig, Hoy, Gunter, Ashley, Barr, et al., 2000). Soon many students and staff members experienced similar symptoms, and the school was evacuated. However, a specific medical or environmental explanation for the illnesses was never found, suggesting that the teacher's reaction led people to believe that they, too, were experiencing such effects. How does that happen? In part because people look to others to see how they should react in a given situation; if others look anxious, "emotional contagion" may occur (Gump & Kalik, 1997).

GREGORY

"Sure, I follow the herd—not out of brainless obedience, mind you, but out of a deep and abiding respect for the concept of community."

views. In turn, as the women spent more time at Bennington, their views became increasingly liberal, in line with the prevailing norms of this college. For example, in the 1936 presidential campaign, 66% of their parents voted for the Republican candidate, as did about 62% of the Bennington freshmen. But only 43% of the sophomores voted for the Republican candidate, and only 15% of the juniors and seniors did. Thus, by the time they graduated, many had become quite liberal. Political views are just one example of the many types of norms we learn from exposure to a given environment. In fact, college students' attitudes become more similar to those living closest to them in a dormitory over the course of a semester, particularly for attitudes that are seen as highly important (Cullum & Harton, 2007).

Interestingly, however, people seem largely unaware of the impact of social influence (Nolan, Schultz, Cialdini, Goldstein, & Griskevicius, 2008). In one study, researchers asked 810 Californians about their frequency of energy conservation measures, their motivation for that behavior, and their beliefs about other people's energy conservation behavior. Although beliefs about others' energy conservation behavior were highly correlated with individuals' own behavior, participants saw such norms as much less important in determining their behavior than other factors, such as protecting the environment. This research suggests that even in cases in which our behavior is influenced by our perception of social norms, we aren't necessarily aware of this type of influence.

ERRORS IN PERCEIVING SOCIAL NORMS

pluralistic ignorance a particular type of norm misperception that occurs when each individual in the group privately rejects the group's norms, but believes that others accept these norms

Although people are generally motivated to adhere to the norms of their group, at times they make errors in perceiving these norms. The term **pluralistic ignorance** refers to a misperception that occurs when each individual in the group privately rejects a group's norms but believes that the other members of the group accept these norms (Miller & McFarland, 1987). They may go along with the norm because they falsely assume that others' behavior has a different cause (acceptance of the norm) than one's own behavior (fear of embarrassment). The study described at the start of this section described how pluralistic ignorance is demonstrated in many college classes. Often a professor will ask, "Are there any questions?" and no one raises his or her hand. Each person assumes that everyone else in the class really understands the material, which is why no one is asking any questions. But many individuals actually do have questions and believe that they are the only ones not raising a hand due to embarrassment and fear of looking stupid.

In one study to test the factors that can impede the initiation of dating relationships, Jackie Vorauer and Rebecca Ratner (1996) conducted a study to find out why students often fail to "make the first move" in initiating a romantic relationship. They gave college students a series of questionnaires that assessed how frequently fear of rejection had been an obstacle in their pursuit of a relationship, as well as how often they believed such fear inhibited others from pursuing a relationship with them. For example, in one questionnaire, participants were asked to imagine that they were at a party and were introduced to a single person who could be a potential romantic partner, and that they talked alone with this person toward the end of the evening. Then the students were asked to imagine that neither person specifically expressed interest in a romantic relationship, and to explain this lack of expressed interest. Although 74% of the students reported that fear of rejection would explain why they failed to express direct interest in the other person, 71%

believed that lack of interest on the part of the other person would best be explained by his or her lack of interest in them. This study describes how pluralistic ignorance can interfere with the formation of a romantic relationship: because each person simply assumes that the other isn't interested in a relationship, whereas his or her own (identical) behavior is driven by his or her fear of rejection.

Unfortunately, misperceiving the social norms of one's environment can have substantial consequences. A number of studies have demonstrated that college students often believe that there is too much alcohol use on campus (Prentice & Miller, 1993). They also believe (wrongly) that other students approve of that amount of alcohol. However, people's estimates of the frequency of alcohol use among their peers influences their own use, even if these estimates are inaccurate (Baer & Carney, 1993; Baer, Stacy, & Larimer, 1991; Marks, Graham, & Hansen, 1992). Similarly, men who believe other men believe in rape myths, such as "Women often provoke rape through their appearance or behavior," are more likely to report behaving in a sexually aggressive way (Bohner, Siebler, & Schmelcher, 2006). In Chapter 10, you'll learn about another consequence of pluralistic ignorance—less interaction between members of different ethnic groups because members of each race would like to have more contact with members of other races, but believe that this interest is not shared by members of other races (Shelton & Richeson, 2005). The Health Connections box describes another way in which misperceiving social norms can have negative consequences.

THE PRESSURE TO CONFORM TO SOCIAL NORMS

The pressure to conform to social norms is often very powerful, in part because people who deviate from the norm often experience negative consequences such as embarrassment, awkwardness, and even hostile behavior from others (Kruglanski & Webster, 1991). For example, students who believe that they deviate from the campus norm of alcohol use feel alienated from campus life and report less interest in attending college reunions later on (Prentice & Miller, 1993). Because of the unpleasant consequences of deviating from the norm, we are motivated to learn and adhere to the norms of our group. For example, teenagers may feel pressure to shoplift when they are with a group of friends who are shoplifting. Even if you are worried about the legal consequences of getting caught, you may be more worried about the social consequences of refusing to go along with your group.

? Questioning the Research

Although research demonstrates an association between feeling discrepant from valued social norms and feeling alienated from that environment, can you think of an alternative explanation for these findings? (Hint: is this correlation or causation?)

Why Misperceiving the Thinness Norm Can Lead to Eating Disorders

My research demonstrates that misperceiving the thinness norm can have substantial consequences. In one study, we surveyed 120 freshmen, sophomores, juniors, and seniors on their own eating habits, body image, exercise motivations, and attitudes regarding the campus thinness norm (Sanderson, Darley, & Messinger, 2002). We also asked women about their perceptions of other women at their university on these measures. As predicted, women thought that other women weighed less, exercised more frequently and for more extrinsic reasons, and desired a smaller body than they themselves do. For example, women have an average body-mass index (BMI) of 22 but believe that other women have a BMI of about 20.5. Similarly, women report exercising about four hours a week but believe that other women exercise about five and a half hours a week. Finally, and most importantly, women who feel that they don't meet the campus thinness norm are more likely to experience symptoms of eating disorders, such as an extreme focus on thinness, binge eating,

and purging. These findings indicate that feeling deviant from the norm is associated with a variety of negative consequences.

© ThinkStock/SUPERSTOCK

In a classic study of the consequences of rejecting group norms, Stanley Schachter asked groups of students to engage in a group decision-making task (1951). Students met to discuss the case of Johnny Rocco, a juvenile delinquent who was awaiting sentencing for a minor crime, and were supposed to determine the appropriate punishment for this person. Each group consisted of several actual participants, plus three students who were acting as confederates of the experimenter and were playing particular roles during the group discussion. One confederate was the "mode": he went along with the group position throughout the discussion. Another confederate was the "slider": he initially chose a position of extreme deviation from the group, but then gradually moved toward the group's modal position. The third confederate was the "deviate": he chose a position of extreme deviation and maintained that position throughout the discussion. After the 45-minute discussion, students rated how much they liked each person in the group, with 1 being the person you liked most, and 9 being the person you liked least. Not surprisingly, people liked the deviate least (6.11, compared to 4.47 for the mode and 4.76 for the slider). This research shows that deviation from the norm can have real consequences for people.

Even watching someone else experience rejection can lead to greater conformity. In one study, participants watched one of two humorous videotapes (Janes & Olson, 2000). Some participants watched a videotape in which one person made fun of another person's appearance—such as saying "His acne was so bad as a teenager we used to call him 'pizza face'." Other participants watched a videotape in which a person made fun of himself—such as saying "My acne was so bad as a teenager they used to call me 'pizza face'." Still other participants watched a videotape in which a comedian made jokes that weren't directed at anyone (the control condition). All participants then saw a cartoon and rated how funny they thought it was. However, before providing their rating, participants learned that other students had rated the cartoon as very funny (when in reality it was not funny at all). What did participants' own ratings of the cartoon show? Those who had watched the self-ridicule tape rated the unfunny cartoon as not funny, as did those who had watched the comedian make jokes that weren't directed at anyone (see Figure 8.1). On the other hand, those who had watched the other ridicule tape conformed to what they thought were the ratings of other students and rated the unfunny cartoon as very funny.

Although the examples described thus far have emphasized the negative consequences of feeling discrepant from the social norms of one's group, in some cases people's desire to conform to social norms influence behavior in a positive way. In one study, Bob Cialdini and colleagues compared different types of messages given to hotel guests to encourage reusing their towels—something that is very beneficial in conserving energy costs (Goldstein, Cialdini, & Griskevicius, 2008). In one condition, hotel

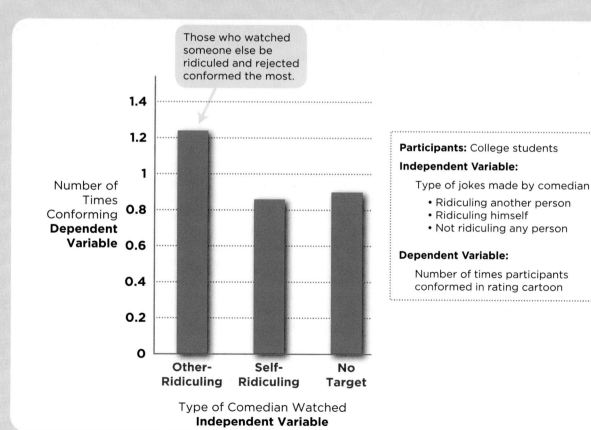

FIGURE 8.1

DO WE CONFORM MORE AFTER SEEING OTHERS REJECTED?

In this experiment, college students were shown two videos. The first showed a comedian telling jokes ridiculing another person, the comedian ridiculing himself, or the comedian making jokes that didn't ridicule anyone. The second video was a cartoon that was not at all funny. Before watching it, the students were told that other viewers had rated the cartoon as very funny. As predicted, those who watched the other-ridicule comedy video conformed more to the other participants' rating of the cartoon than either those who watched the self-ridiculing comedian or those who watched the comedian make jokes that weren't directed at anyone, suggesting that watching someone else be rejected makes us more likely to conform to group norms.

Source: Janes, L. M., & Olson, J. M. (2000). Jeer pressures: The behavioral effects of observing ridicule of others. *Personality and Social Psychology Bulletin, 26*, 474-485.

Those who watched someone else be ridiculed and rejected conformed the most.

Participants: College students

Independent Variable:

Type of jokes made by comedian
- Ridiculing another person
- Ridiculing himself
- Not ridiculing any person

Dependent Variable:

Number of times participants conformed in rating cartoon

Number of Times Conforming **Dependent Variable**

Type of Comedian Watched
Independent Variable

Other-Ridiculing   Self-Ridiculing   No Target

guests received the standard pro-environmental message: "Help Save the Environment: You can show your respect for nature and help save the environment by reusing your towels during your stay." Other guests received a similar message, but with a focus on social norms: "Join Your Fellow Guests in Helping to Save the Environment: Almost 75% of guests who are asked to participate in our new resource savings program do help by using their towels more than once. You can join your fellow guests to help save the environment by reusing your towels during your stay." About 38% of those who received the first message reused their towels. However, about 48% of those who received the second message reused their towels, indicating that learning about other people's behavior was very effective at changing behavior.

Similar norm-based education campaigns have been carried out on many college campuses. For example, campaigns to reduce rates of binge drinking on college campuses have emphasized the message that most students have fewer than five drinks when they party, which can be an effective way of reducing drinking (Perkins, 2002; Perkins & Craig, 2006; Schroeder & Prentice, 1998). Similarly, my own research reveals that telling college women that other women on campus actually eat more and weigh more than they might believe leads to a reduction in symptoms of eating disorders (Mutterperl & Sanderson, 2002). In sum, giving people accurate information about various norms can reduce misperceptions and thereby improve health.

EXAMPLES OF THE INFLUENCE OF SOCIAL NORMS

FACTOR	EXAMPLE
The power of social norms	When Derick's family moves and he must attend a new high school, he suddenly changes his style of dress and music preferences.
Errors in perceiving social norms	Sonja's belief that most other students rarely study until the night before an exam leads her to procrastinate on her own work, sometimes with disastrous consequences.

WHAT FACTORS LEAD TO CONFORMITY?

Think about a time in which you've heard someone say something inappropriate, such as use a racist, sexist, or homophobic slur. How did you respond? Although you may not know it, your response was probably influenced by the presence of other people. To test the impact of other people on individuals' reactions in precisely this situation, researchers in one study asked men (really confederates) to make a sexist remark in front of female participants. For example, in one condition the man said "Yeah, we definitely need to keep the women in shape," and in another, he said, "...one of the women can cook." Women then had a chance to react to this remark (Swim & Hyers, 1999). Only 16% of the women responded with a direct verbal comment, although 91% had negative thoughts about the person who had made the remark, showing that concern about the social pressures and costs of responding directly influenced their behavior. This study demonstrates the power of other people in influencing our behavior, and in particular how we often conform to others' behavior. This section will examine the types of influence that lead to conformity, the factors that lead to conformity, and the role of minority influence in eliciting conformity.

WHY WE CONFORM

Conformity can be produced by two distinct types of influence: informational influence and normative influence. Let's look at each of these.

Informational influence. **Informational influence** refers to influence that produces conformity when a person believes that others are correct in their judgments and that person wishes to be similarly correct (Deutsch & Gerard, 1955; Kelly, Jackson, & Hutson-Comeaux, 1997; Reno et al., 1993). This type of influence might occur when you are new to a situation and therefore look to others for accurate information. For example, if you are trying to decide what course to take next semester, you might ask a senior for his or her thoughts about a given course.

One of the first studies to demonstrate the impact of informational influence on social norms was conducted by Muzafer Sherif (1936). This study used the autokinetic effect: when one is in a dark room and a stationary dot of light is shown on a wall, that dot appears to move even though in reality it does not. When individuals are alone in a room and are asked to guess how far the dot is moving, their guesses differ greatly. But when individuals are in a group, their estimates of how far the dot is moving converge over time. This shows how people can influence one another and thus create a group norm. People therefore use other people's beliefs as a way of getting information about the situation, and believe that these people are correct in their judgments. This study demonstrated **private conformity**, meaning people changed their original view and thus conformed because they believed that others were right.

Normative influence. **Normative influence**, on the other hand, describes influence that produces conformity when a person fears the negative social consequences of appearing deviant (Cialdini et al., 1990; Reno et al., 1993). Let's say you are with a group of friends and someone pulls out a pack of cigarettes, lights a cigarette, and offers cigarettes to everyone in the group. If everyone else accepts a cigarette and begins to smoke, and you don't want to, what do you do? In this case you are not getting factual information ("If I don't smoke I'll get ejected from this party"), but you are receiving information about the norms of the group, and that can be enough to influence your behavior. This is why people often don't react to sexist remarks, as demonstrated in the study at the start of this section (Swim & Hyers, 1999).

In a famous study by Solomon Asch (1955), participants arrived for an experiment on visual discrimination that was being conducted in a group of six or seven people. The design of the experiment is a simple one: participants look at a target line and then at three other comparison lines, and say which line is the same length as the target line (see Figure 8.2). They go through a few sets of lines; the judgments are really easy, and all of the participants identify the same line as being the same length as the target line. On the third set, however, the first person identifies what is clearly a wrong answer. You almost laugh because it is so obvious that it is wrong, but then the next person gives the same (wrong) answer, and so does the next person. At this point, what do you think? More importantly, what do you do? Thirty-seven percent of the time, participants actually gave the wrong answer in order to conform to the rest of the group, with 50% of participants giving the wrong answer at least half of the time. This study revealed **public conformity**, meaning people conformed because they wanted to publicly agree with others, even though in reality they realized that their answer was incorrect. Why do people give the wrong answer when they clearly know it is wrong? This study represents an attribution crisis for participants: first, they must determine why their peers, who are actually confederates of the experimenter, are giving different judgments from their own, and second, they must determine what their own dissent would imply about themselves and their peers.

This study received a great deal of publicity because it seemed like such a remarkable show of conformity: After all, it occurred in a situation in which the people didn't know each other, wouldn't receive rewards for making certain answers, and had no real stake in the study. So, it was feared that the pressure to conform would be even stronger in cases in which the consequences of individuals' behavior really mattered to them. The Media Connections box describes a very dangerous consequence of conformity.

informational influence the influence that produces conformity when a person believes others are correct in their judgments, and they want to be right

private conformity when people rethink their original views, and potentially change their minds

normative influence the influence that produces conformity when a person fears the negative social consequences of appearing deviant

public conformity when people's overt behaviors are in line with group norms

FIGURE
8.2

DOES GROUP PRESSURE INCREASE CONFORMITY?

Participants in Asch's famous experiment joined a group that was shown cards with lines on them, as shown in this figure. Other group members were confederates of the experimenter who sometimes gave the wrong answer when asked which comparison line matched the standard. Even though participants knew the group answer was wrong, they often went along with the group and gave the wrong answer, rather than disagree by providing the correct answer.

Source: Asch, S. E. (1955). Opinions and social pressure. *Scientific American*, 193, 31-35.

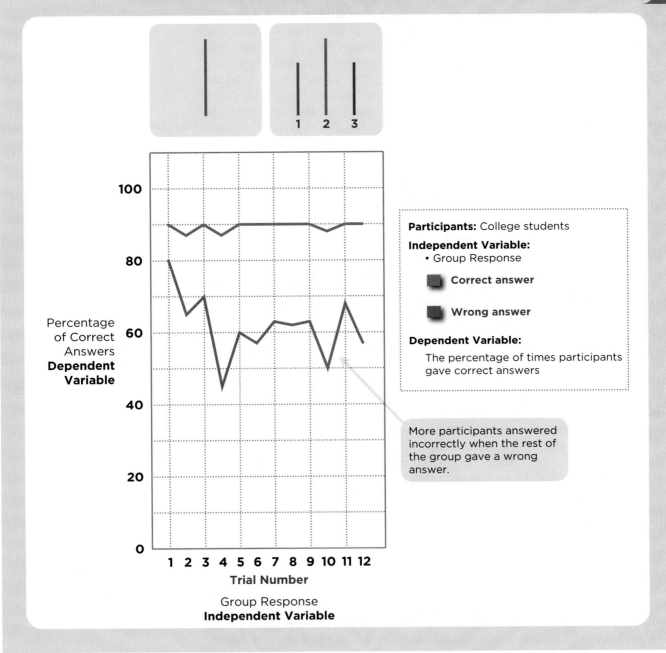

Participants: College students

Independent Variable:
• Group Response

Correct answer

Wrong answer

Dependent Variable:

The percentage of times participants gave correct answers

More participants answered incorrectly when the rest of the group gave a wrong answer.

Percentage of Correct Answers **Dependent Variable**

Trial Number

Group Response **Independent Variable**

FACTORS THAT INCREASE CONFORMITY

Researchers have investigated factors that influence conformity, including group size, standing alone, demographic variables, and motivation for accuracy.

Group size. First, there is the role of *group size* (Asch, 1951; Campbell & Fairey, 1989; Gerard, Wilhelmy, & Conolley, 1968; Knowles, 1983; Mullen, 1983). Common sense suggests that as the size of groups increases, so does their impact.

Why Publicizing Suicides May Be a Bad Idea

After a suicide has made front-page news, rates of suicide increase significantly (Phillips, 1982). Within two months of every front-page suicide story, an average of 58 more people die than in the two months that do not follow such publicity. Similar effects are seen following nationally televised news of feature stories about suicide (Phillips & Carstensen, 1986). Suicides increase only in those places in which the suicide was highly publicized—and the wider the publicity, the greater the increase.

Psychologists and sociologists believe that some people who hear about another's self-inflicted death decide to imitate them in the particular way in which they died. This tendency is particularly strong among adolescents, who tend to be more impressionable and easier to influence toward conformity. For example, in one high school two students committed suicide within four days (Brent, Kerr, Goldstein, & Bozigar, 1989). In the next eighteen days, an additional seven students attempted suicide and twenty-three others reported having thoughts about suicide. This type of conformity occurs even if the suicide occurs on a television show; more suicide attempts occur in the weeks following a

television movie about suicide or a suicide in a soap opera than in the weeks preceding (Gould & Shaffer, 1986). However, the link between fictional suicides and actual subsequent suicides is weaker than the link between publicized suicides and actual subsequent suicides.

NewsCom

In Asch's experiments, when participants responded in the presence of only one confederate, almost no one gave the wrong answer. However, when the opposition increased to two people, the proportion of participants giving the wrong answer on at least one trial jumped to 14%. When the opposition increased to three, 32% of participants bowed to the pressure to conform on at least one trial. Additional increases did not, however, increase conformity; so a group of three is better at producing conformity than a group of two, but a group of seventeen is not better than a group of ten.

The presence of particular *group members* may also influence conformity. As described by **social impact theory**, people we are close to have more impact on us than those who are more distant (Latane, 1981; Latané, Liu, Nowak, Bonvento, & Zhang, 1995). This is why as a college student you are more likely to conform to the norms of your college than those of your high school. We also conform more in the presence of powerful and vocal group members (Miller & McFarland, 1991; Miller & Prentice, 1994; Perrin & Spencer, 1981). For example, Klofas and Toch (1982) found that prison guards and prisoners who held the most hard-line positions—and therefore were not representative of the majority—were likely to define themselves as spokespersons for the group, thereby creating the illusion that all prison guards and prisoners held more hard-line positions than they actually did.

social impact theory a theory that people we are close to have more impact than those who are more distant

Standing alone.   Although both the size of the group and the nature of its members influence rates of conformity, the single biggest predictor of conformity is whether a participant must take the *lone deviant position*, meaning to *stand alone*. In Asch's experiment, when another person in the group gave the truthful answer, the pressure to conform was drastically reduced (Allen & Levine, 1969, 1971; Nemeth & Chiles,

1988). In fact, even when another person in the group gives another—or more extreme—wrong answer, the pressure to conform is drastically reduced. Even if the person who deviates seems to be incompetent (wears thick glasses, complains of being unable to see the lines well, etc.), having anyone else stand up to the majority decreases conformity.

Demographic variables.

Demographic variables, such as age and gender, also influence conformity (Eagly & Carli, 1981; Eagly, Wood, & Fishbaugh, 1981). Conformity is highest in adolescence, when there is real pressure to fit in, and less high in children and older adults (Berndt, 1979; Brown, Clasen, & Eicher, 1986; Gavin & Furman, 1989). Peer pressure, for example, is identified by adolescents as a major predictor of misconduct (e.g., drug/alcohol use, unprotected sex, and

"Gee, Tommy, I'd be lost without your constant peer pressure."

minor delinquent behavior; Brown et al., 1986). Conformity also seems to be stronger overall in women (see Research Focus on Gender).

RESEARCH FOCUS ON GENDER
Do Women Conform More Than Men?

Research indicates that women tend to show higher rates of conformity than men. Specifically, women are more likely than men to agree with others in group decision-making tasks, and are less likely than men to dissent from the group. However, the size of these gender differences in conformity varies across types of situations. First, women are particularly likely to conform in unfamiliar situations (Eagly & Carli, 1981; Eagly et al., 1981). For example, women may conform more in conversations about football, whereas men may conform more in conversations about child-rearing. Women also conform more than men in public situations and those involving direct surveillance by the influencer than in private situations. In public situations, women may feel a need to follow gender stereotypes about women's roles (e.g., be polite, agreeable, supportive), and hence may show more conformity than in more private contexts. In line with this view, people with more masculine gender roles, regardless of their gender, conform less than people with more feminine gender roles (Maslach, Santee, & Wade, 1987).

Motivation. Another factor that can influence conformity is *task importance*: on easy tasks people don't need to look to group members for the answer, whereas on harder tasks they may feel less sure about their answer. In one study, students participated in groups of three (one participant, two confederates) and were asked to serve as eyewitnesses—they saw a crime and then had to identify the perpetrator in a lineup (Baron, Vandello, & Brunsman, 1996). In some cases the task was very difficult (they saw each picture once for only a second). In other cases it was quite easy (they saw each picture twice for a total of 10 seconds). The experimenters also varied the students' motivation to perform well. In some cases they were told that this was only a pilot test, whereas in other cases they were given money for being right. As shown in Figure 8.3, in cases of low motivation (the pilot test), students conformed about one-third of the time, regardless of the difficulty of the task (note that this is very similar to the

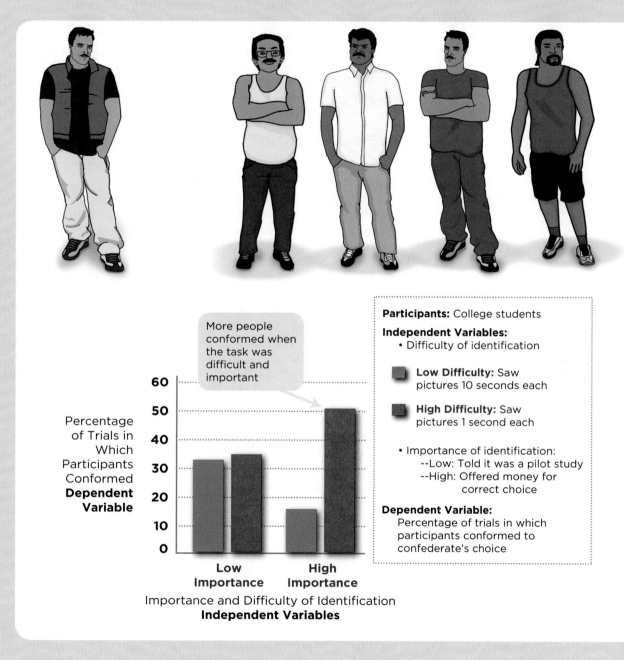

FIGURE 8.3

DOES CONFORMITY INCREASE WHEN THE TASK IS DIFFICULT AND IMPORTANT?

In this study, participants were placed in groups of three, with two confederates of the experimenter. The group witnessed the person on the left commit a crime and had to pick the suspect from a lineup of pictures, like the one shown below on the right. The confederates chose the wrong person from the lineup. As predicted, conformity was highest when the task was difficult and it was important to choose correctly.

Source: Baron, R. S., Vandello, J. A., & Brunsman, B. (1996). The forgotten variable in conformity research: Impact of task importance on social influence. *Journal of Personality and Social Psychology, 71*, 915-927.

More people conformed when the task was difficult and important

Percentage of Trials in Which Participants Conformed **Dependent Variable**

60
50
40
30
20
10
0

Low Importance

High Importance

Importance and Difficulty of Identification
Independent Variables

Participants: College students

Independent Variables:
• Difficulty of identification

Low Difficulty: Saw pictures 10 seconds each

High Difficulty: Saw pictures 1 second each

• Importance of identification:
--Low: Told it was a pilot study
--High: Offered money for correct choice

Dependent Variable:
Percentage of trials in which participants conformed to confederate's choice

rate of conformity in the Asch study). On the other hand, in cases of high motivation (they could win extra cash), they conformed rarely on easy tasks (when they probably felt confident that they knew the right answer) but conformed frequently on difficult tasks (when they probably felt less confident and really wanted to be right).

Social motives seem to influence conformity in different ways for men and women (Griskevicius, Goldstein, Mortensen, Cialdini, & Kenrick, 2006). In one study, researchers measured participants' conformity to the opinions of other members of a group on a task involving rating artistic images. In one condition, participants were asked to imagine an anxiety-provoking situation, such as being in a dark house alone late at night and hearing a noise from an intruder, prior to rating the images. In another condition, participants were asked to imagine a highly romantic situation, such as spending a day at a beach with a desirable partner and kissing that person passionately, prior to rating the images. Compared to those in a control condition (which involved no imagining prior to completing the rating), both men and women who imagined the anxiety-provoking scene showed greater conformity. On the other hand, men and women reacted in very different ways to imagining the romantic situation. For women, imagining a romantic situation increased conformity, but for men, imagining this scene led to lower levels of conformity. The authors propose that men who fail to conform to the norm may be more attractive to potential dating partners, perhaps because they appear independent, and thus being disconforming is a way for men to attract mates. In contrast, conforming to social norms, which indicates agreeableness, may be a way for women to attract mates.

THE POWER OF MINORITY INFLUENCE

minority influence a process in which a small number of people in a group lead to overall change in the group's attitude or behavior

Can individuals who are in the minority on a given view or norm sometimes convince others to go along with them? Although **minority influence** is much less common than majority influence, it does occur. One factor that increases the power of minority influence is the consistency of a person's verbal expression: people who are unwavering in their view attract attention from others and make their argument especially salient (Maass & Clark, 1984, 1986; Nemeth, Mayseless, Sherman, & Brown, 1990; Tanford & Penrod, 1984). Such expression also gives majority group members the idea that the person is not going to yield, which may then put pressure on others to compromise on their own views. When a person is very firm in his or her beliefs (particularly if he or she is in the minority), it can make others think that that individual might actually be right. In fact, majorities usually influence people by eliciting public conformity (because people do not want to appear deviant from the norm), but minorities may lead to private conformity, which occurs when people rethink their original views, and change their minds (Wood, Lundgren, Ouelette, Busceme, & Blackstone, 1994; Wood, Pool, Leck, & Purvis, 1996).

Minority influence can be particularly effective when delivered by a person who is already well established within a group, in part because a certain amount of acceptance has already been granted to him or her (Bray, Johnson, Chilstrom, 1982; Clark & Maass, 1988; Hollander, 1958, 1960). In one study, students with moderate views on abortion were exposed to messages by in-group members (those who attended their university) or out-group members (those who attended a different university; Clark & Maass, 1988). Those who heard minority views expressed by members of their in-group were more likely to be persuaded, in part because in-group members are seen as more credible. Minority opinions expressed by in-group members are also seen more positively and are subjected to less counterargument (Alvaro & Crano, 1997). However, minority influence is weaker in large groups than in small ones, in line with social impact theory (Clark & Maass, 1990).

Questioning the Research
This study examined the power of minority influence by comparing persuasion by students who attended one's own university versus those who attended a different university. Is this distinction a good strategy for measuring minority influence? Why or why not? What might be a better approach to examining influence by a minority member of an in-group versus an out-group?

When minority influence does occur, it can have a beneficial effect on the quality of the decision. Specifically, because minority influence leads to the expression of a wider range of arguments, and more original arguments, from multiple perspectives, hearing about a minority viewpoint leads to newer and more original thoughts (Martin, 1996; Mucchi-Faina, Maass, & Volpato, 1991; Peterson & Nemeth, 1996). Minority messages are also processed more extensively, particularly when they oppose the recipient's attitude (Erb, Bohner, Rank, & Einwiller, 2002). In this way minority influence can improve thinking, as portrayed in the classic film *12 Angry Men*.

THE BENEFITS OF CONFORMITY

You probably wouldn't feel comfortable wearing jeans at a wedding, or a tuxedo or ball gown at a football game. So, although we think of conformity as a bad thing, meaning that people who conform are weak and dependent, conformity is very much a part of our lives. Although many of the salient examples of conformity focus on its dangers (e.g., suicides, fraternity hazing, sexual assault), conformity can also be used for worthwhile purposes. Examples might include a fraternity that mandates community service, or a college campus in which expressions of racist or sexist attitudes are clearly rejected, or a neighborhood in which recycling is the norm (and see the Environment Connections box for another example of the benefits of conformity). In the politically aware college town in which I live (Amherst, Massachusetts), people are given a sticker to wear after voting each election day.

Mark Owens/John Wiley & Sons

"Straight, but not narrow" bumpersticker. Gay, lesbian, and bisexual groups often include "allies," heterosexuals who are supportive of gay rights, in part because mainstream members can increase the likelihood of minority influence.

This sticker then serves as a profound symbol that you have conformed to the (positive) prosocial norm of voting—and presumably may inspire others to get to the polls as well.

Environment
::: CONNECTIONS

Why Conformity Can Decrease Littering

Seeing someone else picking up litter (e.g., a fast-food bag) in a parking lot reduces the percentage of people who throw flyers from their windshields on the ground, from 43% to 9% (Kallgren, Reno, & Cialdini, 2000). In one study, researchers watched participants' behavior in a parking lot that was cluttered with trash, cigarette butts, and paper cups (Reno et al., 1993). In half of the cases, a confederate walked by and threw a piece of paper on the ground. In the other half, the confederate walked by and picked up a piece of trash and put it in a trash can. When the (unknowing) participants reached their cars, they found a "please drive safely" flyer on the windshield. In the control condition, in which there was no confederate, over one-third of the participants littered (38%). Similarly, when the confederate modeled the act of littering, 30% did so. On the other hand, when the confederate instead modeled the act of picking up litter, only 4% littered. This research reveals the power of making certain types of norms salient as a strategy for improving the environment.

Busse Yankushev/Age Fotostock America, Inc.

EXAMPLES OF FACTORS LEADING TO CONFORMITY

FACTOR	EXAMPLE

TYPES OF INFLUENCE

Informational influence	Hassan is trying to decide which candidate to vote for in the upcoming school election. In order make his selection, Hassan asks some of his friends what they think of the different candidates.
Normative influence	Aviva smokes when she is with her high school friends because everyone else is doing it.

INFLUENCES ON CONFORMITY

Group size	Jill always voices her opinion about which type of food she prefers to eat when she is going out to dinner with one or two friends, but when she goes out with a large group of people, she typically defers to whatever the others seem to want.
Standing alone	After Juan saw someone cheating during the final exam in his physics class, he wasn't sure what to do because no one else seemed to be reporting this act. But after hearing that another student had come forward to report the cheating, he decided to go talk to the professor about what he had seen.
Demographic variables	Isabellina, a sophomore in high school, conforms to the behavior of her friends. However, her younger brother, Brian, doesn't conform to Isabellina's friends' behavior or to his own friends' behavior.
Motivation	Allen often agrees with his friends when they are talking about their favorite sports teams, even when he disagrees with their opinions. However, when they are discussing politics, Allen adamantly expresses his opinion even when it goes against those of his friends.
Minority influence	Jasmine's strong views about the importance of distribution requirements at her school were originally opposed by other students, but after she forcefully and consistently described the benefits of her plan, many people came to share her views.

WHAT FACTORS LEAD TO COMPLIANCE?

Imagine that a stranger asks you for a favor—how likely would you be to agree? Would you believe that something as small as sharing the same date of birth as that stranger would increase your willingness to do the favor? In one study, participants signed up for what they believed was a study on astrology (Burger, Messian, Patel, del Prado, & Anderson, 2004). When they arrived for the study, they met another person who they believed was another participant (but who was actually a confederate). As the experimenter began to pass out the questionnaires, she asked for each participant's birthday as a way of determining his or her astrological sign. After the participant responded, the confederate provided her own birthday. In half of the cases, the confederate gave the same birthday as given by the participant (who typically commented on this coincidence). In the other half of the cases, the confederate gave a birthday that was distinct from the participant. After the completion of the questionnaires, the experimenter thanked each person for his or her participation and left the room. The confederate then asked the participant for a favor—that is, to read an eight-page essay for an English class and provide a critique. As predicted, more than 62% of those who believed they shared a birthday with the confederate agreed to provide this critique, compared to only 34% of those who believed they did not share a birthday. This study is one example of how very subtle factors can influence behavior.

This section will examine how strategies can be used to induce compliance, meaning changes in behavior that are elicited by direct requests. These factors include reciprocity, consistency and commitment, and scarcity.

RECIPROCITY

One of the most straightforward strategies that leads to compliance is **reciprocity**, meaning the pressure to reciprocate someone else's behavior. So, if someone does something nice for us, we tend to do something nice for that person (Regan, 1971; Uehara, 1995). Reciprocity explains why if you agree with someone on an initial topic, that person is more likely to agree with you later on a different topic. On the other hand, if you refuse to change your initial position, that person is likely to resist your influence later (Cialdini, Green, & Rusch, 1992). Reciprocity helps explain why many charitable organizations solicit donations by first giving you some type of a "gift," such as address labels or greeting cards, and then asking for a financial contribution. In part due to the norm of reciprocity, after receiving a free gift, we feel obligated to return the favor by making a donation to the organization. Reciprocity explains the effectiveness of both the foot-in-the-door and the "that's not all" techniques.

reciprocity a mutual exchange between two people

Foot-in-the-door Technique. The **foot-in-the-door technique** refers to a two-step technique for inducing compliance in which an influencer first makes a small request, then makes a second, larger request (Beaman, 1983; DeJong & Musilli, 1982; Schwarzwald, Bizman, & Raz, 1983). Sometimes these requests are made by the same experimenter, and sometimes they are made by different experimenters. The percentage of participants who agree to the second, larger request is typically much larger than the percentage of people who would agree to the larger request when it is not preceded by a smaller request. In one study, participants were asked to write a one- or two-sentence message about homelessness on a petition that was supposedly going to their senator (Burger & Caldwell, 2003). Two days later, another experimenter called to ask them to donate two hours of time that weekend helping with a food drive. Thirty-two percent of those who are only asked this larger request agree to help with the food drive, compared to 51% of those who are first asked to sign the petition.

foot-in-the-door technique a two-step compliance technique in which an influencer first asks someone to do a small request, then asks for a larger request

In a classic study of this technique, researchers in Southern California went door-to-door asking people to agree to a small request (Freedman & Fraser, 1966). For example, in one case people were asked to put a small, three-inch-square sign near their front door that said, "Be a Safe Driver"; in another case, they were asked to put up a sign saying, "Keep California Beautiful"; and in two other cases they were asked to sign a petition that was being sent to senators dealing with either safe driving or keeping California beautiful. Most of the people approached by the researchers agreed to these requests. Two weeks later, another experimenter went to the same houses and asked residents to put a public service billboard on their front lawn that said, "Drive Carefully." The sign was very large and poorly lettered, and almost totally blocked the front lawn and their house—as was clearly shown in a photograph they showed to the residents. Who agreed to allow this ugly sign on their front lawn? Only about half of those who had either signed a petition (on a same or different topic) or put a "Keep California Beautiful" sign by their door agreed to the new request. However, 76% of those who had put the

"Be a Safe Driver" sign by their door agreed to the new request. According to Freedman and Fraser, those who agreed with the first request came to see themselves as the type of person who supports safe driving and is willing to put a sign up to help out others. In turn, this new self-image later convinces them to allow the huge sign to be placed on their lawn.

This self-image of being helpful occurs, and influences future behavior, even when the first attempt is not successful (Dolinski, 2000). In one study, random people on the street were approached and asked for help with finding a nonexistent address. Virtually everyone (94%) at least responded (typically "I don't know"), but no one could actually help in this situation (because the street did not exist). Participants were then approached a few blocks later by a woman carrying a huge suitcase and they were asked if they would just watch the bag for a few minutes while she went up to visit a friend who lived on the 5th floor. First, how many people simply walking down the street would agree to such a request? Not that many—about 34%. But what about when they were first asked to help with directions? People who had been asked by the first confederate agreed 58% of the time, suggesting that the foot-in-the-door effect may work in part because it allows people to form an image of themselves as helpful even if their helpful intentions are not carried out.

that's-not-all technique a compliance technique in which the influencer begins with an inflated request, and then decreases its apparent size by offering discounts or bonuses

The That's-Not-All Technique. Another technique that relies on reciprocity is the **that's-not-all technique**. In this strategy, the influencer begins with an inflated request and then decreases its apparent size by offering discounts or bonuses (Pollock, Smith, Knowleds, & Bruce, 1998). In one study, Burger (1986) set up a booth at a college fair to sell cupcakes. Some people who approached the table were told that the cupcakes cost $.75. Others were told that they cost $1, but then the price was quickly reduced to $.75. Seventy-five percent of the people who got the "reduced price" bought the cupcakes, compared to 44% of those who got the (same) regular price. This is in part due to the norm of reciprocity (e.g., someone does something nice for you by lowering the price, so you need to do something nice for them by buying the item).

iStockphoto

The that's-not-all technique is more effective with low-cost items than with higher-cost ones, presumably because we are more likely to be persuaded by subtle cues to spend small amounts of money but think through larger purchases more rationally (Pollock et al., 1998). One study found that the that's-not-all technique led 76% of people to buy a small box of chocolates, compared to only 45% in the control condition. However, this technique had no impact on willingness to buy a large (and more expensive) box of chocolates (18% versus 24%).

CONSISTENCY AND COMMITMENT

Another factor that leads to compliance is people's desire to appear consistent. This factor explains why, once we've committed to engaging in a behavior, we follow through on that, or related, behaviors to appear consistent. This factor explains the effectiveness of the door-in-the-face and lowballing techniques.

door-in-the-face technique a compliance technique in which one first asks for a big request, and then asks for a smaller request

The Door-in-the-Face Technique. The **door-in-the-face technique**, is almost the exact opposite of the foot-in-the-door technique, in which the first request is small, and the second request is large. In using this door-in-the-face technique you first make a big request (a really outrageous one), and then make a smaller request (Cialdini, Vincent, Lewis, Catalan, Wheeler, & Darby, 1975). The beauty of this strategy is that the second request seems pretty reasonable, in comparison to the first request, and thus people are much more likely to comply. You may have used this strategy yourself if you have ever asked your parents for a very outrageous curfew, such as 3 AM, in hopes that they would then agree to a more reasonable—but still late—curfew, such as 1 AM.

In one study on the power of the door-in-the-face technique, Cialdini and his colleagues asked a group of college students to serve as chaperons for a group of juvenile delinquents during a day trip to the zoo (Cialdini et al., 1975). Only 17% agreed. Another group of students was first asked to serve as counselors to juvenile delinquents for two hours a week for two years, an even larger commitment; once again, they all refused. However, these students were then asked to help with the day trip to the zoo. This time, 50% agreed. In this case, spending a day at the zoo with juvenile delinquents didn't seem appealing to most students unless that request was made after something even less appealing—making a two-year commitment to serve as a counselor to juvenile delinquents. This is precisely how the door-in-the-face strategy works, and as you can see in this example, it can be quite effective.

Even knowing about these techniques doesn't make you immune to their influence. A number of years ago, one of my research assistants, Tony, once asked me if I would drive him to the airport (about an hour away) to pick up his girlfriend because he didn't have a car. I wasn't interested in spending two hours on this long errand, so I quickly—and quite easily—declined. Then Tony asked, "Well, could I at least borrow your car?" At that point, lending him my car seemed pretty reasonable; after all, I could stay in the office, and I wasn't planning to use my car that morning anyway, so I agreed. When I thought about this interaction later on, I realized that Tony had clearly mastered the use of the door-in-the-face technique. I probably would have said no if he'd asked to borrow my car initially, but after first rejecting the request to drive him to the airport myself, the subsequent request really did seem quite reasonable.

Lowballing. The term **lowballing** describes a two-step technique in which the influencer secures compliance with a request but then increases the size of that request by revealing hidden costs (Burger & Petty, 1981; Cialdini, Cacioppo, Bassett, & Miller, 1978). Lowballing is commonly used by car dealers. Imagine that you and the car dealer reach an agreement to purchase a particular car at a particular price. But after you've reached the agreement, you learn that the purchase price doesn't include many of the features you might expect (e.g., floor mats, a radio, air conditioning), so the true price is higher. Although the deal has now changed, most people feel compelled to pay the additional fees because they've already committed to buying the car.

The lowball technique works because once someone has agreed to a request, he or she feels committed to follow through, even when the nature of that request changes. In one study, researchers asked students to participate in a psychology study that would begin at 7 A.M. (Cialdini et al., 1978). Only 31% agreed. However, they asked other students just to participate in a psychology study (nearly all agreed). After the students had agreed, the researchers informed them that the study would begin at 7 A.M. In this condition, 56% of the students agreed to participate. Why? Because once they've agreed to the request, it is hard for them to tell the experimenter that they've changed their mind.

Lowballing works only when the same person makes the request both times (Burger & Petty, 1981). People apparently feel some obligation to the person with whom they have initially negotiated, and thus tend to honor that agreement. When research participants are told that they can receive extra credit for completing a series of math problems, most agree (65–70%). However, when they are told that the professor refused to allow such credit and then asked whether they would still be willing to complete the problems, 85% of those who are asked by the same experimenter agree. In contrast, only 21% of those who are asked by a different experimenter agree to complete the problems.

SCARCITY

Yet another factor that leads to compliance is **scarcity**, meaning limiting people's opportunity to act, either in terms of time ("This sale ends on Saturday") or number ("only two left"). This factor explains the effectiveness of the deadline and hard-to-get techniques.

lowballing a two-step technique in which the influencer secures agreement with a request, but then increases the size of that request by revealing hidden costs

scarcity a compliance technique in which the opportunity to act is limited in terms of time or number

Deadline. In a clever demonstration of the power of scarcity by increasing the perceived attractiveness of a given item, Jamie Pennebaker and his colleagues asked people in a bar to rate the average attractiveness of all people of their same gender or the opposite gender (Pennebaker et al., 1979). Some people were asked early in the evening (9 P.M.), some were asked in the middle of the evening (10:30 P.M.), and some were asked at the end of the evening (midnight). The bar closed at 12:30 A.M. Although the attractiveness of the same-gender people showed a slight decrease over the course of the evening, the attractiveness of opposite-gender people rose remarkably as the time remaining in which to meet someone decreased.

Questioning the Research
Can you think of another explanation for the finding that people of the opposite-sex increase in their attractiveness later in the evening? (Hint: What else tends to increase late at night in a bar?)

Many compliance techniques in the real world rely on creating the illusion (often false) of a strict deadline by which you need to act. For example, often when you tour a health club, you are told that if you join right away, you will get the lowest price, but if you don't sign up immediately, you will end up paying more later. Similarly, advertisements for a store selling oriental rugs near my town continually note that the store is going out of business, and hence buying a rug now is essential. Oddly enough, this store continues to be in business ... but continues to use the threat of going out of business to motivate sales.

Most home-shopping programs feature some type of countdown until a given item will no longer be available—even though the same item will undoubtedly appear for sale again in the next few days. But showing viewers that the item will not be for sale much longer leads to an increase in the appeal of the object, and thereby increases sales.

©AP/Wide World Photos

Hard-to-get. In other cases, the perceived scarcity of an object leads people to act more quickly or to pay more because of their concern that the desired object will soon be unavailable (Worchel, Lee, & Adewole, 1975). As a mother, I've noticed a consistent pattern of scarcity of popular toys emerging every year at Christmas, which invariably leads frantic parents to wait long hours for new shipments to arrive and drives up the price of that year's coveted toy.

The hard-to-get effect is quite effective in part because it leads such objects to appear more desirable. One research study demonstrated the power of scarcity in increasing the appeal of an object: people rated a chocolate chip cookie as tasting better when they saw it being taken from a jar containing only two cookies than when they saw it being taken from a jar containing ten cookies (Worchel et al., 1975). Similarly, companies that advertise that only a few job vacancies are left are perceived as paying a higher salary than those advertising many job vacancies (Highhouse, Beadle, Gallo, & Miller, 1998).

THE SERIOUS CONSEQUENCES OF COMPLIANCE

Although most of this section has focused on the power of compliance to elicit relatively inconsequential behaviors, this type of social influence can also elicit much more serious behaviors. As described in the Law Connections box, compliance pressures can even lead people to confess to crimes they did not commit. One of the most famous examples of compliance leading to false confessions occurred in 1990, when five African American and Hispanic teenagers living in Harlem were found guilty of the rape and assault of a 28-year-old investment banker who was jogging in Central Park. Four of the five defendants had made lengthy videotaped confessions to the crime. Thirteen years later, a serial rapist who was in prison for another crime confessed to this crime. After a DNA match was made connecting this person to the crime, the defendants' convictions were vacated and they were released from prison.

Law
:::: CONNECTIONS

The Impact of Compliance on False Identifications and False Confessions

In the legal system, compliance pressures can lead to false identifications. Specifically, when eyewitnesses are asked to identify a suspect in a lineup, the instructions they receive influence their response (Malpass & Devine, 1981). Those who are asked to choose a person from a lineup are much more likely to wrongly identify a person (when the actual suspect is not in the lineup) than those who are asked to choose someone but are specifically told that the suspect may not be in the lineup. Moreover, eyewitnesses who receive confirming feedback—namely, those who hear "Good, you identified the suspect" following their identification—overestimate how good a look they had at the suspect as well as how clearly they were able to make out facial details (Wells, Olson, & Charman, 2003). This increase in confidence about their identification can make them even more compelling witnesses when they later appear in a trial.

Compliance pressures can even lead people to wrongly identify themselves as guilty of an offense they did not commit (Kassin, 2005; Kassin & Kiechel, 1996). In one study of the power of pressure on eliciting false confessions, researchers asked participants to perform a relatively simple computer task that was supposedly designed to test spatial awareness. Before the beginning of the task, they were warned not to press a particular button on the keyboard because doing so would cause the computer to crash and the data to be lost. About one minute after the participant began the task, the computer screen suddenly went blank and the experimenter rushed in and accused the participant of pressing the forbidden key. Although in reality not a single person had touched this key, over 69% of the participants ultimately were willing to sign a confession saying that they had done so. When participants were working on the task in a high-speed condition and their mistake was supposedly seen by an eyewitness, then 100% of the participants agreed to sign the confession. This study provides strong evidence that compliance pressure can have dangerous real-world consequences, as shown in this photo of one of the falsely convicted teenagers in the famous Central Park jogger case. Researchers are currently examining strategies for reducing this type of compliance pressure to avoid convicting people—based on a false confession—for crimes they didn't commit.

Malcolm Clarke/©AP/WideWorld Photos

EXAMPLES OF STRATEGIES FOR INDUCING COMPLIANCE

STRATEGY	EXAMPLE

RECIPROCITY

Foot-in-the-door

Glenda asks her neighbor to buy a box of Girl Scout cookies. After she agrees, Glenda asks if she'd like to contribute $100 to the annual Girl Scout Fundraiser.

That's-not-all

As Alton is standing in a store trying to decide whether to buy a new television, the salesperson comes over to him and whispers that there is an overstock of this particular model and he can give him 10% off the price. Alton quickly agrees to the purchase and hands the clerk his credit card.

CONSISTENCY AND COMMITMENT

Door-in-the-face

Vivian asks her parents if they will buy her a car when she graduates from college. When they say no, she asks if they will give her $1,000 as a down payment on a car.

Lowballing

Aden's friend asks if he would let him borrow his notes because he was sick one day and missed class. After Aden agrees and gives him the notes, the friend remarks that he is going to copy Aden's notes from the entire semester because they are so much more complete than his own.

SCARCITY

Deadline

Monisha is looking for an apartment. After touring an apartment, the landlord tells her that he gives a $100 discount to tenants who put down a deposit the same day they see the apartment. Although Monisha originally intended to spend the next week looking at different apartments, she decides to sign a lease for this apartment today.

Hard-to-get

Pedro is trying to decide if he should go to a NASCAR race with his friends when suddenly he learns that the race only has two spaces remaining. Although he really isn't sure whether he wants to spend the money, he quickly buys a ticket because he is worried that the race will soon sell out.

HOW DO SOCIAL PRESSURES INFLUENCE OBEDIENCE?

The term obedience describes behavior changes produced by the commands of people in authority. In some cases, very subtle cues to authority can lead to obedience. Bickman (1974) studied obedience by asking people on the street to comply with some type of request, such as picking up a paper bag, standing on the opposite side of a sign, or giving someone a dime. In half of the cases the requester

The Nazi government of Germany in the 1930s and 1940s committed horrible acts of cruelty on millions of innocent people. How do we attribute this behavior?

Associated Press

wore ordinary clothes. In other cases he wore a security guard's uniform. Regardless of the request, many more people obeyed the request when the person was wearing a uniform (92%) than when he was wearing street clothes (42%), presumably because the uniform signifies legitimate authority. This section will examine factors that increase obedience, as well as the ethical issues involved in conducting scientific research on obedience.

FACTORS THAT INCREASE OBEDIENCE

In the early 1960s Stanley Milgram at Yale University began a series of experiments to examine the factors that predict obedience to authority (1963, 1974). This study, which marked Milgram's first line of research as a new professor, was based on Milgram's interest in discovering the processes that led to the Nazi Holocaust, in which millions of innocent victims were killed, or sent to their death, by people who were simply obeying orders. He was interested in what led people to be willing to obey such orders, and whether similar levels of obedience could be found in the United States.

In a series of experiments, Milgram brought ordinary men into his lab to participate in what was supposedly a study of memory. After participants arrived at the lab, they were greeted by Milgram and introduced to another person, who was supposedly another participant but in reality was a confederate of Milgram's. The experimenter then explained the study, which they were told was designed to test the impact of punishment on speed of learning. The participants were told that one person would serve as the "teacher" and administer shocks to another person (the "learner") when the learner gave a wrong answer.

Public Announcement

WE WILL PAY YOU $4.00 FOR ONE HOUR OF YOUR TIME

Persons Needed for a Study of Memory

*We will pay five hundred New Haven men to help us complete a scientific study of memory and learning. The study is being done at Yale University.

*Each person who participates will be paid $4.00 (plus 50c carfare) for approximately 1 hour's time. We need you for only one hour: there are no further obligations. You may choose the time you would like to come (evenings, weekdays, or weekends).

*No special training, education, or experience is needed. We want:

Factory workers	Businessmen	Construction workers
City employees	Clerks	Salespeople
Laborers	Professional people	White-collar workers
Barbers	Telephone workers	Others

All persons must be between the ages of 20 and 50. High school and college students cannot be used.

*If you meet these qualifications, fill out the coupon below and mail it now to Professor Stanley Milgram, Department of Psychology, Yale University, New Haven. You will be notified later of the specific time and place of the study. We reserve the right to decline any application.

*You will be paid $4.00 (plus 50c carfare) as soon as you arrive at the laboratory.

– –

TO:
PROF. STANLEY MILGRAM, DEPARTMENT OF PSYCHOLOGY, YALE UNIVERSITY, NEW HAVEN, CONN. I want to take part in this study of memory and learning. I am between the ages of 20 and 50. I will be paid $4.00 (plus 50c carfare) if I participate.

NAME (Please Print)..

ADDRESS ....

TELEPHONE NO. .... Best time to call you ....

AGE........ OCCUPATION..................... SEX ......
CAN YOU COME:

WEEKDAYS .... EVENINGS ......WEEKENDS........

Psychology Archives – The University of Akron

This announcement was placed in various newspapers to attract participants from a variety of backgrounds.

The shock generator used in Milgram's research was designed to look very realistic and thereby convince participants that they were truly giving electric shocks to another participant.

Archives of the History of American Psychology - University of Akron

The learner was always a confederate who would receive the "shocks." The "teacher" was told to start by giving the learner the lowest level of shock (15 volts) and to increase the shock level each time the learner made a mistake.

As the study progressed, the learner continued to give wrong answers and the teacher continued to increase the intensity of the shocks. At the 75 volt level, the learner began to cry out after each shock, and by 150 volts the learner asked to be let out of the experiment (see Table 8.1). Moreover, he began claiming that his heart was bothering him, suggesting a major negative consequence of continuing the experiment. But each time the participant hesitated or turned to the experimenter for advice, he received a prompt that prodded him to continue. These prompts continued until the teacher simply refused to continue or reached the highest level of volts (450, which was marked "XXX dangerous").

Much to Milgram's surprise, the vast majority of the participants in his study were willing to give another innocent participant the maximum level of electric shocks; in fact, 65% of the participants fully obeyed the experimenter's orders. As Milgram himself observed,

"With numbing regularity good people were seen to knuckle under the demands of authority and perform actions that were callous and severe. Men who are in everyday life responsible and decent were seduced by the trappings of authority, by the control of their perceptions, and by the uncritical acceptance of the experimenter's definition of the situation, into performing harsh acts. A substantial proportion of people do what they are told to do, irrespective of the content of the act and without limitations of conscience, so long as they perceive that the command comes from a legitimate authority."

(1965)

TABLE 8.1	THE "LEARNER'S" PROTESTS	
VOLT LEVEL	**LEARNER'S PROTEST**	**PERCENT WHO STOPPED**
75 volts	Ugh!	0
95 volts	Ugh!	0
105 volts	Ugh (louder)	0
120 volts	Ugh! Hey, this really hurts.	0
135 volts	Ugh!	0
150 volts	Ugh!! Experimenter! That's all. Get me out of here. I told you I had heart trouble. My heart's starting to bother me. Get me out of here, please. My heart's starting to bother me. I refuse to go on. Let me out.	0
165 volts	Ugh! Let me out! (Shouting)	0

VOLT LEVEL	LEARNER'S PROTEST	PERCENT WHO STOPPED
180 volts	Ugh! I can't stand the pain. Let me out of here! (Shouting)	0
195 volts	Ugh! Let me out of here. Let me out of here. My heart's bothering me Let me out of here! You have no right to keep me here! Let me out! Let me out of here! Let me out! Let me out of here! My heart's bothering me. Let me out! Let me out!	0
210 volts	Ugh!! Experimenter! Get me out of here. I've had enough. I won't of here. I've had enough. I won't be in the experiment any more.	0
225 volts	Ugh!	0
240 volts	Ugh!	0
255 volts	Ugh! Get me out of here.	0
270 volts	(Agonized scream) Let me out of here. Let me out of here. Let me out. Do you hear? Let me out of here.	0
285 volts	(Agonized scream)	0
300 volts	(Agonized scream) I absolutely refuse to answer any more. Get me out of here. You can't hold me here. Get me out. Get me out of here.	12.5
315 volts	(Intensely agonized scream) I told you I refuse to answer. I'm no longer part of this experiment.	10
330 volts	(Intense and prolonged agonized scream) Let me out of here. Let me out of here. My heart's bothering me. Let me out, I tell you. (Hysterically) Let me out of here. Let me out of here. You have no right to hold me here. Let me out! Let me out! Let me out! Let me out of here! Let me out! Let me out!	5
345 volts	(No response)	2.5
360 volts	(No response)	2.5
375 volts	(No response)	2.5
390 volts	(No response)	0
405 volts	(No response)	0
420 volts	(No response)	0
435 volts	(No response)	0
450 volts	(No response)	65

Participants in the Milgram study were faced with a very unwilling learner and forced to choose whether to obey the authority figure (the experimenter) who was telling them to continue, or the learner, who was insisting that they stop.
Source: Milgram, S. (1974), *Obedience to Authority: An Experimental View*. New York: Harper Collins.

This extremely high rate of obedience—in which only 14 of the original 40 participants defied the experimenter and stopped giving shocks at any point-was very surprising, even to Milgram himself. Before starting the experiment, Milgram asked psychiatrists, graduate students, and faculty to guess how long average participants would continue to obey orders to harm another person in this study (as measured by the level of shocks administered). Virtually everyone predicted that most participants would refuse giving additional shocks at the 150 volt level, in which the learner specifically complains of chest pain and asks to be released from the study.

To examine the factors that led to this high rate of obedience, Milgram conducted a series of follow-up studies that varied different factors in his original study. Which of those factors did and did not affect rates of obedience?

Person factors. First, although initially Milgram and many others assumed that only people who were cruel and sadistic would give high levels of shocks, this study provided little evidence that *person* factors mattered. Most people in the Milgram study did show full obedience, but the vast majority of those who did so really struggled with obeying the researcher: they pleaded with the experimenter, they perspired, they trembled, and so forth. It is not that they were enjoying it or finding it easy. As Milgram describes,

> I observed a mature and initially poised businessman enter the laboratory smiling and confident. Within 20 minutes he was reduced to a twitching, stuttering wreck, who was rapidly approaching a point of nervous collapse. He constantly pulled on his earlobe and twisted his hands. At one point he pushed his fist into his forehead and muttered, "Oh God, let's stop it." And yet he continued to respond to every word of the experimenter, and obeyed to the end.

(Milgram, 1963, p. 377).

The original Milgram study included only male participants, and many people have wondered whether women, who are generally seen as more empathetic, would be less likely to continue obeying orders to give shocks to the learner. However, an identical study with women participants showed that 65% also reached the 450-volt level.

Although most descriptions of the Milgram study emphasize the high rates of obedience, even in this study a sizable minority of people did not give the highest levels of shocks, indicating that the nature of the person does matter. So who is most likely to obey authority? One personality factor that predicts obedience is *authoritarianism*, a trait that describes people who are submissive and uncritical in their acceptance of the morality of authority (see Rate Yourself) (Blass, 1991).

Rate Yourself

How Much Do You Believe in Obeying Authorities?

INSTRUCTIONS: *Rate your agreement with each of the following statements on a scale of 1 (strongly disagree) to 7 (strongly agree).*

☐ **1.** Obedience and respect for authority are the most important virtues children should learn.

☐ **2.** What this country needs most, more than laws and political programs, is a few courageous, tireless, devoted leaders in whom the people can put their faith.

☐ **3.** Most of our social problems would be solved if we could somehow get rid of the immoral, crooked, and feebleminded people.

☐ **4.** People can be divided into two distinct classes: the weak and the strong.

☐ **5.** What the youth needs most is strict discipline, rugged determination, and the will to work and fight for family and country.

SCORING: Add up your scores on each of these items.

INTERPRETATION: This scale measures the degree of authoritarianism, meaning people's belief in and support of the policies and decisions made by powerful authorities. People with higher scores have a greater belief in the power of authorities than those with lower scores (Adorno, Frenkel-Brunswick, Levinson, & Sanford, 1950).

As you might imagine, people who were high in authoritarianism did show higher rates of obedience in the Milgram studies. Although some personality characteristics may increase obedience, this behavior is not primarily a function of the person (Elms & Milgram, 1966).

Authority factors. A factor that did influence rates of obedience was the nature of the *authority*. Although a scientist is not typically seen as a significant authority figure (e.g., compared to a military leader or work supervisor), apparently in this context he was seen as the definitive authority. When Milgram ran this study in a run-down lab in Bridgeport, Connecticut, that was not associated with Yale, the rate of obedience dropped to 48%. When the experimenter was an ordinary person (supposedly just another participant), the rate of obedience dropped to 20%. In other cases, obedience occurs based on even more subtle cues, such as the person's dress—as described in the study at the start of this section (Bushman, 1988). It is important to remember that participants were not simply willing to obey orders to deliver shocks to another person no matter who made the request. Most participants were only willing to obey such orders when they believed that the person making the request was truly knowledgeable about the experiment and thus able to take responsibility for any harm that might occur.

In the NEWS **McDonald's.** In April of 2004, workers at a McDonalds restaurant in Mount Washington, Kentucky, obeyed a series of orders delivered over the phone by a person they believed was a police officer. This officer was supposedly investigating whether a McDonalds' worker had stolen a customer's purse. Following the officer's instructions, the store manager ordered an 18-year-old female employee to remove all her clothing in an effort to find the stolen items. The victim later sued McDonald's for failing to protect her during her ordeal; in October 2007, she was awarded over $5 million in punitive damages and expenses.

Procedure factors. Another factor that contributed to the high rate of obedience in Milgram's studies was the *procedure* used, including the location of the victim and the experimenter (Miller, Collins, & Brief, 1995). When the learner was in the same room as the teacher, only 40% of the participants reached the 450-volt level. When the teacher was required to force the learner's hand onto a metal shock plate, the rate of obedience dropped to 30%. And when the experimenter was not in the same room but instead gave his instructions by telephone, the rate of obedience was only 21% (some participants even lied and stayed at the 15-volt level).

People are also much more willing to convey orders to harm someone else than to actually carry out such orders (Kilham & Mann, 1974). In this case the person's responsibility is reduced even more. When a supposed participant disobeyed, so did most others (90%). Moreover, when participants are given the option of whether to give a shock or not, most do not. People also refuse to continue when two experimenters disagree. And they refuse to obey another participant who tells them to continue.

Although these findings show that some aspects of the procedure and the nature of the authority decrease obedience, a lot of people are still willing to obey. Why? In part because Milgram's procedure was designed to yield obedience. First, the participants did not have personal responsibility for the victim—the researcher was giving the orders (Blass, 1996; Tilker, 1970). As described previously, the experimenter took full responsibility for what was occurring, and thus the participant could absolve himself of blame.

Second, there was a gradual escalation of shock levels, meaning that people could initially feel fine about obeying the request, and obey repeatedly before the frightening implications of the procedure were clear (Gilbert, 1981). Most people would not initially give a 450-volt shock, but once you've given 15 volts, and then 30 and then 45, how do you decide when to stop? This is like the "foot-in-the-door" technique in that participants had no easy way to justify a decision to stop giving shocks at a certain point. In line with this view, people who defy authority tend to do so early on; that is, those who ultimately disobey tend to resist authority more quickly (Modigliani & Rochat, 1995). Interestingly, in all variations of Milgram's studies, participants were most likely to stop obeying orders at the 150-volt level (Packer, 2008). What is unique about this voltage level? This was the first time at which the victim asked to be released.

Third, although the participant could *hear* the victim, he couldn't see *him*; people who have more feedback (audio and visual) are more likely to behave in a responsible way (Tilker, 1970). Nevertheless, people generally ignore such situational factors and attribute evil to the person—right in line with people's tendency to make the fundamental attribution error (Safer, 1980).

ETHICAL ISSUES

The Milgram studies (he conducted a total of twenty-one variations of his original experiment) generated a tremendous amount of interest among social psychologists for several reasons. First, these results were completely unexpected—even experts predicted that very few people would go along with the authority figure to such a dangerous extent. Second, the variations of the experiment that Milgram conducted provide considerable information about the influence of various factors in producing obedience, and therefore enabled researchers to distinguish among the effects of the participant, the procedure, and the authority. Perhaps most important, these studies have generated considerable debate about the ethics of such experiments. Many researchers were horrified that this study was even conducted; it obviously exposed people to psychological harm during the experiment, and it is certainly possible that such effects lingered, perhaps permanently (Baumrind, 1985).

However, Milgram claimed that the debriefing following his study was very thorough and was designed to leave the participants feeling good about themselves and their behavior. In a follow-up questionnaire returned by 92% of the participants, 44% claimed that they were "very glad to have participated in the experiment" and 40% said that they were "glad to have participated." Only 1% were "sorry" or "very sorry" to have participated. Milgram sent each participant a five-page report describing the value of this study. Moreover, an independent psychiatrist examined the 40 participants who were thought to be at greatest risk of experiencing harm, and none of them showed any signs of long-term damage. Nevertheless, the full extent of the harm, or even potential harm, of having participated in this study remains unknown.

For ethical reasons, research of this nature can't be done today. Some evidence suggests that if researchers conducted similar studies they would find similar results. In a more recent series of experiments, researchers asked participants to read various test questions over a microphone to a supposed job applicant, who was actually a confederate of the researcher (Meeus & Raaijmakers, 1995). They were told that if the man did well, he would get the job, whereas if he did not, he would fail. The researchers told the participants that they were interested in examining how job applicants would react under pressure, so they wanted them to harass the applicant by saying things like "If you continue like this, you will fail" and "This job is much too difficult for you." As the "interview" continued, the applicant protested. He pleaded with them to stop, then refused to tolerate the abuse, and was clearly showing signs of tension. He eventually just stopped answering the questions. How many of the participants continued to read the 15 stress statements? Not one did

Questioning the Research

This study was designed to examine rates of obedience while avoiding the ethical constraints of the Milgram study. Do you think this study provides important information about people's willingness to obey authority that is comparable to what was found in the Milgram study and other real-life examples of obedience to authority? Why or why not?

so in a control group (which lacked an authority urging them to continue), but 92% did so when the experimenter prodded them along (and took responsibility for the results).

REAL-WORLD EXAMPLES OF OBEDIENCE

One of the most frightening acts of obedience during recent years occurred in the 1970s in Jonestown, Guyana. The People's Temple was a cult-like organization that was based in San Francisco and drew its members mostly from poor people in that city. In 1977, the Reverend Jim Jones, their leader, moved the group to a remote jungle settlement in South America, and most of his followers joined him. They lived in relative obscurity until 1978, when Congressman Ryan of California came to Guyana to investigate the cult's activities at the urging of relatives of some of its members. Three members of Ryan's party, including a member of the cult who was trying to defect, were shot and killed as they tried to leave Jonestown. Since this act would clearly lead to the arrest and imprisonment of Jones, and hence the abolition of the cult, he decided to require his followers to commit mass suicide. He prepared large vats of strawberry Kool-Aid laced with cyanide, and ordered his followers to drink the Kool-Aid. Although a few people escaped or resisted, virtually all of the 910 followers complied with his order and killed themselves. In one particularly dramatic case, a young woman helped her baby drink some of the poison and then drank some herself.

Associated Press

Social psychological principles explain why more than 900 people obeyed the order to kill themselves at Jonestown.

When the mass suicide at Jonestown occurred, most people questioned why so many people would willingly kill themselves. But social-psychological principles clearly tell us why (Osherow, 2004). First, Jim Jones was very charismatic, a powerful leader who had obviously convinced all of those people to leave their homes and live in the jungle. Second, most of the people were poor and uneducated, and may have appreciated the safety of having someone else control many aspects of their lives in exchange for the security and salvation Jones promised. Third, and probably most important, they were in a place that was totally alien, both physically and socially. They were isolated from others. And as we know from research on the power of norms, people are most likely to look to others for guidance in their own behavior when they are in unfamiliar situations. Those who may have had doubts probably considered the situation, and when they saw other people drinking the poison, seemingly without question, they probably assumed that it was the right thing to do.

Obedience has led to dangerous consequences in many other real-life cases, such as the Nazi's concentration camps in World War II, the My Lai Massacre during the Vietnam War (see insert), and terrorist groups, such as Al Qaeda. Obedience also plays a role in fraternity initiation, as described at the start of this chapter. In the last few years alone, alcohol poisoning as part of a fraternity hazing ritual killed all of the following students:

- 18-year-old Lynn Gordon "Gordie" Bailey, Jr., a student at the University of Colorado at Boulder, on September 17, 2004;
- 18-year-old Phanta "Jack" Phoummarath, a student at the University of Texas, on December 10, 2005;
- 18-year-old Gary DeVercelly, a student at Rutgers University, on March 30, 2007;
- 18-year-old Johnnny Smith, a student at Wabash College, on October 4, 2007.

Although these real-world examples of obedience may seem very different from one another, they actually share many common features that likely contributed to the obedience shown in each. First, the people in many of these situations are in very uncertain, and isolated, surroundings, which increases their dependence on the group. In turn, any doubts about the actions of the group are quelled, and a mindset of "us versus them" (group members versus those outside the group) is created. These strategies for creating obedience are used regularly by leaders of cults (as we saw in the case of Jim Jones) and in military settings (as we saw in the case of prisoner abuse in the Abu Ghraib prison in Iraq). These situational factors can then lead seemingly normal people to behave in really atrocious ways, as you learned about from

UPI Photo/Sajjad Ali Qurehsi/NewsCom

In the NEWS **Terrorism.** On September 28, 2008, a suicide bomber detonated a truck carrying explosives in front of the Islamabad Marriott Hotel in Pakistan. Fifty-four people were killed and at least 266 people were wounded, both in the initial explosion and as the blast caused a natural gas leak which led to a fire throughout the hotel.

THE MY LAI MASSACRE

Some of the most horrible acts of obedience have occurred during times of war. During the Vietnam War, a group of American soldiers approached a Vietnamese village and proceeded to round up men, women, and children. The following interview by Mike Wallace of the TV program *60 Minutes* describes one soldier's view of this event, known as the My Lai Massacre.

Mike Wallace: How many people did you round up?

Soldier: Well, there was about forty, fifty people that we gathered in the center of the village. And we placed them in there, and it was like a little island, right there in the center of the village, I'd say.

Mike Wallace: What kind of people—men, women, children?

Soldier: Men, women, children.

Mike Wallace: Babies?

Soldier: Babies. And we huddled them up. We made them squat down and Lieutenant Calley came over and said, " You know what to do with them, don't you?" And I said yes. So I took for granted that he just wanted us to watch them. And he left, and came back about ten or fifteen minutes later and said, "How come you ain't killed them yet?" And I told him that I didn't think you wanted us to kill them, that you just wanted us to guard them. He said, "No. I want them dead." So...

Mike Wallace: He told this to all of you, or to you particularly?

Soldier: Well, I was facing him. So, but the other three, four guys heard it and so he stepped back about ten, fifteen feet, and he started shooting them. And he told me to start shooting. So I started shooting. I poured about four clips in the group.

Mike Wallace: You fired four clips from your ...

Soldier: M-16.

Mike Wallace: And that's how many clips— I mean, how many ...

Soldier: I carried seventeen rounds to each clip.

Mike Wallace: So you fired something like sixty-seven shots?

Soldier: Right.

Mike Wallace: And you killed how many? At that time?

Soldier: Well, I fired them automatic, so you can't ... You just spray the area on them and so you can't know how many you killed cause they were going fast. So I might have killed ten or fifteen of them.

Mike Wallace: Men, women, and children?

Soldier: Men, women, and children.

Mike Wallace: And babies?

Soldier: And babies.

60 Minutes, Mike Wallace, 1969.

As this interview describes, people can commit horrible acts when they are ordered to do so by an authority figure. Obedience to an authority is especially likely during times of war, in which soldiers must rely on their commanders for guidance, are isolated from family and friends, and experience constant stress.

Zimbardo's prison study that was described in Chapter 2 (Haney et al., 1973; Haney & Zimbardo, 1998). As Nasra Hassan, a Muslim from Palestine who spent four years studying terrorists describes, "What is frightening is not the abnormality of those who carry out the suicide attacks, but their sheer normality" (2001). Her research reveals that members of terrorist groups are typically young men, who have often had a friend or relative killed by the other side. Unfortunately, these findings mean that eliminating terrorism is not as simple as identifying mentally dysfunctional people, but rather changing the situational factors that create terrorists.

STRATEGIES FOR RESISTING OBEDIENCE

What can we do to help people defy unjustified demands by authority figures? Are people who defy authority different in some way from those who obey? Although several researchers have examined factors in the participants who defied the experimenter in Milgram's studies, there are no associations between defiance and personality factors or religious beliefs (Modigliani & Rochat, 1995). Participants who defied the authority in the Milgram studies are simply ordinary people who choose to deliberate about what they are being asked to do—and that deliberation allows them to defy the situational pressures and disobey.

This description of the participants who disobeyed in the Milgram study is very similar to that used to describe people who defied authorities' orders during Nazi Germany and helped the target people (Rochat & Modigliani, 1995). Many of these helpers were ordinary people who recognized a need to help people who were being persecuted. They often began helping by performing a very small action, and these early modest steps escalated to larger and more risky acts of assistance.

One factor that can help people stand up to the pressure exerted by authorities is knowing about the power of influence (Richard et al., 2001). You should therefore be better able to defy unjustified authority after taking a social psychology class. People who are aware of the situational pressures that lead people to obey authorities are more likely to stand up to such authorities themselves—they are willing to act as whistleblowers even in the face of a strong authority. People who are better educated are more likely to disobey military orders, for example (Hamilton, Sanders, & McKearney, 1995).

Another factor that helps people defy authority is having another person who disobeys with them. As we saw in the case of the Asch study, because people do not like to "stand alone," having other people on their side (as a group, or even just one other person) helps those who wish to defy authority (Rochat & Modigliani, 1995). It may not have been enough for the soldier at My Lai to defy the Lieutenant, but if the soldier spoke up, would other soldiers have joined him, making it much less likely that the massacre would have occurred? It's possible. There is power in numbers, and this means that if you disagree with something, you should speak out.

People are especially likely to disobey authority if they see such acts modeled by other authority figures. In a variation of the original study, Milgram examined how people would respond when two experimenters disagreed about whether the "teacher" should continue shocking the "learner." As predicted, virtually no one chooses to continue shocking the learner when one authority disagrees with the other.

In a famous real-world example of conflicting authorities, the pastors of a village in France gave a sermon in response to Hitler's request that all refugees be turned over to the police and sent to Germany (Rochat & Modigliani, 1995). In this sermon, they noted, "We appeal to all our brothers in Christ to refuse to cooperate with this violence, and in particular, during the days that will follow, with the violence that will be directed at the British people...We shall resist whenever our adversaries demand of us obedience contrary to the orders of the Gospel" (p. 199). The initial act of public resistance on the part of two pastors initiated a confrontation between members of Hitler's Third Reich and the people of the La Chambon village that lasted four years—until the day of the German Army's surrender in Paris on August 25, 1944.

Finally, although this section has focused on the hazards of obeying an *unjustified* authority, we should remember that obeying an authority can, in many cases, be good. Nurses may have to obey orders to give a patient an injection or other medical procedure. Prison guards may need to obey orders to place a prisoner in solitary confinement. In these cases, obedience can lead to benefits for society in general, even if at a cost to some individual members.

EXAMPLES OF FACTORS LEADING TO OBEDIENCE

FACTOR	FINDING
Participant	Very little evidence suggests that participant characteristics have a strong influence on obedience, although people who are high in authoritarianism are somewhat more obedient than others.
Authority	The nature of the authority figure clearly affected obedience in the Milgram studies. Although rates of obedience were quite high when the authority figure was seen as an expert, they dropped substantially when another participant served as the authority.
Procedure	Another factor that contributed to the high rate of obedience in the Milgram studies was the *procedure* used. When the participant and the learner were in the same room, and when the experimenter simply gave instructions by phone, obedience dropped substantially.

CULTURE
HOW DOES CULTURE IMPACT SOCIAL INFLUENCE?

To examine cultural differences in the desire for uniqueness, Heejung Kim and Hazel Markus of Stanford University conducted an unusual naturalistic study (Kim & Markus, 1999). Researchers went to San Francisco airport and asked both European Americans and Chinese Americans who were waiting for a flight if they would complete a brief survey. They told them they would receive a pen in exchange for helping. After they completed the survey, the researcher reached into a large bag and pulled out five pens for the participants to select from. In some conditions three of the pens were one color and two were the other color, and in other conditions four of the pens were one color and the fifth was a different color. The researcher simply noted which color the participants chose. The researchers hypothesized that European Americans would tend to choose a more uncommon color pen (e.g., the pen which there were only 1 or 2 of, depending on the condition) than would Chinese Americans. As predicted, European Americans picked the more uncommon color 74% of the time, whereas Chinese Americans only chose the unique color 24% of the time. This study reveals the impact of culture on people's desire to conform to others' behavior. This section will examine this and other ways in which culture impacts social pressure, including conformity, compliance, and obedience.

CONFORMITY

One of the major differences between individualistic and communalistic cultures is the emphasis and value they place on conformity (Markus & Kitayama, 1994). In individualistic cultures, conformity is seen as a sign of weakness (e.g., giving in to others, ignoring one's own opinions and beliefs). In individualistic cultures, conformity is often seen as a bad thing; people want to stand out and be different, and we admire people who differentiate themselves from the crowd. A common expression used is "The squeaky wheel gets the grease," meaning that people should complain in order to get their needs met. This expression epitomizes the admiration people have for sticking out from the crowd.

In contrast, people in collectivistic cultures often place a particular value on fitting in with others and conforming to social norms, and therefore conformity is seen as a sign of self-control, maturity, tolerance, and respect for others (Markus & Kitayama, 1994). The Korean word for conformity means maturity and inner

How do you order a drink at Starbucks? In individualistic cultures, people's orders are often very specific (and personal), whereas this type of precise order is much less common in collectivistic cultures.

strength (Kim & Markus, 1999). In line with this value, a common expression in Japan is "The nail that stands out gets pounded down," clearly indicating the importance of conforming. Kim and Markus point out that people in the United States regularly order precisely what they want in restaurants and even in coffee shops (e.g., "I'll have a decaffeinated latte with skim milk"). However, ordering in such a specific manner in Korea is unheard of—and doing so would convey that this person does not get along with others well and is not sensitive to the needs of his/her waiter.

Not surprisingly, studies reveal that the rates of conformity on an Asch-type paradigm are even higher in collectivistic countries than in the United States (Bond & Smith, 1996). A meta-analysis of 133 studies from 17 different countries revealed that collectivistic countries tend to show higher rates of conformity than individualistic countries. Among the Bantu tribe of Zimbabwe, 51% of participants conformed in this paradigm, nearly double the 30% conformity rate in the United States. One examination of conformity rates across cultures revealed a range of 18% to 60%. Similarly, Chinese and Japanese participants are more likely to use the midpoint of rating scales than are Americans and Canadians (Chen, Lee, & Stevenson, 1995). This reflects a tendency to express individual preferences versus fitting in with the group.

Because people in collectivistic cultures pay more attention to their own and others' behavior to ensure conformity to valued norms, they are less influenced by question wording than are those in individualistic cultures (Ji, Schwarz, & Nisbett, 2000). For example, in one study American and Chinese students were asked how frequently they engaged in various behaviors, such as going to the library, catching a cold, and having a nightmare. In some conditions participants gave open-ended answers. In other conditions they responded based on a low frequency or high frequency scale. As predicted, Americans' responses were much more impacted by the frequency scale used than were the Chinese's responses. The explanation for this result is that collectivistic cultures value monitoring one's own and other's behavior, and hence Chinese students pay more attention to their behavior and have a more accurate recall of their behavior. Autobiographical memory is therefore more accurate in collectivistic cultures.

COMPLIANCE

The rates and predictors of compliance also differ as a function of culture (Bontempo, Lobel, & Triandis, 1990). In one study with students from the United States and Brazil, researchers asked how they would respond to various hypothetical situations involving helping others, such as helping a sick friend, loaning someone money, or encouraging someone to change an unhealthy behavior. Although in both cultures people report a similar willingness to help others, the Brazilians reported a sincere enjoyment of providing such assistance whereas Americans report little satisfaction. Moreover, Brazilians are equally likely to engage in the helping behavior whether it would be done anonymously or in public (see Figure 8.4). The Americans are much more likely to say they would do the behavior in a public situation than in an anonymous one.

People from individualistic cultures are more likely to help someone else under conditions of public scrutiny than alone, whereas those in collectivistic cultures are equally likely to help someone under private or public situations.

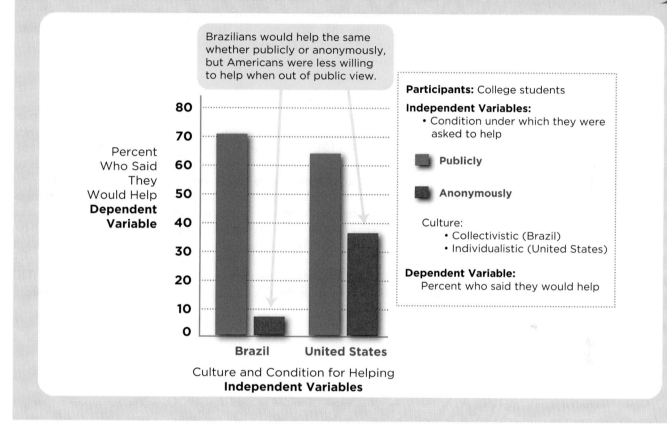

FIGURE 8.4

HOW DOES CULTURE IMPACT COMPLIANCE?

Researchers in this experiment asked students in Brazil and the United States how they would respond to various requests for help. As predicted, Brazilians are equally likely to engage in the helping behavior whether it would be done anonymously or in public, whereas Americans are much more likely to perform helping behavior in a public situation than in an anonymous one.

Source: Bontempo, R., Lobel, S., & Triandis, H. (1990). Compliance and value internalization in Brazil and the U.S.: Effects of allocentrism and anonymity. *Journal of Cross-Cultural Psychology, 21*, 200-213.

Brazilians would help the same whether publicly or anonymously, but Americans were less willing to help when out of public view.

Percent Who Said They Would Help **Dependent Variable**

Culture and Condition for Helping
Independent Variables

Participants: College students

Independent Variables:
- Condition under which they were asked to help

■ **Publicly**

■ **Anonymously**

Culture:
- Collectivistic (Brazil)
- Individualistic (United States)

Dependent Variable:
Percent who said they would help

Once again, Americans apparently help out of obligation, particularly if they might receive public scrutiny for not helping, whereas the Brazilians help out of an intrinsic desire to help their group members.

Attitudes and norms are more in line with one another in collectivistic cultures than in individualistic ones. In one study, university students in the United States and Poland (a collectivistic culture) were asked about their willingness to complete a marketing survey without pay (Cialdini et al., 1999). Half of the students in each group were first asked to consider their own prior history of compliance with requests, whereas the other half were first asked to consider information regarding other students' compliance. Although both own prior history and others' history influenced compliance in students in both countries, own history had a greater impact on compliance for Americans, whereas others' compliance had a greater impact on Polish students.

Subtle differences in wording have a greater impact on compliance in collectivistic cultures than in individualistic ones. In one study, participants from the United States and Korea imagined what they would say in various situations in which they were asked to make a request (e.g., borrowing money, asking for the time, etc.; Holtgraves & Yang, 1992). Although Americans were overall more polite than Koreans, the Koreans' use of language was more responsive to the specific features of the situation (e.g., power of the target of the request, degree of acquaintance between themselves and the target, etc.). This may be because in collectivistic cultures, strong distinctions are drawn between people in different groups, and therefore there is more variability overall in social interactions. In turn, people in collectivistic cultures are more sensitive and attuned to the situation.

Similarly, subtle differences in the way a request is phrased have a greater impact on perceptions of the request by Koreans than by Americans (Holtgraves & Yang, 1990). For example, Americans see the statements "You'll go get the mail, won't you?" and "I'd like you to go get the mail," as relatively similar. Koreans see these small wording changes as somewhat different.

Finally, Koreans' usage of politeness strategies is more sensitive to relational cues, whereas Americans' usage of politeness strategies is more sensitive to the content of the message (Ambady, Koo, Lee, & Rosenthal, 1996). These findings emerge because the content of communications is very important in cultures that focus on directness and accuracy, and relationships are based on equality. On the other hand, in cultures that pay particular attention to hierarchies and relationships, the roles of the target and speaker also convey meaning, and hence people are less focused on the content of the message.

OBEDIENCE

Finally, rates of obedience also differ as a function of culture. In one study, participants from the United States, Russia, and Japan read surveys that described different acts of obedient behavior in the workplace (Hamilton & Sanders, 1995). These acts included things like obeying orders to dump fertilizer, which leads to a toxic waste spill, and obeying orders to not carry out adequate tests of a new drug due to time pressure. Participants then rated how responsible the person was for engaging in the behavior. As predicted, participants from collectivistic cultures (Japan, Russia) were more likely to excuse the person for engaging in the behavior than those from individualistic cultures (the United States). These findings are in line with those you've learned about earlier in this book, such as the greater emphasis placed on the role of the situation in collectivistic cultures compared to the greater emphasis placed on the role of the person in individualistic cultures.

The Big Picture

SOCIAL INFLUENCE

This chapter included many applications of the three "big ideas" studied in social psychology. The examples below should help you see the connection between persuasion and these big ideas and contribute to your understanding of the big picture of social psychology.

THEME	EXAMPLES
The social world influences how we think about ourselves.	• We believe we're less comfortable with the amount of drinking on campus than are other students. • We believe fear of looking stupid inhibits us from asking questions in class, and we believe that other students don't ask questions because they don't have questions. • We admit to making an error we didn't make if we are under time pressure and another person claims to have seen us commit the error.
The social world influences our thoughts, attitudes, and behaviors.	• We adopt the political attitudes of our friends. • We pay more for a car than we should—due to the necessary "add-ons" the dealer describes. • We laugh at offensive jokes, even though we don't find them funny.
Our attitudes and behavior shape the social world around us.	• When we feel strongly about a given position, we convince others to support our view. • We eat less than we want to in public settings (to conform to the perceived thinness norm), which then strengthens the prevalence of that (false) norm for others. • We ask our parents for an outrageous curfew, and thereby are granted a later curfew than we typically have.

WHAT YOU'VE LEARNED

This chapter has examined four key principles of social influence, including social norms, conformity, compliance, and obedience, as well as the impact of culture on each of these types of social influence.

YOU LEARNED **How do social norms influence behavior?** This section examined how social norms influence behavior in multiple ways. You learned about the power of social norms, the pressure people feel to conform to norms, and the errors people make in perceiving norms. You also learned why it is probably a good idea to ask a professor a question when you don't understand the course material.

YOU LEARNED **What factors lead to conformity?** This section described factors that influence conformity. You learned about the two types of influence: informational influence and normative influence. Next, you learned about different influences on conformity, including group size, standing alone, demographic variables, and motivation. Finally, you learned about minority influence, and the benefits of conformity. You also discovered that people can find jokes offensive, but fail to confront the joke-teller for fear of the consequences.

YOU LEARNED **What factors lead to compliance?** This section described five strategies used to gain compliance. You learned about the foot-in-the-door technique, the door-in-the-face technique, lowballing, scarcity, and reciprocity. You also learned that we are more likely to comply with requests from those who are similar to ourselves—such as if they share our birthday.

YOU LEARNED **What factors lead to obedience?** This section described factors that lead to obedience. You learned about the factors that led to obedience in the Milgram study, and that subject factors have little to do with whether we obey, but that procedure and authority factors have significant impact. You learned about ethical issues in conducting research on obedience, real-world examples of obedience, and strategies for resisting obedience. You also learned that most people will obey an order from a person in a uniform—even when that person gives an order that has nothing to do with his or her position of authority.

YOU LEARNED **How does culture impact social influence?** The last section in this chapter described the impact of culture on social influence. You learned that people in collectivistic cultures place a greater value on fitting in with and conforming to social norms than people in individualistic cultures. You learned that the factors that motivate compliance, and the rates of obedience, differ in different cultures. You also learned that Americans prefer pens that are unique in their color, whereas Koreans prefer pens that are common in their color.

KEY TERMS

compliance 250
conformity 250
descriptive norms 251
door-in-the-face technique 266
foot-in-the-door technique 265
informational influence 257
injunctive norms 251

lowballing 267
minority influence 262
normative influence 257
obedience 250
pluralistic ignorance 252
private conformity 257
public conformity 257

reciprocity 265
scarcity 267
social impact theory 259
social norms 250
that's-not-all technique 266

QUESTIONS FOR REVIEW

1. Describe the impact of social norms on behavior, including the power of social norms and errors we make in perceiving norms.
2. What are four influences on conformity?
3. Explain the factors that lead to compliance?
4. Describe two factors that increased obedience in the Milgram studies and one factor that did not.
5. How does culture influence conformity, compliance, and obedience?

TAKE ACTION!

1. Your roommate is depressed because she feels stupid in her classes (when no one else has questions about the material that she is really not understanding) and because the man of her dreams has not asked her out (even though they have talked intimately together on several occasions). How would you cheer her up by describing the potential role of pluralistic ignorance in these two problems?
2. You are on the school board committee, and the committee has been asked to reach a decision about how to balance the school budget. Your own ideas for how to accomplish a balanced budget differ from those of the other people on this committee. How best could you convince others to adopt your proposed strategies?
3. You are trying to recruit volunteers for a community service fair at your university. Describe three approaches that you could use to induce compliance. Which approach do you think would be most effective and why?
4. Your younger sister calls you because she's worried about her upcoming sorority initiation. She has heard that upperclass students often command pledges to obey orders to engage in embarrassing tasks. How could you advise her to handle this situation?
5. Your cousin has just been hired to work in China following graduation. What might you tell him about the importance of conforming to social norms in this culture to help him fit in?

RESEARCH CONNECTIONS

Try some of these research activities to gain experience in conducting and evaluating research, and to increase your understanding of research methods and techniques in social psychology.
Visit WileyPLUS for more activities and interactve research tools!
(www.wileyplus.com)

Participate in Research

Activity 1 **The Power of Social Norms:** This chapter has described how people often feel compelled to act in ways that are in line with the norms of their group. Think about various norms in your social group or culture and rate how much pressure you feel to conform to these different norms.

Activity 2 **The Impact of Normative Influence:** One factor that influences conformity is normative influence, meaning our beliefs about what other people think or feel. Go to WileyPLUS to test how your responses to a situation might be influenced by your perceptions of others' attitudes.

Activity 3 **Strategies of Compliance:** This chapter describes a number of different strategies of compliance that are often used in daily life. Think about times in which you've received these compliance techniques. How did you respond?

Activity 4 **The Impact of the Situation on Obedience:** You learned in this chapter about factors that influence obedience, and how we often underestimate the power of situational factors in leading to such obedience. Go to WileyPLUS to read a description of a person obeying an authority, and then rate what you see as the cause of his or her behavior.

Activity 5 **The Impact of Culture on Social Influence:** The final section of this chapter describes how people from different cultures vary in how they are impacted by social influence. Go to WileyPLUS to rate your agreement with various statements about conformity; then see how other students, including those from other cultures, rate their own agreement.

Test a Hypothesis

One of the common findings in research on social influence is that women tend to conform more than men (at least on some topics). To test whether this hypothesis is true, create a survey that describes different types of norms and the extent to which people feel compelled to conform to particular norms. Give this survey to both men and women, and see if there are indeed gender differences.

Design a Study

To design your own study testing the impact of different factors on conformity, go to WileyPLUS. You'll be able to choose the type of study you want to conduct (self-report, observational/naturalistic, or experimental), choose your own independent and dependent variables, and form your own hypothesis.

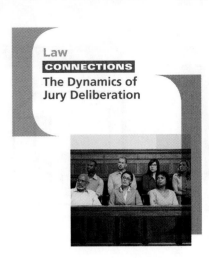

9

Group Influence: The

WHAT YOU'LL LEARN

How do groups influence behavior?

How does the group process influence decision-making?

 RESEARCH FOCUS ON GENDER
How Are Women as Leaders?

How do groups handle conflict?

How do groups handle social dilemmas?

How does CULTURE impact group influence?

Did you ever wonder?

On the morning of January 28, 1986, the space shuttle Challenger blasted off from the Kennedy Space Center in Florida. Seventy-three seconds after lift-off, the Challenger exploded, killing all seven astronauts on board. An investigation into why the Challenger exploded identified the primary cause of the accident as a failure in the joint between two stages of the rocket that allowed hot gases to escape during lift-off and burn a fuel tank. Following the explosion of the Challenger, considerable information came to light about the faulty decision-making processes within the National Aeronautics and Space Administration (NASA) that led to the decision to launch. Some engineers had expressed concerns about the design of the O-ring seal in the solid-fuel rocket, which could allow hot gases to leak through the joint and thereby spark an explosion. However, in the pressure to launch the shuttle as scheduled, these concerns were ignored by management. As Engineering Vice President Bob Lund was told when he urged NASA to gather additional data about the effects of cold temperature on

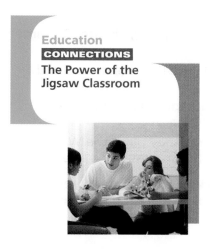

Education
CONNECTIONS
The Power of the
Jigsaw Classroom

Business
CONNECTIONS
Using Mediation
and Arbitration to
Resolve Conflict

Health
CONNECTIONS
Why Not Vaccinating
Your Child Can Be
Good for You, but Bad
for the Community

Impact of Group Processes

the O-ring seal before launching the shuttle, "Take off your engineering hat and put on your management hat."

Unfortunately little was learned from this tragic accident because many of these same errors contributed to the loss of the Columbia space shuttle, and its seven astronauts, on February 1, 2003. Research now shows that prior to the Columbia disaster, some NASA engineers had grave concern about the shuttle's ability to return to earth following some damage it experienced on lift-off. On January 28, just days before the Columbia tragedy, a landing gear specialist at NASA sent an email expressing his concerns about the tile damage, writing, "Any more activity today on the time damage, or are people just relegated to crossing their fingers and hoping for the best?" However, high-level NASA administrators viewed the damage to the shuttle as minor—not a serious threat—and refused to respond to requests from engineers for particular pieces of data on the level of damage the shuttle experienced. This chapter will examine group processes such as the types of processes that may have led to both the Challenger and the Columbia space shuttles disasters. In addition, you'll find out ...

Associated Press

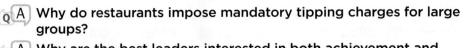

Q A Why do restaurants impose mandatory tipping charges for large groups?

Q A Why are the best leaders interested in both achievement and personal relationships?

Q A Why are people on the pro-choice and pro-life sides of the abortion issue more similar than they realize?

Q A Why are people less cooperative when they play "the Wall Street game" than when they play "the community game"?

Q A Why are Chinese Americans more likely to cooperate with friends after seeing a picture of a Chinese dragon than an American flag?

PREVIEW

We all interact in groups on a regular, even daily, basis. Sometimes these interactions are informal—we watch a movie with other people in the theater, we attend a concert with a group of friends, we spend a day at a crowded beach. Other times these interactions are more formal and structured— we collaborate on projects with coworkers, we play sports in front of large crowds, we serve on a jury and reach a verdict. In turn, these group settings influence our attitudes, decisions, and behavior, and can lead to both positive and negative outcomes. The 1980 men's Olympic hockey team overcame tremendous odds to win a Gold Medal, demonstrating the importance of team cohesion. The 2004 9/11 Commission report describes how ineffective group work made the United States more susceptible to terrorist attacks. This chapter will describe ways in which both informal and formal groups influence people's behavior for better and for worse.

HOW DO GROUPS INFLUENCE BEHAVIOR?

Think about a time in which you've had dinner in a restaurant with a group of people. How did you tip? According to research in social psychology, probably not very well. In one study, researchers examined the impact of group size on the size of the tip left at a restaurant (Lynn & Latané, 1984). Groups of diners were surveyed as they left an International House of Pancakes restaurant. Researchers asked them how many people were in the size of their group, the amount of their bill, and the size of the tip left. As predicted, single people were the most generous (tipping an average of 19%) and parties of four or more were the least generous (tipping an average of 11%). This phenomenon is precisely why many restaurants impose a "mandatory tip" on large parties: as the group size increases, each individual person slightly reduces the size of his or her tip, expecting that others will pick up the slack. (If you've ever worked as a waiter, this finding will not be surprising.) This section will examine this and other ways in which groups influence behavior, including social facilitation, social loafing, deindividuation, and cohesion.

Q A

SOCIAL FACILITATION

Although research on deindividuation describes the dangers of the group setting on individuals' behavior, in other cases individuals' behavior can benefit from the presence of a group. This phenomenon was first noticed by Norman Triplett (1898), a psychologist who noticed that cyclists were faster when they raced with other cyclists than when they raced alone. In one of the first experimental studies to test this idea, Triplett asked children to wind string on a fishing reel as fast as they could. Children who performed this task in the presence of other children wound the string significantly faster than those who performed this task alone.

However, other researchers noticed that the presence of other people can also lead to worse performance (Bond & Titus, 1983). For example, people who perform a difficult task (such as typing their name backwards with various letters interspersed between the letters) do so more slowly in front of other people than they do alone (Schmitt, Gilovich, Goore, & Joseph, 1986). In one unusual study, researchers examined how long it took men at a urinal to start urinating based on how close another man was standing to them (Middlemist, Knowles, & Matter, 1976). As you might predict, men took an average of 4.9 seconds to start urinating when they believed they were alone in the bathroom (the researcher was hidden inside a stall), but a much longer 8.4 seconds when they were standing immediately beside another person.

How can the presence of others lead to better performances in some cases and worse performance in others? According to Robert Zajonc's theory of **social facilitation**, the mere presence of other people increases our physiological arousal (meaning energy or excitement), and this arousal enhances whatever a person's dominant tendency is on a particular task (Blascovich, Mendes, Hunter, & Salomon, 1999; Bond & Titus, 1983; Zajonc, 1965; Zajonc & Sales, 1966). On well-learned or easy tasks, the dominant response is the correct one—to make that foul shot, to solve the simple addition problems, or to solve easy anagrams. High arousal therefore leads to better performance on tasks that are simple or well-learned (see Figure 9.1). On the other hand, high arousal leads to worse performance on tasks that are difficult or less familiar. This theory therefore explains why people perform better on some tasks in the presence of a group compared to when they are alone, but worse on others.

social facilitation a phenomenon in which people do better on particular tasks in the presence of a group compared to when they are alone

FIGURE 9.1

MODEL OF SOCIAL FACILITATION

According to social facilitation theory, the presence of other people in our environment increases our arousal, which in turn leads to better performance on well-learned and/or easy tasks, but worse performance on difficult tasks.

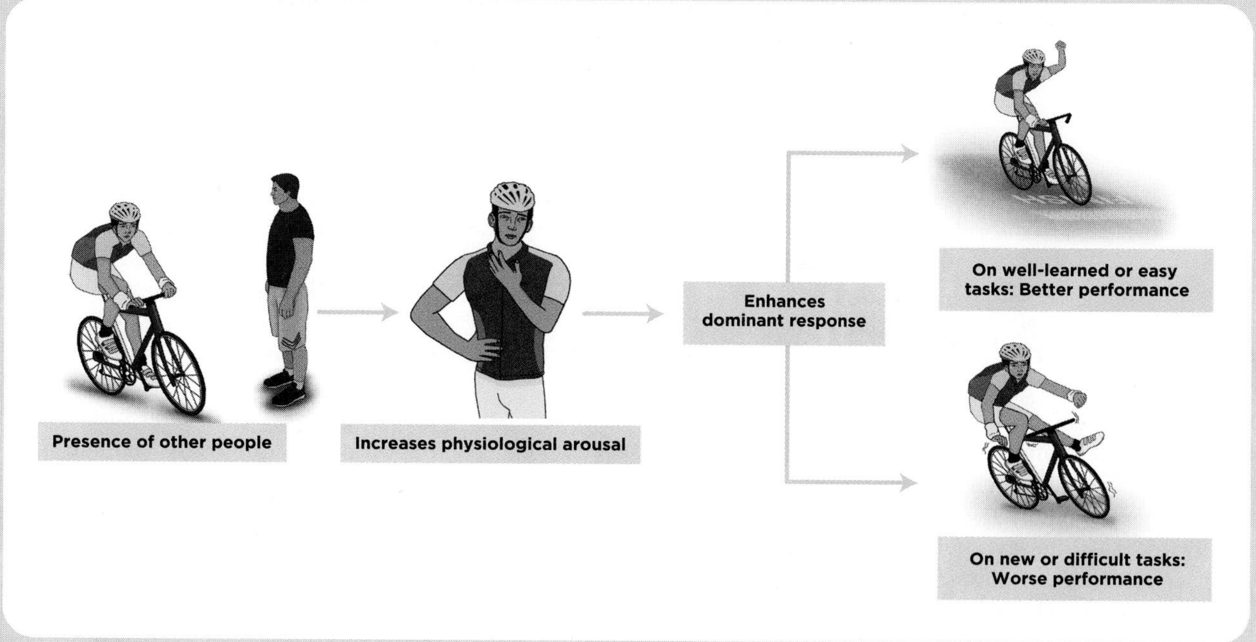

Presence of other people → Increases physiological arousal → Enhances dominant response → On well-learned or easy tasks: Better performance / On new or difficult tasks: Worse performance

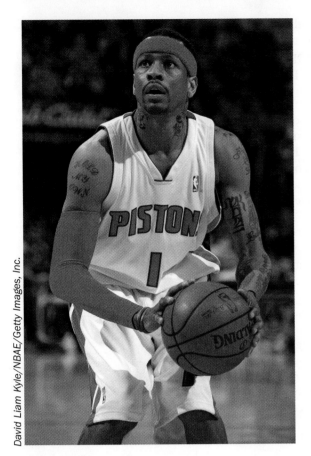

David Liam Kyle/NBAE/Getty Images, Inc.

Allen Iverson and other NBA athletes should perform better at foul shots in front of a larger crowd than when alone, whereas less-skilled basketball players should show the reverse.

Why does the presence of others lead to arousal? Research points to three explanations: mere presence, evaluation apprehension, and distraction.

Mere presence. One explanation for social facilitation is that the mere presence of other people is energizing (Zajonc, 1965). For example, you might prefer to take an aerobics class with other people than do aerobics to a video in your living room. In this case, you simply feel more energetic in their presence than you would by exercising alone.

A classic study on social facilitation was conducted using cockroaches as participants (Zajonc, Heingartner, & Herman, 1969). Researchers conducted two mazes: one was very simple (a straight path from one end of the box to another), and the other was more complex (it included multiple paths that led in different directions). In one condition, the cockroaches were alone as they scurried from one end of the maze (with a bright light which they disliked) to the other (which was darkened). In the other condition, the cockroaches were observed by other cockroaches as they completed the maze (the other cockroaches were placed in "audience boxes" that lined the maze). As predicted by social facilitation, cockroaches performed the simple maze faster in the presence of other cockroaches than they did alone. However, the presence of other cockroaches disrupted performance on the more complex maze: they were slower in the presence of other cockroaches than they were alone. This study provides some support for Zajonc's idea that the mere presence of others can lead to social facilitation.

Evaluation apprehension. Other researchers believe that social facilitation is caused not simply by the mere presence of other people in an environment, but rather by people's concern about being evaluated by this audience (e.g., evaluation apprehension; Henchy & Glass, 1968). In one of the first studies to test this explanation for social facilitation, Cottrell and colleagues asked people to pronounce various nonsense words (a relatively easy task) under one of three conditions (Cottrell, Wack, Sekerak, & Rittle, 1968). Participants in one condition were alone, participants in another condition were in front of an audience of two confederates (who could see the words that the participant was trying to pronounce), and participants in the third condition were in front of an audience of two confederates who were blindfolded (and thus could not see the words). As predicted, participants were more accurate in the audience condition than in either the alone or mere presence condition. This finding indicates that the presence of an evaluating audience is a stronger influence on performance than the mere presence of others.

Unfortunately, the presence of a supportive audience can lead to worse performance on difficult or unfamiliar tasks. In one study, students took a math test while either a friend or a stranger watched (Butler & Baumeister, 1998). Although students felt less stress when taking the test in front of a friend, they made more errors and took longer to complete it. This research suggests that we may "choke under pressure" of our audience's high expectations. Similarly, female students who are taking a stressful math test show lower blood pressure when in the presence of a friend, as long as that friend is not evaluating their performance (Kors, Linden, & Gerin, 1997). The Would You Believe Box describes a real-world case in which people's concern about how others will evaluate them impacts performance.

WOULD YOU BELIEVE... The "Homefield Advantage" Can be a Disadvantage? You've probably heard of the "homefield advantage." But do you know that playing at home can in some cases be a *disadvantage*? Research demonstrates that teams usually perform better at home, but they play badly when they must play decisive home games at home (Baumeister & Steinhilber, 1984; Schlenker, Phillips, Boniecki, & Schlenker, 1995a, 1995b). Under these unique conditions, such as having to win a game to win a championship series, the intense pressure from supportive fans may disrupt performance. In baseball's World Series, home teams tend to win the early games, but lose decisive (final) games. Choking is especially likely if the home team has the opportunity to win the championship at home.

Distraction.   Another explanation for the effect of arousal on performance is that the presence of other people is distracting—even in cases in which they are not evaluating our performance. This distraction decreases our ability to focus on a particular task (Baron, Moore, & Sanders, 1978; Groff, Baron, & Moore, 1983; Huguet, Galvaing, Monteil, & Dumas, 1999). If we are performing an easy task, this distraction isn't a problem. However, if we are performing a complex task, this distraction impairs our performance. For example, people who are leaving a parking space take longer to leave when someone is waiting for their spot than when no one is waiting (Ruback & Juieng, 1997). More importantly, teenage drivers, who are likely to find driving more difficult than more experienced older drivers, show significantly more crashes when they are driving with passengers than when driving alone (Chen, Baker, Braver, & Li, 2000).

In one study, researchers asked participants to perform either a difficult or an easy task supposedly in preparation for a task they would be completing with other participants (Markus, 1978). The easy task was tying their shoes. The difficult task was tying an apron behind their backs. In some conditions people performed the task alone, whereas in others they performed the task in front of the experimenter. In all conditions, participants were not aware that they were being timed, and believed that they were performing the task only in preparation for engaging in the real task of the experiment. As predicted, people took less time completing the easy task in front of a watching audience than they did alone, but took more time completing the difficult task in front of others than alone (see Figure 9.2). Because participants were not aware that their performance was being timed, and hence should not have experienced evaluation apprehension, this study suggests that the distraction caused by the presence of others can lead to social facilitation.

? Questioning the Research
Distraction caused by the presence of other people in the car is one explanation for teenagers' higher rate of accidents when driving with others than when driving alone. But can you think of an alterative explanation for this finding?

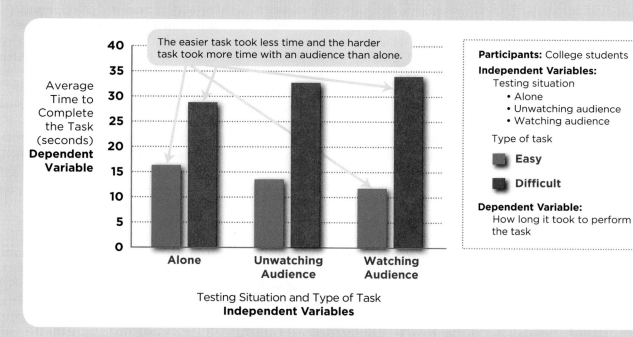

FIGURE 9.2

HOW DOES THE PRESENCE OF OTHERS EFFECT TASK SPEED?

In this experiment, students were unaware that they were being timed while doing either an easy task (tying their shoes) or a hard task (tying an apron behind their backs). As predicted, the mere presence of an audience, whether or not they were watching, made participants take less time to perform an easy task and more time to perform a difficult task, providing support for the social facilitation theory.

Source: Markus, H. (1978). The effect of mere presence on social facilitation: An unobtrusive test. *Journal of Experimental Social Psychology, 14*, 389-397.

The easier task took less time and the harder task took more time with an audience than alone.

Average Time to Complete the Task (seconds) **Dependent Variable**

Alone **Unwatching Audience** **Watching Audience**

Testing Situation and Type of Task
Independent Variables

Participants: College students
Independent Variables:
Testing situation
• Alone
• Unwatching audience
• Watching audience

Type of task
■ **Easy**
■ **Difficult**

Dependent Variable:
How long it took to perform the task

SOCIAL LOAFING

In social facilitation, an individual is completing a task in the presence of others. His or her individual performance is being evaluated. But what happens when people work together in a group toward producing a common group goal and the individuals' own performance is not measured or evaluated? Individuals experience less arousal in this situation. What is the effect of this relaxation on performance? When only the overall group performance is noticed, we experience a reduced drive and arousal because we no longer fear a negative evaluation of our own performance. Just think about a time in which you worked with other people on a group project. Did each person pull his or her own weight, or did some people slack off? In group situations, each person's contribution seems dispensable, and hence people are often tempted to reduce their effort.

The term **social loafing** describes this group-produced reduction in individual output on tasks where contributions are pooled (Hoeksema-van Orden, Gaillard, & Buunk, 1998; Karau & Williams, 1993; Kerr, 1983). In one study, students alone or in groups of two, four, or six were put in soundproof rooms and asked to clap and cheer as loudly as possible (Latane, Williams & Harkins, 1979). Each student made the most noise when alone, and the least noise when in a group of six. When students were alone, they felt compelled to make as much noise as possible, in line with the instructions they were given. But when students were in groups (even groups as small as five other people), they reduced their effort and made considerably less noise. Similarly, and as described at the start of this section, restaurants often impose a mandatory tip when people are dining in a group of five or six people, precisely because of the (realistic) concern that social loafing will lead to lower tips (Boyes, Mounts, & Sowell, 2004; Lynn & Latane, 1984).

What factors influence social loafing? According to the **collective effort model**, people are motivated to exert effort in group tasks only when they believe their distinct efforts are identifiable, that these efforts will make a difference in the group's success, and when they will experience positive outcomes (Jackson & Williams, 1985; Karau & Williams, 1993; Kerr, 1983; Williams & Karau, 1991). Let's examine each of these factors.

Identifiable contributions. First, one factor that influences social loafing is whether people believe that their own contribution will be recognized (Shepperd, 1993; Weldon & Gargano, 1988; Williams, Harkins, & Latané, 1981). People socially loaf in part because they can "hide-in-the-crowd." Making their outputs identifiable decreases the tendency to withdraw effort even in a group setting. In turn, people do not socially loaf when their own outputs will be evaluated, especially if these outputs will be compared to that of others', or if they will receive individual feedback about their efforts (Harkins & Jackson, 1985; Hoeksema et al., 1998). For example, if you are working on a group project, but each person takes responsibility for writing a separate part of the report—and the professor will know which part each group member did—you will be more motivated to expand your effort than if your effort is pooled together with everybody else's efforts and your own distinct, contribution will not be known. This finding helps explain why swimmers on a relay team post faster times than when swimming individual events when their own time is identified, but slower when simply the relay team's time is identified (Williams, Nida, Baca, & Latane, 1989).

Contributions' impact. Another factor that influences social loafing is whether you believe your efforts will have an impact on the group's performance; in other words, if you work harder, better performance will result (Kerr & Bruun, 1983). People who must perform a difficult and unique task don't withdraw effort, even when their individual output won't be evaluated. In this case, they feel they can make a unique and important contribution to group effort (Harkins & Petty, 1982; Karau & Williams, 1993; Shepperd, 1993b; Shepperd & Taylor, 1999b). On the other hand, people who believe their efforts aren't necessary for the suc-

social loafing a group-produced reduction in individual output on easy tasks where contributions are pooled

collective effort model a model that describes people's motivation to exert effort in group tasks only when they believe their distinct efforts are identifiable, these efforts will make a difference in the group's success, and they will experience positive outcomes

cess of the group tend to display less effort. People who believe their partner is capable of good performance but is lazy (and therefore is just choosing not to expend effort) are particularly likely to reduce their own effort (Kerr, 1983). After all, nobody wants to be the "sucker" who does all the work while others rest. (This is one reason why many students fear group projects—they are concerned that they will end up being the one who does all the work for the group.)

Task importance. People are also motivated to work hard on a group task if the task is highly important to them (Karau & Williams, 1993; Shepperd, 1993b; Shepperd & Taylor, 1999b). If you are working on a group lab report for your social psychology class, and you hope your professor will write a letter of recommendation for you for graduate school, you are likely to work hard on the project even if others in your group are not contributing much. In one study, students who were told to evaluate a proposal for implementing mandatory senior comprehensive exams were much more likely to loaf if the proposal would not be implemented for six years, or would be implemented at a different school, than if the proposal could be implemented at their own school next year—and thereby effect them personally (Brickner, Harkins, & Ostrom, 1986).

Although only the group's total speed in a relay race determines which team wins, each individual swimmer's time is recorded. This should decrease social loafing.

In cases in which the task is very important, people can be highly motivated to work hard even when their own contributions won't be identifiable, especially when they believe that other group members aren't going to work to produce a high quality product. In this case, **social compensation** occurs, meaning people work harder on a project to compensate for poor performance or social loafing by others (Williams & Karau, 1991). In one study, college students were told that they would work with a partner on either a math test or a verbal test (Plaks & Higgins, 2000). In some cases this partner was a female student, in other cases this partner was a male student, and in still other cases participants were not told the gender of the partner. As shown in Figure 9.3, participants worked harder on a group task when they had low expectations about their partner's competence than if they had high expectations about their partner's competence. These findings suggest that people try to compensate when they expect their partner to perform poorly.

social compensation the notion that if a project is important to you, you may work even harder to compensate for poor performance or social loafing by others

DEINDIVIDUATION

Another way in which groups influence individuals' behavior is through **deindividuation**. Deindividuation occurs when a person loses a sense of him- or herself as a distinct individual, and is thus less compelled to follow normal rules of behavior (Diener, 1979; Festinger, Pepitone, & Newcomb, 1952; Mullen, 1986; Postmes & Spears, 1998). Deindividuation is more likely to occur in group settings, and contributes to the tendency of groups of people to engage in highly destructive actions. For example, lynchings, riots, and acts of vandalism occur in group settings (Mullen, 1986; Watson, 1973). In some cases, groups of people have even encouraged disturbed persons to commit suicidal acts, such as jump off a bridge, building, or tower (Mann, 1981). We'll discuss the role of deindividuation in leading to aggression toward others in detail in Chapter 11.

What factors lead to deindividuation? Research points to three contributing factors: anonymity, accountability, and decreases in self-awareness.

deindividuation a phenomenon in which a person loses the sense of him or herself as a distinct individual, and in turn feels less compelled to follow normal rules of behavior

FIGURE
9.3

HOW DOES SOCIAL COMPENSATION IMPACT TASK PERFORMANCE?

Researchers in this experiment told college students that they would work with a partner on a test. Some students were told they would work with a male partner, some with a female partner, and others were not told the gender of the partner. As predicted, participants worked harder on a group task when they had low expectations about their partner's competence (e.g., a woman working on a math test, a man working on a verbal test) than if they had high expectations about their partner's competence (e.g., a man working on a math test, a woman working on a verbal test).

Source: Plaks, J. E., & Higgins, E. T. (2000). Pragmatic use of stereotyping in teamwork: Social loafing and compensation as a function of inferred partner-situation fit. *Journal of Personality and Social Psychology, 79,* 962-974.

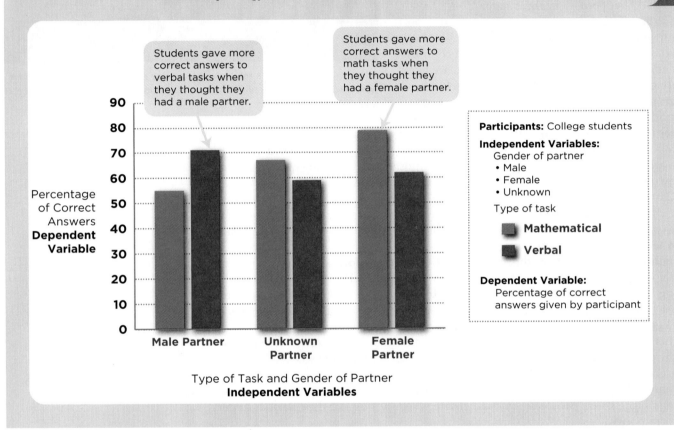

Anonymity.

Anonymity. One factor that contributes to deindividuation is *anonymity* (Rehm, Steinleitner, & Lilli, 1987). Anonymity is provided by a group setting, because each individual is less distinguishable. Anonymity is also enhanced in situations where people wear uniforms, which makes each individual less identifiable. For example, women who wear identical white coats and hoods give longer electric shocks to another participant than those who wear their own clothes and are identified with a large name tag (Zimbardo, 1970).

In one study, researchers observed over 1,000 children trick-or-treating on Halloween night (Diener et al., 1976). Some of these children were alone, and others were in groups. In half of the conditions, the researcher greeted the children and asked for their name and where they lived. In the other half of the conditions, researchers greeted the children, but did not request any personal information. The researcher then invited the children to take *one piece of candy*, and left the room. Which children were most likely to take more than one piece? Over 50% of those who were in groups and were anonymous took more than one piece of candy. In contrast, fewer than 10% of those who were alone and identified took more than a single piece.

Associated Press

Deindividuation. After major sports championships, acts of vandalism by both excited and disappointed fans in large groups are quite common. Following the University of Maryland victory over Indiana in the 2002 NCAA basketball championship, Indiana fans broke windows of local shops, threw bottles at police officers, and lit bonfires.

Accountability. Another factor that contributes to deindividuation is *accountability*, meaning whether a person expects to be held responsible for his or her actions (Nadler, Goldberg, & Jaffe, 1982). Because people in group settings are less likely to be identified, they feel less self-conscious and inhibited in their behavior, compared to individuals who are acting alone. You might normally feel uncomfortable engaging in vandalism or other types of destructive behaviors, but if everyone else in your group is doing so, these constraints may fade away. In line with this view, as the size of the group increases, so does its level of violence (Leader, Mullen, & Abrams, 2007).

Decreases in self-awareness. Group settings also lead to a decrease in *self-awareness*, which in turn leads to deindividuation (Diener, 1979; Prentice-Dunn & Rogers, 1980, 1982). People who are in a group have less of a sense of themselves as distinct individuals. As described in Chapter 3, this decrease in self-awareness leads people to be less focused on matching their behavior to their normal standards (Duval & Wicklund, 1972; Wicklund & Frey, 1980).

In one study, researchers told participants that they needed help with two tasks, and that they would do one task and that another student would do the other task (Batson et al., 1999). One of these tasks was very appealing—and allowed participants to earn raffle tickets toward a desirable prize. The other task was very boring, and had no positive rewards. Students were given a coin to flip, if they wanted, to choose which person would do each task. About two-thirds of the students chose to flip the coin in order to determine which person would do which task (most of the other one-third simply assigned the more appealing task to themselves). However, 24 of the 28 students who performed the supposedly fair coin toss were assigned to do the appealing task—a very unlikely event. However, when participants who chose to flip the coin were asked to do so in front of a mirror, the results of the coin toss became fair. In this condition, exactly half of the participants were assigned the appealing task and the other half were assigned the boring task. This research points to the impact of self-awareness on people's behavior—and our willingness to engage in less moral behavior when self-awareness is low.

COHESION

Although this section has focused on how group processes can lead to negative behaviors, in some cases groups lead to positive effects. For example, highly cohesive groups perform better than less cohesive ones (Cota, Evans, Dion, Kilik, & Longman, 1995;

Questioning the Research

This research suggests that creating a highly cohesive team will lead to better performance. Can you think of an alternative explanation for the cohesion-performance link? (Hint: Does this research distinguish between correlation and causation?)

Mullen & Copper, 1994). One study examined level of cohesion and attitudes about the Army among members of 60 military platoon leadership teams (Mael & Alderks, 1993). Squad members' perceptions of cohesion of their platoon were related to greater job involvement, higher motivation to perform well, a stronger intent to continue one's career with the Army, and greater confidence in the effectiveness of the platoon. Most importantly, cohesion was also associated with higher ratings of performance, including planning, preparing, and executing eight practice combat missions. Higher cohesion is also associated with better performance for sports teams (Patterson, Carron, & Loughead, 2005).

The cohesion-performance link is stronger for tasks that require high levels of interaction and interdependence between group members than for those that simply require high levels of individual performance (Carron, Colman, Wheeler, & Stevens, 2002). In one study, researchers asked 320 male varsity high school soccer and baseball players to complete measures of team cohesion at the start of the season and then again at the end of the season (Murray, 2006). The researchers examined the association between team cohesion and team performance during the season. Interestingly, cohesive soccer teams were more successful than less cohesive soccer teams, but more cohesive baseball teams were actually less successful. This finding points to the difference between the two types of sports: in soccer, all players on the field at a given time are likely to influence the play in some way. In contrast, baseball games may be won by a small number of players who are particularly good at one task, such as pitching or hitting. Thus, in more interactive sports, cohesion is likely to be a stronger predictor of success than in less interactive ones.

Jasper Juinen/GettyImages, Inc.

Athletic teams may be highly cohesive. Everyone is pulling together for the same goal (winning), and there is often great pride in the group (jackets, uniforms, etc.). The group meets frequently and often under intense circumstances.

EXAMPLES OF THE INFLUENCE OF GROUPS ON BEHAVIOR

Concepts in Context

FACTOR	EXAMPLE
Social loafing	As part of a community service project, Lucia's sorority is spending a day cleaning up a local park. Because there are so many women in her group, Lucia figures that no one will really notice if she shows up late and leaves early.
Social facilitation	When Caitlyn bowls (a game at which she excels), she perform even better when in front of her friends than when alone, but when she is playing pool (a game at which she is pretty weak), she performs much better alone than in front of anyone.
Deindividuation	Sports fans in a large group may vandalize property following a big loss by their team.
Cohesion	Miller's softball team has won its last seven games. He feels very close and connected to all of the people on the team, and believes that this close bond led to the strong team performance. However, the team wasn't particularly close prior to the start of the current winning streak.

HOW DOES THE GROUP PROCESS INFLUENCE DECISION MAKING?

Think about a group you are in—a student government organization, a community service program, an athletic team—and the leader of that group. Was this person an effective leader? If so, what was he or she like? Researchers examined the characteristics of effective group leaders by asking students to participate in a series of group interaction tasks (Sorrentino & Field, 1986).

First, students attended five weekly sessions consisting of group problem-solving activities, such as planning a project and ordering materials they would need to survive in a desert. These sessions were recorded so that researchers could rate each participant's interaction.

In addition, participants rated their impressions of their own and other group members' contributions to the problem-solving tasks. Participants who were oriented toward both achievement and interpersonal dynamics scored the highest on all measures. These students took pride in accomplishment, had high self-confidence, and established friendly relations with and approval by other group members.

Participants with both of these characteristics were rated higher on objective behavioral measures, such as the quantity of verbal participation, and were most likely to be chosen as the leader of the group by other participants.

This section examines how the group process influences decision making. We'll look at two factors that lead groups to err in their decisions: group polarization and groupthink. We'll also discuss the impact of leadership on group decisions.

GROUP POLARIZATION

Group polarization occurs when the initial tendencies of group members become more extreme following group discussion (Isenberg, 1986; Moscovici & Zavalloni, 1969; Myers & Kaplan, 1976; Teger & Pruitt, 1967). This process can lead groups to make riskier decisions than individuals would make alone, a phenomenon described as the **risky shift** (Wallach, Kogan, & Bem, 1962). For example, when people must choose between a relatively safe choice or a risky choice (e.g., making a particular chess move, trying a difficult play in the last seconds of a football game, etc.), groups are much more willing to take a risky choice than are individuals who must act alone.

Why does group discussion lead group members to become more extreme, and riskier, in their views? Research points to two explanations.

Hear more persuasive arguments. First, group members hear more persuasive arguments that support their own views, including points they had not previously considered, which can intensify these views (Isenberg, 1986). For example, you may enter a discussion with the opinion that you are opposed to changing the distribution requirements at your school. After hearing additional persuasive arguments that support your original view, you are likely to be even more strongly opposed. Simply repeating arguments during group discussion can lead to greater attitude polarization (Brauer, Judd, & Gliner, 1995).

Groups are particularly likely to hear more persuasive arguments because they deliberately search out such views. In one study, researchers asked managers from banks and industrial companies to read a case study about a company that was deciding whether to invest a considerable sum in starting production in a developing company (Schulz-Hardt, Frey, Lüthgens, & Moscovici, 2000). Participants were put in small groups and asked to discuss this situation and reach a group decision. These groups were told that additional information about the decision was available, including articles both in favor of and opposed to the investment. These articles were written by experts on the economy, and groups were given a list of these articles. Groups could request any articles that they wanted. What type of information did groups want? As predicted, groups that consisted of individuals with the same view were more interested in receiving articles that supported their decision than that opposed it (3.33 versus 0.92). In contrast, groups

Q A

group polarization a phenomenon in which the initial tendencies of group members become more extreme following group discussion

risky shift a process by which groups tend to make riskier decisions than individuals would make alone

that consisted of individuals with more discrepant views showed less interest in receiving articles that supported their decision and more interest in receiving articles that opposed it (2.08 versus 1.42).

Learn group norms. Group polarization can also occur following discussion because such discussion leads us to more accurately assess the norms of our group (Isenberg, 1986). Prior to group discussion, we may underestimate group members' views about a given topic, and therefore such discussion increases our accuracy of these views. However, because most people want to fit in with, but also be "better than," other members of their group, we may express even more extreme attitudes as a way of demonstrating that our views are strong and in the right direction. Therefore, we get more confident in our own views because we know the group norms.

To examine the effects of group discussion on individuals' own attitudes, researchers asked women to privately (in writing) rate the attractiveness of men in magazine photos (Baron, Hoppe, Kao, & Brunsman, 1996). Then women read their ratings aloud in the presence of other women (actually confederates of the experimenters) who had performed the same task. In one condition, the confederates agreed with the participants' view, in another condition they disagreed with the confederates' view, and in a third condition, the confederates didn't provide their responses aloud. Next, participants were told they could look at the photographs again for a longer period of time, and that they could change their ratings if they found their views had changed. As shown in Figure 9.4, women's

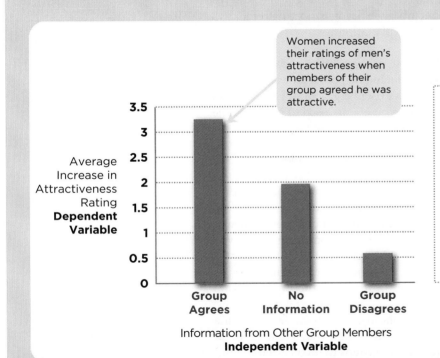

FIGURE 9.4

HOW DOES LEARNING GROUP NORMS IMPACT ATTITUDES?

In this experiment, female college students rated the attractiveness of magazine photos of men. Then they shared their rating with a group of others, who were all confederates of the experiments. As predicted, woman's ratings of the attractiveness of people in magazine photos became more extreme after learning that others share the same opinion as they do, suggesting that learning we agree with group norms reinforces and polarizes our opinions.

Source: Baron, R. S., Hoppe, S. I., Kao, C. F., & Brunsman, B. (1996). Social corroboration and opinion extremity. *Journal of Experimental Social Psychology, 32*, 537-560.

Women increased their ratings of men's attractiveness when members of their group agreed he was attractive.

Average Increase in Attractiveness Rating **Dependent Variable**

Information from Other Group Members **Independent Variable**

Group Agrees | No Information | Group Disagrees

Participants: Female college students

Independent Variable:
Information from other members of the group:
- Group agrees with participant
- No information
- Group disagrees with participant

Dependent Variable:
Average increase in participants' ratings of men's attractiveness after they learn how other group members have rated the pictures

The Dynamics of Jury Deliberation

Many of the same errors in group decision making described thus far can have a major impact on jury deliberations. For example, group discussion may exaggerate initial biases among individuals in a jury (Kaplan & Miller, 1978; Myers & Kaplan, 1976). Information that is consistent with the members' initial preferences is more likely to be discussed, whereas non-confirming information is more likely to be ignored (Stasser & Titus, 1985). In one study, juries spent more time discussing information that supported their preferred outcome, and less time discussing information that disputed this outcome (Sommer, Horowitz, & Bourgeois, 2001). Jurors may also weigh information that favors their preferred outcome more heavily than non-confirming information as a way of supporting their desired verdict. They may even ignore information that contradicts their preferred verdict.

What can help jury decision making? Interestingly, juries that include both White and Black members are more likely to have in-depth discussions than all-White juries (Sommers, 2006). In one study, researchers compared the quality of deliberation in all-White versus diverse mock juries. Diverse groups discussed a wider variety of information than all-White groups. In addition, compared to those in all-White groups, Whites in diverse groups cited more case facts, made fewer errors, and were more likely to discuss the impact of racism on the trial. These findings suggest that diverse juries engage in better decision-making processes than those in all-White juries.

© Image Source/SUPERSTOCK

ratings changed more after learning that other women disagreed with their views or receiving no information about other women's views. The Law Connections box describes a real-world example of the hazards of relying on group norms.

GROUPTHINK

Another common problem with group decision making is the development of **groupthink**, which describes a group decision-making style characterized by an excessive tendency among group members to seek concurrence, consensus, and unanimity, as opposed to making the best decision (Janis, 1972, 1982; Tetlock, Peterson, McGuire, Chang, & Feld, 1992). Groups who show this decision-making style overestimate the morality and invulnerability of their group, and ignore or even stifle discrepant views. This decision-making style can in turn lead group members with discrepant views to avoid stating them for fear of rejection from the group. As described at the beginning of this chapter, groupthink contributed to the loss of both the Challenger space shuttle in 1986 and the Columbia space shuttle in 2003. Groupthink also contributed to the decision to invade Iraq, as described in Table 9.1, and the collapse of the energy company Enron.

groupthink a group decision-making style characterized by an excessive tendency among group members to seek concurrence, consensus, and unanimity, as opposed to making the best decision

Overestimate invulnerability and morality. As mentioned, the groupthink decision-making style is more likely to occur when groups overestimate their invulnerability and morality (Janis, 1982). Groups may see their chosen course of action as highly likely to succeed, and as based in the group's fundamental goodness and morality. For example, one of the factors that led to the escalation of the Vietnam War was the belief that democracy was inherently better than Communism, and hence Americans were bound to win the war.

TABLE
9.1

USING GROUPTHINK TO EXPLAIN THE DECISION TO INVADE IRAQ

SYMPTOM OF GROUPTHINK	EXAMPLE
Illusion of invulnerability	The war was presented by Defense Secretary Colin Powell and others in the Bush administration as an easy, fast, and certain victory for the United States. Deputy Secretary of Defense Paul Wolfowitz promised that American troops would be welcomed with "chocolates and flowers."
Collective rationalization	The Bush administration continued to speak about Iraq's intense seeking, developing, and/or hiding of various weapons of mass destruction. Each story was eventually discredited, but Bush continued to claim that weapons of mass destruction could be found in Iraq.
Belief in inherent morality	President Bush labeled Iraq, North Korea, and Iran an "axis of evil" in his 2002 State of the Union address. He repeatedly referred to Saddam Hussein as an "evil-doer," and that "you are either with us, or you are with the terrorists."
Stereotyped views of out-groups	Saddam Hussein was presented as an evil dictator of oppressed people who, once this leader was removed from power, would welcome the troops and the freedom of democracy.
Direct pressure on dissenters	Many people who spoke against the Bush administration's policies, including evidence supporting the decision to invade Iraq, were fired. For example, Richard Clarke, the president's chief adviser on terrorism on the National Security Council, was fired after writing a memo stating that there was no link between al-Qaeda and Saddam Hussein.
Self-censorship which creates the illusion of unanimity	By keeping a strong distance from the press, the Bush administration kept information from the public. As described by Christiane Amanpour, CNN's top war correspondent, the press muzzled itself during the Iraq war and was intimidated by the Bush administration's climate of fear and self-censorship.
Self-appointed "mindguards"	Members of the Bush administration have kept contradictory information hidden from the public, such as a memo written on August 6, 2001, that described an imminent terrorist attack involving hijacking.

Many of the factors that led the Bush administration to declare war on Iraq, and to continue to fight that war, fit perfectly into Janis's model of the eight symptoms of *Groupthink*.

Source: http://www.salvationinc.org/archives/000339.html

Closemindedness. Another factor that contributes to groupthink is closemindedness, meaning that group members can't hear dissenting views from outgroup members (Tetlock et al., 1992). This type of group isolation means that no efforts are made to seek information from out-group members, and any information that is received is dismissed as unimportant. Some evidence suggests that high-level administrators at NASA were dismissive of information received from lower-level employees about the potentially disastrous consequences of foam hitting the space shuttle Columbia at lift-off. Groups with a strong and rigid leader are at greater risk of closemindedness, in part because such leaders may be unwilling to seek outside information.

Pressure toward uniformity. The third factor that contributes to groupthink is pressure toward uniformity (Janis, 1982; Kameda & Sugimori, 1993). This pressure is especially common among groups that are highly cohesive, meaning those that are composed of people from similar backgrounds (Hogg, Hains, & Mason, 1998). As described by Ken Auletta of *The New Yorker*, "This is a cohesive White House staff, dominated by people whose first loyalty is to Team Bush."

Unfortunately, this cohesiveness can hurt performance in some cases, such as when creative, innovative ideas are needed. In one study, groups of participants were asked to recommend a solution for an automobile production problem—productivity (Turner, Pratkanis, Probasco, & Leve, 1992). Some assembly workers who produced instrument panels had decreased their productivity. Some of the groups were made highly cohesive (e.g., they wore name tags that displayed their name and their group's name), whereas others were low cohesive, and some groups were under high threat conditions (e.g., they were told that experts would use the videotape of their group's discussion to evaluate dysfunctional group processes), whereas others were not given this threat. As shown in Figure 9.5, high cohesive groups made somewhat higher quality decisions than non-cohesive groups under conditions of no threat, but much lower quality decisions under conditions of high threat.

Solutions to groupthink. Although this section has focused on the various factors that lead groups to make faulty decisions, people in groups can work together to make good decisions. First, group members, and in particular group leaders, need to encourage open contributions from all group members as well as to emphasize the importance of open criticism. Groups with a norm of engaging in constructive criticism make better decisions (Postmes, Spears, & Cihangir, 2001), and criticism from in-group members is often easier for people to accept than criticism from out-group members (Hornsey & Imani, 2004). Encouraging open contributions and criticism is particularly important in cases in which not all group members

"*All those in favor say 'Aye.*'"
"*Aye.*"   "*Aye.*"   "*Aye.*"   "*Aye.*"   "*Aye.*"

Questioning the Research
In the Turner et al. (1992) study, the groups consisted of strangers, who were brought together to participate in a psychology study. How do you think the results would be different if this study were done with a real group, in which people expected to interact in the future and could experience consequences for the quality of their decision?

In the NEWS **Groupthink.** A classic example of the hazards of groupthink was seen on the board of Enron, a Houston-based company with revenues of over 100 billion dollars a year as of 2000. Unfortunately, directors on the Enron board showed many of the signs of groupthink, such as deferring to company executives instead of challenging them and discouraging debate, so that nearly every board vote was unanimous. This poor decision-making process ultimately destroyed the company: Enron declared bankruptcy in 2001, after it was revealed that its reported financial condition was sustained substantially by accounting fraud.

FIGURE
9.5

HOW DOES GROUP COHESIVENESS IMPACT DECISION MAKING?

In this experiment, groups were asked to recommend solutions for increasing the productivity of automobile production workers. It was hypothesized that pressure toward uniformity in highly cohesive groups would lead to poorer quality solutions. The results partly supported this hypothesis: when threat levels were high, cohesive groups did make poorer suggestions, but under a low threat level, cohesive groups made higher quality suggestions

Source: Turner, M. E., Pratkanis, A. R., Probasco, P., & Leve, C. (1992). Threat, cohesion, and group effectiveness: Testing a social identity maintenance perspective on groupthink. *Journal of Personality and Social Psychology, 63*, 781-796.

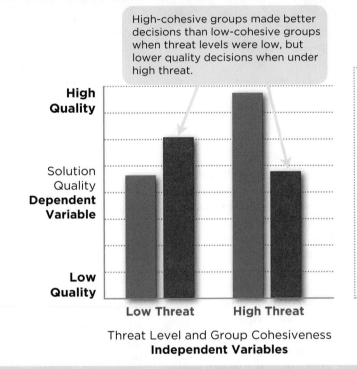

High-cohesive groups made better decisions than low-cohesive groups when threat levels were low, but lower quality decisions when under high threat.

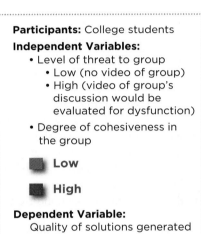

Participants: College students

Independent Variables:
- Level of threat to group
  - Low (no video of group)
  - High (video of group's discussion would be evaluated for dysfunction)
- Degree of cohesiveness in the group

  ▇ **Low**

  ▇ **High**

Dependent Variable:
  Quality of solutions generated

have the same information. For example, in the case of the Challenger explosion, engineers had access to information that managers lacked about the likelihood of O-ring failure at colder temperatures. Group members also need to regularly seek input from non-group members.

Second, groups should deliberately recruit diverse members. Although groups that consist of people from diverse backgrounds (e.g., race, gender, religion, culture) can have problems with miscommunication and misunderstanding, such groups have a broader range of opinions, attitudes, and thoughts. This diversity can lead to greater flexibility and creativity as well as better decisions (as long as the group has good communication). Researchers examined the content of group discussion between groups consisting of all Caucasian college students versus those consisting of a majority of Caucasian college students and one African American college student (Antonio, Chang, Hakuta, Kenny, Levin, & Milem, 2004). As predicted, the presence of an African American student in the group led to a greater integration of different perspectives and viewpoints.

Finally, training a person in the group about the dangers of biased group decision making and having him/her inform other group members about these issues can also be effective (Larson, Foster-Fishman, & Keys, 1994). Even forewarning participants about who knows what information increases accuracy (Stasser, Stewart, & Wittenbaum, 1995; Stewart & Stasser, 1995). All of these factors can help avoid the likelihood of groupthink—a phenomenon described by the *New*

York Times as showing "the ways that smart people working collectively can be dumber than the sum of their brains."

THE POWER OF LEADERSHIP

One important influence on the group decision-making process and outcome is the group leader (Albright & Forziati, 1995; Chemers, Watson, & May, 2000; Kaiser, Hogan, & Craig, 2008). Group leaders play a very important role in guiding and motivating the group. In some cases group leaders are chosen in a formal process, such as an election by group members, or an appointment by those in higher-up positions. In other cases, leaders emerge informally and gradually as the group interacts over time.

What is a good leader? Theory and research points to three models: the trait (or "great person") model, transactional versus transformational leadership, and the contingency model.

Diversity isn't just politically correct and fair to people who have traditionally faced discrimination: it leads to better decision making.

Trait or "great person" model. The trait (or "great person") model of leadership describes good leaders as emerging based on specific personality traits, such as intelligence, dominance, and extraversion (Zaccaro, 2007). As described at the start of this section, students who are oriented toward both achievement and interpersonal dynamics receive the highest leadership scores. In line with this view, people with particular leadership characteristics (e.g., initiative, planning, delegation) were rated by judges as more effective at leading groups on diverse tasks, including an artistic task, a logical/spatial task, a social task, and a creative task (Albright & Forziata, 1995). Similarly, one study on leadership effectiveness in military cadets demonstrated that individuals who were high in leadership efficacy (e.g., skills in initiative, decisiveness, judgment, communication, and so on) were rated higher in leadership potential by both their supervisors and their peers (Chemers et al., 2000).

Transactional versus transformational leaders. Other models of leadership describe the difference between transactional and transformational leaders. Transactional leaders reward desirable behaviors by group members and act once mistakes or problems occur (Burns, 1978). In contrast, transformational leaders foster trust among group members, build identification with and excitement about higher-level group goals, and examine new approaches for problem solving. Although both transactional and transformational leaders can be successful, groups with transformational leaders tend to have better performance (Bass, Avolio, Jung, & Berson, 2003). Transformational leadership may be more effective because it creates intrinsic motivation (Charbonneau, Barling, & Kelloway, 2001). Sports teams with transformational coaches, for example, create higher levels of intrinsic motivation in their players, which in turn leads to better performance (as you might remember from Chapter 3).

Contingency models. Contingency models of leadership emphasize the importance of having a match between the leader's specific traits and the demands of a particular situation (Kaplan & Kaiser, 2003; Peters, Hartke, & Pohlmann, 1985; Vroom & Jago, 2007). According to this model, some people are *task-oriented*, meaning they focus on organizing projects, setting standards, and achieving goals. Task-oriented leaders are very good at keeping others focused on the work at hand and maintaining group effort. Other leaders are described as *people-oriented* or *relationship-oriented*, meaning they focus on building a supportive, caring, and democratic work environment. People-oriented leaders seek out feedback and contributions from group members, validate people's contributions, and facilitate teamwork.

People tend to have less favorable attitudes toward women leaders than men leaders, which makes it harder for women to be viewed as effective leaders (Biernat, Crandall, Young, Kobrynowicz, & Halpin, 1998; Eagly & Karau, 2002; Sczesny & Kühnen, 2004). In one study, male and female confederates were trained to give specific comments and arguments during a group discussion in which they served as leaders (Butler & Geis, 1990). Women leaders received more negative responses and fewer positive responses than men who offered the same suggestions and arguments; men received generally the same number of positive and negative responses. Women leaders are also devalued compared to men when they use stereotypically male leadership styles, including autocratic and directive styles, and occupy male-dominated roles (Eagly, Makhijani, & Klonsky, 1992). These negative evaluations are more pronounced when given by men than women. Finally, women who express anger in a professional context are seen in a much more negative way than men who express such anger; in fact, men who express anger are seen as more powerful and as higher in status, whereas women are seen as lower in status and as less competent (Brescoll & Uhlmann, 2008). All of these factors point to the challenges women face in being seen as effective leaders.

Other research suggests that both men and women can be effective leaders, although they tend to adopt different leadership styles. Women tend to act in a more democratic or participatory style, and men tend to act in a more autocratic or directive style (Eagly & Johnson, 1990). People are most effective in leadership roles that fit their gender (e.g., men in masculine roles—those requiring ability to direct and control people, and women in feminine roles—those that require the ability to cooperate and get along; Eagly, Karau, & Makhijani, 1995). Even in natural group settings, men tend to emerge as leaders in groups with a focus on a specific task, and in short-term groups. Women tend to emerge as leaders in groups that require more complex social interaction (Eagly & Karau, 1991). Finally, female leaders are more likely than men to use contingent rewards (rewards for good performance), which is a highly effective leadership strategy (Eagly, Johannesen-Schmidt, & van Engen, 2003). Research indicates that women are as effective as men in leadership roles, and in some cases can even be more effective than men.

Can Hilary Clinton be an effective leader in her role as Secretary of State? According to research in social psychology, yes, but she may be more effective using a democratic or participatory leadership style than an autocratic or directive style.

EXAMPLES OF HOW THE GROUP PROCESS INFLUENCES DECISION MAKING

Concepts in Context

FACTOR	EXAMPLE
Group polarization	At the start of the discussion, Justin thought that requiring high school students to do mandatory community service was probably not a great idea. But after the discussion, Justin was strongly opposed to this requirement.
Groupthink	The board of trustees met in secret to develop a plan to renovate the college museum at a cost of $2 million dollars, a plan they believed would be welcomed by the college community. When the plan was announced, both faculty and students were very upset that these much-needed funds were not being used to hire more professors and provide more scholarships to students. Faculty and students engaged in public protest again the planned renovation.
Leadership	Caroline is intelligent, assertive, and extraverted. Whenever she is in a group meeting, she seems to naturally emerge as the group leader.

HOW DO GROUPS HANDLE CONFLICT?

The prior section examined how people in a given group work together to make decisions. However, in some cases people in different groups compete against each other over a resource, such as land, money, or power. Unfortunately, biased perceptions often lead to escalating conflict between groups, even in cases in which true differences are relatively small. Researchers asked both pro-choice and pro-life participants a series of questions about abortion (Robinson, Keltner, Ward, & Ross, 1995). These questions included:

- sympathy they felt for women undergoing abortion in different situations,
- medical and scientific facts about abortion,
- factors that influenced their own feelings about abortion, and
- consequences they believed would result from restrictions to legal access to abortion.

Participants were also asked about how they thought other pro-life and pro-choice participants would respond to these questions. As predicted, participants who were pro-choice reported feeling more sympathy for women undergoing abortion than those who were pro-life. However, the gap in sympathy between pro-choice and pro-life participants was much smaller than either pro-choice or pro-life participants assumed. Pro-life participants felt more sympathy for a woman undergoing abortion than either pro-choice or pro-life participants assumed they would. Similarly, although pro-choice participants believed that restricting access to abortion would result in more deaths to women from illegal abortions than did pro-life participants, the actual gap between estimates from pro-choice and pro-life participants was much smaller (18.2%) than either pro-choice or pro-life participants assumed (61.2% and 41.6%, respectively). This research demonstrates one way in which people's biased perceptions lead to the overestimation of differences between groups, which in turn can escalate conflict. This section will describe this and other factors that can lead to **conflict**, the presence and/or perception of incompatible goals between two people or groups. We will also examine strategies for resolving conflict.

conflict the presence and/or perception of incompatible goals between two people or groups

FACTORS LEADING TO CONFLICT

What factors lead to conflict between groups? This section will address several factors that contribute to intergroup conflict, including competition for resources, societal beliefs, and entrapment.

In the NEWS

Conflict. Although people on opposing sides of the abortion debate often see their own views as directly opposed to those of the other side, these two sides may be less different than is often believed. People on both sides of this issue probably agree that abortion should be rare, and that preventing unplanned pregnancy is a very good idea.

Competition for resources. One factor that leads to conflict between groups is the competition for resources, a theory described as **realistic group conflict theory** (Correll & Park, 2005; Coser, 1956; Sherif, 1966). People in different groups often compete for scarce resources, such as land, jobs, and power. (In Chapter 10, we'll talk about the impact of this competition on stereotypes and prejudice.) This competition leads to conflict between groups.

A classic study by Muzafer Sherif examined the role of competition on creating conflict using a sample of 11-year-old boys at a summer camp. The boys arrived at camp and were randomly divided into two groups. The groups interacted completely separately: they did their own activities, created their own names (Rattlers and Eagles), etc. Then, the two groups participated in competitive activities, such as football, tug-of-war, and a treasure hunt. An intense rivalry quickly developed. Group flags were burned, cabins were ransacked, and food fights in the dining hall were commonplace. This demonstration reveals just how quickly competition can lead to conflict, even among groups of very similar people with no prior history of conflict.

Biased perceptions. One of the major factors leading to conflict is that each side holds *biased perceptions* about both themselves and those in the out-group (Bronfenbrenner, 1961; Rouhana & Bar-Tal, 1998). First, groups see their own goals as just and fair, and attribute positive traits and values to their own side. Both Israelis and Palestinians see their goals (e.g., establishing a Jewish state in their ancient homeland, establishing a Palestinian state in the West Bank and Gaza, respectively) as crucially important and inherently just.

At the same time, groups view people in the out-group in a simplistic and stereotyped way (Pettigrew, 2003; Rouhana & Bar-Tal, 1998). Groups tend to believe that they are victims of harms and atrocities committed by the other side, and to minimize, or even ignore, their own role in contributing to the problem. As the mother of three children, I recognize this tendency well: each child invariably insists that the other one started the fight. This tendency can also be seen on a more global level: both Israelis and Arabs see the other side as the aggressor in each of the four major wars between these countries (1948, 1956, 1967, 1973). However, both Israel and Palestine technically fired first in two of the wars.

This simultaneous view of our own side as just and fair and those on the other side as evil and selfish, even when the outward behavior may be identical, describes the phenomenon of **mirror-image perception** (Bronfenbrener, 1961; Pettigrew, 2003; Tobin & Eagles, 1992). As described at the start of this section, in mirror-image perception, each group sees its own behavior as caused by the same factor—that is, the actions of the other side (see Table 9.2).

Another example of the biased perceptions between groups is that we see the views of our own side as reflecting reality, but see others' views as biased and particularly extreme (Keltner & Robinson, 1997; Robinson et al., 1995; Rouhana & Bar-Tal, 1998). These biased perceptions are particularly strong when we think about values that are central to our own side's position (Chambers, Baron, & Inman, 2006). In one study, researchers asked both Democrats and Republicans to rate their agreement with a series of statements (Chambers & Melnyk, 2006). They were also asked to estimate how members of the other side would rate their agreement with each statement. Democrats and Republicans did tend to disagree about the relative truth of each statement, with Democrats perceiving more disagreement with Republicans about liberal issues than about conservative issues, and Republicans perceiving more disagreement with Democrats about conservative issues than about liberal issues. However, the actual disagreement between Democrats and Republicans was considerably smaller than the perceived disagreement. These perceptions of greater disagreement than actually exists contribute to increased conflict. This explains the very negative views expressed by both Democrats and Republicans about the other side: Democrats claim Republicans don't care about poor people or about the environment, whereas Republicans claim Democrats are attacking traditional family values and the free market.

TABLE 9.2

EXAMPLES OF MIRROR-IMAGE PERCEPTIONS ABOUT THE NUCLEAR ARMS RACE

BELIEF	UNITED STATES LEADER	SOVIET LEADER
We prefer mutual disarmament.	We want more than anything else to join with them in reducing the number of weapons.	We do not strive for military superiority; we want termination, not continuation of the arms race.
We must avoid disarming while the other side arms.	We refuse to become weaker while potential adversaries remain committed to their imperialist adventures.	Our country does not seek superiority, but it also will not allow superiority to be gained over it.
Unlike us, the other side aims for military superiority.	For the Soviet leaders peace is not the real issue; rather, the issue is the attempt to spread their dominance using military power.	The main obstacle ... is the attempts by the U.S. and its allies to achieve military superiority.

Statements by both American and Soviet leaders reveal that both sides prefer mutual nuclear disarmament over all other options, but each side perceives the other side as trying to "trick" them into disarming while they arm. This misperception, not surprisingly, leads to the build-up of nuclear arms.

Source: Plous, S. (1985). Perceptual illusions and military realities: A social psychological analysis of the nuclear arms race.

This tendency to see the other side as biased, but our own side as purely objective, explains the **hostile media phenomenon**, meaning the belief that media coverage of events is biased against the side we favor. In one study, 144 Stanford students watched six segments of national news coverage of a wide-spread Israeli move into West Beirut, Lebanon (Vallone, 1985). Members of pro-Arab and pro-Israeli student organizations were recruited to participate in this study. After watching the videotape, students rated the fairness and objectivity of the news programs. First, each side saw the news programs as biased for the other side: pro-Arab subjects gave a rating of 6.7 (1 is biased against Israel, 9 is biased in favor of Israel), and pro-Israel subjects gave a rating of 2.9. Similarly, they saw the focus on Israel as too much (2.9) if they were pro-Israel, and too little (5.9) if they were pro-Arab. Finally, they saw the proportion of Israeli favorable information as low if they were pro-Israel (22%) and high (62%) if they were pro-Arab. This study demonstrates that even supposedly objective information from the media is seen as biased against our own side—likely because our own views are hardly objective.

The phenomenon of entrapment can be used to explain why countries continue fighting wars they are losing as a way to justify resources already devoted to this cause.

ALI YUSSEF/Stringer/Getty Images, Inc.

hostile media phenomenon the tendency to believe that media coverage of events is biased against the side we favor

Entrapment. Another factor that can increase conflict is **entrapment** (Brockner & Rubin, 1985). Entrapment describes the common situation in which groups escalate commitment to failing courses of action, in part to justify investments already made. There are many real-world examples of entrapment: banks increase their commitment to problem loans (Staw, Barsade, & Koput, 1997), coaches grant more playing time to higher drafted NBA players (Staw & Hoang, 1995), and venture

entrapment the common situation in which groups escalate commitment to failing courses of action, in part to justify investments already made

capitalists continue investing in unprofitable projects (Antonides, 1995). Many people now see the war in Iraq as an example of the problem of entrapment (e.g., we must stay in the war to justify all the people who've already been killed).

What motivates someone to continue to pursue a losing course of action? One factor is egotism. In one study, participants were told they would play a gambling game in which they could potentially win a jackpot of $10 (Zhang & Baumeister, 2006). In order to continue playing the game (and have a chance to win the jackpot), participants needed to continue investing small amounts of money on each trial. Some participants were randomly assigned to the ego-threatening condition, in which the researcher suggested that if they tended to choke under pressure, they should probably "play it safe" in the task. Participants in the control condition did not receive any mention of choking. Researchers then examined how much money participants in each condition had gambled (and lost). As predicted, threatened participants consistently lost more money than nonthreatened participants, presumably because they feared being seen as giving up and thus continued in the game longer than they should have. This research demonstrates that the desire to preserve self-esteem can have detrimental effects on a person's financial well-being.

Questioning the Research

This study suggests that people who are afraid of appearing to "choke" lose more money because they are playing to preserve self-esteem. Can you think of an alternative explanation for their findings? (Hint: is there another factor that could lead those who are reminded of "choking" to stay in the game too long?)

STRATEGIES FOR RESOLVING CONFLICT

Although you've just learned about several factors that can lead to conflict between groups, other factors are effective in reducing such conflict. Let's examine some of these strategies for resolving conflict.

Equal status contact.   According to Allport's *contact hypothesis*, one of the simplest and most effective ways to resolve group conflict is to increase interaction between people in different groups (Dixon, Durrheim, & Tredoux, 2005; Gaertner, Dovidio, et al., 1999; Slavin & Madden, 1979). Bringing different groups together to work on a cooperative task is an effective strategy for resolving conflict. However, bringing people from different groups together to interact in unequal ways, such as members of one group tutoring or working for members of another group, can further conflict between groups. Thus, reducing conflict between groups needs to involve *equal status contact*, meaning that each group member contributes to that interaction on a level playing field. The Education Connections box describes a unique approach to creating this type of equal status interaction in the classroom.

Common ground.   Finding *common ground* between two groups can also lead to a reduction in conflict (Cohen & Insko, 2008; Gaertner et al., 1999; Slavin & Madden, 1979; Swaab, Postmes, Van Beest, & Spears, 2007). As described by Gaertner and Dovidio's *Common Ingroup Identity Model*, when group members believe they have shared identity (a sense of belonging that encompass both groups) or are working on a shared goal, the attractiveness of out-group members increases while biases and discrimination decreases (Sherif, 1966). In these cases everyone benefits from belonging to a larger group. For example, countries that are at odds with each other may realize they can work together on common goals, such as the safety of their citizens, the management of terrorism, and the reduction of the threat of nuclear war (Rubin, Pruitt, & Kim, 1994).

The counselors at the summer camp for boys described previously used the strategy of finding common ground to end violence between the groups (Sherif et al., 1961). The counselors initiated a series of situations that required the use of superordinate goals, meaning goals that can be achieved only through cooperation among all members of both groups. In one case the camp truck "broke down" and required the strength of everyone to help pull it up the hill. In another case, counselors offered to rent a very desirable movie for all campers to see—but the movie was so expensive that contributions from both groups were needed to pay for it. This focus on superordinate goals decreased the barriers between

Associated Press

In World War II, the United States and Russia, two countries that had previously been in conflict, came together to defeat Germany. This pursuit of a common goal reduced conflict between these two former enemies.

Education

The Power of the Jigsaw Classroom

The "jigsaw" classroom is a technique designed by Eliot Aronson and his colleagues to bring children from different backgrounds together to work toward a common goal (Aronson & Bridgeman, 1979; Slavin & Cooper, 1999; Weigel, Wiser, & Cook, 1975). This technique involves dividing students within a classroom into small learning groups, and then giving each child in that small group one piece of information to learn.

For example, as part of a history lesson, each child in the group might be given information about a different stage of a historical figure's life. Because each member of the group only has one piece of information, group members need to work together to learn the information possessed by each student. This process gives each child a chance to explain his or her material to the other students, and helps students focus on asking questions and listening to one another. In this way, the jigsaw technique changes the classroom environment into one in which children cooperate together toward the common goal of mastering the material, instead of competing against one another to share the right answer.

Research on cooperative learning programs reveals that this approach can be very effective (Blaney, Stephan, Rosenfield, Aronson, & Sikes, 1977; Lucker, Rosenfield, Sikes, & Aronson, 1976). Children in jigsaw classrooms show greater liking for their classmates and greater increases in self-esteem than those in other classrooms. Jigsaw classrooms led to greater academic performance on the part of minority students (both Mexican American and African American children), and no differences in the academic performance of Caucasian students. In fact, after two weeks of the jigsaw technique the gap between performance by Caucasian and minority students dropped from 17 percentage points to about 10 percentage points.

What leads to the beneficial effects of the jigsaw technique? First, children who participate in jigsaw groups tend to increase their participation and interest in school activities (Blaney et al., 1977). Second, children gain in empathy and perspective-taking. Finally, children may change the attributions they make for others' behavior (Stephan, Presser, Kennedy, & Aronson, 1978). They may begin to give others credit for their successes (e.g., he really is smart) and to remove blame for failures (e.g., that was a ridiculously hard question). In other words, they start to use the same attributions to explain others' successes and failures that they use to explain their own.

© Corbis/SUPERSTOCK

the two groups of campers remarkably, and by the end of the camp, the groups were fully integrated and very friendly.

Members of different groups can experience greater cooperation and forgiveness if they think about the commonality of their experience, as opposed to the differences. Researchers asked Jewish college students to reflect on one of two statements (Wohl & Branscombe, 2005). In one condition, students thought about the Holocaust as an event in which the Germans behaved aggressively toward Jews. In the other condition, students thought about the Holocaust as an event in which some people behaved aggressively toward other people. Participants then rated their willingness to forgive Germans for the Holocaust. As predicted, Jewish students who reflected on the Holocaust as an event that involved aggression by some people toward other people were much more willing to forgive Germans for this tragedy than Jewish students who reflected on the Holocaust as an event that involved aggression by German people toward Jewish people.

GRIT (Graduated and Reciprocated Initiatives in Tension Reduction) a strategy to create unilateral and persistent efforts to establish trust and cooperation between opposing parties

GRIT. The **GRIT (graduated and reciprocated initiatives in tension reduction)** strategy refers to a particular approach to creating unilateral and persistent efforts to establishing trust and cooperation between opposing parties (Lindskold & Han, 1988; Osgood, 1962). In this case, one party announces its intention to reduce conflict, and invites the other party to reciprocate. Then you carry out your tension-reducing activities as planned, even if there is no immediate response. This increases your credibility and may put pressure on the other party to respond accordingly. Once the other party acts, you quickly reciprocate. If the other party retaliates, you quickly and *at the same level* retaliate.

Participants who use the GRIT strategy are more likely to reach optimal agreements and feel differently about their interaction partner than those who use competitive strategies. In one study, 90% of those who used this strategy reached an agreement, as compared to 65% of those in a typical competitive interaction (Lindskold & Han, 1988). Participants who use GRIT also reach agreements faster and form more positive expectations regarding future interactions.

The most significant attempt at GRIT was the so-called "Kennedy experiment" (Etzioni, 1967). President Kennedy announced that the United States would stop all atmospheric nuclear tests, and would not resume them unless another country did. This speech was published in the Soviet Union, and five days later, the Soviet leader reciprocated by announcing that he had halted production of strategic bombers. The United States then agreed to sell wheat to Russia, which had previously been forbidden, and in turn, the Soviets agreed to a "hot line" between the two countries. These efforts ultimately led to a test-ban treaty, and warmer relations between the two countries.

bargaining seeking an agreement through direct negotiation between both sides in a conflict

Bargaining. **Bargaining** means seeking an agreement through direct negotiation between both sides in a conflict, and is commonly used to resolve conflict. When you are buying a car or a house, you often negotiate the price, with each side having opposing goals (e.g., you want to pay less, the seller wants to receive more). Bargaining is difficult because you need to strike the right line between being tough (and getting the other side to compromise) and being reasonable (not suggesting a price that is unreasonable so that the other party walks away).

People who appear tough during negotiations are more likely to secure a good deal. In one study, participants acted as sellers who negotiate the price and warranty of cell phones with a buyer (Van Kleef, De Dreu, & Manstead, 2004). In some cases, participants were told that the buyer was very angry (e.g., he supposedly said, "This is a ridiculous offer, it really pisses me off."). In other cases, participants were told that the buyer seemed happy with the offer (e.g., he supposedly said, "This is going pretty well, I can't complain."). Researchers then measured how information about the buyers' moods influenced participants' negotiating demands. As predicted, participants who believed the buyer was angry offered better prices than those who believed the buyer was happy.

One problem with using bargaining to resolve conflict is that people who misrepresent their needs can gain a real advantage in bargaining situations (O'Connor & Carnevale, 1997; Schweitzer, DeChurch, & Gibson, 2005; Steinel & De Dreu, 2004). People who misrepresent their own motives can trick others into making bad decisions—decisions that hurt themselves and take advantage of the other person. For example, a father who wants his wife to have sole custody and to pay low alimony may pretend to want joint custody as a way of then compromising on custody to get lower alimony. About 28% of people in negotiations misrepresent what they want, and these people tend to get better outcomes. However, the overall joint outcome is better when both people are honest.

Business CONNECTIONS

Using Mediation and Arbitration to Resolve Conflict

Mediation is a commonly used strategy for resolving conflict between labor-management in business disputes (Brett, Goldberg, & Ury, 1990; Emery & Wyer, 1987; Shapiro & Brett, 1993). Mediators first help parties rethink the conflict so that they understand the costs of continuing it (e.g., people will lose their jobs, businesses will lose money) and the benefits of ending the conflict. Mediators also try to decrease misperceptions, and help people on opposing sides find common ground, such as finding superordinate goals that everyone wants to achieve. Because a key factor in successful mediation is trust between the parties, a mediator can be useful in getting each side to identify and rank their goals, and then ideally reach a compromise. Because the use of a mediator can lead to greater flexibility and perspective-taking, as well as collaboration (e.g., seeing the conflict as a joint problem that must be solved), this approach can often lead to beneficial outcomes for both parties.

People see mediation as more just and fair than many other forms of negotiation (Shapiro & Brett, 1993). One study found that 77% of those who participated in mediation to resolve a dispute were satisfied with the procedure, compared to 45% of those who used arbitration (Brett & Goldberg, 1983). This greater satisfaction is due in part to people's ability to help control and develop the outcome of mediation decisions.

As in mediation, arbitration uses a neutral third party to help two sides reach an agreement. However, in arbitration, this third party studies both sides and

then imposes a settlement (Lind, Kanfer, & Earley, 1990). Arbitration is commonly used to resolve contract disputes between players and management of professional sports teams. People are generally less satisfied with arbitration than mediation because each party has little control over the outcome. However, combining these two strategies can be an effective way of resolving disputes. In some cases people first use mediation, and then follow with arbitration if an agreement is not reached (McGillicuddy, Welton, & Pruitt, 1987). This approach leads to more problem solving and less competition and hostility than those in straight mediation, in which negotiation just ends if an agreement is not reached.

Associated Press

The Business Connections box describes two other approaches to resolving conflict: **mediation**, in which a neutral third party tries to resolve a conflict by facilitating communication and offering suggestions, and **arbitration**, in which a neutral third party studies both sides and then imposes a settlement.

Integrative solutions. An **integrative agreement** is a negotiated resolution to a conflict. All parties obtain outcomes that are superior to what they would have obtained from an equal division of the contested resources (De Dreu, Koole, & Steinel, 2000). Although it seems as if this approach would be relatively easy to reach—because both parties benefit—misperceptions often hinder such agreements. One review of research found that in over 20% of agreements that could have resulted in integrative agreements, the participants agreed to terms that were worse for each.

mediation a particular type of bargaining situation in which a neutral third party tries to resolve a conflict by facilitating communication and offering suggestions

arbitration a resolution of a conflict by a neutral third party who studies both sides and imposes a settlement

integrative agreement a negotiated resolution to a conflict in which all parties obtain outcomes that are superior to what they would have obtained from an equal division of the contested resources

Imagine that you are negotiating the terms for a new job, and that you are most interested in having a large number of vacation days, and less concerned about salary. When you are dissatisfied with the offer the company proposes, you suggest a compromise of a small increase in salary and one additional vacation day. However, you would in reality prefer no increase in salary but three additional vacation days. Why don't you make this suggestion? Because you believe the company would not agree to such terms—although the company might prefer precisely this option (but misperceive your desire for vacation days over salary). When the company agrees to your suggested compromise, both you and the company are less satisfied than if you had agreed on three extra vacation days (the integrative solution).

How can integrative agreements be reached? One of the best ways is letting both sides honestly discuss their goals and needs (Swaab et al., 2007; Thompson & Hrebec, 1996; Thompson, Peterson, & Brodt, 1996). Through open communication and trying to understand the other party's point of view, people may come to see that there are opportunities for joint benefits. Although we often think that what we want is very clear, sometimes these goals are not so obvious to the other side (Vorauer & Claude, 1998). In fact, people often fail to realize they have compatible interests and settle for a choice that is less good for both (e.g., a lose-lose agreement) simply because they don't share information. This failure to recognize the presence of integrative agreements is particularly likely when people negotiate under time pressure, and thus focus more on the immediate consequences of a negotiation than the longer-term outcomes (Henderson, Trope, & Carnevale, 2006).

Another factor that can lead to integrative agreements is perspective-taking, meaning understanding the viewpoint of the other side (Galinsky, Maddux, Gilin, & White, 2008). People who are better at perspective taking, such as those who agree with the statement, "I believe that there are two sides to every question and try to look at them both," are more likely to reach creative agreements that benefit both sides.

Finally, experienced negotiators are more successful at helping people reach this type of agreement than inexperienced negotiators (Thompson, 1990, 1995). In the mid-1970s, President Carter helped President Sadat of Egypt and Prime Minister Begin of Israel reach an integrative agreement regarding a long-standing conflict about how to divide the Sinai Desert (Rubin et al., 1994). Instead of continuing their argument about dividing the land, both leaders agreed to return the land to its historical owner (Egypt) and to demilitarize the area to provide Israel with its need for security.

CONFLICT RESOLUTION IN THE REAL WORLD

One of the major goals of research on conflict is to reduce major conflicts worldwide. Although there are no easy solutions to long-standing conflicts, such as that between Israelis and Palestinians, some psychologists have proposed specific steps for reducing such conflict (Kelman, 1997; Rouhana & Bar-Tal, 1998). Herbert Kelman of Harvard University created an interactive problem-solving approach in which unofficial representatives of different communities come together to openly describe their perspective, and thereby help groups understand each other's concerns, fears, priorities, and constraints. Following this open description, both parties are encouraged to work together on creating joint solutions to the conflict. This approach is designed to increase communication and perspective-taking, and to help parties see the possibility of working together on a common goal (e.g., a nonviolent future for their country). Although these workshops are specifically carried out with unofficial representatives of each group (e.g. not government officials), the participants are often politically influential and thus might bring a new understanding and openness to later discussion within members of their own community.

EXAMPLES OF FACTORS LEADING TO CONFLICT AND CONFLICT RESOLUTION

FACTOR LEADING TO CONFLICT	EXAMPLE
Competition for resources	Bart hates students who attend his rival high school in part because they've won the state football championship three years in a row.
Biased perceptions	Hana sees her own behavior in a real estate negotiation as motivated by good will and respect, but sees the other party's behavior as motivated by power and greed.
Entrapment	Government officials in one city voted to spend a certain amount of money on a new transit system, which is now only halfway complete at double the original estimate. Instead of cutting their losses and giving up on this new plan, they commit more and more resources to this new system to justify the considerable expense they've already incurred.

STRATEGIES FOR RESOLVING CONFLICT	EXAMPLE
Equal status contact	Organizing elementary school children on athletic teams with children from different backgrounds on each team can help to reduce prejudice and conflict.
Finding common ground	Bringing opposing campus groups together to lobby for a new student center can reduce group conflict.
GRIT	In an effort to reach out to her grumpy neighbor, Rhea makes the first effort to be friendly. When her neighbor responds with a similarly friendly gesture, she quickly reciprocates by engaging in yet another friendly outreach.
Bargaining	Colin is trying to negotiate a price for a new car from a car dealer. In order to secure the best deal, he angrily rejects the first price suggested.
Integrative agreement	A brother and sister are fighting over possession of a bat and ball. Their wise father points out that if each child takes one of the toys, they could play baseball together, with one person throwing the ball and the other person batting.

HOW DO GROUPS HANDLE SOCIAL DILEMMAS?

The previous section described conflict—and conflict resolution—between different groups. But in some cases, the conflict is not between groups but rather
between the group and an individual in that group. What factors lead to conflict
and conflict resolution in this situation?   Q A

Researchers asked college students to play a game in which they can win some
money (Liberman, Samuels, & Ross, 2004). In this game, each person plays with

a partner, and on each trial a person can choose to cooperate with his or her partner, or to compete with the partner. If both people cooperate, each person wins $.40. If both people compete, each person receives nothing. However, if one person cooperates and the other competes, the person who cooperates loses $.20 and the person who competes wins $.80.

Although all participants play this same game, it is described in different ways. Half of the participants are told this game is "the Wall Street game," which is designed to increase the tendency to compete. The other participants were told that this game is "the community game," which is designed to increase the tendency to cooperate. As predicted, participants were much more likely to cooperate when they were playing the "community game," than when they were playing "the Wall Street game."

Why does a simple group label change people's behavior? These labels create expectations about how one's partner will behave in the situation, and our own behavior is thus influenced by these expectations. This example illustrates a **social dilemma**, a situation in which what is best for the individual is in conflict with what is best for the group. This section will describe factors that influence social dilemmas, situations in which the interests of the group and the individual conflict, as well as some solutions to such dilemmas.

social dilemma a situation in which a self-interested choice by everyone creates the worst outcome for the group

TYPES OF SOCIAL DILEMMAS

In all social dilemmas, what is best for the individual is not best for the group (and vice versa). However, the specific nature of the dilemma can differ, including whether the dilemma is between groups or individuals and whether the dilemma involves reducing a common resource or sustaining a common good or service. This section will describe three types of social dilemmas: common resource dilemma, public good dilemma, and prisoner's dilemma.

common resource dilemma a social dilemma in which each person can take as much as he or she wants of a common resource, but if everyone takes as much as he or she wants, the resource will eventually be completely depleted

Common resource dilemma. A **common resource dilemma** is a type of social dilemma in which a resource, such as water, land, or oil, can be reduced—and even eliminated—by overuse (Edney, 1980; Komorita & Parks, 1995). In this case, each person can take moderate amounts of a common resource, but if everyone takes as much as he or she wants, the resource will eventually be depleted. For example, during times of drought, people in affected communities are urged to take short showers, wear clothes for longer periods of time without washing them, and flush the toilet less frequently. However, each person may be reluctant to comply with these recommendations in part because they believe that their own use of water is relatively minimal. But if everyone chooses to ignore the water restriction recommendations, eventually the water could run out, leading to serious problems for everyone.

Garrett Hardin (1968), an ecologist, described a resource dilemma that occurred when New England sheepherders allowed overgrazing on common lands. When herders were on their own private pastures, they were very careful to allow only a limited number of animals to graze on the land, given their concerns about overgrazing leading to the destruction of the grass—and in turn, the potential to run out of food for their flock. However, when herders brought their sheep to public lands, they freely allowed many sheep to graze on a single pasture, which led to the destruction of the grass. This situation is referred to as the *tragedy of the commons*.

In a famous demonstration of a resource dilemma in action, several participants sat around a table on which there was a bowl of 60 nuts (Edney, 1979). The experimenter explained that every ten seconds he would double the number of nuts in the bowl, and that each participant's goal was to get as many nuts as possible. Any participant could reach

© Comstock/SUPERSTOCK

Libraries could save a lot of money by simply providing books for people to borrow for as long as they would like—but without the structural regulation of checking out books and imposing fines on those that are kept too long, some people would not return books on time, thereby reducing other people's access to them.

into the bowl and grab nuts at any time in order to get nuts. Participants should have managed their resources best by removing only 30 nuts, and then waiting for the experimenter to double the nuts (returning to the original amount), so every 10 seconds they could take 30 nuts (in theory forever). But 65% of the groups never got past the first 10 seconds—someone instantly grabbed the nuts, which then led the other participants to follow suit, and at 10 seconds, no nuts remained in the bowl to be doubled (remember, zero times zero equals zero).

Public goods dilemma. Another type of a social dilemma is a **public goods dilemma**, in which a public good or service needs to be sustained over time (Komorita & Parks, 1995). This type of dilemma refers to a situation in which each person can take freely of the resource, and must decide whether and what to contribute to the common pool of resources. If a sufficient number of people contribute to the common pool, than others can benefit because the resource will be available to them even if they don't contribute. However, if not enough people contribute to the common pool, the resource can disappear completely. In fact, the best choice for each individual is to not contribute, but hope that others do.

There are many real world examples of public goods dilemmas.

"Leave some shells for less fortunate children."

"Leave some shells for less fortunate children."

- Many people watch the Public Broadcasting Station (PBS) but do not donate money to pay for these shows (which depends on financial contributions to fund its programs, unlike other stations that are funded by paid commercials).
- Many people take for granted blood would be available for them if they ever need a transfusion, but haven't chosen to donate their own blood for others' use.
- Many people don't contribute to the American Cancer Society but could benefit from research on cancer treatment funded by those who do donate.

public goods dilemma social dilemmas in which each person must decide what to contribute to a common pool of resources. But if people do not all contribute, these public goods will not be available

Prisoner's dilemma. The **prisoner's dilemma** refers to the situation in which two people may choose to either cooperate with each other or compete (Pruitt & Kimmel, 1977). In the classic situation, each person is better off competing with his or her partner, but only if the partner cooperates. Let's say two men are caught robbing a liquor store. They are separated, and each is told that if he confesses and the other one does not, he will go free whereas his partner will get 10 years. On the other hand, if his partner confesses and he does not, he gets the 10 years. What's the worst option? If both people confess, each person could get 5 years. In contrast, the best option for the group (meaning both people together) is for both people to cooperate and plead not guilty. This choice could lead each person to receive a relatively short prison sentence (not as good as having no prison sentence, but certainly better than receiving a 10-year sentence). The prisoner's dilemma paradigm therefore describes a situation in which the best outcome for each individual person leads to the worst outcome for his or her partner.

prisoner's dilemma the situation in which two people may choose to either cooperate or compete with each other

The prisoner's dilemma represents a dilemma (not surprisingly) for participants because each person's best option depends on the option chosen by the other person. If you trust your partner, the best option is for you to cooperate. However, if you don't trust your partner, the best option is for you to compete. Because people often doubt how much they can trust their partner, choosing to compete often seems like the safest option. Unfortunately, when both people choose to compete, they both lose (see Figure 9.6).

FIGURE 9.6

SAMPLE PRISONER'S DILEMMA PAYOFF MATRIX

In prisoner's dilemma paradigms, the best outcome for each person is to compete (plead guilty) while their partner cooperates, (pleads not guilty) whereas the worst outcome is to cooperate while their partner competes. However, both people jointly are best off if they both cooperate and plead not guilty.

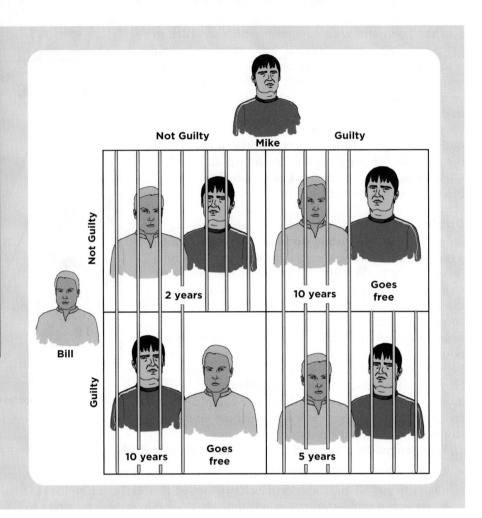

SOLUTIONS TO SOCIAL DILEMMAS

Social dilemmas involve a conflict between what is best for a person and what is best for his or her group. Social dilemmas are challenging issues to solve, but these problems can be successfully resolved:

- by regulating the use of resources,
- engaging in open communication,
- activating altruistic motives
- creating small groups, and
- creating consequences for competition.

Let's examine each of these approaches.

Regulate the use of resources.   One strategy is to set up a formal way to *regulate* the use of limited resources (Messick, 1983; Samuelson, Messick, Rutte, & Wilke, 1984; Sato, 1987; van Dijk, Wilke, & Wit, 2003). These solutions often involve creating a structural system, such as an organization or a leader, to allocate resources fairly. For example, the Environmental Protection Agency is in charge of setting rules about pollution, because we don't trust companies to regulate their own pollution levels. We are especially interested in setting up formal ways to regulate access to limited resources when we think others are overusing a resource and we don't trust them to stop. The Health Connections box describes why many countries have compulsory vaccinations in part because parents are less likely to have children vaccinated without such regulations.

Setting up ways to regulate the use of resources is particularly important because people often overconsume resources due to biased perceptions about their fair share (Herlocker, Allison, Foubert, & Beggan, 1997). Researchers assigned

Why Not Vaccinating Your Child Can Be Good for You, but Bad for the Community

Many countries, including the United States, have compulsory immunization requirements. For example, babies in the United States are required to have vaccinations for small pox, diphtheria, and polio to avoid the spread of deadly diseases. Although these vaccines are very effective at preventing disease, they pose a very small risk to each individual baby: a few babies each year suffer seizures and even death as a result of receiving a vaccination.

As a parent, the ideal choice is clearly to have all other babies vaccinated but not to have your own baby vaccinated. After all, if all other babies are vaccinated, there is no way your child can acquire one of these diseases, and you could then avoid exposing your child to even the very small risk of such a vaccination. But think about what would happen if each parent chose to refuse the vaccination for his or her own child; many babies would then develop these diseases, leading to the death of many children. This is another example of the dilemma that results when what is good for the community is not necessarily what is best for the individual (Salmon & Omer, 2006).

participants to either 3-person or 12-person groups. Participants were then told that the group needed to share resources (such as blocks or sand), and that each group member could take as many units of a given resource as he or she desired. After participants selected the amount of resources they wanted, they were asked to estimate how much of the total pool of resources they selected. Although participants admitted to intentionally taking more of the resources than was their fair share, they also underestimated the proportion of the resources they took.

Communication. Another strategy that groups can use to solve solution dilemmas is communication, especially face-to-face (Bornstein, Rapaport, Kerpel, & Katz, 1989; Dawes, 1980; Drolet & Morris, 2000; Kerr & Kaufman-Gilliland, 1994). Face-to-face group discussion helps increase cooperative behavior in social dilemmas, in part because such discussion leads group members to see others as wanting to cooperate and enables people to make commitments to cooperate (Bouas & Komorita, 1996; Kimmel, 1980; Orbell, Van de Kragt, & Dawes, 1988). Communication can also clear up misunderstandings that could impede cooperation (Tazelaar, Van Lange, & Ouwerkerk, 2004).

Communicating about one's intentions to behave cooperatively is an especially effective strategy for solving social dilemmas. One study found that repeating one's intention to cooperate in a prisoner's dilemma interaction led to more cooperation, greater liking, and more trust (Lindskold, Han, & Betz, 1986). Moreover, people who expect cooperation from a partner are more creative and flexible problem-solvers; 58% of those who expect cooperation in a negotiation reach a solution, compared to only 25% of those who expect conflict (Carnevale & Probst, 1998).

One reason why communication increases cooperation is that group discussion can lead group members to develop an internalized personal norm for behaving cooperatively. For example, if group members discuss the advantages of limiting how many fish a person can catch, some people will follow this agreement based on their own internalized norms, even without a clear monitor for such behavior (Kerr, Garst, Lewandowski, & Harris, 1997). Even subtle cues can lead to cooperation, such as knowing that someone similar to you cooperated (Parks, Sanna, & Berel, 2001), or, as described at the start of this section, describing a prisoner's dilemma game as "the community game" instead of "the Wall Street game" (Liberman et al., 2004).

Activate altruistic or moral motives.   Another approach to solving social dilemmas is to get people to activate altruistic or moral motives, meaning the motive to help others and behave in a moral way (Dawes, 1980; Lynn & Oldenquist, 1986). As shown in Figure 9.7, people who identify with their community use low amounts of water regardless of whether they pay a fixed rate for water (in which case their own personal use doesn't influence how much they pay) or a variable rate (in which case they are charged for the water they consume; Van Vugt, 2001). In contrast, people who don't identify as part of their community use significantly more water when they pay a fixed rate than when they pay a variable rate. Simply feeling respected by other people in your group increases cooperation, especially for those who are most concerned about fitting in with others in the group (De Cremer, 2002).

FIGURE 9.7

HOW DOES COMMUNITY IDENTIFICATION IMPACT COOPERATION?

This study measured how much water people used in a community that encouraged water conservation. The hypothesis was that people who identify strongly with community goals would conserve water, regardless of whether tax rates penalized them for high water use or not. As predicted, people with a variable tax rate use about the same amount of water regardless of their community identification, whereas, under a fixed tax rate, people who identify highly with their community use much less water than those who do not identify as strongly.

Source: Van Vugt, M. (2001). Community identification moderating the impact of financial incentives in a natural social dilemma: Water conservation. *Personality and Social Psychology Bulletin, 27*, 1440-1449. Used by permission of Sage Publications.

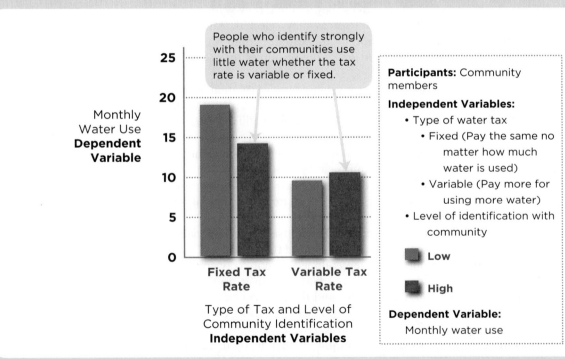

Create small, connected groups. Creating small, connected groups is yet another strategy that reduces competition and increases cooperation in social dilemmas (Dawes, 1980; Edney, 1980). People in small groups are less selfish than those in large groups, perhaps because we can more directly see the consequences of our good (and bad) behavior in small groups (Brewer & Kramer, 1986). For example, you are probably more willing to toss litter on a public highway than you are to toss litter on a street in your neighborhood. We also behave more cooperatively when our choices will be identified to other group members (Schopler, Insko, Drigotas, Wieselquist, Pemberton, & Cox, 1995). As you learned at the start of this chapter, people who are individually identified tend to behave in a more prosocial way than those who behave anonymously.

How can social dilemmas be solved when groups are very large, such as people who live in a given town or attend a specific college? In these cases, it may be difficult for people to directly see the benefits of cooperation, but other strategies can work to increase cooperation. One approach is making a superordinate group identity salient. This involves creating a focus on what all people in the group have in common (e.g., we are all members of this college community; Kramer & Brewer, 1984). Another effective approach is to divide the larger community into subgroups. For example, colleges could increase recycling efforts by reporting the percent of trash recycled by each dorm instead of simply reporting the overall percent of recycling at the school.

Creating consequences for competition. One way to create consequences for competing is to use the **tit-for-tat** strategy. This strategy involves starting with cooperation, and then doing whatever one's partner does on each interaction (e.g., cooperate after a cooperate and compete after a compete). Although cooperators can be taken advantage of, and competition has the potential for greater rewards, the tit-for-tat strategy leads to better overall outcomes for both members in a social dilemma, in part because it helps people protect themselves. After all, people who always cooperate are likely to be exploited by their partners (Komorita, Chan, & Parks, 1993).

tit-for-tat a strategy that involves starting with cooperation, and then doing whatever one's partner does on each interaction (e.g., cooperate after a cooperate and compete after a compete)

Creating consequences for competition as well as rewards for cooperation can increase cooperation in social dilemmas, particularly among those who are initially competitive (Komorita & Barth, 1985; Komorita, Parks, & Hulbert, 1992; Sheldon, 1999). For example, people who receive a bonus for cooperating show more cooperation than those who receive a negative incentive. The Research Focus on Neuroscience describes how cooperation even seems to be rewarding on a neurological level.

RESEARCH FOCUS ON NEUROSCIENCE
How Cooperation Looks in the Brain

Although you might imagine that cooperation is simply something we learn through experience, some research suggests that there are neurological benefits to engaging in cooperating behavior. In one study, researchers examined the areas of the brain that are activated when people are cooperating (Rilling, Gutman, Zeh, Pagnoni, Berns, & Kilt, 2002). Thirty-six women played multiple rounds of Prisoner's Dilemma Game with another woman. On each trial, participants could cooperate with their partner or compete with their partner. As is typical in Prisoner's Dilemma games, participants received the best outcomes for themselves when they competed and their partner cooperated. Researchers used fMRI (functional Magnetic Resonance Imaging) to scan the brains of the participants throughout these trials. When both participants cooperated, the scans revealed consistent activation in brain areas that are associated with reward processing. This type of activation was not present during any of the other pairings of cooperative/compete behavior. This finding suggests that cooperating with someone, even at some cost to one's self, is positively reinforcing at a neurological level: in other words, cooperating with someone else feels good in the brain.

However, there is a downside to creating negative consequences as a strategy for encouraging cooperation: the use of such consequences can undermine people's trust that others are internally motivated to cooperate (Mulder, van Dijk, De Cremer, & Wilke, 2006). In turn, people may trust other group members less when they believe their cooperative behavior is motivated by the external fear of the consequences of failing to cooperate. This is particularly likely when trust within a group is initially high.

Concepts in Context

EXAMPLES OF TYPES OF SOCIAL DILEMMAS AND THEIR SOLUTIONS

FACTOR	EXAMPLE
TYPES OF SOCIAL DILEMMAS	
Common resource dilemma	If each person waters his or her lawn during a drought, soon there won't be enough water for anyone to shower.
Public goods dilemma	Neil always takes a few cents from the "take a penny, leave a penny" jar to help pay his order at the local coffee shop. However, Neil has never left any change in the jar for others.
Prisoner's dilemma	A student is accused of cheating on an exam, and is told that he or she will receive a lesser punishment by identifying another person who also cheated. However, he or she will receive the maximum punishment if he or she chooses not to identify another student who cheated and that person then identifies the first student.
SOLUTIONS TO SOCIAL DILEMMAS	
Regulate use of resources	Tollbooths are used to require people to pay for use of the road.
Communication	Bringing two groups together who both want access to a local park on a given day may help them reach a compromise that will work well for both sides.
Activate prosocial motives	Reminding people at holiday times of those who are less fortunate may lead them to contribute more money to charitable organizations.
Create small groups	Creating a competition between different classrooms in an elementary school for picking up litter can lead each classroom to work together for the common good.
Create consequences for competition	When Taylor and Connor argue over their shared toys, their mother takes the toys away for one week.

HOW DOES CULTURE IMPACT GROUP INFLUENCE?

To examine the impact of priming different types of cultural symbols on cooperation in a prisoner's dilemma task, researchers recruited Chinese American participants (Wong & Hong, 2005). Participants in one condition were primed with Chinese cultural symbols (such as a dragon and a person performing kung fu). Participants in the other condition were primed with American icons (such as the American flag and a scene at a football game). Then the participants played the Prisoner's Dilemma game with either a friend or a stranger. As predicted, participants were more likely to cooperate toward friends when Chinese cultural knowledge was activated than when American cultural knowledge was activated: 77% versus 53%. In contrast, participants showed a similarly low level of cooperation toward strangers after both Chinese and American culture priming (63% versus 59%). These findings indicate that priming different cultures influences people's behavior, and in particular their willingness to cooperate with a friend. This research demonstrates the impact of culture on cooperation in a social dilemma. This section will examine this and other ways in which culture impacts social influence in group settings including social loafing, group decision making, conflict, and social dilemmas.

SOCIAL LOAFING

As described earlier in this chapter, social loafing occurs frequently when groups of people work together on tasks in which each person's individual input is not measured: each person withdraws effort in this situation due to an expectation that their contribution doesn't really matter. However, in collectivistic cultures, individuals may be particularly motivated to have their group seem competent, regardless of whether their own individual input is identified (Karau & Williams, 1993). For people in collectivistic cultures, group harmony and success may be even more important than individual performance (and they could even be evaluated poorly by group members for socially loafing).

The greater ability to see multiple perspectives on an issue by those from collectivistic cultures can lead to better negotiation outcomes compared to the outcomes reached by those from individualistic cultures.

In order to examine the impact of culture on social loafing, researchers assigned 80 Chinese and 72 American children in 6th and 9th grades to complete a task either alone or in pairs (Gabrenya, Wang, & Latané, 1985). This task involved listening to a series of tones that were played through stereo headphones, and noting whether the tones were played to the left ear, right ear, or both. Although there was no effect of culture on rate of social loafing for sixth graders, culture did impact performance for the ninth graders. Specifically, American ninth graders had fewer errors when working on the task alone than when working in pairs, demonstrating their tendency to socially loaf when working in pairs. In contrast, Chinese ninth graders had fewer errors when working on the task in pairs, showing "social striving," meaning they performed better when working with a partner than when working alone.

CONFLICT

Culture may also impact how individuals view the causes of conflict as well as the strategies used to resolve conflict. In one study, researchers asked both American and Chinese students to read several hypothetical scenarios involving conflict (e.g., mother-daughter disagreement, decision to go to school or have fun; Peng & Nisbett, 1999). Then students rated how they would resolve this situation. Seventy-four percent of Americans give an answer that assigns exclusive fault to one side. In contrast, only 28% of the Chinese people responded in a way that assigned fault to one side. Americans also have trouble making sense of contradictions when reading opposing sides of an argument (e.g., family connections are good or bad) and choose a side, whereas Chinese are comfortable believing both.

Does this ability to see both sides in a conflict lead people in collectivistic cultures to achieve better resolutions to conflict? In a word, yes. Participants from the United States and Hong Kong participated in two-party negotiations (Arunachalam, Wall, & Chan, 1998). Hong Kong negotiators achieved higher joint outcomes as well as higher individual outcomes than American negotiators. Similarly, research examining differences in decision-making strategies used by managers in America, Japan, and Hong Kong reveals that Japanese leaders are more willing to listen to different perspectives on a problem than Americans (Cosier, Schwenk, & Dalton, 1992). In addition, compared to American leaders, Japanese leaders tend to exert less control over the decision-making process, which in turn, leads to better decision making.

Cultural differences may also impact the effectiveness of negotiations between people from different cultures. Because people from individualistic and collectivistic cultures may vary in the assumptions they make about others' perspectives, these misunderstandings could make it difficult to reach compromise (Kimmel, 1994). Individualistic cultures typically assume others see negotiation as a business activity, as primarily a form of verbal communication, and that time and deadlines are important. On the other hand, those from collectivistic countries such as Asia and the Middle East may see negotiation as a social activity that is built on a trusting relationship, that communication is often nonverbal, and that because building a relationship takes time, deadlines are not particularly important. In line with this view, Asians pay less attention to verbal expressions and more attention to nonverbal expressions than do Americans (Ambady et al., 1996; Ishii, Reyes, & Kitayama, 2003; Markus & Kitayama, 1991).

People in different cultures also vary in the extent to which they focus on verbal content versus verbal tone (Ishii et al., 2003). In one study with Americans and Japanese, Americans had more trouble ignoring vocal content than vocal tone, showing that Americans focus more on content (e.g., see it as more important, relevant, etc.). In contrast, Japanese people showed greater difficulty ignoring vocal tone than verbal content. This different preference can lead to misunderstandings, when information in cultures is conveyed in different ways.

Think about the numerous ways you could say the word "yes"—with great excitement (yes!), resignation (yes...), confusion (yes?). If Americans rely on content more than tone, all of the "yeses" would be largely understood in the same way. In contrast, if Japanese people rely more on tone, they would ignore the verbal content, and interpret the verbal answer in very different ways.

SOCIAL DILEMMAS

Given the greater emphasis on fulfilling individuals' needs in individualistic cultures compared to collectivistic ones, research on how people solve social dilemmas reveals considerable differences across cultures. In one study, researchers examined rates of cooperation among groups in Japan and in the United States (Wade-Benzoni, Okumura, Brett, Moore, Tenbrunsel, & Bazerman, 2002). Participants in both countries completed a social dilemma exercise in which they needed to manage a real-life crisis in the shark fishing industry. This crisis involved overfishing, meaning that fishers were catching sharks faster than the sharks could reproduce, and thus the resource was being rapidly depleted. The groups were asked to allocate resources between different interests, such as commercial fishers and recreational fishers. As predicted, groups of Japanese decision makers agreed to harvest less and more equally allocate resources than groups of American decision makers. What led to these differences? One factor was expectation: Americans expected others to act more competitively than the Japanese did, and this expectation contributed to Americans' less cooperative behavior. Similarly, and as described at the start of this section, simply reminding Chinese Americans of their American identity led to more competition than reminding them of their Asian identity.

The Big Picture

GROUP INFLUENCE

This chapter included many applications of the three "big ideas" studied in social psychology. The examples below should help you see the connection between group influence and these big ideas and contribute to your understanding of the big picture of social psychology.

THEME	EXAMPLES
The social world influences how we think about ourselves.	• People are less self-aware when in a group than when alone. • In conflict situations, we see our own goals as just and fair. • People underestimate the proportion of resources they take from a common pool.
The social world influences our thoughts, attitudes, and behaviors.	• We make more errors on a math test when we take the test in front of a friend than in front of a stranger. • We exert more effort on a task when working with a low ability partner, if our contributions will be pooled together. • We get more extreme in our views following discussion with others.
Our attitudes and behavior shape the social world around us.	• We see people in other groups in a simplistic and stereotypical way. • We feel more positively towards others once we have worked together on a common goal. • We take goods from a common pool even when we don't contribute to that pool.

This chapter examined factors in group influence, and in particular the power of groups on influencing behavior, decision-making, social dilemmas, and conflict.

YOU LEARNED How do groups influence behavior? This section examined ways in which groups influence behavior. You learned about social facilitation, and three explanations for this effect (distraction, evaluation apprehension, mere presence). This section described social loafing, and the impact of identifiable contributions, contributions' impact, and task importance on this process. This section also examined deindividuation and the role of accountability, anonymity, and decreases in self-awareness in leading to deindividuation. Finally, this section examined the link between cohesion and group performance. You also learned why most restaurants impose a mandatory tip on groups of five or more.

YOU LEARNED How can the group process influence decision making? This section examined how the group process influences decision making. You learned about group polarization and the factors that contribute, including hearing more persuasive arguments and learning group norms. This section also describes the factors leading to groupthink, including overestimating the group's invulnerability and morality, closemindedness, and pressure toward uniformity. You also learned about three models of leadership: the trait or "great person" model, transformational versus transactional leadership, and the contingency model. You also learned that people who are oriented toward both achievement and interpersonal dynamics are the most effective leaders.

YOU LEARNED How do groups handle social dilemmas? This section examined how groups handle social dilemmas, in which the needs of the individual conflict with the needs of the group. You learned about types of resource dilemmas, including the common resource dilemma, the public goods dilemma, and the prisoner's dilemma. This section also described solutions to social dilemmas, including regulating resources, communication, and creating small and connected groups. You also learned that describing a prisoner's dilemmas game as "the Wall Street game" leads to higher levels of competition than describing it as "the community game."

YOU LEARNED How do groups handle conflict? This section examined how groups handle conflict, including the factors leading to conflict and strategies used to resolve conflict. You learned about factors that lead to conflict, including societal beliefs, biased perceptions, mirror-image perceptions, and entrapment. You also learned about strategies for resolving conflict, including equal status conflict, common ground, GRIT, bargaining, mediation, and arbitration. You also learned that people on both sides of the abortion debate see the differences between people in these two groups as more extreme than they actually are.

YOU LEARNED How does culture impact group influence? This section examined the impact of culture on group influence. You learned about the impact of culture on social loafing, conflict, and social dilemmas. You also learned why Chinese Americans are more likely to cooperate with friends after seeing a picture of a Chinese dragon than an American flag.

KEY TERMS

arbitration 313

bargaining 312

collective effort model 294

common resource dilemma 316

conflict 307

deindividuation 295

entrapment 309

GRIT (graduated and reciprocated initiatives in tension reduction) 312

group polarization 299

groupthink 301

hostile media phenomenon 309

integrative agreement 313

mediation 313

mirror-image perception 308

prisoner's dilemma 317

public goods dilemma 317

realistic group conflict theory 308

risky shift 299

social compensation 295

social dilemma 316

social facilitation 291

social loafing 294

tit-for-tat 321

QUESTIONS FOR REVIEW

1. What are four ways in which groups influence behavior?
2. Describe three factors that influence group decision making.
3. Describe two factors that lead to conflict between groups, and two ways of reducing conflict.
4. What are two types of social dilemmas, and what are some solutions to such dilemmas?
5. Describe how culture influences social loafing, decision making, conflict, and social dilemmas.

TAKE ACTION!

1. You are a professor assigning a group project. What do you do to make sure all students give the project their all?
2. You are the president of a student group that must make recommendations to the college administration about strategies for improving the quality of education and student life. What strategies could you use to avoid problems associated with group decision making, such as group polarization and groupthink?
3. You have just been hired as a divorce mediator by a local law firm. What two things could you do to reduce conflict between opposing spouses?
4. You are a senator from California, a state with some consistent problems with water conservation. What three things could you do to try to encourage Californians to conserve water?
5. You are working with people from different cultures on a negotiation project. How might you work to avoid misperceptions that can lead to conflict between people from different backgrounds?

RESEARCH CONNECTIONS

Try some of these research activities to gain experience in conducting and evaluating research, and to increase your understanding of research methods and techniques in social psychology.

Visit WileyPLUS for more activities and interactive research tools! (www.wileyplus.com)

Participate in Research

Activity 1 The Impact of Task on Social Facilitation: This chapter has described how physiological arousal can lead us to perform better on some tasks, but worse on others. Think about how arousal has influenced your performance on different types of tasks in the past.

Activity 2 The Importance of Leadership: One factor that influences how well groups function is the style and characteristics of the group leader. Think about the different groups you are in. What types of leadership strategies would work for each of these groups and why?

Activity 3 The Hazards of Biased Perceptions: You learned in this chapter about how people see the gap between their own and others' attitudes as larger than it actually is, which in turn can lead to greater conflict. Go to WileyPLUS to rate your agreement with various political statements, and your perceptions of how those with the opposite view would rate such statements.

Activity 4 **Strategies for Resolving Conflict:** This chapter described how creating consequences for competition can reduce conflict. You can go online to see how your behavior influences another person's behavior in ways that can either escalate or reduce conflict in a prisoner's dilemma game.

Activity 5 **The Impact of Culture on Conflict:** The final section of this chapter described how culture impacts social interaction in group settings. Go online to rate the effectiveness of different strategies of conflict resolution. Then you can see how people from different cultures would rate these distinct strategies.

Test a Hypothesis

One of the common findings in research on group processes is that individuals in groups exert less overall effort than individuals working alone. To test whether this hypothesis is true, recruit some friends to work on a brainstorming task. Tell half of your friends to come up with various ideas as a group, and tell others to come up with ideas individually. This approach will let you see whether people in groups do socially loaf, and thereby come up with fewer ideas than those who work individually.

Design a Study

To design your own study testing the factors that can lead to groupthink, go to WileyPLUS. You'll be able to choose the type of study you want to conduct (self-report, observational/naturalistic, or experimental), choose your own independent and dependent variables, and form your own hypothesis.

10 Stereotypes, Prejudice,

What factors contribute to stereotyping and prejudice?

RESEARCH FOCUS ON GENDER
The Hazardous Impact of Stereotypes on Women's Achievement in the Workplace

What are the consequences of being stereotyped?

What factors make stereotyping inevitable?

RESEARCH FOCUS ON NEUROSCIENCE
How the Brain Responds to In-Group and Out-Group Faces

How can social and cognitive interventions help overcome stereotypes?

How does CULTURE influence prejudice and stereotypes?

Did you ever wonder?

On August 23, 2005, Hurricane Katrina formed as a tropical depression over the southeastern Bahamas. By the time Hurricane Katrina reached Mississippi and Louisiana, its heavy winds and storm surges severely weakened the city of New Orleans's levee system and damaged most of the major roads traveling into and out of the city. Katrina also caused widespread loss of life—an estimated 1,836 people died during the storm and its immediate aftermath.

Within days of Katrina's August 29, 2005 landfall, widespread public criticism arose about the government's response to Hurricane Katrina, including condemnations of mismanagement and lack of leadership in the relief efforts in response to the storm and its aftermath. Some people believed that race and class contributed to delays in government response. New Orleans, with a population that is 67% Black, is one of the poorest cities in the United States, with 34% of households living below the federal poverty line. Most of the affluent (and largely White) people in New Orleans were able to

Education
CONNECTIONS
Reducing the Effects
of Stereotype Threats
in the Classroom

Health
CONNECTIONS
The Impact of Racism
on Physical Health

Business
CONNECTIONS
Examining the Effects
of Affirmative Action
Policies

and Discrimination

flee Hurricane Katrina in their own cars. In contrast, the poorer (and largely Black) people had no way to escape, and many remained in New Orleans without water, food, or shelter. As noted by the Reverend Jesse Jackson, race was "at least a factor" in the slow response. "We have an amazing tolerance for Black pain," he told CNN.

This chapter will examine how social psychological factors may have contributed to the government's response—or lack thereof—to Hurricane Katrina. In addition, you'll find out...

Q A Why can discriminating against someone else make you feel good?

Q A Why can watching television ads lead women to avoid math and science careers?

Q A Why does a shooter fire faster when seeing a Black man than a White man?

Q A Why does adopting more tolerant views about women and gay people reduce discrimination against gay people?

Q A Why do older Americans experience more hearing problems than older Chinese people?

Associated Press

We all hold beliefs about groups of people, and beliefs that associate a whole group of people with certain traits are called **stereotypes**. You probably have a stereotype for what type of person drives a BMW convertible, a Lincoln Town Car, and a Honda Accord. Most of us rely on stereotypes on a regular basis, typically to describe people who differ from ourselves in some way. You may believe that blondes have more fun, left-handed people are creative, or Miss America contestants are not so bright.

Although stereotypes may sometimes be relatively harmless, they can lead to **prejudice**, meaning hostile or negative feelings about people based on their membership in a certain group, and **discrimination**, meaning behavior directed against persons solely because of their membership in a particular group. And prejudice and discrimination are certainly not harmless. This chapter will examine how social psychological factors contribute to stereotyping, prejudice, and discrimination, the consequences of being stereotyped, and strategies for overcoming these harmful effects.

HOW DO SOCIAL PSYCHOLOGICAL FACTORS CONTRIBUTE TO STEREOTYPING AND PREJUDICE?

stereotypes beliefs that associate a whole group of people with certain traits

prejudice hostile or negative feelings about people based on their membership in a certain group

discrimination behavior directed against persons because of their membership in a particular group

Think about a time in which you've behaved badly to someone of a different race or gender, and what factors might have motivated your behavior. Research in psychology suggests that we may engage in negative behavior toward others when we feel badly about ourselves. Steve Fein and Steve Spencer (1997) designed a study to examine whether people whose self-esteem is threatened are more likely to use stereotypes. Participants came into the lab and were given either positive or negative feedback about their intelligence. Then participants were asked to evaluate a job candidate, based on her resume, a photograph, and a videotape of her interview. In half of the cases, the woman was named Maria D'Agnostino and portrayed as Italian. In the other half, she was named Julie Goldberg and portrayed as Jewish. (This study was conducted at a school in which there was a strong negative stereotype about Jewish American women, but not about Italian American women.)

As predicted, participants who had received negative feedback about their own intelligence rated Julie Goldberg's personality more negatively (even though all of the materials were the same) than those who rated Maria D'Agnostino. There were no differences in ratings of the candidates for those who received positive feedback. Second, those who had rated the Jewish woman more negatively had a greater boost in self-esteem following the experiment.

These results indicate that receiving a blow to one's own self-esteem motivates the expression of prejudice, and that the expression of this prejudice then boosts one's own self-esteem. This section will discuss this and other ways in which social psychological factors contribute to stereotypes and prejudice, including social learning, social categorization, realistic conflict theory, social identity theory, and cognitive errors.

SOCIAL LEARNING

As we learned in Chapter 6, people form attitudes through broad learning principles, such as classical conditioning, operant conditioning, and modeling (Bandura, 1986). Children may receive rewards and punishments for expressing particular attitudes or engaging in particular behaviors toward others. For example, a child who is punished for using a derogatory term for gays or lesbians learns that using this type of stereotypical expression is unacceptable, and should be less likely to use such a term again. Similarly, children often form their attitudes about people in different groups from watching (and listening) to their parents. If a child hears a parent express negative attitudes about people who hold different religious beliefs from their own, or avoid interactions with people with such beliefs, the child is likely to form negative beliefs about people in this group and potentially to act themselves in a more biased way (Towles-Schwen & Fazio, 2001).

Parents aren't the only people who can serve as models—we often look to our peers for guidance in forming our own attitudes and behaviors. Hearing someone express prejudiced attitudes, watching someone engage in discrimination, or observing someone respond favorably to a joke regarding a stereotype all contribute to the formation and maintenance of stereotypes (Crandall, Eshleman, & O'Brien, 2002). For example, Whites who hear someone express racist views express less strong antiracist positions than those without such exposure (Blanchard, Crandall, Brigham, & Vaughn, 1994). Simply hearing someone use an ethnic slur regarding a Black person leads to especially low evaluations of this person (Greenberg & Pyzszczynski, 1985; Kirkland, Greenberg, & Pyszczynski, 1987; Simon & Greenberg, 1996).

Parents who have friends from different backgrounds and express tolerant and accepting attitudes toward other groups model non-prejudicial attitudes for their children.

Social learning is one explanation for why people are often willing to express certain types of prejudice, but not others (Crandall et al., 2002). For example, many people feel relatively comfortable expressing prejudice against racists, drug addicts, KKK members, child molesters, terrorists, and ex-convicts. However, they are unlikely to feel comfortable expressing prejudice against people in other stigmatized groups, such as people who are blind, elderly, or Latinos. People therefore learn to avoid discriminating against those in the "not acceptable" category, but may show a high level of prejudice to people in those groups for whom there is social support for such discrimination. Similarly, many people who consider themselves non-prejudiced because they consciously avoid discriminating against people based on their race or gender may feel comfortable telling a joke about a pedophile or a "red-neck."

Believing that other people agree with our stereotypes also increases their strength and accessibility, and thereby makes them more resistant to change (Stangor, Sechrist, & Jost, 2001; Wittenbrink & Henly, 1996). In one study, White students rated their attitudes toward Blacks (Sechrist & Stangor, 2001). Some students were then told that these beliefs were common—that 81% of the students at their school shared their beliefs. Other students were told that these beliefs were uncommon—that only 19% of the students at their school shared their beliefs. Receiving information about the normality of their views influenced participants' beliefs about the percentage of Blacks who possessed positive traits (such as athletic, hardworking, musical, and emotionally expressive) as well as negative traits (such as poor, violent, irresponsible, and uneducated). Specifically, students who were high in prejudice who received information that their views were shared by others believed that a greater percentage of Blacks possessed more negative traits and fewer positive traits compared to those who received information that their

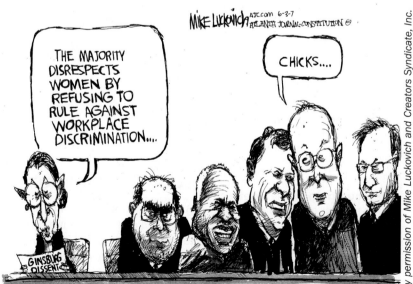

"Chicks..." *(Luckovich – Atlanta Journal-Constitution, 2007).*

FIGURE
10.1

DOES CONSENSUS WITH PREJUDICED BELIEFS AFFECT BEHAVIOR?

In this study, White students rated their attitudes toward African Americans, and were then told either that these beliefs were common or uncommon. Participants then sat in a waiting room with an African American student. High-prejudiced White students who received information that many others shared their views (high consensus) sat farther away from an African American student than those who learned that many others disagreed with their views (low consensus). Low-prejudiced White students showed the opposite patterning, and sat closer to an African American after learning others shared their views than after learning others did not.

Source: Sechrist, G. B., & Stangor, C. (2001). Perceived consensus influences intergroup behavior and stereotype accessibility. *Journal of Personality and Social Psychology, 80*, 645-654. Copyright © 2001 by the American Psychological Association. Reproduced with permission. The use of APA information does not imply endorsement by APA.

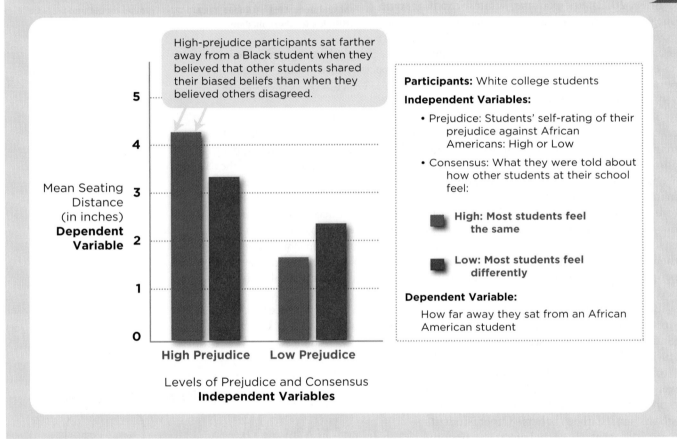

views were not shared by others. Receiving information about the normality of their views also influenced behavior, such as how close they sat next to a Black student (see Figure 10.1).

SOCIAL CATEGORIZATION

Another factor that contributes to stereotyping and prejudice is our tendency to quickly classify people into groups on the basis of common attributes, meaning into in-groups (e.g., people like us) versus out-groups (e.g., people not like us; Billig & Tajfel, 1973). This type of **social categorization** can even be done on meaningless grounds, such as your eye color, shoe size, or the state where you were born. This classification of people into two groups has two consequences that contribute to stereotyping—the **out-group homogeneity effect** and **in-group favoritism**.

social categorization the tendency for individuals to classify people into groups on the basis of common attributes

out-group homogeneity effect people's tendency to underestimate the variability of out-group members compared to the variability of in-group members

in-group favoritism the tendency to discriminate in favor of those in your in-group versus your out-group

Out-group homogeneity effect. The out-group homogeneity effect refers to people's general tendency to see out-group members as very similar to one another, while seeing members of our in-group as more diverse (Judd & Park, 1988; Judd, Ryan, & Park, 1991; Mullen & Hu, 1989; Ostrom & Sedikides, 1992). For example, we may see students who attend a different school as a single group of very similar people (e.g., students at *that other school*), but divide people at our school into athletes, musicians, artists, etc. Students in my classes make this mistake frequently when they describe students who attend a rival college as all fitting a single stereotype, yet see students who attend their own (virtually identical) college as all having unique and distinct qualities.

Why do people hold such different beliefs about in-group versus out-group members? One reason is that we typically have less exposure to and familiarity with people in the out-group than those in our in-group (Harasty, 1997; Park, Ryan, & Judd, 1992). Greater familiarity with a group leads to greater perceived differentiation and variability within that group (Linville, Fischer, & Salovey, 1989). For example, women who join sororities see less variability in women in other sororities later in the semester than earlier, presumably as they spend more time with women in their own group (Ryan & Bogart, 1997). In fact, babies as young as nine months are better at discriminating between faces within their own ethnic group than those from other ethnic groups, suggesting that this same-race effect occurs quite early in life (Kelly, Quinn, Slater, Lee, Ge, & Pascalis, 2007). In line with this view, Korean children who are adopted by White families between the ages of three and nine are better at recognizing White faces than Asian ones (Sangrigoli, Pallier, Argenti, Ventureyra, & de Schonen, 2005). In contrast, Korean children who grow up in Korea recognize Korean faces better than White ones. The Law Connections box describes another real-world example of the hazards of the out-group homogeneity effect.

In-group favoritism. Social categorization also leads to the tendency to discriminate in favor of those in your in-group versus your out-group (Brewer, 1979; Chatman & von Hippel, 2001; Reynolds, Turner, & Haslam, 2000). For example, jurors give shorter sentences to those in their same ethnic group who are accused of crimes (Sommers & Ellsworth, 2000). Amazingly enough, this in-group favoritism occurs even when groups are based on meaningless criteria, such as the number of dots people see in a picture or the letters they choose at random from a bag (Crisp, Hewstone, & Rubin, 2001).

What factors contribute to in-group favoritism? One factor is self-interest: We are motivated to favor those in our in-group because those people are more likely to favor us in return (Vivian & Berkowitz, 1992, 1993). This preference for those in our in-group is acquired early in life and remains fairly stable: although self-reported prejudice decreases over time, White six-year-olds show the same pro-White, anti-Black bias on subtle tests as older children and adults (Baron & Banaji, 2006). We even rate words referring to our in-group (us, we) more positively than those referring to out-groups (e.g., they, them), suggesting that this preference for those in our in-group occurs at an automatic level (Otten & Wentura, 1999; Perdue, Dovidio, Gurtman, & Tyler, 1990).

In-group favoritism is also more likely when people heavily identify with the group, and when group norms are salient (Gagnon & Bourhis, 1996; Levin & Sidanius, 1999; Marques, Abrams, Paez, & Martinez-Taboada, 1998). Whites who identify strongly with their White racial identity and think about how an affirmative action policy will impact Whites are less supportive of such a policy than those who identify less strongly with their racial identity or who think about how this policy will impact Blacks (Lowery, Unzueta, Knowles, & Goff, 2006).

Another factor that contributes to in-group favoritism is a person's level of **social dominance orientation**, a personality variable which refers to the extent to which one wants his or her in-group to dominate and be superior to out-groups (see Rate Yourself; Guimond, Dambrun, Michinov, & Duarte, 2003; Pratto, Sidanius, Stallworth, & Malle, 1994; Whitley, 1999). Not surprisingly, people who

social dominance orientation
a personality variable describing the extent to which one wants his or her in-group to dominate and be superior to out-groups

Law

The Hazards of Cross-Race Identification

In the early morning hours in June 1982, a Florida woman reported that two Latino men broke into her home and sexually assaulted her. After the men left, she called the police, who issued an all-points bulletin with general descriptions of two Latino men, one of whom had no shirt and no hair (which is how the woman described the man in her bedroom). Within minutes, an officer stopped several Cuban American men in a nearby convenience store parking lot; only one of them (Orlando Bosquete) had little or no hair and was not wearing a shirt. The victim was taken to the area to see whether she could identify her attacker; from 20 feet away, in a police car in the middle of the night, she identified Bosquete as the man who had attacked her. She was shown a photograph of Bosquete the night before she testified in court, when she repeated this identification, which led to his conviction. Orlando Bosquete was sentenced to 65 years in prison for rape based solely on an identification by the victim, a white woman. After serving 23 years in prison, he was released in 2006 after DNA tests revealed that he was not the attacker. This is just one example of a case in which white witnesses have identified a person of a different race as the perpetrator of a crime, and were later found to have identified the wrong person.

Why does this misidentification occur? One explanation is that people engage in deeper processing when seeing a same-race person than a cross-race person (Chance & Goldstein, 1981). Another factor could be familiarity. For example, Whites tend to be less accurate in recognizing Blacks (the out-group) than they are recognizing members of their in-group. People tend to see out-group members as looking very similar to one another, and they show greater accuracy for recognizing in-group members than out-group members. This phenomenon is called the cross-race identification bias (Anthony, Cooper, & Mullen, 1992; Slone, Brigham, & Meissner, 2000; although see Bothwell, Brigham, & Malpass, 1989).

However, it's surprising to note that accuracy is similar for Blacks' out-group and in-group (Ryan, 1996). One explanation for this difference is that Whites, who are in the majority group (there are more Whites in the United States than Blacks), have less familiarity with Blacks than Blacks do with whites. Another explanation is that members of groups who are low in power and social status need to know more about members of high-power groups than those in high-power groups need to know about members of low-power groups. Regardless of the process that leads to cross-race identification bias, this perceptual error can lead to significant problems in eyewitness identification, which is a serious issue. Psychologists now testify in court about the dangers of relying on eyewitness testimony, especially in the absence of other corroborating evidence.

Associated Press

are high in social dominance orientation are more likely to engage in-group favoritism, in part because those who want to maintain the superior position of their own in-group are particularly motivated to derogate out-group members and reward in-group members as a way of maintaining their superiority.

In turn, those who believe that their own group should be dominant over other groups are more prejudiced against people in lower-status groups, including women, homosexuals, and minority group members. This prejudice may come, at least in part, from a strong motivation to internalize beliefs that legitimize the group differences (e.g., men are motivated to believe that women are less intelligent than they themselves are; Guimond, 2000). In one study, White participants rated the percentage of Blacks who they believed held various traits (e.g., poor, violent, intelligent; Strube & Rahimi, 2006). Those who were high on social dominance orientation held the least positive views of Blacks, and moreover, believed that other students held the same views.

REALISTIC GROUP CONFLICT THEORY

Another explanation for why people tend to favor in-group members and derogate out-group members is self-interest due to direct competition for limited resources (Esses, Jackson, & Armstrong, 1998; Jackson, 1993). Specifically, **realistic group conflict theory** posits that the animosity between different groups, such as that between Blacks and Whites, men and women, and Arabs and Israelis, is a result of individuals' self-interest motives, in terms of competition for jobs, land, and power. For example, people have a more positive attitude toward Asian Americans when they believe they will be working with an Asian American student on a chemistry project—in which case this partner should be seen as an advantage—than when they believe they will be working with an African American partner and competing against an Asian American student (Maddux, Galinsky, Cuddy, & Polifroni, 2008). In the second case, Whites are concerned about being out-performed by an Asian student, who indeed represents a realistic threat to their own achievement, and thus show more prejudiced beliefs.

Although group competition can lead to prejudice and conflict, people who have not been directly impacted by group conflict over resources also show prejudicial attitudes and behaviors. This points to other factors in leading to conflict between groups— symbolic racism and relative deprivation.

realistic group conflict theory
the theory that competition between groups for resources leads to conflict

Modern racism. **Modern racism** describes cases in which people's negative feelings about out-group members are not rooted specifically in their group membership (e.g., race, gender), but rather in more general beliefs about people's moral values (Haddock, Zanna, & Esses, 1993; Sears & Henry, 2003; Stephan et al., 2002). For example, people could see discrimination against Blacks as caused not by racism per se, but rather by the belief that Blacks often fail to work hard enough to succeed, expect too much too fast, and have gotten more than they deserve. In one study, researchers examined voting patterns in two mayoral elections in Los Angeles that pitted a White candidate against a Black candidate (Kinder & Sears, 1981). Feelings of symbolic racism were the major factor influencing voting against the Black candidate. Direct racial threats to Whites' lives, such as jobs, schools, neighborhoods, and safety, had little effect.

modern racism an underlying prejudice in which people's negative feelings about out-group members are not rooted specifically in their group membership (e.g., race, gender), but rather in more general beliefs about people's moral values

Both liberal and conservative Whites express prejudice toward Blacks, but do so in distinct ways (Nail, Harton, & Decker, 2003). On the one hand, conservatives know that it is not appropriate to express prejudiced attitudes, given the social norms against appearing racist, and therefore show public compliance to such norms. However, they continue to hold negative beliefs about Blacks, which manifest themselves in subtle ways. For example, conservatives are more likely to oppose affirmative action programs, and are more lenient in their views regarding a European American who is facing criminal charges than a Black in the same situation.

On the other hand, liberals have generally internalized non-prejudiced values and social norms, and truly support a society with greater opportunities for all. Nonetheless, many White liberals hold negative feelings toward Blacks at an unconscious and emotional level. These types of negative feelings and beliefs about Blacks conflict with liberals' desire to maintain their view that all people are equal, and thereby create feelings of discomfort or uneasiness in the presence of Blacks. For example, White liberals show greater physiological arousal, such as sweat and heart rate, when they are touched by a Black experimenter compared to a European American experimenter. This combination of an endorsement of non-prejudiced attitudes and beliefs coupled with unconscious negative attitudes toward Blacks is called aversive racism (Gaertner & Dovidio, 1986).

Relative deprivation. Another aspect of realistic group conflict theory that can lead to prejudice is **relative deprivation**, meaning discontent caused by the belief that one fares poorly compared to people in other groups (Ellemers & Bos, 1998; Olson, Herman, & Zanna, 1986). This prejudice can occur even in the absence of *absolute deprivation* (when one's own resources are directly threatened by people in other groups). In line with this view, people who experience relative deprivation have more negative attitudes toward out-group members, as do participants who believe they are more advantaged than others (Guimond & Dambrun, 2002). Students who are told they will have either a much more difficult or a much easier time finding jobs in the future are more likely to hold prejudicial attitudes toward immigrants and express support for restrictive immigration policies. These findings suggest that prejudice can be caused by intergroup competition for resources (in line with relative deprivation

relative deprivation the feeling of discontent caused by the belief that one fares poorly compared to people in other groups

theory), but can also be used to justify the preferential treatment of one's own-group.

SOCIAL IDENTITY THEORY: THE ROLE OF SELF-ESTEEM

social identity theory a theory that posits that each person strives to enhance his or her self-esteem, which is composed of two parts: a personal identity and a social identity

Prejudice can also occur when people are trying to improve their own feelings of self-worth. According to **social identity theory**, each person strives to enhance his or her self-esteem, which is composed of two parts: a personal identity and a social identity (Tajfel, 1982). Because our group memberships impact our thoughts, feelings, and behavior, we are motivated to affiliate with successful groups as a way of increasing our own feelings of self-worth (Smith & Henry, 1996; Smith & Tyler, 1997; Snyder, Lassegard, & Ford, 1986). In turn, people can feel good about themselves by calling attention to their connection to successful groups (e.g., people from Texas after Bush is elected president, Blacks after Serena Williams wins Wimbledon, and so on). In sum, people favor their in-groups over their out-groups in order to enhance their self-esteem.

Social identity theory also posits that threats to one's self-esteem increase the need for in-group favoritism (Tajfel, 1982). Therefore, people whose group is threatened and those who feel bad about themselves develop more in-group identification and are more likely to derogate out-group members (Branscombe & Wann, 1994; Esses & Zanna, 1995; Forgas & Fiedler, 1996; Marques et al., 1998). For example, White students who receive negative feedback from an experimenter are more likely to make stereotypic word completions related to Black stereotypes— meaning to complete word fragments in a stereotypic way (e.g., —ITOR is more likely to be completed as JAN-itor than MON-itor) than those who receive positive or no feedback (Spencer, Fein, Wolfe, Fong, & Dunn, 1998). Similarly, and as described at the start of this section, people who feel badly about themselves are more likely to derogate a Jewish applicant than those who do not feel badly (Fein & Spencer, 1997).

According to social identity theory, derogating out-group members also enhances one's own self-esteem, especially for those who strongly identify with

Questioning the Research

People who receive negative feedback are more likely to complete word fragments in a stereotypic way. But this research doesn't explain why negative feedback leads to stereotyping. What process might account for this association? How could you test your hypothesis?

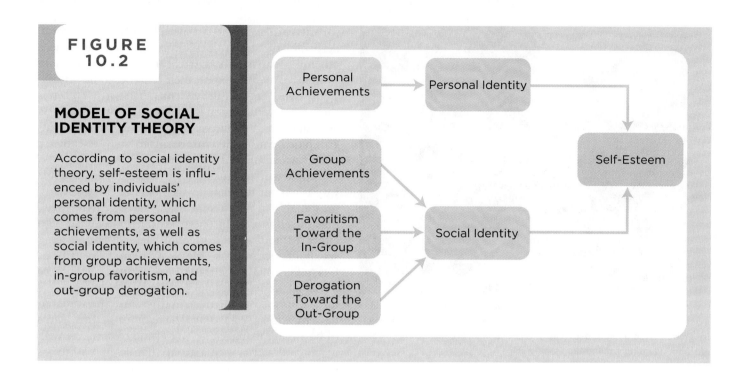

FIGURE
10.2

MODEL OF SOCIAL IDENTITY THEORY

According to social identity theory, self-esteem is influenced by individuals' personal identity, which comes from personal achievements, as well as social identity, which comes from group achievements, in-group favoritism, and out-group derogation.

Personal Achievements → Personal Identity → Self-Esteem

Group Achievements

Favoritism Toward the In-Group → Social Identity → Self-Esteem

Derogation Toward the Out-Group

the in-group (Gagnon & Bourhis, 1996; Tajfel, 1982). In line with this view, people who discriminate in favor of the in-group report higher self-esteem than those who are not given this opportunity, suggesting that intergroup discrimination increases self-esteem (Oakes & Turner, 1980). In fact, people with high self-esteem are more likely to respond to threats by derogating the out-group and enhancing the in-group than those with low self-esteem (Crocker & Luhtanen, 1990; Crocker, Thompson, McGraw, & Ingerman, 1987).

Social identity motives, including in-group favoritism as well as out-group derogation, are particularly likely to occur under specific conditions—that is, being part of a small group, having marginal status within the group, and the status of the in-group. Let's examine each of these conditions.

Group size. The size of the in-group needs to be small enough for people to feel unique, which is why minority groups tend to have greater group loyalty than majority groups (Brewer & Pickett, 1999). This is one reason why groups of minority students are much more commonly formed (such as the Black Student Union, Women's Center, Gay and Lesbian Alliance) than those of majority groups (a reason why you probably haven't heard about a White Student Union, or a Heterosexual Alliance).

Status within group. People who have a marginal status in the in-group are more likely to derogate out-group members, particularly in the presence of in-group members (Noel, Wann, & Branscombe, 1995). Fraternity and

Associated Press

People who believe that liberal immigration policies will make it more difficult for themselves, or members of their group, to find jobs tend to hold more negative attitudes toward immigrants and support more restrictive immigration policies.

Gay/lesbian/bisexual/transgender (GLBT) alliance groups often provide much needed support to members of minority groups. Members of majority groups, such as heterosexuals in this example, are less likely to benefit from adopting such group memberships.

sorority pledges, who are peripherally in the group, derogate other fraternities/sororities when they believe other in-group members will hear their responses more so than when they expect their remarks to be private. Those who are full-fledged members of the groups show no differentiation in their out-group derogation as a function of public versus private expression. Out-group derogation therefore seems to work to enhance one's own status in an in-group.

People who feel their identity is threatened in some way often act hostilely to members of other groups, presumably in an attempt to increase their own feelings of self-worth. In one study, men interacted with either a traditional or a feminist female partner on a social interaction task (Maass, Cadinu, Guarnieri, & Grasselli, 2003). The traditional partner wants to be a teacher, and decides not to be a lawyer because it is more appropriate for men, and because she wants to have time to have a family. The feminist partner wants to be a bank manager, is "not afraid to compete with men," and works with a group that defends women's rights. As part of the study, participants were asked to send each other photographic images (including pornographic or neutral images) and to respond to these images. Men sent more pornographic images to the feminist woman than to the traditional woman, presumably because they felt threatened by that person's success and ambition.

Status of the in-group. Groups that are threatened with inferiority also take particular pleasure at another group's failure—even if that failure will not directly benefit them in any way. In one study, researchers examined how Dutch soccer fans felt after their German rivals lost to the Croatian team in the 1998 Soccer World Cup (Leach, Spears, Branscombe, & Doosje, 2003). Dutch soccer fans who first thought about how poorly their team typically did in the World Cup experienced greater pleasure with the German loss than fans who did not think about their chronic inferiority.

COGNITIVE BIASES

As described in Chapter 5, people often use shortcuts in their thinking, and these faulty problem-solving strategies can lead to stereotyping. These biases include illusory correlation, tokenism, the ultimate attribution error, the contrast effect, and perceptual confirmation.

Illusory correlation. One cognitive bias that contributes to stereotyping is **illusory correlation**, which describes an overestimation of the association between variables that are only slightly or not at all correlated (Hamilton & Gifford, 1976; Hamilton & Rose, 1980; Johnson & Mullen, 1994; McConnell, Sherman, & Hamilton, 1994). Because people pay particular attention to things that are novel or unique, people who are distinctive are more salient—they basically stick out more. In turn, behaviors committed by members of small or rare groups receive more attention and are more memorable than the same behaviors committed by members of common groups (Risen, Gilovich, & Dunning, 2007). People then overestimate how frequently that behavior is performed by that group. As Anne Frank wrote in her diary, "What one Christian does is his own responsibility, what one Jew does is thrown back at all Jews" (Frank, 1993, p. 239).

Here's a real-world example of the impact of illusory correlation. Fewer people in the world are homosexual than heterosexual, and child molestation is (fortunately) a relatively rare behavior. However, because both homosexual orientation and child molestation are unique, people often see them as going together more

illusory correlation the tendency to see a correlation between two events when in reality, no such association exists

frequently than they actually do (e.g., holding the belief that homosexuals are particularly likely to engage in inappropriate sexual behavior with children). In reality, of course, heterosexual men are statistically the most likely to abuse children.

Tokenism. The cognitive bias of *tokenism* describes the case in which individuals serve as the only representative of their group in a larger setting (Cohen & Swim, 1995). Because members of minority groups are distinct and highly salient, their behaviors get blown out of proportion (Taylor, Crocker, Fiske, Sprinzen, & Winkler, 1979). The token person is seen as having a greater impact on whatever happens in the group, is evaluated more extremely, and is more likely to be remembered. For example, observers recall more information said by the token than by other group members (Lord & Saenz, 1985).

What are the effects of tokenism? Being in the token position can make people feel uncomfortable. Women who expect to be the only woman in a group are more likely than nontoken women to prefer a different group and to desire a change in the gender composition of the group (Cohen & Swim, 1995). These effects are particularly strong if the women are less confident about the upcoming task. Similarly, my husband experienced the uncomfortable feeling of serving as a token when he took a class on feminist theories of the law. He was the only man in the class, and thus was constantly called upon, by the teacher as well as other students, to give the "male perspective" on whatever topic they were discussing. This feeling of discomfort may help explain why people who are the only representative of their group in a given situation can experience worse performance (see Figure 10.3; Sekaquaptewa & Thompson, 2002).

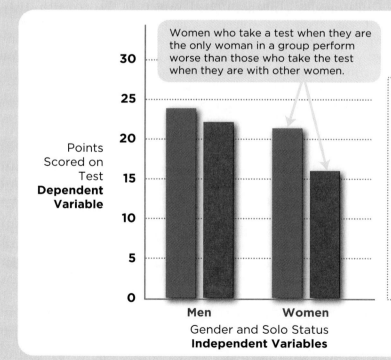

FIGURE 10.3

DOES BEING A TOKEN MEMBER OF A GROUP AFFECT PERFORMANCE?

Students took a math test either in a group of entirely members of the other sex or in a group with both men and women. For women, being the token member of their gender in a group led to lower scores. Men's performance was not influenced by the composition of the group.

Source: Sekaquaptewa, D., & Thompson, M. (2002). The differential effects of solo status on members of high- and low-status groups. *Personality and Social Psychology Bulletin, 28*, 694-707.

Women who take a test when they are the only woman in a group perform worse than those who take the test when they are with other women.

Points Scored on Test
Dependent Variable

Men   Women
Gender and Solo Status
Independent Variables

Participants: College students

Independent Variables:
- Gender: Male or Female
- Solo status:

  Non-Solo: There are others of same gender in the group.

  Solo: Student is only one of his or her gender in the group

Dependent Variable:
Number of points scored on an oral exam

ultimate attribution error an error in which people make dispositional attributions for negative behavior and situational attributions for positive behavior by out-group members, yet show the reverse attributions for successes and failures for in-group members

belief in a just world the phenomenon in which people believe that bad things happen to bad people and good things happen to good people

How do you see former Vice Presidential candidate Sarah Palin? People's views of strong women can be colored by their expectations that women will be generally passive and gentle.

Ultimate attribution error. Another cognitive bias that can lead to stereotypes and prejudice is the **ultimate attribution error** in which people make different attributions for success and failure for in-group versus out-group members (Hewstone, 1990; Hewstone & Ward, 1985; Pettigrew, 1979). Specifically, people tend to make dispositional, or internal, attributions for negative behavior by those in an out-group, whereas they tend to make situational, or external, attributions for the same behavior if committed by someone in their in-group. In one study, Black and White college students read a scenario in which a Black or a White person was fired (Chatman & von Hippel, 2001). Both Blacks and Whites showed in-group attribution biases, judging the firing as caused by internal factors, such as personality and intelligence, for out-group members but by external factors, such as situational pressures and circumstances beyond the person's control, for in-group members.

Why do we make these different attributions for negative things that occur to people in our in-group versus those in our out-group? In part because these attributions help us feel safe in an often unpredictable world. So, if we believe that women who are raped have "asked for it" in some way, perhaps due to drinking alcohol, wearing skimpy clothing, or walking alone late at night, we can feel that this type of bad thing won't happen to us. This phenomenon describes **the belief in a just world**, meaning we assume bad things happen to bad people and good things happen to good people (Lerner, 1980).

Unfortunately, this tendency to make different attributions for in-group versus out-group members can lead to scapegoating and "blaming the victim" (Lerner & Miller, 1978). In one study, participants read about the behavior of a young woman who was friendly to a man at a party (Janoff-Bulman, Timko, & Carli, 1985). Half of the participants then read that she had been raped by that man later in the evening. All participants then rated how appropriate her behavior at the party had been. Those who did not read about the rape saw her behavior as appropriate, whereas those who learned she had been raped saw the same behavior as inappropriate. This research shows the power people have to interpret the same information differently, in this case in a way that makes them feel that the victim's behavior caused the attack.

Contrast effect. As you learned in Chapter 5, people perceive stimuli that are different from expectations as more different than they actually are (Fiske, Bersoff, Borgida, Deaux, & Heilman, 1991; Jussim, Coleman, & Lerch, 1987). For example, if you expect that women will be passive and gentle, when you encounter a woman who is assertive and strong, she may seem especially tough and aggressive. As Stephen Carter, a Black man and a law professor at Yale University, describes in his book *Reflections of an Affirmative Action Baby*, "...like a flower blooming in winter, intellect is more readily noticed where it is not expected to be found" (p. 54, Carter, 1993). Similarly, if you believe that football players are dumb, when you encounter one who gets an A on an exam, you may see him as even smarter than another student with the same grade.

What accounts for these overly positive (or negative) perceptions of average behavior? According to the *shifting standards model*, people within a group are compared to others within that group more than they are compared to people in other groups (Biernat, 2003; Biernat & Manis, 1994; Biernat, Manis, & Nelson, 1991). For example, a woman may be described as a great athlete because her skills are better than those of most other women even if these skills are only average compared to men's. One study revealed that softball managers respond with greater enthusiasm for good performance by a woman—such as hitting a single—than the same performance by a man (Biernat & Vescio, 2002). However, they also favor men over women with comparable skills for favored infield positions and batting order.

However, while it is easier for minority group members to make minimum standards (due to shifting standards), these positive evaluations based on lowered standards can, not surprisingly, be insulting (Biernat, 2003). As described by one Black employee working in a largely White environment: "They were

Associated Press

astonished that I could write a basic memo. Even the completion of an easy task brought surprised compliments" (p. 55). Minority group members also must work harder to prove that their performance is based on ability (Biernat et al., 1998; Biernat & Kobrynowicz, 1997). As Carter (1993) eloquently describes, Blacks "really do have to work twice as hard to be considered half as good" (p. 58). Members of minority groups, including women and Blacks, are required to "jump through more hoops" to prove their worth.

Perceptual confirmation.   Another factor that can lead to stereotyping is **perceptual confirmation**, meaning the tendency to see things in line with one's expectations. Perceptual confirmation occurs in part because we interpret ambiguous information as supporting our stereotypes, and thereby see the same behavior in a very different way depending on our expectations (Hilton & von Hippel, 1990; Kunda & Sherman-Williams, 1993; Kunda, Sinclair, & Griffin, 1997). Perceptual confirmation leads people to see mental patients' behavior as abnormal (Rosenhan, 1973), view other athletic teams as more unfairly aggressive than their own (Hastorf & Cantril, 1954), and underestimate 11-month-old girl infants' crawling ability and overestimate such behavior in boys (Mondschein, Adolph, & Tamis-LeMonda, 2000).

perceptual confirmation the tendency for people to see things in line with their own beliefs and expectations

CATHY © 1986 Cathy Guisewite. Reprinted with permission of UNIVERSAL PRESS SYNDICATE. All rights reserved.

lead people to recall certain information about a person
their expectations, they interpret and encode that informa-
(e.g., stereotypical) ways. In one study, all participants saw a video
(Hannah) who was either from a poor background or a rich back-
(Darley & Gross, 1983). Half of the participants were also given additional information by watching her answer a series of academic problems in an inconsistent way (she got some right and some wrong). Then all participants rated Hannah's academic ability. Although those who did not watch Hannah's academic performance seemed reluctant to judge her ability simply on the basis of her socioeconomic status, those who saw the video of her academic performance readily judged her ability, even though the video provided ambiguous information. Specifically, those with negative expectations (e.g., those who thought Hannah was poor) rated her lower on work habits, motivation, and cognitive skills than if they had not seen the video. Those with positive expectations (e.g., those who thought Hannah was rich) rated her somewhat higher if they had seen the video. In this case, stereotypes did not have a direct effect on performance expectations, but clearly made subjects more willing to use irrelevant information to interpret behavior in line with their stereotype.

We also require fewer examples to confirm our beliefs about a trait that is highly stereotypical of a person in a given out-group than for a person in our in-group (Biernat & Ma, 2005). For example, if a young person misplaces his or her keys, we assume that person is just being forgetful. But if an older person misplaces his or her keys, we assume that person may be experiencing serious memory loss.

confirmation bias a tendency to search for information that confirms one's existing beliefs and to avoid information which contradicts these beliefs

Confirmation bias. **Confirmation bias** describes the tendency to search for information that supports one's initial view. When people have expectations about a particular person, they address few questions to that person, and hence acquire relatively little information that could disprove their assumptions (Trope & Thompson, 1997). People may also ask questions that are designed to confirm their expectations, which protects them from gaining and using disconfirming information. So, if you are meeting a person from Canada for the first time, you might ask him about his love of ice hockey and cold weather, whereas if you are meeting a person from Mexico for the first time, you might ask him or her about his or her love of spicy foods and festive music. Do you see the confirmation bias at work here?

We also ignore information that disputes our expectations. We are more likely to remember (and repeat) stereotype-consistent information and to forget or ignore stereotype-inconsistent information, which is one way stereotypes are maintained even in the face of disconfirming evidence (Lyons & Kashima, 2003; O'Sullivan & Durso, 1984). If you learn that your new Canadian friend hates hockey and loves sailing, and that your new Mexican friend hates spicy foods and loves rap music, you are less likely to remember this new stereotype-inconsistent information.

What's the good news? People who are unprejudiced pay more attention to stereotype-disconfirming information than stereotype-confirming information (Wyer, 2004). In one study, participants read four brief descriptions of a target person, and then selected one person to learn more about in a subsequent task. Some of these descriptions included stereotypical information (e.g., a Black person who is uneducated and has a job doing menial labor). Others included information that disconfirmed stereotypes (e.g., a Black person who is educated and has a White collar job). Of those who were unprejudiced (as assessed by scores on a racism scale), 68% chose to receive more information about a stereotype-disconfirming person. Of participants who were prejudiced, 77% chose to receive more information about a person who was stereotype-confirming. People who are unprejudiced also make different attributions for behavior—seeing stereotype-confirming behavior as situational rather than internal, and stereotype-disconfirming behavior as dispositional.

RESEARCH FOCUS ON GENDER

The Hazardous Impact of Stereotypes on Women's Achievement in the Workplace

Although a growing number of women are now succeeding in traditionally male-dominated fields such as law, medicine, and business, women still face numerous hurdles in achieving success in some domains. This infamous "glass ceiling" impairs women's achievement in often subtle ways (Eagly & Steffen, 1984; Fiske et al., 1991).

First, people see female-dominated occupations, such as nurse, teacher, and secretary, as requiring feminine personality traits and physical attributes for success, and see male-dominated occupations, such as doctor, lawyer, and business executive, as requiring male personality traits for success (Cejka & Eagly, 1999). In turn, both males and females show a bias toward male applicants in high-prestige positions (Kanekar, Kolsawalla, & Nazareth, 1989; Van Vianen & Willemsen, 1992). Therefore, even when males and females have the same qualifications, interviewers are more likely to hire a man because he is likely to have more masculine characteristics.

Second, even after women are hired for high-prestige jobs, such as in financial services, women and men have different experiences: women report having less authority, less international mobility, and fewer stock options than men (Lyness & Thompson, 1997). Women also report less satisfaction with future career opportunities, and report more obstacles to success, than do men. One study of male and female managers at 20 Fortune 500 corporations revealed that women lagged behind men with respect to salary progression and frequency of job transfers, even though men and women were equally well-educated, worked in similar industries, and had the same commitment to the work force (Stroh, Brett, & Reilly, 1992). As shown in Table 10.1, women receive less pay than men in the same job across many occupations.

TABLE 10.1	WEEKLY SALARY FOR THE SAME JOB AS A FUNCTION OF GENDER
TYPE OF JOB	**RATE OF PAY FOR WOMEN COMPARED TO MEN**
Physicians and surgeons	$681 less
Lawyers	$366 less
Professors	$189 less
Nurses	$157 less
Elementary/middle school teachers	$123 less
Food service managers	$111 less
Waiters and waitresses	$69 less
Office and administrative support	$61 less

Source: Bureau of Labor Statistics (2009).

ASSESSING STEREOTYPES

In order to examine the prevalence of stereotypes about different groups, as well as the factors that contribute to stereotypes, researchers need to be able to assess such beliefs. This section will examine three ways in which researchers in psychology measure stereotypes: self-report measures, the Implicit Association Test, and the bogus pipeline.

Self-report measures. As you learned in Chapter 2, self-report measures are commonly used to examine people's attitudes, beliefs, and behaviors. This approach is direct, and can be cost-effective since it is possible to gather data from many people relatively quickly. Many self-report measures of stereotypes exist, including the Modern Racism Scale (McConahay, 1986), the Homosexuality Attitudes Scale (Kite & Deaux, 1986), and the Modern Sexism Scale (Swim, Aikin, Hall, & Hunter, 1995). The Rate Yourself box provides an example of a scale that can be used to assess people's willingness to rely on stereotypes.

Although self-report measures of stereotypes can provide useful information, these measures are also problematic for testing something as sensitive as stereotypes. As you can probably imagine, people are often reluctant to express stereotypes about people in other groups, and thus may deliberately misreport their answers as a way of appearing more accepting and tolerant than they actually are. Many researchers who study stereotypes therefore rely on covert, or indirect, methods of testing such assumptions.

How Much Do You Accept Stereotypes?

Acceptance of Stereotypes Scale

INSTRUCTIONS: *Rate each item on a scale of 0 (strongly disagree) to 6 (strongly agree).*

☐ **1.** Stereotypes are useful in daily life even though they are not always correct.

☐ **2.** Stereotypes can be harmful but they are essential for interacting with members of real groups.

☐ **3.** To hold a stereotype does not necessarily mean that you are looking down on someone.

☐ **4.** In daily life, there's so much to pay attention to, it helps if you can make a few assumptions about a person.

☐ **5.** People differ so much from one another, it is impossible to generalize about them.

☐ **6.** If we did not stereotype each other, there would be a lot less conflict in the world.

☐ **7.** If you hold a stereotype about people, you'll never be able to see them for who they really are.

☐ **8.** Stereotypes have too much influence on our behavior toward others.

SCORING: First, add up your points on items 1, 2, 3, and 4. Then add up your points on items 5, 6, 7, and 8. Subtract your summed score on the second set of items from your summed score on the first set of items to get your final score.

INTERPRETATION: This scale assesses people's general acceptance of stereotypes. People with higher scores on this scale have a greater willingness to rely on stereotypes when interacting with other people, whereas those with lower scores on this scale are less willing to rely on such beliefs (Carter, Hall, Carney, & Rosip, 2006).

Covert measures. Because people are often unwilling to express prejudiced beliefs, researchers who study stereotypes and prejudice have developed covert methods of assessing such beliefs. One such method is the bogus pipeline, which is just a fake lie-detector test. Participants are told that they are hooked up to a mechanical device that assesses their true beliefs, and thus any false information will be detected. Participants are therefore more likely to give honest responses to avoid getting caught in a lie.

The Implicit Association Test (IAT) is another commonly used covert method of testing people's stereotypes about individuals in different groups. This test is based on the assumption that it is easier—and therefore faster—to make the same response to concepts that are strongly associated with each than those that are weakly associated (Nosek et al., 2005). In this test, people respond to two different types of stimulus words: the first set is attitudinal words (e.g., pleasant, peace, ugly, happy, etc.), and the second set is the list of stereotypic target words (e.g., women's names and men's names, Black leaders and White leaders, etc.). People press one key when they see a pleasant word and another key when they see an unpleasant word. Because people are faster at responding to the compatible blocks than the incompatible ones, it is often assumed that these two concepts are implicitly linked. For example, students often respond more quickly to the pairing of the words "fat" and "bad" (which are often closely linked in people's mind) than the words "thin" and "bad" (which are typically less closely linked). Although the IAT is the most widely used covert method for assessing people's attitudes toward members of different groups, some researchers have criticized the validity of the IAT, particularly when it is used to provide specific information about a given person's degree of prejudice (Blanton & Jaccard, 2006).

FACTORS LEADING TO STEREOTYPING

FACTOR	EXAMPLE
Social learning	J.D. is in 2nd grade and has a good friend, Tomika, who is a girl. After J.D. is ridiculed by children on his bus for liking a girl, he refuses to play with Tomika anymore.
Social categorization	Yvette just joined a sorority, and is having fun getting to know other women in this sorority. She feels very glad to have joined this sorority, which includes a wide range of women with different interests, as opposed to one of the other sororities, in which she hears that the women are all very similar to one another.
Realistic group conflict theory	Myles learns that his brother was rejected from a state university, and that many Latino students with lower academic qualifications were admitted. Myles now sees Latinos in a much more negative way due to his anger about his brother's college rejection.
Social identity theory	Liza just received a C- on her geology term paper and is very upset. Later, when she is giving a tour of her college to prospective students, she is particularly negative about a local rival school.
Cognitive biases	Sierra volunteers at a local senior citizens center one afternoon a week. In this role, she insists on carrying groceries for Mr. Maglione, even after he insists he is perfectly capable of carrying the groceries himself. Sierra sees Mr. Maglione's white hair and wrinkled skin, and assumes that he must need assistance.

WHAT ARE THE CONSEQUENCES OF BEING STEREOTYPED?

Unfortunately, stereotypes can have real consequences. In one study, researchers randomly assigned female college students to watch one of two sets of television commercials (Davies, Spencer, Quinn, & Gerhardstein, 2002). Some women watched gender-stereotypic television commercials, in which a woman jumped on her bed with joy after discovering a new acne product or drooled in anticipation of trying a new brownie mix. Other women watched counterstereotypic commercials, in which a woman impressed someone with her knowledge about automotive engineering or spoke intelligently about her concerns about health care. All women then completed a math test. As predicted, women who watched the gender-stereotypic commercials performed worse on the math test than those who watched the counterstereotypic commercials (19% correct compared to 31% correct). This research demonstrates just one example of the negative, and at times lasting, consequences of being stereotyped. This section will examine how the use of stereotypes leads to this, and other negative consequences, including self-fulfilling prophecy, stereotype threat, reduced psychological well-being, and reverse discrimination.

SELF-FULFILLING PROPHECY

self-fulfilling prophecy the process by which people's expectations about a person lead them to elicit behavior that confirms these beliefs

People's expectations not only lead them to see things in line with their beliefs (i.e., perceptual confirmation), but also to interact with the person in ways that elicit the expected behavior (see Figure 10.4; Darley & Fazio, 1980). As described in Chapter 5, **self-fulfilling prophecy** refers to the tendency to seek, interpret, and create information that verifies our own beliefs. If you believe that a person is not so bright, you are likely to ask questions that elicit these expectations ("Who do you think the *American Idol* winner will be?"). On the other hand, if you think

FIGURE 10.4

MODEL OF A SELF-FULFILLING PROPHECY

In the cycle of self-fulfilling prophecy, people's expectations about a person lead them to engage in behaviors that, in turn, elicit behavior from the target person that supports initial expectations.

you are talking to a smart person, you might ask about other topics (e.g., "What is your favorite novel?").

In a classic study, researchers asked white Princeton students to interview both black and white Princeton undergraduates for a job (Word, Zanna, & Cooper, 1974). As predicted, interviewers who interacted with black applicants interacted in very different ways than those who interacted with white applicants, including sitting farther away, making more speech errors, and having less eye contact. Next, the researchers trained students to interview job applicants using the distinct styles shown by those who had interviewed whites versus blacks. In other words, some students were trained to interview in the style used when people had interviewed the white students (using correct grammar, sitting closer to the applicant, and having good eye contact). Others were trained to interview in the style used when people had interviewed the black students (making frequent speech errors, sitting farther away, having little eye contact). These students then interviewed a new group of all white job applicants. Can you predict the findings?

Those who were interviewed by someone using the style used with black applicants in the first part of the study performed worse than those who were interviewed in the style used with white applicants. Specifically, those who were interviewed "as if black" made more speech errors, sat farther away from the interviewer, and were seen as less calm and composed than those who were interviewed "as if white." Most importantly, applicants who were interviewed "as if black" were seen by independent judges as less adequate for the job. This study demonstrates that people's expectations about a person can lead them to engage in behaviors that in turn elicit behavior that supports these expectations—a vicious, and dangerous, cycle.

How do people's expectations about others elicit the behavior they expect? People who have negative expectations about another person may treat that person more negatively. This path toward eliciting negative behavior was shown in the study just described about the differences in how people interview students who are black versus white. Similarly, men in high-power positions ask subordinate women, compared to men, fewer questions that describe their strengths, assign women to fewer tasks, and estimate less success from women (Vescio, Gervais, Snyder, & Hoover, 2005; Vescio, Snyder, & Butz, 2003). Not surprisingly, women who are in this low expectation condition feel angrier, are less confident, and actually perform less well. These findings indicate that when powerful people hold stereotypes about those in subordinate positions, their behavior can elicit the negative behavior they expect.

Questioning the Research
This classic study was conducted in 1974. Do you think researchers today would find the same differences in terms of how white interviewers interact with black versus white job applicants? Why or why not?

© Blend Images/SUPERSTOCK

A man who has a negative expectation about whether a women is suited for a particular job could treat her more negatively, which in turn could elicit a more negative response.

STEREOTYPE THREAT

Another negative consequence of stereotyping is **stereotype threat**, in which minority group members experience an apprehension that they may behave in a manner that confirms existing cultural stereotypes (Steele, 1997). This apprehension, in turn, interferes with their ability to perform well, and thus leads them to confirm the negative stereotype about their group. For example, if I as a woman am told that I am about to take a test on spatial reasoning that women typically do poorly on, that awareness may make me nervous, and so I will do less well on the test.

In the first study to demonstrate the stereotype threat effect, Claude Steele and Joshua Aronson (1995) randomly assigned black and white college students at Stanford University to one of three groups before taking a verbal SAT test. Some received diagnostic information ("this test examines the factors associated with high versus low ability"), and some received nondiagnostic information ("this test examines methods of problem solving"). Findings indicated, as predicted, that blacks did just as well as whites when the test was nondiagnostic, but did much worse than

stereotype threat an apprehension that an individual may experience when he or she believes he or she may behave in a manner that confirms existing cultural stereotype, which in turn disrupts performance

whites when the test was presented as diagnostic. All of these students were smart—they were Stanford students—but the black students may have felt more nervous about taking a diagnostic test, given the stereotypes of Blacks as underachievers.

The impact of stereotype threat on academic tasks has been demonstrated by people in a variety of different types of stereotyped groups, including high school girls and college women taking math tests described as diagnostic of math ability (Keller & Dauenheimer, 2003; Spencer, Steele, & Quinn, 1999). In addition, stereotype threat effects on performance are found for:

- white males who take a math test after comparing their math ability to that of Asian males (Aronson, Lustina, Good, Keough, Steele, & Brown, 1999);
- Latino men and women who take a math test described as diagnostic of their ability (Gonzales, Blanton, & Williams, 2002); and
- children from low socioeconomic backgrounds who take intellectual tests described as diagnostic of their overall intellectual ability (Croizet & Claire, 1998).

Stereotype threat can also impact the same person in different ways, depending on which aspect of their identity is made salient. One study by Margaret Shih at Harvard University found that Asian women do better on math tests when their ethnic identity is primed, but worse when their sex is primed (see Figure 10.5; Shih, Pittinsky, & Ambady, 1999).

Although in many cases researchers create stereotype threat by describing a test as diagnostic of one's true aptitude, it can also be activated in more subtle ways, as

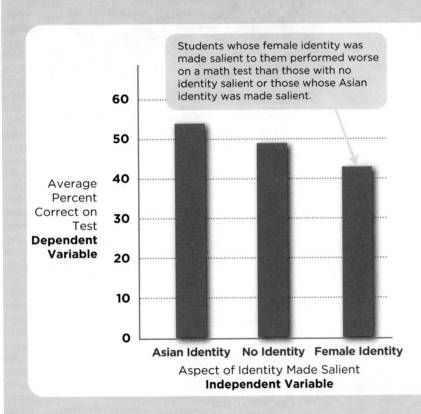

FIGURE 10.5

CAN IDENTITY SALIENCE IMPACT PERFORMANCE?

In this study, Asian American students wrote about an aspect of their identity (either their Asian or their female identity), and then took a math test. When students' attention was focused on their female identity, they performed worse on the test than when their attention was focused on their Asian identity.

Source: Shih, M., Pittinsky, T. L., & Ambady, N. (1999). Stereotype susceptibility: Identity salience and shifts in quantitative performance. *Psychological Science, 10*, 80-83.

Students whose female identity was made salient to them performed worse on a math test than those with no identity salient or those whose Asian identity was made salient.

Average Percent Correct on Test **Dependent Variable**

Asian Identity   No Identity   Female Identity

Aspect of Identity Made Salient
Independent Variable

Participants: Asian American female college students

Independent Variable:

Which aspect of their identity was made salient to them

- Asian identity
- None
- Female identity

Dependent Variable:

How well they did on a math test

will be described. As indicated at the start of this section, women who see gender-stereotypic commercials perform worse on a math test than those who watched the counterstereotypic commercials (Davies et al., 2002). Women who watched the gender-stereotypic commercials also show less interest in careers requiring quantitative skills (such as engineer, mathematician, computer scientist, accountant) than those who watched the counterstereotypic ads. Simply being the only person of your gender or race in a group can activate stereotype threat, and thus disrupt performance, particularly for members of disadvantaged or stereotyped groups (Inzlicht & Ben-Zeev, 2000; Sekaquaptewa & Thompson, 2002). However, and as described in the Education Connections, subtle manipulations can also minimize the negative effects of stereotype threat.

"Ah, Harding—perhaps you can give us some input from the straight community."

Education
::: CONNECTIONS

Reducing the Effects of Stereotype Threats in the Classroom

Considerable research points to a gender gap in math achievement in the United States: although high school girls tend to earn higher grades than boys in most subjects (and thus are more likely to graduate in the top 10 percent of their class), scores on standardized tests show that boys tend to get significantly higher scores. For example, in 2007 girls' average score on the math portion of the SAT was 499 points (out of 800), compared with 533 for boys, out of a possible 800 (College Board, 2007). Men also outperform women on the quantitative section of the GRE (Educational Testing Service, 1999), and math achievement tests (College Entrance Examination Board, 1994). What causes these

OJO Images/Superstock

dramatic differences? Many psychological factors may help explain some of these differences, including behavioral confirmation (treating girls as if they are less intelligent and capable in math), lowered expectations (assigning girls to lower level math classes), and perceptual confirmation (seeing girls as less capable in math). Yet another possibility is that stereotype threat leads to lower performance.

Encouragingly, some recent evidence points to strategies for reducing the impact of stereotype threat on standardized test performance. In one study, both men and women completed difficult math problems that were either described as a problem-solving task or a math test (Johns, Schmader, & Martens, 2005). In addition, students in a third condition were told that they would complete a math test, but were also told that stereotype threat could interfere with women's performance on the test. Although women who were told they would complete a math test and were not told about the potential impact of stereotype threat on their performance performed worse than men on these tests, there were no gender differences on the scores when the test was simply described as a problem-solving task or when they were informed about the potential impact of stereotype threat on performance. This finding suggests that simply making people aware of the hazards of such a threat can reduce its effect.

Researchers are now investigating how stereotype threat leads to decreased performance. One explanation is that stereotype threat leads to lower working memory capacity. In line with this view, Latino students who are told that a memory test is highly predictive of intelligence recall fewer words on a memory task than those who are not given this information (Schmader & Johns, 2003). Another explanation is that such a threat increases anxiety, which in turn disrupts performance (Inzlicht & Ben-Zeev, 2003). Support for this explanation is found in research demonstrating that being the only representative of one's group in a situation leads to lower levels of performance. More recent research has examined how stereotype threat is associated with the activation of particular parts of the brain (Krendl, Richeson, Kelley, & Heatherton, 2008). This work indicates that although women who are solving math problems usually show activation in a part of the brain that controls mental math tasks (not surprisingly), those who are under conditions of threat instead show activation in a part of the brain that regulates emotions. This finding suggests that women under conditions of stereotype threat may focus more on the social and emotional consequences of confirming negative stereotypes about their group, and less on successfully computing the math problems.

REDUCED PSYCHOLOGICAL WELL-BEING

Members of low-status groups are, not surprisingly, more likely than those in high-status groups to report experiencing personal discrimination (Major, Gramzow, McCoy, Levin, Schmader, & Sidenius, 2002; Schmitt, Branscombe, Kobrynowicz, & Owen, 2002). According to the **rejection-identification model**, perceiving prejudice and discrimination negatively impacts psychological well-being. People who attribute others' negative behavior toward them (e.g., receiving a speeding ticket, failing to get a desired job, being told an apartment you want to rent is unavailable) to prejudice experience depression, sadness, and helplessness (Branscombe, Schmitt, & Harvey, 1999; Schmitt & Branscombe, 2002). Observing blatant discrimination toward a member of our own group can also lead to impaired cognitive abilities (Salvatore & Shelton, 2007). As described in Health Connections, experiencing discrimination can lead to negative effects on physical health as well.

Although minority group members overall report experiencing more personal and group discrimination than majority group members, those who strongly identify with their group report feeling more discrimination, as well as psychological distress, than those who do not strongly identify (Operario & Fiske, 2001; Sellers & Shelton, 2003). For example, women who believe gender discrimination is likely experience lower psychological well-being, especially if they strongly identify with their in-group (Schmitt et al., 2002). In contrast, men show no effect of perceiving gender discrimination on well-being, regardless of in-group identification.

Social costs of attributions to prejudice. People who attribute poor behavior to prejudice can also experience social costs. For example, Blacks who attribute failing grades to discrimination are seen less favorably than those who take responsibility for their poor performance, suggesting that the social costs of making attributions on discrimination are substantial (Kaiser & Miller, 2001). Minority group members are often aware of the personal costs of reporting discrimination to majority group members. For example, both women and Blacks are more likely to report that a failing grade assigned by a majority group member was caused by discrimination, rather than their own lack of ability, when they make the judgment privately and in front of another stigmatized group member than publicly and in front of a nonstigmatized group member (Stangor, Swim, Van Allen, & Sechrist, 2002).

Strategies for minimizing effects of prejudice. Although people in stigmatized groups can develop low self-esteem, minority group members often avoid internalizing negative stereotypes about their own group and thereby protect

Health
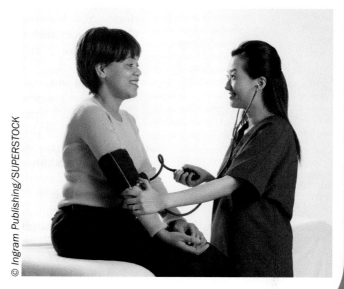

CONNECTIONS

The Impact of Racism on Physical Health

One of the most dangerous consequences of prejudice and discrimination is its impact on physical health. Blacks have higher rates of coronary heart disease (CHD) and hypertension than do White Americans, and these differences may be caused in part by the constant exposure to discrimination and racism (Clark, Anderson, Clark, & Williams, 1999; Mendes, Major, McCoy, & Blascovich, 2008). In one study, African American men and women who reported experiencing racial discrimination and accepting unfair treatment had significantly higher blood pressure than those who reported experiencing such discrimination but challenging unfair treatment (Krieger & Sidney, 1996; Krieger, Sidney & Coakley, 1998). However, this association between accepting racial discrimination and high blood pressure was found in working class Blacks, but not among professional African Americans. This finding suggests that stress may be greatest among those who are trying to overcome adversity, but have limited socioeconomic resources to do so.

Perceived discrimination is also associated with other negative health effects. Blacks who report experiencing discrimination have more difficulty sleeping and thus feel considerable fatigue (Thomas, Bardwell, Ancoli-Israel, & Dimsdale, 2006). Blacks who perceive racial discrimination are also more likely to report depression, anxiety, and substance use, including alcohol, smoking, and drugs (Gibbons, Gerrard, Cleveland, Wills, & Brody, 2004). Those who perceived frequent discrimination reported more anxiety, depression, and substance use nearly two years later, compared to those who perceived infrequent discrimination. Finally, Latinos who believe they are discriminated against due to their ethnicity show higher resting blood pressure, which may lead to greater risk of cardiovascular disease (Salomon & Jagusztyn, 2008). In sum, experiencing discrimination is associated with negative physical as well as psychological well-being.

© Ingram Publishing/SUPERSTOCK

their self-esteem (Crocker & Major, 1989; Guimond, 2000). How can they avoid the negative effects of prejudice? Research points to several effective strategies.

1. People can disengage from and ignore negative feedback (Crocker, Voelkl, Testa, & Major, 1991; Major, Spencer, Schmader, Wolfe, & Crocker, 1998). The correlation between self-esteem and academic outcomes increases over time among White adolescents, but decreases among Black adolescents, suggesting a separation between feelings about the self and academic feedback (Osbourne, 1995).

2. Members of low-status groups compare their outcomes to those of others in their in-group as opposed to those in their out-group. Women executives, for example, may be aware that they are not receiving the same salary or promotions as their male counterparts, but may feel encouraged about their career prospects when they compare themselves to women who are secretaries.

3. People may devalue the dimensions on which their group doesn't do so well and value those dimensions in which their group excels. Athletes are likely to emphasize the positive effects of physical abilities and downplay the importance of musical aptitude, whereas members of singing groups are likely to show the reverse pattern.

4. People in low-status groups may increase their identification with the in-group, perhaps as a way of increasing self-esteem and thereby well-being (Branscombe et al., 1999; Major et al., 2002; Schmitt et al., 2002). For example, people with body piercings who feel discriminated against by the mainstream report greater group identification, which in turn leads to higher self-esteem (Jetten, Branscombe, Schmitt, & Spears, 2001). This identification also influences how people react to discrimination. People who identify with their group (women, ethnicity, etc.) react to discrimination by feeling angry at the out-group, whereas people who don't really identify with their in-group often feel angry at themselves following discrimination (Hansen & Sassenberg, 2006).

REVERSE DISCRIMINATION

Reverse discrimination occurs when people show preferential treatment to those in stereotyped groups (Fajardo, 1985; Harber, 1998). In some cases, colleges and businesses have used different standards for admitting or hiring people from historically nondominant groups (typically students of color and women) than for those from historically dominant groups (typically White students and men). Opponents of such policies fear that such practices result in underqualified members of minority groups being admitted or hired instead of more qualified members of majority groups. For example, in one state, White males seeking promotion to Sergeant in the police department were required to score 92 or above on the Sergeant's exam, while minorities and females were required to score only 83 and above. In many highly publicized court cases, White students have filed suit against schools that use different standards for admitting students from different racial backgrounds (see In the News).

Reverse discrimination can lead people to prefer candidates from under-represented groups over those from other groups, and to justify such preferences on seemingly objective criteria. In one study, people were asked to choose between two college applicants (Norton, Vandello, & Darley, 2004). White participants favored Black candidates over White ones for admission to college, and biased the criteria they use to favor these applicants. Fifty-six percent of Whites rated grade-point average (GPA) as the most important criterion for college admissions when they believed a White candidate had a higher GPA than the Black candidate (or when they were given no information about the candidate's race). However, 84% of Whites rated GPA as the most important criterion when they believed a Black candidate had the higher GPA.

Although in some cases members of disadvantaged groups may be seen as especially good, they can also be seen as especially bad; in sum, they are often evalu-

AL GOLDIS/Associated Press

In the NEWS

Reverse discrimination. In 1995, Jennifer Gratz was denied admission to the University of Michigan despite placing 12th in her graduating class, with a 3.8 GPA along with numerous extracurricular activities including serving as Student Council Vice President and Honor Roll Student for consecutive years. After a lengthy investigation, spearheaded by a University of Michigan professor, it was discovered that the University was using a dual-admissions system with completely different standards depending on one's race. On June 23, 2003, the U.S. Supreme Court struck down the preference programs in place for the past decade at the University of Michigan.

ated more extremely, or as especially good if good, but especially bad if bad (Branscombe et al., 1993; Linville & Jones, 1980). In one study, participants were instructed to give a certain number of shocks to another subject (who was either Black or White), but they could choose the intensity of the shocks (Rogers & Prentice-Dunn, 1981). When the confederate was friendly, Blacks received lower severity shocks than Whites, showing that participants "bend over backwards" to show how "not racist" they are. However, when the confederate is hostile, Blacks receive shocks of much greater intensity than Whites. Thus, reverse discrimination may benefit members of stereotyped groups, but can also be detrimental.

THE HAZARDS OF POSITIVE STEREOTYPES

Recent research suggests that stereotypes consist of two basic dimensions—competence and warmth (see Table 10.2; Fiske, Cuddy, Glick, & Xu, 2002; Fiske, Xu, Cuddy, & Glick, 1999).

- People who belong to high-status groups (e.g., rich people, Asians, Jews) are seen as highly competent (e.g., intelligent, aggressive, competitive), but not as particularly warm (e.g., honest, warm, sensitive; Fiske et al., 2002; Lin, Kwan, Cheung, & Fiske, 2005).
- People who belong to low-status groups (e.g., elderly people, housewives) are seen as incompetent but warm (Fiske et al., 1999; Fiske et al., 2002).
- People who belong to very-low-status groups (e.g., poor people, homeless people) are seen as low in competence and low in warmth (Fiske et al., 2002).

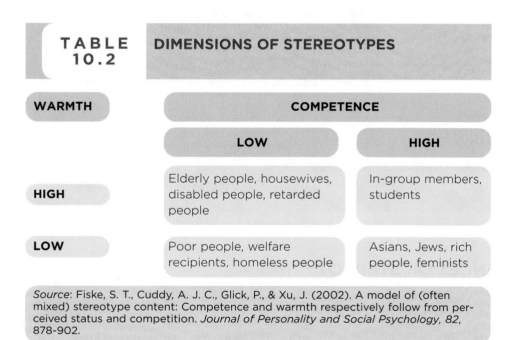

TABLE 10.2	**DIMENSIONS OF STEREOTYPES**	
WARMTH	**COMPETENCE**	
	LOW	**HIGH**
HIGH	Elderly people, housewives, disabled people, retarded people	In-group members, students
LOW	Poor people, welfare recipients, homeless people	Asians, Jews, rich people, feminists

Source: Fiske, S. T., Cuddy, A. J. C., Glick, P., & Xu, J. (2002). A model of (often mixed) stereotype content: Competence and warmth respectively follow from perceived status and competition. *Journal of Personality and Social Psychology, 82*, 878-902.

We also react differently to people in the different groups (Cuddy, Fiske, & Glick, 2007). We pity those who are in low-competent but warm groups, and envy those who are in low-warmth and high-competence groups. Thinking of people in groups seen as low in warmth and low in competence, such as drug addicts and the homeless, even activates the portions of the brain that are responsible for encoding disgust (Harris & Fiske, 2006). Perceptions of disgust, in turn, suggest that we dehumanize members of certain groups, which can help explain atrocities, such as hate crimes, genocide, and prisoner abuse (as you will learn about in Chapter 11).

Although positive stereotypes may seem harmless, they can have detrimental effects. Researchers Peter Glick and Susan Fiske developed a theory of sexism that distinguishes between different types of attitudes that people could have about women (see Table 10.3; Glick & Fiske, 1996, 2001). **Hostile sexism**, which

hostile sexism a feeling of hostility toward women based on their threat to men's power

benevolent sexism a view of women as needing protection and affection

describes feelings of hostility toward women based on their threat to men's power, is what we more typically think of as prejudice against women. People who are high in hostile sexism have negative attitudes toward women, such as believing that women are inherently less intelligent than men. On the other hand, **benevolent sexism** describes holding positive, but patronizing, views of women. People who are high on benevolent sexism have seemingly positive attitudes toward women, such as believing that women need protection and are better listeners. Although men tend to be higher on hostile sexism than women, both men and women commonly endorse benevolent sexism (Glick et al., 2000).

TABLE 10.3 | **HOSTILE VERSUS BENEVOLENT SEXISM**

HOSTILE SEXISM STATEMENTS	BENEVOLENT SEXISM STATEMENTS
Most women interpret innocent remarks or acts as being sexist.	Many women have a quality of purity that few men possess.
Most women fail to appreciate all that men do for them.	Women should be cherished and protected by men.
Women seek to gain power by getting control over men.	Women, as compared to men, tend to have a more refined sense of culture and good taste.
Women exaggerate problems they have at work.	Men should be willing to sacrifice their own well-being in order to provide financially for the women in their lives.
Once a woman gets a man to commit to . her, she usually tries to put him on a tight leash.	Every man ought to have a woman whom he adores.

These items illustrate the distinction between hostile and benevolent sexism.

Source: Glick, P., & Fiske, S. T. (1996). The Ambivalent Sexism Inventory: Differentiating hostile and benevolent sexism. *Journal of Personality and Social Psychology*, 70, 491-512.

THE CONSEQUENCES OF STEREOTYPING

Concepts in Context

FACTOR	CONSEQUENCE
Self-fulfilling prophecy	Professor Gonzales believes that athletes are less intelligent than other students. He therefore avoids calling on athletes in class, and uses more simplistic examples when discussing course material with athletes during office hours. Professor Gonzales' views about athletes' intelligence are confirmed when these students perform less well on the final exam.
Stereotype threat	Vira is taking her engineering exam in a room with 10 male students, and not another female student. She feels quite nervous during the test, and is disappointed when she receives a very low score on the exam even though she had performed at a much higher level on her practice tests.

Reduced psychological well-being	Dr. O'Connor is initially bothered that her salary is somewhat lower than the salary received by her male counterparts. However, she feels better when she realizes how much higher her salary is than the female secretaries in her medical practice.
Reverse discrimination	Jonas is meeting with his chemistry lab partner, Traci, for the first time. She seems to have an adequate knowledge of most of the techniques they need to use, although she struggles a bit with remembering some of the formulas they are supposed to use. Jonas later raves to another friend about Traci's high intelligence and great skill.
The hazards of positive stereotypes	When Pieta learns that her new roommate is Asian American, she is disappointed. She had hoped that her roommate would be social and outgoing. However, Pieta at least hopes this roommate will serve as a good role model for increasing her own studying.

IS STEREOTYPING INEVITABLE?

Can stereotypes influence behavior, even among people who believe they are non-prejudiced? On November 25, 2006, Sean Bell, an unarmed 23-year-old black male, was shot and killed by plainclothes New York City Police Department detectives while leaving a nightclub early one morning (see In the News). This news story shows the results of stereotyping, and research in social psychology helps explain why such tragedies occur. In one study, researchers asked both white and black participants to play a videogame (Correll, Park, Judd, & Wittenbrink, 2002). Participants were told to shoot armed targets and to not shoot unarmed targets. Results revealed that both black and white participants made the right decision to shoot an armed target more quickly if the target was black than white, and made the right decision to not shoot an unarmed target more quickly if the target was white than black.

This study points to the influence of stereotypes on real-life situations, in which police officers must decide almost instantly whether to shoot a potential suspect—and may partially explain why Blacks are at greater risk of being accidentally shot, as you learned at the start of this section. This section will examine evidence that stereotyping is inevitable, including the automatic activation of stereotypes, the difficulty of suppressing stereotypes, the active maintenance of stereotypes, and the persistence of subtle forms of discrimination.

SHANNON STAPLETON/Reuters/Landov

In the NEWS **Sean Bell** was shot and killed by plainclothes New York City Police Department detectives on November 25, 2006. Bell and two friends were leaving Bell's bachelor party at a strip club in Jamaica, Queens, when they were shot. Three of the five detectives involved in the shooting have been indicted by a grand jury for the incident.

STEREOTYPES ARE ACTIVATED AUTOMATICALLY

Stereotypes are activated automatically and without conscious awareness, even among people who describe themselves as non-prejudiced (Bargh & Chartrand, 1999; Greenwald & Banaji, 1995). Patricia Devine (1989) at the University of Wisconsin at Madison conducted one of the first studies demonstrating this automatic activation of stereotypes. Participants were exposed at an unconscious level to words (or "primes") related to stereotypes of Blacks (e.g., poor, slavery, Harlem, jazz), and then read a paragraph about a man, Donald, who engaged in several ambiguously hostile behaviors, such as demanding his money back from a store clerk and refusing to pay the rent until his apartment is painted. Participants who had been primed with the stereotypically Black words judged Donald's behavior as more aggressive than those who are primed with neutral words, suggesting that unconscious priming of Black stereotypes activated the general Black stereotype, which in turn led the ambiguous behavior to be seen in a negative way.

Questioning the Research

Can you think of another explanation for why people who are unconsciously exposed to stereotypes of Black people then judge another person's behavior as more hostile? Does this study *prove* that exposure to these words activates the general Black stereotype?

This type of automatic activation of stereotypes occurs not just for race, but for other characteristics, including age (Kawakami, Young, & Dovidio, 2002; Perdue & Gurtman, 1990) and gender (Banaji & Greenwald, 1995; Ito & Urland, 2003; Rudman, Ashmore, & Gary, 2001). As you learned in Chapter 5, college students who are subliminally primed with words that cue elderly people take longer to walk to the elevator than those students who are primed with neutral words (Bargh et al., 1996). Similarly, and as shown in Figure 10.6, people who are induced to act in a way that cues obesity (by asking them to wear a heavy life vest and ankle weights while they perform a series of movements) rate a target person as having more traits associated with obesity (such as unhealthy, sluggish, lazy) than those who perform such movements without wearing the life vest and ankle weights (Mussweiler, 2006). Research Focus on Neuroscience describes how techniques in neuroscience can be particularly useful in examining how the brain responds to pictures of people from different backgrounds.

RESEARCH FOCUS ON NEUROSCIENCE
How the Brain Responds to In-Group and Out-Group Faces

Some of the most recent research examining issues in stereotypes, prejudice, and discrimination has been conducted using the tools of neuroscience (Eberhardt, 2005). These techniques are particularly well-suited for examining these issues, given people's tendency to express less prejudicial attitudes than they might feel. Neuroscience techniques can therefore be extremely useful in answering questions about whether prejudiced responses occur automatically and how responses can be reduced.

Allen Hart and his colleagues showed photos of Blacks and Whites to both Black and White participants (Hart et al., 2000). Researchers then examined neural activity in the amygdala, a part of the brain responsible for interpreting emotional responses. During the initial presentation of the faces, participants showed no differences in how they reacted to in-group versus out-group faces. However, during later presentations, activity in the amgydala declined more for in-group faces than for out-group faces, indicating greater familiarity with these faces.

The impact of this differential brain activity in response to in-group versus out-group faces may reflect biased evaluations of out-group members. In line with this view, research by Phelps and colleagues (2000) reveals that White participants with the greatest brain activation in response to Black faces also show more negative attitudes toward Blacks. However, when they repeated this study using pictures of famous, positively regarded Black and White men, the association between brain activity and prejudiced responses disappeared. This finding

FIGURE 10.6

CAN BEHAVIOR LEAD TO STEREOTYPING?

In this study, people were induced to wear a heavy life vest and ankle weights while they performed a series of movements (and thus were induced to act in a way that cued obesity) or to perform such movements without wearing the life vest and ankle weights, and to then rate a target person. As predicted, participants who were induced to act in a way that cued obesity described the target person as having more traits associated with obesity (such as unhealthy, sluggish, lazy) than those who did not wear the vest and weights.

Source: Mussweiler, T. (2006). Doing is for thinking! Stereotype activation by stereotypic movements. *Psychological Science, 17*, 17–21.

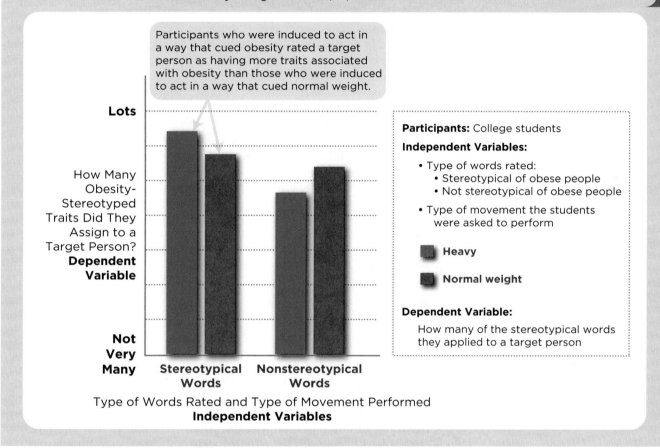

Participants who were induced to act in a way that cued obesity rated a target person as having more traits associated with obesity than those who were induced to act in a way that cued normal weight.

How Many Obesity-Stereotyped Traits Did They Assign to a Target Person?
Dependent Variable

Lots

Not Very Many

Stereotypical Words   **Nonstereotypical Words**

Type of Words Rated and Type of Movement Performed
Independent Variables

Participants: College students

Independent Variables:

- Type of words rated:
  - Stereotypical of obese people
  - Not stereotypical of obese people
- Type of movement the students were asked to perform

■ Heavy

■ Normal weight

Dependent Variable:

How many of the stereotypical words they applied to a target person

suggests that different levels of brain activity to faces of in-group and out-group members may simply reflect familiarity with different racial groups.

However, greater brain activity in response to out-group members is not necessarily automatic. First, Whites who view African American faces incidentally as part of another task don't show any differences in brain activation compared to those who view White faces (Wheeler & Fiske, 2005). Some type of deeper level processing is required to show differences in brain activation. Second, although when Whites see Black faces very briefly, the amygdala is activated more strongly than when they see White faces, the difference in activation for Black versus White faces is drastically reduced when the faces are shown for a longer period of time (Cunningham, Johnson, Raye, Gatenby, Gore, & Banaji, 2004). This finding suggests that if time permits, Whites attempt to actively control initial prejudiced responses. In other words, stereotyping may be automatic, but with time, these reactions may be able to be brought under conscious control.

Not surprisingly, this automatic activation of stereotypes can have real and very dangerous consequences. The study described at the start of this section demonstrated that participants made the right decisions to shoot an armed target more quickly if the target was Black than White, but made the right decision to not shoot an unarmed target more quickly if the target was White than Black (Correll et al., 2002). People also identify guns faster and misidentify tools as guns more often when they are primed with Black faces than White faces (Payne, 2001, 2006). Similarly, Whites who are primed with Black faces (at an unconscious level) are faster to recognize crime-related objects (guns, knives) than those who are primed with White faces, and Whites who view abstract concepts that cue Blacks (e.g., basketball, free throw, guns, knives) show a faster recognition of Black male faces than White male faces (Eberhardt, Goff, Purdue, & Davies, 2004).

STEREOTYPES ARE HARD TO SUPPRESS

You might think that one effective strategy for reducing the negative effects of stereotypes and prejudice would be to try to actively suppress them. Unfortunately this approach is quite ineffective. For example, elderly people, who report a stronger desire than younger people to control prejudiced reactions, rely more on stereotypes, even when instructed not to (von Hippel, Silver, & Lynch, 2000). Suppressing stereotypes also uses up considerable energy and effort, so someone who initially resists using stereotypes later performs worse on cognitive tasks (Gailliot, Plant, Butz, & Baumeister, 2007).

Trying to inhibit initially prejudicial responses can also lead someone to show more prejudice later (Liberman & Förster, 2000; Monteith, Sherman, & Devine, 1998; Wegner, 1997; Wyer, Sherman, & Stroessner, 2000). Benoit Monin and Dale Miller (2001) conducted a study to examine whether people who have the opportunity to show how non-prejudiced they are in one situation show increased use of stereotypes later on. In this study, students rated five applications for a starting position at a large consulting firm. Each candidate was briefly described (e.g., GPA, major, college, photo), and in all cases the "best candidate" was clear (one person had attended the best school and had the highest GPA). In some cases this candidate was a White woman. In other cases this candidate was a Black man, and in other cases this person was a White man (the control condition). Students overwhelmingly chose this "best candidate" in all conditions (regardless of the race/gender of this person).

Next, participants were told that they had one more hiring task to solve. The situation was that a police chief in a small town in a rural area had to hire a new police officer for a department that was racist (or sexist). A prior officer (who was Black or female, depending on the condition) had complained of a hostile work environment and had quit, and the police chief knows that a White male would be the best blend with the other officers. Should this reason allow you to use ethnicity (or gender) as one factor in hiring a new position? Students who had been able to show how non-prejudiced they were in the first task by recommending the Black or female applicant were more likely to agree that race (or sex) should be a factor in this second condition than those who had recommended the white man in the first case.

DISCONFIRMING EVIDENCE IS IGNORED

Even when people meet others who disconfirm their stereotypes, they can maintain the prior stereotypes by creating a separate category for them, a process called **subtyping**, which impedes stereotype change (Hewstone, Macrae, Griffiths, & Milne, 1994; Kunda & Oleson, 1995). For example, one study with high school students found that even after the creation of a police-schools liaison program designed to change adolescents' negative stereotypes about police officers, students became more positive about those officers who participated in the program (Hewstone, Hopkins, & Routh, 1992). Unfortunately, these beliefs did not generalize to other police officers. They simply categorized their school police officer differently from other police in general.

subtyping a phenomenon decribing how when people meet individuals who disconfirm their stereotypes, they can maintain the prior beliefs by creating separate categories for them

However, encountering stereotype-inconsistent information can decrease the strength of stereotypes if this information is dispersed across different group members as opposed to being concentrated in a small number of people (Hewstone et al., 1994; Kunda & Oleson, 1997; Queller & Smith, 2002). In one study, participants received three pieces of information (one stereotype-consistent, one stereotype-inconsistent, and one neutral) about a number of corporate lawyers, and then rated how stereotypical this group of lawyers was (Weber & Crocker, 1983). Some participants read descriptions in which the inconsistent information was distributed across all the lawyers, whereas others read descriptions in which this information was clustered in a small number of lawyers. Those who read about lawyers all of whom had some stereotype-inconsistent information revised their general stereotype of the lawyer group. In contrast, those who read about totally atypical members just dismissed those as flukes, and hence did not change their overall impression of lawyers. In sum, people who see high dispersion among group members are therefore less confident in holding stereotypes about particular individuals (Ryan, Judd, & Park, 1996). Stereotype-inconsistent behavior is especially effective in reducing stereotypes if it is attributed to stable internal causes (Wilder, Simon, & Faith, 1996).

SUBTLE DISCRIMINATION PERSISTS

Although stereotypes of Blacks, women, and gay people are less prevalent today than they have been in the past (Diekman & Eagly, 2000), more subtle types of discrimination remain (Devine & Elliot, 1995; Dovidio & Gaertner, 2000; Swim et al., 1995). For example, subtle discrimination based on race and class may have led to the delays in the government response following Hurricane Katrina. Similarly, and as described in Business Connections, while blatant sexism against women has largely disappeared, people continue to engage in more subtle forms of sexism, such as denying that women continue to experience discrimination, feeling antagonistic toward women's demands, and opposing policies designed to help women in education and work settings.

Learning that the tough guy football player in your calculus class loves to play the cello would probably change your football player stereotype. Learning that this football player is required to play in the school orchestra in order to maintain his athletic eligibility would likely not change your stereotype.

Stereotypes can influence how people are treated, albeit often in subtle ways. In one study, confederates applied for jobs at local stores, and wore a hat saying either "Gay and Proud" or "Texan and Proud" (Hebl, Foster, Mannix, & Dovidio, 2002). Although those wearing the "Gay and Proud" hats were not discriminated against in formal ways (e.g., were not more likely to be told there were no jobs available or to be hired), they were responded to more negatively in informal ways: the average interaction length was nearly 6 1/2 minutes with the nonstigmatized applicants, but only a little over 4 minutes for the gay and lesbian applicants.

People may also justify acts of discrimination in creative ways to avoid appearing prejudiced. In one study, male and female participants read a description of an applicant—either "Michael" or "Michelle"—who had applied for a position as a police chief (Uhlmann & Cohen, 2005). Half of the participants in each of these conditions read that the applicant was *streetwise*, meaning tough, had worked in rough neighborhoods, and got along well with other officers. The other half of the participants read that the applicant was *educated*, meaning well-schooled and experienced in administration. Participants then rated the strength of the applicant's credentials as well as the importance of both streetwise and educated characteristics in hiring.

The results revealed that the criteria used to evaluate the candidate differed depending on the candidate's gender. If the male applicant was described as educated, educated criteria were seen as more important than when the female applicant was described as educated. In contrast, if the female candidate was

Examining the Effects of Affirmative Action Policies

Affirmative action policies, meaning policies designed to combat discrimination and promote equal opportunity for members of all groups, have received considerable attention in the legal system as well as in the field of psychology (Crosby & Franco, 2003). Affirmative action is used in hiring employees as well as in admitting students to schools. The benefits of such policies include increasing diversity, which can be beneficial to both majority and minority group members, and improving minority group members' access to jobs and education.

Affirmative action policies can also, however, lead to costs for precisely those people they are designed to help. For example, women who believe they were hired as managers because of their gender have less organizational commitment, less satisfaction with their work, and less satisfaction with their supervisor and co-workers (Chacko, 1982). Women who believe they were selected to be team leaders because of their gender also perform worse than those who are selected at random or who believe they were selected based on a combination of gender and random selection (Brown, Charnsangavej, Keough, Newman, & Rentfrow, 2000).

The negative effects of affirmative action are also apparent in school settings: students who believe they were admitted to college based on race preferences in admissions have lower GPAs than those who believe such criteria did not impact their admissions (Brown et al., 2000). Finally, the affirmative action label also affects the perceived competence of female and minority group hires, meaning that other people see those who potentially benefited from such policies as less capable than those who are assumed to have been hired based entirely on their own merits (Crosby, Iyer, Clayton, & Downing, 2003; Heilman, Block, & Lucas, 1992).

Does this mean that affirmative action policies should be eliminated? No: most research suggests that overall, affirmative action programs benefit both majority and minority group members, and that the potential negative costs of such policies can be eliminated or at least reduced (Crosby et al., 2003). First, affirmative action policies need to take into account an individual's distinct qualifications as well as his or her race and/or sex, which reduces the potential negative effects the beneficiaries of such policies may experience (Heilman et al., 1992). Second, emphasizing the substantial institutional and societal barriers many members of minority groups face, and thereby portraying such policies as simply "leveling the playing field," can serve to reduce negative feelings about such programs on the part of majority group members. In fact, even people who strongly endorse principles of merit, and thereby typically reject affirmative action programs, are supportive of such programs in cases of high levels of workplace discrimination, which therefore deprive minority group members of merit-based opportunity (Son Hing, Bobocel, & Zanna, 2002).

© MediaMagnet / Stockbroke/SUPERSTOCK

described as streetwise, educated characteristics were seen as much more important in the hiring decision than when the male candidate was described as streetwise. This study reveals that stereotypes do influence hiring decisions—and that male applicants are typically preferred—but that people justify these decisions using other factors. In sum, we've clearly come a long way, but there is still progress to be made.

PERSPECTIVES ON WHETHER STEREOTYPING IS INEVITABLE

FACTOR	EXAMPLE
Stereotypes are activated automatically	Jeanine is reading a newspaper article about a woman who is on welfare. She immediately assumes the woman is black, and is surprised to later read that she is white.
Stereotypes are hard to suppress	Ryan is working late, and is very tired. When evaluating a set of job applications, he rates the male applicants as more qualified than the female applicants, although their overall qualifications are virtually identical.
Disconfirming evidence is ignored	Yu Peng's new co-worker, Mary Jo, is from Alabama. Yu Peng has assumed that people from the South are all football fans, and thus is surprised to learn that Mary Jo doesn't follow football. Yu Peng now sees Mary Jo as an odd exception, and continues to believe that all people from the South are football fans.
Subtle discrimination persists	Eleanor and Mabel are trying to get a sales clerk's attention at a department store. They notice that the clerk helps other people who have not been waiting as long before she helps them.

HOW CAN SOCIAL AND COGNITIVE INTERVENTIONS HELP OVERCOME STEREOTYPES?

Although the last section described stereotypes as inevitable, the use of stereotypes can be reduced. In one study, researchers examined the effect of beliefs that men and women are equal, on reducing antigay prejudice (Dasgupta & Rivera, 2006). Participants read some information about a college student who they were told would be interviewing them about their attitudes toward politics. Some participants read that this interviewer was a member of the university's gay students alliance. Other participants read that the interviewer was a member of a fraternity. Participants were then interviewed by a student (who was really a confederate of the experimenter). Students who held traditional beliefs about the roles of women and homosexuals in our society showed discriminatory behavior—less eye contact, less smiling, and overall less comfort. Those with more tolerant views about the role of women and homosexuals showed more positive behavior. This section will examine this, and other ways, in which social and cognitive interventions can help people overcome their reliance on stereotypes, including increasing contact between groups, providing education and training, and being motivated to avoid stereotyping.

INCREASE CONTACT

Informal contact with people from different backgrounds is one effective strategy for reducing prejudice and is associated with more positive feelings, and reduced prejudice, toward members of a variety of out-groups (Pettigrew, 1997).

- White students who are randomly assigned to a Black roommate show more positive attitudes and reduced anxiety toward Blacks than those who have a White roommate (Shook & Fazio, 2008).
- Heterosexuals who have friendships with gay men have more positive attitudes toward gay men (Vonofakou, Hewstone, & Voci, 2007).

Providing opportunities for teenagers and older adults to work collaboratively on a shared project should lead to more positive attitudes toward both groups by in-group members.

- College students who have good relationships with their grandparents have more positive attitudes toward older adults (Harwood, Hewstone, Paolini, & Voci, 2005).
- Christians who have more contact with Muslims have stronger intentions to have future contact with members of the out-group (including living near members of the out-group, marrying a member of the out-group, and working for a member of the out-group; Henry & Hardin, 2006).

Even people who *know* an in-group member who has an out-group friend have less negative attitudes toward that group, as do those who observe an in-group/out-group friendship (Wright, Aron, McLaughlin-Volpe, & Ropp, 1997).

Increasing contact between people in different groups is an especially good strategy for reducing prejudice, given research showing that both Blacks and Whites want more interracial interaction, but believe that those in the out-group don't want contact with them (Shelton & Richeson, 2005). Both Whites and Blacks also attribute different motives for the lack of contact by members of their own versus other groups. Specifically, when people don't initiate contact with those in the out-group, they attribute their own behavior to fear of rejection. But they believe that when members of the out-group don't initiate contact with them, it is because of lack of interest. These biased perceptions, in turn, lead people to avoid inter-group contact during their first semester of college. (Does this phenomenon sound familiar? It should—remember the discussion of pluralistic ignorance in Chapter 8?)

Increasing contact between people from different groups is particularly beneficial when other conditions are met, including providing equal status contact and forming a common group identity. Let's look at these factors.

Provide equal status contact. Contact between people in different groups is most effective in reducing prejudice when the interaction occurs with two groups of equal status who work cooperatively (Desforges, Lord, Pugh, Sia, Scarberry, & Ratcliff, 1997; Dixon et al., 2005; Dovidio, Gaertner, & Validzic, 1998). For example, people who engage in a cooperative interaction with a person they believe was formerly a patient hospitalized for psychiatric illness adopt more positive attitudes and less prejudiced attitudes toward people who were psychiatric patients later on (Desforges et al., 1991). Similarly, and as described in Chapter 9, cooperative learning programs can help reduce prejudice by providing students with opportunities to talk with students from different backgrounds, learn from each other, and develop a shared social identity (Aronson & Bridgeman, 1979; Slavin & Cooper, 1999; Weigel et al., 1975).

Contact with people from different groups is especially beneficial when people see this contact as important, meaning they see it as personally relevant, valuable, and important (Van Dick et al., 2004). People who see inter-group contact as important in helping to broaden their horizons and gain insight into other cultures experience greater reductions in prejudice from having this contact. So it's not just having the contact, but having it with the right goals. In other words, reducing prejudice occurs not just having friends from out-groups, but seeing the presence of these friends as important to one's self.

Form a common group identity. A reduction in prejudice is also more likely when members of both groups develop a common group identity (Gaertner et al., 1999; Gaertner, Mann, Dovidio, Murrell, & Pomare, 1990; Gaertner, Mann, Murrell, & Dovidio, 1989). Simply emphasizing a superordinate category (e.g., instead of emphasizing the specific college one attends but rather the broad category of "college student") can reduce biases (Hornsey & Hogg, 2000). In one study, Whites read about a terrorist threat, and then watched a videotape

Questioning the Research

Although one study is described as showing that college students who have good relationships with their grandparents have more positive attitudes toward older adults, can you think of an alternative explanation for this finding? Hint: Does it show correlation or causation?

Dennis MacDonald/PhotoEdit

(Dovidio et al., 2004). In one condition the threat was described as "against all Americans." In the other condition, the threat was described as "against White Americans." Participants who read about the common threat (to all Americans) showed reduced prejudice toward Blacks, presumably because in this condition, participants experienced a "same group" feeling with a common identity of Americans, regardless of race.

One strategy for helping people in different groups adopt a common group identity is to have members of both groups pursue common goals (Gaertner et al., 1999; Slavin & Madden, 1979). As described in Chapter 9, a classic study by Sherif reduced prejudice between two groups of boys at a summer camp by creating a series of problems that required the use of goals that could be achieved only through cooperation among all members of both groups (Sherif et al., 1961). For example, in one case the camp truck "broke down" and the strength of everyone was needed to pull it up the hill. Developing this type of common goal, that requires the cooperation of members of both groups, is an effective way of breaking down stereotypes.

PROVIDE TRAINING AND EDUCATION

Stereotypes can also be controlled through education and training. Let's examine a few approaches: taking another person's perspective, learning considerable information about a person, and receiving training in statistical reasoning.

Take another person's perspective. Taking the perspective of a person in a stereotyped group can help decrease the prevalence of stereotyping (Esses & Dovidio, 2002). In one study, participants were asked to write about a day in the life of an elderly man (Galinsky & Moskowitz, 2000). Some were asked to suppress their stereotypes of the elderly whereas others were asked to take the perspective of the man while they wrote. Later, in a second task, those who had taken the perspective of the elderly man were less likely to recall stereotypes than those who had tried to suppress their stereotypes. Similarly, White participants who watched a videotape showing examples of racial discrimination and imagined the victim's feelings showed greater decreases in prejudice than those who didn't engage in this perspective-taking (Dovidio et al., 2004).

In a clever demonstration to help children experience how discrimination feels, Jane Elliott, an elementary school teacher in Iowa, told her students that "blue-eyed people were better than brown-eyed people." (On a later day this was reversed so that brown-eyed people were better than blue-eyed people.) She described numerous positive features of the high-status group (e.g., "George Washington had blue eyes"), gave students in this group preferential treatment (e.g., let them sit in the front of the classroom), and forbade students in the different groups from playing with each other at recess. This exercise helped students understand how it feels to be the target of prejudice and discrimination.

As you might expect, Elliott very quickly created a divided classroom. Children in the majority group ridiculed the kids in the other group, refused to play with them, and behaved aggressively toward them on the playground. Children in the minority group became depressed, withdrawn, and self-conscious. Perhaps most importantly, children performed worse on tests when they were members of the minority group than when they were members of the majority group.

Is this type of demonstration an effective technique for reducing prejudice? It is, but only if a person actually participates in the exercise; simply hearing a lecture or watching a video do not appear to reduce prejudicial attitudes (Byrnes & Kiger, 1990).

Learn considerable information about a person. People who have considerable personal information about a person also tend to rely less on stereotypes than those who are unable to make clear individualistic distinction among different group members (Locksley, Borgida, Brekke, & Hepburn, 1980; Postmes & Spears, 2002). For example, when you hear only that a person is a male or female,

DG/Associated Press

Jackie Robinson was recruited in 1947 by Branch Rickey, the owner of the Brooklyn Dodgers, who felt that integrating baseball would be good for the game and was the moral thing to do. Branch Rickey was assured by a social scientist friend that a baseball team had a number of features that could lead to successful integration—equal status among teammates, personal interactions, and pursuit of a common goal. Although Jackie Robinson faced racism throughout his career, this hiring was the start of the integration of baseball (and American sports).

you rely much more on the use of stereotypes than when you have more information about the person's actions.

Learning information about one member of a group can also help people think about a group in a more diverse way, and thereby decrease reliance on stereotypes (Wolsko, Park, Judd, & Wittenbrink, 2000). For example, exposing people to admired Black people (e.g., Denzel Washington) and disliked Whites (e.g., Jeffrey Dahmer) as well as positive Black stereotypes (e.g., a family barbecue, a church) reduces prejudice (Dasgupta & Greenwald, 2001; Wittenbrink, Judd, & Park, 2001). Similarly, exposing people to information about famous female leaders as well as seeing women in leadership positions decreases automatic stereotypes (Dasgupta & Asgari, 2004).

Provide training in statistical reasoning. Training in statistical reasoning, including gaining knowledge about how we can erroneously think certain things go together, reduces the formation of stereotypes (Schaller, Asp, Rosell, & Heim, 1996). As described previously, police officers are initially more likely to mistakenly shoot (on a computer simulation task) unarmed Blacks compared with unarmed White suspects (Plant, Peruche, & Butz, 2005). But, after repeated training with the computer program that reveals the race of the suspect is unrelated to whether a weapon is present, officers are able to eliminate their biases. This study demonstrates that training reduces police officers' biases toward shooting unarmed Blacks—a finding with very important real-world implications.

Even a simple shift, such as in how people think about inequality, can impact stereotypes. Whites who think about racial inequality as White privilege show lower racism than those who think about it as Black disadvantages (Powell, Branscombe, & Schmitt, 2005). Framing inequality as a Black disadvantage lets Whites interpret it as an out-group issue with little self-relevance. But focusing on White privilege may help focus people on the advantages of in-group membership, leading to more guilt and lower racism.

BE MOTIVATED TO AVOID STEREOTYPING

Stereotypes are, at least to some extent, within our control, meaning that people who are motivated can reduce their reliance on stereotypes (you can test your own motivation to avoid prejudice in the Rate Yourself exercise on the next page; Legault, Green-Demers, Grant, & Chung, 2007). For example, women tend to express less prejudice toward gay men and lesbians than do men (Ratcliff, Lassiter, Markman, & Snyder, 2006). This gender difference is largely a function of women's greater internal motivation to respond without prejudice. Similarly, Patricia Devine's research reveals that individuals can stop stereotyping or acting biased on stereotypes (Plant & Devine, 1998). People who are high on internal motivation to respond without prejudice (e.g., "I attempt to act in non-prejudiced ways toward Black people because it is personally important to me") and low on external motivation (e.g., "I attempt to appear non-prejudiced toward Black people in order to avoid disapproval from others") show lower levels of race bias on implicit tests as well as on self-reports (Amodio, Harmon-Jones, & Devine, 2003; Devine, Plant, Amodio, Harmon-Jones, & Vance, 2002).

So, what factors can help people avoid stereotyping? Let's review a few strategies, including increasing in self-awareness, adopting egalitarian goals, being motivated to be accurate, and avoiding trying too hard.

Increase self-awareness. People who do not want to hold prejudiced attitudes feel guilty when they believe they are engaging in a discriminatory way (Devine, Monteith, Zuwerink, & Elliot, 1991; Son Hing, Li, & Zanna, 2002; Macrae et al., 1998). In turn, pointing out their stereotypical attitudes leads to self-reflection, which can motivate them to change such beliefs. For example, telling White people that they had negative reactions to pictures of Blacks leads them to feel guilty and to inhibit such reactions later on (Monteith, Ashburn-Nardo, Voils, & Czopp, 2002). Similarly, activating straight people's self-discrepancies

How Motivated Are You to Avoid Prejudice?

Motivation to Be Non-prejudiced Scale

INSTRUCTIONS: *Rate each item regarding the extent to which each reason corresponds to your ultimate reason for avoiding prejudice on a scale of 1 (does not correspond at all) to 7 (corresponds exactly).*

- ☐ **1.** I am motivated to avoid prejudice because I would feel guilty if I were prejudiced.
- ☐ **2.** I am motivated to avoid prejudice because biased people are not well-liked.
- ☐ **3.** I am motivated to avoid prejudice because I am tolerant and accepting of differences.
- ☐ **4.** I am motivated to avoid prejudice because striving to understand others is part of who I am.
- ☐ **5.** I am motivated to avoid prejudice because I would feel bad about myself if I were prejudiced.
- ☐ **6.** I am motivated to avoid prejudice because I get more respect/acceptance when I act unbiased.
- ☐ **7.** I am motivated to avoid prejudice because I value non-prejudice.
- ☐ **8.** I am motivated to avoid prejudice because tolerance is important to me.

SCORING: Sum up your total number of points on all of these items.

INTERPRETATION: This scale measures individuals' motivation to avoid prejudice. People with higher scores are more motivated to avoid prejudice toward others, whereas those with lower scores are less motivated (Legault et al., 2007).

between their attitudes and behaviors regarding gay people leads low-prejudiced people to exert greater control over their prejudiced responses; once these discrepancies are activated, people who are low in prejudice feel bad and inhibit their response to a gay joke (Monteith, 1993). In sum, heightened self-focus reduces the expression of stereotypes, at least in participants who have a personal desire to avoid using stereotypes.

Adopt egalitarian goals. People with egalitarian goals, meaning a focus on avoiding the use of stereotypes, are able to control automatic stereotype activation (Moskowitz, Gollwitzer, Wasel, & Schaal, 1999). As described at the start of this section, people who held traditional beliefs about the roles of women and homosexuals in our society showed discriminatory behavior when they believed they were interacting with a gay student (Dasgupta & Rivera, 2006). In contrast, those with more tolerant views about the role of women and homosexuals avoided engaging in such behavior. In sum, stereotypes may be the dominant response, but they can be controlled in some situations and by some people.

Be motivated to be accurate. Because stereotypes are shortcuts that let us focus our energy on other things, we are especially likely to use stereotypes when we are under time pressure. This is one reason why powerful people, who tend to have more responsibility and thus are more likely to use cognitive shortcuts, often rely more on stereotypes (Fiske, 1993). People make immediate stereotypes about a person when they interact with them only briefly, but interactions as long as 15 minutes (when they are coupled with more information) lead to the inhibition of stereotypes (Kunda, Davies, Adams, & Spencer, 2002). This shows stereotypes are automatically and quickly activated, but that they are short-lived.

However, when you need to form an accurate impression of someone, you won't simply rely on quick and easy judgment rules such as stereotypes (Neuberg, 1989; Pendry & Macrae, 1994; Weary, Jacobson, Edwards, & Tobin, 2001).

You may initially categorize someone in a wheelchair largely based on what you see as his or her disability. However, if you are motivated to form an accurate impression of that person, you will focus more on that person's actual characteristics and rely less on stereotypes.

© Photodisc/SUPERSTOCK

Those who are motivated to be accurate gather more information and do so in a less biased way, which in turn improves their performance. For example, if you are told that you will work with this person on a joint task and that you can win money for performing well on the task, you pay more attention to the person's actual characteristics and rely less on the stereotypes (Neuberg & Fiske, 1987).

Avoid trying too hard. In some cases, people's efforts to appear nonbiased can backfire, and lead people to behave in a more distant manner to members of other groups (Norton, Sommers, Apfelbaum, Pura, & Ariely, 2006; Vorauer, 2005). In one study, White participants believed they would discuss either racial profiling or love and relationships with either a White or a Black partner (Goff, Steele, & Davies, 2008). White participants sat closer to Black partners than White partners when they expected to discuss love and relationships, but sat farther away when they expected to discuss racial profiling. Just the threat of appearing racist may lead Whites to stand farther away from Blacks.

Ironically, people who are high in prejudice can overcompensate for this bias and therefore seem especially nice or even nicer than those who are low in prejudice (Shelton et al., 2005). In one study, some people were told that the study focused on how they act toward someone from a different ethnic group (Vorauer & Turpie, 2004). Others did not receive this information about the study's focus. Findings indicate that people who are low in prejudice and who believe the study focuses on how they act toward those in a different ethnic group are less warm and responsive to their partner than those who did not receive this information. Those who are low in prejudice may be anxious about appearing racist, and this concern may lead them, ironically, to act in a more distant and controlled manner. On the other hand, those who are high in prejudice treat their interaction partner better if they are told about the evaluation than if they are not. Once again, efforts to show "color blindness" can backfire, meaning that people who are high in prejudice can at times appear less prejudiced than those who are actually low in prejudice.

Concepts in Context

WAYS IN WHICH SOCIAL AND COGNITIVE INTERVENTIONS CAN HELP OVERCOME STEREOTYPES

FACTOR	EXAMPLE
Increase contact	The "nerds" and "jocks" at Nathan's high school rarely interacted, and saw members of the out-group in very stereotyped ways. After the school worked together to win a city-wide recycling contest, these divisions between groups largely disappeared.
Provide training and education	Allison, a Methodist, thought of Jewish people as being very different from herself. But after reading Anne Frank's diary in school, she learned that Jewish girls shared many of her same hopes and fears.
Be motivated to avoid using stereotypes	Rosalina was surprised to learn that she responded differently to photographs of other Latinas than she did to photos of Blacks. She now makes a conscious effort to respond in a similar way to people of all ethnicities.

HOW DOES CULTURE INFLUENCE PREJUDICE AND STEREOTYPES?

You are probably familiar with the stereotype that older people experience memory loss. But would you believe that the mere presence of this stereotype can *cause* such memory loss? Researchers examined whether the negative American stereotypes about aging would impact memory scores in older Americans, but not among older people in groups in which this stereotype was not present (Levy & Langer, 1994). Participants were from three groups: Americans who could hear, Americans who were deaf (who presumably would be less aware of cultural stereotypes), and Chinese who were hearing (and who live in a culture in which older people are considered in a very honored way). In each of these three groups, half of the participants were younger adults (ages 15 to 30) and half were older adults (ages 59 to 91). All participants completed several memory tests. As predicted, memory scores did not differ across the three groups for the younger participants, indicating that memory was equally good across Americans who could hear, Americans who were deaf, and Chinese people who were hearing. However, in the older age group, memory scores among the Americans who were deaf and Chinese people were significantly higher than among the Americans who could hear.

These findings suggest that the negative American stereotypes about memory in older adults may actually create a self-fulfilling prophecy in which memory loss is greater than in cultures in which a negative stereotype does not exist. This section will examine the impact of culture on the reliance on cognitive biases as well as the types of stereotypes.

RELIANCE ON COGNITIVE BIASES

People in collectivistic cultures are less likely than those in individualistic cultures to show the ultimate attribution error, in which they attribute positive behavior within one's group to oneself, and to attribute negative behavior within one's group to external factors (Pettigrew, 1979). In one study, researchers asked Malaysian men (half from the Chinese ethnicity, and half from the Malay ethnicity) to read a series of descriptions about a person's behavior (Hewstone & Ward, 1985). Some scenarios described a positive behavior, such as a person helping someone who had fallen off a bicycle. Other scenarios described a negative behavior, such as a person refusing to shelter someone who had been caught in a rainstorm. In addition, some of these paragraphs featured a Chinese person, whereas others described a Malay person. The participants then chose an explanation for the behavior.

These findings indicated that culture influenced people's use of **in-group favoritism.** As you would expect, members of the Malay ethnic group tended to explain positive behaviors on the part of the Malay actor as having internal causes, and negative behavior as having external causes, more than when the actor was Chinese. This finding is in line with prior research on in-group favoritism and attributional biases.

Interestingly, however, Chinese people actually favored the out-group. They made more internal attributions for negative behavior, and fewer internal attributions for positive behavior, by the Chinese person than the Malay person. This research points to the important role of culture in influencing the attributions we make for behavior by in-group versus out-group members.

People in collectivistic cultures also show more evidence of in-group favoritism. In one study, researchers asked Korean sixth graders to resolve a conflict between two people with different goals (Han & Park, 1995). Children with a collectivistic orientation were much more likely to show greater discrimination between in-groups and out-groups than those with an individualistic orientation.

TYPES OF STEREOTYPES

As described at the start of this section, cultures vary in the stereotypes they hold about different people. These stereotypes then influence how we see members of different groups. For example, the negative American stereotypes about memory problems in older adults may lead to greater memory loss in older adults in the United States than in countries in which such a stereotype does not exist. Two other stereotypes that show difference across cultures are beliefs about people who are overweight and beliefs about women.

Stereotypes about people who are overweight.   As described in Chapter 5, collectivistic cultures emphasize the role of situations, not just dispositions, in influencing behavior. In turn, people in collectivistic cultures put less blame on obese people for their weight, and thereby show lower levels of prejudice and discrimination than people in individualistic cultures, who place great emphasis on the role of personal responsibility in determining weight.

People in individualistic cultures (such as the United States) versus collectivistic cultures (such as Mexico) differ in how they attribute the causes of obesity to internal versus external factors.

In one study, Chris Crandall and his colleagues examined anti-fat prejudice and attributions of controllability of weight in nearly 1000 people from six different countries (United States, Australia, India, Poland, Venezuela, and Turkey; Crandall, D'Anello, Sakalli, Lazarus, Wieczorkowska, & Feather, 2001). As predicted, among individualistic cultures, the tendency to see fat as controllable led to greater prejudice, in part because people place more emphasis on individuals' autonomy and choice. As predicted, Americans report much greater prejudice against fat people than do Mexicans, in part because Americans are more likely to hold individual people responsible for their weight and to see weight as controllable (see Figure 10.7; Crandall & Martinez, 1996).

Stereotypes about women.   As described previously, researchers Peter Glick and Susan Fiske developed a theory of sexism that distinguishes between **hostile sexism** and **benevolent sexism**, and this theory has been tested in 19 different countries (Glick & Fiske, 1996, 2001; Glick et al., 2000; Glick et al., 2004). In some ways, sexist beliefs are very similar across different cultures:

- hostile and benevolent sexism are correlated in all cultures, with hostile sexism predicting negative traits and benevolent sexism predicting positive traits;
- although women show more rejection of hostile sexism than do men, both men and women commonly endorse benevolent sexism; and
- both men and women see men in more negative ways, but also as having more power.

These hostile and benevolent attitudes toward women reflect and support gender inequality by describing men as inherently dominant.

In other ways, cross-cultural comparisons reveal different beliefs about women. Specifically, mean scores on both types of sexism in a given culture are inversely related to gender equality, including women's empowerment (e.g., representation in high-powered roles in a society) and development (e.g., longevity, education, standards of living; Glick et al., 2004). In highly sexist cultures, women endorsed benevolent sexism even more than did men. This finding suggests that women may accept benevolent sexism as the lesser of two evils when they are in a culture with generally negative attitudes toward women, and may be motivated to endorse this type of sexism as a way of gaining protection from men. Unfortunately, benevolent sexism can legitimize hostile sexism by allowing men to hold condescending

FIGURE
10.7

HOW DOES CULTURE INFLUENCE ANTI-FAT ATTITUDES?

Researchers asked students from a collectivistic culture, Mexico, and an individual-istic one, the United States, about their attitudes toward fat people and being fat. As predicted, Americans report much greater prejudice against fat people than do Mexicans, in part because Americans are more likely to hold individual people responsible for their weight and to see weight as controllable.

Source: Crandall, C. S., & Martinez, R. (1996). Culture, ideology, and antifat attitudes. *Personality and Social Psychology Bulletin, 22,* 1165-1176.

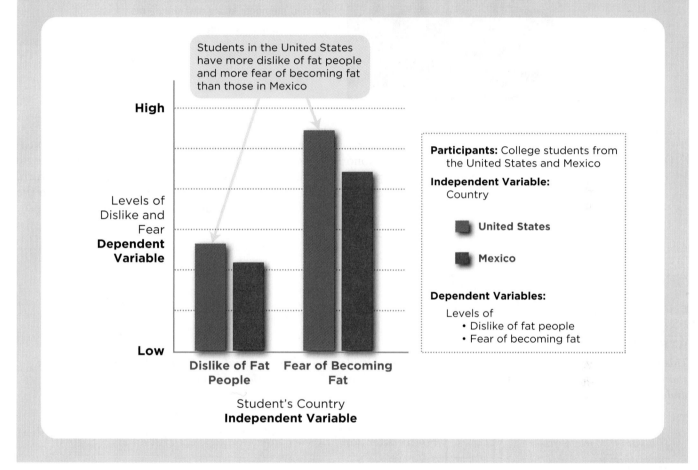

attitudes toward women, and can thereby undermine women's efforts to achieve true equality.

This perception of women as needing protection, and as part of the property of their families, can have dangerous, and even deadly, consequences. The term "honor killing" refers to an act of violence, usually murder, committed by male family members against female family members, who are seen as having brought dishonor upon the family (see In the News). This dishonor can be caused by refus-ing to enter into an arranged marriage, dating or marrying a person outside of her family's ethnic and/or religious community, seeking a divorce, or committing adultery. These killings are supported not only by men in the family, but also by other women, due to the perception in these cultures that the family is the prop-erty and asset of men.

© AP/Wide World Photos

In the NEWS **Honor Killing:** In 2006, **Banaz Mahmod**, a 20-year-old Muslim woman living in England, was strangled with a boot lace, stuffed into a suitcase, and buried in a garden after her father learned she had fallen in love with the "wrong man." Her father, who planned the honor killing and hired a man to carry it out, was sentenced to life in prison.

Honor killings can occur even in cases in which the woman has no responsibility for the "dishonoring" behavior. For example, in some cultures a single woman who is raped will be unable to garner a bride price if she marries. In turn, women who are raped are seen as worthless burdens that bring dishonor to the family—and may even be killed for this act of "allowing" themselves to be raped.

The Big Picture

STEREOTYPES AND PREJUDICE

This chapter included many applications of the three "big ideas" studied in social psychology. The examples below should help you see the connection between stereotypes and prejudice and these big ideas and contribute to your understanding of the big picture of social psychology.

THEME	EXAMPLES
The social world influences how we think about ourselves.	• People who call attention to their connection to successful others feel good about themselves. • Women who see gender-stereotypic commercials see themselves as less suited for careers that require quantitative skills. • People who attribute others' negative behavior toward them to prejudice feel sad and depressed.
The social world influences our thoughts, attitudes, and behaviors.	• Children whose parents express prejudiced attitudes and behaviors are likely to form those attitudes themselves. • Men who have prejudiced attitudes toward women ask female job applicants fewer questions about their strengths than they ask male job applicants. • People who are primed with black faces are more likely to misidentify tools as guns than those who are primed with white faces.
Our attitudes and behavior shape the social world around us.	• We see people in our in-groups as different and unique, but see people in out-groups as very similar to one another. • White students who interview job applicants "as if they are black" elicit worse performance than those who interview applicants "as if they are white." • People who are told that they will work with another person on a joint task and can win money for performing well pay more attention to the person's actual characteristics and rely less on the stereotypes.

This chapter examined social psychological factors that contribute to stereotyping, prejudice, and discrimination.

YOU LEARNED **How do social psychological factors contribute to stereotyping and prejudice?** This chapter examined a number of social psychological factors that contribute to stereotyping and prejudice. These factors include social learning from parents and peers, social categorization, realistic group conflict theory, social identity theory, and cognitive biases, such as illusory correlation, solo status, the ultimate attribution error, the contrast effect, perceptual confirmation, and confirmation bias. You also learned why discriminating against another person after you've received negative feedback about your intelligence can make you feel better.

YOU LEARNED **What are the consequences of being stereotyped?** This chapter examined various negative consequences of being stereotyped. These consequences include behavioral confirmation or self-fulfilling prophecy, stereotype threat, reduced psychological well-being, reverse discrimination, and the hazards of positive stereotypes. You also learned that women who watch gender-stereotypic commercials underperform on a math test.

YOU LEARNED **Is stereotyping inevitable?** This chapter reviewed evidence that stereotyping is inevitable. Stereotypes can be seen as inevitable in part because such stereotypes are activated automatically and are hard to suppress. In addition, disconfirming evidence is ignored, and even when blatant prejudice is rare, subtle discrimination persists. You also learned that both Black and White participants correctly shoot an armed target more quickly if the target is Black than White, and refrain from shooting an unarmed target more quickly if the target is White than Black.

YOU LEARNED **How can social and cognitive interventions help overcome stereotypes?** This chapter examined several ways in which stereotypes can be overcome. These strategies include increasing contact between members of different groups, providing training and education, and being motivated to avoid using stereotypes. You also learned that people who have egalitarian motives act more positively toward a homosexual person than those without such motives.

YOU LEARNED **How does culture influence prejudice and stereotypes?** This chapter examined the impact of culture on prejudice and stereotypes. First, we examined the reliance on cognitive biases, such as the ultimate attribution error and in-group favoritism, across different cultures. Next, we examined the prevalence of different stereotypes in different cultures, and specifically the prevalence of fat bias and sexism. You also learned why older hearing Americans perform worse on memory tests that older Chinese people or deaf Americans.

KEY TERMS

QUESTIONS FOR REVIEW

1. Describe four social psychological factors that lead to stereotypes.
2. What are three negative consequences of stereotypes?
3. Describe two pieces of evidence suggesting that stereotypes occur automatically.
4. What are four strategies for helping reducing stereotypes, prejudice, and/or discrimination?
5. Describe cultural differences in the prevalence of different stereotypes.

TAKE ACTION!

1. Your sister recently had twins and wants very much to raise them to have tolerant and accepting attitudes toward people from different backgrounds. What advice would you give her?
2. After you overheard a friend tell a sexist joke, you have an argument about whether stereotypes are truly harmful to members of low-status and disadvantaged groups. What information could you give him about the dangers of stereotyping?
3. Your father is attending a male friend's commitment ceremony to another man this weekend. He is not very comfortable with the idea of two men getting married. What advice would you give him about overcoming his negative attitudes and behavior?
4. Think about your high school and identify some examples of discrimination. Based on your knowledge of social and cognitive interventions to reduce stereotypes, what strategies could you implement to help reduce prejudice and discrimination?
5. Your grandparents are planning a trip to Egypt. What might you tell them to expect about stereotypes and prejudice toward women?

Try some of these research activities to gain experience in conducting and evaluating research, and to increase your understanding of research methods and techniques in social psychology.

Visit WileyPLUS for more activities and interactive research tools!
(www.wileyplus.com)

Participate in Research

Activity 1 **The Power of Social Categorization:** This chapter has described how quickly and easily we divide people into those who are like us (our in-group) and those who are different from us (our out-group). Go online to rate which types of people you would place into each category.

Activity 2 **The Hazards of Positive Stereotypes:** You've learned in this chapter about the hazards of even positive stereotypes about individuals in particular groups. Rate the characteristics of different groups you know to see what types of positive and negative stereotypes you hold.

Activity 3 **The Automatic Activation of Stereotypes:** This chapter described how stereotypes are activated at an automatic and unconscious level. Visit WileyPLUS to test how readily your stereotypes toward others can be activated using a version of the IAT test.

Activity 4 **Strategies for Reducing Stereotypes:** You learned in this chapter about factors that reduce people's reliance on stereotypes. Rate how effective you think these different strategies could be in reducing stereotypes.

Activity 5 **The Impact of Culture on Stereotypes:** The final section of this chapter described how people from different cultures vary in the types of stereotypes they hold. Go to WileyPLUS to rate your views about people in different groups.

Test a Hypothesis

One of the common findings in research on stereotypes and prejudice is that we learn stereotypes from what we see in the media. To test whether this hypothesis is true, watch several children's television programs and count the number of sex-stereotyped behaviors in which boys and girls engage. What do your findings reveal?

Design a Study

To design your own study testing the factors that contribute to stereotyping and prejudice, go to WileyPLUS. You'll be able to choose the type of study you want to conduct (self-report, observational/naturalistic, or experimental), choose your own independent and dependent variables, and form your own hypothesis. Then, you can share your findings with other students.

11

Aggression

Health
CONNECTIONS
The Link Between Alcohol Use and Aggression

WHAT YOU'LL LEARN

How do biological factors influence aggression?

RESEARCH FOCUS ON GENDER
Explaining Gender Differences in Aggressive Behavior

How do social psychological factors influence aggression?

How does the media influence aggression?

RESEARCH FOCUS ON NEUROSCIENCE
The Impact of Violent Media on the Brain

How can we reduce aggression?

How does CULTURE influence aggression?

Did you ever wonder?

On October 2, 2006, Charles Carl Roberts IV walked into a tiny Amish schoolhouse in Lancaster County, Pennsylvania, carrying tools, guns, and ammunition. He allowed the 15 boys and three women with infants to leave and then barricaded the doors to the one-room schoolhouse. Roberts told the remaining 10 female students, ranging in age from six to 10, to line up in front of the blackboard, and tied the girls' feet together. As the police began to surround the building, Roberts called his wife to tell her that he would not be coming home. He then began shooting the girls in the head at close range before killing himself, as police began to enter the schoolhouse. Five girls died in the attack, including sisters, Mary Liz Miller, age eight, and Lena Miller, age seven. The other five girls were critically wounded.

How did the Amish community react to this tragedy? They reached out to the families of the victims, but they also reached out to the family of the man who committed these acts. The evening of the attacks a group of Amish people organized a horse and buggy to visit the family of Charles Carl Roberts with food

376

Business
CONNECTIONS
The Dangers of Sexual Harassment

Media
CONNECTIONS
The Hazards of Violent Pornography

Education
CONNECTIONS
The Problem of Bullying

and sympathy. They invited the killer's widow to the family funerals, and established two memorial funds, one for the families of the dead girls, one to provide for the killer's family. This type of forgiveness and empathy is remarkable in today's world, in which many acts of violence are followed by violence.

This chapter will describe factors that may have contributed to Roberts' decision to commit this horrible crime, as well as factors that led members of the Amish community to reach out to his family following the tragedy. You'll also find out...

Q A Why are prisoners who are high in testosterone more likely to violate prison rules?

Q A Why does the mere presence of a gun lead to more aggression?

Q A Why does watching violent television lead you to see other people as evil?

Q A Why is saying you are sorry often a good idea?

Q A Why is hurting someone who insults your sister more understandable in the Southern United States than in the North?

NewsCom

Although people use the word aggression regularly in daily life, it can be surprisingly hard to define exactly what this word means. Is accidentally hurting someone aggressive? Is crashing into someone during a hockey game aggressive? Is yelling at someone aggressive? In social psychology, **aggression** refers to physical or verbal behavior that is intended to hurt another person who does not want to be injured. According to this definition, it would not include accidental acts (e.g., unintentionally hitting someone with an errant golf ball), or assertive acts (e.g., asking for a refund for your new broken television).

Researchers also distinguish between different types of aggression. **Emotional or hostile aggression** refers to aggression in which one inflicts harm for its own sake. Examples of hostile aggression including a jealous lover striking out in a rage or soccer fans having a brawl in the stands after a game. In contrast, **instrumental aggression** describes inflicting harm in order to obtain something of value. People who kill others in self-defense, or to gain money or attention, are motivated by instrumental aggression.

HOW DO BIOLOGICAL FACTORS INFLUENCE AGGRESSION?

One of the most basic and fundamental factors that influences aggression is biological makeup: including instincts and evolution, genetics, and hormones. Jim Dabbs and his colleagues at Georgia State University examined rates of testosterone and misbehavior in male prison inmates (Dabbs, Carr, Frady, & Riad, 1995). Researchers collected saliva samples from 692 male inmates to measure levels of testosterone. They also examined data on the type of crime for which each inmate was serving time (robbery, assault, drug offenses, and so on), and whether the inmate had received a disciplinary report for violating prison rules during his incarceration.

These data revealed that men who had committed violent crimes, such as rape and assault, had higher testosterone levels than men who had committed property crimes, such as burglary and theft. In addition, men with higher testosterone levels had violated more rules while in prison. This study suggests that testosterone levels are associated with men's aggression behavior, including the type of criminal activity that led to their incarceration as well as patterns of misbehavior while incarcerated.

This section will examine the role of biological factors in predicting aggressive aggression, including instinct and evolutionary explanations as well as genetic and hormonal explanations.

INSTINCT AND EVOLUTIONARY THEORIES

Innate theories of aggression share a common link in that they describe something within the person that is responsible for aggressive tendencies, and that this is not a learned behavior. Let's examine two of the most famous theories.

Freud's death wish. Sigmund Freud (1930) believed that people possess a powerful death wish or drive, which is caused by the struggles and tensions of daily life. In order to cope with this unconscious desire, people need to channel this energy in some direction. One possibility is that they can turn this energy inward—and thereby engage in self-destructive behavior. Another option is to turn this energy outward—and thereby engage in aggression against other people.

Freud (1933) also saw aggression as a type of energy that builds up over time until it is released, a process called **catharsis**. This view of aggression was accepted for a long time, and led to considerable practical advice. For example, the idea that people should "blow off some steam" to relieve built-up tension is based in

aggression physical or verbal behavior that is intended to hurt another person who does not want to be injured

emotional (or hostile) aggression aggression in which one inflicts harm for its own sake on another

instrumental aggression aggression in which one inflicts harm in order to obtain something of value

catharsis the belief that aggression is a type of energy that builds up over time until it is released

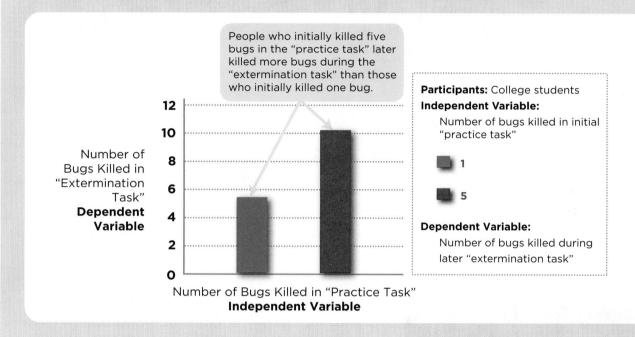

FIGURE 11.1 — DOES CATHARSIS INCREASE AGGRESSION?

Researchers in this experiment asked participants to kill bugs in a "practice task," then gave them the opportunity to kill bugs again in a later "extermination task." The results did not support the catharsis theory: people who expressed a large amount of aggression engaged in more, not less, aggression later on.

Source: Martens, A., Kosloff, S., Greenberg, J., Landau, M. J., & Schmader, T. (2007). Killing begets killing: Evidence from a bug-killing paradigm that initial killing fuels subsequent killing. *Personality and Social Psychology Bulletin*, 33, 1251-1264. Used by permission of Sage Publications.

People who initially killed five bugs in the "practice task" later killed more bugs during the "extermination task" than those who initially killed one bug.

Number of Bugs Killed in "Extermination Task" **Dependent Variable**

Number of Bugs Killed in "Practice Task" **Independent Variable**

Participants: College students
Independent Variable: Number of bugs killed in initial "practice task"
1
5
Dependent Variable: Number of bugs killed during later "extermination task"

the idea of catharsis. A billboard in Texas emphasized the belief in catharsis using the slogan, "Hit a pillow, hit a wall, but don't hit your kids." This view is often promoted by the mass media and accepted by the general public. In the movie *Analyze This*, a psychiatrist played by Billy Crystal tells his mafia client, "You know what I do when I'm angry? I hit a pillow. Try that." People who are angry are advised to "blow off steam," "get it off your chest," and "don't bottle up anger inside." In sum, the popular view is that releasing one's anger is beneficial.

However, catharsis is not generally seen as an effective way of dealing with aggressive feelings. Scientific evidence suggests that engaging in aggressive behavior does not reduce aggressive feelings, and in some cases may even increase them (Bushman, Baumeister, & Phillips, 2001; Bushman, Baumeister, & Stack, 1999). For example, participants who are asked to kill one bug initially as part of a "practice task" later kill fewer bugs during a timed "extermination task" than those who are asked to kill five bugs during the practice task, suggesting that higher levels of initial aggressive behavior can lead to increasing levels of aggression later on (see Figure 11.1; Martens, Kosloff, Greenberg, Landau, & Schmader, 2007). Why is catharsis so ineffective? In part because imagining or observing aggression may actually feel good, which can then become rewarding.

Lorenz's instinct theory. Konrad Lorenz also saw aggression as a natural and instinctual motivation (Lorenz, 1966, 1974). According to Lorenz's **instinct theory**, people's innate desire to live leads to our desire to aggress against others. This instinct to aggress would develop because only those animals that were aggressive would ensure that they (and their offspring) would survive (e.g., by securing food, shelter, protection from predators, etc.).

instinct theory a theory that describes people's innate desire to live as leading to the desire to aggress against others

"My first choice, of course, is to solve things amicably."

Aggression may be evolutionarily advantageous in some situations, but it's hard to see how yelling at other drivers can help survival.

Lorenz's theory, and other theories of sociobiology and evolutionary psychology, propose that the drive for aggression is evolutionarily adaptive because those who are aggressive have a greater likelihood of living (for themselves and their offspring). These theorists suggest that this is why in virtually all societies men are more aggressive than women (because aggression is how men obtain status and hence the best females). This theory also explains why parents are much more likely to abuse and murder stepchildren, with whom they don't share genes, than biological children (Daly & Wilson, 1996). It also explains why sexual jealousy, caused by men's concern that they will expend resources on another man's child, often leads to aggression (Buss, 1995; Buss & Shackleford, 1997; Wilson & Daly, 1996).

GENETICS

Considerable research points to the role of genetic factors in influencing aggression (DiLalla & Gottesman, 1991). One meta-analysis suggests that up to 50% of the variance in aggression may be caused by genetic factors (Miles & Carey, 1997). In support of the view that genetics influences aggression, marked individual differences in rates of aggression are seen even by age three (Deluty, 1985; Olweus, 1979). In one study, researchers examined interpersonal behavior during school over an 8-month period in 50 children (22 boys, 28 girls) in 3rd, 4th, and 5th grade (Deluty, 1985). Researchers were trained to identify and count particular types of aggressive behavior, such as physical attacks (biting, hitting), verbal attacks (teasing, ridiculing), shouting, and bossing other children. The children were then watched by the observers (in unobtrusive ways) in a number of different types of school settings, including reading silently during class, taking tests, rehearsing for a play, participating in art and music classes, and playing at recess. Findings revealed that boys showed remarkable consistency in their expression of aggression, meaning that boys who engaged in more of one type of aggression also engaged in more of other types of aggression. Although girls showed less consistency in the types of aggressive behavior they engaged in than did boys, relatively consistent associations between different types of aggressive behavior were also seen in girls. These findings reveal that the frequency of aggressive behavior is quite high across different types of school situations as well as in different measures of aggression, and suggest that genetic factors may be associated with the frequency of aggressive behavior. (See Rate Yourself to test your own level of aggression.)

Other evidence that suggests a role of genetics in predicting aggressive behavior comes from longitudinal research indicating that children who are highly aggressive early in life are more likely to be aggressive later. For example, both boys and girls who are rated as aggressive by their teachers at age 13 are more likely to engage in delinquent law-breaking behavior by age 26 (Stattin & Magnusson, 1989). In one study, Rowell Huesmann and his colleagues examined over 600 eight-year-olds, and then followed these children 22 years later (Huesmann, Eron, Lefkowitz, & Walder, 1984). People who were the most aggressive at the beginning of the study were also the most aggressive

WOULD YOU BELIEVE... Aggression is Often Caused by a Loved One? According to the National Clearinghouse on Child Abuse and Neglect, an estimated 872,000 children are abused each year. Of these, 62.4% suffer neglect, 17.5% are physically abused, 9.7% are sexually abused, 7% are emotionally or psychologically maltreated, 2.1% are medically neglected, and the remaining 14.5% experience other types of maltreatment such as abandonment or threats of harm. Experiencing abuse and neglect can lead to long-lasting problems, including aggression, dating violence, criminal behavior, substance abuse, emotional problems, and even suicide. In some cases, abuse can be fatal: an estimated 1400 children die of abuse or neglect each year.

Perhaps most surprisingly, abuse and neglect are often perpetrated by a child's parents. In fact, 79% of deaths from abuse or neglect are caused by a parent. These deaths can be caused by a single act of abuse, such as suffocation or drowning, or repeated abuse over time, such as extended malnourishment, repeated beating, or shaking. What could possibly lead a parent to abuse his or her child? Parents who abuse and neglect their children are often normal psychologically, but are under severe stress, perhaps due to financial pressures, crowded living conditions, and inadequate social support (Belsky, 1993; Malinosky-Rummell & Hansen, 1993; Peterson & Brown, 1994). They may also have been abused themselves.

Women are also at substantial risk of experiencing aggression at the hands of a loved one. An estimated two to three million women are physically assaulted by a male partner each year in the United States, and between 21% and 34% of all women experience such an assault during adulthood (Browne, 1993). Women who experience abuse often suffer long-term emotional and physical health consequences. These include effects of physical injury, such as traumatic brain injury, and emotional problems, such as depression (Jackson, Philip, Nuttal, & Diller, 2002; Rennison & Welchans, 2000).

A particular type of aggression that women may experience is rape, and college women are at particular risk. One survey of over 6,000 students at 32 colleges across the United States revealed that 27.5% of women reported experiencing an act that met the legal definition of rape (Koss, Gidycz, & Wisniewski, 1987). Although people often think about rape as a crime committed by a stranger, women are four times as likely to be raped by someone they know than by a stranger (Koss, 1992). As high as these estimates are, they are undoubtedly low because many date or acquaintance rapes go unreported.

Robert A. Sabo/Getty Images, Inc.

In the NEWS **Aggression by Loved Ones.** On January 11, 2006, 7-year-old Nixzmary Brown was found dead in her New York City apartment. Her mother and step-father were charged with second-degree murder and child endangerment, with each one claiming the other ultimately committed the final blow that killed the small girl. Her step-father was convicted of manslaughter and was sentenced to 25 years in prison; her mother was also convicted of manslaughter and was sentenced to 43 years in prison.

at the end of the study, showing that aggression is remarkably stable. Those who were aggressive as children were more likely to be involved in more serious aggressive acts later on, including criminal behavior, spouse abuse, and traffic violations.

Although research on the stability of rates of aggression over time can be interpreted as providing support for a genetic view of the causes of aggression, environmental factors are also very likely to stay stable over time. In other words, children who observe and/or experience aggressive behavior in their parents at one point in time are likely to continue to observe and/or experience such aggression later on (and you'll learn about the role of modeling, and other social psychological factors, in leading to aggression in the next section). Thus, merely finding stability in rates of aggression is not enough to prove that genetics alone explains aggressive behavior.

HORMONES

In virtually all societies, males are more aggressive than females. One theory about the causes of these gender differences in aggression is the presence of the male sex hormone testosterone (Mazur & Booth, 1998; Olweus, Mattsson, Schalling, & Löw, 1988; Susman, Inoff-Germain, Nottelman, & Loriaux, 1987). In line with this view, people who are highly aggressive have higher levels of testosterone than those who are less aggressive: boys ages 5 to 11 who are aggressive show higher levels of testosterone (Chance, Brown, Dabbs, & Casey, 2000); delinquent and violent people have higher testosterone levels than do college students (Banks & Dabbs, 1996). Among inmates who commit homicide, those high in testosterone more often knew their victims and planned their crimes ahead of time (Dabbs, Riad, & Chance, 2001). As described at the start of this section, men with higher levels of testosterone are more likely to commit personal crimes than property crimes, and are more likely to violate rules while they are in prison (Dabbs et al., 1995).

Testosterone rates are also correlated with level of violence in women. Researchers examined rates of testosterone and levels of aggression in female prison inmates (Dabbs & Hargrove, 1997). As predicted, women who were rated as highly aggressive by guards (such as behaving physically aggressive to others and repeatedly breaking rules) had higher rates of testosterone than those who were neutral or passive in their behavior. Research Focus on Gender describes other gender differences in aggression.

Rate Yourself

How Aggressive Are You?

The Aggression Questionnaire

INSTRUCTIONS: *Rate each item on a scale of 1 (extremely uncharacteristic of me) to 5 (extremely characteristic of me).*

☐ **1.** Once in a while I can't control the urge to strike another person.
☐ **2.** I have become so mad that I have broken things.
☐ **3.** Given enough provocation, I may hit another person.
☐ **4.** If I have to resort to violence to protect my rights, I will.
☐ **5.** I tell my friends openly when I disagree with them.
☐ **6.** I often find myself disagreeing with people.
☐ **7.** My friends say that I'm somewhat argumentative.
☐ **8.** When people annoy me, I may tell them what I think of them.

SCORING: Sum up your total number of points on the first four items. Then sum up your total number of points on the second four items.

INTERPRETATION: The first four items measure physical aggression, whereas the next four items measure verbal aggression. People with higher scores on the first four items have higher levels of physical aggression than those with lower scores. People with higher scores on the next four items have higher levels of verbal aggression than those with lower scores (Buss & Perry, 1992).

Explaining Gender Differences in Aggressive Behavior

Who is more aggressive, men and boys or women and girls? Most of us see this as an easy question—surely boys and men are much more aggressive than girls and women. And research evidence generally supports this view; men commit the vast majority of homicides (Knight, Fabes, & Higgins, 1996), and even among small children, boys show more physical aggression, meaning acts intended to inflict physical harm, than girls (Hyde, 1984; Loeber & Hay, 1997). This gender difference may be due in part to genetic and evolutionary factors, including men's higher levels of testosterone and their historical role in protecting women (especially during periods of pregnancy and nursing).

But biology and evolution are not the only explanations for gender differences in aggression. According to **social learning theory**, males and females are taught different things about the costs and benefits of aggression (Eagly & Steffen, 1986). Specifically, boys who use their fists to fight may receive social rewards (admiration from parents and peers) whereas girls who engage in this behavior may be punished (Rodkin, Farmer, Pearl, & VanAcker, 2000). In fact, highly aggressive boys are often seen as cool and athletic, and may be among the most popular children in elementary school classrooms.

social learning theory a theory that describes behavior as learned by observing or modeling others' behavior as well as by the presence of punishments and rewards, or reinforcements

Although men usually are more aggressive than women, these gender differences are not large, and the differences are smaller in more recent studies than in older ones (Hyde, 1984). Gender differences in aggression differ substantially for distinct types of aggression. Men and boys are much higher than women and girls on rates of physical aggression, but only slightly higher on rates of verbal aggression (meaning verbal expressions intended to hurt someone else) and are lower on rates of relational aggression (meaning behaviors intended to disrupt relationships; Archer, 2004; Archer & Coyne, 2005; Buss & Perry, 1992; Crick, Casas, & Mosher, 1997; Crick & Grotpeter, 1995). Similarly, men aggress more than women in cases of aggression caused by physical injury or pain, but women aggress more in cases in which aggression produces psychological or social harm, suggesting that gender differences in aggression are caused largely by social roles and learning (Archer, 2000; Eagly & Steffen, 1986; Jenkins & Aubé, 2002).

Gender differences in aggression are also larger in more naturalistic studies than in experimental ones, and when behavior is measured through observation as opposed to self-report (Hyde, 1984). A meta-analysis by Bettencourt & Miller (1996) revealed that unprovoked men are more aggressive than women, but differences among provoked men and women are small, indicating that provocation reduces the impact of gender role norms on aggression. Similarly, Lightdale and Prentice (1994) found that gender differences in aggression appear when people are identifiable in a given situation, but not when they are anonymous, suggesting that girls appear less aggressive than boys only when they believe their specific behavior will be noticed.

Although gender differences in rates of physical aggression are relatively large, gender differences in rates of verbal aggression are relatively small.

How do high testosterone levels create aggression? High testosterone leads to an increased readiness to respond assertively to provocation and threats, and makes people more impatient and irritable, which can lead to aggression (Olweus et al., 1988). People high in testosterone experience more arousal and tension, and higher levels of frustration, in daily life (Dabbs, Strong, & Milun, 1997). In one study, participants were asked to keep daily records of their

Questioning the Research

Although these studies describe high levels of testosterone as leading to aggressive behavior, can you think of an alternative explanation for this association? (Hint: Can they tell causation or only correlation?)

thoughts and activities for a four-day period (Dabbs et al., 1997). People who were high in testosterone reported experiencing more arousal and tension than those who were low in testosterone, and felt frustrated when they were unable to accomplish their goals.

Some evidence suggests that it may not be testosterone alone that leads to higher rates of aggression, but rather the presence of testosterone along with some other variable (Dabbs & Morris, 1990). In line with this view, men with high income levels have relatively low rates of adult delinquency regardless of their level of testosterone, whereas men with low income show low delinquency if they have low levels of testosterone, but high rates of adult delinquency if they have high levels of testosterone. Why? Perhaps because men with high income can dominate people in other ways (e.g., driving a nicercar, wearing nicer clothes, living in a nicer house, etc.). Similarly, men who are high in testosterone and high in fearlessness are the best at fighting fires, suggesting that personality and hormone levels together interact to produce the aggressiveness necessary to perform effectively under this unique type of pressure (Fannin & Dabbs, 2003).

Health
CONNECTIONS

The Link Between Alcohol Use and Aggression

The link between alcohol use and aggression is consistent in both field and laboratory research (Bushman & Cooper, 1990; Hull & Bond, 1986). For example, 50% of murderers had been drinking prior to committing the act (Bushman, 1993), and men who abuse alcohol are also at increased likelihood of abusing their spouse (Coker, Smith, McKeown, & King, 2000; Murphy & O'Farrell, 1996). Similarly, people who are intoxicated give higher levels of shocks to an opponent, even when not provoked, than do sober people (Bailey & Taylor, 1991).

Why does alcohol use lead to such high levels of aggression? One reason is that alcohol use leads to disinhibition, meaning a weakening or removal of inhibitions that normally restrain people from acting on their impulses (Ito, Miller, & Pollock, 1996; Steele & Southwick, 1985). For example, people may normally be inhibited from acting aggressively due to fear of the consequences and/or the belief that they have responsibility to act in a controlled manner, but intoxication reduces such concerns. Alcohol use also interferes with information processing by impairing people's ability to think straight, draw accurate conclusions, and integrate pieces of information (Bailey & Taylor, 1991; Laplace, Chermack, & Taylor, 1994; Steele & Josephs, 1988). In line with this view, men who have been drinking have trouble seeing their dating partner's side of a conflict, and hence feel more anger toward her (MacDonald, Zanna, & Holmes, 2000).

Alcohol exposure may also lead to more aggression at a subconscious level. In one study, participants were primed with alcohol-related images (e.g., beer bottle, martini glass), weapon images, or plant images (Bartholow & Heinz, 2006). Next, they had to recognize a series of aggression and neutral words. Participants who were primed with alcohol-related images or weapon images recognized aggressive words faster than neutral words, whereas those who were primed with plant images showed no difference in the speed of recognizing these distinct types of words. Similarly, exposure to alcohol advertisements, compared to neutral advertisements, led people to interpret the behavior of a target person as more hostile. These findings suggest that exposure to alcohol-related images, even in the absence of alcohol consumption, can increase aggressive thoughts, and in turn, can potentially lead to aggressive behavior.

© ACE STOCK LIMITED/Alamy

Other evidence suggests that the link between aggression and testosterone is cyclical. In other words, testosterone can increase levels of aggression, but aggression, or even aggressive cues, can also lead to increases in testosterone levels. In line with this view, some intriguing research indicates that men who handle a gun for 15 minutes show higher increases in testosterone, and behave more aggressively toward another participant, than those who handle a child's game (Klinesmith, Kasser, & McAndrew, 2006).

But testosterone is not the only hormone that may be associated with aggression. Other evidence points to the role of the neurotransmitter *serotonin* on aggression (Bernhardt, 1997; Davidson, Putnam, & Larson, 2000). Animals who are aggressive have been shown to have low serotonin levels, and low serotonin levels have been shown to make animals overreact to aversive stimuli; therefore they are at a greater risk of experiencing frustration and aggression (Bernhardt, 1997). A portion of the brain responsible for emotion regulation is damaged in those who show impulsive violence, suggesting that they can't appropriately regulate their feelings and therefore engage in aggression (Davidson et al., 2000). As described in Health Connections, another factor that can influence aggressive behavior is alcohol use.

Concepts in Context

BIOLOGICAL FACTORS LEADING TO AGGRESSION

FACTOR	EXAMPLE
Instinct and evolutionary theories	Hong Li sees life as "kill or be killed," and wants to make sure that he comes out ahead. He reacts angrily when he sees his girlfriend talking to other men, and tries to quickly interrupt such conversations.
Genetics	As a child, Matt was aggressive—he was always fighting with other children on the playground and frequently came home with black eyes and a bloody nose. Matt is now 16 and has just been arrested for assault.
Hormones	Carla is high in testosterone. She experiences high levels of tension in daily life, is easily frustrated, and responds very assertively to even mild provocation.

HOW DO SOCIAL PSYCHOLOGICAL FACTORS INFLUENCE AGGRESSION?

Given the limitations of the theories explaining aggression as a function of genetic and biological factors, researchers have also examined how social psychological factors influence aggression. In one study, participants were told the researchers were examining how liking for sports was related to attitudes and personality (Dienstbier, Roesch, Mizumoto, Hemenover, Lott, & Carlo, 1998).

In the weapon condition, participants watched a brief video of a fishing program, and then practiced casting with a fishing rod. Next, participants watched a brief video of target shooting, and then practiced holding and aiming a rifle and a pistol.

In the sport condition (the control condition), participants watched a three-minute video of gymnastics, and then held a football and imagined throwing it. Next, participants watched a video of an exciting basketball slum-dunk contest, and then held and imagined dunking a basketball.

All participants then read several scenarios about first-offense crimes, such as vandalism, robbery, and drug offenses, and recommended a sentence for the offense. As predicted, participants who completed the survey in a room with a weapon recommended longer sentences than those who were in a room with a piece of sporting equipment: an average of 4.4 years compared to 3.4 years. Apparently the presence of such an object serves to "prime" aggression, or basically increase the likelihood of an aggressive act.

This section will examine several theories that explain how psychological factors influence aggression, including frustration-aggression theory, cognitive-neoassociation theory, excitation transfer theory, social learning theory, and the general aggression model.

FRUSTRATION-AGGRESSION THEORY

frustration-aggression theory a hypothesis that frustration always leads to the desire to aggress, and that aggression is caused by frustration

displacement people's tendency to aggress against others when the person who has frustrated them is unavailable

The **frustration-aggression theory** is one of the earliest social psychological theories regarding aggression (Berkowitz, 1989; Dollard, Doob, Miller, Mowrer, & Sears, 1939; Geen, 1968). This theory states that frustration always leads to the desire to aggress, and that all aggression is caused by frustration. Frustration is caused when people are prevented from having something they want. For example, if I drive to a store because I want ice cream, but the store has just closed when I arrive, I will feel frustrated, and should be motivated to aggress in some way (e.g., write an angry letter to the store management about the hours the store is open, or act in a hostile way to people I see eating ice cream outside the store).

In line with the predictions of this theory, frustrating events lead to aggression. In one study, researchers hired students to call strangers on the phone to request donations to a charity (Kulik & Brown, 1979). Half of the students was led to believe that most people would contribute. The other half was led to believe that most people would refuse to contribute. Students who expected most people to contribute showed much higher levels of aggression (e.g., slamming the phone down, using a harsher tone) in response to a negative response than those who expected few people to contribute. Students who had high expectations for donations were more frustrated because they were unable to fulfill the goal they expected to achieve—and thus they showed higher levels of aggression than those who initially had low expectations and hence didn't experience the same frustration caused by failing to meet one's goals.

Displacement. Frustration-aggression theory states that when people are frustrated, they have a need or drive to aggress against the object of their frustration. However, it also states that when the target of one's frustration is not available, people transfer their anger to whatever target is available, a phenomenon known as **displacement** (Marcus-Newhall, Pedersen, Carlson, & Miller, 2000). So if you have a fight with your mother, you could kick the dog.

NEW LISTINGS FROM
FRUSTRATION HOUSE

#397 –
This picture-perfect hat can be yours! Guaranteed to make you look like a million bucks for only...
$2.99
SORRY, NONE LEFT

#421 –
The most interesting, witty, inspiring, entertaining, and enlightening book ever written on this planet!
Just $3.11
SOLD OUT

#599 –
World-famous L'Escargot© cookware. Impossible to make a mistake, even if you are the world's worst cook.
$5.29
DISCONTINUED ITEM

#758 –
Elegant one-family town house on N.Y.C.'s historic upper East Side. Lots of light, space; garden in back.
$79.89
LAST ONE

r. Chast

Unfortunately, this displacement is particularly likely to take place on particular people—"designated victims"—in a given society, such as immigrants, the unemployed, welfare recipients, and so on. Ervin Staub (1996) of the University of Massachusetts at Amherst suggests that mass killings, such as those observed during the Holocaust, are often rooted in frustration caused by economic and social difficulties. These frustrations lead to scapegoating and a "blame the victim" mentality in which people blame those in a particular group and thereby both discriminate and aggress against them. Following World War I the Germans blamed the Jews for the loss of the war and the severe economic problems and political instability that followed.

To examine the factors that led people to displace anger toward one person onto another, researchers created a situation in which participants were deliberately provoked (Pedersen, Gonzales, & Miller, 2000). Participants listened to either mild or irritating music, completed either easy or difficult anagrams, and were given either neutral or negative feedback (as a manipulation of the provocation). Then, they interacted with a confederate who gave them either negative or neutral feedback about their performance. Finally, they were asked to rate the confederate.

As predicted, participants who completed a difficult task and were given negative feedback by the experimenter, and received negative feedback from the confederate, gave the highest level of negative ratings of the research assistant. Although participants did not show aggression when they received only negative feedback from the experimenter, when such feedback was followed by negative feedback from the confederate, participants displaced their anger caused by the feedback onto the research assistant (see Figure 11.2). Displacement of aggression is particularly common when one is provoked, and then given the opportunity to think about this provocation—which maintains, and could even increase, one's negative mood (Bushman, Bonacci, Pedersen, Vasquez, & Miller, 2005).

Associated Press

One factor that contributed to the horrors of the Holocaust was the Germans' frustration at the economic troubles their country faced after World War I, which was blamed on Jewish people.

The impact of relative deprivation.

Frustration can also result from feelings of perceived injustice and **relative deprivation**, meaning that you have fewer resources than those to whom you are comparing yourself (Wenzel, 2000; Wood, 1989). This is why professional athletes who make millions of dollars a year may feel angry about their salary—they are not comparing what they make to what most people in America make, but rather to what many of their highly publicized teammates may be making. In fact, decreasing the income discrepancy in a country—meaning the difference in income between the very wealthy and the very poor—increases the overall happiness in a country, in part by reducing the negative effects of social comparison (Hagerty, 2000). Similarly, some researchers believe that the increase in television watching leads to increases in violent crime, in part due to the impact of relative deprivation (e.g., seeing what other people had; Hennigan, Heath, Wharton, Del Rosario, Cook, & Calder, 1982). This is especially true because television often shows middle- and upper-class people.

In line with this view, aggressive behavior increases when people are in difficult financial situations. In an early test of this relationship, Carl Hovland and Robert Sears (1940) examined the link between the price of cotton in 14 Southern states from 1882 to 1930 and the number of lynchings of African Americans. As predicted, there was a strong negative correlation between the price of cotton (a major aspect of the economy during this time) and the number of lynchings, meaning that the more financial pressure people were under, the more lynchings occurred.

relative deprivation the feeling of discontent caused by the belief that one fares poorly compared to people in other groups

FIGURE
11.2

DOES PROVOCATION LEAD TO ANGER DISPLACEMENT?

In this experiment, researchers provoked some participants by making them do a difficult task and then giving them negative feedback on it. Participants then met a confederate who offered some of them a trigger for aggression by also giving negative feedback. As predicted, people who were provoked displaced their frustration onto a new person who triggered their aggression, supporting the theory that we displace our anger.

Source: Pedersen, W. C., Gonzales, C., & Miller, N. (2000). The moderating effect of trivial triggering provocation on displaced aggression. *Journal of Personality and Social Psychology*, 78, 913-927. Copyright © 2000 by the American Psychological Association. Reproduced with permission. The use of APA information does not imply endorsement by APA.

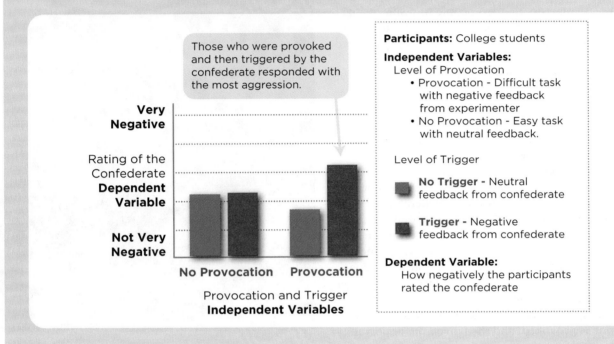

This research suggests that people displace their frustration caused by poor economic conditions onto minority group members. A more recent study using complex statistical procedures revealed that the rate of lynching was particularly high when a period of poor economic growth followed a period of strong growth (Hepworth & West, 1988). Although some researchers have questioned the conclusions of the studies showing a link between economic conditions and lynchings (Green, Glaser, & Rich, 1998), other work finds that people who lose their jobs, and therefore experience economic hardships, show higher rates of violence (Catalano, Novaco, & McConnell, 1997; Steinberg, Catalano, & Dooley, 1981). As shown in the Business Connections box, this frustration may be particularly likely to be displaced onto women in the workplace.

Critiques of frustration-aggression theory. Although frustration can and does lead to aggression, more recent research has called into question some aspects of this theory (Berkowitz, 1989).

I'm pretty sure Jason Kidd makes more money than you or I do... but he may still feel angry that he makes less money than some of his basketball-playing peers.

The Dangers of Sexual Harassment

Sexual harassment against women in the workplace is unfortunately a relatively common problem in our society (Fitzgerald, 1993). Although people often think of sexual harassment as physical and/or sexual violence against women, in most cases harassment is more subtle, such as intrusive, unwanted, and coercive sexual attention. One large-scale study of female government employees revealed that 33% of the women heard repeated sexual remarks, 25% experienced physical touching, 15% received pressure for dates, and nearly 10% experienced direct pressure for sexual cooperation. Women who are in male-dominated and nontraditional occupations are at particular risk of experiencing sexual harassment, but such harassment can and does occur in very diverse settings. However, when women are working in nontraditional settings (e.g., as steelworkers or forklift operators), people are less likely to perceive sexually coercive behavior as sexual harassment than when women are working in more traditional settings (Burgess & Borgida, 1997). Not surprisingly, the consequences of sexual harassment are severe: they include job loss, absenteeism, decreased job satisfaction and morale, and physical symptoms (e.g., depression, headaches, sleep disturbance, and nausea).

What can be done to reduce the incidence of sexual harassment? Louise Fitzgerald of the University of Illinois at Urbana-Champaign suggests a number of strategies (1993). First, employers need to develop clear policies against harassment, and to notify all employees of such policies. Second, encourage the awarding of large damages to victims of sexual harassment to motivate employers to eliminate such problems. Third, revise unemployment compensation policies so that women who quit their jobs due to sexual harassment are eligible to receive benefits. Fourth, extend the statute of limitations for filing sexual harassment charges, because many victims take considerable time before feeling able to press charges. Finally, ensure that victims of sexual harassment are treated fairly by the legal system and are not forced to defend themselves for experiencing this behavior.

altrendo images /Getty Images, Inc.

Male boss behaving inappropriately toward a female subordinate.

One limitation of this theory is that frustration does not have to lead to aggression, but could lead to other emotions, such as disappointment, sadness, and depression. Therefore, aggression represents only one of the possible responses to frustration.

A second limitation of this theory is that not all aggression stems from frustration (Berkowitz, 1989). Most researchers now make the distinction between emotional/hostile aggression and instrumental aggression (although see Bushman & Anderson, 2002, for an exception). Frustration is much more likely to lead to emotional or hostile aggression than to instrumental aggression.

COGNITIVE-NEOASSOCIATION THEORY

Another theory explaining aggression suggests that experiencing a negative mood or affect activates anger-related thoughts and feelings as well as aggressive behavior (Berkowitz, 1984, 1990). This **cognitive-neoassociation theory** proposes that any event that leads to negative affect, such as heat, pain, unpleasant noises and odors, crowding, and so on, can lead to aggression. For example, if you are in a bad mood because you've recently failed an exam, you might be more likely

cognitive-neoassociation theory a theory that describes aggression as caused by experiencing negative affect of any kind, which in turn evokes aggressive-related thoughts, memories, feelings, and ideas

to respond angrily to a salesman who knocks on your door. Such triggers to aggressive behavior could include observing the following types of aggression:

- aggression in daily life (e.g., watching two children fight on a playground),
- aggression in the media (e.g., watching a television show in which cartoon characters behave aggressively),
- reading a story containing aggressive acts (e.g., an action comic book).

Let's review the evidence for how different factors can lead to negative mood or affect and thereby increase aggression.

Hot temperatures. Numerous studies demonstrate that as the temperature increases, so does the incidence of aggressive acts, including murder, rape, domestic violence, and assault (Anderson, 1989, 2001; Anderson & DeNeve, 1992; Cohn, 1993). In one study, Anderson and colleagues examined the association between the number of hot days (days the maximum temperature reached 90 degrees) in a given summer and the rate of violent crimes in 50 different American cities (Anderson, Bushman, & Groom paper, 1997). As predicted, hotter summers were associated with more violent crimes, including assault, property crime, and rape. Research in laboratory settings reveals similar findings: participants are more hostile to confederates when they are in 90-degree rooms versus rooms at a more comfortable temperature (Griffit, 1970; Griffit & Veitch, 1971). Why do high temperatures increase aggression? Research suggests that high temperatures lead to increased hostile feelings and thoughts, as well as physiological arousal, all of which may increase the likelihood of aggression (Anderson, Deuser, & DeNeve, 1995).

More batters are hit in major league baseball games when the temperature is above 90 degrees than below 90 degrees (Reifman, Larrick, & Fein, 1991).

AFP/Getty Images, Inc.

However, some research suggests that the link between heat and aggression is curvilinear, meaning that at extremely high temperatures aggression does decrease. Although warmer cities have higher violent crime rates than cooler ones, at very high levels of heat, violence decreases somewhat (Anderson & Anderson, 1996; Bell, 1992). Cohn and Rotton (1997, 2000) tried to explain this evidence by analyzing the relationship between heat and aggression during the day (when temperatures are at their highest) versus in the evening. Using data from both Minneapolis, Minnesota, and Dallas, Texas, evidence showed that most assaults happen in the late evening/early morning, when temperatures are somewhat lower. This suggests a curvilinear function, with assaults reaching a peak at moderately high temperatures, but then decreasing.

However, other researchers have criticized Cohn & Rotton's conclusions, noting that these data ignore time of day, which is likely to have a strong impact on the frequency of aggression (Bushman, Wang, & Anderson, 2005a, 2005b). In line with this view, a re-analysis of the data used by Cohn and Rotton reveals that over night (between 9 PM and 3 AM), increasing temperature was associated with increasing frequency of assault. On the other hand, there was no association between temperature and frequency of assault during the day (3 AM to 9 PM).

Other unpleasant conditions. Aggression is also produced when people experience other bad conditions (e.g., pollution, threatened self-esteem, crowding, pain, noise, poverty, etc.; Baumeister, Bushman, & Campbell, 2000; Fleming, Baum, & Weiss, 1987). For example, people who are experiencing pain (by holding one of their hands in a bucket of painfully cold water) report having higher feelings of irritation and annoyance toward another student (Berkowitz, Cochran, & Embree, 1981). Various environmental factors, including ozone levels, cigarette smoke, wind speed, and humidity, are associated with rates of aggression, as evidenced by calls to police for assistance in assaults (Rotton & Frey, 1985; Zillman, Baron, & Tamborini, 1981). Feeling personally rejected or ostracized can also lead to more aggressive behavior (Twenge, Baumeister, Tice, & Stucke, 2001).

Cues to aggression. According to the cognitive-neoassociation theory, another factor that can trigger aggressive behavior is the mere presence of an object associated with aggression (Berkowitz, 1984). In a classic demonstration of the power of a weapon to elicit aggression, Berkowitz and LePage (1967) conducted a study in which male participants were provoked and then delivered shocks to a confederate. In one condition, sporting items (racquet, balls) were in the room. In the other condition, a revolver and rifle were in the room. In which case did the participant aggress more? The one in which the guns were present. Similarly, and as described at the start of this section, participants who handle a rifle and pistol give higher sentencing recommendations than those who held a basketball and football.

Obviously this finding has dangerous implications, particularly given the prevalence of guns in our society. Thus, although it is true that "guns don't kill; people do," the mere presence of a gun seems to be able to elicit aggressive responses from others, particularly if they are ready to aggress and do not have strong inhibitions against such behavior. A study in the *New England Journal of Medicine* reported that having a gun in one's home triples your risk of being killed (Kellermann, Rivara, Rushforth, & Banton, 1993). Similarly, John Sloan and colleagues examined the rate of murder in two Northwestern cities (Seattle, Washington, and Vancouver, British Columbia; Sloan, Kellerman, Reay, & Ferris, 1988). Although these two cities are very similar in numerous respects, including population, climate, economy, and overall crime rate, Seattle has twice the murder rate of Vancouver. One possible explanation? Vancouver severely limits handgun ownership. Similarly, after the 1976 Firearms Control Regulations Act was carried out in Washington, DC, which required restrictive licensing of handguns, the number of homicides and suicides committed with firearms in Seattle declined (Loftin, McDowall, Wiersema, & Cottey, 1991). Other research indicates that following the purchase of a handgun, risk of suicide is significantly higher— and as much as 57 times as high as the rate in the general population (Wintemute, Parham, Beaumont, Wright, & Drake, 1999).

"Or maybe you're at the office and you discover that somebody has been using the copy machine for personal purposes."

Questioning the Research
The correlation between owning a gun and the likelihood of killing someone— or oneself—with the gun is clear. But is there an alternative explanation for this association? (Hint: Are people randomly assigned to have guns?)

EXCITATION TRANSFER THEORY

According to the **arousal-affect/excitation transfer model**, aggression is influenced by both the intensity of the arousal and the type of emotion produced by the stimulus (Zillman, 1983). In other words, any type of arousal can be interpreted as aggression if a person is in a situation that cues aggression. (Does this theory ring a bell? It should: it is based on Schachter and Singer's two-factor theory of emotion, as you read in Chapter 3.) In one study, researchers randomly assigned some men to engage in mild exercise (a slow ride on a stationary bike) and others to engage in strenuous exercise (a more strenuous bike ride; Zillman, Katcher, & Milavsky, 1972).

arousal-affect/excitation transfer model a model describing aggression as influenced by both the intensity of the arousal and the type of emotion produced by the stimulus

Those who engaged in strenuous exercise and were provoked by a confederate delivered higher intensity shocks to the confederate than those who engaged in mild exercise and hence were less aroused. In sum, if we are physiologically aroused (for whatever reason), and if our environment tells us we are angry, we act aggressively.

Why does arousal lead to aggression? People misattribute their feelings of arousal caused by other sources to the situation, and hence if there are cues to aggression in the situation, they interpret their arousal as aggression. For example, you'll learn in the next section that watching pornography can lead to increased aggression because people interpret their sexual arousal as aggression.

SOCIAL LEARNING THEORY

As you learned in Chapter 6, Bandura's (1973, 1983) social learning theory posits that behavior is learned by observing or *modeling* others' behavior as well as by the presence of punishments and rewards, or *reinforcements*. Both of these factors can lead to aggressive behavior.

Modeling. Children can learn to engage in aggressive behavior through watching such behavior, either in real life or through television and movies (Bandura, Ross, & Ross, 1963). As described in Chapter 2, Al Bandura conducted a classic study of the power of modeling on aggression in children (Bandura et al., 1963). In this study, children were shown a video of an adult throwing around, punching, and kicking an inflatable Bobo doll. The video was very unusual and specific in terms of the behavior and words modeled (e.g., the adult sat on the doll, punched it in the nose, hit him with a wooden mallet, and said "Sock him in the nose" and "Hit him down"). The researcher then observed the children's behavior following a frustrating event (being shown some very attractive toys but then being told that these toys were being saved for another child, and given some less good toys to play with). As expected, children who'd watched the adult aggress against the Bobo doll replicated much of that behavior, even using the exact same words and actions. To educate parents about the ease with which children model aggressive behavior, the Adults and Children Together (ACT) Against Violence created a national media campaign.

Reinforcement. In addition to learning how to model specific behaviors through observation, children may also receive positive reinforcement for being aggressive (Bandura, 1973, 1983). For example, a young child who grabs a toy from another is positively rewarded because he has won the toy. The same is true when the grade school bully takes other children's lunch money. The bully has been rewarded (he has the lunch money) for being aggressive. A child who learns that aggression leads to a good outcome (e.g., the aggressive child succeeds in getting the desired toy away from a classmate) should be more likely to engage in such behavior in the future than a child who sees aggression as having negative consequences (e.g., the aggressive child received a time-out; Boldizar, Perry & Perry, 1989). In turn, aggressive children are more confident that aggression will lead to tangible rewards, such as reducing aversive treatment by others, and are less concerned about aggression leading to negative

EVERY TIME YOU YELL AT YOUR SPOUSE, SHE LEARNS A LESSON.

You're always teaching. *Teach carefully.*

www.ACTAgainstViolence.org

Ad Council

MetLife Foundation

act against violence

This type of public service advertisement is designed to remind parents that their behavior serves to model behavior for their children—and thus will hopefully serve to decrease acts of aggression around their children.

outcomes, such as experiencing peer rejection (Boldizar et al., 1989; Perry, Perry, & Rasmussen, 1986).

In one study, participants played one of three versions of a race-car video game (Carnagey & Anderson, 2005).

- In one version, violence was rewarded—participants received points for killing pedestrians and race opponents.
- In another version, violence was punished—participants lost points for killing pedestrians and race opponents.
- In the third version, there was no violence—killing others was not an option.

Participants who were rewarded for violence showed increased hostile emotions, aggressive thinking, and aggressive behavior. Punishment (losing points) had no effect on aggressive thinking or behavior, but did increase hostile emotions.

GENERAL AGGRESSION MODEL

To integrate the various theories on factors that increase the likelihood of aggression, Craig Anderson and colleagues have combined these factors into an overall model called the **general aggression model** (GAM: Anderson, Anderson, & Deuser, 1996; Lindsay & Anderson, 2000). As shown in Figure 11.3, this model proposes that both individual difference variables (e.g., genetic factors, personality traits, hostility) and situational variables (e.g., presence of guns, frustration, negative affect, exposure to violence in the media) can lead to aggressive-related thoughts, aggressive-related feelings, and/or physiological arousal. In turn, these thoughts, feelings, and arousal can lead to aggressive behavior, depending on how people appraise or interpret the situation.

What is the evidence for this model? First, people do vary in their general tendency toward aggression. In one study, pairs of participants competed in a reaction time task, in which they gave and received punishment—a loud blast of unpleasant

general aggression model a model proposing that both individual differences and situational factors lead to aggressive-related thoughts, feelings, and/or physiological arousal

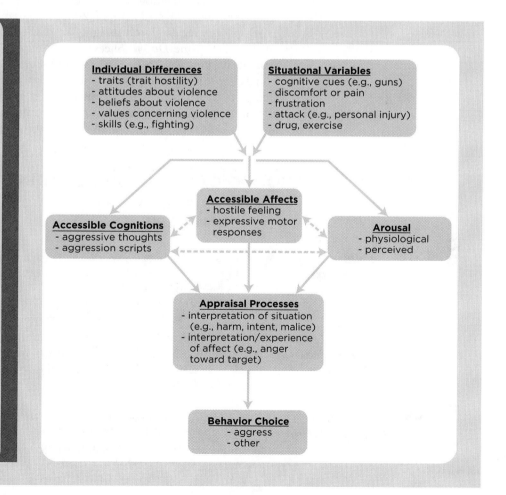

FIGURE 11.3

THE GENERAL AGGRESSION MODEL

The General Aggression Model describes the role of both individual differences (such as traits, beliefs, and skills) and situational factors (such as pain, frustration, and the presence of guns) in leading to aggressive-related thoughts, mood, and arousal. In turn, the presence of such thoughts, mood, and arousal can lead people to appraise situations in ways that lead to aggressive behavior.

Source: Anderson, C. A. (1997). Effects of violent movies and trait hostility on hostile feelings and aggressive thoughts. Aggressive Behavior, 23, 161-178.

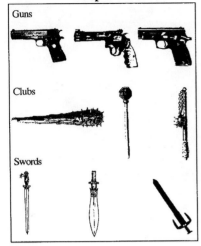

Weapon Primes

Guns

Clubs

Swords

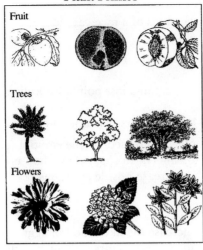

Plant Primes

Fruit

Trees

Flowers

Participants who see a weapon prime are much faster at recognizing aggressive words than those who see a plant prime.

Source: Anderson, C. A., Benjamin, A. J. J., & Bartholow, B. D. (1998). Does the Gun Pull the Trigger? Automatic priming effects of weapon pictures and weapon names. *Psychological Science, 9,* 308-314.

noise—to each other (Anderson, Buckley, & Carnagey, 2008). Participants who were higher on trait aggressiveness gave louder noise blasts than did those who were lower in aggressiveness. Those who are high in aggressiveness are also more likely to interpret neutral words (e.g., alley, police, animal) as having an aggressive component (Bushman, 1996).

Second, exposure to cues to aggression, such as an aggressive word, a photo of a weapon, a violent movie or video game, or even songs with violent lyrics, can trigger aggressive thoughts and feelings (Anderson, 1997; Anderson et al., 2003; Anderson, Carnagey, & Eubanks, 2003). People who watch a violent movie, or play a violent video game, interpret neutral stories in a more aggressive way and recognize aggressive words more quickly compared to people who watch a nonviolent movie (Bushman, 1998; Giumetti & Markey, 2007). Male undergraduates with frequent experience playing violent video games interpret their partner's behavior in a competitive game as more aggressive than those without such exposure, and this perception, in turn, leads them to behave more (Bartholow, Sestir, & Davis, 2005). Similarly, and as shown in the illustration of the weapon and plant primes, people who see pictures of weapons recognize aggressive words more quickly compared to those who see pictures of plants (Anderson, Benjamin, & Bartholow, 1998).

Finally, this activation of aggression thoughts and feelings can lead to aggressive behavior (Anderson & Bushman, 2001; Bushman & Anderson, 2002). In one study, participants were randomly assigned to play either a violent or a nonviolent version of the video game *Doom* (Sheese & Graziano, 2005). After completing the video game task, they were asked to play a prisoner's dilemma type game in which they could choose to either cooperate with their partner for moderate mutual gain or compete with their partner for the possibility of greater personal gain. As predicted by the GAM, participants who had first played the violent video game were much more likely to choose to compete than those who had played the nonviolent video game.

SOCIAL PSYCHOLOGICAL FACTORS LEADING TO AGGRESSION

Concepts in Context

FACTOR	EXAMPLES
Frustration-aggression theory	Luis has just finished writing a 10-page paper when his computer crashes. In his frustration at losing all that work, he throws his stapler across the room, breaking a window.
Cognitive-neoassociation theory	Maria is driving to work behind a car displaying a bumper sticker featuring a handgun. When the car in front of her at a light doesn't move when the light turns green, Maria honks her horn loudly.
Excitation transfer theory	After running for 30 minutes on the treadmill, Lawrence's heart is beating quickly. As he heads to the locker room to shower, a woman accidentally bumps into him in the hall. Lawrence rudely snaps, "Watch where you are going, lady!"

Social learning theory	Katya's older sister, Lena, threatened to hit anyone who sat in "her seat" at the back of the school bus. Katya now makes the same threat to ensure that she can sit in her favorite seat.
General aggression model	Anirudh enjoys playing violent video games. After playing such games, he tends to interpret other people's behavior as hostile, which in turn leads him to act aggressively toward them.

HOW DOES THE MEDIA INFLUENCE AGGRESSION?

The average one-hour program in the United States contains eight acts of verbal aggression and nine acts of physical aggression, meaning that by the end of elementary school, a typical child has seen 8,000 murders and more than 100,000 acts of violence on television (Huston et al., 1992). Not surprisingly, exposure to aggressive acts in the media is associated with aggression in daily life: it is estimated that exposure to television is related to approximately half of all homicides in the United States each year (Centerwall, 1989). In fact, the relationship between watching television and aggression is as strong as the link between smoking and cancer (Bushman & Anderson, 2001).

Both lab studies and longitudinal field research suggest that exposure to violence on television contributes to aggression (Anderson, 1997; Christakis & Zimmerman, 2007; Friedrich-Cofer & Huston, 1986; Wood, Wong, & Chachere, 1991). In one study to examine the effects of media violence on aggression, men and women were randomly assigned to play either a violent video game (*Mortal Kombat*) or a nonviolent game (*PGA Tournament Golf*; Bartholow & Anderson, 2002). After playing one of these two games for 10 minutes, participants competed with a confederate in a reaction time task that allowed for punishment and retaliation (a burst of loud noise through headphones). Participants who played the violent game chose higher intensities of noise levels than those who played the nonviolent game, and this effect was particularly strong for men.

This study describes one way in which exposure to violence in the media can lead to aggression in daily life. This section will examine several factors that contribute to the link between media violence and aggression, including modeling aggression, priming aggressive thoughts and emotions, creating physiological arousal, and reducing reactions to aggression.

MODELS AGGRESSION

One clear way in which exposure to violence on television can lead to aggression is via modeling (Huesmann, 1986; Josephson, 1987). As described in the previous section, people who are exposed to media violence learn aggressive ways to act as well as the rewards for this behavior. One study with over 2000 high school students revealed that students who watch wrestling on television are more likely to engage in fighting with peers (DuRant, Champion, & Wolfson, 2006). In several tragic cases, attempts to mimic aggressive events seen on television and in the movies have led to death.

Why does exposure to violence in the media lead to aggression in real life? One explanation is that television shows and movies portray the world as full of people who are evil and violent (Berkowitz, 1984; Bushman, 1998). This view, in turn, creates a suspicious and cynical worldview, which can increase the likelihood of aggressive behavior. People who have a sinister worldview may feel more fearful and distrustful of others (e.g., assume others will hurt them), and so take steps to protect themselves (e.g., buy a gun). They may also interpret ambiguous situations in a more aggressive way (e.g., shoot a masked teenager who comes to the door to ask for directions to a Halloween party).

Questioning the Research
Although considerable research shows that children who watch more violent television engage in greater aggression, does this show that media viewing causes aggression? Why or why not?

In one study, third and fifth grade children were randomly assigned to watch either an aggressive or a nonaggressive television show (Thomas & Drabman, 1978). Then they heard descriptions of conflict situations and asked how they believed the average child would act in these situations. Children who had first seen an aggressive television show were more likely to believe that other children would act aggressively than those who had seen a nonaggressive show.

PRIMES AGGRESSIVE THOUGHTS AND FEELINGS

As described earlier in the description of the GAM, exposure to violence in the media primes aggressive thoughts and feelings, which in turn can lead to aggressive behavior (Anderson & Bushman, 2001; Anderson & Dill, 2000; Zillman & Weaver, 1999). As described at the start of this section, participants who played *Mortal Kombat* behaved more aggressively (based on noise level they gave to their partner) than those who played the nonviolent game (Bartholow & Anderson, 2002).

In one study, male participants were told they would assist with two different market surveys—one about music preferences and one about taste preferences (Fischer & Greitemeyer, 2006). First, participants listened to either a song that contained anti-women lyrics (such as "Superman" by Eminem) or more neutral lyrics (such as "It's My Life" by Bon Jovi). Next, as part of the taste preferences study, participants were asked to prepare a sample of hot sauce for another participant to sample. Participants heard another student (a confederate of the experimenter's) express his or her dislike of hot spices, and then prepared a sample of hot sauce for this person to taste. Participants were told that the other person would have to consume all of the sample, and that they should administer however much hot sauce they wanted.

As shown in Figure 11.4, participants who heard the anti-women lyrics gave more hot sauce to female confederates than to male confederates. Type of lyrics had no impact on the amount of hot sauce given to male confederates, suggesting that the lyrics specifically modeled aggressive behavior toward women, as opposed to aggression in general.

Even the media publication of real-world events can have a substantial influence on aggression (Phillips, 1977, 1979). Sociologist David Phillips has conducted several studies examining the link between boxing matches and murder rates (Phillips, 1983, 1986). Using archival data, Phillips analyzed the change in rate of homicides following heavyweight championship prize fights. These data reveal that immedi-

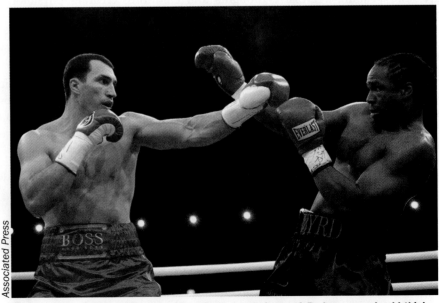

Associated Press

Do you think of boxing matches as harmless entertainment? Perhaps you should think again.

FIGURE 11.4 — DO ANTI-WOMEN LYRICS PRIME AGGRESSION TOWARDS WOMEN?

Experimenters primed male college students with song lyrics, then gave them the opportunity for aggression against a confederate: making that person eat hot chili sauce. As predicted, men who listened to anti-woman lyrics poured more hot sauce for women confederates than those who listened to neutral lyrics, suggesting that song lyrics can prime us for aggression toward targeted group members.

Source: Fischer, P., & Greitemeyer, T. (2006). Music and aggression: The impact of sexual-aggressive song lyrics on aggression-related thoughts, emotions, and behavior toward the same and the opposite sex. *Personality and Social Psychology Bulletin, 32,* 1165-1176.

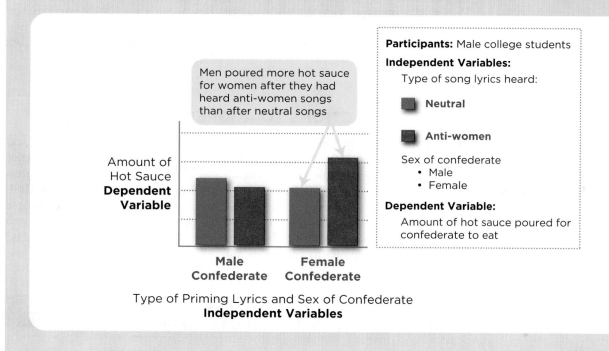

ately after prize fights, homicides increase 12.5%, and these increases are largest after heavily publicized fights. Not only do murders increase following fights, but also murders of the race of the person who lost the fight show a particularly sharp increase—if a Caucasian person loses the fight, more Caucasian people are killed, whereas if an African American person loses the fight, more African American people are killed. Why would heavily publicized fights lead to increases in aggression? Phillips theorizes that people match their behaviors to those that they see publicized in the media. This doesn't mean that seeing these behaviors in the media leads people to do something they wouldn't ordinarily have done (e.g., commit homicide), but rather that this exposure prompted or triggered preexisting aggressive impulses (in line with several of the theories of aggression described earlier in this chapter).

CREATES PHYSIOLOGICAL AROUSAL

Watching highly violent television leads to physiological arousal for most people (Bushman & Geen, 1990). Exposure to violence in the media leads to increase in heart rate, blood pressure, and the skin's conductance of electricity, which in turn can increase aggression. In one meta-analysis, researchers examined the impact of video game violence on physiological arousal (Anderson & Bushman, 2001). These studies revealed that exposure to violence in video games does increase physiological arousal, including blood pressure and heart rate.

How does physiological arousal lead to aggression? First, arousal can energize, or heighten, whatever a person is already feeling, and thus increase the likelihood that a person will act on his or her feelings. Second, arousal can lead someone to misattribute the cause of this arousal, and thus react more strongly if provoked by another person. (This process was discussed in detail in Chapter 3.) These factors explain why someone who is watching an aggressive sporting event (and thus feeling some arousal) may act aggressively toward other fans at the slightest provocation—for example, when another person accidentally spills beer on him.

To examine the effect of watching aggression on physiological arousal, participants in one study watched one of three videotapes (Bushman & Geen, 1990). Two of the videotapes featured violent clips, including fistfights and gun battles. The third videotape featured no violence. Researchers measured participants' blood pressure and pulse rate before starting the videotape, three times (at two minute intervals) during the videotape, and again at the end of the videotape. As predicted, the violent videotapes increased participants' blood pressure.

REDUCES REACTIONS TO AGGRESSION

desensitization (disinhibition)
the state in which physiological reactions to violence are reduced due to repeated exposure to violence

Although exposure to violence in the media can initially lead to physiological arousal (and in turn, increased levels of aggression), repeated exposure to violence over time can reduce people's psychological and physiological reactions to aggressive images (Geen, 1981). This process is called **desensitization or disinhibition**. Researchers believe that repeated exposure to violence in the media leads people to become accustomed to such images, which decreases their impact. Research Focus on Neuroscience describes how such exposure to aggression can decrease brain activity in response to violent stimuli.

RESEARCH FOCUS ON NEUROSCIENCE
The Impact of Violent Media on the Brain

Recent research in neuroscience reveals how exposure to violence in the media can have an impact on brain activity (Carnagey, Anderson, & Bartholow, 2007). In one study, researchers examined event-related potentials (ERPs) in the brain while participants were watching either violent or nonviolent photographs (Bartholow, Bushman, & Sestir, 2006). Participants with a high history of exposure to violent video games had lower brain reactivity in response to violent photographs, presumably because they were desensitized to such images. Unfortunately, reduced brain activity in response to violent stimuli predicted increased aggression in a later task. Other research suggests that playing violent video games leads to decreased activity in the portion of the brain that inhibits behavior and suppresses emotional reactions (Weber, Ritterfeld, & Mathiak, 2006). These findings suggest that exposure to violence in the media could lead to increased rates of aggression over time, at least in part because such exposure may decrease neurological responses to such images.

In line with this view, people who are repeatedly exposed to violence in the media show lower levels of arousal in response to aggression images (Berkowitz, 1984). In fact, people who watch two violent films in a row become less aroused during the second one than do adults who watch a violent film after first watching a nonviolent film (Drabman & Thomas, 1974, 1975). Exposure to violence can even lead people to show little physiological arousal while engaging in aggressive behavior: Participants who are angered by a confederate and watch a 15-minute aggressive television program show the highest levels of aggression but the lowest pulse rates (Thomas, 1982).

Desensitization can also reduce people's inhibitions about engaging in aggressive behavior. Research with children (ranging from kindergarten to fifth grade) reveals that those who watch a violent film are more tolerant of real-life aggression than those who watch a nonviolent film (Drabman & Thomas, 1974, 1975). In one study, third graders watched either a detective film or a nonviolent baseball movie. They then were asked to watch a supposedly real classroom and to seek adult assistance if any problems emerged. When problems occurred—meaning the younger children became disruptive and aggressive—children who had watched the violent detective film took longer to seek adult help than those who had watched the nonviolent film. Similarly, and as described in Media Connections, exposure to sexually explicit images of women desensitizes men to such images, which in turn can lead to aggression against women.

Media
:::: **CONNECTIONS**

The Hazards of Violent Pornography

Although exposure to pornography is often described as relatively harmless, watching violent pornography, meaning materials that portray women as "enjoying" being victimized, can lead to aggression toward women (Linz, Donnerstein, & Penrod, 1988; Malamuth & Cheek, 1983). Why? In part because men who watch sexually violent movies become desensitized to the images of violence against women. In one study, men watched three violent R-rated slasher films—showing violence against women as well as sexual images—over the course of a week (Mullin & Linz, 1995). Participants then watched a videotape featuring a victim of domestic violence describing her assault and injury, and rated their beliefs about the victim of domestic violence, including the degree of her injuries and the extent to which her own behavior had caused the assault. Compared to those who had not seen the violent movies, men who had watched these films expressed less sympathy for this victim of domestic violence. Men who see a sexually violent movie show more acceptance of violence against women, less sympathy for women who are the victims of such violence, and more acceptance of rape myths (see Table 11.1; Donnerstein & Berkowitz, 1981; Linz, Donnerstein, & Penrod, 1984, 1988; Malamuth & Check, 1985). When offered the opportunity, they also give more shocks to female confederates compared to those who watch neutral or erotic pornography (Donnerstein, 1980).

What's the good news? Men differ in how they respond to sexually explicit and violent films: some men show greater sexual arousal when watching aggressive portrayals of sexual situations, but most do not (Malamuth, Check, & Briere, 1986). Men who show greater sexual arousal in response to violent pornography often show a desire to experience dominance during sex, an overall hostility toward and conflict with women, as well as positive attitudes toward violence against women (Malamuth, 1983, 1986; Malamuth, Linz, Heavey, Barnes, & Acker, 1995). Narcissistic men also enjoy films showing consensual affection followed by rape more than other men (Bushman, Bonacci, Van Dijk, & Baumeister, 2003). On the other hand, some men who imagine engaging in sexual aggression are able to resist acting on these urges (Dean & Malamuth, 1997). Men who are sensitive to others' feelings are able to inhibit their desire to aggress, whereas those who are more self-centered do not.

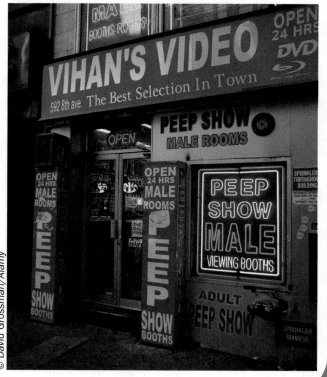

© David Grossman/Alamy

TABLE 11.1   RAPE MYTHS

1. Any healthy woman can successfully resist a rapist if she really wants to.

2. Many women have an unconscious wish to be raped, and may then unconsciously set up a situation in which they are likely to be attacked.

3. If a girl engages in necking or petting and she lets things get out of hand, it is her own fault if her partner forces sex on her.

4. One reason that women falsely report a rape is that they frequently have a need to call attention to themselves.

5. When women go around braless or wearing short skirts and tight tops, they are just asking for trouble.

Men who watch sexually aggressive films are more likely to agree with these statements than those who watch more neutral films.

Source: Burt, M. R. (1980). Cultural myths and support for rape. *Journal of Personality and Social Psychology, 38*, 217–230.

FACTORS LEADING TO THE MEDIA-AGGRESSION LINK

Concepts in Context

FACTOR	EXAMPLE
Models aggression	Betty watches World Wide Wrestling Federation on television every Friday night. She later performs some of these wrestling moves on her brother when they are fighting.
Primes aggressive thoughts and feelings	Austin enjoys listening to rap music, including music that contains anti-women lyrics. After listening to such music, Austin acts more aggressively toward his female friends.
Creates physiological arousal	Devon just went to see the *Texas Chain Saw Massacre*, and feels his heart racing. When another driver cuts him off leaving the parking lot of the movie theater, Devon lays on his horn and makes a rude gesture.
Reduces reactions to aggression	Lucinda used to find violent movies very scary and upsetting. But now that she's gone to a few violent movies with her friends, she realizes they aren't really so scary.

HOW CAN WE REDUCE AGGRESSION?

Aggression is prevalent in the real world and in the media, and is triggered by a number of distinct biological and psychological factors. In spite of this, aggressive behavior can be controlled. In one study, college students performed poorly on some difficult tasks, due to errors made by the research assistant when providing instructions (Ohbuchi, Kameda, & Agarie, 1989).

- In one case the assistant apologized for the wrong directions,
- in another case the director of the project told the students he knew their poor performance was caused by administrative errors (thus removing their responsibility for the poor performance), and
- in a third case there was no apology at all.

Not surprisingly, students were considerably less angry when the assistant apologized, regardless of whether they were going to be held responsible for their poor performance. What does this study show? Basically that just saying you're sorry does help. This section will examine this and other ways of reducing aggression, including punishing aggressive behavior, modeling nonaggressive responses, training in communication and problem-solving skills, focusing on the person, and creating positive feelings.

punishment the provision of unpleasant consequences to try to reduce a negative behavior

PUNISHING AGGRESSIVE BEHAVIOR

Punishment, meaning providing unpleasant consequences, is one of the most common ways people try to reduce aggression. Punishment can refer to giving a child a time-out giving a driver a speeding ticket, or suspending a high school student.

Although punishment may sometimes reduce aggression, it also models the use of aggression. Parents who use more harsh discipline techniques during their children's early years have more aggressive children, in part because children are more likely themselves to use aggressive responses in future interactions (Weiss, Dodge, Bates, & Pettit, 1992). One meta-analysis on the consequences of corporal punishment, such as spanking, revealed several negative outcomes, including increased delinquency and antisocial behavior for children and increased likelihood of abusing one's own child or spouse as an adult (Gershoff, 2002). Spanking also led to less internalization of moral standards of behavior, presumably because children attribute their positive behavior to fear of punishment as opposed to intrinsic motives.

As described in Chapter 6, cognitive dissonance theory predicts that implementing severe punishment for an offense can lead people to believe the only reason they are not aggressing is due to the fear of punishment (as opposed to a true concern with avoiding such behavior).

Questioning the Research
Research suggests that children who are spanked show higher levels of aggressive behavior than those who are not. Does this mean that spanking children leads to aggressive behavior? Can you think of an alternative explanation for this association?

Gemstone Images/Getty Images, Inc.

MODELING NONAGGRESSIVE RESPONSES

Although children can learn aggressive responses from watching various models, they can also learn and model nonaggressive responses. This approach is what has led parenting books to emphasize the use of "time-outs" and other nonaggressive approaches of discipline. Exposing children to compelling prosocial television programs can help reduce aggression.

Parents can also help discuss problems of television modeling (Huesmann, Eron, Klein, Brice, & Fischer, 1983). In one study, 169 first and third grade children who watched a lot of violent television were randomly assigned to receive a control condition or education about the unrealistic nature and unacceptable nature of television violence. Two years later, children who received this education were rated as less aggressive by their peers than those in the control condition. Although children in both groups showed an increase in aggression over time, those in the education group showed a significantly smaller increase.

TRAINING IN COMMUNICATION AND PROBLEM-SOLVING SKILLS

Training in communication and problem-solving skills can reduce aggression. Because much of what we see in the media shows destructive and violent ways of handling aggression, one way to reduce aggression is to show people how to respond constructively to frustrating situations (DuRant, Treiber, Getts, & McCloud, 1996).

The Peaceful Conflict Resolution and Violence Prevention Program was designed to reduce violence in school settings by training children in identifying situations that could result in violence, gaining skills in problem-solving, communication, and conflict-resolution, and providing strategies for effective anger without fighting (DuRant, Barkin, & Krowchuk, 2001). Schools that implemented this program showed decreases in the use of violence by students, whereas those without such programs showed increases. Education Connections describes another school-based approach to preventing aggression.

One of the most effective communication strategies for reducing aggressive behavior is apologizing, in which one person acknowledges wrongdoing and expresses regret (Ohbuchi et al., 1989; Weiner, Amirkhan, Folkes, & Verettte, 1987). Receiving a direct apology from a person who criticizes you dramatically minimizes aggressive tendencies, especially if you are able to attribute such criticism to external factors (e.g., the person being in a bad mood) and uncontrollable

Education
:::: CONNECTIONS

The Problem of Bullying

Bullying is a serious problem in many schools in the United States and other countries (Nansel, Overpeck, Pilla, Ruan, Simons-Morton, & Scheidt, 2001). Research by the Secret Service and the U.S. Department of Education reveals that many of those who commit school shootings have been bullied, threatened, or attacked by others (Anderson et al., 2001). Bullying likely contributed to the Columbine massacre in 1999, when Eric Harris and Dylan Klebold carried out a shooting rampage at their high school, killing 12 students and a teacher and injuring 24 others before killing themselves, as shown in the photo below.

A report in the *Journal of the American Medical Association* revealed that 30% of sixth to tenth grade children reported some involvement in bullying, with
• 13.0% acting as a bully,
• 10.6% being bullied, and
• 6.3% both bullying and being bullied (Anderson et al., 2008).

Males were more likely than females to both bully and be bullied, although females were more likely than males to be psychologically or verbally bullied. Bullying was more common in younger children, grades sixth to eighth than in older children, grades ninth and tenth. Bullies and victims of bullying had trouble adjusting to their environment, both socially and psychologically, and showed distinct patterns of poor adjustment. Bullies tended to be poorer students and to engage in substance abuse, whereas the victims of bullies tended to have difficulty making friends and feel lonely. So-called "cyberbullying" is also increasing at dramatic rates, as teenagers spend more time interacting in chat rooms, instant-messaging, and socializing on MySpace and Facebook (Ybarra, Mitchell, Wolak, & Finkelhor, 2006).

Although the problem of bullying has been largely ignored, researchers are now beginning to examine some strategies for coping with this serious problem, in part due to people's grave concern over school violence in general (Olweus, 1995). Dan Olweus developed a school-based intervention program that includes:
• creating greater awareness of bullying as a problem,
• developing class rules against bullying,
• increasing supervision of children during lunch and recess, and
• holding serious talks with bullies and victims.

When this program was used in middle and junior high schools in the Netherlands, bully-related problems decreased 50%, as did other antisocial behavior (e.g., vandalism, fighting, stealing, etc.). This program also led to more positive attitudes toward school, improved social relationships, and greater order and discipline in the classroom.

Associated Press

factors (e.g., car broke down; Baron, 1990; Weiner et al., 1987). As described at the start of this section, people are considerably less angry when someone apologizes for the errors he or she made.

Although expressing anger in an aggressive, violent, and destructive manner leads to increased aggression, letting someone know that you are angry can also be an effective way of reducing anger. The benefit of opening up to someone is due at least in part to the insights and self-awareness that often comes from such self-disclosure. Thus, processing intense feelings helps to reduce one's need to aggress. And ruminating about a problem increases anger, whereas distracting oneself from it reduces anger (Rusting & Nolen-Hoeksema, 1998). In one study, participants were angered, and then hit a punching bag while they either thought about the person who upset them (rumination group) or thought about becoming physically fit (distraction group; Bushman, 2002). Compared to people in the no punching bag control condition as well as those in the distraction condition, those in the rumination condition felt angry, and engaged in more aggressive behavior in a later task.

INCREASING EMPATHY

Another factor that can help reduce aggression is to increase empathy for others (Bandura, Barbaranelli, Caprara, & Pastorelli, 1996; Miller & Eisenberg, 1988). As you read at the start of this chapter, the Amish people felt empathy for Charles Carl Roberts IV, which helps explain their forgiveness for the murders he committed. People find it difficult to inflict pain purposely on another human being, which is why we dehumanize people in times of war. Thus, if we feel empathy toward others, we feel guilty if we hurt them, and therefore find it much harder to aggress against them (Baumeister & Campbell, 1999). For example, people give less severe shocks to a person who has just self-disclosed to them, indicating that feeling empathy reduces the need to aggress (Ohbuchi, Ohno, & Mukai, 1993). Similarly, children with greater empathy for others are less likely to use aggressive actions toward others, and hence training children in perspective taking can be a useful way of reducing aggression.

In one study to test the power of empathy on reducing aggression, participants were told they would be interacting with their partner in a series of tasks (Konrath, Bushman, & Campbell, 2006). Participants in one condition were told that they shared a birthday with their partner; participants in the other condition were not given any information indicating their similarity to their partner. All participants then wrote an essay about abortion (endorsing whichever side they preferred). In both conditions, this essay received harsh criticism from their partner, including statements such as "this is one of the worst essays I have ever read." Participants then engaged with their partner in a reaction time task in which the slower person received an unpleasant blast of noise (a reliably, and subtle, way of measuring aggression). Participants chose the level of noise their partner would receive. Those who believed they shared a birthday with their partner chose significantly softer levels of noise than those who weren't given information about their similarity to their partner.

Learning information about a person's situation, indicating that he or she should not be held fully responsible for his or her actions, can also reduce people's desire for aggression, in part because such information helps us understand and empathize with the person (Kremer & Stephens, 1983). For example, people who learn information that helps explain a person's aggressive behavior *before* being insulted by this person show less physiological arousal and less annoyance than those who learn about such circumstances only after receiving the insult (Johnson & Rule, 1986). Similarly, learning that a person's aggressive behavior was unintentional or was provoked leads to lower levels of aggression and anger.

FACTORS THAT REDUCE AGGRESSION

FACTOR	EXAMPLE
Punishing aggressive behavior	Dr. Vernon is a high school principal. At the start of the year, she instituted a policy in which any student who fights on school grounds receives a mandatory one-week suspension. Fighting has been dramatically reduced.
Modeling nonaggressive responses	Ella and her sister Sophie frequently fight—about who is faster, who sits in which seat in the car, and who is better at hopscotch. Their father suggests they watch *Sesame Street* to learn some effective ways of cooperating. After just a few weeks, Ella and Sophie are getting along much better.
Training in communication and problem-solving skills	Donovan was very angry after his boss, Lianne, was critical of his performance during a meeting. His anger disappeared after Lianne apologized for her negative remarks, explaining that she was in a bad mood that day.
Increasing empathy	Pearl was upset when her friend, Ling, failed to respond to two invitations to a party, and vowed not to call her again. When Pearl learned that Ling had been very busy taking care of her sick mother, she immediately called Ling and offered to run errands for her.

CULTURE

HOW DOES CULTURE INFLUENCE AGGRESSION?

Cultural and subcultural factors are strongly associated with the frequency of and motivation for aggression. In a clever study to test regional differences in views about the appropriateness of types of aggression, researchers sent letters to employers all over the United States (Cohen & Nisbett, 1997). This letter was from a fictitious job applicant who admitted having been convicted of a felony, and asked for an application for employment from their organization. In some of the cases the applicant reported having *accidentally* killed a man who had been having an affair with his fiancée and then bragged about it in a bar (an "honor killing"), and in other cases the applicant had stolen a car to sell in order to pay off debts. Researchers then measured whether the organization responded, and if so, how encouraging and understanding the response was. As predicted, the theft letters were responded to with about the same tone in the North, South, and West, but honor killing letters were responded to with much more warmth in the South and West than in the North. This section examines cultural differences in the prevalence of aggression, rates of domestic violence, and subcultural differences in the prevalence of aggression.

PREVALENCE OF AGGRESSION

Rates of aggression differ substantially across different cultures—as shown in Table 11.2—the rate of aggression is much higher in the United States than in other similar Western countries, including Canada, Australia, and virtually every European country (Lore & Schultz, 1993). The homicide rate is

- three times greater in the United States than in Australia,
- four times greater in the United States than in Canada, and
- seven to ten times greater in the United States than in most other European countries.

Some other countries show extremely low rates of aggression (Bonta, 1997). These societies are found throughout the world, such as the Paliyan people in India, the !Kung children of Namibia and Botswana, and Amish people in the United States. These societies share certain common principles, including an intense focus on intergroup cooperation, avoidance of competition, and the inhibition of emotions. Similarly, in certain cultures in Tahiti and in Eskimos of Canada, there are no words for aggression or aggressive acts, and children are taught that violent acts are unacceptable. Disputes are handled via alternative means, such as singing abusive songs about the other, or engaging in contests in which the first one who breaks a stick with a rock is considered the braver.

Some cultures have more peaceful approaches to handling disputes.

Does orientation toward individualism versus collectivism influence rates of aggression? It is difficult to determine. Some data suggest that collectivistic cultures show higher rates of aggression, including total violent crime and homicide (Bond, 2004). Higher rates of aggression may be due to the greater distinctions drawn between in-group and out-group members in collectivistic cultures.

However, other data suggest that peer-directed aggression is lower in collectivistic cultures than in individualistic ones (Bergeron & Schneider, 2005). In one study, researchers examined rates of aggression across a range of studies collected in 28 countries with over 42,000 participants. These data revealed that countries that are high on individualism have higher rates of aggression. Apparently people in societies that place a high value on the needs of the group as opposed to the needs of the individual show lower levels of aggression.

PREVALENCE OF DOMESTIC VIOLENCE

Although the data on rates of aggression in collectivistic cultures versus individualistic ones are mixed, data on rates of domestic violence strongly indicate that this type of behavior is substantially higher in collectivistic cultures (Archer, 2006; Vandello & Cohen, 2003). Women in collectivistic countries are more likely to experience physical violence by their husbands.

What leads to higher rates of domestic violence in collectivistic cultures? One explanation is that collectivistic cultures are lower on gender equality, which is highly related to attitudes regarding aggression toward women (Acher, 2006). For example, in Egypt, a country with a low gender empowerment, 70% of people believe that a man is justified in beating his wife if she refuses to have sex. In contrast, only 1% of people believe that this act would be justified in New Zealand, a country with high gender empowerment.

Another explanation is that collectivistic cultures tend to hold more traditional values, including an emphasis on loyalty and self-sacrifice as well as unquestioned acceptance of religion (Archer, 2006). In turn, a "good wife" is one who is obedient to her husband; a woman who remains in an abusive relationship would therefore be seen as strong and loyal. In an individualistic culture, a woman who stays in an abusive relationship would be seen as passive and foolish.

These differences in rates of domestic violence are also seen within subcultures of the United States. In one study to examine the impact of subculture on perceptions about domestic violence, researchers recruited participants from both Northern and Southern states as well as participants from Hispanic backgrounds

TABLE 11.2 — RATES OF HOMICIDE IN DIFFERENT COUNTRIES

COUNTRY	HOMICIDE RATE PER 100,000	COUNTRY	HOMICIDE RATE PER 100,000
South Africa	55.86	England & Wales	1.61
Russia	22.05	Italy	1.50
United States	5.56	Ireland	1.42
Finland	2.86	Greece	1.38
Czech Republic	2.52	Germany	1.15
New Zealand	2.50	Spain	1.12
Romania	2.41	Switzerland	1.12
Hungary	2.34	Sweden	1.11
Poland	2.05	Japan	1.05
Australia	1.87	Denmark	1.02
Canada	1.77		

Homicide rates differ dramatically across different countries, from a low of 1.02 per 100,000 in Denmark to more than 50 times this amount in South Africa.

Source: Barclay, G., & Tavares, C. (2003). International Comparisons of Criminal Justice Statistics, 2001. London, UK: Home Office, Research Development Statistics.

(within the United States, Southerners and Hispanics are more collectivistic than Northerners; Vandello & Cohen, 2003). Participants overheard a physical confrontation between a student (supposedly another participant in the same study) and her boyfriend. The confrontation ended with the boyfriend aggressively slamming his partner against a wall, which the participant overheard. The victim (a confederate) then walked into the room to complete the study, and remarked on the abuse, saying, "He really cares about me. I guess that's just how he shows it, you know?" The confederate then noted the participants' response, and specifically whether she expressed tolerance for the abuse. As predicted, 29% of Southern participants and 24% of Hispanic participants expressed some tolerance for the abuse, in contrast to only 10% of Northern participants. These findings suggest that people in different cultures differ in how they view abuse against a dating partner.

SUBCULTURAL DIFFERENCES IN AGGRESSION: THE CULTURE OF HONOR

Even within the United States, rates of some types of aggression are higher in the South than in the Northeast and Midwest (Cohen, 1996; Nisbett, 1993). People in the South are more likely than those in other parts of the country to have a gun in their home, and to see having a gun as an important aspect of protection: Southerners see having a gun as making their home safer more than dangerous, whereas Northerners see *not* having a gun as making their home safer. In fact, 67% of Southerners have guns/revolvers in their homes, compared to 50% of non-Southerners, and 40% of Southerners keep guns for protection, compared to only 23% of non-Southerners. Southern states are also more likely to carry out the death penalty than Northern states: 94% of Southern states allow capital punishment, versus only 43% of Northern states, and between 1977 and 1991, 69% of Southern states carried out an execution, compared to only 13% of Northern states.

One explanation for such differences is that the culture of honor in the American South promotes certain types of aggressive acts, meaning those that serve to protect oneself and defend one's honor (Cohen & Nisbett, 1994). This culture may have developed due to the prevalence of herding animals as a means of economic support. Because animals are difficult to patrol over large plots of land, people need to be able to use force to protect their animals from theft, and developing a reputation as someone who would use force to protect his or her livelihood would be an important strategy for protecting such an investment.

In line with this view, Southerners do not endorse violence more generally than Northerners but do see defending one's honor (with aggression) as necessary following insults and for protection. Compared to people from the North, those from the South are more likely to agree that a person has the right to kill in order to "defend his home" and to hit a drunk who bumps into a man and his wife. Similarly, and as described in the study at the start of this section, employers in the South and West respond more positively to letters describing an honor killing letters than employers in the North.

Although much of the evidence for the link between Southern culture and aggression relies on correlational research, experimental research also suggests subcultural differences in how people understand types of aggression. In one study, letters were sent to college newspapers across the country giving information about a story (Cohen & Nisbett, 1997).

- In one condition, the letter described a fight that occurred between Victor Jensen and Martin Shell at a party. Shell had dated Jensen's sister for about a month, but they had broken up several weeks before. At the party, Shell spelled beer on Jensen's pants, and then shouted that Jensen's sister was a "slut." Jensen tried to fight Shell, but was restrained by his friends. As Jensen was leaving the party later that night, Shell shouted that both Jensen's mother and sister were "sluts." Jensen then demanded that Shell take these comments back, "or else." When Shell refused, Jensen pulled a knife out of his pocket and stabbed Shell twice.
- In the other condition, the letter described an altercation between Robert Hansen and John Seger. Seger was working at a 7–11 convenience store when Hansen entered the store, showed a gun, and demanded that Seger open the safe. Seger said that he did not know the combination and instead offered Hansen $75 from the cash register. Seger tried to open the safe, but when he could not do so, Hansen struck Seger five times in the head with his gun. When Seger fell to the ground, Hansen spit at him, swore at him, and kicked him in the stomach.

Researchers then coded the articles that were written by reporters from different colleges to see how these stories were described in different ways in different parts of the country.

Southern and Western newspapers described the honor crime in a much more sympathetic and understanding way than did Northern newspapers. There was no subcultural difference in description of the other crime.

Subcultural differences also directly impact people's interpersonal behavior. In one study, researchers examined how culture impacted how men responded to an insult (Cohen, Nisbett, Bowdle, & Schwarz, 1996). They recruited male students who had grown up in the North or the South to participate in a study supposedly on "human judgment." The participant completed a brief questionnaire and was then supposed to bring the questionnaire to a table in the hall. To get to the table they had to pass a person standing in the hall filing papers into a file cabinet, and that person had to shut the cabinet in order to allow the participant to pass. After the participant passed the second time (after dropping off the questionnaire to the experimenter), that person said "asshole" and deliberately bumped the participant with his or her shoulder.

At the conclusion of the study the participant then walked down that hall toward another confederate. The dependent variable was how close the participant came to bumping into the confederate before yielding (e.g., a game of chicken). As shown in Figure 11.5, Southerners moved sooner in the control condition than when they'd been insulted. In sum, whereas Northerners' behavior was relatively similar regardless of whether they'd been insulted, Southerners were more polite (e.g., yielded sooner) in the control condition, but reacted more aggressively when provoked.

FIGURE 11.5

DOES SUBCULTURE IMPACT AGGRESSION FOLLOWING PROVOCATION?

Experimenters insulted some men from Northern and Southern backgrounds, and then measured how close they came to bumping into another person before turning away. As predicted, Southerners came closer than Northerners to bumping someone after they had been called an "asshole," supporting the idea that a culture of honor in the South permits aggression in response to insults.

Source: Cohen, D., Nisbett, R. E., Bowdle, B. F., & Schwarz, N. (1996). Insult, aggression, and the southern culture of honor: An 'experimental ethnography'. *Journal of Personality and Social Psychology*, 70, 945-960.

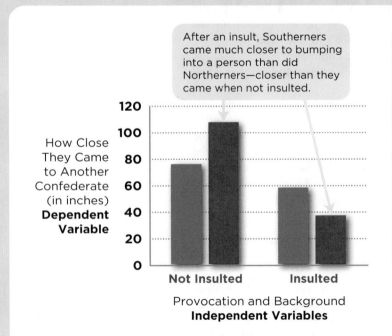

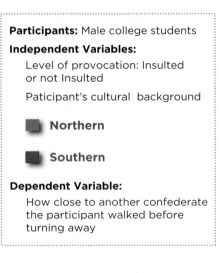

After an insult, Southerners came much closer to bumping into a person than did Northerners—closer than they came when not insulted.

How Close They Came to Another Confederate (in inches) **Dependent Variable**

Provocation and Background
Independent Variables

Participants: Male college students
Independent Variables:
Level of provocation: Insulted or not Insulted
Paticipant's cultural background
■ **Northern**
■ **Southern**
Dependent Variable:
How close to another confederate the participant walked before turning away

The Big Picture

AGGRESSION

This chapter included many applications of the three "big ideas" studied in social psychology. The examples below should help you see the connection between aggression and these big ideas and contribute to your understanding of the big picture of social psychology.

THEME

EXAMPLES

> *The social world influences how we think about ourselves.*

- Boys learn that engaging in physical aggression makes them seem cool, athletic, and popular.
- Professional athletes who make millions of dollars a year feel underpaid when they compare themselves to other professional athletes.
- Children who are spanked are less likely to internalize moral standards of behavior than those who receive other forms of punishment.

> *The social world influences our thoughts, attitudes, and behaviors.*

- When we are frustrated, we act aggressively.
- When we are hot, we act aggressively.
- Children who see aggression on television act aggressively.

> *Our attitudes and behavior shape the social world around us.*

- Children who are highly aggressive are more likely to engage in spouse abuse, criminal behavior, and traffic violations as adults.
- When we feel empathy for someone, we are less likely to aggress against them.
- Children who are exposed to violent films are less likely to seek adult assistance when other children behave aggressively.

WHAT YOU'VE LEARNED

This chapter has described factors that influence aggression as well as factors that can be used to reduce aggression.

YOU LEARNED How do biological factors influence aggression? This section examined the role of biological factors in influencing aggression. You learned about two instinct and evolutionary theories that predict aggression: Freud's death wish and Lorenz's instinct theory. This section also examined the impact of genetics and hormones on rates of aggression. You also learned that male inmates with higher levels of testosterone are more likely than those with lower levels of testosterone to have committed crimes against a person than property crimes, and are more likely to have violated rules in prison.

YOU LEARNED How do psychological factors influence aggression? This section described the role of psychological factors in influencing aggression. You learned about the frustration-aggression theory, including the role of displacement and the relative deprivation, as well as critiques of this theory. This section also described the impact of negative affect, including heat, arousal, other negative conditions, and aggressive cues, on aggression. Finally, this section described how social learning theory explains aggression, and in particular the influence of modeling and reinforcement. You also learned that people who complete a survey in a room with a weapon recommend longer sentences than those who were in a room with a piece of sporting equipment.

YOU LEARNED How does the media influence aggression? This section examined four factors that explain the link between media exposure and aggression. You learned about modeling, priming of aggressive thoughts and feelings, physiological arousal, and desensitization. You also learned that playing violent games leads to more aggression than playing the nonviolent games, especially for men.

YOU LEARNED How can we reduce aggression? This section examined strategies for reducing aggression. These strategies include punishing aggressive behavior, modeling nonaggressive responses, training in communication and problem-solving skills, focusing on the person, and creating positive feelings. You also learned that simply saying you're sorry to someone you've harmed (even unintentionally) reduces aggression.

YOU LEARNED How does culture influence aggression? This section examined cultural differences in aggression. First, you learned that the prevalence of aggression differs dramatically across different cultures. Next, you learned that rates of aggression against women differ across cultures. Finally, you learned that subcultures differ in their perception of different types of aggression, and specifically whether aggression is more acceptable if it protects one's honor. You also learned that stabbing someone who insults your sister is more understandable in the South than in the North.

KEY TERMS

aggression 378
arousal-affect/excitation transfer model 391
catharsis 378
cognitive-neoassociation theory 389
desensitization (disinhibition) 398
displacement 386
emotional (or hostile) aggression 378
frustration-aggression theory 386

general aggression model 393
instinct theory 379
instrumental aggression 378
punishment 401
relative deprivation 387
social learning theory 383

QUESTIONS FOR REVIEW

1. Describe how types of biological factors, including instinct and evolutionary factors, genetics, and hormones, can influence aggression.
2. What are three psychological factors that influence aggression?
3. Describe four ways in which the media influences aggression.
4. What are four effective ways of reducing aggression?
5. Describe cultural differences in the prevalence and causes of aggression.

TAKE ACTION!

1. Your next door neighbor's eight-year-old son is impatient, irritable, and aggressive. What would you predict about his level of aggression as a teenager?
2. Your roommate has just jogged on the treadmill for 45 minutes while watching a boxing match on television and is now driving home. How will he react when a driver cuts him off?
3. Given what we know about the effects of media violence on aggression, should we adopt limits on violence in television, music, movies, and video games? Why or why not?
4. You want to discipline your child for hitting a friend. What approaches might work, and what approaches might not?
5. You are from Alabama, a Southern state, and your co-worker is from New York, a Northern state. What differences in views about aggression would you expect to find?

RESEARCH CONNECTIONS

Try some of these research activities to gain experience in conducting and evaluating research, and to increase your understanding of research methods and techniques in social psychology.
Visit WileyPLUS for more activities and interactive research tools! (www.wileyplus.com)

Participate in Research

Activity 1 **The Risk of Aggression by a Loved One:** This chapter has described how children are most at risk of experiencing violence from parents. Search your local newspaper for instances of aggression against a child, and count the percentage of acts carried out by a parent versus a stranger.

Activity 2 **The Impact of Frustration on Aggression:** One influence on rates of aggression is thought to be frustration. Go to WileyPLUS to read a series of scenarios and rate how likely you would be to behave aggressively in each situation.

Activity 3 **The Impact of Media Violence:** This chapter described the impact of violence in the media on rates of aggression. To examine the prevalence of acts of aggression in the media, watch several children's television programs and count the number of acts of aggression.

Activity 4 **Reducing Aggression:** You learned in this chapter about factors that reduce aggression. Go online to read about various strategies for reducing aggression, and then rate how effectively you believe each approach would work.

Activity 5 **The Impact of Culture on Aggression:** The final section of this chapter described how culture influences the definition and prevalence of aggression. Go online to rate how aggressive you find different behaviors; then compare your ratings to how other students, including those from different cultures, might rate such behaviors.

Test a Hypothesis

One of the common findings in research on aggression is that children's programs frequently portray acts of aggression, which in turn can lead to aggressive behavior. To test whether this hypothesis is true, watch several children's television programs geared to different groups (such as age or gender) and count the number of acts of aggression.

Design a Study

To design your own study testing how aversive circumstances can lead to aggression, go to WilyPLUS. You'll be able to choose the type of study you want to conduct (self-report, observational/naturalistic, or experimental), choose your own independent and dependent variables, and form your own hypothesis. Then, you can share your findings with other students across the country!

12

Interpersonal Attraction

Did you ever wonder?

In 2009, single dad Jason Mesnick proposed
to Melissa Rycroft during the final episode of
The Bachelor. Melissa was selected over the
24 other contestants following a courtship
played out almost entirely on national
television. However, six weeks after making
this decision, Jason revealed that following
their engagement, he continued to have
strong feelings for runner-up Molly Malaney.
In front of more than 17 million television
viewers, Jason announced that their
engagement was off, and expressed his
strong interest in pursuing a relationship with
Molly (and this interest was reciprocated).
This event was the culmination of the 17th
season of *The Bachelor* or *The Bachelorette*,
and although many of these shows have
ended in proposals, Trista Rehn and Ryan
Sutton are still the only couple to have
actually gotten married after meeting on this
type of reality television show. One problem
with finding true love in such a setting is that
the arousal caused by meeting and dating in
front of cameras and a large television
audience may be misinterpreted as romantic

and Close Relationships

interest and even love. This chapter will describe how this and other factors impact interpersonal attraction and close relationships. In addition, you'll find out...

Q A Why are secret affairs often very exciting?

Q A Why do we feel different about those we "love" versus those with whom we are "in love"?

Q A Why are students with greater commitment and investment in their dating relationships less likely to stray during spring break?

Q A Why are men more concerned about their partner having sex with someone, and women are more concerned about their partners falling in love with someone?

Q A Why do Israeli children have very good best friends, and Arab children have very good friendship networks?

These questions can all be answered by social psychology research on factors that impact interpersonal attraction and close relationships.

© Matt Klitscher/ABC/Retna

The need to form close interpersonal bonds with others is a fundamental part of human nature (Baumeister & Leary, 1995; Reis & Collins, 2004; Reis, Collins, & Berscheid, 2000). As noted by William James, "Human beings are born into this life span of which the best thing is its friendships and intimacies" (1920). We care about what other people think of us, we want to form close and intimate relationships, and we feel sad when these relationships end. And in fact, close relationships can have a number of psychological as well as physical benefits; people who are in a close relationship are happier and even live longer than those who are not. Although we all have many types of close relationships (e.g., friends, family members, romantic partners), most people report feeling closest to a romantic partner (Berscheid, Snyder, & Omoto, 1989). In this chapter we will generally focus on romantic relationships.

WHAT PREDICTS INTERPERSONAL ATTRACTION?

Have you, or someone you know, ever tried to hide a romantic relationship from others? If so, you probably know that just trying to keep this secret makes the relationship more exciting and romantic. Dan Wegner and his colleagues at the University of Virginia conducted a series of studies to examine the special allure of "secret relationships" (Wegner, Lane, & Dimitri, 1994). They hypothesized that keeping a secret may increase relationship excitement because people have to exert time and energy suppressing their desire to talk about the relationship to others. To test this hypothesis, unacquainted students were told that they would play a communication game with a partner. Some students were told that they should communicate with their partner using their feet (e.g., tapping feet under a table to convey information) so that they could beat the other couple seated with them at the table. In one condition, all four subjects were told that one couple would be communicating in this way. In the other condition, the other subjects were not told about this secret form of communication. Researchers then measured attraction for the partner. As predicted, participants who played "footsie" with their partner and kept this communication secret showed higher levels of attraction for each other than the couples that simply sat near each other, but did not touch. Couples who played "footsie" also reported higher levels of attraction for each other than those who played "footsie" in cases in which others at the table were aware of this behavior. These findings suggest that keeping a secret with one's partner leads to an obsessive preoccupation with not revealing the secret, which, in turn, increases attraction. This section will examine this and other factors that influence interpersonal attraction: physical attractiveness, relationship factors, and situational factors.

PHYSICAL ATTRACTIVENESS

You probably aren't surprised to learn that we find physically attractive people attractive. However, you might be surprised to learn that people from diverse backgrounds and cultures generally agree on what is physically attractive—and that physical attractiveness is associated with many benefits.

The consistency of facial attractiveness. Although you may believe that different people find different things attractive, what people find beautiful is quite consistent. For example, prominent cheekbones, thin eyebrows, and big eyes are commonly viewed as attractive. These preferences are found among people in different ethnic groups within a given culture (e.g., Caucasians, Hispanics, Asians, and African Americans within the United States) (Langlois, Ritter, Roggman & Vaughn, 1991). They are also found across different cultures. In one study, researchers examined ratings of beauty made by American college students and foreign college students who had newly arrived in the United States from a variety of different countries (Japan, China, Guatemala, Panama, etc.; Cunningham et al.,

1995). Ratings of beauty were very similar across students from different backgrounds.

One reason for this consistency in what is seen as attractive is that people prefer faces that are "average" as opposed to "distinct" (Langlois & Roggman, 1990; Rhodes, Halberstadt, Jeffery, & Palermo, 2005). This may seem like an odd finding—after all, we don't exactly see Jennifer Aniston's face or Brad Pitt's face as "average." But people find composite photos (those that are made up of multiple different photos) more attractive than the individual faces that make up the composite (although the most attractive single faces are still seen as more attractive than the composite). Do you find this difficult to believe? See how you'd rate these photos. Moreover, our preference for "average" faces is not unique; people even find average dogs and birds more attractive than more unique ones (Halberstadt, 2006; Halberstadt & Rhodes, 2000).

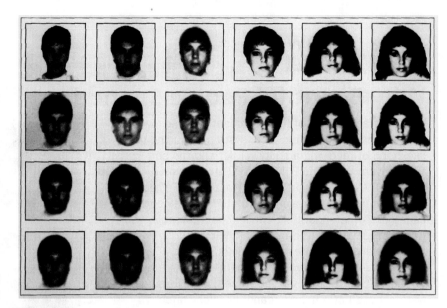

Which faces do you find most attractive? Most people find the photos in the bottom row, which average 32 different faces, more attractive than the faces in the top row, which average four faces. *Source*: Langlois, J. H., & Roggman, L. A. (1990). Attractive faces are only average. *Psychological Science 1*, 115-121.

One explanation for people's preference for composite photos is that these pictures tend to be more symmetrical, because they average the slight differences between people. People do find symmetry attractive (Halberstadt & Rhodes, 2000; Rhodes, Sumich, & Byatt, 1999). For example, Shackelford and Larsen (1997) found that people with symmetrical faces were rated as more physically attractive, as well as healthier and more dominant/extroverted. Even within pairs of identical twins, the more symmetrical twin was more attractive (Mealey, Bridgstock, & Townsend, 1999).

The benefits of physical attractiveness. Not surprisingly, the attractiveness of the other person plays a large role in determining attraction in interpersonal relationships. Physically attractive people experience many benefits, including greater likelihood of being hired for a job, higher starting salaries, and bigger raises (Biddle & Hamermesh, 1998; Frieze, Olson, & Russell, 1991; Hamermesh & Biddle, 1994; Marlowe, Schneider, & Nelson, 1996). For example, each point one rises on a 1 to 5 scale of attractiveness, a woman earns an additional $2,100 per year, and a man earns an additional $2,600 a year—suggesting that plastic surgery could eventually pay off (Frieze et al., 1991). Attractiveness can also contribute to job security. Researchers in one study examined teaching evaluations for 463 courses taught by 94 faculty members at the University of Texas at Austin (Hamermesh & Parker, 2005). Professors who were the most attractive received, on average, evaluations of about 4.5 (on a 1 to 5 scale). Those who were the least attractive received evaluations of about 3.5. Because tenure in universities is determined in part by teaching evaluations, these findings mean that attractive professors have a distinct advantage in maintaining their jobs! Attractive people who are accused of crimes even get lower bail and smaller fines, as described in Law Connections (Downs & Lyons, 1991).

Explanations for the physical attractiveness effect. Why does physical attractiveness lead to attraction? First, aesthetic appeal is desirable, and leads to positive affect (Kenrick, Montello, Gutierres, & Trost, 1993). We like to look at things that we find visually appealing, and hence people show a general preference for objects they find attractive. This preference therefore influences not only the people we choose to date, but also the cars we buy, the paintings we like to look at, and the clothes we wear. Remarkably, infants as young as two to three

Why Beautiful People Spend Less Time in Jail

The attractiveness of the defendant impacts decisions made in the legal system, including the likelihood of receiving a guilty verdict and the sentence given (DeSantis & Kayson, 1997; Downs & Lyons, 1991; Lieberman, 2002; Mazzella & Feingold, 1994). In one study, researchers studied the court cases of 74 defendants in criminal court. People who were attractive received significantly lower penalties than those who were less attractive (Stewart, 1980, 1985). In another study, researchers examined the fines and bail set for over 2,000 people in Texas who were accused of a misdemeanor or felony offense. (Downs & Lyons, 1991). Once again, the attractiveness of the defendant (as rated by outside observers) influenced the sentencing decision: the mean fine for a highly unattractive person was $1,384.18 versus $503.74 for a highly attractive person. What causes this relationship? Research points to a number of possibilities: the tendency for unattractive people to commit more crimes, the perception that crimes are committed by attractive people must be less serious, and the belief that attractive people are "good" and hence would not commit such crimes.

© Corbis/SUPERSTOCK

months of age show a preference for looking at pictures of attractive, compared to unattractive, people (Langlois et al., 1991). In addition, both men and women focus on, and remember, attractive females, suggesting that we pay particular attention to information about physical attractiveness (Maner et al., 2003). Some recent research even suggests that when men see photos of highly attractive women, a particular part of the brain is more strongly activated than when they see photos of average-looking women (Aharon, Etcoff, Ariely, Chabris, O'Connor, & Breiter, 2001). Most intriguingly, the part of the brain that is activated in response to beautiful faces is also activated in response to rewarding behaviors (e.g., money, drugs, etc.), suggesting that for men, seeing beautiful women is very rewarding.

A second explanation for our strong preference for attractive partners is that people hold a "what is beautiful is good" stereotype. In other words, we see attractive people as also having a variety of other positive traits (Eagly et al., 1991; Feingold, 1992; Langlois et al., 2000). Attractive people are rated as higher in intelligence and social competence, and are seen as better adjusted and more extroverted/dominant. They are also expected to have better lives (e.g., happier marriages, more prestige, more social success, etc.). So, for better or for worse (perhaps depending on your own level of attractiveness), people do judge books by their covers.

But do attractive people really have more desirable traits? In a word, yes. Attractive people are less lonely, less anxious, more popular, more sexually experienced, and even smarter (Diener, Wolsic, & Fujita, 1995; Feingold, 1992; Langlois et al., 2000). Not surprisingly, they also feel better about themselves.

Third, attractive people possess greater social skills, so they may be more fun to be around. One explanation for this link between attractiveness and social skills is that people who are attractive are consistently treated better, including having more positive interactions, less negative interactions, and more help, attention, and reward (Zebrowitz, Collins, & Dutta, 1998). As described in Chapter 4, women who are called by men who believe they are attractive (based on a photograph they are given) are much more socially engaging and friendly on the phone compared with women who are called by men who believe they are unattractive (Snyder et al., 1977). In turn, these frequent and positive interactions could lead attractive individuals to develop greater social skills. In one study, pairs of unacquainted male and female college students were asked to have a conversation (Stiles, Walz, Schroeder, & Williams, 1996). Those who were attractive *and* who were interacting with an attractive partner engaged in more self-disclosure.

Fourth, people may want to associate with attractive people because such relationships could lead to social profit (e.g., you look good if your date is good-looking; Geiselman, Haight, & Kimata, 1984). In fact, people who are standing with others who are attractive seem more attractive than those who are standing with others who are unattractive. This is one reason why attractive people have more dating and sexual experience (Langlois et al., 2000).

"Would you mind taking a picture of me with your girlfriend?"

The value of resources.

Although people in general show a preference for physically attractive dating partners, men and women differ in the extent to which they prefer attractive partners (Buss & Schmitt, 1993; Feingold, 1990, 1991; Fletcher, Tither, O'Loughlin, Friesen, & Overall, 2004). As you might expect, men place more importance on physical attractiveness in a dating partner than do women. One out of every three men advertising in personals requests an attractive partner, whereas only one in seven women make such a request (Koestner & Wheeler, 1988; Rajecki, Bledsoe, & Rasumussen, 1991). Similarly, women's ads tend to offer physical attractiveness (e.g., describe what they look like), suggesting that they are aware of what men are hoping to find in a dating partner. Men also prefer partners who are younger than themselves (Buss, 1989; Rajecki et al., 1991). These preferences for a physically attractive partner are generally found in homosexual as well as heterosexual men (Bailey, Gaulin, Agyei, & Gladue, 1994; Kenrick, Keefe, Bryan, Barr, & Brown, 1995).

In contrast, women give more weight than men to traits that signify resources, such as wealth, ambitiousness, character, and status (Buss & Schmitt, 1993; Feingold, 1992). Compared to men, women are more willing to date and marry someone who is not good-looking, is older by 5+ years, earns more, and has more education (Buss, 1989; Rajecki et al., 1991; Sprecher et al., 1994). In line with this preference, women's personal ads are much more likely than men's to request professional status in a partner (Koestner & Wheeler, 1988; Rajecki et al., 1991). Women are also attracted to men who are confident (another potential cue to resources), but men don't really care about women's dominance (Sadalla, Kenrick, & Vershure, 1987).

What accounts for the sex differences in resource preferences? Evolutionary psychologists believe that men and women evolve different mate preferences because these preferences maximize their reproductive success (Buss, 1989; Buss & Schmitt, 1993). Specifically, women who are pregnant or nursing may have difficulty in securing their own resources; they need to have partners with resources to provide for them and their child. In turn, women are motivated to look for, and maintain relationships with, men with high levels of education and well-paying jobs (Buss & Shackelford, 1997). This is why men may go out of their way to emphasize the resources they could provide to a potential partner, such as saying they intend to go to law school, drive an expensive car, or will pay for dinner. Some intriguing

Questioning the Research
If people seem more attractive when they are with people who are highly attractive, how does this explain the contrast effect, which would predict being with a highly attractive person would make others fall short in comparison?

Women's preference for men with resources may be particularly strong during times of peak fertility, in which conception is most likely to occur. One recent study examined women's preferences for different men as a function of whether they were currently in a fertile versus a non-fertile time during their menstrual cycle (Gangestad, Simpson, Cousins, Garver-Apgar, & Christensen, 2004). In this study, women saw brief segments of videotaped interviews with various men, who varied on a number of characteristics, including social presence (e.g., athletic presentation, eye contact, composure, lack of self-deprecation, and lack of nice-guy self-presentation) and direct competitiveness (e.g., derogation of other men, lack of mentioning a nice personality, lack of laughing). Then the women rated each man in terms of his attractiveness for a short-term mate (meaning he would be appealing for a short-term sexual affair) as well as a long-term mate (meaning he would be appealing in terms of a long-term relationship). In line with predictions from evolutionary theory, women who are in a fertile period of their cycle prefer men with both social presence and direct competitiveness when they are imagining a short-term mate. However, fertility is not associated with such preferences when women are considering a longer-term mate. Women at times of peak fertility are also more concerned with the attractiveness of potential mating partners, suggesting that those who are most likely to conceive are more focused on how physically attractive their partners are (Beaulieu, 2007). These findings suggest that during times of fertility, women show a particular preference for sexual partners with traits that indicate masculinity, dominance, and attractiveness.

Research also indicates that women may behave in particularly appealing ways during times of fertility, perhaps in an attempt to attract a desirable mate. In one unusual study, researchers calculated the tips earned by strippers through lap dancing during different times of their monthly cycle (Miller, Tybur, & Jordan, 2007). As predicted, strippers earn more tips during the time in their monthly cycle in which they are ovulating (about $15 an hour more than women at other points in their cycle), presumably because this is when women are most interested in having sex. Moreover, women who were taking birth control pills—which work by inhibiting ovulation—don't have an earning peak halfway through their cycle.

research even suggests that women's preferences for resources may vary depending on their likelihood of becoming pregnant, as described in Would You Believe....

Because men can produce children with many different women, they prefer partners who are most likely to produce healthy children (Buss & Shackelford, 1997). They also devote more time and energy to finding —and keeping—partners who are young and healthy, because these traits are seen as cues of health and more fertility. In support of this evolutionary argument, men do show a preference for women with particular types of bodies (those whose waists are narrower than their hips), perhaps because this "hourglass figure" is associated with fertility (Singh, 1993, 1995). For example, men judge women with a low "waist-to-hip ratio" (meaning larger hips in comparison to waists) as more attractive than those with higher ratios. They also rate these figures as higher in attractiveness, health, and reproductive fitness.

Critiques of the evolution perspective.

Although these evolutionarily based explanations for gender differences in attraction may seem to "make sense," some researchers point out flaws of this theory. First, these gender differences are much more pronounced when you ask people for their preferences in short-term and casual dating situations than in long-term and more committed ones (Kenrick, Sadalla, Groth, & Trost, 1990; Kenrick, Groth, Trost, & Sadalla, 1993). For example, both men and women prefer physical attractiveness in a short-term mate (Li, Bailey, Kenrick, & Linsenmeier, 2002; Li & Kenrick, 2006), and both men and women are pickier when selecting a long-term partner than a short-term partner (Stewart, Stinnett, & Rosenfeld, 2000). Moreover, some recent research suggests that people report sex differences in the importance of attractiveness and earning potential, but their actual interest in real-life partners shows no sex differences on these traits (Eastwick & Finkel, 2008). The Research Focus on Gender box describes both gender similarities and differences in terms of sexual behavior. Finally, some research suggests that preferences in terms of women's body shape and size have changed rather dramatically over time, indicating that societal preferences, and not just evolutionary factors, clearly also influence how we think of attractiveness (see Figure 12.1).

RESEARCH FOCUS ON GENDER

How Different Are Men and Women in Sex-Related Behaviors?

According to evolutionary theory, men's short-term sexual strategy is based on obtaining many partners. Meeting a person who might be good for a short-term affair (easy sexual access) could intensify men's short-term romantic desires, but could lead to the reverse for women. In a series of studies to test this hypothesis,

FIGURE 12.1

CHANGING MODELS OF PHYSICAL ATTRACTIVENESS OVER TIME

As shown in this figure, what is seen as attractive varies considerably over time, from the rather heavy woman portrayed in the painting, to Marilyn Monroe, who was seen as a paragon of attractiveness in the 1950s, to the very thin model who may be seen as representing attractiveness today.

Source: (a) Helena Fourment in a Fur Wrap, 1636-38 by Peter Paul Rubens (1577-1640) Kunsthistorisches Museum, Vienna, Austria/ The Bridgeman Art Library; (b) Sunset Boulevard/Sygma/©Corbis; (c) Wendell Teodoro/Wire Images/Getty Images, Inc.

men's and women's attraction to various partners was tested as a function of the type of partner (e.g., easy sexual access versus relationship exclusivity; Schmitt, Couden, & Baker, 2001). During some interviews, participants were exposed to an experimental confederate exhibiting cues to easy sexual access (e.g., "I'm kind of a flirt really. Lately, though, my dates have been calling me too much, you know what I mean; especially the 'night after'). In other cases, they were exposed to a person cueing more difficult sexual access (e.g., "I don't like to waste time on dates, though, unless it's with someone interested in the same thing I am—a long-term, exclusive relationship"). Targets who exhibited cues to easy sexual access were rated more desirable by men than women in the context of short-term mating.

However, there is no real difference between what men and women want in long-term contexts—both prefer exclusive partners. Similarly, there are no gender differences in desirability as a marriage partner based on sexual experience. In terms of dating potential, women valued men more highly who had moderate sexual experience. On the other hand, men placed the highest value on women with high sexual experience (presumably because these women will be more willing to have sex early in a new relationship; Sprecher, McKinney, & Orbuch, 1991).

Data on gender differences in preferences for sexual partners also reveal mixed results. For example, if you ask men and women for their desired number of lifetime sexual partners, there are large differences—men want an average of 7.69, compared to women, who want an average of 2.78 (Pedersen, Miller, Putcha-Bhagavatula, & Yang, 2002). These general findings about gender differences in desire for sexual variety are found across diverse cultures, again providing support for an evolutionary theory (Schmitt et al., 2003). However, the majority of both men and women report the ideal number of partners over the next 30 years is one, and 99% of both men and women say they want to ultimately settle down (in the next five years) with a single partner. In sum, although men are more interested than women in having multiple sexual partners, if you ask people to think about the number of sexual partners they'd like to have over the next 30 years, these gender differences largely disappear.

Another critique of the evolutionary argument is that women generally don't prefer men who have stereotypically masculine traits and high levels of resources. Specifically, both men and women see androgynous dating partners as more desirable, and feminine characteristics as better than masculine ones (Green & Kenrick, 1994; Ickes, 1993). For example, prosocial men (those who are willing to help others) are rated higher in physical and sexual attractiveness, social desirability, and dating desirability than non-prosocial men (Jensen-Campbell, Graziano, & West, 1995). On the other hand, dominant men are not rated higher than prosocial men on any measures of attraction.

Women aren't just interested in men with resources—they also want men who are caring.

Relatedly, women don't just want men with resources—they want men with particular character traits, such as talent and ambition, that in turn may lead to resources (Hanko, Master, & Sabini, 2004). In one study, participants read about a man who had a net worth of $14 million dollars. Some people read that he had earned this fortune through winning the lottery. Others read that he had earned this money through selling a dot-com company. Women, but not men, rated the lottery winner as less attractive than the dot-com creator. These findings suggest that even when women show a preference for men with resources, this preference is heavily influenced by their assumptions about the link between these resources and other character traits.

Still other researchers point to a sociocultural explanation for these gender differences in mate preferences (Eagly & Wood, 1999). Alice Eagly and Wendy Wood believe these preferences simply reflect long-standing gender differences in societal roles, in which men are given greater opportunities to pursue economic resources (such as education and jobs). Therefore, women have traditionally needed to look for men with such resources, because they don't have access to these benefits. In line with this view, men and women were more similar in their mate preferences in the 1990s than they were earlier (Buss, Shackelford, Kirkpatrick, & Larsen, 2001). Both sexes, but especially men, increased the importance they place on finding a partner with good financial resources. Both men and women also increased the importance they place on finding a physically attractive partner. So, while women may have originally needed to find men with high resources, they now have the luxury of looking for partners with other traits.

Yet, more evidence for the role of sociocultural differences in influencing mate preferences is found in research showing that gender differences in mate preferences differ across different societies (Eagly & Wood, 1999). In societies in which women have little access to resources, such as Kenya, Pakistan, and Haiti, they continue to show a strong preference for wealthy, well-educated, and high status men. But in societies in which women have considerable access to resources, such as Norway, Australia, and the United States, such preferences are minimal. For example, when researchers examine societies in which women participate equally with men in economic, political, and decision-making roles, women are less concerned about how much their partners make. These data indicate that as women gain power and resources, they are less focused on choosing mates with these needs.

RELATIONSHIP FACTORS

Thus far the chapter has focused on physical attractiveness as a factor that influences one's attraction toward another. However, in many cases, attraction is not only a function of the other person, but also of the interaction between that person and the other person. This section will describe relationship factors that impact interpersonal attraction: similarity, complementarity, and reciprocity.

Similarity.   We like people who are similar to ourselves, including those who share our attitudes, values, and interests, as well as those who share demographic characteristics (e.g., age, race, religion, economic background; Botwin, Buss, & Shackelford, 1997; Caspi & Herbener, 1990). In one study, students were given fictional data about another student's attitudes, and were then asked to rate how much they liked this other student (Byrne, 1997). Those who thought the other person shared none of their attitudes rated them a 4.41 (on a 2- to 14-point scale). Those who thought they shared half of their attitudes rated them a 7.20. Finally, those who thought they shared all of their attitudes rated them a 13.00. We also tend to seek and find partners who are at roughly our own level of physical attractiveness: this is referred to as the **matching hypothesis** (Feingold, 1988; Kalick & Hamilton, 1986).

Why does similarity lead to attraction? In part because people who share our important traits and values make us feel good about ourselves. After all, we like ourselves and our views, so it is rewarding when someone else feels the same way. We also see similar people as more likeable and attractive (Moreland & Zajonc, 1982), in part because we believe similar others will like us (Condon & Crano, 1988). Having a partner who shares our valued attitudes also reduces the potential for conflict. Just imagine the consequences of dating a person who disagreed with your major political and religious beliefs.

Similarity in a romantic partner also leads to happiness (Botwin et al., 1997; Byrne, 1997; Luo & Klohnen, 2005). In one study, 93 cohabiting and married couples described their attitudes and relationship satisfaction (Aube & Koestner, 1995). When researchers asked these couples to report their relationship satisfaction 15 months later, those who were similar in attitudes had greater satisfaction.

matching hypothesis the hypothesis that people tend to seek and find partners who are roughly our own level of physical attractiveness

Complementarity.   Although similarity is a strong predictor of attraction, can *complementarity* also lead to attraction? Despite the proverb "opposites attract," little research shows that people are attracted to those who are fundamentally different from themselves. In fact, qualities in a partner that are different from one's own quality are initially arousing and exciting, but can later be strongly disliked (the "fatal attraction" effect; Felmlee, 1995, 1998). Students who rated traits in their partner as "different" and "exciting" are more likely to experience

"We laugh at the same things."

© The New Yorker Collection 1998 Bernard Schoenbaum/cartoonbank.com. All Rights Reserved dissatisfaction later on than those who rated their partners as similar in personality and/or interests. In sum, qualities that we initially see as unusual and exciting can eventually cause irritation.

reciprocity a mutual exchange between two people

Reciprocity. Another strong predictor of attraction is **reciprocity**, meaning believing the other person likes us (Aron, Dutton, Aron, & Iverson, 1989). People often report starting a friendship or dating relationship because the other person liked them; we all like to be liked, and therefore we are attracted to those who like us. Interestingly, having someone grow to like you more over time can lead to especially strong feelings of attraction. In one study by Aronson and Linder (1965), groups of two "subjects" (one a true "subject" and the other a confederate) talked over seven sessions, and the subject then received the confederate's rating of the subject's personality after each session. Those who were told that the person (confederate) never liked them (28 negative things were said) and those who were told that the person used to like them but didn't now (8 positives, 14 negatives) don't like the confederate very much. However, those who were told the confederate always liked them (28 positives) liked the person quite a bit, and those who were told the confederate used to not like them but now did (8 negatives, 14 positives), liked the person the most. This is true even though there are fewer positive things said and more negative things said than in the "always liked" condition.

Believing that someone likes you can also lead to greater self-disclosure over time (Collins & Miller, 1994). This is the quid pro quo of mutual exchange. We feel happy when people share things with us because it implies trust and respect in the relationship (Miller, 1990; Taylor, Gould, & Brounstein, 1981). In turn, we disclose more to people who disclose to us. We also like people who disclose to us, and like them even more after we disclose to them. In one study, 202 college students engaged in brief, get-acquainted conversations with a stranger (Vittengl & Holt, 2000). Students who engaged in greater self-disclosure during the conversation showed a more positive mood after the conversation, including greater happiness and excitement, as well as greater liking for their conversation partner.

You may be questioning these findings about the power of reciprocity—after all, doesn't conventional wisdom tell us that it is better to play "hard to get"? Well, playing hard to get means walking a very fine line: We are indeed *more* interested in dating people who seem selective or choosy in their partner selections than those who seem nondiscriminating, but we are *less* interested in pursuing potential dating partners who seem "impossible to get" (Walster, Walster, Piliavin, & Schmidt, 1973). But be careful in the use of this strategy—it can backfire. In one study, male college students read information about five women who were potential dating partners. One woman appeared to everyone as a very difficult person to date. (She had given all of the prospective dating partners she evaluated low ratings). One appeared very easy for all men to date (she had given all of the men high ratings), and one appeared easy for the subject to date, but hard for others to date (had rated only the subject high). The majority of subjects see the "selectively hard" woman as more friendly and warm as well as less problematic to date, and 59% chose this woman from the five options they were given.

SITUATIONAL FACTORS

You may not want to believe it, but interpersonal attraction can be influenced by very non-romantic factors, such as the situation. This section will describe three situational factors that impact interpersonal attraction: proximity, physiological arousal, and the contrast effect.

Proximity. Some of the earliest research on the predictors of interpersonal attraction revealed that people are attracted to those who are familiar to us (Festinger, Schachter, & Back, 1950). One reason why proximity tends to lead to attraction is simply that you are more likely to meet and get to know—and therefore become attracted to—people who live or work near you. I met my husband because he lived on my hall during my sophomore year of college. We could easily have never met if one of us had chosen to live in a different building that year. Physical distance from another person is strongly associated with the number of "memorable interactions" (Latané, Liu, Nowak, Bonevento, & Zhang, 1995). Of course people can—and do—have meaningful interactions with people who live far away, but most meaningful interactions occur with those who we are near.

The attraction caused by proximity is not simply due to the opportunity to meet and interact with people, but also due to the familiarity that comes with seeing these people over time (Bornstein, R. F. (1989); Harmon-Jones & Allen, 2001; Moreland & Zajonc, 1982). In fact, the more we are exposed to something, the more we like it, a phenomenon called **mere exposure** (as you may recall from Chapter 6). Richard Moreland and Scott Beach (1992) conducted a very clever study to test the power of mere exposure on interpersonal attraction. Four women who were similar in age and appearance were randomly assigned to attend a certain number of class sessions of a social psychology course. One of the women attended the class 5 times, another attended 10 times, a third attended 15 times, and the fourth never attended the class. Each time the woman attended the class, she entered the back of the classroom and walked to the front to take a seat so that a majority of students could see her. During the last week of class, all of the students in the class rated the attractiveness of each of the four women. As they predicted, women who attended the class more times were rated as more attractive.

Yet another explanation for the impact of proximity on attraction is ease of maintaining the relationship. It simply takes less effort to manage a friendship with someone who lives next door or across the hall than with someone who lives in a different city or state. Relationships can indeed persist over great distances, but usually only important ones (e.g., relatives, very close friends).

Physiological arousal.

Another situational predictor of attraction is physiological arousal, which can lead to excitation transfer (Allen, Kenrick, Lindner, & McCall, 1989; Foster, Witcher, Campbell, & Green, 1998; Zillman, 1972). **Excitation transfer** occurs when the arousal caused by one stimulus is added to the arousal from a second stimulus and the combined arousal is attributed (erroneously) to the second stimulus. For example, if I have a big cup of coffee in Starbucks (which leads my heart to race), and then I meet an attractive guy (which might also lead my heart to race), I will likely think I am very attracted to him because I attribute my now very rapidly beating heart entirely to this second stimulus (the hot guy), while ignoring the effect of the hot coffee (caffeine). This misattribution of arousal from one source to a second source (two-factor) is based on Schachter's two-factor theory of emotion (as described in Chapter 3; Schachter & Singer, 1962).

In one study to test this hypothesis, Gregory White and colleagues asked college men to run in place for 15 seconds or for 120 seconds as a way of creating high and low arousal (White, Fishbein, & Rutstein, 1981). They then watched a videotape of a potential date, who was either an attractive

© Comstock/SUPERSTOCK

According to research on the impact of proximity on liking, people find those they see frequently more attractive.

mere exposure the phenomenon by which the greater exposure we have to a given stimulus, the more we like it

excitation transfer a phenomenon in which the arousal caused by one stimulus is added to the arousal from a second stimulus and the combined arousal is erroneously attributed to the second stimulus

"Gee, but I miss the heightened eroticism of those five and a half years of conjugal visits."

woman (wearing tight clothes, makeup, saying how she wanted to meet someone) or an unattractive woman (wearing baggy clothes, awful makeup, a scarf over her head, saying that she had a bad cold). The men then rated how attracted they were to each woman. Not surprisingly, everyone was more attracted to the attractive woman. However, men who had also just exercised for 120 seconds found her even more attractive than those who had not exercised for so long, and they found the unattractive woman even less attractive (and perhaps even repulsive).

Donald Dutton and Art Aron (1974) conducted a very clever study on the impact of physiological arousal on attraction. College men were asked to complete a questionnaire, and then to return it to a male or a female experimenter who was standing on a bridge. In some conditions the bridge was very firm and stable. In other conditions the bridge was quite narrow and shaky—presumably leading to some fear and hence physiological arousal. After the men crossed the bridge to return the questionnaire, they were given the experimenter's phone number so that they could contact him/her if they had any questions about the experiment later on. As shown in Figure 12.2, men who crossed the shaky bridge to the female experimenter were much more likely to call than those in any of the

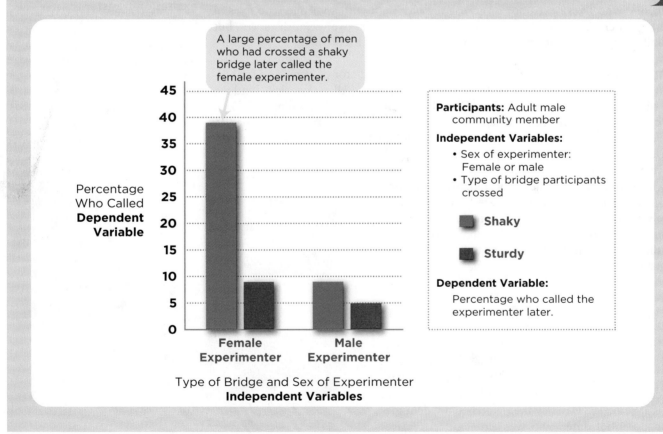

FIGURE 12.2

DOES PHYSIOLOGICAL AROUSAL IMPACT ATTRACTION?

Men completed a questionnaire, and then walked across either a sturdy or a shaky bridge to give it to the experimenter. The experimenter thanked them for their participation, and then gave participants his or her phone number to call with any questions about the study. Although men who cross either bridge are quite unlikely to later call a male experimenter with questions, men who cross a shaky bridge to the female experimenter are quite likely to later call her—perhaps because they misattribute their physiological arousal that is caused by the shaky bridge to feelings of attraction to this woman.

Source: Dutton, D.G., & Aron, A.P. (1974). Some evidence for heightened sexual attraction under conditions of high anxiety. *Journal of Personality and Social Psychology*, 30, 510-517.

A large percentage of men who had crossed a shaky bridge later called the female experimenter.

Percentage Who Called **Dependent Variable**

Participants: Adult male community member

Independent Variables:
- Sex of experimenter: Female or male
- Type of bridge participants crossed

  Shaky

  Sturdy

Dependent Variable:
Percentage who called the experimenter later.

Female Experimenter

Male Experimenter

Type of Bridge and Sex of Experimenter
Independent Variables

other conditions. These men misattributed the physiological arousal caused by the situation (ie., the shaky bridge and their fear of falling) to the female experimenter, and hence were probably calling to act on their feelings of attraction.

The misattribution of physiological arousal is evident in many real-life situations. One of the most poignant examples of this effect was seen in the years following the 9-11 terrorists attacks. Many firefighters who survived these attacks came to the aid of women who lost their firefighter husbands. This support was intended to provide these widows with the type of assistance their husbands would have provided, such as managing home repairs, mowing the lawn, and helping with the children. But in several cases, the firefighters ultimately left their own wives and families and began romantic relationships with the widows of their former colleagues. These relationships can be explained at least partially by the misattribution of arousal caused by grief and sadness, which then gets misinterpreted as deep romantic love.

Contrast effect. Another situational factor that can influence interpersonal attraction is the attractiveness of the people to which you are comparing a potential dating partner (Kenrick & Gutierres, 1980; Kenrick et al., 1989; Kenrick, Neuberg, Zierk, & Krones, 1994). In other words, a particular dating partner might look very attractive when you are comparing him or her to other college students, but could somehow seem less attractive when you are comparing him or her to movie stars and models. As you read in Chapter 5, our evaluations of a given object are often influenced by the objects to which you are comparing it; a $100 sweater may not seem like a bargain, unless you see that it was marked down from $300.

The contrast effect can have a strong impact on ratings of attractiveness (Kenrick et al., 1994). In one study, men were asked to rate the attractiveness of a woman they could supposedly go on a blind date with (Kenrick & Gutierres, 1980). Half of the men rated the prospective blind date candidate as they were watching *Charlie's Angels* (a television show featuring three highly attractive crime-fighting women who often wore bikinis). The other half rated this woman while they were watching a television show that featured less attractive actors. As predicted, the same blind date candidate was rated much more highly when the men were watching the neutral show than when they were watching *Charlie's Angels*. Similarly, men who look at centerfolds from *Playboy* and *Penthouse* then rate their own partners as lower in attractiveness (Kenrick et al., 1989). And the contrast effect can have consequences for relationship longevity: among men who are in dating relationships, commitment decreases when they see a group of attractive women (Kenrick et al., 1994).

The contrast effect can also influence women's ratings of their own partners. Women's commitment to their current relationship decreases once they see a group of dominant men (Kenrick et al., 1994). (As noted earlier in this chapter, women are particularly interested in partners with resources, and dominant men are seen as more likely to have resources.) In sum, how attractive a person finds his or her own and other potential partners is a function not only of the target's desirability, but also the desirability of other people in the environment to which they are compared.

PREDICTORS OF ATTRACTION IN FRIENDSHIP

Although this section has focused on the predictors of interpersonal attraction in romantic relationships, many of these factors also predict attraction in friendships. For example, similarity is a strong predictor of attraction and satisfaction in friendships (Cash & Derlega, 1978; McKillip & Reidel, 1983; Morry, 2005). In one study,

"Don't forget to click Reply."
© The New Yorker Collection 2003 William Haefeli/cartoonbank.com.
All Rights Reserved

FIGURE 12.3

DOES PROXIMITY INFLUENCE ATTRACTION?

Students were randomly assigned to sit next to someone, or in the same row as someone, in a psychology class for a semester. Researchers then measured the liking for that student a year later. As predicted, students who were assigned to sit in neighboring seats for a semester felt friendlier toward each other than those who sat farther apart.

Source: Back, M.D., Schmukle, S., C., & Egloff, B. (2008). Becoming friends by chance. *Psychological Science, 19*, 439–440.

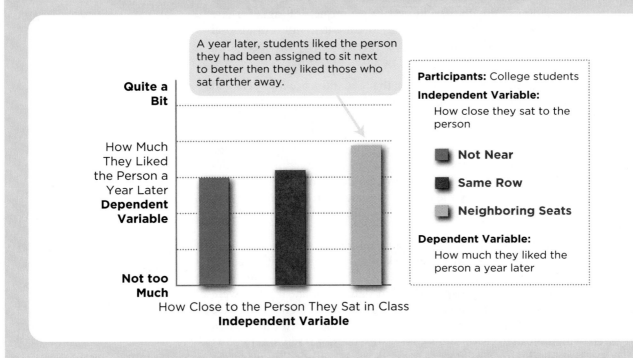

researchers examined satisfaction in randomly assigned roommate relationships (Carli, Ganley, & Pierce-Otay, 1991). People with roommates who were similar to themselves in personality and physical attractiveness were more likely to choose to room again with them the following year. Similarly, Kuperschmidt and colleagues found that as similarity across age, gender, academic, and social attributes increased in 3rd and 4th graders, so does friendship (Kuperschmidt, De Rosier, & Patterson, 1995).

Proximity is another strong predictor of attraction in friendships. In one of the first studies to examine the role of proximity, Leon Festinger and his colleagues (1950) investigated friendship patterns in a large apartment complex in which residents were simply given apartments as they became available—they did not choose where exactly they would live within the building. Many more people reported developing friendships with those who lived near them, such as next door to them or on their hall in college housing, than with those who lived farther away. For example, 41% of the residents said a next-door neighbor was their best friend. Only 22% of those chose a best friend who was two doors away and 10% chose someone at the end of their hall. More recently, and as shown in Figure 12.3, students who were randomly assigned to sit next to someone, or in the same row as someone, in a psychology class for a semester liked that person more a year later than those who sat in a space without physical proximity (Back, Schmukle, & Egloff, 2008). Once again, proximity breeds attraction—even in friendships. The Media Connections box describes how long-distance proximity—via the Interne—impacts interpersonal relationships.

Does the Internet Facilitate Intimacy or Inhibit It?

Over the last 20 years, with the increased reliance on the Internet for communication, researchers have started examining how Internet use influences interpersonal relationships. Some people are concerned that the Internet can discourage real relationships; people may spend time on-line (e.g., "talking" in chat rooms, sending emails, shopping, etc.) instead of spending time interacting with real people and thereby forming real relationships. One study found that people who begin using the Internet show higher rates of loneliness and depression two years later (Kraut, Patterson, Lundmark, Kiesler, Mukophadhyay, & Scherlis, 1998). Greater Internet use was also associated with declines in family communication (because they are online as opposed to interacting), and may lead to weakened social ties as people invest less time and energy in their real-life relationships in favor of more time with the Internet relationships.

Does time on the Internet lead to gaining relationships? Not really. One national survey found that only 22% of respondents (all of whom had been using the Internet for two or more years) had made a new friend— and, as you might imagine, more than 22% of people make a new friend in real life during this amount of time. The Internet may also have different effects on different people. For example, some evidence suggests that greater Internet use is associated with positive outcomes, such as increased community involvement and decreased loneliness, for extroverts, but the reverse for introverts (Kraut, Kiesler, Boreua, Cummines, Helgewn, & Crawford, 2002). Similarly, adolescents who are lonely and socially anxious are more likely to use the Internet to interact with strangers as opposed to close friends (Gross, Juvonen, & Gable, 2002). This means the Internet may be serving as a means to connect with those who are not part of one's daily life, which in turn could impair the formation of normal social relationships.

On the other hand, other research points to the value of the Internet in helping people meet and form relationships (Bargh, McKenna, & Fitzsimons, 2002; McKenna & Bargh, 1998, 2000; McKenna & Green, 2002). For example, McKenna and colleagues found that 63% of respondents had spoken on the telephone with someone they'd met on the Internet, and 54% had met in person. Of those who began a romantic relationship via the Internet, 71% were still in these relationships two years later. And, surprisingly, people who first meet online express greater liking for one another than those who first meet in person (McKenna, Green, & Gleason, 2002).

Jupiter Images/Getty Images, Inc.

Concepts in Context

FACTORS THAT INFLUENCE ATTRACTION

FACTOR	EXAMPLE
Physical attractiveness	Sarah's roommate, Jeanine, is very attractive. She receives much attention from others, including frequent invitations to parties, numerous phone calls, and even several job offers.
Relationship	Your brother just got engaged to his long-time girlfriend, Cheryl. You are certain they will have a great marriage because they have so much in common: they both love bowling, dogs, the beach, and movies.
Situation	Norman and Melba live in adjoining apartments. They met one day on the elevator on the way to the laundry room and have been dating ever since.

WHAT IS LOVE?

Think about different relationships in your own life—parents, siblings, friends, dating partners. How would you describe the type of love you feel for each person? To examine this question, researchers in one study asked participants to list all of the people in their social worlds who fit into one of two categories: *love* and *in love* (Meyers & Berscheid, 1997). As predicted, participants saw these different types of relationships in very different ways. First, they listed more people in the "love" category (9 to 10 people) than in the "in love" category (about one person). Second, although both men and women reported being "in love" with the same number of people, women reported "loving" more people than did men. So, what exactly is love, and how is it defined differently by different people? This section will examine three distinct theories about love: the passionate-companionate model, triangular theory, and the love styles theory.

PASSIONATE-COMPANIONATE LOVE

One of the earliest theories of love focused on the difference between passionate love and companionate love (see Rate Yourself; Hatfield & Sprecher, 1986). **Passionate love** is an intense, exciting, and all-consuming type of love, which includes cognitions (e.g., constant thoughts about the person), emotions (e.g., a powerful physical attraction), and behavior (e.g., intense communication). People who are high on passionate love also tend to experience high levels of sexual desire for their partner (Regan, 2000). Passionate love describes your first crush and initial stages of love in new relationships—when you can't get the person out of your mind.

On the other hand, **companionate love** is a more stable, calm, and dependable type of love (Hatfield, 1988). This type of love is basically an extension and intensification of liking. It may include quiet intimacy, predictability/stability, shared attitudes/values/life experiences, and high levels of self-disclosure. Companionate love describes the type of love people have in very long-term relationships—perhaps your parents or grandparents have this type of love.

The evolution of types of love over time. As you might expect, passionate love tends to be highest in the early stages of romantic relationships, and

passionate love an intense, exciting, and all-consuming type of love that may include constant thoughts about the person, powerful physical attraction, and intense communication

companionate love a stable, calm, and dependable kind of love that may include quiet intimacy, stability, shared attitudes/values/life experiences, and high levels of self-disclosure

---

Rate Yourself

How Strongly Do You Feel Passionate Love?

The Passionate Love Scale

INSTRUCTIONS: *Rate each item on a scale of 1 (strongly disagree) to 6 (strongly agree).*

☐ **1.** I sense my body responding when ___ touches me.

☐ **2.** I would feel deep despair if _____ left me.

☐ **3.** I possess a powerful attraction for _____ .

☐ **4.** _____ always seems to be on my mind.

☐ **5.** I eagerly look for signs indicating _____'s desire for me.

☐ **6.** I would rather be with _____ than anyone else.

☐ **7.** I melt when looking deeply into _____'s eyes.

☐ **8.** No one else could love _____ like I do.

☐ **9.** For me, _____ is the perfect romantic partner.

☐ **10.** Sometimes I feel I can't control my thoughts; they are obsessively on _____.

SCORING: Sum up your total score on these 10 items.

INTERPRETATION: This scale measures passionate love, meaning the cognitive, emotional, and behavioral reactions we have toward a person we love (Hatfield & Sprecher, 1986). Higher scores indicate more intense feelings, whereas lower scores indicate less intense feelings.

then shows a small decline over time (Baumeister & Bratslavsky, 1999). In one study, couples completed measures of love types two months before and eight months after each of three life transitions: from engagement to marriage, from childlessness to parenting, and from children at home to empty nest (Tucker & Aron, 1993). Passionate love decreased over each of the three transitions, although the overall decreases were small. In contrast, companionate love tended to increase over time, as couples knew each other better and engaged in more self-disclosure.

The impact of love type on relationship satisfaction. How are these different types of love associated with relationship satisfaction? Couples who have greater companionate love experience greater relationship satisfaction and longevity (Berg & McQuinn, 1986; Hendrick, Hendrick, & Adler, 1988; Kim & Hatfield, 2004; Sprecher, 1987). Greater passionate love is also associated with higher levels of satisfaction. In one study of 100 married couples, passionate love was correlated with greater relationship excitement, less relationship boredom, more shared activities, and more kissing (Aron & Henkemeyer, 1995).

TRIANGULAR THEORY

According to Robert Sternberg (1986, 1997), there are three distinct components of love: *passion*, *intimacy*, and *commitment*. The component of love that Sternberg calls passion is very similar to passionate love described previously. Sternberg's passion consists of deep physical attraction to the person as well as constant thoughts about—and even obsession with—the person. This type of love is also related to sexual desire (Regan, 2000). On the other hand, the component of intimacy consists of great liking and emotional closeness to another person (again, this component is similar to companionate love). Finally, the third component, commitment, refers to your degree of connection and responsibility to the other person.

As shown in Figure 12.4, the three components of love lead to eight possible types of love: people can experience love as only one of the three components, as any two of the components, or as all three of the components. Romantic love, such as that shown in many movies, includes the components of passion and intimacy. Companionate love includes the components of intimacy and commitment (similar to what is described in the passionate-companionate model described previously).

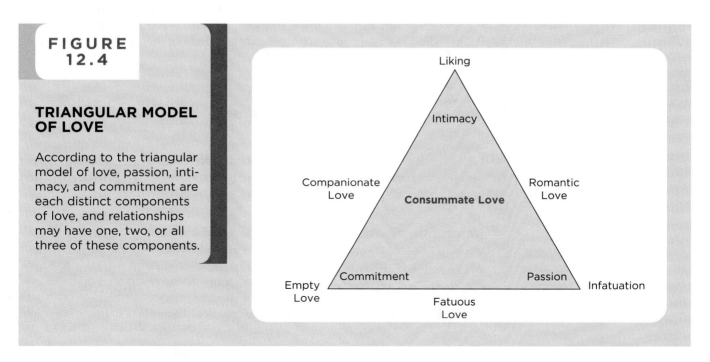

FIGURE 12.4

TRIANGULAR MODEL OF LOVE

According to the triangular model of love, passion, intimacy, and commitment are each distinct components of love, and relationships may have one, two, or all three of these components.

The value of consummate love.   Although the triangular theory of love describes all three components of love as defining complete love (*consummate love*), people can experience other types of love that have only one or two of the three components (Sternberg, 1986). A relationship with only passion and intimacy is a type of fleeting romantic love (such as a brief but intense summer fling), and a relationship with intimacy and commitment is described as companionate love (and may represent some marriages that have lasted for considerable time). However, relationships that include all three components are the happiest and most long-lasting (Whitley, 1993).

Questioning the Research

This research indicates that the experience of love is different for those in different types of relationships. But does this finding indicate correlation or causation? Can you think of some alternative explanations for this association?

Changes in love across relationship stage.   Scores on each of the love components tend to change over time in a relationship. In one study, researchers examined scores on each of the three components over time in 446 individuals in a romantic relationship (Lemieux & Hale, 2002). As predicted by the triangular model, intimacy and passion scores were lowest for those who were casually dating. These scores were higher for participants who were engaged, but lower again for those who were married. Not surprisingly, commitment scores increased at each of these three levels of relationship seriousness.

LOVE STYLES

The love styles theory classifies types of love in yet a different way (Hendrick & Hendrick, 1986, 1993, 1995; Lee, 1988). The love styles theory (as shown in Table 12.1) includes six distinct love styles. These styles are *eros* (passionate love), *ludus* (uncommitted love), *storge* (friendship love), *mania* (obsessive love), *pragma* (practical love), and *agape* (selfless love). People with an eros love style are drawn to romantic partners with specific physical qualities (the "type" they prefer), have an intense focus on their dating partners, and tend to be high in self-esteem (Campbell, Foster, & Finkel, 2002). The ludus style views romantic relationships as a playful sort of game in which everyone has fun and no one gets too serious. The storge love style is similar to companionate love—it describes love as a secure and trusting friendship. Pragma is a very practical, or pragmatic, type of love. People who have this love style aren't looking for great excitement and passion, but rather security and the appropriate "fit." Mania, or manic love, is similar in some ways to our concept of romantic love, including passion. But this type of love also includes negative elements, such as jealousy and obsession, and is seen most commonly in those with low self-esteem. Finally, agape, the rarest of the love styles, describes love as giving and selfless. People who have agape love are more concerned about their partner's well-being than their own well-being.

Gender differences.   As you might expect, men and women differ in the extent to which they focus on each of these types of love. Men generally score higher than women on ludus (Hendrick & Hendrick, 1995). On the other hand, women generally score higher than men on storge, mania, and pragma. However, it is difficult to tell whether these differences are caused by inherent differences between men and women or, alternatively, by societal roles and expectations.

Impact on relationships.   These love styles are also associated with relationship preferences interaction, satisfaction, and longevity. First, people tend to prefer dating partners who have similar love styles to their own (Davis & Latty-Mann, 1987; Hahn & Blass, 1997). Participants in one study read brief descriptions of potential dating partners. Each of these partners described themselves as having characteristics of one of the six love styles. Then participants were asked

TABLE 12.1   LOVE STYLES

TYPE OF LOVE	EXAMPLE
Eros (passionate love)	My lover and I were attracted to each other immediately after we first met.
Storge (friendship love)	It is hard for me to say exactly when our friendship turned into love.
Ludus (uncommitted love)	I try to keep my lover a little uncertain about my commitment to him/her.
Mania (obsessive love)	When things aren't going right with my lover and me, my stomach gets upset.
Pragma (practical love)	I considered what my lover was going to become in life before I committed myself to him/her.
Agape (selfless love)	I try to always help my lover through difficult times.

The love styles model describes the three primary styles of love (eros, storge, and ludus) and the three secondary styles (pragma, mania, and agape).

Source: Hendrick, C., & Hendrick, S. (1986). A theory and method of love. *Journal of Personality and Social Psychology*, 50, 392-402.

which person they preferred to date. As predicted, people generally preferred dating partners who were similar to themselves on love styles.

Love styles also influence interaction within on-going dating relationships. In one study, members of 57 college student dating couples completed measures of the love styles as well as relationship satisfaction (Hendrick et al., 1988). For men, high scores on eros and low scores on ludus were associated with high satisfaction. For women, high scores on eros and low scores on mania were associated with high satisfaction. Findings from the two-month follow-up revealed that couples that stayed together were higher on eros and lower on ludus. In sum, lasting relationships involved both passionate and committed love.

WHY DOES LOVE MATTER?

Experiencing love, however we define it, is very important for psychological as well as physical well-being (Reis & Aron, 2008). Being in love makes us feel better about ourselves, which translates into higher levels of self-esteem and self-efficacy (Aron, Paris, & Aron, 1995). Just thinking about a close relationship helps people cope with threatening information about themselves (Kumashiro & Sedikides, 2005). On a more practical note, marriage seems to lead to higher income—at least for men. One recent study by economists Kate Antonovics and Robert Town found that men who were married earned about 19% more than those who were unmarried (2004).

Developing loving close relationships is also good for our physical well-being. One study of over 1,000 patients with confirmed heart disease found that those

Why We Get By with a Little Help from Our Friends (and Pets)

You probably already know that close relationships make you feel happy. Did you also know that these relationships can make you healthier? People who have close interpersonal relationships experience positive health outcomes, including greater psychological well-being, greater physical well-being, faster recovery from illness, and, most importantly, lower rates of mortality (Allen, 2003; Stroebe & Stroebe, 1996). For example, among men who received heart surgery, those who were married requested less pain medication and recovered more quickly (Kulik & Mahler, 1989). Married patients who received high support were also released an average of 1.26 days sooner than those who received low support.

But we don't just benefit from having social support from people. Even pets can provide us with helpful support (Allen, Blascovich, Tomaka, & Kelsey, 1991). In one study, 938 people age 65 or older were interviewed by telephone about their health status, social support, pet ownership, and frequency of doctor visits (Siegel, 1990). People with pets had fewer doctor visits. Pet ownership was particularly beneficial for those who experienced many stressful events. Those who had experienced many stressful events and did not have a pet had an average of 10.37 doctor visits during the year compared to 8.38 for those who had a pet. These studies all point to the benefit of social support, even that from our pets, for psychological and physical well-being.

Burke/Triolo Productions/Getty Images, Inc.

with a spouse or close confidant had lower rates of mortality (Williams et al., 1992). Eighty-two percent of those who were married or had a close confidant lived for at least five years, compared to only 50% of those without such support. Similarly, women in highly satisfying marriages experienced better health than those in marriages with low satisfaction or who were single, widowed, or divorced (Gallo, Troxel, Matthews, & Kuller, 2003). Health Connections describes the benefits of a particular type of relationship—with our pets—on our physical well-being.

Finally, love even seems to be processed at a neurological level. Participants who are asked to think about their romantic partner while they are in an fMRI machine show distinct patterns of brain activation (Aron, Fisher Mashek, Strong, Li, & Brown, 2005; Bartels & Zeki, 2000; Fisher et al., 2002). In this way, feelings of romantic love may neurologically seem like the impact of a drug, which could help explain the intensity of romantic feelings. It could also help explain the intensity that occurs when love goes awry—stalking, spousal homicide, and jealousy.

Concepts in Context

THEORY	EXAMPLE
Passionate versus companionate love	Howard has been dating Brooks for nearly six months He thinks about her all the time and feels very sexually attracted to her.
Triangular theory	Kent and Rory have been married for six years. They share great intimacy, and are highly committed to the relationship. But after the birth of their second child, they feel lower levels of passion.
Love styles	Alexandra and Adrian were close friends in college. They continued to talk and see each other frequently after graduation, and over time their friendship evolved into a romantic relationship.

WHAT PREDICTS RELATIONSHIP SATISFACTION?

How happy are you in your current (or most recent) romantic relationship? Do you know what makes you happy? Some research in social psychology suggests that one important predictor may be the amount of time and energy we have put into the relationship. In a research study designed to test the importance of investment in predicting infidelity, 38 heterosexual college students in dating relationships completed measures regarding their investment in and commitment to their partner at the start of their spring break (Drigotas, Safstrom, & Gentilia, 1999). These students then completed daily diary entries each night of spring break. Findings indicated that 80% of the participants had some type of emotional intimacy with a person of the opposite sex, and 43% had some physical intimacy. Moreover, people with lower levels of commitment and investment were more likely to engage in physical and emotional intimacy with other people over the spring break week. Because our relationships have a significant impact on our psychological—and even physical—well-being, we want to be in happy and healthy relationships. This section will examine three models of relationship satisfaction and maintenance: social exchange theory, attachment styles, and positive illusions.

Q A

social exchange theory a theory that people's satisfaction in a relationship is determined by the costs and rewards of this relationship

SOCIAL EXCHANGE THEORY

Social exchange theory is a very rational and practical approach to relationship satisfaction that is rooted in principles of economics (Bui, Peplau, & Hill, 1996; Clark & Grote, 1998; Le & Agnew, 2003; Rusbult, Martz, & Agnew, 1998). According to this theory, people are happiest in their relationships when the benefits of these relationships are greater than their costs. What are the rewards of close relationships? These benefits include companionship, sex, happiness, economic support, and intimacy (Sedikes, Oliver, & Campbell, 1994). In contrast, the costs of close relationships include time, energy, lack of freedom to date other people, feelings of dependence, and stress and worry regarding the relationship.

"I've done the numbers, and I will marry you."
© The New Yorker Collection 2000 William Hamilton/cartoonbank.com.
All Rights Reserved

TABLE 12.2 CALCULATING THE COSTS AND BENEFITS OF A RELATIONSHIP

BENEFITS	COSTS
Juan is considerate when she is feeling sad.	Juan gets jealous when she spends time with friends.
Juan cooks her dinner regularly.	Juan is always borrowing money from her.
Juan shares her interest in NASCAR racing.	Juan is pretty messy.

This table describes how Jenny might decide whether to stay in a relationship with Juan. According to social exchange theory, Jenny would calculate the costs and benefits of her relationship, and stay with Juan if the benefits outweigh the costs, or exit the relationship if the costs outweigh the benefits. In addition, people who experience greater benefits and fewer costs have a low comparison level and a low comparison level for alternatives. These are people who are highly invested in their relationships and who will experience greater satisfaction and relationship longevity.

comparison level the expected outcome of a relationship, meaning the extent to which a given person expects his or her relationship to be rewarding

comparison level for alternatives (CLalt) a calculation regarding the expected benefits and costs a person could receive from having a relationship with various other partners

The predictors of relationship satisfaction are very similar for heterosexual and same-sex couples: relationships with many benefits and fewer costs are more satisfying for everyone.

The impact of comparison level.   Social exchange theory also proposes that relationship success or failure is influenced not only by the overall costs and benefits in the relationship, but also by the expectations people have regarding the costs and benefits of intimate relationships (Thibaut & Kelley, 1959). The term **comparison level** refers to the expected outcome of a relationship, meaning the extent to which a given person expects his or her relationships to be rewarding (see Table 12.2). A person who has had many unpleasant relationships could have a very low comparison level—and in turn, might be happy even in relatively poor relationships. In contrast, a person who has a high comparison level has high expectations for the quality of his or her close relationships, and would exit relationships that do not meet these expectations.

Social exchange theory also proposes that people make a similar type of calculation regarding the expected benefits and costs they could receive from having a relationship with various alternative partners, called the **comparison level for alternatives,** or **CLalt** (Thibaut & Kelley, 1959). Individuals will be committed to their relationships when the overall benefits and costs of their current relationship are greater than that provided by alternative relationships, but will choose to leave the relationship if their alternative options are more appealing (Drigotas & Rusbult, 1992). In line with this theory, a study by Caryl Rusbult and John Martz (1995) found that battered women who had few alternatives in life (due to low levels of education, little money, and/or no job) were more likely to feel committed to their relationship and to return to their abusive partner.

Although most of the research testing the social exchange model of relationship satisfaction was conducted on heterosexual couples, research with same-sex couples points to very similar findings (Kurdek, 1992, 2000). In one study, researchers examined relationship quality in four types of couples: heterosexual married couples, non-married heterosexual couples, male homosexual couples, and female homosexual couples (Kurdek & Schmitt, 1986). All couples lived together and did not have children in the home. Findings revealed that heterosexual married couples, gay couples, and lesbian couples all reported greater love for their partner and more relationship satisfaction than cohabiting heterosexual couples. For each of the couples types, greater relationship satisfaction was associated with seeing few alternatives to the relationship, reporting many attractions of the

Janet Kimber /Getty Images, Inc.

relationship, feeling high attachment to one partner, and engaging in high levels of shared decision making. These findings provide further evidence that the factors that predict satisfaction in homosexual relationships are the same ones that predict satisfaction in heterosexual relationships (Gottman et al., 2003).

The impact of investment. Finally, social exchange theory also includes the component of **investment**, meaning the resources devoted to a relationship that cannot be retrieved (e.g., time, energy, self-disclosure; Le & Agnew, 2003; Rusbult, 1980, 1983). These investment factors influence individuals' commitment to their present relationship, and thereby their willingness to tolerate costs. For example, if you have been in a relationship for only a few weeks—and hence have little investment in this relationship—you would be quite likely to end the relationship in the face of a substantial problem (e.g., finding evidence of your partner's infidelity). On the other hand, if you have been in a relationship for many years, and have great investment in this relationship (e.g., own a house with a person, have children with this person, etc.), you should be more likely to try to maintain the relationship even if the costs of the relationship are greater than their benefits at a particular point in time. As described at the start of this section, couples with lower levels of investment in a dating relationship are more likely to engage in infidelity.

investment the resources devoted to a relationship that cannot be retrieved

But is it really equity that matters? According to social exchange theory, satisfaction is largely a function of each person's costs and benefits in the relationship. But according to **equity theory**, the ratio of costs and benefits for each partner is a better predictor of satisfaction than simply the overall costs and benefits (Hatfield, Greenberger, Traupmann, & Lambert, 1982; Walster, Walster, Walster, & Traupman, 1978). People are most satisfied with a relationship when the ratio between benefits and contributions is similar for both partners. In other words, I could be equally happy in a relationship in which I give little to my partner and receive little from my partner and one in which I give a lot and receive a lot—because in both of these cases, the equity between the two partners is equivalent.

equity theory a theory that relationship satisfaction is determined by the ratio of costs and benefits in a relationship for each partner

However, relationships that lack equity are associated with distinct types of dissatisfaction (Van Yperen & Buunk, 1990; Walster et al., 1978). People who feel they give more than their partners (underbenefited) often feel (understandably) angry and resentful. Just think about a relationship you might have had in which you found yourself having to always be the one who initiates plans, offers assistance, and pays for dinner—you probably felt somewhat resentful. On the other hand, people who are in a relationship in which they receive more than they give (overbenefited) may feel guilty and uncomfortable (see Figure 12.5).

FIGURE 12.5

EQUITY THEORY

Equity theory proposes that relationship satisfaction is a function of the relative costs and benefits of the relationship for each partner, and that couples in which both partners experience a similar ratio of costs to benefits experience greater satisfaction.

$$\frac{\text{Person A's costs}}{\text{Person A's benefits}} = \frac{\text{Person B's costs}}{\text{Person B's benefits}} \qquad \begin{array}{ccc} \text{Person A's costs} & > & \text{Person B's costs} \\ \text{Person A's benefits} & < & \text{Person B's benefits} \end{array}$$

Equitable Relationship

Inequitable Relationship
(Person A is underbenefiting and Person B is overbenefiting)

Interestingly, some recent research on the impact of social support in intimate relationships reveals that men and women react in distinct ways to relationships that lack equity (Väänänen, Buunk, Kivimaki, Pentti, & Vahtera, 2005). Researchers examined the amount of support given and received in a relationship as well as the frequency of missing work due to illness. For women, giving more support than they received (remember, an underbenefited relationship) was associated with fewer sick days. In contrast, for men, receiving more support than they gave (an overbenefited relationship) was associated with fewer sick days. This research suggests that the impact of equity on satisfaction may be different for men and women.

ATTACHMENT STYLES

attachment styles the expectations people have about their relationship partners, based largely on early experiences with their caregivers

Research in developmental psychology demonstrates that children form close attachments to their parents and those who care for them (Bowlby, 1982, 1988). These attachment bonds give children a sense of security, and thereby provide reassurance in unfamiliar and upsetting situations. However, the precise nature of these **attachment styles**, meaning the expectations children have about their relationships with others, varies with some children forming a secure attachment and others forming an insecure attachment bond (Ainsworth, Blehar, Waters, & Wall, 1978). Children with a secure attachment bond have parents who are available and responsive to their children's needs; and hence the children feel comfortable depending and relying on their parents and comfortable with exploring new situations.

In contrast, children who form an insecure attachment bond can have an anxious/ambivalent attachment or an avoidant attachment. Children with an anxious/ambivalent attachment have parents who are inconsistent in how they respond to their child's needs; they are available, and even intrusive, at times, but are unavailable at other times. These children have difficulty trusting and relying on others, although they want very much to have intimate and close relationships. On the other hand, children with an avoidant attachment have parents who are consistently unavailable, and may even be rejecting or dismissive of the child. These children, not surprisingly, seem to not need or desire close relationships, and may reject such closeness even when it is offered.

Children with a secure attachment bond have parents who are available and responsive to their needs, which lets them feel comfortable exploring new situations.

Some intriguing research reveals that individuals also report having different attachment styles toward romantic partners in adulthood (see Table 12.3; Brennan & Shaver, 1995; Feeney, 1996; Feeney & Collins, 2001; Hazan & Shaver, 1987). Approximately 59% of adults classify themselves as secure, about 25% classify themselves as avoidant, and only 11% classify themselves as ambivalent (with the remaining 5% showing roughly equal scores on two attachment styles; Mickelson, Kessler, & Shaver, 1997). Adults with a secure attachment style feel comfortable getting close to others, and don't worry about becoming overly dependent or about being abandoned by their partners. Those with an anxious attachment style want desperately to have close relationships, but they are less trusting of others and fear their partner will leave them, and hence can become jealous and possessive. Individuals with an avoidant attachment style are less interested in and invested in close relationships. They rarely seek support from their dating partners and pull away from them in stressful situations. Attachment styles are fairly stable across different relationships, meaning that people who are secure in one relationship are likely to be secure in all of their relationships (Brumbaugh & Fraley, 2006).

The impact of attachment styles on dating interaction. Individuals' attachment styles are associated with their interactions and experiences in dating relationships (Carnelley, Pietromonaco, & Jaffe, 1996; Davila, Bradbury, & Fincham,

TABLE 12.3   MODELS OF ATTACHMENT STYLES

ATTACHMENT STYLE	DESCRIPTION
Secure	I find it relatively easy to get close to others and am comfortable depending on them and having them depend on me. I don't often worry about being abandoned or about someone getting close to me.
Avoidant	I am somewhat uncomfortable being close to others; I find it difficult to trust them completely, difficult to allow myself to depend on them. I am nervous when anyone gets too close, and, often, love partners want me to be more intimate than I feel comfortable being.
Anxious	I find that others are reluctant to get as close as I would like. I often worry that my partner doesn't really love me or won't want to stay with me. I want to merge completely with another person, and this desire sometimes scares people away.

Which of the following descriptions best describes you? The attachment style model links research in developmental psychology to research in social psychology and is one of the most studied theories in the field of close relationships (Hazan & Shaver, 1987).

1998). For example, individuals with secure attachment styles give more support to their partners during anxiety-provoking situations. In contrast, individuals with anxious attachment styles give little support to their partners, perhaps because they are so focused on their own needs (Collins & Feeney, 2000). Although most of the work on attachment styles has examined heterosexual couples, recent research suggests that secure attachment is also associated with greater relationship satisfaction in gay and lesbian couples (Elizur & Mintzer, 2003).

Not surprisingly, individuals' attachment styles are associated with the experience of and strategies for managing conflict. People who are securely attached are more open and supportive when discussing a conflict with their dating partner (Creasey & Ladd, 2005; Simpson, Rholes, & Phillips, 1996; Simpson, Rholes, & Nelligan, 1992). People who are securely attached:

- are less anger-prone,
- endorse more constructive anger goals,
- report more adaptive responses and more positive affect in anger episodes,
- attribute less hostile intent to others, and
- expect more positive outcomes than insecure people.

For example, one study with both dating and married couples found that those with secure attachment models were more likely to forgive their partner for misbehavior, which in turn predicted relationship satisfaction (Kachadourian, Fincham, & Davila, 2004). People who are securely attached seem to have a functional response to anger, which is rooted in a rational analysis of the situation (rather than a paranoid or uncontrollably hostile reaction), and have more constructive responses to anger.

On the other hand, people with insecure attachment styles have much more difficulty managing interpersonal conflict. In a study of 123 dating couples, researchers examined how individuals with different attachment styles respond to major problems in their relationships (Simpson et al., 1996). As predicted, those with an anxious orientation perceived their partner and their relationship less positively after discussing a major conflict. Observer ratings also revealed that anxious women had greater stress and anxiety, whereas avoidant men were rated as less warm and supportive. Insecure attachment is also associated with more negative attributions for one's partner's behavior, which in turn led to poorer communication (Pearce & Halford, 2008). People with insecure attachment styles also experience greater physiological stress reactions to interpersonal conflict than securely attached people (Powers, Pietromonaco, Gunlicks, & Sayer, 2006).

People with an anxious attachment style also perceive more conflict with their dating partner than do others, which can escalate the severity of conflict (Campbell, Simpson, Boldry, & Kashy, 2005). In one study, participants read about a negative behavior by a hypothetical dating partner (Collins, Ford, Guichard, & Allard, 2006). These behaviors included "didn't respond when you tried to cuddle" and "left you standing alone at a party where you didn't know anyone." Those with an anxious attachment style saw these negative behaviors more negatively than did those with secure or avoidant attachment styles. They also responded to these negative behaviors by acting more negatively themselves, which in turn is likely to lead to conflict. In turn, these perceptions lead to decreased satisfaction over time. This is one reason why people with an anxious attachment style are more likely to be unsatisfied in their dating relationships. Research Focus on Neuroscience describes the impact of attachment style on how people regulate negative thoughts regarding their relationships.

RESEARCH FOCUS ON NEUROSCIENCE
The Impact of Attachment Styles on Suppressing Negative Thoughts

Recent research in neuroscience suggests that attachment styles influence the ability to suppress negative thoughts about interpersonal interactions (Gillath, Buget, Shaver, Wendelken, & Mikulincer, 2005). In this study, 20 women completed measures of attachment styles, and then participated in a functional magnetic resonance imaging (fMRI) procedure. They were asked to think about—and stop thinking about—various negative relationship scenarios. These scenarios included breaking up with one's dating partner, having a fight with one's dating partner, and experiencing the death of one's dating partner. In line with the predictions, people who had anxious models of attachment showed greater activation in the area of the brain that is associated with sadness when they were thinking about the negative events compared to people who were less anxious. Anxious participants also showed lower levels of activation in the area of the brain responsible for regulating emotions. These findings suggest that people who have an anxious attachment style react more strongly to thoughts of loss and are less able to regulate these negative emotions.

The impact of attachment styles on sexual experience. Attachment styles are associated in distinct ways with both the types of sexual experiences people have as well as their motives for having sex (Davis, Shaver, & Vernon, 2004; Gentzler & Kerns, 2004; Schachner & Shaver, 2004; Schmitt, 2005). Those with anxious models of attachment tend to have sex as a way of reducing insecurity and fostering intense intimacy (Schachner & Shaver, 2004). For example, they are likely to report engaging in sex to make their partner love them more and to feel valued.

On the other hand, those with avoidant models of attachment tend to have sex to increase their status and prestige among peers (Schachner & Shaver, 2004). They tend to report engaging in sex in response to peer pressure, including fitting in with others and bragging about it. Individuals with avoidant attachment have more sexual experiences: they are more accepting of casual sex and are less likely to engage in sex within the context of a committed relationship (Gentzler & Kerns, 2004).

POSITIVE ILLUSIONS

As described in Chapter 3, people tend to see themselves in an overly positive light (e.g., as more athletic, intelligent, attractive than others—than they actually are). According to research on close relationships, people extend these idealized self-views to both their relationships and their relationship partners (Klohen & Mendelsohn, 1998; Martz, Verette, Arriaga, Slovik, Cox, & Rusbult, 1998; Murray & Holmes, 1998; Murray, Holmes, & Graffia, 1996; Neff & Karney, 2005). Specifically, people see their romantic partners as particularly attractive and intelligent, and rate them even more highly on these traits than their partners rate themselves. Even when people recognize a negative trait in a partner, they miraculously see this trait in a positive way (e.g., stubbornness is seen as "conviction"; Murray & Holmes, 1996).

People also describe their own romantic relationships as better than other people's relationships. They are more optimistic in their expectations about their dating relationships than their roommates or their parents are about those relationships. In addition, people list fewer current or future "relationship challenges" than their parents see in their children's relationships (Buunk & van der Eijnden, 1997; MacDonald & Ross, 1999; Rusbult, Van Lange, Wildshut, Yovetich, & Verette, 2000). People who engage in this type of "perceived superiority" are happier and are more likely to have their relationship last. Holding such idealized views of one's relationship partner is actually associated with increased satisfaction and relationship longevity.

Why positive illusions can be good.
How can holding such positive illusions lead to happy relationships? First, people may deliberately ignore "the bad," and thereby minimize conflict (e.g., not recognize when their partner is attracted to someone else). In one study, dating couples were asked to rate and discuss pictures of six opposite-sex people with whom they might interact in a dating context (Simpson, Ickes, & Blackstone, 1995). These discussions were videotaped, and then each partner viewed the tape and reported what he or she was thinking and what he or she thought the partner was thinking at each point in the discussion. As hypothesized, dating partners who were close and secure about their relationship were the least accurate in assessing their partners' thoughts during this potentially relationship-threatening task, suggesting that inaccuracy can be a defense (e.g., "head protecting the heart").

People who are in relationships also tend to ignore or devalue other potential partners, which in turn helps protect them from threats to their relationship (Lydon, Fitzsimons, & Naidoo, 2003; Miller, 1997). For example, college students who are in dating relationships rate attractive people (who could presumably threaten their current relationship) as less physically and sexually attractive than do college students who are single (Simpson, Gangestad, & Lerman, 1990). Similarly, Bazzini and Shaffer (1999) found that people who are in dating relationships and are asked to rate the attractiveness of an available dating partner rate that person as lower in attractiveness when they are told that the person is interested in them (and hence represents a potential threat to their relationship) than when they are told the person is not attracted to them. In contrast, single people rate the target person as higher in attractiveness when that person is supposedly attracted to them (see Figure 12.6).

The downside of positive illusions.
But illusions aren't always beneficial. In fact, Bill Swann and his colleagues at the University of Texas at Austin found that dating couples experience greater satisfaction when their partner sees them in an idealized way, but married couples are happiest when their spouse sees them as they see themselves (Swann, De La Ronde, & Hixon, 1994). Couples in both types of relationships completed measures describing their own attributes (e.g., intelligence, attractiveness, athletic skills, etc.) and their partner's

You might expect that people in a relationship would be more accurate about its future than those outside of it—but in reality, dating couples are more optimistic in their expectations about their dating relationship than their friends or their parents are about these relationships.

FIGURE
12.6

DOES RELATIONSHIP THREAT DECREASE RATINGS OF ATTRACTION?

People in both serious and casual dating relationships were asked to rate the attractiveness of an available dating partner after being told either that the person is interested in them or that the person is not attracted to them. As predicted, people who are in casual dating relationships were more interested in a potential partner when they learned that this person was interested in them (a high threat condition), whereas those who were in exclusive relationships were actually less interested in the face of this threat to their relationship.

Source: Bazzini, D.G., & Shaffer, D.R. (1999). Resisting temptation revisited: Devaluation versus enhancement of an attractive suitor by exclusive and nonexclusive daters. *Personality and Social Psychology Bulletin*, 25, 162-176.

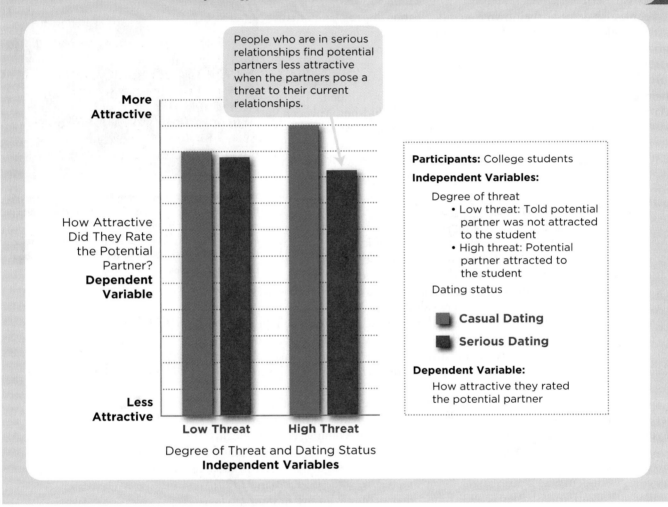

attributes, as well as measures of intimacy. Individuals in dating relationships who saw their partners in a favorable light (regardless of how partners viewed themselves) had greater satisfaction. And individuals in marital relationships who saw their partner as they saw themselves had greater satisfaction. Seeing one's partner in a positive light seems to be an important predictor of satisfaction early in a relationship, but accuracy seems to be more important over time. Why? Probably because it is good and relaxing to be with someone who likes us for who we are, and understands us (De La Ronde & Swann, 1998). It is also probably good for marital functioning to recognize your spouse's weaknesses (so you don't have a spouse who is bad with numbers balancing the checkbook, for example). In line with this view, more recent research reveals that individuals with greater accuracy about their spouse's strengths and weaknesses are less likely to get divorced (Neff & Karney, 2005).

Positive illusions can also lead to greater disappointment when these high expectations don't pan out. Researchers James McNulty and Benjamin Karney (2004) examined expectations, satisfaction, and problem-solving skills in newly married couples over four years. Their findings reveal that couples whose expectations matched their problem-solving skills were more satisfied over time. Those who had high expectations and strong skills did experience high levels of satisfaction, as did those with lower expectations and weaker skills. However, those with high expectations and low skills experienced the lowest levels of satisfaction.

STRATEGIES FOR INCREASING RELATIONSHIP SATISFACTION

So, what can you do to experience greater satisfaction in your interpersonal relationships? First, increase the number of rewarding and positive behaviors in the relationship (Gottman & Levenson, 1992). This seems like a very simple strategy, but it works: even if the relationship has some problems, increasing the number of positives or rewards about the relationship will enhance satisfaction, in part by changing the costs-benefits ratio (in line with social exchange and equity theories). Couples with many rewarding interactions are less likely to break up, and couples who show increases in rewards in their relationship experience greater satisfaction (Berg & McQuinn, 1986; Gottman & Levenson, 1992; Rusbult, 1983). So, to increase satisfaction in your own relationship, do something nice for your partner: cook dinner, bring home flowers or a present, pay a compliment, and go dancing.

What else might you do to make your relationship more satisfying? Engage in new and arousing activities with your partner to maintain relationship excitement over time. Many surveys reveal that marital satisfaction decreases over time—with sizeable drops occurring after the first year of marriage and after the seventh/eighth years—perhaps because people simply get bored (Kurdek, 1999). Some recent research by Art Aron and his colleagues suggests that people need to combat the boredom that may arise in a relationship after the newness and exhilaration has decreased (Aron, Norman, Aron, McKenna, & Heyman, 2000). In one study, married couples were randomly assigned to one of three conditions: one group did no activity (control condition), one group rolled a ball back and forth (mundane task), and one group did unusual activities such as tying partners legs and arms together and having them crawl across a floor carrying a pillow between their legs (the novel task). Oddly enough, couples that struggled and laughed their way through the novel task reported more satisfaction in their relationship than did those in the other two groups. Why did engaging in these tasks lead to greater satisfaction? Perhaps it was cognitive dissonance ("I look really stupid, so this must be worth it") or arousal-excitation theory ("My heart is beating fast so I must love my partner").

Last, but not least, remember that relationships can be very rewarding, but they take considerable attention and energy to maintain (Harvey & Omarzu, 1997). We need to "mind our relationships," and not simply take them—and our partners—for granted. As Leo Tolstoy (1877) described in *Anna Karenina*, "On entering into family life he saw at every step that it was not at all what he had imagined. At every step he felt as a man might feel who, after admiring the smooth, cheerful motion of a boat on a water, actually gets into the boat himself. He saw that apart from having to sit steadily in the boat without rocking, he also had to keep in mind, without forgetting for a moment where he was going, that there was water beneath his feet, that he had to row, that his unaccustomed hands hurt, and that it was easy only when you looked at it, but that doing it, though it made you very happy, was very hard."

THEORIES OF RELATIONSHIP SATISFACTION

FACTOR	EXAMPLE
Social exchange theory	Jose and Charlene have been happily married for 15 years. Their relationship is not perfect—they at times have vigorous fights—but they both see the benefit of love and stability that their relationship provides as far outweighing its costs.
Attachment styles	Tabitha has been dating Russ for one year, but she is not very happy with their relationship. She becomes very worried if Russ is even a few minutes late to pick her up for a date. Tabitha then becomes convinced that he doesn't really love her, and this concern often leads to an intense fight.
Positive illusions	Beth has recently started dating Eric. She feels so lucky to be dating someone who is just perfect in many ways. Eric sometimes is a little cheap (he insists on eating only in fast food restaurants), which Beth sees as a wonderful sign of how concerned he is about saving for their future.

WHAT ARE COMMON PROBLEMS IN CLOSE RELATIONSHIPS?

Although the previous section described how relationships bring us much joy and happiness (as well as better health), people also experience various problems and challenges in their relationships. Let's take a look at an example of one problem: jealousy. In one study on jealousy, participants imagined their dating partner flirting with someone else at a party (Dijkstra & Buunk, 1998). Some participants were asked to imagine their partner flirting with someone who is very physically attractive. Others were asked to imagine their partner flirting with someone who is high in dominance, meaning a person who is self-confident, influential, and powerful. Participants then reported how jealous they would feel. As predicted, men are more jealous when they imagine their partner flirting with someone who is high in dominance than someone who is highly physically attractive. Women show the reverse pattern: they experience greater jealousy when they believe their partner is flirting with someone who is highly attractive. This section will examine the predictors of jealousy in interpersonal relationships, as well as three other common problems in close relationships: conflict, loneliness, and relationship dissolution.

CONFLICT

One of the most important things couples have to manage in close relationships is conflict, because naturally all close relationships will involve some conflict (Holmes & Murray, 1996; Jensen-Campbell & Graziano, 2000). Married couples have an average of two to three disagreements per month (McGonagle, Kessler, & Schilling, 1992), and adolescents report having one to two conflicts per day—usually with a friend, sibling, or parent (Jensen-Campbell & Graziano, 2000). Although conflict is a part of all close relationships, people handle relationship conflicts in very different ways—and how they handle conflict is a major predictor of relationship satisfaction and longevity. Let's examine some common strategies couples use in managing conflict.

TABLE
12.4

RESPONSES TO RELATIONSHIP DISSATISFACTION

RESPONSE TYPE	STRATEGY	EXAMPLE
Voice	Discussing problems, seeking help from a friend or therapist, suggesting solutions, changing oneself or attempting to change a partner.	"We talked things over and worked things out"; "I tried my hardest to make things better."
Loyalty	Praying for improvement, supporting a partner in the face of criticism, continuing to wear symbols of a relationship (a ring, a locket).	"I loved her so much that I ignored her faults"; "I prayed a lot and left things in God's hands."
Neglect	Letting things fall apart, ignoring a partner or spending less time together, criticizing a partner for things unrelated to the problem.	"Mostly my response was silence to anything he might say, ignoring him if we were around other people"; "we seemed to drift apart; we might have exchanged five to ten words in a week."
Exit	Separating, actively abusing a partner, threatening to leave, screaming shrewishly at a partner.	"I told him that I couldn't take it any more and that it was over"; "I slapped her around a bit, I'm ashamed to say."

Not surprisingly, people who have high relationship investment and satisfaction are more likely to use a constructive strategy for resolving conflicts.

Source: Drigotas, S. M., Whitney, G. A., & Rusbult, C. E. (1995). On the peculiarities of loyalty: A diary study of responses to dissatisfaction in everyday life. *Personality and Social Psychology Bulletin*, 21, 596-609.

Typology of responses. Carol Rusbult and her colleagues at the University of North Carolina at Chapel Hill describe four major types of responses that people use in handling conflict (Drigotas, Whitney, & Rusbult, 1995; Rusbult & Zembrodt, 1983; Rusbult, Zembrodt, & Gunn, 1982). One constructive strategy is **voice**, meaning talking things over with your relationship partner to try to solve the conflict (see Table 12.4). For example, if your partner continually comes home late from the office, you could discuss with your partner how his/her tardiness makes you upset, and try to reach a solution to this problem (e.g., perhaps he/she could bring work home from the office).

Other strategies used to handle relationship problems are destructive. **Neglect**, meaning giving up on the relationship and withdrawing from it emotionally, is one type of destructive strategy, and **exit**—leaving the relationship—is another. **Loyalty**, defined as remaining committed to the relationship and simply waiting patiently for things to get better, is the final strategy described by this model. Loyalty sounds as if it could be a good strategy, but this approach is not associated with favorable consequences, possibly because it is a less visible and more indirect strategy (Rusbult et al., 1982).

voice talking things over with a relationship partner to try to solve the conflict

neglect giving up on a relationship and withdrawing from it emotionally

exit leaving the relationship altogether

loyalty remaining committed to a relationship and simply waiting patiently for things to get better

The Four Horsemen of the Apocalpyse.
John Gottman, a professor at the University of Washington, has conducted extensive research on relationship conflict (Gottman & Levenson, 2002). His research uses a variety of measures (physiological, nonverbal, verbal, and questionnaire), and large samples of couples that

are followed over time. This research has revealed four styles of conflict that are particularly destructive in a marriage:

- *criticism*: complaining about some features of the spouse or the relationship,
- *contempt*: acting as if sickened or repulsed by one's partner,
- *defensiveness*: protection of the self, and
- *stonewalling*: emotional withdrawal and refusal to participate in conversation.

All of these strategies can lead to increased isolation and withdrawal; in fact, Gottman calls these messages the "Four Horsemen of the Apocalypse" (meaning that the end of a relationship—the apocalypse—will be brought on—riding in on four horses—by these four negative styles of conflict). In support of this model, Huston and Vangelisti (1991) found that relationships in which there are high levels of negative behavior by either spouse, including criticizing, complaining, and becoming angry and impatient, lead to lower satisfaction over time in wives (though not husbands).

The stonewalling approach is part of another commonly observed conflict behavior called the **demand/withdraw interaction pattern**. This pattern refers to the relatively common situation in which one partner attempts to start a discussion by criticizing, complaining, or suggesting change (Christensen & Heavey, 1990; Verhofstadt, Buysee, De Clercq, & Goodwin, 2005). The other partner then attempts to end this discussion—or avoid the issue—by maintaining silence or withdrawing from the situation. In a heterosexual relationship, the man is more likely to withdraw from conflict and the woman is more likely to take a leading role in initiating conflict and discussion of conflict. This gender difference is explained in part due to socialization pressures that lead women to have higher expectations for closeness in a relationship than do men. Other researchers explain this gender difference by noting the typical power imbalance in marriage, in which men tend to receive more benefits than women—and therefore have less interest in making changes. And sadly, avoiding communication and withdrawing from conflict leads to relationship dissatisfaction (Bodenmann, Kaiser, Hahlweg, & Fehm-Wolfsdorf, 1998; Weger, 2005).

Jupiter Images

Which of the strategies of resolving conflict is this couple using: voice, contempt, criticism, or defensiveness?

demand/withdraw interaction pattern a situation in which one partner is nagging, critical, and insistent about discussing the relationship problems while the other partner is withdrawn, silent, and defensive

Negative attributional traps. The attributions people make for events in their relationships can also be classified as constructive, or relationship-enhancing, or destructive to the relationship (Bradbury & Fincham, 1992; Bradbury, Beach, Fincham, & Nelson, 1996; Karney & Bradbury, 2000). As described in Chapter 5, people readily make attributions, or create explanations, for events they observe in the world, and people usually make beneficial attributions for the events that happen to themselves and their loved ones. In turn, people in happy relationships make beneficial attributions for their partners' behavior, such as creating external excuses for misbehaviors and internal explanations for positive behavior. So, when your partner comes home late (again), you could attribute this behavior to an external factor (e.g., her boss is so demanding), and when your partner surprises you with a special gift, you could attribute this behavior to an internal factor (e.g., he is so thoughtful).

negative attributional traps an approach in which a person explains his or her partner's behaviors in negative ways

In contrast, **negative attributional traps** occur when people explain their partner's positive behavior in negative ways (Graham & Conoley, 2006; McNulty & Karney, 2001). In one study, married couples rated their trust in their partner, discussed a common relationship problem, and then rated the beliefs about their partner's behavior during the discussion (Miller & Rempel, 2004). Researchers then contacted the couples again two years later and showed them the same videotape. Once again, they rated their beliefs about their partners' motives. As predicted, people who made negative attributions initially reported less trust in their partner two years later. Similarly, people who reported lower trust initially made more negative attributions later on. People who make negative attributions for their partner's behavior experience lower marital satisfaction, in part because this type of explanation for behavior tends to increase relationship conflict (Fincham & Bradbury, 1992; Kubany, Beaver, Muraoka, & Richard, 1995). Negative attributional traps can therefore have a significant and lasting impact on relationship satisfaction.

Strategies for effective conflict resolution Because conflict and disagreements are part of all close relationships, couples need to learn strategies for managing conflict in a healthy and constructive way (Honeycutt, Woods, & Fontenot, 1993). Some couples just avoid and deny the presence of any conflict in a relationship. However, denying the existence of conflict results in couples failing to solve their problems at early stages, which can then lead to even greater problems later on. Not surprisingly, expressing anger and disagreement initially leads to lower marital satisfaction (Gottman & Krokoff, 1989). However, these patterns predict increases in marital satisfaction over time. This research suggests that working through conflicts is an important predictor of marital satisfaction.

"O.K., we'll try it your way—let's ignore any problems that come up in the next twenty years and see what happens."

So, what can you do to manage conflict in your own relationships? First, try to understand the other person's point of view and put yourself in his or her place (Honeycutt et al., 1993). People who are sensitive to what their partner thinks and feels experience greater relationship satisfaction. For example, Arriaga and Rusbult (1998) found that among people in dating relationships as well as marriages, those who can adopt their partner's perspective show more positive emotions, more relationship-enhancing attributions, and more constructive responses to conflict.

Second, because conflict and disagreements are an inevitable part of close relationships, people need to be able to apologize to their partner for wrongdoings and receive forgiveness from their partner for their own acts (Fincham, 2000; McCullough, Rachal, Sandage, Worthington, Brown, & Hight, 1998; McCullough, Worthington, & Rachal, 1997). Apologies minimize conflict, lead to forgiveness, and serve to restore relationship closeness. In line with this view, spouses who are more forgiving show higher marital quality over time (Paleari, Regalia, & Fincham, 2005). Interestingly, apologizing can even have positive health benefits (Witvliet, Ludwig, & Vander Laan, 2001). For example, when people reflect on hurtful memories and grudges, they show negative physiological effects, including increased heart rate and blood pressure, compared to when they reflect on sympathetic perspective-taking and forgiving.

JEALOUSY

Jealousy is a common problem in relationships because people naturally fear threats—real or perceived—to their relationships (Parrot & Smith, 1992). We react with more jealousy to high levels of threat (e.g., your partner finds someone attractive) than low levels of threat (e.g., your partner has a work colleague he spends time with), and with more jealousy to threats to our self-esteem (e.g., your partner sees someone wearing clothes like yours and comments on how good they look; DeSteno, Valdesolo, & Bartlett, 2006; Sharpsteen, 1995).

Gender differences in the causes of jealousy. Although both men and women experience jealousy, they differ in exactly when or what causes jealousy (Buss, Larsen, Westen, & Semelroth, 1992). According to the evolutionary psychology perspective, jealousy is an adaptation to the different reproductive issues faced by men versus women. Men, on the one hand, should be more concerned about a partner's sexual infidelity, because they could end up raising another man's child. In line with this view, most research suggests that men's jealousy is a primary cause of aggression toward women. In the words of O.J. Simpson, accused of the murder of his ex-wife, "Let's say I committed this crime. Even if I did do this, it would have to have been because I loved her very much, right?" (Farber, 1998). Women, on the other hand, should be more concerned about a partner's emotional infidelity, because men who are emotionally involved with a different partner could start devoting resources to this new relationship. In other words, if a man becomes involved in a new relationship, he would likely provide support for the children in this new relationship and therefore have less (if any) support available to help children from an earlier relationship.

In turn, men and women react in different ways to sexual versus emotional infidelity (Buss et al., 1999; Buunk, Angleitner, Oubaid, & Buss, 1996). In a series of studies to test this hypothesis, men and women were asked whether they would be more upset if their romantic partner formed a deep emotional attachment or had sexual intercourse with someone else (Buss et al., 1992). Sixty percent of the men would be more upset by a partner's sexual infidelity whereas 83% of the women felt that emotional infidelity would be worse (see Figure 12.7). As described at the beginning of this section, men and women also report feeling jealous in response to different people who threaten the relationship: men are more concerned when their partner is talking to someone highly dominant, and women are more concerned when their partner is talking to someone highly attractive.

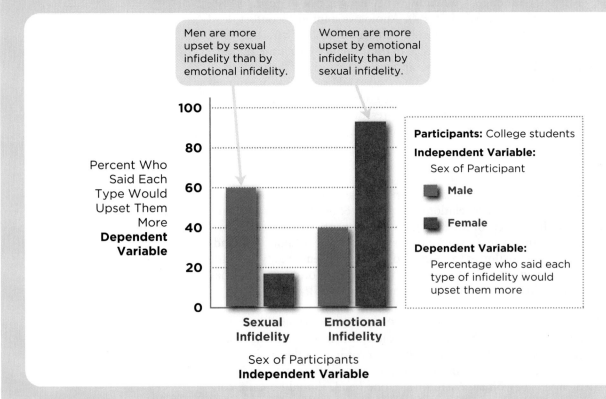

FIGURE 12.7

DO MEN AND WOMEN DIFFER IN THEIR RESPONSES TO DIFFERENT TYPES OF INFIDELITY?

Men and women were asked whether they would be more upset if their romantic partner formed a deep emotional attachment or had sexual intercourse with someone else. As predicted, a higher percentage of men said they would be more upset by a partner's sexual infidelity than emotional infidelity, whereas a higher percentage of women felt that emotional infidelity would be more upsetting.

Source: Buss, D.M., Larsen, R.J., Westen, D., & Semmelroth, J. (1992). Sex differences in jealousy: Evolution, physiology, and psychology. *Psychological Science*, 3, 251-255.

Social roles and pressures in our society, such as men's motive to appear more concerned about sexual transgressions, could account for these findings from Buss. However, research using measures of physiological arousal, such as heart rate and sweat, reveals similar gender differences when imagining sexual infidelity versus emotional infidelity. Moreover, cross-cultural research reveals similar patterns (Buss et al., 1999; Buunk et al., 1996), again suggesting that evolutionary factors are responsible for this discrepancy.

Critiques of the evolutionary perspective.   Some recent research contradicts some of the gender differences in reactions to infidelity (sexual and emotional) found by Buss and his colleagues. First, some researchers suggested that these gender differences in jealousy are a result of the different expectations men and women have about the pairings of emotional and sexual infidelity (Harris & Christenfeld, 1996; DeSteno & Salovey, 1996). According to this *"double-shot" hypothesis*, men believe that if their partner is engaging in sexual infidelity, she is also very likely to have some type of emotional commitment to that relationship; yet they do not assume that a partner who is emotionally involved with someone is necessarily involved in a sexual relationship. In contrast, women who learn that their mate is emotionally involved with someone are very likely to assume that he is also sexually involved, whereas they do not assume that a man who is sexually involved with someone is also emotionally involved.

Other recent challenges to the evolutionary explanation for the gender differences call into question the method used. Buss finds strong gender differences when people answer hypothetical scenarios (e.g., which would bother you more?), but when participants recall actual incidents of infidelity by a partner, both men and women are more focused on a partner's emotional, as compared to sexual, infidelity (Harris, 2002). Moreover, gender differences in jealousy aren't found in people who've actually experienced infidelity (Berman & Frazier, 2005). This research suggests that hypothetical accounts are very different than what people actually experience. Still other research reveals that the gender differences on jealousy emerge only when participants are given the forced choice phrasing (that is, "which of the two types of infidelity would be worse?"). In contrast, when participants are asked to rate each type of jealousy on a 1 to 7 scale, both men and women report greater jealousy in response to sexual infidelity (DeSteno, Bartlett, Braverman, & Salovey, 2002; Sabini & Green, 2004). All of these findings suggest that the method used to assess reactions to infidelity may influence whether gender differences in response to types of infidelity are found—in turn suggesting that such differences may reflect the method used, and not fundamental differences in reactions.

Researchers have even raised concerns about how to interpret the findings from studies that use physiological measures, which are used in part to eliminate the problems associated with biased self-report. As noted previously, compared to women, men tend to show greater physiological reactivity, such as heart rate and blood pressure, when they imagine sexual infidelity (Harris, 2000, 2002). However, this greater physiological reactivity also occurs when men imagine sexual scenes that do *not* include infidelity. In other words, and perhaps not surprisingly, the increases in physiological arousal seen in men who think about sexual infidelity may simply measure increases in arousal caused by thinking about sex in general, not infidelity in particular.

Still other research points to the impact of the sample studied on the conclusions researchers reach. Gender differences in reactions to jealousy are more common in the college student population than in non-student samples (Sabini & Green, 2004). These findings therefore call into question the idea that gender differences in jealousy are rooted in evolutionary factors.

LONELINESS

Another common problem in interpersonal relationships is actually the absence of such relationships, which can lead to a state of loneliness. People who are lonely feel left out of social events, isolated from others, and lacking in close interpersonal

Rate Yourself

How Lonely Are You?

The UCLA Loneliness Scale

INSTRUCTIONS: *Rate each item on a scale of 1 (never) to 4 (often).*

- ☐ **1.** I lack companionship.
- ☐ **2.** There is no one I can turn to.
- ☐ **3.** My interests and ideas are not shared by those around me.
- ☐ **4.** I feel left out.
- ☐ **5.** I am no longer close to anyone.
- ☐ **6.** I feel isolated from others.
- ☐ **7.** No one really knows me well.
- ☐ **8.** My social relationships are superficial.
- ☐ **9.** I am unhappy being so withdrawn.
- ☐ **10.** People are around me but not with me.

SCORING: Sum up your total number of points on all 10 items.

INTERPRETATION: This scale assesses the extent to which a person is experiencing loneliness. People with higher scores feel more lonely, whereas those with lower scores feel less lonely (Russell, Peplau, & Cutrona, 1980).

relationships (see Rate Yourself; Archibald, Bartholomew, & Marx, 1995; Berg & McQuinn, 1989; Berg & Peplau, 1982). Researchers often distinguish between different types of loneliness. *Social loneliness* describes people who lack the presence of close others and a social network. People who are socially lonely don't get invited to parties, rarely have plans for dinner with friends, and can't easily call on a friend for assistance with moving or other practical tasks. In contrast, *emotional loneliness* refers to the lack of a romantic partner (Green, Richardson, Lago, & Schatten-Jones, 2001). People who are emotionally lonely may have a strong friendship network, but lack a very close and intimate romantic relationship. Although social and emotional loneliness are moderately correlated, a person can experience one type of loneliness without the other.

Loneliness is associated with major consequences, including lower immune competence, higher blood pressure, and higher levels of stress hormones (Hawkley, Burleson, Berntson, & Cacioppo, 2003; Uchino, Cacioppo, & Kiecolt-Glaser, 1996). One recent study with college students revealed that students who have high levels of loneliness have a weaker immune response to the flu vaccine, meaning they are at greater risk of developing the flu even following a vaccination (Pressman, Cohen, Miller, Barkin, Rabin, & Treanor, 2005).

What leads to loneliness? Research points to three main factors: poor social skills, negative self-views, and negative expectations. Let's examine each of these explanations.

The impact of poor social skills. People who are lonely often have poor social skills, which impairs the formation of positive interpersonal relationships (Berg & Peplau, 1982; Jones, Carpenter, & Quintana, 1985). People who are lonely also engage in less open self-disclosure and react negatively to other people's self-disclosure, which in turn inhibits self-disclosure from their partner (Rotenberg, 1997; Solano, Batten, & Parish, 1982). In turn, people who do not reciprocate self-disclosure appropriately experience more discomfort and less liking from their interaction partners. Interestingly, heterosexual people who are lonely engage in very little self-disclosure with opposite-sex others (impairing the natural quid pro quo of self-disclosure in close friendships), but inappropri-

Digital Vision/Getty Images, Inc.

People who are lonely often have poor social skills, and hence have trouble meeting people and engaging in appropriate levels of self-disclosure.

ately high self-disclosure with same-sex others. For example, in conversations in the lab with strangers, lonely people chose very superficial topics to discuss with opposite-sex strangers (e.g., "The toothpaste I use") but very personal topics to discuss with same-sex strangers (e.g., "My worst experience in school").

The impact of negative self-views.   Lonely people generally have negative self-views (Christensen & Kashy, 1998). They often experience other negative emotions, including anxiety, depression, and shyness (Jones et al., 1985). They have trouble trusting others and a fear of intimacy (Rotenberg, 1994; Sherman & Thelen, 1996), suggesting that they may have insecure attachment models (Duggan & Brennan, 1994). For example, lonely people show a greater accuracy for remembering negative feedback about themselves (Frankel & Prentice-Dunn, 1990). In contrast, non-lonely people show a greater accuracy for remembering positive feedback.

MODEL OF A SELF-FULFILLING PROPHECY

People who are lonely may expect rejection in social interactions, and hence may act in ways that elicit this behavior.

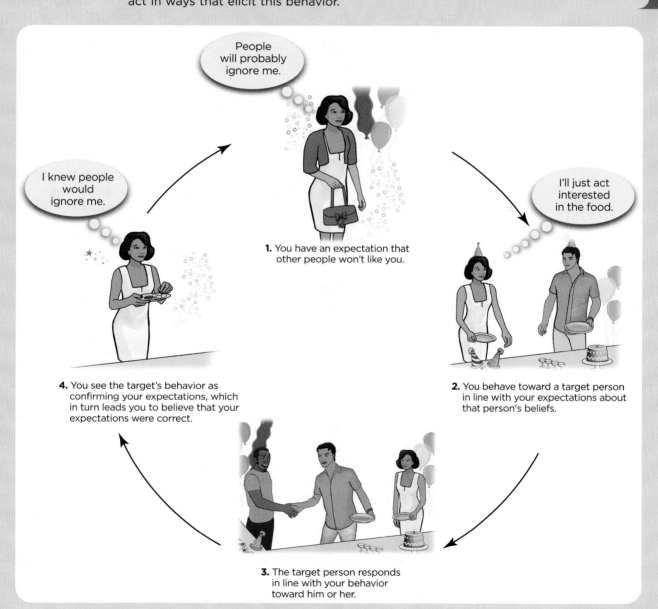

People will probably ignore me.

I knew people would ignore me.

I'll just act interested in the food.

1. You have an expectation that other people won't like you.

4. You see the target's behavior as confirming your expectations, which in turn leads you to believe that your expectations were correct.

2. You behave toward a target person in line with your expectations about that person's beliefs.

3. The target person responds in line with your behavior toward him or her.

Given the negative effects of observing high levels of conflict between parents, children who are in families with constant conflict between the parents may in fact be best served by divorce.

The impact of negative expectations. Lonely people also have extremely negative expectations about their interactions with others as shown in Figure 12.8 (Bruch, Hamer, & Heimberg, 1995; Melshko & Alden, 1993). They often feel nervous and inhibited during social interactions, in part because they expect that others are forming a negative impression of them, and hence interact in a highly self-protective way. In one study, both lonely and non-lonely people watched videotapes of their own interactions with friends (Duck, Pond, & Leatham, 1994). Compared to non-lonely people, lonely people tended to evaluate the communication quality lower and draw more negative conclusions about their own friendships. In sum, lonely people may be extremely critical of their own communication patterns, which in turn leads to dissatisfaction with their behavior in relationships.

RELATIONSHIP DISSOLUTION

Romantic breakups are understandably difficult—the end of such a relationship is stressful and disruptive. These breakups can lead to negative psychological outcomes, including sadness, depression, and anger (Sbarra & Emery, 2005). People who are left or "dumped" typically experience increased distress, compared to those who initiate the breakup.

Negative impact of divorce. Relationship dissolution is particularly hard when it involves children. Children who experience their parents' divorce experience negative outcomes, including higher conflict in their own marriages, more negative attitudes toward marriage, and a decreased likelihood of being in a close relationship (Segrin, Taylor, & Altman, 2005).

Why do children of divorce experience such negative, and lasting, consequences? One explanation is that divorce is disruptive to children's lives in a number of ways, including changes in the family's economic status and adjusting to living in a single-parent home. Thus, some people have argued that couples need to "stay together for the sake of the children," and that people should try to stay together if at all possible in order to avoid the disruption for the children. (Keep reading to find out whether this is actually a good idea or not.)

Another explanation is that divorce may lead children to develop negative beliefs about relationships. After all, findings indicate that the children of divorced parents are themselves more likely to experience a divorce, and thus it may be that children whose parents divorce develop more negative attitudes about marriage in general and about their potential spouse in particular.

Children whose parents get divorced (or have high levels of conflict) may also model their own relationships on such patterns, and thereby experience negative marriages themselves. After all, children who grow up and observe their parents' frequent fights may experience negative consequences and beliefs about relationships regardless of whether the parents eventually choose to divorce. In one study, researchers examined 297 parents and their adult married children (Amato & Booth, 2001). Findings indicated that children whose parents' marriage had a lot of conflict also had a lot of conflict (and less happiness and more problems and instability) in their own marriages. What accounts for this relationship? Children's perceptions of their parents' marriage were a significant predictor of their own marital problems (e.g., probably due to observational learning). This is true regardless of whether parents ultimately got divorced. Similarly, research with adolescents indicates that parental marital status is not strongly related to children's psychological adjustment (Enos & Handal, 1986), but instead the level of perceived conflict is a strong predictor of children's well-being. In sum, children who are in families in constant conflict may in fact be best served by divorce.

Benefits of relationship break-up.   Encouragingly, however, people with secure attachment models experience less distress than those with anxious or avoidant attachment (Davis, Shaver, & Vernon, 2003; Sbarra, 2006). And other people see some benefits as well (see Table 12.5).

Even divorce can have some positive outcomes. For example, individuals whose parents divorced report more positive relationships with their mothers, greater social support, and more independence (Riggio, 2004). Divorce may therefore bring some benefits to children, as they struggle with their mother to adapt to changes brought on by the divorce and take on greater responsibility at an earlier age. Interestingly, individuals who experience the divorce of their parents also report less anxiety about their own personal relationships than those whose parents' marriage is still intact. In this way, they may come to understand that relationships do not last forever, and that people may still be happy even if a valued relationship ends.

TABLE 12.5	POSITIVE CHANGES CAUSED BY RELATIONSHIP BREAK-UPS
CATEGORY	**EXAMPLE**
Person positive	Through breaking up I found I can handle more on my own.
	I am more self-confident.
Other positives	I've learned what I do and don't want in a relationship partner.
	I am a lot more cautious in choosing a romantic partner.
Relational positives	I know not to jump into a relationship too quickly.
	I learned many relationship skills that I can apply in the future (e.g., the importance of saying you're sorry).
Environment positives	I rely on my friends more. I forgot how important friends are when I was with him.
	Concentrate on school more: I can put so much more time and effort toward school.

Although relationship break-ups typically cause tremendous sadness, they also can teach us valuable things about ourselves that will help us in our future relationships.
Source: Tashiro, T., & Frazier, P. (2003). 'I'll never be in a relationship like that again': Personal growth following romantic relationship breakups. *Personal Relationships*, 10, 113–128.

COMMON RELATIONSHIP PROBLEMS

FACTOR	EXAMPLE
Conflict	Kayla is very eager to discuss the problems in her marriage. But every time she tries to start a discussion with her husband, Jack, he simply walks away.
Jealousy	Al's girlfriend Elizabeth is on a trip with some friends. He knows that these friends enjoy going out dancing and drinking at bars, and he is worried that Elizabeth may become interested in dating someone she meets on the trip.
Loneliness	Naomi is just starting college, and she very much wants to make new friendships. But Naomi feels pretty bad about herself. She doubts that most other people would even want to be her friend.
Dissolution	After 12 years of marriage, Jessemie and John have just decided to divorce. They are worried about the effects of this decision on their son, Clark. After talking with a counselor, however, they realize that their constant fighting may already be causing him problems. They agree that an environment with less conflict would be better for him, and they start working on an amicable divorce.

CULTURE

HOW DOES CULTURE INFLUENCE INTERPERSONAL ATTRACTION AND CLOSE RELATIONSHIPS?

Q A Think about your own friendships. Would you say you are more satisfied with your best friendship, or with your friendships in general? Research in social psychology suggests that your culture may influence the answer to this question. In one study, researchers examined friendships among both Arab (more collectivistic) and Jewish (more individualistic) fourth- and fifth-graders in Israel (Scharf & Hertz-Lazarowitz, 2003). Arab students tended to have better quality peer relationships in general. In contrast, Jewish students tended to have a better quality of best-friend relationships. These findings make sense, given the relative importance placed on connectedness and reciprocity in collectivistic cultures (and hence, strong social networks), as well as the relative importance placed on independence, autonomy, and personal relationships in individualistic ones. This study demonstrates that the predictors of friendship satisfaction are different for people in different cultures. This section will examine this and other ways in which culture impacts people's views about attraction and close relationships, including the definition of beauty, the nature of love, and definitions of friendship.

DEFINING BEAUTY

On the whole, people across different cultures agree on what is attractive (Cunningham et al., 1995; Langlois et al., 2000). People from diverse cultures show a consistent preference for faces that are "average" as opposed to "distinct," and for those with "baby faces" (McArthur & Berry, 1987). People across cultures also show particular gender differences in what they want in a mate, with men preferring young and attractive partners and women preferring older and wealthier partners (Buss & Schmitt, 1993; Feingold, 1992). These findings suggest there are some universal features that we look for in mates.

But cultures do vary in the stereotypes they hold about attractiveness. Although the "what is beautiful is good" stereotype holds true across different cultures, the precise meaning of "what is good" varies from culture to culture (Wheeler & Kim, 1997). In Korea, people who are beautiful are seen as higher in integrity and concern for others. In the United States, on the other hand, people who are beautiful are seen as higher in dominance and assertiveness.

THE NATURE OF LOVE

Cultures have very distinct views about the importance of different types of love (Dion & Dion, 1993, 1996; Simmons, vom Kolke, & Shimizu, 1986). Compared to Americans, Chinese people focus more on practical and selfless love (Goodwin & Findlay, 1997). On the other hand, Americans focus more on passionate or romantic love.

Cultures may even differ in how they define love. For example, people in individualistic cultures, such as the United States and Italy, overwhelmingly see "passionate love" as exciting and positive. On the other hand, those in China see "passionate love" as both positive and negative—a type of "sad love." In one study, researchers examined lyrics of popular love songs in the United States and China (Rothbaum & Tsang, 1998). Then they rated these songs on several dimensions, such as degree of intense desire, negative outcomes, suffering, and dependence. American love songs were more likely to focus on the two lovers as isolated from others (e.g., "There is nobody here, it's just you and me, the way I want it to be"). In contrast, Chinese love songs were more likely to include negative views of love, such as love connected to suffering (e.g., "Not knowing that tragedy has been predestined ... Can't forget the commitment we had made ... I call to you with the endless pain in my heart").

Importance of love for marriage. Cultures also differ considerably in the importance (or lack thereof) of love in leading to marriage, with people in individualistic cultures seeing love as a more important component of marriage than people in collectivistic cultures (see Table 12.6; Dion & Dion, 1996; Levine, Sato, Hashimoto, & Verma, 1995; Sprecher, Sullivan, & Hatfield, 1994). People in individualistic cultures also expect more from marital relationships (Hatfield & Sprecher, 1995). Individualistic cultures emphasize personal fulfillment in marriage, and thus focus on the impact of individual factors, such as personality and attractiveness, on relationship satisfaction (Goodwin & Findlay, 1997). They are choosy in their preferences for dating and marriage partners, and see individuals as having an inherent right to choose a spouse on their own, even if this choice conflicts with the wishes of one's family and friends (Sprecher et al., 1994).

TABLE 12.6	HOW WOULD YOU HANDLE A PARENT-FIANCÉ CONFLICT?			
APPROACH	USA	AUSTRALIA	GREECE	HONG KONG
Nothing	28%	52%	14%	3%
Tell fiancé that he/she should make a greater effort to "fit in with the family"	28%	26%	76%	79%

People in different cultures vary considerably on how they would handle conflicts between their parents and their fiances, with Australians and Americans most likely to do nothing, whereas the Greek and Hong Kong responses are to tell the fiancé to fit in.

Source: Triandis, H. C., Chen, X. P., & Chan, D. K. (1998). Scenarios for the measurement of collectivism and individualism. *Journal of Cross-Cultural Psychology, 29*, 275-289.

TABLE 12.7 — WHO MARRIES FOR GOOD QUALITIES, BUT NOT FOR LOVE?

RESPONSE	INDIA	PAKISTAN	UNITED STATES	ENGLAND	AUSTRALIA
YES	49.0%	50.4%	3.5%	7.3%	4.8%
NO	24.0%	39.1%	85.9%	83.6%	80.0%
UNDECIDED	26.9%	10.4%	10.6%	9.1%	15.2%

Students were asked "If a man (woman) had all the other qualities you desired, would you marry this person if you were not in love with him (her)?" About half of those in the collectivistic cultures of India and Pakistan would agree to marry this person. In contrast, very few of those in the individualistic cultures of the United States, England, and Australia would agree to do so.

Source: Levine, R., Sato, S., Hashimoto, T., & Verma, J. (1995). Love and marriage in eleven cultures. *Journal of Cross-Cultural Psychology, 26,* 554-571.

In contrast, collectivistic cultures emphasize the importance of intimacy across a network of family relationships, not just the marriage (Dion & Dion, 1993; Simmons et al., 1986). For example, while only about 5 to 10% of Americans, English, and Australians would marry a person they did not love, this is true for 50% of those from India and Pakistan (see Table 12.7).

Chinese people also value social or parental conformity moreso than do Americans. Family approval of a relationship influences individuals' commitment to that relationship in Indonesia, but not in Australia (MacDonald & Jessica, 2006). Again, both a partner and a partner's family influence the future of a romantic relationship more in collectivistic cultures than in individualistic ones.

These differences in views about the importance of love in marriage lead to different views about the cause of relationship dissolution. In individualistic countries people are more willing to dissolve a marriage that is not working, because the predominant goal of marriage should be to make both spouses feel happy and fulfilled (Hatfield & Sprecher, 1995; Sprecher et al., 1994). On the other hand, in collectivistic countries marriage may be seen as a way to join two families in order to benefit them both, and hence the happiness of the spouses may be less important. A famous historic example of this joining is Marie Antoinette, who was Austrian and married off by her family to French royalty, with the hopes that this marriage would improve relations between the two countries.

Satisfaction in arranged marriages. Almost all marriages in the United States and other Western cultures are chosen by the two people most directly involved. But in many other cultures, marriages are initiated instead by family members. Not surprisingly, couples in arranged, or family-initiated, marriages report some differences in patterning and interaction than those in couple-initiated marriages. A study of couples in Turkey revealed that those in family-initiated marriages reported fewer interactions alone with their

Questioning the Research

Although this research suggests that love is more important for marriage in individualistic than collectivistic cultures, can you think of an alternative explanation for this association? Hint: What else might differ across these different cultures?

partner, and lower levels of disclosure in their relationships, compared to those in couple-oriented relationships (Hortacsu & Oral, 2001).

How does the type of marriage impact relationship satisfaction? Some research indicates that marital satisfaction is lower in arranged marriages than in couple-initiated ones. For example, one study with over 500 Chinese women compared marital satisfaction in those from arranged marriage and those in "love matches" (Xiaohe & Whyte, 1990). Women in love matches reported greater satisfaction than those in arranged marriages. However, other research indicates no differences in relationship satisfaction between those living in arranged marriages and marriages of choice (Myers, Madathil, & Tingle, 2005).

Managing conflict   People in different cultures rely on different types of strategies for managing conflict. For example, Yum (2004) examined the typology of responses to conflict in both individualistic (American) and collectivistic (South Korean) samples. Members of collectivistic cultures tend to enact more relationship-maintaining strategies (e.g., loyalty, voice) but use fewer relationship-destructive strategies (e.g., exit, neglect) than those in individualistic cultures. These findings make sense, given the great focus on maintaining relationships and showing loyalty and respect in communalistic cultures. Individualistic cultures, on the other hand, emphasize the importance of engaging in behaviors to satisfy one's own personal needs and goals.

THE NATURE OF FRIENDSHIPS

Friendships in individualistic cultures often include concepts describing personal stimulation, such as creative, active and energetic, and directs activities (Maeda & Ritchie, 2003). People in individualistic cultures tend to want friends who are independent (e.g., "not a whiner"). In fact, too much dependence in a friendship is seen as a sign of personal weakness.

People in individualistic cultures tend to distinguish between types of friendships (Adams & Plaut, 2003). As described at the start of this section, people in individualistic cultures report having high quality "best friendships," and are likely to depend heavily on a small number of friends. Emotional reliance on friends, meaning willingness to confide in and rely on our friends, is higher in the United States and Russia and lower in South Korea and Turkey (Ryan, La Guardia, Solky-Butzel, Chirkov, & Kim, 2005).

In contrast, friendships in collectivistic cultures often emphasize comfort and ease (Maeda & Ritchie, 2003). For example, research on friendships in Ghana revealed that such relationships focus on practical support, advice, and interdependence (Adams & Plaut, 2003). Similarly, studies of friendships in Japan suggest an emphasis on providing self-esteem support (e.g., "encourages me"). As described in Business Connections, people in collectivistic cultures also tend to focus on interpersonal concerns that impact larger social networks, including workplace relationships.

Andreanna Seymore/Getty Images, Inc.

Love is a more valued component of marriage in individualistic cultures than in collectivistic ones.

The Impact of Culture on Workplace Relationships

Latinos (Mexicans and Mexican Americans) are much more concerned with the socioemotional aspects of workplace relationships than are Americans (Sanchez-Burks, Nisbett, & Ybarra, 2000). For example, when watching a videotape of a workplace interaction, Mexicans are more likely to suggest improvements related to feelings, and to believe that a greater focus on emotional concerns would benefit the workgroup. Moreover, when participants are asked to choose which student advisory committee to join, 87% of Anglo Americans choose the task committee compared to only 55% of Mexican Americans. On the other hand, 46% of the Mexican Americans choose to work on the task committee plus the interpersonal concerns committee, compared to only 12% of the Anglo Americans. Finally, after listening to a group discussion, Mexican Americans remember nearly twice as many feelings-related events as do Anglo Americans.

Jenny Acheson /Getty Images, Inc.

The Big Picture

INTERPERSONAL ATTRACTION AND CLOSE RELATIONSHIPS

This chapter included many applications of the three "big ideas" studied in social psychology. The examples below should help you see the connection between interpersonal attraction and close relationships and these big ideas and contribute to your understanding of the big picture of social psychology.

THEME	EXAMPLES
The social world influences how we think about ourselves.	• Thinking about a close relationship helps us cope with threatening information about ourselves. • People with a secure attachment style feel comfortable getting close to others and don't worry about becoming overly dependent or being abandoned by their partners. • Married couples feel happiest in their relationships when their partner sees them as they see themselves.
The social world influences our thoughts, attitudes, and behaviors.	• Attractive professors get higher teaching evaluations. • Men who run on a treadmill for two minutes find an attractive woman more attractive than those who run for only 15 seconds. • Women who are in an inequitable marriage are more likely to have an affair.
Our attitudes and behavior shape the social world around us.	• Men who look at centerfold pictures rate their own partners as less attractive. • People with an anxious attachment style see negative behaviors as worse than do those with secure or avoidant attachment styles. In turn, they respond to these negative behaviors by acting more negatively themselves, which leads to conflict. • People who are lonely engage in less open self-disclosure, which in turn inhibits self-disclosure from their partner.

This chapter has examined five key principles of interpersonal attraction and close relationships.

YOU LEARNED What predicts interpersonal attraction? This section examined different predictors of interpersonal attraction. Physical attractiveness influences attraction, as do relationship factors (similarity, complementarity, and reciprocity) and situational factors (physiological arousal, proximity, and the contrast effect). You also learned why "secret relationships" can lead to particularly high levels of attraction.

YOU LEARNED What is love? This section described three distinct models of love, and the distinct components of each approach. These models include passionate versus companionate love, the triangular theory (passion, intimacy, commitment), and the love styles model (ludus, eros, mania, agape, storge, pragma). And you learned that we see relationships with people we "love" as different from those with people we are "in love" with.

YOU LEARNED What predicts relationship satisfaction? This section described three models predicting satisfaction in relationships. These models include social exchange theory (the costs and benefits of a given relationship), attachment styles model (secure, anxious, avoidant), and the positive illusions approach. You also learned that dating couples who have higher levels of investment in their relationship are less likely to cheat during spring break than those with lower levels of investment.

YOU LEARNED What are common problems in close relationships? This section described several common problems that emerge in close relationships. These topics included constructive and destructive approaches to managing conflict, gender differences in reactions to infidelity, the causes and correlates of loneliness, and the hazards and benefits of relationship dissolution. You learned that men are more jealous when they imagine their partner flirting with someone who is high in dominance than someone who is highly physically attractive, whereas women experience greater jealousy when they believe their partner is flirting with someone who is highly attractive.

YOU LEARNED How does culture influence interpersonal attraction and close relationships? The last section in this chapter described the role of culture in influencing interpersonal attraction and close relationships. We examined cultural differences in defining beauty, the nature of love, and the nature of friendship. Finally, you learned that people in individualistic cultures report having higher quality "best friend" relationships, and those in collectivistic cultures report having higher quality peer relationships in general.

KEY TERMS

attachment styles 436
companionate love 428
comparison level 434
comparison level for alternatives
 (CLalt) 434
demand/withdraw interaction
 pattern 444

equity theory 435
excitation transfer 423
exit 443
investment 435
loyalty 443
matching hypothesis 421
mere exposure 423

negative attributional traps 444
neglect 443
passionate love 428
reciprocity 422
social exchange theory 433
voice 443

QUESTIONS FOR REVIEW

1. Why do most people prefer to date attractive partners? Provide four specific reasons.
2. Explain how each of the three models of love conceptualizes the distinct types of love.
3. Describe each of the three models predicting relationship satisfaction.

4. What are four common problems in close relationships?
5. Describe how culture influences how people see love and marriage.

TAKE ACTION!

1. Let's say your roommate is interested in dating a woman in his history class. What three things would you suggest to help him establish a relationship with her?
2. Your aunt and uncle have been married for 30 years. Based on your knowledge of triangular theory, what love components are likely to be highest in their relationship right now?
3. Your older sister recently started a new dating relationship. According to social exchange theory, what types of things should she do to increase her relationship satisfaction?

4. Imagine that you are getting married. What two approaches might you use when managing conflict in this relationship, and what two approaches would it be good for you to avoid?
5. Your co-worker has a friend from India who is planning on having an arranged marriage. Your co-worker makes a number of rude remarks about her friend's approach to marriage. What could you tell her about the cultural differences in marriage as well as the predictors of satisfaction?

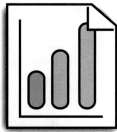

RESEARCH CONNECTIONS

Try some of these research activities to gain experience in conducting and evaluating research, and to increase your understanding of research methods and techniques in social psychology.
Visit WileyPLUS for more activities and interactive research tools! (www.wileyplus.com)

Participate in Research

Activity 1 Are Average Faces Most Attractive?: This chapter has described how people see composite faces, meaning those that are made up of many different faces, as more attractive than single faces. Go to WileyPLUS to look at different faces and rate how attractive you find each; then use your results to determine whether you also see composite photographs as more attractive.

Activity 2 Testing the Triangular Theory of Love: This chapter examined the three distinct components of love, according to the triangular theory. Go online to rate your feelings of intimacy, passion, and commitment to see what type of love you have in your current (or more recent) relationship.

Activity 3 The Impact of Attachment Styles on Dating Patterns: This chapter described the impact of attachment styles on patterns of dating as well as interactions in romantic relationships. You can go online to test your own attachment style and see how this style may influence your dating patterns and interactions.

Activity 4 Gender Differences in Jealousy: You learned in this chapter about the impact of gender on reactions to different types of infidelity. Go online to read about different types of infidelity, and then rate how upset you would be in each situation.

Activity 5 The Impact of Culture on Love: The final section of this chapter described how people from different cultures vary in how strongly they believe that love is an essential part of marriage. Go online to rate your agreement with the importance of love in leading to marriage, and the absence of love in leading to divorce.

Test a Hypothesis

As you've learned in this chapter, men and women tend to look for different characteristics in dating partners. To test whether this hypothesis is true, find personal ads for dating in a local newspaper, and calculate the percentage of men and women who are looking for particular traits (such as attractiveness, wealth, or intelligence). Then, report your findings to other students.

Design a Study

To design your own study testing factors that predict interpersonal attraction, go online. You'll be able to choose the type of study you want to conduct (self-report, observational/naturalistic, or experimental), choose your own independent and dependent variables, and form your own hypothesis.

13

Altruism and Prosocial

WHAT YOU'LL LEARN

How do personal factors influence helping?

 RESEARCH FOCUS ON GENDER
Are Men or Women More Helpful?

How do situational factors influence helping?

Does pure altruism exist?

 RESEARCH FOCUS ON NEUROSCIENCE
How Perspective-Taking Looks in the Brain

Who gets help when they are in need?

How does CULTURE influence helping?

Did you ever wonder?

On September 11, 2001, police officers and firefighters rushed into the burning World Trade Center towers in New York City to save workers who were trapped. Many people who behaved altruistically on 9/11 lost their lives. Three hundred and seventy-two firefighters died trying to save others; many were still inside the World Trade Center trying to rescue trapped office workers when the towers collapsed. Civilians who acted altruistically also lost their lives helping others. One man, Abe Zelmanowitz, refused to abandon his friend, Ed Beyea, who was in a wheelchair. Both men died when the North Tower collapsed.

In the days following these attacks, in which terrorists hijacked United States airplanes and deliberately flew them into the World Trade Center towers, other people helped in different ways. Some people donated money to provide support to family members of the nearly 3,000 victims. Other people helped with recovery efforts at the World Trade Center site, provided much-needed supplies to rescue workers, or simply stood on the side of

Education
CONNECTIONS
What Are the
Consequences of
Requiring Volunteerism?

Media
CONNECTIONS
Does Watching
Sesame Street Lead to
Prosocial Behavior?

Law
CONNECTIONS
The Impact of
Similarity of Race on
Guilt

Behavior

the road and expressed their appreciation to the recovery workers as they left the site each day. What would motivate people to run into a burning building to help those they don't even know, or refuse to leave a burning building? Why would someone donate money, or time, to help people they didn't know? You'll find out in this chapter. In addition, you'll find out...

Q A Why does seeing the word "God" increase prosocial behavior?

Q A Why are you less likely to get help in an emergency when you are surrounded by many other people than with only a few people?

Q A Why can selfish motives help increase volunteering at an HIV clinic?

Q A Why is it better for women to ask for directions than for men to ask for directions?

Q A Why are people in India as willing to donate bone marrow to strangers as to family members, but Americans are much more willing to donate to family members?

Associated Press

What do these questions have in common? They can all be answered by findings from research in social psychology on factors that impact **prosocial behavior,** meaning any type of action intended to benefit someone other than oneself, such as cooperating, sharing, and comforting (Batson, 1998). In some cases, such behavior is motivated by a desire to improve one's own circumstances. For example, if a child shares a favorite toy with a sibling because her father has promised her a cookie, the child's motivation for helping is not to improve her brother's well-being, but rather to improve her own well-being. Other times, helping behavior can be motivated by a desire to improve another person's well-being with no thought of benefit to the self. For example, a man who jumps onto a subway track to save a stranger who has fallen and is about to be hit by a train is clearly concerned only with the other person's welfare (a true story that you'll learn about later in this chapter). This type of helping is called **altruism**. This chapter will examine how both personal and situational factors influence helping, whether true altruism actually exists, the people who are most likely to get help, and the impact of culture on helping.

HOW DO PERSONAL FACTORS INFLUENCE HELPING?

Many people do things to help other people with some regularity: they give money to benefit schools, religious organizations, and social and political causes; they volunteer their time with animal shelters, foster children, and soup kitchens; they jump into cold water, burning buildings, and crushed cars to save people. But what motivates people to provide such help? You might be surprised that even very small things can motivate prosocial behavior. In one study, researchers asked participants to unscramble 10 five-word sentences (Shariff & Norenzayan, 2007). In one condition, these sentences contained words that cue religion, such as God, prophet, and sacred. In the other condition, these sentences contained neutral words that were unrelated to religion. Participants then completed a game with another participant (actually a confederate of the experimenter's) in which they could reward their partner with anywhere from zero to ten one-dollar coins (and keep any remaining coins for themselves). As predicted, people who unscrambled the sentences containing cues to religion were more altruistic than those who solved the sentences with the neutral words: they left, on average, $4.22, compared to $1.84, and 64% left $5.00 or more, compared with only 12% leaving $5.00 or more in the neutral condition. This study demonstrates that just cueing religious words can increase helping, which suggests that people who are more religious might be more likely to engage in prosocial behavior. This section will examine the role of personal factors, including evolutionary factors, personality, and religion, in predicting helping.

EVOLUTIONARY FACTORS

According to the evolutionary perspective, people sometimes act in altruistic ways to help someone else even at great personal cost (see Rate Yourself). When is this likely to happen? When such behavior will help ensure the survival of their genes, which can then be passed on (Burnstein, Crandall, & Kitayama, 1994). In other words, your act of altruism might lead to your own death, but if this act resulted in the survival of your child, your genes would live on. Remember, evolutionary theory views behavior as shaped by the desire to ensure the survival of one's genes. Therefore, it explains why people might engage in behavior that is costly to themselves—in terms of time and effort and even personal safety—but helps ensure the welfare of someone else who shares their genes. An "altruistic gene" would continue to be passed on, because parents who lacked this gene would be less likely to have children who survived to pass on their own "selfish genes." In sum, this

prosocial behavior any behavior that has the goal of helping another person

altruism the desire to help another person

theory of **kinship selection** is used to explain why parents may self-sacrifice (that is, put themselves in positions of great danger) for the benefit of their children.

kinship selection the idea that we are more likely to help those we are genetically related to

Evidence for kinship selection.

If altruistic behavior is motivated at least in part by the desire to have one's own genes survive, we should find that people behave more altruistically to those who could potentially reproduce and pass on their own genes (Kruger, 2003; Segal, 1993). Is there evidence that people are more likely to help those who are closely related to them (and share more genes) than people who are distantly related (and share fewer genes)? If a grizzly bear is attacking your family group, are you more likely to help your children and your siblings than your cousins and uncles? Are identical twins (who share all the same genes) more helpful to one another than fraternal twins (who share only 50% of their genes)? Let's look at what the research says.

AFP/Getty Images, Inc.

In one study, college students responded to a series of hypothetical dilemmas in which someone needed help (Korchmaros & Kenny, 2006). In some cases these dilemmas involved life-or-death situations. For example, two of the participants' family members were asleep in a burning building, and there is time to save only one of them. Other cases involved everyday-favor situations. For example, two of the participants' family members needed help running errands, and there is time to help only one of them. Researchers also manipulated the type of relationship between the participants and the person who needed help: degree of genetic relatedness, emotional closeness, perceived similarity, and frequency of interaction. Findings indicated that relationship factors, including emotional closeness and similarity, influence helping in part because genetic factors lead to these relationship factors. In other words, we feel similar and close to our relatives, which leads to our desire to help them.

Moreover, people should also be more likely to help those who are likely to reproduce and pass on their genes, as opposed to those who are in poor health (and therefore unlikely to survive) and those who are very old (and therefore unlikely to reproduce; Burnstein et al., 1994). A series of studies by Eugene Bernstein and his colleagues provides support for this hypothesis.

Questioning the Research

This study suggests that people are more likely to help those with whom they are emotionally close and similar, and therefore provides support for the kinship selection model of helping. But can you think of another explanation for these findings? (Hint: How reliable is self-report in this case?)

In life-or-death situations, people chose to give help to those who are closely related more often than to distantly related, to the young over the old, the healthy over the sick, and premenopausal women over postmenopausal women.

Evidence for reciprocal altruism.   But people do show altruistic behavior even to non-relatives. You probably help your friends and neighbors, even though you share no genetic material. What explains this type of helping? According to the **reciprocal altruism** perspective, people help others to increase the odds that they, in turn, will help you (Kruger, 2003; Trivers, 1971, 1985). In other words, you are probably willing to loan your class notes or give a ride to your friend because you'd like to depend on that person for help at some other time. This tendency to help those who help us is shown even among animals that live in social groups, such as monkeys, cats, and fish. In sum, because helping others leads them to reciprocate, this type of cooperation among group members, regardless of their genetic connection, increases survival. Research Focus on Gender describes how men and women differ in the types of help they provide.

reciprocal altruism the idea that we are motivated to help others due to the expectation that they will then help us in return later on

RESEARCH FOCUS ON GENDER
Are Men or Women More Helpful?

Men and women vary considerably in their likelihood of helping in different types of situations (Becker & Eagly, 2004; Eagly & Crowley, 1986; Eagly, 1987). Men are more likely than women to help in situations that call for heroic, brave behavior (e.g., rescuing someone from a burning building). For example, men receive 91% of the Carnegie Hero Medals, which specifically are given to people who risk their lives to save a stranger. Similarly, the vast majority of people who are publicly recognized in the media for some type of heroic behavior, such as stopping a robbery or rescuing a drowning child, are men (Huston, Ruggiero, Conner, & Geis, 1981). Moreover, these gender differences in helping are found across a range of cultures, including Australia, Egypt, and Korea (Johnson, Danko, Danvill, & Bochner, 1989).

© Blend Images/SUPERSTOCK

Although both men and women will help in life-threatening situations, men are more likely to engage in heroic acts, and women are more likely to engage in long-term caring for those in need.

x

© Ashley Cooper/©Corbis

Why are men more likely to help in these dramatic life-and-death cases? One explanation is that men experience fewer costs for helping than do women; men who help are larger and have more training than men who don't help, suggesting that they expect to experience fewer costs of helping. Men may also benefit from some behavior: women prefer risk-prone brave males over risk-averse non-brave males, and men are well aware of this preference (Kelly & Dunbar, 2001).

Another explanation for this supposed gender difference is that women help in different ways. An analysis of those who assisted the Jews during the Nazi Holocaust, a clearly life-threatening act, revealed that women were as likely as men to provide help (Becker & Eagly, 2004). Women are also more likely than men to donate a kidney to a close relative. In addition, women are more likely than men to volunteer for both the Peace Corps and Doctors of the World, organizations designed to provide much-needed on-going volunteer services.

PERSONALITY

We often assume that people who engage in highly altruistic behavior, such as spending tremendous amounts of time volunteering, making substantial donations to charitable organizations, and especially risking one's life to help others, have distinct personality characteristics. For example, Oskar Schindler, a German man who rescued over 1,300 Jews during the Holocaust, literally risked his life by hiding Jewish people from the Nazis. In general, people show an increase in empathy and prosocial behavior as they mature, but individuals also vary considerably in their frequency and types of helping (Davis, Luce, & Kraus, 1994; Matthews, Batson, Horn, & Rosenman, 1981; Rushton, Fulker, Neale, Nias, & Eysenck, 1986; Zahn-Wexler, Radke-Yarrow, Wagner, & Chapman, 1992). Health Connections describes another example of a very helpful, even life-saving, behavior some people engage in—organ donation.

Health
::: CONNECTIONS

The Amazing Generosity of Living Organ Donors

One of the major medical advances in the 1900s has been the ability of doctors to transplant organs, including kidneys, livers, lungs, and hearts, from one person to another (Dowie, 1988; Fox & Swazey, 1992). Although organ transplantation has allowed many people who have malfunctioning organs to live, the number of people who need organs is consistently much, much higher than the number of organs available for donation; 11 to 12 people who are on a waiting list die each day, before an organ comes available. Although in most cases organ donations come from people who have died, living people can also donate some organs, such as a kidney (because we have two), or a portion of an organ, such as a piece of their liver. What could motivate someone to perform this type of selfless act? Several factors increase people's intent to donate their own organs (Morgan, Miller, & Arasaratnam, 2003). These include positive attitudes toward organ donation, a general desire to help others, and knowing someone who has donated or received an organ.

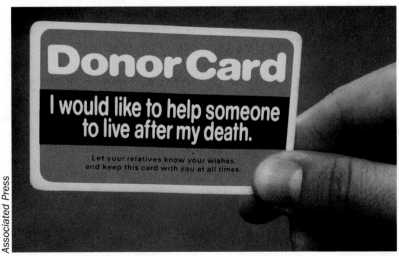

Associated Press

How Empathic Are You?

Emotional Empathy

INSTRUCTIONS: Rate each item on a scale of −4 (very strong disagreement) to +4 (very strong agreement).

☐ **1.** It makes me sad to see a lonely stranger in a group.

☐ **2.** I tend to get emotionally involved with a friend's problems.

☐ **3.** Seeing people cry upsets me.

☐ **4.** I become very involved when I watch a movie.

☐ **5.** I am very upset when I see an animal in pain.

☐ **6.** I really get involved with the feelings of the characters in a novel.

☐ **7.** The people around me have a great influence on my moods.

☐ **8.** I cannot continue to feel OK if the people around me are depressed.

SCORING: Sum up your total number of points on these eight items.

INTERPRETATION: This scale measures emotional empathy, meaning the extent to which people understand other people's perspectives and respond emotionally to others' experiences. Higher scores indicate higher levels of emotional empathy, whereas lower scores indicate lower levels of emotional empathy (Mehrabian & Epstein, 1972).

empathy the ability to understand other people's perspectives and respond emotionally to other people's experiences

Empathy.　People who are generally altruistic share some common traits. First, they are high in **empathy**, meaning they tend to understand other people's perspectives, and respond emotionally to other people's experiences (Batson & Oleson, 1991; Dovidio, Piliavin, Gaertner, Schroeder, & Clark, 1991; Eisenberg et al., 2002; Eisenberg & Miller, 1987). As shown in Rate Yourself, people vary in how much empathy they have for other people, and those who are empathic are more likely to take the perspective of others (e.g., those who are suffering), and therefore to try to help ease the suffering.

In turn, people with higher levels of empathy engage in more prosocial behavior, including donating money to charitable causes (Davis, 1983) and spending time helping people in need (Otten, Penner, & Altabe, 1991). For example, Carlo and colleagues found that people who were high in empathy were much more likely to agree to switch places with another subject who was doing an upsetting task than those who were low on empathy (Carlo, Eisenberg, Troyer, Switzer, & Speer). Individual differences in empathy and altruism appear even in children: children who feel sad when they see others feeling sad or being picked on are more helpful to children in a hospital burn unit than those who show less empathy for others (Knight, Johnson, Carlo, & Eisenberg, 1994).

What makes some people more empathic than others? Some evidence points to a genetic link (Davis et al., 1994; Rushton et al., 1986). The link between empathy and behavior is more similar in identical twins—who share all of their genes—than fraternal twins—who share only half of their genes. In fact, research comparing empathy in response to others' distress using identical and fraternal twin samples suggests that as much as 70% of people's response to distressing situations may be rooted in genetics.

moral reasoning a personality factor that describes the extent to which a person's willingness to help is a function of his or her own needs and expected consequences versus larger moral standards

Moral reasoning.　Another personality factor that influences helping is an individual's level of **moral reasoning** (Eisenberg & Miller, 1987). When deciding whether to engage in a particular action, some people focus on their own needs and the concrete consequences of their actions (e.g., whether they will avoid punishment or receive a reward). Others are more concerned about adhering to moral standards regardless of external social controls (e.g., whether their actions will help someone else, even if they conflict with a person's own motives).

Consider the following dilemma: "A girl named Mary was going to a friend's birthday party. On her way, she saw a little girl who had fallen down and hurt her leg. The girl asked Mary to go to her house and get her parents so the parents could take her to the doctor. But if Mary did run and get the child's parents, she would be late for the birthday party and miss the ice cream, cake, and all of the games. What should Mary do? Why?" (Eisenberg, 1982, p. 231). Research using this and other moral dilemmas shows that the use of higher-level reasoning is associated with greater empathy and altruism. For example, children who use higher-level moral reasoning are more likely to choose to anonymously donate part of their earnings from participating in a study to children seen in a UNICEF poster (Eisenberg, Shell, Pasternack, Lennon, Beller, & Mathy, 1987).

In another study, four- and five-year-old children saw a film about two children who fall from a jungle gym and get hurt (Miller, Eisenberg, Fabes, & Shell, 1996). Then they had the option of playing on their own with some very attractive toys or putting loose crayons into boxes to be packed up and sent to the hospital for the injured children. Children who are high on both empathy and moral reasoning are the most likely to help the injured children and forego their own playing time.

Children whose parents use positive behavior and teach prosocial behavior are more likely to engage in prosocial behavior, such as sharing themselves.

Parents' direct teaching of prosocial behavior can influence children's moral reasoning (Eisenberg, Fabes, Schaller, Carlo, & Miller, 1991; Fabes, Eisenberg, & Miller, 1990). Parents who teach their children about helping using perspective taking and empathy are more likely to foster higher levels of moral reasoning than those who focus on helping as a way of gaining rewards or avoiding punishment. For example, a parent can foster moral reasoning by saying, "If you don't share your toys with that child, he/she will feel sad." It's less effective for a parent to say, "If you don't share your toys with that child, I will not give you candy" or "I will be disappointed."

Martin Hoffman (1994) believed that parents who point out the effects of a child's behavior on others are more likely to develop empathy and moral reasoning in that child than parents who use other strategies, such as love withdrawal or power assertion. Similarly, parents who use positive behavior, including positive feelings toward their child as well as positive discipline strategies (e.g., firmness, reasoning, calm), create more prosocial behavior in their children over time (Knafo & Plomin, 2006).

RELIGION

How does religion influence prosocial behavior? Some religious teachings emphasize the importance of engaging in cooperative and prosocial behavior (Batson, 1983). Other religions emphasize the importance of "brotherly love," and encourage people to treat others as they'd like others to treat them ("do unto others"). Religious beliefs are also associated, in some studies, with more altruistic behavior. For example, college students who describe themselves as more religiously committed spend more time volunteering with various campus organizations (Benson et al., 1980; Hansen, Vandenberg, & Patterson, 1995). As described at the start of this section, even cueing people with religious words can increase prosocial behavior.

But religion does not always lead to more helping. In fact, people who hold strong and conservative religious beliefs are very likely to help those who they believe deserve help, but not to help those who are undeserving (Skitka & Tetlock, 1993). Jackson and Esses (1997) found that religious fundamentalists are more likely to help some people (e.g., those who are seen as deserving of help), but less likely to help those whose behavior contradicts that of their religion (e.g., homosexuals, single mothers). Similarly, people who are highly religious are less likely to provide help to someone who is gay (Batson, Floyd, Meyer, & Winner, 1999).

Concepts in Context

FACTOR	EXAMPLE
Evolution	Domingo and his 10-year-old son, Jerome, were trapped in their house during a fierce hurricane. Rescuers finally came, but they had room for only one more person in the boat. Domingo immediately put his son in the boat.
Personality	Pilar has volunteered once a week at a nursing home for the past two years. She recognizes the loneliness of the patients she visits, and believes that her visits really help them.
Religion	Eduardo regularly attends a Baptist church in which the minister encourages church members to provide help to those in need of assistance. Eduardo therefore decides to volunteer at a soup kitchen one Saturday morning a month.

HOW DO SITUATIONAL FACTORS INFLUENCE HELPING?

On March 13, 1964, a young woman named Kitty Genovese was returning home after work to her apartment in New York City at 3 AM (Rosenthal, 1964). She was 28 years old. She was stabbed and raped within 35 yards of her apartment building, on the street. Two times the attacker ran away, in fear that someone was coming, and both times he came back and continued to stab her. It was a loud, long, tortured death. Although it was 3 o'clock in the morning, 38 neighbors in her building were awakened by her screams, and watched what was happening (lights went on, windows were open). After 30 minutes, one person called the police. But by then, it was too late—Kitty Genovese was dead. This case created headlines across the nation, as people searched for a cause for this apparent indifference on the part of her neighbors. Was it because it occurred in a big city? Was it because the people in her building were cruel or thoughtless? This incident led to a series of studies in social psychology that examined how situational factors can influence helping behavior at an unconscious level. This section will examine two models that describe how situational factors influence whether help is given—the decision-making process model and the arousal/cost-reward model—as well as the influence of three additional situational factors that may influence helping behavior—mood, modeling, and the environment.

DECISION-MAKING PROCESS MODEL

decision-making process model a model describing helping behavior as a function of five distinct steps

According to the **decision-making process model** developed by Latané and Darley (1970), there are a number of features of emergencies that make it difficult to get help. First, because emergencies are rare and unusual events, people do not have lots of experiences in handling emergencies, and therefore they may not have direct personal experience in how to cope. As you may recall from Chapter 6, the link between attitudes and behavior is stronger when you have direct personal experience with something, and therefore people's good intentions (e.g., "I would step in and save the person") may go awry.

Second, because emergencies themselves differ widely, even when people have direct experience in handling one type of an emergency, they are not likely to have experience in handling other types of emergencies, all of which require different types of help. For example, saving someone who is drowning requires jumping into water, swimming to them, and dragging them out. Helping someone with a

NewsCom

In the NEWS **Failure to Help.** **Esmin Elizabeth Green**, age 49, died in a waiting room at a Brooklyn hospital on June 19, 2008. What is remarkable, however, is that she fell to the floor, and lay there twitching while several strangers sat nearby. Two other patients were in the waiting room with her. A guard saw her on the floor. At one point, a hospital staff person even nudged the woman with her foot. She lay there for more than an hour before a staff member put her on a gurney and took her away—but by that time she had died.

FIGURE 13.1

MODEL OF HOW WE DECIDE TO HELP

According to the model of the decision-making process proposed by Latane and Darley, helping behavior occurs only when a person takes five distinct steps. If, at any point, a person fails to take a particular step, he or she will not provide aid.

Source: Latane, B., & Darley, J. M. (1970). *The Unresponsive Bystander: Why Doesn't He Help?* Upper Saddle River, NJ: Prentice Hall.

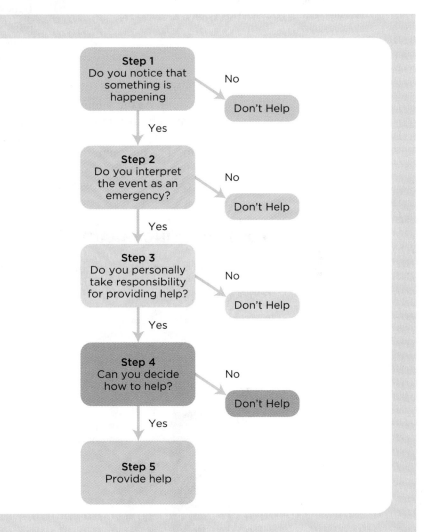

flat tire requires assisting with changing the tire (or perhaps just making a phone call to AAA or a tow truck).

Third, emergencies are unforeseen. Because they emerge suddenly, people are not able to think through various options and develop plans of action.

According to the model of the decision-making process proposed by Latane and Darley (see Figure 13.1), helping behavior occurs only when a person takes five

THE PARABLE OF THE GOOD SAMARITAN

A man was going down from Jerusalem to Jericho and fell into the hands of robbers, who stripped him, beat him, and went away, leaving him half dead. Now by chance a priest was going down that road; when he saw him, he passed by on the other side. So likewise a Levite, when he came to the place and saw him, passed by on the other side. But a Samaritan while traveling came near him; and when he saw him, he was moved with pity. He went to him and bandaged his wounds, having poured oil and wine on them. Then he put him on his own animal, brought him to an inn, and took care of him. The next day he took out two denarii [a type of money], gave them to the innkeeper, and said, "Take care of him; and when I come back, I will repay you whatever more you spend" (Luke 10:30–35).

distinct steps; if at any point a person fails to take a particular step, he or she will not provide aid. These five steps are: notice something is happening, interpret it as an emergency, take responsibility for providing help, decide how to help, and provide help.

Notice something is happening. First, you need to *notice that something is happening.* This can actually be surprisingly hard to do, because people are often self-focused. Noticing an event may be particularly difficult for people who live in a big city, and therefore are used to blocking out all kinds of stimuli (e.g., noise, strangers, etc.). So, in some cases people simply aren't paying attention and are not aware of emergencies that may be occurring.

In one clever study showing the extent of people's ability to not notice, John Darley and Daniel Batson (1973) asked seminary students, who by nature should be motivated to help others, to give a speech at a nearby building. This speech was on a parable from the Bible, "the Good Samaritan," and specifically describes a person who altruistically gives time and care to a wounded man lying on the side of the road (see example box). As the seminary students walked to the building where they would give the speech, they passed a stranger (who was actually a confederate of the experimenters) who was slumped in a doorway, coughing and groaning. Who provides help? The only significant factor predicting help was time pressure: as shown in Figure 13.2, men who were in a hurry were very unlikely to help, yet those who were not in a hurry were quite likely to provide help. People are also more likely

---

FIGURE 13.2

DOES HURRYING IMPACT HELPING?

Experimenters observed whether seminary students on their way to give a speech about the Good Samaritan would stop to help someone in need. As predicted, fewer students who were in a hurry stopped to help a person in need.

Source: Darley, J.M., & Batson, C.D. (1973) From Jerusalem to Jericho: A study of situational and dispositional variables in helping behavior. *Journal of Personality and Social Psychology*, 27, 100-108.

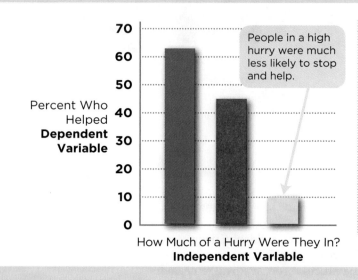

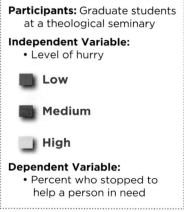

to give help when they witness a clear and vivid emergency than when they see something less clear (Piliavin, Piliavin, & Broll, 1976). In one study, 89% of people helped when they directly saw a person fall down a flight of stairs or slump to the floor in a faint, but only 13% of people helped when they saw only the aftermath of such an event (e.g., a person holding and rubbing their ankle).

Interpret it as an emergency. Second, even if you notice an event, *you need to interpret it as an emergency* in order to provide help. But people often interpret events as "non-emergencies" and so fail to act. In 1993 two 10-year-old boys in England took a two-year-old from a shopping mall, and carried him two miles away. The little boy was fighting the older kids the entire time, and many people witnessed the children walking away, but interpreted the scene as siblings fighting, and did not try to intervene. Sadly, the older boys beat the toddler to death. One study found that more than three times as many people try to stop a man from assaulting a woman if they think they are strangers (e.g., the woman yells "Get away from me; I don't know you") than if they think they are a romantically involved couple (e.g., the woman yells "Get away from me; I don't know why I ever married you"; Shotland & Straw, 1976). In sum, situations with greater ambiguity lead to less help (Shotland & Heinold, 1985).

People often look to the crowd to see how others are responding, and therefore fail to interpret the event as an emergency themselves (Latane & Darley, 1968; Latane & Rodin, 1969). As described in Chapter 8, when people are in a new or unfamiliar situation, they often look to see how other people are responding. So, if you are unsure whether a person is truly in need of help, you may look to see what other people are doing to decide how you should act. Unfortunately, this can lead to a state of **pluralistic ignorance**, in which people look to each other's public behavior to determine how they should act. But if each person is looking to others to judge how to interpret the situation, and no one wants to be seen as the person who overreacts (and thus feels embarrassed), the person in need may receive no help at all—simply because each person may assume that because others are not reacting, there is no emergency.

pluralistic ignorance a particular type of norm misperception that occurs when each individual in the group privately rejects the group's norms, but believes that others accept these norms

John Darley and Bibb Latane (1968) conducted one of the first studies on the impact of situational factors on people's interpretation of emergencies. They brought students into the lab to participate in a simple questionnaire study. Some of the students were placed in a room alone to complete the questionnaire. Others were placed in the room with two other subjects. A few minutes after starting the questionnaire, an unusual event occurred: smoke started pouring into the room. The researchers then examined what students would do in the face of this seemingly obvious "emergency." Of the participants who were alone in the room, virtually all of them stood up to investigate the source of the smoke, and then left the room to report it to the experimenter. But what happened when three subjects were together in the room? In most cases, no one reported the smoke during the next six minutes (when the researchers officially ended the study)! In fact, among the 24 people in the eight groups, only one person reported the smoke within the first four minutes. And remember, this smoke was not a subtle effect: by the end of the six-minute trial, the smoke was so thick that the subjects were constantly having to wave the smoke away from their faces just to read the questionnaires!

What types of things help people label events as an emergency? One clear sign is a direct cry for help, such as a scream. Clear cues to distress increase the likelihood that the person will get help (Clark & Word, 1972; Gaertner & Dovidio, 1977; Yakimovich & Saltz, 1971). In one study, researchers created either an ambiguous emergency, in which participants heard a loud crash but no verbal cues indicating pain, or an unambiguous emergency, in which participants heard a loud crash and groans of pain (Clark & Word, 1972). Students who heard the unambiguous emergency helped regardless of whether they were alone or in a group. Those who heard the ambiguous emergency were much more likely to help if they were alone than if they were in a group.

Take responsibility for providing help. Third, you need to *take responsibility for providing help*. Even when people recognize that a situation is indeed an emergency, they may assume that other people in the situation will help, and therefore they do not need to do so themselves. In fact, this diffusion of responsibility means that people are actually less likely to get help when they are with many people than with only one or two other people (Latané & Nida, 1981). This phenomenon is called the **bystander effect**.

John Darley and Bibb Latané (1968) created a clever study to directly test this diffusion of responsibility. Subjects were taken to one of a series of small rooms that were connected by intercoms, and were told that they would be talking about personal problems that college students face, and therefore as a way of protecting confidentiality, the experimenter would not be listening to the conversation. Some subjects talked with just one other person, others were in groups of three, and still others were in groups of six. Early in the conversation, one participant mentioned that he had some trouble with a seizure disorder that was sometimes triggered by stress. Later in the conversation, this person's speech was slurred and he asked for help, saying that he was going to die. So who helped him? Eighty-five percent of the subjects who were alone with that person got help immediately, as did all who were with just one other person (perhaps not wanting that person to think they were mean?), and 62% of those with two others in the group. However, 31% of the subjects in the six-person groups didn't leave the room. Clearly they assumed that someone else would help.

What's the good news? People who believe they are the only one who could provide help to a person are more likely to help, even if they think others are aware of the need for help (Bickman, 1971). For example, if you believe that other people are aware of a person's need for help, but that those other potential helpers are too far away to help, you are much more likely to help than if you think the other people are as available to help as you are. Even arbitrarily giving a person responsibility in a situation can increase his or her likelihood of helping. In one study, a researcher asked people on a beach to watch his radio while they went on a walk (Moriarty, 1975). Only 20% of the bystanders who were not given responsibility later tried to prevent the staged theft, yet 94% of those who had been explicitly asked intervened in some way! Similarly, one study with a group of 177 Halloween trick-or-treaters (ages 4 to 13 years old) manipulated responsibility by asking either one child, each child, or no child to take responsibility for donating some of their candy to hospitalized children (Maruyama, Fraser, & Miller, 1982). Giving a child personal responsibility increased the likelihood of donating any candy and increased the number of candies donated.

Decide how to help. Fourth, you need to *decide how to help*, such as by calling 911, providing CPR, or jumping into a pool. People with relevant skills help more than people without such skills or training. In a study by Cramer and colleagues, participants were either education students or nursing students, and were either alone or with another participant (Cramer, McMaster, Bartell, & Dragna). As they were filling out a questionnaire, they heard a man fall from a ladder outside the room, and scream out in pain. What percentage helped in the education condition? Those who were alone were much more likely to help than those who were with a nonresponding other. The percentage of nursing students who helped was basically the same if they were alone or with others. This doesn't mean that nursing students are simply nicer people; it just means they knew what to do, so they were more willing to get involved even if the other person with them didn't help.

bystander effect the finding that the more people who witness an emergency, the less likely a victim is to receive help

Provide help.   Fifth, you need to actually *provide help*. This step can be difficult due to *audience inhibition*. In other words, people can be reluctant to help for fear of making a bad impression on others, by appearing stupid or overly cautious. One summer during college I had a job working at an inner-city public hospital, and lived in an apartment in a rather seedy neighborhood. My roommate came home from work one day to find an old man lying unconscious on our doorstep. She immediately did the right thing—she called 911, and an ambulance arrived within minutes. But my roommate, Carrie, was horrified—and embarrassed—by the loud laughing of the medical attendants as they quickly recognized the man as a local drunk, who was simply sleeping off a long night of drinking.

How/when do you get rid of audience inhibition? Well, one factor is familiarity of context, and of the others in that context. In one study, students came into the lab in either pairs or groups of four (Rutkowski, Gruder, & Romer, 1983). In half of the cases, the students had 20 minutes to "get to know each other," and were then supposed to work on some problems individually. In the other case, the students did not have such a conversation. As they were working, a workman supposedly fell from a ladder outside, and clearly needed help. Who helped? In line with other findings, those who were in pairs were more likely to help than those in larger groups. But among those in groups, those who had a chance to first talk were much more likely to help than those who were with strangers.

Strategies for getting help.   So, what can you do to make sure you get help if you experience or witness an emergency while you are in a large group?

- First, identify one person in the crowd, and call out to that person directly (e.g., "Hey, the woman in the red dress—I need help"). This strategy eliminates the problems caused by diffusion of responsibility, because that specific person is then identified as the person who needs to provide help.
- Second, clearly label the situation as an emergency (e.g., "I am having trouble breathing"). This approach eliminates the problem caused by misinterpretation of the situation.
- Finally, give instructions on how exactly the person should help (e.g., "Hey, you in the red shirt, call 911").

Can this approach help people in need get help? Absolutely. In fact, I mentioned this technique to my mother one night on a vacation a few summers ago, and the very next day she used it. She and my stepfather were out in a sailboat in the ocean, and they tipped the boat over (this was not an unusual occurrence for them, so luckily they were wearing life jackets). My stepfather managed to get back in the boat, but unfortunately it sailed away and he wasn't able to steer it back to her. So my mother was in fairly deep water in the ocean. She saw a guy going nearby on a windsurfer and yelled, "Hey, you on the windsurfer, I need some help." The man on the windsurfer came over to my mother, and she rested on the board until my stepfather got the boat back to her.

AROUSAL/COST-REWARD MODEL

The **arousal/cost-reward model** is a rational, cost-benefit analysis to predicting prosocial behavior. According to this model, people experience arousal when they see other people who are experiencing pain and suffering, and so they are motivated to behave altruistically to help decrease their own arousal (Dovidio et al., 1991; Piliavin, Dovidio, Gaertner, & Clark, 1981; Piliavin, Rodin, & Piliavin, 1969). If you hear a baby crying, you might be motivated to pick up the baby so that it will stop crying, not due to any particular concern about the child, but rather to avoid having to hear the unpleasant sobbing.

One study found that people who reported feeling shock, terror, or horror when hearing about a major fire in Australia donated significantly more money to the victims than did those who did not experience such intense emotions (Amato, 1986). Similarly, people whose physiological responses show they are

arousal/cost-reward model a model describing helping behavior as caused by the physiological arousal resulting from seeing someone in need of help, but also the calculation of the costs and rewards of providing such help

FIGURE
13.3

THE AROUSAL/COST-REWARD MODEL OF HELPING

According to this model, people who see an emergency will experience unpleasant arousal (due to seeing others in distress), and then weigh the anticipated costs and benefits of helping to determine whether they will act.

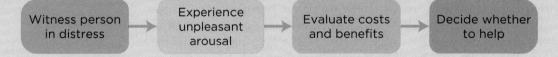

Witness person in distress → Experience unpleasant arousal → Evaluate costs and benefits → Decide whether to help

particularly distressed in response to seeing someone else in trouble give the most help (Krebs, 1975). In sum, individuals who experience shock and distress at watching something unpleasant may be motivated to help simply to reduce their own distress.

Even when people experience unpleasant arousal when they see others in pain, they compute the relative costs and benefits of helping before deciding to take action. (This model is similar to the *social exchange model* of relationship satisfaction, as described in Chapter 12.) For example, you may calculate the potential rewards to yourself and the victim (e.g., receiving a reward from the victim, becoming a hero, feeling good about yourself), as well as the potential costs (e.g., you yourself might die, you will lose time, you could be embarrassed; see Figure 13.3).

Impact of costs.   Do the costs of helping influence altruistic behavior? Yes (Piliavin & Piliavin, 1972; Piliavin, Piliavin, & Rodin, 1975; Wagner & Wheeler, 1969). In a study on a subway car in Philadelphia, three confederates watched as another confederate walked to the end of a car using a cane, and then fell on the ground. In some cases he just lay still, but in others, he lay still and started bleeding from the mouth (using some red dye he bit into). The other confederates timed how long it took someone to help him. As predicted, people were significantly less likely to help and took longer to help when he was bleeding than when he was not bleeding. (Given the HIV epidemic, the impact of seeing

Associated Press

In the NEWS   **The Costs of Helping.** On January 2, 2007, **Wesley Autrey**, a 50-year-old construction worker, dived onto the subway tracks to save a man who had suffered a seizure and fallen onto the tracks. Although Mr. Autrey did not know the man who had fallen onto the tracks, he risked his own life by jumping just in front of a subway train to hold the man down as five subway cars rolled just inches above them. "I don't feel like I did something spectacular; I just saw someone who needed help," Mr. Autrey said. "I did what I felt was right." This is a very unusual perspective.

blood at the time of helping would probably be even stronger today.) Although bleeding may imply personal harm, even non-life-threatening costs can decrease helping. As described earlier, Darley and Batson (1973) found that seminary students who were going to give a speech (ironically on the "Good Samaritan") were much more likely to help if they were early for their presentation than if they were late.

Unfortunately, teaching someone about the personal costs of prosocial behavior can lead to a decrease in helping. In one study by Frank and colleagues, students were asked at the beginning of the semester and again at the end how they would respond to a number of helping situations (e.g., if you found an addressed envelope with $100; Frank, Gilovich, & Regan, 1993). Of students in an astronomy class, 10% became less helpful over the course of the semester (not a very large decrease in helpfulness). Of those in an economics class, who presumably learned about the financial and personal costs of helping as part of course material, 28% became less helpful (a much more substantial drop in rate of helping).

Impact of benefits. Although the costs of prosocial behavior decrease the likelihood of helping, the benefits or rewards of prosocial behavior work to increase helping. That is why your parents give you an allowance—to reward helping around the house. Even hearing "thank you" can be a reward. One study found that subjects who were told "thank you" for exchanging roles with another subject (who was really a confederate) continued to be more helpful throughout the experiment than did those who did not receive this appreciation (McGovern, Ditzian, & Taylor, 1975). Similarly, more than 93% of those who received a kind thank you for giving a person directions later helped another person who had dropped a small bag (Moss & Page, 1972). In contrast, only 40% of those who were treated rudely when they were giving directions (the confederate interrupted them and said they'd just ask someone else) later helped. Children seem to be especially motivated by rewards; in one study, children who received praise for generosity were still more generous two weeks later (Rushton & Teachman, 1978).

But receiving certain types of rewards for prosocial behavior can actually lead to a decrease in helping. In one study, children were given either a few pennies or praise for helping (Smith, Gelfand, Hantman, & Partlow, 1979). When the children were later asked *why* they helped, those who received pennies reported it was to get the money. In contrast, those who simply received praise reported they had helped due to concern about another person's welfare.

Similarly, Richard Fabes and his colleagues examined altruistic behavior in children whose mothers said they often used rewards to get their child to engage in prosocial behavior (Fabes, Fultz, Eisenberg, May–Plumlee, & Christoper, 1989). The researchers gave half of the children a reward for helping children in a hospital (by making games for them). The others did not receive such a reward. When the children were then given a second chance to help these sick children, all of those who did not receive a reward helped compared to 44% of those who received a reward.

What causes this difference in helping behavior? Research suggests that when a reward is given, it undermines children's spontaneous helping (again, this is the phenomenon of *overjustification*, as you learned about in Chapter 3). In other words, giving a reward leads children to attribute their altruistic behavior to external, as opposed to internal, factors. My sons' preschool teachers experienced an unintended consequence after they instituted a "Peace Watch" in which teachers wrote down acts of generosity and cooperation displayed by the children (such as "Andrew handed Jade her lunch box," and "Zora and Brandon shared the trucks"). Although creating this list initially led to an increase in prosocial behavior, the teachers quickly found that after the children engaged in any type of helping, they raced over to a teacher and demanded that this behavior be added to the chart! Education Connections describes another way in which creating rewards can deter prosocial behavior.

What Are the Consequences of Requiring Volunteerism?

Did your high school require you to volunteer in order to graduate? An increasing number of schools are doing just that. Proponents of these programs describe the advantages for students and the community: students gain exposure to people who are often less fortunate than themselves, and learn skills for interacting with people from different backgrounds and with different experiences. Community organizations, including hospitals, nursing homes, and homeless shelters, gain valuable and much-needed support. But mandatory volunteer programs can also have significant drawbacks. The main problem with these programs is that requiring students to engage in altruistic behavior can lead people to make extrinsic, as opposed to intrinsic, attributions for this behavior. For example, a person who had always enjoyed volunteering on his or her own could now come to see volunteering as something one does only if it is mandated.

Arthur Tilley /Getty Images, Inc.

MOOD

Another situational factor that influences prosocial behavior is mood. Interestingly, both good and bad moods can lead to helping, as you'll see in this section.

Good mood effect. The *good mood effect* refers to the finding that helping behavior increases when people are in a good mood (Carlson, Charlin, & Miller, 1988). For example, people are more helpful after they are offered a cookie (Isen & Levin, 1972), are told they are especially intelligent (Weyant, 1978), find a dime (Isen & Levin, 1972), listen to a tape that makes them feel good about themselves (Rosenhan, Salovey, & Hargis, 1981), or listen to uplifting music

(North, Tarrant, & Hargreaves, 2004)! In fact, tipping is better on sunny days, presumably because we are happier on those days (Cunningham, 1979).

In one study, researchers approached people in a shopping mall and asked them for change for a dollar (Baron, 1997). In some cases the people were asked right in front of a "good-smelling" store (e.g., Cinnabon, Mrs. Fields). In other cases they were asked in front of a "neutral-smelling" store (e.g., Gap, Old Navy). Fifty-six percent helped when they were in front of a good-smelling store, as compared to only 19% of those in a neutral-smelling store.

What is it about a good mood that leads to helping? First, people who are in good moods want to maintain them, and seeing someone else who is in need could destroy the mood (Isen & Levin, 1972; Wegener & Petty, 1994). We therefore help other people in need in part to maintain our own good mood. Another reason why a good mood leads to helping may be that people who are in a good mood focus more on positive aspects of situations, such as the benefits of helping, rather than the negative aspects, such as the costs (Isen & Simmonds, 1978). So, being in a good mood may make the benefits of helping much more salient than the costs. A third possibility for why a good mood leads to helping is that people who are in a good mood experience increased self-awareness, which in turn leads them to try to match their behavior to their internal values (as you learned about in Chapter 3; Carlson et al., 1988; Duval et al., 1979; Hoover, Woods, & Knowles, 1983). For example, people who are looking at themselves in a mirror are more helpful than those who are not (Batson et al., 1999).

Bad moods.   Although good moods can increase the likelihood of prososical behavior, so can *bad moods* (Regan, Williams, & Sparling, 1972). In one study, an experimenter stopped a woman on the street and asked her to take his picture with a very expensive-looking camera (Cunningham, Steinberg, & Grev, 1980). He mentioned that the camera was sensitive, but that all she needed to do was aim and push one button. However, when she pushed the button, the camera did not work. In some cases, he dismissed the problem by saying "The camera acts up a lot." In other cases, he tried to make the woman feel guilty by saying she had jammed the camera by pushing too hard. Then, as the woman walked down the street, she noticed another person whose groceries were falling from a shopping bag. Who took advantage of this new opportunity to help? Only 15% of those who did not feel guilty compared to 55% of those who believed they broke the camera.

One reason why bad moods increase helping is our desire to make up for whatever we did that caused this negative feeling. In the case of the Cunningham et al. (1980) study in which participants thought they'd broken an expensive camera, helping someone else allows them to restore their positive self-image. Similarly, people who have been told they did badly on an IQ test help more, presumably to raise their self-esteem (Yagi & Shimizu, 1996).

But bad moods can also increase helping even when we aren't trying to make up for our own wrongdoing. For example, people who are asked to imagine the grief and worry one of their close friends would experience from dying of cancer later help more (Thompson, Cowan, & Rosenhan, 1980). We can simply want to make ourselves feel better by doing something good to counteract any overall bad feeling, regardless of its cause.

However, there is an important exception to this tendency for bad moods to increase helping: when we have been socially excluded, we are less likely to help (Twenge, Baumeister, DeWall, Ciarocco, & Bartels, 2007). In a series of studies, Jean Twenge and her colleagues have examined how people who believe other participants in a psychology study have rejected them as potential interaction partners react when later they are asked to help. Socially rejected people donate less money to a student fund, cooperate less in a game with another student, are less likely to volunteer for future psychology studies, and are less helpful when a researcher drops a bunch of pencils. These findings point to the negative impact of social rejection on likelihood of helping in many different ways.

MODELING

Questioning the Research

Several studies demonstrate that people who perform major acts of altruism, such as saving Jewish people during the Holocaust, report having very altruistic parents. But can you think of a problem with this type of research method? (Hint: Can we trust their self-reports?)

People can increase their altruistic behavior when such behavior is modeled for them by their parents, peers, or even media figures (Grusec & Skubiski, 1970; Hornstein, Fisch, & Holmes, 1968; Rushton, 1975; Sprafkin, Liebert, & Poulos, 1975). As described in Chapter 6, children learn much about social behaviors by watching—and imitating—others' behavior (Bandura, 1986). Many Germans who helped the Jews during World War II and many civil rights activists in the 1960s reported having parents who had very high moral standards, suggesting that this brave altruism was caused, at least in part, by modeling (Schroeder, Penner, Dovidio, & Piliavin, 1995). Many of the firefighters killed in the World Trade Center attacks on 9/11 had fathers, grandfathers, uncles, and brothers who were firefighters. These models probably helped them see the importance of risking their lives to help others.

Seeing other people engage in helping behavior gives us role models to follow, shows us the rewards of helping, and reminds us of the positive societal value of helping. In one study, a woman stood beside a car with a flat tire in a neighborhood in California (Bryan & Test, 1967). In some cases, the experimenters had put a man changing a flat tire for a woman 1/4 mile earlier in the road. Although most people didn't stop in either condition, 10 times as many people stopped after seeing the model. Similarly, watching another person donate to a Salvation Army kettle increased donations by seven percent (Bryan & Test, 1967). As described in Media Connections, exposure to positive models on television can lead to prosocial behavior.

But exposure to highly altruistic models can also decrease helping in some cases. People who see moderately helpful models and are then asked to help may agree to the request, but judge their motivation for such behavior to be externally based (e.g., due to social pressure; Thomas, Batson, & Coke, 1981). In turn, people who see highly altruistic models actually see themselves as less altruistic than those who are exposed to more moderately helpful models. Similarly, you may see yourself as very helpful if you volunteer at a homeless shelter one Sunday afternoon while your roommate watches National Football League (NFL) football...but you probably see yourself as much less helpful if your other roommate volunteers all day every Saturday. Finally, and as you learned earlier in this section, people who see an emergency in the presence of other people who do not react are particularly unlikely to act themselves.

ENVIRONMENTAL FACTORS

Environmental factors, such as the location of an emergency, influence prosocial behavior. Folk wisdom tells us that people are friendlier in rural towns than in large cities. We often think of people who live in country settings as more helpful and cooperative, and think of those who live in urban environments as more aloof and egocentric. But do these stereotypes give an accurate portrayal of these opposing environments? In large part, yes. People in small towns are more likely than those in urban areas to help others in a variety of small ways, including giving the time of day, participating in a survey, providing directions, returning a lost letter, and giving change (Amato, 1981, 1983; Levine, Martinez, Brase, & Sorenson, 1994; Steblay, 1987). People in small towns are also more likely to provide help in more serious situations, including helping an injured person and a lost child. In one study, a man limped down the street and then fell down with a cry of pain. He lifted the leg of his pants to reveal a heavily bandaged leg that was bleeding profusely. When this incident was staged in a small town, about half of the pedestrian witnesses helped. But when this incident was staged in a large city, only 15% of those helped.

Does Watching *Sesame Street* Lead to Prosocial Behavior?

Much evidence points to the hazards of exposing young children to violent and aggressive television. But can watching positive models on television lead children to engage in prosocial behavior? To answer this question, researchers conducted a meta-analysis, meaning a summary of the findings from multiple studies examining this issue (Mares & Woodard, 2005). The researchers gathered data from many studies in which children were exposed to positive behavior on television. Then they measured the effects of this exposure on four behaviors:

- positive interactions (friendly play or peaceful conflict resolution),
- altruism (sharing, donating, offering help, and comforting),
- stereotype reduction (exposure to counter-stereotypic portrayals of gender and ethnicity), and
- aggression (verbal and/or physical aggression).

As predicted, children who watched prosocial content behaved more positively as measured by all four behaviors. Males and females were equally affected by exposure to prosocial content. However, the older children in these studies (around age seven) benefited more than the younger children (as young as age three). For example, six-year-olds who see a

television show modeling helping behavior, such as a boy helping a dog, are much more likely to help in a later task than those who see a different episode of the same show (Sprafkin et al., 1975). Younger children may lack the cognitive ability to understand the nature of prosocial acts. This research suggests that television has the potential to lead to positive social interactions and outcomes.

©BananaStock/SUPERSTOCK

Why do people in cities help less? According to the **urban overload hypothesis** (Milgram, 1970), people in cities help less as a result of the greater stimulation they are exposed to. So, they have a desire to keep to themselves more (e.g., they learn to block things out). For example, people who see a person wearing a large cast on his or her arm drop several boxes of books are much less likely to help the person when there is lots of noise from a power lawn mower than when there is no such competing stimulus. Only 15% help in the first case, as compared to 80% in the second (Mathews & Canon, 1975). In addition, people who live in cities are likely to be less similar to each other (given the greater diversity of cities), to be more anonymous (so less accountable for their actions/inactions), and to be greater in number (so diffusion of responsibility occurs). It does not appear that people in cities are generally meaner or have been raised differently (e.g., people who are raised in cities versus small towns are equally likely to help/not help, depending on where they live when the help is required)!

Another environmental factor that can influence helping behavior is the region of the country. Table 13.1 shows the regions of the country where people are more likely to receive different types of help. Across many of these measures, people in the South were more likely to give help than those in the Northeast or West (Levine et al., 1994). However, people in the North central are as likely as those in the South to give change and help a blind person, and are more likely than those in other parts of the country to help mail a lost letter.

urban overload hypothesis a hypothesis that people who live in urban areas are constantly exposed to stimulation, which in turn leads them to decrease their awareness of their environment

TABLE 13.1 PERCENTAGE OF PEOPLE WHO HELP IN A GIVEN SITUATION BY REGION OF THE COUNTRY

	PICKED UP AND RETURNED A DROPPED PEN	PICKED UP MAGAZINES FOR A PERSON WITH A HURT LEG	HELPED A BLIND PERSON CROSS A STREET	GAVE CHANGE FOR A QUARTER	MAILED A LOST LETTER
South	57	69	57	78	76
North Central	43	59	56	78	87
Northeast	53	60	45	59	75
West	45	53	40	65	72

This table shows regional differences in the percentage of people who help in a given situation.

Source: Levine, R. V., Martinez, T. S., Brase, G., & Sorenson, K. (1994). Helping in 36 U.S. cities. *Journal of Personality and Social Psychology, 67*, 69-82.

HOW SITUATIONAL FACTORS INFLUENCE HELPING

Concepts in Context

MODEL	EXAMPLE
Decision-making model	Chris and Joilene are walking across campus late at night. They hear screams coming from an open window. At first they discuss whether they should call the police. Then they notice several other people walking near them who have clearly also heard the screams and have not reacted at all to the noise. So, they decide the screams must just be someone having some fun, and continue on home.
Arousal/cost–reward model	Cindy walks out of a store and notices a small puppy playing near a busy road. She goes over to the dog to see if it is wearing a tag so she can contact its owner. But the dog is not wearing a collar, and clearly seems to be lost. Cindy knows she should take the dog to a shelter, but she's running late for a job interview. She gets into her car and drives away.
Mood	Ji Ling has just received a compliment from her boss about a proposal she submitted, and is feeling very happy. When a man on the subway asks her for change to buy food, she hands him a dollar.
Modeling	Ray hates to donate blood. But after his roommate announces his own intention to donate (following a televised plea for more blood from a local hospital), Ray reluctantly agrees to donate.
Environment	Leandra has recently moved to Boston from a small town in Maine. After she drops a stack of papers on the street, she is surprised that no one stops to help her pick them up—which she is certain would have happened in the town where she grew up.

DOES PURE ALTRUISM EXIST?

Q A

Think about a time in which you've helped someone else. Was this helping motivated by a genuine desire to help, or a desire to make yourself feel better? Researchers in social psychology disagree about the factors that motivate prosocial behavior. In one study, researchers examined the motivations of volunteers who worked at an AIDS service organization (Stürmer, Snyder, & Omoto, 2005). These volunteers completed questionnaires prior to starting their volunteer training, after completing their training but before starting their volunteer work, and again after three months and six months of service. These questionnaires examined volunteers' motivations for helping, level of empathy, and amount of help actually provided. Findings indicated that for heterosexual volunteers, the best predictor of helping was their feelings about the person they were helping—meaning whether they liked this person and enjoyed spending time with him or her. On the other hand, for homosexual volunteers, the best predictor of helping was their empathy for the person they were helping—meaning their feelings of concern, warmth, and compassion toward this person. Because all of the clients who were receiving help were homosexual men, this study shows that people who identify with this person (that is, the homosexual volunteers) are more motivated to help out of feelings of empathy. In contrast, those who do not identify with this person are primarily motivated to help out of feelings of personal benefit. So, do people help out of true empathy for others, or to help themselves? This section will compare two distinct hypotheses: the empathy-altruism hypothesis and the negative-state relief hypothesis.

EMPATHY-ALTRUISM HYPOTHESIS

According to the **empathy-altruism hypothesis**, some helpful actions are genuinely motivated by a desire to do good for others (Batson, 1981). Infants cry more when they hear another infant crying, suggesting that empathy may be a natural part of human nature (Hoffman, 1981). For example, even one-day-old infants cry in response to hearing other infants cry, and this noise produces even more distress than hearing tapes of their own cries (Martin & Clark, 1982). In turn, empathic concern for a person in need produces an altruistic motive for helping.

empathy-altruism hypothesis a hypothesis that when we feel empathy for a person, we will help that person even if we incur a cost by doing so

If someone does not adopt the other's perspective but notices that the person is in distress, he or she may still be motivated to relieve that person's distress to relieve his or her own concern. However, this type of motive for helping would not be altruistic, but rather egoistic, because the goal of the behavior is not easing the other person's burden, but relieving one's own distress. Daniel Batson (1991) believes that most helping is motivated by self-focused concerns, but that true altruism does exist.

As shown in Figure 13.4, when individuals take the perspective of the person in need, they will feel concern and therefore be motivated to help relieve the person's distress. As described at the start of this section, gay men help people who are HIV-positive due to feelings of empathy, presumably because they identify with them. Heterosexual men, on the other hand, help largely due to their own feelings of

"Here I was, all this time, worrying that maybe I'm a selfish person, and now it turns out I've been suffering from compassion fatigue."

FIGURE
13.4

THE ROLE OF DIFFERENT MOTIVATIONS IN HELPING

According to Batson's model, people can help for either egoistic or altruistic motives, depending on whether they adopt the other person's perspective and therefore feel empathy.

Source: Batson, C. D. (1991). The Altruism Question: Toward a Social-Psychological Answer. Hillsdale, NJ: Erlbaum.

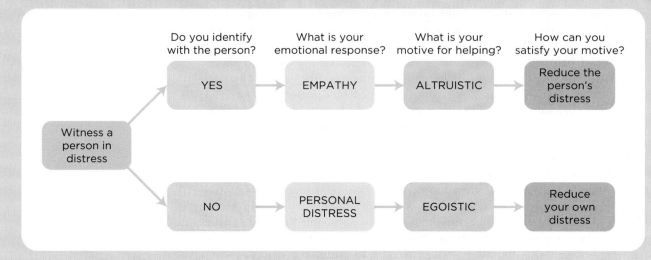

| Do you identify with the person? | What is your emotional response? | What is your motive for helping? | How can you satisfy your motive? |

Witness a person in distress

YES → EMPATHY → ALTRUISTIC → Reduce the person's distress

NO → PERSONAL DISTRESS → EGOISTIC → Reduce your own distress

Even children can feel empathy, and thus may feel sad themselves when they see another child who is sad.

stockbyte/Getty Images, Inc.

satisfaction. Research Focus on Neuroscience describes how different portions of the brain are activated when imagining your own experience of an emotion versus taking someone else's perspective.

RESEARCH FOCUS ON NEUROSCIENCE
How Perspective-Taking Looks in the Brain

According to the empathy-altruism hypothesis, one key factor that influences whether a person engages in prosocial behavior is whether that person can adopt someone else's perspective. Recent research in neuroscience examines whether different parts of the brain process emotions when we are imagining ourselves experiencing them compared to when we are imagining other people experiencing them. In one study, participants were given short written statements that described social emotions (Ruby & Decety, 2004). These social emotions included

- shame (someone opens the toilet door that you have forgotten to lock),
- irritation (someone knocks over a coffee cup on your clothes), and
- pride (a job promotion is promised to you).

Then the participants were asked to imagine how they would feel if they were in those situations, and how their mothers would feel in those situations. Researchers used PET (positron emission tomography) scans of their brains to show which portions of the brain were activated when participants imagined each type of social emotion from both their own and their mothers' perspective. When participants adopted their mothers' perspective, portions of the brain that are associated with perspective-taking processes were activated. This research provides evidence that different portions of the brain process different types of emotion-relevant stimuli, depending on whether we are thinking about these emotions from one's own perspective or from another person's perspective.

Batson and his colleagues have conducted several studies to distinguish between people's motivations to help to make themselves feel better (e.g., egoism) versus to make others feel better (e.g., altruism). What determines which motivation a person will have in a given situation? People may feel empathy with a person based on their own personality (i.e., whether they are generally high in empathy). People may also feel empathy due to something about the other person (i.e., feeling a special connection to the person in need of help, such as sharing similar interests). Let's examine research on each of these processes.

Impact of empathic motives.   In one of the earliest studies to test the empathy theory of helping, Miho Toi and Daniel Batson (1982) played a tape for students describing another student, Carol Marcy, who had broken both of her legs in a car accident. Carol needed a tutor for her psychology class so she could graduate on time. In some cases, students were told that regardless of their decision, they would continue to see Carol over the course of the semester, making the costs of not helping (that is, feeling guilty and ashamed) relatively high. In other cases, students were told that it was unlikely they would ever see Carol again, making the costs of not helping quite low.

So, who chose to help Carol? Students with generally empathic motives helped at about equal levels regardless of whether the costs of helping were high or low—81% and 71%, respectively. Students with generally egoistic motives who thought the costs of not helping would be high were also very likely to help—76%. However, students who were motivated by egoistic concerns and who believed the costs of not helping would be low were very unlikely to help: only 33% of the students in this condition agreed to serve as a tutor.

Empathic motives can also be created simply by imagining one's self in another person's place, which in turn creates helping behavior (Batson et al., 2003). In one study, participants were asked to assign both themselves and another student to research tasks. In each case, one task was more desirable than the other, and participants were given the option of simply choosing the task they preferred or flipping a coin to choose which person did which task. Before making the decision about which task each person would do, participants in one condition were asked to complete a perspective-taking exercise, in which they were told to "Imagine how the other participant will likely feel when told which task he or she is to do." Participants in the control condition were not asked to complete this imagination task. In line with predictions, 75% of students in the control condition assigned the more desirable task to themselves. In contrast, only 42% of those in the perspective-taking condition assigned the more desirable task to themselves. This study provides compelling evidence that imagining yourself in someone else's shoes can increase prosocial behavior.

Impact of feeling similar.   Feeling similar to someone else also increases empathy and, in turn, helping. In one of the first studies to test the empathy-altruism hypothesis, Daniel Batson and his colleagues at the University of Kansas conducted a study to examine the impact of empathy on altruism (Batson, Duncan, Ackerman, Buckley, & Birch, 1981). The subject is told that this study involves the effect of unpleasant conditions on task performance, and that one person will be randomly chosen to be the learner and one will be the observer. The "subjects" draw lots, and the real subject is always the observer. While in the observing room, you see the confederate hooked up to some scary equipment. She "receives some shocks" and seems uncomfortable. Then she tells the experimenter about a frightening experience she had as a child in which she was thrown from a horse onto an electric fence. Elaine, the confederate, is willing to continue, but the experimenter is not sure if that makes sense. So the experimenter asks you if you will trade places with her. At the beginning of the study, half of the subjects were told that she and Elaine were very similar in values and interests. The other half was told that they were very different. In addition, half of the subjects were told that they could leave after witnessing two of the ten trials during which Elaine would receive random shocks, and the others were told they would need to watch all ten trials.

So who switched places? As shown in Figure 13.5, for those who felt little or no empathy for Elaine, the difficulty of the escape made all the difference. Specifically, those who were in the difficult escape condition were moderately likely to switch, and those in the easy escape condition were very unlikely to help. In contrast, most of the high-empathy (similar) subjects helped, regardless of whether they had an easy or difficult escape.

Research also reveals that empathy is a particularly strong predictor of helping behavior when the helper and the target belong to the same cultural group (Stürmer, Snyder, Kropp, & Siem, 2006). In this case, feeling similar to the person who is in need of help increases feelings of empathy, which in turn increases helping behavior. For example, students who themselves have been through a difficult romantic break-up feel more empathy for another person who has

FIGURE 13.5

HOW DOES EMPATHY IMPACT HELPING?

In this experiment, participants were asked to trade places with a person who was receiving electrical shocks. As predicted, a higher percentage of participants who were similar to the victim helped regardless of whether they are able to leave the experiment quickly or remain through all the trials, suggesting that their behavior is truly motivated by empathic concern for the victim.

Source: Batson, C.D., Duncan, B.D., Ackerman, P., Buckley, T., & Birch, K. (1981). Is empathic emotion a source of altruistic motivation? *Journal of Personality and Social Psychology, 40,* 290-302.

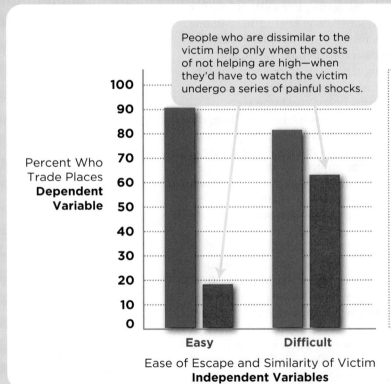

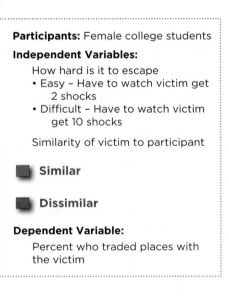

People who are dissimilar to the victim help only when the costs of not helping are high—when they'd have to watch the victim undergo a series of painful shocks.

Percent Who Trade Places **Dependent Variable**

Easy   Difficult

Ease of Escape and Similarity of Victim
Independent Variables

Participants: Female college students

Independent Variables:

How hard is it to escape
• Easy – Have to watch victim get 2 shocks
• Difficult – Have to watch victim get 10 shocks

Similarity of victim to participant

■ **Similar**

■ **Dissimilar**

Dependent Variable:

Percent who traded places with the victim

experienced such a break-up (Batson, Sympson, Hindman, & Decruz, 1996). Similarly, students who feel similar in terms of personality and beliefs to a young woman who they are told is a cancer patient are more supportive and warm toward her than those who feel less similar (Westmaas & Silver, 2006).

NEGATIVE-STATE RELIEF HYPOTHESIS

In contrast to the empathy-altruism model, the **negative-state relief hypothesis or egoistic-altruism hypothesis** describes people's altruistic behavior as motivated by their expected benefits in terms of mood (Cialdini, Kenrick, & Baumann, 1982; Cialdini, Schaller, Houlihan, Arps, Fultz, & Beaman, 1987). According to this model, prosocial behavior can be motivated by selfish motives, such as making yourself feel better, gaining respect from others, or even for tangible rewards (Batson, 1998). For example, you may be motivated to help build a Habitat for Humanity house because it will give you something to write about on a college application, or be motivated to donate to a local hospital because your name will be publicized to others. In other words, people help because it makes them feel better about themselves (not to make other people feel better), and hence helping is based in egoistic factors.

This motive for prosocial behavior is illustrated by a famous story about Abraham Lincoln (Sharp, 1928). As Lincoln was in a carriage crossing over a bridge, he noticed a number of baby pigs who were in great danger of drowning. He quickly jumped out of the carriage, ran to the pigs, and carried them to safety. When he returned to the carriage and was praised for his generosity, he remarked that "...that was the very essence of selfishness. I should have had no peace of mind all day had I gone on and left that suffering old sow worrying over those pigs. I did it to get some peace of mind..." (Sharp, 1928, p. 75).

"Hey, there's Sara, padding her college-entrance résumé!"

Although helping for selfish reasons doesn't really fit our definition of true altruism, this type of motivation may ironically lead to providing more help (Omoto & Snyder, 1995). Allen Omoto and Mark Snyder examined the motivations of people who volunteered to help persons with AIDS, and then measured how long the volunteers continued to work. People who were motivated to work for more altruistic motives (e.g., wanting to help others, wanting to contribute to their community) were less likely to continue volunteering than those who were motivated by more selfish concerns (e.g., wanting to make friends, wanting to learn more about HIV prevention). Would You Believe describes a perhaps surprising way in which helping other people increases our own happiness.

According to the negative-state relief, or egoistic, model of helping, helping occurs under two conditions: if one is in a bad mood, and if helping can lead to improvement in mood. Let's examine each of these two conditions.

Helping occurs to relieve one's own bad mood.

Although this hypothesis predicts that people who are in a bad mood will be motivated to help to make themselves feel better, if they can feel better in some other way, they will not help. To test this aspect of the negative-state relief hypothesis, Bob Cialdini and his colleagues made participants believe they had accidentally ruined a graduate student's data (Cialdini, Darby, & Vincent, 1973). Some of the participants

WOULD YOU BELIEVE... Spending Money on Other People **Makes Us Happy?** The egoistic model of helping suggests that helping others makes us happy, and thus helping is motivated by our own desire to feel better. In line with this view, recent research reveals that helping others may make us happier than helping ourselves. In one study, researchers asked a national sample of American adults to rate their general happiness, and to report how much they spent in a typical month on four distinct types of items: bills and expenses, gifts for themselves, gifts to others, donations to charity (Dunn, Aknin, & Norton, 2008). Although the amount people spent on themselves was not related to overall happiness, people who spent more money on other people (either through gifts to those they knew or contributions to charities) reported higher levels of happiness. Next, these researchers examined how employees spent an unexpected profit-sharing bonus from their company, and whether their spending decisions predicted happiness six to eight weeks later. As predicted, employees who spent this money on other people (buying something for someone else or donating it to charity) experienced greater happiness than those who spent this money on themselves (paying bills or the mortgage or buying something for themselves). Finally, researchers conducted a very clever experimental study. In this study, participants were given an envelope containing $20.00 and were told they needed to spend the money by 5 PM that day. Some participants were told they needed to spend this money on a bill, expense, or a gift for themselves; others were told they needed to spend this money on a gift for someone else or as a donation to a charity. Researchers then asked participants to return to the psychology department that day at 5 PM to report their happiness. As predicted, participants who spent the money on someone else were happier than those who spent the money on themselves. All of this research points to what may be a surprising conclusion: spending money on other people makes us happier than spending money on ourselves.

later participated in a positive event (received praise for doing well), and others did not. As predicted, more than 70% of those help when they feel guilty and have no other way of making themselves feel better. In contrast, fewer than 30% of those who receive praise for their performance on a subsequent task help. Those who receive praise for their performance don't need to help because they already feel better. Even the expectation that you will soon feel better can decrease helping. For example, people who feel sad due to their empathy for another person but who believe their sadness will soon be alleviated by listening to a comedy tape are less likely to help than those who do not see their mood as soon ending (Schaller & Cialdini, 1988).

Developmental psychology offers additional evidence for the negative-state relief model of helping. As described earlier in the chapter, young children do not yet understand that helping can increase one's own mood, and therefore have egoistic benefits (Eisenberg & Miller, 1987). Therefore, children should be less motivated to help due to the expectation of improving their own mood than would teenagers, who understand the personal benefit of helping. To test this hypothesis, Cialdini and Kenrick (1976) asked children (ages 6 to 8) and teenagers (ages 15 to 18) to think of something very sad (such as the death of a favorite pet) or something neutral. They were then given a chance to help other students by sharing some of the prizes they had won in a game. As predicted, young children, who did not yet see the connection between helping others and feeling good themselves, donated about half as many prizes in the sad condition as in the neutral condition. In contrast, teenagers, who understand that behaving altruistically can feel good, donated over four times as many coupons in the sad condition as in the neutral condition.

Questioning the Research

This study suggests that teenagers understand that helping can lead to improvements in one's own mood, which in turn leads older children to engage in higher levels of helping behavior than younger children. But can you think of another explanation for the findings? (Hint: Could teenagers just be more motivated to appear good than younger children?)

Helping won't occur if mood improvement is impossible.

Another egoistic explanation for helping behavior is that empathic people feel sad when they see others in need, and so the empathic person is motivated to help purely to relieve this unpleasant state (Cialdini et al., 1987). In turn, people will be motivated to help others only when they believe that helping will relieve their bad feelings; in other words, why should people go to the trouble of helping if they aren't going to feel better?

To test this proposition, researchers asked some students to remember their most personally distressing memories (to put them in a sad mood), and others to remember the route they had taken to school (to put them in a neutral mood, and still others to remember a positive memory (to put them in a happy mood; Manucia, Baumann, & Cialdini, 1984). They then drank a cup of "memory drug" called Mnemoxine (it was actually flat tonic water). The researchers then told half of the students in each condition that the drug would have no mood-related side effects, and told the others that a standard side effect of the drug was to preserve chemically for 25 minutes whatever mood you are in when you take the drug. The experimenter then left the room to get some forms, at which point a

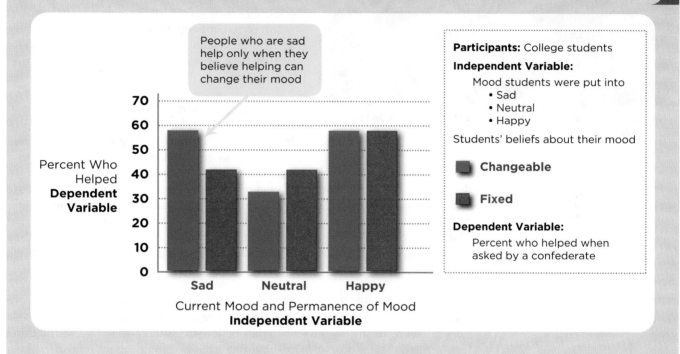

FIGURE 13.6

HOW DOES MOOD IMPACT HELPING?

Experimenters put students in sad, neutral, or happy moods, and then led them to believe their mood could either change or be stuck the same way for the next 25 minutes, before giving them an opportunity to help. A higher percentage of sad participants helped than happy or neutral mood participants when they believed helping could lead to mood improvements, suggesting that we help in order to reduce our own negative feelings.

Source: Manucia, G.K., Baumann, D., J., & Cialdini, R.B. (1984). Mood influences on helping: Direct effects or side effects? *Journal of Personality and Social Psychology, 46*, 357-364.

confederate appeared and asked the students to make some calls seeking blood donors. The dependent variable was the percent of the students who agreed to help make the calls. As shown in Figure 13.6, students who were in a sad mood and believed the drug would help their mood were much more likely to help than those who believed that helping would not improve their mood.

COMPARING THE MODELS

There is considerable debate among social psychologists about the presence of true altruism. Researchers continue to examine the conditions that lead to altruistic behavior, and whether such behavior is motivated by egoistic or altruistic factors. One study by Bob Cialdini and his colleagues found that the conditions that lead to empathy also lead to a greater sense of overlap with other people. In turn, empathy for others may really be aimed at helping one's self (Cialdini, Brown, Lewis, Luce, & Neuberg, 1997). Not surprisingly, Batson and his colleagues dispute this (Batson, Sager, Garst, Kang, Rubchinsky, & Dawson, 1997). Is the debate on egoistic versus altruistic motivations for helping settled? Not at all.

Although these models may seem to contradict one another, they do agree that at times people engage in helping for egoistic reasons. The main difference between these models is that the empathy-altruism model describes the self-benefits of helping as unintended consequences, yet the negative-state relief hypothesis describes these benefits as the primary motivation for helping. What are these benefits to the self? They can be grouped into three categories: reduction of aversive arousal, fear of punishment for not helping, and desire for reward. Let's examine each of these categories.

Seeing people who are in need of help can make us feel bad, and thus we may help in part to reduce our feelings of arousal in this situation.

©BananaStock/SUPERSTOCK

Reduction of aversive arousal.
The most common egoistic explanation for helping is that people want to reduce the unpleasant arousal they experience when hearing or seeing someone who is in distress. This is why Abraham Lincoln helped the drowning pigs, and why even strangers want to comfort crying babies on airplanes. However, Batson and his colleagues (1981) argue that people who feel empathy for the person in distress help even when they could avoid hearing the person in distress by leaving. Although people who do not feel such connection to the victim help only when they are forced to continue listening to the suffering, people who feel genuine empathy help regardless of whether they have an easy or difficult escape from the situation.

Fear of punishment for not helping.
Another egoistic explanation for helping is that people know that helping is "the right thing to do," and hence are worried about feeling guilty or ashamed if they do not help. Once again, in this case, helping would really be motivated by a desire not to feel lousy about one's own behavior, and not by a true desire to improve another person's welfare (Schaller & Cialdini, 1988). Although this is a tough question to directly test, Batson and his colleagues created a clever study to do just that (Batson et al., 1988). They specifically told participants that most people in their situation did *not* help. Did this knowledge decrease helping behavior? Not at all, for people who felt empathy for the victim.

Desire for reward.
Finally, and as discussed earlier in the chapter, people learn fairly early in life that they can receive rewards for helping. In turn, people may behave altruistically only when they believe that others will notice—and think less of them if they do not help—and therefore helping is again motivated by a self-focused concern (Fultz, Batson, Fortenbach, McCarthy, & Varney, 1986). To test this explanation for helping behavior, some students were made to feel empathy for a person in distress and others were not. Then, some students were given an opportunity to help this person. Regardless of whether anyone, including the person who was in trouble, would know that they declined to help, people who were high in empathy were much more likely to offer help. This finding showing that people demonstrate the same kind of altruistic behavior regardless of whether they believe someone else is watching provides strong evidence that the helping is not simply motivated by an expectation of personal benefits.

PREDICTING LONG-TERM HELPING

Although helping may be motivated by either empathic or egoistic factors, helping motivated by empathy is most likely to lead to long-term helping. In December 2001, researchers at the University of Tennessee conducted a study to examine the frequency of helping and the motivation for helping following 9/11 (Piferi, Jobe, & Jones, 2006). In this sample of college students, 62% reported giving some type of aid to those involved in the attacks. The most common types of support provided were sending money (66%), praying (35%), and donating blood (24%). What motivated this aid? (Remember, this study took place in Tennessee, and only 7% of the sample even knew someone who lived in New York or Washington.)

- Thirty-four percent of those who gave support reported they were motivated to relieve their own personal pain due to the event.
- Twenty-two percent reported they were motivated to give because they would expect others to help them if the roles were reversed.

- Approximately 20% reported providing help because they recognized that other people were suffering.
- Another 19% felt it was the patriotic thing to do.
- Fifteen percent felt it was their duty to give.
- Approximately 12% helped because they knew someone who was involved.

However, when researchers followed up with these participants one year later and asked whether they were still giving, 80% of those who helped for other-focused reasons (that is, they recognized that others were suffering) were still giving. Fewer than half of those who were helping for any other reason were still giving one year later.

DOES PURE ALTRUISM EXIST?

Concepts in Context

MODEL	EXAMPLE
Empathy-altruism model	Ryder's seven-year-old sister, Amanda, is very scared of the dark. Ryder has an important chemistry test to study for, but chooses to stay in Amanda's room with her until she falls asleep. He remembers when he was younger and was also scared of the dark.
Egoistic-altruism model	Vicky is leaving a very depressing movie with some friends when she notices a woman struggling to change a flat tire. Vicky decides to stop and help because she hopes engaging in this act of kindness will improve her mood.

WHO GETS HELP WHEN THEY ARE IN NEED?

Think about a time in which a stranger has asked you for help. Maybe he or she needed directions, or change for a dollar, or the time. Did you help? If not, why not? Research in social psychology suggests that aspects of the person as well as your relationship influence whether help is provided. In one study, both male and female researchers asked people for help in 120 bus stations across the United States (Pearce, 1980). The requests for help were relatively minor: "Do you have the time?" and "Where can I stay in this city?" Some of the people who requested help were "familiar strangers," meaning they had ridden on the bus with the people they asked for help and so they looked familiar. Others who requested help were "unfamiliar strangers"—they asked for help from people who had never seen them before.

Who was most likely to receive help? Familiar strangers were helped more than total strangers. Females were helped significantly more often than males. This section will describe why both familiarity and gender influence getting help. In addition, we'll examine how person factors, social norms, and relationship factors influence getting help.

PERSON FACTORS

Some people are much more likely to receive help than others. This section will examine the impact of person factors, including gender, age, attractiveness, and personality, on help received.

Gender. Gender has a strong influence on who gets help, with women being more likely than men to receive help (Bruder-Mattson & Hovanitz, 1990; Good, Dell, & Mintz, 1989). As described at the start of this section, strangers are more likely to respond to simple questions (e.g., what time is it, where's the nearest post office) posed by females than males (Pearce, 1980).

"We've been wandering in the desert for forty years. But he's a man—would he ever ask directions?"

But this gender difference doesn't mean that people aren't willing to help men, but rather that men may be less interested in or even willing to receive help than women (Barbee, Cunningham, Winstead, & Derlega, 1993; Eagly & Crowley, 1986). The often-cited example of men's failure to ask for directions illustrates this point. Seeking help is more threatening to men, and in this way has more costs. In line with this view, men are more likely than women to worry about how people will react if they request help (Bruder-Mattson & Hovanitz, 1990). The potential costs of helping for men—admitting weakness, depending on others—may simply be too high.

Age. Another demographic factor that influences how much help we want as well as how much help we get is age (Shell & Eisenberg, 1992). As you might expect, children are very willing to seek help, in part because they legitimately need a lot of help, and in part because they do not see asking for help as a sign of weakness. However, as children get older, they become aware that requesting help can show weakness and dependence on others, and therefore they become more reluctant to seek help.

Attractiveness. Perhaps not surprisingly, attractive people get more help (Benson, Karabenick, & Lerner, 1976). Attractive people are more likely to receive directions, assistance mailing a letter, and change for a dollar (Wilson, 1978; Wilson & Dovidio, 1985). People also spend more time giving directions to attractive people than to unattractive people (Harrell, 1978).

These cases have described helping in a direct situation, in which the potential rewards for helping an attractive person are clear. For example, an attractive person might appreciate the help, and the helper might benefit by getting future interactions with that person. But attractive people also get more help in situations in which there is no possibility of future interaction. In one study, a stamped, completed application to psychology graduate school was left in a phone booth (Benson et al., 1976). There was a photo of the applicant, who in some cases was very attractive and in some cases was very unattractive. The attractive applicant got helped 47% of the time versus 35% of the time for the unattractive applicant.

Personality. Personality factors, such as shyness, anxiety, and self-esteem, also influence the likelihood of receiving help (DePaulo, Dull, Greenberg, & Swaim, 1989). For example, people who are socially anxious receive lower levels of social support from their friends (Caldwell & Reinhart, 1988). Bella DePaulo and colleagues found that shy people were less effective than non-shy people at getting people to return a questionnaire (1989). When they make phone calls, they sound less warm and confident, and speak less fluently. This behavior elicits fewer responses. Although shy and non-shy people did not differ in their frequency of asking for help, shy people were especially reluctant to ask for help from a member of the opposite sex.

Self-esteem has a mixed effect on likelihood of receiving help. On the one hand, people who are high in self-esteem are generally less willing to ask for help, in part because they do not want to feel weak or dependent (Nadler, Mayseless, Peri, & Chemerinski, 1985). Also, people who are high in self-esteem and get unsolicited help feel particularly bad (Nadler, Altman, & Fisher, 1979)!

Questioning the Research

This study suggests that people who are socially anxious receive little social support from their friends. Can you think of an alternative explanation for this association? (Hint: Is this link correlation or causation?)

On the other hand, people with high self-esteem are more likely to receive, and benefit from, social support One study with college students found that those with high self-esteem were more likely to receive social support from their families than those with low self-esteem (Caldwell & Reinhart, 1988).

SOCIAL NORMS

Social norms also influence helping. Let's examine two norms that are associated with prosocial behavior: The norm of reciprocity and the norm of social responsibility.

Norm of reciprocity. As you learned in Chapter 8, according to the **norm of reciprocity**, people usually give back to people who have given to them (Wilke & Lanzetta, 1970, 1982). Social marketers, who use commercial marketing techniques to promote the adoption of positive health or social behaviors, often rely on the norm of reciprocity to motivate people to make donations they might otherwise not have made. For example, charitable organizations often send out small "gifts," such as greeting cards, address labels, and wrapping paper. This organization hopes that, in return for this gift, people will feel obligated to give a donation to thank them for their generosity. Similarly, waiters often use the norm of reciprocity to encourage better tipping: customers who receive a small piece of candy with their check tip more than customers who don't receive candy (Strohmetz, Rind, Fisher, & Lind, 2002).

One clever study by Dennis Regan (1971) examined the norm of reciprocity in an experimental setting. Two students (one subject and one confederate) worked on a task, and were then given a short break. In one condition the confederate returned from the break with two sodas—one for himself and one for his partner. At the end of the study, the confederate asked the subject whether he would like to buy some raffle tickets, which could earn the confederate a nice prize. Subjects who received the soda bought twice as many tickets as those who did not receive the soda—and in fact, they spent nearly five times as much as the confederate did buying the soda!

> **norm of reciprocity** the idea that we should help those who are in need of assistance, because they will then help us in the future

Norm of social responsibility. The **norm of social responsibility** describes people's obligation to help those who are in need of assistance, even if you have no expectation that you will later receive help from them (Berkowitz & Daniels, 1963). For example, are you motivated to give money to a person who is homeless, or to hold a door open for a person in a wheelchair? If so, you have a sense of social responsibility. According to Bierhoff, Klein, and Kramp (1991), people with a greater sense of social responsibility are more likely to help victims of a traffic accident than those who are lower on this measure.

> **norm of social responsibility** the idea that we have an obligation to help those who are in need of assistance, even if we have no expectation that we will later receive help from them

We are especially likely to help other people if we see their need for help as caused by something beyond their control. For example, in 2005, Americans gave an estimated $260 billion dollars to charity, including 1.93 billion to help the victims of a South Asian tsunami and 5.3 billion to help the victims of Hurricane Katrina.

But we don't always help people who need help. In situations in which we hold the person responsible for his/her predicament, we may be much less likely to help (Meyer & Mulherin, 1990; Schmidt & Weiner, 1988). For example, in the early years of the AIDS epidemic, people were much more motivated to donate money to groups for persons with HIV who were not seen as responsible for acquiring the disease (e.g., people who became infected through a blood transfusion, infants who were infected through their mothers) than to groups supporting

AFP /Getty Images, Inc.

Professional tennis player Arthur Ashe died of AIDS in 1993. He acquired HIV through a blood transfusion, and thus was seen as a "blameless victim," unlike those who acquire HIV in other ways.

other people with HIV (e.g., IV drug users, gay men; see Weiner, Perry, & Magnusson, 1988).

Why do people see some people as "deserving" of help, and others as not? As you read in Chapter 4, the attributions people make about why a person has a need for help influence whether they give help (Weiner, 1980, 1986). The phenomenon known as **belief in a just world** describes our tendency to assume that good things happen to good people and bad things happen to bad people (Lerner, 1980; Lipkus et al., 1996). In turn, we are more likely to help someone if we don't see that person as responsible for his or her current situation (Skikta, 1999). For example, conservatives generally see poverty as caused by a lack of intelligence and moral standards, whereas liberals tend to see poverty as caused by unjust social practices and structures. These differing views on the causes of poverty help explain why liberals tend to favor, whereas conservatives tend to oppose, increased spending on social programs.

belief in a just world the phenomenon in which people believe that bad things happen to bad people and that good things happen to good people

The attributions we make even for people's minor requests can influence whether, and how much, we help. Schmidt and Weiner (1988) presented students with a scenario about a classmate asking to borrow their lecture notes. Students were much more likely to help the person who was wearing an eye patch and dark glasses, presumably because this person was unable to take his own notes due to circumstances beyond his control, than the person who admitted he missed class to go to the beach!

RELATIONSHIP FACTORS

Although thus far the chapter has focused on personal factors that influence helping, in many cases such behavior is not simply a function of aspects of the other person, but also of the connection between that person and ourselves. This section will examine the impact of relationship factors on who we help, including similarity and friendship.

Similarity. We are most likely to help those who are similar to us—in dress, gender, nationality, and attitudes (Dovidio & Morris, 1975; Holloway, Tucker, & Hornstein, 1977; Krebs, 1975). In a series of studies in Boston, Paris, and Athens, researchers examined helping behavior for natives of the country, foreigners who spoke the language, and foreigners who did not speak the language (Feldman, 1968). Types of helping behavior included giving directions, mailing a letter, and being correctly charged for a cab ride. Results consistently showed that people help those who are most similar. For example, 24% of the time natives were not given directions and natives were never given wrong directions. Foreigners were not helped in 35% of the instances when they asked for help, and were given wrong directions 10% of the times they asked. So, only about half of the time do foreigners get useful help. As described in Law Connections, we also give shorter sentences to people who are of our same race, a particularly salient type of similarity (Sommers & Ellsworth, 2000).

Even similarity based on relatively superficial characteristics—such as the sports team one roots for—can lead to greater helping. In one study conducted in England, participants who were soccer fans were recruited to take part in a study (Levine, Prosser, Evans, & Reicher, 2005). Unbeknownst to the participants, only those who had specifically identified themselves as fans of the Manchester United soccer team were invited to participate in the study. Participants came into the psychology department to complete a series of questionnaires, and were then told to walk to another part of the building to complete the next part of the study. As the participants rounded a hallway, they saw another person (really a confederate of the experimenter) slip and fall, and then cry out while holding his ankle. In some conditions, this person was wearing a soccer jersey for Manchester United. In other conditions, he was wearing a soccer jersey for Liverpool (a rival team). In the third (control) condition, he was wearing a shirt with no team name on it. Researchers then examined whether participants stopped and helped the injured person. As predicted, participants were much more likely to help someone who was wearing a Manchester United

The Impact of Similarity of Race on Guilt

Jury decision making is a complex process that requires people to process diverse pieces of information—often some pointing to the defendant's guilt and others point to innocence—and ultimately reach a decision with substantial consequences. So, we'd like to believe that this process is fair and just—that jurors make decisions based purely on the stated facts of the case. However, individuals often show a bias in their decision making, and in particular, they tend to favor defendants of their own race (Sommers & Ellsworth, 2000). In a series of studies, Sam Sommers and Phoebe Ellsworth at the University of Michigan gave White and African American college students identical trial summaries and asked the students to rate the defendant's guilt. White students were more likely to see the Black defendant as guilty than the White defendant. African American students showed the opposite pattern. This research points to the powerful impact of similarity on a particular type of helping—helping people avoid a jail term!

© Image Source/SUPERSTOCK

shirt than either of the other shirts. Ninety-two percent of those wearing a Manchester United shirt got help, compared to only 33% of those wearing a rival team's shirt and 30% of those wearing a shirt without a team name. This study provides compelling evidence that we are more likely to help those who are similar to ourselves.

Friends. Not surprisingly, people are more likely to help those they know and care about than strangers, and are more likely to help those who they are in a **communal relationship** with, meaning a relationship in which people expect mutual responsiveness to one's needs. In contrast, we are much less likely to help those with whom we are in an exchange relationship, meaning a relationship in which people desire and expect strict reciprocity. In one study, participants were paired with either a friend or a stranger for a study on task performance (Clark, Mills, & Powell, 1986). Participants in one condition (the "needs" condition) were told that the lights in the room would change whenever the other person needed help (although these lights were totally irrelevant for the subject and could be ignored). Participants in the "inputs" condition were told that the lights would change whenever the other person had made a substantial contribution to their task (which the subject could also ignore). The dependent variable was how often the subject looked at the lights. In support of the hypotheses, participants looked more at the lights in the "needs" condition when the person was a friend, and more at the lights in the "inputs" condition when the subject was a stranger.

We also help friends create the distinct impressions they want to present to others. In one study, people were asked to describe a friend to another person (Schlenker & Britt, 1999). When talking about the friend to an attractive, opposite-sex individual, the friend was described consistent with the qualities this person preferred. On the other hand, when talking about the friend to an unattractive, opposite-sex individual, the friend was described as lacking the qualities this person preferred.

communal relationships those relationships in which people expect mutual responsiveness to one's needs

self-evaluation maintenance model a model positing that one's own self-concept can be threatened if someone else performs better on a self-relevant task

But not always. Although we tend to behave more altruistically to people we are close to, in some cases closeness can backfire. According to the **self-evaluation maintenance model**, we sometimes feel bad about ourselves when a friend outperforms us (Tesser, 1980). Therefore we help our friends in cases in which their achievement is not relevant to ourselves (and in fact, then we can *BIRG*, or *bask in reflected glory*, as described in Chapter 3). But we are less likely to help our friends in cases in which their doing well will make us look (and feel) bad.

In one study, people came in to participate in the study either with a friend or with a stranger (Tesser & Smith, 1980). The subject always went first, and was told they did "a little below average." Then they were asked to help their partner do well on this task by giving them some clues (that were either quite helpful or not very helpful). When you have been told you did poorly on a task that you don't really care about, you give more helpful clues to your friend than to a stranger, but when you care about the task, you actually give less helpful clues to your friend!

Although there may be times when we don't help our friends enough (in an effort to protect our own feelings of self-worth), at other times we overhelp our friends, meaning we provide more help to another person than is really needed (Gilbert & Silvera, 1996). This type of *overhelping* can make you appear altruistic, but also makes the other person seem needy, weak, and dependent. For example, giving a job candidate a series of very easy questions (e.g., "softballs"), such as "Are you an honest person?" and "Do you generally get along with co-workers?" can undermine this person's true job potential, because he or she is not given the opportunity to "show what they can do." This type of hindering of a person's performance leads observers to attribute success to external, as opposed to internal, factors. For example, after you give your roommate extensive feedback on her essay for medical school, others may interpret her admission as a result of your substantial assistance with her application as opposed to her strong grades and scores.

"Daddy's way of helping you with your homework is not to help you."

THE DOWNSIDE OF RECEIVING HELP

In most cases, receiving help is good. When people are in need of help, they want to receive it. Supportive help—help given by a non-similar other in a way that does not make us feel inferior or dependent—leads to positive reactions (Fisher, Nadler, & Whitcher-Alagna, 1982). For example, when you ask your parents to loan you money to buy a car or proofread your resume before a big job interview, you are probably pleased when they provide this assistance. This type of help can lead to increases in self-esteem and positive mood, and make us feel good about ourselves as well as the person who helped us (Deci, La Guardia, Moller, Scheiner, & Ryan, 2006). We are especially appreciative of help when we believe that the decision to help was made based on positive feelings about us on the part of the helper (Ames, Flynn, & Weber, 2004).

However, we react negatively to receiving help when it makes us feel inferior to and dependent on the helper (Ackerman & Kendrick, 2008; Nadler & Fisher, 1986; Reinhardt, Boerner, & Horowitz, 2006; Searcy & Eisenberg, 1992; Seidman, Shrout, & Bolger, 2006). For example, African American students experience a substantial drop in self-esteem if they are offered unsolicited (and unneeded) help, yet White students do not (Schneider, Major, Luhtanen, &

Crocker, 1996). African American students probably experience this drop because they are concerned that their partner assumed they would need help because of their race. Similarly, for older adults, receiving social support, such as physical assistance, is associated with depressive symptoms and vision problems (Reinhardt et al., 2006). These adults may recognize the need for support, but aren't happy to need it. Social support therefore seems to be most helpful when it was invisible, meaning when it is accomplished outside of the person's awareness, or when it can be reciprocated, thereby making us feel less dependent on the support giver (Bolger & Amarel, 2007; Gleason, Iida, Bolger, & Shrout, 2003).

We also react negatively to receiving help if the help comes from people who are similar to ourselves, especially if they are helping us with a task that we really care about (Nadler, 1987; Nadler, Fisher, & Itzhak, 1983). So, if you are a varsity tennis player and your teammate offers to help you with your serve, you may feel uncomfortable about receiving this unwanted help. However, you might be very willing to have this same teammate help you with your chemistry lab report (assuming you are not a chemistry major, of course). This is one of the main drawbacks to peer tutoring programs; because students are on a similar level, it can be difficult for one person to help another.

Finally, people react negatively to receiving help when they don't believe they'll have a way of repaying the help (Nadler & Fisher, 1986). As discussed earlier in this chapter, the norm of equity states that people like to be involved in relationships in which both people give and receive at roughly equal levels. If you receive considerable help, but have no way of repaying the helper, you may feel guilty, which in turn can have a negative impact on that relationship.

WHO GETS HELP WHEN THEY ARE IN NEED

Concepts in Context

FACTOR	EXAMPLE
Person	Lucy just agreed to buy four boxes of Thin Mint Girl Scout cookies. Although Lucy is on a diet and doesn't really want cookies in the house, the little girl who sold her the cookies was very cute. Lucy just didn't see how she could say no.
Social norms	Benjamin really had no need for a new calendar. But after he received a free one as a gift from a local charity, he felt compelled to make a small donation.
Relationship	Tate is walking in a large city. He is asked several times for money by older and disheveled homeless people. Each time he refuses. Then a young man comments that he also roots for the team on Tate's baseball hat before he asks Tate for a few dollars. Tate gives him two dollars.

CULTURE
HOW DOES CULTURE INFLUENCE HELPING?

Remember the information about the generosity of organ donors, described earlier in this chapter in Health Connections: The Amazing Generosity of Living Organ Donors? One of the factors that influences people's willingness to donate is culture. In one study, both Indian and American college students read a hypothetical scenario (Baron & Miller, 2000). This scenario described a person who needed a bone marrow transplant, and the participant was told that he or she was a potential donor. Both Americans and Indians felt obligated to help members of their own families by providing bone marrow (67% of Americans and 72% of Indians feel they should donate in this case). However, 76% of Indians saw donating as "morally required," even if the person in need was a stranger. Only 29% of Americans saw donating to a stranger as "morally required." This study demonstrates that norms for helping behavior are different across cultures. This section will examine differences in these cultural social norms for helping behavior, including the frequency of helping, norms for helping, motivations for helping, and factors increasing helping.

FREQUENCY OF HELPING

To examine differences in likelihood of helping across cultures, Robert Levine and his colleagues examined three types of helping behavior in large cities in 23 countries (Levine, Norenzayan, & Philbrick, 2001). The three types of helping behavior measured were assisting a blind person across the street, retrieving an "accidentally" dropped pen, and picking up a pile of magazines for a person with a hurt leg. As shown in Table 13.2, rates of helping differ dramatically across different countries, from a high rate of overall helping in Brazil to a low rate of overall helping in Malaysia (with the United States a close second in least helpfulness).

What factors generally predicted helping across countries? The most consistent predictor of helping was economic productivity, meaning that countries in which people earned *more* actually helped *less*. People from countries with high rates of economic stability may have more negative attitudes about helping others than those from countries in which more people experience stressful financial situations and hence empathize more with those who need assistance. The most helpful countries (Brazil, Costa Rica, Malawi, and India) are all third-world environments.

On average, people in cities from Latin America and Spain were more helpful than those in other international cities. Spanish and Latin American cultures are defined by their concern with the well-being of others, which includes a focus on being friendly, polite, and helpful to strangers (Levine et al., 2001). These cities also have primarily Roman Catholic populations, which may also lead to higher rates of helping.

However, in some cases people from collectivistic cultures are less likely to seek help—and therefore less likely to receive help—than those from individualistic cultures. Specifically, people from collectivistic cultures may be less willing to seek social support when dealing with stressful events, precisely because they are worried about the negative implications of support seeking on their interpersonal relationships (Kim, Sherman, Ko, & Taylor, 2006; Taylor, Sherman, Kim, Jarcho, Takagi, & Dunagan, 2004). For example, support seeking could lead to burdening others with one's own problems, feeling embarrassed and losing face, or receiving criticism and poor evaluations by others. In line with this view, research reveals that Asian Americans and Koreans seek social support less frequently, and find such support less helpful, than do European Americans. This research indicates that cultural norms regarding relationships influence the use of social support as a method for handling stress.

NORMS FOR HELPING

These differences in rates of helping are partly a result of the different norms for helping in different cultures. In one study, Americans and people from India were asked whether people in different situations have an obligation to help others (Miller, Bersoff, & Harwood, 1990). In some conditions, the help needed was minimal, such as giving directions or providing a ride to the train station. In other conditions, the help needed was extreme, such as donating blood or driving someone to the hospital. Although when the need to help was extreme or moderate, both Americans and people from India felt that help must be offered, people from

TABLE 13.2 — RATES OF HELPING ACROSS CULTURES

COUNTRY	BLIND PERSON	DROPPED PEN	HURT LEG
Brazil	100%	100%	80%
Costa Rica	100%	79%	95%
Malawi	100%	93%	65%
India	92%	63%	93%
Austria	75%	88%	80%
Spain	100%	76%	63%
Denmark	67%	89%	77%
China	63%	75%	92%
Mexico	92%	55%	80%
El Salvador	92%	89%	43%
Czech Republic	100%	55%	70%
Sweden	58%	92%	66%
Hungary	67%	76%	70%
Romania	92%	66%	48%
Israel	83%	67%	54%
Italy	75%	35%	80%
Thailand	42%	75%	66%
Taiwan	50%	65%	62%
Bulgaria	80%	69%	22%
Netherlands	58%	54%	49%
Singapore	50%	45%	49%
USA	75%	31%	28%
Malaysia	53%	26%	41%

Rates of helping for each type of situation differ considerably across cities, from a high rate of overall helping in Brazil to a low rate of overall helping in Malaysia.

Source: Levine, R. V., Norenzayan, A., & Philbrick, K. (2001). Cross-cultural differences in helping strangers. *Journal of Cross-Cultural Psychology*, 32, 543-560.

India were much more likely than Americans to say that help must be offered in cases in which the need to help was mild (see Figure 13.7). Similarly, and as described at the start of this section, people from India are much more likely than Americans to see donating bone marrow as "morally required," even if to a stranger.

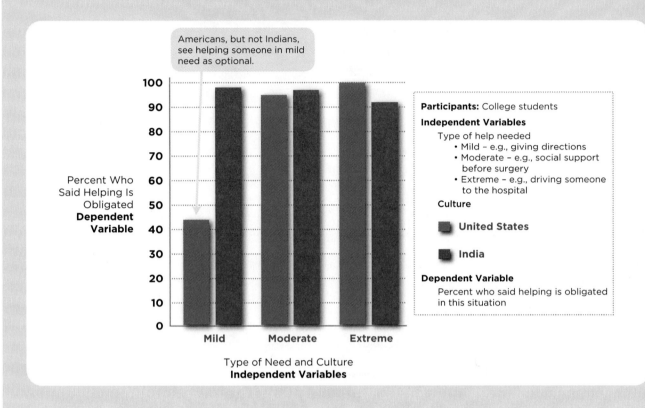

**FIGURE
13.7**

HOW DOES CULTURE IMPACT NORMS FOR HELPING?

Researchers asked students from a collectivist culture, India, and an individualistic
one, the United States, how obligated they felt to help people with various needs.
As predicted, in collectivist cultures people viewed helping as required in more
situations than in individualistic cultures.

Source: Miller, J.G., Bersoff, D.M., & Harwood, R.L. (1990). Perceptions of social responsibilities
in India and in the United States: Moral imperatives or personal decisions? *Journal of
Personality and Social Psychology*, 58, 33-47.

Cultures also differ in how they view the norm of reciprocity, and specifically
on how much concerns about reciprocity of helping influence prosocial behavior
(Miller & Bersoff, 1994). Americans see reciprocity (e.g., helping someone who
has helped them) as a matter of personal choice. In contrast, those in collectivistic cultures see reciprocity as a moral imperative: when a given person has received
help from another person, he or she then feels obligated to offer help to that person later on. On the other hand, people from India give less weight than Americans
to rewards, payments, and self-interest in explaining altruistic behavior.

MOTIVATIONS FOR HELPING

People in different cultures also vary in their motivations for helping. Researchers
in one study compared motivations for helping in children in Iceland and in China
(Keller, Edelstein, Schmid, Fang, & Fang, 1998). Children read a story in which a
child had to choose between spending time with a long-time friend and going to a
movie with a new friend. Then they answered a series of questions about the choice
the child in the story should make, and why this choice was the right one. Compared
to those from China, participants from Iceland focused more on self-interest concerns (e.g., a desire to see the movie) and obligation (e.g., she's made a promise).
Those from China focused more on altruistic and relationship concerns, such as taking the other person's needs into account (e.g., the new child doesn't know anyone
else) and the quality of the friendship (e.g., they have been friends a long time).

The Big Picture

ALTRUISM AND PROSOCIAL BEHAVIOR

This chapter included many applications of the three "big ideas" studied in social psychology. The examples below should help you see the connection between altruism and prosocial behavior and these big ideas and contribute to your understanding of the big picture of social psychology.

THEME	EXAMPLES
The social world influences how we think about ourselves.	• Children who receive money for helping then describe their helping as motivated by this reward. • We give our friends less help in cases in which their doing well makes us look (and feel) bad. • Older adults who receive physical assistance experience higher rates of depression, because they are concerned about the perception that they need such support.
The social world influences our thoughts, attitudes, and behaviors.	• We tip more when we receive candy with our dinner check. • We are more likely to change a flat tire when we've just seen another person model this behavior. • People in small towns get help faster than those in big cities.
Our attitudes and behavior shape the social world around us.	• People with higher levels of empathy engage in more prosocial behavior, including donating money to charitable causes and spending time helping people in need. • We help other people so that they will follow the norm of reciprocity and help us when we need help. • People who are with other people when they see smoke pouring into their room act as if they don't recognize this emergency—thereby leading other people to ignore the emergency as well.

WHAT YOU'VE LEARNED

This chapter has examined five key principles of altruism and prosocial behavior.

YOU LEARNED **How do personal factors influence helping?** The first section examined how personal factors influence helping behavior. We examined three factors that explain why people help those in need, including evolutionary factors, personality, and religion. You also learned that cueing people with religious words can increase prosocial behavior.

YOU LEARNED **How do situational factors influence helping?** We described several different situational factors that influence helping. You learned about the decision-making tree, which views helping as influenced by five distinct steps, and the arousal/cost-reward model, which describes helping as influenced by the arousal caused by seeing someone in need as well as the costs and benefits of providing that help. In addition, this section described the impact of mood, modeling, and environmental factors on prosocial behavior. You also learned that the large number of people who watched Kitty Genovese's attack partially explain why she did not receive help.

YOU LEARNED **Does true altruism exist?** This next section examined two competing views on whether true altruism exists. You learned about the empathy-altruism model, which describes helping as motivated, at least at times, from true feelings of empathy with a person in need. This section also described the egoistic model, which describes helping as emerging from individuals' own selfish motives. You also learned that self-interested motives drive volunteerism with HIV patients for heterosexual people, and empathy-based motives drive such volunteerism for homosexual people.

YOU LEARNED **Who gets help when they are in need?** This section described factors that impact whether a person gets help when her or she is in need. These factors include person factors (such as gender, age, attractiveness, and personality), social norms (such as reciprocity and social responsibility), and relationship factors (such as similarity and friendship). You also learned that women are more likely to get help than are men.

YOU LEARNED **How does culture influence helping?** The final section examined the impact of culture on helping. You learned how culture impacts prosocial behavior, including the frequency of helping, motivations for helping, and factors that increase helping. You also learned why people in India are as willing to donate bone marrow to a stranger as to a family member, but people in the United States are much more willing to donate to a family member than to a stranger.

KEY TERMS

altruism 462
arousal/cost-reward model 473
belief in a just world 492
bystander effect 472
communal relationships 493
decision-making process
   model 468

empathy 466
empathy-altruism hypothesis 481
kinship selection 463
moral reasoning 466
negative-state relief/egoistic-
   altruism hypothesis 485
norm of reciprocity 491

norm of social responsibility 491
pluralistic ignorance 471
prosocial behavior 462
reciprocal altruism 464
self-evaluation maintenance
   model 494
urban overload hypothesis 479

QUESTIONS FOR REVIEW

1. What are two personal factors that lead people to help those in need?
2. Describe each of the steps in the decision-making tree and the arousal/cost-reward model predicting when people get help.
3. What are the empathy-altruism and egoistic models of helping? Which theory of altruism do you find more convincing, the egoistic or the empathetic perspective, and why?
4. Describe two types of people who are more likely to get help, and then two types of people who are less likely to get help.
5. What is the impact of culture on the frequency, norms, and motivations of helping?

TAKE ACTION!

1. You are the parent of a 3-year-old girl. Describe two things you could do to help make her more altruistic to others.
2. Based on your knowledge about the decision-tree model of helping, describe three things you would tell people to do if they need help in an emergency.
3. You are in charge of a blood drive for your sorority. How could you encourage people to show up to donate blood by relying on empathy motives and by egoistic motives? Which approach should be more effective and why?
4. Your roommate, Bill, is writing a laboratory report for his social psychology class. He would like a friend to read it over before he turns it in, and wonders whether it would be better to ask Susie (a friend who is a psychology major and is also in this same class) or Cindy (a friend who is a biology major). Whom would you recommend, and why?
5. Your brother is traveling abroad to Japan for the first time. What would you tell him about his likelihood of receiving help, if he needs it, and the factors that would motivate such help?

RESEARCH CONNECTIONS

Try some of these research activities to gain experience in conducting and evaluating research, and to increase your understanding of research methods and techniques in social psychology. Visit WileyPLUS for more activities and interactive research tools! (www.wileyplus.com)

Participate in Research

Activity 1 The Impact of Relatedness on Helping: This chapter has described how we are more likely to help those with whom we share genes, and thus close relatives are more likely to be helped than distant relatives or nonrelatives. Go to WileyPLUS to read about various people who need help, and rate how likely you would be to help in each situation.

Activity 2 Testing the Arousal/Cost-Benefit Model of Helping: One model that predicts helping behavior is the arousal/cost-benefit model, which describes how the decision to help is influenced in part by the potential costs and benefits of helping in a given situation. Go online to rate the costs and benefits of helping in different situations to see how these factors may influence your own prosocial behavior.

Activity 3 The Impact of Empathy on Helping: This chapter described the importance of feeling empathy with another person in leading to helping. You can go online to read about various people who are in need of help, and then rate how much you empathize with each—and how likely you'd be to help in each situation

Activity 4 Examining the Factors that Impact Who Gets Help: You learned in this chapter about the types of people who are more, and less, likely to receive help. Go online to read several descriptions of people, and then rate how likely you would be to help each person.

Activity 5 The Impact of Culture on Helping: The final section of this chapter described how people from different cultures vary in how likely they are to help in different situations. Go online to rate how likely you would be to offer different types of help to a stranger; then see how other students might rate their own likelihood of helping in these different situations.

Test a Hypothesis

One of the common findings in research on altruism is that people who are in a good mood are more likely to help than those who are in a neutral mood. To test whether this hypothesis is true, design a study in which you create a good mood in some people, and not in others (for example, through giving people a piece of candy, or smiling at them). Then, measure whether those who are in a good mood are more likely to help someone. Then report your findings to other students.

Design a Study

To design your own study testing the factors that influence helping behavior, go online. You'll be able to choose the type of study you want to conduct (self-report, observational/naturalistic, or experimental), choose your own independent and dependent variables, and form your own hypothesis.

GLOSSARY

A

actor-observer effect the tendency to see other people's behavior as caused by dispositional factors, but see our own behavior as caused by the situation

affective forecasting the process of predicting the impact of both positive and negative events on mood

aggression physical or verbal behavior that is intended to hurt another person who does not want to be injured

altruism the desire to help another person

anchoring and adjustment a mental shortcut in which we rely on an initial starting point in making an estimate but then fail to adequately adjust from this anchor

arbitration a resolution of a conflict by a neutral third party who studies both sides and imposes a settlement

archival research a research approach that uses already recorded behavior

arousal-affect/excitation transfer model a model describing aggression as influenced by both the intensity of the arousal and the type of emotion produced by the stimulus

arousal/cost-reward model a model describing helping behavior as caused by the physiological arousal resulting from seeing someone in need of help, but also the calculation of the costs and rewards of providing such help

attachment styles the expectations people have about their relationship partners, based largely on early experiences with their caregivers

attitudes positive and negative evaluations of people, ideas, objects, and events

automatic thinking a type of decision-making process that occurs at an unconscious or automatic level and is entirely effortless and unintentional

availability heuristic a mental shortcut in which we make a judgment based on the ease with which we can bring something to mind

B

bargaining seeking an agreement through direct negotiation between both sides in a conflict

base-rate fallacy an error in which people ignore the numerical frequency, or base-rate, of various events in estimating their likelihood

basking in reflected glory (BIRGing) associating with successful others to increase one's feelings of self-worth

behaviorism a theory of learning that describes people's behavior as acquired through conditioning

belief in a just world the phenomenon in which people believe that bad things happen to bad people and good things happen to good people

belief perseverance the tendency to maintain, and even strengthen, beliefs in the face of disconfirming evidence

benevolent sexism a view of women as needing protection and affection

bystander effect the finding that the more people who witness an emergency, the less likely a victim is to receive help

C

catharsis the belief that aggression is a type of energy that builds up over time until it is released

central or systematic route a type of processing of persuasive messages that occurs when people have the ability and motivation to carefully listen to and evaluate the arguments in a persuasive message

classical conditioning a type of learning in which a neutral stimulus is repeatedly paired with a stimulus that elicits a specific response, and eventually the neutral stimulus elicits that response on its own

cognitive dissonance theory a theory that describes attitude change as occurring in order to reduce the unpleasant arousal people experience when they engage in a behavior that conflicts with their attitude or when they hold two conflicting attitudes

cognitive-neoassociation theory a theory that describes aggression as caused by experiencing negative affect of any kind, which in turn evokes aggressive-related thoughts, memories, feelings, and ideas

collective effort model a model that describes people's motivation to exert effort in group tasks only when they believe their distinct efforts are identifiable, these efforts will make a difference in the group's success, and they will experience positive outcomes

collectivistic a view of the self as part of a larger social network, including family, friends, and co-workers

common resource dilemma a social dilemma in which each person can take as much as he or she wants of a common resource, but if everyone takes as much as he or she wants, the resource will eventually be completely depleted

communal relationships those relationships in which people expect mutual responsiveness to one's needs

companionate love a stable, calm, and dependable kind of love that may include quiet intimacy, stability, shared attitudes/values/life experiences, and high levels of self-disclosure

comparison level the expected outcome of a relationship, meaning the extent to which a given person expects his or her relationship to be rewarding

comparison level for alternatives (CLalt) a calculation regarding the expected benefits and costs a person could receive from having a relationship with various other partners

compliance changes in behavior that are caused by a direct request

confirmation bias a tendency to search for information that confirms one's existing beliefs and to avoid information which contradicts these beliefs

conflict the presence and/or perception of incompatible goals between two people or groups

conformity the tendency to change our perceptions, opinions, or behaviors in ways that are consistent with perceived group norms

consensus information about whether other people generally behave in the same way toward the stimulus as the target person

consistency information about whether a person's behavior toward a given stimulus is the same across time

contrast effect the tendency to perceive a stimulus in different ways depending on the salient comparison

controlled or effortful thinking thinking that is effortful, conscious, and intentional

correlation a technique that examines the extent to which two or more variables are associated with one another

correspondent inference theory the theory that people infer whether a person's behavior is caused by internal dispositions of the person by looking at various factors related to that act

counterfactual thinking the tendency to imagine alternative outcomes to various events

covariation theory a theory explaining how people determine the causes of a person's behavior by focusing on the factors present and absent when a behavior does and does not occur, and specifically on the role of consensus, distinctiveness, and consistency

covert measures measures that are not directly under a person's control

D

debriefing a disclosure made to participants after research procedures are completed in which the researcher explains the purpose of the study, answers questions, attempts to resolve any negative feelings, and emphasizes the contributions of the research to science

deception false information given to participants in a research study

decision-making process model a model describing helping behavior as a function of five distinct steps

deindividuation a phenomenon in which a person loses the sense of him or herself as a distinct individual, and in turn feels less compelled to follow normal rules of behavior

demand characteristics the features introduced into a research setting that make people aware they are participating in a study

demand/withdraw interaction pattern a situation in which one partner is nagging, critical, and insistent about discussing the relationship problems while the other partner is withdrawn, silent, and defensive

dependent variable the factor that is measured to see if it is affected by the independent variable

descriptive norms norms that describe how people behave in a given situation

desensitization (disinhibition) the state in which physiological reactions to violence are reduced due to repeated exposure to violence

discrimination behavior directed against persons because of their membership in a particular group

displacement people's tendency to aggress against others when the person who has frustrated them is unavailable

distinctiveness information about whether a person's behavior is generally the same toward different stimuli

door-in-the-face technique a compliance technique in which one first asks for a big request, and then asks for a smaller request

downward social comparison comparing ourselves to people who are worse than we are on a given trait or ability in an attempt to feel better about ourselves

E

elaboration likelihood model (ELM) a model describing two distinct routes of persuasion (central and peripheral) that are used to process persuasive messages

emotional (or hostile) aggression aggression in which one inflicts harm for its own sake on another

empathy the ability to understand other people's perspectives and respond emotionally to other people's experiences

empathy-altruism hypothesis a hypothesis that when we feel empathy for a person, we will help that person even if we incur a cost by doing so

entrapment the common situation in which groups escalate commitment to failing courses of action, in part to justify investments already made

equity theory a theory that relationship satisfaction is determined by the ratio of costs and benefits in a relationship for each partner

event-recording measure a particular type of self-report or survey data where participants report various experiences they have at regular time intervals

excitation transfer a phenomenon in which the arousal caused by one stimulus is added to the arousal from a second stimulus and the combined arousal is erroneously attributed to the second stimulus

exit leaving the relationship altogether

experimental methods a research approach that involves the manipulation of one or more independent variables and the measurement of one or more dependent variables

experimental realism the extent to which participants are engaged in a particular study and hence act in more spontaneous and natural ways

experimenter expectancy effects a phenominon in which an experimenter's expectations about the results of the study influence participants' behavior and thereby affect the results of the study

external attribution an explanation of a person's behavior as caused by situational, or external, factors

external validity the degree to which there can be reasonable confidence that the same results would be obtained for other people in other situations

F

facial feedback hypothesis the hypothesis that changes in facial expression can lead to changes in emotion

false consensus effect the tendency to overestimate the extent to which other people share our opinions, attitudes, and behaviors

false uniqueness effect the tendency to underestimate the extent to which other people are likely to share our positive attitudes and behaviors

field experiments experiments that are conducted in natural settings

foot-in-the-door technique a two-step compliance technique in which an influencer first asks someone to do a small request, then asks for a larger request

forewarning making people aware that they will soon receive a persuasive message

framing the tendency to see an issue differently based on the way it is presented

frustration-aggression theory a hypothesis that frustration always leads to the desire to aggress, and that aggression is caused by frustration

fundamental attribution error the tendency to overestimate the role of personal causes, and underestimate the role of situational causes, in predicting behavior

G

general aggression model a model proposing that both individual differences and situational factors lead to aggressive-related thoughts, feelings, and/or physiological arousal

Gestalt psychology a theory that proposes objects are viewed holistic

GRIT (Graduated and Reciprocated Initiatives in Tension Reduction) a strategy to create unilateral and persistent efforts to establish trust and cooperation between opposing parties

group polarization a phenomenon in which the initial tendencies of group members become more extreme following group discussion

groupthink a group decision-making style characterized by an excessive tendency among group members to seek concurrence, consensus, and unanimity, as opposed to making the best decision

H

heuristics mental shortcuts often used to form judgments and make decisions

hindsight bias the tendency to see a given outcome as inevitable once the actual outcome is known

hostile media phenomenon the tendency to believe that media coverage of events is biased against the side we favor

hostile sexism a feeling of hostility toward women based on their threat to men's power

hypothesis a testable prediction about the conditions under which an event will occur

I

illusory correlation the tendency to see a correlation between two events when in reality, no such association exists

implicit personality theory the theory that certain traits and behaviors go together

impression management strategies that people use to create positive impressions of themselves

impression management theory a theory that individuals are not motivated to be consistent, but rather to appear consistent

in-group favoritism the tendency to discriminate in favor of those in your in-group versus your out-group

independent variable the variable that is manipulated in experimental research

individualistic a view of the self as distinct, autonomous, self-contained, and endowed with unique attributes

informational influence the influence that produces conformity when a person believes others are correct in their judgments, and they want to be right

informed consent all participants must sign a form stating their deliberate, voluntary decision to participate in research

ingratiation a strategy in which people try to make themselves likeable to someone else, often through flattery and praise

injunctive norms norms that describe what people ought to do in a given situation, meaning the type of behavior that is approved of in a given situation

inoculation the idea that exposure to a weak version of a persuasive message strengthens people's ability to resist that message later on

instinct theory a theory that describes people's innate desire to live as leading to the desire to aggress against others

instrumental aggression aggression in which one inflicts harm in order to obtain something of value

integrative agreement a negotiated resolution to a conflict in which all parties obtain outcomes that are superior to what they would have obtained from an equal division of the contested resources

inter-rater reliability the extent to which two or more coders agree on ratings of a particular measure

internal attribution an explanation of a person's behavior as caused by dispositional, or internal, factors

internal validity the degree to which one can validly draw conclusions about the effects of the independent variable on the dependent variable

intuition a decision-making shortcut in which we rely on our instinct instead of relying on more objective information

investment the resources devoted to a relationship that cannot be retrieved

K

kinship selection the idea that we are more likely to help those we are genetically related to

L

lowballing a two-step technique in which the influencer secures agreement with a request, but then increases the size of that request by revealing hidden costs

loyalty remaining committed to a relationship and simply waiting patiently for things to get better

M

matching hypothesis the hypothesis that people tend to seek and find partners who are roughly our own level of physical attractiveness

mediation a particular type of bargaining situation in which a neutral third party tries to resolve a conflict by facilitating communication and offering suggestions

mere exposure the phenomenon by which the greater exposure we have to a given stimulus, the more we like it

meta-analysis a literature review that also analyses data from many different studies

minority influence a process in which a small number of people in a group lead to overall change in the group's attitude or behavior

mirror-image perception the phenomenon in which we view those on our own side as just and fair and those on the other side as evil and selfish, even when the outward behavior may be identical

modern racism an underlying prejudice in which people's negative feelings about out-group members are not rooted specifically in their group membership (e.g., race, gender), but rather in more general beliefs about people's moral values

moral reasoning a personality factor that describes the extent to which a person's willingness to help is a function of his or her own needs and expected consequences versus larger moral standards

mundane realism the extent to which the conditions of the study resemble places and events that exist in the real world

N

negative attributional traps an approach in which a person explains his or her partner's behaviors in negative ways

negative-state relief/egoistic-altruism hypothesis a hypothesis that people are motivated to help others in order to relieve their own negative feelings

neglect giving up on a relationship and withdrawing from it emotionally

norm of reciprocity the idea that we should help those who are in need of assistance, because they will then help us in the future

norm of social responsibility the idea that we have an obligation to help those who are in need of assistance, even if we have no expectation that we will later receive help from them

normative influence the influence that produces conformity when a person fears the negative social consequences of appearing deviant

O

obedience behavior change produced by the commands of authority

observational learning/modeling a type of learning in which people's attitudes and behavior are influenced by watching other people's attitudes and behavior

observational/naturalistic methods a research approach that involves the observation and systematic recording of a particular behavior

operant conditioning a type of learning in which behavior that is rewarded increases whereas behavior that is punished decreases

operational definition a specific procedure or measure that one uses to test a hypothesis

out-group homogeneity effect people's tendency to underestimate the variability of out-group members compared to the variability of in-group members

overjustification the phenomenon in which receiving external rewards for a given behavior can undermine the intrinsic motivation for engaging in that behavior

P

passionate love an intense, exciting, and all-consuming type of love that may include constant thoughts about the person, powerful physical attraction, and intense communication

perceived control the tendency to see uncontrollable events as at least partially under our control

perceptual confirmation the tendency for people to see things in line with their own beliefs and expectations

peripheral or heuristic route a type of processing of persuasive messages that occurs when people lack the ability and motivation to carefully listen to and evaluate a persuasive message, and hence are influenced only by superficial cues

persuasion communication that is designed to influence one's attitudes

pluralistic ignorance a particular type of norm misperception that occurs when each individual in the group privately rejects the group's norms, but believes that others accept these norms

positive psychology a recent branch of psychology that studies individuals' strengths and virtues

prejudice hostile or negative feelings about people based on their membership in a certain group

primacy the tendency for information that is presented early to have a greater impact on judgments than information that is presented later

priming the process by which recent experiences increase the accessibility of a given trait or concept

prisoner's dilemma the situation in which two people may choose to either cooperate or compete with each other

private conformity when people rethink their original views, and potentially change their minds

prosocial behavior any behavior that has the goal of helping another person

prototype/willingness model a model that describes the role of prototypes, or social images of what people who engage in the behavior are like, in influencing their willingness to engage in the behavior in a given situation

public conformity when people's overt behaviors are in line with group norms

public goods dilemma a social dilemma in which each person must decide what to contribute to a common pool of resources. But if people do not all contribute, these public goods will not be available

punishment the provision of unpleasant consequences to try to reduce a negative behavior

R

random assignment a technique used in experimental research meaning every participant has an equal opportunity of being selected for any of the conditions in a particular experiment

reactance the idea that people react to threats to their freedom to engage in a behavior by becoming even more likely to engage in that behavior

realistic group conflict theory the theory that competition between groups for resources leads to conflict

reciprocal altruism the idea that we are motivated to help others due to the expectation that they will then help us in return later on

reciprocity a mutual exchange between two people

relative deprivation the feeling of discontent caused by the belief that one fares poorly compared to people in other groups

representative sample a sample that reflects the characteristics of the population at large

representativeness the tendency to classify someone or something based on its similarity to a typical case

risky shift a process by which groups tend to make riskier decisions than individuals would make alone

S

scarcity a compliance technique in which the opportunity to act is limited in terms of time or number

schemas mental structures that organize our knowledge about the world and influence how we interpret people and events

scientific method a technique for investigating phenomena, acquiring new knowledge, and/or correcting previous knowledge

self-affirmation theory a theory that describes how people can reduce the arousal caused by cognitive dissonance by affirming a different part of their identities, even if that identity is completely unrelated to the cause of the arousal

self-awareness theory a theory that when people focus on their own behavior, they are motivated to either change their behavior (so their attitudes and behavior are in line) or escape from self-awareness (to avoid noticing this contradiction)

self-concept an individual's overall beliefs about his or her own attributes

self-discrepancy theory a theory that our self-concept is influenced by the gap between how we actually see ourselves and how we want to see ourselves

self-esteem our evaluation of our own self-worth, meaning the extent to which we see ourselves as good and worthwhile

self-evaluation maintenance model a model positing that one's own self-concept can be threatened if someone else performs better on a self-relevant task

self-fulfilling prophecy the process by which people's expectations about a person lead them to elicit behavior that confirms these expectations

self-handicapping a strategy in which people create obstacles to success, so that potential failure can be blamed on these external factors

self-monitoring the extent to which one adjusts one's self-presentation in different situations

self-perception how we think about ourselves

self-perception theory the theory that people infer their attitudes by simply observing their behavior

self-presentation how people work to convey certain images of themselves to others

self-promotion a strategy that focuses on making other people think you are competent or good in some way

self-serving attributions the tendency to blame failure on external factors while crediting success on internal factors

self-standards model a model that proposes people experience discomfort whenever they see their behavior as deviating from some type of important personal or normative standard, but that the strategy they use to reduce this dissonance will depend on what thoughts about the self are currently accessible

self-verification theory a theory that people want others to perceive them as they perceive themselves, regardless of whether they see themselves in a positive or negative light

sleeper effect the phenomenon by which a message that is initially not particularly persuasive becomes more persuasive over time

social categorization the tendency for individuals to classify people into groups on the basis of common attributes

social cognition how we think about the social world, and in particular how we select, interpret, and use information to make judgments about the world

social comparison theory a theory that people evaluate their own abilities and attributes by comparing themselves to other people

social compensation the notion that if a project is important to you, you may work even harder to compensate for poor performance or social loafing by others

social dilemma a situation in which a self-interested choice by everyone creates the worst outcome for the group

social dominance orientation a personality variable describing the extent to which one wants his or her in-group to dominate and be superior to out-groups

social exchange theory a theory that people's satisfaction in a relationship is determined by the costs and rewards of this relationship

social facilitation a phenomenon in which people do better on particular tasks in the presence of a group compared to when they are alone

social identity theory a theory that posits that each person strives to enhance his or her self-esteem, which is composed of two parts: a personal identity and a social identity

social impact theory a theory that people we are close to have more impact than those who are more distant

social influence the impact of other people's attitudes and behaviors on our own thoughts, feelings, attitudes, and behavior

social learning theory a theory that describes behavior as learned by observing or modeling others' behavior as well as by the presence of punishments and rewards, or reinforcements

social loafing a group-produced reduction in individual output on easy tasks where contributions are pooled

social neuroscience a subfield of social psychology examining how factors in the social world influence activity in the brain, as well as how neural processes influence attitudes and behavior

social norms unspoken but shared rules of conduct in a formal or informal group

social perception how people form impressions of and make inferences about other people and events in the social world

social psychology the scientific study of how people's thoughts, attitudes, and behaviors are influenced by factors in the social world

sociocultural perspective a perspective describing people's behavior and mental processes as shaped in part by their social and/or cultural contact, including race, gender, and nationality

spotlight effect the tendency to overestimate the extent to which one's own appearance and behavior are obvious to others

stereotype threat an apprehension that an individual may experience when he or she believes he or she may behave in a manner that confirms existing cultural stereotype, which in turn disrupts performance

stereotypes beliefs that associate a whole group of people with certain traits

subliminal persuasion a type of persuasion that occurs when stimuli are presented at a very rapid and unconscious level

subtyping a phenomenon decribing how when people meet individuals who disconfirm their stereotypes, they can maintain the prior beliefs by creating separate categories for them

T

that's-not-all technique a compliance technique in which the influencer begins with an inflated request, and then decreases its apparent size by offering discounts or bonuses

theory an organized set of principles used to explain observed phenomena

theory of planned behavior a theory that describes people's behavior as caused by their attitudes, subjective norms, and perceived behavioral control

tit-for-tat a stratey that involves starting with cooperation, and then doing whatever one's partner does on each interaction (e.g., cooperate after a cooperate and compete after a compete)

trait negativity bias the tendency for people to be more influenced by negative traits than by positive ones

two-factor, or cognitive-arousal, theory of emotion a theory that the experience of emotion is determined by two distinct factors: the presence of some type of physiological arousal and the cognitive label a person gives to that arousal

two-stage model of attribution a model in which people first automatically interpret a person's behavior as caused by dispositional factors, and then later adjust this interpretation by taking into account situational factors that may have contributed to the behavior

U

ultimate attribution error an error in which people make dispositional attributions for negative behavior and situational attributions for positive behavior by out-group members, yet show the reverse attributions for successes and failures for in-group members

unrealistic optimism a phenomenon in which people see themselves as more likely than other people to experience good events, and less likely than other people to experience bad events

urban overload hypothesis a hypothesis that people who live in urban areas are constantly exposed to stimulation, which in turn leads them to decrease their awareness of their environment

V

voice talking things over with a relationship partner to try to solve the conflict

REFERENCES

Aaker, J. L., Benet-Martínez, V., & Garolera, J. (2001). Consumption symbols as carriers of culture: A study of Japanese and Spanish brand personality constucts. *Journal of Personality and Social Psychology, 81,* 492-508.

Aaker, J. L., & Williams, P. (1998). Empathy versus pride: The influence of emotional appeals across cultures. *Journal of Consumer Research, 25,* 241-261.

Abrahamson, A., Baker, L., & Caspi, A. (2002). Rebellious teens? Genetic and environmental influences on the social attitudes of adolescents. *Journal of Personality and Social Psychology, 83,* 1392-1408.

Abrams, R., & Greenwald, A. (2000). Parts outweigh the whole (word) in unconscious analysis of meaning. *Psychological Science, 11,* 118-124.

Ackerman, J. M., & Kenrick, D. T. (2008). The costs of benefits: Help-refusals highlight key trade-offs of social life. *Personality and Social Psychology Review, 12,* 118-140.

Adams, G., & Plaut, V. C. (2003). The cultural grounding of personal relationship: Friendship in North American and West African worlds. *Personal Relationships, 10,* 333-347.

Adams, H., Wright, L., & Lohr, B. (1996). Is homophobia associated with homosexual arousal? *Journal of Abnormal Psychology, 105,* 440-445.

Adorno, T. W., Frenkel-Brunswik, E., Levinson, D. J., & Sanford, R. N. (1950). *The Authoritarian Personality.* New York: Harper & Row.

Aharon, I., Etcoff, N., Ariely, D., Chabris, C.F., O'Connor, E., & Brieter, H.C. (2001). Beautiful faces have variable reward value: fMRI and behavioral evidence. *Neuron, 32,* 537-551.

Ainsworth, M. S., Blehar, M. C., Waters, E., & Wall, S. (1978). *Patterns of Attachment: A Psychological Study of the Strange Situation.* Oxford, UK: Erlbaum.

Ajzen, I., & Fishbein, M. (1977). Attitude-behavior relations: A theoretical analysis and review of empirical research. *Psychological Bulletin, 84,* 888-918.

Akimoto, S., & Sanbonmatsu, D. (1999). Differences in self-effacing behavior between European and Japanese Americans: Effect on competence evaluations. *Journal of Cross-Cultural Psychology, 30,* 159-177.

Albarracín, D., Cohen, J. B., & Kumkale, G. T. (2003). When communications collide with recipients' actions: Effects of the post-message behavior on intentions to follow the message recommendation. *Personality and Social Psychology Bulletin, 29,* 834-845.

Albarracín, D., & Wyer, R. (2000). The cognitive impact of past behavior: Influences on beliefs, attitudes, and future behavioral decisions. *Journal of Personality and Social Psychology, 79,* 5-22.

Albright, L., & Forziati, C. (1995). Cross-situational consistency and perceptual accuracy in leadership. *Personality and Social Psychology Bulletin, 21,* 1269-1276.

Albright, L., Kenny, D., & Malloy, T. (1988). Consensus in personality judgments at zero acquaintance. *Journal of Personality and Social Psychology, 55,* 387-395.

Alicke, M., & Largo, E. (1995). The role of the self in the false consensus effect. *Journal of Experimental Social Psychology, 31,* 28-47.

Alicke, M., LoSchiavo, F., Zerbst, J., & Zhang, S. (1997). The person who out performs me is a genius: Maintaining perceived competence in upward social comparison. *Journal of Personality and Social Psychology, 73,* 781-789.

Allen, J. B., Kenrick, D. T., Linder, D. E., & McCall, M. A. (1989). Arousal and attraction: A response-facilitation alternative to misattribution and negative-reinforcement models. *Journal of Personality and Social Psychology, 57,* 261-270.

Allen, K. (2003). Are pets a healthy pleasure? The influence of pets on blood pressure. *Current Directions in Psychological Science, 12,* 236-239.

Allen, K. M., Blascovich, J., Tomaka, J., & Kelsey, R. M. (1991). Presence of human friends and pet dogs as moderators of autonomic responses to stress in women. *Journal of Personality and Social Psychology, 61,* 582-589.

Allen, V. L., & Levine, J.M. (1969). Consensus and conformity. *Journal of Experimental Social Psychology, 5,* 389-399.

Allen, V. L., & Levine, J. M. (1971). Social support and conformity: The role of independent assessment of reality. *Journal of Experimental Social Psychology, 7,* 48-58.

Allport, F. H. (1924). *Social Psychology.* New York: Houghton, Mifflin.

Alvaro, E. M., & Crano, W. D. (1997). Indirect minority influence: Evidence for leniency in source evaluation and counter-argumentation. *Journal of Personality and Social Psychology, 72,* 949-964.

Amabile, T., Hennessey, B., & Grossman, B. (1986). Social influences on creativity: The effects of contracted-for reward. *Journal of Personality and Social Psychology, 50,* 14-23.

Amabile, T., Hill, K., Hennessey, B., & Tighe, E. (1994). The Work Preference Inventory: Assessing intrinsic and extrinsic motivational orientations. *Journal of Personality and Social Psychology, 66,* 950-967.

Amato, P. R. (1981). The effects of environmental complexity and pleasantness on prosocial behaviour: A field study. *Australian Journal of Psychology, 33,* 285-295.

Amato, P. R. (1983). Helping behavior in urban and rural environments: Field studies based on a taxonomic organization of helping episodes. *Journal of Personality and Social Psychology, 45,* 571-586.

Amato, P. R. (1986). Emotional arousal and helping behavior in a real-life emergency. *Journal of Applied Social Psychology, 16,* 633-641.

Amato, P. R., & Booth, A. (2001). The legacy of parents' marital discord: Consequences for children's marital quality. *Journal of Personality and Social Psychology, 81,* 627-638.

Ambady, N., & Rosenthal, R. (1993). Half a minute: Predicting teacher evaluations from thin slices of nonverbal behavior and physical attractiveness. *Journal of Personality and Social Psychology, 64,* 431-441.

Ambady, N., Koo, J., Lee, F., & Rosenthal, R. (1996). More than words: Linguistic and nonlinguistic politeness in two cultures. *Journal of Personality and Social Psychology, 70,* 996-1011.

American Psychological Association (1995). *Ethical Principles of Psychologists and Code of Conduct.* Washington, DC: Authors.

Ames, D. R., Flynn, F. J., & Weber, E. U. (2004). It's the thought that counts: On perceiving how helpers decide to lend a hand. *Personality and Social Psychology Bulletin, 30,* 461-474.

Amodio, D. M., Harmon-Jones, E., & Devine, P. G. (2003). Individual differences in the activation and control of affective race bias as assessed by startle eyeblink response and self-report. *Journal of Personality and Social Psychology, 84,* 738-753.

Andersen, A., & DiDomenico, L. (1992). Diet vs. shape content of popular male and female magazines: A dose-response relationship to the incidence of eating disorders? *International Journal of Eating Disorders, 11,* 283-287.

Anderson, C. (1989). Temperature and aggression: Ubiquitous effects of heat on occurrence of human violence. *Psychological Bulletin, 106,* 74-96.

Anderson, C. A. (1997). Effects of violent movies and trait hostility on hostile feelings and aggressive thoughts. *Aggressive Behavior, 23,* 161-178.

Anderson, C. (1999). Attributional style, depression, and loneliness: A cross-cultural comparison of American and Chinese students. *Personality and Social Psychology Bulletin, 25,* 482-499.

Anderson, C. A. (2001). Heat and violence. *Current Directions in Psychological Science, 10,* 33-38.

Anderson, C. A., & Anderson, K. B. (1996). Violent crime rate studies in philosophical context: A destructive testing approach to heat and southern culture of violence effects. *Journal of Personality and Social Psychology, 70,* 740-756.

Anderson, C. A., Anderson, K. B., & Deuser, W. E. (1996). Examining an affective aggression framework: Weapon and temperature effects on aggressive thoughts, affect, and attitudes. *Personality and Social Psychology Bulletin, 22,* 366-376.

Anderson, C. A., Benjamin, A. J. J., & Bartholow, B. D. (1998). Does the gun pull the trigger? Automatic priming effects of weapon pictures and weapon names. *Psychological Science, 9,* 308-314.

Anderson, C. A., Berkowitz, L., Donnerstein, E., Huesmann, L. R., Johnson, J. D., Linz, D., et al. (2003). The influence of media violence on youth. *Psychological Science in the Public Interest, 4,* 81-110.

Anderson, C. A., Buckley, K. E., & Carnagey, N. L. (2008). Creating your own hostile environment: A laboratory examination of trait aggressiveness and the violence escalation cycle. *Personality and Social Psychology Bulletin, 34,* 462-473.

Anderson, C. A., & Bushman, B. J. (2001). Effects of violent video games on aggressive behavior, aggressive cognition, aggressive affect, physiological arousal, and prosocial behavior: A meta-analytic review of the scientific literature. *Psychological Science, 12,* 353-359.

Anderson, C., Bushman, B., & Groom, R. (1997). Hot years and serious and deadly assault: Empirical tests of the heat hypothesis. *Journal of Personality and Social Psychology, 73,* 1213-1223.

Anderson, C. A., Carnagey, N. L., & Eubanks, J. (2003). Exposure to violent media: The effects of songs with violent lyrics on aggressive thoughts and feelings. *Journal of Personality and Social Psychology, 84,* 960-971.

Anderson, C. A., & DeNeve, K. M. (1992). Temperature, aggression, and the negative affect escape model. *Psychological Bulletin, 111,* 347-351.

Anderson, C. A., Deuser, W. E., & DeNeve, K. M. (1995). Hot temperatures, hostile affect, hostile cognition, and arousal: Tests of a general model of affective aggression. *Personality and Social Psychology Bulletin, 21,* 434-448.

Anderson, C. A., & Dill, K. E. (2000). Video games and aggressive thoughts, feelings, and behavior in the laboratory and in life. *Journal of Personality and Social Psychology, 78,* 772-790.

Anderson, C., Lepper, M., & Ross, L. (1980). Perseverance of social theories: The role of explanation in the persistence of discredited information. *Journal of Personality and Social Psychology, 39,* 1037-1049.

Anderson, C., & Sedikides, C. (1991). Thinking about people: Contributions of a typological alternative to associationistic and dimensional models of person perception. *Journal of Personality and Social Psychology, 60,* 203-217.

Anderson, K., Cooper, H., & Okamura, L. (1997). Individual differences and attitudes toward rape: A meta-analytic review. *Personality and Social Psychology Bulletin, 23,* 295-315.

Anderson, M., Kaufman, J., Simon, T.R., Barrios, L., Paulozzi, L., Ryan, G., Hammond, R., Modzeleski, W., Feucht, T., Potter, L., and the School-Associated Violent Deaths Study Group (2001). School-associated violent deaths in the United States, 1994-1999. *Journal of the American Medical Association, 286,* 2695-2702.

Anderson, N. (1975). On the role of context effects in psychophysical judgment. *Psychological Review, 82,* 462-482.

Anthony, T., Copper, C., & Mullen, B. (1992). Cross-racial facial identification: A social cognitive integration. *Personality and Social Psychology Bulletin, 18,* 296-301.

Antonides, G. (1995). Entrapment in risky investments. *The Journal of Socio-Economics, 24,* 447-461.

Antonio, A. L., Chang, M. J., Hakuta, K., Kenny, D. A., Levin, S., & Milem, J. F. (2004). Effects of racial diversity on complex thinking in college students. *Psychological Science, 15,* 507-510.

Antonovics, K., & Town, R. (2004). Are all the good men married? Uncovering the sources of the marital wage premium. *American Economic Review, 94,* 317-321.

Archer, J. (2000). Sex differences in aggression between heterosexual partners: A meta-analytic review. *Psychological Bulletin, 126,* 651-680.

Archer, J. (2004). Sex differences in aggression in real-world settings: A meta-analytic review. *Review of General Psychology, 8,* 291-322.

Archer, J. (2006). Cross-cultural differences in physical aggression between partners: A social-role analysis. *Personality and Social Psychology Review, 10,* 133–153.

Archer, J., & Coyne, S. M. (2005). An integrated review of indirect, relational, and social aggression. *Personality and Social Psychology Review, 9,* 212-230.

Archibald, F. S., Bartholomew, K., & Marx, R. (1995). Loneliness in early adolescence: A test of the cognitive discrepancy model of loneliness. *Personality and Social Psychology Bulletin, 21,* 296-301.

Ariely, D., & Norton, M. (2007). Psychology and experimental economics: A gap in abstraction. *Current Directions in Psychological Science, 16,* 336-339.

Aron, A., Dutton, D. G., Aron, E. N., & Iverson, A. (1989). Experiences of falling in love. *Journal of Social and Personal Relationships, 6,* 243-257.

Aron, A., Fisher, H., Mashek, D. J., Strong, G., Li, H., & Brown, L. L. (2005). Reward, motivation, and emotion systems associated with early-stage intense romantic love. *Journal of Neurophysiology, 94,* 327-337.

Aron, A., & Henkemeyer, L. (1995). Marital satisfaction and passionate love. *Journal of Social and Personal Relationships, 12,* 139-146.

Aron, A., Norman, C. C., Aron, E. N., McKenna, C., & Heyman, R. E. (2000). Couples' shared participation in novel and arousing activities and experienced relationship quality. *Journal of Personality and Social Psychology, 78,* 273-284.

Aron, A., Paris, M., & Aron, E. N. (1995). Falling in love: Prospective studies of self-concept change. *Journal of Personality and Social Psychology, 69,* 1102-1112.

Aronson, E., & Bridgeman, D. (1979). Jigsaw groups and the desegregated classroom: In pursuit of common goals. *Personality and Social Psychology Bulletin, 5,* 438-446.

Aronson, E., & Carlsmith, J. (1963). Effect of the severity of threat on the devaluation of forbidden behavior. *The Journal of Abnormal and Social Psychology, 66,* 584-588.

Aronson, E., & Linder, D. (1965). Gain and loss of esteem as determinants of interpersonal attractiveness. *Journal of Experimental Social Psychology, 1,* 156-171.

Aronson, E., & Mills, J. (1959). The effect of severity of initiation on liking for a group. *The Journal of Abnormal and Social Psychology, 59,* 177-181.

Aronson, E., Wilson, T., & Brewer, M. (1998). Experimentation in social psychology. *The Handbook of Social Psychology, Vols. 1 and 2 (4th Ed., pp. 99-142).* New York: McGraw-Hill.

Aronson, J., Lustina, M. J., Good, C., Keough, K., Steele, C. M., & Brown, J. (1999). When White men can't do math: Necessary and sufficient factors in stereotype threat. *Journal of Experimental Social Psychology, 35,* 29-46.

Arriaga, X. B., & Rusbult, C. E. (1998). Standing in my partner's shoes: Partner perspective taking and reactions to accommodative dilemmas. *Personality and Social Psychology Bulletin, 24,* 927-948.

Arunachalam, V., Wall, J., & Chan, C. (1998). Hong Kong versus U.S. negotiations: Effects of culture, alternatives, outcome scales, and mediation. *Journal of Applied Social Psychology, 28,* 1219-1244.

Asch, S. (1946). Forming impressions of personality. *The Journal of Abnormal and Social Psychology, 41,* 258-290.

Asch, S. E. (1951). Effects of group pressure upon the modification and distortion of judgment. In H. Guetzkow (Ed.) *Groups, Leadership and Men: Research in Human Relations* (pp. 177-190). Pittsburgh, PA: Carnegie Press.

Asch, S. E. (1955). Opinions and social pressure. *Scientific American, 193,* 31-35.

Aube, J., & Koestner, R. (1995). Gender characteristics and relationship adjustment: Another look at similarity-complementarity hypotheses. *Journal of Personality, 63,* 879-904.

Aune, K., & Aune, R. (1996). Cultural differences in the self-reported experience and expression of emotions in relationships. *Journal of Cross-Cultural Psychology, 27,* 67-81.

Axsom, D. (1989). Cognitive dissonance and behavior change in psychotherapy. *Journal of Experimental Social Psychology, 25,* 234-252.

Axsom, D., & Cooper, J. (1985). Cognitive dissonance and psychotherapy: The role of effort justification in inducing weight loss. *Journal of Experimental Social Psychology, 21,* 149-160.

Axsom, D., Yates, S., & Chaiken, S. (1987). Audience response as a heuristic cue in persuasion. *Journal of Personality and Social Psychology, 53,* 30-40.

Back, M. D., Schmukle, S. C., & Egloff, B. (2008). Becoming friends by chance. *Psychological Science, 19,* 439-440.

Baer, J. S., & Carney, M. M. (1993). Biases in the perceptions of the consequences of alcohol use among college students. *Journal of Studies on Alcohol, 54,* 54-60.

Baer, J. S., Stacy, A., & Larimer, M. (1991). Biases in the perception of drinking norms among college students. *Journal of Studies on Alcohol, 52,* 580-586.

Bahrick, H., Hall, L., & Berger, S. (1996). Accuracy and distortion in memory for high school grades. *Psychological Science, 7,* 265-271.

Bailey, D. S., & Taylor, S. P. (1991). Effects of alcohol and aggressive disposition on human physical aggression. *Journal of Research in Personality, 25,* 334-342.

Bailey, J. M., Gaulin, S., Agyei, Y., & Gladue, B. A. (1994). Effects of gender and sexual orientation on evolutionarily relevant aspects of human mating psychology. *Journal of Personality and Social Psychology, 66,* 1081-1093.

Balcetis, E., & Dunning, D. (2007). Cognitive dissonance and the perception of natural environments. *Psychological Science, 18,* 917-921.

Banaji, M. R., & Greenwald, A. G. (1995). Implicit gender stereotyping in judgments of fame. *Journal of Personality and Social Psychology, 68,* 181-198.

Bandura, A. (1973). *Aggression: A Social Learning Analysis.* Englewood Cliffs, NJ: Prentice-Hall.

Bandura, A. (1983). Self-efficacy determinants of anticipated fears and calamities. *Journal of Personality and Social Psychology, 45,* 464-469.

Bandura, A. (1986). *Social Foundations of Thought and Action: A Social Cognitive Theory.* Englewood Cliffs, NJ: Prentice-Hall.

Bandura, A., Barbaranelli, C., Caprara, G. V., & Pastorelli, C. (1996). Mechanisms of moral disengagement in the exercise of moral agency. *Journal of Personality and Social Psychology, 71,* 364-374.

Bandura, A., Grusec, J. E., & Menlove, F. L. (1967). Vicarious extinction of avoidance behavior. *Journal of Personality and Social Psychology, 5,* 16-23.

Bandura, A., O'Leary, A., Taylor, C., Gauthier, J., & Gossard, D. (1987). Perceived self-efficacy and pain control: Opioid and nonopioid mechanisms. *Journal of Personality and Social Psychology, 53,* 563-571.

Bandura, A., Ross, D., & Ross, S. (1963). Imitation of film-mediated aggressive models. *The Journal of Abnormal and Social Psychology, 66,* 3-11.

Banks, S., Salovey, P., Greener, S., Rothman, A., Moyer, A., Beauvais, J., et al. (1995). The effects of message framing on mammography utilization. *Health Psychology, 14,* 178-184.

Banks, T., & Dabbs, J. M. J. (1996). Salivary testosterone and cortisol in delinquent and violent urban subculture. *Journal of Social Psychology, 136,* 49-56.

Barbash, T. (2003). *On Top of the World: Cantor Fitzgerald, Howard Lutnick, & 9/11: A Story of Loss & Renewal.* New York: Harper Collins.

Barbee, A. P., Cunningham, M. R., Winstead, B. A., & Derlega, V. J. (1993). Effects of gender role expectations on the social support process. *Journal of Social Issues, 49,* 175-190.

Barclay, G. & Tavares, C. (2003). *International Comparisons of Criminal Justice Statistics, 2001.* London, UK: Home Office, Research Development Statistics.

Bargh, J. A., & Chartrand, T. L. (1999). The unbearable automaticity of being. *American Psychologist, 54,* 462-479.

Bargh, J. A., Chen, M., & Burrows, L. (1996). Automaticity of social behavior: Direct effects of trait construct and stereotype activation on action. *Journal of Personality and Social Psychology, 71,* 230-244.

Bargh, J., Gollwitzer, P., Lee-Chai, A., Barndollar, K., & Trötschel, R. (2001). The automated will: Nonconscious activation and pursuit of behavioral goals. *Journal of Personality and Social Psychology, 81,* 1014-1027.

Bargh, J. A., McKenna, K. Y. A., & Fitzsimons, G. M. (2002). Can you see the real me? Activation and expression of the 'true self' on the Internet. *Journal of Social Issues, 58,* 33-48.

Bargh, J., & Pietromonaco, P. (1982). Automatic information processing and social perception: The influence of trait information presented outside of conscious awareness on impression formation. *Journal of Personality and Social Psychology, 43,* 437-449.

Baron, A. S., & Banaji, M. R. (2006). The development of implicit attitudes: Evidence of race evaluations from ages 6 and 10 and adulthood. *Psychological Science, 17,* 53-58.

Baron, J., & Miller, J. G. (2000). Limiting the scope of moral obligations to help: A cross cultural investigation. *Journal of Cross-Cultural Psychology, 31,* 703-725.

Baron, R. A. (1990). Countering the effects of destructive criticism: The relative efficacy of four interventions. *Journal of Applied Psychology, 75,* 235-245.

Baron, R. A. (1997). The sweet smell of . . .helping: Effects of pleasant ambient fragrance on prosocial behavior in shopping malls. *Personality and Social Psychology Bulletin, 23,* 498-503.

Baron, R. S., Hoppe, S. I., Kao, C. F., & Brunsman, B. (1996). Social corroboration and opinion extremity. *Journal of Experimental Social Psychology, 32,* 537-560.

Baron, R. S., Logan, H., Lilly, J., Inman, M., & Brennan, M. (1994). Negative emotion and message processing. *Journal of Experimental Social Psychology, 30,* 181-201.

Baron, R. S., Moore, D., & Sanders, G. S. (1978). Distraction as a source of drive in social facilitation research. *Journal of Personality and Social Psychology, 36,* 816-824.

Baron, R. S., Vandello, J. A., & Brunsman, B. (1996). The forgotten variable in conformity research: Impact of task importance on social influence. *Journal of Personality and Social Psychology, 71,* 915-927.

Bartels, A., & Zeki, S. (2000). The neural basis of romantic love. *Neuroreport: For Rapid Communication of Neuroscience Research, 11,* 3829-3834.

Bartholow, B. D., & Anderson, C. A. (2002). Effects of violent video games on aggressive behavior: Potential sex differences. *Journal of Experimental Social Psychology, 38,* 283-290.

Bartholow, B. D., Bushman, B. J., & Sestir, M. A. (2006). Chronic violent video game exposure and desensitization to violence: Behavioral and event-related brain potential data. *Journal of Experimental Social Psychology, 42,* 532-539.

Bartholow, B. D., & Heinz, A. (2006). Alcohol and aggression without consumption: Alcohol cues, aggressive thoughts, and hostile perception bias. *Psychological Science, 17,* 30-37.

Bartholow, B. D., Sestir, M. A., & Davis, E. B. (2005). Correlates and consequences of exposure to video game violence: Hostile personality, empathy, and aggressive behavior. *Personality and Social Psychology Bulletin, 31,* 1573-1586.

Bass, B. M., Avolio, B. J., Jung, D. I., & Berson, Y. (2003). Predicting unit performance by assessing transformational and transactional leadership. *Journal of Applied Psychology, 88,* 207-218.

Batson, C. D. (1991). *The Altruism Question: Toward a Social-Psychological Answer.* Hillsdale, NJ: Erlbaum.

Batson, C. D. (1983). Sociobiology and the role of religion in promoting prosocial behavior: An alternative view. *Journal of Personality and Social Psychology, 45,* 1380-1385.

Batson, C. D. (1998). Altruism and prosocial behavior. In D. Gilbert, S. Fiske, & G. Lindzey (Eds.), *Handbook of Social Psychology* (pp. 282-316). New York: McGraw-Hill.

Batson, C. D., Duncan, B. D., Ackerman, P., Buckley, T., & Birch, K. (1981). Is empathic emotion a source of altruistic motivation? *Journal of Personality and Social Psychology, 40,* 290-302.

Batson, C. D., Dyck, J. L., Brandt, J. R., Batson, J. G., Powell, A. L., McMaster, M. R., et al. (1988). Five studies testing two new egoistic alternatives to the empathy-altruism hypothesis. *Journal of Personality and Social Psychology, 55,* 52-77.

Batson, C. D., Floyd, R. B., Meyer, J. M., & Winner, A. L. (1999). 'And who is my neighbor?:' Intrinsic religion as a source of universal compassion. *Journal for the Scientific Study of Religion, 38,* 445-457.

Batson, C. D., Lishner, D. A., Carpenter, A., Dulin, L., Harjusola-Webb, S., Stocks, E. L., et al. (2003). '...As you would have them do unto you': Does imagining yourself in the other's place stimulate moral action? *Personality and Social Psychology Bulletin, 29,* 1190-1201.

Batson, C. D., & Oleson, K. C. (1991). Current status of the empathy-altruism hypothesis. In M. S. Clark (Ed.), *Review of Personality and Social Psychology* (Vol. 12, pp. 62-85). Newbury Park, CA: Sage.

Batson, C. D., Sager, K., Garst, E., Kang, M., Rubchinsky, K., & Dawson, K. (1997). Is empathy-induced helping due to self-other merging? *Journal of Personality and Social Psychology, 73,* 495-509.

Batson, C. D., Sympson, S. C., Hindman, J. L., & Decruz, P. (1996). 'I've been there, too': Effect on empathy of prior experience with a need. *Personality and Social Psychology Bulletin, 22,* 474-482.

Batson, C. D., Thompson, E. R., Seuferling, G., Whitney, H., & Strongman, J. A. (1999). Moral hypocrisy: Appearing moral to oneself without being so. *Journal of Personality and Social Psychology, 77,* 525-537.

Baumeister, R. (1982). A self-presentational view of social phenomena. *Psychological Bulletin, 91,* 3-26.

Baumeister, R. F., Bushman, B. J., & Campbell, W. K. (2000). Self-esteem, narcissism, and aggression: Does violence result from low self-esteem or from threatened egotism? *Current Directions in Psychological Science, 9,* 26-29.

Baumeister, R. F., & Bratslavsky, E. (1999). Passion, intimacy, and time: Passionate love as a function of change in intimacy. *Personality and Social Psychology Review, 3,* 49-67.

Baumeister, R., Bratslavsky, E., Muraven, M., & Tice, D. (1998). Ego depletion: Is the active self a limited resource? *Journal of Personality and Social Psychology, 74,* 1252-1265.

Baumeister, R. F., & Campbell, W. K. (1999). The intrinsic appeal of evil: Sadism, sensational thrills, and threatened egotism. *Personality and Social Psychology Review, 3,* 210-221.

Baumeister, R. F., & Leary, M. R. (1995). The need to belong: Desire for interpersonal attachments as a fundamental human motivation. *Psychological Bulletin, 117,* 497-529.

Baumeister, R. F., & Steinhilber, A. (1984). Paradoxical effects of supportive audiences on performance under pressure: The home field disadvantage in sports championships. *Journal of Personality and Social Psychology, 47,* 85-93.

Baumeister, R., & Tice, D. (1984). Role of self-presentation and choice in cognitive dissonance under forced compliance: Necessary or sufficient causes? *Journal of Personality and Social Psychology, 46,* 5-13.

Baumeister, R., & Vohs, K. (2004). Sexual economics: Sex as female resource for social exchange in heterosexual interactions. *Personality and Social Psychology Review, 8,* 339-363.

Baumrind, D. (1985). Research using intentional deception: Ethical issues revisited. *American Psychologist, 40,* 165-174.

Bazzini, D. G., & Shaffer, D. R. (1999). Resisting temptation revisited: Devaluation versus enhancement of an attractive suitor by exclusive and nonexclusive daters. *Personality and Social Psychology Bulletin, 25,* 162-176.

Beaman, A. L. (1983). Fifteen years of foot-in-the-door research: A meta-analysis. *Personality and Social Psychology Bulletin, 9,* 181-196.

Beaman, A., Klentz, B., Diener, E., & Svanum, S. (1979). Self-awareness and transgression in children: Two field studies. *Journal of Personality and Social Psychology, 37,* 1835-1846.

Beaulieu, D. A. (2007). Avoiding costly mating mistakes: Ovulatory shifts in personal mate value assessment. *Journal of Social and Personal Relationships, 24,* 441-455.

Beauregard, K., & Dunning, D. (1998). Turning up the contrast: Self-enhancement motives prompt egocentric contrast effects in social judgments. *Journal of Personality and Social Psychology, 74,* 606-621.

Becker, S. W., & Eagly, A. H. (2004). The heroism of women and men. *American Psychologist, 59,* 163-178.

Bell, P. A. (1992). In defense of the negative affect escape model of heat and aggression. *Psychological Bulletin, 111,* 342-346.

Belsky, J. (1993). Etiology of child maltreatment: A developmental-ecological analysis. *Psychological Bulletin, 114,* 413-434.

Bem, D. (1967). Self-perception: An alternative interpretation of cognitive dissonance phenomena. *Psychological Review, 74,* 183-200.

Bem, D. J. (1972). Constructing cross-situational consistencies in behavior: Some thoughts on Alker's critique of Mischel. *Journal of Personality, 40,* 17-26.

Benedetti, F., & Amanzio, M. (1997). The neurobiology of placebo analgesia: From endogenous opioids to cholecystokinin. *Progress in Neurobiology, 52,* 109-125.

Bensley, L. S., & Wu, R. (1991). The role of psychological reactance in drinking following alcohol prevention messages. *Journal of Applied Social Psychology, 21,* 1111-1124.

Benson, P. L., et al. (1980). Intrapersonal correlates of nonspontaneous helping behavior. *Journal of Social Psychology, 110,* 87-95.

Benson, P. L., Karabenick, S. A., & Lerner, R. M. (1976). Pretty pleases: The effects of physical attractiveness, race, and sex on receiving help. *Journal of Experimental Social Psychology, 12,* 409-415.

Berg, J. H., & McQuinn, R. D. (1986). Attraction and exchange in continuing and noncontinuing dating relationships. *Journal of Personality and Social Psychology, 50,* 942-952.

Berg, J. H., & McQuinn, R. D. (1989). Loneliness and aspects of social support networks. *Journal of Social and Personal Relationships, 6,* 359-372.

Berg, J. H., & Peplau, L. A. (1982). Loneliness: The relationship of self-disclosure and androgyny. *Personality and Social Psychology Bulletin, 8,* 624-630.

Berglas, S., & Jones, E. E. (1978). Drug choice as a self-handicapping strategy in response to noncontingent success. *Journal of Personality and Social Psychology, 36,* 405-417.

Bergeron, N., & Schneider, B. H. (2005). Explaining cross-national differences in peer-directed aggression: A quantitative synthesis. *Aggressive Behavior, 31,* 116-137.

Berkowitz, L. (1984). Some effects of thoughts on anti- and prosocial influences of media events: A cognitive-neoassociation analysis. *Psychological Bulletin, 95,* 410-427.

Berkowitz, L. (1989). Frustration-aggression hypothesis: Examination and reformulation. *Psychological Bulletin, 106,* 59-73.

Berkowitz, L. (1990). On the formation and regulation of anger and aggression: A cognitive-neoassociationistic analysis. *American Psychologist, 45,* 494-503.

Berkowitz, L., & Daniels, L. R. (1963). Responsibility and dependency. *The Journal of Abnormal and Social Psychology, 66,* 429-436.

Berkowitz, L., & LePage, A. (1967). Weapons as aggression-eliciting stimuli. *Journal of Personality and Social Psychology, 7,* 202-207.

Berkowitz, L., Cochran, S. T., & Embree, M. C. (1981). Physical pain and the goal of aversively stimulated aggression. *Journal of Personality and Social Psychology, 40,* 687-700.

Berman, M. I., & Frazier, P. A. (2005). Relationship power and betrayal experience as predictors of reactions to infidelity. *Personality and Social Psychology Bulletin, 31,* 1617-1627.

Bernard, M. M., Maio, G. R., & Olson, J. M. (2003). The vulnerability of values to attack: Inoculation of values and value-relevant attitudes. *Personality and Social Psychology Bulletin, 29,* 63-75.

Berndt, T. J. (1979). Developmental changes in conformity to peers and parents. *Developmental Psychology, 15,* 608-616.

Bernhardt, P. C. (1997). Influences of serotonin and testosterone in aggression and dominance: Convergence with social psychology. *Current Directions in Psychological Science, 6,* 44-48.

Berry, D. (1991). Accuracy in social perception: Contributions of facial and vocal information. *Journal of Personality and Social Psychology, 61,* 298-307.

Berscheid, E., Snyder, M., & Omoto, A. M. (1989). The Relationship Closeness Inventory: Assessing the closeness of interpersonal relationships. *Journal of Personality and Social Psychology, 57,* 792-807.

Bersoff, D. (1999). Why good people sometimes do bad things: Motivated reasoning and unethical behavior. *Personality and Social Psychology Bulletin, 25,* 28-39.

Bettencourt, B. A., & Miller, N. (1996). Gender differences in aggression as a function of provocation: A meta-analysis. *Psychological Bulletin, 119,* 422-447.

Bickman, L. (1971). The effect of another bystander's ability to help on bystander intervention in an emergency. *Journal of Experimental Social Psychology, 7,* 367-379.

Bickman, L. (1974). The social power of a uniform. *Journal of Applied Social Psychology, 4,* 47-61.

Biddle, J. E., & Hamermesh, D. S., (1998). Beauty, productivity, and discrimination: Lawyers' looks and lucre. *Journal of Labor Economics, 16,* 172-201.

Biek, M., Wood, W., & Chaiken, S. (1996). Working knowledge, cognitive processing, and attitudes: On the determinants of bias. *Personality and Social Psychology Bulletin, 22,* 547-556.

Biener, L., & Heaton, A. (1995). Women dieters of normal weight: Their motives, goals, and risks. *American Journal of Public Health, 85,* 714-717.

Bierhoff, H. W., Klein, R., & Kramp, P. (1991). Evidence for the altruistic personality from data on accident research. *Journal of Personality, 59,* 263-280.

Biernat, M. (2003). Toward a broader view of social stereotyping. *American Psychologist, 58,* 1019-1027.

Biernat, M., Crandall, C. S., Young, L. V., Kobrynowicz, D., & Halpin, S. M. (1998). All that you can be: Stereotyping of self and others in a military context. *Journal of Personality and Social Psychology, 75,* 301-317.

Biernat, M., & Kobrynowicz, D. (1997). Gender- and race-based standards of competence: Lower minimum standards but higher ability standards for devalued groups. *Journal of Personality and Social Psychology, 72,* 544-557.

Biernat, M., & Ma, J. E. (2005). Stereotypes and the confirmability of trait concepts. *Personality and Social Psychology Bulletin, 31,* 483-495.

Biernat, M., & Manis, M. (1994). Shifting standards and stereotype-based judgments. *Journal of Personality and Social Psychology, 66,* 5-20.

Biernat, M., Manis, M., & Nelson, T. E. (1991). Stereotypes and standards of judgment. *Journal of Personality and Social Psychology, 60,* 485-499.

Biernat, M., & Vescio, T. K. (2002). She swings, she hits, she's great, she's benched: Implications of gender-based shifting standards for judgment and behavior. *Personality and Social Psychology Bulletin, 28,* 66-77.

Billig, M., & Tajfel, H. (1973). Social categorization and similarity in intergroup behaviour. *European Journal of Social Psychology, 3,* 27-52.

Blanchard, F. A., Crandall, C. S., Brigham, J. C., & Vaughn, L. A. (1994). Condemning and condoning racism: A social context approach to interracial settings. *Journal of Applied Psychology, 79,* 993-997.

Blaney, N., Stephan, C., Rosenfield, D., Aronson, E., & Sikes, J. (1977). Interdependence in the classroom: A field study. *Journal of Educational Psychology, 69,* 121-128.

Blankenship, K. L., & Wegener, D. T. (2008). Opening the mind to close it: Considering a message in light of important values increases message processing and later resistance to change. *Journal of Personality and Social Psychology, 94,* 196-213.

Blanton, H., & Jaccard, J. (2006). Arbitrary metrics in psychology. *American Psychologist, 61,* 27-41.

Blanton, H., VandenEijnden, R., Buunk, B., Gibbons, F., Gerrard, M., & Bakker, A. (2001). Accentuate the negative: Social images in the prediction and promotion of condom use. *Journal of Applied Social Psychology, 31,* 274-295.

Blascovich, J., Mendes, W. B., Hunter, S. B., & Salomon, K. (1999). Social 'facilitation' as challenge and threat. *Journal of Personality and Social Psychology, 77,* 68-77.

Blass, T. (1991). Understanding behavior in the Milgram obedience experiment: The role of personality, situations, and their interactions. *Journal of Personality and Social Psychology, 60,* 398-413.

Blass, T. (1996). Attribution of responsibility and trust in Milgram's obedience experiment. *Journal of Applied Social Psychology, 26,* 1529-1535.

Bless, H., Bohner, G., Schwarz, N., & Strack, F. (1990). Mood and persuasion: A cognitive response analysis. *Personality and Social Psychology Bulletin, 16,* 331-345.

Bochner, S. (1994). Cross-cultural differences in the self concept: A test of Hofstede's individualism/collectivism distinction. *Journal of Cross-Cultural Psychology, 25,* 273-283.

Bodenmann, G., Kaiser, A., Hahlweg, K., & Fehm-Wolfsdorf, G. (1998). Communication patterns during marital conflict: A cross-cultural representation. *Personal Relationships, 5,* 343-356.

Bogart, L., & Helgeson, V. (2000). Social comparisons among women with breast cancer: A longitudinal investigation. *Journal of Applied Social Psychology, 30,* 547-575.

Bohner, G., Siebler, F., & Schmelcher, J. (2006). Social norms and the likelihood of raping: Perceived rape myth acceptance of others affects men's rape proclivity. *Personality and Social Psychology Bulletin, 32,* 286-297.

Boldizar, J. P., Perry, D. G., & Perry, L. C. (1989). Outcome values and aggression. *Child Development, 60,* 571-579.

Bolger, N., & Amarel, D. (2007). Effects of social support visibility on adjustment to stress: Experimental evidence. *Journal of Personality and Social Psychology, 92,* 458-475.

Bond, C., & DePaulo, B. (2006). Accuracy of deception judgments. *Personality and Social Psychology Review, 10,* 214-234.

Bond, C., Omar, A., Mahmoud, A., & Bonser, R. (1990). Lie detection across cultures. *Journal of Nonverbal Behavior, 14,* 189-204.

Bond, C. F., & Titus, L. J. (1983). Social facilitation: A meta-analysis of 241 studies. *Psychological Bulletin, 94,* 265-292.

Bond, M. H. (2004). Culture and aggression: From context to coercion. *Personality and Social Psychology Review, 8,* 62-78.

Bond, R., & Smith, P. B. (1996). Culture and conformity: A meta-analysis of studies using Asch's (1952b, 1956) line judgment task. *Psychological Bulletin, 119,* 111-137.

Boninger, D., Gleicher, F., & Strathman, A. (1994). Counterfactual thinking: From what might have been to what may be. *Journal of Personality and Social Psychology, 67,* 297-307.

Bonta, B. D. (1997). Cooperation and competition in peaceful societies. *Psychological Bulletin, 121,* 299-320.

Bontempo, R., Lobel, S., & Triandis, H. (1990). Compliance and value internalization in Brazil and the U.S.: Effects of allocentrism and anonymity. *Journal of Cross-Cultural Psychology, 21,* 200-213.

Bornstein, G., Rapoport, A., Kerpel, L., & Katz, T. (1989). Within- and between-group communication in intergroup competition for public goods. *Journal of Experimental Social Psychology, 25,* 422-436.

Bornstein, R. (1989). Subliminal techniques as propaganda tools: Review and critique. *Journal of Mind and Behavior, 10,* 231-262.

Bornstein, R. F. (1989). Exposure and affect: Overview and meta-analysis of research, 1968-1987. *Psychological Bulletin, 106,* 265-289.

Bornstein, R., & D'Agostino, P. (1992). Stimulus recognition and the mere exposure effect. *Journal of Personality and Social Psychology, 63,* 545-552.

Bothwell, R. K., Brigham, J. C., & Malpass, R. S. (1989). Cross-racial identification. *Personality and Social Psychology Bulletin, 15,* 19-25.

Botwin, M. D., Buss, D. M., & Shackelford, T. K. (1997). Personality and mate preferences: Five factors in mate selection and marital satisfaction. *Journal of Personality, 65,* 107-136.

Bouas, K. S., & Komorita, S. S. (1996). Group discussion and cooperation in social dilemmas. *Personality and Social Psychology Bulletin, 22,* 1144-1150.

Bouchard, T. (2004). Genetic influence on human psychological traits: A survey. *Current Directions in Psychological Science, 13,* 148-151.

Bowlby, J. (1982). Attachment and loss: Retrospect and prospect. *American Journal of Orthopsychiatry, 52,* 664-678.

Bowlby, J. (1988). *A Secure Base: Parent-child Attachment and Healthy Human Development.* New York: Basic Books.

Boyes, W. J., Mounts, W. S. J., & Sowell, C. (2004). Restaurant tipping: Free-riding, social acceptance, and gender differences. *Journal of Applied Social Psychology, 34,* 2616-2628.

Bradburn, N., & Sudman, S. (1988). *Polls & Surveys: Understanding What They Tell Us.* San Francisco, CA: Jossey-Bass.

Bradbury, T. N., Beach, S. R. H., Fincham, F. D., & Nelson, G. M. (1996). Attributions and behavior in functional and dysfunctional marriages. *Journal of Consulting and Clinical Psychology, 64,* 569-576.

Bradbury, T. N., & Fincham, F. D. (1992). Attributions and behavior in marital interaction. *Journal of Personality and Social Psychology, 63,* 613-628.

Brafford, L., & Beck, K. (1991). Development and validation of a condom self-efficacy scale for college students. *Journal of American College Health, 39,* 219-225.

Branscombe, N. R., Schmitt, M. T., & Harvey, R. D. (1999). Perceiving pervasive discrimination among African Americans: Implications for group identification and well-being. *Journal of Personality and Social Psychology, 77,* 135-149.

Branscombe, N. R., & Wann, D. L. (1994). Collective self-esteem consequences of outgroup derogation when a valued social identity is on trial. *European Journal of Social Psychology, 24,* 641-657.

Branscombe, N. R., Wann, D. L., Noel, J. G., & Coleman, J. (1993). In-group or out-group extremity: Importance of the threatened social identity. *Personality and Social Psychology Bulletin, 19,* 381-388.

Brauer, M., Judd, C. M., & Gliner, M. D. (1995). The effects of repeated expressions on attitude polarization during group discussions. *Journal of Personality and Social Psychology, 68,* 1014-1029.

Braun, K., Ellis, R., & Loftus, E. (2002). Make my memory: How advertising can change our memories of the past. *Psychology & Marketing, 19,* 1-23.

Bray, R. M., Johnson, D., & Chilstrom, J. T. (1982). Social influence by group members with minority opinions: A comparison of Hollander and Moscovici. *Journal of Personality and Social Psychology, 43,* 78-88.

Brehm, J. (1956). Postdecision changes in the desirability of alternatives. *The Journal of Abnormal and Social Psychology, 52,* 384-389.

Brehm, J. W. (1966). *A Theory of Psychological Reactance.* New York: Academic Press.

Brehm, J. W., & Brehm, S. S. (1981). *Psychological Reactance.* New York: Wiley.

Brennan, K. A., & Shaver, P. R. (1995). Dimensions of adult attachment, affect regulation, and romantic relationship functioning. *Personality and Social Psychology Bulletin, 21,* 267-283.

Brent, D. A., Kerr, M. M., Goldstein, C., & Bozigar, J. (1989). An outbreak of suicide and suicidal behavior in a high school. *Journal of the American Academy of Child & Adolescent Psychiatry, 28,* 918-924.

Brescoll, V. L., & Uhlmann, E. L. (2008). Can an angry woman get ahead? Status conferral, gender, and expression of emotion in the workplace. *Psychological Science, 19,* 268-275.

Brett, J.M., & Goldberg, S.B. (1983). Grievance mediation in the coal industry: A field experiment. *Industrial and Labor Relations Review, 37,* 49-69.

Brett, J. M., Goldberg, S. B., & Ury, W. L. (1990). Designing systems for resolving disputes in organizations. *American Psychologist, 45,* 162-170.

Brewer, M. B. (1979). In-group bias in the minimal intergroup situation: A cognitive motivational analysis. *Psychological Bulletin, 86,* 307-324.

Brewer, M. B., & Kramer, R. M. (1986). Choice behavior in social dilemmas: Effects of social identity, group size, and decision framing. *Journal of Personality and Social Psychology, 50,* 543-549.

Brewer, M. B., & Pickett, C. L. (1999). Distinctiveness motives as a source of the social self. In T. Tyler, R. Kramer, & O. John (Eds.), *The Psychology of the Social Self* (pp. 71-87). Mahwah, NJ: Erlbaum.

Brickner, M. A., Harkins, S. G., & Ostrom, T. M. (1986). Effects of personal involvement: Thought-provoking implications for social loafing. *Journal of Personality and Social Psychology, 51,* 763-770.

Briñol, P., & Petty, R. E. (2003). Overt head movements and persuasion: A self-validation analysis. *Journal of Personality and Social Psychology, 84,* 1123-1139.

Broadstock, M., Borland, R., & Gason, R. (1992). Effects of suntan on judgements of healthiness and attractiveness by adolescents. *Journal of Applied Social Psychology, 22,* 157-172.

Brockner, J., & Rubin, J.Z. (1985). *Entrapment in Escalating Conflicts: A Social Psychological Analysis.* New York: Springer Verlag.

Bronfenbrenner, U. (1961). The mirror-image in Soviet-American relations. *Journal of Social Issues, 17,* 45-56.

Brown, R. P., Charnsangavej, T., Keough, K. A., Newman, M. L., & Rentfrow, P. J. (2000). Putting the 'affirm' into affirmative action: Preferential selection and academic performance. *Journal of Personality and Social Psychology, 79,* 736-747.

Brown, B. B., Clasen, D. R., & Eicher, S. A. (1986). Perceptions of peer pressure, peer conformity dispositions, and self-reported behavior among adolescents. *Developmental Psychology, 22,* 521-530.

Brown, J., & Gallagher, F. (1992). Coming to terms with failure: Private self-enhancement and public self-effacement. *Journal of Experimental Social Psychology, 28,* 3-22.

Brown, J., Novick, N., Lord, K., & Richards, J. (1992). When Gulliver travels: Social context, psychological closeness, and self-appraisals. *Journal of Personality and Social Psychology, 62,* 717-727.

Brown, J., & Rogers, R. (1991). Self-serving attributions: The role of physiological arousal. *Personality and Social Psychology Bulletin, 17,* 501-506.

Browne, A. (1993). Violence against women by male partners: Prevalence, outcomes, and policy implications. *American Psychologist, 48,* 1077-1087.

Brownstein, A., Read, S., & Simon, D. (2004). Bias at the racetrack: Effects of individual expertise and task importance on predecision reevaluation of alternatives. *Personality and Social Psychology Bulletin, 30,* 891-904.

Bruch, M. A., Hamer, R. J., & Heimberg, R. G. (1995). Shyness and public consciousness: Additive or interactive relation with social interaction? *Journal of Personality, 63,* 47-63.

Bruder-Mattson, S. F., & Hovanitz, C. A. (1990). Coping and attributional styles as predictors of depression. *Journal of Clinical Psychology, 46,* 557-565.

Brückner, H., & Bearman, P. (2005). After the promise: The STD consequences of adolescent virginity pledges. *Journal of Adolescent Health, 36,* 271-278.

Brumbaugh, C. C., & Fraley, R. C. (2006). Transference and attachment: How do attachment patterns get carried forward from one relationship to the next? *Personality and Social Psychology Bulletin, 32,* 552-560.

Bryan, J. H., & Test, M. A. (1967). Models and helping: Naturalistic studies in aiding behavior. *Journal of Personality and Social Psychology, 6,* 400-407.

Bryant, F., & Guilbault, R. (2002). 'I knew it all along' eventually: The development of hindsight bias in reaction to the Clinton impeachment verdict. *Basic and Applied Social Psychology, 24,* 27-41.

Bui, K. T., Peplau, L. A., & Hill, C. T. (1996). Testing the Rusbult model of relationship commitment and stability in a 15-year study of heterosexual couples. *Personality and Social Psychology Bulletin, 22,* 1244-1257.

Bureau of Labor Statistics. (2009). *Labor Force Statistics.* Washington, DC: U.S. Bureau of Labor Statistics.

Burger, J. M. (1986). Increasing compliance by improving the deal: The that's-not-all technique. *Journal of Personality and Social Psychology, 51,* 277-283.

Burger, J. M., & Caldwell, D. F. (2003). The effects of monetary incentives and labeling on the foot-in-the-door effect: Evidence for a self-perception process. *Basic and Applied Social Psychology, 25,* 235-241.

Burger, J. M., Messian, N., Patel, S., del Prado, A., & Anderson, C. (2004). What a coincidence! The effects of incidental similarity on compliance. *Personality and Social Psychology Bulletin, 30,* 35-43.

Burger, J. M., & Petty, R. E. (1981). The low-ball compliance technique: Task or person commitment? *Journal of Personality and Social Psychology, 40,* 492-500.

Burgess, D., & Borgida, E. (1997). Refining sex-role spillover theory: The role of gender subtypes and harasser attributions. *Social Cognition, 15,* 291-311.

Burgess, M., Enzle, M., & Schmaltz, R. (2004). Defeating the potentially deleterious effects of externally imposed deadlines: Practitioners' rules-of-thumb. *Personality and Social Psychology Bulletin, 30,* 868-877.

Burkley, E. (2008). The role of self-control in resistance to persuasion. *Personality and Social Psychology Bulletin, 34,* 419-431.

Burns, R. B. (1978). The relative effectiveness of various incentives and deterrents as judged by pupils and teachers. *Educational Studies, 4,* 229-243.

Burnstein, E., Crandall, C., & Kitayama, S. (1994). Some neo-Darwinian decision rules for altruism: Weighing cues for inclusive fitness as a function of the biological importance of the decision. *Journal of Personality and Social Psychology, 67,* 773-789.

Burt, M. R. (1980). Cultural myths and support for rape. *Journal of Personality and Social Psychology, 38,* 217-230.

Bushman, B. J. (1988). The effects of apparel on compliance: A field experiment with a female authority figure. *Personality and Social Psychology Bulletin, 14,* 459-467.

Bushman, B. J. (1993). Human aggression while under the influence of alcohol and other drugs: An integrative research review. *Current Directions in Psychological Science, 2,* 148-152.

Bushman, B. J. (1996). Individual differences in the extent and development of aggressive cognitive-associative networks. *Personality and Social Psychology Bulletin, 22,* 811-819.

Bushman, B. J. (1998). Priming effects of media violence on the accessibility of aggressive constructs in memory. *Personality and Social Psychology Bulletin, 24,* 537-545.

Bushman, B. J. (2002). Does venting anger feed or extinguish the flame? Catharsis, rumination, distraction, anger and aggressive responding. *Personality and Social Psychology Bulletin, 28,* 724-731.

Bushman, B. J., & Anderson, C. A. (2001). Media violence and the American public: Scientific facts versus media misinformation. *American Psychologist, 56,* 477-489.

Bushman, B. J., & Anderson, C. A. (2002). Violent video games and hostile expectations: A test of the general aggression model. *Personality and Social Psychology Bulletin, 28,* 1679-1686.

Bushman, B., & Baumeister, R. (1998). Threatened egotism, narcissism, self-esteem, and direct and displaced aggression: Does self-love or self-hate lead to violence? *Journal of Personality and Social Psychology, 75,* 219-229.

Bushman, B. J., Baumeister, R. F., & Phillips, C. M. (2001). Do people aggress to improve their mood? Catharsis beliefs, affect regulation opportunity, and aggressive responding. *Journal of Personality and Social Psychology, 81,* 17-32.

Bushman, B. J., Baumeister, R. F., & Stack, A. D. (1999). Catharsis, aggression, and persuasive influence: Self-fulfilling or self-defeating prophecies? *Journal of Personality and Social Psychology, 76,* 367-376.

Bushman, B. J., Bonacci, A. M., Pedersen, W. C., Vasquez, E. A., & Miller, N. (2005). Chewing on it can chew you up: Effects of rumination on triggered displaced aggression. *Journal of Personality and Social Psychology, 88,* 969-983.

Bushman, B. J., Bonacci, A. M., van Dijk, M., & Baumeister, R. F. (2003). Narcissism, sexual refusal, and aggression: Testing a narcissistic reactance model of sexual coercion. *Journal of Personality and Social Psychology, 84,* 1027-1040.

Bushman, B. J., & Cantor, J. (2003). Media ratings for violence and sex: Implications for policymakers and parents. *American Psychologist, 58,* 130-141.

Bushman, B. J., & Cooper, H. M. (1990). Effects of alcohol on human aggression: An intergrative research review. *Psychological Bulletin, 107,* 341-354.

Bushman, B. J., & Geen, R. G. (1990). Role of cognitive emotional mediators and individual differences in the effects of media violence on aggression. *Journal of Personality and Social Psychology, 58,* 156-163.

Bushman, B. J., & Stack, A. D. (1996). Forbidden fruit versus tainted fruit: Effects of warning labels on attraction to television violence. *Journal of Experimental Psychology: Applied, 2,* 207-226.

Bushman, B. J., Wang, M. C., & Anderson, C. A. (2005a). Is the curve relating temperature to aggression linear or curvilinear? Assaults and temperature in Minneapolis reexamined. *Journal of Personality and Social Psychology, 89,* 62-66.

Bushman, B. J., Wang, M. C., & Anderson, C. A. (2005b). Is the curve relating temperature to aggression linear or curvilinear? A response to Bell (2005) and to Cohn and Rotton (2005). *Journal of Personality and Social Psychology, 89,* 74-77.

Bushman, B., & Wells, G. (2001). Narrative impressions of literature: The availability bias and the corrective properties of meta-analytic approaches. *Personality and Social Psychology Bulletin, 27,* 1123-1130.

Buss, A. H., & Perry, M. (1992). The Aggression Questionnaire. *Journal of Personality and Social Psychology, 63,* 452-459.

Buss, D. M. (1989). Sex differences in human mate preferences: Evolutionary hypotheses tested in 37 cultures. *Behavioral and Brain Sciences, 12,* 1-49.

Buss, D. M. (1995). Evolutionary psychology: A new paradigm for psychological science. *Psychological Inquiry, 61,* 1-30.

Buss, D. M., Larsen, R. J., Westen, D., & Semmelroth, J. (1992). Sex differences in jealousy: Evolution, physiology, and psychology. *Psychological Science, 3,* 251-255.

Buss, D. M., & Schmitt, D. P. (1993). Sexual Strategies Theory: An evolutionary perspective on human mating. *Psychological Review, 100,* 204-232.

Buss, D. M., & Shackelford, T. K. (1997). From vigilance to violence: Mate retention tactics in married couples. *Journal of Personality and Social Psychology, 72,* 346-36.

Buss, D. M., Shackelford, T. K., Kirkpatrick, L. A., & Larsen, R. J. (2001). A half century of mate preferences: The cultural evolution of values. *Journal of Marriage & the Family, 63,* 491-503.

Buss, D. M., Shackelford, T. K., Kirkpatrick, L. A., Choe, J. C., Lim, H. K., Hasegawa, M., et al. (1999). Jealousy and the nature of beliefs about infidelity: Tests of competing hypotheses about sex differences in the United States, Korea, and Japan. *Personal Relationships, 6,* 125-150.

Butler, D., & Geis, F. L. (1990). Nonverbal affect responses to male and female leaders: Implications for leadership evaluations. *Journal of Personality and Social Psychology, 58,* 48-59.

Butler, J. L., & Baumeister, R. F. (1998). The trouble with friendly faces: Skilled performance with a supportive audience. *Journal of Personality and Social Psychology, 75,* 1213-1230.

Buunk, B. P., Angleitner, A., Oubaid, V., & Buss, D. M. (1996). Sex differences in jealousy in evolutionary and cultural perspective: Tests from the Netherlands, Germany, and the United States. *Psychological Science, 7,* 359-363.

Buunk, B. P., & van der Eijnden, R. J. J. M. (1997). Perceived prevalence, perceived superiority, and relationship satisfaction: Most relationships are good, but ours is the best. *Personality and Social Psychology Bulletin, 23,* 219-228.

Byrne, D. (1997). An overview (and underview) of research and theory within the attraction paradigm. *Journal of Social and Personal Relationships, 14,* 417-431.

Byrnes, D. A., & Kiger, G. (1990). The effect of a prejudice-reduction simulation on attitude change. *Journal of Applied Social Psychology, 20,* 341-356.

Cacioppo, J., Amaral, D., Blanchard, J., Cameron, J., Carter, C., Crews, D., et al. (2007). Social neuroscience: Progress and implications for mental health. *Perspectives on Psychological Science, 2,* 99-123.

Cacioppo, J. T., Berntson, G. G., Lorig, T. S., Norris, C. J., Rickett, E., & Nusbaum, H. (2003). Just because you're imaging the brain doesn't mean you can stop using your head: A primer and set of first principles. *Journal of Personality and Social Psychology, 85,* 650-661.

Cacioppo, J., Marshall-Goodell, B., Tassinary, L., & Petty, R. (1992). Rudimentary determinants of attitudes: Classical conditioning is more effective when prior knowledge about the attitude stimulus is low than high. *Journal of Experimental Social Psychology, 28,* 207-233.

Cacioppo, J. T., & Petty, R. E. (1982). The need for cognition. *Journal of Personality and Social Psychology, 42,* 116-131.

Caldwell, R. A., & Reinhart, M. A. (1988). The relationship of personality to individual differences in the use of type and source of social support. *Journal of Social & Clinical Psychology, 6,* 140-146.

Campbell, D., Carr, S., & MacLachlan, M. (2001). Attributing 'third world poverty' in Australia and Malawi: A case of donor bias? *Journal of Applied Social Psychology, 31,* 409-430.

Campbell, J. D., & Fairey, P. J. (1989). Informational and normative routes to conformity: The effect of faction size as a function of norm extremity and attention to the stimulus. *Journal of Personality and Social Psychology, 57,* 457-468.

Campbell, J., Trapnell, P., Heine, S., Katz, I., Lavallee, L., & Lehman, D. (1996). Self-concept clarity: Measurement, personality correlates, and cultural boundaries. *Journal of Personality and Social Psychology, 70,* 141-156.

Campbell, L., Simpson, J. A., Boldry, J., & Kashy, D. A. (2005). Perceptions of conflict and support in romantic relationships: The role of attachment anxiety. *Journal of Personality and Social Psychology, 88,* 510-531.

Campbell, W. K., Foster, C. A., & Finkel, E. J. (2002). Does self-love lead to love for others?: A story of narcissistic game-playing. *Journal of Personality and Social Psychology, 83,* 340–354.

Carli, L. (1999). Cognitive reconstruction, hindsight, and reactions to victims and perpetrators. *Personality and Social Psychology Bulletin, 25,* 966-979.

Carli, L. L., Ganley, R., & Pierce-Otay, A. (1991). Similarity and satisfaction in roommate relationships. *Personality and Social Psychology Bulletin, 17,* 419-426.

Carlo, G., Eisenberg, N., Troyer, D., Switzer, G., & Speer, A. L. (1991). The altruistic personality: In what contexts is it apparent? *Journal of Personality and Social Psychology, 61,* 450-458.

Carlson, M., Charlin, V., & Miller, N. (1988). Positive mood and helping behavior: A test of six hypotheses. *Journal of Personality and Social Psychology, 55,* 211-229.

Carnagey, N. L., & Anderson, C. A. (2005). The effects of reward and punishment in violent video games on aggressive affect, cognition, and behavior. *Psychological Science, 16,* 882-889.

Carnagey, N. L., Anderson, C. A., & Bartholow, B. D. (2007). Media violence and social neuroscience: New questions and new opportunities. *Current Directions in Psychological Science, 16,* 178-182.

Carnelley, K. B., Pietromonaco, P. R., & Jaffe, K. (1996). Attachment, caregiving, and relationship functioning in couples: Effects of self and partner. *Personal Relationships, 3,* 257-277.

Carnevale, P. J., & Probst, T. M. (1998). Social values and social conflict in creative problem solving and categorization. *Journal of Personality and Social Psychology, 74,* 1300-1309.

Carroll, J., & Russell, J. (1996). Do facial expressions signal specific emotions? Judging emotion from the face in context. *Journal of Personality and Social Psychology, 70,* 205-218.

Carron, A. V., Colman, M. M., Wheeler, J., & Stevens, D. (2002). Cohesion and performance in sport: A meta analysis. *Journal of Sport & Exercise Psychology, 24,* 168-188.

Carter, J. D., Hall, J. A., Carney, D. R., & Rosip, J. C. (2006). Individual differences in the acceptance of stereotyping. *Journal of Research in Personality, 40,* 1103-1118.

Carter, S. L. (1993). *Reflections of an Affirmative Action Baby.* New York: Basic Books.

Cash, T. F., & Derlega, V. J. (1978). The matching hypothesis: Physical attractiveness among same-sexed friends. *Personality and Social Psychology Bulletin, 4,* 240-243.

Caspi, A., & Herbener, E. S. (1990). Continuity and change: Assortative marriage and the consistency of personality in adulthood. *Journal of Personality and Social Psychology, 58,* 250-258.

Catalano, R., Novaco, R., & McConnell, W. (1997). A model of the net effect of job loss on violence. *Journal of Personality and Social Psychology, 72,* 1440-1447.

Ceci, S., Huffman, M., Smith, E., & Loftus, E. (1994). Repeatedly thinking about a non event: Source misattributions among preschoolers. *Consciousness and Cognition: An International Journal, 3*, 388-407.

Cejka, M. A., & Eagly, A. H. (1999). Gender-stereotypic images of occupations correspond to the sex segregation of employment. *Personality and Social Psychology Bulletin, 25*, 413-423.

Centerwall, B.S. (1989). Exposure to television as a cause of violence. In G. Comstock (Ed.), *Public Communication and Behavior* (pp. 1-58), New York: Academic Press.

Chacko, T. I. (1982). Women and equal employment opportunity: Some unintended effects. *Journal of Applied Psychology, 67*, 119-123.

Chaiken, S. (1980). Heuristic versus systematic information processing and the use of source versus message cues in persuasion. *Journal of Personality and Social Psychology, 39*, 752-766.

Chaiken, S., & Eagly, A. H. (1983). Communication modality as a determinant of persuasion: The role of communicator salience. *Journal of Personality and Social Psychology, 45*, 241-256.

Chaiken, S., & Maheswaran, D. (1994). Heuristic processing can bias systematic processing: Effects of source credibility, argument ambiguity, and task importance on attitude judgment. *Journal of Personality and Social Psychology, 66*, 460-473.

Chamberlain, L. J., Wang, Y., & Robinson, T.M., (2006). Does children's screen time predict requests for advertised products? Cross-sectional and prospective analyses. *Archives of Pediatrics & Adolescent Medicine, 160*, 363-368.

Chambers, J. R., Baron, R. S., & Inman, M. L. (2006). Misperceptions in intergroup conflict: Disagreeing about what we disagree about. *Psychological Science, 17*, 38-45.

Chambers, J. R., & Melnyk, D. (2006). Why do I hate thee? Conflict misperceptions and intergroup mistrust. *Personality and Social Psychology Bulletin, 32*, 1295-1311.

Chance, S. E., Brown, R. T., Dabbs, J. M. J., & Casey, R. (2000). Testosterone, intelligence and behavior disorders in young boys. *Personality and Individual Differences, 28*, 437-445.

Chance, J. E., Goldstein, A. G. (1981). Depth of processing in response to own- and other-race faces. *Personality and Social Psychology Bulletin, 7*, 475-480.

Chang, E., & Asakawa, K. (2003). Cultural variations on optimistic and pessimistic bias for self versus a sibling: Is there evidence for self-enhancement in the West and for self-criticism in the East when the referent group is specified? *Journal of Personality and Social Psychology, 84*, 569-581.

Chang, E., Asakawa, K., & Sanna, L. (2001). Cultural variations in optimistic and pessimistic bias: Do Easterners really expect the worst and Westerners really expect the best when predicting future life events?. *Journal of Personality and Social Psychology, 81*, 476-491.

Chaplin, W., Phillips, J., Brown, J., Clanton, N., & Stein, J. (2000). Handshaking, gender, personality, and first impressions. *Journal of Personality and Social Psychology, 79*, 110-117.

Charbonneau, D., Barling, J., & Kelloway, E. K. (2001). Transformational leadership and sports performance: The mediating role of intrinsic motivation. *Journal of Applied Social Psychology, 31*, 1521-1534.

Chatman, C. M., & von Hippel, W. (2001). Attributional mediation of in-group bias. *Journal of Experimental Social Psychology, 37*, 267-272.

Chemers, M. M., Watson, C. B., & May, S. T. (2000). Dispositional affect and leadership effectiveness: A comparison of self-esteem, optimism, and efficacy. *Personality and Social Psychology Bulletin, 26*, 267-277.

Chen, H. C., Reardon, R., Rea, C., & Moore, D. J. (1992). Forewarning of content and involvement: Consequences for persuasion and resistance to persuasion. *Journal of Experimental Social Psychology, 28*, 523-541.

Chen, L.H., Baker, S.P., Braver, E.R., & Li, G. (2000). Carrying passengers as a risk factor for crashes fatal to 16- and 17-year-old drivers. *Journal of the American Medical Association, 283*, 1578-1582.

Chen, C., Lee, S., & Stevenson, H.W. (1995). Response style and cross-cultural comparisons of rating scales among East Asian and North American students. *Psychological Science, 6*, 170–175.

Chen, S., English, T., & Peng, K. (2006). Self-verification and contextualized self-views. *Personality and Social Psychology Bulletin, 32*, 930-942.

Choi, I., & Choi, Y. (2002). Culture and self-concept flexibility. *Personality and Social Psychology Bulletin, 28*, 1508-1517.

Choi, I., & Nisbett, R. (1998). Situational salience and cultural differences in the correspondence bias and actor-observer bias. *Personality and Social Psychology Bulletin, 24*, 949-960.

Choi, I., & Nisbett, R. (2000). Cultural psychology of surprise: Holistic theories and recognition of contradiction. *Journal of Personality and Social Psychology, 79*, 890-905.

Choi, I., Nisbett, R., & Norenzayan, A. (1999). Causal attribution across cultures: Variation and universality. *Psychological Bulletin, 125*, 47-63.

Christakis, D. A., & Zimmerman, F. J. (2007). Violent television viewing during preschool is associated with antisocial behavior during school age. *Pediatrics, 120*, 993-999.

Christensen, A., & Heavey, C. L. (1990). Gender and social structure in the demand/withdraw pattern of marital conflict. *Journal of Personality and Social Psychology, 59*, 73-81.

Christensen, P. N., & Kashy, D. A. (1998). Perceptions of and by lonely people in initial social interaction. *Personality and Social Psychology Bulletin, 24*, 322-329.

Church, A., Ortiz, F., Katigbak, M., Avdeyeva, T., Emerson, A., Vargas Flores, J., et al. (2003). Measuring individual and cultural differences in implicit trait theories. *Journal of Personality and Social Psychology, 85*, 332-347.

Cialdini, R. B., Borden, R. J., Thorne, A., Walker, M., Freeman, S., & Sloan, L. (1976). Basking in reflected glory: Three (football) field studies. *Journal of Personality and Social Psychology, 34*, 366-375.

Cialdini, R. B., Brown, S. L., Lewis, B. P., Luce, C., & Neuberg, S. L. (1997). Reinterpreting the empathy-altruism relationship: When one into one equals oneness. *Journal of Personality and Social Psychology, 73*, 481-494.

Cialdini, R. B., Cacioppo, J. T., Bassett, R., & Miller, J. A. (1978). Low-ball procedure for producing compliance: Commitment then cost. *Journal of Personality and Social Psychology, 36*, 463-476.

Cialdini, R. B., Darby, B. L., & Vincent, J. E. (1973). Transgression and altruism: A case for hedonism. *Journal of Experimental Social Psychology, 9*, 502-516.

Cialdini, R. B., Green, B. L., & Rusch, A. J. (1992). When tactical pronouncements of change become real change: The case of reciprocal persuasion. *Journal of Personality and Social Psychology, 63*, 30-40.

Cialdini, R. B., & Kenrick, D. T. (1976). Altruism as hedonism: A social development perspective on the relationship of negative mood state and helping. *Journal of Personality and Social Psychology, 34*, 907-914.

Cialdini, R. B., Kenrick, D. T., & Baumann, D. J. (1982). Effects of mood on prosocial behavior in children and adults. In N. Eisenberg-Berg (Ed.), *Development of Prosocial Behavior* (pp. 339-359). New York: Academic Press.

Cialdini, R. B., Reno, R. R., & Kallgren, C. A. (1990). A focus theory of normative conduct: Recycling the concept of norms to reduce littering in public places. *Journal of Personality and Social Psychology, 58*, 1015-1026.

Cialdini, R. B., Schaller, M., Houlihan, D., Arps, K., Fultz, J., & Beaman, A. L. (1987). Empathy-based helping: Is it selflessly or selfishly motivated? *Journal of Personality and Social Psychology, 52*, 749-758.

Cialdini, R. B., Vincent, J. E., Lewis, S. K., Catalan, J., Wheeler, D., & Darby, B. L. (1975). Reciprocal concessions procedure for inducing compliance: The door-in-the-face technique. *Journal of Personality and Social Psychology, 31*, 206-215.

Cialdini, R. B., Wosinska, W., Barrett, D. W., Butner, J., & Gornik-Durose, M. (1999). Compliance with a request in two cultures: The differential influence of social proof and commitment/consistency on collectivists and individualists. *Personality and Social Psychology Bulletin, 25*, 1242-1253.

Clark, M. S., & Grote, N. K. (1998). Why aren't indices of relationship costs always negatively related to indices of relationship quality? *Personality and Social Psychology Review, 2*, 2-17.

Clark, M. S., Mills, J., & Powell, M.C. (1986). Keeping track of needs in communal and exchange relationships. *Journal of Personality and Social Psychology, 51*, 333-338.

Clark, R., Anderson, N. B., Clark, V. R., & Williams, D. R. (1999). Racism as a stressor for African Americans: A biopsychosocial model. *American Psychologist, 54*, 805-816.

Clark, R. D., & Maass, A. (1988). The role of social categorization and perceived source credibility in minority influence. *European Journal of Social Psychology, 18*, 381-394.

Clark, R. D., & Maass, A. (1990). The effects of majority size on minority influence. *European Journal of Social Psychology, 20*, 99-117.

Clark, R. D., & Word, L. E. (1972). Why don't bystanders help? Because of ambiguity? *Journal of Personality and Social Psychology, 24*, 392-400.

Clark, R., & Hatfield, E. (1989). Gender differences in receptivity to sexual offers. *Journal of Psychology & Human Sexuality, 2*, 39-55.

Cohen, D. (1996). Law, social policy, and violence: The impact of regional cultures. *Journal of Personality and Social Psychology, 70*, 961-978.

Cohen, D., & Gunz, A. (2002). As seen by the other... Perspectives on the self in the memories and emotional perceptions of Easterners and Westerners. *Psychological Science, 13*, 55-59.

Cohen, D., & Nisbett, R. E. (1994). Self-protection and the culture of honor: Explaining Southern violence. *Personality and Social Psychology Bulletin, 20*, 551-567.

Cohen, D., & Nisbett, R. E. (1997). Field experiments examining the culture of honor: The role of institutions in perpetuating norms about violence. *Personality and Social Psychology Bulletin, 23*, 1188-1199.

Cohen, D., Nisbett, R. E., Bowdle, B. F., & Schwarz, N. (1996). Insult, aggression, and the southern culture of honor: An 'experimental ethnography.'. *Journal of Personality and Social Psychology, 70*, 945-960.

Cohen, G. L., Garcia, J., Apfel, N., & Master, A. (2006). Reducing the racial achievement gap: A social-psychological intervention. *Science, 313*, 1307-1310.

Cohen, G. L., Garcia, J., Purdie-Vaughns, V., Apfel, N., & Brzustoski, P. (2009). Recursive processes in self-affirmation: Intervening to close the minority achievement gap. *Science, 324*, 400-403.

Cohen, L. L., & Swim, J. K. (1995). The differential impact of gender ratios on women and men: Tokenism, self-confidence, and expectations. *Personality and Social Psychology Bulletin, 21*, 876-884.

Cohen, S., Doyle, W. J., Skoner, D. P., Rabin, B. S., & Gwaltney, J. M., Jr. (1997). Social ties and susceptibility to the common cold. *Journal of theAmerican Medical Association, 277*, 1940-1944.

Cohen, T. R., & Insko, C. A. (2008). War and peace: Possible approaches to reducing intergroup conflict. *Perspectives on Psychological Science, 3*, 87-93.

Cohn, E. G. (1993). The prediction of police calls for service: The influence of weather and temporal variables on rape and domestic violence. *Journal of Environmental Psychology, 13*, 71-83.

Cohn, E. G., & Rotton, J. (1997). Assault as a function of time and temperature: A moderator-variable time-series analysis. *Journal of Personality and Social Psychology, 72*, 1322-1334.

Cohn, E. G., & Rotton, J. (2000). Weather, seasonal trends and property crimes in Minneapolis, 1987-1988. A moderator-variable time-series analysis of routine activities. *Journal of Environmental Psychology, 20*, 257-272.

Coker, A. L., Smith, P. H., McKeown, R. E., & King, M. J. (2000). Frequency and correlates of intimate partner violence by type: Physical, sexual, and psychological battering. *American Journal of Public Health, 90*, 553-559.

College Board. (2008). *College-Bound Seniors: Total Group Profile Report.* New York: The College Board.

College Entrance Examination Board. (2004). *College-Bound Seniors, 1994: SAT Profile, Profile of SAT and Achievement Test Takers.* Princeton, NJ: Educational Testing Service.

Collins, N. L., & Feeney, B. C. (2000). A safe haven: An attachment theory perspective on support seeking and caregiving in intimate relationships. *Journal of Personality and Social Psychology, 78*, 1053-1073.

Collins, N. L., Ford, M. B., Guichard, A. C., & Allard, L. M. (2006). Working models of attachment and attribution processes in intimate relationships. *Personality and Social Psychology Bulletin, 32*, 201-219.

Collins, N. L., & Miller, L. C. (1994). Self-disclosure and liking: A meta-analytic review. *Psychological Bulletin, 116*, 457-475.

Colvin, C., Block, J., & Funder, D. (1995). Overly positive self-evaluations and personality: Negative implications for mental health. *Journal of Personality and Social Psychology, 68*, 1152-1162.

Condon, J. W., & Crano, W. D. (1988). Inferred evaluation and the relation between attitude similarity and interpersonal attraction. *Journal of Personality and Social Psychology, 54*, 789-797.

Conley, T., & Collins, B. (2002). Gender, relationship status and stereotyping about sexual risk. *Personality and Social Psychology Bulletin, 28*, 1483-1494.

Cooper, J. (1980). Reducing fears and increasing assertiveness: The role of dissonance reduction. *Journal of Experimental Social Psychology, 16*, 199-213.

Cooper, J., & Fazio, R. H. (1984). A new look at dissonance theory. In L. Berkowitz (Ed.), *Advances in Experimental Social Psychology* (Vol. 17, pp. 229-266). New York: Academic Press.

Cooper, J., Fazio, R., & Rhodewalt, F. (1978). Dissonance and humor: Evidence for the undifferentiated nature of dissonance arousal. *Journal of Personality and Social Psychology, 36,* 280-285.

Cooper, J., & Neuhaus, I. M. (2000). The 'hired gun' effect: Assessing the effect of pay, frequency of testifying, and credentials on the perception of expert testimony. *Law and Human Behavior, 24,* 149-171.

Cooper, J., & Worchel, S. (1970). Role of undesired consequences in arousing cognitive dissonance. *Journal of Personality and Social Psychology, 16,* 199-206.

Cooper, M., Frone, M., Russell, M., & Mudar, P. (1995). Drinking to regulate positive and negative emotions: A motivational model of alcohol use. *Journal of Personality and Social Psychology, 69,* 990-1005.

Coovert, M., & Reeder, G. (1990). Negativity effects in impression formation: The role of unit formation and schematic expectations. *Journal of Experimental Social Psychology, 26,* 49-62.

Copeland, J. (1994). Prophecies of power: Motivational implications of social power for behavioral confirmation. *Journal of Personality and Social Psychology, 67,* 264-277.

Correll, J., & Park, B. (2005). A model of the ingroup as a social resource. *Personality and Social Psychology Review, 9,* 341-359.

Correll, J., Park, B., Judd, C. M., & Wittenbrink, B. (2002). The police officer's dilemma: Using ethnicity to disambiguate potentially threatening individuals. *Journal of Personality and Social Psychology, 83,* 1314-1329.

Coser, L. A. (1956). *The Functions of Social Conflict.* Glencoe, IL: Free Press.

Cosier, R. A., Schwenk, C. R., & Dalton, D. R. (1992). Managerial decision making in Japan, the U.S., and Hong Kong. *International Journal of Conflict Management, 3,* 151-160.

Cota, A. A., Evans, C. R., Dion, K. L., Kilik, L., & Longman, R. (1995). The structure of group cohesion. *Personality and Social Psychology Bulletin, 21,* 572-580.

Cottrell, N. B., Wack, D. L., Sekerak, G. J., & Rittle, R. H. (1968). Social facilitation of dominant responses by the presence of au audience and the mere presence of others. *Journal of Personality and Social Psychology, 9,* 245-250.

Cousins, S. (1989). Culture and self-perception in Japan and the United States. *Journal of Personality and Social Psychology, 56,* 124-131.

Cramer, R. E., McMaster, M. R., Bartell, P. A., & Dragna, M. (1988). Subject competence and minimization of the bystander effect. *Journal of Applied Social Psychology, 18,* 1133-1148.

Crandall, C. (1994). Prejudice against fat people: Ideology and self-interest. *Journal of Personality and Social Psychology, 66,* 882-894.

Crandall, C. S., D'Anello, S., Sakalli, N., Lazarus, E., Wieczorkowska, G., & Feather, N. T. (2001). An attribution-value model of prejudice: Anti-fat attitudes in six nations. *Personality and Social Psychology Bulletin, 27,* 30-37.

Crandall, C. S., Eshleman, A., & O'Brien, L. (2002). Social norms and the expression and suppression of prejudice: The struggle for internalization. *Journal of Personality and Social Psychology, 82,* 359-378.

Crandall, C. S., & Martinez, R. (1996). Culture, ideology, and antifat attitudes. *Personality and Social Psychology Bulletin, 22,* 1165-1176.

Crano, W. (1997). Vested interest, symbolic politics, and attitude-behavior consistency. *Journal of Personality and Social Psychology, 72,* 485-491.

Creasey, G., & Ladd, A. (2005). Generalized and specific attachment representations: Unique and interactive roles in predicting conflict behaviors in close relationships. *Personality and Social Psychology Bulletin, 31,* 1026-1038.

Crick, N. R., & Grotpeter, J. K. (1995). Relational aggression, gender, and social-psychological adjustment. *Child Development, 66,* 710-722.

Crick, N. R., Casas, J. F., & Mosher, M. (1997). Relational and overt aggression in preschool. *Developmental Psychology, 33,* 579-588.

Crisp, R. J., Hewstone, M., & Rubin, M. (2001). Does multiple categorization reduce intergroup bias? *Personality and Social Psychology Bulletin, 27,* 76-89.

Crocker, J., & Luhtanen, R. (1990). Collective self-esteem and ingroup bias. *Journal of Personality and Social Psychology, 58,* 60-67.

Crocker, J., & Major, B. (1989). Social stigma and self-esteem: The self-protective properties of stigma. *Psychological Review, 96,* 608-630.

Crocker, J., Niiya, Y., & Mischkowski, D. (2008). Why does writing about important values reduce defensiveness? Self-affirmation and the role of positive other-directed feelings. *Psychological Science, 19,* 740-747.

Crocker, J., Thompson, L. L., McGraw, K. M., & Ingerman, C. (1987). Downward comparison, prejudice, and evaluations of others: Effects of self-esteem and threat. *Journal of Personality and Social Psychology, 52,* 907-916.

Crocker, J., Voelkl, K., Testa, M., & Major, B. (1991). Social stigma: The affective consequences of attributional ambiguity. *Journal of Personality and Social Psychology, 60,* 218-228.

Croizet, J., & Claire, T. (1998). Extending the concept of stereotype and threat to social class: The intellectual underperformance of students from low socioeconomic backgrounds. *Personality and Social Psychology Bulletin, 24,* 588-594.

Crosby, F. J., & Franco, J. L. (2003). Connections between the ivory tower and the multicolored world: Linking abstract theories of social justice to the rough and tumble of affirmative action. *Personality and Social Psychology Review, 7,* 362-373.

Crosby, F. J., Iyer, A., Clayton, S., & Downing, R. A. (2003). Affirmative action: Psychological data and the policy debates. *American Psychologist, 58,* 93-115.

Cross, S., & Madson, L. (1997). Models of the self: Self-construals and gender. *Psychological Bulletin, 122,* 5-37.

Croyle, R., & Cooper, J. (1983). Dissonance arousal: Physiological evidence. *Journal of Personality and Social Psychology, 45,* 782-791.

Cuddy, A. J. C., Fiske, S. T., & Glick, P. (2007). The BIAS map: Behaviors from intergroup affect and stereotypes. *Journal of Personality and Social Psychology, 92,* 631-648.

Cullum, J., & Harton, H. C. (2007). Cultural evolution: Interpersonal influence, issue importance, and the development of shared attitudes in college residence halls. *Personality and Social Psychology Bulletin, 33,* 1327-1339.

Cunningham, M. R. (1979). Weather, mood, and helping behavior: Quasi experiments with the sunshine samaritan. *Journal of Personality and Social Psychology, 37,* 1947-1956.

Cunningham, M. R., Roberts, A. R., Barbee, A. P., Druen, P. B., & Wu, C. (1995). 'Their ideas of beauty are, on the whole, the same as ours': Consistency and variability in the cross-cultural perception of female physical attractiveness. *Journal of Personality and Social Psychology, 68,* 261-279.

Cunningham, M. R., Steinberg, J., & Grev, R. (1980). Wanting to and having to help: Separate motivations for positive mood and guilt-induced helping. *Journal of Personality and Social Psychology, 38,* 181-192.

Cunningham, W. A., Johnson, M. K., Raye, C. L., Gatenby, J. C., Gore, J. C., & Banaji, M. R. (2004). Separable neural components in the processing of black and white faces. *Psychological Science, 15,* 806-813.

Cutler, B., Penrod, S., & Dexter, H. (1990). Juror sensitivity to eyewitness identification evidence. *Law and Human Behavior, 14,* 185-191.

Dabbs, J. M., Carr, T. S., Frady, R. L., & Riad, J. K. (1995). Testosterone, crime, and misbehavior among 692 male prison inmates. *Personality and Individual Differences, 18,* 627-633.

Dabbs, J. M. J., & Hargrove, M. F. (1997). Age, testosterone, and behavior among female prison inmates. *Psychosomatic Medicine, 59,* 477-480.

Dabbs, J. M., & Morris, R. (1990). Testosterone, social class, and antisocial behavior in a sample of 4,462 men. *Psychological Science, 1,* 209-211.

Dabbs, J. M. J., Riad, J. K., & Chance, S. E. (2001). Testosterone and ruthless homicide. *Personality and Individual Differences, 31,* 599-603.

Dabbs, J. M. J., Strong, R., & Milun, R. (1997). Exploring the mind of testosterone: A beeper study. *Journal of Research in Personality, 31,* 577-587.

Dalton, M., Sargent, J., Beach, M., Titus-Ernstoff, L., Gibson, J., Aherns, M., et al. (2003). Effect of viewing smoking in movies on adolescent smoking initiation: A cohort study. *Lancet, 362,* 281-285.

Daly, M., & Wilson, M. I. (1996). Violence against stepchildren. *Current Directions in Psychological Science, 5,* 77-81.

Darley, J. M., & Batson, C. D. (1973). 'From Jerusalem to Jericho': A study of situational and dispositional variables in helping behavior. *Journal of Personality and Social Psychology, 27,* 100-108.

Darley, J. M., & Fazio, R. H. (1980). Expectancy confirmation processes arising in the social interaction sequence. *American Psychologist, 35,* 867-881.

Darley, J. M., & Gross, P. H. (1983). A hypothesis-confirming bias in labeling effects. *Journal of Personality and Social Psychology, 44,* 20-33.

Darley, J. M., & Latane, B. (1968). Bystander intervention in emergencies: Diffusion of responsibility. *Journal of Personality and Social Psychology, 8,* 377-383.

Das, E. H. H. J., de Wit, J. B. F., & Stroebe, W. (2003). Fear appeals motivate acceptance of action recommendations: Evidence for a positive bias in the processing of persuasive messages. *Personality and Social Psychology Bulletin, 29,* 650-664.

Dasgupta, N., & Asgari, S. (2004). Seeing is believing: Exposure to counterstereotypic women leaders and its effect on the malleability of automatic gender stereotyping. *Journal of Experimental Social Psychology, 40,* 642-658.

Dasgupta, N., & Greenwald, A. G. (2001). On the malleability of automatic attitudes: Combating automatic prejudice with images of admired and disliked individuals. *Journal of Personality and Social Psychology, 81,* 800-814.

Dasgupta, N., & Rivera, L. M. (2006). From automatic antigay prejudice to behavior: The moderating role of conscious beliefs about gender and behavioral control. *Journal of Personality and Social Psychology, 91,* 268-280.

Davidson, R. J., Putnam, K. M., & Larson, C. L. (2000). Dysfunction in the neural circuitry of emotion regulation—a possible prelude to violence. *Science, 289,* 591-594.

Davies, M. F. (1997). Belief persistence after evidential discrediting: The impact of generated versus provided explanations on the likelihood of discredited outcomes. *Journal of Experimental Social Psychology, 33,* 561-578.

Davies, P. G., Spencer, S. J., Quinn, D. M., & Gerhardstein, R. (2002). Consuming images: How television commercials that elicit stereotype threat can restrain women academically and professionally. *Personality and Social Psychology Bulletin, 28,* 1615-1628.

Davila, J., Bradbury, T. N., & Fincham, F. (1998). Negative affectivity as a mediator of the association between adult attachment and marital satisfaction. *Personal Relationships, 5,* 467-484.

Davis, C. G., Lehman, D. R., Silver, R. C., Wortman, C. B., & Ellard, J. H. (1996). Self-blame following a traumatic event: The role of perceived avoidability. *Personality and Social Psychology Bulletin, 22,* 557-567.

Davis, C. G., Lehman, D. R., Wortman, C. B., Silver, R. C., & Thompson, S. C. (1995). The undoing of traumatic life events. *Personality and Social Psychology Bulletin, 21,* 109-124.

Davis, D., Shaver, P. R., & Vernon, M. L. (2003). Physical, emotional, and behavioral reactions to breaking up: The roles of gender, age, emotional involvement, and attachment style. *Personality and Social Psychology Bulletin, 29,* 871-884.

Davis, D., Shaver, P. R., & Vernon, M. L. (2004). Attachment style and subjective motivations for sex. *Personality and Social Psychology Bulletin, 30,* 1076-1090.

Davis, K. E., & Latty-Mann, H. (1987). Love styles and relationship quality: A contribution to validation. *Journal of Social and Personal Relationships, 4,* 409-428.

Davis, M. H. (1983). Empathic concern and the muscular dystrophy telethon: Empathy as a multidimensional construct. *Personality and Social Psychology Bulletin, 9,* 223-229.

Davis, M. H., Luce, C., & Kraus, S. J. (1994). The heritability of characteristics associated with dispositional empathy. *Journal of Personality, 62,* 369-391.

Dawes, R. M. (1980). Social dilemmas. *Annual Review of Psychology, 31,* 169-193.

Dawes, R.M. (2001). *Everyday Irrationality: How Pseudoscientists, Lunatics, and the Rest of Us Fail to Think Rationally.* Boulder, CO: Westview Press.

De Dreu, C. K. W., Koole, S. L., & Steinel, W. (2000). Unfixing the fixed pie: A motivated information-processing approach to integrative negotiation. *Journal of Personality and Social Psychology, 79,* 975-987.

De Hoog, N., Stroebe, W., & de Wit, J. B. F. (2005). The impact of fear appeals on processing and acceptance of action recommendations. *Personality and Social Psychology Bulletin, 31,* 24-33.

De La Ronde, C., & Swann, W. B. J. (1998). Partner verification: Restoring shattered images of our intimates. *Journal of Personality and Social Psychology, 75,* 374-382.

De Wit, J. B. F., Das, E., & Vet, R. (2008). What works best: Objective statistics or a personal testimonial? An assessment of the persuasive effects of different types of message evidence on risk perception. *Health Psychology, 27,* 110-115.

Dean, K. E., & Malamuth, N. M. (1997). Characteristics of men who aggress sexually and of men who imagine aggressing: Risk and moderating variables. *Journal of Personality and Social Psychology, 72,* 449-455.

DeBono, K. G. (1987). Investigating the social-adjustive and value-expressive functions of attitudes: Implications for persuasion processes. *Journal of Personality and Social Psychology, 52,* 279-287.

De Cremer, D. (2002). Respect and cooperation in social dilemmas: The importance of feeling included. *Personality and Social Psychology Bulletin, 28,* 1335-1341.

Deci, E., Koestner, R., & Ryan, R. (1999). A meta-analytic review of experiments examining the effects of extrinsic rewards on intrinsic motivation. *Psychological Bulletin, 125,* 627-668.

Deci, E. L., La Guardia, J. G., Moller, A. C., Scheiner, M. J., & Ryan, R. M. (2006). On the benefits of giving as well as receiving autonomy support: Mutuality in close friendships. *Personality and Social Psychology Bulletin, 32,* 313-327.

DeJong, W. (1980). The stigma of obesity: The consequences of naive assumptions concerning the causes of physical deviance. *Journal of Health and Social Behavior, 21,* 75-87.

DeJong, W., & Musilli, L. (1982). External pressure to comply: Handicapped versus nonhandicapped requesters and the foot-in-the-door phenomenon. *Personality and Social Psychology Bulletin, 8,* 522-527.

Deluty, R. H. (1985). Consistency of assertive, aggressive, and submissive behavior for children. *Journal of Personality and Social Psychology, 49,* 1054-1065.

DePaulo, B. (1992). Nonverbal behavior and self-presentation. *Psychological Bulletin, 111,* 203-243.

DePaulo, B. M., Dull, W. R., Greenberg, J. M., & Swaim, G. W. (1989). Are shy people reluctant to ask for help? *Journal of Personality and Social Psychology, 56,* 834-844.

DePaulo, B., & Kashy, D. (1998). Everyday lies in close and casual relationships. *Journal of Personality and Social Psychology, 74,* 63-79.

DePaulo, B., Kashy, D., Kirkendol, S., Wyer, M., & Epstein, J. (1996). Lying in everyday life. *Journal of Personality and Social Psychology, 70,* 979-995.

Deppe, R., & Harackiewicz, J. (1996). Self-handicapping and intrinsic motivation: Buffering intrinsic motivation from the threat of failure. *Journal of Personality and Social Psychology, 70,* 868-876.

des Jarlais, D. C., Friedman, S. R., Casriel, C., & Kott, A. (1987). AIDS and preventing initiation into intravenous (IV) drug use. *Psychology & Health, 1,* 179-194.

DeSantis, A., & Kayson, W. A. (1997). Defendants' characteristics of attractiveness, race, and sex and sentencing decisions. *Psychological Reports, 81,* 679-683.

Desforges, D. M., Lord, C. G., Ramsey, S. L., Mason, J. A., Van Leeuwen, M. D., West, S. C., et al. (1991). Effects of structured cooperative contact on changing negative attitudes toward stigmatized social groups. *Journal of Personality and Social Psychology, 60,* 531-544.

Desforges, D. M., Lord, C. G., Pugh, M. A., Sia, T. L., Scarberry, N. C., 7 Ratcliff, C. D. (1997). Role of group representativeness in the generalization part of the contact hypothesis. *Basic and Applied Social Psychology, 19,* 183-204.

DeSteno, D., Bartlett, M. Y., Braverman, J., & Salovey, P. (2002). Sex differences in jealousy: Evolutionary mechanism or artifact of measurement? *Journal of Personality and Social Psychology, 83,* 1103-1116.

DeSteno, D. A., & Salovey, P. (1996). Evolutionary origins of sex differences in jealousy? Questioning the 'fitness' of the model. *Psychological Science, 7,* 367-372.

DeSteno, D., Valdesolo, P., & Bartlett, M. Y. (2006). Jealousy and the threatened self: Getting to the heart of the green-eyed monster. *Journal of Personality and Social Psychology, 91,* 626-641.

Deutsch, F., & Lamberti, D. (1986). Does social approval increase helping?. *Personality and Social Psychology Bulletin, 12,* 149-157.

Deutsch, M., & Gerard, H. B. (1955). A study of normative and informational social influences upon individual judgment. *The Journal of Abnormal and Social Psychology, 51,* 629-636.

Devine, P. G. (1989). Stereotypes and prejudice: Their automatic and controlled components. *Journal of Personality and Social Psychology, 56,* 5-18.

Devine, P. G., & Elliot, A. J. (1995). Are racial stereotypes really fading? The Princeton trilogy revisited. *Personality and Social Psychology Bulletin, 21,* 1139-1150.

Devine, P. G., Monteith, M. J., Zuwerink, J. R., & Elliot, A. J. (1991). Prejudice with and without compunction. *Journal of Personality and Social Psychology, 60,* 817-830.

Devine, P. G., Plant, E. A., Amodio, D. M., Harmon-Jones, E., & Vance, S. L. (2002). The regulation of explicit and implicit race bias: The role of motivations to respond without prejudice. *Journal of Personality and Social Psychology, 82,* 835-848.

Dhawan, N., Roseman, I., Naidu, R., & Rettek, S. (1995). Self-concepts across two cultures: India and the United States. *Journal of Cross-Cultural Psychology, 26,* 606-621.

Dickerson, C., Thibodeau, R., Aronson, E., & Miller, D. (1992). Using cognitive dissonance to encourage water conservation. *Journal of Applied Social Psychology, 22,* 841-854.

Diekman, A. B., & Eagly, A. H. (2000). Stereotypes as dynamic constructs: Women and men of the past, present, and future. *Personality and Social Psychology Bulletin, 26,* 1171-1188.

Diener, E. (1979). Deindividuation, self-awareness, and disinhibition. *Journal of Personality and Social Psychology, 37,* 1160-1171.

Diener, E., Fraser, S. C., Beaman, A. L., & Kelem, R. T. (1976). Effects of deindividuation variables on stealing among Halloween trick-or-treaters. *Journal of Personality and Social Psychology, 33,* 178-183.

Diener, E., Wolsic, B., & Fujita, F. (1995). Physical attractiveness and subjective well-being. *Journal of Personality and Social Psychology, 69,* 120-129.

Dienstbier, R. A., Roesch, S. C., Mizumoto, A., Hemenover, S. H., Lott, R. C., & Carlo, G. (1998). Effects of weapons on guilt judgments and sentencing recommendations for criminals. *Basic and Applied Social Psychology, 20,* 93-102.

Dijksterhuis, A. (2004). Think different: The merits of unconscious thought in preference development and decision making. *Journal of Personality and Social Psychology, 87,* 586-598.

Dijkstra, P., & Buunk, B. P. (1998). Jealousy as a function of rival characteristics: An evolutionary perspective. *Personality and Social Psychology Bulletin, 24,* 1158-1166.

DiLalla, L. F., & Gottesman, I. I. (1991). Biological and genetic contributors to violence: Widom's untold tale. *Psychological Bulletin, 109,* 125-129.

Dion, K. K., & Dion, K. L. (1996). Cultural perspectives on romantic love. *Personal Relationships, 3*, 5-17.

Dion, K. L., & Dion, K. K. (1993). Gender and ethnocultural comparisons in styles of love. *Psychology of Women Quarterly*, Gender and culture, *17*, 463-473.

Dixon, J., Durrheim, K., & Tredoux, C. (2005). Beyond the optimal contact strategy: A reality check for the contact hypothesis. *American Psychologist, 60*, 697-711.

Dolinski, D. (2000). On inferring one's beliefs from one's attempt and consequences for subsequent compliance. *Journal of Personality and Social Psychology, 78*, 260-272.

Dollard, J., Doob, L. W., Miller, N. E., Mowrer, O. H., & Sears, R. R. (1939). *Frustration and Aggression.* New Haven, CT: Yale University Press.

Donnerstein, E. (1980). Aggressive erotica and violence against women. *Journal of Personality and Social Psychology, 39*, 269-277.

Donnerstein, E., & Berkowitz, L. (1981). Victim reactions in aggressive erotic films as a factor in violence against women. *Journal of Personality and Social Psychology, 41*, 710-724.

Dovidio, J. F., & Gaertner, S. L. (2000). Aversive racism in selection decisions: 1989 and 1999. *Psychological Science, 11*, 315-319.

Dovidio, J. F., Gaertner, S. L., & Validzic, A. (1998). Intergroup bias: Status, differentiation, and a common in-group identity. *Journal of Personality and Social Psychology, 75*, 109-120.

Dovidio, E. Piliavin, J. A., Gaertner, S. L., Schroeder, D. A., & Clark, R. D. (1991). The arousal: cost-reward model and the process of bystander intervention: A review of the evidence. In M. S. Clark (Ed.), *Prosocial Behavior*, (pp. 86-118). Newbury Park, CA: Sage.

Dovidio, J. F., & Morris, W. N. (1975). Effects of stress and commonality of fate on helping behavior. *Journal of Personality and Social Psychology, 31*, 145-149.

Dovidio, J. F., ten Vergert, M., Stewart, T. L., Gaertner, S. L., Johnson, J. D., Esses, V. M., et al. (2004). Perspective and prejudice: Antecedents and mediating mechanisms. *Personality and Social Psychology Bulletin, 30*, 1537-1549.

Dowie, M. (1988). *"We Have a Donor": The Bold New World of Organ Transplanting.* New York: St. Martin's Press.

Downs, A. C., & Lyons, P. M. (1991). Natural observations of the links between attractiveness and initial legal judgments. *Personality and Social Psychology Bulletin, 17*, 541-547.

Drabman, R. S., & Thomas, M. H. (1974). Exposure to filmed violence and children's tolerance of real life aggression. *Personality and Social Psychology Bulletin, 1*, 198-199.

Drabman, R. S., & Thomas, M. H. (1975). Does TV violence breed indifference? *Journal of Communication, 25*, 86-89.

Drigotas, S. M., & Rusbult, C. E. (1992). Should I stay or should I go? A dependence model of breakups. *Journal of Personality and Social Psychology, 62*, 62-87.

Drigotas, S. M., Safstrom, C. A., & Gentilia, T. (1999). An investment model prediction of dating infidelity. *Journal of Personality and Social Psychology, 77*, 509-524.

Drigotas, S. M., Whitney, G. A., & Rusbult, C. E. (1995). On the peculiarities of loyalty: A diary study of responses to dissatisfaction in everyday life. *Personality and Social Psychology Bulletin, 21*, 596-609.

Drolet, A. L., & Morris, M. W. (2000). Rapport in conflict resolution: Accounting for how face-to-face contact fosters mutual cooperation in mixed-motive conflicts. *Journal of Experimental Social Psychology, 36*, 26-50.

Duck, S., Pond, K., & Leatham, G. (1994). Loneliness and the evaluation of relational events. *Journal of Social and Personal Relationships, 11*, 253-276.

Duclos, S., Laird, J., Schneider, E., Sexter, M., Stern, L., & Van Lighten, O. (1989). Emotion-specific effects of facial expressions and postures on emotional experience. *Journal of Personality and Social Psychology, 57*, 100-108.

Duggan, E. S., & Brennan, K. A. (1994). Social avoidance and its relation to Bartholomew's adult attachment typology. *Journal of Social and Personal Relationships, 11*, 147-153.

Dunn, E. W., Aknin, L. B., & Norton, M. I. (2008). Spending money on others promotes happiness. *Science, 319*, 1687-1688.

Dunning, D., Meyerowitz, J., & Holzberg, A. (1989). Ambiguity and self-evaluation: The role of idiosyncratic trait definitions in self-serving assessments of ability. *Journal of Personality and Social Psychology, 57*, 1082-1090.

Dunning, D., Perie, M., & Story, A. (1991). Self-serving prototypes of social categories. *Journal of Personality and Social Psychology, 61*, 957-968.

DuRant, R. H., Barkin, S., & Krowchuk, D. P. (2001). Evaluation of a peaceful conflict resolution and violence prevention curriculum for sixth-grade students. *Journal of Adolescent Health, 28*, 386-393.

DuRant, R. H., Champion, H., & Wolfson, M,(2006). The relationship between watching professional wrestling on television and engaging in date fighting among high school students *Pediatrics, 118*, 265-272.

DuRant, R. H., Treiber, F., Getts, A., & McCloud, K. (1996). Comparison of two violence prevention curricula for middle school adolescents. *Journal of Adolescent Health, 19*, 111-117.

Durkheim, E. (1951). *Suicide.* New York: Free Press.

Dutton, D. G., & Aron, A. P. (1974). Some evidence for heightened sexual attraction under conditions of high anxiety. *Journal of Personality and Social Psychology, 30*, 510-517.

Duval, S., Duval, V. H., & Neely, R. (1979). Self-focus, felt responsibility, and helping behavior. *Journal of Personality and Social Psychology, 37*, 1769-1778.

Duval, S., & Wicklund, R. (1972). *A Theory of Objective Self Awareness.* New York: Academic Press.

Dweck, C.S. (2006). *Mindset.* New York: Random House.

Eagly, A. H. (1987). *Sex Differences in Social Behavior: A Social-role Interpretation.* Hillsdale, NJ: Lawrence Erlbaum.

Eagly, A. H., Ashmore, R. D., Makhijani, M. G., & Longo, L. C. (1991). What is beautiful is good, but . . .: A meta-analytic review of research on the physical attractiveness stereotype. *Psychological Bulletin, 110*, 109-128.

Eagly, A. H., & Carli, L. L. (1981). Sex of researchers and sex-typed communications as determinants of sex differences in influenceability: A meta-analysis of social influence studies. *Psychological Bulletin, 90*, 1-20.

Eagly, A. H., & Chaiken, S. (1975). An attribution analysis of the effect of communicator characteristics on opinion change: The case of communicator attractiveness. *Journal of Personality and Social Psychology, 32*, 136-144.

Eagly, A. H., & Crowley, M. (1986). Gender and helping behavior: A meta-analytic review of the social psychological literature. *Psychological Bulletin, 100*, 283-308.

Eagly, A., Diekman, A., Johannesen-Schmidt, M., & Koenig, A. (2004). Gender gaps in sociopolitical attitudes: A social psychological analysis. *Journal of Personality and Social Psychology, 87*, 796-816.

Eagly, A. H., Johannesen-Schmidt, M. C., & van Engen, M. L. (2003). Transformational, transactional, and laissez-faire leadership styles: A meta-analysis comparing women and men. *Psychological Bulletin, 129,* 569-591.

Eagly, A. H., & Johnson, B. T. (1990). Gender and leadership style: A meta-analysis. *Psychological Bulletin, 108,* 233-256.

Eagly, A. H., & Karau, S. J. (1991). Gender and the emergence of leaders: A meta-analysis. *Journal of Personality and Social Psychology, 60,* 685-710.

Eagly, A. H., & Karau, S. J. (2002). Role congruity theory of prejudice toward female leaders. *Psychological Review, 109,* 573-598.

Eagly, A. H., Karau, S. J., & Makhijani, M. G. (1995). Gender and the effectiveness of leaders: A meta-analysis. *Psychological Bulletin, 117,* 125-145.

Eagly, A. H., Makhijani, M. G., & Klonsky, B. G. (1992). Gender and the evaluation of leaders: A meta-analysis. *Psychological Bulletin, 111,* 3-22.

Eagly, A. H., & Steffen, V. J. (1984). Gender stereotypes stem from the distribution of women and men into social roles. *Journal of Personality and Social Psychology, 46,* 735-754.

Eagly, A. H., & Steffen, V. J. (1986). Gender and aggressive behavior: A meta-analytic review of the social psychological literature. *Psychological Bulletin, 100,* 309-330.

Eagly, A. H., & Wood, W. (1999). The origins of sex differences in human behavior: Evolved dispositions versus social roles. *American Psychologist, 54,* 408-423.

Eagly, A. H., Wood, W., & Chaiken, S. (1978). Causal inferences about communicators and their effect on opinion change. *Journal of Personality and Social Psychology, 36,* 424-435.

Eagly, A. H., Wood, W., & Fishbaugh, L. (1981). Sex differences in conformity: Surveillance by the group as a determinant of male nonconformity. *Journal of Personality and Social Psychology, 40,* 384-394.

Eastwick, P. W., & Finkel, E. J. (2008). Sex differences in mate preferences revisited: Do people know what they initially desire in a romantic partner? *Journal of Personality and Social Psychology, 94,* 245-264.

Eberhardt, J. L. (2005). Imaging race. *American Psychologist, 60,* 181-190.

Eberhardt, J. L., Goff, P. A., Purdie, V. J., & Davies, P. G. (2004). Seeing Black: Race, crime, and visual processing. *Journal of Personality and Social Psychology, 87,* 876-893.

Edney, J. J. (1979). The nuts game: A concise commons dilemma analog. *Environmental Psychology & Nonverbal Behavior, 3,* 252-254.

Edney, J. J. (1980). The commons problem: Alternative perspectives. *American Psychologist, 35,* 131-150.

Educational Testing Service. (1999). *GRE Guide to the Use of Scores, 1998-1999.* Princeton, NJ: Educational Testing Service.

Edwards, K., & Bryan, T. S. (1997). Judgmental biases produced by instructions to disregard: The (paradoxical) case of emotional information. *Personality and Social Psychology Bulletin, 23,* 849–864.

Edwards, K., & Smith, E. E. (1996). A disconfirmation bias in the evaluation of arguments. *Journal of Personality and Social Psychology, 71,* 5-24.

Egan, L., Santos, L., & Bloom, P. (2007). The origins of cognitive dissonance: Evidence from children and monkeys. *Psychological Science, 18,* 978-983.

Ehrlinger, J., Gilovich, T., & Ross, L. (2005). Peering into the bias blind spot: People's assessments of bias in themselves and others. *Personality and Social Psychology Bulletin, 31,* 680-692.

Eid, M., & Diener, E. (2001). Norms for experiencing emotions in different cultures: Inter- and intranational differences. *Journal of Personality and Social Psychology, 81,* 869-885.

Eisenberg, M.E., Olson, R.E., Neumark-Sztainer, D., Story, M., & Bearinger, L.H. (2004). Correlations between family meals and psychosocial well-being among adolescents. *Archives of Pediatrics & Adolescent Medicine, 158,* 792-796.

Eisenberg, N. (1982). *The Development of Prosocial Behavior.* New York: Academic Press.

Eisenberg, N., Fabes, R. A., Schaller, M., Carlo, G., & Miller, P.A. (1991). The relations of parental characteristics and practices to children's vicarious emotional responding. *Child Development, 62,* 1393-1408.

Eisenberg, N., Guthrie, I. K., Cumberland, A., Murphy, B. C., Shepard, S. A., Zhou, Q., et al. (2002). Prosocial development in early adulthood: A longitudinal study. *Journal of Personality and Social Psychology, 82,* 993-1006.

Eisenberger, N., Lieberman, M., & Williams, K. (2003). Does rejection hurt? An fMRI study of social exclusion. *Science, 302,* 290-292.

Eisenberg, N., & Miller, P. A. (1987). The relation of empathy to prosocial and related behaviors. *Psychological Bulletin, 101,* 91-119.

Eisenberg, N., Shell, R., Pasternack, J., Lennon, R., Beller, R., & Mathy, R. M. (1987). Prosocial development in middle childhood: A longitudinal study. *Developmental Psychology, 23,* 712-718.

Eisenberger, R., & Cameron, J. (1996). Detrimental effects of reward: Reality or myth? *American Psychologist, 51,* 1153-1166.

Eisenberger, R., Rhoades, L., & Cameron, J. (1999). Does pay for performance increase or decrease perceived self-determination and intrinsic motivation? *Journal of Personality and Social Psychology, 77,* 1026-1040.

Ekman, P. (1994). Strong evidence for universals in facial expressions: A reply to Russell's mistaken critique. *Psychological Bulletin, 115,* 268-287.

Ekman, P., & Davidson, R. (1993). Voluntary smiling changes regional brain activity. *Psychological Science, 4,* 342-345.

Ekman, P., & Friesen, W. (1974). Detecting deception from the body or face. *Journal of Personality and Social Psychology, 29,* 288-298.

Ekman, P., & O'Sullivan, M. (1991). Who can catch a liar? *American Psychologist, 46,* 913-920.

Ekman, P., O'Sullivan, M., & Frank, M. (1999). A few can catch a liar. *Psychological Science, 10,* 263-266.

Elfenbein, H., & Ambady, N. (2003). When familiarity breeds accuracy: Cultural exposure and facial emotion recognition. *Journal of Personality and Social Psychology, 85,* 276-290.

Elizur, Y., & Mintzer, A. (2003). Gay males' intimate relationship quality: The roles of attachment security, gay identity, social support, and income. *Personal Relationships, 10,* 411-435.

Elkin, R. A., & Leippe, M.R. (1986). Physiological arousal, dissonance, and attitude change: Evidence for a dissonance arousal link and a 'Don't remind me' effect. *Journal of Personality and Social Psychology, 51,* 55–65.

Ellemers, N., & Bos, A. E. R. (1998). Social identity, relative deprivation, and coping with the threat of position loss: A field study among native shopkeepers in Amsterdam. *Journal of Applied Social Psychology, 28,* 1987-2006.

Elliot, A. J., & Devine, P. G. (1994). On the motivational nature of cognitive dissonance: Dissonance as psychological discomfort. *Journal of Personality and Social Psychology, 67,* 382-394.

Elms, A.C. & Milgram, (1966) Personality characteristics associated obedience and defiance toward authoritative command. *Journal of Experimental Research in Personality 1,* 282-289.

Emery, R. E., & Wyer, M. M. (1987). Child custody mediation and litigation: An experimental evaluation of the experience of parents. *Journal of Consulting and Clinical Psychology, 55,* 179-186.

Ennett, S. T., Tobler, N. S., Ringwalt, C. L., & Flewelling, R. L. (1994). How effective is drug abuse resistance education? A meta-analysis of Project DARE outcome evaluations. *American Journal of Public Health, 84,* 1394-1401.

Enos, D. M., & Handal, P. J. (1986). The relation of parental marital status and perceived family conflict to adjustment in White adolescents. *Journal of Consulting and Clinical Psychology, 54,* 820-824.

Epley, N., & Gilovich, T. (2004). Are adjustments insufficient? *Personality and Social Psychology Bulletin, 30,* 447-460.

Erb, H., Bohner, G., Rank, S., & Einwiller, S. (2002). Processing minority and majority communications: The role of conflict with prior attitudes. *Personality and Social Psychology Bulletin, 28,* 1172-1182.

Esses, V. M., & Dovidio, J. F. (2002). The role of emotions in determining willingness to engage in intergroup contact. *Personality and Social Psychology Bulletin, 28,* 1202-1214.

Esses, V. M., Jackson, L. M., & Armstrong, T. L. (1998). Intergroup competition and attitudes toward immigrants and immigration: An instrumental model of group conflict. *Journal of Social Issues, 54,* 699-724.

Esses, V. M., & Zanna, M. P. (1995). Mood and the expression of ethnic stereotypes. *Journal of Personality and Social Psychology, 69,* 1052-1068.

Etzioni, A. (1967). Toward a theory of societal guidance. *American Journal of Sociology, 73,* 173-187.

Fabes, R. A., Eisenberg, N., & Miller, P. A. (1990). Maternal correlates of children's vicarious emotional responsiveness. *Developmental Psychology, 26,* 639-648.

Fabes, R. A., Fultz, J., Eisenberg, N., May-Plumlee, T., & Christopher, F. S. (1989). Effects of rewards on children's prosocial motivation: A socialization study. *Developmental Psychology, 25,* 509-515.

Fabrigar, L. R., Priester, J. R., Petty, R. E., & Wegener, D. T. (1998). The impact of attitude accessibility on elaboration of persuasive messages. *Personality and Social Psychology Bulletin, 24,* 339-352.

Fajardo, D. M. (1985). Author race, essay quality, and reverse discrimination. *Journal of Applied Social Psychology, 15,* 255-268.

Fannin, N., & Dabbs, J. M. J. (2003). Testosterone and the work of firefighters: Fighting fires and delivering medical care. *Journal of Research in Personality, 37,* 107-115.

Farber, C. (1998). Whistling in the dark. *Esquire, 129,* 54-64, 119-120.

Fazio, R. H., & Zanna, M. (1981). Direct experience and attitude-behavior consistency. In L. Berkowitz (Ed.), *Advances in Experimental Social Psychology* (Vol. 14, pp. 161-202). San Diego, CA: Academic Press.

Feeney, B. C., & Collins, N. L. (2001). Predictors of caregiving in adult intimate relationships: An attachment theoretical perspective. *Journal of Personality and Social Psychology, 80,* 972-994.

Feeney, J. A. (1996). Attachment, caregiving, and marital satisfaction. *Personal Relationships, 3,* 401-416.

Fein, S. (1996). Effects of suspicion on attributional thinking and the correspondence bias. *Journal of Personality and Social Psychology, 70,* 1164-1184.

Fein, S., Hilton, J., & Miller, D. (1993). Suspicion of ulterior motivation and the correspondence bias. *Journal of Personality and Social Psychology, 58,* 753-764.

Fein, S., & Spencer, S. J. (1997). Prejudice as self-image maintenance: Affirming the self through derogating others. *Journal of Personality and Social Psychology, 73,* 31-44.

Feingold, A. (1988). Matching for attractiveness in romantic partners and same-sex friends: A meta-analysis and theoretical critique. *Psychological Bulletin, 104,* 226-235.

Feingold, A. (1990). Gender differences in effects of physical attractiveness on romantic attraction: A comparison across five research paradigms. *Journal of Personality and Social Psychology, 59,* 981-993.

Feingold, A. (1991). Sex differences in the effects of similarity and physical attractiveness on opposite-sex attraction. *Basic and Applied Social Psychology, 12,* 357-367.

Feingold, A. (1992). Good-looking people are not what we think. *Psychological Bulletin, 111,* 304-341.

Feldman, R. E. (1968). Response to compatriot and foreigner who seek assistance. *Journal of Personality and Social Psychology, 10,* 202-214.

Felmlee, D. H. (1995). Fatal attractions: Affection and disaffection in intimate relationships. *Journal of Social and Personal Relationships, 12,* 295-311.

Felmlee, D. H. (1998). 'Be careful what you wish for . . .': A quantitative and qualitative investigation of 'fatal attractions.' *Personal Relationships, 5,* 235-253.

Festinger, L. (1954). A theory of social comparison processes. *Human Relations, 7,* 117-140.

Festinger, L. (1957). *A Theory of Cognitive Dissonance.* Oxford, England: Row, Peterson.

Festinger, L., & Carlsmith, J. (1959). Cognitive consequences of forced compliance. *The Journal of Abnormal and Social Psychology, 58,* 203-210.

Festinger, L., Pepitone, A., & Newcomb, T. (1952). Some consequences of de-individuation in a group. *The Journal of Abnormal and Social Psychology, 47,* 382-389.

Festinger, L., Schachter, S., & Back, K. (1950). *Social Pressures in Informal Groups: A Study of Human Factors in Housing.* New York: Harper.

Fiedler, K., Walther, E., & Nickel, S. (1999). Covariation-based attribution: On the ability to assess multiple covariates of an effect. *Personality and Social Psychology Bulletin, 25,* 607-622.

Fincham, F. D. (2000). The kiss of the porcupines: From attributing responsibility to forgiving. *Personal Relationships, 7,* 1-23.

Fincham, F. D., & Bradbury, T. N. (1992). Assessing attributions in marriage: The Relationship Attribution Measure. *Journal of Personality and Social Psychology, 62,* 457-468.

Fischer, P., & Greitemeyer, T. (2006). Music and aggression: The impact of sexual-aggressive song lyrics on aggression-related thoughts, emotions, and behavior toward the same and the opposite sex. *Personality and Social Psychology Bulletin, 32,* 1165-1176.

Fisher, H. E., Aron, A., Mashek, D., Li, H., & Brown, L. L. (2002). Defining the brain systems of lust, romantic attraction, and attachment. *Archives of Sexual Behavior, 31,* 413-419.

Fisher, J. D., Nadler, A., & Whitcher-Alagna, S. (1982). Recipient reactions to aid. *Psychological Bulletin*, 91, 27-54.

Fiske, S. T. (1993). Controlling other people: The impact of power on stereotyping. *American Psychologist*, 48, 621-628.

Fiske, S. T., Bersoff, D. N., Borgida, E., Deaux, K., & Heilman, M. E. (1991). Social science research on trial: Use of sex stereotyping research in Price Waterhouse v. Hopkins. *American Psychologist*, 46, 1049-1060.

Fiske, S. T., Cuddy, A. J. C., Glick, P., & Xu, J. (2002). A model of (often mixed) stereotype content: Competence and warmth respectively follow from perceived status and competition. *Journal of Personality and Social Psychology*, 82, 878-902.

Fiske, S. T., Xu, J., Cuddy, A. C., & Glick, P. (1999). (Dis)respecting versus (dis)liking: Status and interdependence predict ambivalent stereotypes of competence and warmth. *Journal of Social Issues*, 55, 473-489.

Fitzgerald, L. F. (1993). Sexual harassment: Violence against women in the workplace. *American Psychologist*, 48, 1070-1076.

Flegal, K. M., Carroll, M. D., Kuczmarski, R. J., & Johnson, C. L., (1998). Overweight and obesity in the United States: Prevalence and trends, 1960-1994. *International Journal of Obesity and Related Metabolic Disorders*, 22, 39-47.

Fleming, I., Baum, A., & Weiss, L. (1987). Social density and perceived control as mediators of crowding stress in high-density residential neighborhoods. *Journal of Personality and Social Psychology*, 52, 899-906.

Fletcher, G., Danilovics, P., Fernandez, G., Peterson, D., & Reeder, G. (1986). Attributional complexity: An individual differences measure. *Journal of Personality and Social Psychology*, 51, 875-884.

Fletcher, G. J. O., Tither, J. M., O'Loughlin, C., Friesen, M., & Overall, N. (2004). Warm and homely or cold and beautiful? Sex differences in trading off traits in mate selection. *Personality and Social Psychology Bulletin*, 30, 659-672.

Forgas, J. P., Bower, G. H., & Krantz, S. E. (1984). The influence of mood on perceptions of social interactions. *Journal of Experimental Social Psychology*, 20, 497–513.

Forgas, J. P., & Fiedler, K. (1996). Us and them: Mood effects on intergroup discrimination. *Journal of Personality and Social Psychology*, 70, 28-40.

Foster, C. A., Witcher, B. S., Campbell, W. K., & Green, J. D. (1998). Arousal and attraction: Evidence for automatic and controlled processes. *Journal of Personality and Social Psychology*, 74, 86-101.

Försterling, F., Preikschas, S., & Agthe, M. (2007). Ability, luck, and looks: An evolutionary look at achievement ascriptions and the sexual attribution bias. *Journal of Personality and Social Psychology*, 92, 775-788.

Fox, R. C., & Swazey, J. P. (1992). *Spare Parts: Organ Replacement in American Society*. New York: Oxford University Press.

Fox, S., & Walters, H. (1986). The impact of general versus specific expert testimony and eyewitness confidence upon mock juror judgment. *Law and Human Behavior*, 10, 215-228.

Fragale, A. R., & Heath, C. (2004). Evolving informational credentials: The (mis)attribution of believable facts to credible sources. *Personality and Social Psychology Bulletin*, 30, 225-236.

Frank, A. (1993). *Anne Frank: Diary of a Young Girl*. New York: Bantam.

Frank, M., & Ekman, P. (1997). The ability to detect deceit generalizes across different types of high-stake lies. *Journal of Personality and Social Psychology*, 72, 1429-1439.

Frank, M., & Ekman, P. (2004). Appearing truthful generalizes across different deception situations. *Journal of Personality and Social Psychology*, 86, 486-495.

Frank, R., Gilovich, T., & Regan, D.T. (1993). Does studying economics inhibit cooperation?. *Journal of Economic Perspectives*, 7, 159–171.

Frankel, A., & Prentice-Dunn, S. (1990). Loneliness and the processing of self-relevant information. *Journal of Social & Clinical Psychology*, 9, 303-315.

Frazier, P. (2003). Perceived control and distress following sexual assault: A longitudinal test of a new model. *Journal of Personality and Social Psychology*, 84, 1257-1269.

Freedman, J. (1965). Long-term behavioral effects of cognitive dissonance. *Journal of Experimental Social Psychology*, 1, 145-155.

Freedman, J. L., & Fraser, S. C. (1966). Compliance without pressure: The foot-in-the-door technique. *Journal of Personality and Social Psychology*, 4, 195-202.

Freedman, J. L., & Sears, D. O. (1965). Warning, distraction, and resistance to influence. *Journal of Personality and Social Psychology*, 1, 262-266.

Freimuth, V. S., Hammond, S. L., Edgar, T., & Monahan, J. L. (1990). Reaching those at risk: A content-analytic study of AIDS PSAs. *Communication Research*, 17, 775-791.

Freud, S. (1930). *Civilization and Its Discontents*. New York: W.W. Norton.

Freud, S. (1933). *New Introductory Lectures on Psychoanalysis*. New York: W.W. Norton.

Fried, C., & Aronson, E. (1995). Hypocrisy, misattribution, and dissonance reduction. *Personality and Social Psychology Bulletin*, 21, 925-933.

Friedman, H., Tucker, J., Tomlinson-Keasey, C., Schwartz, J., Wingard, D., & Criqui, M. (1993). Does childhood personality predict longevity? *Journal of Personality and Social Psychology*, 65, 176-185.

Friedrich, J., Fetherstonhaugh, D., Casey, S., & Gallagher, D. (1996). Argument integration and attitude change: Suppression effects in the integration of one-sided arguments that vary in persuasiveness. *Personality and Social Psychology Bulletin*, 22, 179-191.

Friedrich-Cofer, L., & Huston, A. C. (1986). Television violence and aggression: The debate continues. *Psychological Bulletin*, 100, 364-371.

Frieze, I. H., Olson, J. E., & Russell, J. (1991). Attractiveness and income for men and women in management. *Journal of Applied Social Psychology*, 21, 1039-1057.

Fultz, J., Batson, C. D., Fortenbach, V. A., McCarthy, P. M., & Varney, L. L. (1986). Social evaluation and the empathy-altruism hypothesis. *Journal of Personality and Social Psychology*, 50, 761-769.

Fung, H. H., & Carstensen, L. L. (2003). Sending memorable messages to the old: Age differences in preferences and memory for advertisements. *Journal of Personality and Social Psychology*, 85, 163-178.

Furnham, A., & Gunter, B. (1984). Just world beliefs and attitudes towards the poor. *British Journal of Social Psychology*, 23, 265-269.

Gabrenya, W. K., Wang, Y., & Latané, B. (1985). Social loafing on an optimizing task: Cross-cultural differences among Chinese and Americans. *Journal of Cross-Cultural Psychology*, 16, 223-242.

Gabriel, S., & Gardner, W. (1999). Are there 'his' and 'hers' types of interdependence? The implications of gender differences in collective versus relational interdependence for affect, behavior, and cognition. *Journal of Personality and Social Psychology, 77*, 642-655.

Gaertner, S. L., & Dovidio, J. F. (1977). The subtlety of White racism, arousal, and helping behavior. *Journal of Personality and Social Psychology, 35*, 691-707.

Gaertner, S. L., & Dovidio, J. F. (1986). The aversive form of racism. In J.F. Dovidio & S.L. Gaertner (Eds.), *Prejudice, Discrimination, and Racism* (pp. 61-89). San Diego, CA: Academic Press.

Gaertner, S. L., Dovidio, J. F., Rust, M. C., Nier, J. A., Banker, B. S., Ward, C. M., et al. (1999). Reducing intergroup bias: Elements of intergroup cooperation. *Journal of Personality and Social Psychology, 76*, 388-402.

Gaertner, S. L., Mann, J. A., Dovidio, J. F., Murrell, A. J., & Pomare, M. (1990). How does cooperation reduce intergroup bias? *Journal of Personality and Social Psychology, 59*, 692-704.

Gaertner, S. L., Mann, J., Murrell, A., & Dovidio, J. F. (1989). Reducing intergroup bias: The benefits of recategorization. *Journal of Personality and Social Psychology, 57*, 239-249.

Gagnon, A., & Bourhis, R. Y. (1996). Discrimination in the minimal group paradigm: Social identity or self-interest? *Personality and Social Psychology Bulletin, 22*, 1289-1301.

Gailliot, M. T., & Baumeister, R. F. (2007). Self-regulation and sexual restraint: Dispositionally and temporarily poor self-regulatory abilities contribute to failures at restraining sexual behavior. *Personality and Social Psychology Bulletin, 33*, 173-186.

Gailliot, M. T., Plant, E. A., Butz, D. A., & Baumeister, R. F. (2007). Increasing self-regulatory strength can reduce the depleting effect of suppressing stereotypes. *Personality and Social Psychology Bulletin, 33*, 281-294.

Galinsky, A. D., Maddux, W. W., Gilin, D., & White, J. B. (2008). Why it pays to get inside the head of your opponent: The differential effects of perspective taking and empathy in negotiations. *Psychological Science, 19*, 378-384.

Galinsky, A. D., & Moskowitz, G. B. (2000). Perspective-taking: Decreasing stereotype expression, stereotype accessibility, and in-group favoritism. *Journal of Personality and Social Psychology, 78*, 708-724.

Gallo, L. C., Troxel, W. M., Matthews, K. A., & Kuller, L. H. (2003). Marital status and quality in middle-aged women: Associations with levels and trajectories of cardiovascular risk factors. *Health Psychology, 22*, 453-463.

Gallucci, M. (2003). I sell seashells by the seashore and my name is Jack: Comment on Pelham, Mirenberg, and Jones (2002). *Journal of Personality and Social Psychology, 85*, 789-799.

Gangestad, S. W., Simpson, J. A., Cousins, A. J., Garver-Apgar, C. E., & Christensen, P. N. (2004). Women's preferences for male behavioral displays change across the menstrual cycle. *Psychological Science, 15*, 203-206.

Gannon, L., Luchetta, T., Rhodes, K., Pardie, L., & Segrist, D. (1992). Sex bias in psychological research: Progress or complacency? *American Psychologist, 47*, 389-396.

Garcia, S., Tor, A., & Gonzalez, R. (2006). Ranks and rivals: A theory of competition. *Personality and Social Psychology Bulletin, 32*, 970-982.

Garner, D., Garfinkel, P., Schwartz, D., & Thompson, M. (1980). Cultural expectations of thinness in women. *Psychological Reports, 47*, 483-491.

Garrity, K., & Degelman, D. (1990). Effect of server introduction on restaurant tipping. *Journal of Applied Social Psychology, 20*, 168-172.

Gavin, L. A., & Furman, W. (1989). Age differences in adolescents' perceptions of their peer groups. *Developmental Psychology, 25*, 827-834.

Gawronski, B. (2003). Implicational schemata and the correspondence bias: On the diagnostic value of situationally constrained behavior. *Journal of Personality and Social Psychology, 84*, 1154-1171.

Gawronski, B. (2003). On difficult questions and evident answers: Dispositional inference from role-constrained behavior. *Personality and Social Psychology Bulletin, 29*, 1459-1475.

Geen, R. G. (1968). Effects of frustration, attack, and prior training in aggressiveness upon aggressive behavior. *Journal of Personality and Social Psychology, 9*, 316-321.

Geen, R. G. (1981). Behavioral and physiological reactions to observed violence: Effects of prior exposure to aggressive stimuli. *Journal of Personality and Social Psychology, 40*, 868-875.

Geiselman, R. E., Haight, N. A., & Kimata, L. G. (1984). Context effects on the perceived physical attractiveness of faces. *Journal of Experimental Social Psychology, 20*, 409-424.

Gentzler, A. L., & Kerns, K. A. (2004). Associations between insecure attachment and sexual experiences. *Personal Relationships, 11*, 249-265.

Gerard, H. B., Wilhelmy, R. A., & Conolley, E. S. (1968). Conformity and group size. *Journal of Personality and Social Psychology, 8*, 79-82.

Gerrard, M., Gibbons, F., Reis-Bergan, M., Trudeau, L., Vande Lune, L., & Buunk, B. (2002). Inhibitory effects of drinker and nondrinker prototypes on adolescent alcohol consumption. *Health Psychology, 21*, 601-609.

Gershoff, E. T. (2002). Corporal punishment by parents and associated child behaviors and experiences: A meta-analytic and theoretical review. *Psychological Bulletin, 128*, 539-579.

Gibbons, F. X., Gerrard, M., Cleveland, M. J., Wills, T. A., & Brody, G. (2004). Perceived discrimination and substance use in African American parents and their children: A panel study. *Journal of Personality and Social Psychology, 86*, 517-529.

Gibbons, F., & Gerrard, M. (1995). Predicting young adults' health risk behavior. *Journal of Personality and Social Psychology, 69*, 505-517.

Gibbons, F., & McCoy, S. (1991). Self-esteem, similarity, and reactions to active versus passive downward comparison. *Journal of Personality and Social Psychology, 60*, 414-424.

Gibbons, F., Eggleston, T., & Benthin, A. (1997). Cognitive reactions to smoking relapse: The reciprocal relation between dissonance and self-esteem. *Journal of Personality and Social Psychology, 72*, 184-195.

Gibbons, F., Gerrard, M., & McCoy, S. (1995). Prototype perception predicts (lack of) pregnancy prevention. *Personality and Social Psychology Bulletin, 21*, 85-93.

Gibbons, F., Gerrard, M., Blanton, H., & Russell, D. (1998). Reasoned action and social reaction: Willingness and intention as independent predictors of health risk. *Journal of Personality and Social Psychology, 74*, 1164-1180.

Gibbons, J., Hamby, B., & Dennis, W. (1997). Researching gender-role ideologies internationally and cross-culturally. *Psychology of Women Quarterly, 21*, 151-170.

Gibson, B., & Maurer, J. (2000). Cigarette smoking in the movies: The influence of product placement on attitudes toward smoking and smokers. *Journal of Applied Social Psychology, 30*, 1457-1473.

Gibson, B., & Sanbonmatsu, D. (2004). Optimism, pessimism, and gambling: The downside of optimism. *Personality and Social Psychology Bulletin, 30*, 149-160.

Gifford, R. (1991). Mapping nonverbal behavior on the interpersonal circle. *Journal of Personality and Social Psychology, 61*, 279-288.

Gigerenzer, G. (2004). Dread risk, September 11, and fatal traffic accidents. *Psychological Science, 15*, 286-287.

Gilbert, D. T., & Silvera, D. H. (1996). Overhelping. *Journal of Personality and Social Psychology, 70*, 678-690.

Gilbert, D. T., Krull, D. S., & Malone, P. S. (1990). Unbelieving the unbelievable: Some problems in the rejection of false information. *Journal of Personality and Social Psychology, 59*, 601-613.

Gilbert, D. T., Tafarodi, R. W., & Malone, P. S. (1993). You can't not believe everything you read. *Journal of Personality and Social Psychology, 65*, 221-233.

Gilbert, D., & Hixon, J. (1991). The trouble of thinking: Activation and application of stereotypic beliefs. *Journal of Personality and Social Psychology, 60*, 509-517.

Gilbert, D., & Malone, P. (1995). The correspondence bias. *Psychological Bulletin, 117*, 21-38.

Gilbert, D., & Osborne, R. (1989). Thinking backward: Some curable and incurable consequences of cognitive busyness. *Journal of Personality and Social Psychology, 57*, 940-949.

Gilbert, D., & Wilson, T. (2000). Miswanting: Some problems in the forecasting of future affective states. *Feeling and Thinking: The Role of Affect in Social Cognition* (pp. 178-197). New York: Cambridge University Press.

Gilbert, D., Pelham, B., & Krull, D. (1988). On cognitive busyness: When person perceivers meet persons perceived. *Journal of Personality and Social Psychology, 54*, 733-740.

Gilbert, D., Pinel, E., Wilson, T., Blumberg, S., & Wheatley, T. (1998). Immune neglect: A source of durability bias in affective forecasting. *Journal of Personality and Social Psychology, 75*, 617-638.

Gilbert, S. J. (1981). Another look at the Milgram obedience studies: The role of the gradated series of shocks. *Personality and Social Psychology Bulletin, 7*, 690-695.

Gillath, O., Bunge, S. A., Shaver P. R., Wendelken, C., & Mikulincer, M. (2005). Attachment-style differences in the ability to suppress negative thoughts: Exploring the neural correlates. *Neuroimage, 28*, 835-847.

Gilovich, T., Medvec, V., & Savitsky, K. (2000). The spotlight effect in social judgment: An egocentric bias in estimates of the salience of one's own actions and appearance. *Journal of Personality and Social Psychology, 78*, 211-222.

Giner-Sorolla, R., & Chaiken, S. (1994). The causes of hostile media judgments. *Journal of Experimental Social Psychology, 30*, 165-180.

Giner-Sorolla, R., & Chaiken, S. (1997). Selective use of heuristic and systematic processing under defense motivation. *Personality and Social Psychology Bulletin, 23*, 84-97.

Giumetti, G. W., & Markey, P. M. (2007). Violent video games and anger as predictors of aggression. *Journal of Research in Personality, 41*, 1234-1243.

Gladwell, M. (2004). Big and bad: How the S.U.V. ran over automotive safety. *The New Yorker*, January 12, 28-33.

Gleason, M. E. J., Iida, M., Bolger, N., & Shrout, P. E. (2003). Daily supportive equity in close relationships. *Personality and Social Psychology Bulletin, 29*, 1036-1045.

Glick, P., & Fiske, S. T. (1996). The Ambivalent Sexism Inventory: Differentiating hostile and benevolent sexism. *Journal of Personality and Social Psychology, 70*, 491-512.

Glick, P., & Fiske, S. T. (2001). An ambivalent alliance: Hostile and benevolent sexism as complementary justifications for gender inequality. *American Psychologist, 56*, 109-118.

Glick, P., Fiske, S. T., Mladinic, A., Saiz, J. L., Abrams, D., Masser, B., et al. (2000). Beyond prejudice as simple antipathy: Hostile and benevolent sexism across cultures. *Journal of Personality and Social Psychology, 79*, 763-775.

Glick, P., Gottesman, D., & Jolton, J. (1989). The fault is not in the stars: Susceptibility of skeptics and believers in astrology to the Barnum effect. *Personality and Social Psychology Bulletin, 15*, 572-583.

Glick, P., Lameiras, M., Fiske, S. T., Eckes, T., Masser, B., Volpato, C., et al. (2004). Bad but bold: Ambivalent attitudes toward men predict gender inequality in 16 nations. *Journal of Personality and Social Psychology, 86*, 713-728.

Godfrey, D., Jones, E., & Lord, C. (1986). Self-promotion is not ingratiating. *Journal of Personality and Social Psychology, 50*, 106-115.

Goethals, G., Cooper, J., & Naficy, A. (1979). Role of foreseen, foreseeable, and unforeseeable behavioral consequences in the arousal of cognitive dissonance. *Journal of Personality and Social Psychology, 37*, 1179-1185.

Goff, P. A., Steele, C. M., & Davies, P. G. (2008). The space between us: Stereotype threat and distance in interracial contexts. *Journal of Personality and Social Psychology, 94*, 91-107.

Goldstein, A. O., Sobel, R.A., & Newman, R. T. (1999). Tobacco and alcohol use in G-rated children's animated films. *Journal of the American Medical Association, 281*, 1131-1136.

Goldstein, N. J., Cialdini, R. B., & Griskevicius, V. (2008). A room with a viewpoint: Using normative appeals to motivate environmental conservation in a hotel setting. *Journal of Consumer Research, 35*, 472-482.

Gonzales, P. M., Blanton, H., & Williams, K. J. (2002). The effects of stereotype threat and double-minority status on the test performance of Latino women. *Personality and Social Psychology Bulletin, 28*, 659-670.

Good, G. E., Dell, D. M., & Mintz, L. B. (1989). Male role and gender role conflict: Relations to help seeking in men. *Journal of Counseling Psychology, 36*, 295-300.

Goodwin, C.J. (1998). *Research in Psychology: Methods and Design.* New York: Wiley.

Goodwin, R., & Findlay, C. (1997). 'We were just fated together'.....Chinese love and the concept of yuan in England and Hong Kong. *Personal Relationships, 4*, 85-92.

Gordijn, E., Hindriks, I., Koomen, W., Dijksterhuis, A., & Van Knippenberg, A. (2004). Consequences of stereotype suppression and internal suppression motivation: A self-regulation approach. *Personality and Social Psychology Bulletin, 30*, 212-224.

Gordon, R. (1996). Impact of ingratiation on judgments and evaluations: A meta-analytic investigation. *Journal of Personality and Social Psychology, 71*, 54-70.

Gortmaker, S., Must, A., Perrin, J., & Sobol, A. (1993). Social and economic consequences of overweight in adolescence and young adulthood. *New England Journal of Medicine, 329*, 1008-1012.

Gosling, S., Vazire, S., Srivastava, S., & John, O. (2004). Should we trust web-based studies? A comparative analysis of six preconceptions about Internet questionnaires. *American Psychologist, 59*, 93-104.

Gosselin, P., Kirouac, G., & Doré, F. (1995). Components and recognition of facial expression in the communication of emotion by actors. *Journal of Personality and Social Psychology, 68*, 83-96.

Gottman, J. M., & Krokoff, L. J. (1989). Marital interaction and satisfaction: A longitudinal view. *Journal of Consulting and Clinical Psychology, 57*, 47-52.

Gottman, J. M., & Levenson, R. W. (1992). Marital processes predictive of later dissolution: Behavior, physiology, and health. *Journal of Personality and Social Psychology, 63*, 221-233.

Gottman, J., & Levenson, R. W. (2002). A two-factor model for predicting when a couple will divorce: Exploratory analyses using 14-year longitudinal data. *Family Process, 41*, 83-96.

Gottman, J. M., Levenson, R. W., Gross, J., Frederickson, B. L., McCoy, K., Rosenthal, L., et al. (2003). Correlates of gay and lesbian couples' relationship satisfaction and relationship dissolution. *Journal of Homosexuality, 45*, 23-43.

Gould, M. S., & Shaffer, D. (1986). The impact of suicide in television movies: Evidence imitation. *The New England Journal of Medicine, 315*, 690-694.

Graham, J. M., & Conoley, C. W. (2006). The role of marital attributions in the relationship between life stressors and marital quality. *Personal Relationships, 13*, 231-241.

Graham, S. (1992). 'Most of the subjects were White and middle class': Trends in published research on African Americans in selected APA journals, 1970-1989. *American Psychologist, 47*, 629-639.

Graham, S., Weiner, B., & Zucker, G. (1997). An attributional analysis of punishment goals and public reactions to O. J. Simpson. *Personality and Social Psychology Bulletin, 23*, 331-346.

Gray, J., & Silver, R. (1990). Opposite sides of the same coin: Former spouses' divergent perspectives in coping with their divorce. *Journal of Personality and Social Psychology, 59*, 1180-1191.

Green, B. L., & Kenrick, D. T. (1994). The attractiveness of gender-typed traits at different relationship levels: Androgynous characteristics may be desirable after all. *Personality and Social Psychology Bulletin, 20*, 244-253.

Green, D. P., Glaser, J., & Rich, A. (1998). From lynching to gay bashing: The elusive connection between economic conditions and hate crime. *Journal of Personality and Social Psychology, 75*, 82-92.

Green, L. R., Richardson, D. S., Lago, T., & Schatten-Jones, E. C. (2001). Network correlates of social and emotional loneliness in young and older adults. *Personality and Social Psychology Bulletin, 27*, 281-288.

Greenberg, J., & Pyszczynski, T. (1985). The effect of an overheard ethnic slur on evaluations of the target: How to spread a social disease. *Journal of Experimental Social Psychology, 21*, 61-72.

Greenwald, A. G., & Banaji, M. R. (1995). Implicit social cognition: Attitudes, self-esteem, and stereotypes. *Psychological Review, 102*, 4-27.

Greenwald, A. G., Spangenberg, E. R., Pratkanis, A. R., & Eskenazi, J. (1991). Double-blind tests of subliminal self-help audiotapes. *Psychological Science, 2*, 119-122.

Greitemeyer, T., & Weiner, B. (2003). Asymmetrical attributions for approach versus avoidance behavior. *Personality and Social Psychology Bulletin, 29*, 1371-1382.

Griffit, W. B. (1970). Environmental effects on interpersonal behavior: Ambient effective temperature and attraction. *Journal of Personality and Social Psychology, 15*, 240-244.

Griffit, W., & Veitch, R. (1971). Hot and crowded: Influence of population density and temperature on interpersonal affective behavior. *Journal of Personality and Social Psychology, 17*, 92-98.

Griskevicius, V., Goldstein, N. J., Mortensen, C. R., Cialdini, R. B., & Kenrick, D. T. (2006). Going along versus going alone: When fundamental motives facilitate strategic (non)conformity. *Journal of Personality and Social Psychology, 91*, 281-294.

Groff, B. D., Baron, R. S., & Moore, D. L. (1983). Distraction, attentional conflict, and drivelike behavior. *Journal of Experimental Social Psychology, 19*, 359-380.

Gross, E. F., Juvonen, J., & Gable, S. L. (2002). Internet use and well-being in adolescence. *Journal of Social Issues, 58*, 75-90.

Gross, J. (1998). Antecedent- and response-focused emotion regulation: Divergent consequences for experience, expression, and physiology. *Journal of Personality and Social Psychology, 74*, 224-237.

Gross, J., & Levenson, R. (1993). Emotional suppression: Physiology, self-report, and expressive behavior. *Journal of Personality and Social Psychology, 64*, 970-986.

Grove, J., Hanrahan, S., & McInman, A. (1991). Success/failure bias in attributions across involvement categories in sport. *Personality and Social Psychology Bulletin, 17*, 93-97.

Grube, J., & Wallach, L. (1994). Television beer advertising and drinking knowledge, beliefs, and intentions among schoolchildren. *American Journal of Public Health, 84*, 254-259.

Grusec, J. E., & Skubiski, S. L. (1970). Model nurturance, demand characteristics of the modeling experiment, and altruism. *Journal of Personality and Social Psychology, 14*, 352-359.

Guadagno, R. E., & Cialdini, R. B. (2002). Online persuasion: An examination of gender differences in computer-mediated interpersonal influence. *Group Dynamics: Theory, Research, and Practice, 6*, 38-51.

Guéguen, N. (2002). The effects of a joke on tipping when it is delivered at the same time as the bill. *Journal of Applied Social Psychology, 32*, 1955-1963.

Guimond, S. (2000). Group socialization and prejudice: The social transmission of intergroup attitudes and beliefs. *European Journal of Social Psychology, 30*, 335-354.

Guimond, S., & Dambrun, M. (2002). When prosperity breeds intergroup hostility: The effects of relative deprivation and relative gratification on prejudice. *Personality and Social Psychology Bulletin, 28*, 900-912.

Guimond, S., Dambrun, M., Michinov, N., & Duarte, S. (2003). Does social dominance generate prejudice? Integrating individual and contextual determinants of intergroup cognitions. *Journal of Personality and Social Psychology, 84*, 697-721.

Gump, B. B., & Kulik, J. A. (1997). Stress, affiliation, and emotional contagion. *Journal of Personality and Social Psychology, 72*, 305-319.

Gutierres, S., Kenrick, D., & Partch, J. (1999). Beauty, dominance, and the mating game: Contrast effects in self-assessment reflect gender differences in mate selection. *Personality and Social Psychology Bulletin, 25*, 1126-1134.

Haberstroh, S., Oyserman, D., Schwarz, N., Kühnen, U., & Ji, L. (2002). Is the interdependent self more sensitive to question context than the independent self? Self-construal and the observation of conversational norms. *Journal of Experimental Social Psychology, 38*, 323-329.

Haddock, G., Zanna, M. P., & Esses, V. M. (1993). Assessing the structure of prejudicial attitudes: The case of attitudes toward homosexuals. *Journal of Personality and Social Psychology*, *65*, 1105-1118.

Hagerty, M. R. (2000). Social comparisons of income in one's community: Evidence from national surveys of income and happiness. *Journal of Personality and Social Psychology*, *78*, 764-771.

Hahn, J., & Blass, T. (1997). Dating partner preferences: A function of similarity of love styles. *Journal of Social Behavior & Personality*, *12*, 595-610.

Halberstadt, J. (2006). The generality and ultimate origins of the attractiveness of prototypes. *Personality and Social Psychology Review*, *10*, 166-183.

Halberstadt, J., & Rhodes, G. (2000). The attractiveness of non-face averages: Implications for an evolutionary explanation of the attractiveness of average faces. *Psychological Science*, *11*, 285-289.

Hamermesh, D. S. & Biddle, J. E. (1994). Beauty and the labor market. *American Economic Review*, *4*, 1174-94.

Hamermesh, D. S., & Parker, A. (2005). Beauty in the classroom: Instructors' pulchritude and putative pedagogical productivity. *Economics of Education Review*, *24*, 369-76.

Hamilton, D. L., & Gifford, R. K. (1976). Illusory correlation in interpersonal perception: A cognitive basis of stereotypic judgments. *Journal of Experimental Social Psychology*, *12*, 392-407.

Hamilton, D. L., & Rose, T. L. (1980). Illusory correlation and the maintenance of stereotypic beliefs. *Journal of Personality and Social Psychology*, *39*, 832-845.

Hamilton, V. L., & Sanders, J. (1995). Crimes of obedience and conformity in the workplace: Surveys of Americans, Russians, and Japanese. *Journal of Social Issues*, *51*, 67-88.

Hamilton, V. L., Sanders, J., & McKearney, S. J. (1995). Orientations toward authority in an authoritarian state: Moscow in 1990. *Personality and Social Psychology Bulletin*, *21*, 356-365.

Han, G., & Park, B. (1995). Children's choice in conflict: Application of the theory of individualism-collectivism. *Journal of Cross-Cultural Psychology*, *26*, 298-313.

Han, S., & Shavitt, S. (1994). Persuasion and culture: Advertising appeals in individualistic and collectivistic societies. *Journal of Experimental Social Psychology*, *30*, 326-350.

Haney, C., Banks, C., & Zimbardo, P. (1973). Interpersonal dynamics in a simulated prison. *International Journal of Criminology & Penology*, *1*, 69-97.

Haney, C., & Zimbardo, P. (1998). The past and future of U.S. prison policy: Twenty-five years after the Stanford Prison Experiment. *American Psychologist*, *53*, 709-727.

Hanko, K., Master, S., & Sabini, J. (2004). Some evidence about character and mate selection. *Personality and Social Psychology Bulletin*, *30*, 732-742.

Hansen, D. E., Vandenberg, B., & Patterson, M. L. (1995). The effects of religious orientation on spontaneous and nonspontaneous helping behaviors. *Personality and Individual Differences*, *19*, 101-104.

Hansen, N., & Sassenberg, K. (2006). Does social identification harm or serve as a buffer? The impact of social identification on anger after experiencing social discrimination. *Personality and Social Psychology Bulletin*, *32*, 983-996.

Harasty, A. S. (1997). The interpersonal nature of social stereotypes: Differential discussion patterns about in-groups and out-groups. *Personality and Social Psychology Bulletin*, *23*, 270-284.

Harber, K. D. (1998). Feedback to minorities: Evidence of a positive bias. *Journal of Personality and Social Psychology*, *74*, 622-628.

Hardin, G. (1968). The tragedy of the commons. *Science*, *162*, 1243-1248.

Harkins, S. G., & Jackson, J. M. (1985). The role of evaluation in eliminating social loafing. *Personality and Social Psychology Bulletin*, *11*, 457-465.

Harkins, S. G., & Petty, R. E. (1981). Effects of source magnification of cognitive effort on attitudes: An information-processing view. *Journal of Personality and Social Psychology*, *40*, 401-413.

Harkins, S. G., & Petty, R. E. (1982). Effects of task difficulty and task uniqueness on social loafing. *Journal of Personality and Social Psychology*, *43*, 1214-1229.

Harmon-Jones, E. (2000). Cognitive dissonance and experienced negative affect: Evidence that dissonance increases experienced negative affect even in the absence of aversive consequences. *Personality and Social Psychology Bulletin*, *26*, 1490-1501.

Harmon-Jones, E., & Allen, J. (2001). The role of affect in the mere exposure effect: Evidence from psychophysiological and individual differences approaches. *Personality and Social Psychology Bulletin*, *27*, 889-898.

Harmon-Jones, E., Brehm, J., Greenberg, J., Simon, L., & Nelson, D. (1996). Evidence that the production of aversive consequences is not necessary to create cognitive dissonance. *Journal of Personality and Social Psychology*, *70*, 5-16.

Harmon-Jones, E., & Devine, P. (2003). Introduction to the special section on social neuroscience: Promise and caveats. *Journal of Personality and Social Psychology*, *85*, 589-593.

Harmon-Jones, E., & Harmon-Jones, C. (2002). Testing the action-based model of cognitive dissonance: The effect of action orientation on postdecisional attitudes. *Personality and Social Psychology Bulletin*, *28*, 711-723.

Harré, N., Brandt, T., & Houkamau, C. (2004). An examination of the actor-observer effect in young drivers' attributions for their own and their friends' risky driving. *Journal of Applied Social Psychology*, *34*, 806-824.

Harrell, W. A. (1978). Physical attractiveness, self-disclosure, and helping behavior. *Journal of Social Psychology*, *104*, 15-17.

Harris, C. R. (2000). Psychophysiological responses to imagined infidelity: The specific innate modular view of jealousy reconsidered. *Journal of Personality and Social Psychology*, *78*, 1082-1091.

Harris, C. R. (2002). Sexual and romantic jealousy in heterosexual and homosexual adults. *Psychological Science*, *13*, 7-12.

Harris, C. R., & Christenfeld, N. (1996). Gender, jealousy, and reason. *Psychological Science*, *7*, 364-366.

Harris, L. T., & Fiske, S. T. (2006). Dehumanizing the lowest of the low: Neuroimaging responses to extreme out-groups. *Psychological Science*, *17*, 847-853.

Harris, P. R., & Napper, L. (2005). Self-affirmation and the biased processing of threatening health-risk information. *Personality and Social Psychology Bulletin*, *31*, 1250-1263.

Harrison, K., & Marske, A. (2005). Nutritional content of foods advertised during the television programs children watch most. *American Journal of Public Health*, *95*, 1568-1574.

Hart, A. (1995). Naturally occurring expectation effects. *Journal of Personality and Social Psychology*, *68*, 109-115.

Hart, A. J., Whalen, P. J., Shin, L. M., McInerney, S. C., Fischer, H., & Rauch, S. L. (2000). Differential response in the human amygdala to racial outgroup vs ingroup face stimuli. *Neuroreport*, *11*, 2351-2355.

Harvey, J. H., & Omarzu, J. (1997). Minding the close relationship. *Personality and Social Psychology Review, 1*, 224-240.

Harwood, J., Hewstone, M., Paolini, S., & Voci, A. (2005). Grandparent-grandchild contact and attitudes toward older adults: Moderator and mediator effects. *Personality and Social Psychology Bulletin, 31*, 393-406.

Hashish, I., Hai, H. K., Harvey, W., Feinmann, C., & Harris, M. (1988). Reduction of postoperative pain and swelling by ultrasound treatment: A placebo effect. *Pain, 33*, 303-311.

Hassan, N. (2001). An arsenal of believers talking to the human bombs. *New Yorker*, November 19, 77, 36.

Hassin, R., & Trope, Y. (2000). Facing faces: Studies on the cognitive aspects of physiognomy. *Journal of Personality and Social Psychology, 78*, 837-852.

Hastorf, A. H., & Cantril, H. (1954). They saw a game: A case study. *The Journal of Abnormal and Social Psychology, 49*, 129-134.

Hatfield, E. (1988). Passionate and companionate love. In R. J. Sternberg & M. L. Barnes (Ed.), *The Psychology of Love* (pp. 191-217). New Haven, CT: Yale University Press.

Hatfield, E., Greenberger, D., Traupmann, J., & Lambert, P. (1982). Equity and sexual satisfaction in recently married couples. *Journal of Sex Research, 18*, 18-32.

Hatfield, E., & Sprecher, S. (1986). Measuring passionate love in intimate relationships. *Journal of Adolescence, 9*, 383-410.

Hatfield, E., & Sprecher, S. (1995). Men's and women's preferences in marital partners in the United States, Russia, and Japan. *Journal of Cross-Cultural Psychology, 26*, 728-750.

Hawkins, S., & Hastie, R. (1990). Hindsight: Biased judgments of past events after the outcomes are known. *Psychological Bulletin, 107*, 311-327.

Hawkley, L. C., Burleson, M. H., Berntson, G. G., & Cacioppo, J. T. (2003). Loneliness in everyday life: Cardiovascular activity, psychosocial context, and health behaviors. *Journal of Personality and Social Psychology, 85*, 105-120.

Hazan, C., & Shaver, P. (1987). Romantic love conceptualized as an attachment process. *Journal of Personality and Social Psychology, 52*, 511-524.

Heatherton, T., Macrae, C., & Kelley, W. (2004). What the social brain sciences can tell us about the self. *Current Directions in Psychological Science, 13*, 190-193.

Heatherton, T., & Vohs, K. (2000). Interpersonal evaluations following threats to self: Role of self-esteem. *Journal of Personality and Social Psychology, 78*, 725-736.

Hebl, M. R., Foster, J. B., Mannix, L. M., & Dovidio, J. F. (2002). Formal and interpersonal discrimination: A field study of bias toward homosexual applicants. *Personality and Social Psychology Bulletin, 28*, 815-825.

Hedley, A. A., Ogden, C. L., Johnson, C. L., Carroll, M. D., Curtin, L. R., & Flegal, K. M. (2004). Prevalence of overweight and obesity among US children, adolescents, and adults, 1999-2002. *Journal of the American Medical Association, 291*, 2847-2850.

Heider, F. (1958). *The Psychology of Interpersonal Relations*. Hoboken, NJ: Wiley.

Heilman, M. E., Block, C. J., & Lucas, J. A. (1992). Presumed incompetent? Stigmatization and affirmative action efforts. *Journal of Applied Psychology, 77*, 536-544.

Heine, S., Kitayama, S., Lehman, D., Takata, T., Ide, E., Leung, C., & Matsumoto, H. (2001). Divergent consequences of success and failure in Japan and North America: An investigation of self-improving motivations and malleable selves. *Journal of Personality and Social Psychology, 81*, 599-615.

Heine, S., & Lehman, D. (1995). Cultural variation in unrealistic optimism: Does the West feel more vulnerable than the East? *Journal of Personality and Social Psychology, 68*, 595-607.

Heine, S., & Lehman, D. (1997). Culture, dissonance, and self-affirmation. *Personality and Social Psychology Bulletin, 23*, 389-400.

Heine, S., & Lehman, D. (1997). The cultural construction of self-enhancement: An examination of group-serving biases. *Journal of Personality and Social Psychology, 72*, 1268-1283.

Heine, S., & Lehman, D. (1999). Culture, self-discrepancies, and self-satisfaction. *Personality and Social Psychology Bulletin, 25*, 915-925.

Heine, S., Lehman, D., Markus, H., & Kitayama, S. (1999). Is there a universal need for positive self-regard? *Psychological Review, 106*, 766-794.

Heine, S., Lehman, D., Peng, K., & Greenholtz, J. (2002). What's wrong with cross-cultural comparisons of subjective Likert scales?: The reference-group effect. *Journal of Personality and Social Psychology, 82*, 903-918.

Hejmadi, A., Davidson, R., & Rozin, P. (2000). Exploring Hindu Indian emotion expressions: Evidence for accurate recognition by Americans and Indians. *Psychological Science, 11*, 183-187.

Helgeson, V., & Mickelson, K. (1995). Motives for social comparison. *Personality and Social Psychology Bulletin, 21*, 1200-1209.

Henchy, T., & Glass, D. C. (1968). Evaluation apprehension and the social facilitation of dominant and subordinate responses. *Journal of Personality and Social Psychology, 10*, 446-454.

Henderson, M. D., Trope, Y., & Carnevale, P. J. (2006). Negotiation from a near and distant time perspective. *Journal of Personality and Social Psychology, 91*, 712-729.

Hendrick, C., & Hendrick, S. (1986). A theory and method of love. *Journal of Personality and Social Psychology, 50*, 392-402.

Hendrick, S. S., Hendrick, C., & Adler, N. L. (1988). Romantic relationships: Love, satisfaction, and staying together. *Journal of Personality and Social Psychology, 54*, 980-988.

Hendrick, S. S., & Hendrick, C. (1993). Lovers as friends. *Journal of Social and Personal Relationships, 10*, 459-466.

Hendrick, S. S., & Hendrick, C. (1995). Gender differences and similarities in sex and love. *Personal Relationships, 2*, 55-65.

Hennenlotter, A., Dresel, C., Castrop, F., Ceballos Baumann, A. O., Wohlschläger, A.M., & Haslinger, B. (2009). The link between facial feedback and neural activity within central circuitries of emotion: New insights from botulinum toxin-induced denervation of frown muscles. *Cerebral Cortex, 19*, 537-542.

Hennigan, K. M., Heath, L., Wharton, J. D., DelRosario, M. L., Cook, T.D., & Calder, B.J. (1982). Impact of the introduction of television on crime in the United States: Empirical findings and theoretical implications. *Journal of Personality and Social Psychology, 42*, 461-477.

Henry, P. J., & Hardin, C. D. (2006). The contact hypothesis revisited: Status bias in the reduction of implicit prejudice in the United States and Lebanon. *Psychological Science, 17*, 862-868.

Hepworth, J. T., & West, S. G. (1988). Lynchings and the economy: A time-series reanalysis of Hovland and Sears (1940). *Journal of Personality and Social Psychology, 55*, 239-247.

Herlocker, C. E., Allison, S. T., Foubert, J. D., & Beggan, J. K. (1997). Intended and unintended overconsumption of physical, spatial, and temporal resources. *Journal of Personality and Social Psychology, 73*, 992-1104.

Hewitt, P., Flett, G., Sherry, S., Habke, M., Parkin, M., Lam, R., et al. (2003). The interpersonal expression of perfection: Perfectionistic self-presentation and psychological distress. *Journal of Personality and Social Psychology, 84*, 1303-1325.

Hewstone, M. (1990). The 'ultimate attribution error'? A review of the literature on intergroup causal attribution. *European Journal of Social Psychology, 20*, 311-335.

Hewstone, M., Hopkins, N., & Routh, D. A. (1992). Cognitive models of stereotype change: I. Generalization and subtyping in young people's views of the police. *European Journal of Social Psychology, 22*, 219-234.

Hewstone, M., Macrae, C. N., Griffiths, R., & Milne, A. B. (1994). Cognitive models of stereotype change: 5. Measurement, development, and consequences of subtyping. *Journal of Experimental Social Psychology, 30*, 505-526.

Hewstone, M., & Ward, C. (1985). Ethnocentrism and causal attribution in Southeast Asia. *Journal of Personality and Social Psychology, 48*, 614-623.

Higbee, K. L. (1969). Fifteen years of fear arousal: Research on threat appeals: 1953-1968. *Psychological Bulletin, 72*, 426-444.

Higgins, E. (1996). The 'self digest': Self-knowledge serving self-regulatory functions. *Journal of Personality and Social Psychology, 71*, 1062-1083.

Higgins, E., Rholes, W., & Jones, C. (1977). Category accessibility and impression formation. *Journal of Experimental Social Psychology, 13*, 141-154.

Higgins, R., & Harris, R. (1988). Strategic 'alcohol' use: Drinking to self-handicap. *Journal of Social & Clinical Psychology, 6*, 191-202.

Highhouse, S., Beadle, D., Gallo, A., & Miller, L. (1998). Get em while they last! Effects of scarcity information in job advertisements. *Journal of Applied Social Psychology, 28*, 779-795.

Hill, T., Smith, N., & Lewicki, P. (1989). The development of self-image bias: A real-world demonstration. *Personality and Social Psychology Bulletin, 15*, 205-211.

Hilton, J. L., & Darley, J. M. (1991). The effects of interaction goals on person perception. In M.P. Zanna (Ed.), *Advances in Experimental Social Psychology*, Vol. 24, (pp. 235-267). New York: Academic Press.

Hilton, J., & Darley, J. (1985). Constructing other persons: A limit on the effect. *Journal of Experimental Social Psychology, 21*, 1-18.

Hilton, J., Fein, S., & Miller, D. (1993). Suspicion and dispositional inference. *Personality and Social Psychology Bulletin, 19*, 501-512.

Hilton, J. L., & von Hippel, W. (1990). The role of consistency in the judgment of stereotype-relevant behaviors. *Personality and Social Psychology Bulletin, 16*, 430-448.

Hirt, E., Deppe, R., & Gordon, L. (1991). Self-reported versus behavioral self-handicapping: Empirical evidence for a theoretical distinction. *Journal of Personality and Social Psychology, 61*, 981-991.

Hoeksema-van Orden, C. Y. D., Gaillard, A. W. K., & Buunk, B. P. (1998). Social loafing under fatigue. *Journal of Personality and Social Psychology, 75*, 1179-1190.

Hoffman, M. L. (1981). Is altruism part of human nature? *Journal of Personality and Social Psychology, 40*, 121-137.

Hoffman, M. L. (1994).The contribution of empathy to justice and moral judgment. In B. Puka (Ed.), *Reaching Out: Caring, Altruism, and Prosocial Behavior* (Vol. 7, pp. 161-194). New York: Garland.

Hofstede, G. (1991). *Culture and Organizations: Software of the Mind*. London: McGraw-Hill.

Hogg, M. A., Hains, S. C., & Mason, I. (1998). Identification and leadership in small groups: Salience, frame of reference, and leader stereotypicality effects on leader evaluations. *Journal of Personality and Social Psychology, 75*, 1248-1263.

Holland, R., Roeder, U., van Baaren, R., Brandt, A., & Hannover, B. (2004). Don't stand so close to me: The effects of self-construal on interpersonal closeness. *Psychological Science, 15*, 237-242.

Holland, R., Verplanken, B., & van Knippenberg, A. (2003). From repetition to conviction: Attitude accessibility as a determinant of attitude certainty. *Journal of Experimental Social Psychology, 39*, 594-601.

Hollander, E. P. (1958). Conformity, status, and idiosyncrasy credit. *Psychological Review, 65*, 117-127.

Hollander, E. P. (1960). Competence and conformity in the acceptance of influence. *The Journal of Abnormal and Social Psychology, 61*, 365-369.

Holloway, S., Tucker, L., & Hornstein, H. A. (1977). The effects of social and nonsocial information on interpersonal behavior of males: The news makes news. *Journal of Personality and Social Psychology, 35*, 514-522.

Holmes, J. G., & Murray, S. L. (1996). Conflict in close relationships. In E. T. Higgins & A. W. Kruglanski (Eds.), *Social Psychology: Handbook of Basic Principles* (pp. 622-654). New York: Guilford.

Holtgraves, T., & Yang, J. N. (1990). Politeness as universal: Cross-cultural perceptions of request strategies and inferences based on their use. *Journal of Personality and Social Psychology, 59*, 719-729.

Holtgraves, T. M., & Yang, J.H. (1992). The interpersonal underpinnings of request strategies: General principles and differences due to culture and gender. *Journal of Personality and Social Psychology, 62*, 246-256.

Honeycutt, J. M., Woods, B. L., & Fontenot, K. (1993). The endorsement of communication conflict rules as a function of engagement, marriage and marital ideology. *Journal of Social and Personal Relationships, 10*, 285-304.

Hoover, C. W., Wood, E. E., & Knowles, E. S. (1983). Forms of social awareness and helping. *Journal of Experimental Social Psychology, 19*, 577-590.

Horgen, K. B., Choate, M., & Brownell, K. D. (2001). Television food advertising: Targeting children in a toxic environment. In D. G. Singer & J. L. Singer (Eds.), *Handbook of Children and the Media* (pp. 447-461). Thousand Oaks, CA: Sage.

Hornsey, M. J., & Hogg, M. A. (2000). Intergroup similarity and subgroup relations: Some implications for assimilation. *Personality and Social Psychology Bulletin, 26*, 948-958.

Hornsey, M. J., & Imani, A. (2004). Criticizing groups from the inside and the outside: An identity perspective on the intergroup sensitivity effect. *Personality and Social Psychology Bulletin, 30*, 365-383.

Hornstein, H. A., Fisch, E., & Holmes, M. (1968). Influence of a model's feeling about his behavior and his relevance as a comparison other on observers' helping behavior. *Journal of Personality and Social Psychology, 10*, 222-226.

Hortacsu, N., & Oral, A. (2001). Comparison of couple- and family-initiated marriages in Turkey. *The Journal of Social Psychology, 134*, 229-239.

Hoshino-Browne, E., Zanna, A., Spencer, S., Zanna, M., Kitayama, S., & Lackenbauer, S. (2005). On the cultural guises of cognitive dissonance: The case of Easterners and Westerners. *Journal of Personality and Social Psychology, 89*, 294-310.

Hovland, C. I., & Sears, R. R. (1940). Minor studies of aggression: VI. Correlation of lynchings with economic indices. *Journal of Psychology: Interdisciplinary and Applied, 9*, 301-310.

Hovland, C. I., & Weiss, W. (1951). The influence of source credibility on communication effectiveness. *Public Opinion Quarterly, 15*, 635-650.

Howard, D. J. (1997). Familiar phrases as peripheral persuasion cues. *Journal of Experimental Social Psychology, 33*, 231-243.

Huesmann, L. R., Eron, L. D., Klein, R., Brice, P., & Fischer, P. (1983). Mitigating the imitation of aggressive behaviors by changing children's attitudes about media violence. *Journal of Personality and Social Psychology, 44*, 899-910.

Huesmann, L. R. (1986). Psychological processes promoting the relation between exposure to media violence and aggressive behavior by the viewer. *Journal of Social Issues, 42*, 125-139.

Huesmann, L. R., Eron, L. D., Lefkowitz, M. M., & Walder, L. O. (1984). Stability of aggression over time and generations. *Developmental Psychology, 20*, 1120-1134.

Huffman, K. (2009). *Psychology in Action*. Hoboken, NJ: John Wiley & Sons.

Huguet, P., Galvaing, M. P., Monteil, J. M., & Dumas, F. (1999). Social presence effects in the Stroop task: Further evidence for an attentional view of social facilitation. *Journal of Personality and Social Psychology, 77*, 1011-1025.

Hull, J. G., & Bond, C. F. (1986). Social and behavioral consequences of alcohol consumption and expectancy: A meta-analysis. *Psychological Bulletin, 99*, 347-360.

Hull, J., & Young, R. (1983). Self-consciousness, self-esteem, and success-failure as determinants of alcohol consumption in male social drinkers. *Journal of Personality and Social Psychology, 44*, 1097-1109.

Huston, A. C., Donnerstein, E., Fairchild, H. H., Feshbach, N. D., Katz, P. A., Murray, J. P., et al. (1992). *Big World, Small Screen: The Role of Television in American Society*. Lincoln, NE: University of Nebraska Press.

Huston, T. L., & Vangelisti, A. L. (1991). Socioemotional behavior and satisfaction in marital relationships: A longitudinal study. *Journal of Personality and Social Psychology, 61*, 721-733.

Huston, T. L., Ruggiero, M., Conner, R., & Geis, G. (1981). Bystander intervention into crime: A study based on naturally-occurring episodes. *Social Psychology Quarterly, 44*, 14-23.

Hyde, J. S. (1984). How large are gender differences in aggression? A developmental meta-analysis. *Developmental Psychology, 20*, 722-736.

Hyman, I., Husband, T., & Billings, F. (1995). False memories of childhood experiences. *Applied Cognitive Psychology, 9*, 181-197.

Ickes, W. (1993). Traditional gender roles: Do they make, and then break, our relationships? *Journal of Social Issues, 49*, 71-86.

Invernizzi, F., Falomir-Pichastor, J. M., Muñoz-Rojas, D., & Mugny, G. (2003). Social influence in personally relevant contexts: The respect attributed to the source as a factor increasing smokers' intention to quit smoking. *Journal of Applied Social Psychology, 33*, 1818-1836.

Inzlicht, M., & Ben-Zeev, T. (2000). A threatening intellectual environment: Why females are susceptible to experiencing problem-solving deficits in the presence of males. *Psychological Science, 11*, 365-371.

Inzlicht, M., & Ben-Zeev, T. (2003). Do high-achieving female students underperform in private? The implications of threatening environments on intellectual processing. *Journal of Educational Psychology, 95*, 796-805.

Isen, A. M., & Levin, P. F. (1972). Effect of feeling good on helping: Cookies and kindness. *Journal of Personality and Social Psychology, 21*, 384-388.

Isen, A. M., & Simmonds, S. F. (1978). The effect of feeling good on a helping task that is incompatible with good mood. *Social Psychology, 41*, 346-349.

Isenberg, D. J. (1986). Group polarization: A critical review and meta-analysis. *Journal of Personality and Social Psychology, 50*, 1141-1151.

Ishii, K., Reyes, J. A., & Kitayama, S. (2003). Spontaneous attention to word content versus emotional tone: Differences among three cultures. *Psychological Science, 14*, 39-46.

Ito, T., Larsen, J., Smith, N., & Cacioppo, J. (1998). Negative information weighs more heavily on the brain: The negativity bias in evaluative categorizations. *Journal of Personality and Social Psychology, 75*, 887-900.

Ito, T. A., Miller, N., & Pollock, V. E. (1996). Alcohol and aggression: A meta-analysis on the moderating effects of inhibitory cues, triggering events, and self-focused attention. *Psychological Bulletin, 120*, 60-82.

Ito, T. A., & Urland, G. R. (2003). Race and gender on the brain: Electrocortical measures of attention to the race and gender of multiply categorizable individuals. *Journal of Personality and Social Psychology, 85*, 616-626.

Iyengar, S., & Lepper, M. (1999). Rethinking the value of choice: A cultural perspective on intrinsic motivation. *Journal of Personality and Social Psychology, 76*, 349-366.

Izard, C. (1994). Innate and universal facial expressions: Evidence from developmental and cross-cultural research. *Psychological Bulletin, 115*, 288-299.

Jacks, J. Z., & Cameron, K. A. (2003). Strategies for resisting persuasion. *Basic and Applied Social Psychology, 25*, 145-161.

Jackson, H., Philip, E., Nuttall, R. L., & Diller, L. (2002). Traumatic brain injury: A hidden consequence for battered women. *Professional Psychology: Research and Practice, 33*, 39-45.

Jackson, J. M., & Williams, K. D. (1985). Social loafing on difficult tasks: Working collectively can improve performance. *Journal of Personality and Social Psychology, 49*, 937-942.

Jackson, J. W. (1993). Realistic group conflict theory: A review and evaluation of the theoretical and empirical literature. *Psychological Record, 43*, 395-413.

Jackson, L. M., & Esses, V. M. (1997). Of scripture and ascription: The relation between religious fundamentalism and intergroup helping. *Personality and Social Psychology Bulletin, 23*, 893-906.

James, W., & James, H. (1920). *The Letters of William James*. Boston, MA: The Atlantic Monthly Press.

Janes, L. M., & Olson, J. M. (2000). Jeer pressures: The behavioral effects of observing ridicule of others. *Personality and Social Psychology Bulletin, 26*, 474-485.

Janis, I. L. (1972). *Victims of Groupthink*. Boston: Houghton-Mifflin.

Janis, I. (1982). *Groupthink (2nd ed.)*. Boston: Houghton-Mifflin.

Janis, I. L., & Feshbach, S. (1953). Effects of fear-arousing communications. *The Journal of Abnormal and Social Psychology, 48*, 78-92.

Janis, I. L., Kaye, D., & Kirschner, P. (1965). Facilitating effects of 'eating-while-reading' on responsiveness to persuasive communications. *Journal of Personality and Social Psychology, 1*, 181-186.

Janiszewski, C., & Uy, D. (2008). Precision of the anchor influences the amount of adjustment. *Psychological Science, 19*, 121-127.

Janoff-Bulman, R., Timko, C., & Carli, L. L. (1985). Cognitive biases in blaming the victim. *Journal of Experimental Social Psychology, 21*, 161-177.

Jarvis, W. B. G., & Petty, R. E. (1996). The need to evaluate. *Journal of Personality and Social Psychology, 70*, 172-194.

Jemmott, J., & Magloire, K. (1988). Academic stress, social support, and secretory immunoglobulin A. *Journal of Personality and Social Psychology, 55*, 803-810.

Jenkins, S. S., & Aubé, J. (2002). Gender differences and gender-related constructs in dating aggression. *Personality and Social Psychology Bulletin, 28*, 1106-1118.

Jensen-Campbell, L. A., & Graziano, W. G. (2000). Beyond the school yard: Relationships as moderators of daily interpersonal conflict. *Personality and Social Psychology Bulletin, 26*, 923-935.

Jensen-Campbell, L. A., Graziano, W. G., & West, S. G. (1995). Dominance, prosocial orientation, and female preferences: Do nice guys really finish last? *Journal of Personality and Social Psychology, 68*, 427-440.

Jetten, J., Branscombe, N. R., Schmitt, M. T., & Spears, R. (2001). Rebels with a cause: Group identification as a response to perceived discrimination from the mainstream. *Personality and Social Psychology Bulletin, 27*, 1204-1213.

Ji, L., Nisbett, R., & Su, Y. (2001). Culture, change, and prediction. *Psychological Science, 12*, 450-456.

Ji, L., Peng, K., & Nisbett, R. (2000). Culture, control, and perception of relationships in the environment. *Journal of Personality and Social Psychology, 78*, 943-955.

Ji, L., Schwarz, N., & Nisbett, R. E. (2000). Culture, autobiographical memory, and behavioral frequency reports: Measurement issues in cross-cultural studies. *Personality and Social Psychology Bulletin, 26*, 585-593.

Ji, L., Zhang, Z., & Nisbett, R. (2004). Is it culture or is it language? Examination of language effects in cross-cultural research on categorization. *Journal of Personality and Social Psychology, 87*, 57-65.

Johns, M., Schmader, T., & Martens, A. (2005). Knowing is half the battle: Teaching stereotype threat as a means of improving women's math performance, *Psychological Science, 16*, 175-179.

Johnson, C., & Mullen, B. (1994). Evidence for the accessibility of paired distinctiveness in distinctiveness-based illusory correlation in stereotyping. *Personality and Social Psychology Bulletin, 20*, 65-70.

Johnson, J. (2005). Ascertaining the validity of individual protocols from Web-based personality inventories. *Journal of Research in Personality, 39*, 103-129.

Johnson, R. C., Danko, G. P., Darvill, T. J., & Bochner, S. (1989). Cross-cultural assessment of altruism and its correlates. *Personality and Individual Differences, 10*, 855-868.

Johnson, R., Kelly, R., & LeBlanc, B. (1995). Motivational basis of dissonance: Aversive consequences of inconsistency. *Personality and Social Psychology Bulletin, 21*, 850-855.

Johnson, T. E., & Rule, B. G. (1986). Mitigating circumstance information, censure, and aggression. *Journal of Personality and Social Psychology, 50*, 537-542.

Jones, E. (1979). The rocky road from acts to dispositions. *American Psychologist, 34*, 107-117.

Jones, E. E. (1990). *Interpersonal Perception.* New York: WH Freeman.

Jones, E. E. & Davis, K. E. (1965). From acts to dispositions: The attribution process in social psychology. In L. Berkowitz (Ed.), *Advances in Experimental Social Psychology* (Volume 2, pp. 219-266), New York: Academic Press.

Jones, E., Davis, K., & Gergen, K. (1961). Role playing variations and their informational value for person perception. *The Journal of Abnormal and Social Psychology, 63*, 302-310.

Jones, E., & Harris, V. (1967). The attribution of attitudes. *Journal of Experimental Social Psychology, 3*, 1-24.

Jones, E. E., & Nisbett, R. E. (1971). *The Actor and the Observer: Divergent Perceptions of the Causes of Behavior.* New York: General Learning Press.

Jones, J. L., & Leary, M. R. (1994). Effects of appearance-based admonitions against sun exposure on tanning intentions in young adults. *Health Psychology, 13*, 86-90.

Jones, J. T., Pelham, B. W., Carvallo, M., & Mirenberg, M. C. (2004). How do I love thee? Let me count the Js: Implicit egotism and interpersonal attraction. *Journal of Personality and Social Psychology, 87*, 665-683.

Jones, T. F., Craig, A. S., Hoy, D., Gunter, E. W., Ashley, D. L., Barr, D. B., et al. (2000). Mass psychogenic illness attributed to toxic exposure at a high school. *New England Journal of Medicine, 342*, 96-100.

Jones, W. H., Carpenter, B. N., & Quintana, D. (1985). Personality and interpersonal predictors of loneliness in two cultures. *Journal of Personality and Social Psychology, 48*, 1503-1511.

Josephs, R., Markus, H., & Tafarodi, R. (1992). Gender and self-esteem. *Journal of Personality and Social Psychology, 63*, 391-402.

Josephson, W. L. (1987). Television violence and children's aggression: Testing the priming, social script, and disinhibition predictions. *Journal of Personality and Social Psychology, 53*, 882-890.

Judd, C. M., & Park, B. (1988). Out-group homogeneity: Judgments of variability at the individual and group levels. *Journal of Personality and Social Psychology, 54*, 778-788.

Judd, C. M., Ryan, C. S., & Park, B. (1991). Accuracy in the judgment of in-group and out-group variability. *Journal of Personality and Social Psychology, 61*, 366-379.

Jussim, L., Coleman, L. M., & Lerch, L. (1987). The nature of stereotypes: A comparison and integration of three theories. *Journal of Personality and Social Psychology, 52*, 536-546.

Jussim, L., & Eccles, J. (1992). Teacher expectations: II. Construction and reflection of student achievement. *Journal of Personality and Social Psychology, 63*, 947-961.

Kachadourian, L. K., Fincham, F., & Davila, J. (2004). The tendency to forgive in dating and married couples: The role of attachment and relationship satisfaction. *Personal Relationships, 11*, 373-393.

Kahneman, D., & Tversky, A. (1972). Subjective probability: A judgment of representativeness. *Cognitive Psychology, 3*, 430-454.

Kahneman, D., Knetsch, J. L., & Thaler, R. H. (1986a). Fairness and the assumptions of economics. *Journal of Business, 59,* S285-S300.

Kahneman, D., Knetsch, J. L., & Thaler, R.H. (1986b). Fairness as a constraint on profit seeking: Entitlements in the market. *The American Economic Review, 76,* 728-741.

Kahneman, D., Knetsch, J. L., & Thaler, R. H. (1990). Experimental tests of the endowment effect and the Coase theorem. *Journal of Political Economy, 98,* 1325-1348.

Kaiser, C. R., & Miller, C. T. (2001). Stop complaining! The social costs of making attributions to discrimination. *Personality and Social Psychology Bulletin, 27,* 254-263.

Kaiser, R. B., Hogan, R., & Craig, S. B. (2008). Leadership and the fate of organizations. *American Psychologist, 63,* 96-110.

Kalichman, S., & Coley, B. (1995). Context framing to enhance HIV-antibody-testing messages targeted to African American women. *Health Psychology, 14,* 247-254.

Kalick, S. M., & Hamilton, T. E. (1986). The matching hypothesis reexamined. *Journal of Personality and Social Psychology, 51,* 673-682.

Kallgren, C. A., Reno, R. R., & Cialdini, R. B. (2000). A focus theory of normative conduct: When norms do and do not affect behavior. *Personality and Social Psychology Bulletin, 26,* 1002-1012.

Kameda, T., & Sugimori, S. (1993). Psychological entrapment in group decision making: An assigned decision rule and a groupthink phenomenon. *Journal of Personality and Social Psychology, 65,* 282-292.

Kanagawa, C., Cross, S., & Markus, H. (2001). 'Who am I?' The cultural psychology of the conceptual self. *Personality and Social Psychology Bulletin, 27,* 90-103.

Kanekar, S., Kolsawalla, M. B., & Nazareth, T. (1989). Occupational prestige as a function of occupant's gender. *Journal of Applied Social Psychology, 19,* 681-688.

Kaplan, M. F., & Miller, L. E. (1978). Reducing the effects of juror bias. *Journal of Personality and Social Psychology, 36,* 1443-1455.

Kaplan, R. E., & Kaiser, R. B. (2003). Rethinking a classic distinction in leadership: Implications for the assessment and development of executives. *Consulting Psychology Journal: Research and Practice, 55,* 15-25.

Karau, S. J., & Williams, K. D. (1993). Social loafing: A meta-analytic review and theoretical integration. *Journal of Personality and Social Psychology, 65,* 681-706.

Karney, B. R., & Bradbury, T. N. (2000). Attributions in marriage: State or trait? A growth curve analysis. *Journal of Personality and Social Psychology, 78,* 295-309.

Karney, B., & Coombs, R. (2000). Memory bias in long-term close relationships: Consistency or improvement? *Personality and Social Psychology Bulletin, 26,* 959-970.

Karremans, J. C., Stroebe, W., & Claus, J. (2006). Beyond Vicary's fantasies: The impact of subliminal priming and brand choice. *Journal of Experimental Social Psychology, 42,* 792-798.

Kashima, Y., Kokubo, T., Kashima, E., Boxall, D., Yamaguchi, S., & Macrae, K. (2004). Culture and self: Are there within-culture differences in self between metropolitan areas and regional cities? *Personality and Social Psychology Bulletin, 30,* 816-823.

Kashima, Y., Siegal, M., Tanaka, K., & Kashima, E. (1992). Do people believe behaviours are consistent with attitudes? Towards a cultural psychology of attribution processes. *British Journal of Social Psychology, 31,* 111-124.

Kassin, S. M. (2005). On the psychology of confessions: Does innocence put innocents at risk? *American Psychologist, 60,* 215-228.

Kassin, S. M., & Kiechel, K. L. (1996). The social psychology of false confessions: Compliance, internalization, and confabulation. *Psychological Science, 7,* 125-128.

Kassin, S., & Sukel, H. (1997). Coerced confessions and the jury: An experimental test of the 'harmless error' rule. *Law and Human Behavior, 21,* 27-46.

Kawakami, K., Dovidio, J., & Dijksterhuis, A. (2003). Effect of social category priming on personal attitudes. *Psychological Science, 14,* 315-319.

Kawakami, K., Young, H., & Dovidio, J.F. (2002). Automatic stereotyping: Category, trait, and behavioral activations. *Personality and Social Psychology Bulletin, 28,* 3-15.

Keller, J., & Dauenheimer, D. (2003). Stereotype threat in the classroom: Dejection mediates the disrupting threat effect on women's math performance. *Personality and Social Psychology Bulletin, 29,* 371-381.

Keller, M., Edelstein, W., Schmid, C., Fang, F., & Fang, G. (1998). Reasoning about responsibilities and obligations in close relationships: A comparison across two cultures. *Developmental Psychology, 34,* 731-741.

Kellermann, A. L., Rivara, F. P., Rushforth, N. B., & Banton, J. G. (1993). Gun ownership as a risk factor for homicide in the home. *New England Journal of Medicine, 329,* 1084-1091.

Kelley, H. (1950). The warm-cold variable in first impressions of persons. *Journal of Personality, 18,* 431-439.

Kelley, H. (1967). Attribution theory in social psychology. *Nebraska Symposium on Motivation, 15,* 192-238.

Kelly, D. J., Quinn, P. C., Slater, A. M., Lee, K., Ge, L., & Pascalis, O. (2007). The other-race effect develops during infancy: Evidence of perceptual narrowing. *Psychological Science, 18,* 1084-1089.

Kelly, J. R., Jackson, J. W., & Hutson-Comeaux, S. L. (1997). The effects of time pressure and task differences on influence modes and accuracy in decision-making groups. *Personality and Social Psychology Bulletin, 23,* 10-22.

Kelly, S., & Dunbar, R. I. M. (2001). Who dares, wins: Heroism versus altruism in women's mate choice. *Human Nature, 12,* 89-105.

Kelman, H. C. (1997). Group processes in the resolution of international conflicts: Experiences from the Israeli-Palestinian case. *American Psychologist, 52,* 212-220.

Keltner, D., & Robinson, R. J. (1997). Defending the status quo: Power and bias in social conflict. *Personality and Social Psychology Bulletin, 23,* 1066-1077.

Kenrick, D. T., Groth, G. E., Trost, M. R., & Sadalla, E. K. (1993). Integrating evolutionary and social exchange perspectives on relationships: Effects of gender, self-appraisal, and involvement level on mate selection criteria. *Journal of Personality and Social Psychology, 64,* 951-969.

Kenrick, D. T., & Gutierres, S. E. (1980). Contrast effects and judgments of physical attractiveness: When beauty becomes a social problem. *Journal of Personality and Social Psychology, 38,* 131-140.

Kenrick, D. T., Gutierres, S. E., & Goldberg, L. L. (1989). Influence of popular erotica on judgments of strangers and mates. *Journal of Experimental Social Psychology, 25,* 159-167.

Kenrick, D. T., Keefe, R. C., Bryan, A., Barr, A., & Brown, S. (1995). Age preferences and mate choice among homosexuals and heterosexuals: A case for modular psychological mechanisms. *Journal of Personality and Social Psychology, 69,* 1166-1172.

Kenrick, D. T., Montello, D. R., Gutierres, S. E., & Trost, M. R. (1993). Effects of physical attractiveness on affect and perceptual judgments: When social comparison overrides social reinforcement. *Personality and Social Psychology Bulletin, 19*, 195-199.

Kenrick, D. T., Neuberg, S. L., Zierk, K. L., & Krones, J. M. (1994). Evolution and social cognition: Contrast effects as a function of sex, dominance, and physical attractiveness. *Personality and Social Psychology Bulletin, 20*, 210-217.

Kenrick, D. T., Sadalla, E. K., Groth, G., & Trost, M. R. (1990). Evolution, traits, and the stages of human courtship: Qualifying the parental investment model. *Journal of Personality*, Biological foundations of personality: Evolution, behavioral genetics, and psychophysiology, *58*, 97-116.

Kerr, N. L. (1983). Motivation losses in small groups: A social dilemma analysis. *Journal of Personality and Social Psychology, 45*, 819-828.

Kerr, N. L., & Bruun, S. E. (1983). Dispensability of member effort and group motivation losses: Free-rider effects. *Journal of Personality and Social Psychology, 44*, 78-94.

Kerr, N. L., Garst, J., Lewandowski, D. A., & Harris, S. E. (1997). That still, small voice: Commitment to cooperate as an internalized versus a social norm. *Personality and Social Psychology Bulletin, 23*, 1300-1311.

Kerr, N. L., & Kaufman-Gilliland, C. M. (1994). Communication, commitment, and cooperation in social dilemma. *Journal of Personality and Social Psychology, 66*, 513-529.

Kilham, W., & Mann, L. (1974). Level of destructive obedience as a function of transmitter and executant roles in the Milgram obedience paradigm. *Journal of Personality and Social Psychology, 29*, 696-702.

Kim, H., & Markus, H. R. (1999). Deviance or uniqueness, harmony or conformity? A cultural analysis. *Journal of Personality and Social Psychology, 77*, 785-800.

Kim, H. S., Sherman, D. K., Ko, D., & Taylor, S. E. (2006). Pursuit of comfort and pursuit of harmony: Culture, relationships, and social support seeking. *Personality and Social Psychology Bulletin, 32*, 1595-1607.

Kim, J., & Hatfield, E. (2004). Love types and subjective well-being: A cross cultural study. *Social Behavior and Personality, 32*, 173-182.

Kimmel, M. J. (1980). Effects of trust, aspiration, and gender on negotiation tactics. *Journal of Personality and Social Psychology, 38*, 9-22.

Kimmel, P. R. (1994). Cultural perspectives on international negotiations. *Journal of Social Issues, 50*, 179-196.

Kinder, D. R., & Sears, D. O. (1981). Prejudice and politics: Symbolic racism versus racial threats to the good life. *Journal of Personality and Social Psychology, 40*, 414-431.

Kirby, D. (2002). The impact of schools and school programs upon adolescent sexual behavior. *Journal of Sex Research, 39*, 27-33.

Kirkland, S. L., Greenberg, J., & Pyszczynski, T. (1987). Further evidence of the deleterious effects of overheard derogatory ethnic labels: Derogation beyond the target. *Personality and Social Psychology Bulletin, 13*, 216-227.

Kitayama, S., & Karasawa, M. (1997). Implicit self-esteem in Japan: Name letters and birthday numbers. *Personality and Social Psychology Bulletin, 23*, 736-742.

Kitayama, S., Markus, H., Matsumoto, H., & Norasakkunkit, V. (1997). Individual and collective processes in the construction of the self: Self-enhancement in the United States and self-criticism in Japan. *Journal of Personality and Social Psychology, 72*, 1245-1267.

Kitayama, S., Mesquita, B., & Karasawa, M. (2006). Cultural affordances and emotional experience: Socially engaging and disengaging emotions in Japan and the United States. *Journal of Personality and Social Psychology, 91*, 890-903.

Kitayama, S., Snibbe, A., Markus, H., & Suzuki, T. (2004). Is there any 'free' choice?: Self and dissonance in two cultures. *Psychological Science, 15*, 527-533.

Kite, M. E., & Deaux, K. (1986). Attitudes toward homosexuality: Assessment and behavioral consequences. *Basic and Applied Social Psychology, 7*, 137-162.

Klein, J. (1991). Negativity effects in impression formation: A test in the political arena. *Personality and Social Psychology Bulletin, 17*, 412-418.

Klein, W. (1997). Objective standards are not enough: Affective, self-evaluative, and behavioral responses to social comparison information. *Journal of Personality and Social Psychology, 72*, 763-774.

Klein, W., & Kunda, Z. (1992). Motivated person perception: Constructing justifications for desired beliefs. *Journal of Experimental Social Psychology, 28*, 145-168.

Kleinke, C., Peterson, T., & Rutledge, T. (1998). Effects of self-generated facial expressions on mood. *Journal of Personality and Social Psychology, 74*, 272-279.

Klinesmith, J., Kasser, T., & McAndrew, F. T. (2006). Guns, testosterone, and aggression: An experimental test of a mediational hypothesis. *Psychological Science, 17*, 568-571.

Klofas, J., & Toch, H. (1982). The guard subculture myth. *Journal of Research in Crime and Delinquency, 19*, 238-254.

Klohn, L. S., & Rogers, R. W. (1991). Dimensions of the severity of a health threat: The persuasive effects of visibility, time of onset, and rate of onset on young women's intentions to prevent osteoporosis. *Health Psychology, 10*, 323-329.

Klohnen, E. C., & Mendelsohn, G. A. (1998). Partner selection for personality characteristics: A couple-centered approach. *Personality and Social Psychology Bulletin, 24*, 268-278.

Knafo, A., & Plomin, R. (2006). Prosocial behavior from early to middle childhood: Genetic and environmental influences on stability and change. *Developmental Psychology, 42*, 771-786.

Knight, G. P., Fabes, R. A., & Higgins, D. A. (1996). Concerns about drawing causal inferences from meta-analyses: An example in the study of gender differences in aggression. *Psychological Bulletin, 119*, 410-421.

Knight, G. P., Johnson, L. G., Carlo, G., & Eisenberg, N. (1994). A multiplicative model of the dispositional antecedents of a prosocial behavior: Predicting more of the people more of the time. *Journal of Personality and Social Psychology, 66*, 178-183.

Knowles, E. S. (1983). Social physics and the effects of others: Tests of the effects of audience size and distance on social judgments and behavior. *Journal of Personality and Social Psychology, 45*, 1263-1279.

Knowles, E., Morris, M., Chiu, C., & Hong, Y. (2001). Culture and the process of person perception: Evidence for automaticity among East Asians in correcting for situational influences on behavior. *Personality and Social Psychology Bulletin, 27*, 1344-1356.

Koestner, R., & Wheeler, L. (1988). Self-presentation in personal advertisements: The influence of implicit notions of attraction and role expectations. *Journal of Social and Personal Relationships, 5*, 149-160.

Komorita, S. S., & Barth, J. M. (1985). Components of reward in social dilemmas. *Journal of Personality and Social Psychology, 48*, 364-373.

Komorita, S. S., Chan, D. K., & Parks, C. (1993). The effects of reward structure and reciprocity in social dilemmas. *Journal of Experimental Social Psychology, 29*, 252-267.

Komorita, S. S., Parks, C. D. (1995). Interpersonal relations: Mixed-motive interaction. *Annual Review of Psychology, 46*, 183-207.

Komorita, S. S., Parks, C. D., & Hulbert, L. G. (1992). Reciprocity and the induction of cooperation in social dilemmas. *Journal of Personality and Social Psychology, 62*, 607-617.

Konrath, S., Bushman, B. J., & Campbell, W. K. (2006). Attenuating the link between threatened egotism and aggression. *Psychological Science, 17*, 995-1001.

Korchmaros, J. D., & Kenny, D. A. (2006). An evolutionary and close-relationship model of helping. *Journal of Social and Personal Relationships, 23*, 21-43.

Kors, D. J., Linden, W., & Gerin, W. (1997). Evaluation interferes with social support: Effects on cardiovascular stress reactivity in women. *Journal of Social & Clinical Psychology, 16*, 1-23.

Koss, M. P. (1992). The underdetection of rape: Methodological choices influence incidence estimates. *Journal of Social Issues, 48*, 61-75.

Koss, M. P., Gidycz, C. A., & Wisniewski, N. (1987). The scope of rape: Incidence and prevalence of sexual aggression and victimization in a national sample of higher education students. *Journal of Consulting and Clinical Psychology, 55*, 162-170.

Kowalski, R. & Weston, D. (2009). *Psychology.* Hoboken, NJ: John Wiley & Sons, Inc.

Kramer, R. M., & Brewer, M. B. (1984). Effects of group identity on resource use in a simulated commons dilemma. *Journal of Personality and Social Psychology, 46*, 1044-1057.

Kraus, S. (1995). Attitudes and the prediction of behavior: A meta-analysis of the empirical literature. *Personality and Social Psychology Bulletin, 21*, 58-75.

Kraut, R., Kiesler, S., Boneva, B., Cummings, J. N., Helgeson, V., & Crawford, A. M. (2002). Internet paradox revisited. *Journal of Social Issues, 58*, 49-74.

Kraut, R., Patterson, M., Lundmark, V., Kiesler, S., Mukophadhyay, T., & Scherlis, W. (1998). Internet paradox: A social technology that reduces social involvement and psychological well-being? *American Psychologist, 53*, 1017-1031.

Krebs, D. (1975). Empathy and altruism. *Journal of Personality and Social Psychology, 32*, 1134-1146.

Kremer, J. F., & Stephens, L. (1983). Attributions and arousal as mediators of mitigation's effect on retaliation. *Journal of Personality and Social Psychology, 45*, 335-343.

Krendl, A. C., Richeson, J. A., Kelley, W. M., & Heatherton, T. F. (2008). The negative consequences of threat: A functional magnetic resonance imaging investigation of the neural mechanisms underlying women's underperformance in math. *Psychological Science, 19*, 168-175.

Krieger, N., & Sidney, S. (1996). Racial discrimination and blood pressure: The CARDIA study of young Black and White adults. *American Journal of Public Health, 86*, 1370-1378.

Krieger, N., Sidney, S., & Coakley, E. (1998). Racial discrimination and skin color in the CARDIA study: Implications for public health research. *American Journal of Public Health, 88*, 1308-1313.

Krosnick, J. (1989). Attitude importance and attitude accessibility. *Personality and Social Psychology Bulletin, 15*, 297-308.

Krosnick, J. A., & Alwin, D. F. (1989). Aging and susceptibility to attitude change. *Journal of Personality and Social Psychology, 57*, 416-425.

Krosnick, J., Betz, A., Jussim, L., & Lynn, A. (1992). Subliminal conditioning of attitudes. *Personality and Social Psychology Bulletin, 18*, 152-162.

Krosnick, J., Boninger, D., Chuang, Y., Berent, M., & Carnot, C. (1993). Attitude strength: One construct or many related constructs? *Journal of Personality and Social Psychology, 65*, 1132-1151.

Kruger, D. J. (2003). Evolution and altruism: Combining psychological mediators with naturally selected tendencies. *Evolution and Human Behavior, 24*, 118-125.

Krueger, J. (1998). Enhancement bias in descriptions of self and others. *Personality and Social Psychology Bulletin, 24*, 505-516.

Kruger, J., & Dunning, D. (1999). Unskilled and unaware of it: How difficulties in recognizing one's own incompetence lead to inflated self-assessments. *Journal of Personality and Social Psychology, 77*, 1121-1134.

Kruger, J., & Gilovich, T. (2004). Actions, intentions, and self-assessment: The road to self-enhancement is paved with good intentions. *Personality and Social Psychology Bulletin, 30*, 328-339.

Krueger, J., Ham, J., & Linford, K. (1996). Perceptions of behavioral consistency: Are people aware of the actor-observer effect? *Psychological Science, 7*, 259-264.

Kruger, J., Wirtz, D., & Miller, D. (2005). Counterfactual thinking and the first instinct fallacy. *Journal of Personality and Social Psychology, 88*, 725-735.

Kruglanski, A. W., & Webster, D. M. (1991). Group members' reactions to opinion deviates and conformists at varying degrees of proximity to decision deadline and of environmental noise. *Journal of Personality and Social Psychology, 61*, 212-225.

Krull, D. (1993). Does the grist change the mill? The effect of the perceiver's inferential goal on the process of social inference. *Personality and Social Psychology Bulletin, 19*, 340-348.

Krull, D., Loy, M., Lin, J., Wang, C., Chen, S., & Zhao, X. (1999). The fundamental attribution error: Correspondence bias in individualist and collectivist cultures. *Personality and Social Psychology Bulletin, 25*, 1208-1219.

Kubany, E. S., Bauer, G. B., Muraoka, M. Y., & Richard, D. C. (1995). Impact of labeled anger and blame in intimate relationships. *Journal of Social & Clinical Psychology, 14*, 53-60.

Kuchment, A. (2007). Which is better? *Newsweek*, March 19, 79.

Kulik, J. A., & Brown, R. (1979). Frustration, attribution of blame, and aggression. *Journal of Experimental Social Psychology, 15*, 183-194.

Kulik, J. A., & Mahler, H. I. (1989). Social support and recovery from surgery. *Health Psychology, 8*, 221-238.

Kumashiro, M., & Sedikides, C. (2005). Taking on board liability-focused information: Close positive relationships as a self-bolstering resource. *Psychological Science, 16*, 732-739.

Kunda, Z., & Oleson, K. C. (1995). Maintaining stereotypes in the face of disconfirmation: Constructing grounds for subtyping deviants. *Journal of Personality and Social Psychology, 68*, 565-579.

Kunda, Z., & Oleson, K. C. (1997). When exceptions prove the rule: How extremity of deviance determines the impact of deviant examples on stereotypes. *Journal of Personality and Social Psychology, 72,* 965-979.

Kunda, Z., & Sherman-Williams, B. (1993). Stereotypes and the construal of individuating information. *Personality and Social Psychology Bulletin, 19,* 90-99.

Kunda, Z., Sinclair, L., & Griffin, D. (1997). Equal ratings, but separate meanings: Stereotypes and the construal of traits. *Journal of Personality and Social Psychology, 72,* 720-734.

Kunda, Z., Davies, P. G., Adams, B. D., & Spencer, S. J. (2002). The dynamic time course of stereotype activation: Activation, dissipation, and resurrection. *Journal of Personality and Social Psychology, 82,* 283-299.

Kupersmidt, J. B., DeRosier, M. E., & Patterson, C. P. (1995). Similarity as the basis for children's friendships: The roles of sociometric status, aggressive and withdrawn behavior, academic achievement and demographic characteristics. *Journal of Social and Personal Relationships, 12,* 439-452.

Kurdek, L. A. (1992). Relationship stability and relationship satisfaction in cohabiting gay and lesbian couples: A prospective longitudinal test of the contextual and interdependence models. *Journal of Social and Personal Relationships, 9,* 125-142.

Kurdek, L. A. (1999). The nature and predictors of the trajectory of change in marital quality for husbands and wives over the first 10 years of marriage. *Developmental Psychology, 35,* 1283-1296.

Kurdek, L. A. (2000). Attractions and constraints as determinants of relationship commitment: Longitudinal evidence from gay, lesbian, and heterosexual couples. *Personal Relationships, 7,* 245-262.

Kurdek, L. A., & Schmitt, J. P. (1986). Relationship quality of partners in heterosexual married, heterosexual cohabiting, and gay and lesbian relationships. *Journal of Personality and Social Psychology, 51,* 711-720.

LaBrie, J., & Earleywine, M. (2000). Sexual risk behaviors and alcohol: Higher base rates revealed using the unmatched-count technique. *Journal of Sex Research, 37,* 321-326.

Laird, J. (1974). Self-attribution of emotion: The effects of expressive behavior on the quality of emotional experience. *Journal of Personality and Social Psychology, 29,* 475-486.

Lang, F., & Heckhausen, J. (2001). Perceived control over development and subjective well-being: Differential benefits across adulthood. *Journal of Personality and Social Psychology, 81,* 509-523.

Langer, E. (1975). The illusion of control. *Journal of Personality and Social Psychology, 32,* 311-328.

Langlois, J. H., Kalakanis, L., Rubenstein, A. J., Larson, A., Hallam, M., & Smoot, M. (2000). Maxims or myths of beauty? A meta-analytic and theoretical review. *Psychological Bulletin, 126,* 390-423.

Langlois, J. H., & Roggman, L. A. (1990). Attractive faces are only average. *Psychological Science, 1,* 115-121.

Langlois, J. H., Ritter, J. M., Roggman, L. A., & Vaughn, L. S. (1991). Facial diversity and infant preferences for attractive faces. *Developmental Psychology, 27,* 79-84.

LaPiere, R. T. (1934). Attitudes vs. actions. *Social Forces, 13,* 230-237.

Laplace, A. C., Chermack, S. T., & Taylor, S. P. (1994). Effects of alcohol and drinking experience on human physical aggression. *Personality and Social Psychology Bulletin, 20,* 439-444.

Larson, J. R., Foster-Fishman, P. G., & Keys, C. B. (1994). Discussion of shared and unshared information in decision-making groups. *Journal of Personality and Social Psychology, 67,* 446-461.

Lassiter, G., Geers, A., Handley, I., Weiland, P., & Munhall, P. (2002). Videotaped interrogations and confessions: A simple change in camera perspective alters verdicts in simulated trials. *Journal of Applied Psychology, 87,* 867-874.

Lassiter, G., Geers, A., Munhall, P., Ploutz-Snyder, R., & Breitenbecher, D. (2002). Illusory causation: Why it occurs. *Psychological Science, 13,* 299-305.

Lassiter, G., & Irvine, A. (1986). Videotaped confessions: The impact of camera point on view of judgments of coercion. *Journal of Applied Social Psychology, 16,* 268-276.

Latané, B. (1981). The psychology of social impact. *American Psychologist, 36,* 343-356.

Latane, B., & Darley, J. M. (1968). Group inhibition of bystander intervention in emergencies. *Journal of Personality and Social Psychology, 10,* 215-221.

Latané, B., & Darley, J.M. (1970). *The Unresponsive Bystander: Why Doesn't He Help?* Upper Saddle River: Prentice Hall.

Latané, B., Liu, J. H., Nowak, A., Bonevento, M., & Zhang, L. (1995). Distance matters: Physical space and social impact. *Personality and Social Psychology Bulletin, 21,* 795-805.

Latané, B., & Nida, S. (1981). Ten years of research on group size and helping. *Psychological Bulletin, 89,* 308-324.

Latane, B., & Rodin, J. (1969). A lady in distress: Inhibiting effects of friends and strangers on bystander intervention. *Journal of Experimental Social Psychology, 5,* 189-202.

Latané, B., Williams, K., & Harkins, S. (1979). Many hands make light the work: The causes and consequences of social loafing. *Journal of Personality and Social Psychology, 37,* 822-832.

Lau, R., & Russell, D. (1980). Attributions in the sports pages. *Journal of Personality and Social Psychology, 39,* 29-38.

Laumann, E., Gagnon, J.H., Michael, R.T., & Michaels, S. (1994). *The Social Organization of Sexuality: Sexual Practices in the United States.* Chicago, IL: University of Chicago Press.

Le, B., & Agnew, C. R. (2003). Commitment and its theorized determinants: A meta-analysis of the investment model. *Personal Relationships, 10,* 37-57.

Leach, C. W., Spears, R., Branscombe, N. R., & Doosje, B. (2003). Malicious pleasure: Schadenfreude at the suffering of another group. *Journal of Personality and Social Psychology, 84,* 932-943.

Leader, T., Mullen, B., & Abrams, D. (2007). Without mercy: The immediate impact of group size on lynch mob atrocity. *Personality and Social Psychology Bulletin, 33,* 1340-1352.

Leary, M. R., & Jones, J. L. (1993). The social psychology of tanning and sunscreen use: Self-presentational motives as a predictor of health risk. *Journal of Applied Social Psychology, 23,* 1390-1406.

Leary, M., Tchividijian, L., & Kraxberger, B. (1994). Self-presentation can be hazardous to your health: Impression management and health risk. *Health Psychology, 13,* 461-470.

Ledgerwood, A., & Chaiken, S. (2007). Priming us and them: Automatic assimilation and contrast in group attitudes. *Journal of Personality and Social Psychology, 93,* 940-956.

Lee, F., Hallahan, M., & Herzog, T. (1996). Explaining real-life events: How culture and domain shape attributions. *Personality and Social Psychology Bulletin, 22,* 732-741.

Lee, F., Peterson, C., & Tiedens, L. (2004). Mea culpa: Predicting stock prices from organizational attributions. *Personality and Social Psychology Bulletin, 30*, 1636-1649.

Lee, J. A. (1988). Love-styles. In M.H. Barnes & R.J. Sternberg (Eds.). *The Psychology of Love* (pp. 38-67). New Haven, CT: Yale University Press.

Legault, L., Green-Demers, I., Grant, P., & Chung, J. (2007). On the self-regulation of implicit and explicit prejudice: A self-determination theory perspective. *Personality and Social Psychology Bulletin, 33*, 732-749.

Leippe, M., & Eisenstadt, D. (1994). Generalization of dissonance reduction: Decreasing prejudice through induced compliance. *Journal of Personality and Social Psychology, 67*, 395-413.

Lemieux, R., & Hale, J. L. (2002). Cross-sectional analysis of intimacy, passion, and commitment: Testing the assumptions of the triangular theory of love. *Psychological Reports, 90*, 1009-1014.

Lepper, M. R., Greene, D., & Nisbett, R. E. (1973). Undermining children's intrinsic interest with extrinsic reward: A test of the 'overjustification' hypothesis. *Journal of Personality and Social Psychology, 28*, 129-137.

Lerner, J., Gonzalez, R., Small, D., & Fischhoff, B. (2003). Effects of fear and anger on perceived risks of terrorism: A national field experiment. *Psychological Science, 14*, 144-150.

Lerner, J., Small, D., & Loewenstein, G. (2004). Heart strings and purse strings: Carryover effects of emotions on economic decisions. *Psychological Science, 15*, 337-341.

Lerner, M. (1980). *The Belief in a Just World*. New York: Plenum Press.

Lerner, M. J., & Miller, D. T. (1978). Just world research and the attribution process: Looking back and ahead. *Psychological Bulletin, 85*, 1030-1051.

Levesque, M., & Kenny, D. (1993). Accuracy of behavioral predictions at zero acquaintance: A social relations analysis. *Journal of Personality and Social Psychology, 65*, 1178-1187.

Levin, I., Schnittjer, S., & Thee, S. (1988). Information framing effects in social and personal decisions. *Journal of Experimental Social Psychology, 24*, 520-529.

Levin, S., & Sidanius, J. (1999). Social dominance and social identity in the United States and Israel: Ingroup favoritism or outgroup derogation? *Political Psychology, 20*, 99-126.

Levine, G., Halberstadt, J., & Goldstone, R. (1996). Reasoning and the weighting of attributes in attitude judgments. *Journal of Personality and Social Psychology, 70*, 230-240.

Levine, M., Prosser, A., Evans, D., & Reicher, S. (2005). Identity and emergency intervention: How social group membership and inclusiveness of group boundaries shape helping behavior. *Personality and Social Psychology Bulletin, 31*, 443-453.

Levine, R. V., Martinez, T. S., Brase, G., & Sorenson, K. (1994). Helping in 36 U.S. cities. *Journal of Personality and Social Psychology, 67*, 69-82.

Levine, R. V., Norenzayan, A., & Philbrick, K. (2001). Cross-cultural differences in helping strangers. *Journal of Cross-Cultural Psychology, 32*, 543-560.

Levine, R., Sato, S., Hashimoto, T., & Verma, J. (1995). Love and marriage in eleven cultures. *Journal of Cross-Cultural Psychology, 26*, 554-571.

Levy, B., & Langer, E. (1994). Aging free from negative stereotypes: Successful memory in China among the American deaf. *Journal of Personality and Social Psychology, 66*, 989-997.

Li, N. P., Bailey, J. M., Kenrick, D. T., & Linsenmeier, J. A. W. (2002). The necessities and luxuries of mate preferences: Testing the tradeoffs. *Journal of Personality and Social Psychology, 82*, 947-955.

Li, N. P., & Kenrick, D. T. (2006). Sex similarities and differences in preferences for short-term mates: What, whether, and why. *Journal of Personality and Social Psychology, 90*, 468-489.

Liberman, A., & Chaiken, S. (1992). Defensive processing of personally relevant health messages. *Personality and Social Psychology Bulletin, 18*, 669-679.

Liberman, N., & Förster, J. (2000). Expression after suppression: A motivational explanation of postsuppressional rebound. *Journal of Personality and Social Psychology, 79*, 190-203.

Lieberman et al., 2004.

Liberman, V., Samuels, S. M., & Ross, L. (2004). The name of the game: Predictive power of reputations versus situational labels in determining prisoner's dilemma game moves. *Personality and Social Psychology Bulletin, 30*, 1175-1185.

Lieberman, J. D. (2002). Head over the heart or heart over the head? Cognitive experiential self-theory and extralegal heuristics in juror decision making. *Journal of Applied Social Psychology, 32*, 2526-2553.

Lieberman, J., Solomon, S., Greenberg, J., & McGregor, H. (1999). A hot new way to measure aggression: Hot sauce allocation. *Aggressive Behavior, 25*, 331-348.

Lightdale, J. R., & Prentice, D. A. (1994). Rethinking sex differences in aggression: Aggressive behavior in the absence of social roles. *Personality and Social Psychology Bulletin, 20*, 34-44.

Lin, M. H., Kwan, V. S. Y., Cheung, A., & Fiske, S. T. (2005). Stereotype content model explains prejudice for an envied outgroup: Scale of anti-Asian American stereotypes. *Personality and Social Psychology Bulletin, 31*, 34-47.

Lind, E. A., Kanfer, R., & Earley, P. C. (1990). Voice, control, and procedural justice: Instrumental and noninstrumental concerns in fairness judgments. *Journal of Personality and Social Psychology, 59*, 952-959.

Lindsay, J. J., & Anderson, C. A. (2000). From antecedent conditions to violent actions: A general affective aggression model. *Personality and Social Psychology Bulletin, 26*, 533-547.

Lindskold, S., & Han, G. (1988). GRIT as a foundation for integrative bargaining. *Personality and Social Psychology Bulletin, 14*, 335-345.

Lindskold, S., Han, G., & Betz, B. (1986). Repeated persuasion in interpersonal conflict. *Journal of Personality and Social Psychology, 51*, 1183-1188.

Linville, P. W., Fischer, G. W., & Salovey, P. (1989). Perceived distributions of the characteristics of in-group and out-group members: Empirical evidence and a computer simulation. *Journal of Personality and Social Psychology, 57*, 165-188.

Linville, P., Fischer, G., & Fischhoff, B. (1993). AIDS risk perceptions and decision biases. *The Social Psychology of HIV Infection* (pp. 5-38). Hillsdale, NJ: Lawrence Erlbaum Associates, Inc.

Linville, P. W., & Jones, E. E. (1980). Polarized appraisals of outgroup members. *Journal of Personality and Social Psychology, 38*, 689-703.

Linz, D. G., Donnerstein, E., & Penrod, S. (1984). The effects of multiple exposures to filmed violence against women. *Journal of Communication, 34*, 130-147.

Linz, D. G., Donnerstein, E., & Penrod, S. (1988). Effects of long-term exposure to violent and sexually degrading depictions of women. *Journal of Personality and Social Psychology, 55*, 758-768.

Lipkus, I. M., Dalbert, C., & Siegler, I. C. (1996). The importance of distinguishing the belief in a just world for self versus for others: Implications for psychological well-being. *Personality and Social Psychology Bulletin, 22*, 666-677.

Locksley, A., Borgida, E., Brekke, N., & Hepburn, C. (1980). Sex stereotypes and social judgment. *Journal of Personality and Social Psychology, 39*, 821-831.

Loeber, R., & Hay, D. (1997). Key issues in the development of aggression and violence from childhood to early adulthood. *Annual Review of Psychology, 48*, 371-410.

Loftin, C., McDowall, D., Wiersema, B., & Cottey, T. J. (1991). Effects of restrictive licensing of handguns on homicide and suicide in the District of Columbia. *New England Journal of Medicine, 325*, 1615-1620.

Loftus, E., & Palmer, J. (1974). Reconstruction of automobile destruction: An example of the interaction between language and memory. *Journal of Verbal Learning & Verbal Behavior, 13*, 585-589.

Loftus, E., & Pickrell, J. (1995). The formation of false memories. *Psychiatric Annals, 25*, 720-725.

Lord, C. G., Ross, L., & Lepper, M. R. (1979). Biased assimilation and attitude polarization: The effects of prior theories on subsequently considered evidence. *Journal of Personality and Social Psychology, 37*, 2098-2109.

Lord, C. G., & Saenz, D. S. (1985). Memory deficits and memory surfeits: Differential cognitive consequences of tokenism for tokens and observers. *Journal of Personality and Social Psychology, 49*, 918-926.

Lord, C., Scott, K., Pugh, M., & Desforges, D. (1997). Leakage beliefs and the correspondence bias. *Personality and Social Psychology Bulletin, 23*, 824-836.

Lore, R. K., & Schultz, L. A. (1993). Control of human aggression: A comparative perspective. *American Psychologist, 48*, 16-25.

Lorenz, K. (1966). *On Aggression.* New York: Harcourt, Brace & World.

Lorenz, K. (1974). *Civilized Man's Eight Deadly Sins.* San Diego, CA: Harcourt Brace.

Losch, M., & Cacioppo, J. (1990). Cognitive dissonance may enhance sympathetic tonus, but attitudes are changed to reduce negative affect rather than arousal. *Journal of Experimental Social Psychology, 26*, 289-304.

Lowery, B. S., Unzueta, M. M., Knowles, E. D., & Goff, P. A. (2006). Concern for the in-group and opposition to affirmative action. *Journal of Personality and Social Psychology, 90*, 961-974.

Lucker, G. W., Rosenfield, D., Sikes, J., & Aronson, E. (1976). Performance in the interdependent classroom: A field study. *American Educational Research Journal, 13*, 115-123.

Luo, S., & Klohnen, E. C. (2005). Assortative mating and marital quality in newlyweds: A couple-centered approach. *Journal of Personality and Social Psychology, 88*, 304-326.

Luthar, S., & Latendresse, S. (2005). Comparable 'risks' at the socioeconomic status extremes: Preadolescents' perceptions of parenting. *Development and Psychopathology, 17*, 207-230.

Lydon, J. E., Fitzsimons, G. M., & Naidoo, L. (2003). Devaluation versus enhancement of attractive alternatives: A critical test using the calibration paradigm. *Personality and Social Psychology Bulletin, 29*, 349-359.

Lyness, K. S., & Thompson, D. E. (1997). Above the glass ceiling? A comparison of matched samples of female and male executives. *Journal of Applied Psychology, 82*, 359-375.

Lynn, M., & Latané, B. (1984). The psychology of restaurant tipping. *Journal of Applied Social Psychology, 14*, 549-561.

Lynn, M., & Oldenquist, A. (1986). Egoistic and nonegoistic motives in social dilemmas. *American Psychologist, 41*, 529-534.

Lyons, A., & Kashima, Y. (2003). How are stereotypes maintained through communication? The influence of stereotype sharedness. *Journal of Personality and Social Psychology, 85*, 989-1005.

Maass, A., Cadinu, M., Guarnieri, G., & Grasselli, A. (2003). Sexual harassment under social identity threat: The computer harassment paradigm. *Journal of Personality and Social Psychology, 85*, 853-870.

Maass, A., & Clark, R. D. (1984). Hidden impact of minorities: Fifteen years of minority influence research. *Psychological Bulletin, 95*, 428-450.

Maass, A., & Clark, R. D. (1986). Conversion theory and simultaneous majority/minority influence: Can reactance offer an alternative explanation? *European Journal of Social Psychology, 16*, 305-309.

MacDonald, G., & Jessica, M. (2006). Family approval as a constraint in dependency regulation: Evidence from Australia and Indonesia. *Personal Relationships, 13*, 183-194.

MacDonald, G., Zanna, M. P., & Holmes, J. G. (2000). An experimental test of the role of alcohol in relationship conflict. *Journal of Experimental Social Psychology, 36*, 182-193.

MacDonald, T., MacDonald, G., Zanna, M., & Fong, G. (2000). Alcohol, sexual arousal, and intentions to use condoms in young men: Applying alcohol myopia theory to risky sexual behavior. *Health Psychology, 19*, 290-298.

MacDonald, T. K., & Ross, M. (1999). Assessing the accuracy of predictions about dating relationships: How and why do lovers' predictions differ from those made by observers? *Personality and Social Psychology Bulletin, 25*, 1417-1429.

MacDonald, T., Zanna, M., & Fong, G. (1995). Decision making in altered states: Effects of alcohol on attitudes toward drinking and driving. *Journal of Personality and Social Psychology, 68*, 973-985.

MacDonald, T.K., Zanna, M.P., & Fong, G.T. (1996). Why common sense goes out the window: Effects of alcohol on intentions to use condoms. *Personality and Social Psychology Bulletin, 22*, 763-775.

Mackie, D. M. (1987). Systematic and nonsystematic processing of majority and minority persuasive communications. *Journal of Personality and Social Psychology, 53*, 41-52.

Mackie, D. M., Gastardo-Conaco, M. C., & Skelly, J. J. (1992). Knowledge of the advocated position and the processing of in-group and out-group persuasive messages. *Personality and Social Psychology Bulletin, 18*, 145-151.

Mackie, D. M., & Worth, L. T. (1989). Processing deficits and the mediation of positive affect in persuasion. *Journal of Personality and Social Psychology, 57*, 27-40.

MacLeod, C., & Campbell, L. (1992). Memory accessibility and probability judgments: An experimental evaluation of the availability heuristic. *Journal of Personality and Social Psychology, 63*, 890-902.

Macrae, C. N., Bodenhausen, G. V., & Milne, A. B. (1998). Saying no to unwanted thoughts: Self-focus and the regulation of mental life. *Journal of Personality and Social Psychology, 74*, 578-589.

Madden, T., Ellen, P., & Ajzen, I. (1992). A comparison of the theory of planned behavior and the theory of reasoned action. *Personality and Social Psychology Bulletin, 18*, 3-9.

Maddux, J. E., & Rogers, R. W. (1980). Effects of source expertness, physical attractiveness, and supporting arguments on persuasion: A case of brains over beauty. *Journal of Personality and Social Psychology, 39*, 235-244.

Maddux, W. W., Galinsky, A. D., Cuddy, A. J. C., & Polifroni, M. (2008). When being a model minority is good...and bad: Realistic threat explains negativity toward Asian Americans. *Personality and Social Psychology Bulletin, 34*, 74-89.

Madon, S., Guyll, M., Spoth, R., Cross, S., & Hilbert, S. (2003). The self-fulfilling influence of mother expectations on children's underage drinking. *Journal of Personality and Social Psychology, 84*, 1188-1205.

Madon, S., Guyll, M., Spoth, R., & Willard, J. (2004). Self-fulfilling prophecies: The synergistic accumulative effect of parents' beliefs on children's drinking behavior. *Psychological Science, 15*, 837-845.

Madon, S., Jussim, L., & Eccles, J. (1997). In search of the powerful self-fulfilling prophecy. *Journal of Personality and Social Psychology, 72*, 791-809.

Madon, S., Smith, A., Jussim, L., Russell, D., Eccles, J., Palumbo, P., et al. (2001). Am I as you see me or do you see me as I am? Self-fulfilling prophecies and self-verification. *Personality and Social Psychology Bulletin, 27*, 1214-1224.

Maeda, E., & Ritchie, L. D. (2003). The concept of Shinyuu in Japan: A replication of and comparison to Cole and Bradac's study on U.S. friendship. *Journal of Social and Personal Relationships, 20*, 579-598.

Mael, F. A., & Alderks, C. E. (1993). Leadership team cohesion and subordinate work unit morale and performance. *Military Psychology, 5*, 141-158.

Maheswaran, D., & Chaiken, S. (1991). Promoting systematic processing in low-motivation settings: Effect of incongruent information on processing and judgment. *Journal of Personality and Social Psychology, 61*, 13-25.

Major, B., & Gramzow, R. (1999). Abortion as stigma: Cognitive and emotional implications of concealment. *Journal of Personality and Social Psychology, 77*, 735-745.

Major, B., Gramzow, R. H., McCoy, S. K., Levin, S., Schmader, T., & Sidanius, J. (2002). Perceiving personal discrimination: The role of group status and legitimizing ideology. *Journal of Personality and Social Psychology, 82*, 269-282.

Major, B., Spencer, S., Schmader, T., Wolfe, C., & Crocker, J. (1998). Coping with negative stereotypes about intellectual performance: The role of psychological disengagement. *Personality and Social Psychology Bulletin, 24*, 34-50.

Malamuth, N. M. (1983). Factors associated with rape as predictors of laboratory aggression against women. *Journal of Personality and Social Psychology, 45*, 432-442.

Malamuth, N. (1986). Predictors of naturalistic sexual aggression. *Journal of Personality and Social Psychology, 50*, 953-962.

Malamuth, N. M., & Check, J. V. (1983). Sexual arousal to rape depictions: Individual differences. *Journal of Abnormal Psychology, 92*, 55-67.

Malamuth, N. M., & Check, J. V. (1985). The effects of aggressive pornography on beliefs in rape myths: Individual differences. *Journal of Research in Personality, 19*, 299-320.

Malamuth, N. M., Check, J. V., & Briere, J. (1986). Sexual arousal in response to aggression: Ideological, aggressive, and sexual correlates. *Journal of Personality and Social Psychology, 50*, 330-340.

Malamuth, N. M., Linz, D., Heavey, C. L., Barnes, G., & Acker, M. (1995). Using the confluence model of sexual aggression to predict men's conflict with women: A 10-year follow-up study. *Journal of Personality and Social Psychology, 69*, 353-369.

Malinosky-Rummell, R., & Hansen, D. J. (1993). Long-term consequences of childhood physical abuse. *Psychological Bulletin, 114*, 68-79.

Malle, B., & Knobe, J. (1997). Which behaviors do people explain? A basic actor-observer asymmetry. *Journal of Personality and Social Psychology, 72*, 288-304.

Malle, B., & Pearce, G. (2001). Attention to behavioral events during interaction: Two actor-observer gaps and three attempts to close them. *Journal of Personality and Social Psychology, 81*, 278-294.

Malpass, R. S., & Devine, P. G. (1981). Eyewitness identification: Lineup instructions and the absence of the offender. *Journal of Applied Psychology, 66*, 482-489.

Maner, J. K., Kenrick, D. T., Becker, D. V., Delton, A. W., Hofer, B., Wilbur, C. J., et al. (2003). Sexually selective cognition: Beauty captures the mind of the beholder. *Journal of Personality and Social Psychology, 85*, 1107-1120.

Manis, M., Shedler, J., Jonides, J., & Nelson, T. (1993). Availability heuristic in judgments of set size and frequency of occurrence. *Journal of Personality and Social Psychology, 65*, 448-457.

Mann, L. (1981). The baiting crowd in episodes of threatened suicide. *Journal of Personality and Social Psychology, 41*, 703-709.

Manucia, G. K., Baumann, D. J., & Cialdini, R. B. (1984). Mood influences on helping: Direct effects or side effects? *Journal of Personality and Social Psychology, 46*, 357-364.

Marcus-Newhall, A., Pedersen, W. C., Carlson, M., & Miller, N. (2000). Displaced aggression is alive and well: A meta-analytic review. *Journal of Personality and Social Psychology, 78*, 670-689.

Mares, M., & Woodard, E. (2005). Positive effects of television on children's social interactions: A meta-analysis. *Media Psychology, 7*, 301-322.

Marin, B. V., Marin, G., Perez-Stable, E. J., Otero-Sabogal, R., & Sabogal, F. (1990). Cultural differences in attitudes toward smoking: Developing messages using the theory of reasoned action. *Journal of Applied Social Psychology, 20*, 478-493.

Marks, G., Graham, J. W., & Hansen, W. B. (1992). Social projection and social conformity in adolescent alcohol use: A longitudinal analysis. *Personality and Social Psychology Bulletin, 18*, 96-101.

Markus, H. (1977). Self-schemata and processing information about the self. *Journal of Personality and Social Psychology, 35*, 63-78.

Markus, H. (1978). The effect of mere presence on social facilitation: An unobtrusive test. *Journal of Experimental Social Psychology, 14*, 389-397.

Markus, H. R., & Kitayama, S. (1991). Culture and the self: Implications for cognition, emotion, and motivation. *Psychological Review, 98*, 224-253.

Markus, H. R., & Kitayama, S. (1994). A collective fear of the collective: Implications for selves and theories of selves. *Personality and Social Psychology Bulletin, 20*, 568-579.

Markus, H., Uchida, Y., Omoregie, H., Townsend, S., & Kitayama, S. (2006). Going for the gold: Models of agency in Japanese and American contexts. *Psychological Science, 17*, 103-112.

Marlowe, C. M., Schneider, S. L., & Nelson, C. E. (1996). Gender and attractiveness biases in hiring decisions: Are more experienced managers less biased? *Journal of Applied Psychology, 81*, 11-21.

Marques, J., Abrams, D., Paez, D., & Martinez-Taboada, C. (1998). The role of categorization and in-group norms in judgments of groups and their members. *Journal of Personality and Social Psychology, 75*, 976-988.

Marsh, H., Kong, C., & Hau, K. (2000). Longitudinal multilevel models of the big-fish-little-pond effect on academic self-concept: Counterbalancing contrast and reflected-glory effects in Hong Kong schools. *Journal of Personality and Social Psychology, 78*, 337-349.

Marsh, K., Hart-O'Rourke, D., & Julka, D. (1997). The persuasive effects of verbal and nonverbal information in a context of value relevance. *Personality and Social Psychology Bulletin, 23*, 563-579.

Marteau, T. (1989). Framing of information: Its influence upon decisions of doctors and patients. *British Journal of Social Psychology, 28*, 89-94.

Martens, A., Kosloff, S., Greenberg, J., Landau, M. J., & Schmader, T. (2007). Killing begets killing: Evidence from a bug-killing paradigm that initial killing fuels subsequent killing. *Personality and Social Psychology Bulletin, 33*, 1251-1264.

Martin, G. B., & Clark, R. D. (1982). Distress crying in neonates: Species and peer specificity. *Developmental Psychology, 18*, 3-9.

Martin, K., & Leary, M. (1999). Would you drink after a stranger? The influence of self presentational motives on willingness to take a health risk. *Personality and Social Psychology Bulletin, 25*, 1092-1100.

Martin, P. Y., Laing, J., Martin, R., & Mitchell, M. (2005). Caffeine, cognition, and persuasion: Evidence for caffeine increasing the systematic processing of persuasive messages. *Journal of Applied Social Psychology, 35*, 160-182.

Martin, R. (1996). Minority influence and argument generation. *British Journal of Social Psychology*, Minority influences, *35*, 91-103.

Martino, S., Collins, R., Kanouse, D., Elliott, M., & Berry, S. (2005). Social cognitive processes mediating the relationship between exposure to television's sexual content and adolescents' sexual behavior. *Journal of Personality and Social Psychology, 89*, 914-924.

Martz, J. M., Verette, J., Arriaga, X. B., Slovik, L. F., Cox, C. L., & Rusbult, C. E. (1998). Positive illusion in close relationships. *Personal Relationships, 5*, 159-181.

Maruyama, G., Fraser, S. C., & Miller, N. (1982). Personal responsibility and altruism in children. *Journal of Personality and Social Psychology, 42*, 658-664.

Masicampo, E., & Baumeister, R. (2008). Toward a physiology of dual-process reasoning and judgment: Lemonade, willpower, and expensive rule-based analysis. *Psychological Science, 19*, 255-260.

Maslach, C., Santee, R. T., & Wade, C. (1987). Individuation, gender role, and dissent: Personality mediators of situational forces. *Journal of Personality and Social Psychology, 53*, 1088-1093.

Masuda, T., & Nisbett, R. (2001). Attending holistically versus analytically: Comparing the context sensitivity of Japanese and Americans. *Journal of Personality and Social Psychology, 81*, 922-934.

Mathews, K. E., & Canon, L. K. (1975). Environmental noise level as a determinant of helping behavior. *Journal of Personality and Social Psychology, 32*, 571-577.

Matsumoto, D., & Yoo, S. (2006). Toward a new generation of cross-cultural research. *Perspectives on Psychological Science, 1*, 234-250.

Matthews, K. A., Batson, C. D., Horn, J., & Rosenman, R. H. (1981). 'Principles in his nature which interest him in the fortune of others . . .': The heritability of empathic concern for others. *Journal of Personality, 49*, 237-247.

Mayer, J., & Hanson, E. (1995). Mood-congruent judgment over time. *Personality and Social Psychology Bulletin, 21*, 237-244.

Mazur, A., & Booth, A. (1998). Testosterone and dominance in men. *Behavioral and Brain Sciences, 21*, 353-397.

Mazzella, R., & Feingold, A. (1994). The effects of physical attractiveness, race, socioeconomic status, and gender of defendants and victims on judgments of mock jurors: A meta-analysis. *Journal of Applied Social Psychology, 24*, 1315-1344.

McArthur, L. (1980). Illusory causation and illusory correlation: Two epistemological accounts. *Personality and Social Psychology Bulletin, 6*, 507-519.

McArthur, L. Z., & Berry, D. S. (1987). Cross-cultural agreement in perceptions of babyfaced adults. *Journal of Cross-Cultural Psychology, 18*, 165-192.

McAuliffe, T., DiFranceisco, W., & Reed, B. (2007). Effects of question format and collection mode on the accuracy of retrospective surveys of health risk behavior: A comparison with daily sexual activity diaries. *Health Psychology, 26*, 60-67.

McCall, M., & Belmont, H. J. (1996). Credit card insignia and restaurant tipping: Evidence for an associative link. *Journal of Applied Psychology, 81*, 609-613.

McClure, S., Laibson, D., Loewenstein, G., & Cohen, J. (2004). Separate neural systems value immediate and delayed monetary rewards. *Science, 306*, 503-507.

McConahay, J. (1986). Modern racism, ambivalence, and the Modern Racism Scale. *Prejudice, Discrimination, and Racism* (pp. 91-125). San Diego, CA: Academic Press.

McConnell, A. R., Sherman, S. J., & Hamilton, D. L. (1994). Illusory correlation in the perception of groups: An extension of the distinctiveness-based account. *Journal of Personality and Social Psychology, 67*, 414-429.

McCullough, M. E., Rachal, K. C., Sandage, S. J., Worthington, E. L. J., Brown, S. W., & Hight, T. L. (1998). Interpersonal forgiving in close relationships: II. Theoretical elaboration and measurement. *Journal of Personality and Social Psychology, 75*, 1586-1603.

McCullough, M. E., Worthington, E. L. J., & Rachal, K. C. (1997). Interpersonal forgiving in close relationships. *Journal of Personality and Social Psychology, 73*, 321-336.

McGillicuddy, N. B., Welton, G. L., & Pruitt, D. G. (1987). Third-party intervention: A field experiment comparing three different models. *Journal of Personality and Social Psychology, 53*, 104-112.

McGonagle, K. A., Kessler, R. C., & Schilling, E. A. (1992). The frequency and determinants of marital disagreements in a community sample. *Journal of Social and Personal Relationships, 9*, 507-524.

McGovern, L. P., Ditzian, J. L., & Taylor, S. P. (1975). The effect of one positive reinforcement on helping with cost. *Bulletin of the Psychonomic Society, 5*, 421-423.

McGuire, W. (1964). Inducing resistance to persuasion: Some contemporary approaches. In L. Berkowitz (Ed.), *Advances in Experimental Social Psychology* (Vol. 1, pp. 191-229). New York: Academic Press.

McKenna, K. Y. A., & Bargh, J. A. (1998). Coming out in the age of the Internet: Identity 'demarginalization' through virtual group participation. *Journal of Personality and Social Psychology, 75,* 681-694.

McKenna, K. Y. A., & Bargh, J. A. (2000). Plan 9 from cyberspace: The implications of the Internet for personality and social psychology. *Personality and Social Psychology Review, 4,* 57-75.

McKenna, K. Y. A., & Green, A. S. (2002). Virtual group dynamics. *Group Dynamics, 6,* 116-127.

McKenna, K. Y. A., Green, A. S., & Gleason, M. E. (2002). Relationship formation on the Internet: What's the big attraction? *Journal of Social Issues, 58,* 9-31.

McKillip, J., & Reidel, S.L. (1983). External validity of matching on physical attractiveness for same and opposite sex couples. *Journal of Applied Social Psychology, 13,* 328-337.

McNulty, J. K., & Karney, B. R. (2001). Attributions in marriage: Integrating specific and global evaluations of a relationship. *Personality and Social Psychology Bulletin, 27,* 943-955.

McNulty, J. K., & Karney, B. R. (2004). Positive expectations in the early years of marriage: Should couples expect the best or brace for the worst? *Journal of Personality and Social Psychology, 86,* 729-743.

Mealey, L., Bridgstock, R., & Townsend, G. C. (1999). Symmetry and perceived facial attractiveness: A monozygotic co-twin comparison. *Journal of Personality and Social Psychology, 76,* 151-158.

Medvec, V., & Savitsky, K. (1997). When doing better means feeling worse: The effects of categorical cutoff points on counterfactual thinking and satisfaction. *Journal of Personality and Social Psychology, 72,* 1284-1296.

Meeus, W. H. J., & Raaijmakers, Q. A. W. (1995). Obedience in modern society: The Utrecht studies. *Journal of Social Issues, 51,* 155-175.

Mehrabian, A., & Epstein, N. (1972). A measure of emotional empathy. *Journal of Personality, 40,* 525-543.

Meleshko, K. G., & Alden, L. E. (1993). Anxiety and self-disclosure: Toward a motivational model. *Journal of Personality and Social Psychology, 64,* 1000-1009.

Mendes, W. B., Major, B., McCoy, S., & Blascovich, J. (2008). How attributional ambiguity shapes physiological and emotional responses to social rejection and acceptance. *Journal of Personality and Social Psychology, 94,* 278-291.

Menon, T., Morris, M., Chiu, C., & Hong, Y. (1999). Culture and the construal of agency: Attribution to individual versus group dispositions. *Journal of Personality and Social Psychology, 76,* 701-717.

Messick, D. M. (1983). Individual adaptations and structural change as solutions to social dilemmas. *Journal of Personality and Social Psychology, 44,* 294-309.

Meyerowitz, B., & Chaiken, S. (1987). The effect of message framing on breast self-examination attitudes, intentions, and behavior. *Journal of Personality and Social Psychology, 52,* 500-510.

Meyer, J. P., & Mulherin, A. (1980). From attribution to helping: An analysis of the mediating effects of affect and expectancy. *Journal of Personality and Social Psychology, 39,* 201–210.

Meyers, S. A., & Berscheid, E. (1997). The language of love: The difference a preposition makes. *Personality and Social Psychology Bulletin, 23,* 347-362.

Mickelson, K. D., Kessler, R. C., & Shaver, P. R. (1997). Adult attachment in a nationally representative sample. *Journal of Personality and Social Psychology, 73,* 1092-1106.

Middlemist, R. D., Knowles, E. S., & Matter, C. F. (1976). Personal space invasions in the lavatory: Suggestive evidence for arousal. *Journal of Personality and Social Psychology, 33,* 541-546.

Miles, D. R., & Carey, G. (1997). Genetic and environmental architecture on human aggression. *Journal of Personality and Social Psychology, 72,* 207-217.

Milgram, S. (1963). Behavioral study of obedience. *The Journal of Abnormal and Social Psychology, 67,* 371-378.

Milgram, S. (1970). The experience of living in cities. *Science, 167,* 1461-1468.

Milgram, S. (1974). *Obedience to Authority: An Experimental View.* New York: Harper Collins.

Millar, M., & Millar, K. (1996). The effects of direct and indirect experience on affective and cognitive responses and the attitude—behavior relation. *Journal of Experimental Social Psychology, 32,* 561-579.

Miller, A. G., Collins, B. E., & Brief, D. E. (1995). Perspectives on obedience to authority: The legacy of the Milgram experiments. *Journal of Social Issues, 51,* 1-19.

Miller, A. G., McHoskey, J. W., Bane, C. M., & Dowd, T. G. (1993). The attitude polarization phenomenon: Role of response measure, attitude extremity, and behavioral consequences of reported attitude change. *Journal of Personality and Social Psychology, 64,* 561-574.

Miller, A., Ashton, W., & Mishal, M. (1990). Beliefs concerning the features of constrained behavior: A basis for the fundamental attribution error. *Journal of Personality and Social Psychology, 59,* 635-650.

Miller, C. T., Rothblum, E. D., Barbour, L., Brand, P. A., & Felicio, D. (1990). Social interactions of obese and nonobese women. *Journal of Personality, 58,* 365-380.

Miller, D. T., & McFarland, C. (1987). Pluralistic ignorance: When similarity is interpreted as dissimilarity. *Journal of Personality and Social Psychology, 53,* 298-305.

Miller, D.T., & McFarland, C. (1991). When social comparison goes awry: The case of pluralistic ignorance. In J. Suls & T.A. Wills (Eds.), *Social Comparison: Contemporary Theory and Research* (pp. 287-313). Hillsdale, NJ: Erlbaum.

Miller, D. T., & Prentice, D. A. (1994). Collective errors and errors about the collective. *Personality and Social Psychology Bulletin, 20,* 541-550.

Miller, G., Tybur, J. M., & Jordan, B. D. (2007). Ovulatory cycle effects on tip earnings by lap dancers: Economic evidence for human estrus? *Evolution and Human Behavior, 28,* 375-381.

Miller, J. (1984). Culture and the development of everyday social explanation. *Journal of Personality and Social Psychology, 46,* 961-978.

Miller, J. G., & Bersoff, D. M. (1994). Cultural influences on the moral status of reciprocity and the discounting of endogenous motivation. *Personality and Social Psychology Bulletin, 20,* 592-602.

Miller, J. G., Bersoff, D. M., & Harwood, R. L. (1990). Perceptions of social responsibilities in India and in the United States: Moral imperatives or personal decisions? *Journal of Personality and Social Psychology, 58,* 33-47.

Miller, J., & Krosnick, J. (1998). The impact of candidate name order on election outcomes. *Public Opinion Quarterly, 62,* 291-330.

Miller, L. C. (1990). Intimacy and liking: Mutual influence and the role of unique relationships. *Journal of Personality and Social Psychology, 59,* 50-60.

Miller, P. A., & Eisenberg, N. (1988). The relation of empathy to aggressive and externalizing/antisocial behavior. *Psychological Bulletin, 103*, 324-344.

Miller, P. A., Eisenberg, N., Fabes, R. A., & Shell, R. (1996). Relations of moral reasoning and vicarious emotion to young children's prosocial behavior toward peers and adults. *Developmental Psychology, 32*, 210-219.

Miller, P. J. E., & Rempel, J. K. (2004). Trust and partner-enhancing attributions in close relationships. *Personality and Social Psychology Bulletin, 30*, 695-705.

Miller, R. S. (1997). Inattentive and contented: Relationship commitment and attention to alternatives. *Journal of Personality and Social Psychology, 73*, 758-766.

Mita, T., Dermer, M., & Knight, J. (1977). Reversed facial images and the mere-exposure hypothesis. *Journal of Personality and Social Psychology, 35*, 597-601.

Mitchell, J., Macrae, C., & Banaji, M. (2004). Encoding-specific effects of social cognition on the neural correlates of subsequent memory. *Journal of Neuroscience, 24*, 4912-4917.

Modigliani, A., & Rochat, F. (1995). The role of interaction sequences and the timing of resistance in shaping obedience and defiance to authority. *Journal of Social Issues, 51*, 107-123.

Mondschein, E. R., Adolph, K. E., & Tamis-LeMonda, C. S. (2000). Gender bias in mothers' expectations about infant crawling. *Journal of Experimental Child Psychology, 77*, 304-316.

Monin, B., & Miller, D. T. (2001). Moral credentials and the expression of prejudice. *Journal of Personality and Social Psychology, 81*, 33-43.

Monin, B., & Norton, M. (2003). Perceptions of a fluid consensus: Uniqueness bias, false consensus, false polarization, and pluralistic ignorance in a water conservation crisis. *Personality and Social Psychology Bulletin, 29*, 559-567.

Monteith, M. J. (1993). Self-regulation of prejudiced responses: Implications for progress in prejudice-reduction efforts. *Journal of Personality and Social Psychology, 65*, 469-485.

Monteith, M. J., Ashburn-Nardo, L., Voils, C. I., & Czopp, A. M. (2002). Putting the brakes on prejudice: On the development and operation of cues for control. *Journal of Personality and Social Psychology, 83*, 1029-1050.

Monteith, M. J., Sherman, J. W., & Devine, P. G. (1998). Suppression as a stereotype control strategy. *Personality and Social Psychology Review, 2*, 63-82.

Moreland, R. L., & Beach, S. R. (1992). Exposure effects in the classroom: The development of affinity among students. *Journal of Experimental Social Psychology, 28*, 255-276.

Moreland, R. L., & Zajonc, R. B. (1982). Exposure effects in person perception: Familiarity, similarity, and attraction. *Journal of Experimental Social Psychology, 18*, 395-415.

Morgan, S. E., Miller, J. K., & Arasaratnam, L. A. (2003). Similarities and differences between African Americans' and European Americans' attitudes, knowledge, and willingness to communicate about organ donation. *Journal of Applied Social Psychology, 33*, 693-715.

Mori, D., Chaiken, S., & Pliner, P. (1987). 'Eating lightly' and the self-presentation of femininity. *Journal of Personality and Social Psychology, 53*, 693-702.

Moriarty, T. (1975). Crime, commitment, and the responsive bystander: Two field experiments. *Journal of Personality and Social Psychology, 31*, 370-376.

Morling, B., & Lamoreaux, M. (2008). Measuring culture outside the head: A meta-analysis of individualism-collectivism in cultural products. *Personality and Social Psychology Review, 12*, 199-221.

Morris, M., & Peng, K. (1994). Culture and cause: American and Chinese attributions for social and physical events. *Journal of Personality and Social Psychology, 67*, 949-971.

Morrongiello, B., Corbett, M., & Bellissimo, A. (2008). 'Do as I say, not as I do': Family influences on children's safety and risk behaviors. *Health Psychology, 27*, 498-503.

Morry, M. M. (2005). Relationship satisfaction as a predictor of similarity ratings: A test of the attraction-similarity hypothesis. *Journal of Social and Personal Relationships, 22*, 561-584.

Morse, S., & Gergen, K. (1970). Social comparison, self-consistency, and the concept of self. *Journal of Personality and Social Psychology, 16*, 148-156.

Moscovici, S., & Zavalloni, M. (1969). The group as a polarizer of attitudes. *Journal of Personality and Social Psychology, 12*, 125-135.

Moskowitz, G. B., Gollwitzer, P. M., Wasel, W., & Schaal, B. (1999). Preconscious control of stereotype activation through chronic egalitarian goals. *Journal of Personality and Social Psychology, 77*, 167-184.

Moss, M. K., & Page, R. A. (1972). Reinforcement and helping behavior. *Journal of Applied Social Psychology, 2*, 360-371.

Mucchi-Faina, A., Maass, A., & Volpato, C. (1991). Social influence: The role of originality. *European Journal of Social Psychology, 21*, 183-197.

Mueller, C. M., & Dweck, C. S. (1998). Intelligence praise can undermine motivation and performance. *Journal of Personality and Social Psychology, 75*, 33-52.

Mulder, L. B., van Dijk, E., De Cremer, D., & Wilke, H. A. M. (2006). Undermining trust and cooperation: The paradox of sanctioning systems in social dilemmas. *Journal of Experimental Social Psychology, 42*, 147-162.

Mullen, B. (1983). Operationalizing the effect of the group on the individual: A self-attention perspective. *Journal of Experimental Social Psychology, 19*, 295-322.

Mullen, B. (1986). Atrocity as a function of lynch mob composition: A self-attention perspective. *Personality and Social Psychology Bulletin, 12*, 187-197.

Mullen, B., & Copper, C. (1994). The relation between group cohesiveness and performance: An integration. *Psychological Bulletin, 115*, 210-227.

Mullen, B., & Hu, L. (1989). Perceptions of ingroup and outgroup variability: A meta-analytic integration. *Basic and Applied Social Psychology, 10*, 233-252.

Mullin, C. R., & Linz, D. (1995). Desensitization and resensitization to violence against women: Effects of exposure to sexually violent films on judgments of domestic violence victims. *Journal of Personality and Social Psychology, 69*, 449-459.

Munro, G. D., & Ditto, P. H. (1997). Biased assimilation, attitude polarization, and affect in reactions to stereotyped-relevant scientific information. *Personality and Social Psychology Bulletin, 23*, 636-653.

Muraven, M., Tice, D., & Baumeister, R. (1998). Self-control as a limited resource: Regulatory depletion patterns. *Journal of Personality and Social Psychology, 74*, 774-789.

Murphy, C. M., & O'Farrell, T. J. (1996). Marital violence among alcoholics. *Current Directions in Psychological Science, 5*, 183-186.

Murphy, S., & Zajonc, R. (1993). Affect, cognition, and awareness: Affective priming with optimal and suboptimal stimulus exposures. *Journal of Personality and Social Psychology, 64*, 723-739.

Murray, N. P. (2006). The differential effect of team cohesion and leadership behavior in high school sports. *Individual Differences Research, 4,* 216-225.

Murray, S. L., & Holmes, J. G. (1996). The construction of relationship realities. In G. Fletcher & J. Fitness (Eds.), *Knowledge Structures and Interaction in Close Relationships: A Social Psychological Approach* (pp. 91-120). Hillsdale, NJ: Lawrence Erlbaum Associates, Inc.

Murray, S. L., & Holmes, J. G. (1997). A leap of faith? Positive illusions in romantic relationships. *Personality and Social Psychology Bulletin, 23,* 586-604.

Murray, S. L., Holmes, J. G., & Griffin, D. W. (1996). The benefits of positive illusions: Idealization and the construction of satisfaction in close relationships. *Journal of Personality and Social Psychology, 70,* 79-98.

Mussweiler, T. (2006). Doing is for thinking! Stereotype activation by stereotypic movements. *Psychological Science, 17,* 17-21.

Mussweiler, T., & Rüter, K. (2003). What friends are for! The use of routine standards in social comparison. *Journal of Personality and Social Psychology, 85,* 467-481.

Mussweiler, T., & Strack, F. (2000). The use of category and exemplar knowledge in the solution of anchoring tasks. *Journal of Personality and Social Psychology, 78,* 1038-1052.

Mutterperl, J. A., & Sanderson, C. A. (2002). Mind over matter: Internalization of the thinness norm as a moderator of responsiveness to norm misperception education in college women. *Health Psychology, 21,* 519-523.

Myers, D. G., & Kaplan, M. F. (1976). Group-induced polarization in simulated juries. *Personality and Social Psychology Bulletin, 2,* 63-66.

Myers, J. E., Madathil, J., & Tingle, L. R. (2005). Marriage satisfaction and wellness in India and the United States: A preliminary comparison of arranged marriages and marriages of choice. *Journal of Counseling & Development, 83,* 183-190.

Nadler, A. (1987). Determinants of help seeking behaviour: The effects of helper's similarity, task centrality and recipient's self esteem. *European Journal of Social Psychology, 17,* 57-67.

Nadler, A., Altman, A., & Fisher, J. D. (1979). Helping is not enough: Recipient's reactions to aid as a function of positive and negative information about the self. *Journal of Personality, 47,* 615-628.

Nadler, A., & Fisher, J. D. (1986). The role of threat to self-esteem and perceived control in recipient reaction to help: Theory development and empirical validation. In L. Berkowitz (Ed.), *Advances in Experimental Social Psychology* (Vol. 19, pp. 81-121). Orlando, FL: Academic Press.

Nadler, A., Fisher, J. D., & Itzhak, S. B. (1983). With a little help from my friend: Effect of single or multiple act aid as a function of donor and task characteristics. *Journal of Personality and Social Psychology, 44,* 310-321.

Nadler, A., Goldberg, M., & Jaffe, Y. (1982). Effect of self-differentiation and anonymity in group on deindividuation. *Journal of Personality and Social Psychology, 42,* 1127-1136.

Nadler, A., Mayseless, O., Peri, N., & Chemerinski, A. (1985). Effects of opportunity to reciprocate and self-esteem on help-seeking behavior. *Journal of Personality, 53,* 23-35.

Nail, P. R., Harton, H. C., & Decker, B. P. (2003). Political orientation and modern versus aversive racism: Tests of Dovidio and Gaertner's (1998) integrated model. *Journal of Personality and Social Psychology, 84,* 754-770.

Nansel, T. R., Overpeck, M., Pilla, R. S., Ruan, W. J., Simons-Morton, B., & Scheidt, P. (2001). Bullying behaviors among US youth: Prevalence and association with psychosocial adjustment. *Journal of the American Medical Association, 285,* 2094-2100.

Nasco, S., & Marsh, K. (1999). Gaining control through counterfactual thinking. *Personality and Social Psychology Bulletin, 25,* 556-568.

Nattinger, A., Hoffmann, R., Howell-Pelz, A., & Goodwin, J. (1998). Effect of Nancy Reagan's mastectomy on choice of surgery for breast cancer by US women. *Journal of the American Medical Association, 279,* 762-766.

Neff, L. A., & Karney, B. R. (2005). To know you is to love you: The implications of global adoration and specific accuracy for marital relationships. *Journal of Personality and Social Psychology, 88,* 480-497.

Nelson, L., & Simmons, J. (2007). Moniker maladies: When names sabotage success. *Psychological Science, 18,* 1106-1112.

Nemeth, C., & Chiles, C. (1988). Modelling courage: The role of dissent in fostering independence. *European Journal of Social Psychology, 18,* 275-280.

Nemeth, C., Mayseless, O., Sherman, J., & Brown, Y. (1990). Exposure to dissent and recall of information. *Journal of Personality and Social Psychology, 58,* 429-437.

Neuberg, S. L. (1989). The goal of forming accurate impressions during social interactions: Attenuating the impact of negative expectancies. *Journal of Personality and Social Psychology, 56,* 374-386.

Neuberg, S. L., & Fiske, S. T. (1987). Motivational influences on impression formation: Outcome dependency, accuracy-driven attention, and individuating processes. *Journal of Personality and Social Psychology, 53,* 431-444.

Neuberg, S., Judice, T., Virdin, L., & Carrillo, M. (1993). Perceiver self-presentational goals as moderators of expectancy influences: Ingratiation and the disconfirmation of negative expectancies. *Journal of Personality and Social Psychology, 64,* 409-420.

Newcomb, T. M. (1961). *The Acquaintance Process.* New York: Holt, Rinehart and Winston.

Newman, M., Pennebaker, J., Berry, D., & Richards, J. (2003). Lying words: Predicting deception from linguistic styles. *Personality and Social Psychology Bulletin, 29,* 665-675.

Nichter, M., & Nichter, M. (1991). Hype and weight. *Medical Anthropology, 13,* 249-284.

Nickerson, C., Schwarz, N., Diener, E., & Kahneman, D. (2003). Zeroing in the dark side of the American Dream: A closer look at the negative consequences of the goal for financial success. *Psychological Science, 14,* 531-536.

Nisbett, R. E. (1993). Violence and U.S. regional culture. *American Psychologist, 48,* 441-449.

Nisbett, R., Peng, K., Choi, I., & Norenzayan, A. (2001). Culture and systems of thought: Holistic versus analytic cognition. *Psychological Review, 108,* 291-310.

Noel, J. G., Wann, D. L., & Branscombe, N. R. (1995). Peripheral ingroup membership status and public negativity toward outgroups. *Journal of Personality and Social Psychology, 68,* 127-137.

Nolan, J. M., Schultz, P. W., Cialdini, R. B., Goldstein, N. J., & Griskevicius, V. (2008). Normative social influence is underdetected. *Personality and Social Psychology Bulletin, 34,* 913-923.

Norenzayan, A., Choi, I., & Nisbett, R. (2002). Cultural similarities and differences in social inference: Evidence from behavioral predictions and lay theories of behavior. *Personality and Social Psychology Bulletin, 28,* 109-120.

Norenzayan, A., & Nisbett, R. (2000). Culture and causal cognition. *Current Directions in Psychological Science, 9,* 132-135.

Norman, W., & Goldberg, L. (1966). Raters, ratees, and randomness in personality structure. *Journal of Personality and Social Psychology, 4,* 681-691.

North, A. C., Tarrant, M., & Hargreaves, D. J. (2004). The effects of music on helping behavior: A field study. *Environment and Behavior, 36,* 266-275.

Norton, M., Monin, B., Cooper, J., & Hogg, M. (2003). Vicarious dissonance: Attitude change from the inconsistency of others. *Journal of Personality and Social Psychology, 85,* 47-62.

Norton, M. I., Sommers, S. R., Apfelbaum, E. P., Pura, N., & Ariely, D. (2006). Color blindness and interracial interaction: Playing the political correctness game. *Psychological Science, 17,* 949-953.

Norton, M. I., Vandello, J. A., & Darley, J. M. (2004). Casuistry and social category bias. *Journal of Personality and Social Psychology, 87,* 817-831.

Nosek, B. A., Greenwald, A. G., & Banaji, M. R. (2005). Understanding and using the Implicit Association Test: II. Method variables and construct validity. *Personality and Social Psychology Bulletin, 31,* 166-180.

Oakes, P. J., & Turner, J. C. (1980). Social categorization and intergroup behaviour: Does minimal intergroup discrimination make social identity more positive? *European Journal of Social Psychology, 10,* 295-301.

O'Connor, K. M., & Carnevale, P. J. (1997). A nasty but effective negotiation strategy: Misrepresentation of a common-value issue. *Personality and Social Psychology Bulletin, 23,* 504-515.

Oettingen, G., & Seligman, M.E.P. (1990). Pessimism and behavioral signs of depression in East versus West Berlin. *European Journal of Social Psychology, 20,* 207-220.

Ohbuchi, K., Kameda, M., & Agarie, N. (1989). Apology as aggression control: Its role in mediating appraisal of and response to harm. *Journal of Personality and Social Psychology, 56,* 219-227.

Ohbuchi, K., Ohno, T., & Mukai, H. (1993). Empathy and aggression: Effects of self-disclosure and fearful appeal. *Journal of Social Psychology, 133,* 243-253.

Oishi, S. (2002). The experiencing and remembering of well-being: A cross-cultural analysis. *Personality and Social Psychology Bulletin, 28,* 1398-1406.

Olson, J. M., Herman, C. P., & Zanna, M.P. (1986). Relative deprivation and social comparison: An integrative perspective. In J.M. Olson, C.P. Herman, & M.P. Zanna (Eds.), *Relative Deprivation and Social Comparison: The Ontario Symposium* (Vol. 4., pp. 1-15). Hillsdale, NJ: Erlbaum.

Olson, J., Vernon, P., Harris, J., & Jang, K. (2001). The heritability of attitudes: A study of twins. *Journal of Personality and Social Psychology, 80,* 845-860.

Olweus, D. (1979). Stability of aggressive reaction patterns in males: A review. *Psychological Bulletin, 86,* 852-875.

Olweus, D. (1995). Bullying or peer abuse at school: Facts and interventions. *Current Directions in Psychological Science, 4,* 196-200.

Olweus, D., Mattsson, Å., Schalling, D., & Löw, H. (1988). Circulating testosterone levels and aggression in adolescent males: A causal analysis. *Psychosomatic Medicine, 50,* 261-272.

Omoto, A. M., & Snyder, M. (1995). Sustained helping without obligation: Motivation, longevity of service, and perceived attitude change among AIDS volunteers. *Journal of Personality and Social Psychology, 68,* 671-686.

Operario, D., & Fiske, S. T. (2001). Effects of trait dominance on powerholders' judgements of subordinates. *Social Cognition, 19,* 161-180.

Orbell, J. M., Van de Kragt, A. J., & Dawes, R. M. (1988). Explaining discussion-induced cooperation. *Journal of Personality and Social Psychology, 54,* 811-819.

Orne, M. (1962). On the social psychology of the psychological experiment: With particular reference to demand characteristics and their implications. *American Psychologist, 17,* 776-783.

Osbourne, J. W. (1995). Academics, self-esteem, and race: A look at the underlying assumptions of the disidentification hypothesis. *Personality and Social Psychology Bulletin, 21,* 449-455.

Osgood, C. E. (1962). *An Alternative to War or Surrender.* Urbana, IL: University of Illinois Press.

Osherow, N. (2004). Making sense of the nonsensical: An analysis of Jonestown. In E. Aronson (Ed.), *Readings About the Social Animal* (pp. 80-97). New York: Worth.

Ostrom, T. M., & Sedikides, C. (1992). Out-group homogeneity effects in natural and minimal groups. *Psychological Bulletin, 112,* 536-552.

O'Sullivan, C. S., & Durso, F. T. (1984). Effect of schema-incongruent information on memory for stereotypical attributes. *Journal of Personality and Social Psychology, 47,* 55-70.

O'Sullivan, M. (2003). The fundamental attribution error in detecting deception: The boy-who-cried-wolf effect. *Personality and Social Psychology Bulletin, 29,* 1316-1327.

Ottati, V., Riggle, E., Wyer, R., Schwarz, N., & Kuklinski, J. (1989). Cognitive and affective bases of opinion survey responses. *Journal of Personality and Social Psychology, 57,* 404-415.

Otten, C. A., Penner, L. A., & Altabe, M. N. (1991). An examination of therapists' and college students' willingness to help a psychologically distressed person. *Journal of Social & Clinical Psychology, 10,* 102-120.

Otten, S., & Wentura, D. (1999). About the impact of automaticity in the Minimal Group Paradigm: Evidence from affective priming tasks. *European Journal of Social Psychology, 29,* 1049-1071.

Ouellette, J.A., Hessling, R., Gibbons, F.X., Reis-Bergan, M.J., & Gerrard, M. (2005). Using images to increase exercise behavior: Prototypes vs. possible selves. *Personality and Social Psychology Bulletin, 31,* 610-620.

Packer, D. J. (2008). Identifying systematic disobedience in Milgram's obedience experiments: A meta-analytic review. *Perspectives on Psychological Science, 3,* 301-304.

Paleari, F. G., Regalia, C., & Fincham, F. (2005). Marital quality, forgiveness, empathy, and rumination: A longitudinal analysis. *Personality and Social Psychology Bulletin, 31,* 368-378.

Park, B., Ryan, C. S., & Judd, C. M. (1992). Role of meaningful subgroups in explaining differences in perceived variability for in-groups and out-groups. *Journal of Personality and Social Psychology, 63,* 553-567.

Parks, C. D., Sanna, L. J., & Berel, S. R. (2001). Actions of similar others as inducements to cooperate in social dilemmas. *Personality and Social Psychology Bulletin, 27,* 345-354.

Parks-Stamm, E., Heilman, M., & Hearns, K. (2008). Motivated to penalize: Women's strategic rejection of successful women. *Personality and Social Psychology Bulletin, 34*, 237-247.

Parrott, W.G., & Smith, R.H. (1993). Distinguishing the experiences of envy and jealousy. *Journal of Personality and Social Psychology, 64*, 906-920.

Patrick, H., Neighbors, C., & Knee, C. (2004). Appearance-related social comparisons: The role of contingent self-esteem and self-perceptions of attractiveness. *Personality and Social Psychology Bulletin, 30*, 501-514.

Patterson, M. M., Carron, A. V., & Loughead, T. M. (2005). The influence of team norms on the cohesion—self-reported performance relationship: A multi-level analysis. *Psychology of Sport and Exercise, 6*, 479-493.

Paulhus, D. (1998). Interpersonal and intrapsychic adaptiveness of trait self-enhancement: A mixed blessing? *Journal of Personality and Social Psychology, 74*, 1197-1208.

Paulhus, D., Bruce, M., & Trapnell, P. (1995). Effects of self-presentation strategies on personality profiles and their structure. *Personality and Social Psychology Bulletin, 21*, 100-108.

Payne, B. K. (2001). Prejudice and perception: The role of automatic and controlled processes in misperceiving a weapon. *Journal of Personality and Social Psychology, 81*, 181-192.

Payne, B. K. (2006). Weapon bias: Split-second decisions and unintended stereotyping. *Current Directions in Psychological Science, 15*, 287-291.

Pearce, P. L. (1980). Strangers, travelers, and Greyhound terminals: A study of small-scale helping behaviors. *Journal of Personality and Social Psychology, 38*, 935-940.

Pearce, Z. J., & Halford, W. K. (2008). Do attributions mediate the association between attachment and negative couple communication? *Personal Relationships, 15*, 155-170.

Pechmann, C. (1997). Do anti-smoking ads combat underage smoking? A review of past practices and research. In M.E. Goldberg, M. Fishbein, & S. Iddlestadt (Eds.), *Social Marketing: Theoretical and Practical Perspectives* (pp. 189-216). Hillsdale, NJ: Lawrence Erlbaum Associates.

Pechmann, C., & Shih, C. (1999). Smoking scenes in movies and antismoking advertisements before movies: Effects on youth. *Journal of Marketing, 63*, 1-13.

Pedersen, W. C., Gonzales, C., & Miller, N. (2000). The moderating effect of trivial triggering provocation on displaced aggression. *Journal of Personality and Social Psychology, 78*, 913-927.

Pedersen, W.C., Miller, L.C., Putcha-Bhagavatula, A., & Yang, Y. (2002). Evolved sex differences in the number of partners desired? The long and the short of it. *Psychological Science, 13*, 157-161.

Pelham, B., Carvallo, M., DeHart, T., & Jones, J. (2003). Assessing the validity of implicit egotism: A reply to Gallucci (2003). *Journal of Personality and Social Psychology, 85*, 800-807.

Pelham, B., Mirenberg, M., & Jones, J. (2002). Why Susie sells seashells by the seashore: Implicit egotism and major life decisions. *Journal of Personality and Social Psychology, 82*, 469-487.

Pelphrey, K., Viola, R., & McCarthy, G. (2004). When strangers pass: Processing of mutual and averted social gaze in the superior temporal sulcus. *Psychological Science, 15*, 598-603.

Pendry, L. F., & Macrae, C. N. (1994). Stereotypes and mental life: The case of the motivated but thwarted tactician. *Journal of Experimental Social Psychology, 30*, 303-325.

Peng, K., & Knowles, E. (2003). Culture, education, and the attribution of physical causality. *Personality and Social Psychology Bulletin, 29*, 1272-1284.

Peng, K., & Nisbett, R. E. (1999). Culture, dialectics, and reasoning about contradiction. *American Psychologist, 54*, 741-754.

Pennebaker, J. W. (1989). Confession, inhibition, and disease. In L. Berkowitz (Ed.), *Advances in Experimental Social Psychology* (Vol. 22, pp. 211-244). New York: Academic Press.

Pennebaker, J. W., Dyer, M.A., Caulkins, R.S., Litowitz, D.L., Ackreman, P.L., Anderson, D.B., & McGraw, K. (1979). Don't the girls get prettier at closing time? A country and western application to psychology. *Personality and Social Psychology Bulletin, 5*, 122-125.

Pennebaker, J. W., & Sanders, D. Y. (1976). American graffiti: Effects of authority and reactance arousal. *Personality and Social Psychology Bulletin, 2*, 264-267.

Pennebaker, J., & Skelton, J. (1981). Selective monitoring of physical sensations. *Journal of Personality and Social Psychology, 41*, 213-223.

Perdue, C. W., & Gurtman, M. B. (1990). Evidence for the automaticity of ageism. *Journal of Experimental Social Psychology, 26*, 199-216.

Perdue, C. W., Dovidio, J. F., Gurtman, M. B., & Tyler, R. B. (1990). Us and them: Social categorization and the process of intergroup bias. *Journal of Personality and Social Psychology, 59*, 475-486.

Perkins, H. W. (2002). Social norms and the prevention of alcohol misuse in collegiate contexts. *Journal of Studies on Alcohol*, Supplement 14, 164-172.

Perkins, H. W., & Craig, D. W. (2006). A successful social norms campaign to reduce alcohol misuse among college student-athletes. *Journal of Studies on Alcohol, 67*, 880-889.

Perrin, S., & Spencer, C. P. (1981). Independence or conformity in the Asch experiment as a reflection of cultural and situational factors. *British Journal of Social Psychology, 20*, 205-209.

Perry, D. G., Perry, L. C., & Rasmussen, P. (1986). Cognitive social learning mediators of aggression. *Child Development, 57*, 700-711.

Peters, L. H., Hartke, D. D., & Pohlmann, J. T. (1985). Fiedler's Contingency Theory of Leadership: An application of the meta-analysis procedures of Schmidt and Hunter. *Psychological Bulletin, 97*, 274-285.

Peterson, C., & Seligman, M. (1987). Explanatory style and illness. *Journal of Personality, 55*, 237-265.

Peterson, C., & Seligman, M. (2004). *Character Strengths and Virtues: A Handbook and Classification*. Oxford: Oxford University Press.

Peterson, C., Seligman, M., Yurko, K., Martin, L., & Friedman, H. (1998). Catastrophizing and untimely death. *Psychological Science, 9*, 127-130.

Peterson, L., & Brown, D. (1994). Integrating child injury and abuse-neglect research: Common histories, etiologies, and solutions. *Psychological Bulletin, 116*, 293-315.

Peterson, R. S., & Nemeth, C. J. (1996). Focus versus flexibility: Majority and minority influence can both improve performance. *Personality and Social Psychology Bulletin, 22*, 14-23.

Pettigrew, T. (2004). Justice deferred a half century after Brown v. Board of Education. *American Psychologist, 59*, 521-529.

Pettigrew, T. F. (1979). The ultimate attribution error: Extending Allport's cognitive analysis of prejudice. *Personality and Social Psychology Bulletin, 5,* 461-476.

Pettigrew, T. F. (1997). Generalized intergroup contact effects on prejudice. *Personality and Social Psychology Bulletin, 23,* 173-185.

Pettigrew, T. F. (2003). Peoples under threat: Americans, Arabs, and Israelis. *Peace and Conflict: Journal of Peace Psychology, 9,* 69-90.

Petty, R. E., & Cacioppo, J. T. (1984). The effects of involvement on responses to argument quantity and quality: Central and peripheral routes to persuasion. *Journal of Personality and Social Psychology, 46,* 69-81.

Petty, R. E., & Cacioppo, J. T. (1986). *Communication and Persuasion: Central and Peripheral Routes to Attitude Change.* New York: Springer-Verlag.

Petty, R. E., Cacioppo, J. T., & Goldman, R. (1981). Personal involvement as a determinant of argument-based persuasion. *Journal of Personality and Social Psychology, 41,* 847-855.

Petty, R. E., Schumann, D. W., Richman, S. A., & Strathman, A. J. (1993). Positive mood and persuasion: Different roles for affect under high- and low-elaboration conditions. *Journal of Personality and Social Psychology, 64,* 5-20.

Petty, R. E., Wells, G. L., & Brock, T. C. (1976). Distraction can enhance or reduce yielding to propaganda: Thought disruption versus effort justification. *Journal of Personality and Social Psychology, 34,* 874-884.

Phelps, E. A., O'Connor, K. J., Cunningham, W. A., Funayama, E. S., Gatenby, J. C., Gore, J. C., et al. (2000). Performance on indirect measures of race evaluation predicts amygdala activation. *Journal of Cognitive Neuroscience, 12,* 729-738.

Phillips, D. (1982). The impact of fictional television stories on U.S. adult fatalities: New evidence on the effect of the mass media on violence. *American Journal of Sociology, 87,* 1340-1359.

Phillips, D. P. (1977). Motor vehicle fatalities increase just after publicized suicide stories. *Science, 196,* 1464-1465.

Phillips, D. P. (1979). Suicide, motor vehicle fatalities, and the mass media: Evidence toward a theory of suggestion. *American Journal of Sociology, 84,* 1150-1174.

Phillips, D. P. (1983). The impact of mass media violence in U.S. homicides. *American Sociological Review, 48,* 560-568.

Phillips, D.P. (1986). Natural experiments on the effects of mass media violence on fatal aggression: Strengths and weaknesses of a new approach. In L. Berkowitz (Ed.), *Advances in Experimental Social Psychology* (Vol. 19, pp. 207-250). New York: Academic Press.

Phillips, D. P., & Carstensen, L. L. (1986). Clustering of teenage suicides after television news stories about suicide. *New England Journal of Medicine, 315,* 685-689.

Piferi, R. L., Jobe, R. L., & Jones, W. H. (2006). Giving to others during national tragedy: The effects of altruistic and egoistic motivations on long-term giving. *Journal of Social and Personal Relationships, 23,* 171-184.

Piliavin, I. M., Piliavin, J. A., & Rodin, J. (1975). Costs, diffusion, and the stigmatized victim. *Journal of Personality and Social Psychology, 32,* 429-438.

Piliavin, I. M., Rodin, J., & Piliavin, J. A. (1969). Good Samaritanism: An underground phenomenon? *Journal of Personality and Social Psychology, 13,* 289-299.

Piliavin, J. A., Dovidio, J. R., Gaertner, S. L. & Clark, R. D., III. (1981). *Emergency Intervention.* New York: Academic Press.

Piliavin, J. A., & Piliavin, I. M. (1972). Effect of blood on reactions to a victim. *Journal of Personality and Social Psychology, 23,* 353-361.

Piliavin, J. A., Piliavin, I. M., & Broll, L. (1976). Time of arrival at an emergency and likelihood of helping. *Personality and Social Psychology Bulletin, 2,* 273-276.

Pittman, T. (1975). Attribution of arousal as a mediator in dissonance reduction. *Journal of Experimental Social Psychology, 11,* 53-63.

Plaks, J. E., & Higgins, E. T. (2000). Pragmatic use of stereotyping in teamwork: Social loafing and compensation as a function of inferred partner-situation fit. *Journal of Personality and Social Psychology, 79,* 962-974.

Plant, E. A., & Devine, P. G. (1998). Internal and external motivation to respond without prejudice. *Journal of Personality and Social Psychology, 75,* 811-832.

Plant, E. A., Peruche, B. M., & Butz, D. A. (2005). Eliminating automatic racial bias: Making race non-diagnostic for responses to criminal suspects. *Journal of Experimental Social Psychology, 41,* 141-156.

Plous, S. (1985). Perceptual illusions and military realities: The nuclear arms race. *Journal of Conflict Resolution, 29,* 363-389.

Pollan, M. (2002). An animal's place. *The New York Times Magazine,* November 10, p. 58.

Pollock, C. L., Smith, S. D., Knowles, E. S., & Bruce, H. J. (1998). Mindfulness limits compliance with the that's-not-all technique. *Personality and Social Psychology Bulletin, 24,* 1153-1157.

Pomerantz, E. M., Chaiken, S., & Tordesillas, R. S. (1995). Attitude strength and resistance processes. *Journal of Personality and Social Psychology, 69,* 408-419.

Pope, H., Olivardia, R., Gruber, A., & Borowiecki, J. (1999). Evolving ideals of male body image as seen through action toys. *International Journal of Eating Disorders, 26,* 65-72.

Postmes, T., & Spears, R. (1998). Deindividuation and antinormative behavior: A meta-analysis. *Psychological Bulletin, 123,* 238-259.

Postmes, T., & Spears, R. (2002). Behavior online: Does anonymous computer communication reduce gender inequality? *Personality and Social Psychology Bulletin, 28,* 1073-1083.

Postmes, T., Spears, R., & Cihangir, S. (2001). Quality of decision making and group norms. *Journal of Personality and Social Psychology, 80,* 918-930.

Poston, I., Ericsson, M., Linder, J., Nilsson, T., Goodrick, G., & Foreyt, J. (1999). Personality and the prediction of weight loss and relapse in the treatment of obesity. *International Journal of Eating Disorders, 25,* 301-309.

Powell, A. A., Branscombe, N. R., & Schmitt, M. T. (2005). Inequality as ingroup privilege or outgroup disadvantage: The impact of group focus on collective guilt and interracial attitudes. *Personality and Social Psychology Bulletin, 31,* 508-521.

Powers, S. I., Pietromonaco, P. R., Gunlicks, M., & Sayer, A. (2006). Dating couples' attachment styles and patterns of cortisol reactivity and recovery in response to a relationship conflict. *Journal of Personality and Social Psychology, 90,* 613-628.

Pratkanis, A. R., Greenwald, A. G., Leippe, M. R., & Baumgardner, M. H. (1988). In search of reliable persuasion effects: III. The sleeper effect is dead: Long live the sleeper effect. *Journal of Personality and Social Psychology, 54,* 203-218.

Pratto, F., & John, O. (1991). Automatic vigilance: The attention-grabbing power of negative social information. *Journal of Personality and Social Psychology, 61*, 380-391.

Pratto, F., Sidanius, J., Stallworth, L. M., & Malle, B. F. (1994). Social dominance orientation: A personality variable predicting social and political attitudes. *Journal of Personality and Social Psychology, 67*, 741-763.

Prentice, D. A., & Miller, D. T. (1993). Pluralistic ignorance and alcohol use on campus: Some consequences of misperceiving the social norm. *Journal of Personality and Social Psychology, 64*, 243-256.

Prentice-Dunn, S., & Rogers, R. W. (1980). Effects of deindividuating situational cues and aggressive models on subjective deindividuation and aggression. *Journal of Personality and Social Psychology, 39*, 104-113.

Prentice-Dunn, S., & Rogers, R. W. (1982). Effects of public and private self-awareness on deindividuation and aggression. *Journal of Personality and Social Psychology, 43*, 503-513.

Pressman, S. D., Cohen, S., Miller, G. E., Barkin, A., Rabin, B. S., & Treanor, J. J. (2005). Loneliness, social network size, and immune response to influenza vaccination in college freshmen. *Health Psychology, 24*, 297-306.

Priester, J. R., & Petty, R. E. (1995). Source attributions and persuasion: Perceived honesty as a determinant of message scrutiny. *Personality and Social Psychology Bulletin, 21*, 637-654.

Pruitt, D. G., & Kimmel, M. J. (1977). Twenty years of experimental gaming: Critique, synthesis, and suggestions for the future. *Annual Review of Psychology, 28*, 363-392.

Quattrone, G., & Jones, E. (1978). Selective self-disclosure with and without correspondent performance. *Journal of Experimental Social Psychology, 14*, 511-526.

Queller, S., & Smith, E. R. (2002). Subtyping versus bookkeeping in stereotype learning and change: Connectionist simulations and empirical findings. *Journal of Personality and Social Psychology, 82*, 300-313.

Rajecki, D. W., Bledsoe, S. B., & Rasmussen, J. L. (1991). Successful personal ads: Gender differences and similarities in offers, stipulations, and outcomes. *Basic and Applied Social Psychology, 12*, 457-469.

Ratcliff, J. J., Lassiter, G. D., Schmidt, H. C., & Snyder, C. J. (2006). Camera perspective bias in videotaped confessions: Experimental evidence of its perceptual basis. *Journal of Experimental Psychology: Applied, 12*, 197-206.

Ratcliff, J.J., Lassiter, G.D., Markman, K.D., & Snyder, C.J. (2006). Gender differences in attitudes toward gay men and lesbians: The role of motivation to respond without prejudice. *Personality and Social Psychology Bulletin, 33*, 1325-1338.

Reeder, G., Vonk, R., Ronk, M., Ham, J., & Lawrence, M. (2004). Dispositional attribution: Multiple inferences about motive-related traits. *Journal of Personality and Social Psychology, 86*, 530-544.

Regan, D. T. (1971). Effects of a favor and liking on compliance. *Journal of Experimental Social Psychology, 7*, 627-639.

Regan, D., & Fazio, R. (1977). On the consistency between attitudes and behavior: Look to the method of attitude formation. *Journal of Experimental Social Psychology, 13*, 28-45.

Regan, D. T., Williams, M., & Sparling, S. (1972). Voluntary expiation of guilt: A field experiment. *Journal of Personality and Social Psychology, 24*, 42-45.

Regan, P. C. (2000). The role of sexual desire and sexual activity in dating relationships. *Social Behavior and Personality, 28*, 51-59.

Rehm, J., Steinleitner, M., & Lilli, W. (1987). Wearing uniforms and aggression: A field experiment. *European Journal of Social Psychology, 17*, 357-360.

Reifman, A., Larrick, R., & Fein, S. (1991). Temper and temperature on the diamond: The heat-aggression relationship in major-league baseball. *Personality and Social Psychology Bulletin, 17*, 580–585.

Reinhardt, J. P., Boerner, K., & Horowitz, A. (2006). Good to have but not to use: Differential impact of perceived and received support on well-being. *Journal of Social and Personal Relationships, 23*, 117-129.

Reis, H. T., & Aron, A. (2008). Love: What is it, why does it matter, and how does it operate? *Perspectives on Psychological Science, 3*, 80-86.

Reis, H. T., & Collins, W. A. (2004). Relationships, human behavior, and psychological science. *Current Directions in Psychological Science, 13*, 233-237.

Reis, H. T., Collins, W. A., & Berscheid, E. (2000). The relationship context of human behavior and development. *Psychological Bulletin, 126*, 844-872.

Reis, H.T., & Wheeler, L. (1991). Studying social interaction with the Rochester Interaction Record. In M. P. Zanna (Ed.), *Advances in Experimental Social Psychology* (Vol. 24, pp. 270-318). San Diego: Academic Press.

Reno, R. R., Cialdini, R. B., & Kallgren, C. A. (1993). The transsituational influence of social norms. *Journal of Personality and Social Psychology, 64*, 104-112.

Rennison, C. M., & Welchans, S. (2000). Intimate Partner Violence Special Report, NCJ 178247. Washington, DC: US Department of Justice.

Reynolds, K. J., Turner, J. C., & Haslam, S. A. (2000). When are we better than them and they worse than us? A closer look at social discrimination in positive and negative domains. *Journal of Personality and Social Psychology, 78*, 64-80.

Rhee, E., Uleman, J., Lee, H., & Roman, R. (1995). Spontaneous self-descriptions and ethnic identities in individualistic and collectivistic cultures. *Journal of Personality and Social Psychology, 69*, 142-152.

Rhodes, G., Halberstadt, J., Jeffery, L., & Palermo, R. (2005). The attractiveness of average faces is not a generalized mere exposure effect. *Social Cognition, 23*, 205-217.

Rhodes, G., Sumich, A., & Byatt, G. (1999). Are average facial configurations attractive only because of their symmetry? *Psychological Science, 10*, 52-58.

Rhodewalt, F., Sanbonmatsu, D., Tschanz, B., Feick, D., & Waller, A. (1995). Self-handicapping and interpersonal trade-offs: The effects of claimed self-handicaps on observers' performance evaluations and feedback. *Personality and Social Psychology Bulletin, 21*, 1042-1050.

Richard, F. D., Bond, C. F. J., & Stokes-Zoota, J. J. (2001). 'That's completely obvious...and important': Lay judgments of social psychological findings. *Personality and Social Psychology Bulletin, 27*, 497-505.

Richards, J., & Gross, J. (1999). Composure at any cost? The cognitive consequences of emotion suppression. *Personality and Social Psychology Bulletin, 25*, 1033-1044.

Rigby, K., Brown, M., Anagnostou, P., Ross, M. W., & Rosser, B.R.S. (1989). Shock tactics to counter AIDS: The Australian experience. *Psychology & Health, 3*, 145-159.

Riggio, H. R. (2004). Parental marital conflict and divorce, parent-child relationships, social support, and relationship anxiety in young adulthood. *Personal Relationships, 11,* 99-114.

Rilling, J., Gutman, D., Zeh, T., Pagnoni, G., Berns, G., & Kilts, C. (2002). A neural basis for social cooperation. *Neuron, 35,* 395-405.

Risen, J. L., Gilovich, T., & Dunning, D. (2007). One-shot illusory correlations and stereotype formation. *Personality and Social Psychology Bulletin, 33,* 1492-1502.

Robinson, R. J., Keltner, D., Ward, A., & Ross, L. (1995). Actual versus assumed differences in construal: 'Naive realism' in intergroup perception and conflict. *Journal of Personality and Social Psychology, 68,* 404-417.

Rochat, F., & Modigliani, A. (1995). The ordinary quality of resistance: From Milgram's laboratory to the village of Le Chambon. *Journal of Social Issues, 51,* 195-210.

Rodkin, P. C., Farmer, T. W., Pearl, R., & Van Acker, R. (2000). Heterogeneity of popular boys: Antisocial and prosocial configurations. *Developmental Psychology, 36,* 14-24.

Roese, N. (1994). The functional basis of counterfactual thinking. *Journal of Personality and Social Psychology, 66,* 805-818.

Rogers, R. W., & Prentice-Dunn, S. (1981). Deindividuation and anger-mediated interracial aggression: Unmasking regressive racism. *Journal of Personality and Social Psychology, 41,* 63-73.

Rosenberg, M. (1965). *Society and the Adolescent Self-image.* Princeton, NJ: Princeton University Press.

Rosenfeld, P., Giacalone, R., & Tedeschi, J. (1984). Cognitive dissonance and impression management explanations for effort justification. *Personality and Social Psychology Bulletin, 10,* 394-401.

Rosenhan, D. (1973). On being sane in insane places. *Science, 179,* 250-258.

Rosenhan, D. L., Salovey, P., & Hargis, K. (1981). The joys of helping: Focus of attention mediates the impact of positive affect on altruism. *Journal of Personality and Social Psychology, 40,* 899-905.

Rosenthal, A.M. (1964). *Thirty-Eight Witnesses: The Kitty Genovese Case.* Berkeley, CA: University of California Press.

Rosenthal, R. (1994). Interpersonal expectancy effects: A 30-year perspective. *Current Directions in Psychological Science, 3,* 176-179.

Rosenthal, R., & Fode, K. (1963). The effect of experimenter bias on the performance of the albino rat. *Behavioral Science, 8,* 183-189.

Rosenthal, R., & Jacobson, L. (1968). *Pygmalion in the Classroom: Teacher Expectation and Pupils' Intellectual Development.* New York: Holt, Rinehart & Winston.

Ross, L., Amabile, T., & Steinmetz, J. (1977). Social roles, social control, and biases in social-perception processes. *Journal of Personality and Social Psychology, 35,* 485-494.

Ross, L., Greene, D., & House, P. (1977). The false consensus effect: An egocentric bias in social perception and attribution processes. *Journal of Experimental Social Psychology, 13,* 279-301.

Ross, L., Lepper, M., & Hubbard, M. (1975). Perseverance in self-perception and social perception: Biased attributional processes in the debriefing paradigm. *Journal of Personality and Social Psychology, 32,* 880-892.

Ross, M., & Sicoly, F. (1979). Egocentric biases in availability and attribution. *Journal of Personality and Social Psychology, 37,* 322-336.

Rosselli, F., Skelly, J., & Mackie, D. (1995). Processing rational and emotional messages: The cognitive and affective mediation of persuasion. *Journal of Experimental Social Psychology, 31,* 163-190.

Rotenberg, K. J. (1994). Loneliness and interpersonal trust. *Journal of Social & Clinical Psychology, 13,* 152-173.

Rotenberg, K. J. (1997). Loneliness and the perception of the exchange of disclosures. *Journal of Social & Clinical Psychology, 16,* 259-276.

Rothbaum, F., & Tsang, B. Y. (1998). Lovesongs in the United States and China: On the nature of romantic love. *Journal of Cross-Cultural Psychology, 29,* 306-319.

Rothman, A., & Hardin, C. (1997). Differential use of the availability heuristic in social judgment. *Personality and Social Psychology Bulletin, 23,* 123-138.

Rothman, A., & Salovey, P. (1997). Shaping perceptions to motivate healthy behavior: The role of message framing. *Psychological Bulletin, 121,* 3-19.

Rothman, A., Salovey, P., Antone, C., & Keough, K. (1993). The influence of message framing on intentions to perform health behaviors. *Journal of Experimental Social Psychology, 29,* 408-433.

Rotton, J., & Frey, J. (1985). Air pollution, weather, and violent crimes: Concomitant time-series analysis of archival data. *Journal of Personality and Social Psychology, 49,* 1207-1220.

Rouhana, N. N., & Bar-Tal, D. (1998). Psychological dynamics of intractable ethnonational conflicts: The Israeli-Palestinian case. *American Psychologist, 53,* 761-770.

Rowatt, W., Cunningham, M., & Druen, P. (1998). Deception to get a date. *Personality and Social Psychology Bulletin, 24,* 1228-1242.

Ruback, R. B., & Juieng, D. (1997). Territorial defense in parking lots: Retaliation against waiting drivers. *Journal of Applied Social Psychology, 27,* 821-834.

Rubin, J. Z., Pruitt, D. G., & Kim, S. H. (1994). *Social Conflict: Escalation, Stalemate, and Settlement* (2nd Ed.). New York: McGraw-Hill.

Ruby, P., & Decety, J. (2004). How would you feel versus how do you think she would feel? A neuroimaging study of perspective-taking with social emotions. *Journal of Cognitive Neuroscience, 16,* 988-999.

Ruder, M., & Bless, H. (2003). Mood and the reliance on the ease of retrieval heuristic. *Journal of Personality and Social Psychology, 85,* 20-32.

Rudman, L. (1998). Self-promotion as a risk factor for women: The costs and benefits of counterstereotypical impression management. *Journal of Personality and Social Psychology, 74,* 629-645.

Rudman, L. A., Ashmore, R. D., & Gary, M. L. (2001). 'Unlearning' automatic biases: The malleability of implicit prejudice and stereotypes. *Journal of Personality and Social Psychology, 81,* 856-868.

Rudman, L., & Borgida, E. (1995). The afterglow of construct accessibility: The behavioral consequences of priming men to view women as sexual objects. *Journal of Experimental Social Psychology, 31,* 493-517.

Rudman, L., Phelan, J., & Heppen, J. (2007). Developmental sources of implicit attitudes. *Personality and Social Psychology Bulletin, 33,* 1700-1713.

Rule, N., & Ambady, N. (2008). The face of success: Inferences from chief executive officers' appearance predict company profits. *Psychological Science, 19,* 109-111.

Rusbult, C. E. (1980). Commitment and satisfaction in romantic associations: A test of the investment model. *Journal of Experimental Social Psychology, 16*, 172-186.

Rusbult, C. E. (1983). A longitudinal test of the investment model: The development (and deterioration) of satisfaction and commitment in heterosexual involvements. *Journal of Personality and Social Psychology, 45*, 101-117.

Rusbult, C. E., Van Lange, P. A. M., Wildschut, T., Yovetich, N. A., & Verette, J. (2000). Perceived superiority in close relationships: Why it exists and persists. *Journal of Personality and Social Psychology, 79*, 521-545.

Rusbult, C. E., & Martz, J. M. (1995). Remaining in an abusive relationship: An investment model analysis of nonvoluntary dependence. *Personality and Social Psychology Bulletin, 21*, 558-571.

Rusbult, C. E., Martz, J. M., & Agnew, C. R. (1998). The Investment Model Scale: Measuring commitment level, satisfaction level, quality of alternatives, and investment size. *Personal Relationships, 5*, 357-391.

Rusbult, C. E., & Zembrodt, I. M. (1983). Responses to dissatisfaction in romantic involvements: A multidimensional scaling analysis. *Journal of Experimental Social Psychology, 19*, 274-293.

Rusbult, C. E., Zembrodt, I. M., & Gunn, L. K. (1982). Exit, voice, loyalty, and neglect: Responses to dissatisfaction in romantic involvements. *Journal of Personality and Social Psychology, 43*, 1230-1242.

Rushton, J. P. (1975). Generosity in children: Immediate and long-term effects of modeling, preaching, and moral judgment. *Journal of Personality and Social Psychology, 31*, 459-466.

Rushton, J. P., Chrisjohn, R. D., & Fekken, G. C. (1981). The altruistic personality and the Self-Report Altruism Scale. *Personality and Individual Differences, 2*, 293-302.

Rushton, J. P., Fulker, D. W., Neale, M. C., Nias, D. K. B., & Eysenck, H. J. (1986). Altruism and aggression: The heritability of individual differences. *Journal of Personality and Social Psychology, 50*, 1192-1198.

Rushton, J. P., & Teachman, G. (1978). The effects of positive reinforcement, attributions, and punishment on model induced altruism in children. *Personality and Social Psychology Bulletin, 4*, 322-325.

Russell, D., Peplau, L. A., & Cutrona, C. E. (1980). The revised UCLA Loneliness Scale: Concurrent and discriminant validity evidence. *Journal of Personality and Social Psychology, 39*, 472-480.

Russell, J. (1995). Facial expressions of emotion: What lies beyond minimal universality? *Psychological Bulletin, 118*, 379-391.

Rusting, C. L., & Nolen-Hoeksema, S. (1998). Regulating responses to anger: Effects of rumination and distraction on angry mood. *Journal of Personality and Social Psychology, 74*, 790-803.

Rutkowski, G. K., Gruder, C. L., & Romer, D. (1983). Group cohesiveness, social norms, and bystander intervention. *Journal of Personality and Social Psychology, 44*, 545-552.

Ryan, C. S. (1996). Accuracy of Black and White college students' in-group and out-group stereotypes. *Personality and Social Psychology Bulletin, 22*, 1114-1127.

Ryan, C. S., & Bogart, L. M. (1997). Development of new group members' in-group and out-group stereotypes: Changes in perceived variability and ethnocentrism. *Journal of Personality and Social Psychology, 73*, 719-732.

Ryan, C. S., Judd, C. M., & Park, B. (1996). Effects of racial stereotypes on judgments of individuals: The moderating role of perceived group variability. *Journal of Experimental Social Psychology, 32*, 71-103.

Ryan, R. M., La Guardia, J. G., Solky-Butzel, J., Chirkov, V., & Kim, Y. (2005). On the interpersonal regulation of emotions: Emotional reliance across gender, relationships, and cultures. *Personal Relationships, 12*, 145-163.

Ryckman, R., Robbins, M., Kaczor, L., & Gold, J. (1989). Male and female raters' stereotyping of male and female physiques. *Personality and Social Psychology Bulletin, 15*, 244-251.

Sabini, J., & Green, M. C. (2004). Emotional responses to sexual and emotional infidelity: Constants and differences across genders, samples, and methods. *Personality and Social Psychology Bulletin, 30*, 1375-1388.

Sadalla, E. K., Kenrick, D. T., & Vershure, B. (1987). Dominance and heterosexual attraction. *Journal of Personality and Social Psychology, 52*, 730-738.

Safer, M. A. (1980). Attributing evil to the subject, not the situation: Student reaction to Milgram's film on obedience. *Personality and Social Psychology Bulletin, 6*, 205-209.

Sagarin, B. J., Cialdini, R. B., Rice, W. E., & Serna, S. B. (2002). Dispelling the illusion of invulnerability: The motivations and mechanisms of resistance to persuasion. *Journal of Personality and Social Psychology, 83*, 526-541.

Salganik, M. J., Dodds, P. S., & Watts, D. J. (2006). Experimental study of inequality and unpredictability in an artificial cultural market. *Science, 311*, 854-856.

Salmon, D. A., & Omer, S. B. (2006). Individual freedoms versus collective responsibility: Immunization decision-making in the face of occasionally competing values. *Emerging Themes in Epidemiology, 3*, 13.

Salomon, K., & Jagusztyn, N. E. (2008). Resting cardiovascular levels and reactivity to interpersonal incivility among Black, Latina/o, and White individuals: The moderating role of ethnic discrimination. *Health Psychology, 27*, 473-481.

Salvatore, J., & Shelton, J. N. (2007). Cognitive costs of exposure to racial prejudice. *Psychological Science, 18*, 810-815.

Samuelson, C. D., Messick, D. M., Rutte, C., & Wilke, H. (1984). Individual and structural solutions to resource dilemmas in two cultures. *Journal of Personality and Social Psychology, 47*, 94-104.

Sanchez-Burks, J., Nisbett, R. E., & Ybarra, O. (2000). Cultural styles, relationship schemas, and prejudice against out-groups. *Journal of Personality and Social Psychology, 79*, 174-189.

Sanderson, C. A., Darley, J. M., & Messinger, C. S. (2002). 'I'm not as thin as you think I am': The development and consequences of feeling discrepant from the thinness norm. *Personality and Social Psychology Bulletin, 28*, 172-183.

Sanford, A., Fay, N., Stewart, A., & Moxey, L. (2002). Perspective in statements of quantity, with implications for consumer psychology. *Psychological Science, 13*, 130-134.

Sangrigoli, S., Pallier, C., Argenti, A. M., Ventureyra, V. A. G., & de Schonen, S. (2005). Reversibility of the other-race effect in face recognition during childhood. *Psychological Science, 16*, 440-444.

Sanitioso, R., & Wlodarski, R. (2004). In search of information that confirms a desired self perception: Motivated processing of social feedback and choice of social interactions. *Personality and Social Psychology Bulletin, 30*, 412-422.

Sanna, L., & Turley, K. (1996). Antecedents to spontaneous counterfactual thinking: Effects of expectancy violation and outcome valence. *Personality and Social Psychology Bulletin, 22*, 906-919.

Sato, K. (1987). Distribution of the cost of maintaining common resources. *Journal of Experimental Social Psychology, 23*, 19-31.

Saulnier, K., & Perlman, D. (1981). The actor-observer bias is alive and well in prison: A sequel to Wells. *Personality and Social Psychology Bulletin, 7*, 559-564.

Savitsky, K., Epley, N., & Gilovich, T. (2001). Do others judge us as harshly as we think? Overestimating the impact of our failures, shortcomings, and mishaps. *Journal of Personality and Social Psychology, 81*, 44-56.

Savitsky, K., Medvec, V., Charlton, A., & Gilovich, T. (1998). 'What, me worry?' Arousal, misattribution and the effect of temporal distance on confidence. *Personality and Social Psychology Bulletin, 24*, 529-536.

Sbarra, D. A. (2006). Predicting the onset of emotional recovery following nonmarital relationship dissolution: Survival analyses of sadness and anger. *Personality and Social Psychology Bulletin, 32*, 298-312.

Sbarra, D. A., & Emery, R. E. (2005). The emotional sequelae of nonmarital relationship dissolution: Analysis of change and intraindividual variability over time. *Personal Relationships, 12*, 213-232.

Schachner, D. A., & Shaver, P. R. (2004). Attachment dimensions and sexual motives. *Personal Relationships, 11*, 179-195.

Schachter, S. (1951). Deviation, rejection and communication. *Journal of Abnormal and Social Psychology, 46*, 190-207.

Schachter, S., & Singer, J. (1962). Cognitive, social, and physiological determinants of emotional state. *Psychological Review, 69*, 379-399.

Schaller, M., Asp, C. H., Rosell, M. C., & Heim, S. J. (1996). Training in statistical reasoning inhibits the formation of erroneous group stereotypes. *Personality and Social Psychology Bulletin, 22*, 829-844.

Schaller, M., & Cialdini, R. B. (1988). The economics of empathic helping: Support for a mood management motive. *Journal of Experimental Social Psychology, 24*, 163-181.

Scharf, M., & Hertz-Lazarowitz, R. (2003). Social networks in the school context: Effects of culture and gender. *Journal of Personal Relationships, 20*, 843-859.

Scheier, M., & Carver, C. (1993). On the power of positive thinking: The benefits of being optimistic. *Current Directions in Psychological Science, 2*, 26-30.

Scher, S., & Cooper, J. (1989). Motivational basis of dissonance: The singular role of behavioral consequences. *Journal of Personality and Social Psychology, 56*, 899-906.

Schkade, D., & Kahneman, D. (1998). Does living in California make people happy? A focusing illusion in judgments of life satisfaction. *Psychological Science, 9*, 340-346.

Schlenker, B. R., & Britt, T. W. (1999). Beneficial impression management: Strategically controlling information to help friends. *Journal of Personality and Social Psychology, 76*, 559-573.

Schlenker, B. R., Phillips, S. T., Boniecki, K. A., & Schlenker, D. R. (1995a). Championship pressures: Choking or triumphing in one's own territory? *Journal of Personality and Social Psychology, 68*, 632-643.

Schlenker, B. R., Phillips, S. T., Boniecki, K. A., & Schlenker, D. R. (1995b). Where is the home choke? *Journal of Personality and Social Psychology, 68*, 649-652.

Schlenker, B., & Trudeau, J. (1990). Impact of self-presentations on private self-beliefs: Effects of prior self-beliefs and misattribution. *Journal of Personality and Social Psychology, 58*, 22-32.

Schmader, T., & Johns, M. (2003). Converging evidence that stereotype threat reduces working memory capacity. *Journal of Personality and Social Psychology, 85*, 440-452.

Schmidt, G., & Weiner, B. (1988). An attribution-affect-action theory of behavior: Replications of judgments of help-giving. *Personality and Social Psychology Bulletin, 14*, 610-621.

Schmitt, D., & Allik, J. (2005). Simultaneous administration of the Rosenberg self-esteem scale in 53 nations: Exploring the universal and culture-specific features of global self-esteem. *Journal of Personality and Social Psychology, 89*, 623-642.

Schmitt, B. H., Gilovich, T., Goore, N., & Joseph, L. (1986). Mere presence and social facilitation: One more time. *Journal of Experimental Social Psychology, 22*, 242-248.

Schmitt, D. P., Alcalay, L., Allik, J., Ault, L., Austers, I., Bennett, K. L., et al. (2003). Universal sex differences in the desire for sexual variety: Tests from 52 nations, 6 continents, and 13 islands. *Journal of Personality and Social Psychology, 85*, 85-104.

Schmitt, D. P. (2005). Is short-term mating the maladaptive result of insecure attachment? A test of competing evolutionary perspectives. *Personality and Social Psychology Bulletin, 31*, 747-768.

Schmitt, D. P., Couden, A., & Baker, M. (2001). The effects of sex and temporal context on feelings of romantic desire: An experimental evaluation of sexual strategies theory. *Personality and Social Psychology Bulletin, 27*, 833-847.

Schmitt, M. T., & Branscombe, N. R. (2002). The internal and external causal loci of attributions to prejudice. *Personality and Social Psychology Bulletin, 28*, 620-628.

Schmitt, M. T., Branscombe, N. R., Kobrynowicz, D., & Owen, S. (2002). Perceiving discrimination against one's gender group has different implications for well-being in women and men. *Personality and Social Psychology Bulletin, 28*, 197-210.

Schneider, M. E., Major, B., Luhtanen, R., & Crocker, J. (1996). Social stigma and the potential costs of assumptive help. *Personality and Social Psychology Bulletin, 22*, 201-209.

Schopler, J., Insko, C. A., Drigotas, S. M., Wieselquist, J., Pemberton, M., & Cox, C. (1995). The role of identifiability in the reduction of interindividual-intergroup discontinuity. *Journal of Experimental Social Psychology, 31*, 553-574.

Schreiber, G., Robins, M., Striegel-Moore, R., Obarzanek, E., Morrison, J.A., & Wright, D.J. (1996). Weight modification efforts reported by black and white preadolescent girls: National Heart, Lung, and Blood Institute Growth and Health Study. *Pediatrics, 98*, 63-70.

Schroeder, C. M., & Prentice, D. A. (1998). Exposing pluralistic ignorance to reduce alcohol use among college students. *Journal of Applied Social Psychology, 28*, 2150-2180.

Schroeder, D. A., Penner, L. A., Dovidio, J. F., & Piliavin, J. A. (1995). *The Psychology of Helping and Altruism: Problems and Puzzles.* New York: McGraw-Hill.

Schütz, A. (1999). It was your fault! Self-serving biases in autobiographical accounts of conflicts in married couples. *Journal of Social and Personal Relationships, 16*, 193-208.

Schultz, T., Léveillé, E., & Lepper, M. (1999). Free choice and cognitive dissonance revisited: Choosing 'lesser evils' versus 'greater goods.' *Personality and Social Psychology Bulletin, 25*, 40-48.

Schulz-Hardt, S., Frey, D., Lüthgens, C., & Moscovici, S. (2000). Biased information search in group decision making. *Journal of Personality and Social Psychology, 78,* 655-669.

Schwarz, N. (1998). Accessible content and accessibility experiences: The interplay of declarative and experiential information in judgment. *Personality and Social Psychology Review, 2,* 87-99.

Schwarz, N., Bless, H., Strack, F., Klumpp, G., Rittenauer-Schatka, H., & Simons, A. (1991). Ease of retrieval as information: Another look at the availability heuristic. *Journal of Personality and Social Psychology, 61,* 195-202.

Schwarz, N., Hippler, H., Deutsch, B., & Strack, F. (1985). Response scales: Effects of category range on reported behavior and comparative judgments. *Public Opinion Quarterly, 49,* 388-395.

Schwarz, N., Strack, F., & Mai, H. (1991). Assimilation and contrast effects in part-whole question sequences: A conversational logic analysis. *Public Opinion Quarterly, 55,* 3-23.

Schwarzwald, J., Bizman, A., & Raz, M. (1983). The foot-in-the-door paradigm: Effects of second request size on donation probability and donor generosity. *Personality and Social Psychology Bulletin, 9,* 443-450.

Schweitzer, M. E., DeChurch, L. A., & Gibson, D. E. (2005). Conflict frames and the use of deception: Are competitive negotiators less ethical? *Journal of Applied Social Psychology, 35,* 2123-2149.

Sczesny, S., & Kühnen, U. (2004). Meta-cognition about biological sex and gender-stereotypic physical appearance: Consequences for the assessment of leadership competence. *Personality and Social Psychology Bulletin, 30,* 13-21.

Searcy, E., & Eisenberg, N. (1992). Defensiveness in response to aid from a sibling. *Journal of Personality and Social Psychology, 62,* 422-433.

Sears, D. O. (1986). College sophomores in the laboratory: Influences of a narrow data base on social psychology's view of human nature. *Journal of Personality and Social Psychology, 51,* 515-530.

Sears, D. O., & Henry, P. J. (2003). The origins of symbolic racism. *Journal of Personality and Social Psychology, 85,* 259-275.

Sechrist, G. B., & Stangor, C. (2001). Perceived consensus influences intergroup behavior and stereotype accessibility. *Journal of Personality and Social Psychology, 80,* 645-654.

Sedikides, C. (1993). Assessment, enhancement, and verification determinants of the self-evaluation process. *Journal of Personality and Social Psychology, 65,* 317-338.

Sedikides, C., & Anderson, C. (1994). Causal perceptions of intertrait relations: The glue that holds person types together. *Personality and Social Psychology Bulletin, 20,* 294-302.

Sedikides, C., Campbell, W., Reeder, G., & Elliot, A. (1998). The self-serving bias in relational context. *Journal of Personality and Social Psychology, 74,* 378-386.

Sedikides, C., Oliver, M. B., & Campbell, W. K. (1994). Perceived benefits and costs of romantic relationships for women and men: Implications for exchange theory. *Personal Relationships, 1,* 5-21.

Segal, N. L. (1993). Twin, sibling, and adoption methods: Tests of evolutionary hypotheses. *American Psychologist, 48,* 943-956.

Segrin, C., Taylor, M. E., & Altman, J. (2005). Social cognitive mediators and relational outcomes associated with parental divorce. *Journal of Social and Personal Relationships, 22,* 361-377.

Seidman, G., Shrout, P. E., & Bolger, N. (2006). Why is enacted social support associated with increased distress?: Using simulation to test two possible sources of spuriousness. *Personality and Social Psychology Bulletin, 32,* 52-65.

Seiter, J. S., & Gass, R. H. (2005). The effect of patriotic messages on restaurant tipping. *Journal of Applied Social Psychology, 35,* 1197-1205.

Sekaquaptewa, D., & Thompson, M. (2002). The differential effects of solo status on members of high- and low-status groups. *Personality and Social Psychology Bulletin, 28,* 694-707.

Sellers, R. M., & Shelton, J. N. (2003). The role of racial identity in perceived racial discrimination. *Journal of Personality and Social Psychology, 84,* 1079-1092.

Seta, C., Hayes, N., & Seta, J. (1994). Mood, memory, and vigilance: The influence of distraction on recall and impression formation. *Personality and Social Psychology Bulletin, 20,* 170-177.

Shackelford, T. K., & Larsen, R. J. (1997). Facial asymmetry as an indicator of psychological, emotional, and physiological distress. *Journal of Personality and Social Psychology, 72,* 456-466.

Shapiro, D. L., & Brett, J. M. (1993). Comparing three processes underlying judgments of procedural justice: A field study of mediation and arbitration. *Journal of Personality and Social Psychology, 65,* 1167-1177.

Shariff, A. F., & Norenzayan, A. (2007). God is watching you: Priming God concepts increases prosocial behavior in an anonymous economic game. *Psychological Science, 18,* 803-809.

Sharp, F. C. (1928). *Ethics.* New York: Century Company.

Sharp, M., & Getz, J. (1996). Substance use as impression management. *Personality and Social Psychology Bulletin, 22,* 60-67.

Sharpe, D., Adair, J., & Roese, N. (1992). Twenty years of deception research: A decline in subjects' trust? *Personality and Social Psychology Bulletin, 18,* 585-590.

Sharpsteen, D. J. (1995). The effects of relationship and self-esteem threats on the likelihood of romantic jealousy. *Journal of Social and Personal Relationships, 12,* 89-101.

Sheeran, P., Abraham, C., & Orbell, S. (1999). Psychosocial correlates of heterosexual condom use: A meta-analysis. *Psychological Bulletin. 125,* 90-132.

Sheese, B. E., & Graziano, W. G. (2005). Deciding to defect: The effects of video-game violence on cooperative behavior. *Psychological Science, 16,* 354-357.

Sheldon, K. (1996). The Social Awareness Inventory: Development and applications. *Personality and Social Psychology Bulletin, 22,* 620-634.

Sheldon, K. (2005). Positive value change during college: Normative trends and individual differences. *Journal of Research in Personality, 39,* 209-223.

Sheldon, K. M. (1999). Learning the lessons of tit-for-tat: Even competitors can get the message. *Journal of Personality and Social Psychology, 77,* 1245-1253.

Sheldon, K., Ryan, R., Deci, E., & Kasser, T. (2004). The independent effects of goal contents and motives on well-being: It's both what you pursue and why you pursue it. *Personality and Social Psychology Bulletin, 30,* 475-486.

Shell, R. M., & Eisenberg, N. (1992). A developmental model of recipients' reactions to aid. *Psychological Bulletin, 111,* 413-433.

Shelton, J. N., & Richeson, J. A. (2005). Intergroup contact and pluralistic ignorance. *Journal of Personality and Social Psychology, 88,* 91-107.

Shelton, J. N., Richeson, J. A., Salvatore, J., & Trawalter, S. (2005). Ironic effects of racial bias during interracial interactions. *Psychological Science, 16,* 397-402.

Shepperd, J. (1993a). Student derogation of the Scholastic Aptitude Test: Biases in perceptions and presentations of college board scores. *Basic and Applied Social Psychology, 14,* 455-473.

Shepperd, J. A. (1993b). Productivity loss in performance groups: A motivation analysis. *Psychological Bulletin, 113,* 67-81.

Shepperd, J., & Taylor, K. (1999a). Ascribing advantages to social comparison targets. *Basic and Applied Social Psychology, 21,* 103-117.

Shepperd, J. A., & Taylor, K. M. (1999b). Social loafing and expectancy-value theory. *Personality and Social Psychology Bulletin, 25,* 1147-1158.

Sherif, M. (1936). *The Psychology of Social Norms.* New York: Harper.

Sherif, M., Harvey, O. J., White, B. J., Hood, W. R., & Sherif, C. W. (1961). *Intergroup Conflict and Cooperation: The Robbers Cave Experiment.* Norman, OK: University of Oklahoma Book Exchange.

Sherif, M. (1966). *The Psychology of Social Norms.* Oxford, England: Harper Torchbooks.

Sherman, D. A. K., Nelson, L. D., & Steele, C. M. (2000). Do messages about health risks threaten the self? Increasing the acceptance of threatening health messages via self-affirmation. *Personality and Social Psychology Bulletin, 26,* 1046-1058.

Sherman, M. D., & Thelen, M. H. (1996). Fear of Intimacy Scale: Validation and extension with adolescents. *Journal of Social and Personal Relationships, 13,* 507-521.

Sherman, R., Buddie, A., Dragan, K., End, C., & Finney, L. (1999). Twenty years of PSPB: Trends in content, design, and analysis. *Personality and Social Psychology Bulletin, 25,* 177-187.

Sherr, L. (1990). Fear arousal and AIDS: Do shock tactics work? *AIDS, 4,* 361-364.

Shih, M., Pittinsky, T. L., & Ambady, N. (1999). Stereotype susceptibility: Identity salience and shifts in quantitative performance. *Psychological Science, 10,* 80-83.

Shook, N. J., & Fazio, R. H. (2008). Interracial roommate relationships: An experimental field test of the contact hypothesis. *Psychological Science, 19,* 717-723.

Shotland, R. L., & Heinold, W. D. (1985). Bystander response to arterial bleeding: Helping skills, the decision-making process, and differentiating the helping response. *Journal of Personality and Social Psychology, 49,* 347-356.

Shotland, R. L., & Straw, M. K. (1976). Bystander response to an assault: When a man attacks a woman. *Journal of Personality and Social Psychology, 34,* 990-999.

Sidanius, J., & Pratto, F. (2001). *Social Dominance: An Intergroup Theory of Social Hierarchy and Oppression.* New York: Cambridge University Press.

Siegel, J. M. (1990). Stressful life events and use of physician services among the elderly: The moderating role of pet ownership. *Journal of Personality and Social Psychology, 58,* 1081-1086.

Siegel, J. T., Alvaro, E. M., Crano, W. D., Lac, A., Ting, S., & Jones, S. P. (2008). A quasi-experimental investigation of message appeal variations on organ donor registration rates. *Health Psychology, 27,* 170-178.

Silverstein, B., Perdue, L., Peterson, B., & Kelly, E. (1986). The role of the mass media in promoting a thin standard of bodily attractiveness for women. *Sex Roles, 14,* 519-532.

Silvia, P. J. (2005). Deflecting reactance: The role of similarity in increasing compliance and reducing resistance. *Basic and Applied Social Psychology, 27,* 277-284.

Simmons, C. H., vom Kolke, A., & Shimizu, H. (1986). Attitudes toward romantic love among American, German, and Japanese students. *Journal of Social Psychology, 126,* 327-336.

Simon, D., Krawczyk, D., & Holyoak, K. (2004). Construction of preferences by constraint satisfaction. *Psychological Science, 15,* 331-336.

Simon, L., & Greenberg, J. (1996). Further progress in understanding the effects of derogatory ethnic labels: The role of preexisting attitudes toward the targeted group. *Personality and Social Psychology Bulletin, 22,* 1195-1204.

Simon, L., Greenberg, J., & Brehm, J. (1995). Trivialization: The forgotten mode of dissonance reduction. *Journal of Personality and Social Psychology, 68,* 247-260.

Simpson, D., & Ostrom, T. (1976). Contrast effects in impression formation. *Journal of Personality and Social Psychology, 34,* 625-629.

Simpson, J. A., Gangestad, S. W., & Lerman, M. (1990). Perception of physical attractiveness: Mechanisms involved in the maintenance of romantic relationships. *Journal of Personality and Social Psychology, 59,* 1192-1201.

Simpson, J. A., Ickes, W., & Blackstone, T. (1995). When the head protects the heart: Empathic accuracy in dating relationships. *Journal of Personality and Social Psychology, 69,* 629-641.

Simpson, J. A., Rholes, W. S., & Nelligan, J. S. (1992). Support seeking and support giving within couples in an anxiety-provoking situation: The role of attachment styles. *Journal of Personality and Social Psychology, 62,* 434-446.

Simpson, J. A., Rholes, W. S., & Phillips, D. (1996). Conflict in close relationships: An attachment perspective. *Journal of Personality and Social Psychology, 71,* 899-914.

Singelis, T., Triandis, H., Bhawuk, D., & Gelfand, M. (1995). Horizontal and vertical dimensions of individualism and collectivism: A theoretical and measurement refinement. *Cross-Cultural Research: The Journal of Comparative Social Science, 29,* 240-275.

Singh, D. (1993). Body shape and women's attractiveness: The critical role of waist-to-hip ratio. *Human Nature, 4,* 297-321.

Singh, D. (1995). Female judgment of male attractiveness and desirability for relationships: Role of waist-to-hip ratio and financial status. *Journal of Personality and Social Psychology, 69,* 1089-1101.

Skelton, J. A. & Pennebaker, J. W. (1982). The psychology of physical symptoms and sensations. In G. S. Sanders & J. Suls (Eds.), *Social Psychology of Health and Illness* (99-128). Hillsdale, NJ: Lawrence Erlbaum Associates.

Skinner, B. (1938). *The Behavior of Organisms: An Experimental Analysis.* Oxford, England: Appleton-Century.

Skitka, L.J. (1999). Ideological and attributional boundaries on public compassion: Reactions to individuals and communities affected by a natural disaster. *Personality and Social Psychology Bulletin, 25,* 793-808.

Skitka, L. J., Bauman, C. W., & Sargis, E. G. (2005). Moral conviction: Another contributor to attitude strength or something more? *Journal of Personality and Social Psychology, 88,* 895-917.

Skitka, L. J., & Tetlock, P. E. (1993). Providing public assistance: Cognitive and motivational processes underlying liberal and conservative policy preferences. *Journal of Personality and Social Psychology, 65,* 1205-1223.

Slavin, R. E., & Cooper, R. (1999). Improving intergroup relations: Lessons learned from cooperative learning programs. *Journal of Social Issues, 55,* 647-663.

Slavin, R. E., & Madden, N. A. (1979). School practices that improve race relations. *American Educational Research Journal, 16,* 169-180.

Sloan, J. H., Kellermann, A. L., Reay, D. T., & Ferris, J. A. (1988). Handgun regulations, crime, assaults, and homicide: A tale of two cities. *New England Journal of Medicine, 319,* 1256-1262.

Slone, A. E., Brigham, J. C., & Meissner, C. A. (2000). Social and cognitive factors affecting the own-race bias in Whites. *Basic and Applied Social Psychology, 22,* 71-84.

Slovic, P., & Fischhoff, B. (1977). On the psychology of experimental surprise. *Journal of Experimental Psychology: Human Perception and Performance, 3,* 544-551.

Smith, A., Jussim, L., & Eccles, J. (1999). Do self-fulfilling prophecies accumulate, dissipate, or remain stable over time? *Journal of Personality and Social Psychology, 77,* 548-565.

Smith, C. L., Gelfand, D. M., Hartmann, D. P., & Partlow, M. E. (1979). Children's causal attributions regarding help giving. *Child Development, 50,* 203-210.

Smith, E. R., & Henry, S. (1996). An in-group becomes part of the self: Response time evidence. *Personality and Social Psychology Bulletin, 22,* 635-642.

Smith, H. J., & Tyler, T. R. (1997). Choosing the right pond: The impact of group membership on self-esteem and group-oriented behavior. *Journal of Experimental Social Psychology, 33,* 146-170.

Smith, S. M., & Shaffer, D. R. (1991). Celerity and cajolery: Rapid speech may promote or inhibit persuasion through its impact on message elaboration. *Personality and Social Psychology Bulletin, 17,* 663-669.

Smith, S. M., & Shaffer, D. R. (1995). Speed of speech and persuasion: Evidence for multiple effects. *Personality and Social Psychology Bulletin, 21,* 1051-1060.

Snibbe, A., & Markus, H. (2005). You can't always get what you want: Educational attainment, agency, and choice. *Journal of Personality and Social Psychology, 88,* 703-720.

Snyder, C. R., Lassegard, M., & Ford, C. E. (1986). Distancing after group success and failure: Basking in reflected glory and cutting off reflected failure. *Journal of Personality and Social Psychology, 51,* 382-388.

Snyder, M. (1974). Self-monitoring of expressive behavior. *Journal of Personality and Social Psychology, 30,* 526-537.

Snyder, M., Berscheid, E., & Glick, P. (1985). Focusing on the exterior and the interior: Two investigations of the initiation of personal relationships. *Journal of Personality and Social Psychology, 48,* 1427-1439.

Snyder, M., & DeBono, K. G. (1985). Appeals to image and claims about quality: Understanding the psychology of advertising. *Journal of Personality and Social Psychology, 49,* 586-597.

Snyder, M., & Gangestad, S. (1986). On the nature of self-monitoring: Matters of assessment, matters of validity. *Journal of Personality and Social Psychology, 51,* 125-139.

Snyder, M., & Haugen, J. (1994). Why does behavioral confirmation occur? A functional perspective on the role of the perceiver. *Journal of Experimental Social Psychology, 30,* 218-246.

Snyder, M., Simpson, J., & Gangestad, S. (1986). Personality and sexual relations. *Journal of Personality and Social Psychology, 51,* 181-190.

Snyder, M., & Swann, W. (1978). Behavioral confirmation in social interaction: From social perception to social reality. *Journal of Experimental Social Psychology, 14,* 148-162.

Snyder, M., Tanke, E., & Berscheid, E. (1977). Social perception and interpersonal behavior: On the self-fulfilling nature of social stereotypes. *Journal of Personality and Social Psychology, 35,* 656-666.

Solano, C. H., Batten, P. G., & Parish, E. A. (1982). Loneliness and patterns of self-disclosure. *Journal of Personality and Social Psychology, 43,* 524-531.

Sommer, K. L., Horowitz, I. A., & Bourgeois, M. J. (2001). When juries fail to comply with the law: Biased evidence processing in individual and group decision making. *Personality and Social Psychology Bulletin, 27,* 309-320.

Sommers, S. R. (2006). On racial diversity and group decision making: Identifying multiple effects of racial composition on jury deliberations. *Journal of Personality and Social Psychology, 90,* 597-612.

Sommers, S. R., & Ellsworth, P. C. (2000). Race in the courtroom: Perceptions of guilt and dispositional attributions. *Personality and Social Psychology Bulletin, 26,* 1367-1379.

Son Hing, L. S., Bobocel, D. R., & Zanna, M. P. (2002). Meritocracy and opposition to affirmative action: Making concessions in the face of discrimination. *Journal of Personality and Social Psychology, 83,* 493-509.

Son Hing, L. S., Li, W., & Zanna, M. P. (2002). Inducing hypocrisy to reduce prejudicial responses among aversive racists. *Journal of Experimental Social Psychology, 38,* 71-78.

Sorrentino, R. M., & Field, N. (1986). Emergent leadership over time: The functional value of positive motivation. *Journal of Personality and Social Psychology, 50,* 1091-1099.

Spencer, S. J., Fein, S., Wolfe, C. T., Fong, C., & Dunn, M. A. (1998). Automatic activation of stereotypes: The role of self-image threat. *Personality and Social Psychology Bulletin, 24,* 1139-1152.

Spencer, S. J., Steele, C. M., & Quinn, D. M. (1999). Stereotype threat and women's math performance. *Journal of Experimental Social Psychology, 35,* 4-28.

Sprafkin, J. N., Liebert, R. M., & Poulos, R. W. (1975). Effects of a prosocial televised example on children's helping. *Journal of Experimental Child Psychology, 20,* 119-126.

Sprecher, S. (1987). The effects of self-disclosure given and received on affection for an intimate partner and stability of the relationship. *Journal of Social and Personal Relationships, 4,* 115-127.

Sprecher, S. (1999). 'I love you more today than yesterday': Romantic partners' perceptions of changes in love and related affect over time. *Journal of Personality and Social Psychology, 76,* 46-53.

Sprecher, S., McKinney, K., & Orbuch, T. L. (1991). The effect of current sexual behavior on friendship, dating, and marriage desirability. *Journal of Sex Research, 28,* 387-408.

Sprecher, S., Sullivan, Q., & Hatfield, E. (1994). Mate selection preferences: Gender differences examined in a national sample. *Journal of Personality and Social Psychology, 66,* 1074-1080.

Stangor, C., Sechrist, G. B., & Jost, J. T. (2001). Changing racial beliefs by providing consensus information. *Personality and Social Psychology Bulletin, 27,* 486-496.

Stangor, C., Swim, J. K., Van Allen, K. L., & Sechrist, G. B. (2002). Reporting discrimination in public and private contexts. *Journal of Personality and Social Psychology, 82,* 69-74.

Stapel, D., & Blanton, H. (2004). From seeing to being: Subliminal social comparisons affect implicit and explicit self-evaluations. *Journal of Personality and Social Psychology, 87,* 468-481.

Stapel, D., & Suls, J. (2004). Method matters: Effects of explicit versus implicit social comparisons on activation, behavior, and self-views. *Journal of Personality and Social Psychology, 87,* 860-875.

Stasser, G., Stewart, D. D., & Wittenbaum, G. M. (1995). Expert roles and information exchange during discussion: The importance of knowing who knows what. *Journal of Experimental Social Psychology, 31,* 244-265.

Stasser, G., & Titus, W. (1985). Pooling of unshared information in group decision making: Biased information sampling during discussion. *Journal of Personality and Social Psychology, 48,* 1467-1478.

Stattin, H., & Magnusson, D. (1989). The role of early aggressive behavior in the frequency, seriousness, and types of later crime. *Journal of Consulting and Clinical Psychology, 57,* 710-718.

Staub, E. (1996). Preventing genocide: Activating bystanders, helping victims, and the creation of caring. *Peace and Conflict: Journal of Peace Psychology, 2,* 189-200.

Staw, B. M., Barsade, S. G., & Koput, K. W. (1997). Escalation at the credit window: A longitudinal study of bank executives' recognition and write-off of problem loans. *Journal of Applied Psychology, 82,* 130-142.

Staw, B. M., & Hoang, H. (1995). Sunk costs in the NBA: Why draft order affects playing time and survival in professional basketball. *Administrative Science Quarterly, 40,* 474-494.

Steblay, N. M. (1987). Helping behavior in rural and urban environments: A meta-analysis. *Psychological Bulletin, 102,* 346-356.

Steele, C. M. (1997). A threat in the air: How stereotypes shape intellectual identity and performance. *American Psychologist, 52,* 613-629.

Steele, C. M., & Aronson, J. (1995). Stereotype threat and the intellectual test performance of African Americans. *Journal of Personality and Social Psychology, 69,* 797-811.

Steele, C. M., & Josephs, R. A. (1988). Drinking your troubles away: II. An attention-allocation model of alcohol's effect on psychological stress. *Journal of Abnormal Psychology, 97,* 196-205.

Steele, C., & Josephs, R. (1990). Alcohol myopia: Its prized and dangerous effects. *American Psychologist, 45,* 921-933.

Steele, C., & Liu, T. (1983). Dissonance processes as self-affirmation. *Journal of Personality and Social Psychology, 45,* 5-19.

Steele, C. M., & Southwick, L. (1985). Alcohol and social behavior: I. The psychology of drunken excess. *Journal of Personality and Social Psychology, 48,* 18-34.

Steele, C. M., Southwick, L., & Critchlow, B. (1981). Dissonance and alcohol: Drinking your troubles away. *Journal of Personality and Social Psychology, 4,* 831-846.

Steele, C., Spencer, S., & Lynch, M. (1993). Self-image resilience and dissonance: The role of affirmational resources. *Journal of Personality and Social Psychology, 64,* 885-896.

Steinberg, L. D., Catalano, R., & Dooley, D. (1981). Economic antecedents of child abuse and neglect. *Child Development, 52,* 975-985.

Steinel, W., & De Dreu, C. K. W. (2004). Social motives and strategic misrepresentation in social decision making. *Journal of Personality and Social Psychology, 86,* 419-434.

Stephan, C., Presser, N. R., Kennedy, J. C., & Aronson, E. (1978). Attributions to success and failure after cooperative or competitive interaction. *European Journal of Social Psychology, 8,* 269-274.

Stephan, W. G., Boniecki, K. A., Ybarra, O., Bettencourt, A., Ervin, K. S., Jackson, L. A., McNatt, P.S., & Renfro, C.L. (2002). The role of threats in the racial attitudes of Blacks and Whites. *Personality and Social Psychology Bulletin, 28,* 1242-1254.

Stepper, S., & Strack, F. (1993). Proprioceptive determinants of emotional and nonemotional feelings. *Journal of Personality and Social Psychology, 64,* 211-220.

Sternberg, R. J. (1986). A triangular theory of love. *Psychological Review, 93,* 119-135.

Sternberg, R. J. (1987). Liking versus loving: A comparative evaluation of theories. *Psychological Bulletin, 102,* 331-345.

Stewart, D. D., & Stasser, G. (1995). Expert role assignment and information sampling during collective recall and decision making. *Journal of Personality and Social Psychology, 69,* 619-628.

Stewart, J. E. (1980). Defendant's attractiveness as a factor in the outcome of criminal trials: An observational study. *Journal of Applied Social Psychology, 10,* 348-361.

Stewart, J. E. (1985). Appearance and punishment: The attraction-leniency effect in the courtroom. *Journal of Social Psychology, 125,* 373-378.

Stewart, S., Stinnett, H., & Rosenfeld, L. B. (2000). Sex differences in desired characteristics of short-term and long-term relationship partners. *Journal of Social and Personal Relationships, 17,* 843-853.

Stewart, T., Vassar, P., Sanchez, D., & David, S. (2000). Attitude toward women's societal roles moderates the effect of gender cues on target individuation. *Journal of Personality and Social Psychology, 79,* 143-157.

Stice, E., Chase, A., Stormer, S., & Appel, A. (2001). A randomized trial of a dissonance-based eating disorder prevention program. *International Journal of Eating Disorders, 29,* 247-262.

Stice, E., Mazotti, L., Weibel, D., & Agras, W. (2000). Dissonance prevention program decreases thin-ideal internalization, body dissatisfaction, dieting, negative affect, and bulimic symptoms: A preliminary experiment. *International Journal of Eating Disorders, 27,* 206-217.

Stice, E., Trost, A., & Chase, A. (2003). Healthy weight control and dissonance-based eating disorder prevention programs: Results from a controlled trial. *International Journal of Eating Disorders, 33,* 10-21.

Stigler, J., Smith, S., & Mao, L. (1985). The self-perception of competence by Chinese children. *Child Development, 56,* 1259-1270.

Stiles, W. B., Walz, N. C., Schroeder, M. A. B., & Williams, L. L. (1996). Attractiveness and disclosure in initial encounters of mixed-sex dyads. *Journal of Social and Personal Relationships, 13,* 303-312.

Stipek, D., & Gralinski, J. (1991). Gender differences in children's achievement-related beliefs and emotional responses to success and failure in mathematics. *Journal of Educational Psychology, 83,* 361-371.

Stone, A., Hedges, S., Neale, J., & Satin, M. (1985). Prospective and cross-sectional mood reports offer no evidence of a 'blue Monday' phenomenon. *Journal of Personality and Social Psychology, 49*, 129-134.

Stone, J. (2003). Self-consistency for low self-esteem in dissonance processes: The role of self-standards. *Personality and Social Psychology Bulletin, 29*, 846-858.

Stone, J., Aronson, E., Crain, A. L., Winslow, M. P. & Fried, C. B., (1994). Inducing hypocrisy as a means of encouraging young adults to use condoms. *Personality and Social Psychology Bulletin, 20*, 116-128.

Stone, J., & Cooper, J. (2001). A self-standards model of cognitive dissonance. *Journal of Experimental Social Psychology, 37*, 228-243.

Stone, J., & Cooper, J. (2003). The effect of self-attribute relevance on how self-esteem moderates attitude change in dissonance processes. *Journal of Experimental Social Psychology, 39*, 508-515.

Stone, J., Wiegand, A., Cooper, J., & Aronson, E. (1997). When exemplification fails: Hypocrisy and the motive for self-integrity. *Journal of Personality and Social Psychology, 72*, 54-65.

Storms, M. (1973). Videotape and the attribution process: Reversing actors' and observers' points of view. *Journal of Personality and Social Psychology, 27*, 165-175.

Story, M., & Faulkner, P. (1990). The prime time diet: A content analysis of eating behavior and food messages in television program content and commercials. *American Journal of Public Health, 80*, 738-740.

Strack, F., & Mussweiler, T. (1997). Explaining the enigmatic anchoring effect: Mechanisms of selective accessibility. *Journal of Personality and Social Psychology, 73*, 437-446.

Strahan, E. J., Spencer, S. J., & Zanna, M. P. (2002). Subliminal priming and persuasion: Striking while the iron is hot. *Journal of Experimental Social Psychology, 38*, 556-568.

Strauman, T., Lemieux, A., & Coe, C. (1993). Self-discrepancy and natural killer cell activity: Immunological consequences of negative self-evaluation. *Journal of Personality and Social Psychology, 64*, 1042-1052.

Stroebe, W., & Stroebe, M. (1996). The social psychology of social support. In E. T. Higgins & A. W. Kruglanski (Eds.), *Social Psychology: Handbook of Basic Principles* (pp. 597-621). New York: Guilford Press.

Stroh, L. K., Brett, J. M., & Reilly, A. H. (1992). All the right stuff: A comparison of female and male managers' career progression. *Journal of Applied Psychology, 77*, 251-260.

Strohmetz, D. B., Rind, B., Fisher, R., & Lynn, M. (2002). Sweetening the till: The use of candy to increase restaurant tipping. *Journal of Applied Social Psychology, 32*, 300-309.

Strube, M. J., & Rahimi, A. M. (2006). 'Everybody knows it's true': Social dominance orientation and right-wing authoritarianism moderate false consensus for stereotypic beliefs. *Journal of Research in Personality, 40*, 1038-1053.

Stürmer, S., Snyder, M., Kropp, A., & Siem, B. (2006). Empathy-motivated helping: The moderating role of group membership. *Personality and Social Psychology Bulletin, 32*, 943-956.

Stürmer, S., Snyder, M., & Omoto, A. M. (2005). Prosocial emotions and helping: The moderating role of group membership. *Journal of Personality and Social Psychology, 88*, 532-546.

Stukas, A., Snyder, M., & Clary, E. (1999). The effects of 'mandatory volunteerism' on intentions to volunteer. *Psychological Science, 10*, 59-64.

Suh, E. (2002). Culture, identity consistency, and subjective well-being. *Journal of Personality and Social Psychology, 83*, 1378-1391.

Suls, J., & Wan, C. (1987). In search of the false-uniqueness phenomenon: Fear and estimates of social consensus. *Journal of Personality and Social Psychology, 52*, 211-217.

Susman, E. J., Inoff-Germain, G., Nottelmann, E. D., & Loriaux, D. L. (1987). Hormones, emotional dispositions, and aggressive attributes in young adolescents. *Child Development, 58*, 1114-1134.

Sutton, S. R., & Eiser, J. R. (1984). The effect of fear-arousing communications on cigarette smoking: An expectancy-value approach. *Journal of Behavioral Medicine, 7*, 13-33.

Swaab, R., Postmes, T., Van Beest, I., & Spears, R. (2007). Shared cognition as a product of, and precursor to, shared identity in negotiations. *Personality and Social Psychology Bulletin, 33*, 187-199.

Swann, W. (1987). Identity negotiation: Where two roads meet. *Journal of Personality and Social Psychology, 53*, 1038-1051.

Swann, W. B., de la Ronde, C., & Hixon, J. G. (1994). Authenticity and positivity strivings in marriage and courtship. *Journal of Personality and Social Psychology, 66*, 857-869.

Swann, W., & Ely, R. (1984). A battle of wills: Self-verification versus behavioral confirmation. *Journal of Personality and Social Psychology, 46*, 1287-1302.

Swann, W., & Hill, C. (1982). When our identities are mistaken: Reaffirming self-conceptions through social interaction. *Journal of Personality and Social Psychology, 43*, 59-66.

Swann, W., Hixon, J., & de la Ronde, C. (1992). Embracing the bitter 'truth': Negative self-concepts and marital commitment. *Psychological Science, 3*, 118-121.

Swann, W., Pelham, B., & Krull, D. (1989). Agreeable fancy or disagreeable truth? Reconciling self-enhancement and self-verification. *Journal of Personality and Social Psychology, 57*, 782-791.

Swim, J. K., Aikin, K. J., Hall, W. S., & Hunter, B. A. (1995). Sexism and racism: Old-fashioned and modern prejudices. *Journal of Personality and Social Psychology, 68*, 199-214.

Swim, J. K., & Hyers, L. L. (1999). Excuse me—What did you just say?!: Women's public and private responses to sexist remarks. *Journal of Experimental Social Psychology, 35*, 68-88.

Swim, J., & Sanna, L. (1996). He's skilled, she's lucky: A meta-analysis of observers' attributions for women's and men's successes and failures. *Personality and Social Psychology Bulletin, 22*, 507-519.

Tafarodi, R., & Swann, W. (1996). Individualism-collectivism and global self-esteem: Evidence for a cultural trade-off. *Journal of Cross-Cultural Psychology, 27*, 651-672.

Tajfel, H. (1982). Social psychology of intergroup relations. *Annual Review of Psychology, 33*, 1-39.

Tanford, S., & Penrod, S. (1984). Social influence model: A formal integration of research on majority and minority influence processes. *Psychological Bulletin, 95*, 189-225.

Tashiro, T., & Frazier, P. (2003). 'I'll never be in a relationship like that again': Personal growth following romantic relationship breakups. *Personal Relationships, 10*, 113-128.

Taylor, S. (1989). *Positive Illusions: Creative Self-deception and the Healthy Mind*. New York: Basic Books.

Taylor, S. E., Crocker, J., Fiske, S. T., Sprinzen, M., & Winkler, J. E. (1979). The generalizability of salience effects. *Journal of Personality and Social Psychology, 37*, 357-368.

Taylor, S., & Brown, J. (1988). Illusion and well-being: A social psychological perspective on mental health. *Psychological Bulletin, 103*, 193-210.

Taylor, S., & Fiske, S. (1975). Point of view and perceptions of causality. *Journal of Personality and Social Psychology, 32*, 439-445.

Taylor, D. A., Gould, R. J., & Brounstein, P. J. (1981). Effects of personalistic self-disclosure. *Personality and Social Psychology Bulletin, 7*, 487-492.

Taylor, S. E., Sherman, D. K., Kim, H. S., Jarcho, J., Takagi, K., & Dunagan, M. S. (2004). Culture and social support: Who seeks it and why? *Journal of Personality and Social Psychology, 87*, 354-362.

Tazelaar, M. J. A., Van Lange, P. A. M., & Ouwerkerk, J. W. (2004). How to cope with 'noise' in social dilemmas: The benefits of communication. *Journal of Personality and Social Psychology, 87*, 845-859.

Teger, A. I., & Pruitt, D. G. (1967). Components of group risk taking. *Journal of Experimental Social Psychology, 3*, 189-205.

Tesser, A. (1980). Self-esteem maintenance in family dynamics. *Journal of Personality and Social Psychology, 39*, 77-91.

Tesser, A. (1993). The importance of heritability in psychological research: The case of attitudes. *Psychological Review, 100*, 129-142.

Tesser, A., & Smith, J. (1980). Some effects of task relevance and friendship on helping: You don't always help the one you like. *Journal of Experimental Social Psychology, 16*, 582-590.

Tetlock, P. (2005). *Expert Political Judgement: How Good Is It? How Can We Know?* Princeton, NJ: Princeton University Press.

Tetlock, P. E., Peterson, R. S., McGuire, C., Chang, S., & Feld, P. (1992). Assessing political group dynamics: A test of the groupthink model. *Journal of Personality and Social Psychology, 63*, 403-425.

Thaler, R. (1980). Towards a positive theory of consumer choice. *Journal of Economic Behavior and Organization, 1*, 39-60.

Thibaut, J.W., & Kelley, H.H. (1959). *The Social Psychology of Groups.* New York: Wiley.

Thomas, G. C., Batson, C. D., & Coke, J. S. (1981). Do good samaritans discourage helpfulness? Self-perceived altruism after exposure to highly helpful others. *Journal of Personality and Social Psychology, 40*, 194-200.

Thomas, K. S., Bardwell, W. A., Ancoli-Israel, S., & Dimsdale, J. E. (2006). The toll of ethnic discrimination on sleep architecture and fatigue. *Health Psychology, 25*, 635-642.

Thomas, M. H. (1982). Physiological arousal, exposure to a relatively lengthy aggressive film, and aggressive behavior. *Journal of Research in Personality, 16*, 72-81.

Thomas, M. H., & Drabman, R. S. (1978). Effects of television violence on expectations of other's aggression. *Personality and Social Psychology Bulletin, 4*, 73-76.

Thompson, L. (1990). The influence of experience on negotiation performance. *Journal of Experimental Social Psychology, 26*, 528-544.

Thompson, L. (1995). 'They saw a negotiation': Partisanship and involvement. *Journal of Personality and Social Psychology, 68*, 839-853.

Thompson, L., & Hrebec, D. (1996). Lose-lose agreements in interdependent decision making. *Psychological Bulletin, 120*, 396-409.

Thompson, L., Peterson, E., & Brodt, S. E. (1996). Team negotiation: An examination of integrative and distributive bargaining. *Journal of Personality and Social Psychology, 70*, 66-78.

Thompson, S. (1999). Illusions of control: How we overestimate our personal influence. *Current Directions in Psychological Science, 8*, 187-190.

Thompson, W. C., Cowan, C. L., & Rosenhan, D. L. (1980). Focus of attention mediates the impact of negative affect on altruism. *Journal of Personality and Social Psychology, 38*, 291-300.

Tilker, H. A. (1970). Socially responsible behavior as a function of observer responsibility and victim feedback. *Journal of Personality and Social Psychology, 14*, 95-100.

Tobin, R. J., & Eagles, M. (1992). U.S. and Canadian attitudes toward international interactions: A cross-national test of the double-standard hypothesis. *Basic and Applied Social Psychology, 13*, 447-459.

Tobin, S., & Weary, G. (2003). An on-line look at automatic contrast and correction of behavior categorizations and dispositional inferences. *Personality and Social Psychology Bulletin, 29*, 1328-1338.

Todorov, A., Mandisodza, A., Goren, A., & Hall, C. (2005). Inferences of competence from faces predict election outcomes. *Science, 308*, 1623-1626.

Toi, M., & Batson, C. D. (1982). More evidence that empathy is a source of altruistic motivation. *Journal of Personality and Social Psychology, 43*, 281-292.

Tolstoy, L. (1877). *Anna Karenina.* New York: Penguin Books.

Tormala, Z. L., & Clarkson, J. J. (2007). Assimilation and contrast in persuasion: The effects of source credibility in multiple message situations. *Personality and Social Psychology Bulletin, 33*, 559-571.

Tormala, Z. L., & Petty, R. E. (2004). Resistance to persuasion and attitude certainty: The moderating role of elaboration. *Personality and Social Psychology Bulletin, 30*, 1446-1457.

Towles-Schwen, T., & Fazio, R. H. (2001). On the origins of racial attitudes: Correlates of childhood experiences. *Personality and Social Psychology Bulletin, 27*, 162-175.

Trafimow, D., & Finlay, K. (1996). The importance of subjective norms for a minority of people: Between-subjects and within-subjects analyses. *Personality and Social Psychology Bulletin, 22*, 820-828.

Trafimow, D., Silverman, E., Fan, R., & Law, J. (1997). The effects of language and priming on the relative accessibility of the private self and the collective self. *Journal of Cross-Cultural Psychology, 28*, 107-123.

Trenholm, C., Devaney, B., Fortson, K., Clark, M., Bridgespan, L.Q., & Wheeler, J. (2008). Impacts of abstinence education on teen sexual activity, risk of pregnancy, and risk of sexually transmitted diseases. *Journal of Policy Analysis and Management, 27*, 255-276.

Triandis, H. (1989). The self and social behavior in differing cultural contexts. *Psychological Review, 96*, 506-520.

Triandis, H. C., Chen, X. P., & Chan, D. K. (1998). Scenarios for the measurement of collectivism and individualism. *Journal of Cross-Cultural Psychology, 29*, 275-289.

Triplett, N. (1898). The dynamogenic factors in pacemaking and competition. *American Journal of Psychology, 9*, 507-533.

Trivers, R. L. (1971). The evolution of reciprocal altruism. *The Quarterly Review of Biology, 46*, 35-57.

Trivers, R. L. (1985). *Social Evolution.* Menlo Park, CA: Benjamin/Cummings.

Trope, Y., & Thompson, E. P. (1997). Looking for truth in all the wrong places? Asymmetric search of individuating information about stereotyped group members. *Journal of Personality and Social Psychology, 73*, 229-241.

Tsai, J., Simeonova, D., & Watanabe, J. (2004). Somatic and social: Chinese Americans talk about emotion. *Personality and Social Psychology Bulletin, 30,* 1226-1238.

Tucker, P., & Aron, A. (1993). Passionate love and marital satisfaction at key transition points in the family life cycle. *Journal of Social & Clinical Psychology, 12,* 135-147.

Turner, M. E., Pratkanis, A. R., Probasco, P., & Leve, C. (1992). Threat, cohesion, and group effectiveness: Testing a social identity maintenance perspective on groupthink. *Journal of Personality and Social Psychology, 63,* 781-796.

Tversky, A., & Kahneman, D. (1973). Availability: A heuristic for judging frequency and probability. *Cognitive Psychology, 5,* 207-232.

Tversky, A., & Kahneman, D. (1974). Judgment under uncertainty: Heuristics and biases. *Science, 185,* 1124-1131.

Tversky, A., & Kahneman, D. (1981). The framing of decisions and the psychology of choice. *Science, 211,* 453-458.

Twenge, J. M., Baumeister, R. F., DeWall, C. N., Ciarocco, N. J., & Bartels, J. M. (2007). Social exclusion decreases prosocial behavior. *Journal of Personality and Social Psychology, 92,* 56-66.

Twenge, J. M., Baumeister, R. F., Tice, D. M., & Stucke, T. S. (2001). If you can't join them, beat them: Effects of social exclusion on aggressive behavior. *Journal of Personality and Social Psychology, 81,* 1058-1069.

Tykocinski, O., & Pittman, T. (1998). The consequences of doing nothing: Inaction inertia as avoidance of anticipated counterfactual regret. *Journal of Personality and Social Psychology, 75,* 607-616.

Tykocinski, O., Pittman, T., & Tuttle, E. (1995). Inaction inertia: Foregoing future benefits as a result of an initial failure to act. *Journal of Personality and Social Psychology, 68,* 793-803.

Uchino, B. N., Cacioppo, J. T., & Kiecolt-Glaser, J. K. (1996). The relationship between social support and physiological processes: A review with emphasis on underlying mechanisms and implications for health. *Psychological Bulletin, 119,* 488-531.

Uehara, E. S. (1995). Reciprocity reconsidered: Gouldner's 'moral norm of reciprocity' and social support. *Journal of Social and Personal Relationships, 12,* 483-502.

Uhlmann, E. L., & Cohen, G. L. (2005). Constructed criteria: Redefining merit to justify discrimination. *Psychological Science, 16,* 474-480.

Väänänen, A., Buunk, B. P., Kivimäki, M., Pentti, J., & Vahtera, J. (2005). When it is better to give than to receive: Long-term health effects of perceived reciprocity in support exchange. *Journal of Personality and Social Psychology, 89,* 176-193.

Valins, S. (1966). Cognitive effects of false heart-rate feedback. *Journal of Personality and Social Psychology, 4,* 400-408.

Vallone, R., Griffin, D., Lin, S., & Ross, L. (1990). Overconfident prediction of future actions and outcomes by self and others. *Journal of Personality and Social Psychology, 58,* 582-592.

Vallone, R. P., Ross, L., & Lepper, M. R. (1985). The hostile media phenomenon: Biased perception and perceptions of media bias in coverage of the Beirut massacre. *Journal of Personality and Social Psychology, 49,* 577-585.

Vallone et al., 1985.

Van Boven, L., White, K., Kamada, A., & Gilovich, T. (2003). Intuitions about situational correction in self and others. *Journal of Personality and Social Psychology, 85,* 249-258.

van Dick, R., Wagner, U., Pettigrew, T. F., Christ, O., Wolf, C., Petzel, T., et al. (2004). Role of perceived importance in intergroup contact. *Journal of Personality and Social Psychology, 87,* 211-227.

van Dijk, E., Wilke, H., & Wit, A. (2003). Preferences for leadership in social dilemmas: Public good dilemmas versus common resource dilemmas. *Journal of Experimental Social Psychology, 39,* 170-176.

Van Kleef, G. A., De Dreu, C. K. W., & Manstead, A. S. R. (2004). The interpersonal effects of emotions in negotiations: A motivated information processing approach. *Journal of Personality and Social Psychology, 87,* 510-528.

Van Vianen, A. E., & Willemsen, T. M. (1992). The employment interview: The role of sex stereotypes in the evaluation of male and female job applicants in the Netherlands. *Journal of Applied Social Psychology, 22,* 471-491.

Van Vugt, M. (2001). Community identification moderating the impact of financial incentives in a natural social dilemma: Water conservation. *Personality and Social Psychology Bulletin, 27,* 1440-1449.

Van Yperen, N. W., & Buunk, B. P. (1990). A longitudinal study of equity and satisfaction in intimate relationships. *European Journal of Social Psychology, 20,* 287-309.

Vandello, J. A., & Cohen, D. (2003). Male honor and female fidelity: Implicit cultural scripts that perpetuate domestic violence. *Journal of Personality and Social Psychology, 84,* 997-1010.

Vanman, E., Saltz, J., Nathan, L., & Warren, J. (2004). Racial discrimination by low-prejudiced Whites facial movements as implicit measures of attitudes related to behavior. *Psychological Science, 15,* 711-714.

Verhofstadt, L.L., Buysee, A., De Clercq, A., & Goodwin, R. (2005). Emotional arousal and negative affect in marital conflict: The influence of gender, conflict structure, and demand-withdrawal. *European Journal of Social Psychology, 35,* 449-467.

Verplanken, B. (1991). Persuasive communication of risk information: A test of cue versus message processing effects in a field experiment. *Personality and Social Psychology Bulletin, 17,* 188-193.

Vescio, T. K., Gervais, S. J., Snyder, M., & Hoover, A. (2005). Power and the creation of patronizing environments: The stereotype-based behaviors of the powerful and their effects on female performance in masculine domains. *Journal of Personality and Social Psychology, 88,* 658-672.

Vescio, T. K., Snyder, M., & Butz, D. A. (2003). Power in stereotypically masculine domains: A social influence strategy X stereotype match model. *Journal of Personality and Social Psychology, 85,* 1062-1078.

Visser, P. S., & Krosnick, J. A. (1998). Development of attitude strength over the life cycle: Surge and decline. *Journal of Personality and Social Psychology, 75,* 1389-1410.

Visser, P., Krosnick, J., & Simmons, J. (2003). Distinguishing the cognitive and behavioral consequences of attitude and certainty: A new approach to testing the common-factor hypothesis. *Journal of Experimental Social Psychology, 39,* 118-141.

Visser, P., & Mirabile, R. (2004). Attitudes in the social context: The impact of social network composition on individual-level attitude strength. *Journal of Personality and Social Psychology, 87,* 779-795.

Vittengl, J. R., & Holt, C. S. (2000). Getting acquainted: The relationship of self-disclosure and social attraction to positive affect. *Journal of Social and Personal Relationships, 17,* 53-66.

Vivian, J. E., & Berkowitz, N. H. (1992). Anticipated bias from an outgroup: An attributional analysis. *European Journal of Social Psychology, 22,* 415-424.

Vivian, J. E., & Berkowitz, N. H. (1993). Anticipated outgroup evaluations and intergroup bias. *European Journal of Social Psychology, 23*, 513-524.

Vohs, K., & Heatherton, T. (2000). Self-regulatory failure: A resource-depletion approach. *Psychological Science, 11*, 249-254.

Von Arnim, E. (1922). *The Enchanted April*. London: Virago Press.

von Hippel, W., Silver, L. A., & Lynch, M. E. (2000). Stereotyping against your will: The role of inhibitory ability in stereotyping and prejudice among the elderly. *Personality and Social Psychology Bulletin, 26*, 523-532.

Vonk, R. (1993). The negativity effect in trait ratings and in open-ended descriptions of persons. *Personality and Social Psychology Bulletin, 19*, 269-278.

Vonk, R. (1998). The slime effect: Suspicion and dislike of likeable behavior toward superiors. *Journal of Personality and Social Psychology, 74*, 849-864.

Vonk, R. (1999). Differential evaluations of likeable and dislikeable behaviours enacted towards superiors and subordinates. *European Journal of Social Psychology, 29*, 139-146.

Vonofakou, C., Hewstone, M., & Voci, A. (2007). Contact with out-group friends as a predictor of meta-attitudinal strength and accessibility of attitudes toward gay men. *Journal of Personality and Social Psychology, 92*, 804-820.

Vorauer, J. D. (2005). Miscommunications surrounding efforts to reach out across group boundaries. *Personality and Social Psychology Bulletin, 31*, 1653-1664.

Vorauer, J.D., & Claude, S. D. (1998). Perceived versus actual transparency of goals in negotiation. Personality and Social Psychology Bulletin, 24, 371-385.

Vorauer, J. D., & Ratner, R. K. (1996). Who's going to make the first move? Pluralistic ignorance as an impediment to relationship formation. *Journal of Social and Personal Relationships, 13*, 483-506.

Vorauer, J. D., & Turpie, C. A. (2004). Disruptive effects of vigilance on dominant group members' treatment of outgroup members: Choking versus shining under pressure. *Journal of Personality and Social Psychology, 87*, 384-399.

Vorauer, J., & Ross, M. (1999). Self-awareness and feeling transparent: Failing to suppress one's self. *Journal of Experimental Social Psychology, 35*, 415-440.

Vrij, A., Edward, K., & Bull, R. (2001). Stereotypical verbal and nonverbal responses while deceiving others. *Personality and Social Psychology Bulletin, 27*, 899-909.

Vroom, V. H., & Jago, A. G. (2007). The role of the situation in leadership. *American Psychologist, 62*, 17-24.

Wade-Benzoni, K. A., Okumura, T., Brett, J. M., Moore, D. A., Tenbrunsel, A. E., & Bazerman, M. H. (2002). Cognitions and behavior in asymmetric social dilemmas: A comparison of two cultures. *Journal of Applied Psychology, 87*, 87-95.

Wagner, C., & Wheeler, L. (1969). Model, need, and cost effects in helping behavior. *Journal of Personality and Social Psychology, 12*, 111-116.

Wakschlag, L., Leventhal, B., Pine, D., Pickett, K., & Carter, A. (2006). Elucidating early mechanisms of developmental psychopathology: The case of prenatal smoking and disruptive behavior. *Child Development, 77*, 893-906.

Wallach, M. A., Kogan, N., & Bem, D. J. (1962). Group influence on individual risk taking. *The Journal of Abnormal and Social Psychology, 65*, 75-86.

Walster, E., Walster, G. W., Piliavin, J., & Schmidt, L. (1973). 'Playing hard to get': Understanding an elusive phenomenon. *Journal of Personality and Social Psychology, 26*, 113-121.

Walster, E., Walster, G. W., & Traupmann, J. (1978). Equity and premarital sex. *Journal of Personality and Social Psychology, 36*, 82-92.

Walther, E. (2002). Guilty by mere association: Evaluative conditioning and the spreading attitude effect. *Journal of Personality and Social Psychology, 82*, 919-934.

Wang, C. L., Bristol, T., Mowen, J. C., & Chakraborty, G. (2000). Alternative modes of self-construal: Dimensions of connectedness-separateness and advertising appeals to the cultural and gender-specific self. *Journal of Consumer Psychology, 9*, 107-115.

Wang, Q. (2001). Culture effects on adults' earliest childhood recollection and self-description: Implications for the relation between memory and the self. *Journal of Personality and Social Psychology, 81*, 220-233.

Wang, Q. (2006). Earliest recollections of self and others in European American and Taiwanese young adults. *Psychological Science, 17*, 708-714.

Wansink, B., van Ittersum, K., & Painter, J. (2006). Ice cream illusions bowls, spoons, and self-served portion sizes. *American Journal of Preventive Medicine, 31*, 240-243.

Watson, R. I. (1973). Investigation into deindividuation using a cross-cultural survey technique. *Journal of Personality and Social Psychology, 25*, 342-345.

Weary, G., Jacobson, J. A., Edwards, J. A., & Tobin, S. J. (2001). Chronic and temporarily activated causal uncertainty beliefs and stereotype usage. *Journal of Personality and Social Psychology, 81*, 206-219.

Weber, R., & Crocker, J. (1983). Cognitive processes in the revision of stereotypic beliefs. *Journal of Personality and Social Psychology, 45*, 961-977.

Weber, R., Ritterfeld, U., & Mathiak, K. (2006). Does playing violent video games induce aggression? Empirical evidence of a functional magnetic resonance imaging study. *Media Psychology, 8*, 39-60.

Webster, D. (1993). Motivated augmentation and reduction of the overattribution bias. *Journal of Personality and Social Psychology, 65*, 261-271.

Webster, D., & Kruglanski, A. (1994). Individual differences in need for cognitive closure. *Journal of Personality and Social Psychology, 67*, 1049-1062.

Webster, D., Richter, L., & Kruglanski, A. (1996). On leaping to conclusions when feeling tired: Mental fatigue effects on impressional primacy. *Journal of Experimental Social Psychology, 32*, 181-195.

Wechsler, H., Dowdall, G., Davenport, A., & Castillo, S. (1995). Correlates of college student binge drinking. *American Journal of Public Health, 85*, 921-926.

Wegener, D. T., & Petty, R. E. (1994). Mood management across affective states: The hedonic contingency hypothesis. *Journal of Personality and Social Psychology, 66*, 1034-1048.

Wegener, D., & Petty, R. (1995). Flexible correction processes in social judgment: The role of naive theories in corrections for perceived bias. *Journal of Personality and Social Psychology, 68*, 36-51.

Wegener, D. T., Petty, R. E., Detweiler-Bedell, B. T., & Jarvis, W. B. G. (2001). Implications of attitude change theories for numerical anchoring: Anchor plausibility and the limits of anchor effectiveness. *Journal of Experimental Social Psychology, 37*, 62-69.

Wegener, D. T., Petty, R. E., & Smith, S. M. (1995). Positive mood can increase or decrease message scrutiny: The hedonic contingency view of mood and message processing. *Journal of Personality and Social Psychology, 69,* 5-15.

Weger, H., Jr. (2005). Disconfirming communication and self-verification in marriage: Associations among the demand/withdraw interaction pattern, feeling understood, and marital satisfaction. *Journal of Social and Personal Relationships, 22,* 19-31.

Wegner, D. (1994). Ironic processes of mental control. *Psychological Review, 101,* 34-52.

Wegner, D. M. (1997). When the antidote is the poison: Ironic mental control processes. *Psychological Science, 8,* 148-150.

Wegner, D., & Gold, D. (1995). Fanning old flames: Emotional and cognitive effects of suppressing thoughts of a past relationship. *Journal of Personality and Social Psychology, 68,* 782-792.

Wegner, D. M., Lane, J. D., & Dimitri, S. (1994). The allure of secret relationships. *Journal of Personality and Social Psychology, 66,* 287-300.

Wegner, D., Shortt, J., Blake, A., & Page, M. (1990). The suppression of exciting thoughts. *Journal of Personality and Social Psychology, 58,* 409-418.

Wehrle, T., Kaiser, S., Schmidt, S., & Scherer, K. (2000). Studying the dynamics of emotional expression using synthesized facial muscle movements. *Journal of Personality and Social Psychology, 78,* 105-119.

Weigel, R. H., Wiser, P. L., & Cook, S. W. (1975). The impact of cooperative learning experiences on cross-ethnic relations and attitudes. *Journal of Social Issues, 31,* 219-244.

Weiner, B. (1980). May I borrow your class notes? An attributional analysis of judgments of help giving in an achievement-related context. *Journal of Educational Psychology, 72,* 676-681.

Weiner, B. (1986). Attribution, emotion, and action. In R. M. Sorrentino & E. T. Higgins (Eds.), *Handbook of Motivation and Cognition: Foundations of Social Behavior* (pp. 281-312). New York: Guilford.

Weiner, B., Amirkhan, J., Folkes, V. S., & Verette, J. A. (1987). An attributional analysis of excuse giving: Studies of a naive theory of emotion. *Journal of Personality and Social Psychology, 52,* 316-324.

Weiner, B., Perry, R. P., & Magnusson, J. (1988). An attributional analysis of reactions to stigmas. *Journal of Personality and Social Psychology, 55,* 738-748.

Weinstein, N. (1980). Unrealistic optimism about future life events. *Journal of Personality and Social Psychology, 39,* 806-820.

Weinstein, N. (1984). Why it won't happen to me: Perceptions of risk factors and susceptibility. *Health Psychology, 3,* 431-457.

Weinstein, N. (1987). Unrealistic optimism about susceptibility to health problems: Conclusions from a community-wide sample. *Journal of Behavioral Medicine, 10,* 481-500.

Weiss, B., Dodge, K. A., Bates, J. E., & Pettit, G. S. (1992). Some consequences of early harsh discipline: Child aggression and a maladaptive social information processing style. *Child Development, 63,* 1321-1335.

Weldon, E., & Gargano, G. M. (1988). Cognitive loafing: The effects of accountability and shared responsibility on cognitive effort. *Personality and Social Psychology Bulletin, 14,* 159-171.

Wells, G. L., Olson, E. A., & Charman, S. D. (2003). Distorted retrospective eyewitness reports as functions of feedback and delay. *Journal of Experimental Psychology: Applied, 9,* 42-52.

Wells, G., & Bradfield, A. (1999). Distortions in eyewitnesses' recollections: Can the postidentification-feedback effect be moderated? *Psychological Science, 10,* 138-144.

Wenzel, M. (2000). Justice and identity: The significance of inclusion for perceptions of entitlement and the justice motive. *Personality and Social Psychology Bulletin, 26,* 157-176.

Werner, C. M., Byerly, S., White, P. H., & Kieffer, M. (2004). Validation, persuasion and recycling: Capitalizing on the social ecology of newspaper use. *Basic and Applied Social Psychology, 26,* 183-198.

Werner, C. M., Stoll, R., Birch, P., & White, P. H. (2002). Clinical validation and cognitive elaboration: Signs that encourage sustained recycling. *Basic and Applied Social Psychology, 24,* 185-203.

Westen, D., Blagov, P. S., Harenski, K., Kilts, C., & Hamann, S. (2006). Neural bases of motivated reasoning: An fMRI study of emotional constraints on partisan political judgment in the 2004 U.S. presidential election. *Journal of Cognitive Neuroscience, 18,* 1947-1958.

Westmaas, J. L., & Silver, R. C. (2006). The role of perceived similarity in supportive responses to victims of negative life events. *Personality and Social Psychology Bulletin, 32,* 1537-1546.

Weyant, J. M. (1978). Effects of mood states, costs, and benefits on helping. *Journal of Personality and Social Psychology, 36,* 1169-1176.

Wheeler, L., & Kim, Y. (1997). What is beautiful is culturally good: The physical attractiveness stereotype has different content in collectivistic cultures. *Personality and Social Psychology Bulletin, 23,* 795-800.

Wheeler, M. E., & Fiske, S. T. (2005). Controlling racial prejudice: Social-cognitive goals affect amygdala and stereotype activation. *Psychological Science, 16,* 56-63.

White, G. L., Fishbein, S., & Rutsein, J. (1981). Passionate love and the misattribution of arousal. *Journal of Personality and Social Psychology, 41,* 56-62.

White, K., & Lehman, D. (2005). Culture and social comparison seeking: The role of self-motives. *Personality and Social Psychology Bulletin, 31,* 232-242.

Whitley, B. E. (1993). Reliability and aspects of the construct validity of Sternberg's Triangular Love Scale. *Journal of Social and Personal Relationships, 10,* 475-480.

Whitley, B. E. J. (1999). Right-wing authoritarianism, social dominance orientation, and prejudice. *Journal of Personality and Social Psychology, 77,* 126-134.

Wicklund, R. A., & Frey, D. (1980). Self-awareness theory: When the self makes a difference. In D. M. Wegner, & R. R. Vallacher (Eds.), *The Self in Social Psychology* (pp. 31-54). New York: Oxford University Press.

Wilder, D. A. (1990). Some determinants of the persuasive power of in-groups and out-groups: Organization of information and attribution of independence. *Journal of Personality and Social Psychology, 59,* 1202-1213.

Wilder, D. A., Simon, A. F., & Faith, M. (1996). Enhancing the impact of counterstereotypic information: Dispositional attributions for deviance. *Journal of Personality and Social Psychology, 71,* 276-287.

Wilke, H., & Lanzetta, J. T. (1970). The obligation to help: The effects of amount of prior help on subsequent helping behavior. *Journal of Experimental Social Psychology, 6,* 488-493.

Wilke, H., & Lanzetta, J. T. (1982). The obligation to help: Factors affecting response to help received. *European Journal of Social Psychology, 12,* 315-319.

Williams, K. D., Bourgeois, M. J., & Croyle, R. T. (1993). The effects of stealing thunder in criminal and civil trials. *Law and Human Behavior, 17,* 597-609.

Williams, K., Harkins, S. G., & Latané, B. (1981). Identifiability as a deterrent to social loafing: Two cheering experiments. *Journal of Personality and Social Psychology, 40,* 303-311.

Williams, K. D., & Karau, S. J. (1991). Social loafing and social compensation: The effects of expectations of co-worker performance. *Journal of Personality and Social Psychology, 61,* 570-581.

Williams, S., Kimble, D., Covell, N., & Weiss, L. (1992). College students use implicit personality theory instead of safer sex. *Journal of Applied Social Psychology, 22,* 921-933.

Williams, K. D., Nida, S. A., Baca, L. D., & Latané, B. (1989). Social loafing and swimming: Effects of identifiability on individual and relay performance of intercollegiate swimmers. *Basic and Applied Social Psychology, 10,* 73-81.

Williams, R. B., et al. (1992). Prognostic importance of social and economic resources among medically treated patients with angiographically documented coronary artery disease. *Journal of the American Medical Association, 267,* 520-524.

Wilson, D. W. (1978). Helping behavior and physical attractiveness. *Journal of Social Psychology, 104,* 313-314.

Wilson, D., Kaplan, R., & Schneiderman, L. (1987). Framing of decisions and selections of alternatives in health care. *Social Behaviour, 2,* 51-59.

Wilson, M. I., & Daly, M. (1996). Male sexual proprietariness and violence against wives. *Current Directions in Psychological Science, 5,* 2-7.

Wilson, M., & Dovidio, J. F. (1985). Effects of perceived attractiveness and feminist orientation on helping behavior. *Journal of Social Psychology, 125,* 415-420.

Wilson, T., & LaFleur, S. (1995). Knowing what you'll do: Effects of analyzing reasons on self-prediction. *Journal of Personality and Social Psychology, 68,* 21-35.

Wilson, T., Laser, P., & Stone, J. (1982). Judging the predictors of one's own mood: Accuracy and the use of shared theories. *Journal of Experimental Social Psychology, 18,* 537-556.

Wilson, T., Lisle, D., Schooler, J., Hodges, S., Klaaren, K. J., & LaFleur, S. J. (1993). Introspecting about reasons can reduce post-choice satisfaction. *Personality and Social Psychology Bulletin, 19,* 331-339.

Wilson, T., Wheatley, T., Meyers, J., Gilbert, D., & Axsom, D. (2000). Focalism: A source of durability bias in affective forecasting. *Journal of Personality and Social Psychology, 78,* 821-836.

Wilson, T. D., Dunn, D. S., Bybee, J. A., Hyman, D. B., & Rotondo, J. A. (1984). Effects of analyzing reasons on attitude–behavior consistency. *Journal of Personality and Social Psychology, 47,* 5–16.

Windschitl, P., Kruger, J., & Simms, E. (2003). The influence of egocentrism and focalism on people's optimism in competitions: When what affects us equally affects me more. *Journal of Personality and Social Psychology, 85,* 389-408.

Wintemute, G. J., Parham, C. A., Beaumont, J. J., Wright, M., & Drake, C. (1999). Mortality among recent purchasers of handguns. *New England Journal of Medicine, 341,* 1583-1589.

Wiseman, C., Gray, J., Mosimann, J., & Ahrens, A. (1992). Cultural expectations of thinness in women: An update. *International Journal of Eating Disorders, 11,* 85-89.

Wittenbrink, B., & Henly, J. R. (1996). Creating social reality: Informational social influence and the content of stereotypic beliefs. *Personality and Social Psychology Bulletin, 22,* 598-610.

Wittenbrink, B., Judd, C. M., & Park, B. (2001). Spontaneous prejudice in context: Variability in automatically activated attitudes. *Journal of Personality and Social Psychology, 81,* 815-827.

Witvliet, C. V., Ludwig, T. E., & Vander Laan, K. L. (2001). Granting forgiveness or harboring grudges: Implications for emotion, physiology, and health. *Psychological Science, 12,* 117-123.

Wohl, M. J. A., & Branscombe, N. R. (2005). Forgiveness and collective guilt assignment to historical perpetrator groups depend on level of social category inclusiveness. *Journal of Personality and Social Psychology, 88,* 288-303.

Wolsko, C., Park, B., Judd, C. M., & Wittenbrink, B. (2000). Framing interethnic ideology: Effects of multicultural and color-blind perspectives on judgments of groups and individuals. *Journal of Personality and Social Psychology, 78,* 635-654.

Wong, R. Y., & Hong, Y. (2005). Dynamic influences of culture on cooperation in the prisoner's dilemma. *Psychological Science, 16,* 429-434.

Wood, J. V. (1989). Theory and research concerning social comparisons of personal attributes. *Psychological Bulletin, 106,* 231-248.

Wood, W. (1982). Retrieval of attitude-relevant information from memory: Effects on susceptibility to persuasion and on intrinsic motivation. *Journal of Personality and Social Psychology, 42,* 798-810.

Wood, W., & Eagly, A. H. (1981). Stages in the analysis of persuasive messages: The role of causal attributions and message comprehension. *Journal of Personality and Social Psychology, 40,* 246-259.

Wood, J. V., Giordano-Beech, M., & Ducharme, M. J. (1999). Compensating for failure through social comparison. *Personality and Social Psychology Bulletin, 25,* 1370-1386.

Wood, W., Kallgren, C. A., & Preisler, R. M. (1985). Access to attitude-relevant information in memory as a determinant of persuasion: The role of message attributes. *Journal of Experimental Social Psychology, 21,* 73-85.

Wood, W., Lundgren, S., Ouellette, J. A., Busceme, S., & Blackstone, T. (1994). Minority influence: A meta-analytic review of social influence processes. *Psychological Bulletin, 115,* 323-345.

Wood, W., Pool, G. J., Leck, K., & Purvis, D. (1996). Self-definition, defensive processing, and influence: The normative impact of majority and minority groups. *Journal of Personality and Social Psychology, 71,* 1181-1193.

Wood, W., Wong, F. Y., & Chachere, J. G. (1991). Effects of media violence on viewers' aggression in unconstrained social interaction. *Psychological Bulletin, 109,* 371-383.

Worchel, S., Lee, J., & Adewole, A. (1975). Effects of supply and demand on ratings of object value. *Journal of Personality and Social Psychology, 32,* 906-914.

Word, C. O., Zanna, M. P., & Cooper, J. (1974). The nonverbal mediation of self-fulfilling prophecies in interracial interaction. *Journal of Experimental Social Psychology, 10,* 109-120.

Wright, S. C., Aron, A., McLaughlin-Volpe, T., & Ropp, S. A. (1997). The extended contact effect: Knowledge of cross-group friendships and prejudice. *Journal of Personality and Social Psychology, 73,* 73-90.

Wyer, N. A. (2004). Not all stereotypic biases are created equal: Evidence for a stereotype-disconfirming bias. *Personality and Social Psychology Bulletin, 30,* 706-720.

Wyer, N. A., Sherman, J. W., & Stroessner, S. J. (2000). The roles of motivation and ability in controlling the consequences of stereotype suppression. *Personality and Social Psychology Bulletin, 26,* 13-25.

Xiaohe, X., & Whyte, M. K. (1990). Love matches and arranged marriages: A Chinese replication. *Journal of Marriage & the Family, 52,* 709-722.

Yagi, Y., & Shimizu, T. (1996). Helping behavior following a failure experience. *Japanese Psychological Research, 38,* 53-65.

Yakimovich, D., & Saltz, E. (1971). Helping behavior: The cry for help. *Psychonomic Science, 23,* 427-428.

Ybarra, M. L., Mitchell, K. J., Wolak, J., & Finkelhor, D. (2006). Examining characteristics and associated distress related to Internet harassment: Findings from the Second Youth Internet Safety Survey. *Pediatrics, 118,* 1169-1177.

Yik, M., Bond, M., & Paulhus, D. (1998). Do Chinese self-enhance or self-efface? It's a matter of domain. *Personality and Social Psychology Bulletin, 24,* 399-406.

Yum, Y. (2004). Culture and self-construal as predictors of responses to accommodative dilemmas in dating relationships. *Journal of Social and Personal Relationships, 21,* 817-835.

Zaccaro, S. J. (2007). Trait-based perspectives of leadership. *American Psychologist, 62,* 6-16.

Zahn-Waxler, C., Radke-Yarrow, M., Wagner, E., & Chapman, M. (1992). Development of concern for others. *Developmental Psychology, 28,* 126-136.

Zajonc, R. (1968). Attitudinal effects of mere exposure. *Journal of Personality and Social Psychology, 9,* 1-27.

Zajonc, R. B. (1965). Social facilitation. *Science, 149,* 269-274.

Zajonc, R. B., Heingartner, A., & Herman, E. M. (1969). Social enhancement and impairment of performance in the cockroach. *Journal of Personality and Social Psychology, 13,* 83-92.

Zajonc, R., Murphy, S., & Inglehart, M. (1989). Feeling and facial efference: Implications of the vascular theory of emotion. *Psychological Review, 96,* 395-416.

Zajonc, R. B., & Sales, S. M. (1966). Social facilitation of dominant and subordinate responses. *Journal of Experimental Social Psychology, 2,* 160-168.

Zanna, M., Olson, J., & Fazio, R. (1981). Self-perception and attitude-behavior consistency. *Personality and Social Psychology Bulletin, 7,* 252-256.

Zanna, M. P., & Cooper J. (1974). Dissonance and the pill: An attribution approach to studying the arousal properties of dissonance. *Journal of Personality Social Psychology, 29,* 703-709.

Zárate, M., Uleman, J., & Voils, C. (2001). Effects of culture and processing goals on the activation and binding of trait concepts. *Social Cognition, 19,* 295-323.

Zebrowitz, L. A., Collins, M. A., & Dutta, R. (1998). The relationship between appearance and personality across the life span. *Personality and Social Psychology Bulletin, 24,* 736-749.

Zemack-Rugar, Y., Bettman, J., & Fitzsimons, G. (2007). The effects of nonconsciously priming emotion concepts on behavior. *Journal of Personality and Social Psychology, 93,* 927-939.

Zhang, L., & Baumeister, R. F. (2006). Your money or your self-esteem: Threatened egotism promotes costly entrapment in losing endeavors. *Personality and Social Psychology Bulletin, 32,* 881-893.

Zillman, D. (1983). Transfer of excitation in emotional behavior. In J. T. Cacioppo & R. E. Petty (Eds.), *Social Psychophysiology* (pp. 214-240). New York: Guilford Press.

Zillman, D., Baron, R. A., & Tamborini, R. (1981). Social costs of smoking: Effects of tobacco smoke on hostile behavior. *Journal of Applied Social Psychology, 11,* 548-561.

Zillman, D., Katcher, A. H., Milavsky, B. (1972). Excitation transfer from physical exercise to subsequent aggressive behavior. *Journal of Experimental Social Psychology, 8,* 247-259.

Zillman, D., & Weaver, J. B. I. (1999). Effects of prolonged exposure to gratuitous media violence on provoked and unprovoked hostile behavior. *Journal of Applied Social Psychology, 29,* 145-165.

Zimbardo, P. (1970). Modifying the impact of persuasive communications with external distraction. *Journal of Personality and Social Psychology, 16,* 669-680.

Zuckerman, M., Kieffer, S., & Knee, C. (1998). Consequences of self-handicapping: Effects on coping, academic performance, and adjustment. *Journal of Personality and Social Psychology, 74,* 1619-1628.

Zuckerman, M., Knee, C., Hodgins, H., & Miyake, K. (1995). Hypothesis confirmation: The joint effect of positive test strategy and acquiescence response set. *Journal of Personality and Social Psychology, 68,* 52-60.

Zuwerink, J. R., & Devine, P. G. (1996). Attitude importance and resistance to persuasion: It's not just the thought that counts. *Journal of Personality and Social Psychology, 70,* 931-944.

NAME INDEX

Aaker, J. L., 243
Abraham, C., 192
Abrahamson, A., 189
Abrams, D., 297, 335
Abrams, R., 183
Acker, M., 399
Ackerman, J. M., 494
Ackerman, P., 483, 484
Adair, J., 56
Adams, B. D., 367
Adams, G., 455
Adams, H., 42
Adewole, A., 268
Adler, N. L., 429, 431
Adolph, K. E., 343
Adorno, T. W., 273
Agarie, N., 400
Agnew, C. R., 433, 435
Agras, W., 199
Agthe, M., 121
Agyei, Y., 417
Aharon, I., 416
Ahrens, A., 76
Aikin, K. J., 345
Ainsworth, M. S., 436
Ajzen, I., 192–194
Akimoto, S., 105
Aknin, L. B., 486
Albarracín, D., 69, 206, 240
Albright, L., 161, 305
Alden, L. E., 450
Alderks, C. E., 298
Alicke, M., 82, 88
Allard, L. M., 438
Allen, J., 183, 423
Allen, J. B., 423
Allen, K., 432
Allen, K. M., 432
Allen, V. L., 259
Allik, J., 40
Allison, S. T., 318
Allport, F. H., 8
Altabe, M. N., 466
Altman, A., 490
Altman, J., 450
Alvaro, E. M., 240, 241, 262
Alwin, D. F., 229
Amabile, T., 71, 72, 119
Amanzio, M., 165
Amarel, D., 495
Amato, P. R., 450, 473, 478
Ambady, N., 130, 131, 161, 284, 324, 350
American Psychological Association, 54
Ames, D. R., 494
Amirkhan, J., 402, 403
Amodio, D. M., 366
Anagnostou, P., 232
Ancoli-Israel, S., 353
Andersen, A., 76
Anderson, C., 35, 103, 162, 168, 264, 390
Anderson, C. A., 389, 390, 393–398, 402
Anderson, K., 35
Anderson, K. B., 390, 393

Anderson, N., 156
Anderson, N. B., 353
Angleitner, A., 446
Anthony, T., 336
Antone, C., 157
Antonides, G., 310
Antonio, A. L., 304
Antonovics, K., 431
Apfel, N., 208
Apfelbaum, E. P., 368
Appel, A., 199
Arasaratnam, L. A., 465
Archer, J., 383, 405
Archibald, F. S., 448
Argenti, A. M., 335
Ariely, D., 18, 368, 416
Armstrong, T. L., 337
Aron, A., 17, 364, 422, 429, 431, 432, 441
Aron, A. P., 424
Aron, E. N., 422, 431, 441
Aronson, E., 47, 195, 199, 201, 204, 208,
    311, 364, 422
Aronson, J., 349, 350
Arps, K., 485
Arriaga, X. B., 439, 445
Arunachalam, V., 324
Asakawa, K., 103
Asch, S., 159
Asch, S. E., 257, 258
Asgari, S., 366
Ashburn-Nardo, L., 366
Ashley, D. L., 251
Ashmore, R. D., 162, 358
Ashton, W., 119
Asp, C. H., 366
Aube, J., 421
Aubé, J., 383
Aune, K., 137
Aune, R., 137
Avolio, B. J., 305
Axsom, D., 65, 200, 201, 230

Baca, L. D., 294
Back, K., 422, 426
Back, M. D., 426
Baer, J. S., 253
Bahrick, H., 80
Bailey, D. S., 384
Bailey, J. M., 417, 418
Baker, L., 189
Baker, M., 418
Baker, S. P., 293
Bakker, A., 194
Balcetis, E., 200
Banaji, M., 160
Banaji, M. R., 42, 335, 358
Bandura, A., 30, 165, 186, 187, 332, 392,
    403, 478
Bane, C. M., 227
Banks, C., 53
Banks, S., 157
Banks, T., 382
Banton, J. G., 391

Barbaranelli, C., 403
Barbash, T., 152
Barbee, A. P., 22, 414, 490
Barbour, L., 118
Barclay, G., 406
Bardwell, W. A., 353
Bargh, J., 148, 149
Bargh, J. A., 148, 149, 358, 427
Barkin, A., 448
Barkin, S., 402
Barling, J., 305
Barndollar, K., 149
Barnes, G., 399
Baron, A. S., 335
Baron, J., 495
Baron, R. A., 391, 403, 477
Baron, R. S., 233, 260, 261, 293, 300, 308
Barr, A., 417
Barr, D. B., 251
Barrett, D. W., 209
Barsade, S. G., 309
Bar-Tal, D., 308, 314
Bartell, P. A., 472
Bartels, A., 432
Bartels, J. M., 477
Barth, J. M., 321
Bartholomew, K., 448
Bartholow, B. D., 384, 395, 396, 398
Bartlett, M. Y., 445, 447
Bass, B. M., 305
Bassett, R., 267
Bates, J. E., 401
Batson, C. D., 67, 191, 297, 462, 464, 466,
    467, 470, 475, 477, 478, 481–485,
    487, 488
Batten, P. G., 448
Bauer, G. B., 445
Baum, A., 390
Bauman, C. W., 191
Baumann, D. J., 485–487
Baumeister, R., 13, 67, 68, 89, 147, 207
Baumeister, R. F., 68, 292, 310, 360, 379,
    390, 391, 399, 403, 414, 429, 477
Baumgardner, M. H., 226
Baumrind, D., 277
Bazerman, M. H., 325
Bazzini, D. G., 439, 440
Beach, S. R., 423
Beach, S. R. H., 444
Beadle, D., 268
Beaman, A., 66
Beaman, A. L., 50, 265, 485
Bearinger, L. H., 14
Bearman, P., 228
Beaulieu, D. A., 418
Beaumont, J. J., 391
Beauregard, K., 89
Beck, K., 194
Becker, S. W., 464
Beggan, J. K., 318
Bell, P. A., 390
Beller, R., 467
Bellissimo, A., 187

Perdue, L., 76
Perez-Stable, E. J., 243
Peri, N., 490
Perie, M., 83
Perkins, H. W., 256
Perlman, D., 119
Perrin, J., 118
Perrin, S., 259
Perry, D. G., 392, 393
Perry, L. C., 392, 393
Perry, M., 382, 383
Perry, R. P., 492
Peruche, B. M., 366
Peters, L. H., 305
Peterson, B., 76
Peterson, C., 10, 35, 84, 120
Peterson, E., 314
Peterson, L., 381
Peterson, R. S., 262, 301
Peterson, T., 71
Pettigrew, T., 10
Pettigrew, T. F., 308, 342, 363, 369
Pettit, G. S., 401
Petty, R., 146, 183
Petty, R. E., 71, 218–221, 224, 227, 230,
    231, 234, 235, 237, 267, 294, 477
Phelan, J., 187
Phelps, E. A., 358
Philbrick, K., 496, 497
Philip, E., 381
Phillips, C. M., 379
Phillips, D., 35, 259, 437, 438
Phillips, D. P., 259, 396
Phillips, J., 130
Phillips, S. T., 292
Pickett, C. L., 339
Pickett, K., 37
Pickrell, J., 158
Pierce-Otay, A., 426
Pietromonaco, P., 148
Pietromonaco, P. R., 436, 438
Piferi, R. L., 488
Piliavin, I. M., 471, 473, 474
Piliavin, J., 422
Piliavin, J. A., 466, 471, 473, 474, 478
Pilla, R. S., 402
Pine, D., 37
Pinel, E., 64
Pittinsky, T. L., 350
Pittman, T., 153, 204
Plaks, J. E., 295, 296
Plant, E. A., 360, 366
Plaut, V. C., 455
Pliner, P., 44
Plomin, R., 467
Plous, S., 309
Ploutz-Snyder, R., 124
Pohlmann, J. T., 305
Polifroni, M., 337
Pollan, M., 41
Pollock, C. L., 266
Pollock, V. E., 384
Pomare, M., 364
Pomerantz, E. M., 227
Pond, K., 450
Pool, G. J., 262
Pope, H., 76
Postmes, T., 295, 303, 310, 365
Poston, I., 118
Poulos, R. W., 478

Powell, A. A., 366
Powell, M. C., 493
Powers, S. I., 438
Pratkanis, A. R., 226, 238, 303, 304
Pratto, F., 161, 335, 337
Preikschas, S., 121
Preisler, R. M., 227
Prentice, D. A., 7, 253, 256, 259, 383
Prentice-Dunn, S., 297, 355, 449
Presser, N. R., 311
Pressman, S. D., 448
Priester, J. R., 220, 224
Probasco, P., 303, 304
Probst, T. M., 319
Prosser, A., 492
Pruitt, D. G., 299, 310, 313, 317
Pugh, M., 118
Pugh, M. A., 364
Pura, N., 368
Purdie, V. J., 360
Purdie-Vaughns, V., 208
Purvis, D., 262
Putnam, K. M., 385
Pyszczynski, T., 333

Quattrone, G., 91
Queller, S., 361
Quinn, D. M., 347, 350
Quinn, P. C., 335
Quintana, D., 448

Raaijmakers, Q. A. W., 277
Rabin, B. S., 35, 448
Rachal, K. C., 445
Radke-Yarrow, M., 464
Rahimi, A. M., 336
Rajecki, D. W., 417
Rank, S., 262
Rapoport, A., 319
Rasmussen, J. L., 417
Rasmussen, P., 393
Ratcliff, C. D., 364
Ratcliff, J. J., 366
Ratner, R. K., 252
Rauch, S. L., 17
Raz, M., 265
Rea, C., 239
Read, S., 201
Reardon, R., 239
Reay, D. T., 391
Reed, B., 42
Reeder, G., 81, 122, 161
Regalia, C., 445
Regan, D., 190
Regan, D. T., 265, 475, 477, 491
Regan, P. C., 428, 429
Rehm, J., 296
Reicher, S., 492
Reidel, S. L., 425
Reifman, A., 390
Reilly, A. H., 345
Reinhardt, J. P., 494, 495
Reinhart, M. A., 490, 491
Reis, H. T., 38, 39, 414, 431
Reis-Bergan, M., 195
Rempel, J. K., 444
Rennison, C. M., 381
Reno, R. R., 251, 257, 263
Rentfrow, P. J., 362
Rettek, S., 21

Reyes, J. A., 139, 324
Reynolds, K. J., 335
Rhee, E., 97
Rhoades, L., 72
Rhodes, G., 415
Rhodes, K., 50
Rhodewalt, F., 89, 204
Rholes, W., 148
Rholes, W. S., 437, 438
Riad, J. K., 378, 382
Rice, W. E., 239
Rich, A., 388
Richard, D. C., 445
Richard, F. D., 11, 280
Richards, J., 131, 132
Richardson, D. S., 448
Richeson, J. A., 253, 352, 364
Richman, S. A., 234
Richter, L., 146
Rigby, K., 232
Riggio, H. R., 451
Riggle, E., 40
Rilling, J., 321
Rind, B., 491
Ringwalt, C. L., 232
Risen, J. L., 340
Ritchie, L. D., 455
Rittenauer-Schatka, H., 149
Ritter, J. M., 414
Ritterfeld, U., 398
Rittle, R. H., 292
Rivara, F. P., 391
Rivera, L. M., 363, 367
Robbins, M., 118
Roberts, A. R., 22, 414
Robins, M., 76
Robinson, R. J., 307, 308
Robinson, T. M., 188
Rochat, F., 276, 280
Rodin, J., 471, 473, 474
Rodkin, P. C., 383
Roeder, U., 149
Roesch, S. C., 385
Roese, N., 56, 154
Rogers, R., 81
Rogers, R. W., 224, 234, 297, 355
Roggman, L. A., 414, 415
Roman, R., 97
Romer, D., 473
Ronk, M., 122
Ropp, S. A., 364
Rose, T. L., 340
Rosell, M. C., 366
Roseman, I., 21
Rosenberg, M., 37, 38
Rosenfeld, L. B., 418
Rosenfeld, P., 207
Rosenfield, D., 311
Rosenhan, D., 166, 343
Rosenhan, D. L., 476, 477
Rosenman, R. H., 464
Rosenthal, A. M., 468
Rosenthal, R., 7, 48, 130, 161, 169, 171,
    284
Rosip, J. C., 346
Ross, D., 30, 392
Ross, L., 82, 85, 119, 124, 168, 228, 229,
    307, 315
Ross, M., 81, 85, 95, 439
Ross, M. W., 232

SUBJECT INDEX

Relationship factors:
  in helping, 492–494
  in interpersonal attraction, 421–422
Relationship-oriented individuals, 305
Relationship problems, 442–452
  conflict, 442–445
  dissolution, 450–451
  jealousy, 445–447
  loneliness, 447–450
Relationship satisfaction, 433–441
  and attachment styles, 436–438
  and counterfactual thinking, 152, 153
  culture's influence on, 454, 455
  and love styles, 431
  and love types, 429
  and positive illusions, 439–441
  social exchange theory, 433–436
  strategies for increasing, 441
Relative deprivation, 338, 387, 388
Reliability, inter-rater, 36
Religion, 364, 462, 467
Repetition, and credibility of persuasive
    sources, 226
Replications, of research studies, 51
Representativeness, in social cognition, 150
Representative samples, 51
Reproductive fitness, of women, 417, 418
Republican National Committee, 238
Requests, culture's influence on, 283–284
Research, cross-cultural, 22–23, 58
Research method(s), 28–59
  confidentiality in, 55
  correlational, 33–43
  culture's influence on, 57–58
  debriefing in, 56
  ethical issues with, 53–57
  experimental, 44–46
  external validity in, 49–51
  informed consent in, 54, 55
  Institutional Review Boards for, 53, 54
  internal validity in, 46–49
  observational/naturalistic, 34–37
  selection of, 51–52
  self-report/survey methods, 37–43
  testing ideas in, 30–33
Research process, 30–33
Resistance, 238–242, 280
Resource preferences, 417–421
Resources, 308, 316–319
Response options, on surveys, 40–41
Responsibility, 202, 276, 472, 491–492
Reverse discrimination, 354–355
Rewards, 67, 306, 487–489
Rewarding interactions, 441
Reward processing, in brain, 321
Reward theory, 198
Rickey, Branch, 365
Risky shift, 299
Robby the Robot study, 199–200
Roberts, Charles Carl, IV, 376, 403
Robinson, Jackie, 365
Rochester Interaction Record, 39
Rock music, 24–25
Romania, 406, 497
Romantic love, 429
Ronald McDonald, 180
Rosenberg Self-Esteem Scale, 37–38
Rosenhan, David, 166
Ross, L., 82, 119, 124
Rotton, J., 390

Rumination, 403
Rural areas, prosocial behavior in, 478
Rusbult, C. E., 434, 443, 445
Russia, 283, 406, 455
Rycroft, Melissa, 412

Sadat, Anwar al, 314
Sadness, 236
Salary, 345, 415
Salience:
  frequency of events vs., 147
  of minority members of groups, 340, 341
  performance and identity, 350
  in social perception, 122–124
  of titles, 146
Same-sex couples:
  attachment styles of, 437
  marriage of, 2, 110–111
  relationship satisfaction for, 434–435
Satisfaction, relationship, see Relationship
    satisfaction
Scapegoating, 342, 386
Scarcity, 267–268
Schachter, Stanley, 78, 254
Schemas, 148
Schindler, Oskar, 464
Schmitt, G., 492
School shootings, 376–377, 402, 403
Schwartz, J., 84
Schwarz, Norbert, 149
Scientific method, 12
Sears, Robert, 387
Secret relationships, 414
Secret Service agents, 132
Secure attachment, 436, 437
The Self, regulation of, 67–69
Self-affirmation theory, 206–208, 233
Self-awareness, 191, 297, 366, 367, 477
Self-awareness theory, 66–67
Self-concept, 62–106
  culture's influence on, 97–101
  defined, 64
  and examining your behavior, 69–71
  helping and, 487–489
  and high perceived control, 83–85
  and ingratiation, 92–93
  and interpreting your motivation, 71–73
  and introspection, 64–65
  maintaining a positive concept of,
      102–104
  overly positive views of, 89
  personal factors in, 64–74
  positive, 80–90
  and social comparison theory, 74–77
  social factors in, 74–79
  and spotlight effect, 95–96
  and two-factor theory of emotion, 77–79
Self-concept clarity, 100
Self-consistency, 100
Self-control, 67–69, 241
Self-destructive behavior, 378
Self-disclosure, 403, 417, 422, 448
Self-discrepancy theory, 66
Self-esteem, 75
  culture's influence on, 104
  and gambling, 310
  and help, 490–491, 494
  and prejudice, 332, 338–340, 353–354
Self-evaluation maintenance model of
    altruism, 494

Self-focus, 470, 488
Self-fulfilling prophecy:
  about prejudice, 348–349, 369
  defined, 7
  and loneliness, 449, 450
  and social cognition, 169–173
Self-handicapping, 88–89
Self-image, 120–122, 266
Self-interest, 225, 335
Selfish reasons, for helping, 485
Self-knowledge, and social perception, 127
Self-liking, 104
Self-monitoring, 93–95, 230
Self-perception:
  and culture, 97–101
  of motivation, 101–102
  in social psychology, 4–5
Self-perception theory, 69–70, 206–207
Self-presentation, 5, 90–96, 105
Self-promotion, 91, 104
Self-reliance, 19
Self-report measures, 37–43, 345–346
Self-sacrifice, 463
Self-serving attributions, 81, 103
Self-serving behavior, 87–88
Self-serving beliefs, 82, 83
Self-serving biases, 80–82
Self-serving comparisons, 86–87
Self-standards model, of cognitive
    dissonance, 205, 206
Self-verification, 92–95
Self-views, negative, 449
September 11, 2001 terrorist attacks, 151,
    168, 290, 425, 460–461, 478, 488
Serotonin, 385
Sex education, 45
Sexism. See also Gender, stereotypes about
  and availability heuristic, 148
  benevolent, 356, 370
  and culture, 370–372
  hostile, 355–356, 370
  social norms about, 256
Sexual assault, 90
Sexual behavior:
  fear-based persuasion about, 232
  and gender, 13, 418–420
  and implicit personality theory, 162
  pluralistic ignorance about, 253
  social norms about, 193
  studies of, 50–51
  and virginity pledges, 228
Sexual education, 45
Sexual experience, 419–420, 438
Sexual harassment, 389
Sexual infidelity, 445–447
Sexual jealousy, 380
Sexually aggressive films, 399, 400
Sexually-transmitted diseases (STDs), 228
Sexual orientation. See also Same-sex
    couples
  predicting, 161
  prejudice based on, 363, 366, 367
  social perception of, 110–111
  stereotypes about, 340–341
Shackelford, T. K., 415
Sherif, Muzafer, 9, 257, 308, 365
Shields, Brooke, 218
Shifting standards model, 342
Shih, Margaret, 350